ROBERT YOUNG PELTON'S

# THE WORLD'S MOST
# DANGEROUS
# PLACES®

# ROBERT YOUNG PELTON'S
# THE WORLD'S MOST
# DANGEROUS
# PLACES®

### 5th EDITION
Completely Revised and Updated

An Imprint of HarperCollinsPublishers

A paperback edition of this book was published in 2003 by HarperResource.

Inquiries to the author may be addressed to: *ryp@comebackalive.com*
For updates, news, and products: http://www.comebackalive.com
Watch "Robert Young Pelton's The World's Most Dangerous Places®" on the Travel Channel®, The Discovery Channel® in Canada and around the world.

First Collins edition published 2005.

Library of Congress Cataloguing-in-Publication Data

Pelton, Robert Young.
    [World's most dangerous places]
    Robert Young Pelton's the world's most dangerous places / [Robert Young Pelton].—5th ed.
        p.   cm.
    ISBN 0-06-001160-2 (pbk.)              ISBN 978-0-06-001160-4 (pbk.)
    1. Travel—Safety measures. 2. Travel—Anecdotes. I. Title: World's most dangerous places. II. title.
II. Pelton, Robert Young. Robert Young Pelton's the world's most dangerous places. III. Title.
G151.P44 2003
910'.2'02—dc21                        2002027484

05   06   07   08   09   RRD   10 9 8 7 6

# To Die-Hard Readers

After September 11, 2001, the need to understand far-flung conflicts and obscure groups was no longer the occupation of a few iconoclasts like myself and adventurers, war journos, aid workers, and military folks. *DP5* would have to wait: It was time to pack my well-worn Becker pack and head out. I resisted the urge at first as thousands of journos descended on Afghanistan waiting for the War on Terrorism to start. Instead I did the obligatory talking-head appearances on the networks to explain what our troops should expect and provide background on the players. When I realized that the world's media was in the wrong place and the war had begun, I could wait no longer. I headed for the Northern Provinces in Afghanistan and hooked up with General Abdul Rashid Dostum and his covert group of Green Berets.

In light of events, I made the uncomfortable decision to be a journo . . . well, at least for a month. I made two calls, to Eason Jordan, the president of *CNN News* gathering, and to David Dunbar, the features editor of *National Geographic Adventure,* and to their credit it took them both less than a minute to say yes. For the first time, *DP* and mainstream journalism were in sync.

Given high-tech gear and an instant audience, the world soon met the type of characters I normally meet when researching this book: This trip included the American Taliban, John Walker Lindh; the "brutal warlord," but in truth earnest peacemaker, General Abdul Rashid Dostum; the "Regulators," the bad boys of the 595 Special Forces "A" Team (among them some hard-core *DP* fans); dour talib mullahs; crazed jihadis; and more. All in all, just a fairly typical trip in the life of *DP* readers and our various contributors, but people seemed surprised that we were able to get to the heart of the story and were invited to hang with the players.

So the rest of the world has caught up with *DP*—but for us, it's business as usual with maybe a few more stops on the street now to chat with enthusiastic readers. That's OK, because keeping it real is what it's all about. Meeting real people has always been the point of *DP:* To show people how to connect, get people thinking about the state of the world, and in the process brush away the fear and the barriers that keep them from traveling, meeting, and learning.

Hard-core readers of *DP* have never been content to let talking heads, video press releases, and spin doctors explain what is going on. We seek the stone-heavy truth of experience and the wisdom-inducing perspective of intense emotional experience, tempered by the cool intellectual framework of research. In short, we want you to make up your own minds.

Maybe that's why *DP* has always been and will continue to be a travel guide instead of a political science manual. It is not *DP*'s intent to opine or lecture, but to guide and to inspire.

And remember, the most dangerous thing in the world is still ignorance.

Welcome to *DP5:* No walls, no barriers, no bull.

*—RYP*

# CONTENTS

# LIST OF MAPS

# THE AUTHOR

## Robert Young Pelton

Pelton, 47, has been a lumberjack, boundary cutter, tunneler, driller, hardware store manager, and blaster's assistant. He spends a good part of his time with combatants in remote regions researching, traveling, and meeting rebel and military groups. His unique contacts and breadth of experience with insurgent, jihadi, rebel, criminal, and terrorist groups bring an unusual insight to his interpretation of world events. In the course of his travels he has survived a plane crash, car accidents, a head-on motorcycle crash, killer bees, typhoons, SCUD attacks, a host of wild animal attacks, Marxist rebels, Russian gunships, Northern Alliance artillery, talib rockets, American B-52s, and other nasty things. Pelton has survived being hunted by death squads in Algeria, an Absolut-soaked jungle party with the leadership of the FARC in Colombia where they discussed his kidnapping, the December '99 siege of Grozny while with the rebels, and the uprising at Qali-i-Jangi in

Mazar-I-Sharif, and still looks forward to every trip with a sense of curiosity and enthusiasm.

Pelton's adventures and opinions have long been free filler for print, radio, Internet, and television journalists, but he insists on writing his own books and producing and hosting his own television series. He also provides insight on current events on television news shows, on the Internet, and to generous groups who put up with his backstage demand for no red M&M's. His philosophy is that as long as there are little old ladies and children in the places he visits, he will tell their story instead of his.

He is also the author of the world's only funny and firsthand survival guide, *Come Back Alive* (Broadway); an intensely personal autobiography, *The Adventurist* (Doubleday); and a prescient collection of stories on the future of warfare in *The Hunter, The Hammer and Heaven: Journeys to Three Worlds Gone Mad* (Lyons Press).

Pelton is a Fellow of the Royal Geographical Society in London and lives in Los Angeles, California. Contact: ryp@comebackalive.com.

For updates to *DP*, products, and to meet fellow *DP*ers at Black Flag Café, go to http://www.comebackalive.com.

## The Contributors

**In Memoriam**
**When the Road Less Traveled Comes to an End**
**Wink Dulles (1956–2001)**

Wink Dulles was killed in Thailand on the morning of June 24, 2001, as he rode his motorcycle to the market. He was hit by another motorcycle and died on the scene. His fiancée, who was riding on the back, was injured in the accident.

Dulles spent hard time in Cambodia, Thailand, and Vietnam, traveling by motorcycle. He covered the elections in Cambodia, interviewed rebel leaders in Myanmar, and led a number of motorcycle tours in Vietnam, Thailand, Laos, and Thailand. Wink also wrote for *Action Asia, Trips Magazine,* and the *Toronto Sun.* He was a passionate adventurer, a great writer, and a good friend. He was a pure and driven man who will be remembered by all those who knew him, and I and many others will miss him greatly.

## Gervaise Roderick (Roddy) Scott (1971- 2002)

Roddy was killed while waving a white flag, trying to change sides in a small town in Ingueshetia on September 26, 2002. He was shot in the face by a Russian soldier. As of press time the Russians have refused to return his body to his family, and he remains buried in the Ingush village of Ordzhonikidziyevskaya. He became the fiftieth "media worker" to be killed in 2002. But Roddy was not a media worker or a journalist. He was his own man. After he graduated, Roddy spent eight years as a freelancer, stringer, and adventurer in Yemen, Kurdistan, Iraq, Afghanistan, Albania, Kosovo, Palestine, Sierra Leone, Ethiopia, and Chechnya.

An ever-active, happy, joking, enthusiastic man, he chose covering wars as a way to support his lifestyle. He wrote stories, shot videos, and was the major force behind updating *DP*4. His stories are kept in this edition as a tribute to his unique style and perspective.

Ever since I met Roddy half a decade ago, he regaled me with tales of being jailed, kidnapped, held at gunpoint, expelled, contracting cerebral malaria, and coming out with only the clothes on his back. These tales weren't intended to impress; only to entertain. He had a number of firsts, partly because he earned the trust of a number of rebel groups that most journalists were hesitant to approach. The Chechens, the RUF, the PKK, and other groups respected and protected Roddy because he burned brightly and fiercely. His choice of covering the most violent and remote conflicts did not earn him money or fame, but he was a member of a very small club. Roddy enjoyed what he did, and he did it well; he was loved and he had good friends. That is all we can ask for.

Despite working in the world's most dangerous places, his work was accurate, funny, enlightening, and important. He was an intellectual with a love for adventure. He will be missed.

## Andrew Mueller

Andrew, 33, has been the main man in my attempts to create sense and order in *DP5*. His rock-and-roll sensibility and complete ignorance of the dangers involved in being a *DP* contributor have added a fresh, sharp feel to this edition. To the enduring amusement of the world's customs officials, Andrew Mueller was born in Wagga Wagga, Australia. Now based in London, he has traveled to more than 50 countries and covered stories including the Taliban's takeover of Afghanistan, the lifting of the siege of Bihac, the handover of Hong Kong, the wartime rock-and-roll scene of Sarajevo, and a transcendentally hapless Elvis Presley festival in Tupelo, Mississippi. He has also rioted in Paris, visited

THE AUTHOR

lost tribes in India, ridden the Cresta Run, sat in Stalin's armchair, toured with U2, Radiohead, and The Cure, among many others, and interviewed a bewildering variety of people, including long-imprisoned Native American activist Leonard Peltier and Northern Irish Loyalist paramilitary-turned-surrealist-painter-and-sculptor Michael Stone. Mueller's first book, a collection of travel writing, foreign correspondence, and music journalism, titled *Rock & Hard Places,* was published by Virgin in 1999 and thundered down the charts, where it now resides peacefully as an obscure work of stunning excellence. His work appears in *The Independent, The Independent on Sunday Review, The Guardian, Time Out, Arena, The Australian,* and *Gear.* Contact: andrew@comebackalive.com.

## James Brabazon

James, 30, read history at Cambridge. Before *Dangerous Places* seemed like a good idea, he worked as a celebrity portrait photographer, snapping everyone from Coolio to the Queen of England (who is now on the *DP* mailing list).

Slightly confused as to where the money went, James travels extensively through Africa and Asia as executive producer for the Nairobi-based television agency, Camerapix. He is also a contributing photographer for Katz Pictures in London and Gamma Presse Images in Paris.

Based in London and Johannesburg, and specializing in conflict and politics, James has worked in over 50 countries, including Eritrea, Kashmir, Kosovo, Israel, Zimbabwe, and Northern Ireland. To date, he is the only journalist ever to have visited LURD rebel-held Liberia. Despite repeated invitations, he politely declined president Taylor's rather persistent offers to visit Monrovia. James's work has appeared on the BBC, ABC, and CNN, as well as in *Newsweek, The Sunday Telegraph,* and *Fortune.* Contact: brabazon@comebackalive.com

## Linda van Wijk

Linda, 35, graduated with a degree in science of communication from the University of Amsterdam. She has been writing, traveling, and photographing exotic locales for ten years and raising a family. She is a scuba diver, snowboarder, skydiver, and off-roader. She won the Fjallraven Polar 1999, a dogsled race in Lapland, participated in two expeditions into the jungles of Borneo, and drove her Land Rover across the Sahara. Contact: vanwijk@comebackalive.com.

## Rob Krott

Rob, 38, is a former officer and paratrooper who attended Harvard (anthropology). His military career has earned him various awards and decorations from 10 foreign governments. Besides his anthropological pursuits (with Richard Leakey's Koobi Fora Project), he finds time to organize parachute jumps for ex-Special Forces and paratroopers around the world and cover conflicts as a correspondent. He has been on the ground in El Salvador, Guatemala, Sudan, Uganda, Somalia, Bosnia, Myanmar, Cambodia, and Angola and continues to work in, or travel on assignment to, the world's most dangerous places. He has served with three foreign armies and lived with a number of rebel groups, including the SPLA in Sudan and the KNLA in Myanmar. He continues to spend a considerable amount of time in Asia, Africa, the Balkans, and Latin America. He is the senior foreign correspondent for *Soldier of Fortune*. He has been published in *Harpers, Explorers Journal,* and *New African*. Rob is often mistaken for Chuck Norris in his travels. He is hoping some day to be confused with Robert Redford. He keeps *DP* honest with his multipage submissions of corrections, illuminations, and anecdotes. He lives in Edmonton, Alberta. Contact: krott@comeback-alive.com.

## Dom Rotheroe

Dom, 36, is a London-based filmmaker who covers hot spots, writes books, and collects odd pictures of things. When the republics of Yugoslavia went through an unamicable divorce, he went off to the war in Bosnia with £1,000 and a Hi-8 camcorder. The resultant documentary, *A Sarajevo Diary,* was nominated for a British Academy Award.

Since Bosnia, Rotheroe has been with the POLISARIO in Western Sahara and under fire in East Timor, and has investigated cop-killing street kids in Rio, crossed the blockade around Bougainville, and covered the earthquake in Turkey. The focus of all Dom's films has been to understand the situation from the point of view of the people and telling their story with feeling. Rotheroe's articles have been published in *Esquire, The Independent,* the *Geographical,* and *Adrenalin* in the United Kingdom and in Australia, Portugal, and the Netherlands. He is currently working on his first feature film, a savage love story about sexually abused teenagers. Contact: dom@comebackalive.com.

In addition to the credited contributors who have worked so diligently to make this book relevant and accurate, I would like to thank the hundreds of people who have risked their lives to make sure I made it into and out of some of the world's most dangerous places. To the families that fed me, the fighters who died protecting me, and the people who took me in when all seemed lost, I thank you. To the families and combatants who fed and sheltered me without hesitation, to the guards, commanders, and villagers who let me pass and who have never demanded to see a single shred of proof of who I am, I thank you. Many of those people are no longer alive and I salute them for making the ultimate sacrifice to help their people and their cause. There is truth, there is good, and there is an unspoken, unwritten, unbreakable human bond among people who risk it all for basic principals of freedom and self-determination. I hope I have repaid you and rewarded your trust.

And a special thank you to Megan Newman and Kathy Huck at HarperCollins, who valiantly and cheerfully publish a thousand-page book knowing full well that as soon as a deadline looms, their favorite author will be pulled away on yet another crazy quest.

# WHAT IS DANGEROUS?

# WHAT IS DANGEROUS?

## No One Gets Out of Here Alive

With all this talk about survival and fascination with danger, why is it that we never admit that life is like watching a great movie and—poof!—the power goes off before we see the ending? Just like every love story ends in sadness, every life has a surprise ending. Death is a natural event that comes to us all . . . so shouldn't we get to know him a little?

It's no big deal. Death doesn't really wear a smelly cloak and carry a scythe . . . it's more likely the attractive girl who makes you forget to look right before you cross that busy intersection in London . . . perhaps it's that Ebola-stricken waiter who hawked a loogie in your safari lunch after you stiffed him on his tip at breakfast, or maybe it's that rancid-smelling Russian pilot who staggered in after a night of partying to captain your ill-fated discount flight to Baku. Or maybe it's that routine cross-country flight to LA . . . but hey . . . lighten up. It's only death. We all get to meet him (or her?) at some point. Why not get to know death a little earlier, buy him a drink, slap him on the back, and fake him out? There are things worse than death, such as a full-compliance tax audit by a dyslexic IRS agent or maybe even discount prostate surgery in Monrovia. It helps to look at the big picture when understanding just what might kill you and what won't. It is the baby boomers' slow descent into gray hair, brand-name drugs, reading glasses, and a general sense of not quite being as fast as they used to be that drives this whole survival thing. Relax: You're gonna die. Enjoy life, don't fear it.

> **I**t's no big deal. Death doesn't really wear a smelly cloak and carry a scythe.

To some, life is the single most precious thing they are given and it's only natural that they would invest every ounce of their being into making sure that every moment is glorious, productive, and safe. So does "living" mean sitting strapped into our Barca Lounger, medic at hand, 911 autodialer at the ready, carefully watching for low-flying planes? Or should you live like those folks who are into extreme, mean, ultimate, eco, survival, death match, adventure stuff like flying used MiGs, ballooning around the world, yanking on snakes, and diving in shark-infested waters? Sorry, that stuff may be fun to talk about at cocktail parties, but not really dangerous . . . not even half as dangerous as driving a cab on the graveyard shift in Karachi.

Living is about adventure and adventure is about elegantly surfing the tenuous space between lobotomized serenity and splattered-bug terror and still being in enough pieces to share the lessons learned with your grandkids. Adventure is about using your brain, body, and intellect to weave a few bright colors in the world's dull, gray fabric. And, hell, man, it's not about you surviving; it's about helping others to survive . . . and doing it in style. So wussup with *DP*? Isn't it a guide that seems to have a "lucid, albeit insane" focus on all the things that can damage you and shorten your very existence? Not at all. If you can avoid the things that kill you, then the good bits pretty much take care of themselves. The purpose of *DP* is to get your head screwed on straight, your sphincter unpuckered, and your nose pointed in the right direction.

When you are done reading, you will realize that instead of thinking that *The Crocodile Hunter* pestering reptiles is "dainjerous," you will get your adrenaline fix by looking for shows like "Tubercular Afghan Refugee," "White Zimbabwe Farmer," or "Hutu Goat Herder." Now *those* would be survival shows.

So let's get to it.

# Tick, Tock: Time

Okay, class, what is the thing most likely to kill you? Killer torna-dos? Crazed terrorists? Latex-proof AIDS? Cher infomercials? Give up? It's Father Time. Humans are genetically supposed to exist on this planet for about 40 years. Cavemen had just enough time to sow their seed and maybe feed their children until they were old enough to catch their own food, gum it down, and hobble around their caves at age 30. Back then you grew up, spawned a few kids, and just as life started to look good and comfortable, blap, you were too slow to outrun a sabre-toothed tiger. So on the genetic survival clock, consider anything more than 35 as karmic gravy. These days there are still people in West Africa and on U.S. Indian reservations who think 50 is a long life. Westerners and first-world folks get downright litigious if they don't make it to 70. Thanks to drugs, plastic surgery, clean living, pay-per-view porno, and third-world body parts, life is long and getting longer. The ugly truth . . . other than the frightening thought of millions of 90-year-olds cruising South Beach in Speedos . . . is that the first world is just about maxed out when it comes to natural human longevity. If it weren't for small cars, dirty bars, unprotected sex, fast food, and rock-and-roll you would never get a spot at the canasta table.

# The Real, Real World: Accidents

In reality, death is pretty weird. It has this random, "Holy shit, did you see that?" kind of feel to it. Like watching *Faces of Death* in real time. In the real world, 1 out of every 15 of us will die accidentally. If you live to 80 you will have survived about 12 million other people who were not that lucky. But keep in mind that means most of us aren't going to get killed accidentally.

So it looks like most of us will cruise into our seventies with a head full of Rogaine-induced hair and a drawer full of unused Viagra. Longevity also depends on where and how you live. Your forefathers' sailing the Atlantic or swimming the Rio Grande was a good health move. According to the National Center for Health Statistics, Ameri-cans should get an average of 77.12 years, but that's already a lie. Men, the weaker sex, get 74.24; the gals get an additional 5.7 years to spend the insurance. That's 2 mortgages, 15 car loans, and a good chance of actually seeing your birthday plugged by Willard Scott for Smuckers.

You want to live long? Be a girl, be rich . . . and be Asian. Wanna die young? Be poor, be black (or indigenous if you really want to live dan-gerously), and move to Central Africa. Overall, things are pretty safe and benign for denizens of the Western world and they are getting better for the rest of the world. Yes, that's right, despite what you see on Sunday morning fund-raisers, life spans around world are getting longer. If you are unlucky enough to be from Sierra Leone, statistically you'll get an average of 45 years to do your thing. But the truth is you can also live to 80, watch satellite TV, find a doctor, drive a Land Cruiser with AC, fire up the Internet, and order an espresso in Freetown if you have the economic wherewithal. So money is also the key to staying alive longer.

So what's the scoop?

Does life really suck in the third world? Not really. Worldwide, things are pretty good. Depending on who you want to believe, most of the world lives in a mud hut, goes to bed hungry, and can't read or write. Worse, the "normal person" lives in a state of perpetual fear of the government, hunger, disease, his neighbor, religion, and even the weather. Like most things you read, it's half-true. Most of the world lives day-to-day, hand-to-mouth, trusting to a religious deity or luck for their long-term survival. Yes, most of the world is poor, slightly nervous, and a little fatalistic about what's around the corner. But the secret is that they make do. Are they living every moment in fear and apprehension? Not really. It's the West that does that. It is only in developed countries and in the last 10 years of baby-boomdom that we have developed this obsession with fear and safety. There isn't really anything to fear. Crime is under control, wages are pretty good, life spans are longer, health is improving, and every segment of society has benefited from the political efforts of bleeding-heart liberals and the business efforts of cold-hearted capitalists. So let's all take a deep breath, have a group hug, and be thankful that if you are reading this book in English, and didn't steal it, you are part of the longest-lived, healthiest, most-protected generation that has ever lived on this planet.

**CDC Fast Stats**
http://www.cdc.gov/nchs/fastats/Default.htm

## So What's the Bad News?

The bad news (for us; we'll get to the third world shortly) is that all this safety labeling, caring and sharing, seat-belted, Special-K eating, nose to the grindstone society can quickly piss away a generation of genetic privilege, medical advances, and peace treaties in a single two-week vacation. Why? We seek danger even when we don't even know it exists. We think nothing of driving our Explorers too fast, screaming our JetSkis too long, and thumping our dirt bikes too hard. We snarf down Churros and Slurpees in our paper-thin Minivans while we chatter on our cell phones at 90 miles per hour. We smoke cigarettes, drink too much booze, bang questionable partners, and pick fights with

## LIVE LONG . . . AND DIE

Humans live until about 70 but begin to age at about age 30, giving us perhaps 15 years of maturity and perfect health. Scientists think that aging is triggered by an aging gene.

A room of wonks was presented with an interesting problem. What if man did not die of natural causes (i.e., old age)? Just how long could a human last before grim statistics caught up with us? They quickly whipped out their actuarial tables and figured that healthy humans who escape the ravages of disease could live until they were 1,200 years old before the law of averages would catch up with them. Some could live until they were 10,000 years. Unfortunately they finally came up with the same grim statistic. All of us would die at some point.

strangers. We order extra whipped cream on dessert, cheese on hash browns, and extra butter for pancakes. Hell, this isn't dangerous—this is living well. Yeah, we generally first-world ourselves to death. Yes, for some of us the world's most dangerous place is not 9/11 but the 7-Eleven.

It's no secret that over here heart disease is the big killer. What if we eat our sprouts, clip the lawn for dessert (hmm, funny how most herbivores never outlive carnivores though), breathe through a HEPA filter, and rent a place on Diego Garcia . . . then just who is the Avis of killers? The one thing that tries harder? We weren't joking in saying that if you want to live longer, stay out of the house. Between 5 and 15 percent of humans will die in an accident of some type (depending on where you live, what you do, or how long you escape disease). If you really want to live dangerously . . . just stay at home or take trips less than five miles from home. Each year, cheap toys, shag-carpeted stairs,

**WHEN YA GOTTA GO, YA GOTTA GO**

| | |
|---|---|
| 1. Heart Disease | 37.8% |
| 2. Cancer | 19.3 |
| 3. Stroke | 10.3 |
| 4. Accidents (Non-auto) | 3.0 |
| 5. Influenza (Pneumonia) | 2.9 |
| 6. Motor Vehicle Accidents | 2.4 |
| 7. Diabetes | 1.9 |
| 8. Liver Disease | 1.7 |
| 9. Arteriosclerosis | 1.5 |
| 10. Suicide | 1.4 |

and slippery bathtubs do more damage than all of the world's terrorists. You even have a one in three chance of dying in bed. (From what? We'll let you get creative with that one.) More people will die from a household appliance than in plane crashes. More people will be scraped off the highways than will die in most war zones. The bottom line when it comes to safety is to keep your eye on the ball and not the bull when it comes to understanding what will kill you. Reality check? Yes, please. Statistics are gathered in first-world countries (i.e., safe ones). Most people spend most of their time within a five-mile radius and, despite what *DP* would have you believe, compared to a mud hut on the slope of the Andes, your home is a pretty safe place. Just make sure you know how to get to the Emergency Room . . . and don't drive too fast.

The most dangerous month for accidents is August, with 9,000 unintentional injuries versus a monthly incidence average of 7,500. The safest month is February with only 5,700. Curious to know the other most dangerous months?

| Cause of Death | Most Dangerous Month | Number of Deaths | Least Dangerous Month | Number of Deaths | Average |
|---|---|---|---|---|---|
| Car Accidents | August | 4,243 | January | 2,869 | 3,628 |
| Falls | December | 1,145 | February | 959 | 1,055 |
| Drownings | July | 886 | November | 147 | 385 |
| Firearms | November | 164 | September | 83 | 120 |
| Fire | January | 539 | June | 194 | 343 |
| Poisoning | August | 572 | January | 412 | 475 |

*Source:* National Center for Health Statistics, National Safety Council, http://www.nsc.org

## "Adventure" Travel . . . Isn't

So this is working out fine, we have you worried about sitting around doing nothing in your home. The fear of sitting at home watching a Lakers game is putting big dark stains under your arms. It is now time for an "adventure," "a bold, uncertain, and risky enterprise," "to take a chance," and so on.

You've read *Come Back Alive* cover to cover, you ordered a full "too many damn pockets/ain't I rugged" adventure outfit from REI, you have a backpack bigger than you are, round-the-world tickets, and you can feel adrenaline coursing through your Starbucks-clogged veins!

Sorry, but that's not adventure travel. How about those wild-eyed travelers dragging themselves up snow-covered mountains or rafting down thundering canyons? Sorry, not dangerous. Hey, come on, isn't adventure travel dangerous? Not really. Statistically, you might assume that in order to earn the moniker "adventure," the adventure travel market must be sending a large percentage of their customers back in wheelchairs or cardboard boxes. Although there are no industry-wide statistics available, one study of 143 adventure-tour operators in New Zealand showed that the biggest dangers to adventure travelers were falling from a moving vehicle or animals. Only about 5 percent of foreign travelers have a mishap on vacation. The chance of having a real adventure on an adventure trip is . . . well, pretty remote. Well, okay, if you insist on pressing us for lurid details, there is one mishap you can be pretty sure of experiencing on your next adventure vacation. Now sit down, because chances are, that's what you will be doing a lot of. . . .

The only guaranteed discomfort adventurers will experience is that mad dash to sit and ponder the world's great and varied selection of porcelain evacuation devices, a hacking cough picked up from sucking Pakistani bus exhaust, and maybe the occasional sunburn. (How come James Bond and Indiana Jones never have the runs?)

Where are the destinations that deliver on the promise of adventure? When it comes to where you can get Delhi Belly, Tut's Trot, or Montezuma's revenge, there are no surprises here. India (60% of travelers), Egypt (53%), and Mexico (40%) are the best places to get the runs. The most likely problems affecting travelers to tropical places are diarrhea or intestinal problems, with about 25 to 40 percent of travelers

## TRAVEL ILLNESSES

A 2-year survey of 784 Americans traveling overseas in 123 countries discovered that 64 percent had some kind of illness. Oddly, women were more likely to get ill. And each day of travel increased the chance of getting ill by 3 to 4 percent.

| | |
|---|---|
| Diarrhea | 46% |
| Travelers' Diarrhea | 34 |
| Respiratory Illness | 26 |
| Skin Disorder | 8 |
| Acute Mountain Sickness | 6 |
| Motion Sickness | 5 |
| Accidents and Injuries | 5 |

*Source: Journal of Travel Medicine*
http://www.istm.org

being afflicted. Sunburn affects about 10 percent, with the Caribbean and Mexico being the most likely places to get fried. Malaria affects a minuscule number of travelers. Only about 1,036, or about .0000345 percent, of the 30 million U.S. residents who travel abroad have contracted the mosquito-borne parasite. About 3 percent of those cases were fatal. Interesting statistic: Out of the 600 million people who travel, only about 8 percent actually seek pre-trip health advice.

How about buying the farm while on vacation? The Canadians did a study and found that the Canadians who died abroad were likely to be male (71.2%), around 43 years old, and, naturally, most suffered heart attacks (62.1%). A quarter of the deaths were from accidents, 7.8 percent were from murder, and 5.2 percent were suicides. Now compare that to the average of 18 million outbound tourist trips by Canadians in an average year and you have the proverbial fly on the drive-in movie screen statistic. Want to improve your odds of staying healthy and alive? . . . Go on vacation.

*Travel Medicine*
http://www.travmed.com

*Centers for Disease Control and Prevention*
http://www.cdc.gov

*Morbidity and Mortality Weekly Report*
http://www.cdc.gov/mmwr

*World Heath Organization*
http://www.who.int/en

*WHO Weekly Epidemiological Record*
http://www.who.int/wer

*Travel health resources and links*
http://info.dom.uab.edu/gorgas/geomed/links.html

## IN A DANGEROUS PLACE: PAMPLONA

### RUNNING WITH THE BULLS

*What the hell,* I thought.

"BAM." I heard it again. They were shooting rockets.

I slowly sat up, rubbing my eyes and trying to remember. Where was I? I looked around and saw bodies everywhere, lying in the grass, lying on the benches, lying in the streets, and a few were starting to move. Why were there dead corpses all around me? Why was everyone covered in blood? Why was I covered in blood? My mind was racing from a very, very long night.

Then I remembered. It wasn't a war zone. It was Pamplona. The bodies were not dead. They were passed-out partyers stealing sleep wherever they could, and the blood was red wine spilled from the canvas bags the night before.

I shoved my friend next to me. "Wake up, wake up, the bulls are going to run." He barely moved. Ouch! I tried to stand up only to find that my shoes had somehow been lost in the night and my feet were caked with blood and mud. I didn't care. It was Pamplona and I was going to run with the bulls.

With the burst of the rockets signaling the beginning of the traditional bull run, the bodies lying throughout the city park came to life as if I were watching the raising of the dead. But this was different. Everyone woke with a smile and everyone woke with a drink in hand. Everyone wore the same traditional white attire with red bandanas around their necks. We were all dirty, stinky, and exhausted, but we didn't care. This was Pamplona. The singing and dancing started immediately and soon we were caught up in a tidal wave of people making their way to the cobblestone streets to get a prime viewing spot.

Should we or shouldn't we? We came here to run; we're going to run, we decided. But the last 12 hours of drinking was catching up with us and doubt began to shake my confidence. Fortunately for fate, unlucky for me, we had wasted so much time contemplating that all the viewing spots were gone and we were in the middle of the bare cobblestone street. Looking up in the early morning sun, I could see people, bodies everywhere—hanging from the lampposts, from doorways, sitting on fences, everywhere—but none were in the street. Only the two of us. There was nowhere left to hide. I guess we're running.

Suddenly a wave of screaming people came running up the street behind us. "Run!" my friend shouted. The pressure of sweaty bodies, the stench of stale wine and beer, and my bloody feet just got my adrenaline rushing. We ran, but not fast enough. With the crowd cheering and fellow runners diving for cover, I looked behind me. The bull was gaining on us! I dove for cover under a wood barricade just as the bull came near. As I dove, the bull came crashing down, having slipped on the cobblestone street, sliding close enough that I could touch its leg. I didn't dare. It stood up slowly, getting separated from the pack. The runners remaining stood still surrounding the bull, but he had his eye on me as I lie on the ground halfway under the wooden barricade.

Secure in his safety, high above the street, the man on the fence above me threw a bottle at the bull. This was no ordinary bull; I decided it was the fiercest of the bunch. The provoker was safely out of the bull's reach. I was not.

*Only me, this could only happen to me,* I thought. I frantically tried to get up. The crush of people was too much. I couldn't move. I could have gone back out into the street, but I didn't dare. I was fascinated by the sight of the bull, yet absolute terror enveloped me. For a moment in time, it seemed as though it was him versus me. There was nobody else around. As he lowered his massive neck and blew out his nostrils, I knew I was doomed. He ran toward me and WHAM, he hit the barricade right above my head with such force it knocked the bottle-thrower off the barricade and onto my back. The bull pulled back as if to charge again, people screamed, but I was still facedown in the cobblestone street. Just as the bull was going to charge again, something else caught his attention and he turned, giving us all enough time to reorganize our positions.

Somewhere in those few minutes, a policeman grabbed me and pulled me up with a pat on the back and a smile. "Pamplona," he said. He was right. This was Pamplona. I felt myself breathe again.

*—Ellen Mai*

# WHAT DANGER AWAITS THE WEARY TRAVELER?

## Be Afraid, Be Very Afraid . . . Not

So is travel dangerous? Not really. It's hard to sell people on the idea of weekend expeditions to your local Wal-Mart as the most dangerous form of travel, but it's true. If you believe the doom and gloom of the statistics, Death is not a Chechen terrorist but instead comes up softly on the bunny-slippered. Your mother was right . . . always wear clean underwear 'cuz you never know how, when, or where you are going to meet your maker. But chances are, you will die at home.

When it comes to travel, common sense usually prevails (I said, usually). Strangely, people still buy bus tours to Yemen, there are still sex tourists in Thailand, and both Uganda's gorillas and guerrillas are still amused by hordes of Tilley-hatted ecotourists. The message is that travel can be dangerous if you want it to be, and it can be very safe if you want it to be. Even in a war zone, which these days seems to be everywhere except New Zealand or Greenland.

The frightening statistics and stories of tourist misfortune we are bombarded with must be compared with the staggering numbers of tourists out there at any one time. Even in a down year, well over half a billion tourists or travelers wander around the world. That's a lot of money belts, white shoes, toaster-sized video cameras, and cream-of-mushroom legs. In the mid-1800s, Thomas Cook started the package tour and the race to despoil and photograph our Earth was on. Railroads, steamships, buses, hotels, restaurants, and prices sprang up to accommodate strangers, and, other than a couple of World Wars, tourism was rapidly growing to become the world's largest industry. Oddly enough, before Cook perfected tourism, travel guides had a remarkable similarity to *DP*, providing tips on how to load muskets, tie up prisoners, and slaughter pack animals.

In 1955, there were only 46 million people traveling from one country to another. Most of them were well-heeled folks "doing the Continent" or "taking the sun." Ninety percent of tourists visited just 15 countries back then, and all were considered "civilized." People like Eugene Fodor, Temple Fielding, and Arthur Frommer braved cheap hotels, pushy gondoliers, and bad breakfasts in an attempt to take the adventure out of travel.

Ten years later, there were 144 million, and today, there are almost 700 million. By 2010 the number is supposed to top 1 billion. That's a lot of wheeled luggage. These travelers spend an annual fortune of $455 billion. This massive horde also means you read a lot more about misfortune, illness, and death. It also looks like it's only going to get more crowded out there, so c'mon, everybody, let's move to the rear of the bus to make some room, and pass me that article on "Vacations from Hell." The truth? An average of 26 Americans have been killed per year by terrorists overseas. This doesn't even come close to the number of Americans killed in the U.S. by terrorists. September 11 reduced global travel by a minuscule 0.6 percent, according to the WTO.

> **Y**our mother was right... always wear clean underwear 'cuz you never know how, when, or where you are going to meet your maker.

Besides overcrowding, what do those half a billion people worry about when they travel? Most worry about high prices, dirty accommodations, and safety, in that order. There are plenty of guides that talk about price and quality, but how come they never talk about safety? I don't mean reminding you to lock your door at night, but exactly how many tourists are killed, raped, robbed, thumped, stabbed, infected, crashed, burnt, or drowned? Well, stupid . . . publicizing that information is bad for tourism. Yes, there are travel guides that don't mention the rebel bombing campaign, ignore the crime wave, and conveniently omit the corrupt cops. Well, actually *most* of them sluff off the ugly stuff because . . . that's right . . . you get the point by now. It's bad for tourism. Egypt lost an estimated $1 billion in tourist revenue after the attacks on tourists.

The European Travel Monitor estimates that 3 percent of all travelers had been victims of serious offenses. The most common incidents were car break-ins, handbag thefts, money-exchange rip-offs, and plain old theft. When visitors to Australia were queried about their fears, 43 percent said they would be concerned in New York (pre-9/11) and only 2 percent had any concerns about safety when visiting Australia. Yet the chances are higher for death from drowning and road accidents in Australia than in Disney-clean New York. The truth? A minuscule 2.3 percent experienced any problems, with harassment as the major crime in Oz, and the large percentage experienced it in Sydney and King's Cross, an area known for nightclubs and drunken carousing. So apply the "Duh" factor when fearing a place.

Younger independent travelers seem to be more at risk than older bus tourists or families—and hotels are safer than hostels or other forms of lodging. Back in the bad old days of '93 when the media decided that Southern Florida was the American version of Somalia, they still figured that you still had only a .01 percent chance of getting into trouble.

The sad fact is that there are no comparative statistics on country or travel safety, so there is no way for a traveler to learn the relative safety of a destination. In addition, many tourists do not report crimes and even fewer ever return to prosecute. Sure, you can call up our beloved government, or the government of the country of destination, and even high-priced, think-tank, security companies such as Pinkerton or Control Risks, but you will draw a blank. You'll get a helpful list of oil workers kidnapped in Colombia, Germans who contracted HIV, English travelers who came down with malaria, and so forth, but no one can give you the big picture. There is even a disturbing trend of crooks who follow the directions supplied in popular Western guidebooks because they know they will meet plenty of rubbernecking yuppies with bulging money belts at the ends of remote trails. Don't feel too bad: I lost all my luggage when it was stolen from my parked car at . . . the Vatican. So consider theft as your part to stimulate the economy from the bottom up.

Tourism means money. Money means overdevelopment. Massive overdevelopment means plenty of unemployed. Unemployment breeds crime. Tourists bring lots of money, are easier to hunt than pigeons with popcorn, and have that goofy, cross-eyed, deer-in-the-headlights look when you wave a kitchen knife under their nose. Cheap hotels, cheap bars, and even cheaper tourists now crowd the south of Europe, Mexican beaches, budget Caribbean islands, and even meccas like Torremolinos, Daytona Beach, Cancun, Las Vegas, and Branson. The migratory arrival of pendulous grannies, knob-kneed welders, screaming kids, and haggard housewives now creates an instant feeding frenzy. Every gaggle of tourists seems to have a remora-like retinue of snotty-nosed beggars, clapped-out hookers, gold-toothed cops, nimble-fingered teenagers, and math-challenged bartenders. Tourism breeds crime. You won't find any statistics on crime against tourists in Antigua, Barbuda, Cuba, Jamaica, or Haiti 'cause it's bad for tourism. So understand a basic premise of tourist crime: Tourists are walking cash machines and the only place you are ever going to see crime statistics against tourists is where you are least likely to find crime.

http://www.fbi.gov/hq/cjisd/ucrstat.htm
http://www.lawlink.nsw.gov.au/bocsar1.nsf/pages/media160299
http://www.touristvictimsupport.ie/statistics.html
http://www.safetymaps.com

## BY CRIKEY, WATCH IT, MATE, THAT'S DAINJUHRUS!

Australians state that tourists are more likely than locals to die in car accidents. Twice as likely, according to the Ministry of Transport and Regional Services. Fifty percent didn't wear their seatbelts, compared to 38 percent of locals. Still, out of the 4 million overseas visitors, only 70 are expected to die in on-road accidents. The other killer? Drunk tourists who step off the curb expecting traffic to be coming from the opposite direction. Most of these accidents are associated with alcohol use by either party.

*Source:* Australian Transport Safety Bureau at 1-800-020-616; atsbinfo@atsb.gov.au.

**NUMBER OF DEATHS PER BILLION BASED ON ONE HOUR OF RISK EXPOSURE**

The University of Oregon thought they would get cute and figure out what your chances of dying would be based on length of exposure to various activities.

| Activity | Deaths |
|---|---|
| Being vaccinated | 1.3 |
| Living in an area where snakes are present | 3.8 |
| Traveling by rail or bus travel in the United States | 10 |
| Traveling by rail or bus travel in Britain | 50 |
| Sleeping in a crib (child) | 140 |
| Boxing in an amateur match | 450 |
| Climbing stairs | 550 |
| Mining coal | 910 |
| Hunting | 950 |
| Traveling by car | 1,200 |
| Traveling by airplane | 1,450 |
| Smoking a cigarette | 2,600 |
| Boating | 3,000 |
| Swimming | 3,650 |
| Riding a motorcycle | 6,280 |
| Serving in Vietnam | 7,935 |
| Canoeing | 10,000 |
| Racing a motorcycle | 35,000 |
| Climbing a mountain | 40,000 |
| Boxing professionally | 70,000 |
| Being born | 80,000 |

*Source:* University of Oregon

# Stylin' by the Deadly Mile

Now, despite the lack of stats on tourist crime, there is a preponderance of studies on the relative safety of transportation methods. Once you get to that crime-infested place, you are on your own. Usually these studies focus on countries where they don't have to clear the livestock off the runways before you land, or regions where the white things in the middle of the road aren't the corpses of dead people. Once again, this is akin to conducting STD surveys in convents. But at least it gives you an idea of the relative safety of various modes of transportation, although keep in mind that the relative safety of a bus trip through Wisconsin cannot quite be matched up with taking the bus through Afghanistan.

It is still important to do the math on the relative dangers of travel. The very definition of *travel* requires you to choose between some form of transportation. These are official U.S. statistics, numbers that reflect one of the safest transportation systems in the world. But what about the more typical forms of transportation that adventurers will be forced to use? Here are some U.S. statistics.

| Type of Passenger Transport | Death Rate (per billion passenger miles) | Passenger Miles (in billions) |
|---|---|---|
| Passenger Cars | .89 | 2393.2 |
| Intercity Buses | .03 | 23.7 |
| Transit Buses | .01 | 20.6 |
| Trains | .02 | 13.5 |
| Airplanes | .01 | 354.3 |

**Association for Safe International Road Travel**
http://www.asirt.org

**Comparison of International Fatality Rates**
http://www.general.monash.edu.au/muarc/fatals/fatals.htm

**U.N. Traffic Safety Report (Europe and North America)**
http://www.unece.org

**National Transportation Safety Board**
http://www.ntsb.gov

**Road Safety Statistics—Europe**
http://www.unece.org/trans/roadsafe/rslin.html

**United Kingdom Department for Transport—Road Accidents**
http://www.transtat.detr.gov.uk/roadsafe

## Minibuses

I would have to say after a lifetime of having my knees wrapped around my neck and turbaned men drooling sound asleep on my shoulder that the most dangerous form of travel in the third world is the fabled minibus. These are usually small Japanese-made transports that were originally designed to haul a family of 4, but ingenuity and greed prevails, and some will pack up to 16 passengers in one minibus. The minibuses are used primarily for rush-hour transportation of poor people going to work. Unlike the large, regulated buses, minibuses are run by entrepreneurs who make their money by carrying as many

> I would have to say after a lifetime of having my knees wrapped around my neck and turbaned men drooling sound asleep on my shoulder that the most dangerous form of travel in the third world is the fabled minibus.

people as many times as they can. The deadly driving style is a result of drivers who must make their money within the two hours of rush hour in order to make a profit on their rental owner's charge.

So the minibus may look like the one your neighbor drives with Slurpee stains and soccer-cleat marks in the carpet, but in Pakistan it's typically uglier, older, loaded with people, going 60 miles an hour, and weaving through donkeys, cow poop, and trucks. And while we are painting a mental picture here, imagine the driver stoned on hash, the windows covered with stickers, the tires having cords showing through, the brakes having worn out last year, and an identical mechanism of death heading at a higher rate of speed directly toward you.

So when Achmed turns to wave at Abdul, the kabob vendor, he doesn't quite catch Wali heading at a combined 120 miles an hour toward him. Now, at this point, skill, luck, and religion have deserted you. Only the law of physics and anatomy are in charge. As the two buses collide, your body decelerates from 60 miles an hour to zero in 2 milliseconds. Although the buses have stopped, Newtonian physics compel you through the non-safety plateglass window out into the bustling traffic, and into the crowd of the gawking bystanders who quickly surround your battered, bleeding body to scoop up your wallet and valuables. Not a pretty story. Having been at the site of many bus crashes in my travels, I can best compare the scene to putting a dozen mice in a coffee can along with glass and nails, slamming it against a wall, and then shaking it for a few minutes more. Then spray the bloody contents across the path of oncoming traffic.

There is no clear dividing line between minibuses and buses because they all seem to share the same high passenger count, accident rate, and lack of safety features. I'm sure you will never imagine yourself on one of these rickety, belching conveyances, but the first time you need to get from point A to B in countries where gum and deodorant are considered luxury items, you will indeed find yourself on one.

## PERHAPS IF HE HAD JUST HELD UP HIS MIDDLE FINGER . . .

Just outside Capetown, South Africa, a half-naked 21-year-old Welsh tourist was found bruised, scraped, and bleeding on a highway—missing his pants. While being taken to a hospital he said he had fallen out of the rear of the bus while it was traveling at full speed. It appears he had been drinking and decided to pull his pants off to moon passing motorists. The enthusiastic pressure of his rear end against the window popped the emergency-exit device and he suddenly found himself in the middle lane of a busy highway.

A survey by an English paper found 60 "bus plunges" that caused nearly 1,300 deaths, a number equal to all the air-passenger deaths worldwide. A quarter of these accidents were in India. In Peru, where they are called "killer combis," the death toll also includes nonpassengers trying to get out of the way of weaving, speeding vans. A rough estimate puts the chances of a fatality in a minibus, *matatu*, or *combi* at about 30 times the normal U.S. accident rate. To be fair, in the first world minibuses and buses are from two to three times safer than cars, but then again I don't remember a lot of cops, journalists, or statisticians at the bus crashes I have witnessed.

So when you enter the lands of diesel and dung, keep in mind that there is a reason for the multitude of religious symbols, slogans, and prayers painted on third world buses. Once they shove their doors shut and the wobbly wheels start forward, your life is in the hands of a supreme being.

**Bus Plunge!**
http://users.lanminds.com/tcs55

## HOW TO SURVIVE MINIBUSES

If you travel via small buses, remember the following:

- Don't travel at night. Many bus lines run at night because it is cooler and the road is less crowded. Drunks, rebels, livestock, and hidden washouts all seem to be more prevalent. Local drivers also like to sleep at this time, usually while they are driving.
- Avoid mountainous areas and/or winter conditions. Fly if necessary.
- Bring water and food with you; plan for the unexpected, delays, and diversions.
- Ask whether your desired route goes through areas frequented by bandits or terrorist groups. You may be surprised to find out who controls the countryside in between major cities.
- Sit near an exit or on top. At least make sure you are near an open window.
- Follow the *DP* rule: Be friends with everyone: Your seatmate might be a rebel commander.
- There is a reason why you paid only 23¢ to travel halfway across the country. You don't pay for a lot of brake pads and clutches with that pocket change.
- Remember your rooftop luggage is prey for rummagers, slashers, and thieves. Make your luggage less attractive by hiding it in a standard trash bag, a canvas duffle, or under everyone else's.
- Shirt-slashers wait for you to doze off so they can slip out your money pouches. Put your money in your shoes if necessary.

# Taxis

In many traveling destinations, taxis are not necessarily dangerous from an accident point of view, but they can be dangerous from a criminal point of view. We are at our most vulnerable when we take cabs. We look like perfect pigeons at the airport or hotel, dressed like an Eddie Bauer catalog, struggling with our luggage, reading out of a new phrase book, asking stupid questions like, "Senor, how mucha toa da Forum, eh?" The driver simply moves his toothpick to the other side of his stubble-surrounded mouth, does that shrug, and smiles, "As you like."

You have now entered the cabbie zone, where prices, distances, cost, and time have no relationship to reality. Don't even pull out that new currency converter or download that map on your PDA. You're screwed. Had you simply pointed to the address on the map and had him write down the cost next to it, you could have avoided that $500 fine his cousin, the policeman, hit you with for cheating a cabdriver.

Are cabbies bad guys? Sure, if you let them be. Cabdrivers can be your best friend or your worst enemy, so think carefully about how you treat them. I always ask the cabdriver about his family, the weather, and places to see, and compliment him on his rusting place of business—even if I don't speak the language. Also, plenty of people hail cabs in Mexico and get thumped in an alley, and plenty of backpackers jump in trishaws and are delivered straight to the door of armed men. But that's only because they didn't take the time to ask someone at the hotel, airport, food market, or hostel the best way to get around. Those who do find that cabbies will guard their property, wait around all day, take them to lunch, and even act as unpaid tour guides. Or you can keep in mind that walking is 17 times more dangerous than driving.

**Random Transportation Disaster Generator**
http://www.mindspring.com/~atticus/busplunge

**TACTICS: Private Investigations and International Investigator**
http://www.tacticsone.com

## HOW TO SURVIVE TAXIS

- Choose your cab rather than let it choose you. Inspect the car first. Many are just shills for drivers on the outside. Hire the oldest cabbie or the one with the least damage to his car.
- Ask staff at the airport how much the ride should cost to go to your city. Inquire about other methods of transportation.

(continued)

- Always agree on a total fare first and write the price down and show it to the driver. Ask about luggage, airport, or time-of-day surcharges.
- Keep your luggage in the backseat, not in the trunk.
- Memorize the local words for "no," "yes," "stop here," and "how much?"
- Have the hotel doorman or guide negotiate cab fares in advance when seeing the city. Many private cars also function as taxis, so don't be surprised if a kind person who picks you up wants money.
- It is a global law that cabbies never carry change. Change money at the airport or hotel first.
- Many cabbies will rent themselves out for flat fees. Do not be afraid to negotiate the services of a trusted cabby as guide, chauffeur, and protector of baggage.
- Try to establish a rapport with your driver and he may end up being your best tour guide.

## Automobiles

If you believe accident statistics, then you would subscribe to the idea that the place you are most likely to meet misfortune is on the road. You need to know that 70 percent of road accidents happen in developing countries. Worldwide, half a million people are killed and 15 million are injured in traffic and road mishaps. Smart travelers know that traveling from a country where cars have seat belts, air bags, and padded dashes to regions where the safety equipment is reduced to a cracked statue of an indeterminate saint probably increases the risks of having an accident.

International accident rates for travel are clouded by lack of reporting by the large numbers of people who die in vehicle-related accidents and don't have the courtesy to fill out the paperwork after they are dead. Countries like Turkey, Mexico, Pakistan, Australia, India, Egypt,

### SUCK ON THIS!

The World Health Organization, ever eager to come up with a new statistical cause for concern, has decided that more people die from car exhaust than road accidents. In WHO data gathered from Austria, France, and Switzerland alone, it was estimated that exposure to pollution caused an estimated 21,000 deaths a year. The researchers also calculated that car emissions caused 300,000 extra cases of bronchitis in children and 15,000 extra hospital admissions for heart disease exacerbated by pollution.

and China have horrendous accident rates but do not figure prominently in studies.

Countries like Afghanistan, Somalia, Cambodia, and French Guiana wish they had enough cars or roads to have accidents. There is also an odd sleight of hand that compares deaths per mile of road to deaths per population total. Both methods have their pitfalls when determining the dangers on the road.

Here's what your chances are like outside of the country:

## DEATHS (PER 100 MILLION KILOMETERS DRIVEN)

| | | | |
|---|---|---|---|
| Egypt | 43.2 | Bahrain | 3.2 |
| Kenya | 36.0 | New Zealand | 2.2 |
| South Korea | 29.0 | Israel | 2.2 |
| Turkey | 22.0 | Taiwan | 2.0 |
| Morocco | 21.0 | France | 2.0 |
| Yemen | 12.4 | Germany | 1.9 |
| Austria | 10.7 | Japan | 1.7 |
| South Africa | 10.4 | Switzerland | 1.6 |
| Bulgaria | 9.9 | Ireland | 1.5 |
| Portugal | 9.0 | Denmark | 1.5 |
| Hungary | 8.0 | Finland | 1.4 |
| Macedonia | 7.8 | Thailand | 1.3 |
| Poland | 6.3 | Netherlands | 1.3 |
| Czech Republic | 5.9 | Norway | 1.2 |
| Spain | 5.9 | United States | 1.1 |
| Hong Kong | 4.8 | Sweden | 1.1 |
| Belgium | 3.3 | United Kingdom | 1.0 |

*Source:* IRF, NSC, others (various years)

*International Road Traffic and Accident Database (OECD)*
http://www.bast.de/htdocs/fachthemen/irtad/english/we2.html

You can find a number of conflicting and downright wrong traffic death statistics because the places with the worst drivers and roads . . . well, they just don't give a damn. They have more important things to worry about, like eating, so it is important not only to view statistics as sketchy, but also to at least feel confident that what appears to be bad driving is, actually, bad driving. The conditions under which you are driving have more of an influence than the country you are in. Alcohol, nighttime, high speeds, and bad weather are far more dangerous than cabbing it in Egypt or India. Oh, and if you think you are safe at home in the United States, just remember that it is estimated that after

## HOW TO SURVIVE AUTOMOBILES

There is little to be said that hasn't been said in every driver's education class. Speed, booze, bad roads, and other drivers kill. Driving in poor countries is not safe.

- Be familiar with local road warning signs and laws.
- Avoid driving yourself if possible. A local driver may add a few gray hairs but is conversant with local laws, shortcuts, and safety matters. Then again, maybe he isn't.
- Avoid driving in inclement weather conditions, at nighttime, or, especially, on weekends. Fog kills, rain kills, drunks kill, and other tourists kill.
- Stay off the road in high-risk countries. You may think the Italians, Portuguese, and Spaniards display amazing bravado as they skid around winding mountain roads. The accident rate says they are just lousy drivers who haven't been killed yet.
- Reduce your speed. This is your biggest edge in staying alive.
- Wear a seat belt, rent bigger cars, drive during daylight, use freeways, carry a map, and a good road guide, etc. You're not listening, are you?
- Don't drive at night. You would be surprised what sleeps on the road in the tropics. Most locals never venture outside after dark, let alone drive. In many Central Asian and former Soviet republics drinking and driving is common. I could go on, but you've probably skipped this part, haven't you?
- Don't drive when tired or while suffering from jet lag. Don't pull off to the side of the road to nap, don't leave possessions in plain sight, and try to park in lighted areas. I can see you're not listening, so just do whatever the hell you are going to do, but don't say I didn't warn you.

midnight on Friday and Saturday nights in rural America, three out of five drivers on the road have been drinking. That means if you are one of the sober ones, pray that the only other sober driver is coming the other way.

**U.S. State Department—Overseas Road Safety**
http://travel.state.gov/road_safety.html#stats

**National Transportation Safety Board**
http://www.ntsb.gov/Surface/Highway/highway.htm

**Road Rage and Aggressive Driving—Interpretations**
http://www.aloha.net/~dyc/surveys/interpretations.html

**Association for Safe International Road Travel**
http://www.asirt.org

## Boats

Boats are not inherently dangerous; it's what the operators do with them that make them deadly. Most of the problems can be boiled down to bad weather and overcrowding. Some parts of the world offer more waterborne transportation than land-based. Whether it's tropical archipelagoes like Indonesia or the Philippines or ferries in Hong Kong, the United Kingdom, or Senegal, people get around on boats. Unlike those for planes and cars, there are few helpful statistical heads-ups on boat safety. There are some countries that don't even require enough lifeboats for the number of passengers. Others simply convert cargo ships designed for 12 passengers to carry 700. *DP* safety tips? Emergency exits? Sure, just jump over the side. Sleeping in steerage with 500 other people and one unlit exit when the boat sinks? Uh, let me get back to you on that one. Countries like the United States have rules and inspectors. Sort of. You should know that the majority of U.S. passenger vessels that operate within 20 miles of shore and inland waterways are allowed to carry passengers without enough lifeboats and rafts for everyone, should they sink. Some have as few as will carry 20 percent of the maximum number of passengers allowed. There's a sequel for *Titanic* in there somewhere. In Seattle, where Starbucks-sloshed, fleece-decked ferry commuters confidently sail to and from work every day, there is a third-world attitude toward marine safety. Most of the ferries have equipment to keep only 25 percent of the passengers out of the frigid Puget Sound waters should one sink. Luckily, one never has. The Coast Guard says that in the United States there were 88 fatalities on boats carrying 7 or more passengers in a 30-year period.

The conclusion is that Stateside and in Canada there is little to fear other than a rough crossing. Going overseas, things change.

Ferries in places like Estonia, Haiti, the Philippines, and Hong Kong have had major disasters from capsizing due to overloading and collision. In roughly an 8-year period around the world, there were more than 360 ferryboat accidents killing 11,350 people. Yet ocean travel in large ships is so safe they don't even keep death statistics. Over 6 million people travel on 500 or so ships every year without major loss of life or incident.

## WHO YA GONNA CALL?

Next time you take that dive boat out to Dead Man's Key and spot a speedboat of do-ragged, AK-toting squinty-eyes heading your way, don't bother calling 911. Marine Risk Management (MRM) will send in aircraft to drop Rapid Response teams to the site of your next hijacking and make everything nice again. Hoo yah.

**Marine Risk Management, Piracy Rapid Response Service**
Victoria House
Victoria Mount, Oxton
CH43 5TH, UK
Tel.: (44) (0)151 652 5545
Fax: (44) (0)151 652 0040
Information@marinerisk.com
http://www.marinerisk.com

Those who fancy the life of Joseph Conrad should also know that piracy is still a fact of life in Southeast Asia and other parts of the world. Piracy attacks are primarily against large commercial vessels but are becoming more of a threat to both private and commercial sailors every year. Most pirates, armed with submachine guns, use small speedboats to jump the slow-moving vessels and then commandeer the craft to a safe harbor where they unload the tons of cargo. The major activity centers are in the waters around the Philippines, Thailand, Indonesia, Sri Lanka, Nicaragua, Somalia, Brazil, Sierra Leone, and the Mediterranean. Indonesia has the highest number of piracy incidents; Bangladesh is second, Somali, the Indian Ocean, Latin America, and the Caribbean are next on the list.

**Maritime Security**
http://www.maritimesecurity.com

**Project on Insurgency, Terrorism, and Security/Piracy**
http://paladin-san-francisco.com

**United States Coast Guard**
http://www.uscg.mil/uscg.shtm

**National Transportation Safety Board**
http://www.ntsb.gov/Surface/marine/marine.htm

**Modern-Day Piracy Statistics**
http://www.tortuga.myweb.nl/archive/modern/figures.htm

**ICC**
http://www.iccwbo.org

## HOW TO SURVIVE BOATS

It is difficult to provide general safety tips considering the wide range of waterborne craft travelers can take. Large cruise ships have very different safety problems when compared to pirogues. Here is a starting list.

- Know how to swim, or at least how to float. Panic kills.
- Have quick access to a life preserver. Don't assume that the large chest labeled "Life Preservers" actually has usable life preservers in it. Look. And find the unlocked one. (You are always better off in a lifeboat because of cold water or sharks.)

- Do not take overcrowded boats. (Gee, thanks for the tip.) Charter your own or ask when the boat will be less crowded.
- Avoid travel in rough weather, or during monsoon or hurricane season. (Keep it up, you too can write your own survival book.)
- Stay off the water in areas frequented by pirates. This applies even to pleasure excursions in places like the southern Philippines, Somalia, Borneo, and Thailand.
- In cold weather, remember where the covered life rafts are and if there are exposure suits available. Understand the effects and prevention of hypothermia.
- On large ships, pay attention to safety and lifeboat briefings.
- Practice going from your cabin to the lifeboat station with your eyes closed.
- Keep a small carry-on or backpack with your money, papers, and minor survival gear (water, energy bars, hat, compass, and map). Make it waterproof and add a potential life preserver by using one or two garbage bags as a liner. Most rescues occur within 24 hours.
- Prepare and bring items to prevent seasickness, sunburn, glare, and chapped skin.

### AHOY, THERE, MATEY!

*Targets for Pirates*

| | |
|---|---|
| Tankers | 25% |
| Cargo Vessels | 23% |
| Fishing Vessels | 16% |
| Bulk Carriers | 13% |
| Uncategorized Coastal Vessels and Yachts | 12% |
| Container Vessels | 11% |

## THE ORIGINAL SURVIVOR: A GOLD WATCH BUT NO GREEN CARD

Poon Lim spent 133 days drifting around the South Atlantic. Chinese-born Poon was 25 when he was torpedoed on the SS *Ben Lomond,* en route from Cape Town to what is now Surinam in South America. On November 23, 1942, a U-boat sank the *Ben Lomond* off the northern coast of Brazil. Poon jumped in the water with his life vest and after two hours found an empty life raft. The 8-foot-square raft was made from wood and had tins of biscuits, a 10-gallon water tank, flares, and a flashlight.

Poon was passed over by a number of ships and airplanes, so he came up with a survival plan. First, he used the canvas from his life jacket to collect

(continued)

rainwater. Then he used the spring inside the flashlight and nails from the raft to make fishhooks. The biscuits became bait and hemp rope became fishing line. Tired of fish, he then lured seagulls onto the boat with the leftover fish, and then used the seagull carcasses to attract sharks. He then drank the blood of the shark (from its liver) and even took time every day to swim around his raft. He was rescued on April 5, 1943.

Despite being at sea for 133 days, he had lost only 33 pounds and became the star of a U.S. Navy survival film. The British gave him a medal, Truman created a special law to make him a permanent U.S. resident, and he was given a gold watch by his former employer, the shipping line.

After the war Poon wanted to emigrate to the United States but he didn't make it past the 105 quota. He was denied citizenship.

## Flying

A lot people hate flying. In this country, 20 percent are afraid to fly and 7 percent will not fly at all. It is assumed that the other 73 percent are just lying or acting tough. From the moment they grasp their airline seat with sweaty palms, to when their cab rolls to a stop at their front door, most travelers have a nervous feeling that their life has become more dangerous. The reality is quite the opposite. In one year, the same numbers of people are killed by lightning as by plane crashes. Even with the 9/11 crashes, air transportation deaths actually went down. It is even more telling that among the top 10 aircraft disasters, most occurred when the planes were shot or blown out of the skies or while taxiing on the ground. Another interesting statistic from the NTSB says that in 568 commercial-airplane accidents between 1983 and 2000, 96 percent of those on board survived. Even in 26 serious accidents, 56 percent survived.

So view any statistical journey into aircraft danger as proof of the relative safety of this modern marvel. A British study shows that flying is 176 times safer than walking, 15 times safer than car travel, and 300 times safer than riding a motorcycle. Statistically, if you were to take a flight every morning, you would have to fly for 21,000 years before you would have a deadly crash. There are 12,000 (some say 9,000) airliners in the sky making over 15 million flights carrying 1.3 billion passengers. With all that activity, there are only about 40 accidents involving major airlines (including cargo planes) every year. Still, the volume of air traffic and the emerging travel boom in Asia has prompted Boeing to say that there will be a major air crash every week by the year 2010. A dramatic statement, but that still means only 12 more accidents a year at a time when there will be twice as many airliners in operation.

## First-World Roulette

Remember we told you that fewer accidents happen to people when they travel than when they are at home? Why? Well, think of whom you trust your life to when you travel. If you survive the cab ride (do you really fasten your seat belt, and do you really believe your driver has a license?), you'll arrive in a well-designed, safe terminal complete with sprinklers, emergency exits, and in many cases on-site medical staff. (Does your house have this?) When you board the plane, you enter a multimillion-dollar aircraft, the culmination of more than 100 years of aviation-safety engineering. Every element and every part of the craft is regulated, inspected, maintained, and replaced. Up front, you have two pilots who are the best of their kind. Every commercial pilot in America has gone through intensive training and regular retraining to stay in top form. You are given flight safety procedures by individuals trained in emergency situations, first aid, and other life-saving procedures. After you are aloft you are now under the control of a global traffic network that tracks all major aircraft and weather patterns using a network of computers and fail-safe devices.

Here are some more stats: If you fly any first-world airline, your chances of being killed in a crash are 1 in 4.4 million, according to MIT. If you are on a U.S. carrier, flying coast to coast, the odds are even better, 1 in 11 million. When you change from a big bird to a puddle-jumper you have just increased your chances of crashing by a factor of four. Commuter flights (flights with 30 or fewer seats) carry about 12 percent of all passengers. These small planes not only fly lower and take off and land more often, they are piloted by less-experienced, more overworked pilots and are not subject to the same safety standards as large airliners.

Get on a smaller private plane or a charter and the odds multiply again. About 700 people die in small plane crashes each year in the United States. There are so many crashes that the small airplane industry has almost evaporated because of the resultant litigation. There are 650,000 private pilots in the United States and only 700 out of the 13,000 airfields have control towers.

Why do small planes crash? The main reasons include running out of fuel, misjudging altitude, and not being experienced in challenging conditions. The government says pilot error is responsible for over two-thirds of general aviation accidents, killing about 560 people every year. Simply put: Small planes are 24 times more dangerous than commercial planes. And 70 percent of the 219,000 planes in the United States are single-propeller planes. But safety is improving, with only 7 accidents reported for every 100,000 flight-hours. Twice as good as 10 years ago.

## DANGEROUS TRIPS

Things look a little different when you eliminate the miles covered and focus on the accident rate based on the number of hours one is exposed to a form of transportation. Then again, would you rather walk across Somalia or fly over it?

| Means of Transport | Hours Exposed Before Accident Predicted to Occur |
|---|---|
| Motorcycle | 300.0 |
| Bicycle | 60.0 |
| Walking | 20.0 |
| Automobile | 15.0 |
| Airplane | 15.0 |
| Intercity Bus | 6.6 |
| Train | 4.8 |
| Transit Bus | 0.1 |

Source: Royal Society for the Prevention of Accidents
http://www.rospa.co.uk/CMS

Commercial aircraft have an average accident rate of .2 accidents for every 100,000 flight-hours.

# Third-World Roulette

Something's bugging you. It's okay, I know exactly what you are going to say. All this good news about flying . . . and yet it is still covered in *DP*. So what is the bad news? Well, the U.S.-based Flight Safety Foundation says that in the last 10 years, 70 percent of all accidents involved only 16 percent of air-traffic carriers. A similar statistic exists when safety is examined by region. Over 75 percent of air accidents happen in countries that account for only 12 percent of world air traffic. So the rule of "wrong place, wrong airline" is in full effect. More disturbingly, in this age of high-tech aviation, most deaths (over 50%) still occur because the pilots simply fly their plane and their screaming passengers into the ground. Oops. Somebody pass the Windex up front.

Even U.S. puddle-jumpers are as safe as houses compared to third-world airlines. If you are flying anywhere in Africa, the chances of crashing are multiplied by 20—about the same odds as getting killed in an automobile accident in the States. Some experts calculate the odds of being killed in a plane crash are less than 1 in a million for North America, Canada, and Western Europe, versus 1 in 50,000 for the Dark Continent.

Latin America, the Middle East, Asia, and Eastern Europe follow Africa as the most dangerous areas of the world in which to fly. Some number crunchers say that Eastern Europe has the highest accident

## FATAL ACCIDENTS

|  | (per Hundred Thousand Flights) |
|---|---|
| Africa | 21 |
| Asia | 13 |
| South America | 8 |
| Central America | 8 |
| Europe | 5 |
| North America | 2 |
| Caribbean | 2 |

*Source:* Flight Safety Foundation

rate in the world. It's not surprising, considering that poorer countries fly old aircraft, which are usually purchased from major carriers that have already wrung every useful mile from their abused frames.

There is good news on the eastern horizon. Flying in Russia, after a dismal string of air disasters in the mid-'90s, has actually become safer than flying in America. Once dominated by Aeroflot, the industry broke into 300 different companies. Now 53 percent of the airline business is run by foreign companies, 32 percent is Russian owned, and Aeroflot controls 15 percent of the Russian air-traffic market. Now the shock is that the 8,000 planes that buzz through the Russian sky just seem to actually land more often at their destinations. In 1997, 1998, and 1999, the number of plane crashes per 100,000 flight-hours inside Russia was so low that it was rounded down to zero, according to a French aviation safety expert.

Over the same 3-year period, U.S. plane crash statistics were 0.021, 0.006, and 0.012 respectively per 100,000 flight-hours, while the world averages were 0.080, 0.060, and 0.050 respectively.

Russian planes are typically 10.3 years old versus other airlines' average of 8.7 years. The statistics can be misleading. There just aren't

## SURVIVAL TIPS: THE WORLD'S TOUGHEST FEAR-OF-FLYING SCHOOL

Afraid of flying? Well, it seems the "hair of the dog that bit you" is the best way to overcome that fear. Huh? A study by the American Psychological Association has determined that survivors of air crashes are less afraid of flying than normal frequent flyers. Crash survivors experienced lower levels of stress, less depression or anxiety, and more control.

Unfortunately the survey covered only 40 crash survivors, 20 of whom who were too scared to fill out the survey.

that many people flying anymore. Passenger numbers have dropped 76 percent since 1990.

You might be surprised to learn that things are changing for the better in Asia. Now 65 percent of the planes in the Chinese fleet are Boeings and 20 percent are Airbus jets with 8 A-340s and 20 A-320s on order. Elsewhere in Asia things are improving as well. KAL, whose sterling record of a major crash every year for 5 years did little to improve bookings, spent $30 million with Boeing to teach their pilots new tricks . . . like speaking English, the language of air-traffic controllers worldwide. Another safety tip was to teach Asian copilots to speak up when the plane was crashing. Apparently their cultural training leads them to believe that it's rude to point out that your superior is making a mistake.

So is flying getting safer? You bet. As many people die in airline accidents as die in animal-drawn vehicle mishaps, according to the FAA. In 1946, there were 78 general aviation accidents with 7 fatalities per 100,000 hours of flight time. In 1998, there were 7 accidents and 1 fatality per 100,000 hours. In 1998, there was only 1 death in 41 accidents, or 0.3 crashes and 0.006 fatalities per 100,000 flight hours, according to the National Transportation Safety Board.

Things are getting better on the private side, too, despite the JFK Jr. nosedive. Crashes have dropped in half over the last 20 years, down to 350 a year. There were 37 million private pilots in 1998 who put in the 40 hours to get a license. The FAA issued more than 616,000 flight certificates. In 1998, manufacturers shipped 2,220 planes. Although there are commercial flights permitted out of 300 airports in the States, private pilots fly out of 13,000, which means there is a lot more activity (not as many miles) in the private sector. One tip: Planes with tail wheels have fewer accidents than those with nose wheels.

What should you really worry about? Well, every year about 4,500 passengers are injured by objects falling out of overhead bins.

**Aviation Crashes**
http://www.aviationcrashes.com
    And if you like to watch:
http://www.aviationcrashes.com/movies/
    movies.html

**Airline Accident and Airline Safety
    and Security**
http://www.airsafe.com

**Aviation Safety Network**
http://aviation-safety.net/index.shtml

**Royal Society for the Prevention of
    Accidents**
http://www.rospa.co.uk/CMS

**Aerospace Information, Consultancy,
    and Loss-Adjusting Services**
http://www.airclaims.co.uk

**Air Data Research**
http://www.airsafety.com

**Disaster info, movies, and tips**
http://www.airdisaster.com

*National Transportation Safety Board*
http://www.ntsb.gov/aviation/aviation.htm

*Fear of Flying Clinic*
http://www.fofc.com

*FAA Office of Accident Investigation*
http://www.faa.gov/avr/acri/aaihome.
   htm

## HOW TO SURVIVE FLYING

Despite all the unnerving statistics, if you have a choice of transportation when traveling long distances, jump on a plane. This applies even among the most primitive aviation service providers. Yes, it is dangerous—but not as dangerous as enduring the kaleidoscope of misery and misfortune that awaits you on the ground. *DP* tips:

- Stick to U.S.-based carriers with good safety records.
- Fly between major airports on nonstop flights.
- Avoid bad weather or flying at night.
- You can sit in the back if you want (the rear 10 rows are usually intact in the event of a ground impact, but the passengers usually wind up dead), or above the wing (you may get thrown clear, seat and all), or sitting near an exit (easier egress in case of fire or emergency landing) might be just as advisable.
- Avoid small charter aircraft, dirt strips, and noninstrument fields.
- The smaller the plane, the higher the risk. The poorer the country, same deal, except when foreign carriers operate airplanes in third-world countries.
- Avoid national carriers that are not allowed to fly into the United States.
- Avoid military cargo flights, tagging along on combat missions, or flying over active combat areas.
- Avoid older Soviet- or Chinese-made aircraft or helicopters.
- Keep up on what type of aircraft you will be flying on (U.S. and European are better) and keep in mind that you usually get what you pay for.
- After all else, remember that travel by airliner is the safest method of transportation and that your odds of surviving a plane crash are about 50 percent.

If you are still terrified, remember you can buy flight insurance at 150 airports around the United States. You can get half a million dollars of insurance for $16.65 or you can spend the same amount on 4 stiff drinks. We recommend the former, but usually end up doing the latter.

## Trains

Trains are supposed to be safe. After all, they run on rails, are usually pointed in one direction, and are rumored to be immune to the inclement weather that plagues airplanes, buses, and cars. When trains do hit, they hit hard. Statistics are skewed by large wrecks but, for example, in Europe, a commuter is 25 times more likely to be killed on the road than on a train.

What most people don't know is that most deaths attributed to trains are suicides—people who deliberately kill themselves by being hit by a train. In the United Kingdom, where there are historically 25 to 89 deaths caused by trains in a year, there were 250 to 265 deaths of suicides and trespassers. In the United States in 1998, 536 pedestrians were killed on or beside tracks, compared with 431 at crossings. In 1993, there were 626 deaths from crossing accidents and 523 trespassing deaths along the tracks. This is still statistically irrelevant compared to the 40,000 or so motor vehicle deaths (1 killed every 12 minutes, for stat nuts).

Trains tend to run into substantial objects like trucks stalled on crossings or trains coming the other way. But there are very few accidents compared to cars. So the safety lesson here is: Don't jump in front of trains.

Using the death rate per million miles as a guide, American trains are about twice as dangerous as flying, four times safer than driving, and a lot safer than local buses. If they have a bar car, you can quickly douse your fears as you watch the war-ravaged countryside zip by.

**Bureau of Transportation Statistics**
http://www.bts.gov

**National Transportation Safety Board**
http://www.ntsb.gov/Railroad/railroad.htm

**British Trains**
http://www.railways.dft.gov.uk

**Euro Train Accidents**
http://europa.eu.int/comm/energy_transport/etif/transport_safety/railway_fatalities.html

## HOW TO SURVIVE TRAINS

- Ask locals whether the train is a target for bandits (this is appropriate in Eastern Europe, Russia, Asia, or Africa where terrorists, bandits, and insurgents regularly target trains).
- Beware of Eastern European train routes where thieves are known to ride as passengers. Sleep with the window cracked open to avoid being gassed.
- Stash your valuables in secret spots, making it more difficult for robbers to locate your belongings.
- The back of the train is traditionally the safest area in the event of a collision. Unless, of course, your train is rear-ended.
- Keep your luggage with you at all times if possible. Be nice to the conductor and he will keep an eye out for you.
- Trains are preferable to buses or cars when traveling through mountainous areas, deserts, and jungles.

# Making the Best of Nasty Situations

## Roll Up to the Magical Misery Tour

So now that you know something about *what's* dangerous, let's talk about *where* it's dangerous. There is a point when smarmy travel-safety advice and brutal reality collide, like taking your malaria pill faithfully while walking through a minefield or using a condom when boffing a rebel commander's "socio." You know, like those mountain guides on TV shows who wear the latest Goretex stuff but fall off the face of the mountain? Isn't 99.9 percent of safety advice just pure bull poop and the other .1 percent made up?

Do adventurous people who deliberately travel to dangerous places *really* need to worry about safety?

What could possibly possess normal people to end up in the middle of a war zone? Well, how about the normal desire to explore their world? A world without fast-food, hotels, touts, bus tours, concrete dinosaurs, or even pay toilets. Before Thomas Cook invented the tour, people were hesitant to just head out and wander around. After all, it was dangerous out there. There were criminals, wars, diseases, kidnappers . . . well, you get the point. Things haven't changed much once you explore a little farther off the beaten path. When we meet with victims of overseas tragedy, all of them tell us how safe it was, how much research they did, and how unexpected the whole event turned out to be. In other words, they assumed that intelligence, planning, and dropping a few thou for an adventure tour made them immune from political, criminal, and cultural realities. Our favorite tour company slogan is "Expect the Unexpected," and it just happens to be the heading of an ad in an English magazine that attracted a number of tourists to visit Yemen and end up in the middle of a kidnapping and deadly rescue attempt. Hey, they got their money's worth. The ones who survived, that is.

It is our belief that the truly interesting and educational things on this planet occur in areas of high-intensity living. Places where people warn you not to go. But for Pete's sake, go there expecting danger, not thinking that reading a book somehow vaccinates you against it.

## Dying to Meet You

We spend most of our time in places where people are fighting wars. We don't pretend we can make a major difference, but maybe we can keep a few people safe and help people make heads or tails out of the mess. Warfare is not a bad thing for tourists. It keeps them safe. Our government issues long lists of reasons not to go to places that it considers areas of conflict, but surprisingly, you won't find any information about the safety of our own country posted by our government—and this is a country that has been, and continues to be, at war with a number of nations and movements. This logic therefore includes us as people who live (or travel) in a war zone. But you won't find travel advisories for Wall Street, Oklahoma City, or other areas that have seen deadly episodes and civilian casualties based on violent disagreements with our government.

According to the United Nations, of the 85 or so armed conflicts that were fought in the past 3 years, only 3 were between nations. The rest were civil wars or insurgencies. What the wonks call "low-intensity conflicts." As we went to press there were a mere 39 conflicts festering around the world and our government was itching to start more. Over

4 million civilians have been killed in wars since 1990 and the death toll rises every minute. *The Journal of Peace* states that there are 36 conflicts in 31 places. The National Defense Council says there are around 60 nations currently experiencing warfare, insurgencies, and violence. With so much confusion about where and what is dangerous, there is absolutely no guarantee that you might not be the next casualty. If it helps any, the UN also likes to point out that 90 percent of casualties in today's wars are civilians.

So the first lesson is to not think of war zones as places with yellow "Danger, War in Progress" tape wrapped around them. Many of the countries you might get killed in don't even have names yet. There are somewhere around a couple of hundred countries today—but if you realize that there were only 74 after World War II and only a paltry 62 in 1914, it makes sense to expect that plenty more little nations will continue to break off, creating mayhem and confusion in the process. And maybe even while you are on vacation.

The second important lesson is to remember how wars are fought these days. You won't see long, green lines of nicely uniformed soldiers marching proudly into battle. You won't even see a checkpoint keeping you away from the front lines. In places like Afghanistan, Israel, Russia, and Sri Lanka, ever notice that hotels, cities, and airports are battlefields? And guess who gets caught in the cross fire? Yup. You. Usually while you are enjoying the scenery or reading your flowery, out-of-date guidebook at a quaint café. So "ten hut!" soldier and tighten that Eddie Bauer flak jacket. It's gonna get rough out there.

Various liberation groups around the world are looking for a few good victims and that could include you. Your qualifications? Western, liberal, affluent, on vacation, and in the wrong place at the wrong time? Perfect, you'll do just fine.

**Come Back Alive**
http://www.comebackalive.com

**Overseas Security Advisory Council Database**
http://www.ds_osac.or

**U.S. State Department Travel Warnings**
http://travel.state.gov/travel_warnings.html

# War

### The War on Tourism . . . er . . . Terrorism

*War* is defined as an armed conflict between countries that involves killing and destruction, any serious struggle, argument of conflict between people, and an effort to eradicate something harmful. There are a number of peace groups that carefully collect information on warfare in the silly hope that we will stop whacking each other. In the '90s experts figure there were 108 conflicts, of which only seven were "interstate." The rest were inside countries. That means that they could be described as anything from a police problem to a state of civil war. So how come *DP* found a doofus from Marin County in the middle of the bloodiest battle of the Afghan war? A missionary from Kansas on vacation gets kidnapped and then gunned down in the Philippines, and a British businessman gets kidnapped in Georgia . . . all hot spots in our war on terrorism. Well, the only people who are surprised seem to be the media, but certainly not the readers of *DP*.

Don't believe the hype: War these days seems worse than the WWF. It appears that even though the fighting goes on, nobody wins and everybody pays. Welcome to the post–Cold War world. A less kind, less gentle world at war with endless repeats and a never-changing cast of B-movie bad guy characters. Even our own troops seem to be going into places we were too timid to clean up 20 years ago. Will it end? Of course not.

Aging warlords from Nepal to Colombia are still banging away at each other—for communism, if you can believe it. Islamic radicals don't even bother to mention which country they are fighting for. Their battlefield ranges from Seattle to Washington to East Africa to Indonesia to the Philippines. The causes may have changed, the front lines shifted, but damn, are these people ever going to get their stuff together? It seems like we are stuck with the same '80s teams, playing the same game but locked in sudden death as the leaders get grayer and their countries get more ravaged.

In 1900, there were six democracies and warfare was an accepted part of colonial occupation and old-world politics. In 1980, there were 37 democracies and the USSR was backing anyone with a *kaffiyeh* or flip-flops. In 1998, there were 117 democratic nations, with over half

## HAVE A NICE DAY

The UN figures that 140 out of 200 countries have held multiparty elections. Since 1980, 81 countries have become democratic and 33 military governments have vanished. Since 1990, civil wars have killed 3.6 million people. Today, 2.8 billion folks live on less than $2 a day, and 60 countries have lower per capita income than in 1990.

*Source:* www.UNDP.ORG

of the world's population living in democratic countries. So how come
the National Defense Council (which counts 192 nations) says that we
had 60 conflicts going on in 1998? This is a
drop of 7 since 1997, but a lot more than
the 35 conflicts in 1989. The Center for
Defense Information says the number of
conflicts is in the low 20s. In 1998, it
counted 26. The CIA, which should know
these things, says there are about 25, give
or take a few cruise-missile tests here and
there. *DP* lists about 80 conflicts, and we
are too lazy to list all those tongue-twist-

> **T**he real truth is there are no real wars these days. The world is too interconnected by commerce to allow a real slam-bang, roll the tanks, toe-to-toe, do-or-die war.

ing, unpronounceable Trans-Caucasus cockfights, Somali clan bangs,
or Myanmarese muddles. These days it's hard to tell the difference
between a war and a Middle East wedding.

The real truth is there are no real wars these days. The world is too
interconnected by commerce to allow a real slam-bang, roll the tanks,
toe-to-toe, do-or-die war. Sure, we'll run some tanks around Tikriti,
beach our Zodiacs in Zamboango, or drop some smart bombs in Kunduz, but we are not going to let our boys be bayoneted by some brown-
eyed mother's sons anytime soon. So when you get asked why you are
going to a war zone, just remind them that more people die in road
accidents than wars these days. It's safer.

Why are there no real wars these days? Well, ask yourself, what
would either side do if it actually won? Hell, they might have to pave
the roads, fix the schools, and install crossing lights. So war just seems
like a more sustainable option, and it keeps the people's attention off
the ball and off their empty bellies. That also means fighting can erupt
when you least expect it, and often on your vacation. And in the U.S.
War on Terrorism you can count on being on the front lines whether at
home or on the road. So strap on a sack, you whiner, and get out there!

### The Real War

The sad truth unfolds as you review *DP*: you'll see that most wars
are being fought *inside* countries . . . without fancy weapons, without
uniforms, without any press coverage. In many cases, nary a shot
needs to be fired in order to kill civilians. Starvation, impoverishment,
burning villages, no medical care, and plain old stress tactics can force
people into the grim death spiral of poverty, hunger, and disease.

So for now, expect all these tired, dirty wars to continue for the foreseeable future. Unless we pour mountains of cash on the combatants,
expect them to take pot-shots at each other, starve and torture, recruit

## WHATEVER HAPPENED TO THE GOOD OLD DAYS?

*Civilians Killed by Their Own Governments*

| Country | Death Toll | Year |
|---------|-----------|------|
| Soviet Union | 62,000,000 | 1917–1991 |
| China | 35,000,000 | 1949–today |
| Germany | 21,000,000 | 1933–1945 |
| China (Kuomintang) | 10,000,000 | 1928–1949 |
| Japan | 6,000,000 | 1935–1945 |
| Cambodia | 1,000,000 | 1975–1979 |
| Sudan | 500,000 | 1955–today |

and harangue, and generally become part of the dirty laundry that our shiny white morals will not wash. Oh yeah, World Peace Day is November 17.

**Conflict Data Project**
http://www.pcr.uu.se/research/data.htm

**Political reference site**
http://www.polisci.com

**The World at War**
http://www.cdi.org/issues/World_at_War/wwar00.html

**Current Conflicts and Humanitarian Crisis**
http://www.spfo.unibo.it/spolfo/CRISIS.htm

**Links to Conflict Resolution Sites**
http://www.crinfo.org

**List of Wars and Civil Unrest Due to Religious Intolerance**
http://www.religioustolerance.org/curr_war.htm

## AN ARMY OF ONE . . . YOU

How would you like to die for your country? There's no paperwork required, no physical fitness test, no uniform, no parades. Just to go to work every day in a large high-rise. Better yet, go on vacation. Once you arrive, hang out at any U.S.-owned chain hotels, or fast-food restaurants, and boom! The only thing left of you is that stunned look of surprise on your face, now splattered all over the wall behind you. Thanks pal, back home you go in an industrial-sized baggy, no flag, no pension, no eternal flame. Well, it's not too far from the truth. When journos ask me, "Why would anyone go on vacation to a war zone?" I simply say there are no war zones these days and when they do the body counts it is not soldiers who fill the morgue but typically housewives, old men, and kids. If you are a civilian, welcome to the front lines.

The future? Not good. The Center for International Development and Conflict Management at the University of Maryland says that of the 160 countries it evaluated, there are at least 33 at risk of violent conflict and instability for the foreseeable future, mostly in Africa and Central Asia. Only about half are ranked as stable. Africa is the place where there are more wars than anywhere: 25 countries are at risk of being engaged in warfare (if not already) at last count and it's getting worse. The two shining examples of whether Africa can survive: South Africa and Nigeria . . . Oh, well.

## In the Land of the Yankee Pig

You don't have to go to a war zone to get killed. Sometimes belligerents will track you down and kill you without your leaving the hotel. Despite your own political or religious beliefs, you are a symbol to much of the world. Yes, you may be a nice person, but to some folks, your government is not.

Much of the blind anger toward Americans is a direct result of us either (a) ignoring the region's plight or (b) getting involved in their plight. We also support a wide variety of dictators, despots, evil regimes, eco-ugly businesses, and undemocratically elected rulers because we—well, hell—we make money from them. The United States also wages financial, moral, covert (and not so covert) operations against enemies of the state, such as Islamic fundamentalists, drug dealers, unfriendly dictators, and gangsters. We do this by supporting (or sometimes creating) opposition forces in countries by using money, weapons, and military training. This creates a lot of ill will towards "Americans" regardless of beliefs or background. When you travel abroad, remember you are paying for the sins of your uncle. Uncle Sam, that is.

So don't be surprised if on your next vacation you are just what the mullah ordered: to be held hostage, blown up, sacrificed, or made an example of. Bin Laden has a bad habit of giving people permission to kill Americans and Britons "wherever they are found" as payback. So accept the fact that any beefy, freckled tourist can run the risk of confrontation, kidnapping, detainment, or harassment.

> **W**hen you travel abroad, remember you are paying for the sins of your uncle. Uncle Sam, that is.

## HOW TO SURVIVE BEING A YANKEE PIG

Understand that along with your snazzy Timerberland backpack, you carry a different kind of baggage—about 200 years of imperialism, covert action, warfare, occupation, and political interference. A large part of the world resents the fact that you are so damned affluent and healthy, and they're not. You may not have bombed Laos, smart-bombed innocent Iraqi children, overthrown every Latin America dictator, shot Moros in the Philippines, bombed innocent Afghan citizens, or cut down the rain forests to grow cows for your Big Macs, but the chances are good you will be blamed for it.

- Accept the fact that you just aren't going to blend in, no matter how many local stores you visit or backpacker guides and phrasebooks you read. Deal with it and get up to speed on what the locals think of foreign tourists. It could save your life, if not your wallet.
- Dress conservatively, stay away from obvious American brands and logos, and do not wear signs of wealth (expensive watches, jewelry, large cameras, etc.). Nobody loves having their noses rubbed in their poverty and then being told to smile for the camera.
- Don't go too native until you actually have met the natives. Some cultures can be affronted by you dressing like Gunga Din with Reeboks.
- Learn or try to use the local language, even if only to say "Thank you" and "Excuse me." Learning the phrase, "I love your wonderful country" can get you a lot further than, "What the hell are you saying?" Smile a lot.
- Don't think that wearing American flag pins, handing out Uncle Sam decals, or arguing foreign policy impresses anyone beyond the 50 states. Focus on listening rather than expostulating. Be proud of your country, but wait for others to initiate the politics. Then offer the gifts in person.
- Be compassionate, understanding, and noncommittal about the current situation of the country you are in. If you are a target of an anti-American diatribe, ask the person to tell you what he would do if he were the President of the United States. He will probably be too shocked at your calm intellectual response to stay angry.
- Simple items like sunglasses, air-conditioned cars, and lack of language skills can create barriers and misunderstanding.
- Say hello to everyone you meet on the street and in the course of your travels look people straight in the eye and smile. Be polite, patient, and helpful.
- If you wonder how criminals or terrorists choose their victims, they usually tell you they look for the biggest and loudest jerk they can find.

## Viva la Revolution!

Let's play out this scenario: A backward country emerges from decades under a totalitarian regime. Freedom is in the air. Tourist visas are as easy to get as DiTech Mortgage applications. Hotels are hosed out and airlines change their names into English. You, being the adventurous type, are off in a heartbeat, eager to be the first to visit empty temples, pristine beaches, and untouched wonders. One week after you arrive, tanks fill the streets, surly men in cheap uniforms are thumping innocent bystanders, and shots are heard every night. One morning, someone kicks in your door, and it's not room service. You are officially an enemy of the people, and you will not be able to try out that bitchin' new Garmin GPS in the mountains after all. You are eating cockroach soup and watching your bruises turn ten shades of purple. What happened?

Students of history and readers of *DP* could tell you that you screwed up. You forgot that the countries most likely to be plunged into civil warfare are newly emerging democracies. Yes, you raving liberal, the most dangerous countries are the ones that still can't figure out how to operate a ballot box. One only has to look at Afghanistan, Eastern Europe, the CIS, Latin America, even Albania. These are all examples of what happens when you pop freedom out of its push-up bra. Things get heavy and wobbly real fast.

Once the iron hand is lifted, every crackpot faction has a voice and begins organizing. There is no effective way to compromise with these well-meaning folks. They simply make their points clear by using rifles and shovels. Readers of *DP* know that the most dangerous transition is from long-term dictatorship to democracy. Technically, these transitions are caused by special interest groups putting restraints on leaders and not allowing them to deal with minor uprisings. Division is the natural outcome, splitting the military, religious, regional, and business elements into their tiniest elements. Ideally, these newly formed elements form their own spheres of influence, creating the normal political structures found in first-world countries. Unfortunately, they usually adopt the brutal tactics of their former leaders and have the tanks and population fired up within weeks. Other groups, like the Mafia, drug runners, terrorists, and criminals, make good use of the division and confusion to quickly establish wide-ranging criminal organizations and smuggling corridors.

How should you react? Well, stupid, get the hell out of there. Your embassy (if there is one yet) is your best bet; failing that, go to your country's best friend's embassy (don't be too picky). If you had done your homework, you would have already made friends with the local consul and expats at the local bar. If there are no embassies (not uncommon), then you have two choices: nongovernmental organizations (NGOs) and foreign expats. NGOs will have contingency plans for disasters, and naturally you won't be part of it. But they can offer advice or possibly make connections for you. Foreign businesses will have long ago shuttered their doors, but if you hang around the golf course, you can pick up the local scuttlebutt. It's usually all about getting on a plane ASAP. Failing that, you can try to make local airline connections to at least get you to a less violent area. If not, your next choice will be to enjoy the longest, most expensive, most nerve-wracking cab ride you will ever take.

Best advice from the hard core (and those who haven't seen *The Killing Fields*): Get a room at the nicest hotel, put a mattress against the window, stock up on food, water, and batteries for your shortwave, clean out the bar downstairs, and write that Somerset Maugham-esque novel and hope the Marines show up.

## HOW TO SURVIVE REVOLUTIONARY PLACES

Although no one can predict a sudden change in government, there are some things that could keep you from appearing on CNN wearing a blindfold.

- Check in with the embassy or NGOs when you arrive to get to understand the current situation and to facilitate your evacuation if needed. Remember, the local government will typically downplay the danger posed by revolutionary groups. Your government will play it up.
- Stay away from main squares, the main boulevards, government buildings, embassies (yeah, the same one you have to check in at), radio stations, military installations, airports, harbor, banks, and shopping centers. All are key targets during takeovers or coups.
- If trouble starts, call, or have a local contact, the embassy immediately with your location. Stay off the streets, and if necessary move only during daylight hours, and in groups. Stay in a large hotel with an inside room on the second or third floor. Prepare for shops and banks being closed as well as the telephone service shutting down.
- Understand the various methods of rapid departure. Collect flight schedules and train information, and ask about private hires of cars and planes. Do not travel by land if possible.
- Do not rely on ATMs, credit cards, or traveler's checks.
- Do not trust the police or the army. Remember that there will be many summary executions, beatings, and arrests during the first few days of a coup or revolution. In many cases, it is the army fighting against its own government.
- Hire a local driver/guide/interpreter to travel around town and/or to go out at night. Don't be shy about hiring bodyguards for your residence or family.
- Listen (or have your guide listen) to the local radio station or TV station. Have him or her update you on any developments or street buzz. When the embassy has set up transport, make your move with your bodyguards or guides.
- Make sure the press pays you for your thrilling story to cover all the baksheesh you had to splash around to get out alive.

# Fun-da-Mental Oases

There are many countries, like Iran, North Korea, Pakistan, Yemen, and Syria, that would have Rush Limbaugh's head on a stick in less than 15 minutes. These countries might have a Bill of Far Rights, but nothing that would protect your outspoken butt from a lifetime of incarceration or slow execution for sneezing in front of the Big Guy's photo.

These countries fall into two general categories: fundamental and mental places. The first is usually a region where Bic shavers, baseball hats, and women's legs will never see the light of day. The second are places run by men with Ray-Bans and a distinct lack of humor surrounded by a lot of pictures of them looking stern and wearing Ray-Bans. So let's start with surviving fundamentalist places—places where praying is the national pastime, interrupted by the Friday executions.

I should point out that not all fundamentalists are Islamic. We have our own religious hotheads Stateside, Uganda has the Lord's Resistance Army (a Christian group), and Israel has both those guys with the Shirley Temple haircuts (ultraorthodox Nationalists) and the usual Islamic fundamentalists (usually seen burning something with stars and stripes). Just look for a lot of men in basic black, bad haircuts, and beards.

But most fundamentalist countries are Islamic. That doesn't mean that Islam demands that its religion come in one flavor. One billion of the world's inhabitants are Muslims and only 18 percent are found in the Arab world—most live east of Karachi. Thirty percent of Muslims are found on the Indian subcontinent, 20 percent in sub-Saharan Africa, 17 percent in Southeast Asia, and 10 percent in the CIS and China. There are an estimated 5 million Muslims in the United States. Most Muslims are just like Christians and to a certain extent like Jews, Hindus, Buddhists, and whatever. There is a certain purity, elegance, and hospitality to Islamic countries—just as there is in Christian and other regions. Most Muslims will tell you that Jews, Christians, and followers of their own faith are all "people of the Book" and that there is more to bind us than divide us. So how come every time I see the word *terrorist,* it's usually used to describe some bearded guy in a dress knocking his head on the ground? Well, let's get it out in the open. There has always been a historic antagonism between Christianity and Islam, with the line drawn messily through the Balkans and Transcaucasia and epicentering in Jerusalem. There is the same funny line in the Philippines, a place where the Spaniards just about had a heart attack when they discovered Muslims a few years after they kicked the last of the Moors out of Spain.

## HOW TO SURVIVE FUNDAMENTALIST PLACES

When traveling to fundamentalist, religiously zealous countries, remember to smile, mind your own business, learn and respect their customs, and don't judge until you understand exactly what inspires such religious devotion.

Keep in mind that people tend to be more conservative in rural areas and poor countries. Despite other guidebooks' nervous warnings, Muslims really do understand that Westerners have different customs and won't lop your head off the first time you make a faux pas by passing the pilaf with your left hand.

- Do be very careful in the area of contact between sexes (ideally, none), behavior at religious sites, entering homes uninvited, or touching religious objects. Sexually provocative clothes, obscene gestures, defiling the Koran, theft, or insulting the Prophet and women will get you in a lot of trouble.
- Do not proselytize, preach, or conduct religious functions without permission of the local government. Do not wear religious symbols or use expressions that employ the name of Christ, Allah, God, or other religious entities.
- Read and understand other religions. Most religious people will be impressed that you have studied their religion and are pleased if you ask them questions about their religion.
- Stating that you are a "student of all religions" is a good cop-out for the philosophically challenged or timid if they demand your religious affiliation.
- If you are Jewish, and are traveling in a fundamental Islamic country, you are judged not by your religion but by your actions. Also understand that there is strong antagonism between Shi'a and Sunni Muslim sects.
- Do not squeeze hands roughly when shaking hands with Muslim men. Don't shake hands with women. You may touch your chest after shaking hands in the traditional Muslim greeting. The left hand is considered unclean because, yes, rural Muslims wash their nether regions with that hand. Muslims also squat to urinate (to keep the pipe straight) and find the Western habit of urinating with legs akimbo and penis pointing far too theatrical for their tastes. Men typically do not get naked around other men.
- Be clean and dress conservatively. Remove your shoes in mosques and temples. Do not point the soles of your feet toward your host. Expect to be kissed on both cheeks by male friends. Friday is the Muslim holy day, and anything else you need to know will be communicated to you gladly by your hosts or friends.
- Ask permission before taking pictures; do not insist or sneak photos. Do not take photographs of women, the infirm, or the elderly. Don't blow your nose in public. Don't eat while walking around. Don't admire objects in a host's home (he will feel obligated to give them to you). Small gifts are expected when visiting homes. Do not show open affection. Do not show undue attention to women. The list goes on, but don't be paranoid, just be respectful.
- Women are expected to wear some type of headcovering and in some regions there are separate seating sections on buses and in public places. Women are welcome to meet with other women, but men are usually not in rural regions.
- Read up on the cultures of each region and ask permission to do something when in doubt.

This primal distrust between infidel/crusader, Jew/Arab, and West/East is still very much a part of world politics. This creates problems for Westerners when they travel to regions where the government has inflamed people against the West. It creates prejudice when the government has inflamed people against the East.

There continues to be confusion and distrust generated by the media, which seem unable to understand the basic similarities between Islam, Judaism, and Christianity, but seem to grasp the differences immediately. Usually the media zeroes in on the most extreme examples, like the former religious police of the Taliban, yet you have a hard time finding an article on the same religious police in Saudi Arabia, Iran, and Malaysia. Then there is the media's confusion between devout religious faith and criminal elements within those faiths that profess great religious purpose, whether they are blowing up abortion clinics, shooting prime ministers, or taking over embassies.

A government that has conservative views of family values and law and order, and loves guns and pickup trucks, literally goes ballistic against rulers who have conservative interpretations of—you guessed it—law and order and family values (and who love guns and pickup trucks). When was the last time you saw footage of our leaders praying at church intercut with their political speeches? Yet we are shown shots of Mecca intercut with AK-47-waving loonies on tanks. Christian fundamentalism is just as dangerous and skewed as any other hard-core belief, but most Americans head into the Muslim world with a negative and dangerous image of Islam and its followers.

So how do you survive fundamentalist places? Open your mind and learn.

**European Institute for Research on Mediterranean and Euro-Arab Cooperation**
http://www.medea.be/site.html

**Learning Arabic**
http://www.arabic2000.com

## Mental Places

No one is really prepared for the "mental" places. The places decorated by photos of those square-jawed, stern-faced, mustached loonies. These are the squalid, retro-dictatorial hellholes our government warns us against: the Graham Greene places where everyone assumes the leader has syphilis and is insane. So, what's it like when your human rights are left behind at the airport and you enter the twilight zone?

Well, quite nice, actually. Those who visit places like Syria, Libya, Cuba, Iraq, Myanmar, Iran, or even North Korea find them to be quiet, cheap, clean, crime free, and well, a little unsettlingly . . . nice. Yes, countries ruled with a gun tend to be nice backwards oases of unsettling calm.

It's unsettling because, just like Disney World, you expect there to be an underground world full of covert groups making sure everybody smiles and nobody gets any funny ideas. You, of course, are completely right. Those thin men with the sunglasses that follow you around and park outside your hotel at night are there for your protection, right? When you return to your room and find your luggage in a slightly different mess than you had left it, it was just the maid, right?

About 200,000 Canadians descend on Cuba each year (there are no figures for Americans visiting Cuba, because technically you can't go there): They complain about the Americans jacking up the prices. Libya and Syria have some of the nicest uncrowded ruins you'll ever see, and North Korea really does look just like an underbudgeted episode from the "Twilight Zone." Iran and Iraq are a little nervous about outsiders, but the local folks are more desperate to meet you than their government would like. So how do you survive those forbidden places? Just don't look over your shoulder too much, or you'll make the locals nervous.

*Third-World Traveler*
http://www.thirdworldtraveler.com/US_ThirdWorld/dictators.html

## SAVE 'EM, TRADE 'EM, OVERTHROW 'EM

What's the latest rage in the trading-card world? Friendly Dictator Cards! Well, not really, but you can own 36 of "America's most embarrassing friends" for only . . . hmm, you can't actually buy them since the company and the product have long been out of circulation. They were produced by Eclipse Productions, a fancy name for two brothers operating out of a Forestville, California, garage. Maybe the cards that featured all-stars like Ferdinand Marcos, Samuel Doe, Suharto, and Somoza were all bought up by the subjects' families. Quite funny, quite mean, and sometimes insightful. Who says crime and greed don't pay? The company also produced a card series on covert CIA operations and serial killers. Needless to say, by the '90s the card craze and Eclipse disappeared. Or was it another CIA plot?

You decide.

*Friendly Dictators Trading Cards*
Eclipse Enterprises
P.O. Box 1099
Forestville, CA 95436
http://home.iprimus.com.au/korob/fdtcards/Cards_Index.html

## HOW TO SURVIVE MENTAL PLACES

Don't be scared off by all those stern-looking posters of Big Brother staring down at you. These countries are poor, a little wacky, very retro, and usually safer than an Amish backyard. Just remember there will be a few things missing—like toilet paper and your rights if you get arrested.

- Book a tour with local tourist company. They can intervene when you do something stupid—like talking to a local.
- Understand that the local people don't see many tourists and are shy. Having family members in jail does that to folks.
- Be pleasant with the folks who do walk up to you boldly and want to be your friend. You can start talking by leaning toward their lapel pin and saying "Check, one, two . . ." and winking knowingly.
- Don't talk politics, don't talk about sex, don't talk about government, and don't talk about religion too much. Talk about history, weather, geography, or your home country, and you will make plenty of friends.
- Be careful where you point your camera. Pretty much everywhere and everything is a military installation. Always have someone show you around if you are not part of a tour. Remember, going for a long walk here is called defecting.
- Avoid the police. Just kidding. Keep in mind *everyone* is the police in these countries.

# Jackboot Junkets

We might be cutting it too fine here, but you can't say *DP* doesn't give you your money's worth. Dictatorships don't just come in one shade; some of them have the posters, the cops with Ray-Bans, and even the cute slogans. The problem is, nobody is buying it. Welcome to the dark side—the place where coups are more frequent than soccer matches and the job of dictator is listed under "temporary help wanted." Yes, these are the lands of the godless despots, the evil empires run by the gold-braided braggarts—generals all. These are the countries that have the oxymoronic title of Democratic Republic of (insert ancient, tribal name here). You won't find much religion (let alone the Trinity Broadcasting channel) in these paranoid backwaters. Don't confuse these countries with the stern military, extra-gold-braid-on-the-hat-please, ex-commie playgrounds like Iraq, Libya, Cuba, Syria, and North Korea. These are places from which even the Russians left in disgust and where Ché remarked on the drunken disorder of the future ruling party.

These folks allow tourists into their countries only because their relatives own the hotels, airlines, and companies. Countries like Zimbabwe, Liberia, Congo, C.A.R., and other little cranky, tin-pot countries are furiously pushing their domains back into the Stone Age and dragging their neighbors along with them.

Why visit these countries? Where else can you take a time machine back to the '50s, the '20s, or even the turn of the century (we mean the 12th century)? Imagine meeting people who still herd sheep, break rocks, kill other people, and even carve temples, all with no regard for profit, without an education, and while they're on the brink of starvation. Places where evolution is going backwards. Overtly criminal places where tourism is a low-cost way to import kidnap victims. So why go?

The answer is simple. You have to go. Somebody has to show these people that there is a world out there full of Pop Tarts, Chevy Suburbans (without bulletproofing), MTV, rotisserie barbecues, and fat, happy people who actually die of natural causes. It takes a lot of patience, a lot of money, and a lot of *cojones* to travel through the last of the dark kingdoms. Strangely enough, once you connect with the locals, most of these places are quite safe, and once the police stop spraying the crowd with tear gas and turn the corner, a lot of fun.

## Hard Times Hit the Dictator Job Market

Last year *DP* published the Dictator for Life List. Now we couldn't even hold a beach volleyball game with the remaining alumni. It's not just that these postwar, colonial puppets are dying off from old age, it's that the whole dictator business is going to hell faster than the "25-year-old wanted for dot-com CEO job" market. The Congo's Kabila got plugged, ex-NY waiter Slobo is playing pinochle in a Dutch prison. Peru's Uncle Fuji is getting reacquainted with sushi in Japan, and Vlad Montesinos couldn't buy his way into that old dictator haven of Panama. Even Mexico dumped its 71-year-old one-party system. Mullah Omar is on permanent haj and Savimbi was displayed like a side of beef. It seems that their countries are just being damn ungrateful for all the years of economic prosperity (theirs) and political enlightenment they brought. Sure, there are plenty of funny men from Castro to Mugabe to Taylor still sitting up on their thrones, but not for much longer. The smart ones like Jerry Rawlings of Ghana step aside, to be around to spend their "thank-you" money. The secret weapon against dictators is the one that hits them the hardest . . . in their bank accounts. A more liberal banking world has brought corruption charges in both democratic and authoritarian countries. When these dictators

## HOW TO SURVIVE BRUTAL DICTATORSHIPS

Ever want to see George Orwell's *1984,* but for real? Ever imagined what life was like before civilization? You haven't traveled until you've been to the world's worst places. Here are a few tips to keep you safe:

- Although there is some guy's picture on the money and at the airport, it doesn't mean he actually runs the country. Smile at people with guns, keep your valuables with you, and don't drink the water.
- Life sucks here, so get over it and just make friends. Don't rail against the injustice until you get home. Do not discuss politics with anyone. Usually there are no politics to discuss anyway. Yes, you can be paranoid in these places.
- Jails are not for rehabilitating criminals, they are there to induce you to pay the police a lot of money to not end up there. Don't even think about breaking any laws, if there are any.
- Most autocratic countries employ surveillance or encourage spying on foreigners. Do not be surprised if you are not only followed, but your tails even argue over who gets to follow you. At least you won't be mugged or pickpocketed.
- On the downside, expect to have your room and your luggage searched while you are out. Yes, those swarthy men sitting next to you in the restaurant were the same ones outside your hotel last night.
- Telephone and mail are subject to interception and/or monitoring. Be careful what you say. Make sure your room is very secure when you are in it. And yes, there is someone peeping in that hole.
- Any violation of the law (imagined or real) will result in severe penalties. There is very little your consulate, lawyer, or senator can do for you since you are subject to the laws (or lack of laws) of the country you are in. Stay away from drugs. Stay out of nasty bars. Stay away from attractive women. Stay away from these countries if you suffer from paranoia and anxiety attacks. Nice vacation, huh?
- If you are a journalist, activist, eco-activist, or infomercial host you will be considered a threat. Contact the freedom groups listed in the back of the book to understand what the risks are. Any mention of human rights or fair treatment is found only in comedy routines performed at the dictator's palace.
- If you are truly concerned about conditions in these countries, contact the Red Cross, Amnesty International, Human Rights Watch, or Reporters Without Frontiers to see what you can do to help. But please wait until you have left the country. You don't want to be the subject of a future report. (See our reference section in the back.)

fire up the Lear Jet, they quickly find their platinum cards overdrawn as banks now freeze assets. Montesinos, the director of Peru's secret police, had $70 million frozen in 8 different Swiss bank accounts alone. That's some serious mad money.

**Guess the Dictator and/or TV Sitcom Character game**
http://www.smalltime.com/dictator.html

**Dictator Fashion Spotlight**
http://www.visi.com/~sgrantz/dict_fash

# Gimmeyawalletland

Imagine a naked man walking down the street with $100 bills taped to his body. That's pretty much what the typical tourist looks like to the residents of these nasty places. If there weren't any tourists, the locals would have to rob each other, swapping the same few worthless, freshly printed, inflated bills back and forth like election promises. Yes, you can fear the locals because they don't fear you or the law. Sometimes it's good to have a brutal dictator in power, if only to clean up these places.

The fact that you consider yourself the owner of your camera, wallet, luggage, watch, and jewelry is not really a debating point with many of these folks. The concept that you might need to be killed to expedite the transfer of those goods is really a minor detail to some. You don't need to be robbed in these places to lose your money; the police and officials will simply ask for it with a smile when you arrive, your cab driver will extort it from you if you want your luggage back, the hotel will bill you for it, and the local establishments will cry foul if you debate a rudely presented and highly inflated bill for their sneering, greasy-fingered services.

In many war-ravaged, impoverished places such as Somalia, Yemen, C.A.R., or Liberia, the only law is survival of the fittest or the fastest. In countries like Nigeria, Colombia, Bolivia, and Russia, you may need to hire criminals to protect you from the police. In some places like Mexico, DR Congo, or Uzbekistan, you may discover that it was actually the police who robbed you, creating a minor dilemma when filling out the required police report for your insurance company back home.

You demand justice, you say? Well, how much can you afford? Need to pay off a judge? Buy back your stolen car, repurchase your stolen luggage? No *problemo*. Oh, we stole your money, but we'll put you up in jail until your relatives show up with the cash. Nice people, easy to do business with. If you are frustrated or impoverished by the entrepreneurial legal system, there is good news. In most of these places if

# HOW TO SURVIVE CORRUPT PLACES

As one aid worker so eloquently told me, "Theft is just a more efficient form of distributing aid." So shame on you for bringing all that nice stuff and not wanting to share.

- Understand that "bribery" is normal in many countries, but do not confuse it with theft. Oddly, the locals understand the difference. A *bribe* happens when the bribers demand half of your money, nicely, to prevent all of it from being stolen . . . by the same people, of course. *Bluster, negotiate, smile, give,* or *ignore* are the watchwords here. Be pleasant. Carry small bills, have cheap gifts (like Mr. *DP* stickers) on hand, and realize that being indignant will just end up costing you more.
- *Theft* is a normal element of some regions. You snooze, you lose. Study Darwin, cockroaches, and vultures if you can't figure out why.
- Understand that soldiers at checkpoints are often hungry, sick, and impoverished. They will shoot if you don't stop. They can also work themselves into a frenzy if you anger them. Be cool, smile, pass out the trinkets, and just keep talking.
- Meet with and discuss the country's situation with the local embassy staff. Ask them specifically what to do if you are arrested, followed, or hassled. Carry their card or at least number and address on you while in that country. Ask them for names of military commanders, politicians, or anybody important. Write it down. A name on a piece of paper has more weight than just saying the name.
- Stay within well-defined tourist routes, if there are any.
- Lock all luggage and belongings in a secure place. Use a locking canvas duffel or metal box for luggage.
- Never travel in the country alone. Use a local guide to navigate checkpoints and police roadblocks. Always hire a driver recommended by someone you trust.
- Fly between cities and prearrange transportation from the airport to the hotel.
- Prepare for constant intimidation from police and military. Be firm about your innocence and try to lead them to your embassy or a safe place. Find out and remember to drop the name of a local bigwig if you are frog-marched at gunpoint.
- Remember that police will try to keep items that they remove from you during a search. So show them your papers (not in your wallet, I hope), but do not hand anything to them. If the soldier takes your passport into a bunker or building, walk with him.
- Don't overtly demand to know how much money they want. You won't have any left if you do. Always offer your bribe as a gift to show your appreciation, to help out with the family, and so on. And smile.

you really need to resolve a dispute, it's cheaper to hire a hit man than a lawyer.

The only positive note about these places is that you get to leave and you will have a great story to tell later. Most of the residents of these unfortunate lands must endure the same treatment, along with disease, starvation, and brutality and, of course, no ticket out. Our best advice is to go with the flow (see "Bribes"), use credit cards and traveler's checks, carry the appropriate change to satisfy your wolf-like friends, and keep your main money and assets well hidden. See page 59 for a few tips to at least stanch the flow and escape with your body parts intact.

*Transparency International*
http://www.transparency.org

# Impoverished Paradises

Not all countries are full of nasty thieves, brutal despots, or jabbering zealots. There are plenty of places that are really nice—they just seem to have a lot of dead people on the side of the road in the morning. These places have a terminal funk to them. These are the tough places, the hard countries that barely survive. Places too pitiful to make fun of. Many of these places, like India, Egypt, Bangladesh, Kenya, Pakistan, Haiti, China, and Indonesia, are like this because there are just too many people for the resources available. There are a lot of petty thefts, minor muggings, infectious diseases, scams, and an occasional murder.

In 1950, 33 percent of the world's population lived in developed, industrialized nations. Today, that share is approximately 23 percent. By the year 2025, it will fall to 16 percent; Africa then will have 19 percent of the world's inhabitants. Today, Western and Southeast Asia are home to more people than any other part of the world. The population of India will overtake that of China early in the next century. This area is also home to the most diverse mix of languages, religions, and people in the world, many of whom have been feuding for centuries and who will continue to fight over land, religion, and tribal disputes.

As populations grow and standards of living drop, people will live at ever-greater densities, creating more tension. *The World Bank's World Development Report* noted that at the present time only Bangladesh, South Korea, the Netherlands, and the island of Java have population densities of more than 400 people per square kilometer. By the middle of the next century, one-third of the world's people will probably live at these density levels. Given the current trends, the population density of Bangladesh will rise to a hardly conceivable 1,700 people per square kilometer. Population growth on such a large scale is intrinsically

## PERCENTAGE OF POPULATION IN POVERTY

| | | | |
|---|---|---|---|
| Bangladesh | 80% | India | 40% |
| Ethiopia | 60 | Nigeria | 40 |
| Vietnam | 55 | Indonesia | 25 |
| Philippines | 55 | China | 10 |
| Brazil | 50 | | |

destabilizing. Many of the world's most dangerous places will also be the most crowded and impoverished places. So see them while you can still fit inside.

On the African continent, 45 percent of the population is under the age of 15; in South America, it's 35 percent; in Asia, 32 percent. Only 21 percent of the population of the United States and 19 percent of Europe is under 15. Things are not going to get better in our lifetime.

The World Resources Institute reports that only 3 percent of the world's inhabitants lived in urban areas in the mid-18th century. By the 1950s, that proportion had risen to 29 percent. Today, it is more than 40 percent; by 2025, 60 percent of the world's people are expected to be living in or around cities. Almost all of that increase will be in what is now the third world. Young people tend to migrate to major urban centers seeking Western-style jobs instead of staying in the countryside and doing backbreaking menial labor. Once in the city, they find that the competition for jobs is fierce and that petty crime against the more wealthy is the only source of income. But despite this, the cities continue to grow. Mexico City, which had 17 million inhabitants in 1985, is up to approximately 20 million in 2002. São Paulo jumped from 15 million to more than 18 million. Hey, move over, you're using up my oxygen. Tips to survive?

## HOW TO SURVIVE POOR PLACES

There is a whole generation of *Lonely Planet* travelers that loves cheap, cheap, cheap. Poor countries are photogenic, colorful, and damn, they're cheap. Until, of course, you step in it, or smell it, or get to know the people who toil to make those things or services cheap. Understand the cause and effect of poverty, and then you can admire how people deal with it without losing hope or dignity. Here's what to consider:

(continued)

- Get the guilt thing out of the way early. You're rich; they're not. Yes, it is your fault. They make Nikes and Kmart designer clothes, you wear them and throw them away. Then they get to wear them. Accept it or change it.
- You can help. People who live in poor regions are just as nice, intelligent, witty, and interesting as you are. Find out what would make a difference in their lives and go for it.
- Be aware of "Poverty Tourism": Locals who bring in Westerners first to do things the locals are completely capable of doing themselves and then to pass around old Scooby Doo T-shirts as if they were Versace.
- Don't wait until you get home and donate your fortune to charitable groups. Many eat up your kind dollars in fund-raising and infrastructure. Think of ways you can help the people you meet by getting your dollars directed to them. And it's not always money that brings a smile.
- If you care, meet with the local aid organizations, schools, or government; you will be surprised at how simple their needs can be—from pencils, to batteries, to 20-cent textbooks.
- Be aware that even money and charity cannot fix the root of the problem. Spend some time looking into just how your government can efficiently get involved.
- Think about simple, elegant gifts that will be treasured forever: Take photos of their family, or leave your phrase books, guidebook, or something from your country. Even teaching someone a song can be a lasting gift.

## Terrorist Places

Enough of the feel-good, we-are-the-world, drum-circle stuff. At least those folks are still alive to hate being poor. What about those countries run by evil bastards who just want to kill you? The irredeemable, hard-core punks who want to stick a grenade up your shorts to see how far your head pops off? The slit-eyed bastards who dream of cutting you up like a goat and bathing their faces in your spraying blood? Oh yeah, baby. Darth Vader and Hannibal Lecter are pussies. There are some really bad cats out there. How do we know? Well, our government trained many of them. Terrorists, criminals, thugs, rogue nations, whatever you call them, they are waiting to bring a little misery and mayhem into your backpacking see-the-world-on-two-grand life.

Damn, you say, just show me where these places are on a map and I'll avoid them. Sorry, not so simple. Most of these groups and regions aren't on maps. Some are "transnational criminal groups" like bin Laden and his ever-angry, ever-threatening, Egyptian/Saudi/Yemeni/Algerian/Afghan insane clown posse. Some are Russian-sponsored gangs that kidnap aid workers in the Caucasus. Some are "Marxist Narco-Guerrillas" that make Colombia's national parks "extreme" destinations.

## HOW TO SURVIVE TERRORIST PLACES

There is no real epicenter to terrorism against travelers. It occurs in the Middle East, North America, Latin America, Europe, even Australia. Okay fine, go to the Antarctic for your vacation then. Terrorists will seek you out wherever they can. Here are at least a few pointers:

- Understand what is going on in the world. Open-source databases, Yahoo's news, and other free-security news sources are ideal.
- Despite spending billions on intelligence, our government still doesn't have much of an idea of when and where attacks will happen. They have very poor intelligence inside extremist and fundamentalist groups. Feel better?
- High-traffic tourist areas in countries with poor security are ideal for attacks. There are over two dozen groups actively seeking to harm Americans or our interests. If you are Canadian or European, don't get smug. They don't ask to see passports before they blow up buses or hotels.
- Stay away from group tours, expat hangouts, preplanned political events, and U.S.-related businesses, hotels, and installations.

Others are "paramilitary units" that just don't want you around to witness executions or their dirty work in places like Algeria or East Timor.

There is no simple advice to give on how to avoid being the victim of these groups. Stay at home? Well, what if you live in New York, Washington, London, Los Angeles, or even Oklahoma? Oh yeah, almost forgot, huh? Check with your embassy? Probably not a good idea in Nairobi. Take a guided tour? Really not a wise choice if you are in Uganda or Yemen. A random bomb attack or murder attempt is simply the most devastating, sickening thing a human can survive. Whether it's a Sbarro's pizza shop in Israel, a renovated tourist hotel in Kampala, a London train station, or a New York high-rise, bad things are going to happen to innocent people. It doesn't make sense; it's evil and inspires terror in anyone who reads about it. It's not pretty. And you don't forget.

> **D**on't expect to learn anything more on terrorist groups other than that they are out there. Waiting.

Don't expect to learn anything more on terrorist groups other than that they are out there. Waiting. Like a protoplasmic liquid, terrorism flows around the world and reshapes itself according to the pressures mounted against it. Just when the experts figure they have it pegged, it assumes new, more frightening images.

*EmergencyNet News (terrorist news updated daily)*
http://www.emergency.com/ennday.htm

**U.S. State Department Counterterrorism Office**
http://www.state.gov/www/global/terrorism
http://www.state.gov/s/ct

## THE WORST CITIES ON EARTH

*The Economist* figured out the places where an expat would suffer the most. Here is their less-than-surprising list (note that Grozny, Kabul, and Baghdad are missing— also not surprising):

1. Port Moresby, Papua New Guinea
2. Karachi, Pakistan
3. Lagos, Nigeria, and  Dhoke, Bangladesh
4. Phnom Penh, Cambodia
5. Algiers, Algeria
6. Bombay, India
7. Abidjan, Ivory Coast
8. Dakar, Senegal
9. New Delhi, India

*Source:* EIU, *The Economist*

# Into the Killing Zones: Journos

You got a great deal on a white hardskin Suzuki, and swapped your expensive Leica M6s for one of those disposable, idiot-proof cameras. You are on assignment, thanks to an ambiguous commitment from a free counterculture city weekly and a cable access show. Your pack is stuffed with phrase books, Power Bars, cigarettes, and first-aid kits. You are also lugging a blue helmet and flak jacket (not because you need it, but because you think it will look cool on TV and your insurer demands it). Now all you have to do is figure out what the hell is going on and, of course, try to remember what a journalist is supposed to do and say in a war zone. If it's your first time, you're in for a treat. The crackle of gunfire outside your overpriced hotel makes those Gauloises and whiskey "Hemingwayesque." And you swear that chick and/or dude from *The Guardian* was giving you the eye. You probably read about "the emerging conflict" and, after finally convincing your editor, you've arrived about two months too late. You have been working hard to stumble onto a flare-up or get past those damn checkpoints. But the government is making sure you don't get anywhere near the fighting. If only you can beat that rowdy pack of hungover journos that seem to drive up even the price of a hooker to $100. You try to bribe your "Ministry of Information" contact with your last bottle of Johnny

Walker but, screw it, you end up going back to the bar to write up another "human interest" story to shut your editor up. Ah, the life of a journo. Never have so few drunk so much, for such little.

So, okay, exactly how does this gig work? Can you actually cover a story as a journo and stay healthy, wealthy, and wise doing it? The short answer? Absolutely not. But for those hopeless romantics raised on carefully edited, fashion-rag, neo-war "Holy Crap, There I Was!" true-life stories, here goes.

First of all, war doesn't sell. You can make more money photographing a celebrity showing her underwear than photographing all the mass graves combined. Second, the big dogs will quickly turn a war zone into a place that is more expensive than Cannes during the film festival, and finally, even if you do score a hit, the dishonest, parasitic nature of journalism dictates that your story will be quickly and shamelessly stolen within minutes of hitting the news. Then you can look forward to waiting patiently for the promised check for a reduced rate and reading your mangled story. Your one consolation will be the confident knowledge that working for your parents' mortuary is a definite career boost. Still not deterred? Okay, then here we go.

### Rule 1: Get in Quickly

War zones are pretty easy places to understand, as are their players. One side doesn't like the other side so it bums money from a rich backer (which they will pay off in favorable trade deals and political favors later). The first days of the war are pretty fast-paced and fluid, and then within a week or so things start to bog down. There are front lines, kill zones, and safe zones, but before you get to stumble around in any of these areas, you need to get in. These days the military "officially" shuts most borders, specifically to keep journos out. Or they create little quasi–war zone areas where journos cool their heels and file stories about what they ate for breakfast. Usually you are far enough away from the war zones not to get killed but too far to actually see the fighting. You soon find out that no one is impressed by your laminated press card, your reversed New York Yankees hat, or even that snazzy, dirtied-up photo vest. You want to play—you pay. War zones are the epitome of entrepreneurial start-ups. Everything from taxis to bottled water costs. The more journos, the more it costs—guides, generators, security, tips, food, you name it. You can blame the big nets for this evil. But you too must pay for your sins. The U.S. $100 bill is the coin of the realm. And I mean coin.

### Rule 2: Bring Lots of Cash

If you have a real assignment, you'll have to bring in way too much equipment, rent satellite links, order breakfasts, bribe guards, make appointments, pay off officials, and do all that stuff you do back home, except now there is no electricity, phone service, running water, or civilization. Naturally these basic needs are the most expensive services your host country has to offer. You also need to get permission. But not always from the guy whose picture is on their money. So you need a local "fixer" to get you permission. As usual, they are not hard to miss. They will be hovering over you at breakfast the day after your plane arrives. They will rattle off famous journo's names in bad English, thumb through a two-inch stack of greasy business cards, and give you that smile that says, I ain't going away, pal. Large sums of money will exchange hands and from now on the most common phrases you are going to hear are, "No problem!" followed by "How much?" These phrases will always come up when there is a problem, accompanied by a smile and an outstretched palm. Okay, Rambo, let's get going to the front lines.

### Rule 3: Choose Your Fixer Wisely

But how do you get "in"? How do you actually meet up with the "rebels"? How can you avoid them, is a better question. Believe it or not, smart rebels usually have a press office in London, Paris, or Washington, with unlisted offices in Damascus, Tripoli, or Khartoum. To get in, you need permission either from the rebels (who usually are as extraordinarily inefficient and underfunded as they are helpful and incompetent) or the government (which is usually as slick and efficient as it is unhelpful). The rebels will give you a contact name, a place and time to show up, and a letter that just as likely will put you in jail. Naturally, when you show up, there will be no one there to meet you and you will discover that you can just take a bus like everyone else does. It's all about rebels pretending to have infrastructure. This is where your fixer comes in. In most cases he is directly related to the people back in London, or wherever you got your "official" permission, and he is completely useless unless large amounts of currency are liberally applied. If you find yourself feeling less than generous, it doesn't take a mathematical genius (or your fixer) to discover that he can make more money handing you over to kidnappers, or robbing you . . . or both.

### Rule 4: Don't Believe a Single Word Anyone Tells You

If you are lucky, you will have arrived early and have descended into complete chaos. That means you'll get good stuff: Summary executions, frontal assaults, atrocities, severed heads, all the details that makes editors squeal with glee. If you arrive too late, you'll have to do it the official way, complete with guide, bodyguard, and driver. Then you'll need to be a bona fide journalist. That means you'll spend most of your time interviewing dull-witted officials, visiting hospitals, and watching PowerPoint presentations. Your hosts will load you up with

# HOW TO SURVIVE WAR ZONES

Remember that small wars are not carefully planned or predictable activities. More importantly, land mines, shells, stray bullets, and booby traps have no political affiliations or mercy. So keep the following in mind:

- Contact people who have returned from or are currently in the hot zone. Do not trust the representations of rebels or government contacts. Check it out yourself.
- Avoid politics, do not challenge the beliefs of your host, be firm but not belligerent about getting what you need. Talking politics with soldiers is like reading *Playboy* with the Pope.
- Think about how similar journalism is to spying. Make sure you have a rock-hard story. They still shoot spies.
- Travel only under the permission of the controlling party. In many cases you will need multiple permissions from officers, politicians, and the regional commander. The wrong permission handed to the wrong party can get you shot.
- Check in with the embassy, military intelligence, local businessmen, and bartenders. As for the local touts who offer to take you across the border, just remember they would probably make more money selling you down the river than taking you there.
- Carry plenty of identification, articles, letters of recommendation, and character references. Your kidnappers will enjoy reading them while they wait for your ransom to be paid.
- Bring photographs of your family, friends, house, dog, or car. If your portfolio sucks, these will inspire them to take pity on you.
- Do not misrepresent yourself, exaggerate, or tell white lies. Keep your story simple and consistent. Remember, not only do rebels use the Internet, every journo in the world will blow your cover by publicizing who you are when you get abducted.
- Dress and act conservatively. Be quietly engaging and affable, and listen a lot. Your actions will indicate your intentions as the locals weigh their interest in helping you. It may take a few days for the locals to check you out before they offer any assistance.
- Meet with journalists and photographers (usually found at the bar in the most expensive hotel in town) to understand the local threats. Don't be surprised if NGOs are not thrilled to see you or if your new friends mislead you. It is, after all, about making money.
- Carry a lot of money hidden in various places, and be ready to leave or evacuate at any time. This means traveling very light. Choose a place to sleep that would be survivable in case of a rocket or shell attack.
- Visit with the local Red Cross, UN, embassy, and other relief workers to understand the situation. They are excellent sources of health information and may be your only ticket out. However, they also are busy, so don't expect too much.

(continued)

- If warranted, buy and wear an armored vest or flak jacket. Carry your blood type and critical info (name, country, phone, local contact, allergies) on a laminated card or write it on your vest. Wear a Medic-Alert bracelet. Have evac insurance.
- Carry a first-aid kit with syringes, antibiotics, IV needles, anesthetics, and painkillers as well as the usual medication. Remember it is the people you are with who will be using the kit on you so bring a pocket manual for the kit and tell them where your kit is.
- Understand and learn the effect, range, and consequences of guns, land mines, mortars, snipers, and other machines of war. After you see your first vacuum-bomb or land-mine victim, you may decide to stay home.
- Get life and health insurance (and KRE—kidnap, rescue, and extortion—insurance, if relevant) and don't lie. Tell your insurers the specific country you will be traveling to. Also check with the emergency evacuation services to see if they can go into a war zone to pull you out.
- Keep in mind that for the vast majority of war journalists there is no money, no fame, and very little long-term personal peace or satisfaction in being exposed to fear, death, violence, and mayhem on a regular basis. Although the risk of death or injury is low, many suffer from posttraumatic stress syndrome (PTSS), hearing loss, broken marriages, and nightmares, just as combatants do. Just ask any war journalist if anything they ever did changed anything. Most will say no . . . but at least they tried.

official studies, contact names, military transportation in-country, and a tour of what may or may not be the front lines. You will of course hark back to your misspent youth and sneak around to do a couple of stories on corruption, atrocities, and incompetence, but you will find your permission suddenly revoked once they hit the clipping service. So the seasoned pros toe the line, while the young ones look for other wars to cover, until of course they become old war correspondents who have learned to do things the official, easy way.

Naturally, you see more bloodletting and violence at the front row of a Mike Tyson fight than on these official tours, which usually consist of more briefings, deserted rebel camps, and captured prisoners. But hey, it's a living. The real pros, of course, are back at the cushy media centers, staying at real hotels, drinking hot coffee, retyping official releases hours before you hear of anything, and probably spending less than you are in the field.

### Rule 5: Just Because People Are Firing Guns, It Doesn't Mean There's a War On

If you think you'll be the only journo in the thick of things, good luck. These days journos get to godforsaken places like Afghanistan

# TIPS FOR NOVICE JOURNALISTS

- Remember that people in wartime are highly stressed and conditions are confusing. Many young fighters often can have a lust for blood or irrational behavior. Maintain your cool at all times. Patience and a smile are the secrets here.

- Journalists can be specifically targeted for execution. In many areas journos are considered spies (which in the new era of open-source intelligence, they technically are).

- Crime is an unfortunate element of war zones. Journos are a perfect target because they carry expensive equipment and large amounts of cash. Locals whom you have angered may come back that night. Keep it cool and friendly. Never show your "wad" to anyone.

- Travel with an open mind and do not criticize or judge. Things change quickly and "the evil enemy" could be "the good guy" in the morning.

- Do not lie or suggest any affiliation you don't have. In wartime, people form alliances based on their gut feelings and the look in your eyes, but eventually you will be checked out via Internet or phone and the other people you have met along the way. There are no secrets in a war zone.

- Try to use a simple notebook and write in your own handwriting as illegibly as possible. Use medium-priced autofocus digital cameras that are not too painful to replace. Do not make drawings or maps. Ask permission before taking pictures or point to your camera and give an inquiring thumbs-up. A camera with a long lens can look very similar to a weapon to a trigger-happy rebel.

- Keep a blank roll of film or videotape handy. When soldiers demand your film or tape, you make the switch and then reload the original.

- Snipers like to hone in on lights, bright colors, and even decals. Things like cigarettes, head flashlights, video eyepieces, strobe-ready lights, and press decals can become targets.

- When you go up to the front lines, do not assume that a B-52 knows the difference between the good guys and the bad guys. More good guys than ever die from friendly-fire incidents and accidents in today's remote-control high-tech wars (in Afghanistan there was a point at which more journalists had been killed than U.S. troops—they actually outnumbered the U.S. troops).

- Just because the war is over doesn't mean danger has passed. Land mines, booby traps, snipers, and terrorist attacks continue long after the fighting has ended. If a journalist is kidnapped, contact the Red Cross Journalist Hotline, part of the International Committee of the Red Cross, 19 Avenue de la Paix, CH-1202 Geneva, Switzerland, Tel.: (41) 22 734-6001, Fax: (41) 22 734-8280. http://www.icrc.org

faster than the troops do. And with all those journos around, there is an instant need to control them. So these days expect to be corralled into official press centers and to be fire-hosed with nonstop press releases, videos, and show-and-tells. Your editor will berate you for wasting time, for not going out into the field to get the scoop, and the military will abuse you for not playing fair. Information, after all, is a weapon these days.

The world of war is a shadowy world of lies, propaganda, and circumstantial evidence. So if you think you will benefit by actually learning the truth from rebel leaders and crawling along trenches . . . forget it. When you emerge six months later from inside the rebel camps, your editor will turn to you and say, "Man, where've you been? That's history, not news."

**Rule 6: You'll Make a Lot More Money Stalking Celebs Than Dodging Rockets**

So enjoy it and then get a job covering movie openings.

***Centurion Risk Assessment Services***
http://www.centurion-riskservices.co.uk

***The Rory Peck Trust***
http://www.oneworld.org/rorypeck

## IN A DANGEROUS PLACE: NORTHERN ALBANIA

### SOMETHING FOR NOTHING

For Albania's bandits, payday had come at last. As a thousand journalists, aid workers, and international observers rushed to the north of the country, the poorest bandits in the poorest country in Europe declared open season on the multitude of rich and—more importantly—unarmed foreigners venturing into the country. And a most profitable time they had of it, too. The international media lost cars, satphones, cameras, cash, and anything else they happened to be carrying with them when Kalashnikov-wielding figures stopped their cars in the northern Tropoje region of Albania. In one instance, a London staffer of a news agency that had been relieved of its satphone reputedly dialed up the stolen phone number. It was duly answered by a man speaking Albanian. With no one on hand who spoke Albanian, the frustrated hack was reported as shouting in English, "Give us our kit back, you bastards." Needless to say, the kit, worth several U.S. $100,000, has yet to be seen.

The expulsion of hundreds of thousands of Kosovar Albanians from their homeland into northern Albania was covered by scores of hacks operating Betacams and otherwise dripping with cameras. Images of tearful and exhausted refugees duly filled western television screens and people were duly shocked. I, like the other 1,000 or so hacks, had also made the lengthy journey up to Kukes in northern Albania. Beautiful mountain peaks were complemented by potholed roads and impoverished villages. Kukes, with its one main street and two hotels, was suddenly home to an army of journalists and aid workers, not to mention a few hundred thousand Kosovar refugees. Unsurprisingly, prices had gone through the roof, with local flats being let at anywhere between US$100 and $200 a night, the equivalent of a couple of months' wages for the average Albanian.

North of Kukes is Albania's banditland, a vast expanse of rolling wooded hills and dirt tracks, which even the locals think twice about venturing into. The locals certainly won't talk about the gangs who control the dirt tracks that pass for Albania's roads. "Please don't ask me about these people," an old man begged us. "These are bad times for Albania." Just how bad we were about to find out. We set out early one morning for a Kosovo Liberation Army (KLA) training camp in the Helshan region, a couple of hours' drive north of Kukes.

With me are Roger and Bungy, two freelancers for *Sky News*, as well as our interpreter, Donjeta. We hire a local minibus, which is not only cheaper but, we hope, a little less conspicuous than a Mercedes taxi for a drive into Albania's Wild West.

The drive, along narrow roads and winding mountain passes, is uneventful. There are hardly any cars on the road. Partly, of course, because relatively few people have cars, and those who have them are not about to risk them driving through banditland. It's a clear and bright day as we clamber from our minibus and trudge the few meters to the gates of the camp. Milling around outside the camp are dozens of local Albanians. Entrepreneurial as ever, they have set up small stalls to sell food and cigarettes to the numerous KLA recruits who pass through the camp. I briefly notice a tall, thin man hidden behind a large pair of mirror reflector sunglasses, clutching an assault rifle. He takes Donjeta aside and asks her some questions. When I ask her what he wanted, she merely replies, "It's nothing." A short while later we are taken to the camp commander. About 40 years old, slim, with slightly sunken cheeks and graying hair, he introduces himself as Billy and asks what we want. After the usual ritual of identifying ourselves, we first ask if we can journey into Kosovo with the soldiers to the front lines. We can, if we get permission from Piarko, the regional KLA commander. So instead we ask if we can film the training. Billy agrees and a few minutes later we are trekking across the hillside, pushing leafy branches out of our faces as we make our way through the woods around us. I ask if the area is mined: No, comes the reply. Arriving at a clearing we find about 200 camouflage-clad new recruits on a rifle range, learning the basics about shooting and using the weapons they will soon be using on the front lines.

Three recruits are lying on ground mats firing AK-47s at targets about 150 meters away. For the next few hours, we follow the recruits through their daily training as they take turns repeatedly firing at the white boards at the far end of the range, before trooping back to the camp to strip and clean the weapons. A few interviews later, we take our leave for the ride back to Kukes. Our minibus tentatively renegotiates the potholed track as we make our way down the hillside. Reaching flatter terrain, the driver speeds up. Ahead of us, a few hundred meters away, there is a white van parked on the grass. Go around it, Roger tells the driver. Our driver cuts across another track toward the Kukes road. A man comes running from the white van, shouting at our driver in Albanian. Ignore him and drive on, we chorus to the driver, who duly does so, speeding up. "I think those were the guys from the camp gates," Roger says.

We drive on in an uneasy silence, along the deserted approach to the first bend that will take us back along the mountainous route to Kukes. The silence, though, is shattered a few minutes later by the sound of shots behind us. Glancing back, I see the white van we had left behind accelerating to catch up with us. It is only 30 or so meters behind: Leaning out the window is the same man who had briefly questioned Donjeta at the camp. His Kalashnikov is still in his hands, and he is now firing it in the air, just above our vehicle. With a blinding ability to state the obvious I say, "I think we've got some bandits behind us." We tell the driver to stop and the white van pulls to a halt in front of us. Two bandits get out of the van and run toward our minibus. The lanky, sunglasses-clad bandit opens the front door opposite the driver, jabbing the driver hard in the ribs with his assault rifle. Another pistol-wielding bandit with long, dark hair pulls open the driver's door and drags him out, slapping him across the head. Protesting feebly, the driver is dragged to a ditch by the side of the road and a pistol is put to his head. For a split second I think we are soon to be driverless on a permanent basis. A third bandit with blond hair and blue eyes climbs into the driver's seat. Flourishing his pistol at us, he says, "Don't move or we'll kill you." Nice to meet you, too. He tries to turn the ignition key, but it doesn't work. Our driver is eventually brought back to start the bus, using the more traditional method of hot-wiring the engine.

Another van comes up the road. It is just a van full of local people, but they have managed to arrive at the wrong time. Pistols are flourished at the driver and the van is kicked in an effort to encourage the locals to leave the scene of the crime. It's a matter of seconds before the van, with everyone's faces glued to the windows as they briefly catch a glimpse of three Brits being robbed, speeds on its way. The three bandits all climb into our bus and we start driving northward along the road to Bajram Curri, with the white banditmobile following along behind. In all, it's a 40-minute drive through twisting mountain passes.

I sit quietly and ponder the inevitable loss of all my camera equipment and, in more paranoid moments, my life. Immediately to my right are two of the bandits, casually holding their pistols. The third is sitting in the front. Roger is directly behind me and Bungy is at the back of the van. The bandits are relaxed and confident in the knowledge that three feeble journalists are not going to resist. The sad truth is that they are right. Where are we from, they want to know. England, we say, which brings our friendly patter to an end. We pull over on a deserted bend on top of a gorge. "Get out one by one," says the blond-haired bandit. "Leave everything in the van and don't try and hide anything." With a degree of weariness, we clamber out one by one. "If you don't give us US$2,000 now we'll kill you all," says the one bandit. We point out that, much though we would like to give him $2,000, we just don't have the cash on us. Traveling in Albania has taught us not to carry too much cash. Another time, maybe?

We are lined up on the grass and told to empty our pockets. I only have about 200 lek—two dollars or so—in my pocket. "Keep it and have a beer on me," says the blond-haired bandit with a magnanimous smile. "Very generous of you," I mutter as I notice another bandit transfer all of our kit from our van to theirs. "If you want your stuff back, you will have to pay $2,000," says the Kalashnikov-wielding bandit. "If you come back with the police, we'll kill you with heavy machine guns," he says with a wonderful penchant for detail. I wonder if there is any particular difference between being killed by an AK-47 or a heavy machine gun. "We're only doing this for the money," continues the bandit, in what is obviously the standard bandit lecture to idiot foreigners.

While we are herded back into our van, the warnings about the police are reiterated at close-range pistol point. "Don't even think about it," says the blond-haired bandit, cocking his pistol and putting it to my head through the window, sending a brief surge of adrenaline through my body. I wonder why, given the comprehensive uselessness of the Albanian police. With that we are sent on our way back to Kukes. I try to ask the driver if he knows who the bandits are and where they live. Glancing back he says, "Please don't ask me this, I have a wife and children, I can't talk about these people. As you can see, here in Albania we have no state, no law, no police, and no country. . . . We have nothing."

*—Roddy Scott*

# Business Travelers

## Professional Victims

Now you would picture anybody who goes voluntarily and regularly into a war zone as a pretty game-faced macho kinda guy, right? Knife strapped to thigh, grenades across the chest, spare magazines tucked in tight, first-aid kit ready, a bottle of good Scotch, and a sense of *sang froid* that sends ladies into a swoon. So how come when we get to war zones it's all guys with pocket protectors, thin-blue short-sleeved shirts, cheap plastic briefcases, and that just-off-the-bus look?

Believe it or not, the number-one travelers to war zones are businessmen—dull normal people set on selling oil-field supplies, buying bulldozers, hawking medicine, shipping concrete, or even setting up shoe factories. Headbands and biceps are just not "in" with this crowd.

Doesn't it seem that every time you read about someone getting kidnapped, waylaid, or massacred, he's a vice president of something or other working in Getmeouttahereastan? There is a booming industry selling safety to these business travelers. Companies like Pinkerton, Janes, and Kroll will give you a blow-by-blow of every maiming, kidnapping, bombing, and attack. Almost all security services are targeted at businesses and businessmen (we're not being chauvinistic here, most victims are men). Yet when *DP* gives talks on travel in dangerous places, we never meet any. Instead, we run into mostly gung-ho college students and graying, careful spinsters. Selling safety to business travelers is like offering sex education classes for monks. They don't see the need. After all, they are not really traveling. They get on a plane, have a couple of drinks, review the file, and then meet the driver at the airport. They stay in a swank hotel, have a shower, watch a little CNN, have dinner with the customer, and then the driver takes them to the meeting the next day. Okay, maybe a little shopping; buy a souvenir for the kid, a trinket for the wife, and then back home in 10 hours. Hey, no big deal, just another business trip. All these places are the same anyway.

The reality of business travel from the other side is a little different. By flashing that suit, Rolex, Tony Lama boots, and wafting that distinctly American/Aussie/Canuck/Brit accent, you have become the enemy, the victim, and the provider.

Business travel is perhaps the most dangerous form of travel. Most tourists wouldn't consider flying into a Colombian war zone for a week. Yet folks from oil, computer, pharmaceutical, agricultural, and telecom companies do it regularly. By doing business, you tend to frequent establishments and locations where thieves, terrorists, and opportunists seek affluent victims—luxury hotels, expensive restaurants, expat compounds, airports, embassies, and so on.

Business travel also exposes you to frequent car and air travel and other means of transportation in the grittiest industrial areas and slums. Many trips are also undertaken in bad-weather conditions and at congested travel periods. You are handed along very carefully through a chain of businesses that cater to businesspeople and become a high-profile target for criminals who prey on business travelers. You make appointments well in advance with complete strangers and you have no idea where you are going or where you are, and you even tell strangers you are lost. I often shudder when I see oil-field technicians, complete with cowboy hats, pointed boots, and silver Halliburton briefcases, tossing beer-soaked profanities and Ben Franklins around the world's transit lounges. Can you think of a more inviting target?

**Business travel news**
http://usatoday.com/travel/tfront.htm

**iJET Travel Intelligence**
http://www.ijet.com

**Weather**
http://www.weather.com/activities/travel

**Sports**
http://espn.go.com

**How to make a stiff drink**
http://www.bacardi.com

**Entertainment**
http://www.escortservices.com

**Corporate Travel Safety**
http://www.corporatetravelsafety.com

**Kroll Information Services**
http://kins.kroll-ogara.com/index.cfm

Business travel is not more or less dangerous, but people who travel on business tend to be preoccupied with appointments, directions, and preparing for meetings. This sort of travel also exposes travelers to areas where crimes are committed more often, such as nightclubs, downtown areas, banks, expat restaurants, and other high-profile spots.

But cheer up, the chances of being kidnapped and returned home safe are the least of your worries. You could end up dead without even being kidnapped, extorted, or waylaid. According to International SOS Assistance in Geneva, Switzerland—a company that specializes in health, security, and insurance for travelers—a deadly traffic accident is the most likely reason you'll be flown home dead. Cardiac arrest is the second most likely reason. Tropical diseases are the third. Have fun.

**Foreign Embassies of Washington, D.C.**
http://www.embassy.org/embassies/index.html

**Foreign Consular Offices in the United States**
http://www.state.gov/s/cpr/rls/fco
http://www.state.gov/www/travel/consular_offices/fco_index.html

**Important phone numbers when abroad**
http://travel.state.gov/phone_faq.html

**Business travel tips and advice**
http://businesstravel.about.com/smallbusiness/businesstravel/mbody.htm
http://dest.travelocity.com/Tips/Item/0,3295,_TRAVELOCITY_40,00.html
http://www.biztraveler.org

http://www.internationalist.com/welcome.php3
http://www.bisnis.doc.gov/bisnis/bisnis.cfm
http://www.embassy.org/ibc

**U.S. Embassies**
http://usembassy.state.gov

**Yahoo! directory of Embassies and Consulates**
http://dir.yahoo.com/Government/Embassies_and_Consulates

**Diplomatic Missions and Consular Posts**
http://c-d.org/missions

**Online Services for the Diplomatic Corps**
http://www.ediplomat.com

# TIPS ON SURVIVING BUSINESS TRAVEL

Don't feel guilty. Most business travelers have not read *DP,* and the ones who have enjoyed chuckling at the well-intended advice. After all, it's always the other guy who needs it. . . . Right?

- Keep in mind that expats, reps from multinationals, and foreign business-people are the most favored economic targets of criminals and terrorists.
- Have your host set up transportation, hotel, and a driver/bodyguard. This is cheap insurance and insulation from the realities of the third world.
- Don't get too chatty with the locals. All that info about your travel, room, samples, and employer is worth money to evil men.
- Avoid restaurants frequented by expats and tourists. Don't make reservations in your own name. Do not sit outside. If possible, enjoy your host's hospitality.
- Dress in business attire, carry a briefcase, and dress up only when necessary.
- Don't get into arguments. Yeah, the food sucks, the service is pathetic, and you can't get a decent steak, but making enemies is one sure way to end up on a Polaroid, holding the latest newspaper.
- Make copies of important papers. Separate your credit cards in case you lose your wallet. Keep the numbers, expiration dates, and phone numbers to order replacements. Be careful of credit card fraud, business scams, and identity theft.
- Don't reveal home addresses or phone numbers, or show your wallet when meeting people. Use your business address or P.O. box.
- Wear a cheap watch (or just show the band outward). If driving, wear your watch on the arm inside the car. Leave jewelry at home or in the hotel safe.
- Get used to sitting near emergency exits, memorize fire escape routes in the dark, lock your doors, and be aware at all times.
- Kidnappers need prior warning, routine schedules, or tip-offs to do their dirty work. Vary your schedule, change walking routes, and don't be shy about changing hotel rooms or assigned cabs.
- Do not carry unmarked prescription drugs. Expect small gifts like cigars or alcohol to be appropriated by customs officials. Bring something that can be offered instead, like chocolates, small bottles of booze, or tips in small denominations.
- Leave questionable reading material at home (i.e., *Playboy,* political materials, *DP,* or magazines).
- Carry small gifts for customs, drivers, and other people you meet. Personalized pens or small flashlights are ideal. Knockout drugs are very popular.
- When you talk on hotel or business phones, assume someone is listening.
- Watch your drink being poured.
- Do not hang the "Make Up Room" sign on your hotel room door. Rather, use the "Do Not Disturb" sign. Keep the TV or radio on even when you leave the room. Contact housekeeping and tell them you don't want your room cleaned up.

# TOURISTS

## Fodder for Fiends

The fifth of July, 1841, was an auspicious day. It was the day that 570 passengers traveled by Midland rail to Leicester and back in the world's first organized tour, put together by Thomas Cook. The passengers were the local temperance association in Market Harborough on their way to attend a gathering in Loughborough. Tourism is designed to help pack all your troubles and cares away and just have fun. Isn't it?

Let's take a look at *DP*'s summer vacation slide show:

**Slide 1:** Nineteen French tourists drown on ferry
**Slide 2:** Eight tourists hacked to death while guerrilla, er, sorry, gorilla trekking in Uganda
**Slide 3:** British tourist killed in bus plunge (love that word . . .)

**Slide 4:** Japanese tourist and his bus driver murdered in Guatemala after locals thought they were buying kids for body parts

**Slide 5:** One hundred and eighty killed in a Bali disco, 90 of them Australians on vacation.

It was quite a vacation, wasn't it? Oh, let's not forget the Venezuelan plane crash, the 2 Spanish trekkers clubbed to death in India, the 10 tourists kidnapped from a Malaysian dive resort, the 20 tourists snatched from a Philippine resort—and of course, the tourists murdered in a Colombian national park . . . Oh, I see you have nodded off. We didn't even get to the tourist rapes, beatings, bombings, shootings, extortions, druggings, and other stuff that never made it into the papers.

Would *DP* be exaggerating if we said that tourists are fodder for fiends? Probably. If your idea of a vacation is two weeks in Orlando and a Howard Johnson, then you probably don't spend too much time worrying about *Interahamwe* unbuckling their pants and slobbering over your wife. We do get a nice little cluster of tourist killings in Florida and some really good bus tour massacres every 5 or 10 years, but the meat and potatoes of terrorist and criminal groups are take-out fare.

Let's examine the modern *touristicus domesticus*. They travel in predictably jabbering gaggles, following well-worn trails. Monolingual, they pay little attention to their environment because they are terrified of being left behind. They usually wear outlandish colorful plumage. Gray walking shoes sprout cream-of-mushroom legs marbled with blue veins topped off by what could be either a spare tire or a bulging, overstuffed money belt. Their necks are usually tilted up with a rhythmic swivel, bent slightly forward by the weight of their JC Penney Camcorder and auto-everything SLR with zoom telephoto, binoculars, and silk-screened vinyl camera bag. Their mouths are in a state of continual movement as they talk, not necessarily to each other, but to ensure that they are having a good time and seeing wonderful things. They usually arrive in swarms in shiny buses and descend like locusts to strip souvenir stands clean and then cluster in tight groups under the watchful eye of an overly pleasant, multilingual guide holding an umbrella.

Tourists are the main source of sustenance for touts, louts, and thugs. Some of these tourists do funny things. They sneak away from those bus tour hotels and migrate to seedy places to watch local women take their clothes off. They drink too much. They make friends too easily. They stay out too late. They stagger home at 4 in the morning singing German drinking songs and get lost. Not bad people, just trusting, naive people in the wrong place at the wrong time. And that is the time when bad things happen.

## AAAH, HOME AT LAST

You are more likely to be robbed or become a victim of crime at home. So after you have memorized *DP* for your next vacation, how do you figure out if you might be living in a *DP*? Well, you can't really. It is the function of police departments to keep statistics even in a relatively civilized place like the United States. But how do you find out the relative safety or danger by region? You can start with the Uniform Crime Report and then work your way down to a state level. You might even work your way down to a neighborhood level, but even that is misleading because the location may be of a crime against businesses and not people. Industrial areas with low population have high crime rates. A number of private companies are now stepping in where the government fails and are providing accurate assessments of crime to the public.

*CAP Index*
http://www.capindex.com

*HomeFair.com*
http://www.homefair.com

*Uniform Crime Report*
http://www.fbi.gov/ucr/ucr.htm

There is a subspecies of the *touristicus domesticus*. It is the fabled *touristicus backpackensius*. Unlike the much derided domestic version, this species is more likely to be solitary, but most likely will be seen with a same-sex partner. The key indicators are hiking boots or Nike ACGs, hairy legs with knobby knees (often with scabs from mountain-bike spills), T-shirts with politically correct slogans, hiking outerwear (with ski tags still attached), and UV-block sunglasses. The older members of this subspecies will have gray ponytails. Their mates will have a gray brushcut and fishing lures for earrings. They like to think they are independent, even though they bunch up at the same youth hostels and flophouses each night. These folks are college educated, worldwise, and, in their minds, unlikely to be a victim of any criminal. They are one with the earth and its cultures (they were into world music waaay before Sting or Gabriel), giving them a sense of love and harmony.

So what's to worry about? Could it be that entire year's supply of money in their "secret" neck pouch? How about that new $200 altimeter, stopwatch, or chronometer watch? Those $120 boots are worth a quick $20. And the $400 backpack can fetch another quick 10 bucks. These travelers often enjoy entertainment and souvenirs of the narcotic kind, carry everything on their backs, and wouldn't be noticed missing for at least a month. Good pickings for the charming bandito or even drug-planting *polizia*.

The point of the cheap shots above is to tell you that it doesn't matter who you think you are. You are a primping pigeon in the fox house, a pathetically naive foreigner in a land that is not your own. Go through the thought process. You need a quick hundred bucks, who are you going to go after? Your neighbor or a tourist?

If you are the victim of crime while on vacation, chances are you will hotfoot it to your nearest embassy or the next town to whine to the police. They will look very concerned, have you fill out all kinds of paperwork, and assure you with religious solemnity that this is an outrage against humanity and this case will receive their utmost attention. Of course, a small gratuity to ensure that this case is brought to a speedy conclusion is appreciated. You won't hear them chuckling as they slip your fiver in the tea money chest and slide your smudged police report in the trash.

Why? Well, for starters, you just infused the local economy with a little wealth. The police don't have enough money or time to investigate local murders, let alone petty theft, and you won't be back to file charges or even see the process through. So get over it, consider yourself the ideal victim. And unlike most books that tell you the same dumb stuff, *DP* is going to give you some tricks we don't want you to pass on to your friends.

The good news: The major purpose of crime against tourists is to quickly remove money and other valuables. The perpetrator does not want to hurt you or escalate your brief meeting into assault or murder because the *federales* will be more interested in finding him. The bad news? Same as the above.

Does it get worse? Well, there is rape. Sometimes it's a function of social cultures clashing—usually a result of unaccompanied Western women who travel in rural or sexually frustrated cultures. Other times, it is a violent attack. In a world where *Baywatch* and *The Young and the Restless* are the most-widely syndicated shows, one can do little but hope that they remake and syndicate *Little House on the Prairie* soon, to balance things out.

**L**ook for countries where they make tourist attractions out of skulls (Cambodia) or eat smoked monkeys (Congo) to give you a heads-up that tourists may not be cherished gods.

In the case of homicide or brutal attacks, you have to look at the track record of the country you are going to visit. It is not uncommon for bandits to execute robbery victims simply because they won't get caught. Look for countries where they make tourist attractions out of skulls (Cambodia) or eat smoked monkeys (Congo) to give you a heads-up that tourists may not be cherished gods.

## *DP* Survival Course: Seven Things That Will Save Your Life

### Be Alert

Crooks need you to be distracted, lost, in need of assistance, or simply in the wrong place. Just adopting the habit of stopping and watching people around (and behind you) will arm you against crime. Of course you are on vacation, in a new place and paying attention to everything but being a victim. That's why you'll do just fine as a victim.

### Be Sober

Alcohol, drugs, jet lag, and having too good of a time can fuzz your common sense, making you think for one unfortunate moment that you are with cool cats when you're really among wolves. Even pleasant encounters with the locals in bars can lead to ugly bruises and lost pesos if you don't stay in control. Scams begin when the perpetrator thinks he can overcome your better judgment. Bars and nightclubs are also places where bad people hang out.

### Use It or Lose It

Preventing theft begins when you pack. If you take too much "stuff" and are forced to leave items in your car or hotel, you dramatically increase the chances of losing your "stuff." Travel light; plan on giving away most of the items you bring and perhaps buying local clothes at your destination.

### Insure and Ensure

I know this is something Mutual of Omaha's Marlin Perkins would have told you, but it really does make a difference if your camera, clothes, health, and even life are insured against loss when traveling. You worry less, and if the choice is your new video camera or your life, insurance makes the decision a lot easier. Same goes for cash. Traveler's checks are a pain, but worth it for large blocks of cash. Also, credit cards let you do everything from chartering aircraft to buying blowguns, and even medivac insurance ensures that you can be flown to your local hospital if you get hit by a poisoned dart.

### Trust No One

When you travel, you will meet hundreds of strangers with either pure or impure thoughts. It all depends on the image you present. If you are interested in their kids, their health, and their family, the chances of something evil happening to you decrease. At the same time, understand that financial pressures in some countries might force these same people to finger you to a gang of thugs or pick your pocket. So don't flash your wealth, but do flash your smile.

### Stay Away From Tourists

Tourists attract petty criminals and con artists like dogs attract fleas. It goes without saying that crime occurs at youth hostels, tourist attractions, busy plazas, red-light districts, and other popular spots.

### Prevent Opportunists

Crime generally occurs after you change $2,000 at the Amex office or your wife hitches up her girdle to get $10 to pay for the museum tickets. Other "Rob Me" signs are open zippers on backpacks, luggage endlessly circling on carousels, waterproof cases with lots of stickers on them, papers sticking out of breast pockets, fat purses, and bulging pockets. Places like trunks of rental cars, towels at beaches, and daytime hotel rooms are areas where cameras, money, and just about everything of any value should be expected to disappear.

## Survival Tips for Hard-Core Travelers: Lock 'em, Fake 'em, or Take 'em

### Lock 'em Out

The best defense is preparation. By being careful, you will avoid unfortunate incidents and wonder what all this fuss is about. Most doors to hotel rooms can be flipped open by a 90-pound maid, so it doesn't take much for a 200-pound thug to enter your room at night. Don't open the door if there is a pleasant knock. (That is where you keep all your worldly possessions, isn't it?) That "security latch" is held on to that rotting door frame with two cheap wood screws. God invented pepper spray for this event, if you insist on cracking open the door.

Although it is not as pervasive as street robbery, hotel robbery is more serious. Use a wedge, motion detector, or chair against the door when you go to sleep. During the day, leave a TV or radio on. Take the room key with you and keep your valuables in the hotel safe. In less-developed countries, leave your valuables with the innkeeper or his family.

Use a retractable wire cable to tie the handles of your bags together even when in your hotel. Or, a caribiner can clip two bag handles together or it can clip to something immovable. Buy large combo locks (not those useless luggage locks) and use them on all openings, or use twist ties on zippers to keep them together. The harder you make it to steal your things, the less of a chance they will be stolen. Stick your backpack in a grubby lockable duffel when checking or storing it.

## Fake 'em Out

If you find yourself being trailed by an unshaven man through the back streets, then it's time for Plan B. Strange as it seems, the act of throwing down a decoy pouch or wallet will defuse most pursuit situations. (Unless, of course, the puffing, swarthy man is just trying to catch up to you to return the camera you left at the restaurant.)

Assume that your attacker is just after your money. So give it to him, but not much of it. Carry a moneybelt, pouch, wallet, and neck pouch with a little bit of money in each place. Protest a lot, toss it, and then run like hell in the opposite direction.

When you are being robbed, your attacker may have a weapon. The trick is to keep slowly shuffling backward as you fumble with your decoy pouch or wallet. If you think you can sprint to a safe place, do it. Most thugs will not chase you when other people are around. The attacker is as much of a coward as you are. The difference is, he knows what he is doing and you don't.

If you feel mad as hell and decide you aren't going to take it anymore, try this trick I have used with complete success. Simply stick your hand in your shirt or waistband, turn around and start walking forcefully and directly toward your potential assailant. Never take your eyes off him. When he zigs, you zig and when he zags, you zag. In most cases (I repeat *most*) he will think you are going to pull something on him and will quickly walk in another direction. Anyway, it's more fun than waiting around, knees trembling, to find out what his real intentions are. Oh . . . by the way, I am 6' 4" and 220 pounds. If you are forcibly restrained or bushwhacked, see the "Take 'em Out" section.

Here's a quick overview on how to fake 'em:

- Sew an inside pocket in your shirt under the arm, extend an existing pocket to the inside, or add a panel to your boxers. (You can make an inside pocket or buy the kind that loops over your belt loop and tucks inside your pants.) Use Velcro fasteners.
- Keep your passport and airline tickets in a waterproof freezer bag in an inside pocket.
- Hide money within your various possessions: inside backpack tubes, shoe linings, on the backs of telephoto lenses, sewn into pant cuffs, the lining of your luggage, in books, and so on. You may lose some money, but you'll end up with some, too.
- Save your expired credit cards and *afghanis* to plump up a decoy wallet. Carry it in your inside front pocket.

- Do not carry a purse. If you must, don't carry any money in it since most thieves stay around only long enough to grab the purse and then run away.
- Carry money in concealable holsters, vests, and attachments. You can find most of these items in gun magazines.
- Wear your watch on the arm that is inside a car and away from your window. It is better not to wear a watch at all since it is the first thing a thief (or customs inspector) looks at to judge your eligibility as a victim.

## Take 'em Out

If you are attacked, your attacker will have the advantage. He will either sneak up behind you or boldly walk up to you, or, if you make him nervous, he will hit you with a blunt object. Violent attacks often are performed by groups or gangs. They will typically continue to kick and hit you while they tear off your possessions and empty your pockets. Quite honestly, you are better off shielding your head and stomach and helping them find what they are looking for. Keep in mind that if you choose to fight, you are endangering your life and you must also be prepared to see this through until your attacker becomes the victim.

Any book that tells you how to be like Jackie Chan in these situations is, for lack of a better term, bullshit. Hey, you are on vacation, tough guy, and probably three sheets to the wind when all this is going down. As for women, whoever decides to prey on you probably does this on a nightly basis. People are all animals when attacked. When someone comes at you with an intent to hurt you, the last thing on your mind will be which smooth Kung Fu moves you will use to pulverize your opponent. You can actually watch the amount of time it takes for a happy tourist to slowly realize that he or she is becoming a statistic. It takes at least 20 seconds before they usually wise up—if they are sober.

Typically, the aggressor will stake you out and follow you until you are in the place he wants you to be. At this point, everything you do must be reactive. So learn the basics of self-defense: Boxing, karate, knife fighting, and self-defense training will tell you which parts of the body really hurt when you jab them and a few nasty tricks that will leave your attacker sucking wind through broken teeth.

- Do not carry a weapon. In many countries this will make you subject to criminal charges or imprisonment, and damages your status as a "victim." Instead, learn to use everyday objects like a pen, walking stick, Swiss army knife, flashlight, single-edge razor, and so on.
- Be careful of items like pepper spray, mace, short nonfolding knives, and other offensive weapons. They can be used against you (many

people who use pepper spray or mace often spray themselves or inhale the fumes) and are considered offensive weapons in some countries (like the UK). Airport security will take all of these weapons from you. They won't, however, take away an equally deadly steel pen refill—my favorite weapon.

- One of the best items is the *kubotan* (developed by Takayuki Kubota), who created a system of (believe it or not) pen fighting. The *kubotan* is a five-and-a-half-inch-long rod often attached to a set of keys. The basic principle behind the *kubotan* is to apply pressure and cause intense pain to your opponent.

- Learn to use a sharp object against the groin, upper neck, throat, eyes, and nose. All are useless unless your weapon is free and your arm is unrestrained. The proper thrust is a hard jab "through" the victim followed by as many blows as it takes to incapacitate the victim. If you are in this position, though, things are going to get serious.

- There are a number of books and courses on self-defense. *DP* recommends Tai Kwon Do, karate, boxing, and even Thai kickboxing. Even judo, aikido, and jujitsu will make you comfortable with controlled violence and build your reactive instincts. All are part of street survival and, more importantly, building self-confidence. Once again, consider the consequences of severely beating a stranger in a strange land. You may end up in jail.

- Responses that are always successful in doling out pain, regardless of relative size or strength, are the heel of the hand under the nose, the bowling ball eyeball grip, and the knee in the groin. When in doubt, go for the eyes and run.

## Do Unto Others . . . Then Split

Any violent encounter has an emotional after-effect that may turn your trip into a nightmare. Any criminal act in which a local is injured can lead to accusations, recriminations, and very expensive penalties. Yes, you may have been right when the drunken son of the local police chief tried to rape you and you righteously kicked his butt . . . but . . . "*lo siento señorita*, theeese is no your country." It would be unfair to assume that there are specific forms of tourist crime and specific tips to prevent it. But luckily crime is "relative." You stand a much better chance of being murdered or waylaid by a close acquaintance at home than by a total stranger when you travel.

So before you weld your door locks shut and burn your passport, remember that despite all the efforts of the world's criminals to ruin your vacation, most tourists will complain about cold French fries and lumpy mattresses. Oh, I almost forgot, the most common problems for travelers are diarrhea and sunburn. So, hey, let's be careful out there.

# In a Dangerous Place: Central Asia

### HOTEL TAJIKISTAN

Dushanbe is about the prettiest city in Central Asia with the ugliest buildings. It has wide tree-lined streets with a snowcapped backdrop. The odd German-built apartments, or structures, are in stark contrast to the land-based version of Russian space junk. Massive slabs of blighted aluminum, rusty steel supports, scabby concrete, and stained glass are testament to the Russian talent for blending bad architecture with shoddy construction. Back in the '50s and '60s the Soviets replaced most of the elegant and tumbledown Tajik architecture with their Orwellian/Bauhaus view of the future. Every building must have large slogans and dramatic tableaus of deadly serious workers. But the office and government buildings are Taj Mahals when compared to the epitome of Russian nontechnology: the Intourist hotel.

Here the visitor's first impression of the country is living proof that Russian architecture conspires mightily against Russian construction skills. The abundance of right angles, tile floors, and large plazas are all designed to show up the crooked lines, uneven floors, sloppy construction, and lack of siting. In this cold and gray city, fountains are big. Or, I should say, what should have been fountains are big. Most of them are broken and filled with green slime. Walls of glass doors are bolted or forced shut with chains, hundreds of multiple light fixtures lie empty, with the few that are working containing evil-looking, green flickering tubes.

Russian hotels are square, ugly, large, and dull because they are supposed to be. It makes putting in extra hours at the Gulag much more attractive. Here hotels are designed with heating but no cooling, have no opening windows but balconies, and assume either that all guests will drink themselves unconscious each night or that the Russian businessmen will spend the night with a local hooker and have to turn the lights off because she is so ugly. This philosophy carries over to Russian bars—dark bars, wicked-witch-of-the-east floor ladies with massive chin warts and deflated tractor-tire innertube-sized breasts. These floor ladies were bred to make sure that nothing of value could be stolen or broken because there is nothing of value in a Russian hotel. Even the crushed and scratched water bottles that appeared in my room were reused.

Besides being filthy, dark, and ridiculously expensive, these former Intourist hellholes are models of inefficiency. If a job can't be done slow enough by one glacially moving person, there are usually three immobile people to explain why it can't be done at all . . . ever. If you have a complaint, like the four hookers and the policeman that were sitting on my bed when I came in late, the staff has been trained to slowly lift one eyebrow and tilt their head to the side as if one of my relatives just died. "Sorry. No Heeengleesh." These are the same people that bang on my door at 6 AM to remind me how much I owe them in perfect Queen's diction.

The staff at this hotel are obviously veterans of the hotel business. They have succeeded in ensuring that the hotel is unpopulated except for the drunk Russian soldiers who are forced to live here. If an unwitting adventurer shows up to claim a room, they have an insidious process of paperwork and withheld features (like water or electricity). Naturally, they put me on the top floor because the elevators don't work.

To claim your room, it takes an inordinate amount of thin brown paper, carbon copies, broken pencils, and stamps. I fill out two closely spaced identical forms in triplicate and am handed back four pieces of paper, two receipts, a breakfast chit, and a tiny card with my room number on it. Most of my paperwork has been stamped twice. It takes three people to tear, file, and stamp the paperwork that I never actually get a copy of. I ask if there are other tourists here and the young lady says, "Yes, many." According to the book there are two other Westerners and a group of Chinese businessmen. They're slipping.

The guard shows me how to override the safety lock on the elevator. It works. The elevator groans upward, the floor numbers in the elevator are all akimbo as if someone from Pee-Wee's Playhouse wanted that jumbled effect. The smell is unique: B.O., stale vodka, and cigarettes.

I don't actually get a key. I get two pieces of crinkled paper that I am to hand to the grumpy guardian when I get there. I know she is grumpy before the elevator doors grind open painfully. She looks like she was doing just fine sitting with the lights out, framed by dead potted plants. I hand her my grubby slips of brown paper and she arthritically files them in a drawer in slow motion.

I still don't get a key. As if I really can't be trusted, she just opens the door for me when I need to get in.

My floor lady is a real beauty: a heavy-jowled, gold-toothed scowling matron who jealously guards a box of battered keys (which itself is locked and requires a key that appears magically from beneath her dirty skirts to unlock). She's wearing dayglo pink socks and a fuzzy white sweater, and I can't stop staring at the large fleshy warts on her face. They're the kind that have three or four black hairs on them. The kind you want to snip off while she is not looking. She shuffles off in her soiled slippers in her peculiar hunched-over style, mumbling all the way. Needless to say, my room is filthy in a grubby patina sort of way—the look that film producers yearn for when they do stories about junkies or suicides. Every cheap furnishing or object is worn and broken, every surface is diseased with cracks and brown scabs. As if to add a touch of literary romance, my toilet paper is actually a yellowing Russian novel shoved behind the rusty water pipe. I think it's a novel, but then again it could be the launch instructions to their nuclear missiles. Now I know why the Russians promoted the publication of so much literature.

If you are used to American hotels, where an eager bellhop hustles up your luggage and jumps around showing you how things work, well, you're in for a treat. Here, the floor lady glumly shows me everything that doesn't work. The now-familiar, crossed-arms sign language for "forbidden" or "broken" seems to be the only and most useful word the Russians don't bother using. If she has no memory of it ever working, she waves her hand as if it is beyond her jurisdiction.

The only thing that American and Russian hotel staffs have in common is the outstretched palm at the end of the tour. I give her some coins and she gives that backup harumph and leaves with my key.

So now I can admire my room in solitude. It is decorated with a stained overstuffed chair that takes up too much room, a table with a large dirty glass, a chipped ashtray, and a tiny TV. The bed looks like a stretcher (though not as wide or soft) and it even has a dirty gray blanket to give it that military hospital look. There is also an ancient refrigerator, a heater, a phone, an air conditioner, and a lamp. All are broken except the lamp. I really don't know if the lamp is broken because it doesn't have a bulb. The colors are those '50s "made in China"–style pastels you see in retro stores these days. Out on my balcony I have a stunning view of a public toilet, a trash fire, and a hazy panorama of nondescript box buildings that disappear into the haze.

I was told through sign language and raised fingers that there is hot water between 6:30 and 7:30 in the morning and between 7 and 8 at night. Exactly when people don't need it, I guess. She explained very carefully that the reason I don't have any towels is because there is no hot water. When there is hot water, she will bring the towels. Uh huh.

Right now there is no water at all, so the brown-throated toilet doesn't flush either. I guess, following this logic, she should have taken my Russian novel away and returned it when the water came back on.

I find out that although I paid for a deluxe suite, I was given a cheaper room, which is a common scam in most Russian hotels. The price for this hotel is $80 to $120 if you prepay in America. I pay $35, but I am sure the folks behind the desk pocketed most, if not all, of that money.

Dushanbe's wide and empty streets beckon me, but I find out that it is not wise to be out because of the curfew, the shootings, and the potential for kidnapping. That's okay. I was looking for a reason to visit the disco anyway. Downstairs, things are jumping. It is pitch black and empty except for a sullen bartender. He obviously knows his stuff. The music is that whiny, drank-too-much Russian stuff that they sing before they blow their brains out. Perfect for dancing to. The only good thing is that beer costs 90 cents, but tastes like it should cost less.

The light show is really just two alternating floodlights; one red and one green, both spastically unrelated to the lack of beat in the music. Soon after I enter, the music is drowned out by the blaring TV behind the bar—another stern-faced Russian impassively watching deadly dull news about some disaster destroying the country. The bartender politely stares at me, and after one insipid beer I figure I've had enough partying for one night. I sleep for the first time in two days. There is not much noise after 8 PM in Dushanbe, other than sporadic gunfire.

I am awakened by the hoarse phlegmatic sound of someone trying to hawk up a giant wet loogie. Or is it an oil strike bubbling up under our hotel? Something is coming up from the bowels of the building. I discover the floor lady lied. I have left the tap open by mistake and it would appear that my fantasies are about to be realized—a hot shower after shivering most of the night under my thin, smelly blanket.

There is hot water, although technically the hot water is cold now. There is brown water and foul-smelling gas coming from the hot-water spigot. In bright anticipation of a hot shower, I let the water run in the rusty, blackened shower. It takes precisely 30 of the allotted 60 minutes for the water to turn warm. I crack open my one luxury, the hotel-provided shampoo, a bright red fluid that smells like mold. I don't care. Maybe this is a luxury suite after all. Naturally, my towels never show up, so in an act of defiance, I dry myself on the scratchy, foul-smelling army blanket. Life is good in Tajikistan. At the best hotel in town.

*—RYP*

# BRIBES

## Stand and Deliver

You can't avoid it. The officious smile, the bad breath, the gold tooth. The expression of true remorse for your condition. Yes, my well-traveled friend, it's time to contribute to the health and welfare of law enforcement around the world. Call it payola, mordida, dash, spiffs, baksheesh, cadeau, processing fees, tea money, fines, gifts, or whatever the term, but paying the "bribe" is a regular part of travel in the third world. So don't get upset when the military, police, and government officials expect a gratuity or donation to allow passage, or as payment for minor infractions, or to issue visas. In some cases, when evil child soldiers forget the social niceties part, it may be your money or your life.

But you, you fearless *DP* reader, are no patsy. You don't need no stinking badges, so you say "stuff it where the sun don't shine" in the appropriate language and drive on. You see, you forgot you are playing a game where the other side has already won. Get indignant, yell for your nonexistent consulate, wave your sweat-soaked business card around, and you may find yourself the proud new owner of a mysterious bag of narcotic substance. Your voice goes up an octave, you shriek, "I want a lawyer, this is a frame-up!" You still don't get it, do you? Keep screaming, Papillon, it's only going to cost you more.

So the penalty for not playing the bribery game could be spending some serious time in a very ugly penalty box. You don't have to be a criminal to pay bribes. Criminals take great pride in their ability to extract bribes or "protection money" from honest folks. Moscow has 12 major organized crime groups that have been known to extract up to 30 percent of monthly profits from businesses. So the best way to view bribes is as you would tipping. When a country lowers its wages to its police and officials below the poverty line, they look to you to make ends meet.

Most travelers who are put in jail actually do break the law. Typically they are involved in traffic- or drug-related offenses. Most of them actually broke many more laws, but the severity of their infraction demands retribution.

Keep in mind that it serves no purpose for small or poor countries to incarcerate you for lengthy periods of time. It also does not serve the purpose of policemen to spend their time filling out paperwork when they can resolve the problem and teach you a lesson on the spot. From Minnesota to Malaysia to Mexico, I have been amazed at the solid financial education police officers have been given. (Which is better: $100 in your pocket or in the policeman's pocket?)

But be forewarned, though, there are actually officers who do not accept or want bribes. They will have the nerve to get indignant and throw you in jail. The way to tell is simple. If you are stopped by an officer and he tries to resolve a problem rather than just write you up, handcuff you, or arrest you, you are expected to begin the bribe process. This does not mean stuffing cash into his pockets until he says stop. It's important to add a level of social interaction so that all involved have a good time. Get too indignant and you may hurt the feelings of your scrub-faced, beer-bellied friend.

If you feel an opening gambit has been made, then you are expected to explain to the officer your desire for a speedy and amicable resolution of your problem. In most cases, the officer will share your feelings of injustice about his having to take you all the way back to the station to wait for the judge who is typically out until next week.

If he offers to take the fine back for you or to let you pay it on the spot, then bingo, the chiseling begins. Remember that bribes are a "cash-only" business and the amount you can pay will be limited to the amount of cash you have on you at that moment. Now that you have the rules of the game, please remember that offering any financial inducement to an officer, however innocently, is illegal and can put you in jail.

## Delivering a Bribe

One must never discuss money, the amount, or the reason for the gift. Typically, you will be presented with a "problem" that can be solved but will take time, money, or approval by a higher authority. You will naturally need to have this problem solved. You may ask if there is a fee that will expedite the solution of this problem, or if the local language fails you, you can point out your urgency and present a passport, ticket, or papers with a single denomination of currency tucked inside.

### *DP*'S GUIDE TO BRIBES

| | |
|---|---|
| Minor traffic violations (speeding, imaginary stop signs, burned-out taillights that magically work) | $5–$10 |
| Traffic violations (real stop signs, real speeding tickets) | $10–$50 |
| Serious traffic violations (DUI, very serious speeding or racing) | $50–$500 |
| Very serious traffic problems (accident with no fatalities) | $500–$1,000 |
| Accidents that involve fatalities require the application of funds to a judge, your lawyer, the prosecutor, and probably the police chief | $2,000–$6,000 |
| If you are involved in something shady and need to correct the problem, it is wise to hire a lawyer | $10,000–$45,000 |
| Night out and breakfast at the White House | $500,000 |

## The Price for Doing Bad Things

Bribes might not work if you are caught by the military or happen to be doing something the government is busy eradicating (usually with U.S. funds) at the time. Smuggling drugs, weapons, or people requires the support of a large, covertly sanctioned organization. Freelancers are usually treated roughly with little opportunity to buy their way out. Depending on how big a fish they think you are, you can expect to pay about $12,000 to get out of a South or Central American jail. It is not uncommon to have to pay $30,000 to $120,000 to beat a major drug rap.

The best way to check out bribes is to contact the local embassy, expats who live in the area, local journalists (not foreign journalists), and local lawyers. It should be stated that in many cases a demand for a bribe can be talked down if you are doing nothing wrong. Many junior customs officials will spot first-timers and shake them down for everything from their *Playboys* to their underwear. Feel free to protest, but when the man with the big hat and gold stars agrees with the peon, it's time to start rolling off the twenties.

## IS THAT A ROLL OF TWENTIES IN YOUR POCKET OR ARE YOU JUST HAPPY TO SEE ME?

| Ten Most Corrupt Nations | Ten Most Uncorrupt Places |
|---|---|
| 1. Bangladesh | 1. Finland |
| 2. Nigeria | 2. Denmark |
| 3. Uganda | 3. New Zealand |
| 4. Indonesia | 4. Iceland |
| 5. Kenya | 5. Singapore |
| 6. Cameroon | 6. Sweden |
| 7. Bolivia | 7. Canada |
| 8. Azerbaijan | 8. Netherlands |
| 9. Ukraine | 9. Luxembourg |
| 10. Tanzania | 10. Norway |

http://www.transparency.org

## When It Is Better to Give Than to Receive

Many people view bribery as reprehensible and evil. These are usually the ones who have to pay the bribes. Others view the practice as a normal way to supplement meager government wages (you can guess who they are). All countries including the United States have people who engage in this kind of activity. West and Central Africa are the worst places for bribery, followed by South America and then Central America. South Asia has a kinder, gentler form of bribery, and Russia/CIS and Eastern Europe basically function on extortion and bribery (their problem is that there are few normal functioning services to be corrupted). Northern Europe is the most incorruptible place.

How do you measure corruption? Start with a Russia—a place where foreign-aid money starts with a deluge and ends with a trickle. It evaporates before it reaches the parched ground. It is estimated that $7 billion in early '90s business loans never even reached the government coffers and went straight into off-shore accounts. Work is inflated to double the actual cost. The real money comes in and quickly goes out to a foreign account. Then a loan is floated from a bank to cover the remaining amount and is never paid back. Who says the Russians can't be good capitalists?

In Albania 8 percent of all commerce goes into government officials' pockets. Indonesian businesses slip off 20 percent of income to prevent unnecessary hassles, and in Pakistan shopkeepers kill themselves to protest excessive baksheesh demands. Nigeria has one of the worst reputations for *dash*. What would you expect from an oil-rich country that has to import oil and at the same time make its leaders wealthy? So it's not surprising to expect any minor official in most poor African nations to ask for a *cadeau* in exchange for providing a higher level of service. Expats detest this practice, because they have to go through customs, and refuse to pay it. Tourists are more easily intimidated and usually have much more to lose if they miss a flight, connection, or cruise because of unnecessary delays.

Remember that small bribes are used to facilitate services that can be withheld or denied. Usually tightwads will be processed, but at the back of the line. Obnoxious tightwads who like to make loud speeches about corruption may find themselves with insurmountable visa irregularities ("The stamp in your passport must be green ink for a 15-day visa").

## An Exciting New Franchise Opportunity

With a little help from Friedrich Scheider, an economics professor at the Kepler University in Linz, the *Economist* has estimated that the global GDP is 39 trillion. Another 9 trillion goes unaccounted for, based on how much currency is out there. Based on his study of 76 economies, and assuming that most dirty dealing is in cash, it is estimated that 15 percent of a country's economy is unreported income. In "emerging" economies, the percentage of black-market activity is about a third. When all is said and done, the study figures that almost 80 percent of Nigeria's GDP is black market, followed by Thailand (70%), Egypt (65%), the Philippines (50%), Mexico, and Russia (both at 40%). The most honest country? Switzerland, followed by Japan, the United States, and Austria.

A carton of cigarettes will ensure that you are speedily processed in most African countries. A bottle of Johnny Walker will not get you far in a Muslim country, but will definitely expedite your exit visa in Colombia. Border crossings into most Central American countries can be made for $100, and you can drive as fast as you want in Mexico if you have a good supply of $20 bills. With such gifts, you may not need a visa entering a country and the customs official may forgo even a cursory inspection of your vehicle.

If you need to be smuggled out of a country, it is a little more complicated. First, the "coyote" will demand about twice the normal fee for your departure and there is no guarantee that he will not turn you in for a reward. Second, the matter of securing an exit visa without the benefit of an entry visa will cost you between $100 and $200 in most Asian and Latin American countries. Eastern European and CIS countries can be crossed for as little as $5, with no guarantee that you will not be finked on 10 miles down the road.

> Using bribery is like kissing in junior high school. Both parties must be willing, but you have to be given an opening before you can make your move.

In summary, using bribery is like kissing in junior high school. Both parties must be willing, but you have to be given an opening before you can make your move. If you are brash or unwise, you will be severely rebuked.

# DANGEROUS JOBS

## Danger Live: Nine to Five

Not yet dissuaded from seeing the big, bad world? Don't have time or money for a dangerous vacation? Why not get a dangerous job, see the world, and make money too? Don't get too esoteric in your career goals. There are plenty of dull and dangerous jobs right here. Be a truck driver and get your kicks by being splattered on Route 66. Highway deaths accounted for nearly 25 percent of the 5,915 fatal work injuries in 2000. According to the U.S. Department of Labor, truck drivers had more fatal injuries than any other occupation, with 762 deaths in 2000.

Truck driver sound too romantic? Want your dangerous job closer to home? You could go postal. Homicide was the second leading cause of job-related deaths, accounting for 16 percent of the total. About half of the victims worked in retail establishments, such as grocery stores, restaurants, and bars, where cash is readily available (31,000 convenience store clerks are shot every year and robbery was the primary motive for workplace homicide). Taxicab drivers, police, and security guards also had high numbers of worker homicides. Four-fifths of the victims were shot; others were stabbed, beaten, or strangled. Although highway accidents were the leading manner of death for male workers, homicide was the leading cause for female workers, accounting for 35 percent of their fatal work injuries.

Falls accounted for 10 percent of fatal work injuries. The construction industry, particularly special trade contractors such as roofing, painting, and structural steel erection, accounted for almost half of the falls. One-fifth of the falls were from or through roofs, while falls from scaffolding and from ladders each accounted for about one-eighth. Nine percent of fatally injured workers were struck by various objects, a fourth of which were falling trees, tree limbs, and logs. Other objects that struck workers included machines and vehicles slipping into gear or falling onto workers, and various building materials such as pipes, beams, metal plates, and lumber. Electrocutions accounted for 5 percent of worker deaths in a 1-year span.

Occupations with large numbers of worker fatalities included truck drivers, farm workers, sales supervisors and proprietors, and construction laborers. Industry divisions with large numbers of fatalities included agriculture, forestry, fishing, construction, transportation and public utilities, and mining. Other high-risk occupations included airplane pilots, cashiers, and firefighters.

### THE MOST DANGEROUS JOBS IN AMERICA, OR WHY DON'T WE SEE MORE ACTION/ADVENTURE SHOWS STARRING THESE FOLKS?

| | |
|---|---|
| 1. Truck Driver | 8. Taxicab Driver |
| 2. Farmworker | 9. Timber Cutter |
| 3. Sales Supervisor/Proprietor | 10. Cashier |
| 4. Construction Worker | 11. Fisherman |
| 5. Police Detective | 12. Metalworker |
| 6. Airplane Pilot | 13. Roofer |
| 7. Security Guard | 14. Firefighter |

*Source:* U.S. Labor Department

# Dangerous Occupations

Okay, I am sorry, really sorry, but the image just does not match the reality. Dangerman is not landing on some foreign shore with bombs bursting and flags waving, he is probably fixing the Sno-cone machine just off I-55 at 3 AM. Or he may be ringing your doorbell for a postage-due package. We can all dream: Until you find that perfect high-risk wage job, here are a few other gigs you might consider:

## Army Ranger

The ranger course lasts 68 days and emphasizes patrolling and raiding. The course is being restricted, and very few noninfantry soldiers will be able to attend in the future. Troops from other branches of the army can attend if they are being sent to jobs with a specific need for ranger skills. The ranger school is considered the toughest course in the army.

*U.S. Army*
2425 Wilson Boulevard
Arlington, VA 22210
Tel.: (703) 841-4300
http://www.benning.army.mil/rtb/
rtbmain.htm

*Ranger School*
http://www.benning.army.mil/rtb/ranger/
rangerschool.htm
*Special Operations*
http://www.specialoperations.com/
Army/Rangers/default2.html

## Bicycle Messenger

There are about 1,500 bicycle messengers in New York City. Messengers are paid between $3 and $30 per trip. The average pay is about $7 per trip, with the messenger keeping half. There are, however, higher rates for rush and oversized packages. Messengers also earn bonuses for working in bad weather. A good bike messenger should make about $125 a day and between $500 and $700 a week. The faster you are, the more you can make, especially during rush hour. You have to supply your own bike (usually a $500 to $1,200 mountain bike), safety gear, and health insurance. The messenger company gives you a walkie-talkie and a big bag. Messengers work around the clock and break every rule in the book. Many practice "skitching," or grabbing onto a car or truck to speed up their trip.

*International Federation of Bike*
*Messenger Associations*
P.O. Box 191443
San Francisco, CA 94119-1443
magpie@messengers.org
http://www.messengers.org

*Bicycle Messengers Europe*
http://www.bme.org

*Background on bicycle messengers*
http://www.transalt.org/blueprint/
    chapter14
http://www.messengers.org/travel

*Cycle Messengers*
http://www.angelfire.com/ct/cmwd

*Profile of Messengers*
http://www.transalt.org/blueprint/
    chapter14/chapter14d.html

## Blowout Control

If you like your work hot and dangerous, try containing oil blow-outs. The most famous of these workers is, of course, Red Adair and his group, who inspired a movie starring John Wayne. Despite the dramatic footage of men covered in oil and being roasted, safety comes first. Red is retired, but the company, Global Industries, Inc., lives on.

The general idea is that when oil wells catch on fire, or blow out, there is a lot of money being sprayed into the air. So these people have to work fast. Saddam Hussein overtaxed companies from eight countries when he set the Kuwaiti fields alight. There were 732 oil wells in need of capping, but not before U.S.$60 billion worth of oil had disappeared. Even though the companies can be paid up to a million dollars a job (mostly for equipment and expenses), a more realistic fee is between U.S.$20,000 and U.S.$200,000 to control a blowout. The members of the crew make about U.S.$300 to U.S.$1,000 a day each, plus room and board. The work requires a drilling background. It is tough, hard, and dirty work. You also can't pick your customers, since blowouts happen anywhere, anytime.

*Petroleum Industry Training Service*
Calgary Training Centre
1538 25th Avenue NE
Calgary, Alberta T2E 8Y3
Canada
Tel.: (403) 250-0891
polzin@pits.ca
http://www.pits.ca/internat.html

*Boots & Coots*
11615 North Houston-Rosslyn Road
Houston, TX 77086
Tel.: (281) 931-8884 or (800) BLOWOUT
http://www.bncg.com

*Global Industries, Inc.*
Corporate Headquarters
8000 Global Dr.
Carlyss, LA 70665
P.O. Box 442
Sulphur, LA 70664
Tel.: (337) 583-5000 or (800) 900-4733
Fax: (337) 583-5100
busdev@globalind.com
http://www.globalind.com

# Bodyguard

Not much danger here, but it sounds dangerous. "Big and beefy" works for the low-level celebrity stuff, "spry and deadly" works for the high-level political jobs. You can make about $200 to $300 a day (when you work), and if you think you'll be working on a yacht in Monte Carlo protecting bikini-clad rich gals, wake up and smell the B.O.

Most bodyguards work for businessmen. You can carry a gun, but it'll just wear a hole in your nice dry-cleaned shirts. If you're lucky, you can get a full-time gig where you also get to drive a car, open doors, and other step'n'fetchit stuff. Should something go down, you throw yourself in front of your employer and spend a few months in the hospital if you get shot. Ex's are the preferred folks here: ex-Secret Service, ex-cops, ex-military, and so on. *DP*'s best bet for adventure (but not bucks) is to go south (Latin America), young man, where bodyguarding is serious business. One of our buddies ended up being one of Vesco's bodyguards when he and a pal (ex-navy) were bumming around Costa Rica in the old days. They were hanging out in a bar and were enlisted to make a few *sucres* standing around looking tough.

*Professional Bodyguard Association*
72 New Bond Street
Mayfair–London
W1S1RR UK
xsas@hotmail.com
http://www.bodyguards-pba.com

*International Association of*
*Professional Protection Specialists*
5255 Stevens Creek Blvd., Suite 308
Santa Clara, CA 95051
Tel.: (408) 366-2300
Fax: (408) 343-1209
http://www.iapps.org

*Falcon Global Corporation*
55 Pierce Lane, Suite 204
Montoursville, PA 17754
Tel.: (724) 627-9443

*Anvil Service Group: Crisis Avoidance*
477 Mount Pleasant Road, Suite 400
Toronto, Ontario M4S 2L9
Canada
Tel.: (416) 487-0005
Fax: (416) 487-6264
http://www.anvilgroup.com

*National Bodyguard Association*
*of Russia*
http://www.securityclub.ru/nbga/english.
html

*Nerd World*
http://www.nerdworld.com/nw3373o1o0.
html

# Bounty Hunter

For those of you who can't hold a day job, you might consider bounty hunting. But the romantic notion of men being brought back to jail flopped over their horse is long gone. These days you end up working for bail bondsmen, not the most romantic or even cinematic of employers.

If you are a bounty hunter and you get your man, you get a finder's fee or the bounty. The bigger the fish, the bigger the payout . . . but keep in mind that the big fish are harder to catch. If you do a lot of work with a bail bondsman, you might even get a little expense money up front. Typically the bondsman's insurance can go up if he lets too many get away, so he needs you to handle both little and big jobs.

There are about 7,000 bounty hunters (2,000 make a living and about 50 to 100 make a good living at it) in the United States who return about 20,000 fugitives each year. It is estimated that about 35,000 folks jump bail (don't appear in court after paying a security bond) and about 87 percent are brought back by bounty hunters. Most of these hunters don't make much money. The lower the bail, the less serious the crime. The less money they make, the easier the errant crooks or fugitives (don't forget they are innocent until proven guilty) are to find. Bounty hunters have a better return rate than traditional law enforcement: 87 percent versus 64 percent.

The job does not require much training or even much of anything except a pair of handcuffs, a little macho bluster, and a little skip-tracing education. Yes, there are female bounty hunters, but everyone uses a little backup. Despite the tough guy image, fugitives most often do not put up a fight or even struggle. If you have a permit to carry a gun, you are not always allowed to use it. You need a bondsman's license to operate in Indiana and Nevada, but in other states you are essentially making a citizen's arrest, and if you end up with broken bones or holes in you, it's your problem. There are fewer restrictions on bounty hunters than on the police. You can enter a fugitive's home, cross state lines, and secure and transport a fugitive without all that Miranda, constitutional stuff. How? Well, next time you post bail, read the fine print. If you are a bad guy, you also have some leeway in the legal arena if you feel you were unfairly treated. You can go to school to learn this stuff, but most classes are basically in-person infomercials designed to sell the teacher's books. They do not guarantee work and don't be surprised if the bail bondsman gets a good chuckle when you present your diploma.

**National Institute of Bail Enforcement**
P.O. Box 32230
Tucson, AZ 85751
Tel.: (520) 290-8051
http://bounty-hunter.net

**Western States Bail Enforcement Association**
P.O. Box 352
Los Altos, CA 94023
Tel.: (520) 290-8051
http://www.bounty_hunter.org

# CIA

It's boom time at the CIA. The agency has been given money to hire new case officers and reopen overseas offices. You might almost think that they nuked the Chinese Embassy in Belgrade just to get some attention and a few budget bumps. Despite all that high-tech crap they keep launching into the air, the CIA's job is still to steal secrets. That's why they finally figured they needed more folks on the ground. (You know things are bad when the CIA calls *DP* to demand why the new edition is not out yet.)

The U.S. intelligence community comprises about 100,000 people who work for 28 different organizations. It takes eight agencies just to process and analyze the satellite images sent in by five different intelligence groups. It costs about $28 billion to find out what our friends and enemies are up to. The adventurous, spooky stuff is the clandestine service. If you want to be a clandestine service case officer, only mention your interest in your first interview. They need folks who have language skills and background in Africa and Central Asia (especially former Soviet Republics). The entrance salary is between $31,459 and $48,222 a year. You must be a U.S. citizen with a college degree, and can't be over 35. For super-secret jobs contact:

http://www.cia.gov/cia/employment/ciaeindex.htm

The job category that might attract MBAs/adventurers is what is known as nonofficial cover (NOC). Opportunity is knocking (or NOC-ing) for a few lucky business graduates. Dissatisfied with the traditional foreign-embassy bureaucrat or aid worker as a cover for its operatives, the CIA has decided to get creative. The CIA now recruits young executives through bogus companies usually based in northern Virginia. The ads appear in major periodicals and newspapers and seek recent business-school graduates who want to work overseas. (The CIA has even taken to advertising in the *Economist*.) The job pays well, but requires training. The NOCs are not trained in Camp Peary nor do they ever appear on any CIA database—to keep them safe from moles. Sounds like a great movie plot, so far. If you are exposed or captured, however, you are officially a spy and not protected by a diplomatic passport.

The successful graduates are then posted with real companies overseas. Many large American corporations gladly accept these folks, since they get a real business graduate who works long hours for free. Each NOC has a liaison person who must handle the intel that is provided by his charge. Many of these positions are with banks, import-export firms, and other companies in such nasty places as North Korea, Iraq, Iran, and Colombia. Although the CIA has to cut corners on its $28 billion annual budget and NOCs cost more to train and support, it's hoped they can provide hard information in countries where the embassy is a little light on cocktail party chatter.

To join the clandestine service branch of the CIA you need a bachelor's degree along with strong communication and interpersonal skills. Military experience also helps. The CIA is keen on folks with backgrounds in Central Eurasian, East Asian, and Middle Eastern languages (kind of tells you where the action is, doesn't it?). You need to pass a medical, psychiatric, and polygraph test, too. A lot of the training takes place at the 9,000-acre Camp Peary, outside Williamsburg, Virginia. Here students spend a year at "the farm" learning how to be spies. Former CIA operatives can also sign up with any number of security consultants or groups that provide the private sector with intelligence gathering and security.

## Who Ya Gonna Call?

Although the laws of this country specifically forbid the assassination of other political leaders, it seems that memo never made it to the White House or to the CIA. Our current efforts to redecorate a few foreign caves and palaces confirms what most of the rest of the world thinks we are: greedy, brutal colonialists who like to get involved in poor countries where we can simply scoop up the natural resources . . . after we off whoever is in power. More embarrassing is that the people we off tend to be social reformers who want to redistribute wealth and protect their country from people like us.

Typically, after we dispatch the leader (or instigator), we replace him with a corrupt old-boy ruler who simply hands over whatever we want as long as a few billion stick to his fingers. With friends like Marcos, the Shah, Pinochet, Noriega, Sukarno, Mobutu, the Sauds, and yes, Saddam (when he was at war with Iran), who needs enemies? The question is based on our track record: Are things going to get better or worse for the people we are busy saving?

Okay, enough spook bashing. The real current trend might be the hearts and diapers program under way to sway America's youth to the nefarious dirty work of the CIA.

**CIA Homepage for Kids**
http://www.CIA.gov/cia/ciakids/index.
   html
   Get a disguise for your latest
   assignment.

**CIA Canine Corps**
http://www.CIA.gov/cia/ciakids/dogs/
   index.html
   Make Bo bark! (Ever wonder
   what all those billions in covert
   technology are spent on?)

# THE CIA'S GREATEST HITS

The CIA needs a good press agent. We won't even list the botched coups, uprisings, billion-dollar snapshots of the tops of people's heads, the KLA, Kurds, Castro's beard, or even their own CIA-kids' page. But somebody could base a hit comedy series on the agency. Okay, okay, we will mention the kids' page.

**2/3/02**   CIA drones fire missiles on Afghans collecting scrap metal in Zawar Kili, Afghanistan.

**12/01**   Although Osama bin Laden and his posse are confirmed to be in the Tora Bora area (the same place they have been for five years), the CIA and U.S. military lets him escape.

**12/29/01**   CIA orders air attack on a group of Afghans, killing 52 people on their way to President Karzai's inauguration.

**11/25/01**   CIA agent Mike Spann, 32, becomes the first combat casualty in the war on terrorism at Qali-i-Jangi in Northern Afghanistan. CIA agent Dave Tyson barely escapes with his life.

**9/11/01**   Nineteen foreigners hijack four planes. Two of the planes destroy the World Trade Center, one damages the Pentagon, and one goes down in a Pennsylvania field.

**7/20/99**   U.S. missile hits Sudanese medical factory.

**7/7/99**   U.S. embassies in Kenya and Dar Es Salaam hit by bombs.

**6/7/99**   U.S. missile delivered by B2 bomber hits Chinese embassy in Belgrade.

**6/25/99**   U.S. military gets hit by terrorists in Dhahran. Explosion kills 19 U.S. troops.

**5/11/99**   India tests nuclear bomb. U.S. military is surprised.

**2/13/91**   U.S. smart missile hits Iraqi bunker full of civilians.

**7/3/88**   USS *Vincennes* hits an Iranian Airbus over the Gulf, killing 290 innocent people.

**If you think this is anything new:**

**1970**   The campaign of Chile's Socialist President Salvador Allende is destablished because of his threat to U.S.-owned mining firms. President Nixon demands that the CIA stop him from taking over, but it fails. Allende is toppled by General Augusto Pinochet in 1973.

(continued)

**1966**   President Suharto of Indonesia is put in power due to a CIA-backed coup that ousts President Sukarno.

**1960**   Patrice Lumumba, who freed the Congo from Belgian colonialism, is assassinated by the CIA (with Belgian help). President Eisenhower personally ordered his death and it was carried out by local "rebels." (Katanga is a copper and resource rich area.)

**1959**   The CIA trains and arms 1,300 Cuban exiles to invade Cuba and overthrow Castro. It is the first of many botched attempts to kill Castro.

**1951**   The United States and Britain overthrow Iran's Prime Minister Mohammed Mossadegh after he nationalizes the oil industry. In August 1953, the Shah signs a royal decree, a CIA-drafted royal decree, replacing Mossadegh with puppet General Fazlollah Zahedi.

# War Correspondent

Forget Nick Nolte in *Under Fire*, forget Mel Gibson in *The Year of Living Dangerously*, forget Dennis Hopper in *Apocalypse Now*, forget David Janssen in *The Green Berets*. Real war photographers and writers are crazier, duller, funnier, sadder, richer, poorer, and just about anything more than any cinematic cartoon could portray. For every wild-eyed rich boy, there is a careful, quiet, social scientist. For every gray, wrinkled notetaker there is a naive, heroin-addicted neophyte. The common denominator among war photographers and writers seems to be the desire to be at the cutting edge of history—to make sense out of chaos and ultimately to drift back into the real world with a collection of old press tags, empty cartridges, unit patches, and memories. Fame and self-satisfaction do not pay the rent.

There is not a lot of money to be made in this line of work—stringers might make $75 a story, $100 a photo. Yeah, maybe you'll be the next Amanpour, Morris, Turnley, Nachtwey, or Capa, but don't count on it. War coverage is becoming less and less relevant (and more important) as we head into the video-briefings, police-action, kidnapped-journos world of coverage. Your biggest competitor is a housewife or 14-year-old kid who left their camera on during an earthquake.

Sadly, while you scheme and study to be the next Edward R. Murrow, the news organizations you once worshipped are dissolving. Gone are the days when we gathered around the "telly" waiting for the carefully crafted stories and baritone deliveries. Gone are the big glossy magazines with life-changing photo essays and the newspapers with journalistic integrity. In their place is the happy chattering of coiffed readers wedged in between stock quotes, sports scores, and commercials. News is entertainment, driven by ratings, fattened by rehashed press releases, made over by carefully orchestrated spin doctors, and delivered by earnest-looking "nice people." Nary a bullet wound or ink stain to guide them.

But underneath the saccharin, there is still a subterranean culture of news. There are still people, like you and me, who want to know what the hell is going on. So don't give up. Consider it trench time so that you can gather enough characters and stories to move to Hollywood and then write sitcoms.

The best way for an aspiring war hog to start is to contact one of the many photo or print news agencies to find out who they have in the region and how to file with them. None will pay your way there or provide equipment or expenses at first, but if you set up a rapport and a stream of saleable submissions, you might be on your way. The only advice I can give is *inveniam viam aut facium.*

Writers need to be able to file often and quickly while photographers need reliable ways to modem or courier photos. You'll need the latest Powerbook and digital know-how. It helps to make friends. Call up your favorite writer and tug on his or her coat. Keep your ears open and listen. Trade info, dig hard, bring a bottle of booze and spare whatevers, keep it light back at the hotel, and you'll do fine.

Is this work dangerous? You mean other than the chain smoking, excess drinking, and rabbitlike casual sex that comes with the territory? Not really. There are plenty of stories about journalists gunned down, blown up, or caught in the wrong place. But most journalist/victims are local working stiffs who anger the government or local bad guys, and who have the unfortunate opportunity to experience literary criticism via lead pipe.

**The Associated Press**
International Headquarters
50 Rockefeller Plaza
New York, NY 10020
Tel.: (212) 621-1500
http://www.ap.org

**Reuters**
http://www.reuters.com

**Agence France Presse**
http://www.afp.com

**VII Photo Agency**
http://www.viiphoto.com

**Blackstar**
http://www.blackstar.com

**Corbis**
http://www.corbis.com

**Combat Films**
http://www.combatfilms.com

**Frontline Television**
http://www.frontlinetv.net

## Other Helpful Resources

*NewsLink/JobLink*
http://newslink.org

*Behind the Viewfinder*
http://www.digitalstoryteller.com/BTV99/
    contents.html

*Committee to Protect Journalists*
330 7th Avenue, 12th Floor
New York, NY 10001
Tel.: (212) 465-1004
Fax: (212) 465-9568
info@cpj.org
http://www.cpj.org

*Reporters Sans Frontières*
International Secrètariat
5, Rue Geoffroy Marie—75009
Paris, France
Tel.: (33) 1 44 83 84 84
Fax: (33) 1 45 23 11 51
rsf@rsf.org
http://www.rsf.fr

*Society of Professional Journalists*
3909 N. Meridian Street
Indianapolis, IN 46208
Tel.: (317) 927-8000
Fax: (317) 920-4789
http://www.spj.org

*The Free Lens*
http://www.oneworld.org/rorypeck/
    freelens

*International Federation of Journalists*
Residence Palace
Rue de la Loi 55
B-1040 Brussels, Belgium
Tel.: (33) 2 235 2200
Fax: (32) 2 235 2219
www.ifj.org

In a recent study of 140 war correspondents, it was found that they suffer much higher rates of depression, PTSD, and other problems, compared to their more timid counterparts. Ten percent has post–traumatic stress disorder, 21 percent had experienced severe depression, and 25 percent had PTSD at some time.

*Source:* Anthony Feinstein, University of Texas

## Professional Adventurer

Ha, ha, you say. Indiana Jones U, here I come. Is it possible to get a job as a professional adventurer? You know what's coming—adventure isn't a job, it's, well, an adventure, you moron.

I make a living being a professional adventurer. Jack Wheeler used to do it in the '80s, Cousteau did it for *National Geographic* and then TBS. Michael Palin did it for BBC while I did for it for Discovery. If you are an adventurer and you aren't on TV, something must be wrong with you.

Ranulph Fiennes, Wilfred Thesiger, Sir Richard Francis Burton, Bob Denard, Lawrence of Arabia, Robin Hanbury-Tenison, and Mike

Williams never really made it to television in a big way, or even the news. Most of them never made any money being adventurous. The more hardcore you are, the less time you have to do the cocktail circuit, which ultimately gives you less time and money to do the adventure thing. The bottom line is, don't expect fame or fortune if you are truly adventurous, and if you think someone will actually hire you to be an adventurer, then you are looking at the wrong end of the horse, Tonto.

> **I**f you think someone will actually hire you to be an adventurer, then you are looking at the wrong end of the horse, Tonto.

Career advice? Hang out with like-minded people. Don't spend the rest of your life dreaming about it. Do it . . . but always in your own style.

**Come Back Alive**
http://www.comebackalive.com

**The Royal Geographical Society**
http://www.rgs.org

**Expedition News**
http://expeditionnews.com

## Delta Force

The 1st SFOD-Delta (Delta Force) began in 1977 as Uncle Sam's sharp edge against terrorism. Today it is estimated to employ between 2,500 and 8,000 men (and women). And it has an antiterrorism unit similar to European units like the SAS. There are 3 assault squadrons (A, B, and C) made up of 75 people who are split into 4- to 6-man teams. The Delta Force also has its own small air force made of civilian-dressed aircraft that can be converted once in-country. There is also the Funny Platoon, an intel group that uses female operatives.

A $75 million facility on old Range 19 (on McKellars Road) at Fort Bragg is Delta Force's home. Storming buildings or planes is their specialty, and like the Navy SEALs, they may or may not have been used for a variety of rescue and black ops. The world knows about their botched attempts to rescue the hostages in Tehran and the casualties they suffered trying to take out Aidid in Mogadishu. Delta operatives have spent quite a bit of time cooling their heels in Cyprus trying to rescue hostages or on Howard Air Force Base in Panama.

Delta Force prides itself on being the world's best marksmen under all conditions. The latest thrill ride is being invited to sit in the middle of a Delta Force shooting house during CQB (close-quarter battle) and watch the team storm the buildings, killing all the paper terrorists without messing a single hair on the guests' heads.

Like the Navy SEALs (who often work in conjunction with the Delta Force), the Delta Force can go anywhere, anytime; they just leave the wet jobs to SEAL Team 6—the navy's version of Delta Force. Delta Force operatives are recruited from the army. The average candidate is around 31 years old, has 10 years of service, and has an above-average IQ. Candidates are by invitation only (they are usually recruited from Green Berets and Rangers) and must go through physical and psychological tests. There is an 18-day formal selection course that mimics the SAS course with the addition of rigorous mental tests after periods of physical hardship and sleep deprivation. If accepted, the candidate then goes through a six-month Operators Training Course. The course includes shooting, air assaults, bodyguarding, high-speed driving, mental sharpening, and covert operations. Oh, and those black helicopters everyone hears about—talk to the Delta Force, which conducts urban antiterrorism training. Sorry, you have to start at the bottom.

**Army Recruiting**
GoArmy@usarec.army.mil
http://www.goarmy.com

## Explosives Expert

If Uncle Sam taught you how to blow things up, you might want to try demolishing buildings (no, we don't mean federal buildings). The skill of imploding existing skyscrapers, apartment buildings, and large factories has spawned companies that do nothing but take down buildings in a few seconds flat. Controlled Demolition Group holds the world record for blowing up buildings. Although not a dangerous job with the correct training (hell, even I used to work with explosives), it does demand a certain level of attention.

**Controlled Demolition Group Ltd.**
The Royals
Whitechapel Road
Cleckheaton
West Yorkshire
BD19 6HQ UK
Tel.: (44) (0) 1274 854600
http://www.controlled-demolition.co.uk

## "Green Beret" Special Forces

The Green Berets are the outgrowth of the World War II "Jedburgh teams," special teams that were dropped behind enemy lines to link up with French partisans. They evolved into eight-man (later 12-man) Detachment Alpha or "A" teams. Each team member had multiple and overlapping skills. They were used to train other military or insurgent groups. Despite the shoot 'em, John Wayne image, Green Berets are officially known as U.S. Army Special Forces, and they have always been linked with spook work and covert operations. They were created in 1953 by a veteran of the OSS (the precursor of the CIA), but the Green Beret wasn't officially endorsed until President Kennedy visited Fort Bragg in 1961. To get in, you have to already be a member of the army and pass the three-week selection course at Fort Bragg. Once accepted, there is the Q course, a 3- to 12-month course that teaches the basic skills of counterinsurgency. Today the "Green Beret" label is considered old hat. They prefer to be called Special Forces and they work in ODAs. But after Afghanistan, they have once again proved to be the most efficient and professional team in Uncle Sam's military.

*John F. Kennedy Special Warfare Center and School*
Attn: AMU-SP-R
Fort Bragg, NC 28307
Tel.: (919) 432-1818
http://www.soc.mil/swcs/_home.htm

*101st Airborne Division*
Attn: RCRO-SM-SF-FC
Fort Campbell, KY 42223
Tel.: (502) 439-4390
http://www.goarmy.com/job/branch/
    sorc/index.htm

*Fort Campbell, Kentucky*
Tel.: (270) 956-3481
afzb-kf@emh2.campbell.army.mil
http://www.campbell.army.mil/division.
    htm

## Navy SEAL

Specialists in Naval Special Warfare, the SEALs (SEa, Air, Land) were born on January 1, 1962, when they were created by President Kennedy along with the revitalized Green Berets. Their most recent brush with fame was their less-than-secret invasion of Kuwait City, with the world's press watching and filming with high-powered camera lights. The SEALs go through 27 weeks of intensive basic training, either in Coronado, California, which is near San Diego, or on the East Coast. The training starts with a seven-week exercise and swimming course, just to get them ready for basic training. Then there are nine weeks of extreme physical and mental abuse. The focus is on teamwork and surviving constant harassment. The sixth week is "Hell Week," six days of misery and physical torture with little or no sleep. Then there is extensive classroom and underwater training in SCUBA (Self-Contained Underwater Breathing Apparatus) diving. This phase ends with another serious physical challenge. The final phase is the UDT and above-water training on San Clemente Island. There is also a six-month probation period.

SEAL teams must practice close-quarter battle drills by firing 300 or more rounds of 9mm ammunition weekly. According to the specs on their Beretta 92F pistols, this means they burn out one handgun a year. Their MP5 machine guns last a little longer. The symbol of a SEAL is the gold-plated "Budweiser" pin, the eagle and trident symbol. SEAL Team 6 specializes in antiterrorist operations. They are controlled by NAVSPECWARCOMDEVGROUP out of Coronado, California.

If you just want to look like a SEAL, you can shop at the same place SEALs shop. Be the first on your block to wear a shirt that says "Pain is just weakness leaving your body." Contact: Bullshirts, 1007 Orange Avenue, Coronado, CA 92118.

**U.S. Navy Human Resources**
2531 Jefferson Davis Highway
Arlington, VA 22242-5161
Tel.: (703) 607-3023

**Official SEALs Site**
Public Affairs Office
Naval Special Warfare Command
Naval Amphibious Base Coronado
San Diego, CA 92155-5037
Tel.: (619) 437-3920
http://www.chinfo.navy.mil/navpalib/
    factfile/personnel/seals/seals.html

**SEAL Recruiter East Coast**
NSWC DET Little Creek
1340 Helicopter Rd.
Norfolk, VA 23521-2945
Com. Tel.: (757) 363-4128
DSN Tel.: (757) 864-4128

## Special Operations

On June 6, 1940, Winston Churchill asked General Hastings Ismay to create "a proper system of espionage and intelligence along the whole coasts, to harass the enemy from behind the lines." Churchill knew firsthand the skills of the Boers who fought in "commandos." Since then, there has been a lot of focus on groups such as the Green Berets and the SAS as they get larger and more important to our overall strategy.

Special Operations are considered the best of the best from among the normal rank and file. How do you get to look like the best and the brightest? If you can't swim, can't stomach the thought of jumping out of an airplane, and have "issues" with killing people who live in other countries, why not join one of our homegrown commando units? Yes, folks, the military has come to your hometown. Ever since the INS Commandos played hide-and-seek with Elian Gonzalez, it has became increasingly obvious that just about every branch of our military and police (they are, after all, the same people, aren't they?) has a special operations unit. Yes, you too can wear Kevlar Oakleys, cargo pants, and those cool utility vests for your walkman. And if none of the units want you to join, you can just buy your stuff at Brigade Quartermaster. (Wait . . . do I hear black helicopters approaching?)

**SWAT training, anyone?**
http://www.nasta.ws
http://www.operationaltactics.org
http://www.bad-boys.net
http://www.swattraining.com

**Brigade Quartermaster**
http://www.actiongear.com

**Special Operations**
http://www.specialoperations.com

**USAF Special Operations**
http://www.afsoc.af.mil/index2.shtml

**Marines Special Operations**
http://www.specialoperations.com/
　　USMC/default.html

## HOW MUCH COMBAT PAY DOES WAYNE NEWTON GET?

Military casualties and dangers are surprising. Infantry takes the most casualties, usually 50 to 80 percent in some actions. Units with tanks and artillery have fewer casualties. Artillery kills the most enemy soldiers and is the safest combat group to be in: they typically suffer only 5 to 10 percent of casualties. Support troops make up about 25 to 35 percent of manpower and suffer 1 to 3 percent of the total casualties. Flying can be dangerous: On average, every 100,000 helicopter sorties result in 13 helicopter crashes, and over half are not related to combat. For every hundred helicopters lost in combat, 145 crew members are killed. In noncombat crashes, the average is only 89 lives lost.

Every year, nearly two thousand U.S. military personnel die while on active duty, usually because of accidents. For peacekeepers, the biggest killers are road accidents, with suicides an alarming percentage of deaths. There are no statistics on how many USO entertainers are fragged or shot down by friendly fire.

*Source:* http://www.strategypage.com

# Mercenary

What is it about some jobs that just bring out the weirdoes, misfits, and jackoffs? No, I am not talking about mercenaries, I am talking about people who want to be mercenaries. Every day the e-mail inboxes of every private military company fill up with people wanting to be mercenaries. Their qualifications range from impressive to being naked and holding an airgun. Little do they know that working as a soldier in another army has the same thrill quotient as debugging accounting software.

Most people think being a mercenary is about killing people. Ultimately it is, but if you have real skills, you are not going to be sitting in a filthy trench with a bunch of bug-eyed local recruits. You are probably going to be back at the base, training, coordinating, planning, and not too far out of range of the local nightlife. The only things incoming are going to be memos and the only casualties will be your home life and sense of self-worth. You are, after all, disposable, deniable, and a discomforting dalliance for your employers.

You need to have some pretty impressive skills to get work these days. The files of Sandline, MPRI, Vinnell, and even the local security guard company are flooded with resumes from thousands of eager, underemployed ex-military types. If you are in the Special Forces, worked in an interesting theater, and have a sterling reputation, you might stand a chance. If you have some high tech-skills, some intel, and a dash of language skills, you have an edge. There is a lot of security guard stuff for oil companies, training of armed forces, flying, and large-scale planning, but not a lot of running around in the jungle in sweaty, torn camo yelling, "Hoo ya!" Most of these contracts are through State-side or UK corporations. Most of the gigs are old-boy networks. In other words, if you don't know what's going on and who to call, then don't expect a phone call. Worse case, you can read the chapters on mercenaries and decide to keep that nine-to-five job and live out your fantasies on your vacation instead. After all, aren't tourists more at risk these days?

If you read this and still want to read more, there is an entire chapter devoted to mercenaries, starting on page 243.

**Sandline International**
http://www.sandline.com

**Military Professional Resources, Inc.**
http://www.mpri.com

**Vinnell Corporation**
http://www.vinnell.com

**AirScan, Inc.**
http://www.airscan.com

**Armor Holdings, Inc.**
http://armorholdings.com

**DynCorp**
http://www.dyncorp.com

*Waterborne/Marine Security*
http://www.securitymanagement.com

*Marine Risk Management*
http://www.marinerisk.com

*PISTRIS*
http://www.pistris.com

## Mine Clearance

Land mines kill or maim someone on this planet every hour. There is a big demand for former explosives and munitions experts to clean up these killers. Mine-clearance personnel are paid about U.S.$90,000 a year. There are about 20 companies that specialize in the detection and removal of land mines. Kuwait spent about U.S.$1 billion to clean up the 7 million land mines sown during the 5-month occupation of Kuwait by Iraq; 83 mine-clearance experts have been killed just in Kuwait. If you are looking for big money, get in quick because usually local folks take over the long-term projects. Be aware that local minesweepers in Angola make only U.S.$70 a day, and in Afghanistan they make U.S.$100 a month.

*Mine Action Information Center*
http://www.hdic.jmu.edu

*Ronco Consulting Corporation*
http://roncoconsulting.com

*HALO Trust*
P.O. Box 7712
London
SW1V 3ZA, UK
http://www.britannia.com/newsbits/
    knights.html

*Mines Advisory Group*
47 Newton Street
Manchester
M1 1FT, UK
Tel.: (44) 161 236 4311
Fax: (44) 161 236 6244
maguk@mag.org.uk
http://www.mag.org.uk

*CAMEO Security*
150 Edward Street
Cornwall, Ontario K6H 4G9
Canada
Tel.: (613) 936-6815
Fax: (613) 936-6635
http://www.cameo.org

*Global Training Academy*
P.O. Box 445
Somerset, TX 78069
Tel.: (210) 622-9460 or (800) 777-5984
Fax: (830) 429-3122
http://www.globalcorp.com/
    trainingacademy/index.html

## Smoke Jumper

If the thought of being parachuted into a raging inferno and having to fight your way back until you can be airlifted out appeals to you, then you should try smoke jumping. Smoke jumpers are firefighters who must be in the air within 10 minutes of the start of a fire and parachute into remote areas to fight the fires. Dropped from small planes as low as 1,500 feet in altitude, they quickly must hike to the scene of the fire, and instantly begin to chop and backburn areas to head off forest fires before they get too big. The work is all manual and requires strength, endurance, and an ability to work around the clock if need be.

Most smoke jumpers are attracted by the danger and the camaraderie these jobs afford—although the death of 14 firefighters in Glenwood Springs, Colorado, almost a decade ago reminded people that smoke jumping is dangerous. The fact that there are only 387 smoke jumpers in the United States made those deaths even more significant. The last time any smoke jumpers were killed actually fighting a fire was in 1949 during the Mann Gulch blaze in Montana. During this 45-year period of calm, one jumper pancaked into the ground due to chute failure, and another unintentionally hanged himself when he tried to get out of a tree in which he had landed.

Like most dangerous jobs, the goal is to stay alive and healthy, but you definitely don't do it for the money. Pay for smoke jumpers starts at about $9 an hour, and there is additional pay during fires and with overtime. Most smoke jumpers are part-timers who earn money during the hot summer fire season.

There are nine U.S. Forest Service and Bureau of Land Management (BLM) regional jumper bases in the West. The supervisors react quickly to fires and send in anywhere from two or more jumpers, depending on the size of the fire. If lightning starts a small blaze, fire jumpers can deal with it quickly and effectively before calling in the water bombers. Supplies can be parachuted in as soon as the jumpers are on the ground. Once done, the jumpers then get to hike out with their equipment or can be picked up by helicopter.

Training requires federal certification to fell large trees and to be able to climb in and, more likely, out of trees. Jumpers maintain their own chainsaws and other equipment. Their protective Kevlar suits hold their equipment and protect them when landing in trees. Forest Service jumpers use round chutes and jump at 1,500 feet; BLM smoke jumpers use the more modern rectangular chutes and exit at 3,000 feet.

**National Smokejumpers Association**
http://www.smokejumpers.com

**Alaska Smokejumpers**
http://home.gci.net/~aksmj

**McCall Smokejumpers**
http://www.fs.fed.us/fire/operations/jumpers/mccall

# UN/UN Peacekeeper

The United Nations (UN) was an outgrowth of World War II. It was founded on October 1, 1945, by 51 countries to preserve peace. Well, they meant well. . . . Today the UN includes 189 countries and is the main global agency to promote human rights and international security. It operates thousands of humanitarian, poverty, disaster, ecological, legal, and democratic programs around the world.

Since its deployment in 1948, UN peacekeeping forces have served in 54 successful and not-so-successful missions to stabilize regions. Over 1,600 peacekeepers have died in the line of duty and, as the world gets grittier and nastier, there seems to be no shortage of new problems and projects.

The UN takes a lot of hits as being a bunch of corrupt bureaucratic wonks who live and travel in luxury surrounded by squalor. But when you compare the UN to what it used to be in many of these places, they don't look so bad. The UN now has become a sort of government for hire. They are running things in places like Kosovo, Namibia, and East Timor and they are working hard in Sierra Leone and trying to put the Somalia debacle behind them.

You can't really join the UN as a peacekeeper. Every mission is planned from the ground up, then member states have to donate money, troops, armaments, and other bits and pieces. There is a small staff of UN folks who are all hired on a contract basis. Typically only third-world nations provide troops because, at about a grand a day, only Bangladeshis and Pakistanis can make a profit at supplying troops and pocketing the difference. There are also plenty of opportunities for a little side business for UN-posted officers, so you will see Nigerians, Russians, and other entrepreneurial nations volunteer for diamond areas.

The UN staff tends to be, well, I guess a United Nations of people. Americans are a little short in supply, except when we strong-arm them for political reasons to fill senior posts. If you want to join the UN, they usually want a college degree and some language skills. Despite the frustration of culture clash and stressful work environments it can be a rewarding job. The UN pays well and, although you are pretty much guaranteed a gnarly location, the perks are pretty nice. You get an adjusted allowance for differences in the cost of living and, yes, you get danger pay. The problem is that whenever the UN shows up in force, the cost of rent, food, gas, and other supplies magically skyrockets past even New York prices.

Not many soldiers ask to be UN peacekeepers, and they find it hard to figure out why someone is trying to kill his closest neighbor, or in our case, why we send pimply kids thousands of miles to whomp third-world revolutionaries. Being a UN peacekeeper means wearing silly blue berets and driving around in nice, white trucks. You can be shot at, but you can't shoot back. You can be insulted, but you can't insult back. In fact, you may find yourself actually helping people kill their enemies as you protect war criminals, maintain archaic political boundaries, and provide security for execution squads. You may come under shell fire and gunfire and have to keep up with deadly bureaucratic paperwork. In Bosnia, Canadians were told to return mines they dug up to the armies that planted them. Some scratched their initials on the casings and dug up the same mines weeks later. Peacekeepers must use photodegradable sandbags, and the rules of engagement are so Byzantine that it requires hours to get official clearances to shoot back when they come under fire.

**United Nations**
http://www.un.org/Depts/OHRM/
   brochure.htm

**UN System Staff College**
http://www.unssc.org/unssc1

**UN Peacekeeping**
http://www.un.org/Depts/dpko/dpko/
   home_bottom.htm

**Peacekeeping vacancies**
http://www.un.org/Depts/dpko/field/
   vacancy.htm

**UN Media Accreditation**
Media Accreditation Center
UNITAR Bldg.
801 United Nations Plaza
New York, NY 10017
Tel.: (212) 963-7164 or 963-5934
http://www.un.org/geninfo/malu.htm

# DANGEROUS DISEASES

## Souvenirs from Hell

Infectious diseases kill about 17 million people a year. Approximately 9 million of the victims are children under the age of 5. Infectious diseases are the leading cause of premature death in Africa and Southeast Asia, according to the World Health Organization (WHO). About 70 percent of the deaths attributed to cholera, typhoid, or dysentery can be blamed on contaminated food. To make matters worse, 30 new diseases have sprung up since 1976, among them AIDS and the deadly Ebola virus. Antibiotics are becoming less and less effective in treating many of these diseases because of resistance due to their overuse. Oh, just traveling there for a bit of adventure, you say? Well, bugs don't check passports and for some odd reason normally sane Westerners, who wouldn't think about cruising the wrong side of town after dark, will plunk down thousands to be dumped in a disease-ridden remote hellhole for a little kayaking or hiking.

The odds of coming down with a bug are pretty good once you leave the antiseptic Western world. If you go off on an extended trip (one month or more), you have a 60 to 75 percent chance that you will develop some illness or problem, most likely diarrhea. Only about 1 percent of travelers will pick up an infectious disease. I once thought that the locals had built up resistance to the various bugs that strike down Westerners. But once in-country, you realize what a toll disease takes on the third world. Not only are many people riddled with malaria, river blindness, intestinal infections, hepatitis, sexual diseases, and more, but they are also faced with malnutrition, poor dental care, toxic chemicals, and harsh environmental conditions. WHO recently reported that much of the world's population dies needlessly from preventable diseases due to a lack of access to health care.

I am often asked, "How can you protect yourself against the many health threats that are out there?" The answer is, "You can't." But learn as much as you can about each and every affliction that awaits you and get all the available shots for tetanus, yellow fever, hepatitis B and C, cholera, and others. You can take prophylaxis for malaria and some other strains. All those shots and expensive pills do not guarantee you will not get malaria, dengue, sleeping sickness, and a whole host of resistant, unknown strains of vector-borne diseases. And unfortunately, there are diseases in some places that your doctor does not know about and even baffle the Centers for Disease Control and Prevention. There are diseases that look benign and then make your life a living hell forever. Don't assume that there are safe and unsafe places in the tropics. Talk to your doctor and local doctors, and take a look on the Web if you really are concerned.

Here is the drill if you want to maintain your health, or at least leave a good-looking corpse (with that extra *DP* advice your doctor and trusty guide just don't have the heart to tell you):

- There is a plethora of information available online at the Centers for Disease Control (http://www.cdc.gov). You can check out diseases, outbreaks, travel advice, and precautions, and find plenty of reasons never to leave your house (unless of course your home has radon, toxic waste, carpet mites, etc.).
- Those who find reality shows a little dull can also bone up at WHO's disease outbreak site (http://www.who.int/disease-outbreak-news). Get the latest scoop on legionellosis in Spain or cholera in Chad. Special attention is paid to tourist concerns because tourists have a bad

habit of being the equivalent of poop flies and spreading exotic diseases into not-exotic home regions.

- If you really, really want to find a reason to built a large plastic bubble and live in it, go to http://www.cdc.gov/ncidod/index.htm and search to your heart's content on infectious diseases.

There are plenty of other Web sites that deal with travel health, prevention, and tips. Very few, of course, deal with what the hell to do after blood starts oozing out of your eyes (a symptom of Ebola for you medical-trivia fans).

If you've read up and can deal with the idea of pulling tapeworms out of your butt by rolling them on a stick, and you are now packing, what do you have to do physically

> **W**hen you get the runs, don't freak out and glug down the Immodium—it's a normal readjustment.

before you leave? Meet with a specialist in either tropical disease or travel medicine at least two months before departure. Have a complete checkup; discuss what preventative measures should be taken. Important! Do not do this a week before you leave. Some shots require up to six weeks to take effect. Your doctor should consult with the latest CDC info and give you a lecture on cleanliness, eating, and so on.

What you need to know about food and contamination is simple. Eat lightly and eat as freshly as possible. Disease can be carried by vectors (insects, ticks, animals) and also in the food and fluids you ingest. If you make sure that what goes in your mouth has been boiled, heated to a high temperature, or sealed (as in store bought), you should be okay. Keep in mind that a hermetically sealed bottle of water, handed to you by a diseased vendor, that has been soaking in toxic river water to keep cool, can defeat the purpose of this exercise. Also, do not believe for a second that hotels or large restaurants have any guarantee of cleanliness or sanitation. Usually the opposite is true. Food is left out for long periods of time at low temperatures and water is stored in cisterns on the roof—perfect warm places for bacteria and dead rats. Keep in mind that freshly boiled soups and food that is cooked thoroughly and freshly in front of you are your best bets. Bottled water and tea are the best drinking choices. Strangely, eating in private homes will solve most of your health concerns. So make friends.

When you get the runs, don't freak out and glug down the Immodium—it's a normal readjustment. Just drink plenty of fluids, use the oral rehydration kits to supplement your fluids, and ease off on the food. If you think you don't feel well, see a local doctor. You might be surprised to discover how cheap and knowledgeable they are. Socialized medicine has its advantages.

The next area of concern is simply breathing and existing. Keep your hands clean. Pocket lotion that has an antibacterial element is all the rage, but imagine what kind of things you are breathing in. It might be okay (although an adventure fashion faux pas) to wear a simple surgical mask in places like Karachi or Lagos, but the black-brown residue after a day of wearing one might change your mind. It is quite common to get respiratory ailments in areas with a lot of dust, animals, and traffic.

Another major tip is to forget those adventure morons on TV who wear shorts and T-shirts in the tropics. Cover your damn skin. Wear thick socks (I wear wool) and boots instead of those rafting sandals, and wear a floppy hat. This will protect you from mosquito bites (these tend to occur around your ankles at dusk), the sun, and general scrapes, nicks, and cuts (infection in open cuts is a major danger).

Finally, carry an appropriate first-aid and medical kit. Talk to your doctor about the use of antibiotics, painkillers, and first-aid medications. You can buy pretty much any drug you want in the third world, but there is no guarantee that it will work. Medications like Cipro for intestinal bugs, wound management kits (with gloves!), antibiotics for infections, painkillers, and anti-inflammatories can often require prescriptions. Take hydrogen peroxide for cuts and bruises. Talk to your doctor about a small collection of drugs for "just in case." Don't go overboard because customs is going to want to know just what you are dying of. It is also important to carry a first-aid kit and perhaps a medical manual. Make sure you carry the pills in their original container so you don't get dinged for drug smuggling.

When it comes to medical books, *Where There Is No Doctor* is a good choice. I carry a photo first-aid guide (very gory, but if I have to grunt and point to a Samaritan, I don't have time to teach him English), and a U.S. army first-aid manual. My namesake Robert W. Pelton (no relation, but he writes good books) has a small medical first-aid book for sale, and there are a number of good hiking and military manuals available, too.

Hopefully the worst run-ins you have are sunburn and a great time. Keep in mind that many bugs take time to incubate. You could get bitten on the last day of your trip and wonder why you feel so sweaty and headachy back in Sheboygan. So always have full medical tests upon your return. Give that same doctor a little background on your trip and he will ask for a donation. This means giving a little bit of yourself to the lab to run blood, stool, and urine tests. Your doctor may ask you to come back again because of the long incubation time of some of these nasties. This is not hypochondria, but common sense. Early detection will increase your odds of successful treatment.

## TEN LEAST WANTED

The following top ten killer diseases are primarily third-world, celebrity-free, low-visibility killers of children.

| | |
|---|---|
| Acute Respiratory Tract Infections | 4.4 million |
| Diarrheal Diseases (cholera, typhoid, dysentery) | 3.1 million |
| Tuberculosis | 3.1 million |
| Malaria | 2 million |
| Hepatitis B | 1.1 million |
| HIV/AIDS | 1 million + |
| Measles | 1 million + |
| Neonatal Tetanus | 460,000 |
| Whooping Cough | 350,000 |
| Intestinal Worms | 135,000 |

*Source:* World Health Organization

# Malaria

Malaria is a very dangerous disease, affecting 500 million people worldwide and killing at least 2 million people every year. More than 30,000 European and American travelers will come down with malaria this year.

The mosquito-borne disease is carried by 60 of the 380 types of the anopheles mosquito. It is found in 102 countries (primarily in tropical and subtropical areas) and threatens 40 percent of the world's population. The female anopheles mosquito is small, pervasive, and hungry for your blood, and likes to bite in the cool hours before and after sunset. As the mosquitoes suck out blood to nurture their own procreation, they leave the plasmodium parasites in your blood system.

## MALARIAL CYCLE

- Mosquito bites infected human, ingesting a gametocyte
- Gametocyte breeds internally, creating oocytes
- Sporozoites burst and travel to mosquito's salivary glands
- Mosquito bites another human and sporozoites enter bloodstream
- Within 45 minutes sporozoites penetrate the liver
- Within 9 to 16 days, merozoites develop and invade red-blood and liver cells
- Blood cells rupture, releasing gametocytes and merozoites into the bloodstream, causing the cycle of chills and fevers

Anopheles mosquitoes can be identified by the way they stand head downward when biting, compared to the parallel stance of the benign culex mosquito, and they don't venture more than two miles from where they are bred. Only pregnant females feed on blood, biting every two days to feed eggs.

Malaria continues to become resistant to the drugs used to prevent and treat it. There are resistant strains to Mefloquine (or Larium), though. Malarone, supposed to be the new wonder drug from Glaxo-Wellcome, is a brand name for the drug containing atovaquone and progunil. It is legal in Denmark and used for treatment only in the UK. Keep in mind that 90 percent of the people who contract malaria don't develop symptoms until after they return from their trip. The symptoms can start with a flulike attack, followed by fever and chills, then lead to failure of multiple organs, and can result in death.

Some quick facts:

- Transmission decreases above 200 meters and is rarely found above 3,000 meters.
- Roughly 90 percent of malaria cases occur in Africa.
- Most malaria in Asian and African areas is quinine-resistant and requires multiple or more creative dosages to avoid the horrors often associated with the disease.
- The most vicious strain of malaria *(Plasmodium falciparum)* attacks your liver and red-blood cells, creating massive fevers, coma, acute kidney failure, and eventually death. There are three other types of malaria in the world: *Plasmodium malaria, Plasmodium vivax,* and *Plasmodium ovale* (found only in West Africa).
- The anopheles mosquito is the most dangerous insect in the world, and there are few contenders for its crown.
- Other biting insects that can cause you grief include the *Aedes aegypti* mosquito, which carries yellow fever. His kissing cousins, the *Culex, Haemogogus, Sabethes,* and *Mansonia,* can give you filariasis, viral encephalitis, dengue, and other great hemorrhagic fevers. Next on the list are tsetse flies, fleas, ticks, sandflies, mites, and lice. We won't even bother to discuss wasps, horseflies, African killer bees, deerflies, or other clean biters.

These insects are an everyday part of life in tropical third-world countries. They infect major percentages of the local population, and it is only a matter of time and luck before you become a victim. Prevention is rather simple, but often ineffective. Protect yourself from insects by wearing long-sleeved shirts and long pants. Use insect repellent, sleep under a mosquito net, avoid swampy areas, use mosquito coils, don't sleep directly on the ground, check yourself for tick and insect bites

| Name | Usage | Side Effects |
|------|-------|-------------|
| • Chloroquine (Aralen) | Not effective in areas where chloroquine-resistant malaria is found | Has bitter taste; can cause stomach upset and blurred vision |
| • Mefloquine (Larium) | Commonly prescribed in North America: 2 percent to 5 percent of users have side effects | Usage can cause anxiety, nausea, hair loss, mood changes, and in some cases psychosis |
| • Doxycycline | A common and inexpensive antibiotic | Causes sensitivity to sun but provides protection against infections; can cause stomach upset, thrush, or yeast infections |
| • Chloroquine w/Progunil (Paludrine) | Not as effective as mefloquine or doxycycline | Can cause nausea, loss of appetite, and mouth ulcers |
| • Primaquine | New drug | Effective against *P. vivax* and *P. falciparum*. Can cause nausea and abdominal discomfort |
| • Atovaquone/Progunil (Malarone) | New drug | Effective against chloroquine-resistant malaria; can cause nausea, diarrhea |
| • Fansidar/Fansimef | For self-treatment when malaria is contacted | Serious side effects including skin reactions |

daily, and, last but not least, understand the symptoms and treatment of these diseases so that you can seek immediate care, no matter what part of the world you are in.

http://www.healthscout.com

## THE GIFT THAT KEEPS ON GIVING

| Disease | Annual Deaths |
|---------|---------------|
| Infected by Malaria | 500 million |
| Infected by HIV | 20 million |
| Infected by AIDS | 4.5 million |
| Acute Respiratory Infections | 4.4 million |
| Diarrheal Diseases | 3.1 million |
| Tuberculosis | 3 million |
| Malaria | 2 million |
| AIDS | 1 million |

**DANGEROUS DISEASES**

## Worms

My least favorite infections are the helminthic infections, or diseases caused by intestinal worms. Unlike the more dramatic and deadly diseases, these parasites are easily caught through ingestion of bad water and food and cause long-term damage. Just to let you know what's out there, you can choose from angiostrongyliasis, herring worm, roundworm, schistosomiasis, capillariasis, pinworm, oriental liver fluke, fish tapeworm, guinea worm, cat liver fluke, tapeworm, trechinellosis, and the ominous-sounding giant intestinal fluke (who's eating who here?). All these little buggers create havoc with your internal organs, and some will make the rest of your life miserable as well. Your digestive system will be shot and your organs under constant attack, and the treatment or removal of these nasties is downright depressing. All this can be prevented by maintaining absolutely rigid standards in what you throw or breathe into your body. Not easy, since most male travelers find wearing a biohazard suit a major impediment to picking up chicks or doing the limbo.

Think of yourself as a sponge, your lungs as an air filter, and all the moist cavities of your body as ideal breeding grounds for tropical diseases. It is better to think like Howard Hughes than Pig Pen when it comes to personal hygiene.

## The Fevers

The classic tropical diseases that incapacitated Stanley, Livingstone, Burton, and Speke are the hemorrhagic fevers. Many of these diseases kill, but most make your life a living hell and then disappear. There are so many versions that they are merely named after the places where you stumble across them. Needless to say, these are not featured in any glossy brochures for the various regions. Assorted blood-thinning killers are called Chikungunya, Crimean, Congo, Omsk, Kyasanur Forest, Korean, Manchurian, Songo, Ebola, Argentinian, Hanta, Lassa, and yellow fever.

It is surprising that most of the African explorers lived to the ripe old age that they did. The hemorrhagic fevers are carried by mosquitoes, ticks, rats, feces, or even airborne dust that gets into your bloodstream. These fevers let you die a slow, demented death, as your blood turns so thin it trickles out your nose, gums, skin, and eyes. Coma and death can occur in the second week. Some come back on a regular basis.

The recent outbreaks of the Hanta and Ebola viruses in the United States have proved that North America is not immune from these insect-, rodent-, and airborne afflictions. So far, the Ebola Reston virus

# WHAT'S IN THE BAG?

*DP* reader Dr. Kurt Schultz gives us his pick for his travel meds. The following list is provided to give you a starting point to discuss your ideal travel kit and your own personal needs with your doctor. Many people require instruction on usage of drugs (it's called a medical degree), and most drugs can have side effects, interactions caused by other medications and outside conditions. Many countries prohibit the importation and/or carrying of certain drugs, even for personal use. Warning: Many of these items are available over-the-counter in third-world countries but may be expired, defective, or placebos.

1. Bring prescription antibiotics for internal problems. Get a 20-day supply of Cipro or floxin. These drugs are of the fluoroquinolone class, the "patriot missiles" for traveler's diarrhea/dysentery and infectious diarrhea. They are also the drugs of choice for venereal diseases and will kill gonorrhea, chlamydia, and most causes of wiener drip.
2. Bring antibiotics for external problems (skin infection/cuts). The dirt in the third world is impregnated with 2,000 years of feces. Any trivial break in the skin (nick yourself shaving) can lead to a life-threatening cellulitis (a bacterial skin infection). Examples of drugs to bring: Keflex or Augmentin, a 20-day supply, which is also good for animal bites.
3. Take malaria prophylaxis as directed by the CDC and WHO. The argument rages as to what is best, but taking nothing is dumb. Sometimes this includes doxycycline, a prescription antibiotic.
4. Get all your vaccinations: get the routine tetanus and measles/mumps/rubella shots. Make sure you are up to date on your routine vaccinations. You should get both hepatitis A and B, which are very effective (90% effective in prevention), and also yellow fever, which is often required to even enter most developing countries.
5. Carry lots of over-the-counter, broad-spectrum antibiotic cream like Neosporin.
6. Anti-diarrheals (but go easy) like Immodium, an over-the-counter diarrhea medicine. The runs is a normal part of acclimatization. Let it flow, drink lots of water, eat less food. If it persists, go to internal antibiotics (#1). It helps to have rehydration powders to recover as well.
7. Buy or make first-aid kids for wound management, abrasion, and so on. These kits can be purchased in outdoor stores or over the Internet.
8. Carry lots of Tylenol or Motrin for pain control.
9. Bring tissue-adhesive glue. Cool stuff! It's basically glorified Krazy Glue, modified slightly so the drug companies can charge obscene fees. Literally "glues" wounds together; it's easy to pack.
10. Ketamine. It's hard to score, but it's given as an intramuscular shot. You'll need a syringe and you'll need to know how to inject it. Ketamine disconnects the mind from the body without causing excessive sedation. The military uses this as a "battlefield anesthetic." You can set bones and do

(continued)

major surgery after a single shot. It's related to PCP, but without all the freaky side effects and violence. (Note from *DP:* Although it seems highly altruistic, don't hand out medicines to the locals. Within minutes, the entire village will have a headache and will be lined up outside your tent. If you want to leave medicine for the locals, give it to a doctor or health worker who understands the uses and dangers of your gift.)

http://www.drugs.com
http://www.baproducts.com/fak.htm
http://www.equipped.com/medical.htm

has only been found in monkeys sent by a Philippine supplier. All monkeys exposed to the virus were destroyed, and officials from the Centers for Disease Control reassured the public that Ebola Reston is a different virus from Ebola Zaire (the country is now called the Democratic Republic of the Congo). Ebola Zaire is the strain that killed 244 people in one outbreak. Still, experts warn that the Ebola Reston strain could mutate into a strain that is fatal to humans. The outbreak of plague in India also has travelers a little edgy about the whole concept of adventurous travel. There are real dangers in every part of the world, and the more knowledgeable you are about them, the better your chances for surviving.

## Sex (STDs)

The quest for sexual adventure was once a major part of the joy of travel. Today, the full range of sexual diseases available to the common traveler would fill an encyclopedia. Diseases like HIV, hepatitis A and B, the clap, syphilis, genital warts, herpes, crabs, lice, and others that Westerners blame on the third world, and the third world blames on the West, are very preventable and require parking your libido.

Despite the continual global publicity on the dangers of AIDS, it continues to claim victims at an alarming rate. Of the 34 most affected AIDS countries, 29 are in Africa, where life expectancy has been reduced by an average of 7 years. Yet whorehouses around the world are thriving, junkies still share needles, and dentists in many third-world countries still grind and yank away with improperly sterilized instruments. Other sexually transmitted diseases are also a growing health hazard. According to WHO, 236 million people have trichomoniasis and 94 million new cases occur each year. Chlamydial infections affect 162 million people, with 97 million new cases annually. And these figures don't include the increasing millions with genital warts, gonorrhea, genital herpes, and syphilis. The highest rates for sexually transmitted diseases are in the 20 to 24 age group.

How do you avoid sexually transmitted diseases? Well, keeping your romantic agenda on the platonic side is a good start. The use of condoms is the next best thing. Realistically, the chances of catching AIDS through unprotected sex depends on frequency and type of contact. People infected by blood transfusions, prostitutes, frequent drug users, hemophiliacs, homosexuals, and the millions of people who will get HIV this year from heterosexual sex will continue to make HIV a growing danger.

> **A**lthough it seems highly altruistic, don't hand out medicines to the locals. Within minutes, the entire village will have a headache and will be lined up outside your tent.

## Hepatitis A, B, C

Your chance of getting hepatitis B if you leave the United States is only 5 percent, unless of course you go for a tattoo at the smack-jabbers' rusty-needle convention in the Golden Triangle (and have unprotected sex afterward with a Thai junkie hooker). All macho bull-shit aside, men and women are at equal risk and health workers are at a very high risk for contracting hepatitis B when working in third-world countries. Carrier rates in some undeveloped countries are as high as 20 percent of the total population. Many travelers get hep B without engaging in any high-risk activities because the virus can survive outside the body for prolonged periods. Infection can occur when any infected material comes in contact with mucous membranes or broken skin. The vaccine for hepatitis B is 90 percent effective after three doses. See your doctor or a local health clinic for more information before you travel.

Hepatitis A is a viral infection of the liver transmitted by the fecal, oral route through direct contact with infected people, from water, ice, shellfish, or uncooked food. Symptoms for hep A include fever, loss of appetite, dark urine, jaundice, vomiting, aches and pains, and light stools. You usually get hep A in third-world countries with poor sanitation. It is easy to prevent with a simple vaccination using one of the two vaccines available. For proper protection, the vaccine requires an initial shot (good for three months) and then repeated doses to protect in the long run.

About hep B: *DP* fan and reader Dr. Susan Hou sent us a polite but firm letter demanding that we expand information on this very easy-to-catch and very easy-to-prevent disease. We quote the good doctor (who has knocked around enough to earn a *DP* shirt):

> The majority of people with symptomatic hepatitis B infection don't die, but spend a month wishing they would. One percent develop *fulminate* [*Webster's:* developing or progressing suddenly] disease and die of liver failure. (On the bright side, if you get back to the United States before getting sick, fulminate liver failure moves you to the top of the liver transplant list.) Five to 10 percent of people become chronic carriers, which means they can infect other people. For women this includes 85 percent of the children they carry who don't get treated. Thirty percent of chronic carriers have ongoing liver disease (chronic active hepatitis). Many progress to cirrhosis and require liver transplants (but start out lower on the transplant list). People with chronic active hepatitis develop liver cancer at a rate of 3 percent per year. The bad news if you get a liver transplant: Hepatitis B is usually still in your body and infects the new liver.

# AIDS

Perhaps the most dangerous and publicized disease is AIDS. It strikes right at the heart of American phobia—pain for pleasure. AIDS is the terminal phase of HIV (human immunodeficiency virus). HIV is usually the precursor to AIDS, and then the victim succumbs to death by cancer, pneumonia, or other afflictions that attack the weakened human immune system. AIDS has roughly a nine-year incubation period.

AIDS was supposed to have jumped from animal to man when humans ate simians in Africa. The simian virus that spawned AIDS comes from animals that live in Gabon, Cameroon, and Equatorial Guinea. Other strains have made the crossover from chimpanzee to man.

Initially brushed aside as "the gay plague" or an "African disease," AIDS has in the last few years become the biggest killer of young American men and women. Washington, DC, has the nation's highest AIDS rate, far higher than even New York or San Francisco, according to statistics released by the Centers for Disease Control and Prevention. By 1995, the DC rate was 185.7 AIDS cases per 100,000 residents. Puerto Rico was second with a rate of 70.3 cases per 100,000, followed by New York, Florida, and New Jersey. Nationwide, the rate of AIDS cases is 27.8 cases per 100,000. The CDC says that AIDS is spreading more among women and minorities now, while the epidemic among homosexual white men has slowed. Women accounted for 19 percent of all AIDS cases among adults and adolescents nationwide. A growing number of children are being orphaned by AIDS, which has become the leading cause of death among women of childbearing age in the United States, according to a study in the *Journal of the American Medical Association*. Blacks are six times more likely to have AIDS than whites and twice as likely to have AIDS as Hispanics.

As sobering as the U.S. statistics are, the rate of deaths caused by AIDS in other countries is alarming. WHO says that chronic underreporting and underdiagnosis in developing countries means the actual figure is probably more than the official number of 40 million cases (2.7 million of them are children under 15). More than 70 percent of the estimated cases were in Africa, 9 percent in the United States, 9 percent in the rest of the American hemisphere, 6 percent in Asia, and 4 percent in Europe. (These statistics include only people with active cases of AIDS or those who have died from the disease.)

There are currently 2 million HIV-infected people in Latin America and the Caribbean. The Pan American Health Organization says HIV is increasing among women in the Caribbean and Central America and it is expected to increase rapidly, particularly in areas where injection drug use is prevalent.

According to Italy's statistics institute, ISTAT, AIDS has become as big a killer in Italy as road accidents. An estimated 4,370 Italians died from AIDS last year, compared to 6,000 deaths on the roads. For young males between 18 and 29 in Italy, AIDS has overtaken drugs as the second leading cause of death. ISTAT estimates that the number of HIV-infected Italians is at least 100,000.

AIDS is also on the increase in smaller countries. WHO estimates that at least 400,000, or 1 percent, of Myanmar's citizens are infected with HIV. A high number of injection drug users, social tolerance of prostitution, and large amounts of cross-border trade with nearby nations make Myanmar's populace more vulnerable. Condoms are also costly and rarely used in Myanmar, exacerbating the problem.

Ministry of Health statistics show that more than 100,000 residents of Zimbabwe have died of AIDS-related causes in the past decade. Another 100,000, or 1 percent, of the country's population is expected to succumb to AIDS in the next year and a half. AIDS is expected to slow population growth, lower life expectancies, and raise child mortality rates in many of the world's poorer countries over the next 25 years, according to a report by the U.S. Census Bureau.

In 16 countries—the African nations of Burkina Faso, Burundi, Central African Republic, Congo, Cote d'Ivoire, Kenya, Malawi, Rwanda, Tanzania, Uganda, Congo, Zambia, and Zimbabwe, plus Brazil, Haiti, and Thailand—AIDS will slow population growth rates so dramatically that by 2010, there will be 121 million fewer people than previously forecast. For example, by the year 2010, a Ugandan's life expectancy will decline by 45 percent to 32 years—down from the 59 years projected before AIDS. A Haitian's life expectancy will fall to 44 years, also down from 59 years. Life expectancy in Thailand will drop from a projected 75 years to 45. By the year 2010, Thailand's child-mortality rates are expected to increase from the current 20 deaths per 1,000 children born to 110 deaths. Thailand's population will actually fall by nearly 1 percent because of AIDS deaths. In Uganda, the jump will be from 90 deaths to 175 deaths out of every 1,000 children born. In Malawi, it will soar from 130 to 210 deaths per 1,000. Overall, premature death rates in those countries will double by 2010 compared with 1985 levels.

## "Zoonosis"

According to journalists, AIDS first began near the Congo-Burundi border . . . but did it? A 1992 *Rolling Stone* article by medical journalist Tom Curtis places the blame on polio vaccines grown in primate kidney cells and then injected into humans in 1957 and 1958. Other researchers had injected malaria-tainted blood from chimpanzees and mangabeys into human volunteers. The first AIDS case was reportedly a British sailor (who had never been to Africa) who died in 1959. The case wasn't officially recognized by the Centers for Disease Control until 1981.

There is no hard proof that AIDS came from monkeys or even from Africa, but the preponderance of evidence shows that AIDS may have originated in Central Africa within the past 50 years. AIDS continues to mutate as new strains continue to appear in West Africa and Asia.

## Old-Fashioned Diseases

Don't let the media hype and the fashion models fool you. Diseases like AIDS or Ebola are not only easily avoidable, it's a long shot even if you are in high-risk areas. There are plenty of dull, cocktail-party, free diseases that await you. Many travelers are quite surprised to find themselves coming down with measles or mumps while traveling. Unlike the United States, which has eradicated much of the childhood and preventable viruses through inoculation, the rest of the world is more concerned about feeding than vaccinating their children. Whooping cough, mumps, measles, polio, and tuberculosis are common in third-world countries. Although some of the symptoms are minor, complications can lead to lifelong afflictions. Make sure you are vaccinated against these easily preventable diseases.

But don't just run off to be the next bubble boy and spend the rest of your life in a hermetically sealed dome. For travelers, these diseases are relatively rare and avoidable. To put the whole thing in perspective, the most common complaint tends to be diarrhea, followed by a cold (usually the result of lowered resistance caused by fatigue, dehydration, foreign microbes, and stress). The important thing is to recognize when you are sick versus very sick. Tales of turn-of-the-century explorers struck down by a tiny mosquito bite are now legend. Malaria is still a very real and common threat. Just for fun, bring back a sample of local river water from your next trip and have the medical lab analyze it. You may never drink water of any kind again.

This is not to say that as soon as you get off the plane, you will automatically be struck down with Ebola River fever and have blood oozing out from your eyes. You can travel bug-free and suffer no more than a cold caused by the air-conditioning in your hotel room. But it is important to at least understand the relative risks and gravity of some diseases.

The diseases listed on the following pages are important, and you should be conversant with both symptoms and cures. Please do not assume that this is medical advice. It is designed to give you an overview of the various nasties that possibly await you. Tropical countries are the most likely to cause you bacterial grief. Keep in mind that most of these diseases are a direct result of poor hygiene, travel in infected areas, and contact with infected people. In other words, stay away from people if you want to stay healthy. Second, follow the commonsense practice of having all food cooked freshly and properly. Many books tell you to wash fruit and then forget to mention that the water is probably filled with more bugs than the fruit. Peel all fruits and vegetables, and approach anything you stick in your body with a healthy level of skepticism and distrust. If you are completely paranoid, you can exist on freeze-dried foods, Maggi Mee (noodles), fresh fruit (peeled, remember), and canned food: they can be boring, but are fine . . . unless, hey, didn't you just wash your spoon in the local water?

It is considered wise to ask local experts about dangers that await you. If you do not feel right for any reason, contact a local doctor. It is not advisable to enter a medical treatment program while in a developing country. There are greater chances of you catching worse afflictions once you are in the hospital. Ask for temporary medication and then get your butt back to North America or Europe.

*Hospital Web*
http://adams.mgh.harvard.edu/hospitalwebworld.html

*International health care links*
http://www.healthcareland.com/SOS/embassy_links.htm

*Worst Case, You Can Always Try Humor Therapy*
http://www.humormatters.com

**DANGEROUS DISEASES**

## DOCTOR, DOCTOR

You will hear and read plenty of flippant or useless advice when it comes to health care in dangerous or impoverished countries. That's because often there simply isn't any health care. You might meet a local uncredentialled practitioner, stumble over a dusty apothecary, or even see large buildings that say "hospital." Be careful. If you are concerned about your medical or health needs when abroad, then you should take the time to review your options. When you are run over by a truck and need help fast, you won't really have much time to do research. What is the rule of thumb? Always carry a medical kit on you, including medication and first-aid instructions . . . in the language of the country you are in.

Second, contact an embassy to get complete details of the preferred hospital and doctors who speak your language.

Third, buy a medical-evacuation policy that will get you home on a chartered plane or air carrier as soon as possible.

Worst-case scenarios require knowing the location or contact information for military hospitals, aid groups, missionaries, NGOs, and/or large hotels (who can contact doctors).

Remember that the symptoms of many tropical diseases may not take effect until you are home and back into your regular schedule. It is highly advisable that you contact a tropical disease specialist and have full testing done (stool, urine, blood, physical) just to be sure that you haven't been infected. Very few American doctors are conversant with the many tropical diseases by virtue of their rarity. This is not their fault, since many tourists do not even realize that they have taken trips or cruises into endemic zones. People can catch malaria on a plane between London and New York from a stowaway mosquito that just came in from Bombay. Many people come in close contact with foreigners in buses and subways and on the street from Los Angeles to New York. Don't assume you have to be up to your neck in Laotian pig wallows to be at risk. Many labs do not do tests for some of the more exotic bugs. Symptoms can also be misleading. It is possible that you may be misdiagnosed or mistreated if you do not fully discuss the possible reasons for your medical condition. Now that we have scared the hell out of you, your first contact should be with the Centers for Disease Control in Atlanta.

Dr. Susan Hou recommends that readers take extra medical supplies to leave behind with clinics or doctors where they travel. It is a good rule never to give medication, pills, or even first-aid materials directly to sick people, since most of us do not know the correct usage or are unaware of side effects. She also suggested giving blood (you can bring your own 18-gauge needle), but don't give blood at high altitudes.

**Disease Outbreak News**
http://www.who.int/emc/outbreak_news

**First-Aid Kits**
Adventure Medical Kits
P.O. Box 43309
Oakland, CA 94624
Tel.: (800) 324-3517
Fax: (510) 261-7419
questions@adventuremedicalkits.com
http://www.adventuremedicalkits.com

**Atwater Carey, Ltd.**
339 E. Rainbow Blvd.
Salida, CO 81201
Tel.: (719) 530-0923 or (800) 359-1646
Fax: (719) 530-0928
http://www.atwatercarey.com

**Outdoor Research (OR)**
2203 1st Avenue South
Seattle, WA 98134-1424
Tel.: (888) 467-4327
http://www.orgear.com

**Wilderness Medical Systems**
P.O. Box 584
Absarokee, MT 59001-0301
Tel.: (406) 494-8358 or (800) 858-7430
Fax: (406) 328-6176
http://www.wildernessmedical.com

**Wilderness EMS Training**
http://www.wemsi.org

**Wilderness Professional Training (WPT)**
P.O. Box 759
Crested Butte, CO 81224
Tel.: (970) 349-5939

**Wilderness Medic Outfitters**
2477 County Road 132
Elizabeth, CO 80107
Tel.: (303) 688-5176

**Wilderness Medical Associates (WMA)**
189 Dudley Road
Bryant Pond, ME 04219
Tel.: (207) 665-2707
Fax: (207) 665-2747
http://www.wildernessmedicine.com/welcome.html
http://www.wildmed.com/course_fact_sheets/wfa_facts.html
http://www.wemsi.on.ca/pamph1.html

**Northeastern University, Institute for EMS**
145 South Bedford Street
Burlington, MA 01803
Tel.: (781) 238-8400
http://www.ems.neu.edu

**DANGEROUS DISEASES**

# A Rogue's Gallery of Diseases

This list is a simple and incomplete checklist of what to ask your doctor about when planning your trip. The best single source in the world for information on the various bugs and germs is the Centers for Disease Control and Prevention, available on the Web (http://www.cdc.gov), by phone (404) 639-3311, or reprinted in book form. Always consult with a doctor before traveling and before taking medication to ensure proper precautions are taken. If you are sick within a country, it is wise to have supplementary medical treatment and or evacuation insurance.

### African Sleeping Sickness (African Trypanosomiasis)

*FOUND:* Tropical Africa

*CAUSE:* A tiny protozoan parasite that emits a harmful toxin.

*CARRIER:* Tsetse fly. Tsetse flies are large biting insects about the size of a horsefly found in East and West Africa.

*SYMPTOMS:* Eastern trypanosomiasis: 2 to 31 days after the bite, there are recurrent episodes of fever, headaches, and malaise. Can lead to death in two to six weeks. Western trypanosomiasis: produces a skin ulcer within 5 to 10 days after being bitten, but the symptoms then disappear in two to three weeks. Symptoms reappear six months to five years after the initial infection, resulting in fevers, headaches, rapid heartbeat, swelling of the lymph glands (located in the back of the neck), personality changes, tremors, a lackadaisical attitude, and then stupor leading eventually to death.

*TREATMENT:* Suramin (Bayer 205), pentamidine (Lomodine), melarasoprol (Mel B)

*HOW TO AVOID:* Do not travel to infested areas, use insect repellent, wear light-colored clothing, and cover skin areas.

### AIDS (Acquired Immune Deficiency Syndrome)

*FOUND:* Worldwide

*CAUSE:* Advanced stage of HIV (human immunodeficiency syndrome), which causes destruction of a human's natural resistance to infection and other diseases. Death by AIDS is usually a result of unrelated diseases that rapidly attack the victim. This range of diseases is called ARC (AIDS-related complex).

*CARRIER:* Sexual intercourse with infected person, through use of an infected needle, transfusion of infected blood, or even transmitted from infected mother through breast milk. There is no way to determine if someone has HIV, except by a blood test. Male homosexuals, drug users, and prostitutes are high-risk groups in major urban centers in the West. AIDS is less selective in developing countries, with Central and Eastern Africa being the areas of highest incidence.

*SYMPTOMS:* Fever, weight loss, fatigue, night sweats, lymph node problems. Infection by other opportunistic elements such as Karposi's sarcoma, pneumonia, and tuberculosis are highly probable and will lead to death.

*TREATMENT:* There is no known cure.

*HOW TO AVOID:* Use condoms, refrain from sexual contact, and do not receive injections or transfusions in questionable areas. Avoid live vaccines such as gamma globulin and hepatitis B in developing countries.

### Amebiasis

*FOUND:* Worldwide

*CAUSE:* A protozoan parasite carried in human fecal matter. Usually found in areas with poor sanitation.

*CARRIER: Entamoeba histolyica* is passed by poor hygiene. Ingested orally in water, air, or food that has come in contact with the parasite.

SYMPTOMS: The infection will spread from the intestines and cause abscesses in other organs such as the liver, lungs, and brain.

TREATMENT: Metronidazole, iodoquinol, diloxanide furoate, paromomycin, tetracycline plus chloroquinine base.

HOW TO AVOID: Avoid uncooked foods, drink only boiled water or bottled liquids, be sure that food is cooked properly, and peel fruits and vegetables.

### Bartonellosis (Oroya Fever, Carrion's Disease)

FOUND: In valleys of Peru, Ecuador, and Colombia

CAUSE: *Bartonella bacilliformis*, a bacterium.

CARRIER: Sandflies that bite at night.

SYMPTOMS: Pain in muscles, joints, and bones along with fever occurring within three weeks of being bitten. Oroya fever causes a fever leading to possible death. *Verruga peruana* creates skin eruptions.

TREATMENT: Antibiotics with transfusion for symptoms of anemia.

HOW TO AVOID: Wear high boots, use groundsheets, sleep in hammocks, and use insect repellent.

### Brucellosis (Undulant Fever)

FOUND: Worldwide

CAUSE: Ingestion of infected dairy products.

CARRIER: Untreated dairy products infected with the *brucellosis* bacteria.

SYMPTOMS: Intermittent fever, sweating, jaundice, rash, depression, enlarged spleen and lymph nodes. The symptoms may disappear and go into perma-

nent remission after three to six months.

TREATMENT: Tetracyclines, sulfonamides, and streptomycin

HOW TO AVOID: Drink pasteurized milk. Avoid infected livestock.

### Chagas' Disease (American Trypanosomiasis)

FOUND: Central and South America

CAUSE: Protozoan parasite carried in the feces of insects.

CARRIER: Kissing or Assassin bugs (Triatoma insects or reduviid bugs). Commonly found in homes with thatched roofs. It can also be transmitted through blood transfusions, breast milk, and in utero.

SYMPTOMS: A papule and swelling at the location of the bite, fever, malaise, anorexia, rash, swelling of the limbs, gastrointestinal problems, heart irregularities, and heart failure.

TREATMENT: Nifurtimox (Bayer 2502)

HOW TO AVOID: Do not stay in native villages; use bed netting and insect repellent.

### Chikungunya Disease

FOUND: Sub-Saharan Africa, Southeast Asia, India, and the Philippines in sporadic outbreaks

CAUSE: Alphavirus transmitted by mosquito bites.

CARRIER: Mosquitoes that transmit the disease from the host (monkeys).

SYMPTOMS: Joint pain with potential for hemorrhagic symptoms.

TREATMENT: None, but symptoms will disappear. If hemorrhagic, avoid aspirin.

HOW TO AVOID: Follow the standard precautions to avoid mosquito

**DANGEROUS DISEASES**

bites: Use insect repellent and mosquito nets, and cover exposed skin areas.

## Cholera
FOUND: Worldwide; primarily developing countries

CAUSE: Intestinal infection caused by the toxin *Vibrio Cholerae* O group bacteria.

CARRIER: Infected food and water contaminated by human and animal waste.

SYMPTOMS: Watery diarrhea, abdominal cramps, nausea, vomiting, and severe dehydration as a result of diarrhea. Can lead to death if fluids are not replaced.

TREATMENT: Tetracycline can hasten recovery. Replace fluids using an electrolyte solution.

HOW TO AVOID: Vaccinations before traveling can diminish symptoms up to 50 percent for a period of 3 to 6 months. Cholera is a threat in refugee camps or areas of poor sanitation. Use standard precautions with food and drink in developing countries.

## Ciguatera Poisoning
FOUND: Tropical areas

CAUSE: Ingestion of fish containing the toxin produced by the *dinoflagellate Gambierdiscus toxicus*.

CARRIER: 425 species of tropical reef fish

SYMPTOMS: Up to six hours after eating, victims may experience nausea, watery diarrhea, abdominal cramps, vomiting, abnormal sensation in limbs and teeth, hot–cold flashes, joint pain, weakness, skin rashes, and itching. In very severe cases, victims may experience blind spells, low blood pressure and heart rate, paralysis, and loss of coordination. Symptoms may appear years later.

TREATMENT: There is no specific medical treatment other than first aid. Induce vomiting.

HOW TO AVOID: Do not eat reef fish (including sea bass, barracuda, red snapper, or grouper).

## Colorado Tick Fever
FOUND: North America

CAUSE: Arbovirus transmitted by insect or infected blood.

CARRIER: The wood tick (*Dermacentor andersoni*), also through transfusion of infected blood.

SYMPTOMS: Aching of muscles in back and legs, chills, recurring fever, headaches, eye pain, fear of brightly lit areas.

TREATMENT: Since symptoms only last about three weeks, medication or treatment is intended to relieve symptoms.

HOW TO AVOID: Wear leggings, tall boots, and insect repellent. (Ticks are picked up when walking through woods.)

## Dengue Fever (Breakbone Fever)
FOUND: South America, Africa, South Pacific, Asia, Mexico, Central America, and the Caribbean

CAUSE: An arbovirus transmitted by mosquitoes.

CARRIER: Mosquitoes in tropical areas, which usually bite during the daytime.

SYMPTOMS: There are two distinct periods. The first period consists of severe muscle and joint aches and headaches combined with high fever (the origin of the term "breakbone fever"). The second period is sensitivity to light, diarrhea, vomiting, nausea, mental depression, and enlarged lymph nodes.

TREATMENT: Designed to relieve symptoms. Aspirin should be avoided due to hemorrhagic complications.

HOW TO AVOID: Typical protection against daytime mosquito bites: use insect repellent with high DEET levels, wear light-colored long-sleeve shirts and long pants.

## Diarrhea

FOUND: Worldwide

CAUSE: There are many reasons for travelers to have the symptoms of diarrhea. It is important to remember that alien bacteria in the digestive tract are the main culprits. Most travelers to Africa, Mexico, South America, and the Middle East will find themselves doubled-up in pain, running for the nearest stinking toilet, and wondering why the hell they ever left their comfortable home.

CARRIER: Bacteria from food, the air, water, or other people can be the cause. Dehydration from long airplane flights, strange diets, stress, and high altitude can also cause diarrhea. It is doubtful you will ever get to know your intestinal bacteria on a first-name basis, but *Aeromonas hydrophila*, Campylobacter, *jejuni Pleisiomonas*, salmonellae, shigellae, shielloides, *Vibrio cholerae* (non-01), *Vibrio parahaemolyticus, Yersinia enterocoliticia,* and *Escherichia coli* are the most likely culprits. All these bugs would love to spend a week or two in your gut.

SYMPTOMS: Loose stools, stomach pains, bloating, fever, and malaise.

TREATMENT: First stop eating and ingest plenty of fluids and salty foods; second, try Kaopectate or Pepto Bismol. If diarrhea persists after three to four days, seek medical advice.

HOW TO AVOID: Keep your fluid intake high when traveling. Follow commonsense procedures when eating, drinking, and ingesting any food or fluids. Remember to wash your hands carefully and frequently, since you can transmit a shocking number of germs from your hands to your mouth, eyes, and nose.

## Diphtheria

FOUND: Worldwide

CAUSE: The bacterium *Corynebacterium diptheriae,* a producer of harmful toxins, is usually a problem in populations that have not been immunized against diphtheria.

CARRIER: Infected humans can spread the germs by sneezing, or by contact.

SYMPTOMS: Swollen diphtheritic membrane that may lead to serious congestion. Other symptoms are pallor, listlessness, weakness, and increased heart rate. May cause death due to weakened heart or shock.

TREATMENT: Immunization with the DPT vaccine at an early age (3 years) is the ideal prevention; treat with antitoxin, if not.

HOW TO AVOID: Avoid close contact with populations or areas where there is little to no vaccination program for diphtheria.

### Ebola River Fever

*FOUND:* Among local populations in the Congo

*CAUSE:* A very rare but much publicized affliction.

*CARRIER:* Unknown, but highly contagious. In 1989, the virus was found in lab monkeys in Reston, Virginia. The monkeys were quickly destroyed. Outbreaks in the Congo and Central Africa are a risk.

*SYMPTOMS:* The virus is described as melting people down, causing blood clotting, a loss of consciousness, and death.

*TREATMENT:* None

*HOW TO AVOID:* Unknown

### Encephalitis

*FOUND:* Southeast Asia, Korea, Taiwan, Nepal, Eastern CIS countries, and Eastern Europe

*CAUSE:* A common viral infection carried by insects.

*CARRIER:* The disease can be carried by the tick or mosquito. The risk is high during late summer and fall. The most dangerous strain is tickborne encephalitis, transmitted by ticks in the summer in the colder climates of Russia, Scandinavia, Switzerland, and France.

*SYMPTOMS:* Fever, headache, muscle pain, malaise, runny nose, and sore throat followed by lethargy, confusion, hallucination, and seizures. About one-fifth of encephalitis infections have led to death.

*TREATMENT:* A vaccine is available.

*HOW TO AVOID:* Avoid areas known to be endemic. Avoid tick-infested areas such as forests, rice-growing areas in Asia (which breed mosquitoes), or areas that have a large number of domestic pigs (which are tick carriers). Use insect repellent. Do not drink unpasteurized milk.

### Filariasis (Lymphatic, River Blindness)

*FOUND:* Africa, Central America, the Caribbean, South America, and Asia

*CAUSE:* A group of diseases caused by long, thin roundworms carried by mosquitoes.

*CARRIER:* Mosquitoes and biting flies in tropical areas.

*SYMPTOMS:* Lymphatic filariasis, onchocerciasis (river blindness), loiasis, and mansonellasis all have similar and very unpleasant symptoms. Fevers; headaches; nausea; vomiting; sensitivity to light; inflammation in the legs, the abdomen, and testicles; swelling of the abdomen, joints, and scrotum; enlarged lymph nodes; abscesses; eye lesions that lead to blindness; rashes, itches, and arthritis.

*TREATMENT:* Diethylcarbamazine (DEC, Hetrazan, Notezine) is the usual treatment.

*HOW TO AVOID:* Avoid bites by insects with usual protective measures and use insect repellent.

### Flukes

*FOUND:* The Caribbean, South America, Africa, and Asia

*CAUSE:* The liver fluke (*Clonorchis sinensis*) and the lung fluke (*Paragonimus westermani*), which lead to paragonimasis.

*CARRIER:* Carried in fish that has not been properly cooked.

*SYMPTOMS:* Obstruction of the bile system, along with fever, pain, jaundice, gallstones, and inflammation of the pancreas. There is further risk of cancer of the bile tract after infection. Paragonimasis affects the lungs and causes chest pains.

*TREATMENT:* Paragonimasis is treated with Prazanquantel. Obstruction of the bile system can require surgery.

*HOW TO AVOID:* To avoid liver flukes do not eat uncooked or improperly cooked fish—something most sushi fans will decry. Paragonimasis is found in uncooked shellfish, like freshwater crabs, crayfish, and shrimp.

### Giardiasis

*FOUND:* Worldwide

*CAUSE:* A protozoa, *Giardi lamblia,* that causes diarrhea.

*CARRIER:* Ingestion of food or water that is contaminated with fecal matter.

*SYMPTOMS:* Very sudden diarrhea, severe flatulence, cramps, nausea, anorexia, weight loss, and fever.

*TREATMENT:* Giardiasis can disappear without treatment, but Furazolidone, metronidizole, or quinacrine HCI are the usual treatments.

*HOW TO AVOID:* Cleanliness, drinking bottled water, and strict personal hygiene in eating and personal contact.

### Guinea Worm Infection (Dracontiasis, Dracunculiasis)

*FOUND:* Tropical areas like the Caribbean, the Guianas, Africa, the Middle East, and Asia

*CAUSE:* Ingestion of waterborne nematode *Dracunculus medinensis.*

*CARRIER:* Water systems that harbor *Dracunculus medinensis.*

*SYMPTOMS:* Fever, itching, swelling around the eyes, wheezing, skin blisters, and arthritis.

*TREATMENT:* Doses of niridazole, metronidazole, or thiabendazole are the usual method. Surgery may be required to remove worms.

*HOW TO AVOID:* Drink only boiled or chemically treated water.

### Hemorrhagic Fevers

Some of the more well-known hemorrhagic fevers are yellow fever, dengue, lassa fever, and the horror movie–caliber Ebola fever. Outbreaks tend to be localized and caused by large populations of insects or rats. Don't let the exotic-sounding names lull you into a false sense of security; there was a major outbreak in the American Southwest caused by rodents spreading the disease.

*FOUND:* Worldwide

*CAUSE:* Intestinal worms carried by insects and rodents.

*CARRIER:* Depending on the disease, it can be transmitted by mosquitoes, ticks, and rodents (in urine and feces).

*SYMPTOMS:* Headache, backache, muscle pain, and conjunctivitis. Later on, thinning of the blood will cause low blood pressure, bleeding from the gums and nose, vomiting and coughing up blood, blood in the stool, bleeding from the skin, and hemorrhaging in the internal organs. Coma and death may occur in the second week.

*TREATMENT:* Consult a doctor or medical facility familiar with the local disease.

*HOW TO AVOID:* Avoid mosquitoes, ticks, and areas with high concentrations of mice and rats.

### Hepatitis A, B, Non-A, Non-B
*FOUND:* Worldwide
*CAUSE:* A virus that attacks the liver. Hepatitis A, Non-B, and Non-A can be brought on by poor hygiene; hepatitis B is transmitted sexually or through infected blood.
*CARRIER:* Hepatitis A is transmitted by oral-fecal route, person-to-person contact, or through contaminated food or water. Hepatitis B is transmitted by sexual activity or the transfer of bodily fluids. Hepatitis Non-A and Non-B are spread by contaminated water or from other people.
*SYMPTOMS:* Muscle and joint pain, nausea, fatigue, sensitivity to light, sore throat, runny nose. Look for dark urine and clay-colored stools and jaundice along with liver pain and enlargement.
*TREATMENT:* Rest and a high-calorie diet. Immune globulin is advised as a minor protection against hepatitis A. You can be vaccinated against hepatitis B.
*HOW TO AVOID:* Non-A and Non-B require avoiding infected foods. Hepatitis B requires avoiding unprotected sexual contact, unsterile needles, dental work, and infusions. Hepatitis A requires proper hygiene and avoiding infected water and foods.

### Hydatid Disease (Echinococcosis)
*FOUND:* Worldwide
*CAUSE:* A tapeworm found in areas with high populations of pigs, cattle, and sheep.

*CARRIER:* Eggs of the echinococcosis.
*SYMPTOMS:* Cysts form in the liver, lungs, bones, or brain.
*TREATMENT:* Surgery for removal of the infected cysts. Mebendazole and albendazole are used as well.
*HOW TO AVOID:* Boil water, cook foods properly, and avoid infected areas.

### Leishmaniasis
*FOUND:* Tropical and subtropical regions
*CAUSE:* Protozoans of the genus *Leishmania.*
*CARRIER:* Phlebotomine sandflies in tropical and subtropical regions.
*SYMPTOMS:* Skin lesions; cutaneous ulcers; mucocutaneous ulcers in the mouth, nose, and anus; as well as intermittent fever, anemia, and enlarged spleen.
*TREATMENT:* Sodium stibogluconate, rifampin, and sodium antimony gluconate. Surgery is also used to remove cutaneous and mucocutaneous ulcers.
*HOW TO AVOID:* Use insect repellent, a groundcover when sleeping along with bed nets, and cover arms and legs.

### Leprosy (Hansen's Disease)
*FOUND:* Africa, India, and elsewhere
*CAUSE:* The bacterium *Mycobacterium leprae* that infects the skin, eyes, nervous system, and testicles.
*CARRIER:* It is not known how leprosy is transmitted, but direct human contact is suspected.
*SYMPTOMS:* Skin lesions and nerve damage that progresses to loss of fingers and toes, blindness, and difficulty breathing.
*TREATMENT:* Dapsone, rifampin, and clofazimine

*HOW TO AVOID:* Leprosy is a tropical disease, with over half the cases worldwide occurring in India and Africa. There is no known preventive method.

### Loaisis
*FOUND:* West and Central Africa
*CAUSE:* The loa loa parasite.
*CARRIER:* Chrysops deer flies or tabanid flies in West and Central Africa.
*SYMPTOMS:* Subcutaneous swellings that come and go, brain and heart inflammation.
*TREATMENT:* Diethylcarbamazine
*HOW TO AVOID:* Deerflies are large, and their bites can be avoided by wearing full-sleeved shirts and thick pants. Hats and bandannas can protect head and neck areas.

### Lyme Disease
*FOUND:* Worldwide
*CAUSE:* A spirochete carried by ticks.
*CARRIER:* The Ixodes tick, found worldwide and in great numbers during the summer. Ticks are found in rural areas and burrow into the skin to suck blood.
*SYMPTOMS:* A pronounced bite mark, flulike symptoms, severe headache, stiff neck, fever, chills, joint pain, malaise, and fatigue.
*TREATMENT:* Tetracyclines, phenoxymethylpenicillin, or erythromycin if caught early. Advanced cases may require intravenous penicillin.
*HOW TO AVOID:* Do not walk through wooded areas in the summer. Check for ticks frequently. Use leggings with insect repellent.

### Malaria
Malaria is by far the most dangerous disease and the one most likely for travelers to pick up in third-world countries. Protection against this disease should be your first priority. As a rule, be leery of all riverine, swampy, or tropical places. Areas such as logging camps, shantytowns, oases, campsites near slow-moving water, and resorts near mangrove swamps are all very likely to be major areas of malarial infection. Consult with a local doctor to understand the various resistances and the prescribed treatment. Many foreign doctors are more knowledgeable about the cure and treatment of malaria than domestic doctors.
*FOUND:* Africa, Asia, the Caribbean, Southeast Asia, and the Middle East
*CAUSE:* The plasmodium parasite is injected into the victim while the mosquito draws blood.
*CARRIER:* The female anopheles mosquito.
*SYMPTOMS:* Fever, chills, enlarged spleen in low-level versions, *Plasmodium falciparum,* or cerebral malaria, can also cause convulsions, kidney failure, and hypoglycemia.
*TREATMENT:* Chloroquine, quinine, pyrimethamine, sulfadoxine, and mefloquine. *Note:* Some people may have adverse reactions to any or all of these drugs.
*HOW TO AVOID:* Begin taking a malarial prophylaxis before your trip, as well as during and after your trip (consult your doctor for a prescription). Avoid infected areas and protect yourself from mosquito bites (netting, insect repellent, mosquito coils, long-sleeve shirts, and pants),

especially during dusk and evening times.

### Measles (Rubella)
FOUND: Worldwide

CAUSE: A common virus in unvaccinated areas.

CARRIER: Sneezing, saliva, and close contact with infected or unvaccinated humans.

SYMPTOMS: Malaise, irritability, fever, conjunctivitis, swollen eyelids, and hacking cough appear 9 to 11 days after exposure. Fourteen days after exposure, the typical facial rash and spots appear.

TREATMENT: Measles will disappear, but complications can occur.

HOW TO AVOID: Vaccination or gamma globulin shots within five days of exposure.

### Meliodosis
FOUND: Worldwide

CAUSE: An animal disease (the bacillus *Pseudomonas pseudomallei*) that can be transferred to humans.

CARRIER: Found in infected soil and water, and transmitted through skin wounds.

SYMPTOMS: Various types, including fever, malaise, pneumonia, shortness of breath, headache, diarrhea, skin lesions, muscle pain, and abscesses in organs.

TREATMENT: Antibiotics such as tetracyclines and sulfur drugs.

HOW TO AVOID: Clean and cover all wounds carefully.

### Meningitis
FOUND: Africa and Saudi Arabia

CAUSE: Bacteria—*Neisseria meningitis*, *Streptococcus pneumoniae*, and *Haemophilus influenzae*. Children are most at risk. There are frequent outbreaks in Africa and Nepal.

CARRIER: Inhaling infected droplets of nasal and throat secretions.

SYMPTOMS: Fever, vomiting, headaches, confusion, lethargy, and rash.

TREATMENT: Penicillin G

HOW TO AVOID: *Meningococcus polysaccharide* vaccine. Do not travel to areas where outbreaks occur (the Sahel from Mali to Ethiopia) in the dry season.

### Mumps
FOUND: Worldwide

CAUSE: A virus found worldwide. Common in early spring and late winter and in unvaccinated areas.

CARRIER: Infected saliva and urine.

SYMPTOMS: Headache, anorexia, malaise, and pain when chewing or swallowing.

TREATMENT: Mumps is a self-inoculating disease. There can be complications which can lead to more serious lifetime afflictions.

HOW TO AVOID: Vaccination (MMR)

### Plague
FOUND: India, Vietnam, Africa, South America, the Middle East, and Russia

CAUSE: A bacteria (*Yersinia pestis*) that infects rodents and the fleas they carry.

CARRIER: Flea bites that transmit the bacteria to humans. Ticks, lice, corpses, and human contact can also spread the disease.

SYMPTOMS: Swollen lymph nodes, fever, abdominal pain, loss of appetite, nausea, vomiting, diarrhea, and gangrene of the extremities.

TREATMENT: Antibiotics like streptomycin, tetracyclines, and chloramphenicol can reduce the mortality rate.
HOW TO AVOID: Stay out of infected areas and avoid contact.

### Poliomyelitis (Polio)
FOUND: Worldwide
CAUSE: A virus that destroys the central nervous system.
CARRIER: Occurs through direct contact.
SYMPTOMS: A mild febrile illness that may lead to paralysis. Polio can cause death in 5 to 10 percent of cases in children and 15 to 30 percent in adult cases.
TREATMENT: There is no treatment.
HOW TO AVOID: Vaccination during childhood and a booster before travel is recommended.

### Rabies
FOUND: Worldwide
CAUSE: A virus that affects the central nervous system.
CARRIER: Rabies is transmitted through the saliva of an infected animal. Found in wild animals, although usually animals found in urban areas are most suspect: dogs, raccoons, cats, skunks, and bats. Although most people will automatically assume they are at risk for rabies, there are only about 16,000 cases reported worldwide. The risk is the deadly seriousness of rabies and the short time in which death occurs.
SYMPTOMS: Abnormal sensations or muscle movement near the bite, followed by fever, headaches, malaise, muscle aches, tiredness, loss of appetite, nausea, vomiting, sore throat, and cough. The advanced stages include excessive excitation, seizures, and mental disturbances, leading to profound nervous system dysfunction and paralysis. Death occurs in most cases 4 to 20 days after being bitten.
TREATMENT: Clean wound vigorously; get injections of antirabies antiserum and antirabies vaccine. People who intend to come into regular contact with animals in high-risk areas can receive HDCV (human diploid cell rabies vaccine) shots.
HOW TO AVOID: Avoid confrontations with animals.

DANGEROUS DISEASES

## THE MOST DANGEROUS MAMMAL

Which animal should you truly fear? Forget crocodiles, only about 100 people in Australia have been attacked by crocs and half of them lived . . . over the last century. Forget snakes, only about a dozen people buy it in the States each year. Forget alligators too. The million-plus alligators that come in contact with 15 million Americans can't even do better than 10 deaths in the last 50 years. There are only about 8 to 12 bites each year in the United States. Sharks? A bunch of pussies. Only 50 to 80 attacks worldwide in a year—a pathetic 10 deaths a year. So if you were going to hunt down a dangerous animal and wrestle him every week, what would it be? Well, the family pet, of course.

(continued)

Every year about three-quarters of a million Americans require medical treatment for dog bites. About half of all children are bitten by dogs at some point. The most dangerous animal in our national parks is still the family pet. These pooches are "dainjerous, mate!" Dogs account for more attacks on humans than any wild animal. Around 20 people are killed by Fido every year. Nice doggy, doggy.

In one year dogs cause:

4.5 million injuries
334,000 emergency room visits
20 deaths
670 hospitalizations

*Sources:* Various

**Animal Attack Files**
http://www.igorilla.com/gorilla/animal

## Relapsing Fever

*FOUND:* The louse-borne version is found in poor rural areas where infestation by lice is common.

*CAUSE: Borrelia spirochetes*

*CARRIER:* Lice and ticks. Ticks are found in wooded areas and bite mainly at night.

*SYMPTOMS:* The fever gets its name from the six days on and six days off of high fever. Other symptoms include headaches, muscle pains, weakness, and loss of appetite.

*TREATMENT:* Antibiotics

*HOW TO AVOID:* Avoid infected areas, and check for ticks.

## Rift Valley Fever

*FOUND:* Egypt and East Africa

*CAUSE:* A virus that affects humans and livestock.

*CARRIER:* Mosquitoes, inhaling infected dust, contact with broken skin, and ingesting infected animal blood or fluids.

*SYMPTOMS:* Sudden, one-time fever, severe headaches, muscle pain, weakness, sensitivity to light, eye pain, nausea, vomiting, diarrhea, eye redness, and facial flushing. Blindness, meningitis, meningoencephalitis, and retinitis may also occur.

*TREATMENT:* Seek medical treatment for supportive care.

*HOW TO AVOID:* Avoid contact with livestock in infected areas; protect yourself against mosquito bites.

## River Blindness (Onchocerciais)

*FOUND:* Equatorial Africa, Yemen, the Sahara, and parts of Central and South America

*CAUSE:* The roundworm *Onchocerca volvulus*.

*CARRIER:* Transmitted by blackflies found along rapidly flowing rivers.

*SYMPTOMS:* Itching, skin atrophy, mottling, nodules, enlargement of the lymph nodes (particularly in the groin), and blindness.

*TREATMENT:* Invermectin or Diethyl-carbamazine (DEC), followed by suramin, followed by DEC again.

*HOW TO AVOID:* Insect repellent, long-sleeve shirts, and long pants. Avoid blackfly bites.

### Rocky Mountain Spotted Fever

*FOUND:* Only in the Western Hemisphere

*CAUSE:* A bacterial disease transmitted by tick bites.

*CARRIER: Rickettsial* bacteria are found in rodents and dogs. The ticks pass the bacteria by then biting humans.

*SYMPTOMS:* Fever, headaches, chills, and rash (after fourth day) on the arms and legs. Final symptoms may include delirium, shock, and kidney failure.

*TREATMENT:* Tetracyclines or chloramphenicol

*HOW TO AVOID:* Ticks are found in wooded areas. Inspect your body after walks. Use insect repellent. Wear leggings or long socks or long pants.

### Salmonellosis

*FOUND:* Worldwide

*CAUSE:* A common bacterial infection; *Salmonella gastroenteritis* is commonly described as food poisoning.

*CARRIER:* Found in fecally contaminated food, unpasteurized milk, raw foods, and water.

*SYMPTOMS:* Abdominal pain, diarrhea, vomiting, chills, and fever usually within 8 to 48 hours of ingesting infected food. Salmonella only kills about 1 percent of its victims, usually small children or the aged.

*TREATMENT:* Purge infected food and replace fluids. Complete recovery is within two to five days.

*HOW TO AVOID:* Consume only properly prepared foods.

### Sandfly Fever (Three-Day Fever)

*FOUND:* Africa and the Mediterranean

*CAUSE:* Phleboviruses injected by sandfly bites.

*CARRIER:* Transmitted by sandflies, usually during the dry season.

*SYMPTOMS:* Fever, headache, eye pain, chest-muscle pains, vomiting, sensitivity to light, stiff neck, taste abnormality, rash, and joint pain.

*TREATMENT:* There is no specific treatment. The symptoms can reoccur in about 15 percent of cases, but typically disappear.

*HOW TO AVOID:* Do not sleep directly on the ground. Sandflies usually bite at night.

### Schistosomiasis (Bilharzia)

Bilharzia is one of the meanest bugs to pick up in your foreign travels. The idea of nasty little creatures actually burrowing through your skin and lodging themselves in your gut is menacing. If not treated, it can make your life a living hell with afternoon sweats, painful urination, weakness, and other good stuff. There is little you can do to prevent infection, since the *Schistosoma* larva and flukes are found wherever people have fouled freshwater rivers and lakes. Get treatment immediately, since the affliction worsens as the eggs multiply and continue to infect more tissues. About 250 million people around the world are believed to be infected.

*FOUND:* Worldwide

*CAUSE:* A group of parasitic *Schistosoma* flatworms (*Schistosoma mansoni, Schistosoma* japonicum, and *Schistosoma haematobium*) found in slow-moving, tropical freshwater.

CARRIER: The larvae of *Schistosoma* are found in slow-moving waterways in tropical areas around the world. They actually enter the body through the skin, then enter the lymph vessels, and then migrate to the liver.

SYMPTOMS: Look for a rash and itching at the entry site, followed by weakness, loss of appetite, night sweats, hivelike rashes, and afternoon fevers in about four to six weeks. There will be bloody, painful, and frequent urination and diarrhea. Later, victims become weaker and may be susceptible to further infections and diseases.

TREATMENT: Elimination of *S. mansoni* requires oxamniquine and praziquantel. *S. japonicum* responds to praziquantel alone, and *S. haematobium* is treated with praziquantel and metrifonate.

HOW TO AVOID: Stay out of slow-moving freshwater in all tropical and semitropical areas. This also means wading or standing in water.

### Syphilis
FOUND: Worldwide

CAUSE: A spirochete (*Treponema pallidum*) causes this chronic venereal disease, which if left untreated, progresses into three clinical stages.

CARRIER: Syphilis is spread through sexual contact and can be passed on to infants congenitally.

SYMPTOMS: After an incubation period of two to six weeks, a sore usually appears near the genitals, although some men

and women may not experience any symptoms. Some men also experience a scanty discharge. A skin rash appears in the second stage, often on the soles of the feet and palms of the hands. It may be accompanied by a mild fever, sore throat, and patchy hair loss. This rash generally appears about six weeks after the initial sore. The third phase of the disease may develop over several years if the disease is left untreated and may damage the brain and the heart or even cause death.

TREATMENT: Antibiotics are used to treat syphilis, and infected people should abstain from sex until treatment ends. Blood tests should be performed again in three months after the round of treatment. Sexual partners need to be tested and treated. Victims of syphilis should also be tested for other sexually transmitted diseases.

HOW TO AVOID: Abstain from sexual activities or use a latex condom.

### Tainiasis (Tapeworms)
FOUND: Worldwide

CAUSE: A tapeworm is usually discovered after being passed by the victim.

CARRIER: Ingestion of poorly cooked meat infected with tapeworms.

SYMPTOMS: In advanced cases, there will be diarrhea and stomach cramps. Sections of tapeworms can be seen in stools.

TREATMENT: Mebendazole, niclocsamide, paromomysi, and praziquantel are effective in killing the parasite.

HOW TO AVOID: Tapeworms come from eating meats infected with tapeworm or coming into contact with infected fecal matter.

### Tetanus (Lockjaw)
*FOUND:* Worldwide
*CAUSE:* The bacteria *Clostridiium tetani.*
*CARRIER:* Found in soil and enters body through cuts or punctures.
*SYMPTOMS:* Restlessness, irritability, headaches, jaw pain, back pain and stiffness, and difficulty in swallowing. Then, within 2 to 56 days, stiffness increases with lockjaw and spasms. Death occurs in about half the cases, usually affecting children.
*TREATMENT:* If infected, human tetanus immune globulin is administered with nerve blockers for muscle relaxation.
*HOW TO AVOID:* Immunization is the best prevention, with a booster recommended before travel.

### Trachoma
*FOUND:* Common in Africa, the Middle East, and Asia
*CAUSE:* A chlamydial infection of the eye, which is responsible for about 200 million cases of blindness.
*CARRIER:* Flies, contact, wiping face or eye area with infected towels.
*SYMPTOMS:* Constant inflammation under the eyelid that causes scarring of the eyelid, turned-in eyelashes, and eventual scarring of the cornea and then blindness.
*TREATMENT:* Tetracyclines, erythromycin, sulfonamide, and surgery to correct turned-in lashes.
*HOW TO AVOID:* Trachoma is spread primarily by flies. Proper hygiene and avoidance of fly-infested areas are recommended.

### Trichinosis
*FOUND:* Worldwide
*CAUSE:* Infection of the *Trichinella spiralis* worm.
*CARRIER:* Pig meat (also bear and walrus) that contain cysts. The worm then infects the new host's tissues and intestines.
*SYMPTOMS:* Diarrhea, abdominal pain, nausea, prostration, and fever. As the worm infects tissues, fever, swelling around the eyes, conjunctivitis, eye hemorrhages, muscle pain, weakness, rash, and splinter hemorrhages under the nails occur. Less than 10 percent of the cases result in death.
*TREATMENT:* Thiabendazole is effective in killing the parasite.
*HOW TO AVOID:* Proper preparation, storage, and cooking of meat.

### Tuberculosis
*FOUND:* Worldwide
*CAUSE:* A disease of the lungs caused by the *Mycobacterium tuberculosis* bacteria or *Mycobacterium bovis.*
*CARRIER:* By close contact with infected persons (sneezing, coughing) or, in the case of *Mycobacterium bovis,* contaminated or unpasteurized milk.
*SYMPTOMS:* Weight loss, night sweats, and a chronic cough, usually with traces of blood. If left untreated, death results in about 60 percent of the cases after a period of 2½ years.
*TREATMENT:* Isoniazide and rifampin can control the disease.
*HOW TO AVOID:* Vaccination and isoniazid prophylaxis.

### Tularaemia (Rabbit Fever)

*FOUND:* Worldwide

*CAUSE:* A fairly rare disease (about 300 cases per year) caused by the bacteria *Francisella tularnesis* passed from animals to humans via insects.

*CARRIER:* The bite of deerflies, ticks, mosquitoes, and even cats can infect humans.

*SYMPTOMS:* Fever, chills, headaches, muscle pain, malaise, enlarged liver and spleen, rash, skin ulcers, and enlargement of the lymph nodes.

*TREATMENT:* Vaccination, but streptomycin is primarily used. Tetracycline and chloramphenicol are also effective.

*HOW TO AVOID:* Care when handling animal carcasses, removal of ticks, and avoidance of insect bites.

### Typhoid Fever

*FOUND:* Africa, Asia, and Central America

*CAUSE:* The bacterium *Salmonella typhi*.

*CARRIER:* Transmitted by contaminated food and water in areas of poor hygiene.

*SYMPTOMS:* Fever, headaches, abdominal tenderness, malaise, rash, and enlarged spleen. Later symptoms include delirium, intestinal hemorrhage, and perforation of the intestine.

*TREATMENT:* Chloramphenicol

*HOW TO AVOID:* Vaccination is the primary protection, although the effectiveness is not high.

### Typhus Fever

*FOUND:* Africa, South America, Southeast Asia, and India

*CAUSE:* Rickettsia

*CARRIER:* Transmitted by fleas, lice, mites, and ticks found in mountainous areas around the world.

*SYMPTOMS:* Fever, headache, rash, and muscle pain. If untreated, death may occur in the second week due to kidney failure, coma, and blockage of the arteries.

*TREATMENT:* Tetracyclines or chloramphenicol

*HOW TO AVOID:* Check for ticks, avoid insect bites, attend to hygiene to prevent lice, and avoid mountainous regions.

### Yellow Fever

*FOUND:* Africa and South America

*CAUSE:* A virus transmitted by mosquito bites.

*CARRIER:* The tiny banded-legged *Aedes aegpyti* is the source for urban yellow fever, and the haemogogus and sabethes mosquito carry the jungle version.

*SYMPTOMS:* In the beginning, there is fever, headaches, backaches, muscle pain, nausea, conjunctivitis, albumin in the urine, and slow heart rate. These symptoms are followed by black vomit, no urination, and delirium. Death affects only 5 to 10 percent of cases and occurs in the fourth to sixth day.

*TREATMENT:* Replace fluids and electrolytes.

*HOW TO AVOID:* Vaccination is mandatory when entering or leaving infected areas.

# In a Dangerous Place: The Sahara

## THE SINGING OF THE SANDS

This is a deadly hot place where rain squalls can drop the temperature so quickly they make grown men throw up. Where massive walls of red-brown sand choke and blast everything to a light-brown softness. Where camels walk ghostlike through the desert, carrying dirty white slabs of salt. Where massive mud buildings look about as alien as one can imagine on this planet. A place where paddle-wheelers chug down dirty brown rivers, and faded yellow earthmovers sit dead and picked-over like dinosaur carcasses. It was in this Western, French place that I first became sick. I remember, because I wrote it down as it happened:

I know I am getting weaker. At night I am reduced to lying on the grubby thin mattress. When it gets soaked with my sweat, I roll onto the dusty concrete floor in search of coolness. Puddles of sweat crawl slowly out of me like blood from a sniper victim. I spend days sweating on the cement floor of my windowless room. I am too weak to get up. Too tired to eat. Too stupefied by the fever to think straight. I pull myself to the corner of the room with the stinking drain as fluids pour out of my shivering body. I don't know how many star-filled nights I lay on that hard dirty concrete floor. I could see the stars through the open metal door. I could actually see them move. Like a video being played in slow motion. Time has been disconnected. I can hear the sand whispering as the wind moves it over the ground.

When my head rolls to the side, the puddle formed by my sweat feels cool. I slip in and out of hallucinations interrupted by spasms of pain emanating from inside me. When will it end? What shall I do? There is no one here to answer. They will be back in a week. Deep into the night, in the deadly, godless silence of the Sahara, I think I hear two men approaching slowly. They shuffle slowly, banging the metal doors as I hear them search the rooms of the empty encampment. I can hear them coming closer, but I can't move. In the blackness of my cell, I can't tell if I am awake or dreaming. A few days earlier, a man jumped through my window and was surprised to find me in the room lying in a dark corner. He fled in terror. Has he come back for my life and my money? I wait and listen. My mind and body are wasting away here on the edge of the great Sahara desert. Delirious, sleepless, ill, and sickened, I must get to a doctor or I will die. But how?

The steps are getting closer. I cannot move. I cannot hide. There is no one to call out to. Just the cold stars that move so slowly through the crack in the rusted steel door. The stars watch me with that cruel curiosity you find in Africa.

Too weak to move, I lie in the dark of the moonless night and await my fate. Finally the steps are at my door. I try to make out a shape or form in the darkness. The door clangs open and reveals a silhouette. Looking up, I see what my nemesis is—just an inquisitive donkey.

Africa can do things like that to your mind.

*—RYP*

# DRUGS

## War's Bastard Son

*DP* Drug Law #1: In most of the world, drugs are not a form of recreation. In the rest of the world, drugs are a business. A business that includes peasants, tricksters, smugglers, rebels, police, governments, jailors, the military, and you. Having spent some time helping foreigners get out of jails for drug setups, busts, and extortion, I can never really look at joint, a pill, or a line of powder without seeing the thousands of victims involved.

In an era of travel guides that wink at drug use, is *DP* being uncool in warning travelers about drugs? Guns, bribery, war, crime . . . sure, all those are bad things, but drugs, those are for fun . . . right? Wrong. Those who travel tend to notice that places where you can find guns, bribery, war, crime, and violence are places where you find drugs. We are not talking about the pot places in Amsterdam. We are talking about DRUGS. A Boeing 737, a semitrailer, a cargo ship, or a diplomatic pouch full of drugs. We are talking about a half-a-trillion-dollar industry that can afford to buy entire islands, bribe entire governments, wage private wars, and kill more people than some legitimate conflicts can. Three years ago, the UN estimated the narcotics industry to be a $400 billion business that serviced a hard-core group of 190 million addicts. That's an industry, twice as big as the world's auto industry. Bigger than the oil and gas industry, and bigger than the legitimate drug or chemical category. It is dwarfed only by the world's arms trade, estimated to be $800 billion a year. U.S. sales are estimated to generate $87 billion that requires laundering.

Okay, that's nice, but what do drugs have to with my vacation? Lots, because many Western travelers tend to view drugs as a furtive part of their youth or something that affects only inner cities, but the adventurous traveler quickly learns just how vital a role drugs play in the world's most dangerous places. In fact, in many places, danger is a prerequisite to ensure the smooth flow of illegal goods and profits the drug industry needs to escape interdiction. Whenever there is drug activity there is corruption, AIDS, and organized crime. Here you'll enter a shadowy world where guests are unwelcome.

Typically, narco-regions are run by warlords, corrupt politicians, dirty cops, or criminals, all of whom can be considered tourism-unfriendly. Mexico City's former police chief built a mansion styled after the Parthenon and stashed away between $1 and $3 billion of corrupt profits during his 6-year term. But this is only a small piece of the pie, especially when you consider the Cali cartel made $30 billion last year and the Gulf cartel profited $20 billion (by government estimates).

With the increased presence of U.S. government agents and operatives, the druglords have become more careful and wary of unfamiliar faces—your life could be at risk if you are tagged as someone who should be removed. U.S. government sources spend millions, unsuccessfully, to try to solve the entire world's drug problems. But the problem also may be found within our own borders. The indisputable fact is that the Bolivian peasant who grows coca to feed his family, or Baluchi gunmen who are paid to protect a shipment, are not the criminals. These folks are merely doing something accepted in their own world. We create the drug problem by demanding more and more hard drugs, which keeps a hundred or so drug lords around the world very wealthy.

When *DP* hobnobs with gunmen, warlords, smugglers, fighters, and mafia hoods, it's typical to find that drugs are an integral part of their livelihood and others' not-so-livelihood. In some of these regions, there is no business other than drugs. In the absence of an economy, bribes and guns are used to enslave peasants, couriers, politicians, and entire nations to feed the drug demands of Europe, Russia, Australia, and the Americas.

The drug business would not exist without three major markets, the largest being the United States. Approximately 14.8 million Americans are users of drugs, meaning they used an illicit drug at least once during the month prior to being interviewed for the latest National Household Survey on Drug Abuse—an annual nationwide survey among Americans age 12 and older. About 3.5 million were dependent on illicit drugs; an additional 8.2 million were dependent on alcohol. No biggie, I guess, when comparing the stoners to the boozers. The problem goes deeper, though. In 1998, Americans spent $66.5 billion on these drugs: $39 billion on cocaine; $12 billion on heroin; $2.2 billion on methamphetamine; $11 billion on marijuana; and $2.3 billion on other illegal drugs.

The good and bad news? Crack use is down, heroin use is up (with 20% purer smack available on the streets), and use of marijuana, tweaking (meth), embalming fluid (because it contains PCP), Ecstasy, and mixing prescription drugs, is up. The real bad news is that the drug business is above all a business. Profit and loss, market expansion, recruiting consumers, and supply and demand all drive the industry to create cheaper, more profitable drugs, and get new users on board to replace lost (or jailed) consumers.

**UN drug trends**
http://www.undcp.org/global_illicit_
    drug_trends.html

**National Institute on Drug Abuse**
http://www.nida.nih.gov/NIDAHome.html

**Office of National Drug Control Policy**
http://www.whitehousedrugpolicy.gov

**White House Drug Strategy**
http://www.whitehousedrugpolicy.gov/
    policy/index.html

**U.S. Expenditures on Illicit Drugs**
http://www.whitehousedrugpolicy.gov/
    publications/drugfact/american_
    users_spend2002
http://www.whitehousedrugpolicy.gov/
    policy/ndcs01/tables.html

**DRUGS**

# Heroin

The sticky gum from the *Papaver somniferum,* or Eurasian poppy (or "maker of sleep," for you Latin buffs), was introduced to Asia from the Mediterranean by Arab traders in the twelfth century and was cultivated for its medicinal properties. This innocent little flower has now grown up to become the half-brother of war. India, Myanmar, China, Pakistan, Laos, Thailand, Mexico, Uzbekistan, and Afghanistan are the troubled homes of this gentle, unassuming weed that blows in the wind.

Heroin starts as fields of beautiful-colored poppies. Poppies can be grown in cool plateaus above 500 feet. The plants grow rapidly and propagate easily. Planted at the end of the wet season (in Asia, that's in September and October), the poppy heads are later scraped after the petals fall off. The scraping creates an oozing sap that is removed from the plant and packed tightly into banana leaves. Naturally it doesn't make sense to do all this intensive work in Manhattan or Beverly Hills, so heroin, like coffee and cotton, is a slavery crop. Cheap labor, back-breaking work, and entire families eking out an existence is the general rule for opium farmers. The crude opium is then transported out of the hills via pony or armed convoys to middlemen. Even for those who grow opium, few escape its enticing lure. Hill-tribe growers swiftly become addicts themselves. Up to 30 percent of Southeast Asia's Hmong tribe is addicted to opium. Most of the income of northern Laos is dope money. In fact, small nickel bags, or parakeets as they are called locally, can be used as a form of currency.

Wars have been fought over opium since the 1839 to 1842 Opium War between Britain and China. Today, the battles are taking place on the streets of London, Moscow, Beijing, and even small-town America. Crime experts say that as turf battles among drug lords decline in the cities, America's small towns are becoming the fastest-growing markets. A recent survey found that 47 percent of small-town police chiefs consider drugs a serious problem and two-thirds say drug problems in their area have increased over the last five years. Millions of people are currently enslaved by the byproducts of the opium poppy. And today's heroin's slaves aren't just junkies in back alleys. The media recently has had a field day exposing heroin-addicted movie stars and fashion models. Since the drug can now be snorted like cocaine or smoked rather than injected into veins, and is often used with cocaine to ease the crash, it has begun increasing in popularity.

If you believe the White House, "Club Heroin" includes 3,054,000 Americans who admitted (on a government survey . . . uh, yeah, George, we'll just tick off "Hard-drug user," okay!) to using heroin in their lifetime. Only .1 percent said they used it in the last 30 days. (Funny how they don't get a lot of government surveys filled out in alleys and crack houses.) Down at the morgue, where it's both easy and hard to lie straight, the numbers tell a different story: 41 percent of drug-related deaths in metropolitan areas were linked to heroin or morphine.

The government also estimates that heroin is a $12 billion business in the United States and that there might be just under a million junkies out there. The current purity of heroin found on the street in the United States has jumped from an average of 7 percent in 1984 to

36 percent today, a testament not only to its grip on a nation, but to the seemingly endless world supply of the narcotic. Heroin shipped into the United States comes from at least 11 different countries. The DEA estimates it stops 30 to 40 percent of drugs illegally entering the country.

## The Golden Crescent

Afghanistan had a massive increase in poppy cultivation in the late '90s under the Talibs. It put the country at the top of the list of heroin suppliers and then, poof!, the poppies vanished. Not so much due to the ban on opium cultivation but due more to a deadly drought that made poppies almost impossible to grow.

The bad news is that poppies are hoppin'. In 2002, 30,750 hectares were under cultivation—only half the size of the biggest year's crop, but enough to reestablish Afghanistan as the champs. Most (84 percent) poppies are grown in five southern and eastern provinces. Each hectare will yield 41 kilograms of opium. The 2002 crop is expected to generate over $1 billion at the farmers' level, with prices between $160 and $180 a pound. The United States is investing $75 million to combat the growth in opium production.

Although the Taliban is against the consumption of drugs, it used to tolerate the growing of poppies. In the late '90s the Talib government was estimated to pull in between $10 and $75 million from the taxation of opium.

Most opium transport is via Baluchi trafficking organizations operating out of Quetta, Pakistan. These groups place orders with the Afghani processors and arrange for shipment of the drugs from Afghanistan through Pakistan and to Iranian or Turkish buyers, who move it through Iran and into international drug channels. Most Afghan opium is destined for processing into heroin in Turkey to be sold in the main cities of Western Europe.

## Latin America

Heroin also is an up-and-coming crop in Colombia and Mexico. Forget exotic camel trains, couriers with condoms shoved up nasty places, rusting Chinese cargo ships, or even sweaty tourists at crossing points. Colombia's pure white heroin comes into the United States directly by commercial air, delivered FedEx-style to Miami and L.A. The Mexican "black tar" heroin usually comes over in commercial truck and via entrepreneurs.

## The Golden Triangle

The Golden Triangle is not really a geographic triangle, but a loosely U.S.-defined area that covers eastern Myanmar, northern Laos, and scattered parts of northern Thailand. Under the rigid management of the Chinese (ethnic, gangster, and expat), this region is now number two in opium products. Protection is provided, of course, by the numerous "rebel" armies controlling the region. In smack boomtowns like Mong La, you can find Chinese hookers, Russian dancers, and Australian tourists, all crowding the modern casinos and air-conditioned hotels. Nonstop, high-stakes gambling, ethnic shows featuring Padaung tribeswomen (the giraffe people, as they are called), and side trips to Wa villages are becoming the main attractions. It's not just poppies that fuel this excess. The big news is the shift to chemical drugs like meth, a 400 percent increase over 4 years. You can make a better living through chemistry, according to Thai police. Fifty new *yaba*, or meth factories, have been set up in Myanmar in the last year and another 10 in Laos, cranking out 600 to 700 million yaba tablets at a street price of 50 baht or $1.14 each. Who needs poppies with margins like that?

After reading all the info provided by the CIA, and seeing the industrious efforts of the Chinese in the Golden Triangle, you can't help but wonder how such a destructive industry is so analyzed yet so unfazed. The government of Myanmar says it has nabbed $45 million worth of smack headed our way and over 828 local law enforcement officials have lost their lives in battles with drug lords. It's all part of their 10-year plan to eradicate drugs. So the future of heroin looks good. Over the last 10 years, opium poppy production has been reduced by 17 percent, but the availability and amount of raw opium has increased by 50 percent.

*United Nations Development*
http://www.undcp.org

**DRUGS**

## Cocaine and Crack

In America, heroin is old school; the new drug of choice is cocaine-based crack. It's cheap, available, and delivers what cigarettes, booze, and soft drinks can only hint at. Smoke it, and you may get a groovy high or you may turn into a ruthless brute. Crack is big dollars, big profits, and big trouble. Law enforcement credits much of the body count in the inner cities to gangs fighting over turf to sell the evil stuff. You only have about 5 years to wring every nickel out of the United States's 2.1 million coke and crackheads before they die.

If cocaine hydrochloride [HCl] is the BMW of drugs, then crack is the Yugo. Cocaine costs a lot (about $100 to $150 a gram) and goes fast.

Crack, well, it just makes you crash a lot. Cocaine users tend to be male, white, and in their 30s. Crack is an inner-city, young-kid product with a drive-thru clientele. Crack is cocaine you can smoke, but it is typically cut with anything that grandma left in the cupboard, usually baking soda or sugar. But it can also be cut with pain relievers, such as Novocaine, Anbesol, hell, sometimes rat poison (now that's a pain reliever!). Unlike heroin, which will give you 10 years of hell, cocaine and crack are more addictive and more destructive.

Crack and cocaine enter the United States by the ton. A kilo of cocaine will sell wholesale for between $10,500 and $40,000. But a gram of crack cocaine goes for $20 in Miami and $250 in Honolulu. In order to create low-price entry points, crack even comes in "crumbs" and "kibbles and bits" that sell for around $3 to $5. The cocaine business aims to please, because customer satisfaction is what keeps you coming back, again, and again, and again, and again . . .

Cocaine wasn't always an ugly gutter business. The South American Indians use the coca leave (in a disgusting mixture of lime and betel nut) to keep them alert. But then the German pharmaceutical company Merck discovered that you could make a more refined, potent form of cocaine for medicinal purposes—Sigmund Freud used it on people (including himself)—and the rest is history. The coca bush takes two years to mature, at which point the leaves are picked and ground up. A hectare of mature coca bushes can yield around 2.7 metric tons of dry leaf, which in turn yields about 7.44 kilos of cocaine. It takes about 363 kilos of dry leaves to yield 1 kilo of cocaine. The amount of pure cocaine in the goods depends on the alkaloid level of the leaf. For example, coca leaves in the Chapare region of Bolivia are 0.72 percent alkaloid and you can buy bags of them for pennies. Not much bang for your buck. By the time it is stepped on, or diluted, cocaine goes for about $100 a gram on the street in the United States.

The big players in the cocaine business are the Colombians, along with minor contributions from Peru. Bolivia and Ecuador funnel as much as they can up our noses. The Mexicans have taken over the transportation business and things don't look like they are going to slow down any time soon.

Since coca is used as part of tea, for chewing, and for traditional ceremonies, 12,000 hectares of cultivation are allowed legally. The best coca leaves come from Yungas, while almost all coca grown in the Chapare region is for illegal purposes. Despite efforts to spray the coca bushes into submission, Colombia's potential coca production leaped to 768 metric tons in 2000, forcing local syndicates to expand distribution into Poland and the Czech Republic. Most Colombian cocaine is shipped in huge multiton sea cargo or 8-ton shipments to Mexico, Central

## MANDRAX

Known as "buttons" in the streets of South Africa, and referred to as "ludes" in the States, this now-illegal tablet was first developed as an antimalaria medication in India. It was discovered that the methaqualone, which is the active ingredient responsible for the "rush," or high, when smoked, was an excellent sleeping tablet with a low hangover threshold. Then the druggies in SA found that when you crush the tablets into powder and mix it with dagga (marijuana) and smoke it through a crude pipe, like a broken bottle neck, it has a tremendous kick. This became known as a "white pipe."

Withdrawal can be severe for the serious Mandrax addict. Convulsion, severe headaches, nausea, stomach cramps, insomnia, and bad dreams are quite common among those who've been smoking two and three "guns" daily. Brain damage manifests in short-term memory loss and disorientation, and lung damage can be severe. It is also common for "button heads" to lose their appetite and become apatheic, and they tend to be attracted to Rasta music. . . . Yellow and brown stains on users' hands, especially the palms, are common, because of the manner in which the bottle neck is smoked.

http://clubr.co.za/mx.htm

America, and the Caribbean, where it is broken down into smaller shipments bound for the States or Europe. About 85 percent of the cocaine, and almost all the heroin nabbed in the United States, comes from Colombia. A *DP* check of prices in Peru and Colombia shows that 1 pure kilo of cocaine sells for $1,200 to $1,500 (quantity discounts available) and that same brick in the United States, sold on the street, can garner a stunning $15,000 to $25,000 profit. It's no wonder the jails are full of wannabe importers.

Mexico has increased drug production so much that smugglers have switched from cargo planes to cargo ships to meet the demand. The cargo is picked up by high-speed boats that meet smugglers off the coast. Small planes are also used to drop drugs in-country. The contrabandistas along the border are also eager to smuggle guns, dope, or people, if the price is right.

Nigeria is a major hub for smuggling coke and heroin by virtue of its corrupt customs and the eagerness of its mules, who will carry cocaine either ingested internally in condoms or on their person. The Nigerians leave South America, often via Rio, then bring the cocaine to Nigeria for sale in South Africa.

The Caribbean island of Aruba, off the coast of Venezuela, is a major drug transshipment point. Shipments funnel in from Colombia, Venezuela, and Suriname for transport to the United States and Europe.

Also, Vieques Island (Puerto Rico) and the U.S. Virgin Islands are popular delivery points from the islands of the Lesser Antilles. About 30 percent of the drugs that enter Britain come from the Caribbean. Drugs also flow from these islands into their home protectorate of France and the Netherlands. Cocaine is shipped by sea from South America and then loaded onto aircraft and ships on the ABC Islands. In general, many of the island chains offer ideal smuggling and transfer points due to the large amount of shoreline, number of watercraft, and lack of police in the area.

*International Narcotics Control Board*
http://www.incb.org

## Cannabis/Marijuana/Hashish

It's pretty common to see that little foil pouch of the brown stuff come out in a hostel or city square. It's available to 91 percent of Americans and is considered by most to be a harmless drug and even a medicinal necessity. Who's a stoner? Well, everyone it seems. There is no racial, financial, or regional stereotype. Old ladies, gang bangers, and politicians all do it.

Marijuana can be grown from Alaska to Hawaii and anywhere in between. You are not really smoking the weed, but inhaling the tetrahydrocannabinol (THC) contained in the plant and resin. In America, Mexican commercial grade (with seeds) and sensimilla (without seeds) are the most common variety. Hydroponically grown weed has a high THC content with normal strains having 5 to 30 percent. This type of weed was described scientifically by Drs. Cheech and Chong as "good" shit or "bad" shit. Weed prices are directly related to quality. Hyrdoponic is $1,000 to $2,500 per pound in the big cities. Regular weed is about $500 a pound.

Weed is not really a top priority with the DEA, nor is it a major contributor to criminal activity. It is bulky, has a low margin, and can be homegrown easily by cheapskate customers. In many countries, you will find marijuana plants growing wild in backyards, along roads, and in fields. The benefits of the cannabis trade are that expensive chemicals to create an end product are not needed, and a laissez-faire attitude toward personal consumption in many European and Asian countries. Many countries do not have penalties for the consumption of weed, but do have stiff ones for dealing.

## Pills

A major shift in the drug business is the change from organically grown products (heroin, coke, and weed) to chemical products (meth, Ecstasy, nitrous oxide, Roofies, GHB, LSD, and even cat tranquilizers). The idea is that you can cook these things up anywhere, transport them easily, and sell them for a big markup. Large rural areas guarded by armed men are being replaced with smaller labs in peaceful regions. This actually removes much of the danger associated with travel in dangerous places. Even the buying and selling of pharmaceutical-type pills makes it more difficult for travelers to be detected and put in jail. A dubious plus point in the world of travel.

## Drugs 'n' the Hood

Okay, you sort of know the lay of the land when it comes to drugs, but how do you stay out of their cross hairs? Knowing the players and places can help.

## Europe

Europe is a major consumer of illicit drugs. Lots of junkies live in Germany (150,000) and Russia (80,000), and plenty more are in port cities like Amsterdam, Marseilles, and the Baltics. Poland produces 20 percent of the amphetamines sold in Europe and is a major base for Chinese, Colombian, and other drug groups looking for safe, central places to process drugs. There are about 200,000 drug users in Europe and half of them are addicts.

- **England** has an estimated 100,000 heroin addicts and is a major consumer of soft and hard drugs. Most of the heroin comes from Afghanistan via Pakistani organizations. Marijuana comes from Morocco. Cocaine comes directly from South America via Amsterdam.
- **Italy** is home to three major criminal organizations: The Calabrian ndrangheta, the Neapolitan camorra, and the Sicilian mafia. All work directly with South American cartels to transport and sell cocaine in Europe. Most cocaine comes by sea into mafia-controlled ports. There are around 200,000 cocaine users and 150,000 addicts in Italy.
- **Germany** is the one place where cocaine costs more than in the United States and use is up. Its ports of Hamburg, Bremen, and Rostock are entry points for drugs, and Frankfurt is the main air terminal used by Europe-bound "mules" from Africa and Central Asia.
- **Greece** has 80,000 heroin users and is a major transshipment point into Europe from Turkey, by road, sea, and air.
- **Bulgaria**'s lax airport security allows cocaine smugglers access to Europe. It is also a main route into Europe from Turkey for West Asian drugs.

- **Cyprus** is an important meeting ground and money laundering center for the Russian mafia. There are over 20,000 offshore companies, one-tenth of which are Russian. Its central, neutral location and business infrastructure make it the ideal meeting place for drug deals, payoffs, and discussions.

## The Balkans

The well-maintained roads and compliant customs officials of the former Yugoslavia were the home leg of the long road from the poppy fields of Asia. The war messed up this convenient leg and now most heroin is smuggled through Albania, Macedonia, and Bulgaria. About 70 percent of heroin is smuggled under the direction of the Albanian mafia—stronger than its government—to customers in Germany and Switzerland. The Albanian mafia, primarily members of the Kosovar clan, are bosom buddies with the Italian mafia. Heroin is also processed in Albania by the mafia to increase profits.

Criminals control most major ports and entry areas, making it a free-trade zone for drugs. Cannabis and poppies are also grown domestically. Albanians from the Kosova region are the main smugglers, delivering their wares to retailers in Italy, Turkey, and along the Mediterranean.

## Trans–Caucasus

The rough-and-ready base of Europe is a natural conduit for anything coming from the foggy mountains of Chechnya, Georgia, and other small states. The Chechen *mafyia* backed the original war and provided inside military information from corrupt Russian intelligence officers and a flow of weapons or cash. The Chechen diaspora has criminal and business connections, from the greasy oil fields of Baku to Istanbul, Moscow, and the Middle East. Their only competition seems to be the Russian military, which has a bigger fleet of planes and trucks to move Central and South Asian goods directly to Moscow and sea ports beyond. There is a nasty rumor that after the late Chechnyen leader, Dudayev, unsuccessfully demanded a higher cut of drug monies (as well as oil) from Russian Defense Minister Pavel Grachev, he then began to execute train conductors and confiscate all the drugs, prompting Grachev to invade Chechnya.

## Colombia

Colombia is the world's leading producer and distributor of cocaine. Success in almost eradicating the cocaine business in Peru and Bolivia simply pushed the business into the jungles of Colombia. Now under the ruthless oversight of the "firmas," faceless drug cartels based in the main cities, and the equally brutal FARC rebels who keep the government out of the growing and processing areas, business is booming. The war on drugs is a minor inconvenience to this massive, all-cash, export business.

Colombia is also a major supplier of heroin and marijuana to the Mexican mafia. In the early '70s, Colombia started out primarily as a grower of pot, with cocaine being a small part of the then-$500 million a year export. Pot was mostly cultivated along the Atlantic coast. Today, it is estimated that Colombia's drug industry pockets about $3 billion a year in profits from the drug trade. All this occurs under the protection of the three rebel groups: the ELN, FARC, and the cartels. The ELN generate an estimated $348 million in income linked to drugs through protection of growers, shippers, and labs. FARC makes $900 million in protection money for drug growers. The Colombian cartels, in conjunction with their Mexican and Cuban distributors, have a lock on 75 percent of the world's cocaine, and about 80 percent of the toot goes to Uncle Sam. The DEA figures drug sales pump between $3 and $5 billion into the Colombian economy, making it the country's biggest export earner. To get an idea of what a narcogovernment is, you have to understand that the entire gross domestic product of Colombia is only $5 billion.

Most coca is grown on small plots to escape detection. The Colombian farmers get in three to four harvests a year. Most raspachinos, or "scrapers," are taking the next step and creating coca paste, which sells for about $600 per kilo. Most of the 135,000 acres of coca farms in Colombia are in the far south. It is estimated that there are 35,000 farmers in the business of growing coca and poppies.

## Thailand

Thailand's position in the Golden Triangle is more geographic than economic. It is a net importer of hard drugs and is a major transit route to Western countries. About 50 percent of the opium that enters Thailand from Myanmar heads for the United States. The Thai opium crop is under constant threat by government eradication programs and tough border controls with its northern bad-boy neighbor, Myanmar. Still, the mule trains get through the rough terrain and insurgents keep the Thai soldiers from truly policing or sealing off the area.

## Myanmar

Just under 70 percent of the world's heroin and 60 percent of heroin seized by U.S. law enforcement came from the Golden Triangle. The

## NOT QUITE ON EBAY YET. . . . BUT SOON

The San Diego Narcotic Information Network publishes local drug prices compiled from various drug enforcement agencies in the area. Cocaine in pound or kilo batches has an average purity of 87 percent. Street cocaine runs between 45 percent and 85 percent. Trends show most drugs dropping in price as much as 30 percent from last year. Cheapest prices are quoted below (Hey, this is America, right?):

### Pound Prices

| | |
|---|---|
| Marijuana—low grade, 3% THC | $300 |
| Marijuana—high grade, 30% THC | $4,000 |
| Marijuana—Sinsemilla | $2,000 |
| Hashish | $1,000 |
| Methamphetamine | $3,000 |

### Kilo Prices

| | |
|---|---|
| Marijuana | $1,000–$4,000 |
| Cocaine | $14,000–$20,000 |
| Heroin (black tar) | $40,000–$50,000 |

*Source:* NIN (858) 616-4098

Golden Triangle is not really a geographic triangle but a loosely U.S.-defined area that covers eastern Myanmar, northern Laos, and scattered parts of northern Thailand. The common elements are remoteness and inaccessibility, lack of law enforcement, and the right altitude and climate to permit the cultivation of poppies. It may be more accurate to describe the Golden Triangle as just Myanmar.

Visitors to this area will find the locals decidedly reserved and openly belligerent if pressed for details on their trade. The U.S. State Department estimates that Myanmar exports about 2,300 tons of raw opium a year, primarily from the Kachin and north Shan states. Laos moves about 300 tons and Thailand about 30 tons.

## Mexico

Mexico continues to be the financial and transshipment choice of South American drug cartels due to its lax banking laws, corrupt officials, and the "don't ask, don't tell" policy of its military and government. The drug business in Mexico is sliced into three cartels: the Tijuana, Juarez, and the Gulf. The Tijuana cartel under the Feliz brothers smuggles primarily heroin and marijuana. The Gulf cartel is the coca

DRUGS

express and Amada Carrillo Fuentes' group (before he liposuctioned himself to death) used to cover transborder shipments from El Paso to Brownsville. The Juarez cartel runs drugs to the East Coast. In many cases, the cartels have cut out the beleaguered Colombian middlemen and go right to the source for the coca paste. Cocaine is big business, smuggled in massive bundles complete with exporter logos from South America in multiengine cargo jets and cargo ships. Corrupt customs officials drive new Chevy Suburbans and the ruling class in Acapulco and Tijuana could outbid Bill Gates at any poker game. The downside is that Mexico's border population is coming down with a jones for their product, and the U.S. government is losing patience with our biggest narco-neighbor.

Belize, Costa Rica, El Salvador, Nicaragua, Guatemala, and Honduras are major land, air, and sea transshipment routes for Colombian drugs entering Mexico. Mexico snaps up about 50 to 70 percent of all cocaine from South America. Mexico's corrupt police and long border with the United States make it an ideal entry point for drugs and a major money laundering center.

Mexico also produces about 80 percent of marijuana, 20 to 30 percent of heroin, and a growing amount of methamphetamines.

## Panama

The Darien region of Panama is a hot spot for coca cultivation for the Colombian drug czars. Local Indians are goaded into cultivating crops under the watchful protection of Colombian guerrillas. Panama retains its reputation as an ideal shipment point for drugs and is a major center for laundering drug money.

## Peru

Coca is Peru's second largest crop (after maize), with 930 square miles under cultivation. The major areas are the Huallaga Valley and the Apurimac-Enc Valley east of Lima. The 115,300 hectares of coca leaf (60% of the world's total coca crop) under cultivation is worth 40¢ to 50¢ a kilo (down from $3 in 1994). The drugs are grown by peasants who sell to buyers on behalf of processors.

## Russia

Russia's geographical position makes it a major drug-producing, shipping, and consumption center. Its neighbors make good use of the corrupt and inefficient police and border guards. The Russians quickly motorized the drug business and Russian generals made millions sending drugs back to Russia in lead-lined coffins.

Drugs from the Golden Crescent (Pakistan, Afghanistan, and Iran) are transported to major centers like Tashkent in Uzbekistan, or through the states of Chechnya, Tajikistan, Georgia, and Azerbaijan. There are also major growing areas in southern Russia and the western Ukraine, as well as the states of Uzbekistan, Kazakhstan, and Krygyzstan. The presence of foreign troops during the Balkan War has disrupted the once traditional smuggling routes into Europe, which are being replaced by Afghanistan to Tajikistan to St. Petersburg to Cyprus, and then out through ports on the Baltic Sea and Mediterranean. Russian officials estimate there are about 5.7 million drug users in Russia, with hashish being the drug of choice. A UN report says there may be 100,000 opium poppy fields and more than 2.5 million acres of marijuana under cultivation within the country. Drug-related crime is up 15 percent, and 23 tons of drugs were seized in raids last year. About 80 percent of drug dealers arrested in Moscow are Azerbaijanis; the rest are Chechens. Moscow banks are becoming popular with out-of-town drug dealers like the Sicilian mafia and the Colombian cartels to launder money. The total drug business adds up to an unimpressive US$25 million (compared to our US$500 billion narcotics industry). A kilo of hash in Russia goes for as little as US$15, compared to US$200 in Europe. Accordingly, the profit-savvy and brutal Russian gangs are also expanding into Europe and the United States.

Those drugs that don't end up in Moscow or St. Petersburg go through to the Baltics, where eager Scandinavian and Lowlands customers await.

## Africa

Africa is not a major consumer of drugs, but it is an important transshipment point. Southern Africa is a growing consumer of drugs and producer of meth.

# Getting Arrested

## Oh, Won't You Stay . . . Just a Little Bit Longer

There's a scent of "what the hell" in the air. Rustling palms, blue skies, smiling cops are chatting up girls, street vendors urge the local weed on you, you only have a few days left, and you've been told great and bold stories about the local intoxicants. Anyway, what are you going to do with that bundle of grubby *guidos* when you get home? You roll off half your wad to the smiling beachboy and you are the proud owner of the island's finest herb. Throwing caution to the wind, you invite the local lasses to your $5-a-night fleabag. As if on cue, while you're fully dressed and not even halfway into the carnal depths you intend to plunge into, there is an urgent knock on the door. "*Policia, manos arriba. Tiene armas?*" They go straight to your stash on the dresser and you wonder how it happened so quickly, so cleanly. As you bump your head on the way out, you see your beachboy friend with one of those shit-eating grins. Damn.

There are an average of 6,000 Americans arrested in 90 different countries each year, according to the State Department. About 1,500 are doing time in foreign jails. The majority (about 70 percent) of the cases are drug related. Mexico and Jamaica are responsible for the bulk of the drug-related incarcerations, filing 72 percent of all drug charges against Americans traveling abroad.

The top five destinations for Americans seeking free room and board are Mexico, Germany, Canada, Jamaica, and Great Britain. In one typical year, Mexico had 525 gringos on ice and had arrested 768 that year. Fifty-five of those weren't happy campers and filed complaints of mistreatment. The Mexican judicial system is based on Roman and Napoleonic law and presumes a person accused of a crime is guilty until proven innocent. There is no trial by jury. Trial under the Mexican system is a prolonged process based largely on documents examined on a fixed date in court by prosecution and defense counsel. Sentencing usually takes 6 to 10 months. Bail can be granted after sentencing if the sentence is less than five years. Pretrial bail exists, but is never granted when the possible sentence is greater than five years.

And those folks have it good. In places like Malaysia and Singapore, move dope and die. Zero tolerance. Deal dope and you'll get the rope. Getting beaten up in a Mexican jail may be inconvenient, but at least the *federales* are trying to teach you a lesson, one you might learn from in later life. In Southeast Asia, there is no later life. There are 30 yanquies in Chinese prisons, and China leads the world in executions of prisoners. Not much of an incentive to break the law. It is worth mentioning that the police forces of the third world, who have plenty of thieves, muggers, domestic disputes, and murders to occupy their time, seem to view foreigners caught with drugs as the equivalent to winning the New Jersey lottery. Why? Locals who run over a cow simply provide hours of irritating paperwork and dull, debilitating court appearances and the potential for a dressing down if the accused is related to your boss. However, a whiny backpacker who insists on his rights and other ridiculous fantasies is going to learn very quickly that his arrestors' financial well-being is directly related to how many teeth he retains and how long he calls a damp cell home. The arresting cop will be praised for winning the war on drugs, get to split the booty (and leave a little for the news crews at the bonfire), and everyone will be a hero . . . except you, of course. Remember, there are thousands of reasons why a foreign police officer, military, government, or even private citizen can have you detained and charged. Many seem to be directly related to how many names you call them.

Here are a few survival tips (at the risk of sounding like your mother) for everyone who doesn't want to die as a skinny, frazzled, psychotic wimp in a Pakistani jail:

## Have nothing to do with drugs or the drug culture.

Those pleasant men in tattered uniforms are employed for a single purpose—to find your drugs. Once they've found them, make no mistake, you will be busted. Once you're tried (if you ever are), you will be going away for a long time. And then it will take a lot of money to get you out. A lot of it. And you'll look different, too. Not good.

## Do not take anything illegal through customs, or anything that doesn't belong to you.

Do not be an unwitting mule and carry a package for a friend. Do not think you can sneak a few joints through. Foreign customs officers usually live by two words: "How much?" or "Too bad." How much is it going to cost you to get out of this mess? How much time are you going to do? How much will it cost to repatriate your remains?

## Be careful with unmarked drugs.

Combining drugs or putting prescription drugs into reminder boxes may create questions of legality. Your personal appearance, the quantity of the drugs, and the general demeanor of your inquisitor will determine if you are let off. They can hold you while they test the drugs and their buddy swaps it for something more criminal.

## Avoid driving.

Car accidents are a great way to go to jail. In many countries, the Napoleonic code of justice is utilized. In other words, by law, you are guilty until proven innocent. For instance, if someone smacks into your car in Mexico, you'll go to jail. No witnesses are needed and it may be a long time. Hire a driver and you're off the hook. You may also have a witness when they try to plant anything on you.

## Be judicious in your enthusiasm to photograph military or government facilities.

Soldiers in Africa love camera equipment. Usually yours. If you want it back, you'll have to pay a fine. It's a common scam that teenage boys will walk up sternly and threaten to arrest you unless you pay them something. In most of the former Soviet republics, you will be also be detained or arrested for taking pictures of army bases or airports. *DP* has spent plenty of time fast-talking our way out of jail simply for carrying cameras in countries that demand you have national and regional permits to carry them. It doesn't hurt to check with the local fuzz (not that this will prevent the next cop from shaking you down).

*Get the right kind of help.*

The U.S. embassy will not lift a finger to get you out of jail. They may assist you in communicating with your family, but if you have broken the law in that country, you are expected to do the time. Many countries have legal systems that assume you are guilty and hold you until trial. Since you are a flight risk (you do, after all, have a return ticket home), your bail (if granted) will be astronomical. It may take an extraordinary amount of time for your case to go to trial, and you may even be required to pay your room and board while in jail. Our advice is to ask local U.S. or foreign businesses, not the embassy, to suggest a local lawyer and explore all options for your release. That means bribes, dirty tricks, and being smuggled out. Communicate your case to friends, and tell them to contact journalists in the local and national media. If you really did something stupid and you don't have any money, be prepared for the worst. And, yes, there are people who break people out of jail for a living.

**Getting arrested**
http://travel.state.gov/arrest.html

# In a Dangerous Place: Mali

### C'EST L'AFRIQUE

Paris, France—The next morning at the airport was pandemonium. Africans everywhere waving crumpled tickets, brightly dressed women chattering too loudly and surrounded by acres of crisp shopping bags, all with Parisian designer logos that contrasted with their African block-print dresses. Men in expensive suits with huge tribal scars, mountains of luggage in bursting cardboard boxes and metal "caisses," or coffin-sized steel boxes sealed with large, brass, Chinese-made locks.

Like East Indians with monstrous pastel vinyl suitcases or Asians with their twine-wrapped cardboard boxes, Africans have their metal cases. Not one metal case, but stacks of huge military-looking caskets with giant padlocks covered with first-class stickers. They contain the fruits of kleptocracy, a unique right of the robber rulers of Africa who brutally divert foreign income like damming off a stream.

I have never been to Africa, but I am already learning the class distinctions: The quiet Africans who talk with me while they wait and the noisy garrulous thieves who treat the stewardesses as overpaid waitresses.

The UTA DC-10 traverses the Strait of Gibraltar in seconds: from the French Riviera, over the land of the Moors, and descending into the Dark Continent.

The plane descends through the milky haze that shrouds the Sahel. Slowly, faintly as in a dream, the brown landscape begins to rise toward me. The only signs of habitation are widely spaced, painfully torn trees tied together with thousands of meandering tracks. Then small clusters of brown dots begin to appear. These are the round mud and grass huts of the Bambara. I have never seen a landscape so primitive and exciting.

It begins to hit me as I look past the shiny aluminum wing to the crude huts that this is why I came to Africa. In a microflash I understand the problem of Africa. This 450-miles-per-hour, $10 million aircraft has to land on a flyspeck of broken asphalt in the middle of goats and arid nothingness. I have not come from another country but from another planet.

This, truly, is how the first aliens will appear to Westerners: gleaming, streamlined perfection, landing just long enough to disgorge its sweaty, disorientated passengers into the heat, red dirt, and filth. Above the silver bird is a massive, white, triangular thundercloud, over an ochre runway. I stop, turn, and take a picture.

I am arrested before I can even walk across the hot tarmac to the terminal. Two angry uniformed soldiers run from the terminal and hold me fast.

One of the soldiers roughly grabs for my camera and I hold it away from them. One wags his finger in my face. They smell bad and are not using enough force to convince me to fight back. I am in trouble.

The French UTA ground crew see the commotion and come to my aid. They intervene and use hand motions behind their back to tell me to cool it while they carry on an animated conversation in French with the soldiers. "It is forbidden to take pictures of the airport." This crime is apparently clearly marked inside the terminal that I have yet to enter. The white jump-suited crew asked me if I was taking pictures of the airport, as if to give me an opportunity to say no. I quickly say that I was taking pictures of the giant thunderhead above the plane. A crew member's eyebrow arches. The game is on. They discuss this point in the ongoing shouting match.

Thankfully, Africans are social people even in their suspicion and brutality, and this new interpretation of my crime provokes more heated discussion. This is the first of many times I will be arrested in Africa, but there is no clear resolution to my crime yet. To anger the ground crew is not the goal of my arrest. They expect a direct form of economic penitence from me before I even enter the country. Later, I notice that there are booths to strip-search visitors entering the country.

The pilot of the UTA plane has opened the cockpit window and yells down to see what the commotion is about. I wave at the pilot as if we are old friends. A thought occurs. I explain that I misspoke my bad

French. I now correct my confession to say what I meant to say was that I was taking a picture of the pilot, not the plane or the airport. This slows down my captors. We all agree that the pilot is technically not the airport. This new wrinkle and the support of the pilot and crew is gaining me the upper hand.

Arresting me would now result in more than a backroom interrogation and search. A deal is finally struck. They frogmarch me up the boarding ladder and into the cockpit. The ground crew scoots ahead to prep the pilot. The pilot greets me with a broad smile and asks why they are arresting this poor fellow for taking his picture. Handshakes and apologies all around. As the soldiers leave, the pilot laughs, shrugs and says, "C'est l'Afrique."

*—RYP*

# GUNS

## You Talking to ME?

If you travel to dangerous places you will meet a lot of people with guns. Some gun owners are police in ill-fitting uniforms. They look like they just like to polish their guns as they stroll around staring at the women. Others look a little more serious—stern-faced, giving you enough room to give you a short burst. Others look like they could kill you with either end of the gun. In some dangerous places it seems like you are the only one without a weapon of death and destruction. So what do you do the next time somebody uses a rusty barrel of an AK as a cattle-prod and has that blood-red stare? Why, just relax. Guns don't kill, freaked-out owners do.

Most people are afraid of guns, especially when they are either pointed at them or in the hands of scowling children. That's okay; you are supposed to be scared. Intimidated, fearful, maybe even downright agitated. But don't let it show. Keep eye contact, smile, be laid back, and for God's sake don't make jokes about the gunman's ability to use his weapon.

To acquire this sangfroid to weapons of death, you should know what guns can and cannot do. You should know if the safety is on, what the range of the gun is, and just exactly what that person who is pointing it at you does for a living. Being able to determine rank and training style is also helpful, but difficult if the person is wearing only a loincloth.

You should also know that tension and intimidation are what guns are all about. You are better off respecting guns and acquiescing to their intended role than trying to do a not-quite-as-smooth, Mel Gibson, slap-it-out-of-hand trick to impress your friends and soon-to-be mourners. So once again, relax.

Most people with guns have a very simple logic as to when the trigger should be pulled. Running away from them is one major stimulant. Pissing them off is another. Better yet, forgetting that you are 3,000 miles from the nearest Miranda act and playing tough guy is another. So relax . . .

Okay, smartass, just exactly when should you not relax? Well, think it through, how would you shoot someone? You would probably make them move away from other people, perhaps motion for them to get out of a car and stand by the side of the road, perhaps even check around to see who is watching. Or maybe tie their hands and take them into a back alley. Now you should be getting nervous. Sometimes a good indication is having your boots being fought over and watching the contents of your wallet being divided into equal amounts. What can you do to prevent this?

The first rule is, don't go to places where tourists are arbitrarily shot. I know it sounds odd, but there really aren't that many innocent foreigners shot for no reason. Even the most nihilistic rebels on Earth, the Khmer Rouge and the RUF, went easy on the summary execution stuff. Crime is a big motivation for murder, and so is covering up an incident. Strangely, journos are targets of killings because they know too much. Is there any specific thing you can do to protect yourself against guns? Not really . . . so relax, you stand a much better chance of getting through a tight spot with all your wits about you.

Gun use and ownership is endlessly dissected and debated in the United States. There are more than 220 million guns in the United States; 65 million of those are handguns. About 3 million new ones are made every year. It is estimated that firearm injuries in the States cost about $20 billion in medical costs and lost wages. Firearms send almost 30,000 Americans to their graves each year. Over half would go anyway. Over 18,000 of the 31,000 Americans who kill themselves every year choose guns. Another 18,500 Americans are murdered with a gun, and at least 1,500 more are accidentally shot to death. Around 65,000 people are injured by guns. Gun-related homicides rose 18 percent in the last decade—30 percent among people ages 15 to 24. Gun-control advocates also point out that almost a million violent crimes occur a year. Even in a civilized place like America, gun deaths are second only to traffic fatalities as a cause of injury-related deaths.

Of the 95,000 people who get shot in the average year, about one-third will die. Men are seven times more likely to be shot. Black men between 20 and 24 had the highest fatality rate and are 6 times more likely to be shot than white men.

The most dangerous handheld weapons are rifles, as evidenced in the October 2002 sniper shooting spree in Maryland. Handguns require short ranges and careful aim to be lethal. Handguns tend to be the weapons of choice for domestic violence and robberies. Guns can be a good thing. If you want to see gun love, go to Tombstone, Arizona, where you are allowed to carry a firearm as long as it's visible (and you don't have priors, mental illness, etc.). When we asked the marshal if there had ever been a bank robbery, he smiled and said, "We're waiting for one."

**Gun Safety Articles**
http://www.ncpa.org/pi/crime/crime51.html

**Crime statistics**
http://virlib.ncjrs.org/Statistics.asp

**Handgun Wounding Factors and Effectiveness**
http://www.firearmstactical.com/hwfe.htm

## HAPPY FIRE

In Los Angeles, 39 people have been killed from bullets fired into the air during Independence Day and New Year's Eve shootings. Bullets come down with a velocity of 300 to 500 feet per second. A gun can fire a bullet at 2,700 fps; it travels 2 miles up, and then after a minute lands miles or feet away depending on the angle. Seventy-seven percent of the victims are hit in the head, resulting in a 32 percent mortality rate, according to a study done by the King Drew Medical Center. Bullets usually fall base first. A velocity of 100 fps will penetrate skin, but 200 fps will break bone and penetrate the skull. There are about 600 to 700 reported incidents of happy fire on New Year's Eve in Los Angeles.

## Cops: The Real World

A good indication of what kills out on the streets is represented by the staggering list of 146 law-enforcement officers who were killed in 2001, up from 42 killed in 1999. As expected, firearms did the most damage. Ten were killed with rifles, four with shotguns, three by vehicles, one by a knife, and two officers were killed with their own handguns. Thirty-two of the officers were killed in the South, 13 in the Midwest, four in the West, and two in Puerto Rico. There were no police deaths in the Northeast. The most telling statistic is that 83 officers were killed accidentally while on duty. Thirty of the slain officers were wearing body armor. But that is not the most disturbing statistic. The number of cops who die on the job is dwarfed by the number of police who die by their own hand. Police in the United States are twice as likely as other citizens to end their own lives. According to the National Association of Police Chiefs, about 300 police officers will commit suicide every year.

> **P**olice in the United States are twice as likely as other citizens to end their own lives.

http://www.nlemt.com/FactsFigures/causes.html

### DO YOU FEEL LUCKY, PUNK?

Twenty-three out of 50 states will issue a carry permit to law-abiding citizens. Twenty-three states do not regulate the open carrying of loaded guns in public. John Lott, author of *More Guns, Less Crime,* says that for each year a concealed handgun law is in effect, murders drop an average of 3 percent, robberies by more than 2 percent, and rape by 2 percent.

Between 1876 and 1885 in Dodge City, only 15 people died violent deaths. There was an average of only 1.5 killings per year according to the book *Cattle Towns.* Guns were collected by the sheriff as cowpokes rode into town to get drunk.

## Handguns

You are more likely to encounter handguns than any other weapon almost anywhere, unless you have decided to take a vacation in Central Asia or West Africa. Handguns can hold between 6 and 20 bullets, with an average police automatic packing around 13. The good news is that unless they are in the hands of a highly trained professional (happily absent in most unpleasant places), handguns are very ineffective. They might look cool, but if you can scamper 20 yards away or more, you are usually home free. In fact, the Western movies where men bang away from across the street without hitting anyone are not too far from reality.

Handguns come in a wide variety of calibers, 9mm being the most common. Although they do not travel that far or that fast, many handgun bullets will have an inverted lead nose cone (known as a hollow point) surrounded by a copper jacket. This will spread out like a hot lead pancake on impact, and it will make you wish you were wearing that flak vest after all.

## Rifles and Assault Rifles

Unlike handguns, rifles fire bullets that travel faster than the speed of sound, which is why gunshots sometimes seem to have two bangs. One is the cordite in the cartridge exploding, and the other is the bullet breaking the sound barrier. This means that you will not hear the sound of the bullet that kills you. Apart from the damage caused by the initial impact, any flesh and organs around the wound will be turned into a bloody pulp by the supersonic shockwave following the bullet.

Modern military rifles are usually fully automatic. That means they can be fired in single shots or on full automatic. Full automatic is the least accurate but most intimidating. If a soldier is careful when squeezing off single shots, he is probably trying to kill you. If soldiers are using full automatic (common at night and in attacks), it means you have scared the daylights out of them or they are attacking.

In most armies, rifles are issued to most troops, sometimes without bullets. This is common in Africa. Assault rifles like the M-16 or AK-47 have high burst rates but longer barrels and better accuracy. Most terrorist or liberation movements carry AK-47 assault rifles because they are cheap to buy, easy to fix, and relatively accurate.

Most Asian and African soldiers tend to fire fast and aim high under stress. Middle Eastern and Central Asian countries like Afghanistan and Pakistan breed deadly shots, because they grow up using guns for hunting and engage in warfare at long distances. Jungle fighters like to spray bullets and often use shotguns.

Assault rifles hold between 20 and 40 bullets and go through them pretty quickly on full auto. An Uzi kicks out 600 rounds per minute but has a maximum clip of 40 rounds—10 bullets a second gives you exactly four seconds of looking good until you have to reload. Killing range for rifles can extend to more than 1,000 meters, though most are effective in combat up to 500 yards. Assault rifles (the ones with large clips and short barrels) are designed to be light, possess high rates of fire, and do double-duty as an accurate defensive rifle. They are designed to kill at 20 to 200 yards.

http://www.dmoz.org/Recreation/Guns/Manufacturers

## AK-47 (Avtomat Kalashnikova Obrazets 1947g)

If there is one visual symbol or prop that symbolizes the communist revolutionary influence around the world, it would not be ole Ché smiling down on us but the unmistakable profile of the AK-47. Once it was the hammer and sickle; now it is the banana-shaped clip and pointed barrel of the world's most dangerous rifle.

These weapons are cheap (between $50 and $350), are available around the world, are rock-hard reliable, and are in use from Afghanistan to Zimbabwe. It is estimated that there are about 30 to 50 million copies of the rugged rifle in existence. They can pour out 600 rounds a minute and are designed to be manufactured and repaired in primitive conditions. They use a chromed barrel and the only major defect is the loud click when you change firing rate or go off safety.

In 1941, the 23-year-old tank commander Mikhail T. Kalashnikov was wounded in the battle of Bryansk by the German invaders. While recuperating, he listened to the complaints of Russian soldiers about their archaic bolt-action rifles. Kalashnikov made use of his downtime to copy the current German machine pistol. His pistol never made it into the arsenal of the Russian army, but in 1943 it got him an entry to compete with other Russian gun designers to create the first Soviet assault rifle.

Kalashnikov's design was chosen based on its durability and simplicity. Over 80 million AK-47 and variants thereof have been manufactured in 12 countries from Bulgaria to Yugoslavia. It is actually an AKM you'll be extracting from your ear at most checkpoints around the world. In 1959 the AK-47 was superseded by the "Modernized Kalashnikov" or AKM. Weighing 2½ pounds less than the AK-47, the AKM is an even more durable and accurate development of the original design.

AKs are sighted to 1,000 yards, field-strip down to six parts, fire a 30-round magazine of 7.62 x 39 mm cartridges, and will deliver 3-inch patterns at 25 yards. The rifle is accurate to 200 yards when fired from the shoulder at rest, and accurate to about 50 yards fired from the hip. The AK has inspired countless imitations, the most notable of which are the Israeli Gallil ARM and the South African R4. The newest version of the classic assault rifle is the sophisticated AN-94 (a development of the AK-47 adopted by the Soviets in 1974), which uses a lighter but more accurate 5.45 x 39 mm cartridge. Detested by Kalashnikov himself, the complex AN-94 has so far been issued only to Russian Spetznaz Special Forces.

Kalashnikov was born in the Siberian town of Izhevsk, west of the Ural Mountains. Today, Izhevsk is home to Izhmash, a former major arms manufacturing company that exports hunting rifles under the name Kalashnikov Joint Stock Co. Kalashnikov still designs hunting rifles and has never received a royalty for his innovative design, though he has received many medals for it.

http://kalashnikov.guns.ru
http://www.sovietarmy.com/small_arms/ak-47.html

## The G3

Heckler & Koch are known for high-precision German weapons. A relative newcomer to the arms trade, they were formed in 1949 by three partners; Seidel is the modest one. Originally, the postwar German army used old M-1 Garands and the FAL rifle. The G3 was adopted in 1959 and was the first entirely German-designed and -made rifle (based on the Spanish CETME). The G3 used the standard 7.62 x 51 NATO cartridge, and its accuracy and durability led to it being adopted by more than 50 other countries. The basic rifle design was made in everything from a .22 caliber version to the ultimate H&K version, the PSG1, a $5,000 sniper version for military and police use.

http://www.hecklerkoch-usa.com

## The Uzi

The Uzi is the brainchild of Israeli designer, Major Uziel Gal, borrowing heavily from Czech models 23 and 25. The Uzi is designed to spray a room with bullets or be used as an infantry weapon. The 9mm version has a rate of fire of 10 bullets per second. The magazine inserts through the pistol grip, and the Uzi comes in a 16-inch-long barrel or ultra-compact machine-pistol size. The Uzi is also a favorite of the U.S. Secret Service because of its small size and high rate of fire. Originally designed for 9mm NATO standard ammunition, the Uzi was manufactured in a more powerful .45-caliber format for the U.S. market. Magazines come in 20-, 25-, and 32-round capacity (the .45-caliber version comes in a meager 16-round capacity).

http://www.vectorarms.com/indexframe.html
http://www.tecinfo.com/~jayhawk/uzi.html

## Snipers

The sniper's rifle is the world's most dangerous weapon simply because it is used only to kill. You will never see the sniper who kills you or even hear the high-velocity bullet. Snipers can fire from a mile away and are trained to sit patiently, line up their shot, and make it count. Usually snipers set up before sunrise and will move to a new position after every shot. If they are in a secure area or have no fear of artillery or attack, they may sit all day plinking away at civilians or troops.

The old rules about whether it's best to be first, second, or third are not really true. You can get shot very easily whether you are the first or last to spring across an open area. Snipers usually pick their victims based on seniority, so God help you if you show up at the front lines and the troops suddenly snap to attention. How do you avoid snipers? Well, just like big-game hunting, there is safety in numbers; also, a zigzag motion might give the sniper a few microseconds of hesitation. Their business is sneaking up on you, and that means they have been watching you a lot longer than you have been watching for them.

### CANADIAN WINS MEDAL IN TORA BORA OLYMPICS

The world distance record for a confirmed kill is 2,310 meters, scored by a Canadian sniper during Operation Anaconda in Afghanistan. The kill was made with a MacMillan 50-cal., using AMAX ammo and a Leupold 16t scope. It was the third shot that proved to be a charm. Other kills were made out to be at 2,500 meters, against Taliban and al-Qaeda fighters in March 2002.

http://www.snipersparadise.com

## The Dragunov SVD

Based on the AK-47, the Dragunov is the most common sniper rifle in the third world. Designed by Evgeny Dragunov in the late 1950s, it actually beat several of Kalashnikov's own designs. Recently employed by the Eritreans and mujahideen, this long-barreled killing machine takes a 10-round magazine, and will accurately send a Soviet 7.62 x 54 full-metal jacket 800 yards in your direction—fast enough to ruin your entire day.

# Medium–Range Weapons

When bullets just won't communicate how much an army hates you, the military can whip out some other nasty gizmos to make your life on the front miserable.

Rifles are the brooms of the army, but artillery is the shovel. Most assaults are done in combination with heavy explosive devices that stun and clear large areas before the troops charge it. Or you can be driven by an infantry assault into an area carefully marked and targeted for mortars or artillery bombardment.

## Mortars

Mortars look like tubes with legs on three plates. They are designed to throw shells short distances in a high trajectory. In the military, 5,000 meters is a short distance. The soldier drops the hand-sized missile down the tube and it fires. When it lands, it spreads shrapnel in a 20- to 60-yard perimeter, depending on the shell. The only good things about mortars are that you can tell where they come from and they tend to target specific areas. Being in trenches or inside buildings are your best bets in a mortar attack.

Oh, and if you think your luck is in because the first two bombs have fallen wide (right and left), it isn't: they know where you are, and are triangulating your exact position.

## Artillery

Artillery is another matter. Artillery sends medium to large shells screaming in waves and exploding in a shower of razor-sharp metal and massive concussion. The shells are used either to demoralize troops or create havoc before an attack. Artillery kills more people in warfare than bullets. If you come under artillery attack, it is not a good sign. You should try to change your travel plans in a direction other than toward the guns. Artillery can explode overhead, shredding cowering troops into hamburger meat, or impact on the ground and make nice round craters. You want to be in a trench, facedown, mouth open, and hands over ears when you hear that freight-train sound.

**The Artilleryman**
http://sill-www.army.mil/FA/index.htm

**Russian Artillery**
http://home11.inet.tele.dk/blackice/CIS_ART.htm

## RPGs

Those funny-looking green things on the end of long sticks are RPGs, or rocket-propelled grenades. There are also LAWs, or light antitank weapons. Even the latest Russian T-90 tank can be taken out with a cheap RPG-7. The RPG-7 is 40 years old and still can be used to knock out most armored vehicles and clear bunkers. It is in use by at least 50 armies today. The operator (who usually carries only one extra rocket) aims through the optical site, and fires. The rocket motor kicks in around 11 meters out and then accelerates the warhead. The rocket self-destructs at 920 meters out or 4.5 seconds after launch, and is very accurate.

The new explosive tank armor is easily defeated by the new Basalt-designed PG-7BR that has two charges: one to negate the explosive armor and the second to penetrate the tank. The combination concentrates the explosive charge to cut through tank armor like butter.

LAWs and RPGs give significant range (for the classic guerrilla hit-and-run attack) and cause widespread damage in crowded troop convoys or Sunday schools. RPGs are very much in vogue in Chechnya and West Africa because they were shipped in by the container and can create mayhem for pennies. RPGs are used to attack small- to medium-sized groups of men, trucks, and armored vehicles, and are used against helicopters by mujahideen. A rocket has a range of 1,000 meters, but is used around half that distance for fixed targets and half again for moving vehicles or tanks.

Of the different rockets that the RPG-7 can fire, the most common is the green bulb of an anti-tank shell. These are not particularly effective against troops, but they take apart a house in a direct hit. Smaller anti-personnel rockets are less common, and split into six long shards of white-hot metal—fortunately no one has yet thought of packing them with ball bearings. If you are very lucky, you might encounter a thermo-baric shell. These little beauties act like small fuel-air bombs, and have the same impact on bricks and mortar as a 107 howitzer shell.

There are also the smaller 40mm grenade launcher tubes you see mounted under rifles. These weapons are designed to fire a small explosive, chemical, smoke, illumination, or other type of grenade a few hundred yards away without giving away the location of the shooter.

## Machine Guns

Machine guns were put to good use in the trenches of World War I, where a team of two men with a Maxim could mow down hundreds of attacking troops. The only limitations were how much ammunition they had and if the gun would jam due to the barrel overheating. Travelers will now see the big machine guns only at checkpoints and on top of tanks and bunkers. They are used to pin down or decimate large groups of attacking soldiers. They are also mounted on the back of trucks in places like Somalia. Machine guns fire belt-fed ammunition (great for wearing in bandoliers and posing for bad-guy pictures) and require a tripod (unless you are Arnold Schwarzenegger) for accuracy. They are loud and require someone to make sure the bullets are feeding properly. They are deadly out to 2,500 meters and can also fire armor-piercing bullets. If you are in an area that has a preponderance of these weapons, you can safely assume you are in an active war zone.

http://www.taos-inc.com/smarms.htm
http://www.army-technology.com/contractors/machine_guns

## Long–Range Weapons

Those of you who were lucky enough to see our $5 million cruise missiles go streaking overhead understand why war sucks. Today, there are so many exotic weapons delivery systems that they fill their own *Jane's* book. Travelers won't come across too many of these exotic weapons, unless they are on the wrong side of Uncle Sam. Some groups, like the Chechens, the Afghans, and the Hutus, like to use Stinger surface-to-

### OVERNIGHT DELIVERY, NO SIGNATURE REQUIRED

The toy that gives the medal boys woodies these days is the Tomahawk AGM-86B, a 550-mile-per-hour, flying "smart" bomb that can be launched from air, land, or sea; be programmed onto a target; and then deliver a variety of nasty surprises, including a 250-kiloton thermonuclear device. The Tomahawk is 219 inches long, has a 100-inch wingspan, weighs 2 tons, has a range of 1,553 miles (using a solid booster), and also uses a turbojet engine. It was developed in 1972 and has climbed in price from $50,000 to around $2 million a copy. We used Tomahawks in Yugoslavia, Iraq, Afghanistan, and Sudan because they perform our "don't ask, don't tell, shut up, and roll the video" dirty work of Clintonesque warfare. We used cluster bombs in the camps in Afghanistan, graphite fibers to short-out power lines in Serbia, and 1,000-pound high explosives against hard targets in Iraq. Tomahawks are supposed to be accurate to within 30 feet using GPS (global positioning satellite), TERCOM, or a special terrain way-point radar map and two types of terminal guidance systems: a high-resolution satellite radar image called DSMAC and an infrared mapper. The government says Tomahawks have an 85 percent direct-hit rate. Uh huh, next question.

The Boeing cruise missile uses the same propulsion system but flies faster and smarter. Originally designed to deliver nuclear warheads, the agile cruise missile is now used to accurately deliver high explosives down bunker chimneys or through 3' x 3' windows . . . sometimes.

air missiles, but they are lethal and unexpected, and there is no advice one can give on avoiding them, except take the train.

http://www.milnet.com/milnet/weapons.htm

## The F*** Bomb

Clearly not content with the thousands of millions of tons of weapons already available, military-technical establishments are ever on the look-out for more bizarre and effective ways of ruining *DP* staff holidays. Fuel-air bombs and thermo-baric weapons are a case in point. Your average fuel-air bomb works like this: a warhead filled with aerosol liquid such as ethylene oxide is dropped on the target. A small explosive charge allows the liquid to escape to form a concentrated explosive cloud of vapor that hugs valley floors and sinks into the nooks and crannies of buildings and caves. This cloud is then ignited by a second charge, generating an intense fireball as hot as 3,000 degrees Celsius. The blast wave can travel at approximately 10,000 feet per second.

The Russians used thermo-baric weapons during the 1994–1996 war in Chechnya and in Dagestan in 1999. Not to be outdone by the Ruskies, Uncle Sam, who has been using thermo-baric variants since WWII, dropped the all-new-and-improved BLU-118/B during Operation Anaconda in Afghanistan—a brand new F bomb with the added bonus of a 2,000-pound bunker-busting bombshell. Given the fact that fuel-air explosives are particularly good at vaporizing chemical and biological weapons sites, *DP* suggests that Saddam Hussein's forthcoming BBQ in Baghdad might be a trifle on the warm side.

http://www.fas.org

## Resources

*DP* is a graduate of the Travis Bickle/Dirty Harry school of firearm safety, with plenty of real-world credits to spare. So we are a firm believer of everyone who owns or wants to own a gun being trained and educated no matter what your opinions of guns are. Remember, it's the gun the other guy is holding that is the most dangerous. We do not carry weapons or engage in any hostilities, but it's real nice to know what the range of an AK is versus that of a sniper rifle. The following is a list of resources to expand your knowledge and safe use of weapons. Note: Many of the companies do not deal with the public. Sales of weapons are regulated by state and federal law. These are listings for informational purposes.

*The AK-47*, by Chris McNab, $23.00, Spellmount (ISBN 1-86227-116-X)

*Assault Rifles, Combat Shotguns (including Sniping Rifles)*, by John A. Norris, $29.95 Brassey's (ISBN 1-85753-214-7)

**Eagle Industries**
400 Biltmore Drive, Suite 530
Fenton, MO 63026
Tel.: (636) 343-7547
comments@eagleindustries.com
http://www.eagleindustries.com
Makers of Mr. *DP*'s favorite
pack, loadbearing vests, and also
other military and SWAT gear.

**Knight's Armament Co.**
7750 9th Street, SW
Vero Beach, FL 32968
Tel.: (561) 778-3700
Fax: (561) 569-2955
kacsr25@aol.com
http://www.knightsarmament.com
Manufacturer and designer of
weapons systems including
suppressed 50-cal. sniper rifles.

**Jonathan Arthur Ciener, Inc.**
8700 Commerce Street
Cape Canaveral, FL 32920
Tel.: (321) 868-2200
http://www.m1911.org/ciener.htm
http://www.22lrconversions.com
Manufacturer of sound-
suppressed firearms and
conversion kits.

**AWC Systems Technology**
P.O. Box 41938
Phoenix, AZ 85080
Tel.: (623) 780-1050
Fax: (623) 780-2967
awc@awcsystech.com
http://www.awcsystech.com
Manufacturer of sniper rifles
and silenced weapons.

**Cheaper Than Dirt**
2522 NE, Loop 820
Fort Worth, TX 76106-1809
Tel.: (800) 421-8047
http://www.cheaperthandirt.com

**Brigade Quartermasters, Ltd.**
P.O. Box 100001
1025 Cobb International Drive NW,
Suite 100
Kennesaw, GA 30156-9217
Catalog Order Line: (800) 338-4327
Tel.: (770) 428-1234
http://www.actiongear.com
One of the best sources for
adventure, safari, hunting,
shooting, and military wear.

**TAPCO**
P.O. Box 2408
Kennesaw, GA 30144
Tel.: (800) 554-1445 or (800) 359-6195
customerservice@tapco.com
http://www.tapco.com
Hunting, military surplus, books,
and even bulletproof vests.

## Training Courses

**Tactical Firearms Training Team**
16835 Algonquin Street, Suite 120
Huntington Beach, CA 92649
Tel.: (714) 846-8065
director@tftt.com
http://www.nrawinningteam.com/tftt

**Glock, Inc. (Law-Enforcement and
Military Personnel Training)**
P.O. Box 369
Smyrna, GA 30081
Tel.: (770) 432-1202
http://ericcom.com/glocktalk/contacts.
shtml

**Lethal Force Institute**
P.O. Box 122
Concord, NH 03302-0122
Tel.: (603) 224-6814 or (800) 624-9049
ayoob@attglobal.net
http://www.ayoob.com

GUNS

**190** THE WORLD'S MOST DANGEROUS PLACES

**Thunder Ranch**
HCR 1, Box 53
Mountain Home, TX 78058
Tel.: (830) 640-3138
Fax: (830) 640-3183
http://www.thunderranchinc.com

**H&K International Training Division**
21480 Pacific Boulevard
Sterling, VA 20166
Tel.: (703) 450-1900
http://www.hecklerkoch-usa.com

**Gun and safety training links**
http://www.kuci.org/~dany/links.html

**Yavapai Firearms Academy, Ltd.**
P.O. Box 27290
Prescott, AZ 86312
Tel.: (928) 772-8262
info@yfainc.com
http://www.yfainc.com

**Front Sight Firearms Training Institute**
P.O. Box 2619
Aptos, CA 95001
Tel.: (800) 987-7719
Fax: (831) 684-2137
info@frontsight.com
http://www.frontsight.com

**The Second Amendment Foundation**
http://www.saf.org

**NRA homepage**
http://www.nra.org

**The Firearms Training Site**
aglock45@erols.com
http://www.erols.com/aglock45

**The Citizens Committee for the Right
to Keep and Bear Arms**
http://www.ccrkba.org

# INTELLIGENCE

## What You Don't Know Can Kill You

I say it over and over: "The most dangerous thing in the world is ignorance." The usual sound-bite for kidnapped, blown up, mugged, and
abused tourists on CNN is, "I had no idea. . . ."

The ugly truth about traveling to dangerous places is that you are
solely responsible for your own safety. Despite what you read in this
book, what your government warns you about, what the papers whine
about, what the charming but bored embassy staffer lectures you on, or
even what the locals steer you away from, there is only one true thing:
You, and you alone, are responsible for your own safety. You need to
form your own opinion. Measure the risk, take the precautions, have a
Plan B. Because when the animal waste hits the fan, there is only going
to be you—and that stupid look on your face—to deal with whatever
you got yourself into.

So do you run out and spend thousands of dollars on faux spy situation alerts? Attend Intel briefings by square-jawed spectors, interrupt satellite feeds, or swap missile plans for terrorist calendars? No silly, you use common sense.

Common sense is a very rare commodity these days. It requires that you not get caught up in media hysteria, government posturing, pressure group releases, or PC angst. It means you keep an open mind and then filter it through skepticism, double check it, and then get your info hot and fresh directly from the source.

> **M**easure the risk, take the precautions, have a Plan B. Because when the animal waste hits the fan, there is only going to be you—and that stupid look on your face—to deal with whatever you got yourself into.

Okay, you wanna break that down into baby steps? Sure. Tourism info is your worst bet. Few countries provide murder rates, terrorist phone numbers, and traffic accident statistics with those glossy pamphlets or florid Web sites. So chuck those in the trash. Your first stop should be local or international news sources—the dark side of tourist boards. Keep in mind you are not going to hear about every watch stolen or bum pinched on AP, but it's a start. Too lazy to figure out how to get this info? No-problem news aggregators like Yahoo! do it for you. Even lazier? AOL and other "push" technologies allow you to type in words like "tourist" and "kidnapped" and have any news stories sent directly to your e-mail. Even lazier than that? The OSAC database keeps an ever-churning list of bad things and a simple sort-and-search process to help you find out what bad things are happening out there.

The second step is a little tougher, but can save your life. Contact your native country's embassy in the country you are traveling to (if, of course, they are brave enough to have an embassy) and ask for the security person. Since he (I've never yet met a "she" doing this job) is usually sitting in a little office filling out paperwork, he will be happy to give you specific information (I said specific; having him plan your vacation and recommend hotels is not his balliwick).

Also, get the contact numbers for the following:

- Your embassy
- A Western-level hospital where they speak your language
- A doctor who speaks your language (and doesn't use little pins in dolls)
- A lawyer who handles problems for people just like you
- Any other folks who can help you out

Then have a chat about where you are going and what kind of problems you might encounter. Now don't be shocked if this security guy warns you not to go—let's say if you are a Bible salesman heading to Pakistan or a Frederick's of Hollywood rep going to Saudi Arabia. Finally, ask him if you can buy him a beer when you get there and he will probably set you up with a temporary membership at the embassy watering hole.

Of course, I know none of you are going to do all of the above because, hell, "nothing ever happens to me"—which is absolutely true until something does. Then those bureaucrats can be awfully helpful. You can't blame them for shooing people away so they can focus on the more mundane aspects of their job. Aspects like boxing up dead citizens to ship home, getting messages to jailed tourists, and searching for a daughter who ran off with a snake charmer.

**Main page for U.S. State Department Services**
http://www.state.gov/www/services.html

**Bureau of Consular Affairs**
http://travel.state.gov

**Overseas Security Advisory Council**
http://www.ds-osac.org

**Travel warnings**
http://travel.state.gov/travel_warnings.html

**Consular sections**
http://travel.state.gov/consuls_help.html

**Lists of Doctors/Hospitals Abroad**
http://travel.state.gov/acs.html#medical

So keep all of this in mind when you read our State Department Travel Warnings. They are terribly political, frustratingly vague, and range from being helpful to laughable. Our favorite is the ever-increasing "Worldwide Caution" alerts, that essentially tell us to "maintain a high level of vigilance and to take appropriate steps to increase their security awareness to reduce their vulnerability." Uh, yeah, sure. Hey Earl, pass the ammo and break me off another chunk of that smoked squirrel.

Hey, they're bureaucrats, what do you expect? The fewer people on their turf, the less work they have to do. Also, you might notice one glaring omission—no listing for the United States. In their defense, they are the ones who have to herd you onto the choppers when things go past ugly to apocalyptic. So buy 'em a drink and think about calling the Iraqi embassy the next time you need help.

Now I would have to say that the quality, currency, and comprehensiveness of the U.S.-travel warnings are the best out there. More important, they have responded to pressure groups and added information on aviation, road conditions, children, customs, and other matters. But massive government stupidity can still reign supreme, like

Angola and Eritrea. They still plug in generic information when specific information is at hand and easy to find. As in the condition of roads in the Congo: Poor. Oh, really? Medical conditions in Afghanistan: Not good. Oh, really? And the usual warning: "U.S. citizens in Sierra Leone should review their own personal security situations in determining whether to visit or reside in the country." Sorry, but the bottom line is, once again, it is your job to gather the relevant information regarding your safety (or lack of it) and act on it.

By now you have the cold, clammy feeling that you are pretty much on your own in dangerous places. Don't feel so bad: most people in dangerous places are on their own too. But wait, other than reading this book, where do you find out more about dangerous places?

## Use the Internet

This sounds like mundane advice, but the Internet provides the most up-to-date information on health, problems, internal contacts, and plain old commonsense advice for travelers. Don't assume that because it's on the Net it's fresh, or even right. (Yes, there are mindless generic tourism pages for Somalia, pretty photos of Afghanistan showing Buddhas that haven't been blown up, and smiling Yemenis selling guns.) Use the sites below as a starting point and then search engines and directories like Google to find more. Keep in mind with the size of the Web, that search engines are pretty useless these days and you are better off searching within country, region, or subject-specific databases on dangerous places.

Then use the magic of e-mail and forums to gather more information and even friends. Post specific questions at places like Black Flag Café and get them answered by people who travel or live in dangerous places.

Your best sources are communities specific to the country or activity, news sources from the actual region, and direct e-mail conversations with in-country tour, hotel, and travel operators.

**Google**
http://www.google.com

**Black Flag Café**
http://www.comebackalive.com

**Ed Hasbrouck's Practical Nomad Links**
http://hasbrouck.org/links/index.html

**The Thorn Tree**
http://www.lonelyplanet.com

## Check Things Out

Nag, nag, nag, but accurate knowledge is what separates the quick from the dead. There are a number of sources from NGOs and relief agencies working in remote and dangerous places. They provide weekly reports on incidents and developments. You can also contact them for specific (remember, I said specific) questions relating to regions, events, and activities. Don't be surprised if they adopt the world-weary tone of "piss off, we're busy." They usually are.

Boning up on news reports and incident reports can at least give you a general idea of what is going on, but it won't give you up-to-the-minute information. Remember, things change in war zones about as fast as the fall TV schedule. Check out the Integrated Regional Information Networks and the UN Office for Coordination of Humanitarian Affairs for up-to-the-minute information from war zones and remote regions.

**Yahoo! News by Region**
http://dailynews.yahoo.com/fc/World

**North American Special Operations
  Group**
http://www.nasog.net/intelligence/
  Index.htm

**Relief Web**
http://www.reliefweb.int

**U.N. Integrated Regional Information**
http://www.irinnews.org

**News Trove**
http://www.newstrove.com

**Google News**
http://www.news.google.com

## Expect the Unexpected

Prepare for the worst and then expect the best. Learn about first aid and carry a medical kit, learn about short-term survival and carry a small pocket-sized survival book. Buy a language guide, a good map, and a guidebook if available. Your local travel-specialty store is an excellent place to start. Read my survival guide, *Come Back Alive*, for more information. Most important, understand that the place you are going to will be very different from the place you are coming from and you must develop independence, humor, and resourcefulness to return safely. Anything you need or want to make that job easier should be purchased, and you should become familiar with it, before you leave.

**Professional first-aid kits**
http://www.imsplus.com

**Travel books**
http://www.amazon.com

**Survival books**
http://www.militiaofmontana.com/
  survivbk.htm

**Rough Guide**
http://www.travel.roughguide.com

**Randall's Adventure & Training**
http://www.jungletraining.com

## Train and Learn

How the hell do you *train* for a trip? The upsurge in tourists and journalists being killed, kidnapped, and victimized has spawned a fledgling industry. Crusty old vets of nasty places now can show journalists what to do when guns begin firing and bombs start exploding. They can teach you how to avoid a kidnapping and how to survive one. If that doesn't work, they can teach you how to detect if someone is following you, signal for help, search for car bombs, avoid land mines—basically how to get yourself out of any nasty situation.

**Centurion Risk Assessment Services**
http://www.centurion-riskservices.co.uk

**AKE Group**
http://www.akegroup.com

**CI Centre Counterintelligence Courses**
http://www.cicentre.com/

## Keep Learning

I can safely tell you that 50 to 80 percent of what you just learned before you went to that blasted-to-hell place is wrong or out of date. Why? Because it takes about two years for info to be gathered and published in a traditional guide book, about four to eight months for a magazine story to be published, and up to one to three months for a big newspaper story to run on a remote region. Even radio and TV are usually focused on yesterday's news. Yes, there are live feeds from CNN, but they are not providing background, survival, or travel tips. There is an almost inverse law that says the more helpful and comprehensive the information, the longer it takes to get to market. If you want to cut to the chase, go to the source.

It's not a joke that the most encyclopedic form of information can be found on a barstool. When you first arrive at your destination, find the local watering hole where expats and foreign journos drop in for a chat. It's usually the most expensive hotel in town, an American club (by invitation only, but that's why you were sucking up to the embassy guy, remember?), or a foreign embassy bar. Most expats are surprisingly indifferent or hostile to tourists. They almost resent the fact that you can go back. But many are eager to swap basketball scores or war stories. Ask them pointedly what is going on and what you need to do in case you need Plan B. You will learn that certain aid agencies, NGOs, and foreign embassies are very helpful in case of emergency. Others won't even answer the polished buzzer. Don't ever assume the U.S. embassies are the friendliest, because they aren't. My reception has ranged from being held off at gunpoint to being told to get the hell out of Dodge. On the other hand, once inside, you can see that the staff has reason to be paranoid, and with a few warm-up jokes, they can turn out to be pretty helpful in a pinch. The main reason you want to at least register and say hi is to ensure a spot on the chopper if there is a civilian/noncombatant evac. If you don't sign on, you go to the back of the line.

For some reason, embassies and consulates in every war zone have their own vibe, their own sense of welcome, and to a certain degree their own reason for existing—none of which usually concerns you, the person they were set up to service. They are busy gathering intelligence, twisting local politicians' arms, filling out stupid reports, arranging photo-op trips for our politicians, making business introductions, and keeping Uncle Sam happy.

> **D**on't ever assume the U.S. embassies are the friendliest, because they aren't. My reception has ranged from being held off at gunpoint to being told to get the hell out of Dodge.

How do you survive the hot and harried or cold and disinterested diplomatic shoulder you are likely to get? Well, ignore them. Sometimes the locals outside throwing rocks and chanting slogans are happier to see you than the beleaguered people inside. Remember it's not about what country you are from, it's about the country's politics. You know the stuff that we throw rocks at our own embassy for doing. Once in-country, enlist the help of a local guide, either a friend you meet online, a recommended translator, or even a person recommended by a local aid group. Keep an open mind, learn the language, tour the back streets, stay away from tourists, and try to absorb as much as you can. Travel in difficult places has become surprisingly easy.

## Government Travel Sources

The Overseas Security Advisory Council (OSAC) began in 1985 when a number of businesses demanded information on overseas security. In 1987, a database of incidents and reports was created, including State Department Travel Warnings, terrorist profiles, anniversary dates, special reports on crime, and general information for travelers. The database is free of charge and should be any traveler's starting point for information. They have updated the site to include global news and the latest information on security and links. Keep in mind the information varies widely in quality, currency, and, most important, political perspective. You will need to register and be a business to use the site.

**Overseas Security Advisory Council**
http://www.ds-osac.org

**Bureau of Diplomatic Security**
http://ds.state.gov

**U.S. Department of State**
2201 C Street NW
Washington, DC 20520
Tel.: (202) 647-4000

## Government Travel Sites

Fine, go ahead and say, well, the entire resources of the United States must be worth something, right? But it hasn't prevented embassies from being blown up almost simultaneously in Uganda, Kenya, and Dar Es Salaam. I suggest reading, but more important, questioning, the information that is presented. Another *DP* tip is to simply use the Australian advisory link because they link into U.S. and British government sites.

**U.S. Department of State Travel Warnings and Consular Information Sheets**
http://travel.state.gov/travel_warnings.html

**United Kingdom travel advisories**
http://www.fco.gov.uk/travel

**Canadian government travel advisories**
http://www.voyage.gc.ca/destinations/menu_e.htm

**Australian government travel advisories**
http://www.dfat.gov.au/consular/advice/advices_mnu.html

## Nongovernmental Travel Information

There is no one source of information for dangerous places. You need to search the Web and sift through the blizzard of useless flames and opinions to find useful bits. The technical term for gathering information that is not considered secret is called *open source*. But remember, merely gathering data without generating useful information is simply background noise. There is an entire industry for open source and much information can be found at Robert David Steele's Open Source Solutions (http://www.oss.net) and at the Federation of American Scientists (http://www.fas.org). The idea is that an informed society can make informed decisions and, of course, our own intelligence resources are so wound up in their own little bureaucracies they are functionally dead. In any case, you are not trying to find bin Laden's Swiss bank accounts, just trying to get a clear idea of what dangers to avoid.

There are a number of companies that provide information on dangerous places. For survival-guide stuff, go to this book online (free and available to anyone) at:

**The World's Most Dangerous Places/Dangerfinder**
http://www.comebackalive.com

Keep in mind that the following businesses/organizations are going to charge you a lot more than what you paid for this book, but depending on your needs, it can be money well spent.

## Stratfor Strategic Forecasting
http://www.stratfor.com
info@stratfor.com
Tel.: (512) 744-4300

Stratfor is part of a new trend in open-source information: a private company that gathers, analyzes, and disseminates information on conflict and security for businesses, essentially doing to the CIA what UPS did to the postal service. Stratfor was founded in 1995 in Baton Rouge, Louisiana, by former faculty and students of Louisiana State University, associated with the Center for Geopolitical Studies. The company moved to Austin, Texas, in the summer of 1997, and its staff of 20 has provided generally accurate (albeit desk-bound) open-source information and crystal ball-like predictions since then. You can also have them send you analyses via e-mail. Their Global Intelligence Center is an excellent source of news on regional matters. You can get mini-bits on their mailings or sign on as a media wonk and get more info.

## iJET Travel Intelligence, Inc.
900 Bestgate Road, Suite 400
Annapolis, MD 21401
Tel.: (410) 573-3860
Fax: (410) 573-3869
info@ijet.com
http://www.ijet.com

One of the best ideas in travel safety is based in Annapolis, Maryland. iJET provides very detailed travel information and support packages for travelers. They also provide real-time

travel alerts and a variety of support services. They target their services to corporate clients who stay in major cities and more-traveled countries. One of their better ideas is allowing travelers to buy travel safety reports by region (updated weekly) from Amazon.com.

## Indigo Publications
http://www.intelligenceonline.com

The best source of information on Africa, the Indian Ocean area, and Europe. You can buy articles and information as needed.

## Africa Intelligence
http://www.africaintelligence.com

## International Crisis Group
http://www.intl-crisis-group.org

Provides in-depth analysis of selected conflict areas.

## Pinkerton Global Intelligence Services
4245 N. Fairfax, Suite 725
Arlington, VA 22203
Tel.: (703) 525-6111
Fax: (703) 525-2454
http://www.pinkertons.com

I won't belabor you with the history of Pinkerton, except to say they have been around for awhile. Outside of their thriving business in providing security for businesses, they now offer a sort of intel-lite all the way up to heavy-duty threat analyses. Most travelers will be interested in their Eye on Travel that provides two to five pages of background on more than 210 countries. Information on passport and visa requirements, medical and vaccination information, import/export restrictions, currency and exchange rates, time zones, banking hours, voltage, and commercial holidays. Included are U.S. State Department advisories, consular information reports, and travel notices from the British Foreign Commonwealth Office. It costs money, but you can get information on normal countries not covered in *DP*. Don't expect a lot of original or on-the-ground info, but it is an excellent resource for people who want to get their hands on safety information. You can catch their daily risk assessments free at http://pgis.pinkertons.com.

### Pinkerton U.S. Headquarters
200 South Michigan Avenue
Chicago, IL 60604
Tel.: (312) 322-8800
Fax: (312) 322-8636
mic.coordinator@usa.pinkertons.com

### Strategy Page
http://www.strategypage.com
Good source of news and background on conflict areas.

### Jane's Intelweb
http://intelweb.janes.com
Jane's provides a pricey briefing service (a number of which are written by *DP* contributors), which provides exhaustive background on security, military, and political developments around the world.

### Kroll O'Gara, Inc.
900 Third Avenue
New York, NY 10022
Tel.: (212) 593-1000
Fax: (212) 593-2631
http://www.krollworldwide.com
Kroll provides comprehensive and specific Country Risk Reports designed for expats or companies doing business overseas. Travelers can purchase Kroll's Travel Watch, which covers security and safety information, for about 300 cities (including U.S. destinations). A *DP* tip: Kroll provides quite a bit of content to iJET, which sells their updates on Amazon.com.

# Visas

The world is pretty much your oyster at this point because you've come to the conclusion that (1) things are pretty much screwed up all over, and (2) you are more likely to die within five miles of your house. So what is the next step? Other than putting aside some cash and booking tickets, you will need a visa and shots.

The more third-world your destination, the tougher it is to get clear info on entry requirements. One tip here: Don't wait too long because each embassy will sit on your passport for up to a couple of weeks. I recommend hiring a visa service that hustles around and makes sure you get exactly what you want. Be careful to ask for multiple entries and long-term visas; sometimes they are the same price as single-entry, short-term ones.

*Foreign entry/Visa requirements*
http://travel.state.gov/foreignentryreqs.
  html

*Tourism Offices Worldwide Directory*
http://www.towd.com

*Lonely Planet*
http://www.lonelyplanet.com

*Kim Spy Intelligence and
  Counterintelligence*
http://www.kimsoft.com/kim-spy.htm

*Central Intelligence Agency World
  Factbook*
http://www.cia.gov/cia/publications/fact
  book/index.html

*CIA Search*
http://www.odci.gov/search

*Mario's Cyberspace Station*
http://mprofaca.cro.net

*Global Crisis Control International*
Tel.: (800) 515-9785 (US Toll Free)
     (845) 858-3290 (International)
Fax: (212) 656-1648
International Locations
UK: (44) 207-900-2386
Zurich: (41) 1 274 2906
Sydney: (61) 2 947 54351
info@crisis-control.com
http://crisis-control.com

*Political Resources on the Net*
http://www.politicalresources.net

*Security Intelligence News Service*
http://www.dso.com

*Clandestine Radio Intelligence Web*
http://www.clandestineRadio.com

# News

Accurate news is only as good as the people on the ground. Coverage on esoteric regions and subjects is best sourced from local Web sites, shortwave radio, and newspapers. On a general basis the following are good starting points:

*BBC*
http://news.bbc.co.uk/hi/english/world
  Your best source for world news
  and background online is the
  BBC. Don't forget that the BBC
  also provides much more
  detailed coverage on their shortwave services. So you might
  want to tune in to the regional
  news *before* you leave.

*Yahoo! News*
http://dailynews.yahoo.com/h/wl
  Yahoo! gathers and sorts news
  by subject or country. You can
  also set up alerts if you are
  tracking regions or topics.

*Matt Drudge*
http://www.drudgereport.com
  Forget Drudge's self-serving
  muckraking; bookmark his
  homepage for the best news
  links and columnists he offers.

*The* **New York Times**
http://www.nytimes.com
  You can set up news alerts here
  (you need to sign on for free) or
  buy archived articles.

*Nando Times*
http://www.nandonet.com
  A good general source for news
  that is not necessarily
  mainstream.

**AfricaNet**
http://www.africanet.com
A good source for news from
Africa.

**Associated Press**
http://www.newsday.com/news/
nationworld/wire

**Middle East Network Information
Center**
http://menic.utexas.edu/menic/menic.
html
Excellent background
information with links for the
Arab world.

## For Journalists/Writers

**Project for Excellence in Journalism**
http://www.journalism.org

**Pew Research Center for the People
and the Press**
http://www.people-press.org

**Power Reporting Resources for
Journalists**
http://www.powerreporting.com

**Finding Data on the Internet**
http://nilesonline.com/data

**Federation of American Scientists**
http://www.fas.org

**NewsPlace**
http://www3.niu.edu/newsplace

**Committee to Protect Journalists
Report by Country**
http://www.cpj.org

**Columbia Journalism Review**
http://www.cjr.org

**Conciliation Resources**
http://www.c-r.org

**The Associated Press**
http://www.ap.org

**Sygma (owned by Corbis)**
http://www.sygma.com

**Reuters**
http://www.reuters.com

**Agence France-Presse**
http://www.afp.com

**Blackstar**
http://www.blackstar.com

**Corbis**
http://www.corbis.com

## Other Helpful Resources

**American Journalism Review (JobLink)**
http://newslink.org/joblink

**Behind the Viewfinder**
http://www.digitalstoryteller.com/YITL

**Committee to Protect Journalists**
http://www.cpj.org

**Reporters Sans Frontières**
http://www.rsf.fr/content.php3

**Society of Professional Journalists**
http://www.spj.org

**The Free Lens**
http://www.oneworld.org/rorypeck

## Cool Tools

These URLs might help you do a little planning:

**Maps**
http://www.nationalgeographic.com/
maps/index.html
http://www.immigration-usa.com/maps
http://www.atlapedia.com

**Universal Currency Converter**
http://www.xe.net/currency/full

**Flight tracking**
http://www.trip.com/trs/trip/flighttracker
/flight_tracker_home.xsl

**Visa ATM Tracker**
http://www.visa.com/cgi-
bin/vee/pd/atm/main.html

**The World Clock**
http://www.timeanddate.com/worldclock

**Calendar (for any year)**
http://www.timeanddate.com/calendar

**Measurement converter**
http://www.mplik.ru/~sg/transl

**Concierge.com**
http://www.concierge.com/maps/airport
guides
Best way into town from more
than 100 airports.

**Weather worldwide**
http://www.weather.com

**Online foreign-language dictionaries**
http://www.yourdictionary.com

**Encarta**
http://encarta.msn.com

**Encyclopedia Britannica**
http://www.britannica.com

## Safety Training

Many of these courses and all of this information are available to non-journalists. These days anyone with small DV cameras and adventure gear in a war zone is considered a journo. The courses are expensive but obviously worth whatever you think your hide is worth.

Groups such as Frontline and CPJ have no interest in providing travel-planning tips to civvies, but if you are trying to break into the impecunious business of war reportage, they can offer some advice.

**Centurion Risk Assessment Services**
Reed Cottage, Fleet Road
Elvetham, Hartley Wintney,
Hants
RG27 8AT, UK
Tel.: (44) 01264 355255 or 07000
221221
Fax: (44) 01264 355322 or 07000
221222
http://www.centurion-riskservices.co.uk

P.O. Box 1740
Andover, Hants
SP11 7PE, UK
main@centurion-riskservices.co.uk
Survival training for journalists,
body armor, and helmet rental

**AKE Ltd.**
http://www.ake.co.uk

### AKE Ltd., UK office
AKE Limited
Mortimer House
Holmer Road, Hereford
HR4 9TA UK
Tel: (44) (0) 1432 267111
Fax: (44) (0) 1432 350227
services@ake.co.uk

### AKE Ltd., U.S. office
AKE LLC
1825 I Street, NW, Suite 400
Washington, DC 20006
Tel: (202) 974-6556
services@akellc.com

> Monthly courses on surviving hostile regions in the UK.

### Frontline Television
7 Southwick Mews
London W2 1JG, UK
Tel.: (44) 020 7616
http://www.frontlinetv.com

> Freelance agency for reporters in war zones, also provides armored car rental.

### International Freedom of Expression Exchange
http://www.ifex.org

### FreedomForum
http://www.freedomforum.org

> The Freedom Forum is a non-partisan, international foundation dedicated to free press, free speech, and free spirit for all people. The foundation pursues its priorities through conferences, educational activities, publishing, broadcasting, online services, fellowships, partnerships, training, research and other programs, news of interest to journalists, and a good links page.

### International Federation of Journalists
IPC-Residence Palace
Rue de la Loi 155
B-1040 Brussels
Belgium
Tel.: (32) 2 235 22 00
Fax: (32) 2 235 22 19
ifj@ifj.org
http://www.ifj.org

### IFJ List of Journalists and Media Staff Killed
http://www.ifj.org/hrights/killlist/killoverview.html

### Excellent Links page
http://www.ifj.org/links/links.html

# KIDNAPPING

## You're in Good Hands

The Bani Dhabyan tribe was a little apologetic. They apologized profusely to the government of Yemen for being forced to kidnap the 32-year-old son of the mayor of Sana'a. The reason? There were no suitable foreigners available at the time.

The Bani Dhabyan were trying to use the hostage to gain the release of six of their fellow tribesmen. (The tribesmen were being charged with the kidnapping of a Dutchman in 1997 and four Germans in 1999.) The son of the mayor is being treated well and is still in custody in a place where the leader keeps sons of tribal leaders in jail "so they won't act up." Times are tough in Yemen: only eight foreigners were kidnapped in six incidents in 2000 and only one died. In 1999, 42 were snatched, and 50 became unwilling houseguests in 1997. Thankfully, the Abu Sayyaf group single-handedly revived the homestay program for kidnapped tourists when they snatched 2 large groups of a total of 42 tourists and workers from resorts in Sipadan and Palawan. Things are looking up for the kidnapping business.

Depending on whom you believe, there are between 12,500 and 25,500 people kidnapped every year worldwide. Most of them are local businesspeople or members of prominent families, and most never make the headlines. It is also estimated that only 1 in 10 kidnaps, or only about 7,000 to 12,000, are reported to the police, making the above statistic fuzzy at best. About 1,800 of this list are foreigners, most working or living in a foreign country. In many cases, foreigners and kidnappers demand no publicity, so once again, 1,800 is just the known number.

Kidnapping is an ancient crime and in most cases is designed to generate income or force political or personal favor. In some cases, it is employed as a direct method of terrorism. The victims do not want to advertise that they have paid off kidnappers or been successfully extorted for fear of a repeat instance. Kidnapping can range from child-custody disputes to being a major source of revenue for terrorist groups like the FARC of Colombia. There is also a large business of extorting protection money from targeted victims: sort of kidnap insurance in reverse. In London, over $130 million is paid in KRE premiums (Lloyds collects $70 million).

A typical kidnapping is well planned; the victim is selected for the ability to pay a ransom and is usually grabbed as they leave for work in the morning. Although there is no such thing as a "typical" kidnapping, a recent study of kidnappings of foreign victims showed that 66 percent were released after negotiation, 5 percent escaped on their own, 9 percent were killed or died in captivity, and 20 percent were rescued. Roughly half were kept for 1 to 10 days. One-quarter were held from 11 to 50 days.

Kidnapping is a minor risk in developed countries, but a very real threat in underdeveloped nations. In Latin America, former Soviet Union/Central Asian states, and the Philippines it is a growth industry. About 90 percent of kidnappings took place in the 10 riskiest countries, with Colombia as the country with the most kidnappings. In Colombia, 10 people are snatched away every day. On average, forty percent of hostages are released once the ransom has been paid, about 30 percent are rescued beforehand, and approximately 10 percent are released when kidnappers give up their demands. Kidnappers in the Philippines now demand the names of two other likely victims and an estimate of their net worth before releasing rich children of ethnic Chinese they kidnap. That's cold. These numbers do not include Chechens sold back to their families by Russian soldiers.

## WHEN YOU ARE IN BAD HANDS

The first kidnapping insurance policy was written after the 1932 abduction and murder of aviator Charles Lindbergh's baby boy. At the time, the $50,000 demanded by the kidnappers was the highest amount ever demanded in the United States. Today the KRE business is a $130 million-a-year business for Lloyds. Companies like Hiscox are close mouthed about the policies they sell, the cost, and even who actually has policies.

Another UK-based company, Asset Security Management, say they protect over 1 million individuals with kidnapping insurance. Their site provides the latest info on kidnap events around the world and an electronic quote.

It is important to remember that most kidnappings are not recorded. In the case of Colombia, police estimate that 1,500 hostages are currently being held (150 of them foreigners) and that the actual number is much higher than these official estimates. Across the globe, many kidnappings go unreported because, as mentioned above, insurance companies and victims refuse to admit that they have paid off kidnappers for fear that it will happen again.

**Asset Security Management (ASM) Ltd.**
Tel.: (44) 0207 668 9400
Fax: (44) 0207 481 0351
enquiries@asm-uk.com
http://www.asm-uk.com

**Global List of Kidnapping Events**
http://www.mapreport.com/subtopics/c/k.html

## AN OLD GAME

Think kidnapping in Latin America is a new phenomenon? Wrong. The highest ransom ever paid was for the Incan Emperor Atahualpa in what is now Peru. When Francisco Pizarro invaded the Incan Empire in 1532, he took Atahualpa prisoner. Atahualpa was sentenced to death because he refused to become a Christian. So Pizarro cut him a deal. The king would be spared if the chief's people could fill his prison with gold and silver. Pizarro made off with about $250 million (in present dollars). Then, of course, they killed Atahualpa anyway. Things haven't changed much. Chikao Muramatsu, 52, a vice-president for Yazaki in Colombia, is being ransomed for between $5 and $8 million by the FARC in Colombia. It is indicative of the nature of the business that he was recently kidnapped at a roadblock by a group of armed men disguised as police, and then sold to the FARC for $250,000.

You won't be seeing too many Japanese plant managers on the sides of milk cartons. Statistically, in America the most common kidnapping victim is a child involved in a domestic custody dispute. The big money is when criminals snatch wealthy families or employees of multinationals. The most dangerous scenario is becoming a hostage kidnapped during a violent crime. Kidnaps of business executives are not statistically high, but they are favored targets because the crime usually results in a lucrative payout and little threat of violent retribution or capture afterward. Kidnapping is a crime that can be avoided or, at the very least, the risk can be reduced by simple awareness and preventative measures. Kidnappers will usually monitor a potential victim to determine routine and ease of snatch. If a prospective target is difficult to track, has adequate security, and could pose a problem, criminals will usually shift their attention to another individual.

If an executive is to be posted in a high-risk area, it is also wise to have kidnap and ransom (K&R) insurance, which pays for the careful negotiation and payment of the ransom as well as other losses incurred by the corporation and the individual. Insurance fees are completely dependent on the area of operations, exposure to risk, and number of people insured. It is important to note that some insurers will cancel coverage if the insured divulges that they have K&R insurance. It is assumed that this makes the insured an attractive target. Company or family policies are available with sensible coverage starting at $1 to $5 million.

If there is no insurance, the wisest choice is to contact a security company, like Control Risks Group or the Ackerman Group, which has experience in dealing with hostage and kidnapping situations. These types of companies will negotiate on behalf of the payee and take steps to insure the safety and well-being of the victim. If this option is not used, the kidnappers may resort to a number of well-known tricks to extort additional or multiple payments. Liaison with local police without a reliable and legitimate middleman may also result in kickbacks or additional money being required to free an individual. The purpose of a negotiator is to keep a positive, constructive dialog between the criminals and the contact. The ultimate goal is to ensure the health and return of the victim as well as arrange for a reduction in payment demands. The negotiator typically acts only as an advisor and mediator, using his or her experience in previous events and knowledge of the perpetrators as a guide.

Below are the Hiscox kidnapping statistics from 1992 to 1999.

## KIDNAPPING STATISTICS 1992 TO 1999

| Rank | Country | 1992 | 1993 | 1994 | 1995 | 1996 | 1997 | 1998 | 1999 | TOTAL |
|---|---|---|---|---|---|---|---|---|---|---|
| 1 | Colombia | 464 | 244 | 217 | 469 | 947 | 908 | 960 | 972 | 5,181 |
| 2 | Mexico | 46 | 87 | 31 | 48 | 109 | 275 | 436 | 402 | 1,269 |
| 3 | Russia/SU/C. Asia | 5 | 5 | 13 | 3 | 21 | 41 | 57 | 105 | 250 |
| 4 | Brazil | 94 | 66 | 73 | 56 | 65 | 67 | 43 | 51 | 515 |
| 5 | Philippines | 53 | 56 | 78 | 61 | 113 | 61 | 51 | 39 | 492 |
| 6 | Nigeria | 1 | 0 | 0 | 1 | 0 | 2 | 6 | 24 | 34 |
| 7 | India | 9 | 10 | 13 | 9 | 5 | 8 | 5 | 17 | 76 |
| 8 | Ecuador | 1 | 10 | 15 | 11 | 7 | 5 | 5 | 12 | 66 |
| 9 | Venezuela | 15 | 6 | 7 | 7 | 28 | 24 | 10 | 12 | 109 |
| 10 | South Africa | 0 | 0 | 0 | 1 | 0 | 0 | 0 | 10 | 11 |
| Total | | 683 | 484 | 447 | 666 | 1,295 | 1,391 | 1,573 | 1,644 | 7,773 |

*Source:* Hiscox, April 19, 2000 (http://www.hiscox.com)

If negotiations do not go well, it is not advised that corporations mount rescue attempts. Statistically, if the victim survives the initial snatch, the second most dangerous time is during an armed rescue operation. According to various sources, 40 to 70 percent of fatalities occur during these rescue attempts. More important, it puts the victim in extreme jeopardy and encourages retaliation against the victim since the kidnappers have no further reason to keep him or her alive. In essence, you now have the kidnappers trying to kill you and your rescuers trying to kill the kidnappers. There is also the danger of being wounded by friendly fire during the heated entry, snatch, and recovery. The greatest risk of death comes at the start and/or end of the ordeal when the kidnappers are tense and under extreme stress.

Insurance pays for hostage negotiation and expenses, ransom payment, lost wages, and psychological counseling. Most insurance companies work exclusively with a security company to retrieve their customer.

Each situation must be carefully researched and timely intelligence must be available. There have been a number of successful hostage rescues such as the Lima embassy event in Peru, and then there have been disasters like the Moscow theater debacle, but the common denominator has been patience, planning, practice, speed of execution, and absolute surprise (along with overwhelming force). There are also significant legal, political, local liaison, and ethical problems with conducting such operations on foreign soil. Liaison with local military and police is also fraught with problems of informers and corruption, which is common when large sums of money, criminal organizations, and publicity are involved.

Kidnapping also includes abducting people against their will for a variety of reasons. NGOs estimate that at least 700,000 people become

## AN ADVENTUROUS NEW ALTERNATIVE
## TO THOSE TEDIOUS SPA VACATIONS

Former interior minister for Mexico Fernando Gutierrez Barrios called newspaper editors in Mexico City to insist that he hadn't been kidnapped but had just been "on vacation." He disappeared for six days late in December 1997. Witnesses saw 12 armed men hustle him off the streets in Coyoacan. Officials later discovered a large bank withdrawal for $800,000, presumably for his six days of spa and bar charges.

victims of trafficking every year. Women are grabbed for prostitution, children nabbed for soldiering and portering. Even in ugly divorce settlements, domestic disputes can turn into kidnapping. Domestic disputes are estimated to result in 359,000 kidnappings a year, of which only 4,600 are the result of non-family members being involved in the kidnap.

So just what the heck is going on out there? The truth is, nobody knows. Even the police admit they are informed in maybe only 10 percent of kidnaps. Geography-wise, Latin America is the most dangerous place in the world for kidnappings. More than 7,000 people are kidnapped in Latin America every year. Colombia accounts for over 5,000 of those. Just under half of those kidnappings were carried out by FARC and ELN. Kidnapping is estimated to be a $200 million-a-year, tax-free business in Colombia. And they'll wait for their money. Three missionaries who were snagged in a remote village of southern Panama were held for over five years.

Brazil accounts for 800 kidnappings a year, with 104 in Rio alone. In Mexico, there are as many as 2,000 kidnappings a year where the average ransom is around $5,000 for regular folks, but in the multimillion-dollar range for bankers and businessmen. About 100 people are grabbed in Guatemala—mostly children of wealthy families and foreign workers. Ecuador and Venezuela each report around 200 kidnappings a year, and Peru estimates 100 hostages taken annually. In Honduras, primarily around the city of San Pedro Sula, former Salvadoran guerrillas have formed 10 gangs that kidnap about 120 people a year.

Keep in mind that all these statistics don't represent unreported snatches. Colombian groups are considered to be a major exporter of kidnapping to surrounding countries. Their M.O. is killing the families if they don't get the ransom. If kidnapping slows down, they could always work for a credit-card collection agency. Oh, and the latest twist? Police will kidnap the kidnapper's families: I'll raise you one three-year-old and meet your granny.

Don't assume that Europe is safe. There have been 53 abductions since 1989 in Italy; 19 in the UK; and the same number in Spain. Although the media report the big cases, most victims are ranchers and small businessmen. Foreign executives who work in the oil and energy industries are tops on most kidnappers' wish lists but aren't numerically high because of the security provided. The new trend is to snatch regular folks and then force their relatives to use their cash card to pay the ransom.

These days, Chubb, Fireman's Fund, AIG, and Lloyds of London will write policies designed to make sure you come back alive if you get abducted. The premiums run from US$2,500 to $100,000 a year, depending on where you plan to go and how long you plan to stay. Premiums for coverage of $500,000 to $1 million in most western European countries vary from $3,000 to $5,000 per annum. A policy affording coverage for a Russian family with up to 7 people in the household is $18,500 for $500,000 of coverage and $33,500 for $1 million. If you tell the insurers you are going to Chechnya, you'll get a polite giggle. Lloyds of London has experienced a 50 percent jump in policies written over the last 5 years, and more insurance companies are looking into offering the coverage. What do you get for your money? Actually, quite a bit. Insurers will pay for the ransom payment, medical treatment, interpreters, and even your salary while you are involuntarily detained. The services of a security company to help spring you (sorry, no Rambo for rent here) are included in the coverage.

> **O**h, and the latest twist? Police will kidnap the kidnapper's families: I'll raise you one three-year-old and meet your granny.

Chubb has the best deal in town; annual payments total about US$1,000 for every $10 million of ransom payments released. If you are deemed to be "high profile" or the target of previous kidnapping attempts, the premium skyrockets to US$25,000 a year. Kidnapping and ransom insurance for dangerous countries like Colombia cost around $20,000 a year for a million-dollar policy, but expect to pay $60,000 to $100,000 for a decent-sized policy. Coverage is about half that for Brazil. In addition to insurance, armored cars and armed bodyguards are big in Latin America. Expect to pay between $60,000 and $150,000 for an armor-plated Suburban or Lincoln. Armed bodyguards should run you about $90 to $250 a day, depending on the country

## WHAT, ME WORRY?

Should tourists be worried about being kidnapped? Probably not. Expats who live in foreign countries are at most risk, while the casual tourist or in-and-out business visitor are almost risk-free. Travelers who journey to remote regions in drug areas face a higher risk. Yes, some of the folks in the Philippines, Uganda, Yemen, and Colombia were tourists. But chalk it up to wrong place, wrong time. Yeah, they were looking for tourists, but they attacked with little warning and in areas that had not had serious problems before. On the other hand, all these regions are known for kidnapping and threats against foreigners.

you're in. One alarming development is the increase in kidnapping of small children of wealthy victims. The only positive note is that the ransom for kidnapped children is a cheap $2,000 to $5,000 with usually same-day turnaround to avoid expensive diaper bills.

You will most likely be blindfolded, gagged, and bound. If you squirm or bite, they'll thump you a few times to settle you down. Your first destination is a house or country hideout where you are kept in a room with no windows. To prove their point, they may photograph you with a Polaroid or record your voice on a cheap hand-held recorder. They may interrogate you to find out just how much you're worth. Then you will sit and wait, and wait, and wait. If they don't get their initial demands, they may cause you pain or remove body parts (little fingers are popular) to get their point across. What will eventually happen? It depends.

http://www.mopreport.com/subtropics/c/k.html

## HOW TO SURVIVE A KIDNAPPING

- Force yourself to be calm and compliant; there is little you can accomplish by reacting violently.
- Do whatever your captors tell you to do without argument.
- Communicate with your captors to make them understand that you want to stay alive.
- Take control of your mental and physical state. Develop a routine that will include mental and physical exercise.
- If you think you can escape, do so, but stop if you are under threat of death or being shot.
- If you are being rescued by armed troops or police, stay flat on the ground. Make it difficult for your captors to drag you away, but do not resist. The greatest risk of death is during a rescue attempt.

About 40 percent of all hostages are released safely after the ransom is paid. Not very good odds. Having an insurance policy will make your chances of generating the necessary number of bucks a lot easier. But you won't have a choice should someone try to storm the joint in a rescue effort. About 34 percent of hostages are rescued from their captives before the ransom is paid. Being saved is perhaps a hostage's greatest threat. Let's say your right-wing, NRA-supporting, big-game hunter boss (who voted for Ross Perot) says, "Get my boy outta there now!" He sends in a highly trained team of hand-picked ex-SEALs, kicked into action by a cigar-smoking buzz cut. Oops, he just screwed up.

So, what if your wife won't return the kidnapper's calls and your boss figures he really has no need for you because the temp is generating twice the business you did? Nearly 11 percent of kidnapping victims are released without payment, either through negotiation or the abductors' realization that they will not be paid. In Colombia, a mere 3 percent of kidnappers are convicted compared to 95 percent in the United States.

Want to know how to avoid being kidnapped? Stay away from suspect places, vary your routine, keep a low profile, stay out of the local papers, avoid society bashes, live low-key, use a driver/bodyguard, and stay on top of the local threat assessment.

The most dangerous phases of a hijacking or hostage situation are the beginning and, if there is a rescue attempt, the end. At the outset, the terrorists typically are tense and high-strung and may behave irrationally. It is extremely important that you remain calm and alert and manage your own behavior.

## Hostage Etiquette/Survival

Naturally everyone is an expert on being kidnapped . . . except the actual people who get kidnapped. I don't expect you to remember one single tip if you are kidnapped, but I urge you to adopt the general mantra of "be cool," do what you're told, and take the time to plan your move . . . should you want to make one. Generally, the more you cinematically yell "Help, help!" or "Let me go, you brute!" the less chance you have of thinking clearly.

- Avoid resisting and sudden or threatening movements. Do not struggle or try to escape, unless you are certain of being successful.
- Make a concerted effort to relax. Breathe deeply and prepare yourself mentally, physically, and emotionally for the possibility of a long ordeal.
- Try to remain inconspicuous; avoid direct eye contact and the appearance of observing your captors' actions. Harness your fear to think and plan.

- Consciously put yourself in a mode of passive cooperation. Talk normally. Do not complain, avoid belligerency, and comply with all orders and instructions.
- If questioned, keep your answers short. Don't volunteer information or make unnecessary overtures. Gather information from your captors.
- Don't try to be a hero, endangering yourself and others. They may put an informant in with you to gather information.
- Maintain your sense of personal dignity, and gradually increase your requests for personal comforts. Make these requests in a reasonable, low-key manner.
- If you are involved in a lengthy, drawn-out situation, try to establish a rapport with your captors; avoid political discussions or other confrontational subjects.
- Eat what they give you, even if it does not look or taste appetizing. A loss of appetite and weight is normal.
- Develop routines, mental activities, and challenges. Build a ship, write a book, create a code, learn the language. Keep sharp and active.
- Think positively; avoid a sense of despair. Rely on your inner resources. Remember that you are a valuable commodity to your captors. It is important to them to keep you alive and well.

## Kidnap, Rescue, and Extortion Insurance (KRE)

Who do you call when someone is kidnapped? Don't call Chuck Norris, Steven Seagal, or Jackie Chan. You'll probably end up dead. Don't even call the police; they will jack up the ransom demand and may be in cahoots with the kidnappers. You should call your insurance company, followed by the embassy, and a professional hostage negotiator. *DP* advises that anyone in a hostage situation contact a professional in their home country before they contact the local police. Better yet, educate yourself about the truth of kidnapping before you find out the hard way. You will find that it can be a bigger ordeal for the relatives or loved ones than for the kidnapped. There are also many twists, turns, and scams that can crush you with despair. You will need a strong friend.

Your best bet as an American is to contact the FBI. It is their job to negotiate the release of American kidnapping victims worldwide. They will make sure the country the abductee is in will allow U.S. law-enforcement officers to work there and then the local U.S. embassy must invite the FBI in. This can take time depending on how backwater you get. There have been some cases where the State Department doesn't want the FBI involved. Since 1990, the FBI has secured the release of over 60 victims. If you have purchased KRE, then you get the nongovernmental version with all expenses paid. Keep in mind, the FBI does not pay your ransom.

A typical KRE policy with a $1 million limit covers a family of 11 people. In Latin America, businesses are run by extended families, from grandparents down to grandchildren. An annual policy would cost from $7,000 in Brazil up to a maximum of $26,000 in Colombia. When you cover a business family, you will always schedule each person. Corporations usually buy blanket policies that cover all employees.

In most countries except Mexico and Colombia, unless you work for a large oil company, a $10 million policy for a Fortune 100 company will cost about $350,000 a year. Insurers like Seitlin also can write 1-shot, 1-month, $1 million KRE policies for travelers and business-people for between $2,500 and $3,000. Is it necessary? Well, Seitlin believes you'd be crazy to do business south of Miami without $5 to $10 million in KRE coverage. In Colombia, a ransom less than a million is considered a joke. It is estimated that these days about 65 percent of Fortune 500 companies provide kidnap insurance for their employees working overseas.

## More Kidnap Etiquette and Tips

- Try to avoid countries notorious for kidnapping: Colombia, Mexico, Chechnya, and Yemen are just some. Americans (foreigners) doing business for Fortune 100 oil and mining companies in Colombia are at highest risk; low-key backpackers and travelers are usually at low risk.
- Strange as it sounds, the odds of extracting you are better in areas where kidnapping is done in conjunction with the police. Brazil and Mexico are just two countries where kidnapping is a business conducted in conjunction with the local police. Areas where kidnapping is intertwined with Maoist or Marxist ideology are much harder. If you think these things happen fast, forget it. You better get used to watery bean soup and loose teeth; lengthy negotiations are always preferred over snazzy extractions.
- If someone you know is kidnapped, do not contact the police and do not talk to the press. Contact your embassy, the insurance company, and/or a security consultancy to take the next steps. If you have a KRE policy, someone will be dispatched to act as a counselor within hours.
- Tape-record or write down any messages and do not commit to anything until the counselor or security help arrives.

- Most security counselors will be ex-CIA, Mossad, or other intelligence service pensioners. The British firms pull from their own pool of ex-SAS, Scotland Yard, and MI-5 folks. By all means demand credentials and references. People are highly emotional and financially vulnerable during this period. Don't get taken.
- Your security counselor will not make any decisions, but he will facilitate the process and act as a coach, a mediator, and a go-between. They will usually set up a committee that analyzes input and demands and then makes decisions. Usually the decisions are: pay the money, stall, or negotiate the ransom downward. Not the best of jobs for amateurs or someone with emotional connections to the victim.
- The fatality rate on security-consultant–handled kidnappings is a reassuring 2 percent compared to 9 percent for homemade efforts. Part of the skew is because some kidnap deaths can occur at the attack—the victims may die of illness or heart attack, or they can be killed during rescue attempts.

## KRE Resources

### Insurers

#### Asset Security Managers Ltd.
Tel.: (44) 0207 668 9400
Fax: (44) 0207 481 0351
enquiries@asm-uk.com
http://www.asm-uk.com
> Specialists in kidnap insurance and response. Their site contains statistics, advice, and case studies.

#### The Chubb Corporation
15 Mountain View Road
Warren, NJ 07059
Tel.: (908) 903-2000
Fax: (908) 903-2027
http://www.chubb.com/businesses/ep/kr
> Chubb offers KRE coverage for busy executives with a healthy level of fear. Extortion can also cover computer hackers, contamination, or even a computer virus.

#### Lloyds of London
1 Lime Street
London, EC3M 7HA, UK
Tel.: (44) 020 7327 6272
http://www.lloydsoflondon.co.uk
> Lloyds, according to the *Independent,* is paying out over $10 million in kidnap claims a year. The Hiscox Group at Lloyds writes about 5,000 policies a year, about 60 percent of all KRE business. Lloyds uses Control Risks Group (http://www.crg.com) to handle the dirty work, and they become involved in 30 to 40 kidnappings a year. Ransoms paid can range from about $50,000 to over $30 million.

### Hiscox
1 Great St. Helen's
London EC3A 6HX, UK
Tel.: (44) (0) 20 7448 6000
Fax: (44) (0) 20 7448 6900
http://www.hiscox.com
enquiry@hiscox.com

Hiscox bills themselves as the "world's largest provider of specialist insurance for businesses and individuals at risk of kidnap, detention and extortion, accounting for 60 to 70 percent of worldwide premium income." They provide one of the broadest covers in the market and tailor their product to the client's needs. They include, as standard, insurance protection against: kidnap, bodily injury, extortion, products extortion, property damage extortion, hijack, and malicious detention. Hiscox works with Control Risks Group (http://www.crg.com). And they say that they have handled over 1,100 kidnap/extortion cases in 87 countries.

### American International Group (AIG)
http://www.aig.com

AIG is the second largest KRE insurance provider. They use Kroll O'Gara for the negotiation part. AIG is not as chatty as Lloyds (which maintains a tomb-like silence about the specifics of KRE clients), but would be good for a competing bid.

## Brokers

### Black Fox International, Inc.
P.O. Box 1187
205 Garvin Boulevard
Sharon Hill, PA 19079
Tel.: (800) 877-2445 or (610) 461-6690
Fax: (610) 586-5467
jc@black-fox.com
http://black-fox.com/kidnap.htm

### Seitlin
2001 NW 107 Avenue, Suite 200
Miami, Florida 33172
Tel.: (305) 591-0090
Fax: (305) 593-6993
postmaster@seitlin.com
http://www.seitlin.com

Seitlin is the largest insurance broker in Florida and also does a ripping business in kidnap/ransom insurance. Luckily, Seitlin says they only have to pay out about once or twice a year. Their clients include mostly wealthy Latin American families, corporations that do business south of the border, and employees of multinational corporations. They can provide policies from all the major insurance brokers.

## More Information and Contacts
http://www.insure.com/business/kidnapransom.html

**KIDNAPPING**

## Security Resources

Kidnapping may be big business, but security is bigger. Americans spend about $90 billion on security every year. We only spend $40 billion on public police. In California, there are four times as many private police as there are government police. In countries like Russia and South Africa, people don't even bother calling for the police. Areas affected by kidnapping also have a number of local firms that provide security and protection. Inquire at your local embassy or with other multinational companies about security resources.

### *Pinkerton Service Corporation*
U.S. Headquarters
200 South Michigan Avenue
Chicago, IL 60604
Tel.: (312) 322-8800
Fax: (312) 322-8636
http://www.pinkertons.com

Once on the trail of bank robbers in the Wild West, Pinkerton has gone global and high-tech. Today, you can get risk assessments of over 200 countries online or in person. Pinkerton offers access to a database of more than 55,000 terrorist actions and daily updated reports on security threats. For the nonactive, you can order printed publications that range from daily risk-assessment briefings to a monthly newsletter. Their services are not cheap, but how much is your life worth?

Annual subscriptions to the online service start at about U.S. $7,000, and you can order various risk and advisory reports that run from US$200 to $700 each. Pinkerton gets down and dirty with its counter-terrorism programs, hostage negotiators, crisis management, and travel-security seminars.

The service is designed for companies that send their employees overseas or need to know what is going on in the terrorist world. Some reports are

---

## SEITLIN & COMPANY: WHO YOU GONNA CALL?

Dying to know which security groups are called by insurance companies when you get kidnapped? Here is *DP*'s insider list. If you can correctly guess which ex-affiliations these groups hold (army, air force, CIA, Mossad, SAS, etc.), we'll send you a free Mr. *DP* shirt.

- Chubb uses the Ackerman Group.
- AIG uses Kroll Associates.
- Hiscox (Lloyds) uses Control Risks Group.
- Genesis (Lloyds) uses the Ackerman Group.
- Cigna uses Pinkerton's.

mildly macabre, with their businesslike graphs charting annual maimings, killings, assaults, and assassinations. Others are truly enlightening. In any case, Pinkerton does an excellent job of bringing together the world's most unpleasant information and providing it to you in concise, intelligent packages.

### Control Risks Group, London
1749 Old Meadow Road, Suite 120
McLean, VA 22102
Tel.: (703) 893-0083
Emergency Tel.: (703) 893-0083
Fax: (703) 893-8611
83 Victoria Street
London SW1H OHW, UK
Tel.: (44) 20-7222 1552
Emergency Tel.: London
  (44) 071 222 1552
Emergency Tel.: (Australia)
  (613) 9826-5540
http://www.crg.com

This international management consulting company specializes in political, business, and security risk analysis and assessments, due diligence and fraud investigations, preventative security and asset protection, crisis management planning and training, crisis response, and unique problem solving. With extensive experience in kidnapping, extortion, and illegal detention resolution, they have handled more than 700 cases in 79 countries. Control Risks has 14 offices around the world including Washington, DC, London, New York, Bogota, Mexico City, Bonn, Amsterdam, Manila, Melbourne, Moscow, Paris, Singapore, Sydney, and Tokyo.

Their international, political, and security risk-analysis research department is the largest of its kind in the private sector and has provided hundreds of companies with customized analyses of the political and security risks they may face doing business around the globe. An online Travel Security Guide addresses security issues in more than 100 countries.

### Kroll Risk Consulting Services, Inc
900 Third Avenue
New York, NY 10022
Tel.: (212) 593-1000
Fax: (212) 593-2631
http://www.krollworldwide.com

Kroll Risk Consulting is a security/investigative firm founded in 1972 by Jules Kroll and owned by Equifax (the credit info folks). In addition to gumshoeing on an international and corporate level, Kroll has a travel service that provides warnings about crime, medical concerns, and even such hazards as missing manhole covers (stolen by the thousands in Beijing to be sold as scrap metal). The reports are compiled from about 270 cities in 89 countries (including the United States). The Travel Watch is produced and distributed by Kroll Associates, a firm offering security and "risk-assessment" to corporate clients. The reports fill one 8" x 11" page and are delivered to the computers of about 29,000 travel-agency clients of SABRE, one of the industry's principal electronic reservation systems. Within the first 2 weeks of offering the

**KIDNAPPING**

## YEAH, BUT DID HE USE FUR-LINED HANDCUFFS?

Shannon Marketic, Miss U.S.A. 1992, filed suit against the Sultan of Brunei and others for $90 million, claiming she was held against her will as a "sex-slave" for over 1 month. Marketic took the gig along with six other women, thinking she was being hired for modeling and promo work. Upon arrival, her passport and tickets were taken away and she (and other members of her group) were expected to party with the sultan and his friends. She was released after contacting Jack Kemp, a personal friend, by smuggling a letter to her parents. The sultan's brother, Prince Jefri, is being sued by two former friends for $80 million (and he is countersuing for $100 million). It is alleged that Jefri would fly up to 50 women from around the world to Brunei for sex parties. The suit involved a property deal but interesting tidbits were injected into evidence. For example, Jefri is supposed to have bought 10 gold watches decorated with mechanically copulating couples and a set of 10 pens made by Gerald Genta of Geneva in which the top of the pen appears to be copulating with the bottom. The charges were later dropped.

reports in June, Kroll Travel Watch reported about 10,000 requests. The reports are free through travel agency requests. For more information or a Travel Watch for your destination, contact your travel agent or purchase the reports from Kroll directly. Although purchased by an armor car plating company, they have been spun off as a separate business and returned to the name Kroll.

### Investigative Resources Global, Inc. (IRG)

7621 Little Avenue, Suite 426
Charlotte, NC 28226
Tel.: (704) 341-0101
or (800) 694-2313
http://www.irg_siu.com/IRG/irghome.
htm

Investigative Resources Global (IRG) provides training and assistance in kidnapping prevention and resolution. They have offices in London, Sydney and the United States.

### Ackerman Group

166 Kennedy Causeway, Suite 700
Miami Beach, FL 33141
Tel.: (305) 865-0072
Fax: (305) 865-0072
info@ackermangroup.com
http://ackermangroup.com

Mike Ackerman specializes in crisis resolution or hostage return through providing the financial and security resources required to resolve hostage situations safely.

### TroubleShooters International Inc.

Tel.: (403) 302-1691
Tel.: (403) 885-5273
snowflake@tshooters.com
wfirecan@ccinet.ab.ca
Contact: Bob Ketcheson
http://www.tshooters.com

Ex-U.S.-military folks who freelance for hostage situations and can provide aviation services for overseas extractions. They can provide assistance for executive protection, hostage retrieval, and missing person searches.

### Safenet International (SI)

1835A S. Centre City Parkway
PMB 405
Escondido, CA 92025
Tel.: (760) 207-3103
si@safenetinternational.com
http://www.safenetinternational.com

Safenet International (SI) is a security company dedicated to aggressive, discreet, professional security solutions for corporate and private clients, created for the express purpose of assisting individuals and companies with unique security needs. They provide information concerning worldwide privacy and safety and execute the means to secure and maintain them. The four areas of service that SI provides are:

1. *Hostage Rescue:* pursuing the kidnappers, with the goal of safely recovering the hostage
2. *Ransom Recovery:* providing the means for corporations and insurance companies to re-coup their losses
3. *Corporate Security:* furnishing any unique security needs an organization may have; and,
4. *Private Security:* providing personal security services.

# LAND MINES/UXO

## Boom Times

If there were ever a reason to pay attention in history class, land mines would be it. Why? Because travelers to dangerous places need to know more than the current situation; they must also know why and where wars were fought in the past. There may be peace in Afghanistan, Mozambique, China, Jordan, the Ukraine, or even Belgium, but there are plenty of souvenirs from past wars hiding in the ground. Statistics tell us that someone is killed or injured by a land mine every 15 to 20 minutes. Most land-mine victims die in silent agony, unseen, unknown, and uncounted.

Right now there are 88 nations affected by land mines or unexploded ordnance (UXO). There have been new victims in 71 countries since March 1999. Oddly, 39 of those countries were at peace. The highest number of casualties come from Myanmar, Angola, Chechnya, and Kosovo. There are demining programs in 41 countries and assessments have been made in 24 more nations. From Nepal to Senegal to Colombia to the Congo, new land mines are being planted waiting for the day that you decide to visit.

You might find it a little depressing with all the politically correct posturing of the first world that NATO dumped about 15,000 mines on Kosovo. The Russians are spreading love and joy via tiny air-dropped land mines along the Chechen/Georgia border and plenty of other signatories to the Land Mine Ban Treaty are busy ignoring what they promised. In case you feel smug, Uncle Sam dropped over 20,000 bombs in Afghanistan, and not all of them exploded. Up to 20 percent in some strikes are still waiting to be found.

Last year there were land mines used by 11 governments and 30 rebel groups in 20 conflicts worldwide. Land mines can cost as little as $3 but destroy a person for life, causing untold financial and emotional damage with very little effort. There are supposed to be 80 million land mines still buried in the ground and 24,000 new victims every year.

The truth is nobody actually knows exactly how many mines there are since the people who placed them never bothered to remember their exact location. Yes, sometimes there are detailed maps, but rarely. Consequently, the people who find them remember it for the rest of their lives—if they survive the blast.

Even though land mines maim and kill between 20,000 and 24,000 men, women, and children every year, many governments claim they are not a threat to travelers. Even agencies like Greenpeace and the CDC contend the death toll is more like 9,600. Mine clearance groups estimate that the number is 15,000, with about 80 percent being civilians and a third of those being young children. (Some antimine groups estimate 37,000 are killed every year.) The truth is there are few little red signs in the boonies and even fewer keeping count of the deaths and maimings. Being injured by a land mine is one of the most traumatic experiences, both mentally and physically, a human can live through.

Eighty-five percent of current mine-related casualties are in Afghanistan, Angola, and Cambodia—all sites of past and present dirty little wars where land mines are the perfect weapon. With so many mines, it only takes one false step to be killed or maimed for life. As more and more adventure travelers head into the remote regions of Laos, Vietnam, Cambodia, and other remote regions, they will learn firsthand the effects of land mines and UXO. The numbers of hidden land mines seem to grow exponentially. Depending on whom you believe, it could take up to 1,100 years and $33 billion to remove all the world's land mines. A million people have supposedly been injured by land mines since 1975. Once again, nobody really knows, and in places like Chechyna, Angola, and Afghanistan, mines continue to be planted while groups work to remove them at the same time.

## More Than You Ever Want to Know about Mines

The next time someone tells you that it is those crazy Russians and liberation groups that sprinkle the world with mines, you might want to check the receipts of the countries that are buying land mines. According to *Jane's Intelligence Review,* Iran, Israel, Cambodia, Thailand, Chile, El Salvador, Malaysia, and Saudi Arabia top the list. Tsk, tsk, you say. Well, those folks have good reasons to buy those land mines: Iran had a nasty border war with Iraq, Israel gets grief from all of its neighbors, Cambodia had the Khmer Rouge to contend with, Thailand has drug runners, Chile has Paraguay, El Salvador had jungle insurgents, and Malaysia still has vivid memories of a nasty war with Indonesia back in the early '60s. All this is history to journalists but not to the land mines still sitting patiently in the ground.

So just who are those evil amoral people who make these things and where are those nasty places those mines deserve to be put in? The answers may surprise you.

### Sites on land mines
http://www.icbl.org
http://www.landminesurvivors.org
http://www.clearlandmines.com
http://www.banmines.org
http://www.landmines.org

The most industrious and creative producers of land mines are not the Cold War vassal states but the high-tech Western countries who

### WHO MAKES 'EM

Landmine Monitor estimates that there are more than 250 million antipersonnel mines in the arsenals of 105 nations, with the biggest estimated to be China (110 million), Russia (60–70 million), Belarus (10–15 million), United States (11 million), Ukraine (10 million), Pakistan (6 million), and India (4–5 million). Of the 16 nations who are still producers, eight are in Asia (Burma, China, India, North Korea, South Korea, Pakistan, Singapore, and Vietnam), three are in Europe (Russia, Turkey, FR Yugoslavia), three are in the Middle East (Egypt, Iran, Iraq), and two are in the Americas (Cuba, the United States). There are no producers in Africa. There are over 340 types of antipersonnel landmines (AP) that have been produced by over 100 companies in 52 countries around the world.

make such a big stink about all those little kids who get blown to bits. There are 100 different companies in 55 countries that make land mines. Of the 55 countries who design and manufacture antipersonnel mines (about 75% of all land mines), 36 of the countries allow them to be exported. Keep in mind that many mines are bought through shell companies who import them into "nice" countries and then export them to "nasty" countries. Even Switzerland makes and sells five models, while Iran, Cuba, and Myanmar are able only to make one model of land mine. There are billions of mines stockpiled and ready for export should you need them. So, is anyone not using land mines?

Well, *DP* has been up on the lines and we watch the kids place them as if they were planning for an Easter egg hunt. But Uncle Sam doesn't like us to watch them in use in places like Guantanamo Bay in Cuba or the oddly named DMZ in Korea. So don't believe all that hair-shirt stuff about not using land mines. They are an integral part of military training for every armed force around the world (except maybe the Papal Guards). Here's a list of where you can shop for the more than 300 different models of land mines.

### STUMPS 'R' US: WHO DESIGNS 'EM

| Country | # of Models Sold |
| --- | --- |
| United States | 37 |
| Italy | 36 |
| Russia | 31 |
| Sweden | 21 |
| China | 21 |
| Germany | 18 |
| Vietnam | 18 |
| France | 14 |
| Bosnia-Herzegovina | 16 |
| Austria | 16 |

*Source:* Jane's Intelligence Review

## How Are They Used?

Mines are a defensive and psychological weapon. When you don't want Omar and his brigands disturbing your sleep, you string a perimeter with trip wires, and sleep tight. If you need to control a rebel activity, you mine the waterholes, paths, garden patches, and storehouses. That way, rebels can eat, but only while hopping on one foot using one hand. If you want to mess up an entire country, you just drop mines from planes, shoot them from shells, mine waterways, power stations,

## IT'S A DIRTY JOB, BUT . . .

Princes Diana was one of the first celebrities to lend her time to publicizing the problem of land mines. Her death left a gap that has been filled by the widow of the former King of Jordan. American-born, 47-year-old Lisa Najeeb Halaby, or Queen Noor, has taken up the cause. Queen Noor comes from a country that is dramatically affected by land mines and she has proved to be a tireless supporter of a number of programs around the world designed to aid victims, remove mines, and forever eliminate them.

You can e-mail her at hmqoff@hmrc.gov.jo or visit her web site at http://www.noor.gov.jo/main/ip.htm.

highways, and whatever. This ensures the entire country is plunged back into the Stone Age.

Then, of course, your politicians get bored of whatever political manifesto you were protecting and you go home. During hostilities, your minefields were carefully marked with skull-and-crossbones "Beware of mine" signs and carefully fenced off. You backed up these dangerous places with accurate maps showing placement and layout.

Naturally, your land mines were all laid according to pre-agreed military patterns in a standard defensive area. One such NATO pattern is an A pattern, with one antitank mine surrounded by three antipersonnel mines: one above and one on each side like a triangle with the antitank in the middle—the polite way to kill advancing troops and blow up vehicles.

After the war, your nice troops cleaned up all the land mines and handed over the maps to local leaders. Uh-huh. If you come from a super-nice, super-PC country, you also cleaned up all the dud shells, mortars, chemicals, armories, and cap guns you left lying around. Sure, double uh-huh.

Now the war is over, allowing people to live their lives free from fear, safe in their newly created democracy.

That is wishful thinking, since the most effective way to sow land mines is to drop millions of small plastic mines by shell or from aircraft. Small bomblets, 247 to a pod, are dropped as part of cluster bombs. Most rebel groups will put mines in potholes, in detours, along walking paths, and in fields; they'll even booby trap intriguing items that villagers, soldiers, or children will pick up. Guerrillas don't follow patterns. Nobody knows how many mortar rounds, artillery shells, and discarded ordnance will be discovered by curious children or diligent farmers. No one bothers to keep notes of where mines are planted as booby traps or nightly security perimeters. After the war, whoever loses gets their butts kicked out of the country, booby-traps or blows up every arms cache in sight, and leaves behind mountains of useless weapons and material.

Now the shattered economy creates an instant market for the copper and brass used to make mines. Kids will search all day for bombs, mortars, bullets, and mines. Many of them like to play with these items and see if they can blow them up. I once found a large, shiny, unexploded Urgan missile that some kid had hammered open with a chisel to reveal 12 cluster bombs just waiting to go off.

In the country, mines are used to disrupt agriculture and commerce. When things stop, the mines are sitting in rice paddies, along rivers, in wells, and under houses. The overgrown trails and fields soon give up their deadly harvest to ploughs, shovels, and children playing.

The problem of land mines is not so much the human cost but the destruction of vast areas of vital food growing and pastures.

## How Do They Work?

Most people picture the movie cliché of a careless GI hearing a soft click and then sweating buckets while his buddy slides his knife under his boot to keep the detonator depressed on what should be a plate-sized antitank mine. Close, but not quite real. Yes, mines are essentially dumb explosive devices that are detonated by pressure, but weapons' designers have learned a few tricks since those World War II movies.

Most mines are antipersonnel devices, cheap, small, and designed to maim rather than kill. A wounded soldier is a bigger drain on the enemy than a dead one. Some mines are put just under the ground to blast upward while other mines are used above ground to spray debris or ball bearings. These mines are usually planted to protect camps, set ambushes, or slow down chasing soldiers. In more brutal wars, mines are used to deny locals access to water, food, or agriculture. Typically they use a trip wire and are never marked or documented.

A mine contains extremely explosive material that creates a wall of air and debris that expands outward at almost 7,000 meters per second. Some mines add metal projectiles like ball bearings, sharp flechettes, or even nails that puncture soft flesh and shred bone into a fine spray. The shock waves are so strong that many victims leave their feet still in their boots while their bones are turned into projectiles that kill other people.

If you don't die of blood loss, shock, or as a result of being turned into Swiss cheese, infection is your worst enemy. The explosion will imbed bits of clothing, grass, mud, dirt, and your trusty guide into the shredded mass of meat that used to be your legs. You will need to apply a tourniquet and get to a hospital (yeah, sure, there's probably one around the next sand dune) ASAP. Once you're under medical care,

## LIQUID LUNCH IN A CRUNCH

Many times victims of gunshot wounds, mine blasts, and injuries caused by blood loss don't have to die. In order to create an IV solution to provide minimum nutrition and increase blood pressure, it is important to know how to administer an IV injection. If you do not have a sterile IV solution, one can be made by taking one liter of sterile freshwater (filtered, then boiled for five minutes and cooled while covered). Add 25 grams of glucose and 4.5 grams of table salt. In emergency cases, the juice from a green coconut can be used with just the salt added.

the mashed bits will be quickly amputated and you'll be punched with an IV and given enough morphine to kill a junkie.

Other mines have cute names like Bouncing Betty, because they spring up and explode at eye level, releasing a lethal explosion of ball bearings, killing everything within 25 meters, and wounding everyone else within 200 meters. Road mines are so large and powerful that there is a crater and little else left over. Enough scary stuff; let's get specific. Here are the basic types of land mines used today.

### Scatter Mines

The Soviet-made PFM-1 butterfly-type mine delivers specialized deadly services. These small mines are sprinkled all over Afghanistan by Russians to injure, but not kill, mujahideen. The idea is that a wounded person slows down two healthy people. These mines are dropped from helicopters and burrow into the ground using tiny wings. They explode when twisted or pressed firmly—but not necessarily the first time. These mines have not found wide usage, but are a disturbing use of lethal force. They do not always explode when first handled and can actually be kicked, dropped, and twisted before they explode, leading some people to believe that the Russians designed them to kill curious children. There also are "smart" scatter mines that can arm themselves, detonate without direct pressure, and self-detonate after a specified period. These smart mines are delivered by cannon, airplane, or rocket.

### Antipersonnel, Small

Foot soldiers can't carry big heavy mines, so they make a lot of little plastic mines that can be tucked under footpaths, houses, latrines, and rice paddies. These mines are about the size of an oversized hockey puck and have a pressure-sensitive plate that the victim steps on. These mines are usually not buried but placed under brush, streams, wet pot-holes, rice paddies, and mud. The mine takes very little pressure to set it off, and the victim will usually lose a foot and/or a leg up to the knee. These mines are not designed to kill but to create serious, incapacitat-ing injuries that affect the morale of the other side. No one feels gung-ho when they see the results of a mine. Top sellers in this category are the Chinese Type 72, Italian TS-50, and U.S. M14. These mines are very difficult to find, since many of them use plastic casings and cannot be readily picked up by normal metal detectors.

## Antipersonnel, Large

These killer-blast mines usually pack about 200 grams of explosive (compared to 40 grams in the small category). The best-selling Soviet PMN likes to deliver leg-shattering wounds caused by small mines with higher explosive content. They are used to maim groups of soldiers: severe wounds to groin and buttocks and loss of both legs are common. These and their smaller cousins are the most popular mines. They cost about U.S.$3 each and can be found still killing and maiming people in most third-world war zones. There are also large versions of these pres-sure mines that can kill entire platoons. These mines are typically buried just under the surface and can be found easily if they have metal parts.

## Fragmentation Mines

Mines like the U.S. M18A1 "Claymore" were developed during the Korean War to slow down massive Chinese troop assaults. The curved flat mine is mounted on legs and designed to spray large areas with 700 ball bearings embedded in a sheet of C4 explosives. When detonated, they are deadly up to 50 meters in a 60-degree arc. Other fragmenta-tion mines like the grenade-on-a-stick style Russian POMZ-2 explode into thousands of sharp metal pieces. These mines are set up as booby traps with trip wires and are used to protect camp perimeters or to ambush columns along trails. The mines are placed above ground, on trees, across narrow paths, inside buildings, along roads, or anywhere a group of soldiers would collect. One soldier trips over the wire, and instantly he and his buddies are killed or injured. You can learn how to defuse them at http://www.angola.npaid.org/mine_russia_pomz2.htm.

There are also the Bouncing Betty type of fragmentation mines called "bounding" mines. They are designed to be buried in the ground in open areas, and when one of the whisker-like sensors is triggered, the mine will project upward and explode ball bearings or shrapnel in a lethal 360-degree radius. The Italian-made Valmara-69 is the most famous example of this mine. The explosion occurs at a three- to five-foot height, maximizing the "kill ratio" (a popular term in all military sales films). Some mines have over 1,000 individual pieces of shrapnel, so the chances of surviving by ducking or turning sideways are slim to none.

These mines are designed to be lethal and are left behind to slow down advancing armies, decimate charges, and create maximum casualties.

### Chinese Stick Grenades

Chinese stick grenades are stuck on sticks a foot above ground and have a lethal blast radius of 30 yards. They are often strung together in groups of six, and used as booby traps on roads with trip wires. Birds and a strong breeze can also set them off. The Eritreans used them extensively.

## Antitank Mines

The mines that do the most damage to wartime soldiers and peacetime mine clearance workers are the big plate-sized and plank-size tank killers. These are mines laid down in active war zones to disable vehicles, kill the occupants, and destroy the road. The British L9 and the Italian VS-22 are popular mines used in the Gulf War and in other combat zones. Some, like the VS-22, have less metal than a gum wrapper, so don't be too confident when you see the guards sweep the road.

> **W**hat are your chances of finding one of these millions of mines? Pretty good, if you contribute to *DP*. Not so easy if you stay on the beaten path.

Road mines are also used in convoy ambushes and can be detonated by radio-controlled explosives. Since these mines are easy to detect and are placed around major transportation corridors, they are usually the first ones to be cleared up (or to be run over).

### Other Mines and Hidden Dangers

If you really are kinky about mines, you can pick up a *Jane's* directory or send for brochures. There are many booby traps that are not technically mines. There are also extraordinary amounts of unexploded ordnance in the ground that may not jump up and bite you, but can be found displayed in villager's homes and souvenir shops.

What are your chances of finding one of these millions of mines? Pretty good, if you contribute to *DP*. Not so easy if you stay on the beaten path. Most, if not all, mined areas are known to locals and their victims tend to be children and women working their daily chores. Soldiers are maimed and mine clearance people do have accidents.

## Where Are the Mines?

No one knows. Despite what you read here or elsewhere, no one knows how many mines there are at any one time. Mines are being laid as you read this in any place where defensive positions are being created. Eighteen African countries have between 18 and 30 million mines each (did you ever see anyone count them, though?).

Angola has the most land mines, between 9 and 20 million uncleared mines, and even the "lightly mined" countryside of Mozambique (with about 2 million) has turned many small roads into deathtraps and caused large game to vanish. Somalia has 1 million mines; Sudan has between 1 and 2 million (and growing); and Zimbabwe and Ethiopia have major uncleared minefields (about half a million mines each).

http://www.africapolicy.org/docs01/lm0102.htm
http://www.angola.npaid.org

Bosnia-Herzegovina, Cambodia, and Croatia are the most mined countries in the world, with an average of between 92 and 142 land mines per square mile. This can be misleading, because the mines in Egypt are sitting in the remote northern deserts and the mines in Angola are in small towns and fields. All of East Asia has 15 to 23 million land mines. The Middle East has 17 to 24 million land mines, mainly in Iraq, Iran, Kuwait, and the Israeli border. Saddam Hussein went a little overboard during his brief occupation of Kuwait and turned the entire country into a minefield, most of which has been cleaned up at great expense. Europe is home to 7 million mines, mostly along the former Soviet border. During World War I, 7 countries fired nearly 1.5 billion shells. Ninety-five percent of them were conventional explosives; the rest were chemical shells. It is estimated that 30 percent of the chemical shells landed without ever exploding and have been sitting around since 1918. Most of the shells were used in Belgium. The Ukraine is home to over a million mines. Russia has both new minefields and World War II fields that were never cleared. Bosnia-Herzegovina has many uncleared fields, and new mines were being laid at a rate of 60,000 a week. At last count, there were 152 mines per square mile in this torn-up land.

Up to a million uncleared mines are left in South America. There are mines in Colombia, Chile, and most areas of Nicaragua, Guatemala, and even Cuba. Some areas of the Falklands are permanently off-limits because the British could not spare the men to clear the minefields. There is a lot of splattered mutton every week in the Falklands.

Most countries in southern Africa have large mined areas, as do the entire Horn of Africa, all areas of Middle East conflict, and most border areas from the Cold War. Although there are no mines in North America, we did send a few overseas. If you thought the United States didn't do this type of thing, think again. Remember that Uncle Sam used to empty out bomb loads over Laos, leaving millions of cluster bombs for little Laotians to discover. More than 300,000 tons of bombs were dropped on northern Laos during the Vietnam War. No one has any idea how much unexploded ordnance still lies in the jungles of northern Vietnam. The overly cautious should understand that, along with cigarette butts, ammo containers, and mixed-race children, land mines are just the litter of war.

## How Do You Get Rid of Land Mines?

There are movements by the UN, military, and civilian groups (about 300 groups in total) to ban the manufacture and use of land mines. The Mine Ban Treaty tries to make countries accountable, but both warring and non-warring nations love the nasty leg poppers too much. The chances are good of convincing first-world countries of a ban, but the facts are that the most heavily mined countries are a result of dirty wars, not major conflicts. The majority of land mines have been planted in the last 20 years. Currently, 36 nations export land mines and most countries use them. These countries produce about 10 to 20 million units a year. About 2 million new land mines are laid each year depending on what conflicts are raging. The United States still budgets millions for land mine warfare every year.

### SOME FOLKS GROW POTATOES

Yes, you can adopt your very own minefield. The United Nations Association of the United States of America (UNA-USA) and its Adopt-a-Minefield™ program have raised more than $2.9 million, including contributions from the U.S. Department of State's Office of Humanitarian Demining Programs, since March 1999 to clear minefields in Afghanistan, Bosnia-Herzegovina, Cambodia, Croatia, and Mozambique. For information, visit http://www.landmines.org, e-mail: info@landmines.org, or call (212) 907-1300, or fax: (212) 682-9185.

The first task a newly stabilized country faces is cleaning up land mines. Traditional land mines are cleared in a variety of ways. In large open areas, tracked vehicles with flailing chains can clear most mines. In less accessible or poorer areas, the old-fashioned metal detector is used. Some new Scheibel-type models can detect many plastic versions. Some countries use the old-fashioned method of probing at a shallow angle with knives. Sniffing dogs can be used, along with a raft of new high-tech methods employing radar, sonar, thermal neutron, microwave, and even satellites. For now, most mines are detected and dug up the old-fashioned way, by hand, or the painful way—by foot. Wildly speculative estimates on the costs to remove the world's land mines come in at about $33 billion.

There were 7 million land mines laid in Iraq and Kuwait before and during the Gulf War. Kuwait spent $800 million clearing out land mines after the Gulf War.

It costs between $500 and $2,000 per mine to remove them. A few years ago, 80,000 to 100,000 mines were removed around the world at a cost of $100 million. To remove all the mines in the world, it would cost $58 billion. Unfortunately, 2 to 5 million mines are put in the ground every year.

A *DP* reader who spends much of his time in mined areas while working for the UN Rapid Response Unit has sent in these tips:

## WHEEL OF MISFORTUNE

### HOW TO AVOID LAND MINES

1. Never be the first on the road in the early morning. Most mines are laid at night to surprise regular convoys or patrols. Try to follow heavy trucks. Keep at least 200 yards behind, but do not lose sight of the truck.
2. Never take point. (Let others start walking or driving before you.) Keep a distance of at least 60 to 100 feet to avoid shrapnel. If someone is wounded by a mine, apply a tourniquet immediately to the damaged limbs to prevent death by blood loss. Carry a wound kit and IV equipment if you can.
3. If a mine goes off, DO NOT RUN. Stay where you are, and walk backward in your own tracks. Retrieve the victim by following their tracks, but only if you are feeling lucky.
4. In heavily mined areas, NEVER leave the pavement (even to take a leak). If you must turn your vehicle around, do so on the pavement.

5. If you have a flak jacket or bulletproof vest, wear it when walking and sit on it when driving.
6. Know the local mining strategy of the combatants. Do they place mines in potholes (as in northeastern Somalia) or on the off-road tracks made by vehicles avoiding potholes (as in Rwanda, Burundi, and Congo)? Ask the locals: Do they booby trap? Are they dropped by air? Do they mine rivers? Use trip wires? What about UXO?
7. Mines are usually planted at a shallow depth, with their detonators requiring downward pressure. When trapped in a minefield, and only as a last resort, mines can be probed using a long knife or rod inserted at a very shallow angle and with a very gentle touch. If you live in the area, do not touch or remove the mine, but mark it for later removal or detonation. Red-painted stones or a barrier of sticks with fabric is the third-world method of marking mines.
8. Never touch unusual or suspicious objects. Bodies, money, a camera, or even your own equipment may have been booby-trapped at night or in your absence.
9. Travel with all windows open and preferably with doors off or in the back of a pickup truck. This will relieve some of the blast when you hit a mine.
10. If you have reason to believe that there has been mine activity (new digging, unusual tire tracks, or footprints), mark the area with a skull and crossbones and the local or English word "MINES." Red-painted rocks are another common method of identifying mine areas. Notify local and/or foreign authorities.

## IN A DANGEROUS PLACE: KABUL

### THE MINEFIELDS (MARCH 1997)

They say that Kabul is the most destroyed city on Earth. I am sure it is. I am getting used to driving by mile after mile of destroyed office flats, elegant buildings, and brick houses. The factions of Dostum, Massoud, and Hekmatyar duked it out until the Taliban kicked them out. All you hear now is the odd rocket attack and of course the occasional accidental detonation of a mine.

But that's why I was here, to understand about mines and the people who clear them. I had spent a week with the demining dogs: big, burly German shepherds and Belgium Malanoise handled by big, burly Afghans.

The Afghans had to grow beards under Taliban rule, and they looked odd with their U.S.-army-green uniforms. The demining program used to be run by Americans and when the money and supplies ran out, the Afghans just took the old uniforms to the Pakistani tailors in Peshawar. When we first drove along the trunk road to their head-quarters, my cabdriver's eyes widened at the sight of the great black beards and fearsome-looking dogs.

"Talibs?" he inquired.

I laughed and shook my head, but he disappeared quickly. Here in Peshawar at the Mine Detection Center, or MDC, the Afghans were actually breeding and training their own dogs to clear land mines in Afghanistan. What was once a $12,000 U.S.-bred and -trained police dog had become a $300 Afghan demining dog.

The dogs are trained by one trainer from when they are puppies. The concept is simple. Put a reward with whatever you want the dog to find and he will think he is having fun. In this case a red rubber ball is buried with various explosives, metallic objects, and mines. The dog quickly learns to sniff out the telltale scent and is rewarded by his handler.

Then the dogs are trained to walk straight out, sniff, and come back. If the dog sniffs a mine, he sits and indicates. If they get excited and jump around, they could set off the mine. It's a simple business, but the dog has to know what it is doing.

Crossing the border between Pakistan and Afghanistan is an instant education as to why the MDC crew is based in Pakistan. This morning there has been a shootout. Something silly, but the young slack-jawed Talibs picked up their battered green rocket launcher and hit the top of a building on the Pakistani side. There was machine gunfire, and then pleading from the Pakistanis: "Brothers, please stop shooting." Within minutes, life on the border was back to normal, or as normal as Tor-kham can be.

The flow of bent-over, dirty children carrying burlap bags is a flood of brown between tall Pakistani soldiers who stand like sweatered tele-phone poles above. We are waved through because our presence was aiding the torrent of gunnysack-carrying kids. The kids are carrying scrap, junk, bits of wire, old bullets, tins, anything metal. They are greasy and black and bent over from the weight. You know you are in a poor country when the children smuggle junk.

I spent time in Jalalabad, a few yards down the road from the road to Osama bin Laden's compound. I am warned not to walk around, so I do. I am pulled off the street by another demining crew, one that uses manual methods of finding mines. They invite me for breakfast and say "Only brave men work in the mine fields." They wish they had dogs, but they use metal probes and share a battered mine-detector.

We spend our time in the minefields of Jalalabad finding and blow-ing up Russian and Italian antitank mines. The Italian mines are made of plastic and have only a tiny metal pin in them. There are also antipersonnel mines around each tank mine. Off in the distance, the snow-covered mountains of the Hindu Kush frame the Kuchi nomads wandering through the mined pass. "Why do they not trip the mines?" I ask. I am told, "They do."

Often the mines are covered by years of erosion and dirt. But they are also uncovered by the same process. We pull up a silver canister—a Russian mine that listens and feels and then detonates. The batteries have long since gone dead but it is a truly evil invention. Many of the mines are booby trapped by other mines. That's why they are blown in place. The first land to be cleared is the roads, followed by habitations, then farmlands, and then large areas like this. Things are looking good. They will hand over this area next week. While we blow the antitank mines, the buses and cars don't even stop to admire the 60-meter-high mushroom clouds.

I almost make it to Kabul, but the demining crew must turn back. The Taliban are impounding their vehicles and they warn me we must drive back as soon as possible.

I make my own way back to Kabul, and I arrive at the headquarters of the UN demining program. There are plenty of statistics and hand-outs, but the bottom line is that under the Talibs they are making good headway. There is no more fighting, and other than being told to leave mines on the strategic hilltops and around the airports, progress is good. But Kabul is not doing so well. These ruins I drive by every day used to be someone's home. The children playing in the blasted streets and ruins are being injured by mines and UXO. Part of keeping them alive is to educate children about mines.

Some 55 percent of land-mine victims are children, but about 85 percent of the UXO victims are children. The most at risk are young men collecting the metal from bombs to sell as scrap. Most injuries are not caused by accidents, but occur when kids deliberately seek out weapons of death to sell as scrap for pennies. Now I understand why the Talib checkpoints had mountains of trash along with degutted cassette tapes.

At 3:20 PM, a BM-22 Urgan (Hurricane) missile with high explosives slams into Kabul; there is more to come. You get used to rockets, even when you play volleyball here. People look up, measure the distance to the nearest sandbagged bunker, and wait for the telltale whoosh. If it's outgoing, the game goes on.

Today, it's off to the disposal site to see how they get rid of ordnance. I cruise by the closed U.S. embassy in Najibullah Square. As we drive out of town, a silver Taliban Toyota with mirrored windows and chrome roll bars speeds up beside us. A Taliban rolls down the window and stares inside as he drives by. Satisfied, he speeds up and blasts off, scattering children and old men in front of him.

We go to the Polygon, a former military base and tank-firing range to the east of Kabul. Mohammad Zahir is a former colonel in the Afghan army and head of the disposal unit. He knows firsthand the problem with incoming rockets. He had a Russian Luna rocket land 500 yards from his backyard 2 weeks ago.

On display is a spectrum of ordnance ranging from a 500-kilogram concrete-piercing bomb that would demolish a pillbox or building to a 23-millimeter cannon shell fuse that could take off a hand.

The only items that are here are the ones that are determined to be stable. The more dangerous ordnance is destroyed on-site. To blow up the bombs, they use a ballistic disk to explode into the side casing of the bomb and burn off the explosives.

There is a hodgepodge of ordnance laid out for our inspection. The most ominous sight is an Urgan rocket missile that has been smashed open with a chisel by some local to see what was inside. Inside is a cluster of 9 or 12 high-explosive bomblets. The man in charge here is Andrew McAndrew, a Scotsman. He is supervising the local Afghans in destroying this deadly harvest.

> **A** fight breaks out in the pit, and one teenager hauls off and starts hitting another with a shovel. When they see me taking pictures, they stop, look up, and smile.

Noticing my camera, he points to the hills around the blast range. The hills are spiked with silhouettes like Indians waiting for the settlers. They are the nomads and scrap hunters who are waiting for the big bang. The first batch goes off with a devastating bang. As I watch from the bunker, I see the hills streaming with running children.

They run into the pit after the explosion to grab the red-hot fragments. They are looking for the copper drive bands or even the raw steel scrap on the shell casing. They get 20,000 Afghanis for 7 kilograms. They are risking their lives to get 75¢ for 16 pounds of copper. When I approach them, I notice a still-smoking 500-pound bomb in the crater.

There are about 60 people in the hole frantically digging and jostling. Small children grab the red-hot shell fragments and grimace, while others dig for the tiny pieces that make the tinkling sound of deadly shrapnel. A fight breaks out in the pit, and one teenager hauls off and starts hitting another with a shovel. When they see me taking pictures, they stop, look up, and smile.

I wander over to the Hazardous Area Life Support Organization (HALO) Trust Offices and meet Alex, a 28-year-old former officer in the British army with experience in Bosnia, and with HALO experience in Nagorno Karabakh and now Afghanistan. He is a young, thin man who is the only expat running HALO's Afghanistan operation.

It is the first week of demining after the long winter and Alex is having trouble getting the teams to their northern projects due to fighting. He has a large, plastic-covered map of Afghanistan, and there are a surprising number of green dots for cleared sites and very few red ones.

HALO specializes in mechanical removal of mines and has a selection of heavy equipment that can clear mines in collapsed buildings. They don't work directly with the UN program, but they coordinate their work by slicing up Kabul and other regions. There is a little bad blood between HALO and the UN deminers, who consider the HALO operation a showboat operation with a higher-than-needed casualty rate. They don't outwardly have any animosity, but Alex does not allow us to take pictures of the armada of white Land Rovers in their compound. They also have a bullet-proof Range Rover for crossing enemy lines.

The most famous image of demining is Princess Di in Angola visiting HALO and wearing the trademark body armor and face shield (with large logos). I am issued the same safety getup and hope that any mines I detonate will not explode upward, negating any benefits of my Hollywood-style getup.

I talk about how the statistics thrown around by outsiders do not reflect the actual truths on the ground. Like many deminers here, Alex believes that there are fewer mines in Afghanistan than the press or even the UN reports.

He gives credit to the Taliban for providing a stable region in which to conduct their operations. He points on the map to the infamous road from Mazar and says, "That is an interesting road," referring to the banditry and haphazard safe passage. Alex tells a number of blood-chilling stories about doing business in the lawless regions of Afghanistan. He manages to get through with military bluster and good luck. He remains cheerful despite the daunting task ahead of him.

At the UNICA guesthouse, it's "bar night" and crowded to capacity. There are about 150 foreigners in Kabul and about half of them seem to come for the narrow 2-hour window allowed for drinking on Thursday and Friday evenings. I am told that some of the groups have their own private clubs where they drink a homemade brew called *arak*, made of raisins. Outsiders are not welcome at these clubs because they would draw the attention of the Taliban.

The scene is becoming routine. There is a large contingent of French Red Cross workers who had to flee the fighting in Mazar to the north. They view this work as somewhat romantic and have long hair and earrings, and seem the least affected by stress and conditions. They always sit together, and the rest talk shop or spread rumors. It seems we are CIA spies. There is much talk about the two Americans who are ostensibly here to do something on demining, but are neither journalists nor consultants. We are told quite frankly that there are a number of odd people that come through here. For example, they tell me that the U.S. NGO across the street is a front for the CIA, and there have been an awful lot of British and Americans through the bar, none of whom have very good cover stories. But at least I have progressed from mercenary to spy.

"The Talibar" is the name they give to the small bar at the UNICA guesthouse. It used to be called the "Hard Rocket Cafe" before things eased up here. There is also the "Talibision," which carries CNN and the BBC, and the compound has a "Talibphone," or satellite phone, for UN calls. But back to the discovery.

I discover something interesting. They are drinking ten-year-old booze. The limited selection at the bar of whisky, liquors, and vodka arrived in a container in 1991, and they have been drinking it ever since. The Chablis turned sour and the Scotch doesn't age. The most cherished alcohol is Dortmunder beer, the only beer that has remained pure and tasty in storage after eight years.

The bar is probably one of the best (well, actually the only) place in Afghanistan for a drink and a chat. Gregory, with UN Habitat from London, likes to man the bar, and Andrew, from Aberdeen, likes to anchor the other end. Andrew McAndrew is 55, an EOD expert, and has been here three years. He went into the British army at 18 and came out as a warrant officer. Now he works here to make a difference. His specialty is removing the deadly litter of war—unexploded missiles, bombs, rockets, bullets, fuses, mines, and anything that can go bang. He is a quiet man whose favorite line, delivered in a broad Scottish accent, is, "Ah doo wut ahh doo." He is one of the half-dozen expats who are working with the demining program in Afghanistan.

The next day I go to school for land-mine awareness. The children range in age from 6 to 13. They play a game: They pull blue or red questions (blue cards are regular questions, red cards are about land mines). They get an activity book. When I ask the girls what they want to be when they grow up, I hear doctor, pilot, stewardess, and teacher. When I ask if they think they will ever have those jobs they say, "I will try my best." The children also play a charade about what happens when they collect mines. They all blow up and fall down. The younger children laugh.

After the others go to bed, Andrew, the bomb-disposal expert, is having a final drink with me because he is leaving tomorrow and he doesn't know if he will come back. We talk about making a difference. He feels he has made a difference in this world, as unsung or trivial as it may seem. He has spent three years training Afghans to clear, remove, and dispose of deadly explosive devices, allowing them to rebuild. Something that will never make headlines or make him rich despite risking his life daily, a long way from his wife and home. With the front lines only 12 miles away and the sporadic rocket attacks, he thinks it all might have been a waste. I disagree and encourage him to tell other people how they can make a difference when he gets back to Scotland. Someone has to push back the darkness.

Realizing that he is leaving tomorrow and he is very drunk, he turns to me and says, "Robert, I am so tired."

*—RYP*

# MERCENARIES

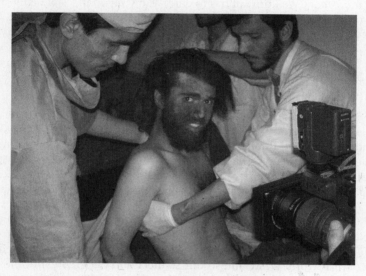

## How to Travel Free, Meet Interesting People, and Then Kill Them

Adventure stirs deep in the loins of youth and before they had low-cost airfares, backpacks, and student discounts, most people got their first trip overseas in uniform. Things have changed.

What can well-trained adventurers do to make this world a better place and tell stories to their grandkids? In the old days, you could ride off to the Crusades, discover the New World, or just raise hell in some wealthy potentate's army. Since then, there have been few noble wars to occupy the heroic and romantic. Between our great and not-so-great wars (when Uncle Sam made you volunteer), poets, thugs, and the bloodthirsty have volunteered for a variety of romantic causes, from the Russian Revolution to the Spanish Civil War.

More important, applying your security, medical, engineering, or military-learned skills to the third world is just as valid as any civilian skills. The most extreme application would be to join a foreign army or a group that is actively fighting for independence, freedom, or any other cause. The KLA was the last manifestation of this age-old tradition, but you will find North American volunteers in Chechnya, Kosovo, Sri Lanka, Kurdistan, Israel, Kashmir, and other conflicts.

Keep in mind that you theoretically can lose your American citizenship if you choose to be a mercenary (although no U.S. contract soldier or mercenary we know of has to date) and your chances of being summarily executed by the side of the road if captured are high. So let's start out with the most PC version of military adventure—the army.

## Happiness Is a Warm Gun:
## The Army/Navy/Marines/Air Force

Today's armed forces look pretty good to the hordes of young men and women who can't find jobs. Some take advantage of the scholarships and benefits and others just figure it's the right thing to do, dammit. The problem is, these days most young men and women have jobs. Recruitment is down, morale is down, the pay sucks, and the idea of being globo-cop is not what most people had in mind when they went in. The world is no longer good versus evil. The world's businesses are just too tightly interwoven and politics too fractured to allow another Axis versus Allies confrontation. A quick look at where Uncle Sam gets to fire guns would result in firing blanks. Sure, there is the quick dash to a third-world wasteland so our soldiers don't get rusty, but most of the current activity of the U.S. military consists of troops sitting on their behinds overseas or polishing their guns back home.

Although the U.S military has officially seen action in Bosnia, Korea, Vietnam, Lebanon, Iraq, Grenada, Panama, Libya, Somalia, and Haiti, none of these have been official wars. Rather, they were primarily police actions or gunboat diplomacy. That said, there has been covert military action in Angola, Cuba, Cambodia, Laos, Nicaragua, Iran, El Salvador, and numerous other areas, and training missions in Uganda, Sri Lanka, Colombia, and with dozens of other "which end does the bullet come out?" armies we call allies. If their countries actually have gas and airlines, we'll train them here. In 1998, Uncle Sam spent $50 million dollars training 9,000 foreign military personnel from over 100 countries.

For data on foreign military training, see:

http://www.us.net/cip/Africa/Demilitarization/FMT_FY2000.htm

Foreign military training costs by the United States per country:

http://www.ciponline.org/facts/fmf.htm#FMF
http://www.ciponline.org/facts/fmtr.htm
http://www.state.gov/www/global/arms/fmtrain/exec_summ.html
http://www.fas.org/asmp/campaigns/training/prog_desc.html

In the past, America could find a big enemy to unleash its big army on. No more. Today's military is killing time instead of bad guys. In places like Bosnia, Iraq, Lebanon, and Somalia, America's finest are now politically correct, overtrained, and underpaid flatfoots. With a lack of clear objectives, or even positive role models, it is no surprise that the U.S. military is having trouble attracting the number or caliber of soldiers it had with the draft. Our current all-volunteer army has lower scores, lower average IQ levels, and gender-modified achievement levels as equipment and technology become more advanced and complicated. Just what would our well-fed, by-the-book, bed-at-night, politically correct, Geneva Convention–style military do against barefoot mujahideen or female suicide bombers? Unlike the days of the Rough Rider, when bar fighters, intellectuals, noblemen, and cowboys joined up to fight the good fight, today's army attracts a totally different crowd. It could be said that today's military, with its too kind, thoughtful, PC nonkillers, does about all it can do to take the adventure out of military service.

What can you expect if you sign up in today's army? The army's 9-week basic training program at Fort Jackson, South Carolina, transforms civilians into soldiers, 60 raw recruits at a time. At bases like Fort Jackson, 70,000 military personnel are trained annually, 3 million since the base's opening in 1917.

Upon arrival, you can expect to fill out horrendous amounts of paperwork. You spend the first 6 days at the Reception Battalion, where you pick up your uniforms, have your head shaved, and are given 16-hour doses of KP, or kitchen patrol. The second week is filled with 12-hour days (with reveille at 4 AM), drill and ceremony movements, classroom work, land and navigation courses, bayonet assault training, and an obstacle course centered around the Victory Tower.

The second month begins with basic rifle marksmanship. You will learn to understand and care for your M-16 like no other physical object you own. You will learn to fire at targets as far as 300 meters away. Based on your performance, you will be called a marksman, sharpshooter, or expert. Toward the end of the second month, the weaponry gets serious, with the M-60 machine gun, AT4 antitank weapon, and hand grenades. Instead of firing your weapon, you get a taste of what it will be like on the receiving end, as you learn how to move around under fire complete with barbed-wire obstacles, exploding dynamite, and M-60 rounds being fired over your head as you crawl 300 meters on your belly.

The last week of training intensifies with PT testing and working with explosives. The climax is a three-day field exercise, where trainees get to play war by digging foxholes and taking eight-mile hikes with full packs. The last few days are spent cleaning barracks in preparation for the next cadets. How tough is it? New recruits will say very; the old salts will say it's not as tough as it used to be. Corporal punishment was banned in the mid-'70s, and sexual harassment has been added to the list of subjects taught. Minor punishment is confined to "smoke sessions," for the less than motivated. These semipunitive periods of intense physical training are designed to remind the errant soldier who is in charge. Soldiers are chewed out using the entire spectrum of profanity.

The front-leaning rest position (a push-up that is never completed) is also used as punishment. There is no form of entertainment, since there technically is no rest time. Television, newspapers, and radios are taboo. Mail and occasional phone calls are allowed. Three washing machines and five showerheads are considered enough to keep 60 active men clean.

Once out of basic training, you can expect to be posted to an area in line with your specialty. The military is still using technology about 10 to 20 years behind what you find on the outside. The main focus in the military is changing from '40s-style ground wars to '70s-style rapid-deployment tactics. The army provides lousy pay, good benefits, excellent training, and a chance to pack in two careers in a lifetime. As for furthering a cause or making the world a better place, one only has to look at Lebanon, Kuwait, Somalia, and Vietnam to see the results of gunboat diplomacy.

## Beau Geste: The French Foreign Legion

The more romantic and politically insensitive might want to consider joining the legion. The legion is, more or less, France's colonial houseworker, oppressing minorities, liberating missionaries, and generally keeping the natives from getting too restless. The legion knows it does France's dirty work and recruits accordingly. They will take all comers, preferably foreigners and men who will not draw too big a funeral procession. The legion is tough and disposable.

The best example of the legion's mind-set is the single most revered object in their possession—the wooden hand of Captain Jean Danjou on display in the museum in Aubagne. Danjou lost his hand when his musket misfired and blew up. He then died with the 59 worn-out survivors defending a hacienda on April 30, 1864, in a small hamlet called Camerone in Mexico. His men, exhausted after a long, forced march to evade the 2,000-strong Mexican army, decided to die rather than surrender. His wooden hand was found by the tardy relief column and enshrined to commemorate his courage. Over 10,000 legionnaires died at Dien Bien Phu in 1954 in a similar debacle. One unit suffered a 90 percent loss at Cao Bang, only to have 576 out of 700 killed 4 years later at Dien Bien Phu.

> **T**he legion is the tough guy's army, tailor-made for Hollywood film scripts, home for intellectuals, criminals, and outcasts.

A normal army would frown upon the lack of reinforcement, bad strategies, and resulting waste of manpower. The legion (like all of French military history) myopically elevates folly into legend and attracts thousands of eager recruits every year. The basic lesson is that with only 75 percent of the legion being French, they are considered disposable.

Despite its notoriety, the legion is still the army of choice when young men dream of adventure. The legion is the tough guy's army, tailor-made for Hollywood film scripts, home for intellectuals, criminals, and outcasts. It's a close-knit band of hardy, brutal men who are either escaping misguided pasts or seeking adventure in exotic places and doing heroic deeds. The lure of the legion is communicated to us via simplistic movies like *Beau Geste* or books that romanticize its violence and bloodshed. What they don't tell you is that the legion has always been brutal and ill-equipped. But you get to learn to be a professional killer and chances are high that you will use those skills on other people.

The legion was created in 1831 by King Louis Phillipe to assist in the conquest of Algeria. The king correctly assumed that paid mercenaries would not complain about the conditions or political correctness in carrying out his orders. Since then, the legion has been used to fight France's dirty little wars in Algeria, Indochina, Africa, and the Middle East. Although there have been many heroic battles fought by the legion in some of the world's most remote and hostile regions, you are better served by reading the multitude of books. The reality today is that the legion has been downsized and specialized.

The legion is one of the few action outfits (like the former Selous Scouts of Rhodesia or Oman's mostly British army) that offers the professional adventurer a steady diet of hardship broken up by short bursts of excitement and danger. This format has attracted many of the world's best-trained soldiers, like the SS after World War II or Special

Forces vets from Vietnam. The world of adventure is shrinking, however. Today the French Foreign Legion is made up of 8,500 officers and men from more than 100 countries. They no longer have any ongoing wars that require constant replacements. They now focus on picking and choosing from among the world's tough guys to enable them to field soldiers who are fluent in many languages and specialties without the religious, political, or ethnic barriers that hamper other peacekeeping or expedition forces.

## How to Get In

There are 16 legion recruiting centers in France, the most popular being Fort de Nogent in Paris. Just ask at the police station for the Legion Etrangere. The more focused head straight for Aubagne, just outside of the dirty Mediterranean port of Marseille. You will be competing with over 8,000 other eager legionnaire-wannabes for the 1,500 slots available. Eastern Europeans make up about 50 percent of the eager candidates these days. Candidates are tested for their intelligence and physical fitness, and special skills are a definite plus. If you just want to escape the IRS or alimony payments, the legion could care less. After all, what better inducement is there to staying after your third year in Djibouti than the thought of spending the same amount of time in jail Stateside?

You won't be required to bring an ID or proof of anything; when you sign up, you will be assigned a nom de guerre and a nationality. Being Canadian is popular, and calling yourself Rambo is definitely an old joke.

You must pass the same general standards as for the French army, but then the legion takes over. They will also run checks on Interpol computers and your home country will get a call. You will learn to march like a mule in hell—long forced marches with heavy packs; jungle, mountain, and desert training. You can bail out during the first four months of training, but from then on, you will speak the thick, crude French of the legionnaire and learn to be completely self-sufficient in the world's worst regions.

There is basic training in Castelnaudary (between Carcassone and Toulouse, just off the A61), commando training in St. Louis near Andorra, and mountain training in Corsica. Four weeks into your training, you will be given the Kepi blanc, the white pillbox hat of the legionnaire. Unlike the Navy SEALs or Western elite forces, the accommodations are simple and the discipline is swift, and other than special prostitutes who service the legion, there is little to look forward to during the mandatory five years of service. Legionnaires can get married after 10 years of service.

Once you pass basic training, you will be trained in a specialized category: mountain warfare, explosives, or any number of trades that make you virtually unemployable upon discharge (except in another mercenary army). French citizens cannot serve, except as officers. Those French officers who sign on do so for a taste of adventure. In troubled times, the legionnaires are always the first to be deployed to protect French citizens in uprisings or civil wars.

With this international makeup, it is not surprising that legionnaires today find themselves employed as peacekeepers, stationed in the tattered shreds of the French empire or with the UN. You may be assigned to protect the European space program in Kourou, in the steamy jungles of French Guiana, or to patrol the desert from Quartier Gaboce, in the hot baked salt pan of Djibouti. When it hits the fan, as in Kolwezi or Chad, you can expect some excitement, a quick briefing, an airdrop into a confused and bloody scene, followed by years of tedium, training, and patrol.

Since the legion attracts loners and misfits, and because many of them spend their time in godforsaken outposts, it is not hard to understand that the legion becomes more than a job. In fact, the motto of the legion is "Legio Patria Nostra," or "The Legion Is Our Homeland," which describes the mind-set and purpose. Many men serve out their full 20 years, since they are unable to find equally stimulating work on the outside.

When you get out, you don't get much, other than a small pension and the opportunity to become a Frenchman (legionnaires are automatically granted French citizenship after five years). After a lifetime of adventure, and divorced from their homeland, the men of the legion can look forward to retirement at Domaine Danjou, a chateau near Puyloubier (12 miles west of St. Maxim, north of the A7) in southern France, where close to 200 legionnaires spend their last years. This is where the legion looks after its own, its elderly, wounded, and infirm. Here the men have small jobs, ranging from bookbinding to working in the vineyards. Later, they will join their comrades in the stony ground of the country that never claimed them but for which they gave their lives. Remember, the legion has always been disposable.

Recruitment centers for the Legion:

*Paris*
Pour la région parisienne 94120
   Fontenay-sous-Bois Fort de Nogent
Tel.: (33) (1) 48 77 49 68

*Lille*
59000 Lille La Citadelle
Tel.: (33) 20 55 40 13

**Marseille**
13007 Marseille La Malmousque
   Chemin du Génie
Tel.: (33) 91 31 85 10
1.RE; 13400 Marseille Quartier Viénot
Tel.: (33) 42 18 82 57

**Rouen**
76038 Rouen Cedex Rue du Colonel
   Trupel
Tel.: (33) 35 70 68 78

**Poitier**
86000 Poitier Quartier Aboville
Tel.: (33) 49 41 31 16

**Bayonne**
64100 Bayonne 18, quai de Lesseps
Tel.: (33) 59 50 14 84

**Nantes**
44000 Nantes Quartier Desgrées-du-
   Loup Rue Gambetta
Tel.: (33) 40 74 39 32

**Bordeaux**
33000 Bordeaux 260, Rue Pelleport
Tel.: (33) 56 92 99 64

**Metz**
57000 Metz Quartier De-Lattre-de-
   Tassigny
Tel.: (33) 87 66 57 12

**Lyon**
69007 Lyon Caserne Sergent Blandan
   37 bis, Rue du Repos
Tel.: (33) 78 58 40 21

**Dijon**
21000 Dijon Caserne Junoy 66, Avenue
   du Drapeau
Tel.: (33) 80 73 54 86

**Nice**
06300 Nice Caserne Saint Jean d'Angely
   Rue des Diables Bleus
Tel.: (33) 93 56 32 76

**Strazbourg**
67000 Strazbourg Quartier Lecourbe
   Rue d'Ostende
Tel.: (33) 88 61 53 33

**Perpignon**
66020 Perpignan Caserne Mangin 8,
   Rue François Rabelais
Tel.: (33) 68 35 05 38

**Reims**
51000 Reims Quartier Colbert 32 bis,
   Avenue de la Paix
Tel.: (33) 26 88 42 50

**Toulouse**
31000 Toulouse Caserne Pérignon
   Avenue Camille Pujol
Tel.: (33) 61 54 21 95

# Working Freelance

All right, you do your 2, 5, or 20 years and you're out. You keep it high
and tight, work out, but selling life insurance or pushing Ralston
Purina to pet stores just doesn't have the same edge. Life outside is dull.
Life inside was dull but at least you got to blow stuff up, party a lot,
shoot at things, jump out of planes, learn cool stuff, hang out with like-
minded manics. You need to get back in.

So who is hiring ex-military experts? Well, technically, nobody.
Although historically many countries like Brunei (which uses Ghurkas),
the Vatican (which has about 100 Swiss guards), and Oman have armies
staffed by paid foreigners (about 360 British officers were "seconded"
to the sultan to fight rebels), you will have to be hired out of an existing army (typically the British army) to be considered. Many foreign

armies are happy to enlist your services and the Israeli, Canadian, British, or Australian armed forces will even give you citizenship when you are finished. But times are tough, so there are plenty of people who like the idea of paid housing and training. You can expect stringent entry requirements and a thorough check of your background.

These days the real action for ex-military is in private military corporations (PMCs), which essentially provide outsourced military skills. But don't hold your breath and pack your bags just yet. Yes, those camel lots, oil rigs, pipelines, expat compounds, and bigwigs need security, but get in line. It's an old boy's network where few if any employees get dropped in the middle of firefights. Watching cheap black-and-white monitors in air-conditioned trailers maybe, but just don't expect a lot of heat and light. If you want to get into the shit, keep in mind that late-night 7-Eleven clerks and bank tellers see more firefights than most of these new mercenaries.

http://www.ambafrance-us.org/atoz/legion/index.asp

## Happiness Is a Hired Gun: PMCs and Mercs

So you did your time in the army and can fieldstrip everything from a Makarov to a Chinese nuclear missile. You can fly an Apache helo or an F-117 blindfolded. You could parachute directly into bin Laden's wife's jacuzzi without tripping the disco-light alarms. You can speak 145 languages (including tribal dialects) and swear in 89 of them. You have been trained to kill a man just by twitching your ears, can make explosives out of Rice Krispies, and can list every LIC and Tango group by acronym alphabetically in Russian. You're under 40, fit, and ready to go private. Congratulations, you can now work at Home Depot in the plumbing department or seek employment as a mercenary. If your girlfriend is not impressed with the term *merc*, then how about "contractor" for a "private military company" or PMC, the new properly spun word for foreign soldiers who work in other people's backyards.

Well, we may be getting a little carried away, but the bottom line is it won't take long before you start discovering that international security companies are forking over $10,000 to $15,000 a month for high-level contract soldiering these days. You only have one problem. Uncle Sam would rather see you work as a Burger King manager than sell your precious skills to the highest bidder. Yes, there are U.S. groups like MPRI, Dyncorp, and Vinnell, which have dull-as-dishwater brochures and do equally dull things like train foreign armies or write operational manuals for esoteric milspec gear, but you are not going to be leading charges on horseback or causing much mayhem. Just the opposite. They like nice quiet folks who can run a laptop as well as an M-50.

## THE *DP* DISCLAIMER

Any U.S. citizen entering a foreign army without prior approval (in writing) from both the secretary of state and the secretary of defense can forfeit U.S. citizenship, although Congress has ruled that enlistment in a foreign army is not a clear enough declaration of intent to voluntarily renounce citizenship.

The 1907 Hague Convention banned operation on the territory of neutral states of offices for recruitment of soldiers (volunteers or mercenaries) to fight in a country at war. In 1977, part of a supplementary protocol to the 1949 Geneva Convention on the Protection of Civilian Population in Time of War made freelancers liable to court trial as criminals if they are taken POW. If found guilty, they can be simply shot on the spot as criminals.

The UN General Assembly reached a consensus in 1989 on the recruiting, training, use, and financing of mercenaries. If you are interested in volunteering, make sure you understand the laws and penalties that will suddenly apply to you. If you think fighting for money will make you popular and chicks will dig you, think again. On the other hand, if Uncle Sam has spent five years and about half a million dollars turning you into all that you can be, there are employment choices other than flipping burgers or working at Jiffy Lube.

## ¿Gringos? No Me Gustan

First, most foreign armies don't want American volunteers. Americans have an image of wanting too much money, complaining too much, and creating too many political overtones when captured or killed. Unless, of course, our CIA has a vested interest in keeping an eye on things. American mercenaries have fought in Angola, Rhodesia, Guatemala, El Salvador, Nicaragua, Sierra Leone, Kosovo, Myanmar, the Congo, Lebanon, Bosnia, and Russia with the blessing and support of the CIA. And keep in mind that more Angolans, Rhodesians, and so forth have fought as mercenaries than Americans. Many are motivated by religion (black Muslims in the Middle East), background (Croats and Muslims in the Balkans), money (Central America), or a misguided sense of adventure (Angola). The United States is not adverse to hiring or supplying mercenaries, starting back when Benjamin Franklin hired the Prussian officer Friedrich von Steuben to instill discipline into the Continental Army, or when Claire Chennault was hired to give Japan grief with his Flying Tigers. And Americans are not adverse to being mercenaries (we are capitalists, after all). In modern times U.S.-hired mercenaries have been as diverse as the Ray-Banned pilots that flew for Air America, the advisers who trained Nung or Montagnard tribes in Vietnam, or the long-haired pilots who spray the coca fields of Colombia. There have been Americans in the Congo, Sierra Leone,

Rhodesia, Myanmar, and Israel. Americans, as far back as fliers in World War I, have been advisers to Haile Selassie in Ethiopia and dozens have fought and died in the Spanish Civil War. We are busy training soldiers in Afghanistan, Sri Lanka, Georgia, the Philippines, and Colombia—so what's the big deal about mercs?

Mercenaries continue to do our dirty, or covert work, but our government does not like the idea of its citizens running off to fight in other people's wars.

The new solution is to legalize mercenary work. Private military companies like MPRI, Sandline, and others are doing a lot of the clean or dirty work countries can't or won't do themselves. Despite what you read in the papers, fighting for a foreign country is a tough business. And we are talking about how getting paid by el jefé may be the toughest part, not the actual fighting.

Today, those who wish to be the traditional "wild geese" or "soldiers of fortune" will find few clear career paths. The e-mail boxes of every PMC fill up daily with Ramboesque CVs and inquiries. You will need the minimum service and training provided by a Western military power. Special Forces members, explosives experts, pilots, and officers with training experience and other specialized skills are in demand.

Although the need for foreign volunteers cannot be predicted, there are certain starting points for employment. The old-boy network is the most reliable. That means you should look up your old buddies to see what is up. Any trade shows that cater to military and security personnel and direct contact with some of the companies listed here can also provide you with information. Just remember, even the best-laid plans go awry, as they did for Sandline in PNG (which sued and won in court for its money) and even in Sierra Leone where Executive Outcomes, technically defunct, but not really, is going after the $20 million it was never paid.

## Employment with a Difference

Getting a job in the merc world is a long way from the "Employment with a Difference" classified ad placed by Mike Hoare in South Africa when he set out to recruit mercenaries to fight in the Belgian Congo. Having neither the budget nor the time to train men, he put together what he called his "Wild Geese," the name of an ancient Irish band of soldiers for hire. He managed to defeat the Simbas, rescue white women, and embarrass the UN. And he received a book and movie deal later. Not bad for a former accountant and car salesman.

Remember, if you find a recruiter in a bar who is looking for "a few good men," they are usually filling grunt and junior-officer levels only for second-tier gigs. The players have already cut their deal up at the top, and they need to fill in the holes to get paid. Top-level giggers like Executive Outcomes, Sandline, and MPRI may get millions to supply expertise, but the ground pounders aren't taking limos to the front lines.

There are also horror stories about hucksters preying on the gullible, as in Angola in the '70s. The U.S. government paid to hire mercenaries out of London in its bid to oust the Cuban-supported MPLA. Four groups of 185 men were sent in to fight with the FNLA. It was a disaster from the start. Psychotic officers (like 25-year-old Costas Georgiou, aka "Colonel Callan") executed their own people, few skirmishes were won, and when it was over, 13 mercenaries were put on trial and 4 were executed by a firing squad (one had to propped up on his stretcher to be shot properly). The high hopes, empty talk, and wasted time continue today. Even if you do find someone who has a gig for you, remember that they get paid by the head count, and once in that country you can be turned down, arrested, or sent into action on your first day without training, weapons, gear, or ammo. The reality is that most experienced mercenaries either use the old-boy network or simply fly to the capital city of an emerging war zone and offer their services directly to the military advisers for whichever side they feel is the most desperate. Their services usually include rounding up cannon fodder, like you.

There is also a lot of home-grown soldiering that usually leads nowhere—groups like the Falangists and Chamounists in Beirut in the '80s who brought in eager French Falangist Party students—but most look for trained, hardened professionals with special skills. Your paycheck is an occasional bad meal and a place in heaven for fighting the good fight. Young Kashmiris are given a few weeks training and humped off across the mountains to Indian Kashmir to raise hell and end up dead in shootouts. There seems to be no age limit. In Africa, young Ugandan schoolboys are rounded up and used as porters for rebel groups while kidnapped young girls become part-time pillows and cooks. Isn't war fun?

## THE UNKNOWN MERCENARIES

It's an interesting gig working as a peacekeeper for the UN. Now, the save-the-world folks will grimace and pout at the word *mercenary* but sorry, folks, they fall right into the technical definition. Most troops don't choose to be stationed in one of the 15 or so peacekeeping missions going on, but they are paid to fight someone else's war. Oh, you say they are not fighting? Well, if you consider long periods of intense boredom interrupted by disorganized panic fighting, then this is pretty close. The reason I bring this up is that if you take a gander at the casualty list of the United Nations, you will quickly surmise that maybe peace is a little dangerous after all.

**UN PEACEKEEPING FATALITIES, 1948–2001**

| Year | Fatalities | Year | Fatalities | Year | Fatalities | Year | Fatalities |
|------|-----------|------|-----------|------|-----------|------|-----------|
| 1948 | 8 | 1949 | 3 | 1976 | 14 | 1977 | 17 |
| 1950 | 5 | 1951 | 0 | 1978 | 28 | 1979 | 30 |
| 1952 | 0 | 1953 | 0 | 1980 | 20 | 1981 | 30 |
| 1954 | 0 | 1955 | 0 | 1982 | 26 | 1983 | 11 |
| 1956 | 2 | 1957 | 17 | 1984 | 14 | 1985 | 16 |
| 1958 | 17 | 1959 | 10 | 1986 | 27 | 1987 | 17 |
| 1960 | 43 | 1961 | 156 | 1988 | 11 | 1989 | 33 |
| 1962 | 46 | 1963 | 35 | 1990 | 24 | 1991 | 16 |
| 1964 | 22 | 1965 | 18 | 1992 | 60 | 1993 | 252 |
| 1966 | 20 | 1967 | 22 | 1994 | 167 | 1995 | 123 |
| 1968 | 7 | 1969 | 6 | 1996 | 51 | 1997 | 48 |
| 1970 | 8 | 1971 | 9 | 1998 | 31 | 1999 | 25 |
| 1972 | 6 | 1973 | 14 | 2000 | 51 | 2001 | 64* |
| 1974 | 41 | 1975 | 17 | 2002 | 47 | | |

*Source:* United Nations

## Soldiers of Misfortune

If you want to skip the whole resume and personality test, and get straight to merc'ing, there are still plenty of opportunities. You could be a volunteer like the ex-Hitler Youth Group turned merc Rolf Steiner or the bike-riding, rich-kid doctor, Argentinian Ché Guevara, who messed around in Uganda and Cuba, and messed up in Bolivia. Just remember that Steiner was tried, imprisoned, and tortured, and Guevara was ventilated by CIA operatives and dumped in a hastily dug Bolivian grave. When it's over in this business, it's over, babe. There is nothing left but the T-shirt sales and memories.

> **W**hen it's over in this business, it's over, babe. There is nothing left but the T-shirt sales and memories.

Be warned that there are plenty of cheap movies and bad books attempting to add the luster of righteousness and adventure to the mercenary life. These books tend to be short on facts and long on gun talk. They provide hard-to-find tips like "never handle explosives carelessly" (from the *Mercenary's Tactical Handbook,* by Sid Campbell) to "take no unnecessary risks" (from the *African Merc Combat Manual,* from Paladin Press).

There are some good books on this nasty business, most long out of print:

*The Brother's War,* by John St. Jorre
*Legionnaire,* by Simon Murray
*Mercenary,* by Mike Hoare
*The Last Adventurer,* by Rolf Steiner
*Mercenary Commander,* by Jerry Puren

Probably the most accurate, well-written, and depressing of the bunch is *The Whores of War: Mercenaries Today,* by Wilfred Burchett and Derek Roebuck. There are also a host of new books attempting to put forth the ideas that mercenaries are either the scum of the earth or the only people who will save countries like Angola and Sierra Leone.

*Whores,* published in 1977, chronicles the misfortunes of 13 American and British mercs in Angola who were captured, tried, and executed or imprisoned. Sobering stuff for wannabes.

Movies like the *Dogs of War* and *The Wild Geese* have some credible origins in real events, and real mercenaries were used as resources to create the scripts as well as advise the filmmakers on location. But somehow, once the cameras rolled, it all turned into pure gun love, complete with sweat, bulging muscles, babes, handheld machine guns, and chomping cigars.

The bottom line is, the visible part of merc business is about 99 percent bullshit and 1 percent reality, and the reality part usually sucks. Despite having to buy your own beret, cigars, and big knife, you will end up spending time in the most godawful parts of the world, and if a land mine doesn't get you, then the bugs will. If the bugs don't get you, the long arm of the law will.

Any time you leave the apron strings of Uncle Sam's army, you are on your own, and even if you are not in violation of any laws, you will be accused of being a *criminal* (actually, *a criminal has rights—you won't*) and dealt with accordingly.

To be fair, we should inject a little romance and adventure into this much-maligned avocation. The true movers and shakers in the mercenary world are the classic megalomaniacs: vicious self-promoters and verbose ex-soldiers who see their role as beyond that of a short-term gun toter—as a potential ruler of faraway kingdoms. So our advice, if you are going to get into this nasty business (the retirement program sucks), is to think big, don't take any checks, and make sure you remember your hat size when you order your crown.

# The Men-Who-Would-Be-King Club

The kingdom-making business has been around for a long time. Men like Englishman (and eventually Rajah) Brooke of Sarawak bought a fast ship with a few naval guns. He used them to chase off pirates in exchange for giant chunks of Borneo. William Walker and a bunch of ne'er-do-wells ran Nicaragua with a Gatling gun and a few Colt navy pistols. Hell, even I was offered in on a deal to take over a Caribbean island, so there still must be opportunities for adventurers out there.

The late '60s and early '70s were the glory years for mercenaries like "Mad" Mike Hoare, "Black" Jacques Schramme, and Bob Denard. They weren't bright or avaricious enough to grab the main bedroom in the royal palace instead of the barracks the first time around, but it didn't take them long to figure things out. Why support a tin-pot ruler so he or she can continue to loot the national treasury to shop in Paris when you could loot the treasury and go shopping in Paris yourself? Here is a short overview of the folks who thought big.

## Equatorial Guinea (1972)

*The Dogs of War*, by Frederick Forsyth, was published in 1974. Forsyth is said to have modeled the lead character in the book after Denard. In the book and in the film, a group of white mercenaries are hired to take over a West African country on behalf of an industrialist who finds it cheaper to take over the country than pay for its mineral resources. The movie ends with the mercenaries suddenly having a change of heart and installing an idealistic and honest leader. Naturally, the book and the film are fiction. Well, not completely, said an investigative report by *London's Sunday Times*. They claimed that *The Dogs of War* was based on a real incident instigated by the author. The *Times* claimed that in 1972 Forsyth allegedly put up just under a quarter of a million dollars ($240,000) to overthrow President Francisco Macias Nguema of Equatorial Guinea. Forsyth was no stranger to the murky world of mercenaries, since he had spent considerable time in Nigeria covering the Biafran civil war. While he was there, he met a Scottish mercenary named Alexander Ramsay Gay. Gay was only too happy to train and equip a small group of men who would set up a homeland for the defeated Biafrans. It is reputed that Gay was able to purchase automatic weapons, bazookas, and mortars from a Hamburg arms dealer, then hire 13 other mercenaries along with 50 black soldiers from Biafra. They then purchased a ship called the *Albatross* out of the Spanish port of Fuengirola. The plot was blown when one of the British mercs shot himself after a gunfight with London police. The mercenaries were denied an export permit for their weapons and ammunition, and the ship and crew were arrested in the Canary Islands en route to their target.

Forsyth denies the story or any participation in the plot and admits to nothing more than writing a solidly researched book.

***Unofficial Frederick Forsyth Web site***
http://frederickforsyth.cjb.net

# The Sudan (1975)

Rolf Steiner was a member of Hitler's Youth (Hitler Jugend). He joined the French Foreign Legion at the age of 17 in 1950. He fought at Dien Bien Phu and in Algeria and made the mistake of joining the anti–de Gaulle OAS—finding himself a drummed-out corporal chief and a civilian.

In the fall of 1967, Biafra was busy spending oil money and French secret service funds on hiring mercenaries from Swedish pilot Count von Rosen (pilots were paid between $8,000 and $10,000 per month in cash to fly in supplies) and paying Swiss public-relations firms to publicize their plight. Money flowed freely; grisly battle-scarred veterans like Roger Faulques were paid UK£100,000 to hire 100 men for six months, but only delivered 49. He was asked to leave, but Steiner, one of the mercenaries he had hired, chose to stay.

In July of 1968, Steiner asked for and was given a group of commando-style soldiers and had great successes against the Russian-backed Nigerians. He was later given the rank of colonel and given command of thousands of soldiers. This created an instant Napoleon complex and Steiner experienced a series of military defeats and routs. He was reined in by removal of his Steiner Commando Division, and after an angry confrontation with the Biafran leader, Sandhurst-educated General Emeka Ojukwa, he was shipped out of the country in handcuffs.

Steiner then showed up in the southern Sudan among the Anya Na fighting the Islamic north. He taught agriculture, defense, education, and other essential civic skills to the animist tribes. For a brief shining moment, he was their de facto leader, until he was captured by the Ugandans and put on trial in Sudan in the mid-'70s. He was released after spending three years in a Sudanese prison, where he was tortured and beaten. His captors' favorite tortures were hanging Steiner by his feet and stuffing peppers up (down?) his anus. Some say he was a crazed megalomaniac; others say he tried to apply his skills to aid a tiny struggling nation. He died in South Africa of a kidney ailment.

## The Comoros (1978–1989)

"Here, feel the hole in my head" is the way Gilbert Bourgeaud, aka Bob Denard, started his conversation. He grabbed my hand and rubbed it against the shallow depression under his silver hair. When *DP* met with this elegant-looking gentleman, it was just before his trial for taking over the Comoros. He had to invade, he says, things were going to hell. He was acquitted.

One of the more successful invasion attempts was made by Bordeaux native Bob Denard, who actually managed to run the Comoros Islands from May 1978 to 1989. The Comoros are an Indian Ocean island group just northwest of Madagascar. The major export of the long-forgotten islands is ylang-ylang, a rare flower used in the production of aromatic oils. On May 13, 1978, 49-year-old Denard landed with 46 men in a converted trawler named the *Massiwa*. He had sailed from Europe with his black-uniformed crew to claim ownership of this tiny but idyllic group of islands.

Denard had been here before to train the soldiers of Marxist ruler Ali Soilih. Soilih was busy kicking out Ahmed Abdallah. Abdallah fled to Paris and later, short on funds but high on ambition, offered to cut Denard in on the deal if he would return him to power. The deal was rumored to be worth $6 million. Denard enjoyed his new role as "man who would be king." Soilih was a young despot who appointed a 15-year-old to run the police department, burned all government records, and after a witch doctor told him he would be killed by a white man with a black dog, killed every black dog on the island. Abdallah took all the political heat as his puppet.

Denard, a former vacuum-cleaner salesman and policeman, had seen what a few trained soldiers could do in his various adventures as a mercenary in Katanga, Yemen, and Benin. This time he was in charge. He landed quietly at night and proceeded to the palace to find Soilih in bed with three girls watching a pornographic movie. Denard shot him, and the next morning drove through town with Soilih's body draped over the hood. (Denard had with him a black Alsatian.) The crowds cheered and Denard became an able leader of the Comoros for 11 years with 12 other white mercenaries. He took a Comoran wife, bought a villa, converted to Islam, and became Said Mustapha Madjoub.

During his reign, South Africa used the Comoros to ship arms to Iraq and monitor ANC training camps in Tanzania, and the French used his islands to ship arms to the right-wing Renamo guerrillas. Finally, after he (or someone else) shot the puppet ruler, Abdallah, in a heated argument, the tide turned against Denard. His presence angered the other

African states to such a degree that the French arranged for Denard's "resignation" in 1989. Denard, disappointed and back in South Africa, spent his evenings planning his return to paradise. Sounds like a great premise for a sequel. The hole? A piece of shrapnel that nicked a chunk of skull. Nothing really, just a flesh wound. During his last attempt to take over the Comoros to put things right, he says he had more engineers than soldiers. Denard was rousted quite amicably by the French military, tried, and acquitted.

## The Seychelles (1981)

When *DP* arrived in the Seychelles, we found it hard to imagine taking over a nicer place. Henry Moore-like granite sculptures frame azure blue seas. Laughing creoles, scrawny Italian tourists, and lush inland jungles would make the perfect tax-free haven. Dublin-born "Mad" Mike Hoare wasn't really there for the scenery or the beaches. He was hired by persons unknown (most say former President James Mancham in cahoots with South Africa) to take over the Seychelles, a nation of 92 islands 1,000 miles off East Africa. Hoare served in the Royal Armored Corps in World War II and left with the rank of major. He emigrated to South Africa after the war and made ends meet by being a safari guide, car dealer, and accountant, until he was hired by Moise Tshombe in 1964 to help him defeat rebels. Hoare put together about 200 white male mercenaries and led probably the last efficient use of a mercenary army in Africa—to save lives and put down a revolt in the Belgian Congo.

Hoare's last big gig (Major Hoare does not work too often due to his high price tag) was a Keystone Kops affair that would seem to be the result of a bad scriptwriter rather than real political intrigue. They were supposed to overthrow the socialist government of President Albert Rene of the Seychelles and to take control of the idyllic Indian Ocean archipelago. In December of 1981 their plan of flying in as a visiting rugby team quickly unraveled when customs inspectors found heavy weapons in the bottoms of their gym bags. A brief shootout between the 52 raiders and police ensued on the tarmac, with the mercenaries' transportation being quickly hijacked and flown back to safety in South Africa. It was not known for whom or why this was done, but suspicion falls on the South African government. Some analysts believe that Hoare backers were South African businessmen looking for a tax haven. A Durban newspaper charged that several of the mercenaries were South African policemen.

The leniency with which the mercenaries were treated back in South Africa adds to that suspicion. The 44 mercenaries who made it back were put on trial (wearing beach shirts and khakis), not for hijacking the Air India aircraft, which would have meant a mandatory 5 to 30 years in jail; they were charged with kidnapping, which requires no mandatory penalty.

The South African cabinet also approved the freeing on bail of 39 of the 44 mercenaries on the condition they keep a low profile and not discuss the coup attempt. Five mercenaries were arrested in the Seychelles, and it is assumed that three others are dead or hiding in the hills.

Others blame ousted Seychelles President James Mancham, who was exiled after Rene's successful 1977 coup. Although Mancham denied the accusation, one of the captured mercenaries had a tape recording of Mancham's victory speech intended for broadcast after the coup. Oops. The soldiers-for-hire were paid $1,000 each and were promised $10,000 if the coup was successful.

You can smell the spices in this languorous paradise. The giant curved dhows look right out of Sinbad. Things hadn't changed much since the last time Denard was here. They say sequels are never as interesting as the originals, and in this case, they're right. It seems that staring out the window got to be too much for Denard, so at the creaky old age of 66, he decided to give it one more go. On October 4, 1995, Denard and a group of 33 mercenaries (mostly French) rented a creaking fishing trawler and sailed back to the Comoros to recapture his little Garden of Eden where he had been king (actually, head of the presidential guard, watching over a puppet ruler) from 1978 to 1989.

They landed at night and quickly sprung their old buddies out of the islands' main jail; then they captured the two airports, the radio station, and the barracks. After that, they rousted the doddering, 80-something Said Mohamed Djohar out of bed. By morning, Denard was on top and Djohar was a criminal charged with misrule and stealing government funds.

Conveniently (too conveniently, some say), two days later, the French government landed 600 troops and after a brief but halfhearted fight, the mercenaries were rounded up and Denard was politely shipped to France where he was tried and acquitted of doing what comes naturally. Depending on what business you have, Hoare lives in the southwest of France or in South Africa.

http://www.contrast.org/truth/html/seychelles.html

# Sierra Leone (1995)

Executive Outcomes came into their own when they leapt into the breach and saved Sierra Leone. Okay, they were paid a million-and-two a month, but it sounds better this way. It wasn't the first time, but it was the best time. The rebels were eating people and smoking ganja in rolled-up Bible paper to get more Jesus in them. There had been other groups in Sierra Leone, like Gurkha Security Guards, who sent in American Robert MacKenzie, son-in-law of the late CIA deputy director Ray Cline. Things got unpleasant when even MacKenzie was killed and had his head put on a stick by the RUF rebels. GSG pulled out and Executive Outcomes appeared. In 18 months, the rebels were hiding in the bush and refugee camps in neighboring Guinea.

> **T**he rebels were eating people and smoking ganja in rolled-up Bible paper to get more Jesus in them.

By March 1996, Sierra Leone went to the polls for the first presidential elections in 28 years. And all was quiet in the British version of Liberia. The happy government figured they didn't need EO around and in less than 100 days things went to hell again. The government was overthrown in a coup and Sierra Leone quickly plunged into chaos.

http://www.sierra-leone.org/heartmatter.html
http://www.africa-confidential.com/special.htm

## The Comoros (1995)

Operation Kaskari was designed to restore Bob Denard (with the help of 33 mercs) to power. So on September 28, 1995, they overthrew President Djohar.

The French were aware of the return of the king but it wasn't until a week later on October 3 that the French launched Operation Azalee, the green light. The French deployed 600 men (with 1,000 in support roles) to overpower the 300-man force Denard had put together to supplement his 33 mercs. It only took a day, but the French overpowered the not-too-crack Comoroan troops and jailed bad-boy Bob in France. Later it was discovered that Bob's mercs were told not to fight. The penalty for taking over his own island again? Well, it seems that the French were upset that he left France without permission. In 1993, the French courts handed down a suspended jail sentence for his role in trying to overthrow the government of Benin.

## Bougainville (1997)

"Your bag makes me nervous," one of the men behind Sandline told *DP* in a private meeting. The elegant man in the Knightsbridge mews townhouse was not most people's idea of a mercenary. He was, after all, an accountant. But he still came from behind his desk, moved the leather case to point in a different direction, and resumed our conversation. Dodgy business, this.

When you hear it from their side, Sandline International and other "private military companies" make perfect sense. No different than 7-Eleven hiring flatfoots or the Pope needing pantalooned police with pig stickers around his country. It was a simple case of economic expediency, if you listen to Sandline when describing what happened in Papua New Guinea. The government needed help and Sandline came to their rescue.

Who else was going to stop the mayhem? The motivation behind the idea was simple as it is denied. Just how does a destitute country come up with millions to put down an uprising? Simple. A few greased palms, handshake agreements, and a contract is drawn up to settle the little insurgency problem in Bougainville once and for all.

You see, there was a copper and gold mine, the second biggest hole in the world, being held hostage by a small group of ragged, fuzzy-haired natives. That same mine used to provide half of Papua New Guinea's folding green, but it has been shut down by locals—some armed with rusty Japanese swords, homemade shotguns, and slingshots. The local army can't do squat with their undertrained, undermotivated soldiers. So hire some locals to squeal on the bosses, do a little low-level intel, fly in a crack squad of commandos, and "ka-ching": no more revolution. This is how the screenplay was written, but $36 million later it didn't quite work out that way.

The man in charge of the PNG military not only wanted the money for his own troops, but it seems that many of his top officers were related and sympathetic to the rebels in Bougainville and there was that less-than-altruistic problem of another UK-based military supplier depositing money in a UK account. Oops. Counterintel supreme. Second boo-boo: white man shows up with lots of used crusty Eastern European gear and things start looking like a bloodbath. Into the slammer and then onto a plane Tim Spicer goes, and the deal is off. Well, not quite. Sandline (which subcontracted to older and less-PC brother EO) sues, gets paid in full, the rebels get a peace deal, and everyone is happy. The price of copper is in the toilet, the mine is still closed, and Francis Ona, or Cranky Franky as he is known these days, is happy to stay up in his mountaintop kingdom. For those who can't get enough of this tale, you can read Tim Spicer's bio, *An Unorthodox Soldier,* or the excellent Aussie version by Mary-Louise O'Callaghan, *Enemies Within.*

http://www.globalpolicy.org/security/issues/sheppard.htm
http://www.wsws.org/news/1997/apr1997/png-a28.shtml

## Zaire/Congo (1997)

The natty-hatted Mobutu of Zaire knew the end of his 31-year-old dictatorship was near. He peeled off $25 million so that Belgian mercenary, Zaire-born, and Belgium national Christian Tavernier could put together the White Legion. Tavernier ("The Indian Cobra" or "Pitchfork") was an old-school merc from Les Affreux days and quickly determined that a pulse and occasional sobriety would be the minimum requirements for an army of about 300 men. He got out his scraper and soon came up with a group of Serbs from the Krajina region of Croatia, a few French legionnaires, and some former Romanian security police. Promised between $5 and $10K a month and paid three months in advance. Pilot Neill Ellis and a handful of South Africans showed up to pilot the two Russian-made Mi-24 gun ships that had flown in Afghanistan, three Aermacchi MB-325 K jets, and even Mirage fighters from the '80s that Mobutu had left in Brest, France. Tavernier tried to hold back the Ugandan- and Rwandan-backed rebels advised by mercenary Colonel Willy Mallants, but it was no use.

Tavernier quickly set up shop in Watsa, a mining town 700-km north of Kisangani, but his 280 men (Serbs, Croats, Russians, Poles, Belgians, Italians, and French) bailed on him. Ellis ended up being almost executed and having to walk barefoot out of Zaire. The last great hurrah.

## Sierra Leone (1999)

Wait . . . didn't you just read this story? Same tune, different orchestra. Or is it? Seems after Executive Outcomes left Sierra Leone things went sideways fast. Lo and behold, President Kabbah is sitting without a pot to piss in and a nasty, mean military junta under Johnny Paul Koroma (who were sprung from jail) is now running his country. So what's a government in exile to do? Well, Rakesh Saxena, an Indian banker on the lam from Thai authorities for embezzling money, is in Vancouver (stay with me here) and figures he will put up $10 million for a mercenary army to retake Sierra Leone and reinstate the democratically elected president. In exchange he will get all kinds of rutile and diamond concessions. So Rakesh Saxena (who is under house arrest in Vancouver) hires Sandline to do the dirty deed. Okay, he gives the money to the government, which then uses the money to hire Sandline. So everything is nice and tidy. Then Tim Spicer comes up with a plan to arm and train whacked-out native kamajors, who think they are invisible to bullets. (Just think of the savings on helmets and flak

## THE MAN WHO WOULDN'T DIE

Okay. Here is a pop quiz. How many times has America tried to kill Castro? Too late. Time's up! (We don't have a lot of prize money here at *DP*.) If you guessed 637 times, you were right. Ever since Castro and a smelly band of guerrillas tossed out Fulgencia Batista in 1959, Uncle Sam has been holding a grudge against the former baseball player and enemy of Bic shavers. Americans fought wars or sent troops to Cuba in 1898, 1917, and 1923, but never had the cojones to go in and drag Castro out by his Marxist-Leninist whiskers. The CIA began funding sabotage of the sugar industry and financing of mercenaries and hit squads to destabilize Cuba. The Eisenhower administration planned an invasion by a mercenary army of 1,500 men that would be called 2506 Brigade. Training began in the United States, Puerto Rico, and Guatemala. This invasion (now under Kennedy) became known as the Bay of Pigs fiasco in April 1961, in which 176 were killed and 300 wounded. The invasion just happened to be in one of Fidel's favorite fishing spots. Since 1960, Uncle Sam has just been enforcing embargoes on trade and travel to Cuba in hopes that Castro will yell "uncle" and give up.

The Cubans say they uncovered 637 separate assassination plots to kill Castro. For more CIA fun and games read:

***CovertAction Quarterly,***
c/o Institute for Media Analysis, Inc.
143 West 4th Street
New York, NY 10012
Tel.: (212) 477-2977
Fax: (212) 477-2977
info@covertaction.org
http://www.covertaction.org

jackets!) Saxena parts with a measly million-and-a-half to get things rolling, and before you can say Bob's-Yer-Uncle, the Nigerian peacekeepers roll up the nasty rebels and soldiers and Kabbah figures he'll keep his concessions and Saxena is out $1.5 mil. In the meantime, the whole "Arms to Africa" thing shows just how stupid the British government is and how bored the media are, and nobody even notices that all those nice greasy weapons disappear (courtesy of the enterprising Nigerian peacekeepers) once they arrive.

## The Players

The good old days are gone. The old Dogs of War business is drying up like blood on a Kinshassa backstreet. Gone are the skull-and-crossbones patches of Steiner, gone are the nicknames like "Black Jack" and "Mad Mike." I mean, c'mon, the former head of Sandline was called "Tim," fer chrissakes. The famous Euro mercs are now silver-haired and moving slow. The South Africans are getting decent jobs and even the Ché Guevaras, Abu Nidals, and Carlos the Jackals are nothing but memories or potbellied retirees. The last attempt at putting together an old-fashioned merc army was with 300 or so drunken Serbs and Europeans shipped in to fight off Kabila. The French put together a motley crew of 300 South Africans, Brits, French, Serbs, Angolans, and other nationalities. The new merc scene (or should we say the international security scene) is taking advantage of thousands of laid-off, well-trained soldiers and the need of oil and mining companies to keep things flowing in Colombia, Angola, the Sudan, Congo, Papua New Guinea, and other unstable regions. For those who like their action raw and gritty, there is no shortage of unpaid volunteer work in Afghanistan, the southern Philippines, and Latin America. For now, it seems the job opportunities for scarred, tattooed mercenaries looking through the classified section for "Make Big Money Killing Insurgents" ads are over. The famous merc bars full of neckless men are quiet. You now need to e-mail your qualifications to bland-looking megacorporations.

But wait. If you are a trained security consultant, there is hope. Believe it or not, you can see many of the major recruiters listed under "Corporate Security" in phonebooks in Jo'burg, London, Washington, Miami, and Paris. You'll find these euphemistically or acronymically named companies in any big mining or oil-center town. These are really the only places where ex- (and current) soldiers are actively recruited for "security" and "training" work overseas. Sometimes you actually will end up staring at a video monitor in an air-conditioned trailer at an African oil refinery or teaching 18-year-olds how to clean a Makarov. With the right credentials, the right background, and the right questions, you'll get work. Even if you do plug into this world, there is no shortage of experienced people.

Other groups, such as the Ghurkas, the Swiss Guards, and the French Foreign Legion, are not your classic Dogs-of-War-type of mercenaries but vanishing anachronisms. Small but oil-rich countries like Oman or Brunei need outside help to keep things quiet, but usually with the queen's troops on hire, the Ghurkas, and the SAS. Even the Pope hires mercenaries to keep the Holy See nice and safe. The good news is that right now, stinking-rich but "security-asset"-poor flyspeck states are eager employers, but usually by contract through their biggest mineral resource company (which, of course, is blessed by the appropriate ex-colonial country).

Despite the military might available for work for hire, it may surprise you that the real movers and shakers behind the new global security firms are very colorful and wealthy individuals. Here's just a peek at some of the players past and present.

## The Back Room

You are more likely to see these guys on the cover of *Fortune* than *Soldier of Fortune*. These are just some of the people who have been linked, however tenuously or incorrectly, with the brave new world of corporate colonialism and the need for private armies. Not that *DP* has any proof or reason to believe that they have anything to do with new trends. They just seem to show up in articles a lot and do business in interesting places.

## Tiny Rowland

Former UK Prime Minister Mr. Edward Heath described Rowland as "the unacceptable face of capitalism." Some would simply say that Tiny Rowland didn't really play the games or keep up the appearances that colonial countries do in the third world. "Tiny" was born Rowland Walter Fuhrhop in 1917 in an internment camp in India. He died of skin cancer in July 1998 at the age of 80 on his yacht. He was worth $405 million from making friends and enemies.

His father was German and his mother Anglo-Dutch. After World War I, the family returned to Germany where Rowland went to school and later joined the Hitler youth movement. They moved to Britain in 1934, and at a private school he joined the Officer Training Corps and achieved the rank of corporal.

He worked for his father but was interned with his father and other German-born immigrants on the Isle of Man. He spent three months in the Peel camp for high-risk Nazi sympathizers (his brother was fighting in the German army). It is alleged that he was an informer inside the camp and that it earned him special status in his business dealings later.

He moved to southern Rhodesia after the war and married into the royal family. His mentor was Angus Ogilvy, who hired him to run London and Rhodesian Mining and Land Company, later renamed Lonrho.

His business style was, to say the least, loose. He would simply bribe leaders of African nations to obtain mining rights. He would provide his Gulfstream to fly rebel leaders to press conferences or meetings. He even bought newspapers in South Africa and the UK to provide positive coverage of his exploits. One of his partners was Mohamed Al-Fayed, whom he later had a falling out with. He spent about $50 million fighting

Al-Fayed for control of Harrods. He also was responsible for the financial collapse of Australian Alan Bond.

Tiny Rowland didn't invent the idea of getting involved in war and politics to make a buck. He just made it respectable. As then-chief executive of the UK-based multinational Lonrho, Tiny made protection payments to Renamo during the early stages of the war to protect Lonrho's agrarian and business investments. When Renamo reneged, Tiny became involved in the political side of things and pushed for a peace agreement.

## Anthony Rowland Buckingham

Tony (born November 28, 1951) could give James Bond a run for his money. Yachtsman, rallyist, ex-SBS/SAS, businessman, self-made oil and mining tycoon, and alleged behind-the-scenes player and author in a number of intriguing scripts, Tony Buckingham is chief executive of Heritage Oil and Gas. He began as a deep-sea diver working on offshore oil-platform support in various parts of the world and then moved on to put together his own offshore oil deals, primarily with Canadian-based Ranger in Angola. Tony would just be another oil tycoon complete with yachts, fast cars, and big houses except for his hobby of introducing mercenary groups to embattled leaders of countries.

Tony also shies away from the spotlight, preferring to have partners and front men. Some of his business partners have included Robert Friedland, Salim Saleh of Uganda (Museveni's half-brother), and Raymond Moi (son of President Daniel Arap Moi).

Tony first hit the radar when, in January 1993, Buckingham suggested to the MPLA that a little company called Executive Outcomes could help clean up the problems at the Soyo complex. It seems Tony had a computerized pumping station that was costing him $20,000 a day to lease and the rebels wouldn't give it back. Buckingham and Simon Mann convinced the MPLA to commission Eeben Barlow to recruit a force of South African veterans to capture Soyo from UNITA. It was tight but less than 100 men took Soyo for long enough to get Tony's gear out. When it was handed over to the Angolan army, they promptly lost it again—proving to the government of Angola that using mercs to take care of business was a good idea. EO took care of business and a week later the Angolan government flew Tony down to discuss the delicate matter of kicking the rebels out of the rest of the country. The bill was $40 million for the first year and the 300 men who ended up staying chucked the pretence of training and went straight into battle and forced the rebels of UNITA to sign a peace treaty. So was born the modern corporate mercenary army.

EO was off and running. Other gigs followed—Sierra Leone, the alleged rescue of kidnapped foreigners from the OPM in Irian Jaya, a few training jobs in sandy places, and the most famous mercenary gig that never happened: Bougainville.

One would never suppose that the April 7, 1996, meeting between Singirok, then-PNG defense minister, Mathias Ijape, and Tony Buckingham at the Cairns Hilton would set the wheels in motion for the Bougainville fiasco, ending up in a very profitable venture for Sandline, a major corruption probe of the PNG government, and peace talks for the rebels. Tony Buckingham can be seen on the yachting scene or you might bump into him at antique car rallies. Trivia for journos hot on the trail: Tony owns an appropriately named yacht, *Bit of a Coup*.

http://www.sandline.com

## Bob Denard

Bob Denard, 73, can never really be accused of working behind the scenes. He is the most flamboyant and unrepentant of the mercenaries. He has always operated in direct linkage with the French government and its interests. Born in Bordeaux in 1929 as Gilbert Bourgeaud, he began his military career at age 16 with the navy, but was thrown out for starting a fight in a Saigon bar. This, according to Denard, is the only official fighting he did in uniform. He worked as a policeman in Tunisia and was fired for conspiring to overthrow the prime minister of France (who was working for Tunisian independence). He tried his hand as a kitchen appliance salesman for Moulinex but in 1960 went to the Congo to join as a mercenary. Here Mad Mike Hoare teamed up with the gregarious Bourgeaud and in the spirit of rapid African military promotion he became "Colonal Robert Denard." He tried fighting for the Biafra against Nigeria and lost, then the communist rebels in Angola and lost, and then lost again in Rhodesia. Losing seems to be something that supports the romantic right-wing image of a mercenary. He likes to brag that he invaded Zaire with 100 men on bicycles. He also messed around in a number of dirty wars from Afghanistan to Yemen. But the event that defines and redeems him is the take-over of the Comoros. In August of 1975, Denard found himself in charge . . . He suddenly found himself the ultimate ruler of a tropical island. Denard deposed Soilih (who was shot 18 times while "trying to escape") and ruled the island for 11 years. He reinstated Ahmed Abdallah and created a 500-man presidential guard. When Abdallah was killed in 1989, the French, under pressure from the other African states, and Bob left on a South African military plane. He lived in South Africa until 1993, by which time he cut a deal to return to France to stand charges for a 1977 Benin invasion rather than his Comoros vacation. He then reinvaded the Cormoros in September 1995 with only 12 men against the 4,000-man Comoroan army.

His recent trial for the 1989 assassination of Comoroan leader Ahmed Abdallah resulted in acquittal, but it was not necessarily due to any hard evidence (there were dramatically conflicting stories of how the leader was shot). Denard has seven wives and has at various times converted to Judaism (in Morocco) and Islam (in the Comoros) and then back to Catholicism.

What is in the future for Bob? His biography *The Last Corsair* awaits translation into English and Clint Eastwood has the film rights to his life, so stay tuned.

## The Congolomerates

You would never know from the corporate brochures, Web sites, and press releases that these companies are involved in military and security activities around the world, many on behalf of Uncle Sam. Nope, they don't hire trigger-pullers, but they do provide infrastructure, information, equipment, and so on.

### Death from Behind a Desk

Because of the old-boy network and need for inside contacts, many soldiers of fortune do not make their money fighting on the ground, but make themselves available for higher-level training and transportation contracts. They might source leased aircraft, arrange weapons transfers, organize rescue attempts, or train eager recruits to shoot guns and blow things up, all the while living in air-conditioned comfort complete with CNN.

Today's mercenary is not a cigar-chomping, muscle-bound adventurer with a bandolier of 50mm bullets and grenades hung like Christmas ornaments. He is more likely to be an unemployed soldier 30 to 35 years of age who can't find work with his specialized skills. The pay is good when you have skills and tepid if you don't (mercenaries make between $2,000 and $15,500 a month, depending on skills, rank, type of job, and benefits); in its glory years, Executive Outcomes took great pains to provide medivac, health, and life insurance as well as one year's pay for those killed in battle. It may surprise you to learn that many of the companies that provide security like DSL and MPRI are actually part of big, fat-bottom conglomerates. Yes, Brewster, if you buy stock in L3 Communications (LLL-N), you too can be a mercenary. L3 snapped up the outstanding stock of MPRI on June 30, 2000, for $35.7 million. Gone are the sword and the smiling generals, to be replaced by the gray-suited dude in a classroom. War will never be the same.

**MPRI**
1201 East Abingdon Drive, Suite 425
Alexandria, VA 22314
Tel.: (703) 684-0853
Fax: (703) 684-3528
http://www.mpri.com/channels/home.
html
Jobs
http://www.mpri.com/subchannels/job_
listings.cfm
http://www.sec.gov/Archives/edgar/data/
1056239/0000950136-01-000717.txt

**ArmorGroup**
100 East Street, SE
Suite 301
Vienna, VA 22180
Tel.: (703) 242-2525
Fax: (703) 242-9020
info@armorgroup.com
http://www.armorgroup.com
ArmorGroup provides turnkey solutions for global security risk management, business information, and intelligence. They work for corporations, government agencies, and nongovernment organizations (NGOs). The company was originally founded in 1969 as American Body Armor & Equipment, Inc. (ABA) and engaged solely in the development, manufacture, and distribution of bullet- and projectile-resistant garments. In 1996, they began buying companies related to security and personal protection—among them the British company Defense Systems Limited. ArmorGroup has about 3,000 employees and operates on 5 continents and has annual revenue of around $156 million.

**Pacific Architects and Engineers (PAE Group)**
888 South Figueroa Street, Suite 1700
Los Angeles, CA 90017
Tel.: (213) 593-3200
Fax: (213) 481-7189
http://www.paechl.com
Established in 1955, PAE has over 6,000 employees and offices in the United States and overseas. They provide support for military operations, government contracts, and infrastructure for Uncle Sam from Liberia to Russia.

**Dyncorp**
Dyncorp World Headquarters
11710 Plaza America Drive
Reston, VA 20190
Tel.: (703) 261-5000
http://www.dyncorp.com
Created in 1946, initially to provide air-cargo services, Dyncorp has $1.8 billion in revenue and a $4.4 billion contract backlog. They focus mainly on information handling with very close links to the CIA, the military, and other law-enforcement agencies.

**International Charter Incorporated of Oregon (ICI Oregon)**
1860 Hawthorne Avenue, NE, Suite 390
Salem, OR 97303
Tel.: (503) 589-1437
Fax: (503) 371-7285
http://www.icioregon.com/index.htm
ICI Oregon provides air support for the U.S. government overseas in places like Liberia, Haiti, Sierra Leone, and Nigeria.

## Halliburton

jobs@halliburton.com

http://www.halliburton.com/kbr/kbr.asp

Founded in 1919, Halliburton is an international company with annual revenues of $16 billion and more than 100,000 employees in 100 countries. Halliburton wants men and women who seek challenges and adapt quickly to new technology and the ever-changing needs of their clients. They believe that providing diverse opportunities is a key to maximizing their employees' talents.

## SAIC

10260 Campus Point Drive

San Diego, CA 92121

Tel.: (800) 430-7629

http://www.saic.com

Science Applications Incorporated (SAIC) began in 1969 in La Jolla, California. It was started by CEO Dr. J. Robert Beyster on February 3, 1969, with two nuke consulting contracts, one from Los Alamos and one from Brookhaven National Labs. SAIC now has 35 companies, subsidiaries, and equity partners. They are now involved in national security programs, non-nuclear energy studies, health-care systems, environment-related businesses, information technologies, high-technology products, telecommunications, transportation, and eBusiness products and services to commercial and government customers.

## Vinnell Corporation

12150 East Monument Dr., Suite 800

Fairfax, VA 22033-4053

Tel.: (703) 385-4544

Fax: (703) 385-3726

http://www.vinnell.com

## ACS Defense, Inc.

5 Burlington Woods Dr., Suite 100

Burlington, MA 01603

Tel.: (781) 272-7910

## AirScan, Inc.

3505 Murrell Road

Rockledge, FL 32955

Tel.: (321) 631-0005

Fax: (321) 631-5811

airscan@airscan.com

http://www.airscan.com

## J&S Franklin Ltd.

Franklin House

151 Strand

London WC2R 1HL, UK

Tel.: (44) (0) 171-836 5746

Fax: (44) (0) 171-836 2784

defence@franklin.co.uk

http://www.franklin.co.uk

## Armor Holdings, Inc.

http://www.armorholdings.com

http://www.armorgroup.com

## The Peanut Gallery

There is a growing list of experts on the wonderful world of mercenary, private military, and private security companies that continue to shape world events both on camera and behind the scenes.

*Doug Brooks*
IPOA
21 E. Bellefonte Avenue #106
Alexandria, VA 22301
Tel.: (202) 297-9717
Fax: (413) 480-2033
dbrooks@ipoaonline.org
http://www.IPOAonline.org

*Dr. Abdel Fatau-Musah*
Centre for Democracy and Development
Unit 6, Canonbury Yard
190a, New North Road
London N1 7BJ, UK
Tel.: (44) (0) 207 288 8666
Fax: (44) (0) 207 288 8672
cdd@cdd.org.uk
http://www.cdd.org.uk

*Dr. Kevin O'Brien*
International Centre for Security
    Analysis (ICSA)
Department of War Studies
King's College, London
Strand Bridge House
138-142 Strand
London WC2R 2LS, UK
Tel.: (44) (0) 20-7848 1098
Fax: (44) (0) 20-7848 2972
icsa@kcl.ac.uk
http://www.kcl.ac.uk/orgs/icsa

*David Shearer*
International Institute for Strategic
    Studies
The International Institute for Strategic
    Studies, Arundel House
13-15 Arundel Street, Temple Place
London WC2R 3DX, UK
Tel.: (44) (0) 20 7379 7676
Fax: (44) (0) 20 7836 3108
http://www.iiss.org

*Center for Defense Information (CDI)*
1779 Massachusetts Avenue, NW
Washington, DC 20036
Contact: Rachel Stohl
Tel.: (202) 332-0600 ext. 105
Fax: (202) 462-4559
rstohl@cdi.org
http://www.cdi.org

# The Traders/Soldiers of Fortune/The Good Old Days

The idea of forming a corporation and then hiring soldiers to provide a little muscle is not a new one. The charter and trade companies are the historical model for the new PMCs. The Dutch East India Company, the Northwest Company, or the British North Borneo Company were given mercantile monopolies to develop and exploit "newly discovered" regions. Even when there wasn't a charter, enterprising men like Brooke of Sarawak or Stanford Raffles just sailed over and set up their own little domains. They are all examples of times when entire regions were carved up, exploited, and run by corporations with ties to distant sponsors. Their economic interests were slowly replaced by their colonial masters, carving much of the world into the mess it's become. In a world where an oil company or mining concerns can provide the majority of a country's cash, one would be a fool to think the government calls the shots, particularly when the populace has no idea how governments become governments.

One idea has resurfaced. Since there are still riches to be had and the local government is irrelevant, why not stake out that which is of value and let the rest of the pieces fall into place? These days the PMCs work within their sphere of influence, providing muscle or assistance that would be delicate or embarrassing for a national army to provide. So the Dyncorps, MPRIs, Vinnells, and AirScans are simply doing what the CIA or army did, just more quietly and at a profit. What could be more American than that?

**IPOA**                                        http://Dyncorp-sucks.com
21 E. Bellefonte Avenue #106
Alexandria, VA 22301
Tel.: (202) 297-9717
Fax: (413) 480-2033

## Gurkha Security Guards (GSG)

Reputedly, GSG was a front for the British government, set up to facilitate sending Ghurkas to Sierra Leone to defend the diamond mines. Lonrho used the GSG boys to guard its mines and they did de-mining in Mozambique. Nick Bell, a former officer in the Gurkha regiment of the British army, managed to provide a few good men (about 50) to Valentine Strasser. The salary is as high as $8,000 a month. Not bad for the durable little men from the mountains.

GSG mainly consists of Brits and Nepalese Ghurkas who have had service with Her Majesty's Forces or other security work. Oddly, the Ghurkas are already technically mercenaries so it isn't much of a career shift. Obviously, they lean toward hiring men from Nick's old outfit. His last client was the government of Sierra Leone, which was fighting an all-out war against RUF, a rebel faction. The leader of the GSG contingent in Sierra Leone, American Bob MacKenzie, was killed in the Malal Hills in February of 1995. He was killed, mutilated, and decapitated (hopefully in that order). After MacKenzie was killed, the Ghurkas returned to Nepal. GSG is now defunct.

## Executive Outcomes (EO)

Nick van der Bergh and Eeben Barlow used to run Executive Outcomes out of Pretoria, South Africa. Executive Outcomes was founded in 1989 by the 17-year veteran and former long-range recon soldiers from South Africa's 32nd Battalion. They began the new trend for corporate mercenaries in March 1993 when UNITA captured an oil-storage area in Soya owned by Heritage Oil, Sonangol, and a number of other oil concerns. The Forcas Armadas Angolanas (FAA) didn't quite know how to oust the rebels without blowing up the precious oil and drilling equipment. Tony Buckingham, who shared some offshore oil blocks and had some pricey equipment at risk, suggested to the powers that be that the state-owned oil company approach Barlow, who despite the impressive-sounding name of Executive Outcomes and paladin logo on his card, was a one-man band training the South African army and advising DeBeers on security.

EO's men attacked with 600 FAA troops and only ended up with three South Africans wounded. The facility was retaken and as soon as EO's men left, UNITA retook the facility. It was an important event because it showed that outside "security" forces could be used because they were politically sterile and provided military skills without jeopardizing the stability of tottering regimes.

When UNITA screamed that white mercenaries were fighting in Angola, the oil company mentioned they were just security guards. UNITA soon found out that they were not up against polyester-suited doughnut munchers, but ex-South African Defense Force men who had fought with UNITA during the 1976–1988 war in Angola. Money changes everything in the merc business.

EO quickly positioned itself as a security service that stabilizes mining operations, allowing governments to write checks based on the smooth flow of raw resources. EO's strength was keeping things aggressive and using local intel as well as creating detailed plans, acquiring and coordinating air support, relying on local militia who knew the turf, and paying close attention to the real sources of money: the mine owners and not the Ray-Banned dictators. Their gig in Soyo led to a much bigger offensive against UNITA until UNITA came to the negotiation table.

After their success in Angola, the beleaguered Valentine Strasser hired EO to replace the 50 Ghurka Security Guards who just left after their leader was killed. EO got busy shortly thereafter. Coincidentally, Buckingham was also doing business in Sierra Leone, making it two for two where a "private military company" showed up to clean up rebels in an oil- and diamond-rich area. The Koidu diamond mine was held 60 percent by Buckingham/Branch Energy, and now by Vancouver-based Diamondworks, with 40 percent held by the government.

The deal to EO was supposed to be worth $35.2 million. The fee started off at $1.2 million per month (supplied by the IMF) and was reduced to $1 million when things cooled down. EO is still owed $19.5 million, but hey, $35 million is a lot of money for a young military dictator to dig up on short notice. Strasser kept promising he would come up with the scratch, but did not pay one cent for the services provided by EO from the time they deployed in April–May 1995 to January 1996 when they made their first payment of $3 million. Despite the dunning war behind the scenes, EO saved the day in Sierra Leone. Troops were in-country by April, and they quickly managed to push back the rebels from 36 to 26 kilometers from the capital in just 9 days. They then pushed the rebels out of the Kono diamonds fields (about 216 kilometers east of Freetown) in just two days using helicopter gunships. Their reward was to be fired by Strasser in an effort to save $3 million in fees. Shortly after EO left Sierra Leone, about 3,000 rebels were invited back to Freetown by coup leader Johnny Paul Koroma.

Dogs of War, Inc., as some called EO, made sure that the world's press knew about this cleaner, brighter, whiter form of pay-as-you-go warfare. The press reacted accordingly and invented hundreds of lurid stories that usually revolved around mercenaries going after mineral concessions. Publicly, governments recoiled in horror, while privately asking if they could please see a brochure and a price list.

But the rotating circle of dictators, mercenaries, and resource companies became a little too obvious. So EO disappeared to avoid looming antimercenary legislation in South Africa and Sandline International adopted the mantle of the nice-guy corporate mercenary army for hire. Sandline quickly took the forefront in the PMC business, negotiating a little deal in Papua New Guinea to get rid of a secessionist movement on an island that used to provide over 40 percent of the country's money. Although Sandline subbed the dirty work to EO, it became apparent that they were kissing cousins, and once again there was a large mine involved on the island of Bougainville. The local military arrested their new protectors and an intensive inquiry revealed that the only war seemed to be outside military contractors fighting for PNG's defense money. EO is no longer, but oddly enough the principals confide that if anybody needs them, they may be willing to stage a comeback tour. *DP* Trivia: Mercenary and EO Founder Eeben Barlow is now a professional horse whisperer on the Diamond Western dude ranch in South Africa.

**Eeben Barlow**
The Cowboy School
Postnet Suite 158
Private Bag X18
Lynnwood Ridge
Republic of South Africa
0040
Tel.: (27) 83 454 6582
sacowboy@mweb.co.za
http://www.sacowboy.com

# Sandline International

The genesis for Sandline (as in "line in the sand") came from the same impetus that turned Executive Outcomes into a multimillion-dollar private army. Oilman Tony Buckingham and business partner and ex-Scots Guard Simon Mann approached Tim Spicer in October 1995 and asked if he was interested in creating a UK-based version of Executive Outcomes. Spicer, working as a Middle East salesman for a UK-investment firm, passed. By April 1996, he was putting together a gig in Papua New Guinea that was referred by another Scots Guard, Alastair Sims at Defense Systems Limited. He was back in London exactly a year later having been arrested, jailed, charged, and questioned in a debacle that left him with $30 million still unpaid for his plan to defeat the rebels in Bougainville.

On December 23 Tim had a contract in hand from the deposed president of Sierra Leone, who needed help to get back in power. Technically, fugitive Rakesh Saxena was footing the $10 million bill but all the paperwork was set up just right. Rakesh peels off $1.5 mil and the Sandline boys get to work: Bernie McCabe, ex-Delta Force; Cobus Claassens, ex-EO; Jamie Farr, ex-SAS; and Bert Saches, ex-SADF—a veritable UN of mercenaries. Project Python gets snakey when the local Nigerian peacekeepers take matters into their own hands and ECO-MOG rolls the rebels and junta soldiers out of Freetown, leaving Sandline in the midst of planning and supporting. Rakesh welshes on the remaining money and President Kabbah stiffs him on the concessions, which leaves Tim with a bit of a shit storm when he returns to the United Kingdom. It seems that the British government has decided that the 30 tons of Bulgarian war toys are a violation of an arms embargo. Naturally the politicians don't know their RUFs from their AFRCs since the ban applied to the rebel government, not Nigeria, aka ECOMOG. Timmy made the mistake of keeping the diplos in the loop all the while. Oops, plenty of egg on the face, legal bills, posturing, and press clippings and nobody even notices that the container of weapons has magically disappeared, and once again mercenaries come to the rescue.

Careful observers would notice that there seem to be more efficient and far more mercenary talents behind the scenes at Sandline. In October of 1998, the government of PNG was forced legally to cough up $25 million for the $18 million in contract fees. It looks like EO may even get the missing $20 million they never collected back in '95 as well. In September of 2000, Tim got his walking papers and is now running his own private military company and Web site at http://www.sci2000.ws.

*Sandline International*
535 King's Road
London SW10 OSZ, UK
Tel.: (44) 171 351 5555
Fax: (44) 171 351 5555
Tel.: (703) 921-9619 (U.S. Representative)
Fax: (703) 921-9621 (U.S. Representative)
http://www.sandline.com

## Happiness Is a Dead Infidel: The Mujahideen

The *muj* have suffered the most dramatic reversal in fortune since Jane
Fonda went to North Vietnam or John Walker Lindh went to
Afghanistan. Our first introduction to *"muj"* was grainy 16mm films
and 8mm video from the war against the Soviets in Afghanistan. They
seemed like likable blokes, if not a little crazy, and it seems like they
were happy that America was their new best friend. Until a guy named
bin Laden came along and the whole story changed . . . but we are getting ahead of ourselves.

A *mujahid* (warrior for god) fights in a *jihad* (struggle). On the surface not much different from any other religious-inspired volunteer
who goes off to a foreign land and fights. A mujahid is a Muslim who is
bound by a set of rules and is rewarded for his death, injury, or service,
not with money but in the afterlife. There are many ways a Muslim can
contribute to jihad, fighting on the front lines being the most well
known.

Jihad and the mujahids started with Mohammed 1,500 years ago
and was really cooking during the Crusades. It died down for five centuries, and then an almost retro enthusiasm hit in 1979, when the
Soviets decided to install a puppet in Afghanistan and flew in troops to
take over the country. As with all foreign invaders who decided to roll
armies into Afghanistan, they forgot that the tribes there love a good
fight. So much so that the Afghans have historically fought among
themselves even after the conquerors have left. So what makes Afghanistan any different from any other Muslim nation fighting a foreign
invader? Well, for starters, a feisty little guy named Azzam and a fat
rich guy named Uncle Sam. The war against the Soviets in Afghanistan
was the unfortunate collision of two highly explosive powers and the
genesis of our current troubles.

Abdullah Yusuf Azzam was a Palestinian born in the village of Seelet
al-Hartiyeh in the West Bank in 1941. Azzam (which means "the call to
prayer") went on to study at Khadorri College near Tul Karem and
then went on to teach in the village of Adder in southern Jordan. He

fought against the Israelis in the '67 war and soon afterward went to Egypt to get his master's degree in Islamic law, or *shariah*, from the University of Al-Azhar.

He was expelled from Jordan in 1970 along with other Islamic militants and began teaching in Saudi Arabia. In 1979, he went to Afghanistan to fight against the Soviets. He tried teaching at the Islamic University in Peshawar but eventually began working full time to support the jihad against the Russians. In March of 1980, he opened an office at 67 Sayed Jamaludin Afghani Road. It was an era and place similar to Haight Ashbury, except the young men came to the area around Peshawar University for war, not drugs. He moved his family to Peshawar and founded the Bait-ul-Ansar, or Mujahadeen Services Bureau. The most popular newspaper was the Arabic language al-*jihadi* and one of the eager young Arabs who helped him at the newspaper office at 77 Jamaludin Afghani Road in Peshawar was Osama bin Laden. They prayed at the Momin Khan mosque in the university town near the 1913 college. He wrote a watershed book called *Join the Caravan*. That book, along with others, encouraged young Muslim men from around the world to travel to Afghanistan to fight in the jihad. He also provided the basic services they needed when they arrived. More important, he elevated the concept of jihad to mythical status. He created a sense of invincibility and mystique by spreading stories of their exploits against the Russians and he also created a pipeline from America to the Philippines that brought young men to be trained.

The first attempt on Assam's life occurred in 1989 when a bomb under the area where he was to speak was found. He, along with his two sons, was finally killed on November 24, 1989, by three car bombs planted along his route to the mosque. The young Saudi who killed him has always been assumed to be Azzam's protégé. His name was Osama bin Laden.

The 12,000 to 15,000 foreign-born and Afghan-trained "Afghans" who fought in the '80s are the direct effect of too much money, training, and weapons being funneled into one of the world's poorest regions—Pakistan and Afghanistan. The United States decided this would be a great time to give the Russians a bloody nose, prompting it to send in massive amounts of money to support the seven dwarfs, or seven *mujahideen* groups that the Pakistanis chose to fight the Russians. All the Afghan groups had to do was provide a head count, a list of weapons, and an area of operations, and they were in business. Naturally, the smart ones happily accepted the weapons and also stockpiled them for sale or use after the Russians left. The foreigners who came to fight were not directly supported by the Americans but the country was awash in cheap weapons, no border controls, and a tolerance for any group that was hostile to the Russians.

The result is that the Gulf states and United States (through the CIA, via the Pakistan ISI or secret service) created a new "franchise" of warrior clans armed to the teeth with the common goal of causing the Russians grief. Simple, gun-happy tribesmen were trained in everything from how to make explosives out of fertilizer to how to use Stinger missiles. The CIA not only provided more than enough money; they created an unholy recruitment and support network where these factions could later swap war skills and business cards. When these fighters went home, they began to create smaller networks that would work to overthrow their own governments. What the Americans didn't notice or care about was that the common enemy of the foreign jihadis was all infidel oppressors of Muslims, which included Israel and its supporter America.

Don't think that all these muj came from the back streets of third-world countries. Recruits and funding were actively sought in 28 states in the United States, but the number of U.S. volunteers was minuscule compared to Azzam's recruits in the Gulf region. Most U.S. jihadis were black and few put up with the austere conditions of the war in Russia. These days you can find the second generation of the Russian jihad fighting in places like Somalia, Yemen, Tajikistan, Algeria, Chechnya, Saudi Arabia, Afghanistan, the Balkans, Sudan, Indonesia, the Philippines, and many more countries.

## How to Get In

Most muj start out as Koranic students from *madrassahs,* or religious schools. Part of being a good Muslim is the need to protect Islam from infidels. Some are more militant about it than others. The concept of jihad is designed to provide a bulwark against oppression or eradication of Islam. There is both defensive and offensive jihad. To be a holy warrior is the highest calling, a straight shot into paradise if you are killed. Don't confuse suicide bombers with holy warriors. It is understood that Allah will choose the time that you will be brought into paradise.

Mullahs who teach in madrassahs will often recruit volunteers for jihads. Your local mosque in Pittsburgh is not necessarily shipping off recruits to Algeria, but there are more militant groups found in the mosques in suburban New York, Istanbul, or London. These days you would have better luck going to a synagogue and asking where you sign up to join the neo-Nazis. Even overseas, the recruiting offices are not looking kindly at eager American muslims, after Jihad Johnny made the news; either way, don't write down "Langley, Virginia" as

## SMITE THE PURPLE ONE!

For those of you who like Jihad-Lite, you can become a holy warrior against the most insidious of evils: Barney (or B'harnii, as his unholy name is translated literally by the site). Enter the dark side with tales of horror about the purple saurian that will boil your blood and make you rise up in indignation.

http://www.jihad.net

your home address. The muj network has become an old-boy network and the stakes are getting much higher after September 11. You would have a hard time convincing anyone that you are a loyal American and a devout Muslim and you want to fight a brutal oppressive regime in a jihad. If you do get in with a group, don't expect much. John Walker Lindh was the exception, not the rule.

Volunteers are usually sent directly to the area of conflict and receive whatever training is required on the spot. The most popular spot for muj to train used to be in Afghanistan, but most camps are now in Azad Kashmir. There are camps in Chechnya, the southern Philippines, Yemen, Russia, Sudan, Iran, East Africa, the Middle East, and other spots, but jihad as an acceptable form of helping people out is going to be out of vogue for a while.

Life in the camps is pretty austere—up before dawn for prayers, religious studies, weapons training, assault drills, explosives, and tactics. Lunch is simple (usually flat bread, sugared tea, rice, bean soup, and the odd goat or cow bits). Basic training is short (about two weeks) equipment is cheap or nonexistent (there are no uniforms), and the only R&R is soccer or volleyball. You live in tents, use pit toilets, pray five times a day, and then get shipped out to a jihad of the trainer's choice. There isn't a lot of ammunition fired or money spent on your training. If you are successful, you become a *shaheed,* or martyr. If you don't get killed, you are still guaranteed a spot in heaven for being a mujahideen. Money? Sorry.

There is no pay, but your hosts will provide simple food, beat-up equipment, transportation, and crude shelter. *DP*'s muj friends recommend that you bring your own gear, especially boots. Some camps will charge for training and room and board. Most will issue you weapons and ammo but any luxuries should be brought in (like rain gear, GPS, first-aid kits, etc.). The life of a muj is usually spent sitting around poorly fortified positions or in hidden camps, drinking tea, and waiting for your commander to put together an ambush. If you get caught, expect what you came for.

http://www.islaam.com/articles/
objectives_of_jihaad.htm
http://www.azzam.com
http://www.qoqaz.com
http://www.jihad.cjb.net
http://www.quraan.com/Bukhari/52.asp
http://www.quraan.com/Muslim/content
19.asp

### Saudia Arabia
BM Box: MIRA
London WC1N 3XX, UK
Tel.: (44) (0) 208 452 0303
Fax: (44) (0) 208 452 0808

### Pakistan/Kashmir
Lashgar-e-Taiba
http://www.jamatdawa.org

Harakat ul Mujahideen (Kashmir)
Herkat-ul-Mujahideen Head Office:
House No. B-154
Khayban-i-Sir Sayad,
Near C.D.A. Bus Stop
Rawalpindi, Pakistan
Tel./Fax: (92) 4414810

### Jamaat-e-Islami
Mansoora, Multan Road
Lahore 54570, Pakistan
Tel.: (92) 42 7844605 9
Fax: (92) 42 5419505
http://www.jamaat.org

### Muslim Brotherhood
http://www.ummah.org.uk/ikhwan
http://www.ikhwanmuslimoon-
jordan.org

### Laskar Jihad (Indonesia)
Jl. Kaliurang Km 15 Tromol pos 08,
Pakem, Sleman
Yogyakarta 55582, Indonesia
Tel./Fax: (62) (0) 274-895790

Jl. Cempaka Putih Tengah XXVIB No. 78
Jakarta 10510, Indonesia
Tel./Fax: (62) (0) 21 4246417
http://www.laskarjihad.or.id

### Truth is stranger than fiction department
http://www.freejohnwalker.net

# TERRORISM

## I Hear You Knockin', But You Can't Come In

*DP* spends a lot of time with "terrorists." We sit around and kill time, drink tea, tell bad jokes, talk politics, show pictures of our kids, discuss foreign policy, and scratch our heads at how our hosts became "terrorists."

Every time we have a chin wag with an air force pilot, talib, Indian major, Palestinian kid, Israeli settler, rebel leader, child soldier, paramilitary, mercenary, or missionary, we are talking to terrorists. A quick search of the word *terrorist* would include everything from the IRS to suicide bombers. If you Google the word "terrorist" you will find 2,750,000 individual mentions on the Internet. So it's easy to lose track of what the most overused term in recent history actually means.

If you have enough money to actually afford this book or read it with the help of a lightbulb, you probably think that terrorism can be

easily defined as "premeditated, politically motivated violence perpetrated against noncombatant targets by subnational groups or clandestine agents usually intended to influence an audience," as it is by
United States Code Section 2656(d).

If you are sitting in a house being bulldozed or being bombed by
those "civilized" nations, you might beg to differ. To you, terror is the
threat or use of violence against noncombatants, and the official adoption of the tactic by a group thus creates a terrorist group. Even a truc-
ulent scholar would be hard-pressed to find a conflict in the last 4,000
years that didn't involve the use of terror. From the Huns through the
Crusades, the Cold War, and the War on Terrorism—all include deliberate acts of violence against noncombatants by both sides.

But before you get your Ché beret in a knot, keep in mind that terrorism is a natural part of war. It uses the idea of force projection—scaring the pants out of your enemy so he thinks you are bigger and
tougher than he is. One army banging away at another army results in
expensive wars of attrition. Most wars have been fought based on a
simple ratio of man-to-man, gun-to-gun, and dollar-to-dollar. Those
with more money, people, and resources ultimately win wars. Until, of
course, you win—then the victor is faced with the problematic conditions called "low-intensity conflict," "asymmetric warfare," and "low-
level insurgencies." When whoever was supposed to be the winner
gets sick and tired, the losers are called "terrorists," and the "victors"
bang away again. Now *there* is an interesting point: Call them criminals
and they are treated carefully, with all their rights intact, grandstanding
lawyers, and Hollywood deals. Call them "tangos" or "terrs," and you
can do all kinds of dark and nefarious things with nary a *60 Minutes*
reporter or human-rights activist being the wiser.

The standard definition of *terrorism* is obviously the work of leaders
of established and recognized countries, most with democratic political
processes. The definition seems to skirt around groups we created who
are magically labeled "freedom fighters" in our press. Terrorists or freedom fighters? It depends on what week it is, who's in charge, and
what's in it for us.

What about the evil, oops, I mean the good: Kurds, Moros, Israelis,
Contras, Tamils, Pakistanis, Afghans, and so on? All have been labeled
both terrorists and noble allies. Sometimes we give them money and
ask them to help. Sometimes we pay other people to kill them. Sometimes we pay them to kill other people. The fact is that the label "terrorist" is simply another weapon designed to make you dumber and less
interested in somebody's plight. Palestinian suicide bombers are terrorists when they blow up innocent victims, but Israeli soldiers assassinat-
ing innocent Palestinians are not. Okay, you get the point. It should be

remembered that the United States of America, Russia, China, France, and Israel, along with numerous other, now respectable, countries, began their road to independence using terrorist methods and actions against their past leaders. Genghis, Alexander, Caesar, Marx, Mao, the Khmer Rouge, and the military leaders of most militant, oppressed groups have all shown that terrorism is just a natural and, sadly, successful element of conflict.

Even today when we fight our remote-control wars with covert operators, proxy armies, smart bombs, AC-130 Specters, and B-52s all slickly presented in video debriefings in Serbia, Afghanistan, and Iraq, we are sowing terror into the minds of the people on the ground. "Premeditated, politically motivated violence perpetrated against noncombatant targets by clandestine agents usually intended to influence an audience," if I remember correctly. I left out subnational groups. It doesn't really matter who is doing the terrorizing these days.

Forgive me and I will put away my soapbox. The point is, labels can blind us to the purpose of a conflict. A war in the shadows can leave a very long, dark stain on a country that insists it has the moral high ground. More important, anyone who chooses to die for something should be listened to very carefully, and possibly corrective action should be taken. Oddly enough, Alexander the Great had a very simple solution to prevent terrorism and festering uprising. He married off his commanders to local lasses and hey, presto, all warfare was contained to the dining table and bedroom. Whether you agree with these groups or not, you do need to pay close attention to what they are saying and why they are being so damn obnoxious about reminding us about it on a regular basis. Remember one aspect of terrorism is putting you and the kids on the front line in your country's hissy fits, and you don't even get a helmet or a gun.

Today, few can argue that terrorism is and will be a legitimate and sadly productive method to gain international attention, demand concessions, and eventually establish legitimate states, legal representation, or political parties. As in Waco, Oklahoma City, and the World Trade Center, a few angry people can change the course of history, not always for the better. Despite what the world's governments espouse, there are few minority or splinter groups that can use the existing political process to gain their independence or freedom without resorting to outrageous tactics.

The less potent the group is as a political force and the thinner the support base, the more likely the group will resort to more dramatic methods to secure world attention. Typically terrorists are not the unshaven, bug-eyed wild men you see on TV and in the movies. Leaders of these groups tend to be male, between 30 and 50, from the upper classes, and are educated, creative, charismatic, and often deeply religious. (They may be religious, but some are unable to remember the basic and very similar codes of conduct found in most religions.) Another fact you don't read too much about: Out of 9,000 terrorist incidents, only about a dozen have resulted in the deaths of more than 100 people. Until Bang!, they get lucky. September 11 was a stunning combination of luck, theatrics, and reality programming; yet, the death toll was insignificant when compared to other less public but equally murderous events in Afghanistan, Central Africa, Iraq, and other regions.

But even the death tolls from Karachi to Wall Street are kid's play compared to what those mainstream governments can do to their own people in places like Iraq or Rwanda. So if these guys are so smart and effective, in the words of Butch and Sundance . . . "Who are these guys?"

## Why Do Terrorists and Rock Stars Have Only One Name?

Well, first off all, terrorists (and rock stars) are never military or Spartacus material. Terrorist leaders tend to be overeducated, effete, egotistical, and flamboyant almost to the point of ridiculousness. Perhaps they should be called "rich kids with issues": Osama, Ché, Arafat, Khattab, Ocalan, Carlos, and Rafael Sebastin Guillen Vicente—aka the much snappier-sounding Subcommandante "Marcos," the pipe-smoking, wisecracking son of a furniture salesman—are not the exception, but the rule. It's all about image, something Madonna, Shakira, Sting, and thousands of rock groups know. You need a snappy one-word name to get good ink. So if you combine terrorists' fame with their lack of effectiveness, you also see another problem. Despite their "gang that couldn't shoot straight" performance and convoluted obscure rants, the media love them, allowing them to pose in front of flags, holding AKs, and getting more airtime on CNN than MTV gives to P-Diddy.

Now you start to see where the terr boys are really working it: your mind. Yes, that old whipped and abused shady craft of publicity is at fault again. Why? Well, the real crime is that terrorist groups play up to the media. It's the ultimate codependency. The media gleefully parrot the terrorists' stern warnings, empty threats, grainy videos, big explosions, funny outfits, cheesy theatrical backdrops, and unwarranted mystique. Reporters proudly trumpet their "exclusive," stage-managed interviews and nobody points out that the content is silly and those outfits are just plain goofy. Terrorism has brought cable-access-quality video and teenage role-playing scriptwriting to the world's highest tech networks.

It's not about content, quality, or performance, it's all about eyeballs. Forget hearts and minds. The terrorists' ultimate goal is TRPs (total rating points) not GNPs (gross national product). One simple act of minor terrorist violence can quickly result in endless replays of footage, mind-numbing "expert" commentary, and even more idle speculation as to who was behind it or why it matters. You could make a convincing case that without the global news networks, Osama bin Laden would have a hard time getting his relatives to watch his home videos. Terrorists are men who carefully play the press like pimps working twitchy crack ho's: withholding and giving access, controlling every frame of footage, and then blaming the same people for demonizing them. The same people who decry terrorism also sell ads, create mythology, and perpetuate the dime-store romance of these tweaked misfits.

## Land of the Lost

So what if you actually want to go meet these people, like we do? According to our government, you will see the roots of evil in Iran, Libya, Sudan, Syria (and its vassal state Lebanon), Pakistan, and Afghanistan. Funny how these are the same places that our government tells you *not* to visit. Like the bogeyman in the woodshed, they don't want you to check it out . . . "just trust us." But anyone who wants to see the roots of terrorism, the tender shoots of violence, and the fruit of its bitter fruit can save a lot of money in his or her quest.

It may surprise you to know that the roots of terrorism are found in Manhattan boardrooms, Asian gas stations, Dutch oil companies, the Pentagon, or even the bedroom of the former president. The dollars that keep the blood flowing and the talking heads tut-tutting is as American as apple pie, as European as latte, and as Japanese as sushi. Yes, it's true, we supply the money that keeps the rogue states roguish and the terrorists terrorizing. "Huh?" you eloquently reply.

Doesn't Shell supply the vast majority of income to Syria via oil payments? Doesn't Japan buy most of the oil that Iran produces? Doesn't Qaddafi keep those Ferraris topped up in Europe and doesn't the United States keep the Saudis in Bentleys? Just who does buy the diamonds plucked out of Angola or Liberia? Where do bin Laden's rich Wahhabist patrons get their oil money from? Carpets, sand sculptures, knick-knacks at the airport? Sorry, you know exactly where. Just how did bin Laden's daddy get so rich? Who injects the heroin that keeps the Chechen mafia in wide-lapelled suits? Who toots the coke that fuels the rebels rebelling in Colombia? I could go on, but you get the point. Most terrorist organizations are fueled by patrons and regimes that are fueled by . . . literally . . . fuel. Most criminal organizations get their cash directly from Western consumers. In other words, the riches from the drug, sex, and smuggling trades keeps terrorists terrorizing.

The next time you see an act of terrorism, stop and think. How the hell did they get money for that?

Everyone is guilty. Everyone is innocent. Terrorism is not that simple.

## Stop, Hey, What's That Sound?

Terrorism is a phenomenon that cannot be moderated by legal purpose, thick sheaves of legislation, or even firm conviction. You can't bomb it, nuke it, burn it, or kill it. Even drum circles, bake-offs, or group hugs have proven terribly ineffective. Aren't innocent but very dead Serbs, Iraqis, Iranians, Afghans, Sudanese, and other impoverished peoples the same as dead and innocent Americans, British, Australians, and Canadians? The difference is that we are right and they are wrong. Right? Wrong? Right . . . ? In the final analysis if any group lives in such conditions that they decide to die for their cause, then it bears some serious looking into. The seeds of revolution are never clear or pretty, but once they take root they are impossible to stop. The way to stop terrorism is to listen. Scrape off the labels and angry rhetoric and listen. You will see that the desperate and calculated acts of terrorists are all based in legitimate grievances, but grievances that are rarely addressed or understood. It doesn't take long for criminal, political, and militant groups to tap into the red-hot flame. Typically most terrorist groups that have morphed into the political mainstream have simply been given what they asked for . . . or have taken it by force. The other option is simply to kill the entire ethnic, religious, or political group behind the disturbance, but this solution is rapidly falling out of fashion. Nothing makes terrorism vanish faster than putting your cash where your mouth was, or your money where your bomb was.

The U.S. State Department estimates that about 21 percent of world terror is directed against the United States. Most of it is a result of our support of Israel and propping up of the Saud regime, oil projects in South America and Africa, attacks on Muslim countries, and just generally being the biggest bully on the block. Of course, the State Department turns a blind eye toward Oklahoma City, Elian, anthrax, Eric Rudolph, Waco, the Unabomber, random snipers, bombers, and assassins grown in our own political garden. And then there's the oddly disturbing fact that most of the people who flew the planes into the buildings on 9/11 had a perfect right to be here, two of them getting their U.S. visas long after they had gone to meet their 72 virgins.

Although most people can recite chapter and verse on bin Laden, 9/11, and Afghanistan, the predominant number of terrorist attacks against U.S. interests occur in Colombia against oil facilities. Yes, even by our own calculations the biggest threat to America is in Colombia, not the Middle East, yet we chose to wage overt war in Afghanistan and keep our covert war down south hush-hush.

But if you look beyond the carefully crafted definitions of terrorism put together by a timid PC-sensitive government, terrorism is a much more pervasive problem. Nuclear weapons, biochemical weapons, cluster bombs, land mines, and other "traditional" forms of warfare generate far more terror amongst the world populations than the people who have turned public transit vehicles into military weapons.

But that is where I leave it. Terrorism is the most feared foe of established democracies because it forces them to subvert the clean ideals that they pride themselves on. It creates a police state, a state of fear, harsh punishments, and tight controls. Does terrorism work? You bet.

## Terrorism 101

Making mountains of severed heads is just sooo time-consuming. Chopping little baby's hands off seems counterproductive, especially if you have to be kissing them when you get your chance to run for office later. Just popping off mid-level politicians doesn't even make the back page of the local paper anymore. Convoluted manifestos with blurred pictures of long-dead idealists will get you round-filed faster than a dot.com prospectus. So to make sure everybody gets it right; there are certain tried-and-true methods to gaining the world's attention. In the old days it was easy: Attend a workers' meeting, look half-intelligent, rattle off some Marxist/Maoist/socialist clichés, and the commie agitators would give you an instant scholarship to Patrice Lumumba U. There you would learn how to blow things up and maybe even sing "Bandera Rosa" in Swahili. Then it's back home to take potshots at the local soldiers. The death of Mother Russia pretty much 86'd that whole retro revolution stuff. There are few commie shindigs going on in Colombia, Nepal, the Philippines, India, and Peru. But will *Das Kapital* ever replace Harry Potter? Puhleeze . . .

> These days terrorism tends to be a little harder to figure out.

These days terrorism tends to be a little harder to figure out. Gone are the easier-to-read Spanish and Portuguese insults, gone are the dashing glamour boys, gone are the poor versus rich, "If I had two shirts, I would give you one" philosophy. Now we are faced with towelheaded geezers jabbering in Arabic, condemning everything and anything, plowing commuter planes into offices full of working stiffs, disassembling suburban kids in pizzerias, vaporizing pensioners on buses, and just generally pissing us off. Well, what gives?

We know somehow the New Crusades have something to do with Afghanistan, beards, the Koran, and chicks wearing blue sacks, but we can't quite put our finger on what that has to do with the Saudis and Egyptians who actually did all the damage. These terrorists have tongue-twisting names, seem to live here, use the Internet a lot, and rely on the local Home Depot to ply their deadly trade. Well, the *DP* cheat sheet should help you out.

## THE TERMINAL MEN (AND WOMEN)

Here are the groups that have come up with a nifty way to reduce pension expenses and jazz up their press releases. These groups specialize in suicide as a form of terrorism or military attacks complete with videos and photos of the bomber:

| | |
|---|---|
| Al Aqsa Brigades | Israel and Occupied Territories |
| Hamas | Israel and Occupied Territories |
| Islamic Jihad | Israel and Occupied Territories |
| Hizbollah | Lebanon |
| Islamic Jihad (EIJ) | Egypt |
| Gamaya Islamiya (Islamic Group) | Egypt |
| Armed Islamic Group (GIA) | Algeria |
| Barbar Khalsa International (BKI) | India |
| Liberation Tigers of Tamil Eelam (LTTE) | Sri Lanka |
| Osama bin Laden network (al-Qaeda) | Worldwide |

Islamic-based terrorism is rooted in three areas. First, the millions of young, poor people who live under autocratic rule form a swirling, angry mass that can be a lethal recruiting ground. They view Islam as a socialist-type movement that provides equality and eliminates privilege based strictly on wealth. The first group finds their outlet in underground political groups, many of whom have military wings. Egypt, Algeria, Yemen, and Indonesia are the main centers for this activity. Their targets tend to be local government and their supporters, more often than not including Uncle Sam.

# The Anti-Crusaders

Then there are the higher profile, less populist groups that seem fixated on Israel, Jerusalem, and the U.S. presence in the Holy Land of Mecca and Medina. These are the anti-Crusaders. These groups are run by disaffected intellectuals usually tossed out of their home country, supported by toasted ex-jihadis. These cranky expats provide connections with wealthy patrons in the Gulf and areas of Islamic diaspora like London and Istanbul. They funnel this money into small, greatly theatrical units who fail more than they succeed. These groups have a sense of fighting back against a united group called Crusaders and leaders of Islamic countries they call "apostates." They specialize in isolated attacks against high-profile targets to satisfy their patrons and to drum up support among the previous group. Much of their support is found in the Elmer Fudd–sounding but very orthodox Muslim Wahhabists found in the Gulf (and in the official belief of the Sauds).

These groups tend to focus on the classic and never-ending Middle East conflict that pits Arab against Jew for control over the Holy Land. This quasi-biblical catfight rehashes ancient enmities, each with a convenient memory for dates, facts, and rationales. Both sides enjoy a polarity of position, use of violence, and abuse of rhetoric that is envied by wrestlers, rappers, and comic-book writers alike. There's the Wahhabist/Salafist groups found in Algeria, Egypt, the Gulf, and sprinkled throughout Asia and South Asia.

# The Down-Home Idealists

Outside of the Middle East, you have a smattering of independence and grievance groups that are working for a political solution as they are slowly being picked off by the host nation's military (usually with our covert support). These groups tend to use whatever works at the time: traditional armed forces, student political wings, terrorist attacks, summary executions, and more. Somehow the idea that people should be given the right to self-determination has vanished and our hatred for Russia has morphed into a pathetic love. Many are aging communist or mainstream Islamic movements that are making little headway but keep the pot boiling. You will find these fractured and long-standing groups in Chechnya, Indonesia, India, the Philippines, Central Africa, and Colombia. None deliberately target the United States since they don't need to contend with two enemies, but given a choice, they will give us or our allies a jab. In many cases these groups work in collusion with the forces that oppose them because they are richer and better supported in the rural areas.

In Africa the concept of terrorism is ingrained into official government policy that most of the world ignores goings-on in Algeria, the Congo, Egypt, Uganda, Zimbabwe, South Africa, and other messy areas. If the media or world community were to apply standards, we would find ourselves just shaking our heads and focusing on finding a cure for cancer.

## A Hard Rain's Gonna Fall

So what is in the crystal ball; what will happen in the War on Terror? Well, things look pretty gloomy out there. As you progress down the evolutionary chain of terrorists, you end up with a frightening forecast. Despite what the U.S. government would have you believe, terrorism is not a well-oiled global conspiracy but rather a hodgepodge of gangs that can't shoot straight. The Crips and Bloods or the Hell's Angels have it together better than public enemy number one. We are not talking about the jihadis who dutifully go off to get killed in skanky little wars, but the wingnuts and rogue elements who indulge in criminal and brutal acts in the name of religion or cause. As their more visible and idealistic leaders get vaporized, you end up promoting the less visionary, and far more desperate, stand-ins.

Real pros quickly learn that terrorism can be a self-funding form of social entrepreneurialism. Just jump in the van or the speedboat, head for the local Hilton or dive resort, and load 'em up. Don't kill 'em, they are worth more alive than dead. About $5 to $25 million each if you can get a conviction (and a check). This will also guarantee you at least 2 to 5 minutes on CNN every night, with 30-minute repeats every half-hour until the situation is resolved. For God's sake, don't kidnap the journos, even they will forget their liberal arts education and call you names. If you can help it, don't grab politicians or military or embassy workers. Because governments are cheap, politicians will bore you to death with speeches and the military will launch a rescue effort making life very short and miserable for everyone concerned. In the end everybody loses, because terrorism is a method of political furtherance that seems to focus on abusing the little people (me and you) and benefiting the fat cats. One disturbing trend is the intractability of terrorist-gone-criminal groups who end up killing their hostages simply for the publicity.

With the demise of the Soviet paymaster and the War on Terrorism shutting down big Middle East players, terrorists are soon going to be a little short on cash. And you know exactly where they will turn to for some quick cash. Kidnapping, extortion, drugs, weapons, people, and protection will be part of every successful terrorist's portfolio. Many have already learned the criminal part and retained the slogans just to recruit chicks. Colombia's FARC seem to be the best example of how to make big money at Marxism. Things do go better with coke, especially insurgencies, so well that FARC really doesn't want to win the war because it would severely mess up its leaders' cash flow.

Abu Sayyaf went from less than a dozen scrawny, ill-fed fundamentalists to a franchise-like kidnapping group in a few months. Foreigners can pretty much look forward to an ecotour from hell if they stay too long south of Zamboango. Using millions in ransom money they blossomed from a raggedy-ass jihadi group into a well-equipped army. Their choice of Americans as kidnap victims quickly became their downfall as Special Forces and SEALs assisted the Philippino army in a culling program. Is it safe in the southern Philippines now? Not even close.

## PARANOIA, INC.

It seems our beloved government has a hard time believing that terrorists know how to use the Internet and computers. Most regular phone and e-mail traffic is exposed to the carnivorous snooping of the NSA, but one can only imagine how many ears are listening to satellite phone calls being beamed out of remote Afghanistan. Okay, so our government denied they were actually rummaging through our e-mail and then came clean on Carnivore (http://www.fbi.gov/hq/lab/carnivore/carnivore.htm), and we always knew we didn't need all those satellites for weather—but hey, the Internet is the medium of the people, right? Sorry, but it wasn't that surprising to learn that terrorist groups are simply using free encryption products to send and receive messages. It's so popular that it's now taught along with Grenade Tossing 101 and Takbir Shouting in the Afghan training camps. Although the FBI and CIA are shouting unfair, demanding backdoor keys, and whining that these codes are "uncrackable," it's a well-known secret that the CIA actually funded a number of encryption start-ups and wants you to believe that terrorists can't crack these codes. These days hackers and computer nerds are among the agencies' best-paid employees as they race to out-geek the geeks in the secrecy biz. What better and more efficient way than to channel all the criminal and terrorist communication through a few encryption sites?

Links to crypto/privacy sites:

http://www.crypto.com
http://www.anonymizer.com
http://www.cdt.org/crypto
http://www.e4m.net

The results of the War on Terror will be a wistful longing to return to the level of personal freedom that, let's say, the Russians enjoyed in the 1960s, and an explosion of random violent acts, all in the name of freedom. New Zealand and Greenland are looking pretty attractive as retirement spots.

If you are tracking statistics to determine whether terrorism is growing or, alternatively, that we are winning the War on Terror, don't waste your time. Depending on what ledger entry you choose, you could say terrorism is up. Body count is up, incidents are down; we are winning the war but require more funding. The bottom line is that a single bombing campaign can accelerate incidents, but one big blast can push the dead and wounded into the stratosphere. In 2000, 17 of the 19 killed in terrorist acts were aboard the USS *Cole* in Yemen during the October 12 attack. The year before was the big triple-header in Uganda (the Kampala bomb didn't go off), Kenya, and Tanzania. The underlying point is that terrorism is not a big threat despite billions being spent to fight it, politicians holding up bags of faux anthrax, and $25 mil being posted for Binny.

Are there any workable solutions for stomping out terrorism out there? Hey, why not suggest that terrorists send an intelligent, polite, well-researched political proposal with workable, fair solutions to the ruling party? No good, huh? You could hunt terrorism down and kill anyone suspected of being a terrorist, but then you are back to the mountain-of-skulls gig, which in itself goes back to the original point about terrorism being a natural part of warfare. Until our government stops kicking the hornet's nests, and of course sending you to do business or visit in the meantime, the world will be a dangerous place.

Sorry for the bad news but it looks like, for the foreseeable future, life as a noncombatant will force you to closely follow world politics and geopolitics before you take your next vacation.

**IntelCenter**
http://www.intelcenter.com

**Patterns of Global Terrorism**
http://www.state.gov/s/ct/rls/pgtrpt/2001

**Global database of terrorist incidents**
http://polisci.home.mindspring.com/
    ptd/itapvi

**Terrorism Research Center**
http://www.terrorism.com

**ICT Terrorism**
http://www.ict.org.il

**St. Andrews Centre for the Study of Terrorism and Political Violence**
http://www.st-and.ac.uk/academic/
    intrel/research/cstpv

**Federation of American Scientists: Directory of Para-States**
http://www.fas.org/irp/world/para/index.
    html

**ERRI Counter-Terrorism Archive: List of Terrorist Acts Since 1989**
http://www.emergency.com/cntrterr.htm

## WHO'S MINDING THE STORE?

Want to know who is really behind that terrorist group? The Web allows you to find out who gets the bill every month for that rabid, foaming-at-the-mouth hate site, or even that odd twisted page. For example http://www.taliban.com is a postal mailbox in Fremont, California. And http://www.binladen.com is registered in Texas while http://www.Saddam.com is registered in Owings Mills, Maryland. Go figure.

To check site information, just type in:

http://www.netsol.com/cgi-bin/whois/whois

*Special Operations.com Guide to*
*International Terrorist*
*Organizations*
http://www.specialoperations.com/Terro
rism/SOCGuide/Default.htm

*Terrorism Links*
http://www.jmu.edu/orgs/wrni/links.html

*Kim-Spy*
http://www.kimsoft.com/kim-spy.htm

*C4i.org*
http://www.c4i.org

*Terrorism Q&A*
http://www.terrorismanswers.com

## The Other Side

The following Web sites produce related material to groups designated by the United States as terrorist groups. They may or may not be related to the groups themselves. Please note that many of these sites have been hacked since 9/11.

*Al-Aqsa Brigades*
http://www.alaqsamartyres.org/atef.htm

*MILF (The Southern Philippines)*
luwaran@eudora.com
http://www.luwaran.com

*Al Fateh (Palestine)*
http://www.fateh.net

*JihadUnspun*
http://www.jihadunspun.com

## The Bad Boys Club

There are a group of organizations that our country deems as terrorist. To join this elite club you have to be foreign, engage in terrorist activity, and must threaten the security of U.S. nationals or national security. What are the specifics of terrorism and American citizens? You can't give them funds or material support, they can't get visas to the States, and financial institutions must block funds and declare it to the Treasury.

**Abu Sayyaf Group (ASG)**
http://www.inq7.net/specials/inside_
abusayyaf

**Armed Islamic Group (GIA) Algeria**
http://www.au.af.mil/au/aul/bibs/tergps/
tgalg.htm

**Autodefensas Unidas de Colombia
(AUC)**
http://www.colombialibre.org

**Aum Shinriykyo**

**FARC—Colombia**
http://www.farc-ep.org

**Free Aceh Movement—Indonesia**
http://acehnet.tripod.com

**Al-Gama'a al-Islamiyya (Islamic
Group, IG)**
http://www.au.af.mil/au/aul/bibs/tergps/
tgegy.htm

**Hizballah (Party of God)**
http://www.hizballah.org

**Al-Ikhwan Al-Moslemoon (Muslim
Brotherhood Movement)**
http://www.ummah.net/ikhwan

**Japanese Red Army (JRA)**
http://www3.tky.3web.ne.jp/~sper/
11TH/11th.html

**al-Jihad**

**New Kach Movement**
http://www.newkach.org

**Liberation Tigers of Tamil Elam
(LTTE)—Sri Lanka**
http://www.eelam.com

**Mujahedin-e Khalq Organization
(MEK, MKO, NCR, and many
others)**
http://www.iran.mojahedin.org

**National Liberation Army (ELN)—
Colombia**
http://www.web.net/eln

**Palestine Liberation Front—Abu
Abbas Faction (PLF)**
http://www.ict.org.il/inter_ter/orgdet.
cfm?orgid=29

**Popular Front for the Liberation of
Palestine—General Command
(PFLP-GC)**
http://news.bbc.co.uk/hi/english/world/
middle_east/newsid_736000/
736490.stm

**Revolutionary Organization 17
November (17 November)**
http://www.terrorismfiles.org/
organisations/revolutionary_
organization_17_november.html

**Revolutionary People's Liberation
Army/Front (DHKP/C)**
http://www.terrorismfiles.org/
organisations/revolutionary_
peoples_liberation_party.html

**Revolutionary People's Struggle (ELA)**
http://www.fas.org/irp/world/para/ela.htm

**Shining Path (Sendero Luminoso, SL)**
http://www.csrp.org

**Tupac Amaru Revolutionary Movement
(MRTA)**
http://burn.ucsd.edu/~ats/mrta.htm

# A SHORT HISTORY OF THE WAR ON TERROR,
# AKA THE HOUSE OF WAR, AKA THE CRUSADES

**AD 570**  Mohammed is born in Mecca. At age 40 (AD 610), the angel Gabriel reveals the Koran to him, and he is told to call his people to worship one god. This creates the Islamic world, or "house of peace," as separate from the rest of the world, or "house of war."

**AD 622**  After being persecuted and chased out of Mecca in what is called the "hijirah," or travels, Mohammed and his followers move to what will be called Medina. There the locals accept Islam, marking the beginning of the Islamic calendar.

**AD 633**  Mohammed dies. The Abbasid dynasty begins when Abu Bakr is chosen as his successor. A period of great expansion of Islamic belief begins.

**AD 732**  The Muslims are defeated in Poitiers, France. Islam spreads from southern Europe to West Africa to South Asia.

**AD 1098**  The First Crusade is launched from Europe to free the tomb of Jesus from the Turks. Jerusalem is conquered on July 14, 1099, and 70,000 Muslims are put to death. The Shi'as or Fatimids, are aligned with the Christians against the Sunni Turks.

**AD 1120**  Islam spreads to Asia.

**12/24/1144**  Zangi launches a jihad and conquers the Crusade state of Essa, launching the Second Crusade. His son, Nureddin, continues the fight and then Nureddin's former follower, Saladin, unites the Sunni and Shi'a forces against the Crusaders.

**AD 1187**  Saladin overcomes the Crusaders at the Horn of Hattin, attacks Jerusalem on September 20, 1187, and conquers the city two weeks later. The Christians are spared. The loss of Jerusalem sparks the Third Crusade.

**AD 1187**  King Louis IX launches the last crusade (for which he is sainted). His forces and his allies are completely destroyed.

**AD 1540**  The Ottoman Empire reaches its zenith, uniting much of the Middle East.

**AD 1703**  Mohammed ibn Abdul Wahhab (1703–1791) founds a movement that urges a return to the golden age of Islam.

(continued)

His followers believe in a strict view of Islam, and conquer most of the Persian Gulf area, as far north as Iraq and the edges of the Ottoman Empire.

**11/2/17** Britain officially supports the Jewish Zionist idea of the creation of a national home for the Jewish people in Palestine.

**1918** The Ottoman Empire is broken up at the end of World War I, creating many smaller Muslim states.

**1929** Hassan al-Banna forms the *ikwhan,* or Society of the Muslim Brotherhood. They seek a pan-Islamic state and a revival of traditional Islam, in reaction to foreign domination of Arab homelands.

**1932** The area jointly controlled by the Wahhabist Saud family and the British military becomes Saudi Arabia.

**1934** The Arabian American oil company is created to exploit the vast petroleum reserves of Saudi Arabia.

**5/14/47** The state of Israel is created in Palestine to coexist with an Arab state of Palestine.

**5/15/47** Egypt, Syria, Transjordan, Lebanon, and Iraq invade Israel, resulting in Israel controlling larger areas of land.

**1947** The Wahhabists support the *fedayeen,* or suicide squads, to push out Jews from Palestine. The Ikwhan send volunteers to fight, as well, and start a campaign of terror and assassination inside Egypt.

**6/67** Egypt blocks Israel's access to the Gulf of Aqaba. Israel attacks and in the Six-Day War claims the area from the Suez Canal, the West Bank, the Gaza Strip, and up to the Golan Heights within Syria.

**2/1/1979** The Ayatollah Khomeini returns to Iran. The Iranian Revolution replaces the shah with an orthodox Islamic government. The U.S. embassy staff is held hostage.

**12/25/1979** The Russians invade Afghanistan to fight terrorism and to support the Afghan government.

**1979** Abdullah Azzam, a Palestinian, travels to Peshawar to create the Office of Services for foreigners coming to Afghanistan to fight in the jihad against the Russians. Over 40,000 volunteers are trained and armed to fight alongside the Afghans, funded by billions of covert U.S. dollars funneled via the Pakistani secret service. Azzam is killed on November 24, 1989 by a car bomb.

**1988** Osama bin Laden forms the Base, or al-Qaeda, using the names of foreigners gathered by Azzam during ten years of fighting against Russia.

| | |
|---|---|
| **1989** | The Soviets withdraw from Afghanistan, leaving the mujahideen to declare victory. Over 25 groups are formed from foreign-trained Afghan veterans, and Afghanistan descends into warfare and chaos. |
| **8/02/90** | Iraq invades Kuwait. |
| **1/17/91** | Allied Western troops (580,000 in all) attack Iraq (540,000 troops). Iraq attacks Israel, but the United States keeps Israel out of the war. On February 28th, Iraq surrenders. |
| **9/1/91** | Bin Laden is expelled from Saudi Arabia and takes up residence in Sudan. |
| **2/26/93** | The World Trade Center is bombed with a rented truck and fertilizer. Six civilians are killed, and 1,000 are injured. The bombing also causes $500 million in damage. |
| **10/3/93** | A group of foreign-trained mujahids ambush U.S. soldiers in Mogadishu, killing 15 Americans. |
| **1994** | Ramsi Yousef comes up with a plan to assassinate the Pope, blow up a series of airliners, and other plots. |
| **2/03/96** | Osama bin Laden declares war on the United States and Israel. |
| **5/96** | Bin Laden leaves Sudan for Afghanistan. |
| **6/25/96** | Bombing of Khobar Towers kills 18 U.S. soldiers in Dhahran, Saudi Arabia. |
| **2/23/98** | Bin Laden and the World Islamic Front (bin Laden along with representatives of Islamic groups from Pakistan, Bangladesh, and Egypt) declare a fatwa, or religious ruling, that insists that Muslims should kill all Americans and their allies in any country in which it is possible, in order to liberate the al-Aqsa mosque and force the Americans out of Saudi Arabia. Bin Laden also professes support for Iraq. |
| **1998** | Osama bin Laden is interviewed on ABC television. |
| **8/7/98** | U.S. embassies in Kenya and Dar Es Salaam are bombed, killing 301 people and injuring over 5,000. |
| **10/12/00** | The USS *Cole* is hit by a boat-driven bomb in Aden, Yemen. Seventeen American sailors are killed. |
| **9/11/01** | Four aircraft are hijacked by Arabs (15 of whom are Saudi nationals). Two are flown into the World Trade Center towers, one into the Pentagon, and the fourth crashes in a field outside Pittsburgh, Pennsylvania. |

(continued)

| | |
|---|---|
| **9/13/01** | President George W. Bush calls for a "crusade" against terrorists. |
| **10/7/01** | The War in Afghanistan starts. |
| **2002** | Terrorist attacks occur from Bali to Kenya to the Middle East. |

# ADVENTURE CALLS

## Life Is Not a Job

Everybody has a different idea of adventure. It could be bird-watching or it could be parachuting into jungles to fight with rebels. It sure as hell ain't moving memos from the "in" to the "out" basket. But most of us spend the large part of our waking lives working to not work. Our puritanical background says that in the typical 2,000 hours of labor we provide each year, we might be able to squeeze out 2 weeks or 336 hours of real living. The Travel Industry Association of America (http://www.tia.org) says that 98 million people took adventure vacations, but how many took adventure jobs? Adventure is not about

> **A**dventure is about living adventurously 24/7, 365 days a year, year after year, until you drop dead with a smile on your face.

papering your gray Herman Miller foxhole with cool pictures ripped out of magazines. Adventure is about pushing yourself, discovering your own worlds, writing your own itinerary. Adventure is about living adventurously 24/7, 365 days a year, year after year, until you drop dead with a smile on your face. Now, get back to work.

http://www.adventuretravel.com

## Expeditions

The first big step for most people is actually creating a cool venture, an expedition. There is no one way to join or organize an expedition. Most expeditions have goals, structures, deadlines, budgets, and so forth, and require more planning than execution. Most are scientific in nature. Many are adventurous or exploratory, with little of the painstaking information recording required of expeditions in the old days. Expeditions are simply formalized trips. Like any great endeavor, they should have an objective, a unique sense of purpose, and maybe a dash of insanity.

An expedition is a way to say, "Here is what we said we would do, and here is what we did." There is little to no reward for climbing Mt. Everest blindfolded or swimming the Atlantic while towing a barge. There is far more reward in being an actor portraying the adventurer. Sigourney Weaver (as Dian Fossey) and Patrick Bergen (as Sir Richard Burton) put more in the bank than their real-life counterparts ever made in a lifetime—a sobering thought. Fame does await the bold. And after that fame comes an endless procession of rubber-chicken dinners and outdoor-store openings. The more literate adventurers will write a book that will grace remainder lists for years to come. So consider an expedition as a good use of your skills and talents, with the only reward being the satisfaction of fellowship, a job well done, and a better understanding of our world. Along the way, you will enter an elite club of men and women who have tested themselves and found themselves to be comfortably mortal.

Now a warning to the adventurous, who view expeditions as an interesting way to see the world. All expeditions have some hardship involved. In fact, more and more of them seem to feature physical discomfort. Ranulph Fiennes' jaunt to the North Pole on skis is an example of this craziness. He could have flown, but he wanted to do something that had never been done before. Other expeditions, like the recent attempt to climb Mt. Kinabalu in Borneo, have turned into fiascoes because a group of men decided to do whatever they felt like and got lost. They were found later, close to starvation, on a mountain that is routinely climbed by schoolchildren. Expeditions are usually led by tough, experienced men who think there is nothing unusual about forcing physical and mental discomfort on others. So it is not surprising that many expeditions tend to be run either by emotionless, sado-masochistic, raving egomaniacs—men who were dressed as girls when they were young or have questionable characters with overstated cre-dentials—who are forced by their lack of job skills to make their living in godforsaken places.

If you can combine all these characteristics into one person, then you stand the chance of mounting a successful expedition. Why would someone want to walk to the North Pole, bake in the Sahara, or pick ticks out of their private parts, you may well ask? The answer is always unsatisfactory. Most expedition junkies are always testing themselves, trying to prove other people wrong, and seeking to top themselves in their next harebrained adventure.

Why do I sound so cynical here? Maybe because I have watched various expedition leaders lose it and seen many of my well-trained friends throw their hands up in disgust. The biggest single enemy of the expedition is bad chemistry, usually caused by the fearless leader's inability to lead men by example rather than brute force.

My more pleasurable expeditions have always seemed leaderless, where the group reacted in unison, allowing creative interpretation of directions, deadlines, and goals. Also, you must truly know your fellow expedition members. Men and women react very strangely under stress. Some revert to childish whining, others become combative, and still others simply lose it both mentally and physically. The key to suc-cess is to keep your humor; black as it may be, it's a better mood than nihilistic gloom. Hey, they might as well find your corpse with a smile on your face, right?

The best way to see if you have picked the right partners in an expe-dition is to have a dry run that includes at least 48 hours without sleep,

## SHARK! SHARK! TARTAR SAUCE! TARTAR SAUCE!

About 50 people will be attacked by sharks in a typical year. The recent feeding frenzy—by the media not by the sharks—may create the impression that swimmers and surfers are the equivalent of chum. The truth is that shark attacks have been declining since 1995, possibly due to the demand for sharks as food rather than TV stars. Divers are 18 percent of victims. Surfers make up 69 percent. Sharks signal their defensive attack through exaggerated, jerky movements. Look for an arched back, lifting of the head, and figure-eight loops. Tips on avoiding attacks: Sure, stay out of the water.

http://www.flmnh.ufl.edu/fish/Sharks/statistics/statistics.htm

in adverse conditions. Sleep deprivation, combined with some mental and physical abuse at the 36-hour stage, will show a person's real mettle. Strangely enough, in my experience, white-collar workers, physical fitness nuts, city dwellers, businessmen, triathletes, and sportsmen do very poorly in the ill-defined, noncompetitive expedition environment. People with military experience, medical personnel, aboriginals, photographers, blue-collar laborers, and folks with rural backgrounds do very well.

The attributes to look for are experience in hard conditions, physical fitness, a sense of humor, a levelheaded approach to stress, pain, and discomfort, and a genuine desire for knowledge and fellowship.

Expedition members should be chosen for specific knowledge, such as medical, language, or bush lore; always get references. Members should never be chosen for prestige, ability to provide funding, or university credentials. And absolutely stay away from taking on journalists, relatives of backers, and good-looking members of the opposite sex.

## HOW TO LAUNCH AN EXPEDITION

1. Pick a region or topic that is newsworthy or beneficial to sponsors.
2. Select a specific task that you will accomplish, and one that will make the world a better place or create publicity.
3. State specifically how you will generate publicity (book, speeches, press releases, photographs, magazine articles).
4. Write a one-page query letter that states your purpose, method of execution, and perceived result. Ask for a written show of support (do not ask for money) and other people who should be made aware of your expedition.
5. Gather letters of support from high-profile politicians, community members, and scientists, and include them in your proposal.
6. Write an expedition plan (much like a business plan), and explain the benefits to the backers and sponsors.
7. Once you have a raison d'etre and your expedition goal figured out, send a one-page press release and your outline to all news organizations, telling them your intentions and that you need sponsors. It is important to set a date to let sponsors know that you are going with or without their funds.
8. Create a sponsorship program. Tell and show the primary sponsor what they will get, tell the secondary sponsor, and so on. As a rule of thumb, ask for twice as much money as you predict you will need, and come up with something to present to a recognized nonprofit charity at the end of your expedition.

9. Gather lists of potential sponsors, and then phone to get the owner, president, or founder's name. Send in your pitch, along with any early PR you generated. If the president or owner likes it, they will delegate it downward. If you send it in blind, most companies will put you in the talk-to-our-PR-company-who-then-promises-to-talk-to-the-client loop.
10. Follow up with a request for a meeting (money is never pledged over the phone), and thrill them with your enthusiasm and vision.
11. Send a thank-you letter with a specific follow-up and/or commitment date. Promise to follow up with a phone call on a certain date and time.

Do this thousands of times, and you will have enough money to do any harebrained thing you want.

Just as Columbus had to sweet-talk Isabella after the banks turned him down, you have to be creative and ever hopeful. Remember, everyone interested wishes they could go with you, and their investment is just a way of saying "I am part of this adventure."

The best sources for tough expeditions are the Royal Geographical Society in London and the National Geographic Society in Washington, D.C. Local newspapers will carry features on "brave young men and women" who are setting out to do whatever has not been done. In most cases, they will be looking for money (always an automatic entrée into an expedition) or someone with multiple skills (doctor, cook, masseuse) to fill out the team. Be careful, since it all comes down to personality. Many people have never spent more than a weekend in close proximity to their spouse, let alone a total stranger; shakedown cruises are well advised, and go with your first impression. Things usually only get worse.

The upside is that you can be the first person on your block to pogostick to the North Pole, balloon across the Sahara, or kayak Lake Baikal. Fame and fortune may await. You will need lots of money, time, and the enthusiasm of a Baptist preacher. Remember that 99 percent of your time will be spent raising funds and planning.

Expeditions are usually funded by universities or governments, and there are no real grapevines other than reading scientific journals, staying in touch with universities, or talking to expeditioners and outfitters. Most participants will be scientists and will often bring interns (for a fee) to help defray costs. The best way to find out what is happening is to contact a university directly to see if any expeditions are being mounted.

## Expedition Web Sites

http://www.raleigh.org.uk
http://www.100gogo.com
http://www.thebmc.co.uk/world.htm
http://www.symbiosis-travel.com
http://expeditiontravel.net
http://www.go-overland.com
http://www.adventuretravel.com
http://www.nationalgeographic.com/
   adventure

http://gorptravel.gorp.com
http://www.yourexpedition.com
http://www.wildlife-
   film.com/travbody.htm
http://www.4x44u.com/pub/k2/
   am4x44u/whats_new/turtle.htm

## Magazines

**Outside**
http://www.outsidemag.com

**Men's Journal**
http://www.mensjournal.com

**Blue**
http://www.blueadventure.com

**National Geographic**
http://www.nationalgeographic.org

**National Geographic Adventure**
http://www.nationalgeographic.org/
   adventure/index.html

*Royal Geographical Society*
http://www.rgs.org

**Index of travel magazines**
http://dir.yahoo.com/Recreation/Travel/
   News_and_Media/Magazines

The august and venerable National Geographic Society has become the best and most popular means for the world to understand itself. Back in 1888, it was simply a group of philanthropists who wanted to increase and diffuse geographical knowledge. Since then, they have funded almost 5,000 expeditions and educated and entertained hundreds of millions, and today they are the largest geographic group of any kind. The council's scope of exploration includes all realms of Earth, from the deepest oceans to the highest mountains and beyond.

They manage to maintain a rough edge and an accessible front. Unlike the tiny, musty adventurer's clubs, the National Geographic Society has gone global. You can sit in your own musty den and travel to more countries, experience more expeditions, and learn more about our world, thanks to their efforts.

Many adventurers were weaned on their yellow tomes. A generation further back was titillated by sights of unclothed natives and exotic locales. If any magazine could be called adventurous, it would be good old *National Geo.*

National Geographic Society has 9.7 million members in almost 200 countries. Over 44 million people read each issue of the magazine, 40 million watch their documentaries on PBS, and 15 million watch *On*

*Assignment* each month. Though not exactly an elite group, being featured in or by a National Geographic publication thrusts you into the mainstream of adventure/entertainment. If you are written up or have an article in the *National Geographic Magazine,* you can work the rubber-chicken circuit for the next decade. If you are featured on any of their television specials, like Jacques-Yves Cousteau (*The Voyages of the Calypso*) or Bob Ballard (*The Search for the Titanic*), you can contemplate licensing and even starting your own TV series.

Despite being the Valhalla for adventurers, the National Geographic does its bit to generate content. The society awarded 6,000 grants for field research and exploration since its founding in 1888.

### National Geographic Society
1145 17th Street, NW
Washington, DC 20036-4688
Tel.: (202) 862-5200 or (800) 638-4077
Fax: (202) 862-5270
*National Geographic Magazine*
P.O. Box 96095
Washington, DC 20090-6095
http://www.nationalgeographic.com/
research

The old standard (requires membership) $34/year subscription is still a great bargain. The editorial stance is getting tougher, with more articles on pollution, politics, and natural threats, in addition to the standard "purty" pictures. The magazine has launched a small but well-traveled group of photographers who capture the world for a handsome fee. You can also buy *Nat Geo* on the newsstands, finally.

### The Royal Geographical Society
1 Kensington Gore
London SW7 2AR, UK
Tel.: (44) (020) 7591 3000
Fax: (44) (020) 7591 3001
info@rgs.org
http://www.rgs.org

The fabled exploration society still requires nomination by an existing member to join. When in London, nonmembers can visit the Map Room in their creaky Victorian headquarters on Hyde Park near Albert Hall. They also have an impressive photo archive and reference-book selection.

### Geographical Magazine
Unit 11, Pall Mall Deposit
124-125 Barlby Road
London, WI0 6BL, UK
Tel.: (44) (0) 208 960 6400
Fax: (44) (0) 208 960 6004
magazine@geographical.co.uk
http://www.geographical.co.uk

A monthly magazine that is a lot drier, less chatty, and a lot less pretty than a *Nat Geo* publication but much tougher and smarter in its editorial focus. It covers expeditions, environment, travel, adventure—all with a scientific bent (U.S.$69 US/Canada).

Also contact the RGS Expedition Advisory Centre. Don't be shy about calling or ordering any one of their excellent (but very British) books on expedition planning. They have an incredible selection of how-to books, and you can also get listings of past expeditions, contact other people interested in expeditions, and get in touch with experts who have been to your area of interest. They do not sponsor expeditions but have a hand-book on how to raise money. Each year they assist more than 500 teams and provide training and advice to anyone thinking of mounting an expedition.

## Expedition Organizers

If you would like to do more than wander around a country, try joining an expedition. Americans haven't quite caught on to this method of travel, but Europeans and the Japanese are crazy about it. Accordingly, they offer a lot more variety than some of their Stateside counterparts.

**South American Explorers Club**
126 Indian Creek Road
Ithaca, NY 14850
Tel.: (607) 277-0488
explorer@saexplorers.org
http://www.saexplorers.org

The nonprofit South American Explorers Club is a source of travel information about South and/or Central America. There are clubhouses in Lima, Peru; Quito, Ecuador; and Ithaca, New York.

**Royal Geographical Society of Australia, Inc.**
c/o State Library of South Australia
North Terrace
Adelaide
5000 South Australia
Postal Address: GPO Box 419
Adelaide
5001 South Australia
Tel.: (08) 207-7265 or 207-7266
Fax: (08) 207-7247
http://www.asap.unimelb.edu.au/asa/
directory/data/301.htm

**Randall's Adventure & Training**
60 Randall Road
Gallant, AL 35972
Tel.: (256) 570-0175
Fax: (256) 538-6418
http://www.jungletraining.com

Jeff Randall runs tours and training into the Amazon basin and Costa Rica from mild to wild: personalized courses for groups, hard-core training for adventure racing teams and, of course, ecotours.

**Ridgefellows Outdoor Training Ltd**
4 The Gatehouse
20 Bargates
Christchurch
Dorset BH23 1QL, UK
Tel.: (44) 7881 912964
ridgefellows@aol.com
http://www.ridgefellows.com

Ex-Royal Marine John Groom runs expeditions and organizes expedition security in Central and South America. John also provides all levels of survival training in personalized courses in the UK, Ecuador, and Belize.

# Adventure Racing

Pity the adventure racer. Once the domain of quirky, super-fit international party animals who never even knew what jogging was, the sport is now filled with grim hatchet-faced triathletes wearing the latest in injection-molded gear. Nowadays fun has been trained out of it. Now there are so many races they might end up tripping over each other. Eco-Challenge tried to wipe out its competition by doing some event shifting and also ended up shifting over to the USA network from Discovery. In any event, there is no shortage of men and women who want to abuse themselves for a couple of weeks, with the only benefit seeming to be ravaged feet, bruises, and sore muscles.

First it was the Hash House Harriers who ran up mountains as an excuse to booze it up, then it was the crazy Kiwis and their Southern Traverse, then it was the wild and woolly Camel Trophy, and then the competitive Raid Gauloises, followed by the PC-sounding Eco-Challenge—now adventure racing has mutated into dozens of weekend events around the world. Events like the Warn Challenge, Trans Borneo, and Trans Pen have come and gone. I will be the first to admit that I have been in a few of these, but ultimately they are not the most rewarding way to learn about yourself and your limits. Like a poorly paid actor in an S&M donkey show, you are expected to destroy yourself for the entertainment of others. Even though the races have exotic locales, you will be well insulated from the locals (other than the cultural show before the awards) and you will end up stuffing more than a little money into the resorts', airlines', and organizers' pockets.

On the good side, many of these events allow you to trample through the jungle, throw trash in exotic paths, erode mist-covered trails, spit into white-water rivers, and ride $2,000 bikes in places where the locals can't afford pushcarts. If you really want to see what you are made of, keep in mind that you are the spandex version of a celebrity lab rat, where each course has been designed to cause just enough grief to make it look good for TV. Probably the most daunting part of these races is wading through the hyperbole.

Large forested areas become "impenetrable," jungles become "green hells," deserts are "blistering," mountains are "forbidding," rivers are "raging" or laid back, tropical paradises become "harsh environments," and even small insects become "deadly killers."

Okay, okay, so we are a little jealous that we might not be superhumans. But everybody wants a free vacation to go hiking, rafting, and running; we just like to do it without the logos and cameras. That's why you'll also find the evil spawn of adventure racing: adventure racing schools.

## Adventure Racing Links

http://www.burnmagazine.com
http://aracer.websitegalaxy.com
http://www.adventure-video.com
http://dmoz.org/Sports/Adventure_
   Racing/Races

http://www.active.com/moresports/
   adventureracing

## Adventure Racing Schools

http://www.adventuretrain.com/index.
   html
http://www3.sympatico.ca/j-nwallace
http://www.conqueradventures.com

### AdventureTime

http://www.adventuretime.com/links/
   index.html
Good links to everything from underwater hockey to street luge.

## Adventure Races

### The Southern Traverse

http://www.southerntraverse.com
   The Southern Traverse began in 1989 and was based on the first Raid Gauloises, or Grand Traverse, held in the southern Alps on the South Island.

### Marathon des Sables (Sand Marathon)

Racing The Planet, Inc.
P.O. Box 38
Hudgins, VA 23076
Fax: (202) 478-0218
info@racingtheplanet
http://www.sandmarathon.com
   Begun in 1986, with about 500 competitors from around 30 countries running across 200 miles of North African sand in April. You carry all your gear, get hot, eat sand, and then go home. There is also a newsletter online.

### The Eco-Challenge

9899 Santa Monica Blvd., Suite #208
Beverly Hills, CA 90212
Tel.: (310) 399-3080, ext. 4000
Fax: (310) 399-3584
info@ecochallenge.com
http://www.ecochallenge.com
   Big TV deal, lots of sponsors, and well-heeled yuppies meets copy of Raid Gauloises. The Beverly Hills–based organizers have grabbed the market for adventure racing. By now the idea of watching hours of young urban professionals complaining about blisters should be old-hat, but people love it. A fee of $12,500 gets 4 into the 6-to 12-day race. Each team of 4, comprised of men and women, races non-stop, 24 hours a day, over a rugged 300-mile (500-km) course. Disciplines include trekking, whitewater canoeing, horseback riding, sea kayaking, scuba diving, mountaineering, and mountain biking. (Don't forget airfare, gear, and supplies.) You can also take one of their training courses, sponsor a team, or take a package/adventure tour.

### Camel Trophy

Worldwide Brands, Inc.
P.O. Box 124
Staines
Middlesex TW18 4LL, UK
http://www.camel-discovery.com
http://www.4x44u.com/pub/k2/
  cameltrophy

### Landrover G4

http://www.landrover.com

## Raid Gauloises

### Raid Gauloises

6, Rue des Près Riants
73100 Aix-les-Bains
France
Tel.: (33) 4 79 88 66 76
Fax: (33) 4 79 88 49 06
info@raidseries.com
http://www.raid-gauloises.com

United States
470 S. Wetherly Drive
Beverly Hills, CA 90211
Tel.: (310) 271-8335
Fax: (310) 271-8365
nfusilraid@earthlink.net
http://www.raid-gauloises.com

Gerard Fusil started the Raid in 1988 because he thought the Camel Trophy was too easy. He introduced the idea of multiple sports instead of the sleep deprivation and brutal pushing of the Camel event. What was lost was the international teamwork and what was gained was a greater sense of athletics (and of course income from paying teams).

After the originator of the event left to start a new race (he bailed to start his own race; see next entry), things got a little loose for the last race. A blizzard of negative articles about organizational snafus may have put the venerated Raid in jeopardy.

## Elf Adventure, aka Gerard Fusil's Supreme Adventure

### Gerard Fusil Company

1, villa Marie Mustine
92100 Boulogne, Paris, France
Tel.: (33) 1 41 31 74 74
Fax: (33) 1 41 31 05 91
Gfusilcy@aol.com
http://www.elf-aventure.com

There is just something magical about oil and cigarette companies sponsoring adventure racing. What's next, the Strip Mining and Waste Management Eco-Adventure? In any case, if you wondered where Gerard Fusil ended up, it's here. Fourteen 7-member coed teams do a 350-mile mazed sports race in an exotic country where "machetes are mandatory equipment" (stop me if you've heard this before). Competitors must brave the elements, not be eaten by wild animals or stung by insects, etc., etc. A memorable line from a press release: "More than one racer has described snake sightings, and the caves house bats." Egads. Elf bailed and it remains to be seen who will sponsor the race.

## Beast of the East

### Odyssey Adventure Racing

1109 Windsor Road
Virginia Beach, VA 23451
info@oarevents.com
http://www.beastoftheeast.com

This Web site automatically takes you to http://www. oarevents.com, which is for Odyssey Adventure Racing.

Their web page is a good link to a number of regional events, including the SEAL Adventure

## REAL ADVENTURE TRAVEL

If you really want to know what adventure travel is all about, try reading a few good travel guides . . . no, not those tasteless, flavorless backpackers. No faux funny re-explorations of Australia or Upper East Side dilettantes on assignment for *Vanity Fair*. I mean the real deal. Germania. Carthage. Punt. Chaldea. Discover what travel was like before American Express . . . hell, before America . . .

***Travelers Accounts***
http://www.fordham.edu/halsall/IHSP-travelers.html

Challenge (yes, people pay $125 to go through a re-creation of military hell week), the beast of Alaska, and others. Beast promises no gimmicks, just plain old-fashioned adventure racing.

## The Salomon X–Adventure

http://www.salomonsports.com
http://www.x-adventure.com
The "cross" adventure is a series of events in Europe and Japan culminating in a fall event some-where in the world. It's the usual man against nature gig: Six sports over a 30-hour period. Salomon also owns Taylor Made. So how come no extreme golf, guys?

## Hi–Tec Adventure Racing Series

http://www.mesp.com/ars.htm
The boot manufacturer sponsors a number of mini-endurance races around the country. A good way to get into the sport.

# Dangerous Places

## DP's Ratings

There is no single reliable source of safety, deaths, casualties, or misfortunes, so don't look for one here. Our ratings are entirely personal and completely changeable depending on when, where, and why you are there. In really dangerous lands there aren't a whole lot of white-coated scientists with clipboards keeping count. The United States has a very comprehensive system of travel warnings but conveniently overlooks the dangers within its own borders. India will be generous in counting Pakistan casualties in Kashmir but be stiff-lipped about its own dead. What about the people who vanish on aircraft, midocean, or in your hometown? Danger cannot be measured, only prepared against.

So we essentially threw all the official statistics in the dumpster and used our own research. How do we rank these places? We base them on our experiences: We travel without a protective shield, we have the ability to compare disparate places within narrow time periods, and we grind through massive piles of documents to determine just what is going on around the world. So with this caveat in mind, here is how you can interpret our ratings:

★★★★★                                      **Apocalypse Wow**

These places combine warfare, banditry, disease, land mines, and violence in a terminal adventure ride. Tattered countries which visitors are "inserted into" and "escape" from.

★★★★                                           **Very Nasty**

Danger here may be more regional, slightly more definable, and maybe even avoidable. Places where you are more likely to stumble across NGOs or stoned backpackers with a 5-year-old *Lonely Planet* guide.

★★★                                                          Dodgy

Popular places where danger is sporadic and usually avoidable. Plenty of budget tourists taking full advantage of the locals' misery and poverty.

★★                                                          Heads-Up

Danger lurks in these places, but is very contained or is easily identifiable.

★                                                          Bad-Rep Lands

Places that are not really dangerous but have a bad rap for isolated incidences or history. But if you try hard enough, you could get waylaid or interred for being a complete idiot.

# Dangerous Places (Short and Sweet)

## The Grim Reaper's Cheat Sheet

We have been noticing that a lot of people never actually read every page of *DP*. We don't blame them. Like the effects of a GE minigun with the trigger stuck, the thousands of insights, tidbits, facts, and sharp-edged quips found within these pages can quickly defoliate your brain. We recommend that *DP* be taken in small doses or saved for those long-haul flights, Central Asian trains, or U.S. customs lines. Yes, the world record is 48 hours to completely read *DP*. Unfortunately the person now has a guide dog. So look at *DP* as an old and slightly offbeat friend. Someone to look up when life gets dull, conversations need a spark, or you need something to replace the ceramic plate in your flak jacket.

Or do like most *DP*'ers do; dive in and out of this book like a box of mental munchies looking for those neat little nuggets hidden inside. Some read it on the subway, trolling for adventurous and intellectual members of the opposite sex. Others keep *DP* carefully laid out on their coffee table, artfully dog-eared and stained from their last trip to Afghanistan. Some cubicle terrorists insert it into their office bookshelf amongst the software manuals and office procedures binders to remind their boss that going postal is only an argument or cancelled weekend away. In candid recognition of this, we have created a very short, highly opinionated, condensed version of the book that will keep you swimming with free lattes and sagacious companionship. If you are in the mortuary or arms business, it might also be a good lead generator. This cheat sheet will give you the dark cynical air of a fired CNN reporter or burned-out State Department spokesperson.

| | |
|---|---|
| **Afghanistan**<br>★★★★<br>page 319 | The new adventure destination . . . and never-ending *DP*. A place where the locals are figuring out how to rob and plunder their new allies . . . where U.S. AC-130s join in to celebrate Afghan weddings. And that most dangerous of countries . . . a tender new democracy. |
| **Algeria**<br>★★<br>page 377 | Fear and loathing in a place that looks disturbingly similar to Southern California except with heads on sticks. The Jihadsicle capital of the world. |
| **The Balkans**<br>★<br>page 397 | Somebody dropped it years ago and the pieces never really fit back together correctly. A place of simmering tensions, unpronounceable place names, bad food, overlapping loyalties, stolen weapons, and beautiful women. A dangerous place, proved by the fact that *DP* gets more irate letters and death threats from Albanians than any other group. |
| **Chechnya (Ichkeria)**<br>★★★★★<br>page 425 | Russia says, "How about two out of three?" The Chechens oblige by making that a Russian kill ratio. Kidnapping replaces homestays as the biggest tourist concept. |
| **Colombia**<br>★★★★★<br>page 447 | The nastiest and nicest place in the Western Hemisphere: hot rebellistas, '80s-era marxists, cheap cocaine, great beaches, kidnapping. The only country with a higher murder rate than a Chuck Norris movie, and an odd, disturbing sense of being in Vietnam . . . circa 1964. |
| **Georgia (Sakartvelo)**<br>★★★<br>page 479 | Broken shard of Soviet Russia crawling slowly into the 1920s. Everyone seems so friendly: Swarthy gangsters in the cities urge you to stay longer and wild-eyed terrorists invite you for a little radiator chain-stay. |
| **The Great Lakes**<br>★★★★<br>page 499 | The place where man began just may be the wellspring for what ends him. War, pestilence, disease, poverty, and some great deals on safaris. . . . |
| **India**<br>★★<br>page 529 | Like a shaken can of ants, India bustles and hustles and occasionally is given to fits of fury. Do you really trust a nuke that says "Made in India?" |

| **Iran**<br>★<br>page 565 | A burgeoning tourist spot depending on which of their neighbors we are bombing at the moment. |
| **Iraq**<br>★★★<br>page 587 | The next big adventure destination for Americans—uniformed ones, that is. For now Iraq is run by a one-man demolition derby with a successor who will make Saddam look like Walt Disney on Prosac. |
| **Israel/Palestine**<br>★★★★<br>page 627 | "This land is my land, that land is my land. . . ." A place where an "eye for an eye " has blinded both sides. |
| **Kurdistan**<br>★★<br>page 675 | Largest group of folks without a country playing musical chairs over Iran, Turkey, Syria, and Iraq. Inner turmoil with slim likelihood of statehood is likened by *DP* to two bald men fighting over a comb |
| **Lebanon**<br>★<br>page 699 | The place where the stuff hits the fan. Syria's bitch with a rolodex of bad people just waiting for Israel to need a little more Liebensraum. |
| **Liberia**<br>★★★★★<br>page 729 | A sweaty place where Jesse Jackson and Pat Robertson like to hang has to be just a little whacked. A chaotic backwater where an escaped prisoner trained by Qaddafi plunders to the sound of American ganster rap. Hey, *c'est l'afrique,* baby. |
| **Nepal**<br>★★<br>page 759 | A beautiful country with the only rebel group that apologizes to tourists for all the killing and violence. |
| **North Korea**<br>★<br>page 777 | This much-maligned Axis of Evil has only one wheel and he might have a nut loose. The last bastion of useless communist ideals. See it before they open a Starbucks. |
| **Pakistan**<br>★★★<br>page 795 | Hot-headed fundamentalist country run by a coup-installed general with nukes, filled with millions of angry unemployed men, and a deep hatred of America. With friends like these . . . |
| **The Philippines**<br>★★★<br>page 827 | Muslims versus Christians in the south. In the north, Commies versus land-owners. Rebels fighting a four-century war who dig Kenny Rogers and Air Supply. Kinda says it all. |

| | |
|---|---|
| **Russia** ★★ page 853 | Discos, limousines, drugs, wide lapels, cheap booze, big cars, gangsters, nightly gunfights. Makes you homesick for 1930s Chicago. |
| **South Africa** ★★★ page 889 | Mandela promised them jobs, homes, and cars; now they're using AKs to help themselves. (See Zimbabwe.) |
| **Sudan** ★★★ page 911 | Black versus Arab, Islam versus Animist Christians, and formerly a great place for terrorists to catch a little R&R. |
| **United States** ★ page 931 | Land of Bush 'n' Son and reality shows that never quite live up to the 6-o'clock news. Over 70 people killed a day and over 220 million guns ready to party. And we tell other people how to run their countries? |
| **Yemen** ★★★ page 959 | The other Afghanistan; jihad with training wheels. More guns per capita than Texas, with their owners tweaked on qat makes. Think *The Greatest Story Ever Told* meets *Scarface,* starring a cast of a thousand mini bin Ladens. |
| **Zimbabwe** ★★★ page 977 | The land of adventure travel just got very adventurous, although the latest travelers seem to be former white farmers. |

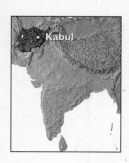

Kabul

★ ★ ★ ★

# AFGHANISTAN

## Tali–Banned, Tali–Bombed, and Tali–Gone

We miss the Taliban here at *DP*. It's not often you get such an obliging bunch of wacky dudes whom you can ridicule so easily. We miss the black turbans, the white flags, the eye patches, Dubai-tagged Toyota Hiluxes, religious edict-o-matic of the week, Friday afternoon reality shows, entertainment, and of course, the no-brainer alliterative abuse of their *talib* moniker. But that's all been Tali-obliterated, hasn't it?

*DP* gets misty-eyed when we think of what the Taliban did for women during their eight-year reign. Oh . . . no . . . not Afghan women: We mean American women. The Taliban gave purpose and focus to millions of bored housewives and documentary makers, empowering them to turn off *Days of Our Lives* and shun PETA flyers in favor of their newly found cause. It was like shooting fish in a barrel. Tupperware and Mary Kay took a back seat to the "We Are the World" horde that adopted Afghan women as the cause du jour. But sadly, that's all Tali-bye-the-bye.

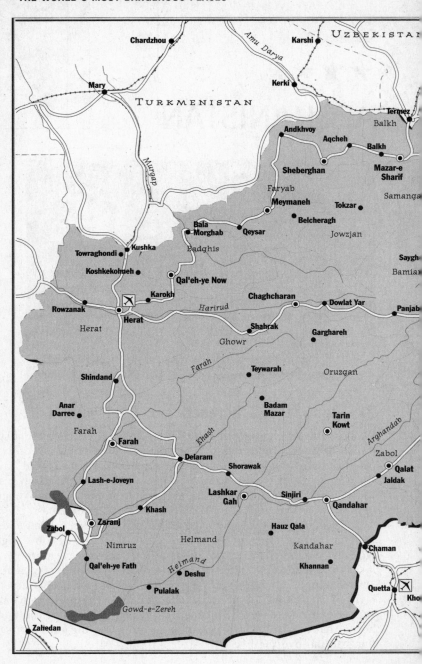

**AFGHANISTAN**

**TAJIKISTAN**

**CHINA**

**Dushanbe**

Kurgan
Tyube

Kulyab

Taxkorgan

Nizhniy
Pyandzh

Khorog

*Pamir*

Langar

**Feyzabad**

**Baharak**

Lasht

Kondoz

Taloqan

*Var Khun*

Konduz

Takhar

**Badakhshan**

Samangan

Warsaj

Skazar

Gilgit

*Indus*

**Baghlan**

Baghlan

Dowshi

Kapisa

Konar

**INDIA**

Charikar

Raqi

Laghman

Srinagar

nian

Parvan

Mehtarlam

Asadabad

Chitral

Kowt-e
Ashrow

**Kabul**

Jalalabad

Khyber
Pass

Vardak

Lowgar

Nangarhar

Landi Kotal

azni

Baraki

Parachinar

Peshawar

**Islamabad**

Jammu

hazni

Gardeyz

Kohat

Rawalpindi

ushaki

Paktia

Thai

Zareh
Sharan

Bannu

*Jhelum*

*Chenab*

b Juy

Paktika

*Indus*

*Ravi*

Tank

Sargodha

Lahore

vargai

Dera Ismail
Khan

Zhob
(Fort Sandeman)

**PAKISTAN**

Multan

Dera Ghazi
Khan

## Afghanistan

⊛ National capital
◉ Province capital
☒ Airport
··········· Province boundary
═══════ Road
┼┼┼┼┼┼ Railroad

0      100      200 km

0            100 mi

Remember those halcyon days when the airwaves were full of Hollywood wives, eternally grumpy RAWAs, whiny women journos, and Hampton hacks fulminating about women's rights, shaking with indignation over a place they had never been, rejecting goofy fatwas, and demonizing the dreaded burqa? God help any male reporter who dared to travel to Afghanistan to do a balanced piece on the two-decade war, the absolute poverty, the deadly drought, the land mines, the natural disasters, or just cover the general state of both Afghan men and women. The Taliban and "denial of women's rights" were being Tali-bitch-slapped . . . big time.

It's too late to mention that the rough-hewn, xenophobic Taliban actually ended most of the factional fighting, stopped crime, ended rape, snuffed out drugs, and put Afghanistan on the map again. Yeah, they went a little crazy up north, but generally things were, dare we say it, almost normal during their ill-formed reign. *DP* readers know that the Taliban tried to issue tourist visas . . . about the same time that they blew up the statues of the Buddhas, their only tourist attraction (so, they have lousy timing). Thirty bucks and you, too, could watch the world's largest Renaissance Faire . . . without the renaissance and without the "fair," of course. The world will miss those slack-jawed, backwoods jokers . . . but for how long, we wonder? What the pass-the-Chardonnay and burn-the-burqa crowd have overlooked is that the seeds of the Taliban are still there. Both Afghan men and women have been screwed equally and continuously since the late '70s and Afghanistan is again slipping back into that quasi-chaotic state of warlords, crime, and attacks against women. Tali-bummer, dude . . . where's the canapés?

The good news? Thanks to all the negative press coverage and the great Crusade, Afghanistan hasn't seen this many tourists for the last two decades. Say what? Tourists?

The tourist boom began in October of 2001. The "boom" part was courtesy of American B-52s and Special Forces on the ground sent in to help Afghan commanders fight the Taliban. The "tourist" part began a few weeks later. Thousands of neophyte journos charged off to make their name in the War on Terror.

Suddenly this bizarre travel guide called *DP* shot up to the top 10 on Amazon's bestseller list. There was a massive run on Domke safari vests, Pakistani-made pakools, and Thuraya satphones, and bang, they were off. Like the climactic moment at Burning Man in Nevada, there were over 2,000 journos waiting for the pyrotechnics to begin. Most of them were stuck in the Panjshir valley waiting for the war to start. Even in the south, dashing Frenchmen, corpulent pommies, and enterprising women had no qualms about donning the dreaded burqa to get into Talib-held Kabul. It would appear that the burqa was now the favorite apparel of indignant journos. After all, it protects from dust and sun and keeps prying Tali-border guards from fondling your packages.

"Kiplingesque" was the order of the day as journos entertained readers with tales of their treacherous mountainous journeys, flights in aging Russian helos, and bad food. Their accounts sounded strangely like runners-up for the "In a Dangerous Place" essay for *DP5*'s Afghanistan chapter. Top prize goes to talk-show host Geraldo for "Mr. Magoo Does Afghanistan." A close second was Ashleigh Banfield for "Gidget Goes Tribal."

> **T**op prize goes to talk-show host Geraldo for "Mr. Magoo Does Afghanistan." A close second was Ashleigh Banfield for "Gidget Goes Tribal."

The journos waited, bored out of their skulls but safely out of harm's way, in the Panjshir (with obligatory trips to see *DP*'s old buddy Commander Baba Jan Bagram to get bang-bang—usually telephoto shots of the bombing—and file those "crouched-in-the-trenches" reports). The less adventurous staked out rebar-adorned hotels in Peshawar. Rooftops sagged under the weight of lights, video gear, and overweight network anchors doing the "war" thing. Pakistanis set Uncle Sam, CNN logos, U.S. flags, and even themselves alight to get a slot on the CBS evening news. Soon it became apparent that all this media was available for a price and within the appropriate rolling report windows. Talking heads artfully choreographed their stand-ups to synchronize with these daily dog-and-pony shows. It was war reporter's heaven . . . without the war, of course, and perhaps without the reporters. Until, of course, the giddy mob started to get killed, murdered, robbed, and shot because they forgot, in their enthusiasm to get to the war, that they were the enemy and that the front lines were right outside their hotel-room doors.

Oh, the war, you ask? It wasn't much to see. Around 25,000 Talibs fought in the north and then quickly cut a deal with General Abdul Rashid Dostum. The less-numerous Talibs in the south never did put up much of a fight: They just went home, leaving behind die-hard clusters of bin Ladenites. They simply shaved, swapped turbans, and changed into something more comfortable, like the 21st century. They did put up a good fight in the Dar-I-Suf valley (where *DP* was, of course) but it wasn't really much of a match. There were a lot of surprised, upward, "what the . . ." looks microseconds before molecular dispersion. Oh, and then there was "Get bin Laden," but the target inconveniently decided not to be got right under the noses of the world's most powerful military/intelligence force.

Yes, the Talibs did exactly the same thing Afghans always do in Afghanistan: crack off a few shots with the AK, throw up their hands, smile a lot, and join the other side. The Taliban . . . er, sorry, the "conservative Pashtun elements," are now our friends again. Like your beret-wearing, Ché-T-shirted, commie, college-kid nephew going back to work at Merrill Lynch in the fall, the Taliban aren't Taliban any more: They are just Tali-been. And to think that Hamid Karzai, the Maryland-restaurant family guy we parachuted in to run their country, not only helped to arm the Talibs but was Mullah Omar's first choice to be their UN rep. But, hey, we are all Tali-buddies, now . . . right?

So exactly where did those "you-so-crazy," prosthetic-knee-slapping, tongue-in-scarred-cheek Talibs go wrong? Well, students of history will remember that we had our noses so far up the Talibs' *patoos* that we even wined and dined them in the United States, just so they would let us build a pipeline. We even wrote them checks because they did such a nice job of getting rid of the opium poppies. We handed them millions of dollars in aid, looked the other way when Pakistan armed and trained them, and even reminisced about the good old days when they used our money to fight the Russians. We were Tali-buds, man.

Then, around 1996 to 1997, the Talibs made three mistakes. They got real mean and ornery when they made it to Mazar, killing thousands of Shi'a Hazaras. They invited Saudi rich-boy-gone-bad Osama bin Laden to be their official mascot, and of course they pissed off Christiane Amanpour, Jay Leno's wife, and a host of other females who successfully reinvented the once-lusty freedom fighters into Amishygonists with AKs. (Quick note to aspiring world leaders: Never piss off a premenopausal female.)

Despite the unwanted publicity and support from bin Laden, the roots of dissent and violence in Afghanistan are as simple as they are obvious: Poverty, abuse, lack of education, and a harsh terrain that happens to be the no-man's land between East and West. A little money and loyalty goes a long way here. This is a fact not lost on Russia, Turkey, and Central Asian dictators and various criminal and terrorist elements. To understand how quickly Afghan loyalties can shift, one needs only to spend five minutes studying the rise and fall of the Taliban.

The Talibs (*talib* means "religious student" or "seeker of truth" in Arabic) appeared as God-fearin', upstandin', rag-headed Gary Coopers who suddenly morphed into cross-eyed, brutal, morose, and wacky Ike Clanton boys. Kipling's "wily Pathans" and Reagan's "noble freedom fighters" were now misogynist mullahs. Perhaps their biggest sin was their absolute indifference to the needs of

**N**GOs and freeloading journos go together like heroin and greasy hair.

journos and their disgust with the wealthy lifestyles of foreign NGOs—a volatile mix, because NGOs and freeloading journos go together like heroin and greasy hair.

Suddenly, gone were the network war-hogs who hiked in over the mountains from Pakistan and wrote stirring tales of muj morality and bravery. During the Talib years, sleek, white UN turboprops off-loaded female journalists into waiting chauffeur-driven black Mercedeses. Over a white-jacket-waited-on lunch at the UN mansion (with exercise room, satellite television, and bar), the well-paid staffers chronicled the horrors of the lack of health care, the treatment of women, and generally how life sucked, and apparently just for women. After an elegantly served lunch, it was off by air-conditioned Land Cruiser to do the standard gender junket. The first stop was to see the deputy head of the religious police at the Department for the Promotion of Virtue and the Prevention of Vice. Here, every writer was assured to get a few giggles from the latest fatwa: no paper bags, no white socks, four fingers of beard, and none of the ultimate media sin . . . picture-taking. Then, to get local color, it was off to a barber for a little four-finger-beard humor, a clandestine visit to a girls' school for a little danger, then pack a lunch and figure out that hidden DV-Cam for the Friday executions. The trip winds up with a few stiff $1.50 Scotches at the "Tali-bar" and a good night's sleep, and then it's off to Peshawar by free Red Cross flight to file the story.

Just what was the centerpiece of their journalist lust? The horrors of war? The impoverishment of a nation? The specter of starvation? No, it was the dreaded burqa, a two-dollar, pleated cotton garment worn by every woman outside of cosmopolitan Kabul for centuries, and of course worn by the vast majority of Afghan women today. No one actually mentioned that it was our best friend, Hekmatyar, who made the burqa mandatory long before the Talibs showed up in Kabul. No one bothered to stray far enough from Kabul to notice that the burqa has long been in common use, not only in the south but also in the cities controlled by the lusty (but equally fundamentalist) freedom fighters of the Northern Alliance, and of course in the tribal areas of Pakistan. The anti-burqa publicity inflamed the world and shut down any aid to the war-torn region, further devastating the country. And then we bombed them just to make sure they stayed that way.

Abusing the Taliban for not providing women's rights is akin to taking Dick Cheney to task for not hosting Greenpeace fundraisers. The draconian and backward views of the Taliban sprang from Pashtun culture (an ethnic group that spreads into and unites Afghanistan with southern Pakistan), in a generation raised during a war caused by outside meddling. And, of course, you have America to thank for the

Taliban. Yes, that's right, the Taliban got that way because we made them that way. We directly supported primarily militant, rural-based, and fundamentalist groups in the '80s because they were the ones who hated the secular, democratic, reconstructive, socialist, urban Afghans whom the Russians relied on to run the country back in the '70s and '80s. Yes, folks, we armed and trained them back then, when they were so eager to go after the Russians. We taught them so well that the minute the Russians left they descended into a maelstrom of infighting and internecine warfare.

Modern Afghan misery began in 1978, when Noor Taraki attempted to import hard-line communism into Afghanistan with the aid of the Soviet Union. Up until this point Afghanistan's economic growth, education, and agricultural advances were courtesy of the Soviet Union— well-intentioned expansionists who built most of what you see lying as rubble in Afghanistan today. It is a credit to the Afghan's negotiating skills that Americans and Euros were shamed into building roads, schools, and airports (for example, we built the airport at Kandahar and Pan Am used to run the Kabul Intercontinental hotel). But the modern reforms in this very traditional country were benefiting the city dwellers, erasing centuries of devout Islamic traditions, and harsh agrarian reforms had the peasants revolting. The tribes and rural villages began to resist this social engineering. Finally, the Russians felt they needed to step in. Taraki's Russian-picked successor, Babrak Karmal, asked Moscow for troops to keep order, thus signaling the beginning of the modern conflict. Marxism was met with mortars, reforms were fought with flintlocks, and the mujahideen, or holy warriors, began as tribal-based rural militia using the mosques and madrassahs as their bases of support. The Afghan army tried to crack down but were poorly trained, poorly equipped, and poorly motivated to do so.

On Christmas of 1989, 85,000 Soviet soldiers were airlifted in to "help" the Afghan government. Their pretext was that the puppet ruler (Afghanistan's friends have a thing for puppets), Karmal, needed help. The official demand for this intervention was sent from Kabul and signed by Karmal, who could not have been in the Afghan capital at the time because he was riding into Kabul with a Soviet army convoy.

The most militant of the muj groups was based out of Peshawar and Quetta and were rural, fundamentalist, and working closely with a Palestinian named Abdullah Azzam and his Saudi sidekick, Osama bin Laden, to encourage foreign fighters to join the fray.

Meanwhile, Gulbuddin Hekmatyar spent the Russian war in safety in Peshawar, squirreling away the massive arms shipments, while Ahmed Shah Massoud was fighting in the mountains of the Panjshir.

Eventually, even regional powerbrokers like Ismail Khan of Herat and General Abdul Rashid Dostum of Mazar-I-Sharif joined the mujahideen to fight the Afghan and Russian army.

The conservative Muslim mujahideen put up an unexpected and bitter resistance to the new government. Soviet troops, armed to the teeth with Moscow's most modern materials of doom, were picked apart on the ground by elusive rebel mujahideen guerrillas, employing antiquated weapons that been modified from 19th-century British army flintlocks. Soon, with CIA money and Pakistan's secret service training, the muj began picking Soviet gunships out of the sky with a couple of thousand U.S.-supplied Stingers and other surface-to-air rockets. The Stingers soon shut down the Russian gunships and supply aircraft. Convoys were easily ambushed. Russia had its very own Vietnam but without the beaches, go-go bars, or palm trees. The muj never technically won the war; they just enjoyed making the Afghan and Soviet troops, and their own villagers, very miserable.

When Afghanistan was first invaded by the Soviets in 1979, President Jimmy Carter provided the mujahideen with US$30 million in covert aid. This manifested itself in the form of the Pakistani secret service, or ISI, supplying selected rebel commanders with old Soviet arms procured from Egypt. The Pakistani military is traditionally a hawkish fundamentalist group who carefully chose their commanders from among southern Pashtuns, an ethnic group that has ties with Pakistanis across the border.

Many of these commanders were virulently anti-American and hard-line Islamics. (Getting nervous yet?) The CIA even knew that once the Russians were gone there was going to be a power grab. It didn't help that many of the muj commanders kept brand-new American-bought weapons in their original containers in large storage yards waiting for the day the Russians would leave. The backdraft caused by the demand for fighters also created a new supply line under Palestinian Abdullah Azzam that pulled in and recruited foreigners from America, northern Africa, the Arabian Gulf, and other Islamic countries as far away as the southern Philippines. The guest house in Peshawar was known as the Base, or *al-Qaeda*.

> **I**t didn't help that many of the muj commanders kept brand-new American-bought weapons in their original containers in large storage yards waiting for the day the Russians would leave.

As covert military aid to the mujahideen increased under the Reagan administration, so did the death toll of Russian as well as Afghan soldiers and civilians. Hundreds of thousands, and then millions, of Afghans fled to Pakistan and Iran to escape the war. By 1985, the

Afghan rebels were receiving US$250 million a year in covert assistance to battle 115,000 Soviet troops in their country. This figure was double the 1984 amount. The annual amount received by the guerrillas reached an incredible US$700 million by 1988. The Americans were even shipping Tennessee mules to Afghanistan to carry all those new weapons into the hills. The "Seven Dwarfs," or the seven muj groups, became the most heavily armed and most powerful groups in Afghanistan. Their main qualification? They hated foreign invaders and they were mostly hard-line Islamists. Now you should be getting really nervous.

Finally, after ten years of both investing in and destroying Afghanistan, the Soviets called it quits in 1989 with 14,453 of their countrymen officially dead (the real number is closer to 35,000 or 50,000). This left Afghanistan with a frightening collection of rural-based, tribally aligned, regionally separated, ethnically pure power groups . . . all armed to the teeth. Even with this *Clockwork Orange* scenario, the U.S. spook-bucks kept flowing. In 1991, anywhere from US$180 million to US$300 million was funneled into Afghanistan by the CIA via the ISI. In all, the CIA spent about US$3.3 billion in rebel aid over the course of the war and no one knew how to turn off the tap. The traditional method of electing leaders based on their social contacts and ability to defend their region was gone. Afghanistan was ruled by the gun and rapidly changing alliances between bitter enemies. The warlords quickly put all those weapons and hatred to use to consolidate their control over trade and commerce. Even small-time commanders now controlled massive arsenals and large numbers of paid "volunteers." These commanders began to consolidate trade, smuggling, and businesses under their control. Traditional law enforcement or tribal control was in disarray. By the early '90s there was no law in Afghanistan except the law of the gun. There were over a dozen checkpoints between Peshawar and Kabul.

By the middle of April 1992, mujahideen guerrillas and other Islamic rebels moved in on Kabul and ousted President Najibullah. A 50-member ruling council comprised of guerrilla, religious, and intellectual leaders was quickly established to create an Islamic republic. A generation of men who had known only killing and war as an occupation were now controlled by a brutal patchwork of Westernized and armed warlords, many of whom had become despots, thieves, and drug lords. Then, like a dust storm from the south, came the movement known as the Taliban.

The Taliban as a combined political, religious, and military movement began in early 1994, during a small border incident in Spin Boldak. The Talibs were originally a small group of Pashtuns from the

Maiwand district of southern Afghanistan, led by a group of 30 former religious students (or *talibs*) who had studied together in the provincial madrassahs from Kandahar and Helmand provinces. Their spiritual leader was one-eyed, 35-year-old Mullah Muhammad Omar. The main leader was the now-deceased Mullah Rabbani. They came from the hard, dry south, and most had been severely victimized by the economic hardships of continual warfare and lawlessness. They had known no traditional schooling, media, or education (other than the madrassahs) and many had fought against the Russians to make a new Afghanistan. Like many rural Afghans, the Talibs viewed the Western-backed brutes as the reason for their misery.

The uprising began when they attacked the highway checkpoints manned by a local warlord under whose rule extortion, robbery, and rape were regular occurrences. These atrocities not only angered the common people but they cut into the business of influential Pakistani Pashtun traders based in Quetta, Pakistan, and Kandahar. These traders (along with the local people) financed the initial campaigns of the Taliban to clear Kandahar of the warlords.

They quickly fought or negotiated their way from the south of Afghanistan all the way to the foothills of the Panjshir valley. The Taliban used bribes, tanks, pickup trucks, suicide charges, and cash to win over region after region. They soon had the patronage of the Pakistani ISI and Pakistani merchants who used the transportation corridors that were now freed from bandits.

In 1996 an old friend showed up—Osama bin Laden. Bin Laden came to stay on a large farm in the Tora Bora (Black Dust), creating for himself a small fiefdom just south of Jalalabad in the scenic Spingar Mountains (the same area in which he had created massive cave complexes during the jihad against the Russians). To show his gratitude to Mullah Omar for letting his posse stay, bin Laden donated around 2,000 Toyota Hiluxes and $300,000 in cash, and worked with the Taliban to defeat their enemies in the north. He counseled Mullah Omar on tactics, government, and even policy. Under bin Laden's influence, the shy and reclusive Omar began to get grand ambitions. Afghanistan was destined to become an emirate and an Islamic state, with Sharia as its law. More important, Afghanistan had become the main training center for international jihadis.

Bin Laden's tactics and military assistance worked. In the summer of 1998 the Taliban finally pushed Uzbek warlord Dostum all the way back to Ankara (for the second time), scared Hekmatyar back to Tehran, and had even walled up Massoud in his scenic Panjshir valley.

By 1999 the Taliban's power base had expanded from its core support in the Durrani and Pashtun provinces of southern Afghanistan and Pakistan to most of Afghanistan. The Taliban had effectively created a Pashtun power base that represented a group of 15 to 17 million people, of which 10 million lived in Afghanistan and the rest in Pakistan. The urban and northern Hazaras (who are Shi'ite) and the northern Tajiks did not see eye-to-eye with the Taliban, and suffered greatly. The Uzbeks were frantic and locked down their borders and invited in the Russians. It was as if the Hatfields and McCoys had simply invaded Washington and set up shop.

> **I**t was as if the Hatfields and McCoys had simply invaded Washington and set up shop.

In the dark years before 2001, Russia (via Tajikistan) and Iran provided covert support to the Tajik, Uzbek, and Hazara elements known as the United Front under Massoud and Rabbani. Massoud tried to alert the world about the foreigners inside Afghanistan who were using his countrymen as live fire targets for other wars. On September 9, 2001, Massoud was assassinated by three men posing as journalists. Two of them, Karim Touzani (alias Abdessar Dahmane) and Kassim Bakkali (alias Bouari El-Ouaer), died in the blast; the third was shot by Massoud's guards. On September 11, 2001, America was attacked, and suddenly Afghanistan and the Taliban were in America's crosshairs.

Back in April of 2001, it was only Iran that supported the United Front. Rabbani had provided $50,000 to bring General Dostum out of exile in Ankara to join in the fight and then in October of 2001 the Iranian advisors magically disappeared as CIA operatives and Green Beret A teams began the war. Reversing the tactics of the Taliban, Uzbek warlord Dostum rolled up the Talibs (with a little help from the world's most powerful air arsenal) from the west, and Tajik warlord Daoud Khan pushed from the east, until the Taliban and their Pakistani and foreign fighters were bottled up in Kunduz. Once the surrender was negotiated (and after the ugly blip of the Qala Jangi uprising), the war was all over as the Talibs faded back into their villages to wait until they are Tali-born again.

For now, Afghanistan awaits reconstruction. And, not to put too fine a point on it, the burqa is still very much in style . . . and the plight of women in the south still sucks.

## The Scoop

Peace has come, the birds are singing, there's a lilt to every Afghan's step, and it's a brand new day in Afghanistan. Twenty-four years of war are over, the fundamentalist Taliban are Tali-busted, and Osama and his multinational geek squad have magically vanished. The warlords have all gone fishing, the AKs have become ploughshares, and a U.S.

lackey rules in isolated splendor. Well, at least that's what you are supposed to believe. The truth is a little less rosy and a little more *DP*'ish.
Afghanistan has become the most dangerous kind of country on earth:
a poor, struggling, new democracy awash with guns, old hatreds, and
plenty of unemployed former soldiers. And, oh yeah . . . exactly where
did those darn Talibs go?

## The Players

### Uncle Sam (Baba Sam)

On October 7, 2001, America returned to Afghanistan and began
bombing. The Great Game was on again. George Bush put his lipstick
on and got into bed with the very people who supported our enemies.
If you watch pre-October videos carefully you will notice that there are
Iranian advisors along with Massoud, Khan, Dostum, Rabbani, and
other anti-Taliban groups. They were quickly replaced by Green Berets
with a lot more cash and gizmos. Now, of course, the same warlords
whom we supplied with A teams, air power, weapons, and serious
money are wondering why their calls don't get returned by the State
Department. Even former Soviet-era General Dostum is quoting Abraham Lincoln and not even getting a penny with Abe's picture on it for
his efforts. The fundamentalist Tajiks have some cushy slots in the new,
pretend government, but will be ousted as soon as the CIA can find some
moderate (hell, we'll even take not-so-moderate, ex-Taliban) Pashtuns
to replace the Iranian-backed fundamentalist Panjshiri Tajiks. Much of
the money promised to rebuild Afghanistan has never appeared, and
large swaths of the country seem to get along just fine without the central government or the influence of Uncle Sam. Will Washington's
complete lack of loyalty, history, or geography push Afghanistan back
into the same state it was in in 1994? The same decentralized, warlord-
run chaos that spawned the Taliban? Probably.

### Hamid Karzai

Karzai (b. December 24, 1957) studied political science at Indiana
University (paid for by big brother Mahmood, who runs a Maryland
restaurant called "Helmand"). Karzai was officially described by *Time*
magazine as "the only Afghan leader with a vision for his country
beyond personal greed and tribal ambitions." Not much of a résumé.
You probably also guessed that Karzai is the recipient of millions in U.S.
PR bucks to shamelessly mold him into his new Gandhi/Mandela/King
image as the present and future leader of the New Improved Afghanistan.

His claim to fame, or rather the presidency, was his father, Abdul
Ahad Karzai, a man who had a mildly illustrative political career in the
'70s when his distant uncle, the king of Afghanistan, was still around.

Coincidentally, Karzai comes from the same Kandahari tribe as the king. Funny how U.S.-sponsored democracy in Afghanistan is still based on the good-old-boy network. Of course, George Bush should appreciate the parallels.

Karzai, the fifth of eight children, was born to privilege. Five of his siblings fled their homeland, but his press releases are careful to note that Hamid "stayed in the region" . . . as in India and Pakistan.

When the Russians invaded, the Karzais moved to Quetta in southern Pakistan. Karzai went to university in Simla, India. He joined the Pakistani-based Afghan National Liberation Front (ANLF) in 1982, and, after the Russians left, joined the muj government.

He soldiered on as deputy foreign minister in the muj government from 1992 to 1994. He left the severely divisive and warring Rabbani muj government due to its internal bickering ("bickering" in Afghan terms means that their disagreements flattened Kabul and killed 50,000 Afghans).

Karzai is a Pashtun and, not surprisingly, was an eager early supporter of the Taliban movement. Although the State Department would rather you didn't know this, Karzai donated $50,000 to the Taliban and gave them a large cache of weapons to get them going. He also met with Mullah Omar several times and was asked by Omar to be their UN envoy in New York. Not quite Gandhi-ish, but close enough.

> **K**arzai is a Pashtun and, not surprisingly, was an eager early supporter of the Taliban movement.

Karzai also initially had a good relationship with the ISI (the Taliban's major benefactor). Karzai says he became suspicious of the Taliban movement around 1994 due to their reliance on the ISI, Pakistani fighters, and covert money (bin Laden would not show up until 1996). Karzai has experience in politicking. His education in political science, diplomatic skills, and language skills came in handy (Karzai speaks Pashto, Dari, Urdu, English, French, and Hindi), and he was seen shuttling back and forth between various embassies during the Taliban years.

After the Karzais' Tali-boosting was over, Hamid and his father campaigned against the Taliban from Quetta. His father was shot while walking home from a mosque in Quetta in July of 2000. Karzai blames the Taliban for the murder. His father's death propelled Hamid to "Khan," with leadership of the 500,000-strong Pashtun Popolzai tribe (his older brothers were in the States). The Popolzai are descendants of Persian warlord Ahmad Shah Durrani, who became the first king of Afghanistan in 1747. Karzai gained major points as a leader when he took his father's body back to Kandahar for burial and the Taliban chose not to interfere.

Come September 11, 2001, Karzai was probably the least-likely candidate to end up running Afghanistan. Karzai had based his organization in Baluchistan since 1998, but was in the process of being ousted by the Pakistani government before September 11. He had never been in combat and was more comfortable running a hotel in Peshawar while acting as a part-time political advisor to muj groups and doing the odd go-between in Islamabad.

The official U.S. PR story is that Hamid, armed with only a satphone and good intentions, hopped on his moped and rode to Afghanistan to start his fight against the Taliban in November 2001. The idea was that he would use silky speeches to convert warlords and, if words failed him, he would perhaps call in the odd air strike on his U.S.-supplied sat. Naturally, the truth is that the CIA and the U.S. military had little use for Hamid "Gandhi" Karzai in the beginning. Karzai was considered a well-meaning but effete lightweight by the U.S. government and never made much headway against the Taliban while in Pakistan. The U.S. ambassador in Islamabad blew off Karzai's initial request for support (the U.S. was working with the ISI, who didn't like Karzai). The unvarnished truth is that Karzai actually entered Afghanistan on October 8, 2001 (the day after U.S. bombing started), with a group of Afghans equipped with few weapons and fewer supplies. He did have a satphone, but no one in Washington (including Colin Powell) was interested in taking his calls. Finally, when the success of Dostum and his A team in the north changed Pentagon strategy (the initial State Department strategy was just to bomb the Taliban until they gave up, and stay out of local politics), the Pentagon and State Department embraced Karzai. During the first week in November, Karzai officially became "our man in Kandahar." Fashion fame followed shortly thereafter.

Kandahari-born Karzai was plucked from third-world obscurity to be America's newest glad-hander/puppet/fashionista. The fact that he had little-to-no political, military, or financial support inside the country was irrelevant to his backers. In the State Department's attempt to show that everything was cool in Afghanistan, they fashioned Karzai into Gandhi-meets-Genghis-Khan. Even Tom Ford of Gucci gushed over his carefully contrived pan-Afghan look: "the most chic man in the world." We never did quite hear that very true story about Karzai being personally asked by Mullah Omar to be the Taliban's UN rep in New York, or even the rumors that he was an ISI stooge long before making the big time in America. We did hear the embarrassing story about how we almost killed him with friendly fire when we tossed him into Afghanistan to make it look like he was leading the fight in the good war. (God forbid that Uncle Sam admits that the effete and educated Karzai couldn't win a game of rock, scissors, paper, let alone a real war.)

On October 8, 2001, Karzai was sent into Uruzgan province with the CIA and a Special Forces ODA to get a little warlord ground-time and to help buy off local commanders. He was almost killed by U.S. bombs (well, OK, he was slightly injured by an errant U.S. bomb) and nearly met the fate of the other CIA stooge, Abdul Haq, who was caught and used as a Pashtun yo-yo by the Taliban. Luckily (and allegedly), U.S. choppers plucked Karzai out of the stew and dropped him inside Pakistan so he could live to vogue again. He initially denied the cut-and-run since it wouldn't look good on his carefully crafted, avenging, warlord-turned-Afghan-president résumé. And, of course, skeptics might have noticed that this carefully positioned pacifist and fan of Gandhi was calling in B-52 air strikes on his fellow tribesmen. Oops. Well, *DP* assumes they were clean, peaceful, and very stylish kills.

Now the hard part begins. Hamid can be seen on the begging circuit wearing a silver *caracol* (attention Tom Ford and the PETA bulemics: the unfashionable Pakistani affectation, the *caracol*, is a hat made from the skin of an aborted baby lamb). He also sports a green-striped *chapan*, the traditional Uzbek horseman's coat—a fashion influence courtesy of Genghis Khan and his Mongol hordes—and a Shalwar Kameez (a reminder of his ties to Pakistan), topped off with an Armani knockoff suit jacket (testament to the fact that although he may be on the CIA payroll, he can't afford a decent suit yet). Karzai makes the brutal polyglot of Central Asian history seem positively chic. Myopic journos gushed over his "Gandhi-like" demeanor, swooning over his chrome dome and maitre d' manners, and ignored his polite but empty speeches. The only thing Gandhi-like about Karzai is, of course, his begging bowl, which he constantly outstretches to the big-talking but short-armed Western countries that insist they are 100 percent committed to rebuilding Afghanistan. It must be tough for a former-royalist-turned-warlord-turned-international-beggar to work up $4 billion in empty pledges and not be able to afford a decent suit.

In any case, on December 22, 2001, Karzai became interim ruler of Afghanistan, which is akin to being given the top job at Enron without a paycheck, desk, phone, or lawyer.

When the *loya jirga* was held in Kabul, Uncle Sam short-circuited the proceedings by announcing in advance that Karzai was their favorite son. Karzai dutifully selected a mishmash of Afghans to form a government. Not that any of the regional rulers paid attention. So, like an epileptic luge team, the new Afghan government slides ever rapidly downward into the abyss with Hamid styling at the helm.

> **S**o, like an epileptic luge team, the new Afghan government slides ever rapidly downward into the abyss with Hamid styling at the helm.

**AFGHANISTAN**

*Hamid Karzai*
President of Afghanistan
Kabul, Afghanistan
*Helmand Restaurant*
A. Qayum Karzai or Assad Jon
806 North Charles Street
North of Mt.Vernon Square
Baltimore, MD 21201
Tel.: (410) 752-0311, or
    (410) 442-2682 (before 1:00 PM)
Fax: (410) 442-2682
helmand@erols.com

The Army's 5th Special Forces Group established a memorial fund to assist the families of Davis, Petithory, and Prosser, who were killed in the Afghan campaign while with Hamid Karzai. Donations can be sent to:

*Chapter 38*
Special Forces Association
Attn: Survivor Fund
P.O. Box 223
Fort Campbell, KY 42223-0223

## The Taliban

When *DP* did a world-exclusive interview with the Talib leadership back in '95, we knew this fundamentalist gig was going to end ugly. They simply put their fate in the hands of God. Six years later, in 2001, we capped it off with another world exclusive with the number-three Talib, Mullah Faizel. He kinda' summed it up: "We fought for an idea and we lost." And of course he put his fate in the hands of God. When pressed, he did admit that the high-tech use of all-weather air power, JDAMs, and laser-guided air strikes had sorta' made any divine intervention to save the Taliban moot.

**W**hen *DP* did a world-exclusive interview with the Talib leadership back in '95, we knew this fundamentalist gig was going to end ugly.

To be kind, the Talibs were about an idea: to create a purely Afghan, Islamic state in which Sharia and Islamic values would rule. Their rejection of outside influences had one lamentable loophole . . . loyalty to an outside meddler called bin Laden, a man who masked his hatred behind religious rhetoric. For now, the Talib mullahs and followers in Pakistan and southern Afghanistan are just biding their time to see how things will turn out. Watch your Tali-bision for developments. You can still contact the Taliban by hanging out in Paktia and Kunar and trying to convince the locals you are not Osama-hunting.

All the Taliban sites have been hijacked or hacked, and if you want "to get yer jihad on," try:

http://www.taliban.com
http://www.jihadunspun.net
http://www.talibanreunited.com

## The Madrassahs

One of the unique elements in Afghan culture is the traditional journey from the Afghan hills to the religious schools in warmer regions in

Pakistan. The Deoband madrassah, or religious school of India, was created in 1866, nine years after the British destroyed the traditional *ulemas,* or schools, that taught the Muslim religious system in 1857. The Deoband school is second in size only to al-Ashar in Cairo. The borders between Afghanistan, Pakistan, and India mean little to religious students, who consider it important to journey to great centers of Islamic learning. It is a long-standing tradition that Afghans are encouraged to seek out knowledge; Talib means "seeker" or "student" in Arabic. The madrassahs are supported by a 2 percent tax or donations supplied by the students, parents, and community. The government does not support the schools and usually only one son in a family, typically the brightest, is accorded the honor of being given a religious education. The largest religious seminary in Pakistan is the Jamiat Ulema-e Islam in Akora Khatak, 65 kilometers east of Peshawar. This madrassah was a favorite recruiting spot for the Talibs and other militant Islamic factions.

The second-largest madrassah in Pakistan is Bionsi Town mosque in Karachi, a Deobandi Sunni school. They have 8,000 students, many of whom supported the basic goals of the Taliban, which was to create an Islamic state free from outside meddling.

In a scenario eerily similar to today, a century ago, when the British were running things, the newly conquered Pashtun, Sindhi, and Punjabi (they were part of India then) Muslims wanted to maintain their traditional religious education and spurned secular and Western influences. In creating a system and method of education outside the political currents, the Deoband school began to turn out activists who were unaligned to the political process and wanted to retain the traditional religious centers in communities, law, medicine, and politics.

Today there are over 8,000 registered religious schools in Pakistan. There are estimated to be another 25,000 that are not registered. Around 30 of these schools have over 2,000 students. Children begin learning at age six and graduate at age 16. In the Arabic tradition of higher learning, students travel to other countries to learn about Islam and its various interpretations. The Afghan empire once spread into the plains of India and across Pakistan, but even today current political boundaries are disregarded, with students encouraged not only to learn abroad but to participate in jihad, or the struggle to protect Islam.

The Talibs drew support from the poor Afghans and Pakistanis who fill the madrassahs in the border refugee camps of Baluchistan and Peshawar. The Pakistani madrassahs in the south were supported by businessmen and religious leaders who had connections with the Pakistani religious party Jamiat Ulema-e Islam, led by a member of Bhutto's government, Fazlur Rahman. The Talib's brand of Islam is the strict, old-fashioned, Sunni Deoband school. It is so strict that the leaders forbade having their pictures taken.

The madrassahs started operating in the northwest frontier regions of British India around the early part of the 20th century. Up until the 1947 partition of India and Pakistan, Afghan religious students dreamed of learning in the Islamic centers in Deoband and Delhi. When it became difficult to travel from Afghanistan through Pakistan to India, some scholars of the Deoband school opened madrassahs in Lahore, Karachi, and Akora Khattak in Northwest Frontier Province. With the establishment of these madrassahs, there was a steady flow of Afghans studying in Pakistan. The process continues to this day and generates the same fervor for religious purity in government and social life.

If you wonder why the Uzbeks are nervous, consider that there's always been a fundamentalist movement to recapture and restore the ancient learning centers of Bukhara, in what is now Uzbekistan.
http://www.madrassah.org

## Toyota Hiluxes

What the hell does a Jap pickup truck have to do with Afghanistan? Well, you can thank Toyota for being the reason we won the war.

Until the mid-'90s, the cars inside Afghanistan were mostly Russian with a smattering of foreign imports; most were ancient vehicles well past their useful life. There were also the Soviet-supplied military vehicles, which could navigate Afghanistan's daunting roads and terrain.

The Taliban captured the Afghan-Pakistani border town of Spin Boldak in October 1994 (it didn't take long, about two to three hours), and after two days of weak resistance the entire city of Kandahar fell to the Taliban. In November and December, the provinces of Uruzgan to the north and Zabol were taken by troops riding in the backs of pickup trucks and waving the Koran and their AKs. What is not generally known is that the Talibs had revolutionized warfare by using second-hand Toyota Hilux pickup trucks bought by Osama bin Laden in Dubai, duty free.

The Taliban had formed a Somali Rat Patrol strategy of loading men, ammunition, and supplies onto the Toyota Hiluxes and backing this up with Gaz trucks and Antonov cargo planes. Within hours, they could surround towns or military positions, or change their own position. Quite a radical departure from the sandals, mules, and "hit-and-run" war that the muj once fought against the Russians in the mountains.

In a strange turn of events, the Talibs' reliance on mechanized columns (they even bolted antiaircraft guns and rocket launchers onto the backs of old beater Russian trucks) made them dependent on roads and airports by the late '90s. This allowed warlords like Dostum (an old hand at Soviet tank tactics, and trained in mechanized warfare) to create mujahideen groups that could live in the hills and attack on horseback. When the U.S. Air Force was set upon these muj groups, the Talibs were easily picked off by Air Force Special Tactics units and Green Berets calling in close air support linked to Afghan cavalry charges.

http://www.4wdonline.com/Toyota/Hilux/Hilux.html

## The Crusaders

Afghanistan has been invaded, burned, raided, conquered, and razed by outsiders ever since Darius of Persia cruised in around 522 BC to do a little sacking and pillaging. For Westerners, the Great Game has been played since 1812 when Napoleon invaded Russia and caused Afghanistan to become a strategic buffer zone. Soon Britain's control of India was threatened by Russian expansionism. The arid wastelands, tortured passes, and walls of mountains created a perfect line of defense against invaders aiming to stream down to the plains of Pakistan and grab the riches of India. Afghanistan's history is full of colorful characters (devotees of George MacDonald Fraser's *Flashman* series can gain insight into this colorful period). Well, that was the basic idea, anyway. Since then, the British, Russians, and now Americans continually relearn the lessons of history courtesy of the same wild and woolly Pathans (or Pashtuns). The joke, of course, is that Afghanistan has absolutely no strategic or economic value other than a handful of emeralds, an occasional blurp of natural gas, and the semiprecious blue stone, lapus lazuli. There are plenty of boring natural resources like iron and copper (the Russians stole all the survey maps), but the landscape and shifting political climate make any investment risky in every sense. Despite this, the British had a go at conquering Afghanistan during the First Afghan War from 1839 to 1842, followed by the Second Afghan War from 1878 to 1881. The Russians tried between 1979 and 1989 and the Americans are the latest to get embroiled in the fight, beginning in October 2001 and with no realistic end in sight. The Great Game continues under the new name, the War on Terror.

> **T**he joke, of course, is that Afghanistan has absolutely no strategic or economic value other than a handful of emeralds, an occasional blurp of natural gas, and the semiprecious blue stone, lapus lazuli.

http://www.afghan-web.com/history
http://www.pangloss.ca/flashman

## Mullah Mohammed Omar

Hulking, bearded, one-eyed Mullah Omar is still the religious leader of the Taliban. He is now assumed to be hiding somewhere in southern Afghanistan. His consistent threats that his followers will oust the invaders are met with the usual yawns. It could be said that Omar doesn't really see things too clearly.

He was born in 1959 in Nodeh, near Kandahar. Fatherless, he had a tough life. He rose to become a village mullah and ran a madrassah before joining the mujahideen to fight the Russians in 1989. He fought for three years, until he lost his left eye, which remains permanently closed. His religious studies were interrupted by the war. He is considered a religious leader, or mullah, although nobody has actually asked to see his diploma. Omar probably made his biggest mistake in offering traditional Afghan hospitality to former jihad buddy Osama bin Laden in 1996. From that point on, the volatile Osama worked the impressionable Omar and encouraged him to play with matches. Eventually, Osama's choice of extracurricular projects burned both him and the Taliban.

Omar is Afghanistan in a microcosm. Wounded war hero, politician, religious leader, visionary shaper of the new Afghanistan, and now a wanted fugitive. He wanted to study the Koran, but the jihad against the Russians interrupted his studies. He was wounded four times in one firefight. His friends say he was a pretty good shot with an RPG. Omar then ascended the ranks to become the chief commander in the Harakat-i-Inqilab-i Islami party of Muhammad Nabi Muhammad. On April 3, 1996, over 1,000 Muslim clergymen chose Mullah Omar to be the "Amir ul Mumineen" (Supreme Leader of the Muslims). The story is that, to capture Kabul, Omar went to the shrine in Kandahar where the cloak of Mohammed is kept and waved it around. That was enough to make Kabul fall on September 26, 1996, after a major siege. The rest is history. For now, Omar is on the lam in southern Afghanistan with his four wives and children.

How would you recognize Omar? He is a big, burly man, speaks very little, is very shy, and is about as much fun as a hung-over undertaker. Omar may be in Afghanistan now, but if you ever get into a cab at JFK and a burly, one-eyed, bearded Afghan is in the driver's seat, say "hi" for us.

## The Northern Alliance/United Front/New Government

The New Government, aka the United Front, aka the Northern Alliance, is an alliance of whoever wasn't Taliban, and now includes some who were Taliban. It's like a frat party where the door security went home and the beer ran out early.

As with any Afghan entity, the United Front was spectacularly un-united, the Northern Alliance was magnificently un-allied, and the new democratic government grandly isn't anything close to democratic. Afghanistan is ruled by an ever-jostling, jockeying, desperate, perfidious hodgepodge of Pashtun, Tajik, Uzbek, Hazari, and other ethnic, religious, and political groups. Occasionally some of the people who actually run Afghanistan are found in the new government and due to the law of statistics sometimes one or two actually agree on things (but not for long, of course). Although they have to check their AKs at the door, and they have scraped enough "intellectuals" (which is newspeak for "former communist," "royalist lackey," "Yankee installed stooge," or "scheming warlord") to kludge together a government, it remains to be seen who the Afghans really want to run their country. The majority probably don't care, because the mostly rural Afghans have seen a ballot box or a government tax dollar about as many times as they have seen the Good Humor man. For now, Afghanistan has a government, whether they like it or not. In less than six months, two senior cabinet members have been sent 7.5mm copper-jacketed retirement notices. It remains to be seen whether "Blind Land Mine Finder" gets more responses in the help-wanted section than "Afghan Politician."

The truth is that Afghanistan is still a factional place with the Tajiks playing screw-your-buddy with the Pashtuns and Uzbeks and outside meddlers. Think *Survivor* on steroids.

**Haron Amin**
Tel.: (212) 972-1212
Fax: (212) 972-1216
AfgWatan@aol.com

**Ahmad Walid Massoud**
Afghan Embassy, London
Tel.: (44) 0171 589 8891

**Embassy of the Islamic State of**
**Afghanistan (UK)**
31 Prince Gate
London SW7 1QQ, UK
Tel.: (44) 0171 589 8891
Fax: (44) 0171 581 3452

**Dr. Abdullah**
Tel.: 873 761 8942 75, or
    873 614 780 73
UK mobile tel.: 0370 890 372

## They Don't Make Warlords Like They Used to Department

*Ahmed Shah Massoud*

After Massoud was killed by suicide bombers on September 9, 2001, there was a stony silence. Some say that September 11th was the other shoe being dropped. Like a scene out of an Afghan version of *The Godfa-*

*ther,* it seems that bin Laden was busy settling scores that fall. The death of Massoud essentially meant that there would be no effective resistance to the Taliban and bin Laden would be protected from any 9/11 repercussions indefinitely. Oh, by the way, the 9/11 score he settled was payback for Sheik Abdel Rachman's imprisonment, and finishing up the job that the blind Egyptian cleric's stooges couldn't pull off.

Massoud's death showed the hand of bin Laden. The same three men posing as a camera crew had interviewed Rabbani without incident, but when they interviewed Massoud they detonated explosives hidden in the camera. Two days later the hijacks and terrorist attacks on the United States occurred. It seemed someone had done a favor for the Talibs and the only man with a large rent bill would be bin Laden.

Massoud remains an important influence in Afghanistan, because his legend and persona capture the self-image of many Afghans. No one will really be able to replace the "Lion of the Panjshir," the darling of adventure journalists, and perhaps the single most famous Afghan in the world after Marwan, the now-deceased, one-eyed lion at the Kabul Zoo. Massoud had become a caricature of himself, always identified by his jaunty *pakool,* the wool hat adopted from his early years in Nuristan that he kept teetering at a ridiculous angle. Massoud was able to project the image of endlessly fighting an enemy that espoused fundamentalism, yet accepting backing from equally fundamentalist Iranian and Afghan supporters. In a smooth PR move, the U.S. media machine forgot to mention that Massoud's greatest enemy was our best new friend . . . Pakistan. Massoud managed to make his neighborhood spat a global icon for freedom fighters. He was described as the Ché Guevara of Afghanistan or, if you're an American journo, the George Washington of Afghanistan.

He was one of those icons that was praised as being morally and financially pure, motivated only by a burning resolve to give his people a democratic government of their own choosing, but oddly pushing a uniquely Panjshiri Tajik Islamist agenda. His influence was so great that the first provisional government ended up with the three main posts filled by fellow Tajiks from the same small village in Panjshir.

## Gulbuddin Hekmatyar

Hekmatyar has been assassinated more times than Leona Helmsley's character. Dumped by the ISI in favor of the Taliban in 1994, he still plays the part of fiery muj leader. Somehow he always pops up alive on the radio a few days later haranguing his detractors. Hek is the late-40-something "rebel without a pause"

**Hekmatyar has been assassinated more times than Leona Helmsley's character.**

from Baghlan who came to prominence as the leader of the most favored of the 12 Afghan rebel factions nurtured by the CIA.

Hek (b. 1947 in Kunduz province) was in the military and then studied engineering for two years at Kabul University. He was imprisoned from 1972 to 1973 for killing a Maoist student. After Daud took over in 1973, Hek went to Pakistan and two years later became leader of Hezb-e-Islami (Islamic Party). He worked as a terrorist for the ISI and after April 1978 his party became one of the largest muj groups fighting against the Russian-backed government and the then-invading Soviets. He became America's darling and received most of the U.S. covert military aid.

Hek tried to overthrow Najibullah and led one of the factions that fought and destroyed Kabul after the Russians left. In 1995 the Taliban ousted him from Char Asiab just southeast of Kabul. He became prime minister in the Rabbani government and he finally fled after the Taliban took over Kabul in September 1996. He turned up in Mashad, Iran, but is now back in Afghanistan fighting against the Karzai government.

### Hezb-e-Islami
http://www.hezb-e-islami.org

### Ismail Khan

Old, canny Ismail (b. 1942 in Shindand) was a Tajik warlord, about to meet the same fate as former warlord Massoud and leader Najibullah at the hands of the Taliban until he escaped from a Talib jail in March of 2000. You may remember a hijacked Ariana Airlines Boeing 727 flight that originated in Kabul with 165 people on board and ended up at Stansted Airport in the United Kingdom. Ismail Khan was the man they were demanding to have released and the reason for the hijacking. Khan managed to convince his jailer that he should be freed, and he escaped to Iran.

Khan was a famous fighter against the Russians and accepted the surrender of the communist Afghan government in western Afghanistan on April 19, 1992. He is the former governor of Herat province, which borders Iran, and rose to become the Amir, or supreme commander, of Herat, Ghor, and Farah provinces. He worked for a peaceful resolution of the warring factions. In 1994, the Talibs attacked Herat and he fled to Mashad, Iran (a popular hang-out for Afghan warlords on the run) to prevent the destruction of his beloved city. When Khan returned on a secret trip with Dostum he was sold out to the Talibs by Malik (who also managed to sell out the Talibs and Dostum and still live). He was arrested and imprisoned in Kandahar until he escaped in March of 2000. He now rules Herat like a pasha. Despite the negative press, Herat is not only free from factional fighting but is a thriving region.

Khan started his career at Kabul Military School and University and was a lieutenant in the Afghan's 17th Division when the communists took over the government. In March of 1979 he left the army and led a rebellion against the communists. He fled to Pakistan and joined Rabbani's Jamaat-e-Islami Party and returned to fight against the Soviets. He became governor and then fought against the Taliban until September 5, 1995. He returned to fight with General Dostum and was turned over to the Taliban when Abdul Malik defected to the Taliban in May of 1997.

## Sayed Jafar Naderi

Jafar is a journo's dream. On the surface he is an Ismaeli who controlled Baghlan province and kept it safe from the turmoil that surrounded it. More colorful insights are that he's a former pizza-delivery boy, Hell's Angel, and rock-and-roll warlord who controlled the strategic and profitable region of Puli Khomri. His father brought him back and he became a general in his twenties. He could barely speak the local language. The Talibs kicked him out in August of 1998 and trashed his luxury compound. He was in town, visiting from his new base in London, when *DP* was in Dushanbe. He's looking for a way to get back into things, no doubt, but we didn't notice any "warlord wanted" ads in the local paper. He used to control a private army of Kayanis who kept things nice and calm.

Sayed is famous for having been a fan of Jon Bon Jovi, sex, drugs, and rock 'n' roll. In a region where you might think that the wheel is a new invention, his snappy interviews, interesting choice of '80s disco decor, and pure love of the game made him the holy grail for rock-and-roll journos doing the Afghan thing.

His most famous attributed statement is his response when asked why he left New Jersey to return to Afghanistan and become a warlord: "Because I can fuck or kill anyone I want." Yeah, baby. For now he runs his phosphate factory and keeps a low profile.

http://www.islandrecords.com/bonjovi/curtain.las

## General Abdul Rashid Dostum

Dostum (actually a nickname which means "our friend") was born in Kwaja da Khool in 1954. Somehow, Dostum attracts bad press like Anna Nicole Smith attracts late-night viewers. Not that there is any basis for truth in most of the stories about him; he just casts the part so well it would be a damn shame if he turned out to really be a smart, savvy politician and military commander. Which, of course, is what *DP* discovered when we spent a month with Dostum during the War on Terror.

Dostum may be the cat with nine lives, having survived intact through the reign of the king, the communists, the Russians, the muj, and now New Afghanistan. The greatest testament to his talent was that after Plan A failed to dislodge the Taliban, Dostum (along with 2,000 mounted horsemen and an A team called "The Regulators") kicked the Talibs all the way to Kunduz and then negotiated a surrender that shut down the Talibs in less than eight weeks.

In keeping with Uncle Sam's history of backing-then-bailing, the State Department never even sent a bouquet and a note thanking Dostum for taking care of their dirty little problem while suffering only one U.S. casualty, CIA paramilitary agent Mike Spann.

Dostum's ability to shift allegiances and pick the winning side (not an unusual Afghan survival trait) has somehow earned him the anger of the Western media while more fashionable and photogenic chameleons and warlords like Karzai and Massoud seem to dodge their criticisms effortlessly. For now, Dostum is assassinated in the press on a regular basis for being a cruel or brutal warlord. (One could only imagine the consequences of the United States backing a "gentle" warlord.) Massoud, who was, of course, literally assassinated by the press on September 9, was the Hollywood and media favorite to front the war against the Taliban, but bin Laden knew how to turn Massoud's love of media against him. Dostum is far more wary. For now, he will stay enigmatic and abused, but alive, thank you.

Dostum was a rough-and-tumble Uzbek farm boy. He played buzkashi and quit school at age 13, first to help his father work the farm and later to work at the natural gas factory in Sheberghan as a laborer. In those days the government would provide an officer commission if you could scrape up enough men to put together a home-defense militia. The elders in Dostum's village gave him 600 men to lead at the age of 23 and Dostum became a government-sponsored commander. His zeal in fighting the rebel and then muj factions quickly brought him to the attention of the central military. He rapidly attained the rank of general and commanded up to 40,000 men in his Jowzhan militia. Although his bills were paid by the Soviet-sponsored government in Kabul, his men would fight to the death for him and swore allegiance to Dostum rather than his backers. That put Dostum into the unique category of being the most powerful man in Afghanistan.

Dostum quickly figured out that Najibullah could not hold onto power against the muj groups for much longer. Dostum threw in his massive army with the mujahideen, complete with their Russian-designed Afghan army uniforms, tanks, and aircraft. His alliance with Massoud and Hekmatyar quickly broke down during the fighting in Kabul, and he returned to the north to mind his own business. His business includes a gas field, urea factory, and even printing his own money at the time. Initially, the Taliban did not mess with Dostum's fearsome army, but in 1997 they began a massive airlift into Kunduz and attacked the Tajiks to the east and Dostum to the west.

Northern Afghanistan (as defined by the flat area north of the Hindu Kush mountains) had always prospered under Dostum's rule. He had been the undisputed ruler, without challenge, and was eager to set up diplomatic and business relationships with outside countries like Russia, Uzbekistan, Turkey, and Iran. The north was progressing until the Taliban attacked in 1997 and Dostum was ousted, not by force, but by treachery.

Dostum got caught in his own game when his second-in-command, Abdul Malik, defected to the Taliban on May 25, 1997, and Dostum had to hightail it to Ankara courtesy of an airplane supplied by a Turkish intelligence officer named Kashif. On September 12, 1997, Dostum blasted his way into Mazar and sent Malik packing. Then of course the Talibs blasted Dostum out of Mazar again and he had to hotfoot it to Ankara yet again. Finally, in April of 2001, Dostum returned with $50,000 (courtesy of Iran via the Northern Alliance) and a handful of men to the Sar-i-Pul region south of Mazar.

The CIA, two Air Force CAS experts, and 12 Special Forces troops showed up on October 19, 2001, and the rest is history. Mazar fell on November 9. The Talibs surrendered to Dostum two weeks later. Not bad for a man with a grade-school education, no money, a dozen Yanks, and a bunch of scrawny horses.

Dostum traditionally controls eight provinces in the north and runs his little fiefdom out of his hometown and western military headquarters of Sheberghan, which is in Jozjan province, 80 miles from Mazar. He can be found just west of his old HQ of Sheberghan or in the industrial development of Khoda Barq just west of Mazar.

*National Islamic Party*
http://www.junbsh.org

## Former President Burhanuddin Rabbani

Rabbani (b. 1942) is a former theology professor from Kabul and the former official political leader of Afghanistan (although his term has legally expired), but one must wonder what country he has been leading. A highly educated man from Faizabad, Rabbani made an attempt to build a bridge between opposing forces when he named Hekmatyar prime minister in 1993 and again in 1996. But there is little room for compromise in this fundamentalist country. He was backed mainly by the Tajiks in the north (3.5 million people, or about 25 percent of Afghanistan's population) and maintained his claim to power only with the former military wiliness of Massoud. His Jamaat-e-Islami party is the only non-Pathan party in Afghanistan. Apparently Rabbani's biggest skill is the ability to put an entire room of feuding warlords to sleep once he starts in on one of his monotonal, marathon speeches. He can usually be found in Faizabad in northern Afghanistan.

http://www.afghan.gov.af

## Pathans, Mujahideen, "Afghans," and the Camps

Afghanistan has always been a vast place ruled by tribal, factional, and local codes of conduct. The Pathans (who are the largest ethnic group) encourage a culture of independence, loyalty, and bellicose reaction to any infringement on their culture.

The wily Pathans (called Pakhtuns in their own language) are not a generic group of evil-looking, bearded men waiting perpetually in ambush along Afghanistan's mountain passes. The Pathans are a group of tribes that make up 40 percent of Afghanistan's populace and 13 percent of Pakistan's. They are primarily rural, clan-based, and aligned in major ethnic or geographic alliances. Their love of freedom, guns, and adventure are probably their most publicized traits, but they are also loyal, honest, and moral, and perhaps above all pragmatic.

In addition to the strong tribal links, years of war and over $3 billion in covert U.S. aid created three new warrior castes in Afghanistan. The first comprises the older generation of Afghans who spent their youth in nomadic columns killing Russians in the early '80s. The second group are the infamous "Afghans"—the Islamic jihadis that the CIA (through the Pakistani ISI or secret service) hired and trained to fight the Russians. They are called "Afghans" because they are not Afghani. They are also called "Arabs" even though they may not be Arab. . . . Stay with me, this stuff is complicated. These "Afghans," estimated to be around 20,000 in all, were primarily Algerians, Egyptians, Saudis, Yemenis, Uihgers, Filipinos, and Palestinians. Most of these men have returned to their home countries and are wreaking havoc everywhere from Basilan, Philippines (Abu Sayyaf) to Algiers, Algeria (GIA), to Manhattan, New York (World Trade Center bombing).

The third group is exclusively Pakistani. These legions of young men felt it was their duty to fight jihad in Afghanistan (against Massoud and the Northern Alliance and in Kashmir against the Indian army). United by religion and ethnicity (Pakistan has strong tribal links to the Pashtuns) they were increasingly used by the Taliban to shore up the front lines and provide firepower.

http://www.clandestineradio.com/intel/afghanistan.htm

## Osama bin Laden

Osama bin Laden, the youngest son of Muhammed bin Laden, was born in the city of Jeddah on March 10, 1957. He was raised in Medina, Munawwara, and Hijaz. He went to school in Jeddah before studying management and economics in King Abdul Aziz University. Although he describes himself as a construction engineer and an agriculturist, bin Laden is most famous for being America's biggest nightmare.

He fought against the Russians in Afghanistan between '79 and '89 and raised a number of volunteers from Arab countries. He also helped build tunnels, roads, and bunkers using heavy construction equipment that he donated. You can visit the huge tunnels he blasted into the Zazi Mountains of Bahktiar Province to use for guerrilla hospitals and arms dumps. He still likes to hang out in air-conditioned, cruise-missile-proof caves.

In 1994 bin Laden was kicked out of Saudi Arabia and hung out with Hassan al-Turabi, leader of the National Islamic Front in Sudan. He built the Port Sudan roads (paid for in sesame seeds), invested in agricultural projects, and built three training camps for mujahideen.

In May 1996 he was expelled from Sudan and hung out in southern Yemen, and some say, Afghanistan as well. He came to the world's attention in April 1996, February 1997, and February 1998 when he gave a round-robin of interviews to the world's press. He has been fingered as the culprit behind the October 12, 2000, attack on the USS *Cole* in Yemen, the first World Trade Center bombing, and the millennium plot to blow up Disneyland, the Space Needle, and LAX airport. He got the attention he wanted after the September 11, 2001, airliner attacks on the Pentagon and the final destruction of the World Trade Center. He is also linked to the November 13, 1995, Riyadh bombing and the June 25, 1998, bombing in Dhahran of the Al-Khobar towers, as well as a number of other events that range from trying to kill the Pope to blowing up 12 airliners from the Philippines to the assassination attempts in June 1995 on Egyptian President Hosni Mubarak in Sudan and in June 1993 on Jordan's Crown Prince Abdullah.

What drives Binny? Well, some say that he always wanted to one-up his older brother Salim, who was killed in a hang-glider accident in Texas in 1989. He is one of 53 children and the only son of one of his father's 10 wives. Technically, he is half Palestinian (on his mother's side) and half Yemeni (on his father's side). Osama was never really taken seriously by the mujahideen in the early days and was even ridiculed as a spoiled brat who expected respect in exchange for his dollars. Osama is no slouch in the toy department—he owns a Gulfstream G-8 business jet. His organization, called "the Base," or al-Qaeda, is unique in that there is no government behind it. Essentially, terrorism meets entrepreneurialism. In 1997, bin Laden's new Terrorists 'R' Us concept was blown apart when moneyman Sidi al-Madani al-Ghazi Mustafa al-Tayyib was busted and squealed. The CIA had been bragging that they have been tracking his satphone calls as well.

What Osama lacks in popularity in the West he makes up for in directness. In his May 26, 1998, ABC interview with John Miller, bin Laden simply said, "Leave Saudi Arabia or die. . . . Allah ordered us in this region to purify the Muslim land of all nonbelievers, and especially in the Arabian Peninsula. . . . We believe that the biggest thieves in the world and the terrorists are the Americans. . . . We do not differentiate between those dressed in military uniforms and civilians; they are all targets in this fatwa." The only thing that bin Laden might have overlooked is that he is not a mullah, since his degree was in economics and agriculture, not religion. It is a bad habit he shares with his close friend, Mullah Omar, who is also technically not a mullah.

A man with 40 brothers, 13 sisters, and wealthy patrons can probably play hide the pickle longer than the State Department can. For now, bin Laden is a right-wing billionaire (or millionaire, or even destitute recluse, or evil empire runner, depending on whom you talk to) who combines industrial activity with political activism. While Binny plays shy, Binny, Jr. is taking care of business. A tip to up-and-comers: Son Muhammed bin Laden (b. 1984) is expected to be the heir apparent. He is currently dead, alive, in hiding, not hiding, in Yemen, Pakistan, or Afghanistan depending, once again, on whom you talk to. *DP* figures he is in the tribal areas or in Yemen. In case you wonder what he thinks of Yanquis, his June and February 1998 pseudo fatwa cut to the chase: ". . . kill[ing] the Americans and their allies—civilians and military—is an individual duty for every Muslim who can do it in any country in which it is possible to do, in order to liberate the al-Aqsa Mosque and the holy mosque [Mecca] from their grip . . ." We like you too, Binny.

**Osama bin Laden**
c/o name withheld by request
Tribal Areas, NWFP
Pakistan
http://www.louisville.edu/library/ekstrom/govpubs/subjects/crime/binladen.html

## Pakistan

Anyone who looks at a map would assume there is a 1,400-mile border between Afghanistan and Pakistan. It even has an official name, "The Durand Line." In reality, anyone with a donkey or a pair of Reeboks can skip over the border and back with the help of friendly smugglers. Things are more difficult now that there are at least five Pakistani border guards napping at each post instead of the usual two. But the seven tribal areas and certain cities are actually a legacy of England's inability to fully conquer the region. Even though the Durand Line was created in the 1900s as an official demarcation between the two countries, it is not recognized by either the Afghanistan or the Pathan tribes whose homeland it divides. And since having a great swath of lawless land benefits all parties involved, it has remained that way. The Pakistani government under General Zia—killed in a plane crash on July 18, 1988—supported the Ghilzai tribe from eastern Afghanistan, where most of the U.S.-backed mujahideen leaders came from. The southern Durranis still support the Afghani royal family of former King Zahir Shah, who lives in splendid luxury in Rome (okay, he has a nice bungalow, which is luxurious by Afghan standards). There is also an intense desire for statehood among the 5.7 million people, or Pathans, who live in the region, for a "Pahktunistan" with a bent toward Afghanistan that might remove most of the NWFP and the tribal areas from the map of Pakistan and destabilize both regions. Although technically Pakistan does not control the region, it is more aligned toward its trade with Afghanistan. The Pak army and police usually intervene in tribal disputes and smuggling busts using the Frontier Crimes Regulations created in 1947. This law allows the Paks to arrest any tribal member without actually needing a reason. Not surprisingly, most disputes (including blood feuds) are solved with the countless weapons found in the region. For now, the official term for the seven tribal areas (Khyber, Kurram, Orakzai, Mohmand, Bajaur, North Waziristan, and South Waziristan) is the Federally Administered Tribal Areas (FATA) of Pakistan's Northwest Frontier Province (NWFP).

http://www.pak.gov.pk/public/govt/basic_facts.html

## The "Afghans"

Any visitor to the Afghan refugee camps can't help but notice thousands of men between 15 and 60 years of age just sitting around in the teahouses. They are out-of-work mujahideen, veterans of the war against the Soviet Union, various Afghan warlords, and the latest fighting between Talibs and Massoud. They are killers with hard, deeply lined faces. None have jobs. Ask anyone what they did in the war and you'll get enough hair-raising stories to write 20 action-movie scripts.

Virtually every male in Afghanistan old enough to lift a rifle fought against the Russians. But Afghanis weren't the only ones. The other "Afghans" included more than 3,000 Algerians, as well as 2,000 Egyptians. Hundreds, if not thousands, of others arrived from Yemen, Sudan, Pakistan, Syria, and other Muslim states.

In all, according to some estimates, 10,000 to 40,000 Arabs received training and combat experience in Afghanistan—of whom nearly half were Saudis (bin Laden was busy for those ten years). A big chunk of the financial backing for the Afghan warlords came, and continues to come from, the fundamentalist Wahhabi sect in Saudi Arabia. A large number of these recruits are Salafists, an austere-minded group that wants to return to the good old days, or rather good old century, of Mohammed.

## Getting In

The race is on. While airlines weigh the economic risk of joining the piles of destroyed Soviet-era aircraft that decorate Afghan airports, the world's backpackers search in vain for train timetables, and the sporadic Kabul bomb attacks still make headlines. The good news is that Afghanistan is open for business. The bad news is the NGOs and peace-keeping forces don't want you there. The Afghans are thrilled, of course, because tourism generates hard dollars . . . in their pockets, and naturally the ex-Talibs love to have more infidels to take potshots at. You can get visas to enter Afghanistan, although some might caution you about land mines, banditry, lack of services, etc. But now really is the time to go . . . as long as you are there to help.

There are flights to Kabul, offered by low-budget Indian and Gulf airlines that go in and out of business faster than a New York electronics store. The UN and Red Cross provide flights from Pakistan into major cities (but only for NGOs, accredited journos, and pals). The World Food program provides three flights a week into Kabul, Herat, Mazar, Faisabad, Termez (Uzbekistan), and Dushanbe (Tajikistan). The pecking order for seats goes: UN personnel, accredited NGOs, donor governments, and then media. Civvies or tourists are not usually allowed, but a convincing reason and a lot of money can get you aboard. The last time we checked, it cost $600 one-way and $1,000 return from Islamabad to Kabul. You fill out the form in advance and you wait for approval.

To learn more, you need to check with UNHAS, House No. 4, Street 51, F-8/3, Islamabad, Pakistan, tel.: (92) 51 226 2842.

The ICRC runs flights but doesn't usually like to take personnel unknown to them. You can always try. Best bet is by land.

### ICRC Delegation
Char Rahi Haji Yaqoob Street
Shar-E-Now
Kabul, Afghanistan

You can also fly on Ariana Afghan Airlines from Frankfurt, the Gulf, or India.

If you come through Pakistan via Peshawar you need to do the Khyber Pass shuffle. Important: Going to Afghanistan is different from just taking a spin out to Torkham and back: one is a tourist junket run by the Khyber agency on Stadium Road; the other requires going through the Home Office.

When you cross from Pakistan to Afghanistan, you have to get a permit from the Khyber Agency on Stadium Road and an Afridi gunman from Peshawar to cross the Khyber (100-rupee tip). Leave plenty of time for your permit. Don't forget you need to hire a car as well. Don't be coy and lie about going into Afghanistan or they will drive to the top of Mechni Hill, let you out to take a leak, and drive you straight back. In Quetta you can get to the border without a guard.

At the border you fill out your name on the Pakistani side and then check in again on the Afghan side. There are usually taxis that will take you to your next stop.

From Iran: There is an Afghan consulate in Mashad on Konsulgari Avenue, tel.: (051) 97551. You take a taxi to Islam Qala (entered from Taybad) and then on to Herat.

From the North: There are Afghan embassies in Turkmenistan's capital of Ashghabat and in Dushanbe, as well as in Tashkent. Entry is by road, and remember you need someone to pick you up on the other side or hope there are taxis.

From the China/Afghanistan border region: Immigration entry point to China from Afghanistan is in Taxkurgan (on the Karakoram Highway) coming from Pakistan. There is usually no Chinese post at the China/Afghanistan border. So, you can use your Pakistani visa to re-enter Pakistan.

Find a complete list of Afghan embassies at http://www.afghana.com/government/embassy.htm.

## *Afghanistan Embassies Worldwide*

### *Pakistan*

Embassy of Afghanistan
176 Shalimar 7/3
Islamabad, Pakistan

The Mall, Saddar Bazaar
Peshawar, Pakistan
Tel.: (91) 285962

Consulate of Afghanistan
Prince Road
Quetta, Pakistan
Tel.: 081 444708

### *Overseas*

Consulate of Afghanistan
P.O. Box 88
Canberra ACT 2601
Australia
Tel.: (61) 2 62868445
Fax: (61) 2 62868446
admin@afghanconsulate.net
http://www.afghanconsulate.net

Embassy of Afghanistan
31 Prince's Gate
London SW7 1QU, UK
Tel.: (44) 20 75898891/2
Fax: (44) 20 75813452

Representative Office of Afghanistan in
  Washington
1021 Arlington Boulevard, Suite 1120
Arlington, VA 22209
Tel.: (703) 469-3946, or (703) 362-9246
Fax: (703) 469-3859

Consulate General of Afghanistan
360 Lexington Avenue, 11th Floor
New York, NY 10017
Tel.: (212) 972-2276, or (212) 972-2277
Fax: (212) 972-9046
consulate@aol.com

Permanent Mission of Afghanistan to
  the United Nations
360 Lexington Avenue, 11th Floor
New York, NY 10017-1890
Tel.: (212) 972-1212, or (212) 972-1213
Fax: (212) 972-1216

Embassy of Afghanistan
Gogol Street 73
700047 Tashkent
Uzbekistan
Tel.: (998) 71 2354112
Fax: (998) 71 2342634

To find out which NGOs are inside Afghanistan, contact: ACBAR: the Agency Co-ordinating Body for Afghan Relief, 2 Rehman Baba Road, University Town, tel.: (91) 44392/40839; open 8:00 A.M. to 4:30 P.M. Monday through Thursday and 8:00 A.M. to 12:30 P.M. on Fridays. Or, get to know somebody at the U.S. embassy to get a pass to the American Club in Peshawar.

http://www.afghana.com/Government/Embassy.htm

## Getting Around

Most Afghanis get around by clinging onto aging Japanese and Russian buses like starving ticks on a hell-bound hound. If you want to travel by taxi, have a local cut the best deal for you. It can take most of the day to get anywhere; even a short distance on a map, like Peshawar to Kabul, is an all-day event. Expect to pay a buck for every 60 miles and one and a half times that for a shared taxi. A private taxi may hit you up for fuel and the five to six passengers he wasn't able to fit into the old Russian clunker.

> **M**ost Afghanis get around by clinging onto aging Japanese and Russian buses like starving ticks on a hell-bound hound.

One of *DP*'s rare hotel rec's is the infamous Intercontinental, not for any practical reason but only to see the battered 1960s time capsule before it gets spruced up.

*Inter-Continental Hotel*
Baghe Bala Road
Kabul, Afghanistan
Tel.: (91) 31851

The telephone number for the (very helpful if you want reasons to stay out of Afghanistan, but are under siege) U.S. Embassy in Islamabad, Pakistan, is (92) 51 826 161 or (92) 51 826 179. There is little they can do for you once you are in Afghanistan.

**U.S. Consulate in Peshawar, Pakistan**
Tel.: (92) 521 279 801; (92) 521 279 802; (92) 521 279 803

**U.S. Embassy in Tashkent, Uzbekistan**
Tel.: (7) 3712 771 407, or (7) 3712 771 081

**U.S. Embassy in Dushanbe, Tajikistan**
Tel.: (7) 3772 21 0356; (7) 3772 21 0360; (7) 3772 21 0457

**U.S. Embassy in New Delhi, India**
Tel.: (91) 11 600 651

## Dangerous Places

The whole damn place.

## Dangerous Things

### Guns

When it comes to gun love, the Afghanis have no equal. Afghanistan has more guns per capita than anywhere else on earth. (Some say Yemen and Somalia vie for this coveted award.) England allowed the Pathans to manufacture their own guns 200 years ago, and the CIA delivered enough weapons to keep the region swimming in weaponry for years to come. But this was all dwarfed by the stockpiles of weapons the Russians abandoned or lost in the ten years of warfare.

> **A**fghanistan has more guns per capita than anywhere else on earth.

http://www.ishipress.com/afghans.htm

### Land Mines

The Russians buried and dropped about 12 million mines in the ground. Some say that at the current removal rate it will take 20,000 years to remove all the mines. HALO figures that 640,000 mines have been laid since 1979. In 1998 they cleared 100,000 individual items of unexploded ordnance, or UXO. HALO has 1,300 Afghan de-miners working under the supervision of only two expats, clearing the towns and countryside. They are working feverishly to de-mine the 95 percent of the country under peace so that more than 3 million Afghans can return to their formerly mined villages. There are currently

300,000 Afghans waiting to rebuild or move back into their homes in Kabul.

Most de-miners will tell you privately that the UN estimate is a little over the top, but it makes them look good when they do it faster. There are more than 50 different kinds of mines, and they are not just Russian-made. There are RAP-2s from Zimbabwe, and even NR-127s made in Belgium. There are neat, battery-powered, multisensored mines that blow up when they feel vibration. According to the UN, 162 of Afghanistan's 356 districts are affected by mines. The most dangerous areas for mines are Helmand, with 5 major fields; Kandahar, with 47; Paktia, with 118; Logar, with 53; and Herat, with 86. The areas affected are grazing lands, irrigation systems, agricultural lands, and cities.

The UN estimates it needs $185 million to carry out all its programs, including de-mining. Afghanistan currently has the world's largest de-mining program and in seven years has destroyed over 200,000 devices, but has cleared only 80 square kilometers. The most heavily mined areas are security zones around the major cities along the Iranian and Pakistani borders (Herat, Kandahar, Jalalabad, and Khost). Follow the basic rules and you will survive: Do not wander off hard surfaces (even when taking a leak). Learn to squat at the edge of the road to urinate like the locals do. Do not travel in snow. Land mines were laid in strength along mountain passes and can be more sensitive with ice and snow cover. Do not turn over or pick up any items. Do not inspect abandoned military vehicles. Do not run up a hill to get a better vantage point . . . and the list goes on.

http://www.mineaction.org

## Getting Sick ————————————————————

Medical care is not Afghanistan's strong point. In a pinch, health care is available in the major cities through aid groups. Many prescription drugs and antibiotics (not opiates) can be bought over the counter, but there is no guarantee you aren't buying Indian and Chinese knock-offs. A traveler with more serious medical needs should seek help in Pakistan or Iran. Better yet, take the next flight home or to London. Malaria (primarily the benign vivax form) is present below 2,000 meters (6,562 feet) between May and November in the southern area, and the *falciparcium* strain occurs in the warmer south. Chloroquine-resistant *falciparcium* has been reported. Rabies, tick-borne relapsing fever, and cutaneous *leishmaniasis* are present.

# Nuts and Bolts

It is not that difficult to figure out Afghanistan. Afghans are skilled at solving any problem for a price. Reconstruction has brought a veneer of civilization that might make old *DP*'ers pine for the old days.

There is new currency (they knocked a zero off and there were actually two *afghanis* with different exchange rates in circulation), and GSM phone service in the major cities, and, yes, there are Internet cafés now. Curfews are being lifted, and by the time you read this it may be positively civilized in Afghanistan. Electricity is European-style (those smoke-blackened receptacles are where you timidly plug in your devices). Weather is hellaciously hot in the summer and numbingly cold in the winter. Farsi (Persian) is the most common language, along with Russian, Pashto, and Uzbek. English is popular in the big towns and there are hotels, restaurants, or guesthouses in most towns. Land mines are common, banditry is practiced with enthusiasm, and journos have permanently warped the Afghan sense of cost versus value. Outside the main cities, there are some very strict cultural taboos against entering homes uninvited, chatting with women, immodest dress, and religious conduct. There is still much suspicion in the south toward Westerners, so keep things up-front and simple.

# Dangerous Days

| | |
|---|---|
| **9/5/02** | Karzai escapes assassination attempt in Kandahar. |
| **11/09/01** | Dostum, Atta, and Mohaqiq enter Mazar-I-Sharif, signaling end of Taliban control of Afghanistan. |
| **10/07/01** | U.S. and British bombing campaign begins against Taliban military targets. |
| **9/11/01** | Aircraft are flown into World Trade Center and Pentagon, and crash in Pennsylvania, triggering the U.S. declaration of war against terrorism and the military attacks on the Talib leadership. |
| **9/09/01** | Ahmed Shah Massoud is killed by three men posing as journalists. |
| **11/9/99** | Mullah Omar offers Massoud a truce if they can join together to fight the Russians in Chechnya. |
| **12/15/98** | New training camps are operational in Khost, Jalalabad, and Kabul. |

| | |
|---|---|
| 8/20/98 | Seventy $1.5 million Tomahawk cruise missiles are dropped on Harakatul Mujahideen camps in Khost (94 miles south of Kabul, near the Pakistani border) in retaliation for the bombings of U.S. embassies in Kenya and Tanzania in August, which killed more than 230. Salvaged cruise missiles are traded to Chinese generals for a mountain of small arms. |
| 8/20/98 | Bill Clinton tells of air strikes against Sudan and Afghanistan while on vacation in Martha's Vineyard. |
| 10/30/97 | Emma Bonino and Christiane Amanpour are beaten and detained by the Taliban for photographing women in a hospital. |
| 9/97 | Over 120 journalists enter Kabul to cover the Taliban's occupation. |
| 9/27/97 | The Taliban enter Kabul. |
| 9/12/97 | Dostum returns to Mazar-I-Sharif after heavy fighting and looting. |
| 5/28/97 | Taliban forces retreat from Mazar-i-Sharif after losing 100 men in 18 hours of fighting. This marks the first retreat in the Taliban's history. |
| 5/24/97 | General Malik Pahlawan turns against warlord Rashid Dostum, opening the city to the Taliban. The Uzbeks and Tajiks revolt when the Taliban try to disarm them. |
| 9/27/96 | The Taliban drive Massoud, Rabbani, and Hekmatyar out of Kabul exactly one year after their founding. |
| 6/19/96 | Pakhtun leader Hekmatyar signs a peace pact with former enemy Rabbani, becoming prime minister in Kabul. |
| 9/11/96 | Hekmatyar's Hezb-e-Islami arms depot is captured in Paktia. |
| 4/3/96 | Mullah Omar is proclaimed Amir-ur-Momineen. |
| 9/5/95 | The Taliban capture Herat and begin imposition of strict Sharia. |
| 9/19/94 | The Taliban emerge from the southern province of Kandahar. |
| 1/19/94 | Hekmatyar lays siege to Massoud and Rabbani in Kabul, turning the city into rubble. |
| 4/15/89 | Najibullah leaves. Rebels begin battle of Kabul as factions war for control. |
| 2/15/1989 | The last Soviet soldier leaves Afghanistan. |
| 1988 | Gorbachev announces Soviet withdrawal from Afghanistan. |

| **1986** | Soviets install Najibullah as the 100,000 Soviet soldiers fight against seven U.S.-backed rebel factions. |
| --- | --- |
| **12/79** | Moscow turfs the socialist government and installs Babrak Karmal. Soviet troops enter Afghanistan to prop up Karmal. |
| **1978** | Socialists under Hafizullah Amin stage a coup in Kabul. Moscow begins to send aid. |
| **1973** | King Zahir Shah is overthrown. |

# IN A DANGEROUS PLACE: AFGHANISTAN

## THE REGULATORS

The Regulators flew in from Uzbekistan at night on a blacked-out Chinook helicopter and landed near a mud-walled compound in a remote valley in northern Afghanistan. As they began unloading their gear, they were met by Afghans in turbans, their faces wrapped. "It was like that scene in *Close Encounters* where the aliens meet humans for the first time," one soldier says later. "Or maybe that scene in *Star Wars:* These sand people started jabbering in a language we had never heard." The Americans shouldered their hundred-pound rucksacks while the Afghans hefted the rest of the equipment. The gear seemed to float from the landing site under a procession of brown blankets and turbans.

The next morning, about 60 Afghan cavalry came thundering into the compound. Ten minutes later, another 40 riders galloped up. General Abdul Rashid Dostum had arrived.

"Our mission was simple," another soldier says. "Support Dostum. They told us, 'If Dostum wants to go to Kabul, you are going with him. If he wants to take over the whole country, do it. If he goes off the deep end and starts whacking people, advise higher up and maybe pull out.' This was the most incredibly open mission we have ever done."

Before heading in-country, the soldiers had been briefed only vaguely about Dostum. They'd heard rumors that he was 80 years old, and that he didn't have use of his right arm. And they'd been told that he was the most powerful anti-Taliban leader in northern Afghanistan.

"I thought the guy was this ruthless warlord," one soldier says. "I assumed he was fricking mean, hard. You know: You better not show any weakness. Then he rides up on horseback with one pant leg untucked, looking like Bluto."

Dostum dismounted and shook everyone's hand, then sat on a mound covered with carpets. He talked for half an hour. Dostum's strategy was now their strategy: to ride roughshod over Taliban positions up the

Dar-I-Suf Valley, roll over the Tingi Pass in the Alborz Range, then sweep north across the plains and liberate Mazar-I-Sharif, Afghanistan's second-largest city. When the council broke up, Dostum stood and motioned toward the horses. America's finest were about to fight their first war on horseback in more than a hundred years.

The rocket howls over the roof of General Dostum's house in Khoda Barq at about 10 PM. It's November 26, my second day in Afghanistan, and already I'm in the middle of a hellacious firefight. Although nighttime gunfire is normal in Afghanistan, there is an urgency to the sound of the deep explosions that come from the 19th-century fortress of Qali-I-Jangi, just over a mile east of Khoda Barq, a Soviet-era apartment complex west of Mazar. The heavy shooting, the worried soldiers, the rapid radio chatter—all signal that something ugly is going on over there.

Meanwhile, I'm hunkered down, waiting for Dostum. I've arranged through intermediaries to spend a month with the general, but for the past week, he has been a hundred miles east, trying to subdue the Taliban forces that control the city of Kunduz. General Abdul Rashid Dostum is a man who has rarely been interviewed, but has often been typecast as a brutal warlord—usually because of his reputation for winning. He is a man who is said by some journalists to define violence and treachery. (In *Taliban*, author Ahmed Rashid reports a tale he heard that Dostum once ordered his men to drag a thief behind a tank until all that was left was a bloody pulp.) Beyond that, all I know is that Dostum, born a poor peasant, grew up to be a brilliant commander, a general, and a warlord—one of the many regional leaders across Afghanistan whose power derives both from ethnic loyalties and from military strength. He is known to be a deft alliance maker—and breaker. He became the first Afghan commander to take over a major city when he entered Mazar-I-Sharif on November 10. It's an irresistible story, made all the more so by a convincing rumor I've been hearing since my arrival: that Dostum triumphed with a little help from his friends—specifically, the Green Berets.

As I wait for Dostum to return, though, the constant chatter of machine guns and the badoom, badoom of cannons from an American gunship bombarding the fort—Dostum's military headquarters—suggest that I might be a bit premature in offering any congratulations on winning the war. I soon learn that yesterday some 400 foreign Taliban prisoners overpowered their guards, broke into arsenals, and took over part of the fortress.

At 3:30 AM, I go to bed. Three hours later, I am awakened by a massive explosion a few yards from the house—another near miss by a rocket fired from inside the fort. The sound of bombing continues without a break, but at a slower pace. Villagers come out in the crisp, golden light of morning, shivering and tired. Some huddle together to watch the gray pillars of smoke rise from the bombing runs. Others begin the work of the day without even paying attention to the nearby fighting.

In the afternoon, when I visit Qali-I-Jangi, bullets sing over my head. Up on the parapets, Dostum's troops stream toward a gap in the ramparts created yesterday by what I've heard was an errant American bomb. Soldiers run up to the bite in the wall, shoot into the fort, and then scurry back down. I watch a fighter go up to the top, then crumple into a black pile of rags. Astoundingly, after two days of bombardment, the prisoners still control the fort.

Late in the afternoon, a convoy of mud-spattered off-road vehicles pulls up, and a dozen dusty Americans in tan camo climb out. They have Beretta pistols strapped to their thighs like gunslingers and short M-4 rifles slung across their chests. They're polite, but wary about having their pictures taken as they set up their night-vision scopes. After a final check of their gear, they head into the fortress. Later, I find out that they've come hoping to retrieve the body of Central Intelligence Agency officer Johnny Michael Spann, who was killed by Taliban prisoners—the first American combat casualty in Afghanistan.

Dostum arrives that night, ducking to avoid banging his head as he strides through the guesthouse door. He takes my hand in a meaty grip and apologizes for being dirty and tired; he has just driven eight hours on a shattered road from Kunduz. He has two weeks of beard, beetling eyebrows, and a graying brush cut. When Dostum frowns, his features gather into a dark, Stalin-like scowl—his usual expression for formal portraits. But when he smiles, he looks like a naughty 12-year-old.

He sits and makes small talk, then excuses himself to take a shower. When he returns, the dark weariness has lifted. Over Chai (tea), he announces good news. He has ended the bloody battle for Kunduz by negotiating with Mullah Faizal and Mullah Nuri, the two most senior Taliban leaders in the north. It seems that the "brutal warlord" has engineered the biggest peaceful surrender in recent Afghan history— more than 5,000 Afghan Taliban fighters and foreign volunteers laid down their arms. He waves the accomplishment aside with a shy smile even as he promises to introduce me to his new trophies—the mullahs. It turns out they're staying next door, guests in Dostum's house.

Dostum proves to be significantly more expansive in conversation than his scant press clippings would suggest, and he's happy to fill me in on his background. (Over the next few weeks, as these conversations work to humanize the warlord, I privately coin for him a nickname:

Heavy D, after the 1980s rapper.) He was born Abdul Rashid in 1954 in the desolate village of Khvajeh Do Kuh, about 90 miles west of Mazar. The most significant tidbit I glean about his childhood is that he was adept at the game of buzkashi, in which teams of horsemen attempt to toss the headless carcass of a calf into a circle. Dating at least to the days of Genghis Khan, this violent game is not so much about scoring as it is about using every dirty trick possible—beating, whipping, kicking—to prevent the opposing team from scoring. Buzkashi is the way Afghan boys learn to ride—and it's the way Afghan politics is played: The toughest, meanest, and most brutal player takes the prize.

After the seventh grade, Dostum left school to help his father on the family farm. At 16, he started working as a laborer in the government-owned gas refinery in nearby Sheberghan, where he dabbled in union politics. When a Marxist government came to power in a bloody coup in 1978, the new regime's radical reforms ignited a guerrilla war with the mujahideen who based themselves in the country's remote mountain ranges. Dostum enlisted in the Afghan military—one of the few ways for poor men to escape lives of labor and hardship in rural Afghanistan.

The people of Dostum's village were so impressed with his leadership that they recruited 600 men for him to command. It was at about this time that Abdul Rashid became "Dostum." In Uzbek, *dost* means "friend"; *dostum* means "my friend." It was a nickname that the young soldier was given for his habitual way of addressing people. When a local singer wrote a song about "Dostum," the name stuck.

In the bewildering matrix of Afghan politics, Dostum has frequently—and nimbly—switched allegiances. In the 1980s, as a young army officer in the Soviet-backed government, he fought against the mujahideen. When the regime fell in 1992, three years after the Soviets departed, Dostum fought alongside the mujahideen and helped the Northern Alliance's legendary Ahmad Shah Massoud battle the fundamentalist Pashtun forces of Gulbuddin Hekmatyar to gain control of the capital. The shelling, raping, pillaging, looting, and house-to-house fighting that then befell Kabul stained the name of every mujahideen commander, including Dostum's, and fueled his reputation for brutality. I show Dostum the chapter in Rashid's book that includes the account of the gruesome execution of the thief. Dostum chuckles and denies the allegation. He freely admits that in two decades of war, abuses have been committed by every commander's troops. "What else do you expect my enemies to say?" he asks. "That I am kind and gentle? I will let what you see be the truth."

In 1996, when the Taliban rolled into Kabul, Dostum was forced to retreat to his stronghold in Mazar as the mullahs instituted their version of a pure Islamic state. "At first I thought, Why not let them rule?" he says. "Power is not given to anyone forever. If the Taliban can rule successfully, let them." A year later, betrayed by his second in command, who had defected to the Taliban, Dostum fled to Turkey.

Those among Dostum's men who had remained in Afghanistan now became guerrilla fighters, holed up in the mountains, attacking the troops of the latest regime. Dostum's lieutenants would call him in Turkey and tell him how difficult life had become. They had to kill their horses for food. They didn't have enough cloth for shrouds, so they had to bury dead comrades in burqas. "People demanded that I do something," says Dostum. "Commanders, clergymen, women—they would all tell me very bitter stories. I was full of emotions. My friends were struggling against the Taliban, and I was sitting there."

Dostum says that to help him get back into the fray, the former president of Afghanistan, Burhanuddin Rabbani, raised about $40,000. The Turks, long staunch enemies of Islamic extremism, contributed a small sum as well, and, on April 22, 2001, General Dostum and 30 men were ferried into northern Afghanistan on Massoud's aging Soviet helicopters. "That," says Dostum, "was when the war against terror began."

Living in caves and raiding Taliban positions, Dostum's men slowly began to harass the well-entrenched Taliban along the Dar-I-Suf. They moved and attacked mostly at night, riding small, wiry Afghan horses well-suited to steep slopes and long desert walks. "The money was hardly enough for feeding my horses," Dostum says. "They had tanks, air force, and artillery. We fought with nothing but hope."

Then came September 11. Using a United Nations envoy as an intermediary, Dostum suggested that the United States might want to give him some help.

The morning after Heavy D's return from Kunduz, he greets me with a deep, booming, "Howareyou?" Today, he tells me, he is eager for me to meet his trophy mullahs.

Next door, in Dostum's pink house, Mullah Faizal and Mullah Nuri sit on pillows in a small room. These are two of the Taliban who chased Dostum out of Mazar in May 1997, but still he treats them more like honored guests than prisoners of war. Faizal has his prosthetic leg off. He is a thick man with a pug nose, bad skin, tiny teeth, and a cruel stare. Nuri has the black look of a Pashtun who has endured a lifetime of war. Wrapped in blankets, members of the mullahs' entourage fix me with soulless stares. Nuri is chatty, although he often looks to the silent Faizal before answering my questions. During the Taliban's reign, thousands of Hazara Shia's were murdered in northern Afghanistan; the mullahs are unrepentant. "We fought for an idea," says Nuri. "We did all that we could. Now we hope that America will not be cruel to the Afghan people."

That afternoon, Dostum and I set off for the fort, where the uprising has been all but quelled. He brings the mullahs along to show them the havoc incited by their foreign volunteers. Perhaps they'll convince any surviving prisoners to surrender.

After four days of bombardment, the interior of the fort is a scene of utter devastation. Blackened, twisted vehicles are perforated with thousands of jagged holes. The crumpled bodies of prisoners, frozen in agony, are scattered everywhere. Most of the fallen look as if they were killed instantly. Some are in pieces; others have been flattened by tank treads. More than 400 prisoners are said to have died; I count only about 50 bodies in the courtyard. The estimated 30 Alliance soldiers who died have already been taken away by their friends. When an American team finally recovered Spann's body, they discovered it had been booby-trapped with a live grenade (which they removed without incident).

It is also rumored that there are many dead and at least two live prisoners holed up in the subterranean bomb shelter. The entrance to the bunker was pierced by cannon shots and is blackened from explosions. Dostum's men have been throwing down grenades and pouring in gasoline and lighting it, but the foreign Taliban refuse to come up. Dostum implores the mullahs to call down to the bunker and tell the remaining men to surrender. Mullah Faizal and Mullah Nuri refuse: They claim they don't know these people.

The trapped Taliban volunteers, it seems, remain hungry for martyrdom. A day later—Thursday, five days since the uprising broke out—they are still firing sporadically at soldiers removing bodies from the courtyard of the fortress. At least two Red Cross workers who descend into the bunker are shot and wounded.

Later that week, Dostum casually mentions that 3,000 other foreign fighters from the surrender at Kunduz are in a Soviet-era prison in the city of Sheberghan, 80 miles west. Anticipating more fireworks, I head there with him and move into another of his residences, a huge, high-walled compound that includes a mosque and, improbably, an unfinished health-club complex.

Some American soldiers are billeted upstairs in the guesthouses; men in camo pants run up and down the stairs. Their rooms are filled with green Army cots, dirty brown packs, and green flight bags. Rifles, night-vision gear, and boots are strewn everywhere. I head downstairs and discover a group of soldiers bantering cheerfully, mostly in southern accents. They've just finished installing a satellite TV. When the television begins to blare, the men stare at the screen. "We haven't seen a TV or news in two months," one soldier says apologetically. Transfixed, they watch the Christmas tree being lit in Rockefeller Center.

These are the soldiers I saw back at Qala-I-Jangi preparing to go in and retrieve the body of the dead CIA agent, Mike Spann. "Don't I know you?" one of them says. "Aren't you the guy who goes to all those dangerous places?"

It feels more than a bit odd to be recognized for my books and TV show—as someone who specializes in traveling to the world's hot spots—while poking around a war in Afghanistan. It feels even odder when I discover that these are Green Berets—soldiers who truly specialize in the world's hot spots. But I never travel without a few "Mr. DP" hats, so I dig them out of my bag and pass them around.

Over the ensuing days, I take every opportunity to spend time in these makeshift barracks, particularly once I discover that this is the very unit of Green Berets I'd been hearing rumors about. This is Dostum's covert support team. At night we sit around talking over stainless-steel cups of coffee. Some details of their mission they can't discuss. Some are provided by Dostum and others. But the story gradually emerges.

There are 12 Green Berets and two Air Force forward air controllers here. Green Berets work in secrecy, so only their first names can be used: There's Andy, the slow-talking weapons expert who is never without his grenade launcher; back home, he keeps the guns in his collections loaded "so they are ready when I am." Both he and Paul, a quiet, bespectacled warrant officer, have been in the unit 11 years. Then there's Steve, a well-mannered southern medic; Pete, the burly chaw spitter; Mark, their blond, midwestern captain; and so on. It's like a casting call for *The Dirty Dozen*. Their motto is "To Free the Oppressed"—something they have done so far in this war with no civilian casualties, no blow-back, and no regrets.

These soldiers, I soon realize, come from much the same background as Dostum's: sons of miners, farmers, and factory workers; men whose only way out of poverty is the military. They range in age from mid-20s to late 30s. They are men with wives, children, mortgages, and bills, men who are the Army's elite, who are college educated and fluent in several languages, yet who are paid little more than a manager at McDonald's. They spend every day training for war, teaching other armies about war, and waiting for the call to fight in the next war.

They are direct military descendants of the Devil's Brigade, a joint Canadian-American unit that fought in Italy during World War II. That group was disbanded and then re-formed in the early 1950s as Special Forces, which John F. Kennedy later nicknamed the Green Berets. The men I'm staying with have dubbed their unit the Regulators, after the 19th-century cowboys who were hired by cattle barons to guard their herds from rustlers. The Regulators have served in the Gulf War, Somalia, Saudi Arabia, the United Arab Emirates, and in other places they can't talk about. Their home base is Fort Campbell, Kentucky, where they spend only a few months of the year. The rest of the time they travel.

On the morning of September 11, the team was returning to base after an all-night training exercise. "The post was in an uproar," says Paul. No one knew just when or where the team would be sent. They cleaned and stowed their gear and waited for the order. And waited. There was talk that the team might be split up; there were rumors of differences with a commanding officer who didn't appreciate the traditional independence of the Green Berets. But toward the end of September, the word came down: "Pack your shit."

Fifteen days later, the team boarded a C-5 Galaxy with a secret flight plan. The Regulators' final destination turned out to be Uzbekistan, where they spent a week building a tent city and waiting for a mission. "We were at the right place at the right time," says Steve. "Fifty tents later, they told us to pack our shit again."

"We had two days to plan," another Regulator says. "The CIA gave us a briefing." Although the Regulators were among the first, other small teams of U.S. forces would soon be airlifted in for similar missions, in response to Dostum's request for American assistance to be sent to other Northern Alliance commanders. Atta Mohammed, for example, would get his own Green Beret escort several weeks later as he raced Dostum to claim Mazar. Once they hit the ground, the Regulators would write their own game plan. "Our commanders said they didn't know what to expect, but at least they were honest enough to admit it," the Green Beret continues. "They said, 'You guys will be on the ground; you figure it out.'"

Within half an hour of meeting Dostum at the mud-walled compound in the Dar-I-Suf, the Regulators swung into action. Some stayed behind to handle logistics and supplies. The rest mounted up and rode north. "It was pretty painful," Paul says. "They use simple wooden saddles covered with a piece of carpet, and short stirrups that put our knees up by our heads. The first words I wanted to learn in Dari were, 'How do you make him stop?'"

Their most important immediate order of business was to establish themselves in Dostum's eyes. "The first thing we wanted to do was to say to Dostum, 'The Americans are here,'" Paul explains, "and to make it a fearsome prospect to mess with us." The Americans set up their gear at Dostum's command post—which overlooked Taliban positions about six miles away—and immediately began the process of calling in close air support, or CAS. "You see the village; you see the bunkers," says a second Steve, one of the two Air Force men attached to the team to help coordinate air strikes. "You call in an airplane; you say, 'Can you see that place? There are tanks. You see this grid? Drop a bomb on that grid.' Pretty straightforward stuff."

It took a few hours for bombers to arrive from their carriers. At first, the planes wouldn't fly below 15,000 feet—the brass was worried about surface-to-air missiles—so targeting was sketchy. But coordination soon improved, and the improbable allies fell into a rhythm: The Americans would bomb; Dostum's men would attack.

A crude videotape made by one of Dostum's men shows a battle in the rolling hills of the Darra-I-Suf,. where the yellow grass contrasts with the deep blue sky. The Americans, up on the ridge, are using GPS units to finalize coordinates. Down below, the small Afghan horses are nipping the dry grass on the safe side of the hill, their riders chatting while waiting for the order to charge. The horses cast long shadows in the late afternoon. The only sign that something is about to happen is a white contrail high in the sky. The radio crackles with call signs and traffic broadcast between bombardiers and the American soldiers. First, a soft gray cloud of smoke rises in a lazy ring. Then the concussion: ka-RUMPH!

The tape now shows Dostum, leaning against a mud wall, watching through large binoculars. The dirty gray mushroom cloud slowly bends in the wind. Dostum stays in contact with the Americans by radio, working to help focus the bombing: a man with a seventh-grade education directing the fire of the world's most powerful military.

Ka-RUMPH! More hits: Tall, fat smoke plumes cast moving shadows on the grass. The riders mount their horses, check their weapons, and begin the one-kilometer sprint to the Taliban front lines. There's the erratic chatter of AK-47s and the deep dut dut-dut-dut of Taliban machine guns. Then the radios are jammed with Dostum's men shouting and celebrating. The Taliban are running.

The videotape cuts to the next morning. Dostum's men are touring the battle scene. The twisted rag-doll bodies of dead Taliban fighters lie heads back, fingers clutched, legs sprawled as if they fell running. Dostum's men kick the corpses into the trenches and cover them with the tan dirt, not bothering to count the dead.

The Regulators were joined by at least three CIA officers kitted in full combat gear, including a 32-year-old ex-Marine named Mike Spann. "We were surprised at how good they were," says Captain Mark. "What we are doing now has not occurred since Vietnam. Up until now the CIA has been hog-tied. Now the CIA and spec ops have been let loose."

Each night, Dostum would sit down with the Americans and lay out the battle plan for the next day. "He would say he is going to attack at about 2 PM," says Air Force Steve. "So we would put in for priority for the planes." The team's primary weapons were not pistols or rifles; they were the most fearsome tools in the American arsenal: F-18s, F-16s, F-14s, and B-52s. They chose not bullets or grenades, but ordnance that ranged from Maverick missiles to laser-guided bombs.

In contrast to the Americans' high-tech warfare, some of Dostum's tactics would have seemed familiar to the British troops who tried and failed to pacify this region in the 19th century. Before the arrival of the Americans, Dostum fought mostly at night. "He couldn't expose his small force to Taliban missile strikes," explains Captain Mark, "so they would hit and retreat. He never sacrificed his men. He would take a village by getting the mounted guys up close. When it looked like they would break the back of the position, he would ride through as fast as he could and keep the Taliban on the run."

With their knowledge of military history, the Regulators appreciated the ironies of this strange war: "The Taliban had gone from the 'muj' style of fighting—in the mountains, on horseback—to working in mechanized columns," says Will, another Green Beret. That heavy reliance on tanks and trucks meant the Taliban wound up fighting a defensive, Russian-style war. "Then, here is Dostum," says Will, "a guy trained in tanks who's using tactics developed in Genghis Khan's time."

The Regulators' job was to invent a new form of warfare: coordinating lightly armed horseback unit attacks with massive applications of American air power—all without hitting civilians or friendly forces. "In an air attack," says Air Force Steve, "you do one of two things. You can bomb until there is no resistance, or you bomb and, as soon as the bomb goes off, you charge. By the time they come up and look, you are on them." The latter approach was well suited to Dostum's style of attack. "A cavalry charge is an amazing thing," Will says. "At a full gallop, it's a smooth ride. The Afghans shoot from horseback, but there is no aiming in this country. It's more like, 'I am coming to get you—whether I hit you is another story.'" It's Old World combat at its finest.

"There's one time I'll never forget," he says. "The Taliban had dug-in, trench-line bunkers shooting machine guns, heavy machine guns, and RPGs [rocket-propelled grenades]. We had an entire 250-man cavalry ready to charge." The Regulators wanted Dostum's right-hand man, Commander Lahl Mohammed, to hold off while they got their aircraft in position, but Lahl had already given the order. In seconds, 250 men on horseback were thundering toward the Taliban position a mere 1,500 meters away.

"We only had the time it takes 250 horses to travel 1,500 meters, so I told the pilot to step on it," Will says. "I looked at Lahl and said, 'Bombs away.' We had 30 seconds until impact; meanwhile, the Afghan horde is screaming down this ridgeline. It was right at dark. You could see machine-gun fire from both positions. You could see horses falling." An outcrop obscured views of the last 250 meters to the target. The lead horsemen disappeared behind the rocks, and the Regulators held their breath, praying the bombs would reach the bunkers before the cavalry did. "Three or four bombs hit right in the middle of the enemy position," says Will. "Almost immediately after the bombs exploded, the horses swept across the objective—the enemy was so shell-shocked. I could see the horses blasting out the other side. It was the finest sight I ever saw. The men were thrilled; they were so happy. It wasn't done perfectly, but it will never be forgotten."

Around eight o'clock on Saturday night, while I'm talking with the Green Berets, one of Dostum's men comes into the house and asks us to follow him outside. Beyond the high steel gates is a confusion of trucks, headlights, and guns, and the sound of men moaning in pain. Lined up against a wall is the most pathetic display of humanity I have ever seen: the survivors of the bunker at Qali-I-Jangi fortress. Dostum's men had finally flooded them out by sluicing frigid water into the subterranean room. Instead of the expected handful of holdouts, no fewer than 86 foreign Taliban emerged after a week in the agonizing dark and cold—starved, deaf, hypothermic, wounded, and exhausted. Their captors brought them here en route to the Sheberghan prison.

They send off steam in the cold night, their brown skin white with dust. Some hide their faces, others convulse and shiver. I talk to an Iraqi, as well as to Pakistanis and Saudis—all of whom speak English. On another truck are the seriously wounded. Some cry out in pain, some are weeping, and others lie still, their faces frozen in deathly grimaces.

They put the prisoners back on the truck. A few minutes later, one of Dostum's men runs up breathlessly, saying there is an American in the hospital. I grab my cameras and ask Bill, a pensive Green Beret medic, to come with me.

The scene at the hospital is ugly. The warm smell of gangrene and human waste hits me as I open the door to the triage room. Shattered, bearded men lie everywhere on stretchers, covered by thin blue sheets. The doctors huddle around a steel-drum stove, smiling and talking, oblivious to the pain and suffering around them. In the back, a doctor leans over a man with a smoke-blackened face, wild black hair, and an unkempt beard. He lies staring at the ceiling. The doctor yells in halting English, "What your name?" He jabs at the half-conscious man's face. "Open your eyes! What your name? Where you from?" The man finally answers. "John," he says. "Washington, DC."

The man is terribly thin and severely hypothermic. At first he is hostile, like a kitten baring its claws. He won't tell me who to contact, or provide any information that would get him out of the crudely equipped hospital. I convince the staff to move him to an upstairs bed, where Bill inserts an IV of Hespan into the man's dehydrated body to increase blood circulation. As Bill checks for wounds, he talks to the young man briefly in Arabic. I tell the prisoner where he is and who he's talking to. Bill finds a shrapnel wound in the emaciated man's right upper thigh and wounds from grenade shrapnel in his back; he also finds that part of the second toe on his left foot has been shot away.

As the Hespan drips into his veins, I fire up the videocamera, and the man begins to tell his story. His name, he says, is John Walker. He studied Arabic in Yemen and then enrolled in a madrassah, or religious school, in northern Pakistan. He says it was an area sympathetic to the Taliban and that his heart went out to them.

Six months ago, he traveled to Kabul with some Pakistanis to join the Taliban. Since he can't speak Urdu, he was assigned to the Arab-speaking branch of Ansar ("the helpers"), a faction that Walker claims is sponsored by Osama bin Laden—whom Walker says he saw many times in the training camps and on the front lines.

He ended up in the Takhar Province, in the northeastern part of the country. Then the war began. After the American bombing campaign decimated their forces, Walker and members of his unit fled on foot nearly a hundred miles west to Kunduz—all for nothing, as it turned out. Mullah Faizal and Mullah Nuri soon surrendered Kunduz to Dostum, and Walker was imprisoned with the other foreign volunteers in the bunker at Qali-I-Jangi.

When I look at the terrible conditions and the predicament that Walker is in, I have to ask him if this is what he expected.

"Definitely."

Was his goal to become martyred?

"It is the goal of every Muslim."

Then the morphine begins to kick in. I suggest to Bill that we remove Walker from the hospital, where he might be killed by other patients, many of whom were fighting against him at the fortress. We transfer him to Dostum's house, and the next day he's spirited away at the same time that his story is being broadcast around the world.

When the videotape of my interview with Walker hits the airwaves back in the United States, the country focuses its white-hot anger on him, and some of that anger spills over onto me. On the right, in the conservative press, I am criticized for being too gentle in my questioning of an obvious traitor, and on the left for cold-bloodedly tricking a helpless boy into incriminating himself.

• • •

If you drive west from Mazar, past Qali-I-Jangi, past Khoda Barq, past the ancient, crumbling city of Balkh, and head south toward a ridge of snow-dusted mountains called the Alborz Range, you will see a gap—the Tingi Pass. This is where the Taliban made their last stand. The Green Berets call it the Gap of Doom.

Two of the Green Berets I've been chatting with—Andy and Paul, the pair with the longest tenure in the company—have decided that I need to see this place for myself, or maybe simply that they need to go see it again one last time. We jump in a Toyota off-road vehicle and set off. Soon we're winding past an ancient brick bridge that crosses a roaring gorge; on the west side are large caves that shepherds have scooped out of the soft rock over the centuries.

As we drive, Paul tells me that back in the United States even the Regulators are subject to a military culture of rules and red tape. Planning a one-day live-ammo training exercise can require six months of paperwork. "If there is no enemy, then bureaucracy is the enemy," he says. But on the ground in Afghanistan, they're on their own. The greatest restrictions they face have been placed on them by Dostum himself. "Dostum was very concerned about us getting too close to the battlefield," Captain Mark told me back at the barracks. "In the last two semi-wars we have been in, every time American soldiers get killed we pull out. That is one of the premises Osama bin Laden operates under." Dostum wasn't about to let an American casualty put a premature end to his battle plan.

Their closest call came toward the end of the campaign, before they'd reached the Tingi Pass; I'd received an account of it last night from Mike, a big, bearded, soft-spoken soldier. The conflict began when several hundred Taliban troops moved into positions on an adjacent hill. Outmanned, the Green Berets decided to move out on horseback. They had gone only about 600 meters when they started taking fire. "I figured I could whip my horse and run across an open area," Mike said. "I whip my horse, it takes three steps, and stops. The rounds are zinging over my head. Somehow I make it across the open area. I get off the horse and say, 'Screw this; I'm walking.'

"We set up in a bomb crater and used it as our bunker. We were receiving more fire. It was somewhere between harassing and accurate— enough to keep our heads down. We called in a couple of bomb strikes. We could see a bunch of Taliban come out of another bunker complex off to the south and disappear behind a hill. It took about an hour to get the aircraft. All the while, we could see troops moving and disappearing. I'm looking through the optics while rounds are zinging all around us." At this point in the tale, Mike nodded toward Paul, who was sitting next to him on the couch at Dostum's guesthouse. "Paul here is busy shooting at guys. What we didn't realize was that the Taliban we saw coming out of the bunker had gone into the low ground and were sprinting up the hills at us in a flanking maneuver.

"Our Afghans are running out of ammo. Their subcommander has told us at least six times over the radio to get out of there. You have to understand: Dostum had told them, 'If an American gets hurt . . . you die.' We were focused on calling in an air strike to take out this truck that had rumbled into view, and now RPG rounds are flying over our heads. We're not about to stand up and watch what's going on. The pilot asked us, 'What's the effect [of the bomb attack on the truck]?' We yell over the radio, 'We don't know! We're not lifting our heads up!'

"When we turn around and notice what's going on, we see our Afghans have split."

The team decided to call in a B-52 strike practically on their own position—a drastic move considering the planes were flying above 15,000 feet. The enemy was 700 meters out and moving quickly. "Matt yelled, 'Duck your head and get down!' And that pilot dropped a shit-load of bombs," Mike said. "You felt the air leave. After the bombs hit, I peeked over the side of the bunker; our horses were gone. We grabbed our stuff and ran."

Paul, Andy, and I drive past villages of round, domed huts, past a checkpoint manned by Dostum's men, and up along the winding road to the Tingi Pass. Three years of drought have broken: A cold rain pours down in gray sheets. We pass the twisted, stripped wrecks of trucks and Toyotas. Afghans in a blue truck are scavenging for parts. The two Green Berets are solemn; they insist on driving through the gap so they can tell their story from the right perspective.

We wind through the tight pass alongside a swollen mountain river, go over the pass, then head one kilometer down the south side of the divide and stop at a freshly mudded house. We get out of the jeep and stand in the rain and slick mud. Paul picks up the story, raindrops dotting his gold-rimmed, government-issue glasses.

"We kept moving north on horseback, but at that point, no one could tell where the front line was anymore. Once we hit Keshendeh-ye Bala, we picked up a road and followed it north in a truck Dostum's men had captured from the Taliban. At eight that night, we pulled in to Shulgareh, which is the biggest town in the valley. We were ready to throw down the mattress and settle in for the night when one of the security guards came up with a radio and said that Dostum needed someone to go up to the front to call in aircraft. We jumped in the back of a truck and drove up to Dostum's HQ here, in this house."

In the courtyard, a soft-eyed cow tries to eat spilled oats just beyond its reach. A hundred yards away, villagers stand against a long compound. They huddle in brown blankets, trying to avoid the soaking rain. Paul points to a misty, triangular peak that forms one side of the gap. It served as Paul's command post.

"When we climbed up to the top of that hill, we could see the Taliban on the other side, regrouping for the final attempt to stop us. They were setting up fixed positions—bunkers with Y-shaped fighting trenches—on the northern side of the gap. It works against tanks, but it's plain stupid in this terrain. We had unrestricted movement into the gap, which gave us the high ground."

Andy chimes in. "Whoever gets the high ground first wins the wars here." From their perch on the east side of the gorge, the Green Berets could shoot directly into the trenches of the Taliban.

"Once the plane got there, it circled about six times," Paul says. "Every time the plane would circle, the Taliban would run behind their bunker. After four times or so, they didn't get bombed, so they just stayed there.

"I targeted a spot right next to this guy's head. I was sick of this guy running back and forth, getting ammo. Then the bombs are dropped, and I look through the scope and see body parts flying everywhere. We moved our targeting up along the ridgeline to the second bunker. Same thing: We identity it and boom! No more Taliban. I target the third bunker. They just can't figure it out. The bomb lands, hits and BAM! After that hit, all of them took off on foot to Mazar. And that ended the resistance." As the three of us climb back into our vehicle, I glance at the battlefield. All I see is grass growing beside abandoned trenches. Only Paul and Andy are able to appreciate what happened here.

Early in the afternoon on November 10, Dostum reached Mazar. His men rounded up vehicles that the Taliban had left behind, and Heavy D entered the city as a conquering hero, standing through the sunroof of a Toyota Land Cruiser. The crowds quickly grew; people threw money in the air for good luck. Dostum's first stop was the blue mosque at the tomb of Hazrat Ali, the revered son-in-law of the Prophet. Men wept as the imam prayed and thanked Dostum for deliverance.

The joy was short-lived. It turned out that 900 Pakistani Taliban had been left behind in a madrassah in the center of a compound about the size of a city block, and they were ready to fight to the death. Dostum and his commanders wanted to negotiate, but the foreign Taliban shot and killed their peace envoys, which left Alliance leaders with little choice. "We had hardened fighters holed up in the middle of an urban area who wanted to die," says Will. "And we were going to oblige them."

The team set up on the roof of a building about 400 meters from the madrassah and called in a strike. When the two aircraft were on location, the Green Berets radioed Alliance commanders to evacuate civilians from the area. The pilots, however, could not lock in on the laser-sighting device that the team was using to identify the target. The madrassah was surrounded for about a mile on each side by identical buildings, which made it difficult for the pilots to pick out the school. "Finally, the pilot says he has the target in sight. I asked him to describe it, just to be sure," says Will. "He described the building we were sitting on to a T." Finally, Air Force Steve guided the pilot to the correct building, and he dropped the ordnance: direct hit.

The team cleared him for immediate re-attack, but the pilot radioed back that he had "hung a bomb"—a bomb had not released. When the pilot radioed that he needed to return to base, the other pilot swung into action. On the next pass, three more bombs went through the hole in the roof made by the first bomb, killing most of the holdouts inside.

Under intense pressure, the Regulators had called in a perfect surgical strike—a bomb drop into a crowded urban area without a single civilian casualty. "This is the first close-air-support strike in years in an urban area," says Air Force Steve. "It was old-fashioned professionalism. The whole team jelled."

The steel gate to the guest house opens, Dostum strolls out, hands in pockets, and is ushered into a black Audi Quattro with tinted windows. Dozens of dark-eyed men in turbans scramble into battered Toyota pickup trucks and assorted four-wheel-drive vehicles. Armored personnel carriers jerk to life in clouds of black diesel exhaust. It's three weeks after the madrassah bombing, and word has come down that 3,000 Taliban are still occupying the city and environs of Balkh, Alexander the Great's old walled capital, a few miles west of Mazar. Dostum has decided to clean up the region's last remaining pocket of Taliban himself.

I ride in the warlord's communications truck, a white Land Cruiser. The Regulators rush to catch up in two mud-covered cars. We roll past weathered villages unchanged in two millennia. Abandoned Soviet-era tanks are scattered about the flat countryside like dinosaur skeletons.

This part of Afghanistan is ancient, arid, windblown—and is the real cradle of its history and wealth. This is where Alexander ruled, where Zoroaster was born, where Buddhists came on pilgrimages, a center of art, poetry, and study where lions were hunted and where Genghis Khan came to conquer. Now, in a scene that has been repeated over and over for the past 2,000 years, a warlord is arriving.

In a village on the outskirts of Balkh, the convoy rumbles to a halt near an ancient castle that is now a rounded mound of tan mud. The truck-mounted ZU antiaircraft guns are cranked down to eye level. Twenty Urgan missiles point toward the village. Dostum's men load RPGs and check their ammo drums. About 200 men have taken up positions around the village, eyeing ragged locals, who stare back from a careful distance. It feels like a scene out of a bad Mexican movie.

After a cinematic pause to allow the implications of his arrival to sink in, Dostum phones the village leadership from the Audi: Send out your weapons and any fighters or we're going in. The deadline is noon.

The general climbs out of the tiny black car and tucks his hands into his belt. He rolls in a John Wayne walk to Commander Lahl, who's in charge of the standoff. The two Afghan leaders study a map with Captain Mark, just in case air strikes are needed. When noon comes and goes, I expect the order to fire. I am surprised, then, to see Dostum wrap his blue turban around his head and chin and stride into the village . . . to talk.

Ironically, it was this sort of diplomatic triumph—the surrender at Kunduz just before my arrival—and not a battle that gave the Regulators their most bitter experience of the war. "We thought Kunduz was [going to be] a full-scale attack," says Captain Mark. "When we got there, we were sitting on our asses." It was while they watched the drawn-out surrender that Mike Spann was attacked at Qal-I-Jangi and the uprising began. "This was a guy who we considered part of our unit," says Mark. "If we had been there, Mike's death would not have happened."

When they got word of the incident, the unit desperately wanted to get back to the prison. "The info I had was that he was MIA," Mark says. "We thought he was wounded. The old creed is that we never leave a guy behind." The Regulators wanted to find the prisoners who had killed Spann and attacked a second CIA man who was questioning the Taliban. "We begged," Mark says, "but we were told to stay away." (In the end, the Regulators wouldn't get clearance to enter Qal-I-Jangi until the uprising was over.)

Commander Abdul Karim Fakir, who was in charge of the fortress while Dostum was in Kunduz, had worked with the Green Berets since they landed in Afghanistan. "I saw this look in Fakir's eyes," says Mark, "like, Why didn't you help?"

Dostum has not been home in five years to the village of Khvajeh Do Kuh. His father is old. Two weeks after Dostum descended on Balkh, things have calmed down, so the warlord climbs into the front passenger seat of a Nissan, and we head across a sandstorm-blasted desert. This time there is no convoy; just a son paying his respects to his father. As we drive through a drought-ravaged wasteland, he points out battlefields and the sites of ambushes and skirmishes. Dostum tells me that he has fought on every inch of Afghan soil and can recite the names of his men who have died, describe each battle in detail, and tell you what he has learned from every encounter. He says it sadly.

A few yards before the turnoff to Khvajeh Do Kuh, he gestures to a place where 180 of his men died fighting the Taliban. All I see are brown dirt and men on donkeys leading camels along the road. Nothing of the war, death, exile, and victory that have shaped the man sitting in the front seat. There is an emotional landscape here I cannot see.

As we approach the village, the men and boys are lined up in a perfect row a hundred yards long, waiting to greet Dostum. The general gets out of the car and goes down the line, trying to embrace and talk to each person, but it is getting dark. The crowd of men follows Dostum into his father's compound.

In a tiny, sparse room are his father, Dostum's former teacher, and a village elder. The old men are frail, with deeply lined faces. The teacher giggles, his white beard shaking with joy. Dostum's father talks to his son as though he were a child, telling him that he and the teacher have been praying for his success. They reach out to shake his hand, to embrace him. The men in the room try to act formally, but as Dostum starts to leave, some begin to cry. An old man yells, "God bless you. We are alive thanks to you." As Dostum stands on the porch, looking at the place of his birth, he chokes up.

He takes me to the hilltop above the village. It's a high, lonely place. When war first came to Afghanistan two decades ago, he built his first stronghold here to guard the village. Dostum points to the fresh dirt of new graves in the cemetery. "The men who first defended this post with me are all dead now. The new graves belong to those who were fighting terrorists." He is silhouetted against the slate-blue sky, the long tails of his silver turban whipping in the wind.

For a brief moment, the general stands triumphant, the conquering hero, the bringer of peace, the warlord who has ended war in the north—and, therefore, perhaps eliminated his own reason for being. As he leans into the Afghan wind, the light falls, and a moment in history fades.

Dostum must now change his focus from fighting to rebuilding his country. (Within a week, he will be named deputy minister of defense for the new interim government of Afghanistan.) Now, on most mornings, Dostum emerges from his house, squinting into a crowd of turbaned men waiting for an audience. They sit patiently for hours, clutching tiny pieces of paper, seeking his aid. Dostum's meetings do not end until well after midnight.

Not long before I'm to leave, Dostum asks for help with a letter of condolence to the widow of Mike Spann. The task inspires him to try to express his feelings about the past two months. He confesses that he had worried at first how the Americans would handle Afghan warfare: "It was cold; the food was bad. The bread we ate was half-mixed with dirt. I wondered if they could adapt to these circumstances. I have been to America and know the quality of life they enjoy. To my surprise, these men felt at home."

And more than that: The Afghan warlord and his tiny band of American soldiers had clearly formed a bond that only men who have been through combat can understand. "I now have a friend named Mark," Dostum says, referring to the Green Beret captain. "I feel he is my brother. He is so sincere; whenever I see him, I feel joy." He pauses for a moment, lost in reflection. "I asked for a few Americans," he says finally. "They brought with them the courage of a whole army."

Down the road at the Regulators' makeshift barracks, a call comes over the Motorola: "Pack your shit." The men quickly gather their gear, as they have so many times before. Within hours, they are gone.

*—RYP*

# ALGERIA

Algiers

## Cutthroat Politics

For almost all of its history, Algeria has been a dreadful waste of Mediterranean coastline. Visitors attempting to enjoy the beaches and cafés have had to snatch their sun and espressos in between the pillaging of Romans, Vandals, Hafsids, Merenids, Spaniards, Turks, French, and pirates of all denominations (this was the home base of Barbarossa, aka Redbeard, and the Barbary pirates). More recently, Algerians have been manufacturing their own problems—indeed, if their actual manufacturing sector was half so industrious, Algerians would be rich enough to fly to work in gold-plated helicopters.

In the last 10 years, more than 120,000 Algerians have died in an Islamist insurgency. This decade has been characterized by brutality, shocking even by the grim standards of African civil wars: Entire villages have been massacred using truck-mounted guillotines. There is also firm suspicion that the body count in these massacres is higher because of right-wing, government-sponsored killers who play tit-for-tat. If

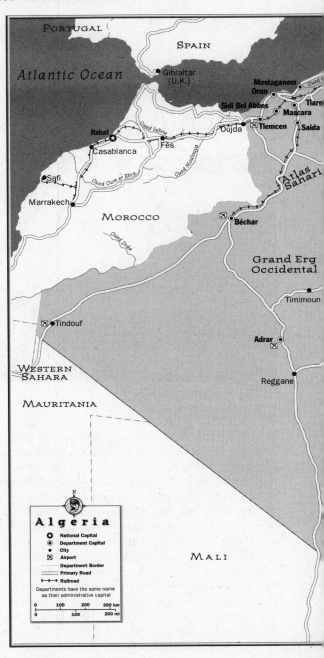

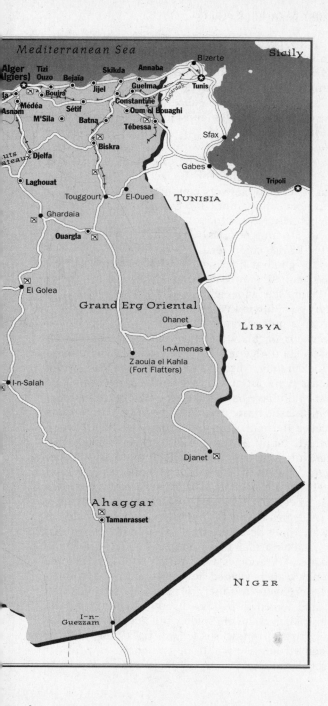

Mediterranean Sea

Sicily

Alger
(Algiers)
Tizi
Ouzo
Bejaïa
Jijel
Skikda
Annaba
Bizerte
Guelma
Tunis
la
Bouira
Constantine
Midridah
Médéa
Asnam
Sétif
Oum el Bouaghi
M'Sila
Batna
Tébessa
Sfax
Biskra
uts
ateaux
Djelfa
Gabes
Laghouat
Tripoli
Touggourt
El-Oued
TUNISIA
Ghardaia
Ouargla
El Golea
Grand Erg Oriental
Ohanet
LIBYA
I-n-Amenas
Zaouia el Kahla
(Fort Flatters)
I-n-Salah
Djanet
Ahaggar
Tamanrasset
NIGER
I-n-
Guezzam

you're wondering why this gets less play on CNN than the comparatively minor fracas in Israel, there are two reasons. One is that dead Muslims just aren't headline news (while the West refused to help Sarajevo during its three-year siege in the '90s, locals joked that the new Bosnian national anthem should be called "Too Many Muslims, Not Enough Oil"). The other reason is that most journalists are terrified of going anywhere near the place.

You'd have thought that the Algerians would have gotten tired of war long before now. Between 1954 and 1962, Algeria was what you could call France's Vietnam, were it not for the fact that Vietnam was also France's Vietnam. The snail-chewers conquered Algeria back in 1830 and managed to hold onto it until 1954, when the natives got caught up in the independence craze that was big in Africa in the '50s and '60s. Say what you will about the British colonizers, they were usually pretty good at figuring out when they weren't wanted. France, by contrast, fought Algeria for Algeria for eight years. By the time they gave up and went home, taking more than a million French settlers (known as *pieds noirs,* or "black feet") with them, 20,000 French troops and more than 350,000 Algerians had been killed. Two hundred of those—Algerians, incidentally—died in Paris in October 1961, when French police attacked a demonstration. One could weep when one thinks of the lives that could have been spared if only France had surrendered with the enthusiastic haste they displayed every time some pointy-hatted bloke called Herman came lumbering over the Rhine.

> **A**lgeria was what you could call France's Vietnam, were it not for the fact that Vietnam was also France's Vietnam.

The manner in which many of these Algerians were killed still causes France to fidget with embarrassment, and rightly so. In 2001, an 83-year-old retired general, Paul Aussaresses, was stripped of his rank and put on trial after writing a book called *Special Services, Algeria 1955–57,* in which he cheerfully admitted torturing and summarily executing prisoners. (Aussaresses and his publishers were convicted of being apologists for war crimes and were fined, though the ex-general was unrepentant: "If I had bin Laden in my hands," he said, "I'd do the same again.") Subsequent interviews with other Algerian veterans conducted by French newspapers yielded similarly unedifying reminiscences: Algerian prisoners were routinely sexually abused, tortured with electric shocks, and forced to fight each other to death for the amusement of French soldiers. One old soldier still dogged by accusations of participating in similar outrages is tedious right-wing buffoon Jean-Marie le Pen, then a volunteer paratroop lieutenant, now leader of the quasi-fascist French National Front.

Algeria's modern, self-inflicted misery began in 1989, when Algeria apparently became infected by the democracy bug that was sweeping Eastern Europe at the time. Algeria had been a one-party state since gaining its independence in 1962, and that one party was the socialist National Liberation Front. One-party socialist states have a poor record of making their people happy for very long, and Algeria was no exception. In 1986 and 1988, there had been serious civil unrest as Algerians got sick of the combination of being broke, unemployed, and living in a country perched on immense lakes of oil. Whether Algeria's leaders were concerned about going the way of Ceausescu, or whether they just felt like being nice guys for a change, they lifted the ban on new political parties. One of 20 groups that took up the offer was the Islamic Salvation Front (FIS).

The FIS were—and, indeed, are—Islamic hard-liners who wanted to turn Algeria into a theocratic Sharia state (they stated, significantly, that any election they won would be Algeria's last). At their first electoral outing, at local elections in 1990, the FIS won 55 percent of the vote. With national parliamentary elections due the following year, the rightly alarmed Algerian government started moving the goalposts. They changed the electoral system to the disadvantage of the FIS, banning campaigning in mosques. They also locked up two prominent FIS leaders, Abassi Madani and Ali Belhadj.

These actions, however, didn't help. In December 1991, the FIS won 188 National Assembly seats, and it seemed certain they would attain the majority they needed to form Algeria's first—and, if they had their way, last—elected government. Sadly for the FIS, Algeria's military, who hadn't been keen on this democracy lark from the off, were not about to submit to the commands of a bunch of rural hairies in silly robes. In January 1992, the army (always the power behind Algeria's throne), suggested to President Chadli that he take a very long holiday. He was replaced with a five-member higher state council, chaired by Mohamed Boudiaf. This new junta called off the election, dissolved 411 FIS-controlled local authorities, and ordered the FIS to disband.

> **S**adly for the FIS, Algeria's military, who hadn't been keen on this democracy lark from the off, were not about to submit to the commands of a bunch of rural hairies in silly robes.

And the FIS did . . . sort of. Tragically for all concerned, the more seriously demented elements of the FIS rebranded themselves as the self-explanatory Armed Islamic Group (GIA). Their first big spectacular was the assassination of Mohamed Boudiaf, which was pulled off by a GIA sympathizer among his own bodyguards. Since then, they've killed thousands. There's not a lot of rhyme or reason to GIA's slaughters. Most of the killing takes place just outside Algiers, and in Algeria's Mitidja Plain. This fertile, and now dirt-cheap, farmland stretches southward from the outskirts of Algiers, and is called the Triangle of Death—an apt name for what may well be the most deadly real estate since Cambodia's Killing Fields. GIA attacks happen at night: the electricity is cut, and convoys of armed masked men arrive and begin killing, house to house. They leave when they get tired.

Algeria's current president, Abdelaziz Bouteflika, has tried a variety of tacks to persuade the Islamic gangs to give it a rest and has had some success. The armed wing of the Islamic Salvation Front is no longer a concern, having responded favorably to a conditional amnesty. Plus, the Algerian military has killed a lot of militants, although they're less happy to discuss the arbitrary imprisonments, dubious arrests, torture of suspects, and plain old "disappearances" that have also been part of the crackdown. But the mayhem continues. And as if that wasn't enough, since April 2001, Algeria's Berber minority (who normally stayed out of violent politics) have gotten uppity, staging several protests and riots.

**Algeria Press Service (French only)**
http://www.aps.dz

**Djazair Online**
http://www.djazaironline.net

**Algeria Interface**
http://www.algeria-interface.com

## The Scoop

Despite the messy divorce, Algeria's 133-year marriage to France has left it more Arabic than French. However, there are much greater risks for the visitor than getting a gobbet of phlegm in your soup. You're safe enough on safari across the Saharan regions of the south (where the sand begins, the security threat ends), but the rest of Algeria can be one of the most dangerous places on earth. Death comes at random if you're a local, and by special delivery if you're a foreigner. You might be safer jogging around downtown Mogadishu wearing 10 gold Rolexes and a stars-and-stripes cape.

> **D**espite the messy divorce, Algeria's 133-year marriage to France has left it more Arabic than French. However, there are much greater risks for the visitor than getting a gobbet of phlegm in your soup.

**Ministry for Tourism and Arts (French only)**
http://www.mta.gov.dz

**Permanent Mission of Algeria to the UN**
http://www.algeria-un.org

# The Players

## Abdelaziz Bouteflika

The man nominally in charge of this blood-soaked sandpit is President Abdelaziz Bouteflika, 65 years old. He is a veteran of Algeria's independence struggle, having served time with both the National Liberation Front and the National Liberation Army. He was the independent Algeria's first-ever Minister for Youth, at the appropriate age of 25, and his curriculum vitae also includes a 14-year stretch as Minister for Foreign Affairs between 1965 and 1979. For all of this period he was the most prominent ally of President Houari Boumediene, the army colonel who overthrew Algeria's first civilian president, Ahmed Ben Bella.

Bouteflika fled Algeria in 1980, after ending up on the wrong side of a power struggle to succeed President Boumediene, who died in 1978. Bouteflika returned to Algeria in 1987, and was elected to the Central Committee of the National Liberation Front, which at the time was Algeria's sole political party. His election to the presidency in April 1999 was a curious business. Though the elections had been loudly billed as democratic, Bouteflika's six opponents withdrew from the race en masse two days before the poll, protesting the refusal of the outgoing President, Liamine Zeroual, to discuss accusations of electoral fraud. The fact that Zeroual refused to let foreign monitors have a peek at the electoral process propped up the crybabies' claims. (It wouldn't have been the first time that Zeroual had put his elbow on the electoral scales—his cancellation of Algeria's 1991 elections set the Islamic Salvation Front off on its campaign of chainsaw manicures in the Algerian countryside.)

Bouteflika's big idea for bringing peace to Algeria is something called the Civil Concord Law. This involved freeing 2,300 jailed militants after their parties offered to call off the armed struggle and offering amnesty, of sorts, to militants who were willing to hand in their guns by a deadline in January 2001. Those who had not directly taken part in massacres, bombings, or rapes were offered freedom on probation; the others were assured that they would not be executed (the maximum sentence was set at 20 years). According to the government, the offer was reasonably successful. Perhaps 80 of Algeria's armed Islamic radicals promised that they'd play nicely from now on. Most remarkably, the Islamic Salvation Army (AIS), the Islamic Salvation Front's military wing, not only accepted the conditions and disbanded but said their now ex-members would be willing to join in the hunt for members of the GIA and the Salafist Group for Preaching and Combat (GSPC), who refused to sign up, calling the AIS "enemies of Islam." So there.

*Presidency of the Republic of Algeria (Arabic and French only)*
http://www.elmouradia.dz

*Ministry of Foreign Affairs*
http://www.mae.dz

## The Algerian Army

The Algerian military has always been, if not Algeria's actual rulers, the people who decide who Algeria's actual rulers are going to be. Not for nothing are Algeria's generals popularly known as Le Pouvoir ("The Power") or Les Decideurs ("The Deciders"). The decideurs-in-chief include top Bouteflika aide General Larbi Belkheir, Chief of Army General Mohamed Lamari, intelligence services director General Toufik Mediene, counter-espionage boss General Smain Laribi, and former Minister of Defense General Khaled

> **N**ot for nothing are Algeria's generals popularly known as Le Pouvoir ("The Power") or Les Decideurs ("The Deciders").

Nezzar. This group promotes themselves as the doughty green line that stands between their people and Islamic terror. The truth may fall somewhat short of the advertising.

In recent years, at least two books have claimed that the military are actively involved in the massacres generally blamed on Islamic militants. The theory here is that the military are deliberately wreaking the carnage in order to justify their continuing control of the country. The first book, *The Dirty War*, by former Algerian special forces officer Habib Souaida, claims that the death toll in Algeria's civil war is more than twice the generally accepted 100,000, and contains eyewitness accounts of mass murders, tortures, and executions by Algerian soldiers. The second text, *Who Killed Bentalha?*, by massacre survivor Nesroulah Yous, accuses the army of slaughtering hundreds of inhabitants of the village named in the book's title. Since the publication of their books, both Souaida and Yous have claimed asylum in France, but Algeria does not seem inclined to let them go lightly. Souaida has been sentenced, in absentia, to 20 years' imprisonment by an Algerian court, and a libel action has been brought against him in Paris by notorious Decideur General Nezzar—himself once the defendant in a torture case in a French court. Yous has received many threats to his life.

In the cities, the army works in groups of 5 to 10 men in plain clothes, while 35,000 troops watch over an "infernal arc" in the Mitidja between Algeria, Blida, Laarba, and Medea. Out in the countryside, small groups of soldiers travel in helicopters and armored personnel vehicles to track down fundamentalists. The annual U.S. Report on

Human Rights noted there was "convincing evidence" of systematic torture and executions of suspected GIA and FIS insurgents. The army also sponsors proxy militias. There are at least 5,000 local so-called "self-defense" or "patriotic" groups in place across the country—these right-wing groups are known more informally as "eradicators." The GIA now almost invariably skips villages where these groups are well organized and well-armed.

Whether the Algerian army are part of the problem, or part of the solution—or, as seems increasingly likely, both—they will continue to rule the roost.

## The Cops

Police and security forces in Algeria consist of three organizations: (1) the national police (DGSN); (2) an agency of the ministry of the interior, Gendarmerie (MOD); and (3) the communal guards, similar to village police with limited training and equipment. There is, however, an ongoing problem with the Islamic terrorist groups infiltrating the ranks of all three. In addition, the terrorists have obtained hundreds of police uniforms and badges and have masqueraded as police to carry out terrorist and criminal operations. Some of these operations have included assassinations of officials by terrorists operating fake police checkpoints. Throughout the war, terrorists have targeted officials, journalists, foreigners, and randomly selected Algerian citizens. But the cops and security forces have borne a large proportion of the targeting and, as such, suffered numerous casualties. The large number of deaths within the police forces, coupled with the uncertainty about fellow officers' loyalties, have resulted in low morale in the police ranks.

## Islamic Salvation Front (FIS)

The FIS are the organization whose surprising success in the 1991 elections prompted the military crackdown, which prompted the Islamic uprising which has prompted massacre, terror, and torture on an epic scale throughout Algeria. FIS is pretty much a busted flush these days: Their military wing, the Islamic Salvation Army, has all but disbanded in response to an offer of partial amnesty from the Algerian government. As a political party, the FIS are as banned as every other political party in Algeria, and even if they weren't, a repeat of their 1991 electoral success would be unlikely. Moderate Islam is in serious decline as a political force in Algeria as elsewhere, and the wild-eyed young men who might once have been attracted to the FIS are instead signing on with the likes of the GIA and GSPC.

The government's policy of attacking and jailing FIS leaders has had the same effect Hercules had on the Hydra. Instead of one unified Islamic group, they now have dozens of smaller groups, each with a different agenda and approach.

**Islamic Salvation Front**
ccfis@yahoo.com
http://www.ccfis.org/english/default.asp

## Armed Islamic Group (GIA)

The GIA is a profoundly unpleasant gaggle of Koran-waving thugs responsible for most of Algeria's mass murders. Locally known as "The Afghans," the GIA can call on several thousand fighters organized into tiny, unrelated, and sometimes warring cells. At the GIA's core are some of the most heartless and cruel men on earth: Algerian veterans of Afghanistan's war against the Soviets. They are hard, brutal, religious zealots, who have racked up a body count clearing six figures in little more than a decade.

The GIA began in 1992 as a radical splinter group of the FIS, founded by Abdul Haq al-Eyadah in the Jijil and Bejiya regions south of Algiers. They want to overthrow the Algerian government—but hey, doesn't everybody?—and replace it with the sort of rigid Islamic theocracy that was such a splendid success in Afghanistan. The GIA's precise structure and leadership is a mystery. One of its more prominent figures, Antar Zouabri, was killed by Algerian security forces in February 2002, and the latest chief, Rachid Abou Tourab, was killed in a raid on July 30, 2002, in Blida, so now it's anyone's guess. It is also known that the GIA contains several hostile factions, whose loathing for each other is frequently murderous, as another GIA founder, Djamel Zitouni, discovered in 1996. The list of dead former GIA grandees is a long one—though not, unfortunately, nearly as long as the list of Algerian civilians murdered in GIA rampages.

The GIA have made occasional forays outside Algeria, hijacking an Air France jet in 1994 and setting off a series of bombs in France in the early '90s. However, quite how these forays were supposed to further the rule of Allah in Algeria was beyond most observers. Mostly, the GIA seems content enough with killing and maiming on their home turf. The big question about the GIA is to what extent, and at what level, they are creatures of the government (trying to pick a way through the claim and counterclaim is made even more difficult by the fact that GIA guerrillas on raids sometimes dress up as Algerian police and soldiers). And, of course, there are those who have claimed that some massacres are conducted by Algerian police and soldiers dressed up as GIA guerrillas.

## Salafist Group for Preaching and Combat (GSPC)

GSPC is a disturbing new offshoot from the GIA. It was founded in September 1998 by a former GIA leader called Hassan Hattab. Hattab was apparently unhappy with the GIA's slaughters of civilians and thought they should be concentrating on slaughtering police and soldiers instead. The GSPC have since pursued this tack with enthusiasm and some success, staging dozens of raids on Algerian security installations and killing hundreds in the process. Their theoretical disdain for attacks on civilians has made them popular in some regions of Algeria, but they have whacked the odd noncombatant.

Hattab's 1,500 fighters are active in the mountains of the Kabylia area about 70 miles east of Algiers and in the west. Though the Algerian authorities are often accused of working in cahoots with the GIA, they're not at all keen on the GSPC. In the wake of 9/11, the Algerian government made loud noises to the effect that the GSPC had been created by Osama bin Laden—as if hoping that America's B-52s might drop by on their way back from Afghanistan.

## Berbers

The green-eyed, fair-skinned Berbers are said to be a mix of European and Arab blood. They make up about 20 percent of Algeria's population, and they're not happy campers. They boycotted Algeria's elections in May 2002, and the region of Algeria they call home, Kabylia, and its major city, Tizi Ouzou, have been convulsed by serious rioting in the last few years. In April 2001, a series of punch-ups between Berbers and Algerian security forces left more than 50 dead.

The Berbers' modern history of discontent dates back to April 1980, when Berber demands for greater rights led to a minirebellion now remembered as "The Black Spring." Their gripes these days are a mixture of political disputes with Algiers and civil rights issues. The April 2001 uproar was sparked by the death in police custody of a young Berber man called Massinissa Guermah. Despite repeated government promises of an inquiry, no prosecutions have been brought.

More recently, the Berbers have been infuriated by a series of government edicts that suggest that Algeria's rulers have been reading from Slobodan Milosevic's "Winning Friends among Your Country's Minorities." In 1998, a law was passed making Arabic Algeria's only official language and imposing fines on anyone caught speaking or writing French, or the Berber language, Tamazight.

This law was overturned by President Bouteflika in 2002, and Tamazight was recognized as a national language, but not an official one. He also compromised on another Berber demand and removed some (but not all) of Algeria's paramilitary gendarmes from the region.

This might not be enough to keep a lid on Kabylia, which continues to simmer. There was more rioting following the boycotted parliamentary elections in 2002, and the region remains under a state of siege.

The principal icon of the Berber unrest is the late singer Lounes Matoub, who was murdered at a roadblock in 1998. The question of who was responsible for Matoub's death remains moot. Matoub's songs had criticized both Algeria's government and Algeria's Islamist weird-beards, so he was killed by either the GIA, by government troops, by government troops dressed as the GIA, by government troops working with the GIA, or by GIA gunmen dressed up as government troops. Whatever; Matoub is no less dead, and the Berbers are no less angry.

**Rally for Culture and Democracy (French only)**
http://rcd-algerie.org

**Berber Associations Worldwide (French only)**
http://www.berbere.com/toutelesassociations.html

# Getting In ————————————————————

Visas are required by citizens of all non-Arab countries, and are a bit of a chore to get hold of. Besides filling in the forms, which you can download from the embassy Web sites, you need a letter from your employer, presumably so that the Algerian authorities may reassure themselves that you're not a freeloading scrounger trying to flee the West to live off the largesse of the Algerian welfare state. You also need something called a *certificate d'heberegement*, which is an invitation to visit Algeria from a travel agent in Algeria. Two travel agencies that might be able to help are Agence Essendilene (touareg@wanadoo.fr) and Agence Tarahist (tarahist.bahedi@caramail.com).

Getting a visa is a little more difficult if you're a journalist, but it will usually come through. After your details have been checked out in Algiers, get an application form from the press office of your local embassy. Upon arrival, you will be provided with an armed security detail. If you decide you'd rather take your chances without it, you'll have to fill in a form absolving the Algerian government of any responsibility should they end up having to post you home in a box (or, as is likely, several boxes). *DP*'s advice is to strike up a relationship with the person in the embassy to understand the best way in for you.

Most visitors will arrive by air at Algiers, but some overland crossings are possible, from Niger, Tunisia, and Libya. The area around the border with Mali is dangerous, and the border with Morocco is closed.

(Algeria supports the Polisario movement in Moroccan-occupied western Sahara, so it's been a while since the last exchange of Christmas cards between Rabat and Algiers.) If you're going to try bringing in alcohol or binoculars, make sure they're damn well hidden.

**Embassy of the Democratic and Popular Republic of Algeria**
2137 Wyoming Avenue, NW
Washington, DC 20008
Tel.: (202) 265-2800
Fax: (202) 667-2174
embalg.us@verizon.net
http://www.algeria-us.org

**Algerian Consulate**
6 Hyde Park Gate
London SW7 5EW, UK
Tel.: (44) 20 7589 6885
Fax: (44) 20 7589 7725
algerianconsulate@yahoo.co.uk
http://www.consalglond.u-net.com

**Embassy of the Democratic and Popular Republic of Algeria**
500 Wilbrod Street
Ottawa, Ontario K1N 6N2
Canada
Tel.: (613) 789-8505
Fax: (613) 789-1406
ambalgcan@rogers.com
http://www.ambalgott.com

## Getting Around

Tourists may be restricted in their movements and either monitored or escorted by the military. Theoretically, tourists are permitted in Algiers, the highway leading to Oran, as well as Oran itself, and other towns along the coast, including Tlemcen. The border area northeast of Nefta on the Tunisian border may also be accessible. Restricted areas include a huge swath of real estate in the Grand Erg Occidental with El Golea as the nucleus.

If a journalist wants to visit an area of the country other than Algiers, travel is restricted to air, via the domestic carrier, Inter-Air Services. Foreign oil workers in the south bypass the north altogether, flying directly into their installations and living in highly secured compounds.

## Dangerous Places

*Everywhere*

Algeria's violence is as random as it is indiscriminate. It is worst in the north and the west, but this shouldn't lead you to believe that the south and the east are going to be a walk in the park.

www.interpol.int/statistics/ICS/downloadlist.asp

## Algiers

Some time ago, a study conducted by an international business body called the Corporate Resources Group rated Algiers the worst city in the world. On a planet that includes Mogadishu, Grozny, and Pittsburgh, that's some accolade.

## Kabylia

The predominantly Berber region has become tense in the last few years as a resurgent Berber nationalism buds. Given a choice between government by a dubious military junta and the rule of violent fundamentalist loons, a lot of Berbers are starting to wonder if they might not be better off on their own.

# Dangerous Things

## Massacres

It is estimated that around 200 Algerians are killed every month, with the holy month of Ramadan the most deadly time. The MO for Muslim rebels is to attack small villages (*mechtas* or *dovars*) with knives and machetes, and go for the jugular. The daily attacks take multiple lives. Children, women, and old folks make the most convenient targets—their throats are slashed like livestock. Besides throat slitting, survivors describe dismemberment by chainsaw, villagers being burned alive, babies being decapitated, and pregnant women being disemboweled. It would be superfluous to get into the incidents, which are clumped together like basketball games during a strike-shortened NBA season: hundreds of villagers are routinely slaughtered during a single massacre. Most massacres are the work of the GIA, though security forces have also participated in their fair share, many dressed as rebels, or working in the GIA under deep cover for the government. Much of the daily carnage takes place southwest of Algiers, in and around Ain Defla Province, Tlemcen, and Relizane. On March 21, 1999, Muslim rebels cut a little deeper with their knives and beheaded four women and then impaled their heads on stakes off a road near Emir Khaled town in Ain Defla. Ouch.

> **B**esides throat slitting, survivors describe dismemberment by chainsaw, villagers being burned alive, babies being decapitated, and pregnant women being disemboweled.

## Buses

The bombers and gunmen of the GIA have learned well from their spiritual kin in the Palestinian Territories: There is nothing like a bus for providing a densely packed mass of humanity who can't run away, and nothing like targeting buses for scaring the bejeebers out of the ordinary folk who have to use them to go about their lives. The difference between the GIA and their Palestinian equivalents is that they have not, yet, embraced suicide bombing; but then, Algerian internal security is not quite as organized as Israel's. It is doubtless that if Hamas had the option of just surrounding Israeli buses and riddling them with AK-47 fire, they'd be absolutely delighted.

### Weather

Proof, were it needed, that Allah is not only not Algerian but actively harboring some obscure grudge against the place, came in November 2001. Weeks of severe drought had led to restrictions on water use in the capital, Algiers. With the city's reservoirs on the verge of evaporating, religious leaders asked the citizens to pray for rain. What followed must have made a few leaders contemplate either atheism or trying to round up two of every animal. Great torrents of flood water, carrying mud, rock, and debris, flowed down from the hills and raged through Algiers. More than a thousand people were killed, and 1,500 families were left homeless.

### Bandits

As if the terrorists weren't enough, there are also numerous incidents of banditry and assault involving foreigners that have been reported in the far southern region of Algeria near the border with Niger. Bandits have robbed, assaulted, kidnapped, and killed travelers in Algeria south of Tamanrasset.

### Criminals

The threat of theft is increasing in Algeria. The most frequent crimes involve the theft of auto parts from parked cars. Car windows and trunk locks are frequently broken in the hope that the thief will find something of value within. Home burglary is an increasingly serious problem, and most residences of foreigners are protected by alarm systems, watchdogs, and/or guards. Foreigners should venture out into the city with only a minimum amount of cash carried in a carefully concealed location. Vehicles are not generally parked in unguarded locations because of theft and vandalism.

### Being a Kid

The GIA likes bombing youth centers and slicing the throats of pop singers and youth idols. The GIA believes that schooling for kids is an "obstacle to the Holy War in Algeria." The youth of Algeria have only two choices in life: join the GIA or join the Algerian military regime. Most just want to find a decent disco. Seventy-five percent of all Algerians are under 30, between 70 percent and 84 percent of whom are unemployed.

## Being a Harki

Harkis are the 250,000 Algerians who fought on the French side in the war of independence, or their descendants. They're not a popular bunch in Algeria, which is why many of them now live in France. Many of them still have family in Algeria that they'd like to visit, but the Algerian government refuses to issue them visas. President Bouteflika has compared the Harkis to the World War II Nazi collaborators of Vichy France.

**Federation of Harki Families (French only)**
merabtisaid@aol.com
http://www.harkis.com

## Journalism

Algeria's press is the most free and critical in Africa or the Middle East, but it pays a dreadful price for its outspokenness. In the last 10 years, more than 100 journalists and media employees have been killed. In Algiers, newspaper journalists work in a guarded complex.

Sad to relate, the fourth estate isn't getting much support from the government. Indeed, in 2001, President Bouteflika threatened to crack down further on Algeria's beleaguered hacks, saying, "We must not confuse freedom of opinion, which is a means of promoting awareness and culture, with abuse." *DP* can't see how promoting Algeria's culture is inconsistent with coming up with creative ways to explain that its president is a jackboot dictator, but maybe that's just us. Army Chief of Staff Mohamed Lamari wasn't best pleased with some of his reviews, either, getting in a fearful huff about "shameless writings, cartoons and so on . . . the obligation we have had until now to show reserve cannot prevent us from regretting the despicable use that is made of freedoms dearly won by our people." *DP* says: Go and play with your tanks, you silly old woman.

Article 144 of Algeria's legal code threatens jail sentences of up to 12 months and fines for "any attack on the state president in terms containing insult or defamation, whether in writing, drawing or speech, irrespective of the medium used: sound, image, electronic, computer or any other." The same law also prevents newspapers, in similarly stringent terms, from blowing raspberries at the parliament, the army, or anything else at all. Several journalists have been imprisoned under Article 144.

*La Tribune (French only)*
http://www.latribune-online.com

*Le Soir d'Algerie (French only)*
http://www.lesoirdalgerie.com

*La Grande Kechfa (French only)*
http://www.elkechfa.com (French only)

*Liberte (French only)*
http://www.liberte-algerie.com

## Singing

When *DP* was in Algeria, we asked about Rai singers. The reply was: "You mean the ones still left alive or the dead ones?" Meaning that Rai singers in Algeria are about as numerous as used Atari Pong games. *Rai* means "opinion"—that alone should tell you why the music is hated by the government and the fundamentalists.

> **W**hen *DP* was in Algeria, we asked about Rai singers. The reply was: "You mean the ones still left alive or the dead ones?"

The Rai music made by the Berbers is a mix of traditional song and weird French Europop—some of the better Rai stuff, in fact, is not a billion miles from fashionable French groups like Air and Daft Punk. In the '80s, Rai became a symbol of protest against the government (as far as Algeria's youth were concerned) and a symbol of Western decadence (in the eyes of Algeria's fundamentalists). The term "Hit Parade" took on new meaning as one singer after another was cleaned up by the hankie-heads: Berber icon Lounes Matoub, Rai superstar Chab Hasni, producer and composer Rachid Baba-Ahmed, and singers Lila Amar and Cheb Aziz.

The GIA cheerfully owned up to being the world's most exacting music critics, faxing *DP* a communique that threatened "Now we will start with the journalists, the poets, and the soldiers. Belly dancing is a prayer to Satan. When Satan's messengers give a direction to people, they dance." In the meantime, we've sent them Sting's address.

*Lounes Matoub Foundation (French only)*
http://www.lounesmatoub.org

# Getting Sick

Take the usual inoculations, plus precautions against malaria. The hospitals and clinics in Algeria are third world and limited in what they can do for you. At the very least, have your embassy's phone number and travel insurance details on hand. If you have the choice or the time, ask to be taken to a military hospital instead of the closest public one (you may find a hand grenade in your bedpan). Your best bet is to ask to be taken to the Ain Naadja Military Hospital in the suburbs of Algiers. If you are seriously wounded, you stand a better chance by being flown out to France, Britain, or Germany. Medicine can be difficult to get and expensive. Don't expect much outside the major cities.

## Nuts and Bolts

Despite the best efforts of various brigades of psychotic Allah-botherers, there are still 31.5 million people in Algeria. More than 99 percent of these people are of Arab or Berber descent—all but a very few of Algeria's European population cleared out when the French did, back in 1962. A similarly overwhelming majority are Sunni Muslims, though there are very, very small Christian and Jewish minorities.

The official language is Arabic, but French is widely spoken. The currency is the Algerian dinar, which trades at around 80 to the dollar—though you'll be better off with euros, which are more happily accepted.

*Embassy of the United States*
4 Chemin Cheikh Bachir El-Ibrahimi
Algiers, Algeria
Tel.: (213) 21 69 1255
Fax: (213) 21 69 3979
amembalg@ist.cerist.dz

*Embassy of Great Britain*
6 Avenue Souidani
Boudiemaa
Algers-Gare 1600
Algiers, Algeria
Tel.: (213) 21 23 0068
Fax: (213) 21 23 0067

*Embassy of Canada*
18, Mustapha Khalef Street
Ben Aknoun
Algiers, Algeria
Tel.: (213) 21 69 1611
Fax: (213) 21 69 3920

## Dangerous Days

| | |
|---|---|
| 7/30/02 | GIA leader Rachid Abou Tourab killed by government troops. |
| 7/5/02 | A bomb kills 35 at a market in Larba. |
| 6/28/02 | GIA gunmen kill 13 in an attack on a bus in Algiers. |
| 6/23/02 | GIA gunmen kill six children playing football in Zeralda. |
| 6/14/02 | GIA gunmen kill 11 in Douera. |
| 6/12/02 | GIA gunmen kill 11 in an attack on a bus in Medea. |
| 5/30/02 | Parliamentary elections are held, but are widely boycotted in Berber regions. |
| 5/29/02 | GIA gunmen kill 23 in Sendjas. |

| | |
|---|---|
| **2/9/02** | GIA leader Antar Zouabri is shot dead by Algerian police in Boufarik. |
| **5/16/02** | A bomb in a market in the Berber-speaking Kabylia region kills four. |
| **5/6/02** | GSPC gunmen kill 15 Algerian soldiers in an ambush near Tizi Ozou. |
| **5/2/02** | GIA gunmen kill 31 in 2 massacres in Ksar Chellala and Sidi Khaled. |
| **4/24/02** | GIA gunmen kill 16 in Tiaret. |
| **4/2/02** | GSPC gunmen kill 20 Algerian soldiers in an ambush near Moulay Larbi. |
| **3/29/02** | Clashes between Berber rioters and Algerian police in the Kabylia region leave dozens injured. |
| **3/6/02** | GSPC gunmen kill 15 progovernment militia troops in a raid on an army barracks in Oum Toub. |
| **2/5/02** | GIA gunmen kill 22 near Sidi Lakhdar. |
| **12/7/01** | GIA gunmen kill 17 in Ain Defla. |
| **11/11/01** | Flash floods kill more than 1,000 in Algiers. |
| **9/27/01** | GIA gunmen kill 22 at wedding in Larba. |
| **9/9/01** | GIA gunmen kill 10 at a funeral in Oran. |
| **9/6/01** | Islamic Salvation Front official Abdel Kader Omar flees Algeria for Europe. |
| **9/4/01** | GIA gunmen kill seven campers on a beach near Annaba. |
| **9/2/01** | GIA gunmen kill 13 in attacks in Algeria's northwest. |
| **8/24/01** | GIA gunmen kill 17 in an ambush on a road in the Beni Chougran mountains. |
| **7/24/01** | GIA gunmen kill three generations of the same family at a holiday camp near Tipeza. |
| **6/19/01** | GSPC gunmen kill 13 Algerian soldiers in an ambush near Chlef. |
| **6/14/01** | Riots by Berbers in Algiers kill two. |
| **5/10/01** | GSPC gunmen kill eight policemen in Tigzirt. |
| **4/28/01** | More than 50 Algerian soldiers are killed in battle with GSPC gunmen in Algeria's northeast. |
| **4/01** | Riots in the Berber region of Kabylia kill at least 60. |
| **2/15/01** | GSPC gunmen kill 13 Algerian soldiers in an ambush near Sidi Bel Abbas. |
| **2/12/01** | GIA gunmen kill 26 near Berrouaghia. |

**12/30/99**   Four hundred people are killed in four villages at the start of Ramadan.

**4/16/99**   Abdelaziz Bouteflika is elected president after six contenders drop out of the race charging widespread election fraud. Massive protests engulf Algiers and other cities.

**6/5/97**   President Liamine Zeroual's government is re-elected; the FIS is banned from participating in the polls.

**5/5/95**   Islamic extremists kill five foreigners working at a pipe mill at an industrial zone in the Ghardaia region of northern Algeria. The victims were identified as two Frenchmen, a Canadian, a Brit, and a Tunisian.

**6/29/92**   Higher State Council Chief Mohamed Boudiaf is assassinated.

**12/91**   Algeria's first ever parliamentary elections are won by Muslim fundamentalists—the Islamic Salvation Front. The elections are annulled by the government, tossing Algeria into civil war.

**4/80**   "The Black Spring": Algeria's ethnic Berbers stage an uprising.

**7/5/62**   Algeria gains independence from France.

**11/1/54**   Algerian independence fighters launch their first armed offensive against French forces in eastern Algeria.

# THE BALKANS
## Kosovo, Macedonia, Bosnia and Herzegovina, Serbia and Montenegro, Albania

## Balkan Bits

Otto von Bismarck, the 19th-century unifier of Germany, made two celebrated and contradictory quips about this beautiful but perpetually unfortunate region of Europe. At various points during the 20th century, thousands of combatants from dozens of countries took the field in defiance of Bismarck's assessment that "The whole of the Balkans is not worth the bones of a single Pomeranian grenadier." Which at least meant that the Iron Chancellor was proved repeatedly to be correct in his other observation, that "If there is another war in Europe, it will come out of some damn silly thing in the Balkans."

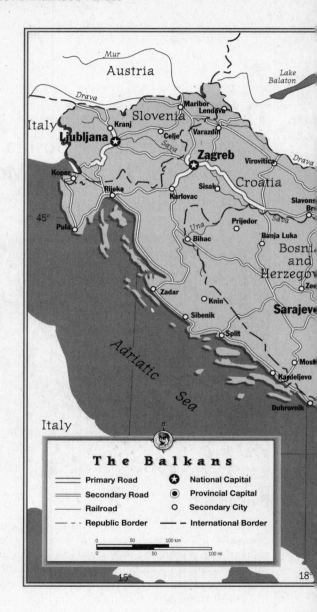

"Damn silly things" have long been a principal export of the Balkans, but the good news since the last edition of *DP* is that the silliest and most damnable of them all got his long overdue comeuppance in 2000. As president of Yugoslavia, Slobodan Milosevic had, in a little over a decade of corrupt, vicious, and idiotic rule, reduced Yugoslavia from a vibrant multiethnic nation, stretching from the borders of Austria to the hinterlands of Greece, to a wretched, bankrupt, mafia-ridden, sanctions-wracked pariah state roughly the size of Maine. Wars in Slovenia, Croatia, Bosnia and Herzegovina, and Kosovo,

> **S**lobodan Milosevic had reduced Yugoslavia to a bankrupt, mafia-ridden, sanctions-wracked pariah state roughly the size of Maine.

all precipitated by Milosevic, killed and maimed hundreds of thousands and displaced millions, replaying scenes that Europe had thought consigned to the flickering memory of World War II newsreels, and finally getting Yugoslavia bombed flat by the most powerful military alliance on earth.

On September 23, 2000, Milosevic put his none-too-impressive record to the popular vote in a presidential election. Though every indication pointed to a convincing victory for his opponent, Vojislav Kostunica, Milosevic refused to concede, insisting on a second round of voting. It was a massive misjudgment by Milosevic of the mood of the country in general, and his capital in particular, where postcard-sellers on Kneza Mihaila Street, the busy pedestrian arcade that winds through the center of Belgrade, were already doing a roaring trade in cartoons of a familiar-looking man in a grey suit holding a pistol to his head, under the caption *Spasi Srbiju, ubij se!* ("Save Serbia, kill yourself!"). On the reverse, the address of the suggested recipient was thoughtfully filled in: Mr. Slobodan Milosevic, 11000 Beograd, Uzicka 16, Srbija.

Whatever arguments may be ultimately advanced about the complicity in Milosevic's crimes of the Serbian people who voted for him over the years—and a few wise heads in Belgrade do acknowledge the need for a national self-examination of the sort undertaken by Germans after 1945—there is no disputing the panache with which Milosevic was removed from office. When the people of Belgrade finally revolted on October 5, 2000, there was no mindless pillaging—targets were hit with a precision that might have been an uncanny echo of NATO's missile strikes of earlier that year, except that the people of Belgrade didn't demolish any foreign embassies by mistake.

After seizing the parliamentary building, they set upon the headquarters of Milosevic's Socialist party, the office of the Yugoslav United Left (the party of Milosevic's ghastly wife, Mira Markovic), the perfume shop—"Scandal"—owned by Milosevic's spoilt gangster son Marko, a couple of police stations, and, most cathartically, the complex that housed Radio Television Serbia (RTS)—the black heart of Milosevic's propaganda machine. (RTS was controversially bombed by NATO in 1999, with the loss of 16 employees—survivors have since claimed that the nightshift was deliberately overstaffed on the orders of Milosevic, in the hope of maximizing the propaganda advantage of civilian deaths.) On October 5, RTS's long-suffering viewers finished what NATO started. The station burned with such apocalyptic fury that the footpath alongside it is now an eerie monochrome mosaic: Soot-stained glass from dozens of shattered windows has melted into the grey asphalt.

It was a hint that even the pathologically obstinate Milosevic could not fail to take. On October 6, he made a bizarrely jaunty concession speech: "Respected citizens, I have just received the official information that Vojislav Kostunica has won the presidential election." Carrying on as if he'd just lost a congressional race in Delaware, and not been chased out of his job by a justly infuriated populace who would certainly have been forgiven by the world at large if they'd hung him by his ankles from a streetlamp in Republic Square, Slobo announced that he was looking forward to spending more time with his family—a statement which in itself might have served as the basis for an insanity plea when the judicial reckoning eventually came.

As it did, inevitably, in June 2001. Milosevic had already made legal history by becoming the first incumbent head of state ever charged with crimes against humanity, and Yugoslavia's first post-Milosevic government noisily insisted that they'd deal with him at home. This resolve lasted about as long as it took the outside world to put together an aid package totalling $1.3 billion—money that was delivered to Belgrade the day after Milosevic was delivered to The Hague.

The country Milosevic once ruled no longer exists: Yugoslavia, or what's left of it, officially adopted the name Republic of Serbia and Montenegro in May 2002. This quaintly titled nation is not without its problems, such as recovering from the bombardment by NATO and the ownership of the local economy to gangsters by Milosevic, but it is heading in the right direction. The outside world is speaking to it and trading with it again, and many of the underworld kingpins who once ran Belgrade are either dead (the most infamous of them all, the paramilitary-turned-"businessman" Arkan, was assassinated in the foyer of Belgrade's Intercontinental Hotel in January 2000) or otherwise departed (Milosevic's son, Marko, has not been seen in some time, but most betting places him in Moscow).

The other budding nations which crawled from the wreckage of Yugoslavia are recovering from Milosevic with varying degrees of success. Slovenia, which won its independence with only a few days of somewhat farcical fighting in 1991, is now a perfectly pleasant, if somewhat dull, exemplar of quiet, stolid *mitteleuropa*. Croatia is another nation which can look upon the Balkan wars of the 1990s as a victory—it got its independence, expelled its intermittently uppity Serb population with the brutal, offensive Operation Storm in 1995, and hasn't even had to suffer the embarrassment of a war crimes–tarnished head of state, given that the president who made modern Croatia possible, the appalling Franjo Tudjman, went to his (doubtless very warm) eternal home in 1999.

For the rest of the region's new countries, things have not been quite so easy. Bosnia and Herzegovina remains uneasily split between its constituent ethnicities; it is supposed to be a single state comprising two entities—the Federation of Bosnia and Herzegovina (Bosnia's mostly Croat and Bosnian areas, including the national capital, Sarajevo), and Republika Srpska (Bosnia's predominantly Serb enclave, with a capital in Banja Luka), separated by a squiggle on the map known as the Inter-Entity Boundary Line (IEBL). Unfortunately, the Serb population of Republika Srpksa, and those of its politicians who don't spend their days huddled in cellars fearful of a sudden involuntary relocation to Holland, still seem to think they're a sovereign nation, even if getting the rest of the world to agree with them is roughly as likely as the Milosevics buying a retirement villa in Sarajevo (or anywhere else, come to think of it).

Republika Srpska remains the last outpost of the boneheaded strain of Serb nationalism that Milosevic encouraged—ask any café patron in Belgrade what they think of their alleged ethnic brethren in the RS, and they'll tell you what Manhattan loft-dwellers would about Montana militiamen. Despite the fact that Republika Srpska is becoming more and more isolated and more and more broke, and even though most of its principal sponsors and idols are either dead, on trial, in jail, or hiding in remote mountain monasteries desperately trying to cultivate extremely thick beards, these hopeless hillbillies won't be told so. Local elections in 2000 resulted in a landslide for the Serbian Democratic Party (SDS)—the party once run by fugitive war-crimes suspect Radovan Karadzic. In May 2001, the SDS staged riots protesting against the rebuilding of historic mosques destroyed during the war, and attacks on returning refugees are still depressingly common. For now, it can only be hoped that one day Republika Srpska will go the same way as the unlamented Herzeg-Bosna—the mythical Croat homeland that militant Tudjmanites once tried to carve out of Bosnia and Herzegovina, and about which little is now heard, outside a few of Mostar's less-savory drinking establishments.

Macedonia flirted with civil war in 2000, when militias from the ethnically Albanian villages in the northwest of the country, arranged under the banner of the National Liberation Army, scrapped with the Macedonian military. By this point, the outside world had assimilated the lesson that the smartest reaction to Balkan conflagrations is to take action, and both parties signed a peace settlement after six months of fighting, each presumably using the hand that wasn't being wrenched behind their backs by the European Union and NATO. In August 2001, NATO launched Operation Essential Harvest to disarm the various ragbag Albanian militias. Like most other disarmament deals, the Albanians handed in as much as they thought was politically expedient and hid the rest in haystacks to await further eventualities. There is certainly still enough loose weaponry available to start a medium-sized war with minimal notice.

Kosovo's current semi-independence came at an immense financial cost to the West, and an incalculable human cost to the Kosovars. Between March 24 and June 10, 1999, a total of 38,008 air sorties were flown by NATO—the total bill, according to *Jane's Defense Weekly*, came to around $4 billion. These raids, we were told, destroyed 30 percent of Serb heavy weaponry in Kosovo—400 Serb artillery pieces, 270 armored personnel carriers, 150 tanks, 100 planes, and 5,000–10,000 Serb soldiers.

That was the estimate until someone had a chance to check the damage on the ground. The actual grand total of all those weeks of bombardment was 13 Serb tanks out of 300. For $4 billion, you'd reckon, Serbia would cheerfully have sold NATO at least 100 tanks, with a year's parts and labor thrown in. It's probably not much consolation to NATO, or to us poor saps whose taxes underwrote this misadventure, that the world's barn doors have, in fact, little to fear from Serbian air defenses. With 38,008 targets to aim at, they managed to bring down two: an American F-16c and F-117 (a Nighthawk "Stealth" fighter.) Remnants of both are on display in the aviation museum next to Belgrade's international airport and, on Kneza Mihaila Street, you can buy badges depicting the F-117 with a caption gloating, "Sorry—we didn't know it was invisible."

> **Y**ou can buy badges depicting the F-117 with a caption gloating, "Sorry—we didn't know it was invisible."

While NATO was refusing to get closer to the conflict than 15,000 feet in the air, dreadful things were happening on the ground—NATO's aerial and technological supremacy weren't much use against a campaign of ethnic cleansing, of which the principal weapon was the cigarette lighter. During the 79 days of war, 1.3 million Kosovars—more than half the total population—became refugees, walking and driving to the borders with whatever they could carry, or shipped out in crammed-full railway cars, hideously reminiscent of World War II. More than 10,000 were killed. Some of these casualties were caused by NATO, which had embarked upon an often-myopic air campaign with the curious proviso that the lives of their volunteer service personnel were worth more than those of the civilians they'd gone to war to protect. The inevitable result of this policy came at Djakovica on April 14, 1999, where, to the ill-concealed delight of Serb authorities, who took busloads of foreign journalists to the gruesome impact site, NATO F-16s demonstrated that, from a distance, convoys of hostile military vehicles and tractors full of refugees can look remarkably similar.

Kosovo today is still something of a basket case. It is liberally riddled with Serb land mines and unexploded NATO ordnance, and tensions between the Kosovars and those Serbs who have been brave or foolish enough to remain are still high. The worst flashpoint remains the northern town of Mitrovica, where the Serbs on the north side of the river and the Kosovars on the south have displayed a marked reluctance to invite each other to their barbecues. The multinational police trying to keep the peace have come under frequent attack. About the only consolation that Kosovo can cling to is that it's not quite as grotesque a shambles as the motherland. Albania, which managed under capitalism every bit as badly as it did under communism, is the poorest country in Europe by a good margin. In fact, it would come as no surprise if a bunch of musicians from Sierra Leone, Rwanda, and the Democratic Republic of Congo got together to do a benefit record for the country.

> **A**lbania is the poorest country in Europe by a good margin. In fact, it would come as no surprise if a bunch of musicians from Sierra Leone, Rwanda, and the Democratic Republic of Congo got together to do a benefit record for the country.

## The Scoop

Most of the former Yugoslavia is now a perfectly safe and thoroughly pleasant place in which to travel. Even during the war, the food was good, the coffee terrific, the beer cold, and the countryside beautiful. The only places where serious caution should still be exercised are the parts of Kosovo in which any Serbs still insist on living: mainly the Presevo Valley region of southern Serbia and the militantly Albanian enclaves of Macedonia.

# The Players

## Slobodan Milosevic

His current landlords at the International Criminal Tribunal for the former Yugoslavia now know him as case IT-02-54. Though Milosevic, a former lawyer, says that he refuses to recognize the court (he is often seen looking theatrically at his watch, as if he has to be someplace else), he is conducting his own defense and generally gives the impression that he's having a whale of a time. Milosevic's basic line is that, far from being an orchestrator of genocide and a chronic fraud who murdered thousands and bankrupted his country, he is the innocent, hapless victim of a conspiracy to promote a global hegemony of American culture and American power. For now Milo seems to be auditioning for admittance to the Hermann Goering/Benito Mussolini School of Misunderstood Dictators, and it remains to be seen how the trial will play out.

**International Committee to Defend Slobodan Milosevic**
http://www.icdsm.org

**Socialist Party of Serbia homepage**
http://www.sps.org.yu

## Dr. Radovan Karadzic and General Ratko Mladic

Karadzic is the former psychiatrist, convicted fraudster, and comically useless poet who, as head of the amusingly named Serbian Democratic Party, presided over the slaughter of tens of thousands of Bosnia's Muslims. Mladic, in his capacity as Commander of the Bosnian Serb army, functioned as Karadzic's attack dog, most notoriously at the woefully misdescribed UN "safe area" of Srebrenica, where more than 7,000 Bosnian civilians were systematically rounded up and slaughtered in the summer of 1995, while the Dutch soldiers who were supposed to be protecting them sat on their rifles and looked the other way. (In April 2002, the entire Dutch government resigned after a damning report of the massacre was published; their sense of honor is commendable, but if doing bugger-all while Bosnians were being butchered is a resigning matter, pretty much every American and European politician who was in office between 1992 and 1995 should start clearing their desks.)

This pair of solid citizens are two men that the International Criminal Tribunal would still most like a word with, and both put up a good fight. One poetic rumor places them in the monasteries of Mount Athos, a semi-autonomous Orthodox Christian religious enclave in Greece—to which, intriguingly, Vojislav Kostunica paid a visit shortly after replacing Milosevic as president of Yugoslavia. However, both are generally believed not to have gone so far from home, if only because it's impossible to believe anyone else would want them.

Karadzic, who may or may not have shaved off his preposterous Hasselhoff-esque bouffant and grown a beard, is believed to drift among the southeast Bosnian towns of Rudo, Visegrad, Foca, Cajnice, and Celibici. In March 2002, an attempt by Stabilization Force (SFOR) troops to arrest Karadzic in Celibici narrowly failed, allegedly as the result of a tip-off by a sympathetic French officer (the French deny this, but it wouldn't have been the first time).

Mladic lived quite openly in Belgrade for a long time prior to Milosevic's demise, even drawing a monthly state pension; armed guards at 119 Blagoja Parovica, a street in the suburb of Banovo Brdo, would politely but firmly explain that the general was not receiving visitors. After the revolution and Milosevic's removal to The Hague, much international pressure was placed upon the new government in Belgrade to hand over Mladic. Belgrade's reaction was to quietly advise him to head for Montenegro, where he is thought to be moving between villages around Niksic.

There's $5 million on offer for anyone who can point NATO in the direction of either Karadzic or Mladic.

http://www.igc.org/wcw/icty/suspects/Radovan_Karadzic.html

**War Criminal Watch**
http://www.wcw.org

## International Criminal Tribunal for the Former Yugoslavia (ICTY)

The ICTY was established in 1993 by UN Security Council Resolution 827. Led by formidable Chief Prosecutor Carla Del Ponte, the ICTY now has a staff of over a thousand and an annual operating budget of more than $90 million. Milosevic aside, other high-profile detainees include General Radislav Krstic, erstwhile deputy commander of the Bosnian Serb army's Drina corps, now serving 46 richly merited years for his role in the Srebrenica massacre; General Tihomir Blaskic, commander of the Bosnian Croat HVO, 45 years for serial ethnic cleansing; Biljana Plavsic and Momcilo Krajisnik, respectively the president and speaker of the Bosnian Serb parliament, both awaiting trial on charges of genocide and crimes against humanity. There is some black-hearted but historically fair merit to the idea of saving the $90 million to do it the "right" way by simply spending the money for a clip of AK-47 bullets and a midnight bus trip to a secluded glen for the defendants. But *DP* will refrain from recommending any further cost-saving ideas. You may submit your ideas to:

**International Criminal Tribunal for the Former Yugoslavia**
Churchillplein 1
2517JW The Hague
Netherlands
Tel.: (31) 70 512 8656
http://www.un.org/icty

## Vojislav Kostunica and Zoran Djindjic

Anyone who would assume that the president of the Republic of Serbia and Montenegro and the prime minister of Serbia would be more or less on the same side doesn't know much about Balkan politics: President Kostunica and Prime Minister Djindjic get on about as well as two rats in a coffee can. While Kostunica is neither a murderous thug nor a pillaging crook—the two crucial differences between him and his predecessor—he is a nationalist, and as such objected to the Dayton peace settlement in Bosnia and Herzegovina, and to the delivery of Milosevic to The Hague. Djindjic, once mayor of Belgrade, is much more pragmatic and pro-Western—it was he who handed Milosevic over to the ICTY—but a lot of people in Serbia haven't forgotten or forgiven Djindjic's decampment to Montenegro during the NATO bombardment in 1999. In Djindjic's defense, Belgrade at the time was a tricky place for anyone who Milosevic perceived as a potential threat—as might be confirmed by the grieving relatives of paramilitary mass-murderer and mafiosi Arkan, Yugoslav Defense Minister Pavle Bulatovic, Yugoslav Airlines general manager Zika Petrovic, provincial politician Bosko Perosevic, newspaper publisher Slavko Curuvija, and, most incredibly, former Serbian president and best man at Milosevic's wedding, Ivan Stambolic, who was last seen jogging near his Belgrade home in August 2000.

Happily for prominent Serbs, the election of Kostunica seems to have reduced the chances of them ending up in the Danube River wearing concrete flippers. When Milosevic-era bigwigs come to any harm these days, it tends to be of their own accord. In 2002, hours after Serbia approved a new law allowing the transfer of war-crimes suspects to The Hague, one such indictee, Milosevic's former interior minister and ethnic-cleanser-in-chief, Vlajko Stojiljkovic, shot himself in front of Belgrade's parliamentary building. This saved the European taxpayer the price of one-way airfare and 30 years of prison meals and, as such, was possibly the first worthwhile and public-spirited act of Stojiljkovic's life.

**Serbian Government**
http://www.serbia.sr.gov.yu

## Vojislav Seselj and Vuk Draskovic

Seselj and Draskovic, the leaders of the Serbian Radical Party and the Serbian Renewal Movement, respectively, are the last of Serbia's prominent old-school politicians still standing. At any given moment, they might be blood brothers or bitter enemies. It's hard to say, given that former paramilitary commander Seselj is described by some as an evil, unprincipled swine whose invitation to The Hague must surely be in the post any day now, and that Draskovic is well and truly at tea with the Mad Hatter. Draskovic, who has been the subject of several assassination attempts, was nearly killed in a suspicious car accident in 1999; Radomir Markovic, Milosevic's former chief of state security, is now facing charges relating to the crash. Just everyday Balkan politics at play.

**Serbian Renewal Movement**
http://www.spo.org.yu

## NATO

NATO is still running three major missions in what used to be Yugoslavia. The Stabilization Force (SFOR) in Bosnia and Herzegovina is being scaled back, and currently comprises 18,000 troops. Nearly 40,000 troops are still in Kosovo with the Kosovo Force (KFOR). Another 2,000 troops are serving in Macedonia.

**NATO**
http://www.nato.int

**NATO in the former Republic of Macedonia**
http://www.nato.int/fyrom/home.htm

**SFOR**
http://www.nato.int/sfor/index.htm

**KFOR**
http://www.nato.int/kfor/welcome.html

## Organization for Security and Cooperation in Europe (OSCE)

Only the OSCE would think of the idea of diffident Euros puttering around poverty-stricken regions in orange Range Rovers as being conducive to security or cooperation. Still, it does keep them off the streets.

**Organization for Security and Cooperation in Europe**
Kärntner Ring 5-7, 4th Floor
1010 Vienna
Austria
Tel.: (43) 1 514 36 0
pm@osce.org
http://www.osce.org

## United Nations Interim Administration Mission in Kosovo (UNMIK)

UNMIK was established in 1999, and has been running the shop in Kosovo ever since. It is now probably the most far-reaching UN mission ever established—UNMIK even runs a newspaper, radio station, and television channel to keep a doubtless-grateful public informed of its activities. It's soon to move to new offices in Pristina, which rather suggests that the "interim" part of UNMIK's name is open to negotiation.

http://www.unmikonline.org

## Office of the High Representative (OHR)

The OHR was the babysitter sent to Bosnia by the international community in 1995 to make sure that all the parties to the Dayton Peace Agreement played nicely. At the moment, the man with the ultimate power to send everyone to bed without pudding is former British politician Paddy Ashdown.

**OHR Sarajevo**
Emerika Bluma 1
71000 Sarajevo
Bosnia and Herzegovina
Tel.: (387) 33 28 3500
Fax: (387) 33 28 3501
http://www.ohr.int

## Radio B92 and Otpor!

Good guys with Serb accents have been thin on the ground over the last decade, and so *DP* would like to do its bit to encourage both of these organizations. B92 was the opposition radio station that functioned throughout the Milosevic years, despite frequent harassment and occasional closures by security forces—B92's full story can be read in Matthew Collin's fine book, *This Is Serbia Calling* (Serpents Tail, 2001). Otpor! (Serbian for "Resistance!") was a student movement that borrowed the humor and tactics of the 1968 French situationists. Otpor!'s nominal leader, Branko Ilic, who was only 19 at the time, described the movement as "guerrillas without guns"—aiming to both embarrass the government and encourage Serbs to contemplate alternate realities. They succeeded in both—but, to their credit, victory didn't make them complacent. Only days after Milosevic had been ejected from power in the revolution that Otpor! helped make possible, a new Otpor! poster appeared around Belgrade. Aimed at the new government, it depicted the bulldozer that Otpor! activists drove into the Belgrade parliamentary building on October 5, and the reminder, "We're watching you."

**Radio B92**
http://www.b92.net

**Otpor!**
http://www.otpor.com

## Kosovars

A question for readers with an interest in semantics: Why was it that when the West couldn't be bothered to help Bosnia between 1992 and 1995, its inhabitants were called Muslims, whereas when we took to the skies in defense of Kosovo, its equally Islamic residents were called Kosovars? Despite the best efforts of Milosevic's goon squads, there are still about two million of them, and they still face a daunting repair job. GDP per capita is an unspectacular $900.

http://www.kosova.com

## Dr. Ibrahim Rugova

The image of the bohemian revolutionary: The return to political pre-eminence of the silk-scarfed, Sorbonne-educated Rugova is one of the few genuinely heartwarming developments in recent Kosovan history—for a long time, he looked like clinching proof that nice guys were always destined to finish last in the Balkans. Exactly who was it that came up with the idea that someone who looked and acted like Francois Truffaut leading a poetry reading somehow would be able to run the toughest neighborhood west of Afghanistan? Probably the same guys who thought Hamid Karzai would whip a fractured, brutalized nation into shape. I mean, for Christ's sake, the man studied not literature . . . but literature theory. It just didn't seem like Milo and his bucked-up goons would be defeated by an overpowering and witty analysis of Jean Paul Sartre.

Rugova had long advocated peaceful resistance to Serbian domination of Kosovo, fearing—quite correctly, as it turned out—that the Serbs would answer violent revolt with yet further violence. Rugova's policy of boycotting Serb institutions and establishing a parallel Albanian infrastructure was popular, and he was twice, in 1992 and 1998, elected president of Kosovo's so-called "shadow government."

Rugova's career looked pretty much over by 1999, when the guerrillas of the Kosovo Liberation Army (KLA) had seized the agenda and Rugova made a sincere but politically tactless effort to negotiate with Milosevic in person. However, the KLA did not win many friends with their behavior following the war, and Kosovo has since returned its loyalty to Rugova and his party, the Democratic League of Kosovo. In elections in 2000, they won 58 percent of the vote. Stay tuned to see if the theory of the pen is mightier than the theory of the sword.

**Kosova Live News Agency**
http://www.kosovalive.com/en/index_en.htm

## Kosovo Liberation Army (Ushtria Clirimtare e Kosoves)

In 1999, the KLA—known at home as UCK—proved the truth of the adage that one man's terrorist is another man's freedom fighter faster than you could say "Northern Alliance." Like America's allies in Afghanistan two years or so later, the KLA had been routinely derided—and not without reason—as a collection of violent, unscrupulous bandits whose business interests would be unlikely to find much favor with the selection committee of the local Rotary club, until it suddenly looked as if they might be useful. Flush with swarthy and eager Albanian volunteers from New Jersey pizza parlors and Detroit car factories; supported with cash, weapons, and training from the CIA; and with comm gear conveniently abandoned by the OSCE, the KLA managed to supplement its normal, grubby drug income with morally clean US$100 bills. When NATO tired of cleaning Kosovar mud off its boots and learned they might actually get killed, the KLA was more than happy to be remade from thuggish militia to plucky defenders of their put-upon people.

The KLA had existed in some shape or form since 1992, but was regarded even by most Kosovars as little more than a feral Boy Scout troop. It owed the status it eventually attained to the 1995 Dayton Peace Agreement, which not only entirely failed to deal with Kosovo, but rewarded the monstrous brutality of the Bosnian Serbs with a Serb quasi-state within Bosnia. A lot of Kosovars began to wonder, not unreasonably, if the nonviolent resistance espoused by Ibrahim Rugova was worth persisting with, if this was the thanks they were going to get. By 1998, the KLA had an estimated strength of 17,000, a ready supply of weaponry liberated during the 1997 meltdown of neighboring Albania, and money coming in from their own drug-running and racketeering as well as from Albanian communities all over the world, and was staging regular raids on Serbian police, military personnel, and installations. The Serbs responded with the same sense of proportion and fair play they had exhibited during the war in Bosnia—one massacre in central Kosovo in February 1998 accounted for the deaths of 80 Kosovar civilians.

That there was some cooperation between NATO and the KLA during the 1999 war is unarguable, but the KLA probably wasn't either as vital or trusted as they wanted to believe at the time and have claimed ever since. Whatever, it was a boom time for the KLA, as young men from the vast Albanian diaspora in Europe and America pledged themselves to the cause and brought their trust funds with them. By now, the KLA seemed under the clear leadership of the 29-year-old Hasim Thaci, with the assistance of a former Croat army brigadier, Agim Ceku, who had been hired as chief of staff to try and turn them into at least a semiprofessional fighting force.

Since the end of the war, the KLA's efforts to ingratiate themselves with the people they helped liberate have been hampered by the fact that their cupboard is so stuffed with skeletons that there's barely room to hang up their uniforms. Agim Ceku, it turned out, had been one of the principal architects of Operation Storm, Croatia's monstrous 1995 onslaught against its ethnically Serb enclave of Krajina. KFOR kept finding KLA arms dumps, despite the KLA's earnest protestations that they'd

> **S**ince the end of the war, the KLA's efforts to ingratiate themselves with the people they helped liberate have been hampered by the fact that their cupboard is so stuffed with skeletons that there's barely room to hang up their uniforms.

given up that line of work, honestly. As a result of all this, the KLA's reinvention as a political party—the Democratic Party of Kosovo (DPK)—failed to excite the affections of the voters, many of whom doubtless recalled the brutality with which the KLA had emphasized their power even among their fellow Kosovars. In local elections in 2000, the DPK won just 27 percent of the vote.

**KLA/UCK**
http://www.geocities.com/MotorCity/Track/4165/kla2.html

### Liberation Army of Presevo, Medvedja and Bujanovac (LAPMB)

Snappily titled, but licensing unfriendly KLA offshoot that took up the Kosovar cause in those predominantly ethnically Albanian enclaves outside Kosovo and inside southern Serbia. The few hundred lightly armed guerrillas of the LAPMB (locally known as UCPMB) had hopes of uniting their region of Serbia with Kosovo in anticipation of statehood for Kosovo as a whole, and perhaps fomenting rebellion among their ethnic brethren in neighboring Macedonia. Unfortunately for them, nobody in the outside world really wanted to know, and they've been pretty quiet for some time. Their goal is to become part of eastern Kosovo, not Western Serbia. Hey, it's a Balkan thing, and of course we guard the border. What's next? Timeshare units with their own liberation armies? There is no official contact, but go there and any one of the 70,000 folks in the Presevo Valley will hook you up with the LAPMB.

**Liberation Army of Presevo, Medvedja, and Bujanovac**
http://www.aacl.com/ucpmb.htm

### National Liberation Army (NLA)

The NLA were routinely, but not altogether accurately, written up as the Macedonian equivalent of the KLA. While the appearances and methods of the two organizations were similar, the motivations were very different. While the KLA wanted an independent Kosovar state, the NLA merely wanted a fair shake for Albanians in Macedonia—despite the paranoid rhetoric of governments in Skopje, Belgrade, and Athens, the Greater Albania conspiracy theory is a crock, for the simple enough reason that not even Albanians want to live in Albania itself.

In September 2001 the NLA's leader, Ali Ahmeti, announced the formal disbandment of the organization after they had handed over nearly 4,000 weapons to troops of NATO's Operation Essential Harvest. Occasional reports of internecine sniping between rival Albanian factions suggest, however, that one or two rifles may have been overlooked.

**Albanians in Macedonia Crisis Center**
http://www.alb-net.com/amcc
http://www.realitymacedonia.org.mk

## The Mujahideen

They were the abominable snowmen of the Yugoslav wars—everyone, especially the Serbs, talked about the Islamic holy warriors imported from Afghanistan, Algeria, Chechnya, and Allah-knows-where-else . . . but had anyone ever seen one? Confirmation that the rumors might have been grounded in truth appeared to come in March 2002, when the Macedonian Interior Ministry claimed that their police had shot dead seven Pakistani "terrorists" in a gun battle north of Skopje. However, eyebrows were raised and chins doubtfully scratched at the evidence the Macedonians claimed to have harvested from the scene—shopfloor-shiny weapons and neatly pressed uniforms with NLA insignia. The true identity of the Skopje Seven remains a mystery, but it seems depressingly likely that they were illegal immigrants who took a wrong turn in their voyage across Europe. *DP* has it on good authority that there were about 600 muj at any one time who made the trip to sort out the mess in the Balkans, but they went home shaking their heads . . . Uncle Sam, of course, stayed. The muj went on to other things. . . .

**The Center for Peace in the Balkans**
http://www.balkanpeace.org/our/our09.shtml

## The Gypsies

If you could find one thing that all residents of the Balkans have in common it would be a hatred for gypsies. The Cigani—or Roma, as gypsies are called here—are an uncounted but ever-present force in the unstable/mysterious/criminal/exotic gestalt of the Balkans. They make the Albanians seem as privileged as East Coast yuppies. Like a strange perfume or wild card they seem to tip the scales of stability every time. Just interrupt a Serb and a Croat argument with a tale of woe caused by a gypsy, and both will unite in their hatred toward this ethnic group.

Three to four million gypsies came to the Balkans in the 1300s (their language is actually related to Sanskrit and Indian languages). Gypsies have always lived on the fringes of respectable society, employed as entertainers and metal workers, and indulge the many activities one would expect of people who never expect to be invited to join the Rotarians.

Despite the injustices perpetrated against these former slaves, the Roma remain largely uncounted, unheralded, and unknown. And they like it that way. Historically, they have been included as a footnote in almost every mass murder, holocaust, and pogrom, but they still endure. They are known for their industriousness in being idle, their raucous violin-playing at 48-hour weddings, and, on a more embarrassing level, for providing many of the babies for the southern European adoption market. Unlike the stolid, dark form of criminality found in polite Balkan society, the gypsies seem to take great pleasure in keeping it at a cottage-industry level. It's almost worth getting scammed just to have the story to tell when you get home.

http://www.greekhelsinki.gr/special-issues-roma.html

## Getting In

There are international airports in all of the capitals of the former Yugoslavia—Llubljana, Zagreb, Sarajevo, Belgrade, and Skopje—but Kosovo is most easily accessible from Skopje. Citizens of Great Britain, Canada, and the United States do not need visas to enter Macedonia, Bosnia and Herzegovina, or the Republic of Serbia and Montenegro as tourists. Journalists theoretically are required to get visas for Serbia and Montenegro, but this measure is not stringently policed; even during the air embargo on Yugoslavia during Milosevic's time, *DP* talked itself across Yugoslavia's border with Hungary by claiming that our bags were full of cameras and notepads because we were part of an international photography and poetry collective.

Road borders can be difficult, though much less so than during the wars in Croatia and Bosnia, when aid trucks were routinely held up for days, and even weeks. Today, Slovenian customs officers in particular are famous for regarding themselves as sentinels defending civilized Western Europe from the barbarian hordes who were, until recently, their compatriots. Entering Republika Srpska from Croatia is predictably tedious, as the border guards will demand an "entrance tax" of whatever they think they can get away with. (There is, of course, no such tax, and you should politely but firmly remind them of this.) Travel from Republika Srpska to Serbia itself is a breeze, as it is from Croatia to Bosnia and Herzegovina, now that Zagreb and Sarajevo are speaking to each other again. Republika Srpska to Montenegro can be odd; Kosovo to Montenegro is usually surprisingly good-natured; and Kosovo to either Macedonia or Serbia is generally tense, dull, and unpleasant. Take a good book—perhaps not General Wesley Clark's *Waging Modern War*—and be patient.

**Embassy of the Republic of Macedonia**
3050 K Street NW, Suite 210
Washington, DC 20007
Tel.: (202) 337-3063
Fax: (202) 337-3093
rmacedonia@aol.com

**Embassy of the Republic of Macedonia**
5th Floor, 25 James Street
London W1U 1DU, UK
Tel.: (44) 207 935 3842
Fax: (44) 207 935 3986
mkuk@btinternet.com

**Embassy of the Republic of Macedonia**
130 Albert Street, Suite 1006
Ottawa, Ontario K1P 5G4
Canada
Tel.: (613) 234-3883
Fax: (613) 233-1852
emb.macedonia.ottawa@sympatico.ca

**Consulate General of Bosnia and Herzegovina**
866 UN Plaza, Suite 580
New York, NY 10017
Tel.: (212) 593-1042
bihconny@aol.com

**Embassy of Bosnia and Herzegovina**
4th Floor, Morley House
320 Regent Street
London W1R 5AB, UK
Tel.: (44) 207 7255 3758
Fax: (44) 207 7255 3760

**Embassy of Bosnia and Herzegovina**
130 Albert Street, Suite 805
Ottawa, Canada K1P 5G4
Canada
Tel.: (613) 236-0028
Fax: (613) 236-1139
bolcan@biosphere.net

**Embassy of the Republic of Yugoslavia**
2134 Kalorama Road, NW
Washington, DC 20008
Tel.: (202) 332-0333
Fax: (202) 332-3933
Yuembusa@aol.com
http://www.yuembusa.org

**Embassy of the Republic of Yugoslavia**
5 Lexham Gardens
London W8 5JJ, UK
Tel.: (44) 207 7370 6105
Fax: (44) 207 7370 3838
londre@jugisek.demon.co.uk

**Embassy of the Republic of Yugoslavia**
17 Blackburn Avenue
Ottawa, Ontario K1N 8A2
Canada
Tel.: (613) 233-6289
Fax: (613) 233-7850
ottambyu@capitalnet.com
http://www.antic.org/ottambyu

**Embassy of Albania**
2100 S. Street, NW
Washington, DC 20008
Tel.: (202) 223-4942
Fax: (202) 628-7342

**Embassy of Albania**
4th Floor, 38 Grosvenor Gardens
London SW1W 0EB, UK
Tel.: (44) 207 730 5709
Fax: (44) 207 730 5747

THE BALKANS

## Getting Around

Bus and rail services throughout the former Yugoslavia are return-ing to prewar levels of efficiency, though comfort is not a priority. The rail network is also slowly coming back to life. You can hire cars, but bear in mind that Bosnians, in particular, still drive like someone is shooting at them.

## Dangerous Places

### The Balkans

Yes, we know it's a little wide-ranging advice-wise, but when was the last time you saw a Web site that proudly offered, instead of weather or fire hazards, color-coded tension indicators with little rotat-ing radar-sweep graphics?

**Balkan Web**
http://www.balkanweb.com

### Mitrovica

This town in northern Kosovo was described by UN envoy Richard Holbrooke as "the most dangerous city in Europe" in 1999, and has hardly improved since. Serbian and Albanian residents glare—and worse—at each other across the river, and the Serb-held northern end of the city is all but a no-go area for UN police, 16 of whom were injured in clashes in March 2002.

http://www.kosovska.mitrovica.s5.com

### Republika Srpska

This dismal swamp is all that remains of the absurd dream of an eth-nically pure Greater Serbia once espoused by Milosevic, Karadzic, and their fellow travelers, and is more depressing than genuinely danger-ous. Citizens of NATO countries are still not tremendously popular here, but you'll be okay as long as you're prepared to endure inter-minable slivovitz-soaked rants from the locals about the perfidies of Americans, Muslims, Britons, Croats, and everybody else who doesn't agree with them, and mercilessly detailed explanations of how nothing that went wrong is at all the fault of anyone who is in any way Serbian.

http://www.srpska.com/

### Albania

To make such a mess of a country in the heart of Europe with direct access to the Mediterranean requires an incompetence that verges on

## DON'T CRY FOR ME ARKAN-TINA

In June 2002, Svetlana Raznatovic Ceca, the widow of assassinated thug Zeljko Raznatovic, aka Arkan, held Serbia's biggest-ever music concert for 100,000 fans in Markana Stadium in Belgrade. Ceca is a "turbo-folk" musician and Serbia's biggest star. Ceca dedicated the show to her late husband. So who exactly was this great man, who inspired such touching sentiment?

Arkan was shot in the left eye (ouch) on January 15, 2000 by a single, masked gunman in the lobby of the Intercontinental Hotel in Belgrade. Arkan was wanted for bank robberies in Western Europe and had been indicted for war crimes. A Serbian, he operated a private militia called the Tigers who terrorized and executed Bosnians and Croats as part of the Serb's policy of ethnic cleansing. He was one of the region's wealthiest individuals—wealth he allegedly acquired from crime and war profiteering. In a fitting tribute, British Prime Minister Robin Cook had this emotional and touching farewell: "Arkan lived violently, so it is no surprise that he died violently."

genius. Among European nations, Albania is at the bottom of the league in every measure, aside possibly from unlicensed gun ownership.

After World War II, Albania became a sort of Balkan North Korea, under the all-pervasive stewardship of the sensationally insane Enver Hoxha. Hoxha, convinced that marauding forces from either west or east were poised to invade Albania—like anyone would want to—dotted more than 150,000 concrete self-defense bunkers around the country, and built lots of statues of himself. He died in 1985, which should have been the more or less perfect cue for Albania to emerge from the grip of communism along with its Eastern European neighbors in the late 1980s.

Instead, things got worse. The succession of crooks, chancers, and outright idiots whom Albanians elected to power managed to make the poorest country in Europe even poorer; all that kept Albania more or less viable was remittances from those of its people who'd done the sensible thing and legged it, legally or otherwise, to America or Europe.

In February 1997, Albania finally stopped being a Balkan North Korea and became a Balkan Somalia instead. Thousands and thousands of Albanians had invested their meager savings in an assortment of pyramid schemes—so many of them that in the mid-'90s, Albania's economy recorded growth rates of between 8.3 and 13.3 percent. It looked great on paper, but paper was about the only asset any of the pyramids owned. The pyramids collapsed. Over half of Albania's GDP—$1.2 billion—vanished into the ether, or into the Swiss bank accounts of some Albanian ministers. The country went berserk.

As Albania's ex-Yugoslav neighbors had already demonstrated, when Balkan nations go berserk, they do it in some style. The people stormed military armories—so many guns were available that an AK-47 could be bought in Tirana for three dollars—and used the spoils to rob anything else they thought might be of value (if they found anything of the sort in Albania, they should have written to Ripley). Not a few of these weapons found their way over the border into Kosovo, to the nascent Kosovo Liberation Army.

The fracas eventually subsided, either due to the presence of Italian peacekeepers or because there was nothing left to steal, and then Milosevic realized there was still one part of the country he'd been elected president of that he hadn't managed to start a war with yet, and set about Albania's kinfolk in Kosovo. When NATO tried to stop him, half a million Kosovars fled over the border into northern Albania, abruptly increasing Albania's population by an eighth, and doing for the national economy what burying does for a corpse—though a few hotel owners in Kukes made a tidy fortune out of the influx of Western media coming the other way, and a few enterprising local hillbillies made sudden and profitable forays into the secondhand laptop, video camera, and outside broadcast-vehicle markets.

Today, Albania is the basket case's basket case—a country that defies solutions or even politically correct supporters. Albania is flat broke and more or less lawless, aside from the ancient rites of tribal loyalty and blood feud set out in the 15th-century Laws of Lek. To the extent that Albania is now run at all, it is by the international community.

To this day *DP* gets dozens of fractured-English death threats from Albanians who insist that our stories of bunny-eared bandits (from wearing panty hose with legs for masks at checkpoints) were not true. We thought the guy with masking tape on his forehead had the best disguise. You'll have to find a copy of *DP4* to get the joke.

http://www.albanian.com/main

## Dangerous Things

### Land Mines

Don't stand on any part of the former Yugoslavia that you are not absolutely sure about—nobody really knows how many mines are scattered about the region, but all the estimates have a lot of zeros on the end of them, and you only have to tread on one for it to ruin your whole trip. NATO's promiscuous use of depleted uranium munitions during the 1999 war hasn't helped. A report by the United Nations Environment Program in 2002 found "widespread, but low-level" contamination—probably not enough to make you glow in the dark, but certainly sufficient to encourage you to stick to bottled water.

## Crime

Organized crime is rampant in Kosovo, and not quite as rampant as it used to be in Serbia. Unless you stick your nose in too far, it shouldn't bother you. There is, however, a fair bit of disorganized crime as well, and a lot of enterprising people who know how to use machine guns. Avoid driving at night, and don't take anything that you absolutely can't live without.

http://www.crisisweb.org/projects/program.cfm?typeid=3
http://www.motherjones.com/total_coverage/kosovo/layne2.html

## Being or Sounding Serbian

There used to be 200,000 Serbs in Kosovo. There are now maybe 20,000. Old scores are still being settled, and angry mobs are not known for their clearheaded common sense: In 1999, a Bulgarian UN worker was beaten and shot dead on Mother Teresa Street in Pristina when a group of teenagers asked him the time and he replied in Serbian. So if you can speak Serbian, don't.

**Official Web site of the Serbian Orthodox Diocese of Raska and Prizren**
http://www.kosovo.com

## Conspiracy Theories

Even liberal Serbs are slow to come to grips with the idea that maybe their country just got bombed because their president was a jerk and everyone else was sick of him. In recent visits to Belgrade, *DP* has been told all of the following by people who appeared to be serious: NATO is the military wing of the Albanian mafia (as if the West went to war to protect the bootleg Marlboros racket of someone called Enver); the whole thing was a romantic overture aimed at KLA commander Hasim Thaci by then-U.S. Secretary of State Madeleine Albright (under Milosevic, Belgrade was covered with abusive, government-sponsored posters of Albright, while Clinton and Blair were ignored); Milosevic

## PHOTO OPPORTUNITIES

In May 2002, the Macedonian interior minister, Ljube Boskovski, wounded four bystanders when he decided to have a go at a grenade-launcher during a public exercise by police commandos. Boskovski fired a grenade into a rock, showering onlookers with shrapnel. "Such things happen," said Boskovski, apparently unaware that everywhere else in the world they really kind of don't.

and/or NATO deliberately flooded Belgrade with weapons-grade Albanian hash to keep the population soft (an idea often floated as another Kalashnikov-sized reefer was being lit, usually without any visible coercion from government agents); Milosevic was working for America all along (a popular anti-Milosevic postcard showed Slobo shaking hands with Albright, above the caption *Vodi ga kuci*—"Take him home."). And, of course, who could forget the West's *Wag the Dog* fever and theories of WWIII, the U.S./oil conspiracy, etc.

http://www.bible-prophecy.com/warbalkans.htm

## Getting Sick

It won't hurt to take your own medical kit, but healthcare throughout the Balkans is pretty good—they've had plenty of practice—and English-speaking doctors aren't too hard to find. The exceptions are Kosovo and Albania. In the former, throw yourself on the mercy of the nearest NGO. In the latter, call your embassy.

## Nuts and Bolts

Take dollars and euros (the latter runs as a currency alongside the Croatian Kuna), Bosnian convertible mark (KM) and the Yugoslav dinar. In Pristina, everyone stays at the Grand Hotel (tel.: (381) 38 20 211). In Belgrade, forsake the standard-issue five-star leviathans (they're all miles out of town anyway) for the Hotel Splendid which, though its rooms and guests are somewhat dilapidated, is cheap and unbeatably located (tel.: (381) 11 323 5444, office@splendid.co.yu, singles from $30). In Sarajevo, the Holiday Inn (tel.: (387) 33 28 8000, holiday@bih.net.ba, singles from around $80) has had most of the more-picturesque shrapnel damage fixed, but retains its mystique as one of the 20th century's definitive war-zone hotels. Electricity is 220V.

http://www.intelbrief.com/balkans.htm

*Embassy Locations*

**U.S. Embassy, Belgrade**
Kneza Milosa 50
11000 Belgrade
Republic of Yugoslavia
Tel.: (381) 11 361 9344
Fax: (381) 11 361 5497
http://www.usemb-belgrade.rpo.at

**British Embassy, Belgrade**
Resavska 46
11000 Belgrade
Republic of Yugoslavia

Tel.: (381) 11 64 5055
Fax: (381) 11 65 9651
ukembbg@eunet.yu

**Canadian Embassy, Belgrade**
Kneza Milosa 75
11000 Belgrade
Republic of Yugoslavia
Tel.: (381) 11 64 4666
Fax: (381) 11 64 1480

**U.S. Embassy, Skopje**
Ilinden
Skopje, Republic of Macedonia
Tel.: (389) 2 116 180
Fax: (389) 2 117 103
http://usembassy.mpt.com.mk
irs@usembassy.mpt.com.mk

**British Embassy, Skopje**
Dimitrija Chupovski 26, 4th Floor
Skopje 1000
Republic of Macedonia
Tel.: (389) 2 116 772
Fax: (389) 2 117 555
info@britishembassy.org.mk
http://www.britishembassy.org.mk

**Canadian Consulate, Skopje**
Udarna Brigada 12
Skopje 91000
Republic of Macedonia
Tel.: (389) 91 23 3453
Fax: (389) 91 11 7550

**U.S. Embassy, Sarajevo**
Hamdije Cemerlica 39
71000 Sarajevo
Bosnia and Herzegovina
Tel.: (387) 33 619-592
Fax: (387) 33 619-593
opabih@pd.state.gov
http://www.usis.com.ba

**U.S. Embassy Branch Office,
   Banja Luka**
Jovana Ducica 5
78000 Banja Luka
Bosnia and Herzegovina
Tel.: (387) 51 21 1500
Fax: (387) 51 21 1775

**U.S. Embassy Branch Office, Mostar**
Mostarskog Bataljona
88000 Mostar
Bosnia and Herzegovina
Tel.: (387) 36 58 0580
Fax: (387) 36 58 0581

**British Embassy, Sarajevo**
8 Tina Ujevica
7100 Sarajevo
Bosnia and Herzegovina
Tel.: (387) 33 44 4429
Fax: (387) 33 66 6131
Britemb@bih.net.ba
http://www.britishembassy.ba

**British Embassy office, Banja Luka**
8 Simeuna Dzaka
Banja Luka
Bosnia and Herzegovina
Tel.: (387) 51 21 2395
Fax: (387) 51 21 6842
beo-bl@inecco.net

**U.S. Embassy, Tirana**
Rruga Elbasanit 103
Tirana
Albania
Tel.: (355) 4 24 7285
Fax: (355) 4 23 2222
http://www.usemb-tirana.rpo.at

**British Embassy, Tirana**
Rruga Skenderbej N12
Tirana
Albania
Tel.: (355) 42 34 973
Fax: (355) 42 47 697

**U.S. gov. office, Pristina**
Nazim Hikmet 30
Pristina
Kosovo
Tel.: (381) 38 54 9516
Fax: (381) 38 54 9890
irc_pristina@pd.state.gov
http://www.usofficepristina.usia.co.at

**British gov. office, Pristina**
Xhemail Kada 37
Dragodani 1
Pristina
Kosovo
Tel.: (381) 38 54 9559
Fax: (381) 38 54 9779
pristina.fco@gtnet.gov.uk

# Dangerous Days

| | |
|---|---|
| **5/31/02** | Yugoslav parliament votes to abolish Yugoslavia and replace it with a confederation to be known as the Republic of Serbia and Montenegro. |
| **6/28/01** | Milosevic extradited to the UN War Crimes Tribunal at The Hague to face charges of crimes against humanity. |
| **4/1/01** | Milosevic arrested and taken for questioning on charges of abuse of power and financial corruption. |
| **10/5/00** | Milosevic forced from office by uprising in Belgrade. |
| **9/23/00** | Presidential election in Yugoslavia. Opposition leader Vojislav Kostunica claims victory. Milosevic insists on second round of voting. Massive protests begin in Belgrade. |
| **1/15/00** | Serbian paramilitary commander and gangster Arkan shot dead in Belgrade's Intercontinental Hotel. |
| **6/12/99** | Russian troops enter Pristina three hours before arrival of NATO troops. |
| **6/10/99** | Serb troops begin withdrawal and bombing campaign is suspended. |
| **6/9/99** | NATO and Serb commanders agree on withdrawal schedule and terms. |
| **6/7/99** | NATO and Serb commanders fail to agree on terms of pullout. Talks suspended. |
| **6/3/99** | Belgrade accepts peace plan proposed by Russian and EU envoys. |
| **5/29/99** | Two Australian aid workers are convicted in Belgrade of spying and are jailed. |
| **5/22/99** | NATO bombs KLA barracks a day after it was visited by the international press. |
| **5/10/99** | Belgrade says it is withdrawing troops from Kosovo. Western powers dismiss the statement. |
| **5/7/99** | NATO bombs Chinese embassy. Three Chinese journalists are killed. |
| **4/14/99** | NATO mistakenly bombs convoy of Kosovar refugees near Djakovica. |
| **4/1/99** | Three captured and bruised U.S. soldiers appear on Serb television. |
| **3/24/99** | NATO launches cruise-missile and bombing attacks over Kosovo and Yugoslavia. |
| **3/23/99** | Serb parliament rejects NATO demands to send peacekeepers into Kosovo. |

| | |
|---|---|
| 3/20/99 | All 1,380 OSCE monitors withdraw from Kosovo. Yugoslav army reinforcements arrive. |
| 3/18/99 | Kosovar Albanians sign international peace deal in Paris. Serbs boycott the event. |
| 3/15/99 | Peace talks resume in Paris. |
| 3/11/99 | U.S. House of Representatives backs deployment of U.S. troops in Kosovo as part of peacekeeping operation. |
| 2/6/99 | Talks held at Rambouillet, France. Milosevic refuses NATO deployment. KLA refuses to disarm. |
| 1/18/99 | UN war-crimes prosecutor Louise Arbour refused entry to Kosovo to investigate. |
| 1/16/99 | 45 ethnic Albanians massacred at Racak by Serb forces. |
| 10/27/98 | Serb security forces withdraw en masse; NATO reverses decision to use air strikes. |
| 10/24/98 | UN Security Council authorizes deployment of OSCE monitors in Kosovo to verify end of fighting. |
| 10/13/98 | U.S. envoy Richard Holbrooke outlines deal to avoid air strikes. NATO gives Milosevic four days to end offensive. |
| 10/1/98 | Series of killings of ethnic Albanians at hands of Serb forces reported. |
| 9/24/98 | NATO issues ultimatum to Milosevic to stop violence in Kosovo or face air strikes. |
| 8/16/98 | Serb forces announce capture of last rebel stronghold, the mountain town of Junik. |
| 3/22/98 | Kosovars vote for president and parliament. Serb authorities dismiss polls as illegal. |
| 2/98 | Milosevic sends troops to Kosovo. |
| 2/97 | Collapse of Albanian pyramid schemes is followed by mass looting of national armories. |
| 12/96 | Three months of street protests in Belgrade follow Milosevic's fixing of municipal elections. Protests evaporate when Milosevic returns the elections to opposition parties, and protestors start arguing among themselves. |
| 12/14/95 | Peace agreement between Serbs, Croats, and Bosnians signed in Paris; four years of war in Bosnia have killed at least 200,000 people and made nearly 6 million homeless. |
| 12/4/95 | First NATO peacekeepers arrive in Sarajevo. |
| 9/21/95 | Peace talks in Dayton to discuss Bosnia and Herzegovina. |
| 9/20/95 | Siege of Sarajevo ends. |

| | |
|---|---|
| **8/30/95** | NATO aircraft begin attacking Serbian positions around Sarajevo. |
| **7/11/94** | Bosnian Serbs seize UN "safe area" Srebrenica. Thousands of Bosnian Muslims subsequently massacred. |
| **3/18/94** | Bosnians and Croats sign peace accord. |
| **2/28/94** | NATO uses force on the battlefield for the first time, shooting down four Serb aircraft over Bosnia. |
| **3/93** | Fighting between Croats and Bosnians breaks out in parts of Bosnia not already held by Bosnian Serbs. |
| **4/92** | Siege of Sarajevo begins. |
| **2/29/92** | Bosnia and Herzegovina declares independence; Bosnian Serbs declare independence from Bosnia and Herzegovina. |
| **12/19/91** | Croatia's Serb population declares its region, Krajina, independent. |
| **6/27/91** | Fighting between Croats and Serbs breaks out in Croatia. |
| **6/25/91** | Croatia and Slovenia declare independence. Yugoslav army attacks Slovenia. |
| **1989** | Kosovo is stripped of its autonomy inside the Yugoslav Federation by Milosevic. |
| **1987** | Little-known Serbian Communist Party hack Slobodan Milosevic makes rabble-rousing speech to Serbs in Kosovo, promising "Nobody will dare to beat you again!" |
| **1980** | Tito dies. |
| **1974** | Yugoslav constitution grants Kosovo autonomy. |
| **1946** | Yugoslavia created under rule of former anti-Nazi partisan leader, Marshal Josip Broz Tito. |
| **1941** | Yugoslavia invaded by Germany and Italy. Croatia becomes pro-Nazi puppet state. |
| **1929** | Kingdom of Serbs, Croatians, and Slovenes changes name to Yugoslavia. |
| **1918** | Kingdom of Serbs, Croatians, and Slovenes founded. |
| **6/28/14** | Archduke Franz Ferdinand of Austria assassinated in Sarajevo by Serbian nationalist Gavrilo Princip, triggering World War I. |
| **1389** | Serbs under the command of Prince Lazar defeated at battle of Kosovo Polje by Ottoman Turks. |

THE BALKANS

★ ★ ★ ★ ★

# CHECHNYA (ICHKERIA)

Grozny

## Howling Wolf

The Chechens have been conquered, neglected, abused, and banished by everyone from the Ak Koyonlu and the Horde of the White Sheep to Georgian-boy-turned-snuffmeister, Joey Stalin. During World War II, Stalin stuffed the Chechens in boxcars and sent them to Siberia and northern Kazakhstan (along with the Tartars) for being German collaborators. Well, they weren't, but, hey, a dictator can never be too careful, you know. So it's not surprising the Chechens have a mean streak as wide as the mountainous border that divides the southern part of their country. After they were repatriated by Kruschev in the '50s, the Chechens, hardened and without any means of earning a living, set about forming the largest criminal gangs in the former Soviet Union.

Keep in mind that in Russia, one has to be careful about calling someone a crook. The Chechens were as far from the Marxist, there-is-no-God, one-size-fits-all Soviet model as a people could have been. And then there is that sense of the world's complete ignorance of the Chechen people because most of the news about them comes from Mother Russia. First, Chechens aren't even Chechen. They are Nuokhchi, or sons of Noah. They speak a unique language, Nakh; they are Muslim; they are more entrepreneurial than Donald Trump; and they are tougher than a hungover hockey team. More important, they have kept their national identity intact. Chechen loyalties are to one of the more than 100 *teips*, or clans, that constitute Chechen society, not to the fat-bottomed thieves in the Kremlin. Think of teips as being similar to the city-states of Athens or mafia families. They are divisive and warring in peacetime and unified and brotherly in war. Left to their own devices, and sitting on the nexus of the east and west, the Chechens have always thought and acted just like the lone wolf that has become their national symbol. The Russians consider them the toughest, baddest ethnic group in the former Soviet Union, so the brutal, duplicitous, and forgetful Russian bear has attacked, raped, and pillaged its way into the Chechen's homeland on a regular basis.

But bears don't kill wolves; packs of wolves kill bears. Russians are quick to accuse the Chechens of blowing up apartments, running drugs, hijacking airliners and school buses, and other crimes, and then hotfooting it back to Chechnya to hide out in their inaccessible mountain villages. So *DP* thought it was strange that the news media were quick to recast the ornery Chechens as the heroic-defenders-of-their-homeland underdogs in the West in the '94–'96 war. Most of the war was simply *contractistyas* hired by the Russian army to start a phony revolution inside newly liberated Chechnya. Despite the underhanded tactics, the Chechens fought back and decided to make good use of the Soviet breakup. Although Russia was eager (or forced) to let other nations go, they wanted Chechnya bad, for the region sits on a fair-sized oil reserve and is a strategic link between the Caspian and Black seas. They lost Georgia, on the other side of the Caucasus Mountains, and they weren't going to lose Chechnya. Russian Defense Minister Pavel S. Grachev boasted that a single paratroop regiment would need only a couple of hours to wipe out the rebellion. Darth Vader he ain't. Outnumbered by five (more likely ten) to one, the Chechen irregulars, along with Islamic volunteers, waged a guerrilla war from the moun-

> **D***P* thought it was strange that the news media were quick to recast the ornery Chechens as the heroic-defenders-of-their-homeland underdogs.

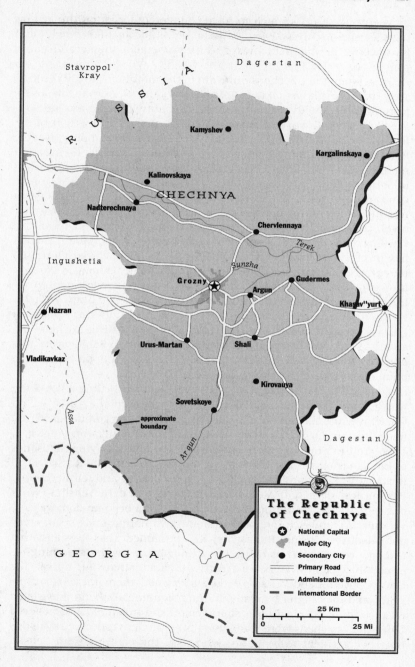

The Republic
of Chechnya

- ⊗ National Capital
- Major City
- ● Secondary City
- — Primary Road
- Administrative Border
- – – International Border

0        25 Km
0        25 Mi

tains. The Russians seemed to have completely forgotten the lessons they learned in Afghanistan, as their forces hid in their newly built forts along the major highways using vulnerable supply and patrol convoys.

Then when the Chechens came out of the mountains to kill the Russians in Grozny, it was all over. It was a story the Western media loved: peasants armed with sticks and shovels defiantly dancing around bonfires in central Grozny, seemingly holding off the entire might of the Russian bear. Wolf-like Chechen fighters, unshaven and dirty, waving their flag while strafing fighters soared overhead, turning their Parliament building into Swiss cheese. Meanwhile, the largest, most powerful army in Europe turned out to be shivering, underfed, stoned, confused, and mostly prepubescent rabble. Although the vastly superior Russian forces eventually took the Chechen capital in February 1995, they faced a low-budget Afghanistan for the next 20 months. The Chechen insurgents—many of them former Soviet soldiers trained in mountain guerrilla fighting—dug into the hills and waged a long and fierce battle of attrition against an undisciplined, underaged band of Moscow's best. The Russian army set up a puppet government while the rebels regrouped in the hills. Around 1,500 to 3,000 Chechen fighters (in three groups) fought this pocket *gazavat*, or holy war. Dzhokhar Dudayev ran his tiny rebel army from his "secret" base in Roshni-Chu, about 45 minutes south of Grozny, until in April 1996 Dudayev was killed by a Russian air-to-ground missile that homed in on his satellite phone in a clearing 20 miles southeast of Grozny.

Despite the loss of the charismatic Dudayev, in February 1995 the Russian army needed 38,000 troops just to keep the rusty lid on Chechnya, and the interior ministry had deployed an additional 15,500 men. But an aggressive drive by the Chechen fighters on August 6, 1996 (Yeltsin's inauguration day), reversed the war, driving thousands of Russian troops and civilians out of Grozny. It seems the Russians had never controlled anything, including their drinking and self-deception. When (now-deceased) Alexander Lebed was sent in by Yeltsin to work out a cease-fire, he found Russian soldiers had become demoralized, vanquished, and lice-ridden weaklings. Two daring raids by Basayev and Raduyev inside Russia quickly reminded the Russians that Moscow was only a bus ticket and a bribe away for these nothing-to-lose holy warriors. A peace treaty was hammered out, but as the Chechen commander told *DP*, Lebed warned them they had three years, and they better be ready. In the meantime all the money slated for rebuilding Chechnya was siphoned off and stolen. So in October of 1999, the Chechens were ready for another underhanded betrayal, this time by president-to-be Putin, who took the controls from Yeltsin.

More than a hundred thousand Russian troops rolled southward, fueled by promises of quick victory and a budget bump from higher oil prices. On paper it looked good: Russian tanks swept through miles of flat northern plains encircling cities, letting innocent civilians escape, pounding them to rubble, and then declaring victory. In reality, the Russian tactic was to declare victory and then pound innocent civilians into rubble.

The second war turned out pretty much like a bigger-budget remake of the first war: a few billion dollars, 150,000 troops, more fireworks, more rhetoric, and more dead. The Russians had learned media spin from ex–CIA director Bush, Sr. and his Gulf War. No journos were allowed (except on escorted military tours) to cover the war. Few, if any, journos dared to cover the war from the rebel side, terrified of very real stories of kidnapping, murder, and deceit. Meanwhile, the Russians pounded their own people (mostly elderly, poor Russians who had retired to cheaper digs in Grozny) while claiming victory against terrorists. *DP* was in the bunkers with the "terrorists," eating pumpkin pancakes and wondering why the media didn't give a damn about "another war in Europe," ethnic cleansing, or even the civilian deaths that happened every day.

> **D**P was in the bunkers with the "terrorists," eating pumpkin pancakes and wondering why the media didn't give a damn about "another war in Europe," ethnic cleansing, or even the civilian deaths that happened every day.

Why would a bankrupt country declare war on its own people? Forget oil, forget the *mafiya*, forget global strategy, forget Islamic fundamentalists, forget all that strategic trans-Caucasian gobbledygook. The war in Chechnya is simply about Putin trying to hold on to the frayed tatters of the Soviet pipe dream. Chechnya is just one of a cluster of tiny southern republics that don't want to be under the skirts of Mother Russia. War has always been the way to keep Russians complaining about something other than the corrupt government.

What is so stunning is the classic Russian skullduggery that supports this war. It took a while (four months) for Yeltsin backers to figure out that Putin needed something more than his lack of charisma to get elected in 2000. So, voilà—nasty apartment bombings (nicely and transparently engineered by Putin's buds at the FSB) and Russian attacks on Dagestani villages designed to flush out Basayev and his trigger-happy volunteers. So it's *Wag the Wolf* time. Ex-spy Putin took a page from ex-spy Bush and ex-caught-in-the-bush Clinton to create the most media-blind event since the Gulf War. Cries were heard of "Smash the Chechen Terrorists!" when in truth it was "Bomb the Old

Russian People!" It became a pathetic game of hyperbole versus reality: Defend Freedom! (lock up the journos), Save Chechens! (mass graves), War without Casualties! (bury the civilians deeper), and so on.

For now, Chechnya is easily the most dangerous place on earth . . . for its citizens. The odd aid workers who dare to operate in the area are usually kidnapped by Russian-directed gangs, and journos, who are immediately thought to be prorebel for risking their lives to enter Chechnya and defy the Russians, are still waiting to tell their tales of misery. For now the Russian army engages in wholesale ethnic cleansing under the guise of their war on terrorism, just like Putin planned.

## The Scoop

In its own badly scripted and acted "War on Terror," Russia now has its own Vietnam and Afghanistan rolled into one. In an eerily parallel universe, Russia squanders lives and money to pursue "bandits" and "terrorists," while its army actually conducts ethnic cleansing, rape, pillaging, and other crimes. Perhaps the biggest crime may be the Russians' continual insistence that they are winning the war. When the second war began in the last three months of 1999, it is estimated that the Russians spent $2 billion. Others say the cost was lower since they were just dumping aging stockpiles of rockets, bombs, and missiles stored during the Cold War on top of old people, women, and children. Most agree that $4 billion has been spent to date.

These days the war costs around $40 million a day, kills around five to 20 people a day, and has made Grozny the most devastated city on earth (an honor once held by Kabul). Putin generously estimated it would cost $80 million to rebuild the country (this was back in 2000 when he also said the war was officially over). The little bit of money that did show up for reparations was stolen. A more accurate estimate was around $13 billion to rebuild just Grozny . . . after the first war. Since then, most major buildings have been reduced to sagging shells or rubble. The truth is nobody has the money to repair the damage caused by Russia in the last two wars.

The Chechen government's blasé pronouncement that "The war with Russia has been going on for centuries, usually every 50 years [with each war lasting] between six to 25 years," should give you some indication of how defeated the Chechens are.

*Newspapers and Weeklies*

**Chechen Press**
http://www.chechenpress.info/english

**Chechen Republic Online**
http://www.amina.com
http://www.qoqaz.com

**Ichkeria.org**
http://www.ichkeria.org/indexen.html

**Radio Liberty/Crisis in Chechnya Group**
http://www.rferl.org/nca/special/chechnya

**Chechnya News**
http://www.chechnyanews.com

**Gazeta.ru**
http://www.gazeta.ru

**Izvestiya**
http://www.izvestia.ru

## The Players

### Vladimir Putin

This is Putin's war. The Russian and Chechen people have long given up on making sense of his brutal and destructive game plan. He is a man described as short, dour, evasive, and far too eager to appear tough. Putin (b. October 7, 1952) sports a rat-like, glowering persona that is the opposite of Yeltsin's corpulent, drunken, "who-wants-to-party?" style. The problem is that they are backed by the same people. Yeltsin was a greedy lush and acted accordingly. Putin ("whore" or "pudding" in a number of languages) was a calculating spy and, accordingly, that guides his actions. Putin sees great treachery in Chechnya and would rather turn it into a parking lot (well, that's not quite accurate; the Russians wouldn't actually pave it) than negotiate. He talks and acts tough, some say so that the military doesn't dump him. Others say he is a mean, vindictive SOB and likes to have an enemy to give him (and the Russian people) something to focus their anger on so they don't realize how miserable their future is. Or, if you would like the Chechen view of Putin (from an avowed and now-dead terrorist), "The problem with Putin, is that he is very small. So the distance from his heart to his asshole is too little." Looks like we won't see many hugs and kisses anytime soon.

http://president.kremlin.ru
http://www.geocities.com/CapitolHill/Parliament/5160/Putin

### Boris Nikolayevich Yeltsin

You can blame much of the misery in Russia on Boris (b. 1931). He was the one who let the new spirit of democracy and capitalism run amok. Yeltsin let the oligarchy rob the government of its assets, and then he robbed the people blind. He was also at the helm when the two wars on Chechnya proved that (round one) the Russian government was militarily bankrupt, and (round two) morally bankrupt.

> **W**ith Boris's liver now looking like the houses in Grozny, it is up to favorite son Putin to eagerly bang the war drum and deflect attention from Russia's muddy slide into oblivion.

The first time he was at the helm, he was mad as hell and wasn't going to take it anymore. But Boris had forgotten that the massive army of Stalin and Brezhnev was long gone. When Boris pushed the button to declare war, all he got was a bunch of sparks and fizzles (he supplied the gas). The second time he took a page right out of former U.S. President Clinton's *Wag the Dog* playbook, except Boris was benched by the money boys and Putin the Punisher was fielded to score the touchdown. Feeling the heat of embezzlement accusations and personal wrongdoing, Boris swapped ex-spook Putin a "Get Out of Jail Free" card and lived to keep his swindled millions. With Boris's liver now looking like the houses in Grozny, it is up to favorite son Putin to eagerly bang the war drum and deflect attention from Russia's muddy slide into oblivion.

http://www.infoplease.com/ce6/people/A0853041.html

## The Chechens

No matter what happens, who wins, or who claims to be in charge, the Chechens will endure. The Chechens say they sprang from Shem, the son of Noah. They are mountain-bred and mean as scorpions when riled up. Normally, the Chechens are an unaligned assortment of major clans that are constantly jockeying for influence and shifting alliances with other clans. They should not be confused with the typical Muslim—they are not predominantly fundamentalists. Each clan is led by a spiritual mystic. Some adhere to a Sufi mystic branch of Sunni Islam called Muridism. This branch of Islam divides its followers into sects led by local feudal leaders. They are united only in their opposition to domination by outsiders. About half of Chechens belong to Sufi brotherhoods, or *tariqas*. The two Sufi tariqas that spread in the North Caucasus were the Naqshbandiya and the Qadiriya.

The Naqshbandiya in the North Caucasus is particularly strong in Dagestan and eastern Chechnya, whereas the Qadiriya has most of its adherents in the rest of Chechnya and Ingushetia. Basayev and his foreign volunteers, formerly led by Khattab, defended and controlled the eastern part of Chechnya. There are plenty of elements of mysticism mingled with Islam in these remote mountain areas.

## The Teips

Above all this are the teips, or clans. The teips are based more on land than on blood and have an uneasy relationship in peacetime, but are bonded together during war. Of course, it's not quite that simple. Commanders can be aligned to teips, religions, political allegiance, governments, business sponsors, mafia groups, relatives, financial deals, or a mixture of all of these. During the war, the Chechens' military chain of command is like a pickup basketball game working toward a grand plan. If units of irregulars met up with each other, it was purely by happenstance. They go out and fight, then come back to eat and sleep. The fighters buy their own weapons, use Russian conscripts for target practice, and are about as coordinated as a demolition derby, but they are also equally as destructive and resourceful. The man with the plan is Aslan Maskhadov, but the man with the juice is Basayev, who makes up for his lack of diplomatic skills by his ability to turn any firefight into a Russian bloodbath. And while you ponder this, also remember that Chechens are Europeans.

**Naqshbandi**
http://www.naqshbandi.org

## Shamil Basayev

Basayev is the million-dollar man and maybe the last man standing (well, limping at least). The Russians think Basayev is worth a million dead or alive; Basayev thinks it's an insult—he figures he is worth much more. Shamil Basayev was born in 1963 in Vedeno. Vedeno is famous for the fortress where the great Chechen leader Iman Shamyl surrendered to Russian forces 100 years earlier. He has two wives and moves around quite a bit. He has three brothers, one of whom was killed during the fighting in Vedeno at the beginning of 1995. An older brother, Shirvani Basayev, was a commandant of the city of Bamut. In 1987, Basayev enrolled at the Moscow Institute of Land-Tenure Regulations Engineers. In August 1991, in one of history's stranger events, he defended Boris Yeltsin with a couple of hand grenades during the takeover of the White House in Moscow. In 1991, he returned to Chechnya from Russia and joined the Confederation of the People of the Caucasus (KHK), working his way up to commander in 1992. In August of that year, Basayev fought in Abkhazia against the Georgians and Russians, and he also fought alongside the Azerbaijanis in Nagorno-Karabakh. He went to Afghanistan between April and July 1994 for training at the Khowst camps. In the summer of 1994, he fought at Dzhokhar Dudayev's side.

Basayev's most famous action was on June 14, 1995, when he took the hospital in the city of Budyonnousk, Russia. His goal was to destroy Yeltsin's credibility at the upcoming June 16 G-7 Summit in Halifax, Canada, but he says he was actually on his way to Moscow but ran out of bribe money. During the standoff with 150 heavily armed Chechens, an old woman walked up to the Chechens in the hospital and asked them the name of the movie they were shooting. It got weirder. On the 18th, Victor Chernomyrdin, the Russian prime minister, appeared live on Russian television to conduct hostage negotiations with Basayev.

Basayev's daring raid worked, and the process of peace negotiations began. In April 1996, he was elected commander of the armed forces of the Chechen Republic.

In December 1996, he left the post of the commander in order to be a candidate for president of the Chechen Republic in forthcoming elections. On January 27, 1997, he pulled in only 23.5 percent of the vote, finishing in second place behind the winner, Aslan Maskhadov. Then, in late 1997, Maskhadov issued a decree appointing Shamil Basayev acting premier for the duration of Maskhadov's trip to Turkey. Shamil Basayev had just resumed his post of first deputy premier. (Since Basayev had submitted his resignation from the post back in the summer, Maskhadov refused to sign the decree on Basayev's resignation.) In early December, President Aslan Maskhadov announced that he would transfer some of his authority as premier to First Vice Premier Shamil Basayev. On January 1, 1998, Maskhadov dismissed his cabinet and tasked Basayev with forming a new government (with 22 ministers instead of the former 45). Maskhadov expected to remain both the president and prime minister of Chechnya. However, Basayev was increasing his powers and influence, and let it be known he preferred to become Chechnya's prime minister. In August of 1999, when Russian units attacked Chechen villages in Dagestan, he and Khattab put together a crusading group of fighters to push back the Russians. This was one of the triggers of the 1999–2000 war, along with the apartment bombings that Moscow blamed on the Chechens (but never actually proved). He lost his right foot in the February 2000 retreat from Grozny and although the Russians regularly report his demise, he is still fighting. In October 2002 Shamil admitted he was the engineer of the bloody Moscow theater takeover. He resigned all other posts and became "Commander of the Martyrs Reconnaissance and Sabotage unit." Stay tuned.

## Tamir Salih Suwailem, aka Omar Ibn-ul-Khattab

Basayev's now-departed commander, a diminutive but fierce bosom buddy (b. 1970 in Ar'ar, Saudi Arabia; d. April 2002), was a curly-locked, dark-skinned Bedouin named Khattab, an Emir (or Commander) of the Foreign Mujahideen Forces in the Caucasus. Khattab (his nom de guerre) had a Dagestani wife living in the settlement of Kara-Makhi in Dagestan. He had come from money. He had lost his last two fingers from his right hand when throwing a homemade grenade. He often wore a bandage or driving glove on his right hand. Although not as well known as Basayev, Khattab was a mujahideen's mujahid. He was also called "one-armed Akhmed" and "the Black Arab."

In 1987, when he was 18, he left the American High School in Jordan to begin his jihad in Jalalabad, Afghanistan. He was originally going to be a surgeon but became a mujahid instead. He fought in Tajikistan from 1993 to 1995 and then returned to Afghanistan, where he met Basayev. Khattab put together a group of volunteers and headed out to Chechnya. He took part in actions in several Persian Gulf countries against French and Israeli citizens. After the Russians retreated in the first war, Khattab set up a training camp during the winter of '96–'97. His training school was near the village of Serzhen-Yurt, Vedeno Rayon, where he and several of his senior veteran "Afghan" and "Bosnian" mujahideen taught black skills. He escaped an assassination attempt in June 1997 while driving a jeep near Benoy, some 70 kilometers south of the capital, Grozny. A remote-control land mine blew up, missing his jeep by seconds. Khattab was not hurt.

But Khattab's luck ran out in 2002. The mainstream Chechen leaders, particularly Maskhadov, had been publicly distancing themselves from Khattab since January 1997 (Khattab once fought under Maskhadov's command). Although he had escaped many a close call, Khattab was finally killed by a poisoned letter delivered by a close confidant.

http://www.qoqaz.net

## Aslan Maskhadov, President of Ichkeria

Born in Kazakstan in 1951 and raised in Zebir-Yurt, Maskhadov moved with his parents at the age of six to the Nadterechny district of the Chechen-Ingush Autonomous Republic. He graduated from the Tbilisi Higher Artillery College in 1972, and from the Kalinin Military Academy in Leningrad in 1981. He was a platoon commander in the Far East, and served in Hungary as a battery commander and then as a regiment commander. Soon he was a colonel in a missile and artillery force during the attempt to capture the television tower in Vilnius in January 1991, which was part of Soviet leader Mikhail Gorbachev's attempts to put down independence in the Baltics. After the breakup of the Soviet Union, Maskhadov served in the Chechen Armed Forces from 1992 to 1996. In December 1993, he was promoted to chief of staff and served as prime minister in the Chechen coalition government from October 1996 until January 1997. He is primarily responsible for hammering out an agreement with the Russians at Nazran in June 1996 and in Novye Atagi from June 28 to July 4, 1996. On August 31, 1996, following talks with former Russian Security Council Secretary Alexander Lebed, he signed the Khasavyurt agreements, buying time for Chechnya. He was unceremoniously replaced in the government during the fall of 1999 as Russian troops invaded what used to be his country.

Maskhadov became Chechnya's president as a result of the January 1997 elections. Maskhadov is a moderate and perhaps the man best suited to restore some semblance of order to Chechnya. Maskhadov was grudgingly endorsed by Moscow as the least of a dozen evils, something that has caused the split between his group and the more militant groups led by Basayev. He is revered by Chechens as a fighter and the man who won the Chechen war, and equally as a diplomat who ended it. Maskhadov is a good military strategist with the personality of a piece of cardboard. *DP* spent a few hours doing the obligatory interview and didn't get too much from him that would be considered profound. He had been elected by a large majority of Chechen voters and controls access into Chechnya, but not the main fighting force. That is when you must talk to the man who calls the shots: Basayev.

## The Lone Wolves

Pretty much every Chechen commander whom *DP* met inside Chechnya during the last war is now dead. They either died in the great retreat, were assassinated, or were killed in prison. *DP*'s host and head of security, Atigirov, died of kidney failure, er, sorry, leukemia, according to the Russians in August of 2002. Probably the last remaining bad boy (serving a life sentence in prison now and probably soon to come down with some terminal affliction) is Salman Raduyev. Raduyev is the poster boy for "Chechen extreme" and the son-in-law of the late Dudayev.

In January 1996, Dudayev led a lone wolf team in taking 3,000 hostages at a hospital in the Dagestan town of Kizlyar. Russian forces surrounded the village and pounded the rebels and hostages for several days before suffering the ultimate humiliation. Raduyev broke through the Russian perimeter with his fighters and 100 hostages and made a successful run for the Chechen town of Pervomayskaya. Although the Russians claimed one of its snipers killed him in March 1996, Raduyev returned to Chechnya in July and claimed responsibility for a series of trolley blasts in Moscow. Reporters noticed that Raduyev had lost his left eye in the March attack—he had been shot in the cheek and the bullet came out his eye (ouch)—and had gotten his mug rearranged by plastic surgeons in Europe after recuperating in the Middle East. He also escaped another assassination attempt in April 1997, although he was badly wounded when his car was blown up. Stallone and Schwarzenegger should take notes.

## Iman Shamyl

You would think Russia would have learned. This war is neither the first nor second conflict in Chechnya. Russia first conquered Chechnya and Dagestan between 1825 and 1859 and had to deal with a fighter named Iman Shamyl. He finally surrendered to Tsar Alexander II, but the fighting went on as Russian columns continued to be attacked in the 1860s. The North Caucasus resisted by force the imposition of Soviet rule between 1917 and 1921, with sporadic clashes continuing into the 1930s. Shamyl was known for daring raids behind Russian lines, fighting against massive odds, and oddly enough, for surrendering and living out his life in comfort in Russia.

## Dzhokhar Dudayev

Looking and acting surprisingly like Boris Badenov of *Rocky and Bullwinkle* fame, Dzhokhar (pronounced Jokar) Dudayev was a Muslim and a former general in the Soviet air force. He, like Massoud to the Afghans, or Ché to the Cubans, is also the latest symbolic martyr of the Chechen people. He was a member of the Myalkhir Hill Clan, a very unpopular clan among other Chechens. The Myalkhir Hill Clan is poor, feisty, and treacherous—sort of the Chechen equivalent of the U.S.'s white trash without the mobile homes.

Dudayev delivered on his promise of a *gazavat,* or holy war, when Moscow invaded his tiny gangster kingdom. Dudayev hated Russians (who weren't too fond of him either—even those opposed to the war and Boris Yeltsin alike). Dudayev's men, led by Basayev, were veterans of the war in Abkhazia, where they are mildly related to and were supportive of the 20-odd clans that are fighting the Russians there. Dudayev's son was killed during the Russian assault on Grozny.

Dzhokar Dudayev was elected president of the self-proclaimed Chechen Republic on a nationalist separatist platform in October 1991, and immediately told Russia to get lost. He knew the strategic and economic value of not only the pipelines but the smuggled contraband that crosses Chechnya. It took a year and a half for Moscow to figure out what to do about Dudayev. In April 1993, Dudayev disbanded the Chechen parliament. The next month, a series of skirmishes developed into war leading to heavy street fighting in Grozny during the summer of 1993. Moscow still hadn't figured out what to do, so they did what they do in all emerging fistfights—they bet on both sides. Both Chechen loyalists and Chechen independence groups used Russian equipment, soldiers, and mercenaries. The alliance that swung the tide was the Chechen mafia, which backed Dudayev and provided intel from corrupt intelligence officers and a flow of weapons. *DP* can confirm that Dudayev is dead, but his spirit is very much alive throughout Chechnya.

http://www.amina.com/article/did_nsa.html

## Monopoly

You know the game where you have to control all the little squares of real estate? . . . Well, it's the same basic idea here. Aslan Maskhadov considers access to the Caspian Sea to be "vitally necessary for Ichkeria." He wants to create an "imamate." The problem is, there is a place called Dagestan in the way. Basayev's attempts to declare Dagestan independent and toss out the Russians didn't work, and it appears the locals weren't too thrilled about being bombed and shelled. The Chechens also like the idea of the Black Sea being part of Ichkeria. The Chechens are cozy with Abkhazian rebels and it's conceivable that they could kick the Russian peacekeepers out.

Now what about Georgia, you say? Well, Georgia hates the Russians more than it hates the Abkhaz rebels or Chechens, so it's conceivable that there could be one fat, happy corridor from the Caspian to the Black Sea. The problem is that Russia has designs on getting Georgia back by hook or by crook. More likely by crook. In September of 2002, Putin had decided that there were "terrorists" in the Pankisi Gorge and timed his invasion/attack speech to coincide with Bush's urgent need to invade Iraq. Whoever wins would create a freeway for drugs, oil, smuggled goods, and whatever else needs to get from Afghanistan through Turkey and into Europe and Russia.

http://www.globalissues.org/Geopolitics/Chechnya.asp

## The Russian Army

The Russian army, since the tsarist era and through the Soviet period, has always relied on brute force and sheer numbers to win wars, which they haven't been doing a lot of recently. Tactically deficient, morally corrupt, and technologically marginal, the army has always relied on overpowering numbers of undertrained, underfed troops to take home battlefield trophies. Even during the Soviet era, there was little need to train elite commando units, as there weren't any uprisings for them to put down. By the time the Russian army was booted out of Grozny, its soldiers were lice-ridden and begging for food in the capital. To get through their roadblocks, all it took was a loaf of bread. If you threw in some Camel cigarettes or vodka, they'd roll out a red carpet and give you an armed escort (big deal). Even *DP*'s muj buddies could pay $1,400 to cross Russian lines to fight, and get a ride in the commander's car tossed in.

> Tactically deficient, morally corrupt, and technologically marginal, the army has always relied on overpowering numbers of undertrained, underfed troops to take home battlefield trophies.

CHECHNYA

# Getting In

Chechnya is currently a republic within Russia, but don't take any bets on how long it will last. Depending on what's going on, you need either a Russian visa or Chechen bodyguards (about 10 is a safe number). Right now it's only volunteers, stringers, and live-fast, die-young types who enter rebel-held Chechnya. *DP*'s Roddy Scott was killed on September 26, 2002, when caught in a Russian operation. Reporters are allowed to work in the country only during trips organized by the Chechen Interior Ministry. So, if you hang with the Russians, you won't get close to much. Ridiculous restrictions and permits are designed to keep journos out. For current information on visa requirements, U.S. citizens can contact the Russian consulates in New York, San Francisco, or Seattle, or the Russian embassy in Washington, DC:

**Russian Embassy Consular Division**
1825 Phelps Place NW
Washington, DC 20008
Tel.: (202) 939-8918, 939-8907, or 939-8913

Entry into Chechnya should only be attempted by journalists or aid groups with heavy protection. Journalists must get permission from the Chechen Interior Ministry, usually through Chechen contacts in Istanbul or Baltic countries. Today, journalists seeking entry into Chechnya or other information should contact one of the following representatives.

**Mr. Lyoma Usmanov**
Official Representative for the Chechen
  Republic in the United States
Tel.: (301) 588-5373
lyomaus@aol.com

**Ms. Dilshad Fakroddin**
ISCA
Tel.: (202) 661-4654
dilshad@islamicsupremecouncil.org

**IHH**
Macar Kardesler Caddesi Hulusi Noyan
Sokak No.23, Fatih Istanbul
Tel.:/Fax: (90) 212 631 3368
http://www.ihhvakf.org

# Getting Around

There is no way to get around safely in Chechnya until things improve dramatically. There is a very high threat of kidnapping (that means journalists). Journalists can only travel in Chechnya on escorted junkets and still run the risk of running into firefights, being bombed by any evil thing, or just being shot by a drunken Russian soldier.

## Dangerous Places ⎯⎯⎯⎯⎯⎯⎯⎯⎯⎯⎯⎯⎯⎯

### The Entire Country (and Then Some)

Military activity is not predictable and occurs in all regions without notice. This includes Dagestan, Ingushetia, and Georgia. The area is under martial law, if you could call it that. For those who like political subtlety, the area north of the Terek River is pro-Russian and does not grumble, the lowland middle of Chechnya is under heavy occupation, and all bets are off in the mountainous southwest. Grozny was blown to hell in the first war, then blown further to hell in the latest war. People do survive here, but only if you consider not being dead as surviving. Chechens are hospitable people and will always offer a stranger hospitality . . . unless, of course, you arrive on the back of a Russian troop carrier.

http://www.amina.com/maps

### Checkpoints

The Russians are fans of checkpoints. Soldiers will inspect your papers and even if they are in order will demand 50 to 100 rubles. If you are a foreigner or missing some magic invisible stamp, expect major grief until Uncle Ben (Franklin, that is) comes to the rescue. Frontline trips usually run a cool $1,000 (it makes no difference if you actually have or don't have official permission).

http://www.memo.ru/eng/memhrc/texts/blockpost.shtml
http://www.hrw.org/reports/2001/chechnya

### Russian Math

As we go to press, the official number of dead from the second (1999) war is approximately 4,500 Russian servicemen killed and more than 12,000 wounded. This tally conveniently does not include the 117 people killed when a giant MI-26 helicopter was shot down by a missile on August 19, 2002. It is also estimated that nearly 14,000 Chechen "terrorists" were killed. The Soldiers' Mothers of Russia group (who seem to have a problem finding their missing sons) say that the actual number of Russian soldiers killed is twice the government estimate.

http://groups.yahoo.com/group/chechnya-sl

### Being a Chechen Civilian

More than 80,000 civilians have been killed in or are missing from the first war. It remains to be seen how many have died in the second. Mass graves are uncovered on a weekly basis. Another 150,000 or so are refugees. Either Russian pilots are bad shots, or they feel the odds are

If you ever doubted that Chechens are tough, try humming a few bars of their national anthem:

## Death or Freedom

We were born at night when the She-wolf whelped
In the morning, under lions' howl, we were given our names
In eagles' nests our Mothers nursed us,
To tame bulls our Fathers taught us.

To people and Native Land we were devoted our Mothers,
And if they need us—we'll bravely rise
We grew up free, together with the mountain eagles,
Difficulties and obstacles we overcame with dignity.

Granite rocks will sooner melt like lead,
Than we shall lose our nobility in life and struggle.
The Earth will sooner be breached in the burning Sun,
Than we will be entombed in soil, our Honor lost,

Never we'll appear submissive before anybody,
Death or Freedom—we can choose only one way.
Our Sisters cure our wounds with their songs,
The eyes of our beloved raise us to the feats of arms.

If hunger gets us down—we'll gnaw the roots.
If thirst takes over us—we'll drink the grass dew.
We were born at night when the She-wolf whelped.
Nation, Native Land, and God,—we serve them only.

better at snuffing slower-moving unarmed civilians. Markets (bazaars), medical facilities, and civilian cars on the roadways (some sites were hit multiple times) were the Russians' favorite targets. The Russians like to attack funeral processions, busloads of children, and even empty roads. There are dozens of well-documented stories of missing people, rapes, robberies, summary executions, and other abuses. The more than 1 million Chechens who live outside of Chechnya (around 5 million that call the Caucasus their native land) provide much of the financial support that keeps the war going.

http://www.amina.com/people

### Being a Russian Civilian

Almost half the 20,000 to 40,000 people trapped and being bombarded inside Grozny in 1999 were Russians. Strangely, the Russian government estimates there were around 100 people. When Basayev took over a Russian hospital in Budyonnovsk in June 1995, the Russian special forces splattered dozens of screaming Russian hostages in their failed efforts to kill terrorists. It was much of the same story when Raduyev got busy in Kizliar in January 1996. Russian forces killed hundreds of Russians in their efforts to win them back.

http://www.hrw.org/wr2k2/europe16.html

## Dangerous Things ─────────────────────────────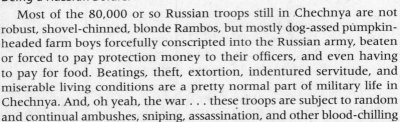

### Being a Russian Soldier

Most of the 80,000 or so Russian troops still in Chechnya are not robust, shovel-chinned, blonde Rambos, but mostly dog-assed pumpkin-headed farm boys forcefully conscripted into the Russian army, beaten or forced to pay protection money to their officers, and even having to pay for food. Beatings, theft, extortion, indentured servitude, and miserable living conditions are a pretty normal part of military life in Chechnya. And, oh yeah, the war . . . these troops are subject to random and continual ambushes, sniping, assassination, and other blood-chilling attacks. Leading of course to staggering numbers of post-traumatic stress syndrome problems once, or, sorry, *if*, they make it home alive.

The sad legacy of both wars is the lack of accurate tracking of casualties and deaths. It is left to distraught mothers to journey to Grozny to meet with the rebels to learn how their children died.

#### Mothers of Soldiers
http://www.soldiersmothers.spb.org
http://www.calguard.ca.gov/ia/Chechnya/Events-Chechnya.htm

### "Zachistkas"

*Zachistkas* is the Russian word for cleanups, or random sweeps by soldiers against villagers. Typically a village is surrounded and the troops go from house to house looking for young men or anyone without papers. A number of Chechens are then dragged off, household items are stolen, and there are numerous reports of murders, rapes, and beatings. The arrested are put in "filtration" camps where they are tortured, beaten, and often forced to confess, pay bribes, or be ransomed back to their families. A disturbing number of Chechens (about 2,000 or so of both sexes and a wide age range) never return from these arrests, and not surprisingly, there are a number of mass graves in Chechnya.

http://tchetchenieparis.free.fr

## BE ALL YOU CAN BE . . . SORTA

Yeah, it's an old American recruiting line, but in the Russian army things are pretty frightening. Take the 58th Army and the 19th Division. Out of 6,351 recruits, the following was found:

- 1,590 were psychologically and intellectually weak or dangerous
- 1,173 had no father at home
- 120 were convicted criminals
- 76 were orphans
- 550 were alcoholics
- 480 were addicted to drugs
- 69 had a tendency toward committing suicide
- 332 were below weight standards
- 669 exhibited some health problem, and
- 930 were determined in need of psychiatric help.

### Kidnapping

Kidnapping here is not pretty. Even well-known aid-maestro and do-gooder Fred Cuny was executed, and his decomposed body was being ransomed for $200,000 to the Soros Foundation. Red Cross workers were shot point-blank in the head with silenced weapons, phone workers were kidnapped and then found decapitated, and, to speed up payments, kidnappers sent videos of victims' fingers and ears being sliced off. Things are ugly in Chechnya. The problem is that most of the kidnapping is done by Russian-hired Chechen gangs. Russians sell back dead Chechen fighters, split ransoms with their victims, snatch journos from Ingushetia, Georgia, and Dagestan, and then keep them in safe houses inside Chechnya. There is even a wholesale business as victims are swapped like baseball cards. So far, about 1,300 people have been officially kidnapped since 1994. Foreigners working for NGOs are now the favorite targets. Russian-backed Chechen warlords make about $8 million from ransoms in a year; some say $20 million. It seems that the film *Prisoner of the Mountain* has turned into an infomercial.

http://news.bbc.co.uk/1/hi/world/europe/1223686.stm

## Getting Sick

There's not much medical help to speak of here. Clean water is a problem and diseases found in refugee camps and destroyed areas are common. There are hospitals with limited supplies and plenty of doctors.

Chechnya is a fairly healthy place, but with very limited medical resources and facilities.

## Nuts and Bolts

Chechnya is a self-proclaimed republic in Russia with a loosely estimated population of 950,000 people lying just to the east of the principal road crossing the central Caucasus, ranging from the plains and foothills into the alpine highlands. Its neighbors are Dagestan to the east, the Turkic-speaking Kumyk people of Russia to the north, the Ingush to the west, and the Southern Ossetians and Georgians to the south. Grozny is the largest city and capital with an official peacetime population of about 400,000, but more like 100,000 these days. The capital was generally depopulated as a result of the Russian bombing. Chechen is the principal language, spoken by some 97 percent of the population. Russian is spoken by all. Ingush is a closely related language understood by most Chechens. Chechens and the Ingush are almost entirely Sunni Muslims of the Hanafi school. The currency is the Russian ruble and the U.S. dollar. The electricity is 220V/50Hz, if you can find it.

## Dangerous Days

| | |
|---|---|
| **12/27/02** | Chechen rebels blow up police station in Grozny, killing 46. |
| **11/03/02** | Putin announces new offensive in Chechnya. |
| **10/23/02** | Rebels (22 males and 19 females) take over Moscow theater. In the attack 129 people are killed, mostly hostages, as a result of the gas used by Russian forces. |
| **9/26/02** | Journalist and DP contributor Roddy Scott is killed by the Russians while covering the war on the rebel side. |
| **4/18/02** | Putin declares war in Chechnya is over. |
| **3/25/02** | Saudi jihadi and famous commander Khattab is poisoned by a letter given to him by friend. |
| **12/31/99** | Boris Yeltsin resigns, putting Putin in charge. |
| **10/1/99** | Russians invade Chechnya . . . again. |
| **9/9/99** | A series of explosions in Moscow apartments is blamed on Chechens. |
| **8/10/99** | Dagestan declares independence after Basayev takes control of selected villages and towns. |
| **7/99** | Basayev and Khattab begin operations in Dagestan. |
| **1/97** | Maskhadov is elected president of the Chechen Republic. |

**8/31/96**  Lebed and Maskhadov sign a peace treaty ending the war in Chechnya.

**1/97**  Two Russian journalists are kidnapped, beginning a long list of kidnap victims in Chechnya. Reconstruction is stopped and aid workers move out.

**8/6/96**  Chechen fighters reverse the war, driving Russian troops out of Grozny.

**3/31/96**  Yeltsin announces a peace plan and says all Russian military operations will be suspended.

**1/16–19/96**  Pro-Chechen commandos hijack a Black Sea ferry at the Turkish port of Trabzon, taking 150 hostages, mostly Russian tourists. Hostages are later released after the hijackers claim their aim of drawing worldwide attention to Russian atrocities in Chechnya is achieved.

**1/17/96**  Russian troops attack Chechen fighters and their hostages die in the village of Pervomayskaya on the Chechnya-Dagestan border. Eighteen hostages are reported missing by Moscow, which also claims killing 153 Chechens and taking 28 prisoner.

**1/9–24/96**  Chechen commandos, led by Salman Raduyev, take 2,000 people hostage at a hospital in Kizliar in the republic of Dagestan.

**6/14–20/95**  Chechen fighters take the southern Russian town of Budyonnovsk and 1,500 hostages in a hospital. Russian forces free 200 people on the 17th, but at least 150 are killed. Talks are held between Chernomyrdin and Shamil Basayev. Negotiations for the withdrawal of Russian troops in Chechnya begin.

**2/9/95**  Former Soviet leader Mikhail Gorbachev describes the campaign as a huge mistake that could cost the country dearly.

**2/4–8/94**  Kidnappers from Chechnya carry out a series of hostage seizures of civilians in southern Russia. Russia blames Dudayev, and calls on Chechens to topple him.

**6/92**  Chechnya and Ingushetia are split. Ingushetia remains part of the Russian Federation.

**11/91**  Yeltsin declares a state of emergency in Checheno-Ingushetia and sends troops to Grozny. Troops are blocked at the airport, Parliament overrules his declaration, and Yeltsin pulls them out after three days.

**10/91**  Dudayev launches a campaign to topple Moscow's temporary administration, attacking government offices and holding mass rallies. He wins 80 percent backing in presidential polls and unilaterally declares Chechnya independent.

| | |
|---|---|
| **9/5/91** | The government of Checheno-Ingushetia, which supports the August hard-line coup against Mikhail Gorbachev, resigns. Soviet Air Force General Dzhokhar Dudayev leaves Estonia and is installed as national leader. |
| **2/26/44** | Hundreds of thousands of Chechens are deported by Soviet dictator Josef Stalin with other Caucasus peoples to Soviet Central Asia. Many die during the journey or while in exile. After Stalin's death, they are allowed to return home in 1957. |
| **1934** | Chechnya merges with neighboring Ingushetia in Checheno-Ingushetia. |
| **1921** | Chechnya becomes part of Russia's Mountain Republic, which is formally incorporated into the Soviet Union in 1924. |
| **1859** | Chechnya is incorporated into Russia. |
| **1817–1864** | Imperial Russia fights a 40-year war to conquer mountainous lands between itself and newly acquired Georgia, defeating the Chechens and other Muslim peoples. |

★★★★★

# COLOMBIA

## Coca Loco Land

When the new president of Colombia, Alvaro Uribe, was inaugurated on August 7, 2002, the people of Bogota celebrated with fireworks. In keeping with the Colombian way, a number of homemade mortars (a nifty IRA design) smashed into the city, including the top edge of the state building, killing 21 people in a nearby slum. This was essentially a freeze-frame of the long-standing problems that plague Colombia. There is no peace, violence is endemic, and the poor people always get screwed . . . mostly by their purported Marxist supporters, the Fuerzas Armadas Revolucionarias de Colombia Ejercito Popular (FARC) and National Liberation Army (ELN).

Welcome to Latin America's most civilized and beautiful country, as well as home to the Western Hemisphere's longest-running insurgency: a nearly four-decade-old war that has cost some 40,000 lives just in the last decade alone. And unlike violent Kenya, which has the romantic fiddle-faddle of *Out of Africa* to attract tourists, Colombia has chainsaw-wielding gangsters out of *Scarface* or *Blow* to fill its hotels and parks. Hey, when the mafia needs a little PR they can point to HBO's miniseries *The Sopranos,* while Colombia has their own U.S.-financed and -costumed remakes of *Apocalypse Now* to show its best side.

To make sure that things spin completely out of control, Colombia has become the United States's third-largest recipient of aid after Israel and Egypt (and we know how calm and peaceful the Middle East is). Uncle Sam has peeled off over a billion dollars in the last two years just to fight drugs (naturally, cocaine production is up), and then tipped the new hard-line government $104 million just to show it cares.

It's not hard to write this chapter every year: When it comes to tracking violence, Colombia (like South Africa and the United States) is cursed with scrupulous record-keeping, vocal human-rights groups, government flacks, and eagle-eyed public defenders. We say cursed because murders, violence, theft, and other nasty crimes are out there for everyone to see. Toss those statistics with a random assortment of machete-wielding rebels, paramilitary massacres, brutal drug lords, and toxic spraying, and voilà, disaster salad.

Obviously, Cali would rather compete with Mogadishu or Grozny for "safest tourist city," but all that U.S. money requires airing your dirty laundry in public. So, to be fair, we are going to focus on the good news. For example, murders in Colombia are down to around 65 per 100,000 people. Of course, even this good news is tempered by the fact that this statistic is still twice as high as any other Latin American country (the rate in the United States is six to seven murders per 100,000 population; Canada can only drum up a pathetic two murders per 100,000 Canucks), and that, folks, is pretty much it for good news. Oh, yeah . . . you are less likely to die of suicide in Colombia than in any other country in the Western Hemisphere. Unfortunately, *DP* doesn't quite know how to make that selling point sing in a travel brochure.

But forget statistics. Despite the grace and hospitality of its people, Colombia is dangerous. While *DP* was in the small southern town of Puerto Asis for six days, 33 people were killed, most of them shot in the head. That means that if things kept up for a full year there would be over 2,000 dead in a town of 40,000 people. Nary a journo was in sight and local folks said that things were only going to get worse. So, if 3,500 people is the official number of deaths in Colombia caused by the war, and this is just one week in a cocaine-rich town . . . you do the math to come up with the real story.

The statistics do little to reveal the entire story of what is happening in Colombia. Colombia is turning into a lawless nation

> **C**olombia is turning into a lawless nation skating on the edge of anarchy.

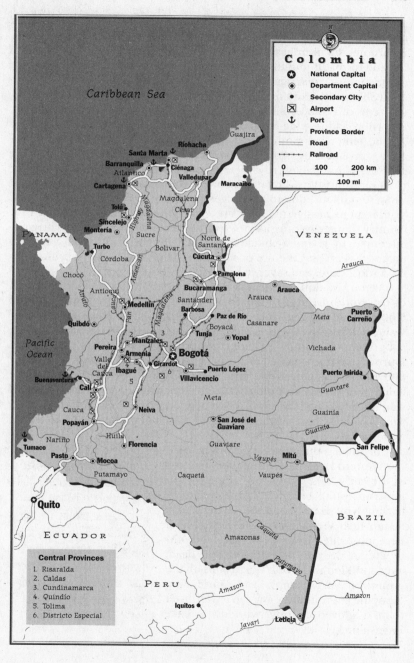

## Colombia

- ⊛ National Capital
- ⊙ Department Capital
- • Secondary City
- ⊠ Airport
- ⚓ Port
- —— Province Border
- —— Road
- +++ Railroad

0   100   200 km
0        100 mi

Caribbean Sea

Guajira

Ríohacha
Santa Marta
Barranquilla        Ciénaga
Atlántico       Valledupar
Cartagena                    Maracaibo

Tolú        Magdalena
Sincelejo       César
Montería
Sucre        Bolívar        Norte de
Turbo                       Santander
Córdoba                     Cúcuta
Chocó                       Pamplona
Antioqui                    Bucaramanga        Arauca
Medellín        Santander
Quibdó          Barbosa        Paz de Río
                Boyacá        Casanare
1  2  3        Tunja
Pereira  Manizales        Yopal
Valle        Armenia        Bogotá
del          Ibagué  Girardot
Cauca                Puerto López
5            Villavicencio
Buenaventura
Cali         Meta
Cauca        Neiva
Popayán                     Puerto Inírida
Narino  Huila        San José del
Tumaco        Florencia        Guaviare
Pasto        Guaviare
Mocoa        Mitú        San Felipe
Putumayo
Caquetá        Vaupés

PANAMA

VENEZUELA

Arauca

Meta        Puerto
Carreño

Vichada

Guaviare

Guainía

Guainía

Pacific
Ocean

Quito

ECUADOR

Amazonas

BRAZIL

PERU

Iquitos        Leticia

Amazon        Amazon

Javari

**Central Provinces**
1. Risaralda
2. Caldas
3. Cundinamarca
4. Quindío
5. Tolima
6. Distrito Especial

skating on the edge of anarchy. Colombia's wealthy, not to mention its intellectuals, have fled to the United States to escape kidnapping, extortion, and murder threats. The drug lords, criminals, revolutionaries, and terrorists join them for weekends in Miami but still have plenty of time to wage war against the government and infrastructure.

In all, the price of the guerrilla war in Colombia since 1990 has been in excess of US$20 billion, or just under 4 percent of the annual GDP. Extortion, kidnapping, oil pipeline attacks, and murders inflicted by a 25,000-plus rebel-strong force (there were a mere 215 insurgents in 1964) have cost the state oil company, Ecopetrol, more than US$600 million—through lost royalties, pipeline attacks, repair and security costs, and ransoms. Private-sector oil companies consider the loss of US$430 million—due to death, destruction, and mayhem—as the cost of doing business here. They are even implementing a war tax in a country that technically is not at war. *DP*'s buddy Mono Jojoy started it, of course, by giving a choice to the people who make over a million dollars a year: pay the tax or face the prospect of being "retained" by the FARC. Cute, and saves on unnecessary paperwork.

Even if you don't make it to the war, Colombia is the kidnap capital of the world. Official numbers say that this year between 3,500 and 5,000 people will get to play hacky sack with their rotting teeth as they wait for relatives to scrape together their ransom. These days it is less about money than it is about publicity as politicians, expats, and journos join the "chained to the plumbing" vacation crowd. More than 800 people (ranging from famous politicians to elderly peasants) are being held captive in Colombia as this ink dries. If you think you can stay out of Colombia's problems when you visit, remember that of all the folks killed here since 1990, more than half of them were innocent bystanders.

Colombia is the most dangerous place in the Western Hemisphere and, like Vietnam in the early '60s, is not considered by our government to be a war zone, which is exactly why some people are saying it may be our next Vietnam. We like it quiet over here in our hemisphere. But facts tell otherwise: A 38-year-old war, 40,000 dead, over a million displaced, U.S. troops on the ground or in swamps, and Uncle Sam pumping more money into the war faster than a gloved granny working a Lake Havasu nickel slot.

**B**ut facts tell otherwise: A 38-year-old war, 40,000 dead, over a million displaced, U.S. troops on the ground or in swamps, and Uncle Sam pumping more money into the war faster than a gloved granny working a Lake Havasu nickel slot.

Even on a global scale, Colombia is a dangerous place. Latin America's longest-running insurgency with one of its last Marxist rebel groups has a special flavor—56 percent of the dead are civilians, with only 5 percent killed with a gun in their hands. To flee the fighting in the countryside, more than 100,000 refugees—or *desplazados*—flood into the capital of Bogota each year. More than 2 million Colombians have been forced from their homes by the war, flooding urban slums and straining civic stability.

The country's rebel groups are at the zenith of their power. Despite losing their Switzerland-size safety zone, they control half of rural Colombia (from 40 to 70 percent). Some 25,000 guerrillas are either fighting in or control 600 of Colombia's 1,061 townships, backed by thousands of informers and quasi-political supporters. Their coffers have been pumped up lately by the proceeds from kidnapping, drug trafficking, and extortion payoffs. Although the Colombian army is 120,000 troops strong, only about 20,000 soldiers are professionally trained, and the lines of young Colombian men lining up to buy their way out of the draft never gets any shorter.

## The Scoop

The new hard-line government in Colombia has shattered the status quo and it remains to be seen just how ugly things will get as right-wing, left wing, and government forces fight for control of the people's hearts and minds and, of course, control of cocaine dollars.

Cities tend to be safe, but all bets are off once you visit Colombia's beautiful but deadly countryside. Despite its previous experience fighting communist insurgents in a jungle, the United States keeps ramping up its not-so-covert involvement in its efforts to create a big-budget Latin remake of Vietnam.

**Colombia Report**
http://www.colombiareport.org

**Colombia Times**
http://www.colombiatimes.com

**El Tiempo**
http://eltiempo.terra.com.co

**Semana**
http://semana.terra.com.co

**Yahoo Colombia News**
http://dailynews.yahoo.com/fc/World/Colombia

## The Players

### President Alvaro Uribe

Legal beagle, professional bureaucrat, and now president, Uribe (b. July 4, 1952, in Medellin), looks suspiciously like a pledging Boy Scout in his campaign poster. But don't be fooled. Within days of being elected, he set about changing the mood from conciliatory to militant, instituting a war tax, shutting down media access, taking a hard-line stance against rebels, paras, and criminals, and arming 15,000 peasants to fight back and demanding that the rest be informers. There is just something about these Putinesque nerdy types that scares *DP*. It doesn't hurt that his new minister of defense, Ingrid Betancourt, is a former fashion model who aims to root out corruption and sloth. He must have rung the bell because he is the first president to get a majority in a long time. He is also the first independent candidate to win since Spain gave Colombia its independence in 1819.

Why is the tiny, bespectacled Uribe so tough? Well, it could be because his father was killed by leftist guerrillas in 1983. And maybe it's because he doesn't have a choice. The FARC have been kidnapping high-level politicos and gunning down public servants without mercy. If it is any comfort, Uribe also studied conflict resolution at Harvard in 1993 and is a darling of the U.S. administration. Colombian presidents are prohibited from serving more than two terms, so Uribe is left with the shards of the previous president's peace plans. Three years of FARC peace talks and their 42,000 square miles of marxist utopia are gone. Reconciliation with the ELN ended in January 2002. The Autodefensas Unidas de Colombia (AUC) is morphing into a political and military power to deal with, and the United States has decided to drop any pretense of political correctness and go after the rebels. And, oh, yeah, did we mention the drugs, civil violence, and corruption?

This former mayor says his favorite pastime is training horses. We will see how he does with the four Colombian Horsemen of the Apocalypse: Drugs, Violence, Crime, and Communism. How gung ho is Alvaro? Well, let's just say one of his two teenage sons is named Jeronimo.

http://www.presidencia.gov.co

## The Colombian Military

A quick trip down memory lane would amuse most foreigners. The Colombian army has fought wars wearing everything from German pig-sticking helmets to straw hats. Now, of course, they are outfitted in the latest in U.S. Kevlar, uniforms, and boots. They still cling to the Gallil rifle and sneak in the odd Russian transport helicopter, but Uncle Sam has successfully hooked Colombia on spending all that U.S. aid on U.S. gear. That's why you will see sleek Blackhawks, shiny Hummers, and snazzy Motorolas amongst the aging C47s, ancient OH 10 Broncos, leased Turbo Thrush spray planes (complete with Midwest-themed nose art), and dozens of honest-to-god Vietnam-era Hueys. You won't see the U.S.-generated maps, NSA intel, or CIA contract mercenaries, but you will see a lot of press shows where millions of dollars are spent on hundreds of troops and dozens of gunships to make a show of setting rudimentary $50 drug labs alight; you might see photos of a few stiff rebels, and of course plenty of *campesinos* looking glum for TV. For now, the entire Colombian military (army, navy, and air force) has about 150,000 men pitted against both Marxist rebels who number about 25,000 and paras who number perhaps 10,000–15,000 (and who don't actually fight against the army since they are fighting both the FARC and ELN).

Americans are busy training those who cannot escape the conscript army (in Colombia it is possible to buy your way out of the military) and things are improving. But, oddly enough, Colombia spends little more on its military (3.4 percent of GDP) than do many of its peaceful neighbors (Chile spends 3.1 percent of its GDP on the military and can't find a darn guerrilla within hundreds of miles). So the United States is taking up the slack.

Why aren't they winning the War on Drugs? Or the War on Terrorism? Or, hell, the War on Anything? As one Colombian rebel put it to *DP,* "The army doesn't like to fight. They also don't like the jungle." The FARC have a point. The army is a conscript army, complete with lousy pay, poor living conditions, and meager resources. They live in fortified bunkers and go on patrol. Most just want to get their military service out of the way and get back to the real world, or they buy their way out to avoid the whole mess. That's not to say that the military is any less prepared or eager to fight this war, but they are spread thin over Colombia's vast landscape and, despite the PR hustle, they barely have the supplies and wherewithal to make a dent.

### Armed Forces of Colombia
http://www.fuerzasmilitares.mil.co
http://www.gwu.edu/~nsarchiv/NSAEBB
    /NSAEBB69/background.html

### Army
http://www.ejercito.mil.co

### Navy
http://www.fac.mil.co

## The Colombian Police

Visitors to Colombia might be taken aback by the site of heavily armed military men circling overhead in minigun-equipped Blackhawk gunships. Don't worry, it's just the cops. Colombian police are probably among the most militarized in the world, thanks to America. The police are given the yeoman's job of not only running traffic and getting kittens out of trees, but also fighting a losing battle with the FARC. It is not uncommon for remote police posts to be surrounded and besieged for days while the military tries to scrape up enough transport to rescue them. Before 9/11, the United States favored the police because of the human rights abuses of the army. The police differ from the military in that they receive more training, are a volunteer professional force, and are besieged by criminal, drug, and political elements.

**Policía Nacional de Colombia**
Avenida el Dorado
CAN Transversal 45 #40-11
Bogotá, Colombia
Tel.: (57) 315 90 00
direccion@policia.gov.co
http://www.policia.gov.co

## Bolivarian Movement for a New Colombia/Revolutionary Armed Forces of Colombia /Fuerzas Armadas Revolucionarias de Colombia Ejercito Popular (FARC-EP)

These are the gum-booted commies who have opposed both political parties and the right-wing death squads, and often the people who are supposed to support them. FARC had its origins after World War II as a Marxist group under the leadership of Manuel Marulanda Vélez (b. May 13, 1930), aka "Tirofijo" (Sure Shot), and the Central Committee of the Communist Party of Colombia (Partido Comunista de Colombia–PCC). Their birth is the direct result of a U.S.-advised attack on May 27, 1964, in Marquetalia, where a group of 46 men and two women led by Manuel Marulanda held out against a massive government attack by 16,000 soldiers . . . or at least that's how the FARC tell it.

FARC officially began in 1966 and had only 500 fighters by the end of the '60s. Outside support (i.e., Soviet) in the '70s allowed FARC to expand, and by the end of the '70s they were *numero uno* with a bullet.

In 1984, FARC went legit as a political party, but hard-liners split off to continue the armed struggle under the Ricardo Franco Front (Frente Ricardo Franco). It didn't help that former revolutionaries turned politicos were being assassinated by government hit squads for their troubles. Burned by this attempt to go legit and seemingly encouraged by attempts to militarily destroy them, FARC is now the largest, oldest, and meanest rebel group operating in Colombia.

The FARC-EP is up made of seven blocks (*bloques*) and 60 *frentes*, or fronts, of varying sizes. Depending on the leader's style, they each have their specialty, which can include assassinations, armed attacks against Colombian targets, bombings of U.S. businesses, extortion, cocaine, kidnapping (including foreigners), and pretty much whatever keeps them in new Land Cruisers and gumboots. They also have urban guerrillas, student political supporters, union reps, and so on.

Their funding comes primarily from extortion . . . er, sorry, "taxation" . . . and protection income from cocaine traffickers. FARC also has begun to cut out the middleman and has been implicated in direct-from-leaf-to-crystal deals. A variety of unsavory customers seen doing business with FARC include IRA members, Iranian fundamentalists, and even Russian gangsters.

FARC is the largest, best-trained, best-equipped (using high-tech gadgetry like cell phones, sophisticated radio equipment, and laptop computers to coordinate attacks) and most effective insurgent organization in Latin America—it's the one Western terrorist group voted "most likely to succeed" by U.S. intelligence services. Many consider FARC to be the "military" arm of the Communist Party of Colombia (PCC). But the truth is that the FARC likes things screwed up. It's good for business, er, we mean social progress. The leadership of FARC is composed largely of disaffected middle- and upper-class intellectuals who recruit/press-gang fighters from the peasant class.

> **T**he FARC likes things screwed up. It's good for business, er, we mean social progress.

FARC also draws support from traditional left-wingers, workers, students, and radical priests. In reality, they have little support due to their brutal tactics and criminal acts. The popularity of FARC has been undermined by the questionable practice of kidnapping peasants and murdering them as "collaborators" and "traitors" if they're not cooperative. Something the paras do as well, just to be sure the *campesinos* don't get too comfortable.

FARC's 47th Front is particularly known for its kidnapping-of-foreigners prowess. The area of Suma Paz just outside Bogota is famous as the place where negotiators go to free hostages. (Bring cash, U.S. dollars please, and leave that *Das Kapital* book back at the hotel.)

The FARC love the jungle and just by a wild coincidence that is where they grow and process coca. Their biggest stronghold is in Meta and Caqueta province, but any military map will reveal that the entire country (and cities) are riddled with FARC guerrillas.

And the group has also publicly admitted to killing at least three Americans. FARC said that members of one of its guerrilla cells executed three U.S. citizens in March 1999. The Americans had been working in Colombia as advocates for the U'wa indigenous tribe when they were abducted and later killed.

On June 15, 1997, FARC, in a major publicity coup, released 70 Colombian soldiers, some of whom had been held for more than nine months and chained to trees. However, hopes for a possible path toward peace were dashed shortly afterward when FARC resumed full-scale offensive operations. In November 1998, FARC was "granted" a Switzerland-sized swath of land in Colombia's south by the government

## SOMETHING TO PROTEST ABOUT
## AT THE NEXT GLOBALIZATION MEETING

On Sept. 7, 2000, a 100-foot-long Russian-designed submarine was discovered in Facatativa, a mountain town (7,500 feet above sea level) a few miles outside of Bogota. The soon-to-be-completed sub was estimated to be able to smuggle 200 tons (that's *tons*) of cocaine drugs. The former Peruvian government, Hizbollah, Russian gangsters, the IRA, and many others have formed lucrative business partnerships with the FARC and Colombian drug cartels. Besides the submarine, 10,000 AK's were intercepted that were bought from Jordan by the Peruvian military in August 2000. Even Vlad Montesino, the intelligence head of the now-deposed Peruvian government, made millions from the drug trade. Colorful folks like Brazilian gangster "Johnny Seashore," Russian gangster Ludwig "Tarzan" Fainberg, and others supply aircraft, subs, and weapons in exchange for that precious white stuff. Hey, get DePalma on the phone.

in an "olive branch" gesture. Government troops were to return to this so-called DMZ after 90 days, but didn't. On April 29, 2000, the FARC launched their secret political wing, the Movimiento Bolivariano por la Nueva Colombia, to the sound of one hand clapping. They also used their zone to train recruits, launch attacks, and perfect their drug business.

On February 20, 2002, former President Pastrana had had enough: The FARC had just kidnapped a senator. He ordered the military in to kick the FARC out. The FARC vanished back into the jungle. Civilization and city life were getting dull anyway.

For now, the main honchos are led by their major domo, "Sureshot" (the world's oldest rebel leader, by the way); his jovial and brutal head of the military, Jorge Briceño Suarez (b. January 1953), alias "Mono Jojoy"; his good-buddy head of the Northwest Block, Luciano Marin Arango (b. June 16, 1955), aka "Ivan Marquez"; chatty but not-quite-accurate FARC spokesman Luis Edgar Devia Velez (b. September 30, 1948), aka "Raul Reyes"; Noel Mata, alias "Efrain Guzmán" Guillermo and former professor and FARC political honcho Leon Saenz Vargas (b. July 22, 1948), aka "Alfonso Cano"; and Rodrigo Londoño Echeverri, aka "Timochenko." All of them came down to say hi to *DP* and chat on camera about what they hell they were doing running a Marxist rebellion in the twenty-first century.

During the heady days of the rebel's government, the press loved the popular spokesman and head of the Caribe block, Juvenal Ovidio Pineda Palmera (b. July 30, 1950), aka Simón Trinidad. Trinidad would artfully present the murderous, self-indulgent acts of the FARC to naïve, fawning reporters as being socially important and helpful. When *DP* asked Mono Jojoy to stop "pumping sunshine up our ass" and answer the question about why they don't even fix the potholes, we were told "that's the government's job." For now, the FARC leaders cruise around in their air-conditioned Land Cruisers followed by their luscious posse of female FARCettes. . . . It's good to be the king. Er, we mean its good to be culturally sensitive, self-sacrificing social reformers and protectors of the proletariat.

For now the FARC has an estimated cash flow of half a billion from protection money, kidnapping, extortion, and even cattle rustling; most of that income is linked to the drug business through protection of growers, shippers, and labs. Their latest gimmick is having bombs carried into urban areas by donkey or horse, or, believe it or not, inside human cadavers. If you think *DP* might be too harsh on these folks, you can always visit the FARC's Web site to read *DP*'s favorite article: "Love Beneath the Intimacy of the Mosquito Netting."

elbarcino@laneta.apc.org
tematicosFarcep@hotmail.com
http://www.fuerzasmilitares.mil.co/ingles/wanted1.htm

## Paramilitary Groups/Autodefensas Unidas de Colombia (AUC)

The newest, most formidable violent force in Colombia is actually the AUC. Although local defense militias are a fixture in Latin America, the paramilitaries are the new vaccine against the FARC. In the '80s, the FARC raised money by kidnapping landowners. One of those kidnapped and killed was the father of Carlos Castano, 34, who owned a 250,000-acre ranch in the north. After the brutal kidnap and murder, Carlos Castano and a number of his brothers became local guides for the Bombona Battalion (XIV Brigade), the military group that trained and armed the first *autodefensas*, or self-defense militias. Fidel Castano (Carlo's older brother) met the Medellin-based Pablo Escobar in 1985, who then put him in touch with José Gonzales Rodriguez Gacha, who ran the Magdalena Medio area. Castano provided protection and also began to actively force out the rebels in Gacha's area. In 1989, the military stopped training and funding these groups when they were discovered also to be working with the drug lords (who happened to be large owners of land and employers of the autodefensas). Fidel decided to simply hire out to the drug lords and fight the guerrillas, unions, and sympathizers on their behalf. Naturally their ties to the army were maintained on a quieter level . . . a charge that remains to this day. In April 1990, the government found half a dozen mass graves on the Castano ranch. Many of the 100-or-so victims showed signs of torture and Fidel became a wanted man. Fidel was killed in a rebel ambush in 1994 and Carlos officially took over the leadership in 1997. Carlos quickly expanded the original 300-man outfit into today's 14,000-man (and growing) nationwide organization.

The AUC was formed when Carlos Castano decided that the various militias, autodefensas, and paramilitary groups needed to have an effective national presence and central command. As its enigmatic spokesman, Castano brought a forthrightness and intensity of purpose that played on the frustration many Colombians have with the government's lack of success against the rebels. Fighting fire with fire, the paras brutally eliminate rebels and their sympathizers and then use protection money from coca growers to fund their group. They quickly monopolize the cocaine market in each region and work in plainclothes to keep FARC informants out by simply shooting them.

The AUC successes of Carlos Castano (some might notice that his name translates into Charlie Brown) have made him a popular hero. Castano has made himself also a recluse by virtue of the war he has declared on the Marxists. He was, however, interviewed and photographed by *DP*'s Steve Salisbury, and he is as lucid and forthright as one expects of a man who has nothing to lose. Despite his Kurtzlike existence in the jungle, he simply wants to rid Colombia of the marxist rebels and restore law and order—something the government and better-off citizens of Colombia have been trying to do for four decades. His recent decision to distance himself from AUC elements who make money from drugs and extortion signals a serious attempt to form a right-wing political juggernaut.

These days the AUC acts much like a franchise, with payments made to a central organization. Trainers and weapons are sent to each franchise, somewhat like Starbucks with waaay too much caffeine and guns involved. They also offer higher pay ($180 a month for new recruits versus from $40 to nothing a month for FARCettes), more holidays, and better working conditions than the FARC. Of course, for the franchise owner there is the added bonus of controlling the coca money in each region.

Castano has admitted that 70 percent of the AUC's income comes from drug-related income. Castano even carries over this truthfulness to his tell-all autobiography, appropriately titled *My Confession*, by journalist Mauricio Aranguren Molina. Castano waxes poetic about his shrapnel wounds (women might be interested to know where they are), loneliness in the jungle, his many acts of violence, links to drug income, and other tidbits that have made him the Jesse Ventura of Colombia. Does he have fans? Well, 15,000 hardcovers sold out in less than two hours and he is up to 60,000 copies in print.

## WEB AT WAR

If you would like to join the war on terror, why not skip over to http://www.accubec.org/juegos/feria.html and play the shooting gallery game that allows you to take potshots at *DP*'s former drinking buddies. Our favorite is the FARCman and ELeNa game. There is also chat, humor, and a strange selection of very pretty touristic and nature shots. Ya' gotta love those wacky paras.

With this kind of popularity, it's not surprising that the umbrella group led by Carlos Castano wants to go legit. You will find plenty of Colombians who think the AUC (pronounced "auk," or called simply the "paras" by the locals) is doing exactly what the government should be doing.

The paras simply move into an area and begin executing rebel sympathizers, harassing armed groups, and imposing penalties for supporting, informing, or working for FARC. *DP*'s driver was shot to death in San Vincente by the paras after the FARC moved out. His car was festooned with FARC flags, stickers, and medallions . . . not exactly a wise move in this deadly, ever-shifting war. The AUC is officially a terrorist group, according to the United States, and the military has token runins with the paras to show their resolve. But for now, AUC continues to find popular, government, and military support. As one Colombian colonel phrased it, "The army sees the enemy of its enemy as its friend."

Castano's number two, 37-year-old Salvatore Mancuso (who has not been photographed in ten years), is the new boss. This U.S.-educated sportsman, who can be found in the jungle camp outside of his hometown of Monteria, was put in charge of the 9-man central command on August 29, 2001. Mancuso is the son of a wealthy Italian immigrant and a Colombian mother. He went to college in Philly, loves to wear designer-label sports gear (hmm . . . no Nike endorsements?), and was kidnapped and held for three days in 1983. On the positive side, on March 12, 2002, Mancuso decided that the AUC will kill no more than three people at a time (the paras were blamed for almost 250 massacres that killed 1,200 people in 2001). The law in Colombia describes more than three deaths at one time as a massacre. Nice touch. On May 30, he resigned from AUC, and in July 2002 Carlos officially disbanded the AUC, conveniently sidestepping their U.S. label as a terrorist group. Any ideas for new, PC-sounding names are welcome. He is currently working on making the AUC legit and escaping a U.S. indictment.

*Autodefensas Unidas de Colombia*
http://www.colombialibre.org

## National Liberation Army/Ejercito de Liberacion Nacional (ELN)

A rural-based, anti-U.S., Maoist-Marxist-Leninist guerrilla group formed in July 1964 by Cuban-inspired Roman Catholic priests, the ELN raises funds by kidnapping foreign employees of large corporations and domestic cattle ranchers and holding them for lofty ransom payments. The ELN draws its support from among students, intellectuals, peasants, and, surprisingly, the middle-class workers of Colombia. The ELN also conducts extortion and bombing operations against U.S. and other foreign businesses in Colombia, particularly the deep-pocketed petroleum industry. The group has inflicted major damage on oil pipelines since 1986.

In 1964 Fabio Vasquez Castano took a page out of Fidel's book and created the Ejercito de Liberacion Nacional, or ELN. Since Colombia is a hell of lot bigger than Cuba, they contented themselves with raising money by robbing banks, holding small towns to show who's boss, and generally destabilizing the area in the Santander Department.

Paramilitaries and the military almost wiped out the ELN in the early '70s, and the government was convinced that they had wiped them out in 1973. A hard core of around 500 fighters rebuilt the ELN by shifting to bank robberies, audacious kidnappings (including the president's brother), and high-level assassinations: most significantly, the inspector-general of the army, General José Ramun Rincun Quiones.

The ELN did not sign the 1984 cease-fire until their hero, Fidel Castro, urged them to do so. The ELN is probably the most aggressive and creative of the three rebel groups in Colombia. Their favorite thing to do on a Friday night is blow holes in the Cano Limon Covenas oil pipeline (over 700 times since 1982).

Depending on what source you believe, the ELN number between 2,000 and 5,000 members, many of whom have been trained and armed by Nicaragua and Cuba. The ELN seeks "the conquest of power for the popular classes," along with nationalizations, expropriations, and agrarian reform. ELN leader Ike de Jesus Vergara was arrested in Bogota in March 1997, and the number-four man, Diego Antonio Prieto, was gunned down by Bogota police in June 1997. ELN leaders Francisco Galan and Felipe Torres were imprisoned as of mid-1999. (Nicolas Rodriguez appears to be calling the shots these days.) But the losses haven't slowed down the ELN. Their kidnappings-for-ransom keep the coffers stuffed. Wealthy ranchers are the bull's-eyes. According to the cattle farmers' organization, 250 of its members were abducted during the first seven months of 1998; 18 ended up dead.

Other operations include assassinations of military officers, airliner hijackings, the offing of labor leaders and peasants, multiple armed robberies, various bombings, raids on isolated villages, weapons grabs on police posts and army patrols, and occupations of radio stations and newspaper offices. The ELN is currently perfecting attacks on petroleum pipelines and facilities, seeking to damage Colombia's economic infrastructure and investment climate. The Cano Limon Covenas pipeline, the largest in Colombia, was attacked no fewer than 40 times during the first half of 1997. When operating normally, the pipeline ships 175,000 barrels of oil a day, about 45 percent of Colombian oil exports. The ELN has sabotaged the pipeline hundreds of times over the last decade, causing more than US$1 billion in damage. The ELN regularly operates near the oil fields in Casanare and neighboring Arauca Departments, looking for foreign hostages to grab.

Perhaps because it thought that FARC was getting too many headlines with its land concessions, the ELN decided to splash some ink of its own. On April 12, 1999, five well-dressed ELN rebels (one attired as a priest!) hijacked an Avianca Airlines domestic flight shortly after it took off from Bucaramanga and forced it to land at a jungle landing strip in southern Bolivar Department, where they, and a waiting force of ELN fighters, whisked the 41 hostages off into the forest. Then, to make the Society page, ELN insurgents kidnapped Diomedes Diaz, the son of a famous Colombian singer, on May 16, 1999. The rebels claimed they seized the plane and cradle-robbed the crooner's kid to show the world they weren't a "spent force." Indeed.

Spanish-born leader and former priest Manuel Perez died in 1998. The group's top commander is Nicolas Rodriguez, who has met with representatives of the Pope . . . one can only wonder what they talked about. Former President Pastrana called off peace talks with the ELN on August 7, 2001, but they are going on secretly with Cuba as the assumed location. For now the ELN is second banana to FARC, and the top military strategist, Antonia Garcia, is busy financing the group through kidnappings.

**Ejercito de Liberacion Nacional**
http://www.web.net/eln

## The U.S. Military

The U.S. government has officially declared war on the rebels and the drug trade in Colombia. The campaign was originally called Plan Colombia, which (surprise) has expanded into the $1.3 billion Andean Regional Initiative (next year it could be called anything). Currently, there are officially from 180 to 200 U.S. advisors in Colombia training troops, and an additional chunk of Americans working through various contracts—everything from 100 workers spraying coca fields (for Dyncorp), to others fixing helicopters, and to still more undisclosed "contract" military workers and "private consultants" on the ground. Visitors to Colombia will also discover a surprising number of CIA, DEA, DOJ, and U.S. military, essentially men with bad haircuts and bad cover stories, running around. You might find it humorous to note that the U.S. Embassy must approve any American journalists who want to go on military operations or drug eradication gigs. Hmm, this is curious: Since when did the U.S. government have authority in Colombia? The truth is that the United States is running much of the antidrug show down there and it's a poorly kept secret that there will be a lot more people with bad haircuts cruising the bars of Bogota soon.

The rebels and drug lords are disturbed by the gringos trying to cramp their style. So it's not surprising that with all the law enforcement and spooky and military Yanquis running around trying to pass as tourists or civvies, you might as well not even bother trying to come up with an alibi if you are kidnapped.

The positive side of having Colombia as our own backyard firing range is that we get to sell them lots of cool stuff, which of course they pay for with our aid money. The police and the military are in love with their Blackhawks, but they could buy five times as many Russian helicopters. The United States sold 12 UH-60L Blackhawk helicopters to Colombia for $169 million, as well as 24 M60D door-mounted machine guns along with 920,000 rounds of 7.62mm ammo. To make sure they need more U.S.-made goodies we are training a U.S.-backed Colombian mobile army battalion specializing in antidrug operations.

**Plan Colombia/Andean Regional Initiative**
http://www.state.gov/p/wha/rt/plncol
http://www.ciponline.org/facts/co.htm

# Getting In

A passport and a return/onward ticket are required for stays up to three months. Minors (under 18) traveling alone, with one parent, or with a third party must present written authorization from the absent parent(s) or legal guardian, specifically granting permission to travel alone, with one parent, or with a third party. This authorization must be notarized, authenticated by a Colombian embassy or consulate, and translated into Spanish. Visas are not required for citizens of the United States, Canada, or Great Britain for stays up to 90 days.

For up-to-the-minute information regarding entry and customs requirements, contact the nearest consulate in Los Angeles, Miami, Chicago, New Orleans, New York, Houston, or San Juan, or the

## HOW TO SURVIVE AN ANACONDA ATTACK

Here is a brief summary of how to survive an anaconda attack, based on the Peace Corps manual for volunteers who work in the Amazon jungle:

1. Do not run. The snake is faster than you are.
2. Lie flat on the ground, put your arms tight against your sides and your legs tight against each other.
3. Tuck your chin in.
4. The snake will begin to nudge and climb over your body.
5. Do not panic.
6. The snake will begin to swallow you feet first.
7. You must lie perfectly still. This will take a long time.
8. When the snake has reached your knees, reach down, take out your knife, slide it into the side of the snake's mouth between the edge of its mouth and your leg. Quickly rip upward, severing the snake's head.
9. Be sure you have your knife.
10. Be sure your knife is sharp.

embassy in Washington, D.C.

An onward ticket is not always requested at land crossings but you may be asked to prove that you have at least US$20 for each day of your stay in Colombia. Thirty-day extensions can be applied for at the DAS (security police) office in any city.

Entering Colombia by land usually presents no problems at the frontiers. But note that when leaving Colombia by land, you'll need to have an exit stamp from the DAS. You may not be able to get this stamp at the smaller frontier towns. Get the stamp in a city; otherwise, you may be detained.

Cities within Colombia are served by a number of regional airlines. The bigger cities are reached on a daily basis, the smaller ones less frequently, sometimes once a week. By air, Avianca and American Airlines fly regularly to Bogota from the United States, Cali, and Barranquilla. There is an airport tax (payable in cash only) when you leave. Prices are higher in the high season (June–August, December). Internal flights are cheap and are preferred over the efficient but potentially risky bus system.

### Colombian Consulate in the United States

10 East 46th Street
New York, NY 10017
Tel.: (212) 949-9898; (212) 370-0004;
    (212) 370-0088
Fax: (212) 972-1725
http://colombia.nosotros.com

**Colombian Embassy**
2118 Leroy Place, N.W.
Washington, DC 20008
Tel.: (202) 387-8338

**Colombian Consulate in Canada**
360 Albert Street, Suite 1002
Ottawa, Ontario K1R 7X7
Canada
Tel.: (613) 230-3760, or (613) 230-3761
Fax: (613) 230-4416
embajada@embajadacolombia.ca
http://www.embajadacolombia.ca/index.
    html

**Colombian Consulate in the UK**
Flat 3A, 3 Hans Crescent
London SW1X 0LN, UK
Tel.: (44) 020 7589 9177, or (44) 020
    7589 5037
Fax: (44) 020 7581 1829

**Colombian Consulate in Australia**
Colombia House, Level 2
101 Northbourne Avenue
Turner ACT 2612
Australia
Tel.: (02) 6257 2027, or (02) 6257 2458
Fax: (02) 6257 1448
emaustralia@iprimus.com.au
http://www.embacol.org.au

**Other embassies:**
http://www.embassyworld.com/
    embassy/incolombia.html

# Getting Around

Cities within Colombia are served by Avianca, Aces, SAM, Intercontinental, Satena, and Aires airlines. The bigger cities are reached on a daily basis, the smaller ones less frequently, sometimes once a week. By air, Avianca and American Airlines fly regularly to Bogota from the United States, Cali, and Barranquilla. There is an airport tax of US$18. Prices are higher in the high season. Purchase intra-Colombia tickets inside the country.

Buses are a great way to get around, but incidents of thefts are increasing. The air-conditioned buses are often quite frigid when the air-conditioning is working. When it isn't, they're hot, because the windows don't open. Bring your own food, as rest stops are infrequent. Additionally, expect the bus to be periodically stopped and boarded by police. Your identity will most likely be checked. Occasionally, a photocopy of your passport will be sufficient. Make one and have it notarized. Buses leave according to schedule, rather than when they are full. Colombia's VELOTAX minibuses are efficient. However, other buses experience frequent breakdowns.

Taxis are plentiful. Take only metered taxis: If one cannot be found, negotiate and set a fixed price before you enter the taxi. Women should not take taxis alone at night (see Dangerous Things).

The roads in Colombia are often dilapidated and unmarked. Avoid driving at night; Colombian drivers are careless and often reckless.

## Dangerous Places

### Everywhere

It is hard to put your finger on the danger pulse of Colombia: although murders are down in big cities, the countryside is becoming more dangerous by the week. There are twice as many murders in Colombia as in the United States. (And remember, there are 40 million people in Colombia versus 285 million in the United States.)

In an average Colombian day, there are two bank robberies, eight highway robberies, 72 murders, and 204 assaults or muggings. Hey, at least you'll have armed guards if you're kidnapped. Colombia is a country where death by homicide outranks the risk of dying of cancer. Since 1990, some 5,000 police officers have been killed. Only about 12 percent of the crimes committed in Colombia ever reach the judicial system. Are tourists a target? . . . Well, a number of national parks are headquarters for FARC, and yes, there are more kidnap and robbery attempts than we have space to list. Suffice it to say that more than 120 U.S. citizens have been kidnapped over the last 20 years, of whom 14 have been killed, and the U.S. embassy in Bogota proudly proclaims that "the U.S. Government's ability to assist kidnapped U.S. citizens is limited."

http://travel.state.gov/colombia.html
http://www.uniandes.edu.co/Colombia/Turismo/turismo.html
http://www.paho.org/English/HCP/HCN/VIO/violence-graphs.htm#external

### The Darien

Pressed against the Panama border, the Darien is a major coca processing and transshipment center. Because it is also the country's richest banana-growing region, it's home to union organizers, leftist guerrillas, and paramilitary outfits who prey on the union organizers and leftist guerrillas. Think of it as a sort of cocaine-fueled Wild Kingdom. How bad is Uraba? Uraba's annual murder rate of 254 per 100,000 people is the highest in Colombia. Local officials are pleading for UN intervention and for a peacekeeping force to be installed. The area around the Darien Peninsula is a major transit point for contraband goods and a center for drug processing. The FARC group provides protection for the drug labs. Two Austrian and two Swiss tourists were kidnapped while visiting a nature preserve in March 1997. Their kidnappers demanded US$15 million, and FARC wasn't going to use that cash to save the rain forest. Two of the victims were killed in the government rescue attempt. Don't forget that malaria is also a problem here.

http://www.outbackofbeyond.com/guide.htm
http://www.4wdonline.com/Places/CentralAmerica/Darien.html

### Cartagena

This is probably the safest place in Colombia, but tourists are fair game for minor hits and scams. Professional pickpockets abound, especially at the beaches. They like to strike in crowded areas. Cameras are a favorite trophy for thieves here. Other crooks pose as tour guides. Some of them can be rather touchy if you turn down their expensive excursion offers. If you're offered a job on a ship bound for the United States or other parts of South America, don't believe it: This is most assuredly a con.

> **I**f you're offered a job on a ship bound for the United States or other parts of South America, don't believe it: This is most assuredly a con.

http://www.cartagenainfo.com/a-z/english

### Medellin

Despite being a major drug traffickers' center and the new murder capital of Colombia, the city is a remarkably friendly place. Medellin had 4,472 murders in 1997, more than 12 a day. However, it's not the drug lords you should be afraid of here, but the petty thieves and street thugs. Medellin has been experiencing a rash of bombings, most attacks being carried out by FARC. On one day alone in June 1997, FARC bombed the union offices of a lingerie maker, two private homes in the Caicedo neighborhood, and five city buses and, for the piece de resistance, guerrillas booby-trapped a FARC flag, which exploded when a man tried to remove it at Antioquia University. Lovers of violent MTV videos and hip-hoppers take note: Over 5,000 juveniles have admitted to being hired to kill in Medellin.

http://www.poorbuthappy.com/colombia

## Dangerous Things ————————————

### Cleaning

There are groups of urban militants who take the law into their own hands. They mostly prey on the "disposables": junkies, street kids, hookers, homosexuals, and bums. One group in Bogota calls themselves "Clean City."

http://www.amnesty.org

### Kidnapping, or "Miracle Fishing"

Some people collect stamps, and others prefer baseball cards. Colombians prefer people. They seem to be easy to collect and they generate big profits when you unload them. Colombia is the kidnap capital of the world (sorry, Yemen) with an official number of 3,040 registered kidnaps. The real number is much higher because publicity just seems to inspire additional attempts. This does not cover the number of Colombians and foreign businesses that are extorted to prevent kidnapping.

> **S**ome people collect stamps, and others prefer baseball cards. Colombians prefer people. They seem to be easy to collect and they generate big profits when you unload them.

Traditional kidnapping is down in 2002 but the numbers retained by "miracle fishing" has skyrocketed. What's the difference, you ask? Normal kidnapping is when a preselected victim is nabbed and ransomed back. Miracle fishing means creating random roadblocks or undertaking mass kidnaps, then sorting through the victims by throwing away the "little fish" and hopefully finding some big catches. About 80 percent of kidnaps are by leftist groups (FARC and ELN) with the top departments for kidnapping being Antioquia, Choco, and Caldas.

In April 2000, FARC's Mono Jojoy issued communiqué 003, which places a voluntary tax of 10 percent on Colombians who have assets of more than a million dollars. Those who do not voluntarily send in the pesos will be retained until they find the scratch. Cynics might note that FARC imposes fewer taxes and penalties than the IRS does. The Colombian GAULAs, or kidnap rescue forces, free about 40 to 50 victims a month. Many victims are ransomed for a few thousand dollars. Ransom demands for Americans start at about $5 million and can go much higher.

Fewer than 1 in 30 kidnappers are ever caught and sentenced. Fewer than half the kidnappings that actually take place are ever reported. Colombians make up the bulk of the victims and most never report the abductions, fearing it would just advertise their culpability.

http://www.antisecuestro.gov.co/principal.htm

## BIRD-WATCHING, ANYONE?

On March 23, 1998, four Americans were abducted at a roadblock in the forests east of Bogota by armed FARC guerrillas. The tourists were armed with DEET, bird-watching guides, and ignorance. They were later released after the guerrillas discerned that they were indeed bird-watchers and not U.S. operatives. For any real U.S. undercover agent, being a birder would be a tough cover. Oh, the ransom for birdwatchers? Five million dollars. That's a lot of binoculars.

### Murder

Colombia has the highest murder rate in the world, with Johannesburg and Washington, D.C., not far behind. For every 100,000 people, 60 to 70 are offed on a national level. That's about nine times the rate in the United States. Although guerrilla groups do have some hand in the slayings, a full 75 percent of the 25,000 annual murders are committed by common criminals. Murder, however, is dropping in the major cities. *DP* chatted with the mayor of Bogota (a former academic who wears a bulletproof vest with the heart cut out) who said that treating murder as an epidemic has worked in isolating some of the violence from the cause.

### Massacres

Normally playing down the significance of grisly statistics, one government official disarmingly admitted that "In Colombia, the notion of the value of human life has largely been lost." The paras have decided that they will not kill more than three people per day (one cadaver below the Colombian definition of a massacre) and we hope they don't have to put too many late hours in to keep up with the couple of thousand people who are victims of political murders every year.

### Flying

In Colombia, many radar and ground tracking stations are damaged by rebels and drug smugglers to protect illegal drug shipments. More than 1,000 people have died in Colombian air accidents since 1986. And, as mentioned earlier, hijacking domestic airliners is becoming a bigger hit with the rebels these days.

One glance at Colombia's topography and airstrips would immediately explain the high number of accidents. *DP* tip: Satena, the military airline, has three flight crew members on each trip and is your best bet for internal flights. Colombia now meets the top FAA standards for air safety . . . there is, however, that nagging problem of hijackings. In

February 2002, hijackers took over an airliner at a major regional hub and forced it to land on a section of road in order to grab a politician traveling on board. Since 1945 there have been 138 fatal air accidents in Colombia and 2,745 deaths, and the country boasts a grim 9.6 percent survival rate. Not really that bad, but not good. The United States has a 27.7 percent survival rate in an airplane accident.

http://www.satena.com
http://aviation-safety.net/database/country/HK.shtml
http://www.aerocivil.gov.co

### Being Mayor

In Colombia there are 1,098 mayors; a tiny group, but a mayor is 25 times more likely to be killed than a regular citizen in a place where a normal citizen is already ten times more likely to be killed than a U.S. citizen. Why? Because both the FARC and the AUC express their political opinions by killing mayors. Since January 1998, 34 elected mayors have been gunned down. Over 300 candidates have quit, 120 mayors have resigned, 100 have been kidnapped, and 26 do business from secure locations using a phone. Family members are intimidated or killed. *DP* has even seen a mayoral candidate gunned down in broad daylight—shot repeatedly in the head outside a hospital for full effect. Some, like the mayor of Bogota, Anatanas Mockus, fight back by refusing to be intimidated. He of course has a slick, high-speed bodyguard detail and bulletproofed Land Cruiser in addition to his trademark bulletproof vest with the heart cut out. The heart cut out . . . his point, as he told *DP*, is that he keeps his heart open to his enemies. Well, ya' gotta give him points for having *cojones* . . .

http://www.alcaldiabogota.gov.co
http://colhrnet.igc.org

### Being the Mayor's Bodyguard

The Office of Administrative Security employs 2,000 men and women as bodyguards for presidents, cabinet ministers, and other government officials. More than 113 of them have been killed in the line of duty over the last ten years. The U.S. Marshall's office (and *DP* fans) are training protectors of the Colombian judicial and mayoral personnel in an effort to even the playing field.

### Sicarios/Quemarropa

*Sicarios* are Medellin's teenage assassins, found typically in the rough-and-tumble north end of town. They were created in the late '80s by now-dead drug boss Pablo Escobar. The idea was to teach kids a skill that would serve them well in later life. Uh, huh. When Pablo bit the bullet on December 2, 1993, his sicar-ios simply rented themselves out to the highest bidder. Their skills in making bombs, coldly gunning down targets, and melting into slums like La Terazza keep them in demand. Perhaps it's their cultlike faith in the Virgin Mary that keeps them going.

> **T**heir skills in making bombs, coldly gunning down targets, and melting into slums like La Terazza keep them in demand. Perhaps it's their cultlike faith in the Virgin Mary that keeps them going.

There are about 4,000 murders a year in Colombia's second-largest city (population around 2 million). Police claim that as many as 2,000 of these prepubescent assassins—typically hired by drug dealers, paramilitaries, businessmen, and even police, to off their rivals—are on the streets of Medellin.

Independent sources say that between 5,000 and 7,000 young people in the city have committed murder for pay at least once. In an odd reversal of fortune, the homeless or orphaned children that Pablo employed and trained as killers are also targets of death squads. The grubby petty thieves are among the 2,000 people that die every year as targets of social cleansing crimes. Their usual fate? *Quemarropa*—execution at point-blank range.

http://www.philly.com/mld/philly/news/special_packages/killing_pablo

## Oil Pipelines

There are 40 foreign oil-producing companies in Colombia. Occidental Petroleum (Oxy) is the country's largest. The Cano Limon oil field (along the border of Venezuela and Colombia) yields Colombia's largest oil deposits. The 470-mile pipeline cost over a billion dollars to build and is the focal point for guerrilla activity. OK, that's boring, but did you know that over half (51 percent) of the world's terrorist attacks (according to the U.S. State Department) are attacks on Colombian oil pipelines?

Nasty men have blown up the pipeline over 600 times since it came online in 1985—over 150 times in 2001 alone. In 1988, an Oxy engineer was kidnapped and sprung for an impressive US$6 million. To make things fair, the government of Colombia took responsibility for the repair of the pipeline every time the bad guys punched a hole in it. It takes about 36 hours to repair the bomb blasts. About 190,000 barrels of crude oil flow through the pipeline every day. The joke is that the rebels claim that the pipeline is robbing the Colombians of their natural resources. The real criminal seems to be the Colombian government, which skims 85 cents from every dollar generated by the oil. There is a $1.20-a-barrel "war tax" to help fight the guerrillas and a tax of 12 percent of all profits taken out of the country. Occidental Petroleum has shut down its Cano Limon oil field because of continual attacks by rebels. They say it costs them $100,000 each day they're offline. Some 11,000 Colombian soldiers are guarding oil installations. The Casanare field run by Oxy has reserves estimated to be worth $40 billion, with the potential daily output of half a million barrels a day. There is just something about oil-rich countries, terrorism, and U.S. involvement, isn't there?

http://usinfo.state.gov/products/pubs/andes/pipe.htm
http://www.ecopetrol.com.co
http://www.oxy.com

## Heroin

With the U.S. appetite for cocaine down to a relative nasal trickle, the Colombian cartels have turned to heroin, making Colombia the world's third-largest exporter of heroin. Of the hauls seized in the United States in 1993, only 15 percent came from Colombia. The figure more than doubled to 32 percent the following year, and doubled again to 62 percent in 1995. Colombian traffickers have tapped their Asian, Italian, and Afghan contacts for expertise in growing poppies and refining opium in the Andes. The Colombian government has spent over $1 billion on drug-eradication programs, some $300 million of which has come from Uncle Sam, with another $1 billion pledged by the UN over the next ten years. That's not much compared to the $3 to $5 billion the drug trade pockets in Colombia. About 50 percent (6.2 metric tons) of U.S.-consumed heroin now comes from Colombia.

http://www.whitehousedrugpolicy.gov/publications/drugfact/heroin_report/part9.html

## Scopolamine

Scopolamine (or burundanga, as it is called locally) is a drug used by Colombian thugs to incapacitate tourists in order to rob them. It's spiked into drinks and cigarettes and sprayed in taxis. The drug renders victims unconscious and causes serious medical problems. Colombian doctors report that hospitals receive an estimated 2,000 scopolamine victims every month in Bogota. Keep an eye on your cocktail.

http://www.infoplease.com/ce6/sci/A0844088.html

## Picking Bananas

Banana growers have been targeted by both ELN and FARC guerrillas for their alleged support of right-wing death squads. And of course the union organizers are targeted by the paramilitaries. Since 1989, more than 3,000 banana workers have been whacked in rebel attacks. A large number of banana workers in the country are members of the

Hope, Peace & Liberty political party, a former radical leftist guerrilla group that gave up its armed struggle in 1990. Many of the slayings are in revenge for the movement giving up the fight. Some days you just can't win.

http://www.bananalink.org.uk

## Doing Good

Missionaries and human-rights activists are some of the favorite victims in Colombia. Nine human-rights activists were murdered in 1999. An American missionary was shot twice in the head in broad daylight as he walked down a street in Bogota. Needless to say, the number of American missionaries stationed long-term in Colombia has dropped from 551 in 1997 to 430 in 2000.

http://www.christianitytoday.com/ctmag/features/international/samerica/colombia.html

## Bombs

Bombs don't drop from the sky here. They usually drive up to you. Car bombs are detonated in crowded, central locations. Buses are bombed, as well as oil pipelines, refineries, hotels, and office buildings. Bombing is a deliberate attempt to capture publicity and strike fear into the populace. Lately guerrillas have used donkeys, horses, and dead bodies to send bombs into villages.

## Driving

Colombia's roads are in poor condition. Many routes aren't marked. Drivers are reckless. Avoid driving at night: Many vehicles have dim headlights, if any at all. Cattle are unpredictable, as they may pause to pee in the middle of the road at midnight. Steer clear of any military vehicles—they are often rebel targets.

## Taxis

Women should never travel alone at night in taxis. Both sexes are subject to popular scams in which the driver feigns a mechanical breakdown. The passenger is asked to get out of the car and help push the taxi in order to "jump-start" it, which separates the passenger from his or her luggage. The driver will then start the car and drive off. Use only well-marked taxis; do not share a ride or enter a cab with more than one person, even though many cabdrivers will tell you that your travel mate is there for protection—remember, you need only be wrong once. Lock the doors and avoid having scopolamine sprayed in your face by keeping alert and a window cracked (but not enough to let people reach in).

## Buses

Bus travel in the south of Colombia can be hazardous. Thieves haunt buses in this area, waiting for passengers to fall asleep. Then guess what they do? Buses between Bogota and Ipiales and between San Augustin and Popayan are frequented by scam artists/thieves who offer doped chewing gum, cigarettes, food, and sweets before taking everything you've got. Theft, druggings, extortion, and kidnapping occur frequently on buses in both the city and rural areas.

## Getting Sick

Medical care is adequate in major cities, but varies in quality elsewhere. Health problems in Colombia include the presence of cholera, although cholera is found mostly in areas outside the cities and usual tourist areas. Visitors who follow proper precautions regarding food and drink are not generally at risk. Doctors and hospitals often expect immediate cash payment for health services. U.S. medical insurance is not always valid outside the United States. In some cases, supplemental medical insurance with specific overseas coverage is considered useful.

If you are the victim of a scopolamine attack, remember to seek medical assistance immediately. Scopolamine is usually mixed with other narcotics and can cause brain damage.

## Nuts and Bolts

Spanish is the official language. English is common in major cities and tourist centers. The Colombians are very helpful and will go out of their way to advise you on staying safe. They also like to party, so expect massive crowds and price hikes during local holidays. Electricity is 110V/60Hz. Local time is the same as New York. The local currency is the peso, about 1,400 to the U.S. dollar at the time of writing.

Temperatures vary widely depending on elevation. It gets cooler and wetter the higher you go. Seaside areas are muggy. Heavy rain falls between April and October.

Business hours are from 8 A.M. till noon and from 2 to 6 P.M. Monday–Friday. Bank hours in Bogota are from 9 A.M. to 3 P.M. Monday–Thursday, and from 9 A.M. to 3:30 P.M. on Fridays, except the last Friday of the month, when they close at noon. In other major cities, businesses are open from 8 to 11:30 A.M. and from 2 to 4 P.M. Monday–Thursday. On Friday, they're open until 4:30 P.M., except the last Friday of the month, when they close at 11:30 A.M.

## Embassy Location/Registration

Upon arrival, U.S. citizens are urged to obtain updated information on travel and security within Colombia and to register with the following:

**Consular Section, U.S. Embassy**
Calle 38 No. 8–61
Bogota, Colombia
Tel.: (57) 1 320-1300

**U.S. Consulate**
Calle 77, Carrera 68
Centro Comercial Mayorista
Barranquilla, Colombia
Tel.: (57) 58 45-8480 or 45-9067

# Dangerous Days

| | |
|---|---|
| **12/12/02** | AUC leader asks UN to join peace talks. |
| **11/29/02** | Carlos Castano and the AUC declare a unilateral cease-fire, ask for protection against the FARC, and abandon links to drug business. |
| **8/11/02** | Uribe declares state of emergency. |
| **8/7/02** | President Alvaro Uribe sworn in; FARC attacks with rockets. |
| **2/22/02** | Army retakes Zona del Despeje, or rebel safe zone. |
| **6/28/01** | FARC releases 242 prisoners. |
| **4/16/01** | Rebels kidnap nearly 100 Occidental Petroleum workers. |
| **11/8/99** | FARC rebels take control of a "demilitarized zone" the size of Switzerland. |
| **10/8/87** | The Simon Bolivar Guerrilla Coordinating Board (CNG) is founded, an umbrella organization under which the Revolutionary Armed Forces of Colombia (FARC), the National Liberation Army (ELN), and a dissident faction of the Popular Liberation Army (EPL) coordinate political positions and organize joint terrorist operations. |
| **4/19/71** | The 19th of April Movement (M-19) originated; leader Ivan Marino Ospina is killed in a clash with government troops. |
| **4/29/67** | Founding of the EPL (Popular Liberation Army). |
| **8/15/64** | The National Liberation Army (ELN) begins its armed struggle. |
| **5/27/64** | Government troops attack the "independent republic" that communist peasant groups set up at Marquetalia, Caldas Department. |

| | |
|---|---|
| **11/11/57** | The Popular Liberation Army (EPL) is founded, a leftist terrorist organization that has since made peace with the government and become a legitimate political party. However, a dissident faction continues the armed struggle against the government. |
| **7/17/30** | Communist Party founded. |
| **8/7/1819** | Battle of Boyacas. |
| **7/20/1810** | Independence Day. |

## In a Dangerous Place: Colombia

### MALAY MERCENARY IN COLOMBIA

"Ismaël"* is a Malay jungle commando who fought last year as a mercenary against the left-wing opposition and drug cartels in Colombia. He sums up the experience: "Fifteen of the twenty men of our unit were shot dead by the FARC. Surrounded and against hundreds of FARC guerrillas, we decided to surrender. . . . Where they came from, I didn't know, but if the drug barons had caught us, we would have been dead within an hour; we were actually glad to be captured by the FARC."

After decades of war the Colombian military still fights the war from heavily armed camps, and controls only the air. In 2001 jungle warfare specialists were brought in to take the War on Drugs to the ground. The most experienced jungle mercenaries are found not in the steaming jungles of Latin America but on the other side of the world. Government commandos in the Southeast Asian nation of Malaysia have built a reputation from the '60s onward based on their struggle against left-wing groups in the jungles of Borneo and on the Malay peninsula. Their reputation equals that of the Ghurkas. Ismaël is one of the ex-commandos who was asked by his government to go to Colombia as a paid mercenary in a covert operation with political deniability. Ismaël has nothing to hide: "I was offered US$50,000 for three months: one third before leaving, one third while entering the plane, and one third on return," he recounts.

Ismaël's mission started in the second half of 2001. "With a group of twenty Malay ex-commandos, we were flown to an American airbase in Germany. Here we received our assignment for the first time and spoke about the tactics. We had to destroy houses, fields, and fabrics of drug barons. Our Malay unit would operate on the basis of First In,

---

*The name of the person interviewed has been changed for security reasons.

First Out, meaning to say that we had to do the dirty work. After this briefing, we flew via the United States and two South American countries to Bogota. Before the start of an operation we received detailed information that the Americans had collected from the air. In this way we knew how many people we could expect. We split up to enter the target from as many different sides as possible, disappeared into the countryside of Colombia, and said we would meet at a certain time at which we opened the attack. Our unit killed the people on and around the target. After that, the Americans—who coordinated the cleaning operation—appeared and burned the site down.

"We had to laugh about the Americans. We had walked already for days in dirty clothes and lightly armed through the lands of Colombia, in order not to attract the attention of the local people . . . a huge contrast with the Americans, who were freshly shaved, smelled like soap, were dressed from head to toe in thick, dark suits and bulletproof vests, and were heavily armed with speakers in their ears and nightviewers on their heads. As soon as the target was destroyed, the Americans left first, after which we disappeared into the jungle pretty much the same way as we came. Just like in Afghanistan, the Americans have the dirty work on the ground done by others. But they put in their newspapers that 'they' booked their next victory." Ismaël smiles bitterly. As a military commando in Malaysia he never received any honor or medals. Dirty operations are kept a secret.

After seven successful operations in Colombia, it all went wrong for Ismaël. "One way or the other, they must have known about our plans. Now that the drug transports don't go by air anymore, they are taking place on the backs of donkeys, with the help of the local farmers, through the countryside. Local farmers, FARC, paramilitaries, and drug lords—they know each other. They talk. Still, I wonder where the leak was. The hundred FARC soldiers who surrounded us, killed fifteen of our men, and captured us couldn't figure us out: Malays look like Colombians, but we don't speak Spanish. When we had to undress, one of them, who had been in a training camp learning about custody, threw something toward us that we had to catch. I caught it with my right hand. They knew now that I did everything right-handed.

"They broke my right ankle, the fingers of my right hand, my right wrist, and kicked the rest of the right side of my body, so that I couldn't escape. They did the same with the other four of our group who were still alive. Pretty smart.

"After that they put me in a knee-high cage made of wood. There was a little stream going through from which I had to drink and which I had to use as a toilet. I am trained for these kind of situations, but it was the first time in my life that I was actually captured."

Although he and his group technically were working as private citizens, Ismaël is glad that it was a government-sponsored operation. "The fact that I worked for the [Colombian] government has saved my life: They paid the ransom money when we were held by the FARC."

Ismaël thinks the Americans will not win the battle against drugs in Colombia. "The situation in Colombia has gone too far. The land is divided between a corrupt government, the FARC, paramilitaries, and other political movements who work together with the drug barons whenever they feel like it and who give the drug barons protection in return for money. One group is even more heavily armed than the other. The drug barons are so rich that the moment you clear something, within weeks it appears again, a couple of kilometers farther down the road.

"I don't want to go back to Colombia. Not only because I think the battle cannot be won. No. There's something else. For me the only way to justify this for myself, that I do this job, is that I am convinced that I fight for the right cause. And I hesitate. Did I fight for the right side? I mean: I am against terrorism, against communism, and against drugs. But if one-third of the people of a country agree with a rebel army that turns itself against the government, then I wonder why they have so many followers? Maybe they do have a legitimate cause for which they are fighting."

*—Linda van Wijk*

### ★ ★ ★

# GEORGIA (SAKARTVELO)

## Breakin' Up is Hard to Do

The former Soviet Republic of Georgia is best thought of as one giant cautionary civics lesson: How Not to Run a Country 101. Over the last century or so, successive bungling rulers (inbred Tsars, murderous communists, and batty nationalists) have surmounted overwhelmingly favorable odds. Georgia has it all; it sits astride a strategic land and sea trade route with a bracing, healthy climate; it boasts scenic beauty that should attract tourists like unwashed dogs attract fleas; it has a poetic history that should spawn epic movies; it is packed with natural resources, including oil and obscene amounts of hydroelectric power; and it has a literate population that you would think would compete with Paris for bohemian bragging rights. But with all these gifts, Georgia is a broken-down, bankrupt ruin whose population shivers in empty buildings without electricity or heating, and where absolutely nothing works, least of all the people. In a country where there is no

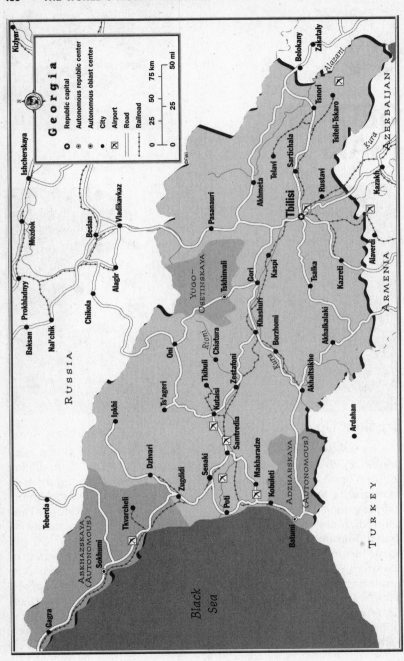

shortage of "Things to Do," almost 15 percent of the labor force is doing nothing. To put an ironic twist to the whole image thing, Georgia's most famous homeboy is Joseph Stalin.

Like most people whose modern times have been less than fun, Georgians are fond of harking back to a bygone golden era. It was here that Jason and his Argonauts chased the Golden Fleece. It is here that wine was perfected. If you squint and give the ancient buildings the benefit of the doubt, you could be in 1920s Paris or 1940s Prague, but you are technically in Asia and realistically in a dump.

Georgia's golden age was 800 years ago, during the reign of King David the Builder. It was David who commissioned the magnificent churches and monuments, which are still pretty much the only structures in Georgia that don't look like they'd come down with a reasonably determined shove. KD the B also freed Georgia from the Turks, whom Georgians still blame for everything wrong with Georgia that they don't blame on Russians, Armenians, or Jews (potential visitors with tender, liberal sensibilities should brace themselves for the fact that saloon-bar talk in downtown Tbilisi, Kutaisi, and Zugdidi can get a little on the unreconstructed side). David's rule also marked, to judge by the state of most of Georgia's public buildings, the last time anyone in Georgia did any dusting, painting, or plumbing.

Since King David passed on to the great toolshed in the sky, not an awful lot has gone right for Georgia. Tbilisi, the capital, has been destroyed 40 times—and, except for the supremely pretty city center, it looks it. In 1801, Georgia's last king, the imaginatively named George, decided that security was better than independence and handed over the keys and pink slips to the Russians—just the people you'd turn to if you were the monarch of a small nation struggling to protect a unique and discrete cultural and linguistic heritage from assorted marauding invaders . . . and you were completely off your rocker.

This arrangement proved so popular with ordinary Georgians that as soon as the Russian royals were distracted by Bolsheviks at their gates, Georgia declared itself independent. The first Republic of Georgia was established on May 26, 1918, presumably in the hope that Russia's new rulers would be too nice or too busy to crush the modest aspirations of a fledgling nation. They weren't. By March of 1921, the Red Army had retaken all of Georgia, and it was forcibly incorporated into the USSR.

Still, by 1929 Georgians could have been forgiven for thinking that it wouldn't be so bad—after all, one of their own was now in charge. Josef Stalin, remembered by fellow residents of the unprepossessing central Georgian town of Gori as cobbler's son Iosif Vissarionovich Dzughashvili. and by the rest of us as one of the most comprehensively appalling people who ever lived, had risen to the exalted position of

General Secretary of the Communist Party. Georgians must have anticipated some special attention from their local boy made good—especially considering that one of his most trusted lieutenants, NKVD
(secret police) chief Lavrenti Beria, was another native son, from the
small Georgian coastal village of Merkheuli.

Georgia most certainly did get special attention from this delightful
pair, though probably not the sort that had been anticipated. Stalin was
as paranoid about Georgian nationalism as he was about everything
else and had tens of thousands of his country folk executed or deported.
Nobody was safe from Stalin's rampages—at a show trial in 1937 the
former premier of Soviet Georgia, Budu Mdvani, was dubiously convicted of plotting to kill Beria and was shot. Mdvani's wife and four
children also fell victim to the purges, as did most of the Georgian Communist Party. Bizarrely, all things considered, Stalin is fondly remembered in Georgia—in Gori, parades commemorate his birthday every
year on December 21, the central square is still dominated by the last
statue of the tyrant standing anywhere in the world, and the town also
contains a vast, and utterly uncritical, museum honoring Stalin's life
and accomplishments. Don't leave without a souvenir key ring.

## BETTER THAN THE WWF

You don't need organized sports or simulated violence to keep busy in Georgia. Here
is just a minor list of what never makes it into the tourist brochures:

| | |
|---|---|
| 12/99 | UNHCR moves Chechen refugees from Shatili (the main gateway) to the remote area of Pankisi. |
| 8/00 | Two ICRC officers kidnapped. |
| 11/30/00 | Two Spanish businessmen kidnapped in Tbilisi and hidden in Pankisi. |
| 5/7/01 | Parliamentarian Petre Tsiskarishvili and his fiancée kidnapped and taken to Pankisi Gorge. |
| 6/7/01 | Two more businessmen escape kidnap attempt right outside their office in Tbilisi. |
| 7/1/01 | 83-year-old father of a Tbilisi restaurant owner kidnapped from Telavi in eastern Georgia. |
| 7/12/01 | Four men kidnap an employee of the State Guard Service from Pshaveli in the Telavi Region. Local villagers start reciprocal kidnappings and form vigilante groups. |
| 7/18/01 | Three villages in the Akhmeta region (Magraani, Agrokhi, and Pichkhovani) create their own Kakheti militia and checkpoints. They claim that the police are behind many of the crimes and kidnapping. |

**7/19/01**   Russia claims that the Pankisi Gorge is harboring bandit groups forced out of Chechnya and the area poses a security threat.

**9/14/01**   Russian Duma representative Boris Nemtsov's announcement that "Russia should annihilate terrorists in the Pankisi Gorge with or without Georgian consent."

**10/7/01**   The wife of Vepkhia Margoshvili, a warlord from Pankisi Gorge, is detained by the police. Margoshvili goes on local television to threaten war if his wife is not released.

**10/14/01**   Georgian citizen kidnapped and released next day ($30,000 ransom not paid).

**10/17/01**   Pankisi warlord Vepkhia Margoshvili is killed by an explosion at his house. He, along with the local police, was linked to the kidnappings of two ICRC officers in summer 2000, the Spanish businessmen, a Georgian MP, and also his fiancée.

**11/13/01**   Four orthodox Christian monks are kidnapped in Pankisi Gorge. Kidnappers demand $1 million.

**11/27/01**   Three of the four kidnapped monks are released in Pankisi Gorge. Police say no ransom was paid.

**11/27/01**   Five Russian helicopters bomb Pankisi Gorge near the villages of Omalo and Birkiani at night. There are no casualties.

**11/28/01**   Two warplanes violate Georgian airspace from Russia.

**11/30/01**   Vladimer Putin denies that the Russian warplanes attacked the Georgian territory and accuses Georgia of harboring Chechen and Arab mercenaries in Pankisi Gorge.

**12/7/01**   Georgian intelligence officers find 33-year-old kidnapped Japanese journalist Kosuke Tsuneoka. He had been missing since July 2001.

**12/9/01**   Two kidnapped Spanish businessmen released near Telavi, eastern Georgia.

**1/14/02**   Internal Affairs Minister Koba Narchemashvili issues a special decree prohibiting negotiations with kidnappers and paying ransom.

**1/15/02**   Georgian police launch operations in Pankisi Gorge to relocate their checkpoint further up the gorge.

**1/15/02**   Georgian government announces an estimate of 600 criminals in Pankisi Gorge.

**2/15/02**   Russian Foreign Affairs Minister Igor Ivanov states at the news briefing in Paris that Osama bin Laden may be in Pankisi Gorge. "Who can prove that this is not true?" the Russian foreign minister asked.

GEORGIA

| 2/17/02 | Following the arrest of a suspect, police checkpoints are attacked in Duisi, Pankisi. Four cops are kidnapped to force release of comrade. |
| 2/19/02 | Four policemen kidnapped on February 17 at a Pankisi checkpoint are released. |

Source: Various news reports; Civil Georgia

After Stalin did everyone the enormous favor of dropping dead, life in Georgia returned to the routine, clammy drudgery of communism, until the Soviet Union stopped answering to its own name in 1991. Georgia's second stab at independence has, at the time of writing, not provoked yet another invasion by Russia, but the hopes that the easing of Moscow's grip might permit Georgia to develop into a Dionysian paradise of wine and song, as portrayed on Intourist posters, have proved forlorn.

In May 1991, Georgia became the first former Soviet Republic to hold a popular presidential election. An extraordinary 86 percent of Georgians voted for Zviad Gamsakhurdia, a well-known university professor who had been jailed during Brezhnev's rule for founding a civil-liberties monitoring group. Unfortunately, Gamsakhurdia seemed to think that his massive mandate gave him license to do as he damn well pleased. (Democracy is a simple idea on paper, but it can take a while to catch on when people aren't used to it.) One of his first bright ideas was to abolish the autonomous status of the province of South Ossetia. When the South Ossetians threatened to go off and start a new country with their friends in North Ossetia, Gamsakhurdia sent in the army. Thousands ended up dead, and thousands more scattered with whatever they could carry (a cease-fire was finally brokered in July 1992).

Not content with provoking tragic and pointless civil wars in the sticks, Gamsakhurdia also started one on his doorstep. He closed newspapers, had everyone he didn't agree with sacked or arrested, and authored economic reforms so ludicrous that even people who'd been governed by Moscow for 70 years noticed how ludicrous they were. They took to the streets, led by several members of Gamsakhurdia's own government. Gamsakhurdia responded with a television address calling on loyal Georgians to turn out in favor of him, and busloads of bumpkins from the boondocks answered the call—the same kind of people who used to turn up in Belgrade for Slobodan Milosevic's sponsored student-thumping away-days for half-witted rent-a-yokels. There was a lot of anger and frustration, and even more weaponry, mostly liberated from Soviet troops still stationed in Georgia and willing to sell pretty much anything for the price of a bottle of vodka. In December 1991, Tbilisi went to war with itself. Gamsakhurdia fled the capital in

January 1992, and in March, the newly formed state council made former Soviet foreign minister Eduard Shevardnadze president—an appointment subsequently confirmed by elections.

Shevardnadze had hardly moved his stuff into the office when fighting broke out in Georgia's northwestern seaside province of Abkhazia. The Abkhazians, egged on by the nefarious Russians, wanted their own country, and the Georgians weren't keen on giving away their coastline. The ensuing war between the Georgian army and Russian-backed separatist militias killed thousands on both sides and displaced 250,000 ethnic Georgians—one Georgian in 20. By September 1993, Georgian troops had been driven out of Abkhazia, and Abkhazia had declared itself independent—there has not, however, been a stampede of nations wanting to open embassies in Sokhumi, the wannabe republic's putative capital.

Gamsakhurdia chose this moment of national humiliation to stage a return. It went, it is fair to say, badly. With the assistance of sympathetic elements of the Georgian army and even some Abkhaz forces, he started off quite well, capturing several towns in western Georgia. Unfortunately, he'd forgotten that his rival for the presidency had a lot more old work buddies in the Kremlin than he did: Shevardnadze asked the Russians for help, and got it. The rebellion folded in January 1994, and Gamsakhurdia killed himself. At his widow's request, he was buried in the Chechen capital, Grozny—the postal address of a lot of the people who'd helped him stage his revolt.

Georgia is now a small and little-regarded front in George W. Bush's War on Terror—U.S. military advisors were deployed in early 2002 to help the Georgian military deal with its lawless Pankisi Gorge region, where guerrillas from neighboring Chechnya were harboring stray jihadi cadres and training foreign terrorists.

## The Scoop

Georgia is a wreck—seriously, the whole country looks like somebody dropped it—but it's a fairly affable one. Despite Georgia's dishevelled state, Russia and America both want it very badly. Russia by whatever underhanded and violent means possible, and America by squandering cash and military training on it. For now the Americans are winning, but don't be surprised if Russia finds a reason to invade (phantom terrorists and questionable crime sprees are the latest excuse for bombing and interfering). Abkhazia, the Pankisi

> **G**eorgia is a wreck—seriously, the whole country looks like somebody dropped it—but it's a fairly affable one.

Gorge, and South Ossetia are more tense than they are dangerous, but the former can escalate into the latter without much warning. Day-to-day existence for most Georgians, and most visitors, is difficult: Utilities and services function erratically, when they function at all.

Probably the most amazing symptom of Georgia's dysfunction is the sight of so many Honda generators being used to power shops in one of the world's most hydroelectric-rich countries.

## The Players

### *Eduard Shevardnadze*

Silver-haired and frequently almost-assassinated, President of Georgia Eduard Shevardnadze's résumé includes stints as a KGB official, communist party apparatchik, and foreign minister of the Soviet Union. Shevardnadze was once enormously popular in Georgia—he was re-elected with 80 percent of the vote at the last election in 2000—but his star is beginning to wane as more and more of the population become less and less patient with Georgia's continuing failure to resemble a modern European country. That said, most Georgians will grudgingly admit that "The Silver Fox," as Shevardnadze is half-admiringly, half-derisively known, might well be the only thing that has prevented this struggling country from going irretrievably to the dogs. Probably only Shevardnadze could have talked down the mutinous soldiers who, in 2001, seized a military barracks near Tbilisi and threatened a coup to protest the fact that they hadn't been paid for a year.

As president, Shevardnadze has adopted a pro-Western outlook, and has done what he can to ameliorate Georgia's prevailing plagues of regional secessionist squabbles, organized crime, and institutional corruption. However, living standards for ordinary Georgians have continued to plummet, and Shervardnadze has shown worrisome signs of resorting, like his Russian counterpart Vladimir Putin, to the favorite Soviet tactic of shooting (or at least harassing) the messenger. In 2001, the privately owned television station Rustavi-2, which had criticized rampant featherbedding by government ministers, was raided by security police on the pretext of financial irregularities (a line also spun by Slobodan Milosevic whenever he sent his head-kickers to shut down broadcasters he didn't like).

Thousands of protestors filled the streets in response, demanding the sacking of the universally loathed minister for internal affairs, Kakha Tarmagadze. Shevardnadze eventually gave Tarmagadze the boot, along with the rest of the government, but his obvious reluctance did nothing to quell rumors that Tarmagadze knows things about Shevardnadze that Shevardnadze would prefer that the rest of us not find out (possibly, according to popular rumor, to do with Gamsakhurdia's death, which is still a subject of conjecture). Perhaps mindful of this, Shevardnadze has announced that he won't run at the next election, due in 2005. He may also be reflecting that, at 74, he's getting a bit old for rough-and-tumble Caucasian politics. Shevardnadze has survived two assassination attempts: a car bomb in 1995, and a grenade attack by sulking Gamsakhurdia fans, known as Zviadists, in 1998. The 1998 attack was masterminded by Gamsakhurdia's finance minister, Guram Absandze, who was later sentenced to 17 years in a labor camp for his troubles.

**Press Office of the President of Georgia**
http://www.presidpress.gov.ge

**Parliament of Georgia**
http://www.parliament.ge

## Vladislav Ardzinba

President of Abkhazia, though neither his position nor his nation are recognized by the rest of the world, Ardzinba was appointed to the post by the parliament in 1994 and eventually elected in 1999 in a landslide victory (which wasn't totally unexpected, given that there were no other candidates). "The elections cannot be called undemocratic just because only one man was running for the presidency," explained Vlad, who is expected to get to page 2 of *Democracy for Beginners* any day now.

http://www.abkhazia.org

## The Abkhazians

It's hard to believe that this former Autonomous Soviet Socialist Republic (founded in March 1921) made money as a tourist resort for Russians. Until, of course, the Russians turned it into a wasteland back in '92 and again in '93. The Russians essentially invented a pro-Russian group that fought against the separatist group, in their classic "If I can't have it, then no one else will" style. The region is a sad testament to the Russian version of Hearts and Minds . . . heartless, mindless destruction. There was also enough Stalinist pushing and shoving between Georgians and Russians to reduce the Abkhazians to only 18 percent of the region's population. Folks here speak Abkhaz instead of Georgian and use the Cyrillic alphabet instead of the squiggly Georgian one. Basically, they're about as different from Georgians as Croats are from Serbs, which is to say both hardly at all and more than enough. There is an ongoing historical debate in Georgian political and academic circles about whether or not the Abkhazians are a pure race quite apart from their Georgian neighbors or kindred descendents of a Georgian tribe; the literature on the subject is highly recommended if you're having trouble sleeping or are about to undergo surgery someplace where there's no anesthetic available. For now, official visits are strictly a UN-chaperoned gig or a sneak in/sneak out affair.

**United Nations Observer Mission in Georgia**
http://www.un.org/Depts/DPKO/Missions/unomig/unomig_body.htm

## The Forest Brothers

No, not the group of banjo-plucking good ol' boys that the name suggests, nor a Caucasian version of the Jungle Brothers, but an organization nevertheless capable of making the unlucky visitor to the Abkhazian border region feel like he's starring in a remake of *Deliverance*. The Forest Brothers are a smallish group of ruffians that evolved from the rather less-pronounceable Mkhedrioni (a private Georgian nationalist militia that formed during the first war with Abkhazia). They are led by someone called Dato Shengalia, about whom little is known beyond the fact that his name is Dato Shengalia.

**Voice of Abkhazia Radio**
http://www.qsl.net/yb0rmi/abkhazia.htm

## The White Legion

Known locally as the Tetri Legioni, the White Legion are another ethnically Georgian rabble with a cause at large in Abkhazia, who finance their activities with kidnapping and banditry. The White Legion was founded in late 1994 by a 46-year-old former physicist called Zurab Samushia—Zoza to his friends—who also serves as chairman of the Committee of the Resistance Movement of Abkhazeti (Abkhazeti is what Georgians call Abkhazia; the Abkhazians have several slightly less-graceful names for Georgia). Samushia's stated ambition is to shoot Abkhazian President Vladislav Ardzinba. Well, all God's children need a dream.

> **S**amushia's stated ambition is to shoot Abkhazian President Vladislav Ardzinba. Well, all God's children need a dream.

**Autonomous Republic of Abkhazeti**
http://www.abkhazeti.org

## The Russian Army

Russian troops are present in large numbers on peacekeeping duties in the fractious provinces of Abkhazia and South Ossetia, and they present a thoroughly wretched spectacle. In late 1998, *DP* was flagged down by a Russian army checkpoint while driving into the mountainous Svaneti region near the border with Abkhazia. Did they want to see our papers? No. Did they want to interrogate us? No. Did they want to hit us up for bribes? No. What they wanted, they explained after a bashful silence, was for us to buy their boots, and any other bits of their dilapidated kit we fancied, because they hadn't been paid for three months and hadn't eaten for three days. So, if you're heading through Russian-patrolled territory, take a few spare loaves of bread and an extra crate of beer. Russian officers make $100 a month and while they are extorting their enlisted men they are also busy selling off AKs, ammo, or any equipment that will get them the price of vodka and cigarettes. Oh, did I tell you that the Russians are in Georgia to help with the security situation?

**Russian-Georgian War**
http://www.geocities.com/shavlego/war_wg_1.htm

## The Mafiya

The neckless, bowling-ball-headed, stripy-, double-breasted–suited brigade are as big in Georgia as everywhere else in the former USSR. They're particularly big in Tbilisi and also in Batumi, the Black Sea port which styles itself as the capital of a would-be banana republic called the Adjaran Autonomous Republic. The flashy discos, 7-series Beemers (no plates, of course), and well-lit restaurants next to dark, empty stores might be a clue to where the money goes in this country. By the way, be careful whom you call *mafiya* in Georgia: the locals usually think you mean the government.

**Human Rights/Corruption in Georgia**
http://www.sakartvelo.com/Files/Rights/human.html

## The Chechens

If you imagine the Caucasus as a junior high school—which, given the politics, shouldn't be difficult—then the Chechens are the gang of glue-sniffers and car thieves that everyone always hopes won't turn up at their party, but who always do. The Pankisi Gorge in Georgia has been a favored R&R location for guerrillas from Chechnya, and, on the other side of the country, Chechens have played a role on either or both sides (depending whom you believe) in the interminable fighting in Abkhazia. In March 2002, Russia's foreign ministry wrote to the Georgian government to insist on the arrest of Chechen commander Ruslan Gelayev, who Moscow claimed was hiding out in Georgia. The truth is, Georgia is home to almost a quarter-million internally displaced persons and about 8,000 refugees—families who have escaped from Chechnya, Abkhazia, South Ossetia, and other regions. Some armed groups from these regions are also present and most have an understanding with the locals that if they buy food and lodging—and protect them from the corrupt police and military—they are welcome.

http://www.refugees.org/world/countryrpt/europe/georgia.htm

## Getting In

Citizens of Russia and of most former Soviet republics, and of Bulgaria (for some reason), can come and go as they please. For everyone else, visas are required, ranging in price from $40 for a two-week single-entry visa to $200 for a multiple-entry visa valid for one year. Unfortunately, the Georgians are still adhering to that infuriatingly pointless and boneheaded relic of Soviet-era, state-sponsored tourism: the letter of invitation. A travel agent will be able to organize this, but independent visitors who don't already know someone in Georgia will have to get creative—try e-mailing companies based in Tbilisi and promising them a bottle of decent Scotch in return for their cooperation. Keep in mind that flying in through the main airport is a piece of cake complete with live entertainment. On our last trip we were entertained by the sounds of screaming: Newly arrived passengers were being hustled into the night by leather-jacketed, gold-chain-adorned secret police. Fun place. . . .

### Georgia Information and News
http://www.eurasianet.org/resource/georgia/hypermail/news/index.shtml
http://dir.yahoo.com/regional/countries/georgia/business_and_economy

Before calling either of the following numbers, brace yourself for the signature telephone manner of all former Soviet peoples, who sound like burned-out telemarketers on horse tranquilizers. In person they are even more charming, adopting the same cheerful demeanor as ticket-sellers at all-night porno houses

### Embassy of Georgia to the United States, Canada, and Mexico
1615 New Hampshire Avenue, NW, Suite 300
Washington, DC 20009
Tel.: (202) 387-2390
Fax: (202) 393-4537
embassyofgeorgia@hotmail.com
http://www.georgiaemb.org

### Embassy of Georgia, London
4 Russell Gardens
London W14 8EZ, UK
Tel.: (44) 207 603 7799
Fax: (44) 207 603 6682
geoemb@dircon.co.uk

## Getting Around

Georgia's travel infrastructure consists of slow trains, unreliable Russian Ladas, ancient buses, and Soviet-era airplanes that one can only hope are more rigorously maintained than everything else in Georgia. By far the best bet is to hire a car and driver, which can usually be done for less than $100 a day through a local travel agent.

Keep in mind that tourism is still a pipe dream here, and restaurants or hotels may magically spring from dormancy when you arrive. Since all the large Intourist hotels are full of refugees, Georgia has one of the nicest and cheapest homestay programs we have seen. Just don't be surprised if the bed is still warm. The usual method is for the hosts to move out of the apartment during your stay (leaving toothpaste, clothes, books, and other personal belongings exactly where they left them), and then move back in when you leave. A good starting point for any ambitious endeavor is:

**Caucasus Travel Ltd.**
P.O. Box 160
380008 Tbilisi
Georgia
Tel.: (995) 32 98 7400
Fax: (995) 32 98 7399
georgia@caucasustravel.com.ge
http://www.caucasustravel.com.ge

**Caucasus Travel Europe Ltd.**
St. Mary's Court
39 Market Place, Henley-on-Thames
Oxfordshire RG9 2AA, UK
Tel.: (44) 1491 410 510
Fax: (44) 1491 413 893
cauceuro@aol.com

# Dangerous Places

## Abkhazia

Abkhazia is in the far northwest, broadly defined by the Black Sea coast, the border with Russia, and the Kodori River. After Georgia became independent from the Soviet Union in 1991, Abkhazia attempted to become independent from Georgia. The war that followed failed to attract much attention in the outside world, but was real enough to the hundreds who ended up dead and the 250,000 (mostly ethnic Georgians) who were displaced—many of Tbilisi's big Intourist hotels are still effectively high-rise refugee camps.

Abkhazia continues to simmer, despite the nonaggression pact signed with Georgia in 2001. Abkhazia has since accused Georgia of encouraging ethnically Georgian guerrillas, ferrying in Chechen jihadis, and carrying out air raids. Georgia blamed the air raids on the Russians, but not too much should be read into this, as blaming the Russians is Georgia's default position on pretty much every subject.

Abkhazia today is fairly safe, aside from the area that you'll have to cross to get into it. The Kodori Gorge—the only part of Abkhazia still under the direct control of the Georgian government—and the Abkhaz side of the Inguri River cease-fire line are prowled by a diverse array of brigands. Kidnappings and hijackings by local bandits are common, and Georgian militias continue to pester Abkhaz military personnel and civilians alike.

Abkhazia is determined to carry on as if it's a normal country, even if nobody else will recognize it as such. Local elections in 2001 were written off as illegitimate by international observers on the not-unreasonable grounds that no provisions were made for getting a vote from the 250,000 ethnic Georgians who have fled Abkhazia since "independence."

http://www.abkhazia.org
http://hypatia.ss.uci.edu/gpacs/abkhazia
http://www.apsny.org

## Zugdidi

The major city on Georgia's frontier with Abkhazia, Zugdidi took a bit of a shellacking during the war, but in a Georgian city nobody really notices a few ruined buildings or the number of potholes. It's now a major base camp for NGOs operating in Abkhazia.

**Horizonti, The Foundation for the Third Sector**
33 Gogebashvili
Tbilisi 380079, Georgia
Tel./Fax: (995) 32 29 2955
presscenter@horizonti.org
http://www.horizonti.org

## South Ossetia

The South Ossetians started flinging their toys out of their prams in 1991, demanding to be united with North Ossetia, in an independent Ossetian state, with all the accoutrements that come with such a thing—their own flag, their own banknotes with dead, bearded, Ossetian blokes on them, a national soccer team doomed to decades of losing 12–0 to Turkmenistan in pointless Central Asian tournaments, and so on. Whatever their national virtues may turn out to be, tact will not be among them. In March 2002, South Ossetia's president, thirty-something former wrestling champion, guerrilla commander, and Moscow businessman Eduard Kokoyev, called on Moscow to react to the deployment of American military advisors in Georgia by sending in more troops of their own.

http://www.kafkas.org.tr/english/BGKAFKAS/bukaf_gosetya.html

## The Pankisi Gorge

This 80-kilometer stretch of Caucasian Wild West on Georgia's northern border has been to the war in Chechnya roughly what the bench is to an ice-hockey match. Moscow has complained long and loud that the Georgian government, if not actively encouraging

Chechen guerrillas to use the Pankisi for training, storing supplies, and recuperation, isn't doing much to discourage them, either. This may not have been just the usual Russian bellicosity—Shevardnadze finally admitted that Chechen commander Khamzat Gelayev and around 300 of his merry men were hiding out in the Pankisi George and went on to describe Gelayev as "an educated man," which might well have done in Shevardnadze's chances of a Christmas card from the Kremlin.

However, Shevardnadze hasn't gotten where he is today by not being able to tell which way the wind was blowing. In March 2002, he welcomed U.S. military advisors whose intended mission was to train Georgian special forces to clean up the Pankisi Gorge—even though journalists had reported there was nothing to clean up. All those nasty terrorists turned out to be simply Chechen refugees trying to escape the fighting in Chechnya. Among them were a few dozen guerrilla fighters on R&R or just visiting family. The United States and Russia decided that this might be the new home of bin Laden, complete with training camps, drive-through dirty-bomb dispensers, and other horrors. If further attempts to change things in Georgia are as successful as previously, it should not make a single ripple. The U.S. government had been training the Border and Customs service. Evidence of this was seen by *DP* when we slipped into Chechnya. We can attest that there was a large, battered guestbook and at least two working pens.

Whatever the truth may be, there is no doubt that the Pankisi Gorge is authentic bandit country. One of the major industries in the region is kidnapping for ransom, generally done by Georgians of Chechen descent, known as Kists.

http://www.tbilisipastimes.com/traveladvice.html

## Dangerous Things

*Roads*

When travelers gather to banter about the foibles of foreigners behind the wheel, the debate about which nation has the world's worst drivers usually focuses on Mediterranean Europe, the Middle East, or the Indian subcontinent—unless someone present has been to Georgia. Georgians have absolutely no idea: On the only decent road in the country, the Georgian Military Highway, the view through your windshield will often be of four cars abreast, each trying to overtake the others, and all heading straight for you. The traditional evasive maneuver is to drive into a ditch by the side of the road, and then wait for someone to stop and tow you out.

http://www.igo.com/Travel/HTML/georgia/06grw.html

## Land Mines

Avoid the temptation to go orienteering where Georgia abuts Chechnya, Ingusetia, Dagestan, or Abkhazia: most of Georgia's border regions are liberally sown with mines, and nobody knows exactly where they are (proof, were it needed, came in 2000, when the brother of Georgia's minister of defense drove over one, with fatal consequences). The Science and Technical Research Department of the Georgian army estimates that 70 percent of the casualties in the Abkhazia war were caused by land mines.

http://www.icbl.org/lm/2001/georgia

## Gorges

Whether it's the Pankisi (east side) or the Kodori (west side) or any other gorge (17 of which are used for major smuggling paths in the mountainous north), you can be assured that the Georgians will tell you they are chock-full of *bandiytis, mafiya,* reprobates, and ne'er-do-wells. When you visit these gorges you will meet the locals who will, of course, warn you about the southern areas which are full of (you guessed it) *bandiytis, mafiya,* reprobates, and ne'er-do-wells. The gorges are supposedly off-limits to outsiders, but a joke, a pack of cigarettes, and a local guide will dispense with national security concerns.

http://www.sarke.com

## Wine, Yogurt, and Centenarians

Georgia invented wine . . . and every scrap of tourism info will herald the quality, the joy, and so on. It is also the home of all those 100-year-olds featured in Dannon's yogurt commercials. Uh, huh . . . sure. The wine? Well, let's just say that Russian vodka has replaced wine and vinegar. The yogurt, old people, and so on, are long gone. Apparently the government stopped paying pensions a few years back in order to save money, and the centenarians simply died because they had no money with which to buy food. It would be a funny joke if it weren't true.

http://www.actr.org/pubs/handbook/georgia.pdf

## Politics

Crime isn't really dangerous here . . . it's more like a natural resource. Tbilisi is a place where there were only 194 cases of property theft and a mere 147 cases of "deliberate assassination." It's the sort of place where the president survives a rocket-propelled grenade launched into his Mercedes and where there have been

> **I**t's politics as usual in a country where Chechens come on holiday, thugs kidnap, and two civil wars flare up and down on a regular basis.

240 documented cases of illegal carrying, storage, manufacturing, and selling of weapons. It's politics as usual in a country where Chechens come on holiday, thugs kidnap, and two civil wars flare up and down on a regular basis.

## Getting Sick

Getting sick is best avoided. Medical care and supplies are limited. Take your own syringes. Also bear in mind that doctors and hospitals often insist on being paid cash on the spot. Thanks to the former Russian system, there are plenty of trained doctors in Georgia and health care is inexpensive. The problem is that the doctors are digging ditches and the hospitals look like horror-movie sets.

## Nuts and Bolts

Georgia's 5 million people speak Georgian, a language with a unique and impenetrable written alphabet. Russian is also widely spoken, and English will get you some way in Tbilisi. The local currency is the *lari,* whose status in international finance markets is a couple of rungs above flat red rocks. Credit cards are next to useless other than in the big hotels in Tbilisi, so you'll need to take lots of cash in American dollars. The locals are well aware of this, so keep it securely stashed. Crime is expected if you are staggering out of a restaurant at 4 A.M., but most taxi drivers and locals will get you back to your guesthouse just fine. Most businesses provide their own power (those Honda generators chained up outside stores are not for sale, silly). Power cuts are frequent, or should we say that electric power is infrequent: take a flashlight. Georgia is the only country where people check their e-mail by candlelight (they use battery backup sources as a norm).

**Crime Reports**
http://www.ceroi.net/reports/tbilisi/issues/population_and_social_conditions/crime.
  htm

### Embassy Locations

**United States Embassy**
25 Atoneli Street
Tbilisi 380026, Georgia
Tel.: (995) 32 98 9967
Fax: (995) 32 93 3759
consulate-tbilisi@state.gov
http://web.sanet.get/usembassy

**British Embassy**
20 Telavi Street
Sheraton Metechi Palace Hotel
Tbilisi 380003, Georgia
Tel.: (995) 32 95 5497
Fax: (995) 32 00 1065
british.embassy@caucasus.net
http://www.britishembassy.org.ge

GEORGIA

## Dangerous Days

| 3/02 | U.S. military advisors arrive in Georgia. |
|------|-------------------------------------------|
| 10/8/01 | UN helicopter shot down by persons unknown over Kodori Gorge region of Abkhazia, killing all nine aboard. |
| 2001 | At a meeting in Yalta, Georgia and Abkhazia sign an accord agreeing not to use force against each other, and to work together to repatriate the refugees created by the war. |
| 9/21/98 | Three UN military observers and their Abkhaz driver wounded in an ambush in Sukhumi. |
| 2/9/98 | Attack on Shevardnadze's motorcade in Tbilisi by Zviadists and Chechens armed with automatic rifles and grenade-launchers. Two of Shevardnadze's security men and one attacker killed in ensuing gunfight. |
| 10/95 | Eduard Shevardnadze elected president. |
| 1994 | Cease-fire in Abkhazia. Russian peacekeepers deployed. |
| 10/93 | Uprising by supporters of Gamsakhurdia in western Georgia put down with help from Russian army, after Georgia agrees to join the Commonwealth of Independent States. |
| 9/93 | Georgian army retreats from Abkhazia. |
| 8/92 | Fighting between Georgian army and secessionist militias in Abkhazia region of Georgia. |
| 3/92 | Former Soviet Union Foreign Minister Eduard Shevardnadze appointed head of newly formed State Council; elected chairman of parliament seven months later. |
| 1/92 | Fighting in Tbilisi between government troops and militias opposed to Gamsakhurdia; Gamsakhurdia deposed. |
| 1992 | Cease-fire signed in South Ossetia; Russian peacekeepers deployed. |
| 1991 | Georgia secedes from Soviet Union; Zviad Gamsakhurdia elected president. |
| 1989 | Clashes between Georgian army and secessionist militias in South Ossetia region of Georgia. |
| 1989 | Nineteen pro-independence demonstrators killed by Soviet troops in Georgia's capital, Tbilisi. |
| 1936 | Transcaucasian Soviet Federated Socialist Republic (TSFSR) dismantled; Georgia becomes a Soviet Socialist Republic in its own right. |

**1921**   Georgia invaded by Red Army and annexed by the USSR along with Armenia and Azerbaijan. The three nations are amalgamated into the TSFSR.

**1918**   Georgia declared an independent state.

# GREAT LAKES
## Burundi, Rwanda, Uganda, and The Democratic Republic of Congo

## Heart of Darkness

This is the information age. You know that because you've read it in newspapers, seen it on television, heard it on the radio, and downloaded it from the Internet. Anything happens anywhere, and we know about it before the dust has settled. News that would once have taken days to reach us by carrier pigeon, cleft-stick-toting messenger, or note in a hopeful bottle is now beamed to our homes as fast as electronic impulses can travel. So how, you wonder as you contemplate this unhappy region of Africa, did we mislay 5 million dead, a great swath of a continent at war, and the biggest conflict of the last 30 years?

The war in the Democratic Republic of Congo—we'll call it DR Congo from here on, partly because it's easier to type, but mostly because it sounds amusingly like it could be the name of a drive-time disc jockey from Oklahoma—has lasted for nearly 10 years, notwith-

GREAT LAKES

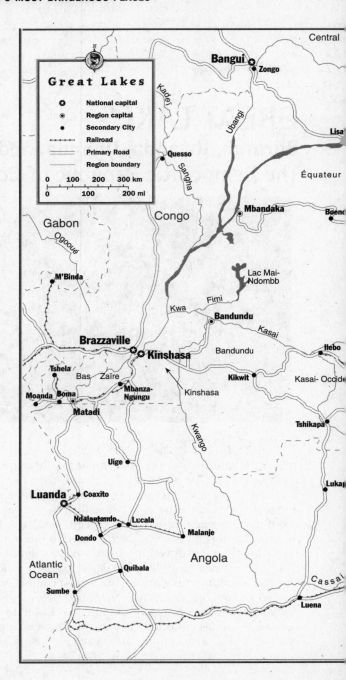

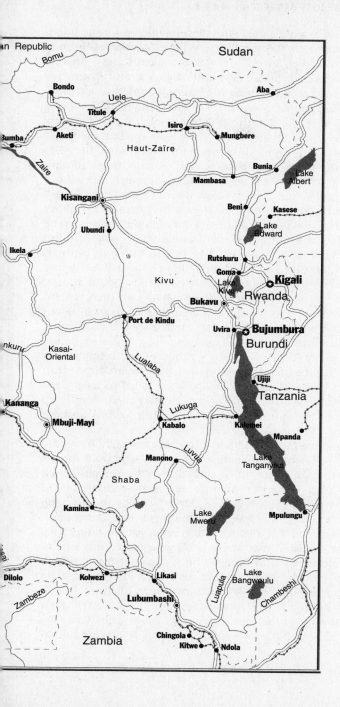

standing a peace agreement, signed with all the same optimistic hopes and intentions focused on Pakistani lottery ticket purchases, in July 2002. The war has sucked in eight neighboring countries—Angola, Namibia, Zimbabwe, Chad, Sudan, Burundi, Uganda, and Rwanda—and killed, according to an estimate by the International Rescue Group, more than 2.5 million people. Some say 5 million. The truth is nobody even bothered counting. Yet the war in DR Congo hardly ever attracts the attention of the news networks, who have been much more interested in the comparatively minor dust-ups in the Balkans and the Middle East. There must be a very good reason for this extraordinary indifference, of which *DP*, at the time of writing, is unaware. It couldn't be because all the protagonists in this colossal conflict are black.

This region's problems go way back—not surprisingly to about the time of the arrival of white men. The record of misery begins in the 15th century, when the Portuguese had an abortive poke around the place, but things really began going to hell in the 19th century, with the arrival of the Belgians. Belgium's King Leopold II is a figure often cited by those who hold European colonialism to be the root of Africa's ills, and not without reason. Leopold pitched his involvement in Congo to the 1885 Berlin conference as an essentially humanitarian mission, to chase Arab slave traders out of the region and do right by the natives. Instead, Leo enslaved the Congolese himself, appropriating the so-called Congo Free State as personal property and ruling with a barbarity that boggled the imaginations of even more infamous African ex-tyrants like Amin and Mobutu: When villages failed to meet their quota of rubber production, Leopold's agents killed them and hung up their heads as a warning to others not to slack off. It paid to read the fine print . . . if you, of course, could read.

Congo finally became independent in 1960, and its neighbors in the Great Lakes region—Rwanda, Burundi, and Uganda—followed shortly afterward, as the Belgians (and, in Uganda's case, the British) furled their flags and toddled off back to their homes, made comfortable, at least in part, by years of exploitation of Africa. Things went wrong almost immediately. The Congolese army mutinied, and the copper-rich southern province of Katanga tried to secede. Patrice Lumumba, Congo's first prime minister, was bumped off with the connivance of the CIA and the Belgians, who thought he was some sort of pinko. Lumumba's shoes—which, seeing how his body was dumped in a vat of acid, were about all that was left of him—were filled by Joseph Mobutu, a deranged autocrat who renamed the country Zaire and spent the '70s, '80s, and most of the '90s shipping as much of its wealth—including foreign aid—into his Swiss bank accounts as he could manage. The CIA, figuring that while Mobutu may have been a five-alarm fruitcake with a stupid hat, at least he wasn't a commie, left him to it.

Things weren't going brilliantly with the neighbors, either. In Uganda, one Ruritanian despot, Milton Obote, was replaced by another, Idi Amin. Amin, now in exile in Riyadh, was a figure no satirical novelist would have dared invent: a bellicose oaf who declared himself Conqueror of the British Empire, among other titles, expelled Uganda's wealthy and educated Indian-born population, and killed 300,000 of his own people, of whom he is said to have eaten several. If that hadn't been enough to make a sane man nostalgic for the colonial certainties, in Rwanda and Burundi the majority Hutu had set about making the minority Tutsi even more of a minority, killing 200,000 of them in 1972 alone. Even when things started looking up for the region—such as when Amin was chased out of Uganda with Tanzanian assistance in 1979—they started looking back down again. Amin was replaced by his no-less-psychotic predecessor, Milton Obote.

The Great Lakes' modern woes began in the early '90s, with ethnic scrapping between Tutsis and Hutus in Rwanda and Burundi. In 1993, a coup attempt left Burundi's president, Melchior Ndadaye, and 30,000 other Burundians dead. In April 1994, the presidents of the two countries at the time, respectively Juvenal Habyarimana and Cyprien Ntaryamira, signed a peace deal in Arusha, Tanzania. On April 6, the plane bringing them both back to the Rwandan capital, Kigali, was shot down as it approached the airport—most likely by an extremist group called Hutu Power, which had long been lurking in Habyarimana's entourage. What followed in Rwanda was the biggest mass killing to have disfigured history since World War II. In just 14 weeks, at least 800,000 people—mostly Tutsis, but including many Hutus who refused to be part of the hysteria—were killed by mobs armed with machetes and rifles.

What made this genocide even worse was that it was predicted, and therefore preventable. On January 11, 1994, the Canadian major general running the UNAMIR mission in Rwanda, Romeo Dallaire, faxed a warning to UN headquarters that preparations were being made for a slaughter of Tutsis. The chief of UN peacekeeping at the time, Kofi Annan, failed to mention it to the Security Council. When Hutu Power unleashed its unholy vengeance, General Dallaire had no mandate to intervene, and

> **W**hat made this genocide even worse was that it was predicted, and therefore preventable.

only a couple of thousand lightly armed troops. Ten Belgians trying to protect Rwanda's moderate Hutu prime minister, Agathe Uwilingiyimana, were among the first to die. On April 21, just two weeks into the butchery, General Dallaire said that with 5,000 well-equipped troops, he could quickly stop Hutu Power's rampage. Instead of doing the decent and obvious—and, according to the UN convention on genocide, legal—thing, the UN Security Council passed a resolution ordering the evacuation of the UNAMIR force, leaving just 270 behind to watch as Rwanda was put to the sword.

The current war in DR Congo is at least in part a result of the insanity that consumed Rwanda in 1994. Many Rwandan Tutsis fled to the DR Congo during Hutu Power's frenzy, and many Hutu Power murderers did likewise when the Tutsis gained the upper hand shortly afterwards, when Paul Kagame's Rwandan Patriotic Front marched to Kigali to pull his enemy out by the roots. Rwanda's troops are in DR Congo theoretically to wipe out Hutu Power leftovers, but it won't have escaped the notice of the canny Kagame that they are doing this in a mineral-rich area of DR Congo—the Congolese rebel group Rally for Congolese Democracy are somewhere between a rowdy Rwandan soccer team and a Rwandan front. Uganda has also waded into DR Congo ostensibly to close down the bases of marauding rebels who support the Allied Democratic Front from across the border, but Uganda's president, Yoweri Museveni, is no fool, and well knows that Congolese real estate is worth owning, so it helps to linger after a cross-border raid.

DR Congo's own civil war continues. Mobutu was followed by half-mad rebel leader Laurent Kabila, a slightly cranky Marxist and undistinguished student of Ché Guevara who'd been adopted and promoted by Kagame in Rwanda and his old pal Museveni in Uganda. However, once in power, Kabila did an about-face on his mates, giving a green light to the Hutu rebels on his territory. Rwanda and Uganda showed up in DR Congo shortly afterward, helping a new rebel group, the Rally for Congolese Democracy, take a whack at Kabila.

Kabila was shot dead by his own bodyguards in January 2001 (that'll teach him not to read résumés properly) and replaced by his son, Joseph. Joseph is now being propped up by Zimbabwe, Namibia, and Angola, none of which—especially Namibia and Zimbabwe, which share no border with DR Congo—can credibly care less who runs DR Congo, but obviously care a great deal about who is allowed to dig for diamonds in it.

In August 2002, the two principal antagonists, DR Congo and Rwanda, signed an accord brokered by Kofi Annan—better late than never, Kofi—and South African President Thabo Mbeki. Under the agreement, the DR Congo government agreed to round up and disarm the Hutu rebels on its turf, and Rwanda agreed to withdraw the tens of thousands of its troops camping out in eastern DR Congo. *DP* only hopes that we're not being unnecessarily pessimistic in noting that the Hutu rebels at the center of this accord haven't signed anything. . . .

## The Scoop

Joseph Conrad wrote *Heart of Darkness* about this fetid, untamed region of Africa more than a hundred years ago, and "The horror, the horror" continues to make the short story a perfect primer on why things just never seem to get all shiny and nice here. Though the genocide in Rwanda and Burundi is apparently over, it's been over many times before, and though they may be talking peace now in DR Congo, African wars are not usually stopped by mere treaties.

**The East African (Uganda)**
http://www.nationaudio.com/news/
    eastafrican

**The Monitor (Uganda)**
http://www.monitor.co.ug

**The New Vision (Uganda)**
http://www.newvision.co.ug

**Le Soft (DR Congo, French only)**
http://www.lesoftonline.net

## The Players

### The Hutus

Hutus, a Bantu race, comprise about 85 percent of the population of Rwanda and Burundi. They got some lousy press following the epic carnage that occurred in Rwanda and Burundi in 1994, but though the attempted genocide of the Tutsis was the work of Hutu Power extremists and the Hutus who followed them, many thousands of Hutus also perished—for not thinking that being born Tutsi is a reason to be hacked to death, or by aggrieved Tutsis, no shrinking violets themselves.

> Joseph Conrad wrote *Heart of Darkness* about this fetid, untamed region of Africa more than a hundred years ago, and "The horror, the horror" continues to make the short novel a perfect primer on why things just never seem to get all shiny and nice here.

### The Tutsis

The Tutsis are originally Nilotic herdsmen from the north. Today, they're about 15 percent of the population of Rwanda and Burundi. The Tutsis were the principal victims of the 1994 genocide that left at least 800,000 corpses stacked up in Rwanda. Tutsis have historically been the elite of Rwanda and Burundi, occupying positions of power out of all proportion to their numbers (the presidents of both countries today are Tutsis, as are 90 percent of Burundian teachers and 80 percent of Burundi's armed forces). This, coupled with a general lack of education and a less-than-sturdy media, has made it easy for the unscrupulous to target them when it's deemed expedient. The Tutsis have also not been above mass murder, killing 200,000 Hutus in Burundi in 1972 alone, following an unsuccessful attempt to restore the monarchy. King Ntare V was among the casualties.

# Burundi

## *Pierre Buyoya*

Major Buyoya's career as Burundi's head of state started in 1987, when then-President Jean Baptiste Bagaza made the mistake of leaving the country to go to a summit meeting in Quebec. While he was out of the building, Buyoya—who was distantly related to Bagaza—seized power in a coup and told Burundi's democrats to come back in five years. Buyoya, a Tutsi, was only a year late in keeping this promise, and to his immense surprise was defeated by a Hutu called Melchior Ndadaye, whose Front Pour la Democratie au Burundi (FRODEBU) was the first Hutu-dominated government in the country's history. It would be nice to able to report that Burundi's Tutsis reacted by collectively saying, "Ah well, fair enough, it's about time they had a go at running the place." And it'd be just as nice to be able to say that the incoming Hutu government didn't bear any grudges at all and were a model of even-handedness. But then this would be a travel guide about Belgium. Ndadaye was assassinated by Tutsi extremist army officers in October 1993.

Buyoya kept his powder dry during the early '90s while Burundi descended into a ghastly burlesque of assassinations, coups, and ethnic massacres—at least some of which Buyoya had advance knowledge of—and helped himself back into the top job in July 1996. He promptly abolished everyone and everything he didn't agree with. Sanctions were imposed by forthright defenders of the democratic ideal such as Ethiopia, Tanzania, Kenya, Uganda, Rwanda, Zambia, Eritrea, and Zaire. These were not entirely effective. Though no commercial flights were permitted into Burundi, planes from Belgium and the United Arab Emirates landed regularly with the staples that Burundians—or, that is, one Burundian—needed to survive: French champagne and cheeses, American bourbons and Scotch whiskeys, Japanese stereos and VCRs, and Celine Dion CDs (as if Burundi wasn't suffering enough). The sanctions did stop food and medicine from reaching ordinary Burundians who desperately needed them, though, so that's something.

Buyoya finally was gently strong-armed into a deal by Nelson Mandela in 2000. At peace talks in Arusha, Tanzania, Buyoya said he'd lead a transitional government for 18 months from November 2001, and then let his Hutu vice president, Domitien Ndayizeye, govern the country for the same amount of time, and then they'd ask Burundi's people what they reckoned. (Burundi's Tutsi-run military was sorely displeased by all this palling up to the Hutus, and staged abortive coups in April and July 2001.) This means that Buyoya is due to start clearing his desk in April 2003—and it remains to be seen whether he'll do that, or contrive some sort of "circumstances" that make an extension of his tenure "vital." For a reasonable idea of how much you should trust Buyoya, spit a housebrick as far as you can, and halve that.

**Government of Burundi**
http://burundi.gov.bi

## Guardians of the Peace

Government-sponsored and Burundian military-trained paramilitary goon squad whose somewhat peculiar method of guarding the peace is to wreak mayhem. Buyoya claims that the Guardians are nothing to do with him. It's presumably just a happy coincidence that the people on the receiving end of the Guardians' preferred tactics—beatings (for men) and pack rape (for women)—are those who Buyoya perceives as potential enemies: mostly restive Hutu in Bururi, Makamba, and Rutana provinces. The Guardians' ranks include a lot of children, press-ganged into service.

## National Council for the Defense of Democracy (CNDD)

The CNDD is the main Hutu rebel group at large in Burundi. It was first wrangled in 1994 by Léonard "The Honorable" Nyangoma, Minister for the Interior under Melchior Ndadaye (Burundi's first Hutu president, subsequently murdered by Tutsi army officers). Nyangoma was stripped of his leadership in 1998 over (rather quaint, all things considered) corruption allegations, and replaced by Colonel John-Bosco Ndayikengurukiye—head of the CNDD's armed wing, the Forces for the Defense of Democracy (FDD). Nyangoma carried on causing havoc with his idea of the CNDD, but it has been Ndayikengurukiye's CNDD-FDD that have been making the running.

The Tanzania-backed CNDD-FDD may be about to go legit, depending on how August 2002 talks with the Burundian government in Dar Es Salaam, mediated by Nelson Mandela, pan out.

**CNDD-FDD**
http://www.burundi-info.com

## National Liberation Front

The National Liberation Front is a Hutu militia based in the northwestern province of Cibitoke. They're not pleased with Buyoya, the current power-sharing initiative in Burundi, white people, or anything else. They've raided Bujumbura on several occasions. In July 2002, they killed several people in a mortar attack launched from near

Bujumbura's airport. They were sitting out the August 2002 talks in Dar Es Salaam.

## Parti Pour la Liberation du Peuple Hutu (PALIPEHUTU)

The PALIPEHUTU is the longest established Hutu rebel group independent from CNDD/FDD. There are regional rivalries between the two groups: CNDD members come from the southern Bururi region and PALIPEHUTU are recruited from the central Muramvya area. PALIPEHUTU, led by Cossan Kabura, has had successes in fighting around Bujumbura. Its armed wing is the Forces Nationales de Liberation (FNL), and it is closely linked to the Front Pour la Liberation Nationale (FROLINA), another Hutu rebel group, whose armed wing is the Forces Armées du Peuple (FAP).

# Rwanda

## Paul Kagame

Major-General and Tutsi poster boy, Kagame was once the commander of the Rwandan Patriotic Army, the armed wing of the Tutsi Rwandan Patriotic Front (RPF). Today, he's president of Rwanda, and the most powerful figure in the Tutsi areas of Burundi—the most powerful figure, in other words, that either of these two precarious states have known since they became independent in 1962.

Kagame was born in Gitarama in 1957. He and his parents fled to Uganda in 1961 to escape the massacres of Rwandan Tutsis that accompanied Rwanda's drive towards independence. Given the fondness for arson of the Tutsi mobs, and the reputation for cannibalism of Uganda's eventual dictator Idi Amin, it was all too literally a case of proceeding from the fire to the frying pan.

In 1979, after Amin had been chased into exile, Kagame signed up with the faction of the new Ugandan army run by Yoweri Museveni—now Uganda's president. When Amin's predecessor, the scarcely less-deranged Milton Obote, staged an unwelcome comeback in 1981, Kagame was one of 27 men who stayed loyal to Museveni, and headed for the bush to plot insurrection. It was a smart move on two levels.

First and most immediately, Obote went to war on Uganda's (overwhelmingly Tutsi) Rwandan population in late 1982, unleashing a campaign of mass murder, rape, and eviction that drove 50,000 of Kagame's people back into Rwanda—where they were either herded into disease-ridden camps or sent back to Uganda by Rwanda's Hutu president, Juvenal Habyarimana. Second and more lasting, when Museveni took power in Uganda in 1986, at least 20 percent of his army were Rwandan Tutsis, who found themselves in a position of real influence. First among these influentials was young Paul Kagame, military intelligence chief. Not a bad gig for a thirty-something Rwandan refugee, but Kagame had his sights set on taking his people home. When Habyarimana announced that no Rwandan refugees would be allowed back into Rwanda, Kagame and his compatriots in Uganda formed the Rwandan Patriotic Front—much to the irritation of Museveni, who wasn't happy about his Rwandan officers deserting, or the kit they took with them. The RPF's military core was Tutsi, but it always had Hutu members—Kagame's politics have generally been commendably free of the tribal sectarian nonsense that was to have such catastrophic consequences for his homeland.

As a member of Uganda's military, Kagame was able to apply for a course in tactics at the U.S. Army Command and General Staff College at Fort Leavenworth, Kansas. In fact (and reflecting in part Tutsi chutzpah), Kagame was in Kansas in October 1990, the very month he and a close comrade, Fred Rwigyema, had planned to invade Rwanda. The invasion went ahead anyway, and though Rwigyema was killed on the second day of fighting, it went well, until France put together a combined force of French, Belgian, and Zairois troops and French-trained Hutu paramilitaries. In 1991, the RPF movement launched its last frustrated invasion. Again, it went well initially, but with the prospect of intervention again on the horizon, Kagame stopped short in the north and agreed to talks. These were to drag on for two years, in the Tanzanian town of Arusha, at the foot of Mt. Kilimanjaro.

President Habyarimana signed a deal in April 1994, and was dead within hours, his plane shot down, presumably by enraged Hutu extremists, as it approached Kigali airport. Genocide followed, as Hutus went on the rampage against Tutsis and moderate Hutus; more than 800,000 were killed, mostly by machete, in just three months. In one province of Rwanda, Kibuye, 200,000 of its 250,000 Tutsis were murdered.

Cometh the hour, cometh Kagame: His RPF reached Kigali on July 4, 1994. By this time, Kagame had turned the RPF into a disciplined outfit, punishing the depressingly common sidelines of African armies—looting, murder, and rape—with flogging and/or execution. He also made his troops take lessons in politics, geography, history, and economics. This is not to say that the RPF behaved absolutely impeccably (looting was commonplace, just better organized than usual) or that no reprisals were taken against Hutu murderers (thousands were shot out of hand), but the RPF's decisive action against Rwanda's genocide puts to shame the behavior of all the Western powers, especially the United States, who could have stopped it with one battalion of Marines, and France—who, it should never be forgotten, aided and abetted those trying to stop Kagame's RPF.

Kagame is by no means perfect, but he's probably the best thing that could have happened to Rwanda. His government has taken steps to erode ethnic divisions, including removing ethnic labels from Rwandan identity cards. Kagame doesn't drink, is married, has four children, and enjoys tennis. In October 2002 Rwanda officially withdrew the last of its troops from the Congo. This did not include the Rwandan Hutus still inside the country.

**His Excellency Paul Kagame**
http://www.rwanda1.com/government/president

**Government of Rwanda**
http://www.rwanda1.com/government

## Army for the Liberation of Rwanda (ALIR)

The ALIR have been raising heck since Kagame's RPF came to power in 1994. They're a mix of former members of the Rwandan Armed Forces and Hutu hard-liners, the Interahamwe—famous internationally chiefly for carving up a party of gorilla-spotting Western tourists in 1999, but remembered in Rwanda as the murderers who hacked up 800,000 of that country's citizens during the blood orgy of 1994. They're pretty much over at this point, having been chased, scattered, and put to the sword by Kagame's RPF since 1994. They're now only as going a concern as DR Congo can be bothered to make them—which will hopefully be less and less as the 2002 truce between Rwanda and DR Congo takes hold.

## International Criminal Tribunal for Rwanda (ICTR)

Though the Western world shagged-all as the genocide in Rwanda was taking place in 1994, it was only too happy to confect an expensive and largely useless legal process to slam the stable door after the Horsemen of the Apocalypse had bolted. In seven years of existence, the ICTR has arrested 60 suspects and managed to convict a total of—drum roll, please, maestro—eight. In a crime scene the size of an entire country, where the victims numbered millions and the eyewitnesses hundreds of thousands, this is a less-than-impressive return—there are Saturday night punch-ups in bars that result in more arrests than this.

The ICTR's biggest scalp to date is that of Jean Kambanda, who was Rwanda's prime minister at the time of the slaughter. Eleven of Kambanda's ministers are also in the ICTR's specially constructed slammer in Arusha, Tanzania, which is assuredly the best place for them. This is to say nothing of the 100,000 or more Hutus currently in jail waiting for Rwanda's own overloaded criminal justice system to pass judgment on their role in the 1994 genocide. Many have already been executed by firing squad—a sanction disdained by the UN court.

*International Criminal Tribunal for Rwanda*
Office of the Prosecutor
Amahoro Hotel
P.O. Box 749
Kigali, Rwanda
Tel.: (250) 84 2661
ictr-press@un.org
http://www.ictr.org

# Uganda

*Yoweri Kaguta Museveni*

Former guerrilla chief Museveni was returned to office in 2001 with 70 percent of the vote. His main opponent, Dr. Kizza Besigye, wasn't happy with the result, and not only because he lost—he claimed that the poll was fixed and that voters were intimidated, and he was probably right (it was an oxymoronic "African election," after all). It was certainly an entertainingly venomous campaign, fueled by the rancor that only former friends can generate—a friendship from back in the '80s, when Museveni was a little-regarded commander of a ragbag guerrilla army hiding in Uganda's dense jungles and Dr. Besigye was his personal physician. They fell out because Dr. Besigye said Museveni's rule had become corrupt and nepotistic. Museveni, in return, accused Besigye of having AIDS and his wife of being "nasty," so there.

Museveni was born in Ankole in 1944. He was a student agitator during his time at the University of Dar Es Salaam in Tanzania, and returned to Uganda in 1971 to join the resistance against Idi Amin, the Ugandan dictator who consistently behaved like the tonnage of gold braid on his hat had mashed his brain. When Amin was finally turfed out of the long-suffering country with the help of Tanzania in 1979, Museveni was briefly minister of defense in a transitional government, but his career took an abrupt turn left when power was seized in 1980 in a comeback coup by Amin's equally loopy predecessor, Milton Obote. In February 1981, Museveni went into the bush with just 27 men (including current Rwandan President Paul Kagame) and formed the National Resistance Army. Five years later, he had the country.

Museveni has become something of a darling of the West—Bill Clinton came calling in 1998—and not without reason. By the none-too-stringent standards of African leadership, he is sane and competent, and Uganda has made progress under his rule—he's kept inflation under control, doubled the country's GDP, started literacy on an upward climb, and, perhaps most impressively, pushed Uganda's rate of HIV infection down—something unique in Africa. Against that, he gets dissed a lot for not doing enough against poverty, suppressing human rights, and calling Uganda's no-party system a "democracy." Museveni's also been helping out the SPLA rebels in Sudan and stirring the large and volatile pot that is DR Congo. But nobody's perfect, right?

**President Yoweri Kaguta Museveni**
http://www.statehouse.go.ug

**Government of Uganda**
http://www.government.go.ug

## The Lord's Resistance Army (LRA)

Arch-dingbats and the only fundamentalist African Christian terrorist group based in Sudan (*Guinness Book of Records*, please note), this cockeyed, ramshackle mob wants to turn Uganda into a theocratic state based on the Ten Commandments—though by *DP*'s admittedly fallible reckoning, their efforts to do so have displayed a frankly appalling lack of respect for commandments two, five, seven, nine, and ten, and we think they should also answer as regards commandments one, three, and four. With Christianity, as with Islam, it is its most fanatical adherents who are also its worst advertisements.

The LRA is largely composed of Acholi tribespeople and is led by a former altar boy and stern-faced lunatic named Joseph Kony. He is the nephew of the LRA's spiritual founder, a prostitute named Alice Lakwena. She founded something called the Holy Spirit Movement back in 1988, and told her fighters she could protect them from bullets (she couldn't, and fled to Kenya). Today, the LRA no longer clings to such primitivism. Now, they think they can deflect bullets with tree oils (they can't, but the LRA keep on coming).

**Yes, eagle-eyed readers will note, this is a fundamentalist Christian terrorist group sponsored by a fundamentalist Islamic regime. It kinda' brings a tear to *DP*'s eye to see teamwork like that.**

The LRA has long been armed and uniformed by northern Sudan, but Khartoum has recently been trying put some distance between themselves and their proteges. Yes, eagle-eyed readers will note, this is a fundamentalist Christian terrorist group sponsored by a fundamentalist Islamic regime. It kinda' brings a tear to *DP*'s eye to see teamwork like that.

Despite either party's religious conviction (or warped view of it), the LRA is believed to have about 4,000 troops under arms—and many of them are under age. Many LRA soldiers are children abducted from refugee camps (6,000 in 1998 alone) or bought from poor families. Boys are turned into soldiers, girls into sex slaves, and both are routinely sold to Sudanese arms dealers. They were also accused of selling kids to bin Laden's drug farms, a story the Kampala edition of the *National Enquirer* seemed to have missed.

Uganda has tried both amnesties and ruthless offensives to bring the LRA to heel, but either God really is watching over the LRA, or—as seems much more likely—just isn't all that keen for the LRA's cranky members to join him. It is essentially an Acholi ethnic movement funded by outsiders to Uganda's detriment, with some very real and brutal reasons for existing.

The LRA is still a serious threat, and 10,000 Ugandan troops are chasing them around southern Sudan to confirm as much.

**Dr. James Alfred Obita, LRM/A Secretary for External Affairs and Mobilisation**
Kacoke Madit
173 Upper Street
London N1 1RG, UK
Tel.: (020) 7288 2768
Fax: (020) 7359 4081
www.km-net.org
admin@km-net.org
http://www.africanprinciples.org/article.asp?cID=4

## Allied Democratic Front (ADF)

*DP* really wishes these guerrilla groups would start showing a bit of imagination with their nomenclature—it's always Allied Democratic this or Popular Front that or Popular Allied Front for Democracy whatever. Just once, it'd be nice if one of these bunches of ratbags called themselves the Grandiose Excuse for Looting, Pillaging, Racketeering, and Rape. Active since November 1996, the ADF are Sudan-backed Muslim nasties based in the Ruwenzori Mountains in DR Congo, but active in the southwest of Uganda, where their antics have displaced more than 100,000 people in Bundibugyo and Kasese districts. The ADF thinks that Museveni is trying to build a Tutsi empire in Central Africa, and is composed of former members of the armies of Rwanda and Zaire, the Salaf Tabliq (Muslim militia), and the no-longer-known-at-this-address National Army for the Liberation of Uganda. This group is also linked to the Bwindi attacks that killed eight tourists in March of '99, and for trying to blow up *DP* at Speke's Hotel in Kampala on April 4 of '98, an attack that resulted in four deaths. The ADF can be credited for creating plenty of great deals on hotels and safaris these days.

**Uganda Tourist Board**
http://www.VisitUganda.com

## Other Armed Groups

These include the West Bank Nile Front, a small but unpleasant group allied with both Sudan; the Ugandan National Rescue Front, a two-men-and-a-dog outfit also operating in the northwest; the Salaf Tabliq, a radical Muslim group now mostly absorbed by the Allied Democratic Front; and unaffiliated members of the Karamojong people, who rustle cattle and children in the northeast.

www.fewer.org/greatlakes

# Democratic Republic of Congo

## Joseph Kabila

The 33-year-old Kabila inherited the job of trying to run DR Congo when his father, Laurent, was assassinated by his own bodyguards in January 2001. Joe Kabila had fought alongside Dad as his rebels had overrun then-Zaire, and after what must have been an exhaustive search, he was rewarded with the prize gig of head of DR Congo's armed forces. Since stepping into his father's boots, he's not exactly been an African Eugene McCarthy, but that thousand-yard stare his father had is mercifully absent. Word on the street is that Joey is . . . well, actually quite normal and lucid. Not at all cut out for Central African Dictatorship duties.

Kabila, Sr. was an unpleasant man, about whom the kindest that could be said was that he wasn't quite as barmy as Joey Mobutu, the dictator he toppled in 1997. Laurent was an old-school revolutionary who'd been trained by Ché Guevara and was fond of trying to inculcate the rudiments of *Das Kapital* in his barely literate fighters. That said, Kabila did a pretty good impression of a sharp capitalist operator as his boys closed on Kinshasa—one U.S. mining firm gave Kabila's government US$50 million as down payment for the right to dig for copper and cobalt, as well as a private jet. Once in power, Laurent Kabila observed the age-old tradition of African revolutionaries made good, and started acting like the kind of guy he'd once have revolted against. He banned political parties and anything else he didn't like, gave jobs to his friends and relatives, and started pulling big bills out of the till.

Kabila, Jr. hasn't been quite so bad so far, but, to be fair, it might just be that he hasn't had time—what with his country hosting an eight-way war, and all. A peace agreement that was being brokered in 2002 might give DR Congo the chance to make the most of its natural gifts. With reserves of diamonds, gold, copper, and especially coltan (a crucial component of chips for mobile phones and such), DR Congo could be a rich and happy place. In July 2000, Laurent Kabila sold the exclusive rights to DR Congo's uncut diamonds to an Israeli company called IDI—the deal was for US$600–700 million, and it remains unclear how much of that plumped up Kabila's mattress.

Kabila, Jr.'s record on human rights and press freedom is awful, but there are signs that his elevator does go all the way up, which would be a welcome change. Once, when asked for his role models among African leaders, he named his father (well, you kind of have to) and Patrice Lumumba (the Congolese leader bumped off by the CIA in 1961), before uttering the very true words, "But what is there in Africa? Total misery. No, there's not really any model." Right on, Joe.

## Rally for Congolese Democracy (RCD)

"First we will take Kinshasa, then we will sort out Congo's political future," promised RCD military commander Jean-Pierre Ondekane after these rebels took up arms against the Kabila regime in August 1998. A year later, Congo's political future was still being sorted out, mostly because of Ondekane's inability to complete even the first task at hand—capturing Kinshasa. At first, it seemed the RCD would have the capital in a matter of weeks. Laurent Kabila was caught with his pants down, and Rwanda and Uganda were providing the RCD with logistical support, weapons, and even the soldiers to go along with them. Kabila fell to his knees, but they were padded with Angola, Namibia, and Zimbabwe, turning Congo's civil war into a good ol'-fashioned African bush rumble. Although RCD got a third of the country in its mitts, they may not be grabbing much more. The guerrillas have been riven from within by defections and splinter groups, and now operate as two different factions.

Sadly, for those of us who like rebel leaders to have names like the titles of Annette Funicello movies, original RCD leader, Ernest Wamba-dia-Wamba, has long since fallen from favor. The torch is now borne in two different directions by Mbusa Nyamisi's Rally for Congolese Democracy (Liberation Movement) and Roger Lumbala's Rally for Congolese Democracy (National). Nyamisi receives support from Uganda and cooperates to an extent with the Movement for the Liberation of Congo (see below), while Lumbala cooperates to an extent with the Movement for the Liberation of Congo (see below) and receives support from Uganda. So, naturally, they spend most of their time fighting each other.

The original Rwanda-backed RCD are still out there, as well, though they've also split into mutually hostile camps: the old-school RCD led by Adolphe Onusumba, and Patrick Masunzu's Banyamulenge Tutsis, who are currently kicking lumps out of each other in DR Congo's southeast. The RCD were left out of the April 2002 talks at Sun City in South Africa that brought the MLC in from the cold.

## Movement for the Liberation of Congo (MLC)

Jean-Pierre Bemba, the leader of the Uganda-backed MLC, reached some sort of agreement with Joseph Kabila's DR Congo government in 2002. Under the terms of the deal, Bemba was supposed to become DR Congo's prime minister, but he has yet to turn up in Kinshasa to claim his keys to the executive washroom.

## The Mai Mai

These young folks would feel right at home in Compton. The Mai Mai are ganja-stoked, witchcraft-practicing, teenage streetfighters of the Hunde, Nande, and Nglima tribes from the villages around Bunia and Uvira. They wear faucets, rosary beads, and garden hoses as jewelry, and worship water. They go into battle wearing a cool grass headdress that they believe makes them invisible, despite an accumulating fly-blown heap of empirical evidence to the contrary.

The Mai Mai are basically local kids letting off a little steam and aren't quite up on the political situation. They were originally part of Laurent Kabila's crusade against Mobutu, but have now joined with the forces fighting the government they fought to install. This is nominally because they think there are too many Tutsis in the DR Congo's new army, but mostly, it has to be suspected, it's because they just like a ruck.

## The Hema and the Lendu

Read as the "Hatfields" and the "McCoys." Two ornery ethnic groups in DR Congo's northeast who've been setting fire to each other's barns for years, the Hema are pastoral farmers, and the Lendu are small-scale crop cultivators. For reasons that passeth all understanding, Uganda has been tooling up the Hema.

## Robert Mugabe

The cranky old clown is apparently not content with just buggering up his own country. He sent 11,000 Zimbabwean troops, nearly a third of his army, into DR Congo in 1998 to help prop up Kabila (and, subsequently, Kabila's son) and, probably more to the point, to get a hold of a share of DR Congo's diamonds and timber. In 1999, Zimbabwe announced that it was setting up a company called Osleg, which would work alongside Comiex—a mining and logging concern whose principal founding shareholder was one Laurent Kabila. The Katanga mines are now about all that is holding Zimbabwe upright—Mugabe has finessed this arrangement with his military by parceling out concessions to the military officers running his Congolese adventure.

When DR Congo and Rwanda buried the hatchet in July 2002, Mugabe muttered something about eventually bringing his boys home, but he won't be hurrying—Zimbabwe can't afford to pay them, and there's only so many journalists Mugabe can have beaten up (see the Zimbabwe chapter). The bad news for DR Congo's long-suffering people is that peace runs directly counter to Mugabe's personal interests.

## The United Nations

There are about 4,000 UN troops from 40-odd countries in DR Congo, under the command of Senegalese Major General Mountaga Diallo. They're spending about US$600 million a year, and have suffered nine fatalities.

**UN Organization Mission in the DR Congo**
http://www.un.org/depts/dpko/monuc/monuc_body.htm

## Mobutu Sese Seko Kuku Ngbenda wa za Banga

Joe Mobutu's a long-dead ex-player, but it would be unfair to readers not to keep him in *DP* just for yuks. The late, self-proclaimed "Redeemer," "Liberator," "Helmsman," "Messiah," "Guide," and the "cock who will jump on anything" (we are not making this up) isn't doing a lot of redeeming, liberating, steering, inspiring, guiding, or jumping anymore. Most of his estimated US$4–8 billion in ill-gotten wealth is safely out of the country and tucked into his family's Swiss bank accounts. The Swiss froze a US$2.75 million villa on Lake Geneva, but the former dictator had 24 other houses around the world to crash at.

How did he get so rich? Well, for example, when the German company OTRAG was looking for a place to test satellite rocket launchers, Mobutu gave them a chunk of his country as big as Belgium. The fee was $50 million, which Joe deposited in his personal account. He creamed off aid money coming in, and sales of raw resources going out. When that wasn't enough, he would simply write himself a check from the main mining concessionaire. In 1978, he made Gecamines write him a check for the entire year's export sales of lead and zinc ($1.2 billion). That's a lot of villas. Most foreign-aid loans or projects benefited him directly—and nobody ever wanted to repossess Zaire. He would siphon CIA money destined for UNITA (which was fighting the MPLA) in Angola to the south, and any money sent to the government to fight communists (aka Kabila) went straight into his pockets.

In the end, his wealth didn't help. He died in Morocco surrounded by about 40 hangers-on and his immediate family. He was 66 years old. Considering that most Congolese don't live to see their 60th birthday, Mobutu Sese Seko did pretty well for the son of a maid from Gbadolite. His Israeli bodyguard, leopard-skin cap, harlequin outfits, and ivory cane became fashion statements among all dictator wannabes and fans of Eddie Murphy. Not a man with an eclectic taste in women, Mobutu's mistress was his wife's twin sister. His numerous offspring will live well on the boulevards of Paris.

## Getting In

Is no exact science. You will most certainly need a passport and all the relevant visas—your nearest embassy will tell you how this works, but a good rule of thumb is to allow roughly twice the amount of time you'd need in a sane world. In theory, visas for Rwanda are handed over without any hassle at the border, but it would be deeply tedious to get there and find out that, in practice, this is not the case. Air connections with the region's capitals are pretty good, via the former colonial overlords of Belgium, France, Great Britain, or South Africa—though many visitors to Uganda arrive by bus or train from the better-connected Kenyan capital, Nairobi. Of course, things can change as fast as the situation on the ground—Bujumbura Airport in Burundi, in particular, opens and closes more often than Roseanne Barr's refrigerator.

Rail services link the Ugandan capital of Kampala with Nairobi in Kenya. Sometimes there are ferries across Lake Victoria to Tanzania and Kenya, and sometimes there aren't. By road, border crossings into Uganda are open at Malaba, Busia Mutuku, Kisoro, Arua, and Lwakhakha. Drivers will need an international license and proof of insurance. There will be a fee for a temporary Uganda license. All things being equal, it should be possible to travel by road between Rwanda, Burundi, and DR Congo—but be sure you've got the latest news and sound, local advice before you attempt it. Brace yourself for searches, hours of unfathomable waiting about, and filling in meaningless forms.

When leaving DR Congo, a special exit permit from Congo's immigration department is required to cross the Congo River from Kinshasa to Brazzaville, in Congo. Unofficially, expect to have a special visa price invented on the spot, and don't be surprised if your money disappears into the same official's pocket. There are three ferry crossing points for overland traffic between DR Congo and the Central African Republic. They are located at Bangui, Mobaye, and Bangassou.

> **F**inally, you should know that the first of 12 conditions for entry and stay in Rwanda is that "proper attire and conduct are required of persons staying in Rwanda." So pull a comb through your hair, already.

Finally, you should know that the first of 12 conditions for entry and stay in Rwanda is that "proper attire and conduct are required of persons staying in Rwanda." So pull a comb through your hair, already.

*Embassy of the Republic of Burundi*
2233 Wisconsin Avenue NW, Suite 212
Washington, DC 20007
Tel.: (202) 342-2574
Fax: (202) 342-2578

*Embassy of the Republic of Burundi*
1000 Bruxelles LE
Square Marie-Louise 46
Brussels, Belgium
Tel.: (322) 230 4548
Fax: (322) 230 7883

*Embassy of the Republic of Burundi*
325 Dalhousie Street, Suite 815
Ottawa, Ontario K1N 7G2
Canada
Tel.: (613) 789-0414
Fax: (613) 789-9537
ambabucanada@infonet.ca

*Embassy of the Republic of Rwanda*
1714 New Hampshire Avenue NW
Washington, DC 20009
Tel.: (202) 232-2882
Fax: (202) 232-4544
rwandemb@rwandemb.org
http://www.rwandemb.org

*Embassy of the Republic of Rwanda*
Uganda House
58-59 Trafalgar Square
London WC2N 5DX, UK
Tel.: (44) 20 7930 2570
Fax: (44) 20 7930 2572
ambarwanda@compuserve.com

*Embassy of the Republic of Rwanda*
121 Sherwood Drive
Ottawa, Ontario K1Y 3V1
Canada

Tel.: (613) 722-5835
Fax: (613) 722-4052
embarwa@sympatico.ca

*Embassy of the Republic of Uganda*
5911 16th Street NW
Washington, DC 20011
Tel.: (202) 726-7100
Fax: (202) 726-1727
ugembassy@aol.com
http://www.ugandaembassy.com

*Embassy of the Republic of Uganda*
Uganda House
58-59 Trafalgar Square
London WC2N 5DX, UK
Tel.: (44) 20 7839 5783
Fax: (44) 20 7839 8925

*Embassy of the Democratic Republic
of Congo*
1800 New Hampshire Avenue NW
Washington, DC 20009
Tel.: (202) 234-7690
Fax: (202) 237-0748

*Embassy of the Democratic Republic
of Congo*
38 Holne Chase
London N2 0QQ, UK
Tel./Fax: (44) 20 8458 0254

*Embassy of the Democratic Republic
of Congo*
18 Range Road
Ottawa, Ontario K1N 8J3
Canada
Tel.: (613) 230-6391
Fax: (613) 230-1945

**GREAT LAKES**

# Getting Around

The trains are unreliable, the roads are a badly loaded dice game with death, and the planes, when they're flying at all, often don't fly quite as far as they're supposed to.

For traveling between towns, four-wheel-drive is preferable in terms of comfort and safety. Vehicles can be hired, along with drivers, in major towns—the guy behind the desk at your hotel will most certainly know someone. In the cities, the usual caveats of third-world taxis must be observed—fix a price first, and don't let them lock anything in the trunk. Otherwise, you can go by bus—likely to be haphazard, but eventually effective, or try to hitch a ride from one of the thousands of NGO vehicles that roam the region.

All four countries are plagued with roadblocks—some official, some not. Bear in mind that whatever the case, they've got guns and you haven't, and the best you can do is be cheerful and courteous and try to get as little stolen as you can. Land mines are another worry, especially away from major roads.

> **B**ear in mind that whatever the case, they've got guns and you haven't, and the best you can do is be cheerful and courteous and try to get as little stolen as you can.

Rwanda Airlines flies internally from Kigali to Gisenyi and Kamembe. However, U.S. embassy staff in the region are not permitted to fly with regional carrier African Airlines, and *DP* is sure that you're as important to you as they are to the State Department. That said, even the grown-up airlines have their problems—in December 2000, two passengers on a flight operated by the Belgian airline Sabena (now SN Brussels Airlines) were injured when the plane was hit with machine-gun rounds as it approached Bujumbura Airport. Unusual, of course, in that no one recently can remember the Rwandans hitting anything unless they were using crudely fashioned and sharpened garden implements at arm's length.

**SN Brussels Airlines**
http://www.brussels-airlines.com

## Dangerous Places ————————————————

### Borders

Dozens of groups of armed militants, refugees, and armed militant refugees wander back and forth between DR Congo, Burundi, and Rwanda. Don't travel at night.

### Roads

All the joys of third-world driving are here for your delectation—bad roads, terrible vehicles, and worse drivers. To pluck just one incident at random from the countless that take place every year, consider the fate of the 70 bus passengers incinerated in Kasese, Uganda, in July 2002 when the brakes on a fuel truck failed, causing it to roll downhill and collect their coach. It was the third major crash involving a fuel truck in Uganda in less than six months.

## Regroupment Camps

Or, as they were called in Europe back in the 1940s, concentration camps. These are a national specialty of Burundi, and are President Buyoya's less-than-constructive response to the civil war pulling his country to pieces. More than 600,000 Burundians, mostly Hutus, have been rounded up at various points into 200 camps dotted around the country. As PR moves go, this rates up there with Disney thinking of adding AuschwitzLand to their theme parks. Nelson Mandela visited one of these dreadful places in 2000 and blew his stack, prompting Buyoya to promise that he'd close them all down.

However, with the obvious exception of the Burundian currency, nothing in this world is worth less than one of Buyoya's promises. In June 2002, the Burundian army forced 30,000 civilians from their homes in Ruyigi province and herded them into camps. The Burundian authorities said that this had been done at the request of the people being moved—presumably the soldiers were just firing into the air to lend an otherwise dreary ethnic cleansing some of the excitement of a major athletics meet.

The camps are dismal places, built from banana leaves and scavenged bits of plastic and metal. There is no sanitation or electricity, but plenty of arbitrary beatings and rapes by Burundian soldiers. Disease, and paramilitary agitation, thrive.

# Dangerous Things

## AIDS/Disease

It's not quite as rampant in the Great Lakes as it is in Zimbabwe, Zambia, or Botswana, but none of those countries are far away, so give it time. Roughly 11 percent of Burundians, 11 percent of Rwandans, and 5 percent of Congolese are HIV-positive. The good news, such as it is, is that Uganda is the only country in Africa to have tamed an HIV epidemic, with its official rate of adult HIV infection falling from 8.3 percent in 1999 to 5 percent in 2001. However, the region's wars and other upheavals can only hinder progress in monitoring and treatment. The bad news, of course, is that NGOs estimate that Uganda has an incident of AIDS of around 25 percent in rural areas in prenatal females.

AIDS may be scary, but it's preventable. Be on the lookout for epidemics of things like Ebola, meningitis, flu, hemorraghic fever, and other highly infectious bugs that flare up periodically.

**Joint UN Program on HIV/AIDS**
http://www.unaids.org
http://www.cdc.gov

## Crime

Not quite as bad as it used to be in Kampala and Kigali, but you still shouldn't wear a Rolex. Really bad everywhere else.

## Curfews

Bujumbura is not a party town: A midnight curfew still operates and is enforced without fear or favor. A Hutu member of Burundi's parliament, Gabriel Gisabwamana, discovered this the hard way in December 1999—out too late one night, he was shot dead at a checkpoint. Once again, the mystery here is how they actually hit him . . .

## Refugees

Hundreds of thousands of the Great Lakes' people spend a lot of time fleeing the hellhole they're stuck in only to find that the country up the road is even worse: There are refugees from Sudan in Uganda and DR Congo, refugees from Rwanda in DR Congo, and refugees from DR Congo in Uganda. About half a million Burundians—the second-largest refugee population in the world—have found an exit from this cycle, however, decamping to relatively civilized Tanzania. All major refugee concentrations are dangerous—for all the usual reasons that concentrations of frightened and desperate people are dangerous, and also for the fact that they serve as both recruitment booths and targets for the various militias on the loose in the region.

**United Nations High Commission for Refugees**
http://www.unhcr.org

## Children

All sides in all the region's wars have used soldiers who shouldn't be playing with real guns. In Uganda, Museveni has admitted that the National Resistance Army that brought him to power was at least partly underage, and the Lord's Resistance Army, the cranky Christian cult that continues to vex the country, is explicitly a children's crusade.

**Coalition to Stop the Use of Child Soldiers**
http://www.child-soldiers.org

## Cults

Something about Uganda in particular seems to attract those who are likely to hand over their life savings to some glassy-eyed nutter in a toga before shedding their human containers to follow a comet to heaven. In 2000, nearly 1,000 members of a Christian cult called the Movement for the Restoration of the Ten Commandments of God were found burned and hacked to death in and around Buhunga and Kanungu, in southwestern Uganda. In the absence of living witnesses, it's a little difficult to figure out what they thought they were accomplishing, but one theory has it that, when the world failed to end at midnight on December 31, 1999—as had been predicted by the sect's leaders—a few of the movement's more uppity members asked for their money back. The movement's overall leader, a manic-depressive called Joseph Kibwitere, decided that a mass murder/suicide was the only solution. Interestingly, he exempted himself from this—he went missing, and the Ugandan police still badly want a word with him.

The movement was born of Kibwitere's devotion to a local hooker called Credonia Mwerinde, who was given to seeing visions of the Virgin Mary. Its 4,000 members wore uniforms, worked in fields, and didn't say much, for fear of breaking one of the Ten Commandments they were seeking to restore (it's tough not to invoke the name of our Lord if you drop a shovel on your foot). It wasn't the first Christian cult to have taken root in Uganda's moist jungle—the Lord's Resistance Army guerrilla group (see "The Players" on page 505) started life as a God-bothering group called the Holy Spirit Movement (whose founding spirit guide was also, interestingly, a woman of dubious repute). Nor was it the last—in September 2000, Ugandan police broke up another bunch of doom-mongering Jesus freaks called the World Message Last Warning group.

**FACTNet**
http://www.factnet.org

### Wildlife

Though the *homo sapien* is by far the most dangerous species in the region, there are others that run him a close second, especially if you sit on them, tease them, or try to pose for a photograph next to one. Make very sure that the branch you're about to tread on is made of wood, and not puff adder, black spitting cobra, Jameson's mamba, black mamba, or Great Lakes bush viper—all detrimental to your travel plans should you get bitten by one.

http://www.fda.gov/fdac/features/995_snakes.html

## Getting Sick

Where do you begin? The Great Lakes region is the devil's own petri dish. Scientists journey here on a regular basis just to figure out why many of the world's nastiest diseases seem to begin in this fetid place.

Get yourself inoculated for yellow fever, cholera, tetanus, typhoid, polio, hepatitis, and meningitis, and take Malarone for malaria. Assume that these precautions don't even begin to protect against the list of woes that await you.

UNAIDS estimates that 3.1 million people die from AIDS-related diseases each year. Every year 5 million join the 40 million people already infected—30 million of those in Sub-Saharan Africa. Fifty-eight percent are female.
*Source:* UNAIDS.

Above all else, get yourself insured for emergency evac, and make sure you read that fine print—many "worldwide" travel insurances have exclusions that mean you're not covered if you go anywhere more dangerous than Rhode Island. You'll need a policy that covers pretty much everything that can possibly go wrong, and includes medical evacuation—in Burundi, for example, there are 14 hospital beds and half a doctor for every 10,000 people. If you do actually visit a hospital in this region, you will quickly want to make room for the fool who wants to linger in a Central African hospital.

If you come down with anything really serious, get the next plane to Johannesburg, at least, or Europe, if possible. Take all the prescription drugs you might need with you, plus extra. Oh, yeah, don't drink the water.

## Nuts and Bolts

Despite years of war, the rampant march of AIDS and other diseases, and occasional all-out ethnic slaughter, there are still 6.2 million Burundians, 7.3 million Rwandans, 24 million Ugandans, and 53.6 million Congolese. However, self-definition in the region is based more on tribe rather than nation. Burundi and Rwanda are both about 84 percent Hutu and 15 percent Tutsi, with tiny minorities of Twa pygmies and South Asian and European expatriates. Uganda's biggest tribes are the Baganda and the Karamojong, comprising nearly 30 percent of the population between them—other minority groups include the Basogo, the Iteso, the Langi, the Bagisu, the Acholi, the Lugbara, the Bunyoro, and the Batoro. DR Congo's population contains over 200 tribes: The four largest—the Bantu groups Kongo, Luba, and Mongo, and the Hamitic group Mangbetu-Azande—include about half the population.

The region's religious leanings are a legacy of the region's colonial past. Around 70 percent of the people in Burundi, Rwanda, Uganda, and DR Congo are Christian, with a slight Catholic majority among them. There is a small Muslim minority of around 10 percent in the region, as well as some adherence to indigenous beliefs. The official languages also reflect bygone European domination—French in Burundi and DR Congo, English in Uganda, French and English in Rwanda. These are spoken mostly among educated, official, and business circles in the cities, while native languages are spoken generally. Literacy in the region varies between 50 percent and 70 percent.

The regional currencies are the Burundian franc, the Rwandan franc, the Ugandan shilling, and the Congolese franc—in DR Congo, be careful you're not palmed off with old Zaires, the imaginatively named currency of Zaire, which is what DR Congo was called until 1998. None of these currencies are big players on international finance markets, and all are in free fall—the Ugandan shilling has gone from about 1,000 to the U.S. dollar to 1,700 in the last six years. Take dollars and euros.

All four countries have climates like the inside of a kettle. The wet season runs from April till October. Basic utilities—water, telephones, electricity—exist, but are erratic. Mobile phone and Internet services are available in the bigger cities, but everywhere else . . . well, it literally is a jungle out there.

**Embassy of the United States**
1720 Avenue des Etats-Unis
Bujumbura, Burundi
Tel.: (257) 22 3454
Fax: (257) 22 2926

**Embassy of Great Britain**
(All Burundi embassy staff operate out
of the embassy in Kigali, Rwanda)

**Embassy of Canada**
(The nearest embassy is in Kigali,
Rwanda)

**Embassy of the United States**
377, Boulevard de la Révolution
Kigali, Rwanda
Tel.: (250) 50 5601
Fax: (250) 50 7143
usisl@rwanda1.com
http://www.usembkigali.net

**Embassy of Great Britain**
Parcelle No 1131
Boulevard de l'Umuganda
Kacyira-Sud
BP 576
Kigali, Rwanda
Tel.: (250) 84 098
Fax: (250) 82 044

**Embassy of Canada**
Rue Akagera
BP 1177
Kigali, Rwanda

Tel.: (250) 73 210
Fax: (250) 72 719
kgali@dfait-maeci.gc.ca

**Embassy of the United States**
Plot 1577
Ggaba Road
Kampala, Uganda
Tel.: (256) 41 25 9791
Fax: (256) 41 25 0314
uscons@infocom.co.ug
http://usembassy.state.gov/kampala

**British High Commission**
10/12 Parliament Avenue
Kampala, Uganda
Tel.: (256) 78 31 2000
Fax: (256) 78 31 2281
bhcinfo@starcom.co.ug

**Canadian High Commission**
Comcraft House
Hailé Sélassie Avenue
Nairobi, Kenya
Tel.: (254) 2 21 4804
Fax: (254) 2 22 6987
nrobi@dfait-maeci.gc.cd

**Embassy of the United States**
310 Avenue des Aviateurs
Kinshasa-Gombe, DR Congo
Tel.: (243) 884 3608
Fax: (243) 884 3467
http://usembassy.state.gov/kinshasa

GREAT LAKES

*Embassy of Great Britain*
83 Avenue de Roi Baudouin
Kinshasa, DR Congo
Tel.: (243) 884 6101

*Embassy of Canada*
17 Avenue Pumbu
Commune de Gombe
Kinshasa, DR Congo
Tel.: (243) 884 1699
Fax: (243) 884 1277

# Dangerous Days

| | |
|---|---|
| **9/27/02** | Rwandan troops leave DR Congo. |
| **7/22/02** | DR Congo and Rwanda agree to a peace deal. |
| **1/19/02** | DR Congo city of Goma destroyed by eruption of Mount Nyiragongo. |
| **7/23/01** | Coup attempt by Tutsi officers in Burundi fails. |
| **4/18/01** | Coup attempt by Tutsi officers in Burundi fails. |
| **3/01** | Fighting between Hutu rebels and Burundian troops in Bujumbura leaves 200 dead. |
| **1/16/01** | President Laurent Kabila of DR Congo assassinated by one of his bodyguards. His son, Joseph, takes over as president. |
| **12/00** | Ebola outbreak in Uganda kills more than 100. |
| **12/00** | More than 10,000 refugees fleeing fighting in DR Congo arrive in Zambia. |
| **6/00** | The DR Congo town of Kisangani set alight by an artillery duel between Rwandan and Zimbabwean forces. |
| **4/14/00** | Explosions caused by electrical faults at Kinshasa Airport kill more than 100 people. |
| **3/00** | Nearly 1,000 members of the Christian cult the Movement for the Restoration of the Ten Commandments hacked or burnt to death in a mass murder/suicide in Uganda. |
| **8/99** | Fighting between rebel factions in the DR Congo town of Kisangani brings Rwandan and Ugandan troops into conflict. |
| **8/4/99** | Sudanese Air Force jets bomb rebel positions in the DR Congo towns of Makanza and Bogbonga. |
| **3/2/99** | Hutu extremists of the Interahamwe kill eight foreign tourists in Uganda. |
| **11/98** | Zimbabwean Air Force jets attack rebel-owned boats in Lake Tanganyika. |
| **10/11/98** | Tutsi rebels backed by Rwanda and Uganda take the DR Congo town of Kindu. |
| **8/27/98** | Namibia joins in the war in DR Congo on Kabila's side, while Angolan UNITA forces shift their alliance to the new Tutsi rebel movement. |

| | |
|---|---|
| **8/23/98** | Rebels take Kisangani. |
| **8/21/98** | First Zimbabwean troops arrive in DR Congo to support Kabila. |
| **8/98** | Several cities in DR Congo seized by Tutsi rebels, who then march on Kinshasa. DR Congo government evacuates to Lubumbashi. |
| **7/99** | Rebels in DR Congo advance on Kabinda and Miba. |
| **5/25/98** | Rwanda puts its forces in DR Congo on cease-fire. |
| **11/28/97** | Fighting between rival factions of the DR Congo army kills 20 in Kinshasa. |
| **10/1/97** | DR Congo forces cross the border into Congo after shelling kills dozens in Kinshasa. |
| **9/7/97** | Mobutu dies, at age 66, in Rabat, Morocco. |
| **5/17/97** | Rebel forces enter Kinshasa. Laurent Kabila proclaims himself president of the Democratic Republic of Congo. |
| **5/16/97** | President Mobutu flees Zaire. |
| **5/97** | Major outbreak of typhus in Burundi's "regroupment camps" for Hutus. |
| **4/16/97** | Sanctions on Burundi eased. |
| **4/97** | Angolan troops invade Zaire in support of Kabila. Angolan UNITA rebels enter on the side of the Zairean government. |
| **3/15/97** | Laurent Kabila's forces occupy Kisangani, Zaire's third-largest city. |
| **1/97** | Burundian troops massacre hundreds of Hutus in central Burundi. |
| **10/30/96** | Rwandan troops cross into eastern Zaire to aid Tutsi rebel forces, and begin a siege of Goma. |
| **10/96** | Serious fighting in Zaire between government forces and the rebels of Laurent Kabila, known as the Alliance of Democratic Forces of Congo-Zaire. |
| **10/96** | Zairean government tells the nation's 300,000 Tutsis that they have a week to leave the country. |
| **8/96** | Sanctions imposed on Burundi by other African nations. |
| **7/96** | Burundian troops massacre more than 1,000 Hutu civilians in Gitega province. |
| **7/25/96** | Major Pierre Buyoya seizes power in a coup d'etat in Burundi. |
| **11/95** | Zairean troops begin a campaign of massacres against Zairean Tutsis. Thousands flee to Rwanda. |
| **7/95** | Ebola outbreak in Kikwit, Zaire, kills more than 200. |
| **4/22/95** | Rwandan government troops kill at least 4,000 Hutu refugees in Kibeho. |

GREAT LAKES

| | |
|---|---|
| 7/4/94 | The Tutsi-led Rwandan Patriotic Front arrive in Kigali. More than 2 million Hutus flee Rwanda for Zaire. The RPF form a new Rwandan government under Paul Kagame. |
| 4/6/94 | President Ntaryamira of Burundi and President Habyarimana of Rwanda are killed when the airplane carrying them both back from peace talks is shot down near Kigali. The Hutu-led Rwandan Armed Forces and a Hutu extremist organisation, the Interahamwe, embark on a genocide that kills more than 800,000 Tutsis and moderate Hutus. |
| 10/93 | Melchior Ndadaye, Burundi's first Hutu president, assassinated by Tutsi extremists. |
| 10/90 | Rwanda invaded by the Rwandan Patriotic Front, an organization of Rwandan exiles based in Uganda. Invasion suppressed with cooperation of troops from Zaire and France. |
| 1990 | The Lord's Resistance Army, a Christian fundamentalist militia based in Sudan, begins attacks against northern Uganda. |
| 1/86 | Milton Obote driven from power in Uganda by the National Resistance Movement of Yoweri Museveni. |
| 4/11/79 | Idi Amin driven from power in Uganda by Ugandan rebels back by Tanzanian troops. Amin flees into exile in Saudi Arabia, while power is retaken by Milton Obote. |
| 1977 | Angola-based rebels stage three-month insurgency in Zaire. |
| 1976 | Ebola virus discovered in Zaire. |
| 4/7/76 | Israeli commandos storm Entebbe airport in Uganda to rescue the passengers of an Air France jet hijacked by pro-Palestinian terrorists. |
| 10/30/74 | Muhammad Ali defeats George Foreman in the "Rumble in the Jungle" in Kinshasa. |
| 1972 | Hutu-orchestrated massacres in Burundi kill approximately 200,000 Tutsis. |
| 10/27/72 | Mobutu renames Congo Zaire. |
| 2/2/71 | Idi Amin seizes power in Uganda, in a coup that deposes Milton Obote. |
| 1965 | Congolese army Chief of Staff Mobutu Sese Seko seizes power. |
| 1962 | Burundi becomes independent from Belgium. |
| 1962 | Rwanda becomes independent from Belgium. |
| 1962 | Uganda becomes independent from Great Britain. |
| 1/61 | Congo's first president, Patrice Lumumba, assassinated with CIA complicity. |
| 1960 | Congo becomes independent from Belgium. |

# INDIA

## Gandhi Pieces

In the previous edition of *DP*, we started out by observing that the land of Mahatma Gandhi, with all its internal diversity and division, was a testament to hope and the potential of postcolonial progress. In the new millennium, it seems as if India is doing its best to make us look bad. India's decades-long confrontation with neighboring Pakistan over the disputed state of Kashmir was escalating to the extent that Western nations were advising their expatriate nationals to get on the next available flight to anywhere. The combination of British military training, North Korean nukes, bombastic Hindi/Pak rhetoric, an inflow of insurgents from Afghanistan, and a bloated, bored army were going to push these uneasy neighbors to the brink. But *DP* has faith that cooler turbans will prevail . . . despite how jerry-rigged the whole country is.

This nation of more than a billion people, and nearly as many ethnicities, religions, and languages—14 official languages and hundreds

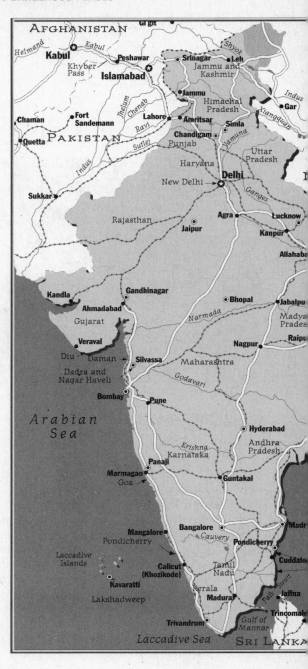

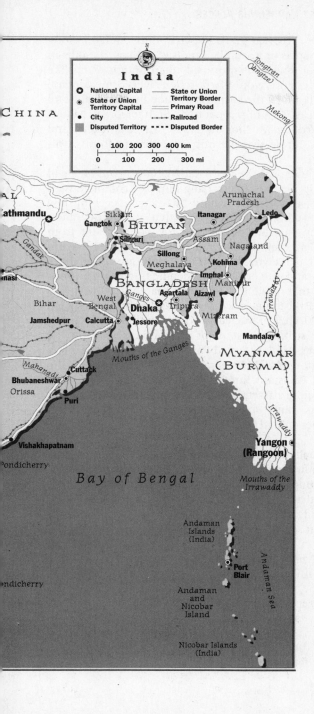

INDIA

of dialects—should have regressed into a bunch of dinky fiefdoms long ago. With Muslim separatists in Kashmir, Tamils in the south, Sikhs in the northwest, and tribal renegades sprinkled all around, it seems like having one big outside enemy would be a relief. Every time a bomb goes off (and they go off a lot), the suspects include Indians, Pakistani agents, Pashtun separatists, Kashmiri separatists, Sikh terrorists, Maoist tribal rebels, Tamil guerrillas, Muslim militants, drug traffickers, and even gangsters. Mother Teresa was the only one exempt from suspicion. And she's dead.

Although the core of India has the worn, faded, industrious bustle of a third-world country, its borders are warring outposts complete with bunkers, artillery duels, terrorist raids, and MiG-21s screeching low overhead. *DP* has been saying for a while now that one of the ugliest imaginable scenarios on the geopolitical horizon could result from India's nuke race with Pakistan, but hey, who listens to us? The world has ignored the standoff, perceiving it as a Hatfield-McCoy stick fight in the boonies. As things stand, the only thing keeping fingers off buttons may be the knowledge that while India may ultimately survive a limited nuclear exchange, Pakistan most certainly would not: India's Agni II missile could lob a 200-kiloton nuclear warhead within 1,000 feet of a target 150 miles away, striking most major Pakistani cities within five minutes of launch. That's a lot of toasted Pakistanis, give or take a few hundred thousand. Unfortunately, it is possible that elements in the upper echelons of the Pakistani military may see the idea of mass national martyrdom as quite attractive. The mind boggles at the thought of crowds of eager Pakistanis dodging and weaving to make it to ground zero, like catcher-mitted baseball fans at a World Series game tracking a homer.

India's history is usually blamed for its troubles. Centuries of warfare, outside cultural influences, and empire-building have made India easily the most interesting country on earth. Reality-show producers would tremble with anticipation at the thought of combining over 700 languages and thousands of castes, tribes, and cultures into one hot, sweaty, tough place. But somehow India gets by. Despite absorbing the worst of each invading culture, they survive. English bureaucracy and motorcars, Afghan driving skills and political rhetoric, third-world weaponry and Hindu militancy, bellicose neighbors and the lowest incarceration rate in the world, a population-busting love fest and a dozen simmering insurgencies . . . what more could the *DP* traveler ask for? To be fair, they may talk tough, but the Indians' most favorite hero is Gandhi, not Rambo.

India's official line is that they wouldn't launch first, but they've not left anyone in much doubt that any Pakistani serve would be returned.

India's prime minister, Shri Atal Bihari Vajpayee, who fancies himself as something of a subcontinental Walt Whitman, ventured into verse to express his feelings:

> Sometimes at night,
> Suddenly, sleep deserts me,
> My eyes open, I begin to ponder
> Those scientists who invented
> nuclear weapons,
> On hearing the gruesome human destruction,
> Of Hiroshima, Nagasaki,
> How did they ever sleep
> at night
>
> Those whose invention,
> Created the ultimate weapon . . .
> Do they even for a moment,
> Feel what was inflicted by them,
> Was monstrous?
> If they do then time will not put
> them in the dock,
> But if they don't,
> Then history will never,
> Ever forgive them.

http://pmindia.nic.in/meetpm/poems.htm

This probably scans better in the original Hindi—we certainly hope so. Whatever, it bespeaks a worrisome moral logic on Vajpayee's part—nuclear war, he seems to be suggesting, is all the fault of the men who built the bomb, not whichever jackass decides to let one rip, to (for example) assert sovereignty over a small corner of one's nation.

India and Pakistan, in their relatively embryonic relationship, have already fought three wars (not counting cricket matches), and Pakistan has gone home crying each time. In between official wars, both countries recruit, train, and field separatist extremists—Pakistan funds the foreign nasties in the Indian-controlled region of Kashmir, while India fans the flames of hatred in Pakistan's Sind area. In the tortured northeast, tribal groups based deep in jungle hideouts fight for freedom and to keep settlers from drowning them out. Bombings, kidnappings, riots, and assassinations are the standard fare.

Not one to miss out on a gang-banging, China is also part of India's multifront diplomatic fray. Just to keep China honest, India fought a brief border war with the Sinos back in 1962. Since then, though, the two countries' relations have improved—if for no other reason than their mutual respect for the size of each others' populations, and the realization that a conventional ground war might take a few hundred years to fight, and still leave each country with populations the size of the United States . . . and with plenty of space for parking.

## The Scoop

India is a relatively safe country with some nasty exceptions, of which Kashmir is the best-known combination of front lines and scenic tourism. Breathing, driving, and hiking can quickly end your life there. Those who seek the traditional sites should be forewarned by the road-side spectacle of mangled buses, lorries, and people; India has the most dangerous road system in the world.

It also has the most maddening bureaucratic inefficiency and cor-ruption. India is home to a billion people, and getting your laundry done or buying a train ticket will necessitate tipping most of the time. In 2001, it was estimated that more than 800 people serving as elected deputies in India's state or national parliaments had criminal records. *DP* figures the system just hasn't gotten around to convicting the rest.

## The Players

### Shri Atal Bihari Vajpayee

Prime minister of India and leader of the Hindu nationalist Bharatiya Janata Party (BJP), the son of a high-caste Brahmin family, born in Gwalior in 1924, Vajpayee spent four decades in India's parlia-ment as an opposition deputy before becoming prime minister for the first time in 1996. However, his coalition government collapsed after 13 days, and Vajpayee was warming the benches again before he'd had time to get new business cards printed. In 1998, he managed to hang on to the top job for a few months before a similarly flaky coalition col-lapsed underneath him, but he was re-elected in 1999.

In a country as vast and diverse as India, it's probably not possible to make much of a career in politics if you have a narrow ideological base, and Vajpayee has covered most of the political spectrum during a long and eventful career. Vajpayee has been a pro-independence activist (he was briefly jailed—er, sorry—"gaoled" by the British in 1942), a com-munist, a right-winger, a moderate, a maker of peace with Pakistan, and a maker of war with Pakistan. He's been criticized by India's Mus-lim population for favoring the Hindu majority and lambasted by Hindu radicals for opposing the destruction of mosques. He also writes poetry, and his favorite color is blue.

*Prime Minister of India*
http://pmindia.nic.in/home.htm
abvajpayee@bjp.org

*Bharatiya Janata Party*
http://www.bjp.org

### The Indian Army

India has a standing army of 1.3 million, on which it spends US$14 billion every year. Nearly half of these troops are deployed in Kashmir—by far the biggest force India has ever fielded against a secessionist insurrection. India subscribes to the domino theory—if Kashmir is allowed to leave India, other states might do the same, and then India's army won't have a country to protect. In a bid to counter the threat from various local militias, and also to keep Pakistan on its toes, India is modernizing its defense forces furiously and cultivating military relationships with Israel and Russia. India recently bought 300 T-90 tanks from Russia, as well as Russian-built warships, and they swap dirty secrets about terrorists.

Handicappers note that although Pakistan has a token 612,000 soldiers, India has a lot more insurgencies than its bellicose neighbor.

*Indian Armed Forces*
http://armedforces.nic.in

*Indian Army in Kashmir*
http://www.armyinkashmir.org

## THE NORTHWEST: KASHMIR AND THE FUNDAMENTALISTS

More than 30,000 people have died since the current insurgency erupted in the disputed northern state of Jammu and Kashmir in 1989. Between 1990 and 2002, the Indian military claim to have killed 14,636 terrorists in Kashmir, of whom 3,914 were foreigners. Well, Pakistanis don't really consider themselves foreigners in Kashmir.

Pakistan has fought two out of three of its last wars over this province of 13 million people, and the situation is expected to remain tense for years to come. The geopolitical volleyball started when Britain divided up India and Pakistan in 1947, based on geographic divisions rather than religious ones; ever since, it has been split between the Indian state of Jammu and Kashmir, with its capital in Srinagar, and the Pakistani entity, Azad (Free) Jammu and Kashmir, with a government of sorts based in Islamabad. At the time, India promised to hold a plebiscite among all Kashmiris to determine whether the territory should be part of India or Pakistan. However, the government backed

**INDIA**

down, and the conflict has been going on ever since. Although most Kashmiris are Muslim they would rather have independence than be part of either India or Pakistan. The losers seem to be the Hindus of the region. At last count, there were about 400,000 Hindus from the Kashmir Valley in refugee camps around the state's winter capital of Jammu.

**Jammu and Kashmir Government**
Opposite Pratap Park
Srinagar 190001, India
Tel.: (91) 194 452 437
Fax: (91) 194 452 227
dipjk@jandk.jk.nic.in
http://jammukashmir.nic.in

**Kashmir Liberation Cell Government of Azad Jammu and Kashmir**
Tel.: (92) 51 445 5222
Fax: (92) 51 441 3620
info@klc.org.pk
http://www.klc.org.pk

**Kashmir News**
http://www.kashmirnews.com

**The Army in Kashmir**
http://www.armyinkashmir.org

**Ministry of Home Affairs (India)**
http://www.mha.nic.in

**Jammu-Kashmir.com**
msadiq@del2.vsnl.net.in
http://jammu-kashmir.com

**Islami Jamiat Talaba (Student Organization)**
1-A Zeldar Park
Ichhra
Lahore, Pakistan
Tel.: (92) 42 7588488
Fax: (92) 42 7572310
jamiatpk@yahoo.com
http://jamiat.org

**Muzaffarabad**
Tasneem Shaheed Manzil
Eidgha Road
Muzaffarabad, Pakistan
Tel: (92) 581 44336

**Kashmiri American Council**
733 15th Street NW, Suite 1100
Washington, DC 20005
Tel.: (202) 628-6789
Fax: (202) 393-0062
info@kashmiri.com
http://www.kashmiri.com

## Pakistan's Inter Services Intelligence (ISI)

The biggest thorn in India's side and the terrorist's best friend. This is Pakistan's version of the CIA—slightly more militarized and crudely transparent. They are no less obvious in their activities than our tow-headed operatives in short-sleeved checkered shirts from J.C. Penney.

The Directorate for ISI was founded in 1948 by British army officer Major General R. Cawthome, then-deputy chief of staff in the Pakistan army. After the British left, the president of Pakistan (General Ayyub Khan) expanded the role of the ISI to include maintaining military rule in Pakistan. This included monitoring opposition politicians. It is a testament to the ISI's efficiency that when Prime Minister Sharif made noises about shutting down ISI training camps in 1999, he suddenly found himself without a job and the military in charge. Staffed by hundreds of civilian and military officers, and thousands of other workers, the agency's headquarters is located in Islamabad. The ISI has about 10,000 officers and staff members.

The ISI began using militants in Kashmir under President Zia Ul Haq in 1988. They are not just busy in Kashmir—they were helping the Taliban in Afghanistan and are still helping Sri Lanka's Liberation Tigers of Tamil Eelam. They're also operating camps near the border of Bangladesh, training groups to fight in the northeastern states: United Liberation Front of Seven Sisters (ULFOSS); National Security Council of Nagaland (NSCN); People's Liberation Army (PLA); United Liberation Front of Assam (ULFA); and North East Students Organization (NESO). The ISI is said to have intensified its activities in the southern Indian states of Hyderabad, Bangalore, Cochin, Kojhikode, Bhatkal, and Gulbarga. They are also supporting groups in Andhra Pradesh, like the Ittehadul Musalmeen and the Hizbul Mujahideen, and are accused of training and supplying Uighur fighters in Xianjang province in western China. They currently train and support at least six different groups in Kashmir, totaling 5,000 to 10,000 fighters, while keeping a lower profile than normal during the West's brief love affair with Mushareff.

**Inter Services Intelligence Directorate**
Near CDA Office
Islamabad, Pakistan
Tel.: (92) 51 920 1456

### The Jammu and Kashmir Liberation Front (JKLF)

The leader of the local JKLF is the oft-jailed, 35-year-old Yasin Malik, and its headquarters are in Anantnag, 44 miles from Srinagar. Founded in 1977, the JKLF wants to make Muslim Kashmir independent from Hindu India. The ball got rolling in 1988 when one of the liberation leaders, Amanullah Khan, got together with the Srinagar-based Islamic Students League. Fighting since 1990, they typically plant bombs and engage in antigovernment activities. It is believed by many that the relatively secular JKLF are not quite the big noise they once were, as more militantly Islamic pro-Pakistani groups emerge as leaders of Kashmir's independence struggle. Yasin spends his time between being jailed and tortured and traveling to Johns Hopkins Hospital for medical treatment.

**Azad Jammu Kashmir**
http://www.kashmiri.com
http://www.klc.org.pk
http://www.geocities.com/jklf-kashmir

INDIA

## The United Jihad Council (UJC)

Possibly because even the ISI had lost track of the number of ratbag organizations they'd tooled up and turned loose in Kashmir, in 1994 they grouped thirteen of them into a more radical umbrella group under the overall command of the Jamiat ul-Mujahideen leader, Commander Manzur Shah.

Among the groups who help make up what must be a swinging annual dinner dance are Harkat ul-Ansar, Hizbul Mujahideen, Ikhwan ul-Mussilmin, al-Jihad, al-Barq, Lashkar-e-Toiba, al-Badar (foreign fighters), and Tehrik-i-Jihad. These organizations (some of which are also umbrella groups) range in size and capability from two toothless hillbillies sharing a rusty Lee Enfield to serious paramilitary outfits with the best kit the Pakistanis can buy them. Members get most of their training in Azad Kashmir and number about 3,000 to 6,000 (depending on how good the aim of the Indian Army is at any one time). The idea is that they are more radical than HUA and the moderate JKLF. Some groups want independence for Kashmir, and others under this umbrella want Kashmir to unite with Pakistan. They squabble with Hindu home defense groups as well as the Indian army.

## Jamiat ul-Mujahideen (JUM)

JUM is a pro-Pakistan separatist group known for its bombings in Jammu and Kashmir. Founded in 1990, it split from the Hizbul Mujahideen when the latter decided to set up shop with Pakistani Islamic party Jamaat-e-Islami. Essentially, JUM is just another angry Boy Scout camp to train scrawny kids to fight in Kashmir. Indian officials claim that the JUM takes its orders from the ISI, and seeing how almost everyone else in Kashmir who can hold a rifle takes their orders from the ISI, there seems no reason not to believe this—though the JUM claim that they, alone among the various paramilitary groups, are a purely Kashmiri organization. The JUM is sucking wind these days because the followers come from the same school as did the Taliban (the Deobandi school).

What remains of the JUM is commanded by Maulana Ghulam Rasool, who escaped from a Srinagar jail in February 2000 (he'd been doing porridge for trying to blow up the residence of Jammu and Kashmir Chief Minister Farooq Abdullah). However, much of the rest of JUM's leadership has been killed or arrested, and they're floundering a bit these days—though their monthly magazine, *Mahaz-e-Kashmir*, is still a real hoot. That said, their capacity for violence should not be underestimated, especially as they try to show the Pakistani new boys who's really in charge. In April 2002, the JUM claimed responsibility for killing five Indian soldiers in an ambush in the Poonch district of Jammu.

## Harkat-ul-Mujahideen (HUM)/Harkat-ul-Ansar (HUA)

Another thorn in India's side, the Harkat-ul-Mujahideen (HUM) started in Pakistan's central Punjab in the early '80s under the name Harkat-ul-Ansar (HUA), with headquarters at Raiwind in Punjab, where it holds an annual conference at which you wouldn't want to be booked as the comedian. The HUM were active in the Afghan resistance of the Soviets, were big mates of the Taliban, and are still friends with Osama bin Laden (they were believed to have a time-share arrangement on some of his training facilities in Afghanistan). Former HUM Grand Poobah Fazlur Rehman Khalil signed bin Laden's February 1998 fatwa calling for attacks against American interests, and the HUM threatened revenge on the United States after some of their members were killed by American cruise missiles during Bill Clinton's Operation Hey Look Over There! (or whatever it was called) in August 1998. HUM's first chief, Parvez Ahmad Gazi, was popped by Border Security Force troopers, as was the new HUM head Peer Baba. And Sanaullah's predecessor, HUA Supreme Commander Arif Hussain Sheikh, was whacked in a crossfire between police and separatists on March 17, 1997. HUM's current leader is Farooq Kashmiri (until, of course, he gets popped).

HUM began their jihad in Kashmir in 1990, under the leadership of Sayyed Afghani Shaheed (literally translated as "Sid Dead Afghan"). The HUM were the people behind the December 1999 hijacking of an Indian airliner that ended up parked on the runway at Kandahar, where the hijackers negotiated the release of former HUA leader Masood Azhar, who had been in prison in India since 1994, along with Sheikh Omar. (Several previous kidnappings of Westerners in Kashmir had also been attempts to open Azhar's coop.) However, rather than returning to the fold, Azhar decided his old pals were no longer quite militant enough and went off to form a new movement, the Jaish-e-Mohammad. There's gratitude . . . after they'd hijacked a plane for him and everything.

HUM is the main recruiter and trainer (with help from the Pakistani Secret Service) of young Kashmiris and out-of-work mujahideen from Pakistan. If you are looking for mujahideen time to add to your resume, they will train you for five weeks in the dark arts of light weapons, land mines, booby traps, and covert operations and then send you marching over the mountains to raise havoc in Indian-occupied

If you are looking for mujahideen time to add to your résumé, they will train you for five weeks in the dark arts of light weapons, land mines, booby traps, and covert operations and then send you marching over the mountains to raise havoc in Indian-occupied Kashmir.

INDIA

Kashmir. The group is also known for sending eager fighters into Bosnia and Herzegovina (all gone home now), Tajikistan (Tajik resistance), Myanmar (training Muslim rebels in the Arakan mountains), and other Muslim holy wars. They claim to have banned Americans from Kashmir, though they're clearly malleable on a case-by-case basis—it was the HUM, for example, who trained Marin County mujahid and not-new-best-friend of *DP*, John Walker Lindh. It may be a testament to the quality of training that the Taliban made Lindh train again at bin Laden's al-Farooq camp, because even the Talibs considered HUM training to be bush league.

**Harkat ul-Mujahideen**
info@harkatulmujahideen.org
http://www.ummah.net.pk/harkat

## Hizbul Mujahideen (Fighters for the Party of God)

The military wing of Pakistan's largest Islamic party, the Jamaat-e-Islami, and the new players and leaders of Kashmir's struggle for independence, the Hizbul Mujahideen are now the largest military force ranged against the Indian government. Commanded by Syeed Salahuddin, whose real name is Syeed Mohammed Yusuf Shah, they claim they are fighting for Azad Kashmir, or Free Kashmir. Currently, there are about 15,000 active rebel fighters with several subfactions among them. The rebels operate in small hit-and-run groups in cities like Srinagar, or from remote bases in Kashmir. Their recent growth can be directly attributed to their patrons' enthusiasm for results.

http://www.kashmirgroup.freeserve.co.uk/links.htm

## All-Party Hurriyat Conference (APHC)

APHC is an alliance of 26 rebel organizations in Indian-administered Kashmir formed by the numerous guerrillas who use secession from India as a common rallying point. Maulvi Mohammad Omar Farooq is both the APHC's leader and the hereditary Mir Waiz of Kashmir, the religious leader of the region's Muslims. The APHC is as close to an internationally acceptable face of Kashmiri militancy as there is: Bill Clinton granted a White House audience to a two-man APHC delegation in 2000. Naturally, all the other Kashmiri militants think the APHC are a bunch of big girls' blouses, which may be why they keep picking on them. In April 2001, two minor militant groups, Mujahidin-e-Haq and Al-Kisas, tossed grenades into a Hurriyat meeting in Srinagar, wounding four. In May 2002, senior Hurriyat member Abdul Ghani Lone was shot dead at a rally in Srinagar.

**All-Party Hurriyat Conference**
**Mirwaiz Manzil**
Rajauri Kadal
Srinagar, Jammu, and Kashmir

## Jaish-e-Mohammad (Army of Mohammad)

This Peshawar-based offshoot of Harkat ul-Mujahideen was formed in 1999 after its founders, Maulana Masood Azhar and British-born Sheikh Omar, were released from Indian jails. HUM members hijacked an Indian Airlines flight to Kandahar in December 1999 to negotiate for the release of Azhar. Up to three-quarters of HUM's membership defected to the new group, which must have made the remaining quarter wonder why they'd bothered with the hijacking lark.

Jaish-e-Mohammad became internationally infamous when they were fingered for the murder of *Wall Street Journal* reporter Daniel Pearl in Karachi in February 2002. Sheikh Omar was arrested days afterward and formally charged with murder. He's also been indicted by a grand jury in Trenton, New Jersey, although they'd be ill-advised to hold their breath waiting for him.

http://www.satp.org/satporgtp/countries/india/states/jandk/terrorist_outfits/jaish_
e_mohammad_mujahideen_e_tanzeem.htm

## Lashkar-e-Toiba (Army of the Pure)

These sons of fun (and their political wing, the Markaz Dawa Al Irshad) are based in the Pakistani Punjab, but increasingly rampant in Indian-administered regions of Kashmir, especially the Srinagar Valley and the districts of Doda, Poonch, and Rajauri. Unlike their fellow strugglers in the cause of Kashmiri independence, the Lahore-based Lashkar-e-Toiba have grander designs: they want to impose Islamic rule over all of India. The fact that they've got about as much a chance as trying to impose Sharia law on Texas hasn't stopped them from pursuing their aims with ruthlessness and undeniable daring.

Led by Professor Hafiz Mohammed Saeed, they first made a name for themselves when they killed four people in an attack on a military complex in Bandipore, near Srinagar, in July 1999. Since then, they have carried out scores of attacks. Among the more noteworthy of these were the raid on the headquarters of India's Kashmir Special Operations Group in December 1999 and the killing of 35 Sikhs in Chattingshpura in March 2000. In December 2000, they took the fight all the way to Delhi, attacking an army camp in the historic Red Fort—once the seat of Muslim rule in India. A year later, they returned to Delhi to launch a suicide attack on India's parliament building, which left all five attackers and seven others dead, and very nearly provoked the full-scale war between India and Pakistan that Lashkar-e-Toiba seems to think desirable. The various muj groups from Pakistan could think of nothing more heartwarming than one of their attacks being the trigger for a nuke attack on Pakistan. The Indian military in Kashmir accused the Lashkar-e-Toiba of trying to "Talibanize" Kashmir, claiming that they wanted to ban television and alcohol and compel women to wear the burqa.

The U.S. State Department isn't a big fan, either: it's added Lashkar-e-Toiba to its list of terrorist organizations and frozen their assets—whatever that means. They've also been outlawed in their native Pakistan. Lashkar-e-Toiba has reacted with the tone of bewildered outrage commonly employed by terrorists who've just been called terrorists: "We are not a terrorist organization," said their spokesman, the splendidly named Yahya Mujahid, "nor does Islam allow acts of terror." A shame, really, that *The Guinness Book of World Records* does not contain a category for ingenuousness.

Under pressure from India, Musharaff banned Lashkar-e-Toiba in January 2002, and arrested its leader, Mohammad Saeed. He was released after three months and then arrested again when he was blamed for an attack on a bus and army barracks in which 34 people were killed.

http://www.jamatdawa.org

### Bit Players: Muslim Janbaz Forc/al-Umar/al-Barq/al-Faran/al-Jolson

These groups are mostly Afghans sent into Kashmir by the ISI. Al-Faran was a nom de guerre of Afghans who took Western trekkers hostage and then killed them after a shoot-out. The rest have the capacity for similar unpleasantness. Incidentally, we've made one of these names up. Using your skill and judgment, can you guess which?

## THE NORTHEAST: TRIBALS

India still tenuously holds onto the glob of mountainous land past the "chicken neck" in the northeast. This tea-growing area has been a hot spot due to the constant displacement of locals by cheap tea-picking labor. Revolutionaries tend to be influenced by China and old-school political thinking. Hey, whatever gets you a free gun and a hot meal.

### Naxalites

The various radical communist groups all are descended from the armed peasants who operated in the 1960s under the banner of Naxalites. They take their name from the Naxalbari, or "chicken neck," the strategic 20-kilometer-wide stretch of land running between Nepal and Bangladesh.

## United Liberation Front of Assam (ULFA)

The area of Assam supplies half of India's oil and 15 percent of the world's tea, but its people have nothing to show for it. The ULFA, formed in 1979 to further sovereignty and drawn from the ranks of those who call themselves Assamese, was supposed to stop its fight for a socialist state when it signed a peace deal with the Indian government in January 1992. The hard-liners said "Screw that" and began a campaign of kidnapping and extortion against the rich tea-growers. The Indian Tea Association quickly put together a 7,000-man private army to protect itself from ULFA thugs. Curious *DP*'ers can find the ULFA's bases in neighboring Bhutan.

There have been reports of large-scale extortion and attacks on police stations throughout Assam by both the ULFA and the National Democratic Front of Bodoland (NDFB), formerly called the Bodo Security Force (the ULFA and the various Bodoland groups don't like each other much). Security forces have stepped up their operations against the militants and rounded up large numbers of both suspects and weapons. In March 2002, the ULFA's monthly newspaper, *Freedom*, carried a call for peace talks with India and discussions on Assamese sovereignty. The Indian government is taking its time about RSVP'ing. Assam state officials, however, are hoping that the government in New Delhi will send in a paramilitary force to end the rebels' kidnappings. For now, Assam is an especially dangerous place if you grow tea. Crumpets, anyone?

## National Democratic Front of Bodoland (NDFB)/Bodoland Liberation Tiger Force (BLTF)

The Bodos comprise some 800,000 people out of Assam's 25 million inhabitants. Bodo tribals living in northwest Assam between the north bank of the Brahmaputra River and the foothills of the Himalayas have been duking it out for 30 years with the Assamese state government and the Indian national government for a homeland that would split Assam in two. The original idea was that cheap labor was needed to pick tea and the Bengalis were it. The Bodos were (and are) pissed at the swarms of Bengali immigrants that have settled on their traditional tribal lands over the past 20 years, as well as the wholesale raping of the environment by illegal loggers. The Bodos like to chop up Bengali villagers and blow things up (trains, bridges, etc.), so the war was on.

The struggle became truly violent, however, only after 1985. The Bodos claim some 1,200 of their people were slaughtered by Indian security forces before the 1993 autonomy agreement. (By the way, the pact was never carried out by the government and the Bodos renounced it in 1996.) However, like all good rebel groups, the Bodos are divided by internal factionalism. The National Democratic Front of Bodoland (NDFB) and the Bodoland Liberation Tiger Force (BLTF) have been hacking up each other with as much fervor as they do immigrants and government security forces. Some 5,500 people have been killed in the insurgency since 1987. Their bases are in Bhutan, leading one to wonder whether Bhutan should invest in nukeproof housing materials.

In 2002, the Assamese state government offered a large measure of autonomy to the Bodo-populated districts of Assam in the hope that this might persuade the NDFB and BLTF to give the mayhem a rest, already. At last report, the NDFB weren't tremendously impressed with the offer.

**Bodoland**
http://www.cidcm.umd.edu/ingcr/mar2/indbodo.htm

## National Socialist Council of Nagaland (NSCN)

The radical Naga movement—and their political wing, the Government of the People's Republic of Nagaland—is considered the godfather of India's rebel factions and includes groups such as the National Socialist Council of Nagaland (NSCN), who've been at it for more than 50 years and are well known for their massacres of civilians and attacks on Indian government officials. (In November 1999, they shot up a convoy carrying Nagaland's chief minister, S.C. Jamir, but missed him.) Naga militants are fighting for a separate Naga homeland—Nagalim, as they call it—composed of Nagaland (in the northeast) and areas in adjacent states where Nagas have settled. Nagas in both Nagaland and adjacent Manipur charge that ethnic Kukis have settled on ancestral Naga land. Other groups at work in the area include United National Liberation Front of Manipur and the National Democratic Front of Tripura.

The NSCN are on cease-fire right now and trying to get respectable, though the squabbling with India continues as the Indian military vacillate about whether they're on cease-fire or not, and if so, which parts of Nagaland they're on cease-fire in. The NSCN's two top dogs, Thuingaleng Muivah and Isak Chishi Swu, met with Indian Prime Minister Vajpayee on neutral ground in Osaka, Japan, in December 2001. It is not known whether Muivah explained to Vajpayee what he'd been doing in January 2000, when he was arrested at Bangkok Airport trying to enter Thailand on a false South Korean passport (the Thais locked him up for a year).

Both sides can talk until the sacred cows come home, but the chances of India freely granting independence to Nagaland, or to any other of its consituent states, must be considered remote.

**National Socialist Council of Nagaland**
nscn_gprh@hotmail.com
http://www.angelfire.com/mo/Nagaland

**Government of Nagaland**
http://nagaland.nic.in

**Nagaland News**
http://www.kuknalim.net


# THE EASTERN AND CENTRAL REGION

## Maoist People's War Group (PWG)/Maoist Communist Center (MCC)

The Scheduled Tribes, also known as *adivasis* (original inhabitants) are 500 or so tribes who were in this part of India before the Aryans turned up in 1500 B.C. The Maoist Peoples' War Group (PWG) and the Maoist Communist Center (MCC)—who, in the grand tradition of revolutionary enterprises the world over, loathe each other with a frequently murderous intensity—are some of the hard-line Maoist-Leninist groups that have taken up their cause in and around Bihar. The PWG, by far the bigger and more important of the two groups, was founded in 1980 by teacher-turned-champion-of-the-landless Kondapally Seetharamaiah. Their aim has always been to create a communist state in tribal areas of Bihar, Andhra Pradesh, and other neighboring states, and they have pursued it by targeting cops and government officials, using homemade, remote-controlled land mines. Six thousand people have been killed in two decades of squabbling between the PWG and security forces.

Though deadly incidents take place on a daily basis, lately there have been some signs that the wheels are beginning to fall off the PWG's bandwagon. One of the PWG's senior commanders, Rudrangi Sudhakar, turned in his rifle, himself, and about three dozen of his followers in December 2001. He apparently complained that nobody was joining the PWG anymore, and that those who were signing on seemed more concerned with such prosaic issues as regional unemployment than establishing a dictatorship of the proletariat in central India. Tch, kids today. Maybe Ché just doesn't resonate in India.

INDIA

*Naxalite*
http://www.naxalite.co.uk

## Ranvir Sena

Ranvir Sena is a death squad bankrolled by landowners—or, as they'd probably prefer to see it, a militia of upstanding citizens formed by upper-caste landlords to deal with the banditry of those damn pinkos in the Peoples' War Group (PWG) and their fellow travellers. Ranvir Sena has not been known to target foreigners; the death squad kills only peasants in remote villages, but it has killed many hundreds of those. It is currently waging what amounts to a caste war against the uppity lower orders in the almost-entirely lawless state of Bihar, figuring that dead people don't demand land. The numbers of active members or of their victims are hard to quantify, Bihar being what it is, but a typical Ranvir Sena outing was the attack staged on a Bihari village called Maipur in June 2000, where 34 men, women, and children were murdered.

http://www.ipcs.org/nmt/milgroups/sena-india.html

# THE PUNJAB

## The Sikhs

The Punjab is the homeland of the Sikhs, and was partitioned between India and Pakistan in 1947. The Sikhs are a proud bunch, with a strong warrior tradition, and all carry the last name Singh, meaning "lion." A small segment of Sikhs want to establish an independent homeland called Khalistan, or Land of the Pure, and India isn't about to let them. The key event in the recent history of the Sikh separatist movement was the storming of the Golden Temple in Amritsar in June 1984. The temple had been occupied by militant Sikh separatists, and India's prime minister, Indira Gandhi, sent the army in. Two months later, she was as dead as the 300 victims of her impetuosity, assassinated by her Sikh bodyguards.

The armed wing of the movement for an independent Khalistan peaked in the '80s, and has more or less fizzled out in the last few years, give or take the odd bus-bombing, leaving the relatives of 30,000 people killed in the conflict wondering what it was all about.

**Council of Khalistan**
1901 Pennsylvania Avenue, NW,
   Suite 802
Washington, DC 20006
Tel.: (202) 833-3262
Fax: (202) 452-9161
khalistan@khalistan.com
http://www.khalistan.com

**Khalistan Government in Exile**
http://www.khalistan.demon.co.uk

**Government of Punjab**
pws@punjabmail.gov.in
http://punjabgovt.nic.in

## OTHER

It would be hard to find an ethnic minority that is not mad as hell and not going to take it anymore. These are just a few more groups who have an unconvincing chance of breaking up India:

**It would be hard to find an ethnic minority that is not mad as hell and not going to take it anymore.**

**Manipur**
http://www.geocities.com/rpf_manipur

**Gujarat**
http://hometown.aol.com/mahagujarat

**Mizoram**
http://www.bsos.umd.edu/cidcm/mar/indmizo.htm

**Mughalstan**
http://www.dalitstan.org/mughalstan

**Tripura**
http://us.geocities.com/CapitolHill/Congress/3519

**Assam**
http://us.geocities.com/CapitolHill/Congress/7434

## Getting In

A passport and visa (which must be obtained in advance) are required for entry into India for tourism or business. Visas range from 15 days to six months and can be had in single-entry or multi-entry versions, but only the six-month visa is extendable. Bear in mind that the celebrated Indian tradition of 19th-century British style bureaucracy and mindless paperwork has been preserved and perfected in most of their missions overseas.

Evidence of yellow-fever immunization is needed if the traveler is arriving from an infected area. Indian customs authorities strictly enforce the laws and regulations governing the declaration, importation, or possession of gold and gold objects. Travelers have sometimes been detained for possession of undeclared gold objects. Those who are convicted of drug offenses and can't figure out how to bribe their way out of it can expect a minimum jail sentence of ten years and heavy fines. For further entry information, contact the following:

**Embassy of India**
2536 Massachusetts Avenue, NW
Washington, DC 20008
Tel.: (202) 939-9806
Fax: (202) 797-4693
http://www.indianembassy.org

At the time of writing, the embassy wasn't accepting visa applications by mail, but there are Indian consulates in Chicago, New York, and San Francisco.

INDIA

**High Commission of India, London**
India House
Aldwych
London WC2B 4NA, UK
Tel.: (44) 207 836 8484 (no visa
    inquiries)
Tel.: (44) 207 240 1012 (passport &
    consular)

**High Commission of India, Ottawa**
10 Springfield Road
Ottawa, Ontario K1M 1C9
Canada
Tel.: (613) 744-3751
Fax: (613) 744-0913
hicomind@sprint.ca
http://www.docuweb.ca/Embassies
    Ottawa/India/index.html

Major international airports in India are at Bombay (Mumbai), Delhi, Calcutta (Kolkata), and Madras (Chennai). Book fixed-price taxis from airports in the arrivals area—you can negotiate cheaper rates with the individual drivers who start pestering you as soon as you've cleared customs, but the savings will be negligible, and it is not completely unheard-of for taxi drivers to deliver hapless rubes into the hands of local bandits. For the same reason, if your flight arrives at night, wait in the airport until the sun comes up before you embark on a needless adventure. There is a departure tax of about US$10, which is sometimes included in the ticket price—and, if it isn't, don't pay until specifically asked, as airport officials often forget to collect it.

Road border-crossings between India and Nepal are at Biranj-Raxaul, Kakarbhitta-Siliguri, and Sunauli-Gorakhpur. Sunauli is the best entry point if traveling from Kathmandu to Delhi or elsewhere in northwestern India. Overland travel between Dhaka and Calcutta is possible. The only border checkpoint open with Pakistan is Lahore-Amritsar. This crossing can also be made by train, but check before you attempt it—India's relationship with Pakistan is turbulent to say the least, and the gate can be shut as easily as it was opened.

## Getting Around

India is serviced by dozens of local airports, ranging from modern Western-style setups to military bases to rusty Nissen huts next to runways on which your aircraft will be competing with the goats grazing on the weeds growing through the cracks in the concrete.

**Indian Airlines**
http://indian-airlines.nic.in

**Jet Airways**
http://www.jetairways.com

India has 63,900 kilometers (37,850 miles) of railway—the largest network in Asia and the second-largest in the world. The rail system is the lifeblood of the Indian people. There are a number of different classes of trains, and the reservation system can be confusing for all classes. You can now book tickets online, but given the utter chaos that reigns in Indian train stations, *DP* recommends that you pay only cash on the nail for a ticket you can hold in your sweaty paw, unless there is absolutely no other option. Train passengers have been subjected to robberies and schedule disruptions due to protest actions.

**Indian Railways Online Passenger Reservation**
http://www.indianrail.gov.in

There are six classes of bus service—from ordinary to deluxe sleeper. The private buses tend to be faster and more comfortable than the state buses. Travel by road after dark is not recommended, and neither is sitting too near the front, or on the side of the bus closest to oncoming traffic.

### Restricted Areas

Permission from the Indian government (from Indian diplomatic missions abroad, or in some cases, from the Ministry of Home Affairs) is required to visit the states of Mizoram, Manipur, Nagaland, Meghalaya, Assam, Tripura, Arunachal Pradesh, Sikkim, parts of the Kulu and Lahual Spiti districts of Himachal Pradesh, border areas of Jammu and Kashmir, areas of Uttar Pradesh, the area west of National Highway 15 running from Ganganagar to Sanchar in Rajasthan, the Andaman and Nicobar Islands (incidentally, before the Andamans became pacified sailors, they ate anyone who washed ashore) and the Union Territory of the Laccadive Islands. This often means that you cannot visit these regions without a recognized tour operator. The permits are sometimes required because the areas are considered dangerous, and sometimes because India's government is trying to protect the way of life of various indigenous people from Nikon-equipped eco-yuppies and crystal-clutching hippies seeking enlightenment. In a specific deterrent to the latter group, a permit to visit the almost-entirely un-Westernized hill tribes of Arunachal Pradesh in India's far northeast will set you back in excess of US$150 for every day you spend there.

## Dangerous Places

### Kashmir

In 1989, the Muslims became violent in opposing Indian rule. Of the approximately 6 million people in Kashmir, 4 million of them are Muslim. Since 1989, about 30,000 people, mostly Muslims, have been killed. Half of the casualties have been civilians, and most were killed in the Kashmir Valley area around the state capital, Srinagar. Kashmir is currently divided, with some parts under the control of Pakistan rebels and others under the auspices of the Indian army. Shootings, bombings, and kidnappings are daily occurrences.

In the 1980s, the Kashmir Valley drew 500,000 to 700,000 tourists a year. No more. Now, each week about 50 people lose their lives in Kashmir due to violence, and there have been incidents in which terrorists have threatened and kidnapped foreigners. (It is even more frightening to know that the executed Norwegian tourist, Hans Ostro, contacted three Indian government tourist offices to inquire about the danger and was told that there was no risk.)

Today, Kashmir is very much a hot insurgency fought in a cold place. The hot spot is the overlapping area that is known as the line of control. Both India and Pakistan claim an area of the Karakoram mountain range that includes a well-armed 50-mile front along the 21,000-foot-high Siachen glacier region. The two countries have established military outposts in the region and armed clashes have occurred. The disputed area includes the following peaks: Rimo Peak, Apsarasas I, II, and III, Tegam Kangri I, II, and III, Suingri Kangri, Ghaint I and II, Indira Col, and Sia Kangri. The line of control was created in July 1972. The UN has one of its oldest and smallest field missions here: the 111-strong United Nations Military Observer Group in India and Pakistan (UNMOGIP). Their job is "to observe and report, investigate complaints of cease-fire violations, and submit its findings to each party and to the Secretary-General." And then what?

Increased violence in Kashmir has brought about a greater likelihood that the two countries will again go to war. India claims that Pakistan is fueling the flames by encouraging and supporting Kashmir secession from India. Of course, rather than seeing Kashmir become an independent entity, Pakistan would like to be the sponge that absorbs it.

Despite a long standing UN presence (and perhaps because of the lack of real outside interest), India and Pakistan have come very close to full-scale war over Kashmir twice in the last few years. In 1999, Pakistan-backed militias crossed the line of control in the Kargil sector, and 400 Indian soldiers died in the ten weeks of fighting that followed before the United States told Pakistan to knock it off. In late 2001, both sides again squared up to each other, dispatching enormous quantities of men and equipment to the front line—though this may have been a none-too-subtle attempt by the Indian government to attract some of the attention that America was then lavishing on its new best friend Pakistan. The violence in Kashmir stopped short of escalating into total, or even nuclear, war, and has since carried on ticking over at its normal steady, depressing clip just as it always has, and just as, barring an unprecedented change of heart in all involved, it always will.

**UNMOGIP**
http://www.un.org/Depts/DPKO/Missions/unmogip.htm

**Jammu Kashmir**
http://www.jammu-kashmir.com

**The Kashmir Times**
http://www.kashmirtimes.com

## Muzaffarabad

This grubby town in Azad Kashmir (or Free Kashmir) is ground zero for war junkies. If push comes to pushing the button, this is where the fireworks will start and the tanks will roll. Although Muzaffarabad technically is in Pakistan, it will be probably be the first place under Indian control when the next war starts. Bring sunglasses and sunblock with an antinuke factor of 5,000. In the meantime, Muzaffarabad is the main center for jihadis and separatist groups and probably the most dangerous place in either country.

> **A**lthough Muzaffarabad technically is in Pakistan, it will be probably be the first place under Indian control when the next war starts. Bring sunglasses and sunblock with an antinuke factor of 5,000.

http://www.tourism.gov.pk/muzaffarabad.html

## Assam and the Northeast

India's northeast is treated like a rich mother-in-law by New Delhi: hit up for its wealth but never invited to dinner. Connected to the rest of India by only a thread of land, but exploited like a pipeline, India's northeast has been wracked by a half-century of tribal wars, separatist insurrections, massacres, terrorism, and guerrilla warfare.

Little wonder—there are some 200 aboriginal groups among the northeast's population. Every day someone is killed due to strife in one of the seven northeast states, at least five of which are suffering from violent insurgencies from the actions of 30 mostly tribal-based armed groups. AIDS and drug smuggling are rampant. The states have been stripped of their oil and tea and have received little in return, spawning separatist groups like the All Tripura Tiger Force, ULFA, the Bodo Liberation Tigers, and the National Democratic Front of Bodoland.

However, India's "chicken neck"—as the 20-kilometer-wide strip of Indian land separating Nepal and Bangladesh is called—doesn't necessarily divide the good guys and the bad guys. The Bodos have been in a slugfest with the Assamese—to protect their language and culture—and even with each other. Meanwhile, Manipur, with a 2,000-year history as a colorful kingdom with a constitution dating from 1180, is better known these days as just another deadly stop along the heroin route from Burma. More than 60 people were killed during a single two-week period in July 1997.

Most of the killing here is related to the Nagas' fight for independence (more than 1,500 people have died in Nagaland alone), the battle for control of Myanmar drug-smuggling routes, and good ol' Hatfield-McCoy shoot-outs. Separatist guerrillas have started enforcing their own antidrug policy: narcotics users are shot in the head after three warnings. In Assam, tea plantation owners are raising a private army of 7,000–8,000 retired soldiers to guard the plantations. The tea estates will also continue to pay protection money to the insurgents.

http://www.assam.org
http://www.assamtribune.com

## New Delhi

The capital and official center of India is an obvious target for all those with a grievance with India's government. And since almost everyone in India seems to have a grievance, it gets knocked about quite a bit. In December 2001, five attackers believed to be affiliated to Kashmiri separatist group Lashkar-e-Toiba launched a suicide assault on Delhi's parliament building, killing seven along with themselves. Lashkar-e-Toiba 'fessed up to a similar raid a year earlier, in which three were killed in a raid on a popular Delhi tourist attraction, the Red Fort. So, when in Delhi, beware of men in balaclavas asking for directions.

## Bombay (Mumbai)

This sweaty Arabian Sea port has attracted a certain type of entrepreneur. There has been an increase in the number of organized criminal gangs operating in Mumbai, and police confirm that the problem exists throughout Maharashtra state. Drug gangs have proliferated in the larger cities, and police report these gangs have moved into some of the most affluent areas of Mumbai. Home burglary still remains the most prevalent crime in Mumbai, often committed by servants or other persons with easy access to the residence involved. However, moves to set up a special court to deal with racketeering and a reintroduction of the death penalty for those convicted reflect the burgeoning fashion for extortion.

http://timesofindia.indiatimes.com

## Gujarat

The most western and parking-lot flat region of Gujarat has suffered disasters of both the natural and man-made kind in recent years. In 2001, the region was hit by an earthquake that killed 20,000 people. Less deadly, but more depressing, was the sectarian rioting that engulfed Gujarat in 2002, when 500 people were killed in four days of rioting, mostly in the commercial capital, Ahmedabad. The trouble started when local Muslims set fire to a train carrying Hindus, killing 58 people. The dead were mostly members of the Hindu nationalist Vishwa Hindu Parishad party, who had been returning from Ayodhya in Uttar Pradesh. The VHP wants to build a temple to the Hindu god Ram in Ayodhya, on the spot where VHP supporters torched a mosque in 1992 (2,000 people died in rioting across India after that escapade). By Indian standards, Gujarat has since been reasonably calm, but India's uncountable ethnic faultlines can be engineered into trouble at a moment's notice by anyone who feels it in their interest to do so. While there, read the newspapers.

**Gujurat Online**
http://gujuratonline.com

## Bihar

The western region of Bihar is, by consensus, the most lawless state in India. Readers who've visited India, or have just read the rest of this chapter, will be aware that this is some accolade—like being the most boring city in Switzerland. Bihar is India's second-largest state, with a population of nearly 90 million. At least half of the populace seems to be driving taxis in Calcutta, and you can't blame them. Bihar is an unholy mess, perpetually broke, and plagued by caste wars betweens Maoist guerrillas and the private militias of rich landlords. It doesn't help that Bihar is run as a personal fiefdom by Laloo Prasad Yadav, a fraud, an election-rigger, and someone who probably keeps a regular executive suite with bars on the windows. When he was finding it difficult to discharge his duties as chief minister in between his frequent, and richly deserved, stays at Beur Prison in the state capital of Patna, he let his wife, Rabri Devi, do the job.

**Honourable Chief Minister of Bihar**
http://bihar.nic.in/governance/cm.htm

**The Bihar Times**
http://www.bihartimes.com

## The South

The tear of India is probably due more to the pain it causes the rest of the country than any romantic attraction. Sri Lanka is a major obstruction in India's nether region because of the ethnic conflict between the Sinhalese majority and Tamil minority. Of course, the Tamils are found in great and generous numbers in the region of Tamil Nadu. When India sent the army in to bring law and order, it, of course, had the opposite effect. Your travel plans may not include Sri Lanka, but members of the Sri Lankan Tamil terrorist group, Liberation Tigers of Tamil Eelam (LTTE), commit their acts of terrorism and violence throughout southern India. Their most famous victim, former Prime Minister Rajiv Gandhi, was killed in Tamil Nadu in May of 1991 by a suicide bomber. In an odd moment of clarity, India has begun the process of unwinding itself from its own little Vietnam. Talks are underway to end the 20-year war that has killed 64,000 people.

http://www.geocities.com/rasida22/tamilnewspaper.htm
http://www.samachar.com

# Dangerous Things

## Insurgents and Separatists

There are more than 100 rebel factions, with 10 being militarily significant, and about 60 intergroup clashes occur each year. Thousands of Kashmiri youths have received rudimentary training in Afghanistan and Azad Kashmir (two weeks to three months). Although there are plenty of weapons supplied by Pakistan, there is little organized fighting. Typically, a mine will be laid across a road and a military convoy will come under attack by small-arms fire from a group of 5 to 10 insurgents. The insurgents then run away and do not press their advantage. The ratio of deaths for insurgents to military is about 5 to 1.

http://www.fas.org/irp/world/india/threat/pakistan.htm

## Nukes

It's a toss-up whether India is more threatened by internal division or by its own nuclear policy. India got nukey when the Chinese got greedy in the '60s. Luckily China has realized the folly of actually taking over India. One could only imagine the convergence of Chinese red politicians and Indian red tape and having to feed a billion hungry mouths. Or perhaps the Chinese know about the terrorizing driving style of the '50s-styled taxis. So China has been sitting on an ice-swept chunk of Kashmir just to pout. Since then India's 150 or so nukes have been realigned or been designed to be dropped on Pakistan—a country that has reciprocated by developing its own Kmart nuke program with about 50 to 60 dirty nukes. The mind boggles at just where these low-budget nukes, propelled by missile, artillery, or aircraft, would actually land and how many casualties would result. The wonks figure 12 to 17 million casualties right off the bat.

It is a measure of the advancement of technology and Brit-style thinking that Indian and Paki artillery (now considered an archaic weapon in today's helicopter and fast-strike wars) were once the sexiest toys in the Pak and Indo arsenals. The new love of the Indian army is their Prithvi (earth), Dhanush (bow), and Agni (fire) ballistic missiles. The Prithvi has a range of around 350 kilometers; the Agni can fly up to 2,500 km; and the Dhanush can be fired from the sea.

http://www.sciam.com/2001/1201issue/1201ramana.html
http://www.tehelka.com/channels/currentaffairs/2002/may/31/ca053102nuke.htm

## The Roads

You haven't seen India until you've sat in an Ambassador taxi going two-wheeled around a blind corner between a sleeping cow and an oncoming cyclist with a bed balanced on his head. It's no wonder that most Indians cling to a religion which offers a pantheon of more than a hundred Gods—the prayers of this many terrified motorists would unfairly clog the to-do list of a single supreme being. For all the activity of India's dozens of rebel groups, revolutionary organizations, insurrectionary militias, and freelance brigands, they do not come close to matching the carnage on India's highways and byways. Granted, these things are always relative, but even in a country of a billion people, an annual road-death toll of 80,000 is pretty spectacular (34 percent occur on major highways) and gruesome.

http://www.asirt.org

## Buses and Trains

Both bus and train stations are popular targets for insurgents and petty criminals alike. Punjab experienced a spate of bus bombings in 2000, blamed on Kashmiri separatists.

## Being Kidnapped

Over 2,500 people have been kidnapped in Kashmir since 1990, including Westerners. Fewer than half of them survived the ordeal.

http://www.ncrbindia.org

## Political Rallies

Various separatist groups, especially the Tamil Tigers, love to send suicide bombers to blow up politicians. The bombs usually contain way

INDIA

## PLACE YOUR BETS

|                 | India     | Pakistan |
|-----------------|-----------|----------|
| Soldiers        | 1,263,000 | 620,000  |
| Aircraft        | 738       | 353      |
| Nukes           | 150       | 50       |
| Warships        | 27        | 8        |
| Subs            | 16        | 10       |
| Recent Wars Won | 3         | 0        |

*Source:* CSIS, *DP*

India may have more, and more powerful nukes, but Pakistan packs more symbolism into their nukes. Technically, a nuclear missile in Pakistan is simply a Scud with a dirty tip that can be up to 35 kilotons. The Indians can deliver 200 kts in a 2,500 km range. With the combination of Pakistani-built quality and a deadly range that spans from Saudi Arabia to Mongolia, the program does cause some concern; once again, skeptics need only to carefully inspect a Mahindra taxi to understand.

Although outnumbered nukewise 3 to 1, the Paks cling to their Shaheen (gentle) and other missiles with 1,500 km ranges as deterrents (does anyone do the math in Pakistan?) and for first-strike capability. Most experts assume that India would attack with land forces and Pakistan would respond with nukes once the Indian troops reached Lahore. But *DP* readers and trivia buffs will be amused and disturbed to know that Pakistan has named their missiles—Ghauri, Ghaznavi, and Adbali—after Afghan warlords who successfully invaded India. Muhammed Ghauri, Mehmood Ghaznavi, and Ahmed Shah Abdali were all Muslim warlords who kicked the Hindus' butts over the last millennium. These days the Pakistanis are so proud of this heritage that reasonable facsimiles are dragged out in ceremonial parades by radical muj groups, decorated with subtle slogans like "Islamic Atom Bomb." Mushareff, of course, made a point of stressing that the oxymoronic "safety of nuclear missiles" was one of his top priorities . . . prompting the United States to immediately send security guards. Pakistan has about 50 uranium nukes and continues to crank out about 5 new ones each year. Hey, who said the Pakistanis carry a grudge?

too much explosive material and nasty things like ball bearings. Needless to say, they bury what's left of the politician in a sandwich bag, and a lot of bystanders die. Political rallies in India are much safer seen on TV.

http://www.tribuneindia.com

## AIDS

There are more than 4 million Indians with HIV—10 percent of the global HIV-positive population. You might want to make war, not love, while in India.

http://www.who.org

## Press Releases

A few years back the Muslim guerrilla group Ikwhan Jammu kidnapped 19 journalists for 10 hours. It was a year after the kidnapping of German Dirk Hasert. The journalists were on their way to a press conference held by Muslim mujahideen in Achabal (40 miles from Srinagar), another guerrilla group. Ikwhan held the journalists because the journalists' editors refused to publish one of the group's press releases or cease publication of the threatened newspapers.

http://www.cpj.org

## Malaria

Calcutta, West Bengal, and northeastern India are once again suffering from serious outbreaks of malaria. Calcutta is reported to be the worst hit of the country's major metropolitan cities. Reports suggest that this is a continuation of a longer trend of higher incidences of malaria in general and of malignant and chloroquine-resistant strains in particular.

http://www.cdc.gov/travel/regionalmalaria/indianrg.htm

## The Weather

India is a land of extremes; even the weather is extreme. In the monsoon season, cities flood in minutes. Cyclones regularly charge up the Bay of Bengal, sweeping all before them. Heat waves kill dozens every year. Keep an eye on weather reports, and take sunblock, a good hat, and a raincoat.

http://weather.123india.com

## Yanni

In March 1997, five Indian farmers threatened to set themselves ablaze to protest a concert in front of the Taj Mahal by Greek-born new-age musician Yanni. The farmers claimed that some 250 acres of crops were destroyed to make way for a stage for the concert . . . or was it because they had heard his music?

http://www.yanni.com
http://www.geocities.com/Hollywood/Boulevard/2616

*China*

With all the hullabaloo about Pakistan, it's easy to forget that China was the original "worst enemy" of India. China has about 300–600 nukes available to solve India's overpopulation problem. It also squats on a desolate, mountainous chunk of Kashmir.

http://www.centurychina.com/plaboard/uploads/1962war.htm

## Getting Sick

Delhi Belly is a bitch here. The chances of seeing India without frequent side-trips to the john are slim. More serious intestinal problems include typhoid, cholera, hepatitis A, and parasites. Don't be shy about consulting an Indian doctor. They know their stuff and they are reasonable. Adequate medical care is available in the major population centers but limited in rural areas of the country. The key is to take preventive measures against malaria, hepatitis, meningitis, and Japanese encephalitis, which also includes taking precautions against mosquito bites. Dengue fever and Japanese encephalitis are mosquito-borne viral diseases that pose a danger in rural areas during the rainy season. Travelers arriving from countries where outbreaks of yellow fever have occurred will be required to furnish a certificate for yellow-fever vaccination. Cholera and gastroenteritis occur during the summer monsoon months, mostly in the poorer areas of India. The best protections include eating only at better-quality restaurants or hotels, drinking only boiled or bottled water, and avoiding ice and dairy products unless you're absolutely sure that the latter have been pasteurized. Whatever you do, you'll get sick anyway, so read up on the free information provided by the Centers for Disease Control and take along medication for intestinal problems.

> **D**elhi Belly is a bitch here. The chances of seeing India without frequent side-trips to the john are slim.

***Centers for Disease Control and Prevention***
http://www.cdc.gov/travel

## Nuts and Bolts

India has three main regions: the mountainous Himalayas in the north; the Indo-Gangetic Plain, a flat, hot plain south of the Himalayas; and the Peninsular Shield in the south, where India's neighbors, Sri Lanka and the Maldives, are located. The coldest months are January and February, and the hottest time is between March and May. The southwestern monsoon season is from June to September. The post-monsoon, or northeast monsoon, in the southern peninsula occurs from October to December.

India is hot, dirty, and humid throughout most of the year. The north is cool in the highlands and alpine regions. If you are looking to latch onto some bacteria, southern India is the place to do it. Bombay may be the dirtiest city on earth and there are plenty of people to pass germs on to you.

There are more than a billion people crammed into India's 3.3 million square kilometers (1.3 million square miles). About 40 percent of India's people live below the poverty line, defined as the resources needed to provide 2,100 to 2,400 calories per person per day. About 70 percent of the population lives in the countryside. The official language is Hindi, but English is the second language and is widely spoken. All official documents are in English. In keeping with India's diverse makeup, 18 languages are recognized for official use in regional areas, of which the most widely spoken are Telugu, Bengali, Marathi, Tamil, Urdu, and Gujarati, each with its own script. Hindus do not eat beef. Muslims avoid pork. Sikhs do not smoke. Strict Hindus are also vegetarian and do not drink.

The rupee (about 31 to the U.S. dollar) is the currency and should be changed only through banks and authorized money changers. Electricity is 230–240V/50HZ.

For reasons that defy rational analysis, the Indian government has, in the last few years, changed the names of some of its most prominent cities. Bombay is now Mumbai, Madras is now Chennai, and Calcutta is now Kolkata. These names are now used on most official documents and many timetables, and by absolutely none of the locals.

## Embassy Locations

**U.S. Embassy**
1 Shantipath, Chanakyapuri
New Delhi 110 021, India
Tel.: (91) 11 419 8000
Fax: (91) 11 419 0017
http://usembassy.state.gov/posts/in1/
    wwwhmain.html

**U.S. Consulates General**
In Bombay (Mumbai):
Lincoln House
78 Bhulabhai Desai Road
Bombay 400026, India
Tel.: (91) 22 363 3611
Fax: (91) 22 363 0350

In Calcutta:
5/1 Ho Chi Minh Sarani
Calcutta 700071, India
Tel.: (91) 33 288 1200
Fax: (91) 33 288 1600

In Madras (Chennai):
Mount Road
Madras 600006, India
Tel.: (91) 44 827 7835
Fax: (91) 44 825 0240

INDIA

**British High Commission**
Chanakyapuri
New Delhi 110021, India
Tel.: (91) 11 687 2161
Fax: (91) 11 687 2882
bhcnpa@w3c.com (Press and Public
    Affairs)
bhcndlib@w3.com (Public Information
    Unit)
nedel.conqry@newdelhi.mail.fco.gov.uk
    (Consular)

**Office of the British Deputy High
    Commissioner in Southern India**
24 Anderson Road
Madras (Chennai) 600006, India
Tel.: (91) 44 827 3136
Fax: (91) 44 820 8790
consular@madras.mail.fco.gov.uk

**Office of the British Deputy High
    Commission in Calcutta**
1A Ho Chi Minh Sarani
Calcutta (Kolkata) 700071, India
Tel.: (91) 33 288 5172
Fax: (91) 33 288 3435
postmaster@calcutta.mail.fco.gov.uk

**British Consular Office in Goa**
302 Manguirish Building
3rd Floor, 18 June Road
Opposite Gulf Supermarket
Panaji 403001
Goa, India
Tel.: (91) 83 222 8571
Fax: (91) 83 223 2828
bcagoa@goatelecom.com

**Canadian High Commission**
7/8 Shantipath
Chanakyapuri
New Delhi 110021, India
Tel.: (91) 11 687 6500
Fax: (91) 11 687 0031
delhi.cs@dfait-maeci.gc.ca
http://www.dfait-maeci.gc.ca/new-
    delhi/government-office-en.asp

**Consulate of Canada, Mumbai**
4th Floor, 41/42 Maker Chamber VI
Jamnalal Bajaj Marg, Nariman Point
Bombay (Mumbai) 400021, India
Tel.: (91) 22 287 6027
Fax: (91) 22 287 5514
mmbai.cs@dfait-maeci.gc.ca

**Office of the Canadian High
    Commission, Chandigarh**
SCO 33-34-35, Sector 17-A
Near Jagat Cinema
Chandigarh 160017, India
Tel.: (91) 17 271 6020
Fax: (91) 17 271 6025
chcchc@glide.net.in

## Other Useful Contacts

**Ministry of Defence**
South Block
New Delhi 110011, India
http://mod.nic.in

**Ministry of External Affairs**
South Block
New Delhi 110011, India
webmasters@mea.nic.in
http://www.meadev.nic.in

**Ministry of Tourism and Culture**
webmaster@tourismofindia.com
http://www.tourismofindia.com

INDIA

## Web Resources

**The Times of India**
http://www.timesofindia.com

**SAPRA (Security and Political Risk Analysis) India**
http://www.subcontinent.com/sapra.html

**India Express**
http://www.indiaexpress.com/news

**India Times**
http://www.indiatimes.com

**The Hindustan Times**
http://www.hindustantimes.com

**Deccan Chronicle**
http://www.deccan.com

**Deccan Herald**
http://www.deccanherald.com

**India Abroad**
http://www.indiaabroad.com

**News India-Times**
http://www.newsindia-times.com

**The Afternoon Dispatch and Courier**
http://www.cybermoon.com

**U.S. State Department Consular Information Sheets**
http://travel.state.gov/india.html

# Dangerous Days

| | |
|---|---|
| 5/27/02 | Musharaff says Pakistan will respond if attacked by India. |
| 5/22/02 | Vajpayee tells India's military to prepare for "a decisive battle" with Pakistan-backed Islamic insurgents in Kashmir. |
| 5/21/02 | Moderate Kashmiri separatist leader Abdul Ghani Lone shot dead in Srinagar. |
| 5/13/02 | Three militants attack a bus and Indian army base in Kaluchak, near Jammu, killing 34 people. Pakistan arrests Lashkar-e-Toiba leader Mohammed Saeed. |
| 2/02 | Sectarian rioting between Hindus and Muslims in Gujurat kills hundreds. |
| 12/25/01 | India and Pakistan both move missiles and troops to their common border. Local civilians on both sides begin leaving their homes. |
| 12/13/01 | Suicide attack on Indian parliament, blamed on Pakistan-based militants. Several police and all five gunmen killed. India imposes sanctions on Pakistan, and Pakistan responds in kind. Both countries mass troops on border. |
| 10/1/01 | State assembly in Kashmir attacked by militants. Initial explosion and subsequent gun battle leaves 29 dead. |

**7/15/01**   Eighteen killed as Indian army fights with militants in Kashmir. Indian Prime Minister Vajpayee meets with Pakistan President Musharaff.

**4/01**   Sixteen Indian and three Bangladeshi troops killed in clashes on India-Bangladesh border.

**1/25/00**   Earthquake in Gujarat kills tens of thousands.

**1999**   More fighting in Kashmir, between Indian military and Pakistan-backed insurgents.

**12/23/99**   Kashmiri separatists hijack an Air India plane in Kathmandu and fly to Kandahar. Taliban refuses to help hijackers.

**5/98**   India carries out nuclear tests, followed shortly afterward by Pakistan.

**11/12/96**   Midair crash of a Saudi 747 and a Kazakh cargo plane kills 349 people in the world's worst midair disaster.

**7/7/96**   Six Indian tourists abducted and murdered in Srinagar.

**8/13/95**   Norwegian Hans Christian Ostro is found beheaded near Anantnag, 37 miles from Srinagar.

**7/4/95**   Al-Faran guerrillas kidnap two Britons and two Americans near Pahalgam, 55 miles from Srinagar.

**10/94**   Rebel leader Shabir Shah released from prison.

**6/94**   Two Brits are kidnapped and released unharmed 17 days later.

**12/6/92**   Hindu extremists destroy the 16th-century Muslim mosque at Ayodhya in India's Uttar Pradesh state. The subsequent rioting and Muslim-Hindu clashes in India, Pakistan, Bangladesh, and other nations result in over 1,000 deaths. Hindus claim the mosque was built on the birth site of the Hindu god Rama, a claim disputed by Muslims.

**8/92**   Two army engineers are kidnapped and killed after the government refuses to release 17 jailed rebels.

**2/92**   India plants mines along border with Pakistan to stop traffic of insurgents between countries.

**9/91**   A former Kashmiri minister, Khemlata Wakhloo, and her husband are kidnapped and freed in a raid one month later. The brother-in-law of an Indian minister, a policeman, an insurance worker, and a bank employee are kidnapped the same month. They are exchanged for imprisoned rebels but not until a hostage's severed thumb is sent as proof.

**6/27/91**   Two Israeli tourists killed in Srinagar. An oil executive is kidnapped and released 53 days later.

| | |
|---|---|
| **5/21/91** | Former Prime Minister Rajiv Gandhi, Indira's son, is assassinated by a Tamil Tigers suicide bomber during a campaign rally in Tamil Nadu state. |
| **3/91** | Two Swedish engineers as well as a daughter and a wife are kidnapped. The wife and child are released but the men are not released until 97 days later. |
| **2/91** | A pregnant 29-year-old is kidnapped and swapped for five rebels. |
| **12/90** | Indian army fires on demonstrators in Srinagar, killing 38. Separatists begin a military campaign for independence. |
| **3/90** | Kashmiri political leader Mir Ghulum Mustafa is kidnapped and killed. |
| **12/89** | Guerrillas kidnap daughter of Indian home minister and swap her for five insurgents. |
| **1/6/89** | Two of Prime Minister Indira Gandhi's Sikh bodyguards are hanged for her assassination on October 31, 1984. |
| **1/3/89** | Muslim Kashmiri militants begin their campaign for independence from India. |
| **7/6/87** | Seventy-two Hindus are killed in an attack by Sikh militants on a bus in the Punjab. |
| **4/29/86** | Sikh militants seize the Golden Temple of Amritsar in Punjab and declare the independent state of Khalistan. They are expelled by government of India forces the next day. |
| **6/23/85** | A bomb explodes on an Air India flight over the North Atlantic following its departure from Canada, killing all 329 passengers on board. A second bomb explodes at Narita Airport in Japan, killing two people. Sikh extremists claim responsibility for both bombings. |
| **12/3/84** | Chemical leak at Union Carbide's Bhopal plant results in 2,000 deaths and nearly 150,000 injuries. |
| **10/31/84** | Indian Prime Minister Indira Gandhi assassinated by her Sikh bodyguards. Anti-Sikh rioting following the assassination results in thousands of Sikh deaths throughout India. |
| **8/9/84** | The head of the Indian security forces that stormed the Sikh golden temple of Amritsar is assassinated by Sikh terrorists. |
| **6/6/84** | Indian troops storm the golden temple of Amritsar, killing 300 Sikhs. |

**2/11/84** Maqbool Butt, founder of the Jammu-Kashmir Liberation Front, is hanged in a New Delhi jail for the 1965 murder of an Indian intelligence agent in Kashmir. Militant Muslims have marked the anniversary of his death with sometimes-violent demonstrations in Jammu and Kashmir.

**1975–77** The Emergency. Political opponents of Prime Minister Indira Gandhi imprisoned, after Gandhi is found guilty of electoral fraud.

**1974** India tests first nuclear device.

**1971** Third war with Pakistan, this time over creation of Bangladesh, formerly known as East Pakistan. It's now India 3, Pakistan 0.

**1965** Second war with Pakistan over Kashmir. India 2, Pakistan 0.

**1962** Border war with China. India 0, China 1.

**1/26/50** India's constitution is promulgated and India becomes a republic within the Commonwealth. (Republic Day is also called Constitution Day.)

**1/30/48** Mahatma Gandhi assassinated.

**1948** First war with Pakistan over Kashmir. India 1, Pakistan 0.

**8/15/47** India becomes an independent nation. Subcontinent partitioned between mainly Hindu India and the new Muslim state of Pakistan. Hundreds of thousands killed in subsequent forced relocations and communal bloodshed.

**1920** Mahatma Gandhi launches campaign of civil disobedience against British rule.

**1858** India placed under direct rule of British crown after failure of Indian Mutiny.

**4/13/1699** Sikh religion was founded by Guru Gobind Singh.

**7/13** Martyr's Day in Kashmir. It commemorates the deaths of Kashmiri nationalists during the British raj.

INDIA

Tehran

★

# IRAN

## Party Like It's 1399

How could you not heed the urge to visit Iran, a country where the United States is warmly referred to as the "Global Arrogance" or where the locals, in their rush to admire Uncle Sam, have amusingly translated his name to sound like "The Great Satan?" Our current leader has further invigorated tourism by insisting that Iran is "the world's most active sponsor of terrorism." This is the same country, by the way, that held spontaneous candlelight vigils after the 9/11 attacks and sent weapons, money, and advisors to the Northern Alliance to help fight the Taliban. Well, I guess you are either for us or against us . . .

Some people insist the Iranians don't like us because of our past assistance in electing new leaders without first consulting the locals. Funny how oil, self-determination, and truth just don't seem to mix in this part of the world. Can't we all just get along?

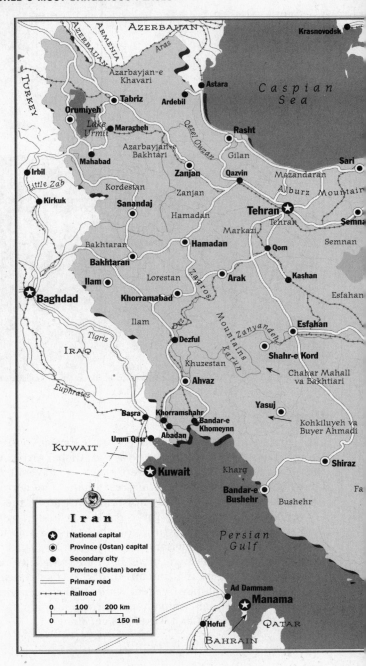

IRAN

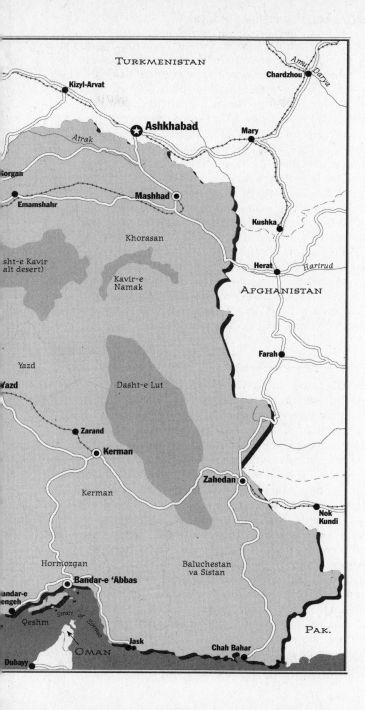

Despite our earnest attempts to replace lefties with righties and democrats with autocrats and arming their enemies, Iranians are eager to let bygones be bygones. They seem a happy bunch, based on observations of their need to get outside and let off a little steam. Just to show there are no hard feelings, when Iranians celebrated the 20th anniversary of the Islamic Revolution on February 11, 1999, thousands of people brought colorful posters and full-size Uncle Sam dolls to Tehran's Freedom Square. The air was filled with happy Iranians singing, shouting, and waving the stars-and-stripes. The only glitch, of course, was that the flags and dolls were on fire and the people were shouting "Death to America." Hmm . . . maybe we should go over there and find out why they are so mad at us. After all, we were so hopping mad at these folks our security advisor Anthony Lake once called Iran "a nest of fleas" in reference to the number of Iran-backed terrorist attacks on the United States.

Okay, so maybe their idea of freedom isn't quite lesbians with babies or tongue piercing, and maybe you won't see *Up with America* touring Isfahan anytime soon. And, of course, having Iran (along with their far-more-realistic enemy Iraq) described by Bush, Jr. as the "Axis of Evil" won't do a lot to encourage drum circles either.

## The Scoop

Evil or medieval? Dangerous or dull? Terrorism or tourism central? I guess it depends on whether you are looking from the inside or the outside. In a country where two-thirds of the population is under 30 and over half is under 20, things are changing fast. On the outside Iran is a poor kissing cousin to Afghanistan and Saudi Arabia, places that have strict penalties for everything from holding hands (someone else's, usually of the opposite sex), drinking (alcohol), and dancing (when not at the end of a rope) to not wearing modest clothing (you better like basic black) and where even today they will demand to view any tapes or videocassettes you bring into the country in their efforts to eliminate Western culture. But they can't kill porn, *Jerry Springer,* and Pamela Lee's silicon implants, and that is where Iran's stern-faced clerics face their biggest threat.

From the inside, young Iranians are desperate to keep up with the latest boy band, lipstick color, slang expression, or even hip-hop expression. Although the underground disco culture has a distinct '80s-ness to it with loud colors and passé rhythms, by the time U.S. troops plow through Iraq and get to the borders of Iran, most young Iranian soldiers should have the lyrics to the latest Eminem CD down pat and be grooving to the latest MTV moves.

We are getting ahead of ourselves. The liberal reformers are the flavor of the day, and although they may enjoy a political superiority, there is still trouble in this "fundamentalist by day, disco king by night" country.

The seeds of democracy in Iran were sown in 1906 when a *majlis*, or elected parliament, was created to balance the autocratic spending of the shah. In the early 1920s, the British began meddling in Iranian politics and, coincidentally, the Qajar dynasty was replaced by the Pahlavi dynasty in 1926, putting the Farmanfarmaian gang in charge and guaranteeing a steady flow of petroleum to the West. Oh, did we mention the oil? Sorry, I suppose we should have. Iran was the first Middle Eastern country to have an oil industry. The dangerous black stuff was first discovered by the English in 1904, about the same time that the former shah's hold on the country became slippery. So you kinda see the picture here? In 1941, Shah Reza Pahlavi was making googly eyes at the Nazis (the goose-steppers seemed to appreciate the oil-rich nation's charms more than the tea drinkers or the baseball players). Shah, Sr. quickly found himself on permanent vacation (thanks to John Bull and Uncle Sam) and a more compliant and U.S. friendly Shah, Jr., was put in charge. Coincidentally Iran was occupied by the Allies and became a base of support for the Russian war effort. Oh, did we mention the oil?

Well, it seemed most of the money for this oil was going to a few compliant shah buds and not the people. (Stop me if you've heard this one before.) So the people started pushing to nationalize the oil industry and reduce the power of the shah. In 1951, pro-Western Premier Ali Razmara was offed at the height of the Cold War and was replaced by a pro-Moscow lefty named Mohammad Mossadeq. He wanted to nationalize the oil industry, limit the powers of the shah, and get into bed with Russia. The shah showed his love for his country by running away and the Americans and British

> The shah showed his love for his country by running away and the Americans and British showed their love for his country by making him go back.

showed their love for his country by making him go back, after the 1953 Operation Ajax defeated the lefty Mossadeq and ensured a hard-line pro-U.S. government. (Oh, did we mention the oil?)

In 1964, the shah and his cronies were sitting on so much black gold that they decided to have the "White Revolution." The idea was to transform Iran from a back-alley Bible pageant to Fifth Avenue Uptown. Money was splashed on everything except, of course, the people, in the shah's attempt to bring Iran into the 18th century. You know the drill: clerics were incensed by the trashing of 2,000 years of culture. Everyone got hot under the turban. The holy men got tossed in and out of jail; among them was Ayatollah Ruhollah Khomeini. In 1965, when Khomeini spoke out against a law giving U.S. servicemen diplomatic immunity from crimes in Iran, he got a vacation, first in Turkey, then in Iraq. In September of 1978 things got ugly

> **M**oney was splashed on everything except, of course, the people, in the shah's attempt to bring Iran into the 18th century.

when Khomeini was trash-talked by an Iranian newspaper. Riots broke out, and on "Black Friday" the shah's forces fired on demonstrators, killing students and igniting the revolution. Because Khomeini was a hot potato, Iraq asked him to move and he ended up in Paris, creating the Islamic Revolution Council in exile.

In January 1979, the shah figured he'd better take a permanent shopping trip overseas and a month later Khomeini returned in triumph. Iran became an Islamic republic in June. History lovers note that this was the first major shift backward (or forward, depending on your viewpoint) of a liberalized state into an Islamic fundamentalist democracy. It was a dramatic shift in world history.

In October the shah came to the United States for cancer treatment and the Iranian hard-liners went ballistic. They seized the U.S. embassy and 52 Americans were held hostage for 444 days. In 1980 President Carter launched Operation Eagle Claw, a hostage rescue attempt that quickly became Operation Desert Disaster. Three of the eight choppers failed and eight servicemen were killed when their helicopter collided with a refueling plane.

That fall, Saddam Hussein felt his oats and decided to launch a series of attacks on Iran. The war quickly settled into a World War I–type trench stalemate that lasted for eight years. (Iraq, of course, became the U.S.'s best new friend.) It was the longest and bloodiest conflict in each country's modern history and it resulted in both sides staggering around bloodied but unbowed. The early '80s was also a period of "whack the politician," as dozens of them were blown up and gunned down. Now, at that point, the Great Satan would have been happy simply to let Iranian politics take care of itself, except that in 1982 our other best friend in the region, Israel, decided to attack Lebanon. As part of the festivities, we decided to support the kidnapping of four high-ranking Iranian Revolutionary Guards. Not surprisingly, this led to a spate of kidnappings and bomb attacks over the next nine years and the rise of Hizbollah as the biggest thorn in Uncle Sam's rear end. Just to ensure that we maintained the lowest possible moral ground, in July of 1988, the USS *Vincennes* accidentally shot down an Iranian passenger plane, killing all 290 souls on board.

In the early to mid-'90s sanctions were slapped on Iran in the feeble hopes that they would once again learn to love and respect us and give us their oil (did we mention the oil?). Since things couldn't get any worse, we decided to make things better. In March of 2000, Madeleine Albright fessed up to the '53 coup and, in a stunning show of solidarity with the Iranian poor, allowed luxury goods to be imported from Iran. The Pashmina craze in New York began and was quickly outré. In 2002, George Bush magically connected Iran, Iraq, and North Korea into the Axis of Evil, and somehow the Iranians weren't one bit surprised. Evil Axes and confusing political agendas aside, Iran has its own problems with being urged on by youthful democratic reformers and held back by crusty rural hard-liners. Iran stopped, started, and staggered into the new millennium. While Europe has never really been bothered by the nattering of fundamentalists (as long as their checks cleared), Uncle Sam is still talking tough, but not as loudly. Seems like George squinted a little and noticed that if we get freaky with Iraq, the little pencil-thin line on his map is going to be awfully hard to patrol that long squiggly border between Iran and Iraq.

## THE ICBM BARBIE

Fans of *DP* will remember that back in January 1995, the Ayatollah Ali Khomeini issued a religious decree apparently banning the consumption of both Coca-Cola and Pepsi. Khomeini's reason was logical and predictable: "Anything that strengthens world arrogance and Zionist circles in itself is forbidden." So when we heard rumors of a homegrown Barbie doll making its debut in Iran, we packed our Zionist baggage and checked our hidden agenda to get the scoop. Well, it seems that Iran's version of the anatomically incorrect Barbie and Ken are twins Dara and Sara. The $15, foot-high dolls (who come with a collection of appropriately modest clothing) are the brainchild of the Institute for the Intellectual Development of Children and Young Adults.

It seems that the Zionist puppet Barbie (the Western one, created by Ruth Handler) was doing quite well in Iran at $40 a pop but was projecting "wanton" values, and there were fears that the Iranian girls who played with them would grow up to reject traditional Iranian family values. The Associated Press interviewed a local toy seller, who warned that the Barbie doll is "more harmful than an American missile."

Although *DP* is pretty sure that Sara and Dara are not romantically involved (they are twins, remember?), we have not determined what the penalties are for peeking under Sara's chador or for being caught with two Dara dolls.

http://answering-islam.org/Women/inislam.html

Despite Iran's woes with unemployment and internal division, the country is one of the most democratic societies in the Middle East—something that Uncle Sam fails to mention when incorrectly stating that Israel is the only democracy in the region. Perhaps that's just a sad reflection of the perilous state of democracy (or lack of it) in the area.

So why don't we get along with Iran? We want their oil, we like Iraq less than Iran, and they have 100-year-old democracy and can make cheaper Barbie dolls. Here is a country that supports family values, fiscal responsibility, and a free press. Well, it seems that Iran sees right through Uncle Sam's rhetoric: We are the Great Satan. We are the ones who propped Saddam Hussein up before we woke up and suddenly realized our mistake.

And yes, Iran does raise hell in Israel, kidnap our spies, blow up our military, work diligently to undermine U.S. efforts in the third world, and also has a homemade nuke program that keeps Israel sleeping with one eye open. But, hey, look how cheap it is to travel there!

We could kiss and make up; after all, Iran has only two demands of the Great Satan: (1) give back our frozen assets, and (2) mind your own business. (*DP* has politely eliminated "burn in hell" as the third request.) But hey, give us a break—America spent only $20 million trying to overthrow their Uncle Ayatollah. That's less than we spend on daily cruise-missile-grams to their neighbor Saddam. Americans are still obsessed with the memory of blindfolded U.S. embassy staffers being paraded along with blazing Uncle Sam piñatas down Tehran's streets. But that was nearly 20 years ago and we're the ones who are still wearing blindfolds. Iran elected a moderate (well, in Iran, he's a moderate) cleric in 1997 and again in 2001 by the name of Mohammad Khatami, who actually wears a nicely cut suit instead of Motel 8 bed sheets. The voter turnout was the highest in Iran since the mullahs came to power in 1979. Americans can now travel freely in this country if they don't mind being shadowed like North Korean agents at a used plutonium sale. For now, Iran is open, the gals are loading up on the Revlon (under the chadors of course), and *Days of Our Lives* via satellite dish is slowly eroding the old Iran we've come to hate.

Oh, and don't forget that hard-liner Ayatollah Ali Khomeini still tosses the lightning bolts in this nation of very heavily clothed people. For now you can go there and form your own opinion.

## The Players

### Ayatollah Mohammed Ali Khomeini

"Ayatollah" means "sign of god," and is Iran's spiritual leader and big cheese. An Ayatollah is essentially the Pope with a turban or maybe

Darth Vader without the plastic helmet. A hard-liner and a fundamentalist to the max, he still holds most of the power after the May 1997 election of Khatami to president. In any case, the *fatwa* stops here, so anything the Ayatollah tells ya goes. He is such a major dude that merely criticizing the bearded one will land you in prison. Funny thing about democracy versus God-given authority, though: Khomeini's hard-line candidate received only 30 percent of the vote a few years back. A failure to communicate, perhaps?

**Government of Iran**
http://www.gov.ir

## The Revolutionary Guards (Pasdaran)

The Pasdaran is a combination army, police, judiciary, training and construction company, and terrorist exporter. This group of 120,000 well-trained, politically indoctrinated soldiers were originally a bearded rabble of zealots run by ad hoc neighborhood groups, or *Komitehs*. On May 5, 1979, they became an armed force that would not be tainted by the old regime and swore to protect the revolution. They earned their reputation for fearlessness in the Iran-Iraq war, and it is a reputation well-justified. These were, after all, the kids who would deliberately walk into minefields, concerned only that their corpses would be in one piece for the funeral.

The man in charge is Major General Yahya Rahim Safavi, who was appointed by hard-liner Ayatollah Ali Khomeini. So if you ever wonder who is large and in charge, it is not the nice, moderate president. And if you wonder who would be your new best friend if you wanted to overthrow Saddam Hussein. . . .

## President Mohammad Khatami

Moderate Khatami overwhelmingly defeated rival Ali Akbar Nateq-Nuri by a margin of 20 million votes in the presidential elections of May 1997. Khatami is being hailed as "Ayatollah Gorbachev," but it remains to be seen what kind of reforming he can do. Khatami was born in 1943 to a fundamentalist cleric and highly vocal critic of Shah Mohammed Reza Pahlavi. Khatami followed in his dad's footsteps, being assigned to Hamburg, Germany, in 1978 to head an Islamic center dedicated to political change in Iran. He returned to Tehran after the shah fled Iran and Khomeini returned from exile in Paris. He was Iran's minister of culture and Islamic guidance in the 1980s, where he gained his reputation as a "cautious liberal." During his tenure at that post, Khatami allowed Western newspapers and magazines into Iran. He also lifted a ban on women singing in public, although the audiences were required to be all-female. (Hey, it's a start.) If Khatami moves at all with reforms, it will be gradually. He was ousted from ministerial power in the early 1990s during a backlash to lipstick and nail polish being worn by women. Sort of shows you what he's up against.

**The President**
Pastor Avenue
Tehran, Iran
Tel.: (98) 21 61 61
khatami@president.ir
http://www.gov.ir/khatami/khbio-e.htm

**Constitution of Iran**
http://www.salamiran.org/IranInfo/State
/Constitution

## Ali Akbar Nateq-Nuri

Ali Akbar Nateq-Nuri may have lost to Khatami, but he's not going to go away. Nateq-Nuri still leads the ultraconservative parliament and remains Khatami's nemesis. Many in Iran believe that Ali Akbar Nateq-Nuri lost the May 1997 polls solely because it was thought that, as president, he would have decreed that women in public wear the long, hooded traditional *chador*, a one-piece garment about as popular in Iran as *The Satanic Verses*. The real fabric of Iran may have been evidenced by the high turnout at the polls.

## Former President Ali Akbar Hashemi Rafsanjani

You may remember him as the patient towel-headed guy who politely endured Mike Wallace's dumb questions on *60 Minutes*. Rafsanjani wanted to talk about how Iran would like to be buddies, but Mike wanted to spank him for something that happened 20 years ago.

What Mike didn't know was that Rafsanjani is the good guy. During his term, he attended to the economy and repaired the damage left by the war with Iraq. He worked to get Iran reacquainted with the international community by expanding world ties and by arranging the release of hostages held by terrorist groups with ties to Iran. Rafsanjani is also credited with persuading Khomeini to finally agree to a cease-fire in the war with Iraq in August 1988. But Rafsanjani has had tougher problems than being grilled by Mike: He has narrowly escaped seven assassination attempts.

http://www.cyberiran.com/government/constitution.html

## Ali Mohammed Besharati

Besharati is Iran's influential interior minister. A former Revolutionary Guard, Besharati was one of the students who seized the U.S. embassy in 1979. His latest action was to unsuccessfully ban Iran's embarrassingly popular satellite dishes—which he views as instruments of Western filth—when he learned that reruns of *Ricki Lake* and *Knight Rider* were getting better ratings than *Muslim Mullahs! Live From Mahabad!* or *Good Morning, Tehran!*

## Mujahideen Khalq Organization (MKO)

The MKO is a 20,000-strong Iranian resistance force based in Iraq. Unlike other liberation groups, 35 percent of the group's soldiers are women, as are nearly three-quarters of its officers. Training at al-Ashraf Camp, just out of reach of Iran's howitzers, the fully armed MKO doesn't collect paychecks and bestows near-deity status on its female leader, Maryam Rajavi, whom the rebel group hopes to install as Iran's next president.

Have these folks got a chance against the mullahs? MKO troops have taken a vow of celibacy until Iran's government is toppled, so at least we know they're motivated. The MKO is one of the few armored liberation groups. The MKO can field 160 T-54/55 tanks (which they probably got from the Moscow military museum) and dozens of rocket launchers, APCs, towed howitzers, and even attack helicopters. Even so, these guys and gals are more talk than action. The organization was 50,000 strong after the Islamic revolution, with nearly half a million supporters. About 5,000 activists have been executed in the government's crackdown, and more than 25,000 imprisoned. They lost a lot of kudos fighting against Iran during the Iran-Iraq war. After the cease-fire in the Iran-Iraq war, the mujahideen invaded Iran but were crushed by the Iranian armed forces.

## National Council of Resistance of Iran (NCR)

Based in the United States, the NCR is the mouthpiece of the MKO. It's all a bit ridiculous, because the MKO is supported by that well-known U.S. ally in the region, Saddam Hussein. Remember him? We can almost sum up U.S. foreign policy in the region: The NCR does lots of lobbying in Congress; the NCR is the political wing of an organization (the MKO) that the State Department has blacklisted as a terrorist organization; the so-called "terrorist" organization operates from Baghdad, but its politicos raise cash to overthrow the mullahs. Yeah, something's definitely wrong here.

## Khomeini Money

In 1989, the Iranian government used its official government presses to print the first of about $10 billion of counterfeit U.S. currency. The U.S. bills of 100-dollar denominations were originally used to finance terrorists in the Bekaa Valley. There were little if any clues to the bills' origin (some say the zeroes have flattened tops).

The U.S. government estimates that there is around $400 billion in bogus U.S. currency outside of the country. The paper used is the same paper used by the U.S. Mint, and, in many cases, the bills cannot be detected even by optical scanners. The bills continue to appear, and have been spotted most recently in North Korea. In dangerous places where U.S. currency is the standard, *DP* has taken to carrying only 20s and not accepting any $100 bills printed in the '80s. If it makes you feel any better, the new $100 bill has already been counterfeited.

http://www.zolatimes.com/V3.22/fifthman2.html

## Getting In

Not only is it legal to travel to Iran, but the country is planning to open its first U.S. tourist office in New York City. The staffers at Iran's UN mission in New York got a little giddy and loosened their guard with *DP* after the elections. "Iran is very safe!" the nameless paper-pusher proclaimed. "We love Americans! Many Iranians want to be just like Americans. Tell me when you're coming. I will tell you how to leave the airport [without being followed]!"

U.S. passports are valid for travel to Iran. However, U.S.-Iranian dual nationals have often had their U.S. passports confiscated upon arrival and have been denied permission to depart the country documented as U.S. citizens. To prevent the confiscation of U.S. passports, the State Department suggests that Americans leave their U.S. passports at a U.S. embassy or consulate overseas for safekeeping before entering Iran. To facilitate their travel in the event of the confiscation of a U.S. passport, dual nationals may obtain in their Iranian passports the necessary visas for countries that they will transit on their return to the United States, and where they may apply for a new U.S. passport. Dual nationals must enter and leave the United States on U.S. passports. The U.S. government does not have diplomatic or consular relations with the Islamic Republic of Iran. The Swiss government, acting through its embassy in Tehran, serves as the protecting power for U.S. interests in Iran and provides only very limited consular services.

*Iran Touring and Tourism*
Deputy Minister for Tourism and Pilgrimage Affairs
Ministry of Culture and Islamic Guidance
Hajj and Pilgrimage Building, Third Floor
Azadi Avenue
P.O. Box 13445-993
Tehran, Iran
Tel.: (98) 21 6423042, or 6432098, or 6432107
Fax: (98) 21 6433842, or 6432088
Telex: 21-2089
info@itto.org
http://www.itto.org

*Information on Iran*
http://tehran.stanford.edu

Visa and passport are required. The Iranian government maintains an interests section through the Pakistan Embassy in Washington, DC: Embassy of Pakistan, 2209 Wisconsin Avenue, NW, Washington, DC 20007, Tel.: (202) 965-4990.

From the Great Satan: The U.S. government does not currently have diplomatic or consular relations with the Islamic Republic of Iran and therefore cannot provide protection or routine consular services to American citizens in Iran. Former Muslims who have converted to other religions, as well as persons who encourage Muslims to convert, are subject to arrest and possible execution. The Iranian government reportedly has the names of all individuals who filed claims against Iran, and who received awards at the Iran–U.S. Claims Tribunal at The Hague pursuant to the 1981 Algerian Accords. There are restrictions on both the import and the export of goods between Iran and the United States. Neither U.S. passports nor visas to the United States are issued in Tehran. That also means that you can't use U.S. traveler's checks at Iranian banks.

> **F**ormer Muslims who have converted to other religions, as well as persons who encourage Muslims to convert, are subject to arrest and possible execution.

http://www.daftar.org/default_eng.htm

## Getting Around

Mehrabad International Airport is seven miles west of Tehran (about a 30-minute drive). Airport facilities include a 24-hour bank, a 24-hour post office, a 24-hour restaurant, a snack bar, a 24-hour duty-free shop, gift shops, 24-hour tourist information, and first-aid/vaccination facilities. Airline buses are available to the city for a fare of RL10 (travel time: 30 minutes). Taxis also are available to the city center for approximately RL1,200–1,500. There is a departure tax of RL1,500. Transiting passengers remaining in the airport are exempt from the departure tax.

Once inside Iran, transportation by private car (with driver) or with a guide (who will be assigned to keep tabs on you) is recommended.

http://www.salamiran.org/Media

## Dangerous Places
*Nowhere/Everywhere*

Forget about crime. A pickpocket would get "two strikes" and then he could audition for *Flipper* sequels. The problem in Iran is that everyone wants to know what you're doing here. U.S. citizens traveling in Iran have been detained without charge, arrested, and harassed by Iranian authorities. Persons in Iran who violate Iranian laws, including Islamic laws, may face penalties that can be severe. Foreigners have been kidnapped.

The eastern and southern portions of Iran are major weapons- and drug-smuggling routes from Pakistan and Afghanistan. Right now, Iran is a brave new world for U.S. travelers and pretty run-of-the-mill for Euro backpackers. Most of the country can be considered safe (that's the good news), but it's still very much a police state (the bad news).

http://www.undcp.org/iran/country_profile_page003.html

## GREASE 'N' GAS

You have figured out by now that the Revolution is fueled by petro dollars. Iran has 9 percent of the world's proven oil reserves and 15 percent of its natural gas. Combine this with the global warming caused by the gas bags who run the country and it's a very flammable mixture. The only thing keeping the brakes on the Iranian Revolution being exported to Omaha is Iran's crippling debt ($21 billion and growing) and unemployment (6 million out of work by 2005). Today Iran relies on oil for 90 percent of all its foreign exchange earnings, bringing in about $24 billion dollars a year.

Iran can pump 3.6 million barrels per day and sell two-thirds of it to foreign customers, Japan being the biggest consumer. Accordingly, the Great Satan wants desperately to reestablish relations with Iran before the damn Euros and Asians get all the lucrative oil contracts. This, of course, makes the tanker ports of Kharg, Sirri, and Lavan very attractive targets for Saddam Hussein.

http://www.eia.doe.gov/emeu/international/iran.html

## Dangerous Things

### Nukes

Iran first got nukey in 1974 under the shah, but the idea was first dropped and then dusted off again by Khomeini in 1984. They didn't actually have any nukes, but they were darn serious about holding off Iraq. Most experts believe that Iran is eagerly pursuing the project while publicly denying it. They better hurry—Israel has had a head start on Iran and has between 75 and 130 weapons.

### Red Tape

The Iranians estimate that within an 8-hour workday, government workers produce an average of 24 minutes of productive labor. In a country where an engineer makes about $250 a month, the average salary for a government employee is about $72 . . . a year. Over 1,100,000 bureaucrats are paid less than $60 a year, with 70 percent living under the poverty line in a country where the poverty line is $138 a year (yeah, that's right, a year). Sally Struthers, are you out there?

http://www.heritage.org/index

## Tourists

Iran has over 2 million full-time tourists, many of whom stay for extended periods of time. At last count there were 1,500,00 Afghans, 390,000 Iraqis and a few thousand others. Some folks say there are an additional half a million Afghans inside Iran. Oh, you say those are refugees . . . ?

Well, okay, Iran wishes those refugees were tourists, but in any case would like them to go back home. The confusion comes from Iran's reluctance to actually call these folks "refugees," or *panahandegan*. The term the Iranians use is *mohageren*, or "involuntary travelers." Iran is so excited about the idea of folks going home that they are handing out 120 pounds of wheat, blankets, and $40 in cash to each. It is estimated that by 2005 the number of "tourists" in Iran will increase from 31 million to 40 million people.

http://www.itto.org/statistics/statics%20of%20Iran.asp
http://www.refugees.org/world/countryrpt/mideast/iran.htm

## The Pepsi Generation

The young generation in Iran have an odd resemblance to the Vietnam-era youth of America, minus, of course, the sex, drugs, and rock 'n' roll. This generation, born in the '70s and '80s, has little economic good news to look forward to (i.e., jobs). Many of these people are educated men and women who have lived through the revolution of 1979 and don't see what's the big deal. They grew up during the eight-year-long Iran-Iraq war in the '80s—a war that killed 286,000 and injured half a million of their parents and siblings. There are 24 million Iranians under 16. The poster child for this generation, Reza Pahlavi, the good-looking, clean-shaven son of the ousted shah, has all the props. Born October 31, 1960, he lives in Maryland, and beams his pearly whites via programs picked up by bootleg satellite dishes. Other than being the son of the shah (who hauled royal butt on January 16, 1979), he doesn't have a whole lot of qualifications. Well, okay, he is good looking, the son of a former leader, trained as a fighter pilot (courtesy of Uncle Sam), and has the backing of wealthy supporters . . . sound familiar?

*Reza Pahlavi*
P.O. Box 566
Falls Church, VA 22040
rpsec@rezapahlavi.org
Tel.: (703) 827-0928
Fax: (703) 827-9101
http://www.rezapahlavi.org/index.htm

## Party! Party! Party!

No, you moron, not the Bud Lite, Jack Black, Dennis Rodman, up-all-night, sleep-all-day kind of party. Political parties. There are a lot of parties going on, but you won't find them in Iran. For now you can find them on the Internet.

http://www.daraee.com/content/Political.html

## Uncle Sam, aka "The Great Satan"

The Iranians (at least those who haven't immigrated to America) have been foaming at the mouth about "Raygun," "Boosh," "Cleen-tun," and now "Leetle Boosh" for so long that they have forgotten we are fairly decent folks. Iranians will, of course, surprise you by asking if you know their relatives in your home state and discussing the acting skills of Pamela Lee's replacement on *Baywatch*.

http://www.freemedia.at/bitter.htm

## Religion

Although Iran is a predominately Muslim society, most are of the Shi'a sect. *Shi'a* means "follower" or "friend" and Shi'as are the followers of the Prophet's son-in-law, not of the leaders chosen after the death of Mohammed. For those who skipped over Comparative Religions 101 for Advanced Barista Choreography, here are the basics. Long ago, Iranians were Persians who were predominately Zoroastrians. When Alexander rolled through, he set up a system that was to protect freedom of religion for years to come, such as freedom for Manichaeists and even Christians. Okay, so they did skin Mani alive and stuff him with straw, and they executed a few Christians. But in any case, the religion of Zoroaster encouraged a rigid social climate that kept the poor poor and the rich rich. Trivia buffs and game-show contestants should know that Iran was actually the birthplace of feudalism long before it came to Europe. Then Islam came along (the first version of socialism) and disrupted the hell out of the status quo. Now a goat herder was every bit as good and noble as a direct descendant of a king. The Persians mulled this over, but didn't actually do much about it, from AD 637 until Ghengis Khan interrupted everything and then the Turks invaded in 1050.

Persia survived the rule of Ghengis and Timur until the Safavid Dynasty brought the luster back to Persia and ensconced the Shi'a version of Islam. The major difference between Shi'as and Sunni Muslims is that Sunnis think the successor to Mohammed can be chosen by man (Mohammed's father-in-law Abu Bakr was chosen as official successor after Mohammed's death), and Shi'as believe that Mohammed appointed his son-in-law Ali. Needless to say, this would be a good time to drop a few cuneiform business cards or stone tablets to sort things out. Well, mere mortals always seem to screw things up when left to their own devices.

Ali b Ali Talib was the husband of Mohammed's daughter Fatima, and it is said that when Mohammed was alive he chose his son-in-law rather than his father-in-law to succeed him. Abu Bakr was chosen by a hastily assembled group of followers, based on the basic idea that a successor chosen by man couldn't possibly interpret the word of God. This divine assignment also meant that Ali and his 11 natural heirs were immune from making mistakes. Until, of course, in 878 when the 12th Imam (the Mahdi) was transferred to a 5-year-old boy, who mysteriously disappeared in AD 939, throwing the whole concept of divine lineage into doubt. Some say there was no Mahdi. Most say he will return. Until then, the Ayatollahs have been collectively making decisions and waiting for the Mahdi to return to erase sin and get things right. With the Mahdi gone, there were splits in the religion that created the sects of the Druze, Kharijites, Ismaelis, Hanafis, and Shafites and Sufis. In the meantime Sunnis, or more Orthodox Muslims, consider all Shi'as to be heretics (and wax poetic about the various ways they should be snuffed). Shi'as traditionally have been victims of persecution around the world, with their archenemy being the fundamentalist Sunni Wahhabis of Saudi Arabia. Their neighbors aren't cutting them any slack either. Iraq has done a fine job wiping out the Marsh Arabs and the Taliban declared open season on the Hazara sect in northern Afghanistan. So, 1,200 years later, you get a general idea why the Iranians can be a little xenophobic and defensive.

http://www.shia.org

## Charity

Iran is a major sponsor of Shi'a resistance groups (like the Hazara in Afghanistan) and militant groups like Hizbollah in Lebanon. They combine missionary zeal with easy access to Russian-made weapons. Although we see the blood-and-guts part, these groups also provide a number of social services. You might find it embarrassing to learn that the original War on Terror in Afghanistan against the Taliban was supported by Iran. When America refused to provide money, advisors, or

## MAKE BIG MONEY IN . . .

No, it's not Amway . . . it's human body parts. Iranians have discovered a brisk market in organs. In a country where religious laws prevent or discourage the removal or implantation of organs from brain-dead or recently dead people, a kidney can go for $4,500 on the black market. Buyers and donors place ads and free-market principles apply. To discourage this trade, the Iranian government has relaxed controls and offers $1,250 (up from a paltry $570) for those who want to voluntarily donate a kidney.

weapons to the embattled United Front (aka Northern Alliance), the Iranians were more than happy to chip in. Readers of *DP* have long known that Iran was the major backer of Ahmed Shah Massoud (before he was assassinated on September 9, 2001). When the various Afghan factional leaders like Dostum, Massoud, and Ismael Khan began their fight back in April of 2001, it was the Iranians, not the CIA, who funded their fight. This led to an awkward point in history in October when the United States found itself fighting on the same side as Iran and at the same time decrying Iran as a supporter of terrorism. Whoops.

http://www.state.gov/s/ct/rls/pgtrpt/2001

### Truth in Politics

Campaign reformers rejoice! President Khatami's election campaign manager was sentenced to six months in jail in June of 2002. His crime was slandering and publishing lies. . . . So, what was the crime again?

http://www.iranian.com

### Dope and the Rope

Despite the button-down appearance of Iran, there are still 1.2 million drug addicts in Iran and 800,000 users. AIDS is now a rapidly growing problem with an estimated 19,000 cases caused primarily by drug injection. Despite its bad rep, Iran is responsible for the majority of drug seizures in the world . . . and does it with only $20 million spent a year on fighting the pervasive problem. In 1 year they netted 180 tons of opium gum and managed to account for 85 percent of the world's drug seizures. Of course it helps to be on the busiest drug highway outside of the U.S.-Mexican/Caribbean border. Iran's border with Afghanistan and southern Pakistan means that there is a continual flow of drugs moving across the border, with large amounts of heroin headed for Turkey and Europe.

Iran has executed nearly 10,000 drug smugglers since the revolution of 1979. Possession of 5 grams of heroin or 3 kilograms of opium will be quite sufficient for you to be turned into a marionette. Execution for drug dealing is usually done in public squares using construction cranes that slowly lift the accused above the crowd while the worked-up masses yell the appropriate slogans, usually starting with: "Death to . . . " Savvy backpackers and touring rock groups should know that the "International Day Against Drug Abuse and Illicit Drug Trafficking" takes place every year on June 26.

You can't blame them for being a little harsh—according to official figures, 3,100 policemen and soldiers have been killed by drug smugglers. We should also tell you that Iran is on Uncle Sam's list of countries that are lax on drug enforcement.

http://www.usdoj.gov/dea/pubs/intel/intel0901.html

## Getting Sick

A yellow-fever vaccination is required for travelers over the age of one year coming from infected areas. Arthropod-borne diseases and hepatitis B are endemic. Malaria is a risk in some provinces from March through November. Food- and water-borne diseases, including cholera, are common, as is trachoma. (Snakes and rabid animals can also pose a threat.) Basic medical care and medicines are available in the principal cities of Iran, but may not be available in outlying areas. There are 3 doctors and 14 hospital beds for every 10,000 people. The international travelers' hot line at the Centers for Disease Control, (404) 332-4559, has additional useful health information.

http://www.cdc.gov/travel/yb/countries/Iran.htm

## Nuts and Bolts

The rial fluctuates on the free market by as much as 15 percent a day. About 3,000 rials are equal to US$1. Inflation is between 60 to 100 percent a year, and a thriving black market takes advantage of outrageous official rates (expect 2 to 3 times the official exchange rate). Government employees make the equivalent of US$60 a month, and many Iranians are forced to take two jobs to get by. Iran is home to more refugees than any other country in the world. There are an estimated 2.2 million Afghans, 1.2 million Iraqis, and 1.2 million others who have fled the strife in Pakistan, Azerbaijan, and Tajikistan. The country is held together by a wide net of informers. But give Iran credit—like most exporters of terrorism, it's a peaceful country.

About three times the size of Arizona, Iran is a constitutional Islamic republic, governed by executive and legislative branches that derive national leadership primarily through the Muslim clergy. Shi'a Islam is the official religion of Iran, and Islamic law is the basis of the authority of the state. Islamic ideals and beliefs provide the conservative foundation of the country's customs, laws, and practices. Shi'ites comprise about 95 percent of the country. Sunnis make up about 4 percent. The literacy rate is at about 75 percent. Iran is a developing country.

The work week in Iran is Sunday through Thursday. Electricity is 220V/50Hz. Languages are Farsi, Turkish, Kurdish, Arabic, and scattered English. Only about half of Iran's population speaks Farsi.

Temperatures for Tehran can be very hot in the summer and just above freezing in the winter. The northern part of the country can experience very bitter winters. Iran has a mostly desert climate with unusual extremes in temperature. Temperatures exceeding 130°F occasionally occur in the summer, while in the winter the high elevation of most of the country often results in temperatures of 0°F and lower. Go in May or October to avoid the extremes.

http://www.tehrantimes.com

There is no U.S. embassy or consulate in Iran. The United States does, however, have an interests section at the Swiss embassy in Tehran.

**Swiss Embassy, U.S. Interests Section**
Africa Avenue
59 West Farzan Street
Tehran, Iran
Tel.: (98) 21 878-2964 and 879-2364
Fax: [98] (21) 877-3265
http://travel.state.gov/iran.html

## Dangerous Days

| | |
|---|---|
| 11/15/02 | Hashem Aghajari, a university professor, refuses to appeal his death sentence for insulting Islam. |
| 1/02 | George W. Bush includes Iran with Iraq and North Korea in defining an "Axis of Evil." |
| 8/8/01 | Khatami is reelected with 77 percent of the popular vote. |
| 2/18/00 | Liberals win control of the *majlis* or parliament. |
| 2/20/99 | 6,800 people run for office in elections. 760 are not allowed to run by the Conservative Council of Guardians. Reformers win big. |
| 5/24/97 | Khatami, a moderate, is elected president with 70 percent of the vote. |

| 5/9/95 | The United States imposes agricultural, oil, and trade sanctions on Iran. |
|---|---|
| 7/3/89 | The Ayatollah Khomeini dies. |
| 2/14/89 | Khomeini announces a death decree on *Satanic Verses* author Salman Rushdie, an Indian national and resident of the United Kingdom. |
| 7/20/88 | Iran announces cease-fire with Iraq. |
| 7/3/88 | The U.S.S. *Vincennes* mistakenly shoots down an Iranian Airbus airliner over the Persian Gulf. |
| 12/4/84 | Four Islamic Jihad terrorists hijack a Kuwaiti airliner bound for Pakistan from Kuwait and order it flown to Tehran. Two U.S. aid personnel are killed during the hijacking, while two others, another U.S. aid official and an American businessman, are tortured during the ordeal. Iranian troops storm the aircraft on December 9, retaking it from the hijackers. |
| 6/28/81 | The prime minister and 74 others are killed in the bombing of the legislature. |
| 1/20/81 | U.S. embassy hostages are released. Fifty-two American hostages are freed after 444 days in captivity, following an agreement between the United States and Iran arranged by Algeria. |
| 9/19/80 | Iran-Iraq war begins. |
| 7/27/80 | Death of the shah of Iran. |
| 4/25/80 | Military plan to rescue American hostages fails in the desert of Iran, due to operational shortfalls and an aircraft accident. |
| 11/4/79 | The U.S. embassy is seized and 63 people are taken hostage. |
| 4/1/79 | Islamic Republic Day, commemorating riots by Islamic fundamentalists in Isfahan. |
| 3/10/79 | Death of Kurdish leader Mullah Mustafa Barzani (Kurdish regions). |
| 2/11/79 | Revolution Day. Celebration of the victory of the Islamic revolution. |
| 2/4/79 | Iranian Revolution begins. Iran's Shi'ite clerics start their takeover of the government. |
| 2/1/79 | Khomeini returns from exile and calls for the start of the "Ten Days of Dawn," commemorating the 10 days of unrest, ending with Khomeini taking power on February 11 (the "Day of Victory"). |
| 1/16/79 | The shah departs Iran. |

| | |
|---|---|
| **11/4/78** | Student uprising against the shah. |
| **9/9/78** | The shah's troops open fire on protesters in Tehran, killing several hundred demonstrators. |
| **11/4/64** | Ayatollah Khomeini is exiled to Turkey. |
| **6/5/63** | The Ayatollah Khomeini is arrested by the shah's police. It is also the Day of Mourning and Revolution Day. |
| **7/22/53** | CIA overthrows nationalist Prime Minister Mohammad Mossadeq. |
| **5/51** | Iran parliament nationalizes the oil industry. |
| **1/22/46** | Kurdish Republic Day. |
| **2/7/1902** | Birth date of the Ayatollah Ruhollah Khomeini. |
| **6/28** | Revolutionary Guards' Day. |
| **3/21** | Persian New Year. Kurdish New Year celebrated. |

Baghdad

# ★★★
# IRAQ

## The Garden of Bleedin'

We promised to bomb them into the Stone Age, but Fred and Barney live much better than the average Iraqi. We called the country's leader nasty names, but he didn't cry; he didn't even spill his champagne when Dubya said Saddam's country was part of an Axis of Evil. We leak about one invasion plan a week to the media, but he doesn't even get flustered. And in case he forgets to turn on CNN, we continue to drop millions of dollars' worth of high-tech hardware on him. Despite the subtle messages we send, Saddam is on a roll. Almost weekly, new palaces and mosques decorate NSA satellite photos and Saddam . . . well, he just doesn't seem to give a damn. Much to the annoyance of Uncle Sam, Saddam Hussein still rules the roost in Baghdad. This sanguine reaction doesn't stop us from firing missiles into radar sites, bunkers, sand dunes, or even at the occasional camel that might be

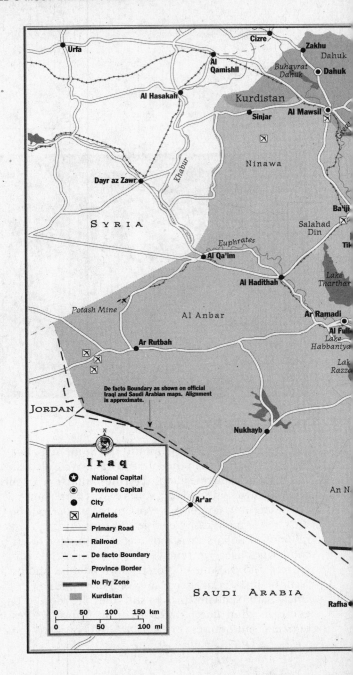

De facto Boundary as shown on official Iraqi and Saudi Arabian maps. Alignment is approximate.

**Iraq**

- ✪ National Capital
- ◉ Province Capital
- ● City
- ☒ Airfields
- Primary Road
- ·····  Railroad
- – – – De facto Boundary
- Province Border
- No Fly Zone
- Kurdistan

| 0 | 50 | 100 | 150 km |
| 0 | 50 | | 100 mi |

Maragheh

Mahabad

Zanjan

Kurdistan

qrah

Rayat

Arbil

Qal'at Dizah

IRAN

Irbil

Little Zab

Kirkuk

As Sulaymaniyah

As Sulaymaniyah

Sanandaj

Ta'mim

Diyala

Hamadan

marra'

Diyala

Khanaqin

Bakhtaran

Tigris

Borujerd

Ba'qubah

Mandali

Ilam

Khorramabad

Baghdad

Baghdad

Simareh

Wasit

Karbala'

Babil

Al Hillah

Al Kut

Tigris

Maysan

rbala

Al Hayy

Dezful

n Najaf

Ad Diwaniyah

Al 'Amarah

Al Qadisiyah

Ahvaz

Euphrates

Jarrah

Dhi Qar

As Samawah

An Nasiriyah

Al Basrah

Khorramshahr

As Salman

Al Muthanna

Al Basrah

Abadan

Makhfar al Busayyah

Umm Qasr

KUWAIT

Persian Gulf

Al Jahrah

Kuwait

employed as a makeshift Scud launcher. It would seem that once again Saddam has us hoist by our own petard.

In 2000, American and British aircraft dropped 155 tons of ordnance—that's heavy explosive things—on Iraq. In 2001, it was only 107 tons—although, intriguingly, there was a huge surge in activity during the time surrounding September 11. A bombardment has been going on since 1991. This is a conflict that has outlasted Saddam's eight-year war with Iran. Wonks in the British and U.S. defense ministries are happy to give the daily score. It is a silly game that has been in overtime for more than a decade, with both sides boasting of stats a paraplegic pentathlete could best. Saddam still insists he is winning. The plucky allies insist they are winning. The problem is that since the name of the game is to get Saddam, we are losing. This dude has more staying power than a rooster on Viagra.

The current American and British onslaught dates back to 1998, when Saddam, to wind the United States and its allies up a bit, kicked out the UN inspection teams searching for weapons of mass destruction. The United States responded with "Operation Desert Fox." (Who thinks up these names? Perhaps we should launch Operation Desert Outfoxed? Operation Desert the Kurds? Oops—America already did that one, back in 1991.) For four days in December 1998, U.S. and British planes blasted the hell out of Iraq, while Bill Clinton justified it on television with his best "this-hurts-me-more-than-it-hurts-you" expression. Bill waged war by remote control, targeting 97 sites throughout Iraq. The United States unleashed 325 Tomahawk missiles, 90 cruise missiles, and dispatched quite a few B-52s from faraway tropical islands. The net result of this fabulously expensive enterprise was that Saddam stayed in his job and the UN stayed out of Iraq—pretty much what could have been accomplished if Clinton had just written him a very rude letter. Since then, the bombing has continued, but it hasn't fazed Saddam a bit. He's put up a bounty of 25 million Iraqi dinars (US$14,000) for anyone who can bring down a U.S. plane, though seeing as Iraq's antiaircraft gunners have been trying for more than a decade and haven't so much as knocked the wing-mirror off an F-16, his money's probably pretty safe.

Saddam made his first big move in 1980. Using a number of minor disputes between Iraq and Iran, he thought he would make his mark in the centuries-old Arab/Sunni versus Persian/Shi'a conflict. Iran had just turfed the Yanks and the shah and relied on U.S. military parts. Their leadership was rudimentary and Saddam rolled in. In an effort to change a few hundred years of mapmakers' work. Saddam didn't get a scratch, but a million Iraqis were killed or wounded. The Iranians were slow off the mark but they held the Iraqis at a stalemate. The Iranians bled Iraq for 8 years until the odd date of 8/8/88, when they signed the peace agreement.

During this war, incidentally, many of the countries that are now loudly proclaiming Iraq Public Enemy Number One supplied Iraq with weapons, in contravention of international conventions and, in some cases, their own laws precluding the supply of arms to countries at war. Here are some of them: the United States, France, Germany, Great Britain, Italy, China, Chile, and Brazil. The government of Great Britain, whose warplanes and rhetoric are now equally lofty where Iraq is concerned, also helped to put that spare tire around Saddam's middle by approving £340 million in extra credits for Iraq shortly after Saddam's murder of 5,000 Kurds in a chemical attack on Halabja. Hey, it was just business back then—now, it's war.

After the Iran-Iraq war, the Iraqis were slowly cluing in to the odd notion that life in Iraq just may suck because of Saddam, not Iran. Saddam quickly disabused them of that notion by finding another enemy. In 1990 Saddam had the brilliant idea of invading Kuwait, partially with the intention of seizing Kuwait's banks, oil refineries, and investment companies to pay for the reconstruction of Iraq. Now, you can't blame him . . . Kuwait historically was part of Iraq . . . and it seems they were slipping their thirsty oil drilling under Saddam's fence. The Kuwaitis, in a brilliant Gallic-like military move, decided to defend their country apparently by setting up their forward control centers in the discos in London. This left any show of protest (other than painting "Down with Saddam" on Kuwaiti cell phones) up to the free world.

It had been almost 15 years since the U.S. military had a good scrap and we had developed an embarrassing habit of leaving just when things got ugly or picking tiny Caribbean islands to invade. What Saddam didn't count on was that his country was obligingly identical to the U.S. terrain where we trained our tankers in California and Texas. And then there was good old American air power itching to try out their new toys.

The events of February 2 to March 3 of 1991 were pretty much textbook "How to Invade Evil Empires," except, of course, someone forgot to write the last chapter entitled "How to Depose Evil Dictators and Ensure Peace and Stability." It seemed that in their haste to get to Baghdad, someone noticed that they might just overshoot into Iran, creating all kinds of ugly scenarios—such as Israel becoming a large smoking hole.

It was also the first live war (although nobody actually covered the "war"). The whole world watched what happened live on CNN: the bombing of Baghdad, Saddam's defending army surrendering en masse to television cameramen, Iraqi soldiers fleeing Kuwait with as much loot as they could cram into stolen Mercedes-Benzes, and their subsequent incineration on the Mittlah Ridge in what was, without doubt, the worst traffic jam in history. And, of course, the destruction of Kuwait's oil fields and ecosystem, as a final "screw you" from the man.

At the end of the 42-day Gulf War, Allied Forces had destroyed, neutralized, or captured 41 of the 42 Iraqi army divisions in the war zone of Kuwait and southern Iraq. Out of half a million Iraqi soldiers positioned in the combat area, the coalition estimated the number of Iraqi prisoners of war at 175,000, and the number of Iraqi casualties at between 85,000 and 100,000. Iraq lost 3,700 of its 5,500 main battle tanks, 1,857 of its 7,500 armored vehicles, and 2,140 of its 3,500 artillery pieces. Ninety-seven of Iraq's 689 combat aircraft and 6 of its 489 helicopters were destroyed—the 160 combat aircraft flown to Iran by terrified pilots were impounded as war reparations. Nine airfields were destroyed, as well as 16 chemical weapons plants, 10 biological weapons plants, and 3 nuclear weapons facilities. Allied deaths in action were 146, of whom 35 were killed in friendly fire incidents.

Iraq had suffered one of the most comprehensive military defeats in history. If Saddam had been managing a football team that had been beaten this badly, the fans would have hung him off the goalposts. A lesser maniac might have panicked. Not Saddam. He knows that the big lie is always more readily believed than the minor fib, so he just told his people that they'd won a tremendous victory. Maybe his people believed him, and maybe they didn't, but another fundamental of governance of which Saddam is well aware is that people will go along with pretty much anything when the alternative is dangling headfirst from meat-hooks or having glass bottles inserted in nether orifices (just two of the amusements popular with Saddam's secret police, the justly feared Mukhabarat). The finer point is that once Saddam did win, of course the Iraqis lost.

Since the Gulf War, Iraq has rebuilt much of its infrastructure, including the phone system, electrical plants, government buildings, bridges, and its contentious chemical weapons facilities. The sanctions still enforced by the Western world have had the effects that sanctions always do—they've made the poor poorer, the sick sicker, the rich richer, and the powerful much more difficult to dislodge.

Oh . . . we almost forgot to tell you . . . we should mention that the Center for Strategic and International Studies estimates Saddam to be almost back to the point where we started this whole thing. Iraq has 400,000 active troops and another 400,000 in reserves. Saddam still has 2,200 tanks and 3,700 armored weapons, 2,200 artillery, 80 helicopters, 316 combat aircraft, and 860 SAM launchers, and CNN will be happy to know that he still has 3,000 very photogenic and wildly inaccurate antiaircraft guns.

The people who will be doing the dying and suffering throughout these medal-thumping and dick-banging displays of toys will be the people of Iraq. Iraq estimates that Western sanctions have killed 1.5 million Iraqi children. Even UNICEF confirms that Western sanctions have killed at least half a million Iraqi children. According to anyone with any sense—a group not including former U.S. Secretary of State Madeleine Albright, who called it "a price worth paying," as if she were the one paying it—Western sanctions have killed way too many Iraqi children. As *DP* goes to press, Saddam sits in any one of his 50 palaces and ponders the content of his next victory speech.

### Voices in the Wilderness
http://www.nonviolence.org/vitw

Why are we going back to Iraq? Although Bush, Jr. secretly gets serious wood thinking about finishing daddy's business, it's really about having a pay-per-view rematch in which everything but the last act has been written. Before Bush runs for re-election, he will need a result. The justification, when war comes, will be Iraq's weapons of mass destruction (and of course their lobbing distance to Israel, not America). The trouble is that nobody knows if they've got any. During the last go-around, when Saddam rained Scuds on the Holy Land, there was nary a nuke or chem warhead to be seen. That's not to say that Iraq hasn't been trying. Before the UN inspectors were first sent packing in 1998, the International Atomic Energy Agency had dismantled 40 nuclear research facilities in Iraq; satellite photos taken since then have shown that some are being rebuilt. UN inspectors also destroyed piles of chemical and biological weapons, developed under the supervision of the British-educated Rihab "Dr. Germ" Taha: 38,500 chemical warheads, 690 tons of chemical agents, and 426 items of chemical weaponry production equipment. They don't know how much they didn't find. They do know there was plenty more where that came from. Even the Iraqi government admits that before the Gulf War they had 8,400 liters of anthrax—which, as you know, is plenty enough.

Iraq's big military initiative right now is the Jaish al-Quds, a people's army with which Saddam reckons he's going to liberate Jerusalem. Iraqi television broadcasts show this mighty force on the march, but it looks suspiciously like the same few hundred blokes marching in circles past one camera. For now Saddam makes sure there are plenty of movies and popcorn in his many bunkers. He can't wait for the show to begin.

## The Scoop

Considering that Baghdad was once the breadbasket of the ancient world and part of the Fertile Crescent, Saddam and his cohorts have done a spectacular job of screwing it up.

Iraq has sufficient oil reserves to make Saudi Arabia look like a dry sump in Lubbock. But instead of basking in its riches, Iraq is hopelessly poor, the consequence of Saddam's maniacal insistence on becoming the superpower of the Middle East. The Gulf War was a laughable attempt by Saddam to shun international diplomacy and snatch oil-rich Kuwait. Either Saddam didn't pay attention during history class or he just likes expensive fireworks, because he qualified his country for the third-world club after a mere three months in 1991. Every time Saddam gets ambitious, the Garden of Eden turns into the Garden of Bleedin'.

> **C**onsidering that Baghdad was once the breadbasket of the ancient world and part of the Fertile Crescent, Saddam and his cohorts have done a spectacular job of screwing it up.

*Iraqi News Agency*
http://www.uruklink.net/iraqnews/eindex.htm

*Iraqi Satellite Channel*
http://www.iraqtv.ws

*Iraq Tourism Board*
http://www.uruklink.net/tourism/eindex1.htm

## The Players

### President Saddam Hussein al-Tikriti

The undisputed ruler of Iraq. Also known as any or all of the following: President, Field Marshal, Chairman of the Revolutionary Command Council, the Anointed One, the Glorious Leader, and a direct descendant of the prophet Mohammed. Saddam Hussein is, along with North Korean dingbat-in-chief Kim Jong Il, the last surviving throwback to the government-by-personality-cult once associated with Hitler, Stalin, Ceaucescu, Amin, Mobutu, and many others whom most of us would regard as slightly dubious role models. Saddam's regime is an immense monument to himself. His capital, Baghdad, is full of pictures of him and things named after him—an airport, a suburb, mosques, and hospitals. He owns at least 50 palaces—the staffs of which cook three complete meals a day, just in case he drops in. He even writes books, or at least has books written on his behalf. In the last few years, he's published two novels, *Zabibah and the King* and *The Fortified*

*Castle*. Perhaps unsurprisingly, they got rave reviews in the Iraqi newspapers (you can take a wild guess as to who controls the press).

Saddam had an early start at being a bastard. He was born out of wedlock on April 28, 1937, in the village of al-Awja near the city of Tikrit, a hundred miles north of Baghdad (al-Awja, amusingly, translates as "crooked"). The man who sired him either died before he was born or simply disappeared, so he's either a very tragic or extremely prescient figure. Saddam was raised from the age of 10 by an uncle, Khairallah Talfah, who was then a teacher but who had once been an army officer—a career that came to a spectacular end when he got five years in the brig for participating in the 1941 Rashid Ali rebellion, during which a group of nationalist colonels failed to overthrow the pro-British regime that surrounded King Faisal II (then all of 6 years old) in favor of a pro-Nazi military government.

The young Saddam was hugely influenced by Uncle Khairallah's somewhat uncompromising politics ("Three whom God should not have created," Uncle K once wrote, "are Persians, Jews, and flies."). In his teens, having moved to Baghdad with Khairallah, Saddam was a regular at demonstrations against the pro-Western monarchy. He developed his understanding of the power of intimidation early, recruiting local thugs to beat up shopkeepers who wouldn't close their businesses in sympathy with the protesters.

Saddam became involved with the Ba'ath Party (Party of Arab Renewal) in 1957, and participated in an assassination attempt on Iraqi President General Qasim on October 7, 1959. The attack was a shambles—though Qasim was wounded, it was more by good luck than good planning. Saddam was hit in the leg, more than likely by one of his co-conspirators firing wildly. (Saddam later had this scene dramatized in an excruciatingly dull, self-commissioned film of his life, appropriately titled *The Long Days*—it's six agonizing hours long and was directed by Terence Young, director of *Dr. No* and *From Russia with Love,* among others.)

Saddam fled to Syria, where he stayed for six months, before going on to study in Egypt. He completed high school in 1961, but dropped out of a law degree program at Cairo University. To the continued vexation of conspiracy theorists, Saddam, like many exiled Iraqi dissidents, was a regular visitor to the U.S. embassy in Cairo, for the U.S. government and the young Saddam had similar views on General Qasim. Saddam returned to Iraq after the February 1963 coup in which his Ba'athist comrades overthrew (and shot) General Qasim.

The same year, Saddam submitted to an arranged marriage to Sajida Talfah, the oldest daughter of Khairallah Talfah, the uncle who raised him (cue "Dueling Banjos"). She went on to bear two delightful sons—

Uday, in 1964, and Qusay, in 1966. To confirm how close fruit falls from the tree in Iraq, Saddam made his wife's brother, Adnan, defense minister, and his wife's father, Uncle Khairallah, the mayor of Baghdad. Of course, in Saddam's Iraq, patronage is a two-way street. Adnan allegedly became quite popular among senior military officers, and ended up dead in a helicopter "accident" in 1989. Khairallah was so obviously corrupt that even his friend in high places couldn't pretend otherwise, and he was eventually eased out of the gig, his consolation prize being to have a few buildings named after him (which, thanks to the intermittent efforts of the USAF, doesn't guarantee a sense of permanence).

## LEGACY OF WAR

It appears that Gulf War veterans are two to three times more likely to suffer from motor-neuron disease than the general population. The University of Texas and a UK-based study has discovered that the brains of a disproportionate percentage of the 130,000 U.S. and British Gulf War veterans may show damage caused by a number of different sources: Pesticides used to kill desert flies and lice, antinerve gas tablets, vaccines, and inhalation of chemicals that occurred after the destruction of an Iraqi chemical weapons depot are some of the agents to blame. The symptoms the men and women exhibit are similar to Parkinson's or Huntington's disease.

The tables turned for Saddam in November 1963, when a split in the Ba'ath government left him dining with the unpopular kids at lunch. Saddam plotted to kill President Arif but was found out and locked up. Saddam escaped in July 1966, after serving 20 months, and was firmly back in business when his fellow Ba'athists deposed General Arif in 1968. Saddam became vice chairman of the ruling Ba'ath Party's Revolutionary Command Council, and chief inquisitor and toe-cutter under the new President—and Saddam's cousin—General Ahmad Hasan al-Bakr. Saddam kept himself busy executing hundreds of Iraqis, and handing out government jobs to fellow Tikritis. Saddam—whose favorite film is *The Godfather*—was building a power base he knew he'd be able to rely on when the time came.

On July 16, 1979, President al-Bakr appeared on Iraqi television to announce his resignation—a decision prompted, in no uncertain terms, by his ambitious cousin. On July 18, 1979, Saddam staked his claim on power with a display of theatrical ruthlessness, which would be utterly unbelievable if its architect had not ensured that the whole thing was recorded on video. Saddam called a meeting of 400 senior party officials. He stood before them and announced the existence of a Syrian-backed conspiracy to undermine or overthrow the Ba'athist regime. He then summoned the Chairman of the Revolutionary Command Council, Muhi Abdel Hussein Mashhadi, who read out the details of the alleged plot while Saddam sat down and puffed diffidently at a huge cigar.

What the audience didn't know was that Mashhadi had been arrested on Saddam's orders three days previously, and tortured into turning against his colleagues. Every time Mashhadi read the name of someone in the audience, armed guards appeared from the wings and escorted them to the door. Some 60 Ba'ath officials left the building in this manner. Not one of them was ever seen again, and it is doubtful in the extreme that their reward for their service to Iraq was a gold watch, a brisk handshake, and a round-the-world plane ticket. The audience members who escaped the purge began applauding, many of them obviously hysterical with fear, and with good reason—over the next few weeks, more than a third of the Revolutionary Command Council were shot, as were scores of students, trades unionists, and anyone else Saddam had taken exception to.

Saddam has not, you'll have noticed, mellowed since. He rules by terror, and everyone in Iraq is well aware that nobody is safe—not even his own family. In 1996, two of Saddam's sons-in-law, the Industry and Minerals Minister General Hussein Kamil Hasan al-Majid, and the Director of the Military Industrialization Organization Saddam Hussein Kamil Hasan al-Majid (who had starred as Saddam in *The Long Days*), defected from Iraq along with their families, and were granted asylum in Jordan. Ignored by the Jordanians and by the CIA, to whom the two brothers had hoped to shop Saddam's military secrets, the pair decided, incredibly, to return to Baghdad, perhaps hoping that not even Saddam was crazy enough to off the husbands of his daughters. They were wrong. Once Saddam's daughters and grandchildren were safely removed to Tikrit, the brothers were killed, along with their father, two sisters, and several nieces and nephews.

Saddam's hold on power in Iraq is absolute. Reports that his people hate him are slightly hopeful. The citizens of dictatorships are not dissimilar to women who stay with violent husbands—they put up with it not out of love, but out of fear and the difficulty of imagining anything different. The Iraq-wide celebrations that marked Saddam's 65th birthday in 2002 were certainly orchestrated, but so were the same year's commemorations of the Golden Jubilee of Britain's Queen Elizabeth II, and both were attended by ordinary people who were there because they wanted to be. The decision by George W. Bush to let the CIA look into means of ushering Saddam into immortality ahead of schedule means that the American president has learned one crucial lesson about his father's nemesis: If and when Saddam goes, it won't be quietly.

*The Iraqi Presidency*
press@uruklink.net
http://www.uruklink.net/iraq/epage1.htm

## Uday Hussein

Eldest son of el presidente, Uday Hussein's principal accomplishment to date has been to make Marko Milosevic look like quite a nice kid.

Uday is 38 years old and runs several newspapers, including the *Daily Babel*; Iraq's top youth radio station, Shebab FM; the Iraqi Olympic Committee; the Iraqi Football Federation; and pretty much anything else he wants to. He has a somewhat unorthodox method of encouraging the athletes he supervises: If they don't perform, they are tortured and beaten.

It's what he gets up to in his spare time, however, that has truly made him infamous. Uday's consuming interests seem to be guns, alcohol, wide allegations of rape, and holding screenings of his vast collection of videos of prisoners being tortured. His behavior is so monstrous that, on one celebrated occasion, even his father thought he'd gone too far: In 1988, he shot dead one of his dad's butlers at a party, for which Uday spent four months in the slammer. To think of all the trouble that might have been saved if Saddam had grounded him for taking the car as a kid.

Accordingly, there were few tears shed when, on December 12, 1996, he got a taste of his own medicine. Uday was speeding to Baghdad's al-Masur Club when six men sprayed his supposedly bulletproof Porsche with machine-gun fire. Uday was hit eight times by bullets coming through the windshield. Uday had a hard time finding anyone who would treat him until Fidel Castro's personal doctor arrived. The upshot was that he lost part of his calf muscle, one lung, and, according to Baghdad bazaar rumor, the portion of his anatomy with which he'd terrorized a generation of Iraq's actresses and singers.

The question of who was responsible remains open, despite thousands of arrests. Lots of people could have done it, and any number of people were delighted someone did it, but most of the smart money is on a group called called Al-Nahda (The Awakening). They are reputedly run by the family of the late Lieutenant General Omar al-Hazzaa, who was punished in 1990 for a thoughtless remark about Uday's old man and had his tongue cut out before he was shot along with his son.

There are some signs that Uday is trying to reinvent himself as a semi-respectable citizen. Aside from his public-spirited work thrashing athletes half to death in pursuit of Iraqi sporting glory, he has made a start on a political career. In March 2000, he stood for a Baghdad constituency in parliamentary elections, receiving 99.9 percent of the vote (hey, you can't please everyone). And, anxious to cultivate some intellectual clout in the succession struggle with his younger brother, Uday has also completed a doctoral thesis on the decline of America's superpower status in the post–Cold War era; *DP* feels curiously certain that it got very good marks indeed. For what it may be worth, Uday reckons America will be overhauled as an economic, cultural, and military power by China, Japan, and the European Union by about 2015, so there.

**Uday Hussein**
udaysaddamhussein@yahoo.com

**Babil (Arabic only)**
http://www.iraq2000.com/babil

## Qusay Hussein

He's Uday's little brother and the second most important man in Iraq, after Dad. Qusay, 37 years old, has beaten his elder brother in the race to succeed Saddam; repeated, though unconfirmed, rumors have it that Saddam has already promised Qusay the keys to the shop. Though Qusay shared the same progressive upbringing—both boys were taken, at an early age, to witness the torture and execution of their father's prisoners—he appears to have emerged from it slightly less deranged than Uday.

This is why Uday has been given all the jobs that enable him to indulge his penchants for fast cars and flash suits, and why Qusay has been given the gigs that matter: Hussein minor runs the military, intelligence, and security services in Iraq. These include organizations such as the Special Security Organization (SSO), the outfit responsible for hiding Dad's nuclear weapons.

*DP* tip: Whenever Qusay thinks Uday is getting too big for his britches, Qusay sends a subtle message to Uday by having his pictures in the soccer clubs replaced with his or pop's. A recent defector told *The Observer* about just who has Dad's favorite knee: "Qusay's the butcher of the family now." On June 9, he survived an assassination attempt on his convoy. Sibling rivalry, perchance?

## Ali Hassan al-Majid (Chemical Ali)

Saddam's cousin and military governor of the Basra and Nasiriyah districts, Ali Hassan al-Majid makes Saddam, Uday, and Qusay look like amateurs when it comes to mass murder. In fact, there are probably quite a few dictators around who could use al-Majid's population disposal services. Al-Majid is known as Chemical Ali because he decided on the best way to solve the Kurdish rebellion: He orchestrated the gassing of Kurdish villages carried out by low-flying helicopters with express orders to kill every living thing in the area, including plants and wildlife. This was all part of Operation "Anvil" at the end of the war with Iran. In March 1988, in the town of Halabja, 5,000 Kurds died writhing in agony and 10,000 were seriously affected when Iraqi jets dropped chemical bombs on the town.

Other highlights on this charmer's résumé include a stint as governor of Kuwait during Iraq's occupation in 1990 and, more recently, overseeing the murders of Saddam's dissident sons-in-law after their ill-advised return to Baghdad.

http://www.kdp.pp.se/chemical.html

## Tariq Aziz

Urbane, clever, and less likely to chew on the furniture than the president, Iraq's deputy prime minister and foreign minister is the man often pushed forward to face the Western press. He is Edith to Saddam's Archie Bunker. Like many educated Iraqis of his generation, the 66-year-old Aziz is a fluent English speaker. He has the very unsettling talent of making Iraqi actions seem quite logical and justifiable, and is equally skilled at pointing out the hypocrisy of America's actions and their effects on the Iraqi people.

He is also a member of Iraq's small—but unharassed—Christian minority, and smart enough to have a permanent diplomatic exit visa.

http://www.pbs.org/wgbh/pages/frontline/gulf/oral/aziz/1.html

**Iraqi Ministry of Foreign Affairs**
foreign@uruklink.net
http://www.uruklink.net/mofa

## The CIA

The CIA has spent some $100 million since 1991 in an effort to bag Saddam Hussein, and they're going to spend more. In 1996, 400 Iraqis died in a failed CIA attempt to overthrow him: The blunder almost cost the United States northern Iraq and was one of the agency's biggest failures in its 50-year history. (This attempt to oust Saddam was spawned by the CIA's belief that Saddam was ripe for a downfall after the defection of his son-in-law Lieutenant General Hussein Kamil Hasan al-Majid in 1995.)

In early 1996, President Bill Clinton approved $6 million for a covert-ops group called the Iraqi National Accord and set up by the CIA. Drafted from the ranks of former Iraqi officers, its mission was to destabilize Baghdad through bombing attacks. Saddam responded by having his tanks roll through Arbil in Iraqi Kurdistan after a Kurdish leader invited him into the region to solve the inter-Kurdish fighting—by crushing the other side.

Saddam took advantage of the invitation to waste every CIA opera-
tive who was unfortunate enough to be in town. Three thousand Iraqis
and Kurds on the CIA payroll had to be evacuated out of Iraq through
Turkey and Guam to the United States—where, we presume, more
than a handful had their faces and fingertips changed. In 2002, Dubya
authorized the CIA to send special-ops teams into Iraq and permitted
them to use lethal force to remove Saddam. (These are the same
geniuses, remember, who've been failing to bump off Castro for 50 years;
who first heard about India's nuclear tests on CNN; and who couldn't
see what was so weird about dozens of young Arab men signing up for
flight training and skipping the "take-off" and "landing" classes.)

***Central Intelligence Agency***
http://www.cia.gov

## The Group of Four

America has taken under its wings a motley crew of rebels, renegades, and refugees in hopes that they will provide an alternative to the
ingrained regime of Saddam Hussein.

### The KDP and the PUK (The Kurds)

Essentially you have the Shi'ites in the south, a bunch of guys who
used to work for Saddam in the middle, and then the Kurds in the north.
To get the complete scoop on the Kurds, see the Kurdistan chapter.

http://www.kdp.pp.se
http://www.puk.org

### Iraqi National Congress (INC)

The CIA met with the INC in the SAS hotel in Vienna in 1992. The
idea was to combine all the anti-Saddam opposition groups at one
postal address so it would be easier to fund them, direct them, and keep
an eye on them. It seemed a good idea at the time, but America hasn't
seemed to know what to do with the INC since. They initially supported the INC to the hilt, then cut off their funding in 1995, leaving
them high and dry in a spectacular fiasco in Kurdistan (see the Kurdistan chapter). In 1998, they changed their minds and authorized $97
million for training pro-INC rebels through the Iraq Liberation Act,
though they still haven't paid up: In 2002, the INC was forced to shut
down its television station, Liberty TV, complaining of a lack of State
Department funding.

For the moment, the INC's top man and the Pentagon's favorite
Iraqi—not that the competition is stiff—is Ahmad Chalabi, a former
banker currently wanted on fraud charges in Jordan. He's not the power
in the INC he once was, though he's now just one member of the

Executive Committee, and the CIA have fallen out of love with him because they think he compromised the 1996 coup attempt led by offi-cers associated with the Iraqi National Accord (see above and below); 400 officers were subsequently executed. And there is also the little matter that they haven't done a damn thing to dent Saddam's popularity.

A more prominent INC spokesman now is Sharif Ali bin al-Hussein, who leads the Constitutional Monarchy Movement within the INC. A cousin of Iraq's last king, Faisal II, this suave former banker wants to be the man who restores the Hashemite throne to Baghdad.

The INC has offices in the Kurdish north of Iraq, but deals with all enquiries through its headquarters in London.

**Iraqi National Congress**
pressoffice@inc.org.uk
http://www.inc.org.uk

### Iraqi National Accord (INA)

The opposition's opposition: The CIA's idea that the INC would pro-vide a united front for all anti-Saddam opposition in Iraq was a nice one, but few things in the world disagree with each other as vehe-mently as Middle Eastern political groups who basically agree with each other. (Sorry to drag out this tired, but deadly accurate, insight; see Monty Python's *Life of Brian* for an accurate depiction of this truth.) The INA are leading lights in the Group of Four, which includes the Kurdish groups, the KDP and PUK (see the Kurdistan chapter), and the Shi'ite group, the Supreme Council for the Islamic Revolution in Iraq (see more about SCIRI later in this chapter).

The Group of Four are believed to have the sympathy of the U.S. State Department, while the Pentagon, for the moment, is sticking with the INC (see Monty Python's *Life of Brian* once again, for a not-so-inaccurate depiction of U.S. foreign policy-making).

**Iraqi National Accord**
wifaq_ina@hotmail.com
http://www.wifaq.com/index_e.html

## And in Case That Fails

### Iraqi National Movement (INM)

Still awake? The Iraqi National Movement are a coalition of exiled Iraqi military bigwigs who were given $315,000 by the State Depart-ment in 2002 to get their show on the road. The Virginia-based group is practically indistinguishable from those of the INC, but at the moment the INM appear to have the better friends in higher places at Foggy Bottom. Their major domo is Brigadier General Fawzi al-Shamari, who once commanded nine battalions in the Iran-Iraq war. The only flaw in this logic seems to be that it would be a better idea to back folks who won. Oh, Shamari is running a restaurant in northern Virginia until he is called to duty. In a *Newsweek* article he laid out his strategy: "You must make people unafraid of (Saddam). Right now he acts like a king in a palace surrounded by a strong fence and stray dogs. If you want to reach Saddam Hussein, the question is: how do I deal with those dogs? Some, you poison. Some, you give a sleeping potion. Some, you don't deal with." Ookay, let's make that order "to go," please. If you are looking for folks to overthrow Saddam, here's a start:

**The Iraqi Constitutional Monarchy Movement**
http://www.iraqcmm.org

**Iraqi National Accord**
http://www.wifaq.com

**Iraqi Turkmen Front**
http://www.turkmencephesi.org

**Iraqi Democratic Union**
http://www.idu.net

**Assyrian Democratic Movement**
http://www.atranaya.org

**Assyrian Patriotic Party**
http://www.zowaa.com

**The Iraqi National Coalition**
http://www.eatlaf.com

## Supreme Council for the Islamic Revolution in Iraq (SCIRI)

Aside from the Kurds in the north, the Shi'ite SCIRI are the only opposition to Saddam with serious numbers on the ground. Though many of their people were killed during the abortive uprising in 1991, they've regrouped and are believed to have about 10,000 men under arms. This military wing is called the Badr Corps, after the late Iraqi Shi'a leader Ayatollah Mohammed Baqir al-Sadr, who was tortured and executed in 1980—according to popular rumor, he was personally strangled by Chemical Ali.

The SCIRI are currently led by Ayatollah Mohammed Baqir al-Hakim. They pursue a two-pronged strategy of light bombing at home (they've claimed several attacks on security installations in Baghdad) and lobbying abroad (sometimes in cooperation with the INC or INA, sometimes not). Their head office is in Tehran, from where, it is safe to assume, they receive some financial assistance—which makes them allies of both Iran and America. However, they field all enquiries at their base in London.

*Supreme Council for the Islamic Revolution in Iraq*
27a Old Gloucester St.
London WC1N 3XX, UK
Tel.: (44) 20 7371 6815
Fax: (44) 20 7371 2886
sciri@btinternet.com
http://www.sciri.org

## Iraqi Officers Movement and Iraqi Free Officers Movement

We promise we're not making this up. These are two Washington-based groups of exiled Iraqi officers, both of whom want to run Iraq, and both of whom appear to be pursuing this strategy by giving interviews to the few who will listen about how unfit the other is to run Iraq. *DP* has the nagging thought that these aging Napoleons trained in third-world, Soviet-style combat may be the exact same folks who used all those brutal tactics against their own people. For now, anyone who has an Iraqi uniform, a few stars, and a plan, please contact the CIA.

http://www.iraqfoundation.org
http://www.iraqfoundation.org/news/2002/cmar/19_exgeneral.html

## Uncle Sam

Yes, Saddam's nemesis is still America. As we go to press, American support of military action in Iraq is flagging. Unlike the Taliban who considered a Toyota Hilux with a muffler the equivalent of a stealth bomber, the Iraqis have a real army. Saddam has been bolstering the army to about 400,000 troops (identical to the size of his army at the beginning of the last Gulf War, and soon to be major consumers of Zip Ties and white flags). Although Saddam's election returns run at about 99 percent, this is also the percentage of the population that U.S. intelligence thinks would turn on him. So the big question is whether it is going to be an internal uprising (an area where Uncle Sam chokes magnificently) or an invasion (an area where we do splendidly in the opening act). The next big question is: Do we want Iran as a next-door neighbor? . . . Stay tuned.

http://travel.state.gov/iraq.html
http://www.state.gov/www/regions/nea/pmiraq.html
http://www.lexisnexis.com/academic/2upa/lmes/sdCentralIraq1.htm
http://www.msnbc.com/modules/new_battlefield/iraq.asp?cp1=1

## Iran

Saddam hates Shi'ite Iran and wasted hundreds of thousands of Iraqis in a bizarre World War I–style retro-war of trenches and artillery duels in the 1980s. He kicked things off on September 22, 1980, when 400,000 Iraqi troops invaded Iran across an 800-mile front. Eight years later, the war ended with no winner, which didn't stop Saddam from erecting a huge monument to his triumph in downtown Baghdad.

http://www.fas.org/man/dod-101/ops/war/iran-iraq.htm

## Getting In

The normal way to enter Iraq is via Jordan—once you have your visas and paperwork together. Entry is difficult for journos at the time of writing, unless you want to do fluff jobs live from the roof of the al-Rasheed Hotel. Since 9/11, visas have only been issued to a few teams from major news broadcasters, and some print journalists. Most people don't realize that tourists can still visit in groups of five. Once you arrive, you are issued a driver and a guide and you get to play tourist. Don't be surprised, though, if you are issued a full-size coach for your tiny group and two guides. You can get the name of a travel agency (which will send you the required invitation, once you pay) from any Iraqi embassy or representative.

Although tourism brings much-needed hard currency (bring small bills for tips), you have to remember a few things: cell- and sat-phones are verboten, and fancy laptops and strange digital devices will encourage inspection and confiscation. Even your film or video could be deemed suspect, based on your guide's reaction to your touristic style.

Swing that DV cam in the wrong direction and, bam . . . out you go. Business visas are easier to get, but you need a sponsor inside Iraq, and pilgrimage visas are pretty straightforward. Saying you just want to look around and take a few pictures would cause a few chuckles. . . . Oh, and if you are American, on February 8, 1991, U.S. passports ceased to be valid for travel to, in, or through Iraq, and may not be used for that purpose unless a special validation has been obtained. For visa information, please contact the Iraqi Interests Section of the Algerian Embassy, 1801 P Street, NW, Washington, DC 20036; tel.: (202) 483-7500; fax: (202) 462-5066. You need to write a letter stating your name, dates of stay, purpose, and guarantee of financial responsibility.

Keep in mind that Iraqis could care less if you have an American passport, and they don't put any stamps inside. One big catch: You need an AIDS test before you enter the country. Not that Iraq is going to become a sex-tourism hot spot any time soon, but you never know what havoc those lonely, poxed journos will wreak on the local population.

Passport Validation: Without the requisite validation, use of a U.S. passport for travel to, in, or through Iraq may constitute a violation of 18 U.S.C. 1544, and may be punishable by a fine and/or imprisonment. Exemptions to the above restriction are granted to Americans residing in Iraq as of February 8, 1991, who continue to reside there, and to American professional reporters or journalists on assignment there.

The categories of individuals eligible for consideration for a special passport validation are set forth in 22 C.F.R. 51.74. Passport validation requests for Iraq should be forwarded in writing to the following address:

**Deputy Assistant Secretary for Passport Services**
U.S. Department of State
2401 E Street, NW, 9th Floor
Washington, DC 20522-0907
Attn: Office of Passport Policy and Advisory Services
Tel.: (202) 663-2662
Fax: (202) 663-2654

The request must be accompanied by supporting documentation according to the category under which validation is sought. Currently, the four categories of persons specified in 22 C.F.R. 51.74 as being eligible for consideration for passport validation are as follows:

1. **Professional Reporters:** This includes full-time members of the reporting or writing staff of a newspaper, magazine, or broadcasting network whose purpose for travel is to gather information about Iraq for dissemination to the general public. Professional reporters or journalists on assignment are specifically exempted from the passport restriction for Iraq and need not apply for a passport validation.
2. **American Red Cross:** The applicant establishes that he or she is a representative of the American Red Cross or International Red Cross traveling pursuant to an officially sponsored Red Cross mission.
3. **Humanitarian Considerations:** The applicant must establish that his or her trip is justified by compelling humanitarian considerations or for family unification. At this time, "compelling humanitarian considerations" include situations where the applicant can document that an immediate family member is critically ill in Iraq. Documentation concerning family illness must include the name and address of the relative, and be from that relative's physician attesting to the nature and gravity of the illness. "Family unification" situations may include cases in which spouses or minor children are residing in Iraq, and dependent on an Iraqi national spouse or parent for their support.
4. **National Interest:** The applicant's request is otherwise found to be in the national interest.

In all requests for passport validation for travel to Iraq, the name, date, and place of birth for all concerned persons must be given, as well as the U.S. passport numbers.

Documentation as outlined above should accompany all requests. Additional information may be obtained by writing to the U.S. Department of State, or by calling the Office of Passport Policy and Advisory Services at (202) 663-2662.

**U.S. Government Economic Sanctions:** In addition to the restrictions on the use of a U.S. passport discussed above, all U.S. persons (defined as "U.S. citizens, permanent resident aliens of the United States, anyone physically located in the United States, and any entity organized under the laws of the United States") are subject to the Iraq Sanctions Regulations administered by the U.S. Department of the Treasury, Office of Foreign Assets Control (OFAC). For up-to-date information about the embargo on Iraq, please consult OFAC's home page on the Internet at http://www.treas.gov/ofac or via OFAC's Info-by-Fax service at (202) 622-0077.

In August 1990, former President Bush issued Executive Orders 12722 and 12724, imposing economic sanctions against Iraq, including a complete trade embargo. OFAC administers the regulations related to these sanctions, which include restrictions on all financial transactions related to travel to Iraq. These regulations prohibit all travel-related transactions, except as specifically licensed. The only exceptions to this licensing requirement are for persons engaged in journalism or in official U.S. government or UN business.

Sanctions regulations prohibit all U.S. persons from engaging in unauthorized travel-related transactions to or within Iraq. Please note, however, that transactions relating to travel for journalistic activity by persons regularly employed in such capacity by a news-gathering organization are exempt from the prohibition. Please note as well that U.S. persons may engage in travel-related transactions for the sole purpose of visiting immediate family members in Iraq, provided that the U.S. persons seeking travel obtain a license from the Office of Foreign Assets Control. The only exceptions to this licensing requirement are for journalistic activity or for U.S. government or UN business.

Questions concerning these restrictions should be addressed directly to:

**Licensing Division**
Office of Foreign Assets Control
U.S. Department of the Treasury
1500 Pennsylvania Avenue, NW
Washington, D.C. 20220
Tel.: (202) 622-2480
Fax: (202) 622-1657

To apply for a travel license, you have to send a fax to your nearest Iraqi diplomatic mission, which they then forward to the Ministry of

Foreign Affairs in Baghdad (or, at least, that's what they will tell you they're doing with it). U.S. passports are not recognized by Iraq unless you're a hack or you've got some other officially sanctioned reason to be there. And, no, "UN Arms Inspector" would not be a great gag. It should go without saying that if you have any Israeli stamps in your passport, there's no point even applying.

*DP* asked one Iraqi mission what would happen if we just turned up at the border and offered the guards a bunch of money, but they got very cross with us. "What kind of people do you think we are?" they thundered. To which we could only reply, "By our experience, among the most polite, hospitable, educated, and civilized people on Earth, aside from your border guards, who are bunch of greedy, grasping pirates who soaked us for $200 last time we came to visit."

If you're still determined to get in, there are a couple of possibilities. One is to go via Kurdistan (see the Kurdistan chapter) and try to sneak your way across the lines into Iraq proper. However, *DP* really wouldn't want to be the guy who gets caught trying to enter or leave Iraq without proper documentation, and is presumed by his captors—as he most certainly would be—to be in the employ of the CIA or Mossad.

The other is to try and bluff your way in. To do this—assuming you've got the visa—you can drive or fly to Iraq from Amman, the capital of Jordan. The 100-mile-an-hour, cannonball run down Expressway 1 takes about 12 hours, and is done in brand-new, air-conditioned Chevrolet vans, which run out of Amman (your concierge will be able to organize this). The border is extremely tedious. The guards get their jobs by bribing the right people in Baghdad, and their salary is whatever they can extort from the poor swine who attempt to visit their country. You'll be charged $20 for someone to lift your bag out of your truck, another $20 for someone to search it (or $40 not to search it), and so on and so on, until you've been robbed of about $200 and three hours of your cruelly finite existence. If the United States must attack *DP* suggests they could strike an early blow by blasting this border post out of the ground.

You may get slightly less grief upon arrival at Saddam Hussein International Airport in Baghdad, but don't bet on it. Royal Jordanian Airlines fly three times a week between Amman and Baghdad. Schedules and prices are irregular, so check ahead.

**Royal Jordanian Airlines**
http://www.rja.com.jo

**Iraqi Interests Section**
Embassy of Algeria
1801 P Street, NW
Washington, DC 20036
Tel.: (202) 483-7500
Fax: (202) 462-5066

***Iraqi Interests Section***
Embassy of Jordan
21 Queen's Gate
London SW7 5JG, UK
Tel.: (44) 20 7584 7141
Fax: (44) 20 7584 7716
iraqyia.london@talk21.com

***Embassy of the Republic of Iraq***
215 McLeod Street
Ottawa, Ontario K2P 0Z8
Canada
Tel.: 1 (613) 236-9177
Fax: 1 (613) 567-1101
iraqyia@on.aibn.com

Iraqi government officials have watched so many soap operas and pay-per-view dirty movies while out of the country that they think all Westerners are fornicators and deviants. Therefore, all visitors over age 12 and under 65 who plan to stay in Iraq for longer than 5 days (official visitors have 15 days) must call on the Central Public Health Laboratory in al-Tayhariyat al Fennia Square between 8:00 AM and 2:00 PM to either present HIV and syphilis (VDRL) certificates or arrange for a local test—take your own needles. HIV and VDRL certificates valid for Iraq may be obtained in the UK by arranging a blood test with a general practitioner.

> **I**raqi government officials have watched so many soap operas and pay-per-view dirty movies while out of the country that they think all Westerners are fornicators and deviants.

The Iraqis really aren't kidding about this—at the border, it seems to be the only "problem" that can't be "solved" by the transfer of American dollars. If your test is not in order, you will be given the option of taking it right there at the border—don't even think about it—or returning to Baghdad. *DP* saw an official delegation from a Japanese corporation turned around and sent on the eight-hour drive back to Baghdad. And while the desert drive is pretty cool, especially at night, it's the kind of thing you don't want to do twice.

## Getting Around

Iraq has 38,402 kilometers of paved roads. Expressway 1—a 1,200-kilometer, 6-lane freeway—connects Baghdad to Kuwait in the south and runs to Jordan and Syria in the west. A 630-kilometer freeway, Expressway 2, runs north from Baghdad to the Turkish border, where it links up with the modern freeway connecting southeast Turkey to Ankara and Istanbul. Another Baghdad-Basra route is planned via Kut and Amarah, and will be known as Expressway 3. Bus services in Iraq are cheap but uncomfortable.

There are 2,032 kilometers of rail network, including the 461-kilometer Baghdad–Kirkuk–Arbil line, the 528-kilometer Baghdad–Mosul–Yurubiyah standard line, and the 582-kilometer Baghdad–Maaqal–

Umm Qasr standard line. The trains do run, but are best avoided if you're in a hurry.

Iraq now has a domestic air service again, though a significant proportion of the national airline's fleet is still parked at Queen Raniah Airport in Amman, where they were stashed for safekeeping in 1990. The planes that are flying don't seem to crash that often, but it might be worthwhile to check that there are no goat-drawn carts going the same way before you book a ticket.

By far the best way to get around in Iraq is in a rented car. You can probably pick one up for less than $50 a day, driver included—ask the taxi drivers outside the Melia Mansur Hotel. Petrol is a negligible expense in oil-soaked Iraq—literally cheaper than water.

## Dangerous Places

### Baghdad

Any pyromaniac would be right at home. While most people have to wait for July 4 to see fireworks, Baghdad residents get a regular eyeful, all for free. The United States and Britain continue to bomb Baghdad whenever Saddam misbehaves (and the rest of Iraq when he doesn't). When wire-guided ordnance isn't raining on it, Baghdad is possibly the safest, and certainly the friendliest, city you'll ever visit. If you want to relive the glory days of CNN and play "journo under the table," stay at the al-Rasheed Hotel.

**Al-Rasheed Hotel**
Tel: (964) 1 8861000
379 Rooms
Price: US$31 to US$39

### The Kuwaiti Border

The Iraqis are sore losers. U.S. citizens and other foreigners working near the Kuwait-Iraq border have been detained by Iraqi authorities for lengthy periods under harsh conditions. Travelers to that area are in immediate jeopardy of detention by Iraqi security personnel whether in Kuwait or not. Journalists and oil workers have been detained. And there are an untold number of land mines waiting to be unearthed. Feeling nervous? Don't be. "We are able to defend our borders with courage and fight to the last soldier and we have a reserve force at the ready that can be on the battlefield in 24 hours," said Kuwait's chief of staff Lieutenant General Ali al-Mounen. It just depends on whether the discos are closed or not.

http://www.kuwait-info.org/Gulf_War/history_kuwait_iraq_border_dispute.html

### Roads

Expressway 1 from Baghdad to Amman, in Jordan, is still the most popular way in or out for foreigners. The problem isn't the cars, which are mostly spanking new, air-conditioned Chevrolet SUVs, or even the road itself, which is as straight as a billiard cue and flat enough to play snooker on, but stray camels and sleepy drivers in oil tankers. But watch what you say about Saddam en route. Your driver might well be a Jordanian who doesn't understand any English other than "stop" and "go," but he might also be a Mukhabarat agent.

http://www.enrp.undp.org/general/travelto.htm
http://www.nonviolence.org/vitw/documents1c.html

## Dangerous Things

### Being a Friend of Uncle Sam

It seems the safest bet you can make these days to ensure longevity is to become an enemy of the United States. Fidel Castro, Muammar Qaddafi, Kim Jong Il, the countries of Russia, China, Germany, and Japan . . . all seem to be very much in one piece and enjoying themselves immensely in their old age, thank you. Although George publicly said "Get Saddam," Saddam should be a lot more worried if he gets an invitation to the Rose Garden for peace talks.

http://usinfo.state.gov/journals/itps/0301/ijpe/ijpe0301.htm

### Losing at Football

Uday Hussein, Saddam's eldest son, head of the Iraqi Football Federation, and the Middle East's master of motivating halftime speeches, had members of the Iraqi national team tortured after they lost a World Cup qualifying match 3 to 1 to Kazakhstan on June 29, 1997. Uday ordered several members of the team to a secret prison at the offices of the Iraqi Olympic Committee, where the players were caned on the soles of their feet and beaten on their backs. Then they were forced to jump into a sewage tank, to help the wounds go septic. As another punishment, they were forced to kick a concrete football around the prison yard. Perhaps unsurprisingly, the Iraq team was conspicuous by its absence from the 2002 World Cup.

http://www.iraqchat.com/irqworld2.htm

### Journalism

The concept of a free press never really caught on in Iraq, where all media is state-run, and where they expect visiting hacks to conform to similar standards. Try not to incur the same fate as Farzad Bazoft, a reporter for the British newspaper *The Observer,* who was hanged in Baghdad in 1990 after being convicted of espionage. All foreign journalists will be assigned a minder from the Ministry of Information. They will be terrifically enthusiastic about taking you to meet small children dying of cancer and to the air-raid shelter in Amiriya, where American missiles killed scores of civilians during the Gulf War, but are absolutely bloody useless at organizing anything else (although this won't stop them dropping endless hints about their "tip," which, as far as possible, you should avoid giving them). The good news is that most of them aren't terribly bright, and can be lost fairly easily in Baghdad's busy streets. If you want a guide, you're much better off hiring a cab driver outside the Melia Mansur or al-Rashid hotels. Many will speak English—many, indeed, will be engineers or doctors trying to earn some real money. Many won't be Mukhabarat informers, but some might be, so be careful.

http://www.rsf.org
http://www.cpj.org

## Getting Sick

The diseases you should be vaccinated against are typhoid, cholera, and hepatitis. Tap water should be sterilized before drinking, and visitors should avoid consuming ice. Milk is unpasteurized and should be boiled. Comprehensive medical insurance covering repatriation is essential, unless you want to get even sicker in an Iraqi hospital. Many doctors have left the country. Stocks of pharmaceuticals are depleted, and there are severe shortages of even nonprescription drugs. If you need, or think you may need, medication or drugs, bring plenty with you. You can always donate what you don't need on your way out.

## Nuts and Bolts

Iraq has a population of 21.5 million. Although 53.5 percent of the population are Shi'a Muslims, the Sunni Muslims (41.5 percent) are politically dominant. Iraq is not, however, an Islamic state—women are not compelled to wear the veil, and the small Christian population isn't hassled. Iraq is, however, a Saddamic state, so try to keep from sniggering at the uncountable silly portraits of Saddam—any trouble you cause will most likely be avenged against any Iraqis you've been seen with, after you're safely back home.

The Iraqi currency is the dinar, which circulates only in blue 250 dinar notes with guess-who featured prominently on them. There's not much point listing an exchange rate, because the dinar long ago slipped behind the Monopoly dollar on international currency markets, and it will probably have gone down another 2 percent by the time you get to the end of this paragraph. You can change your greenbacks for a rucksack full of dinar at any bank or hotel. The dinar is useful for most meals and other incidentals, but hotels, antique stores, and most taxi drivers will want to be paid in real money. If you can't get rid of all your dinars (and you can't), the individual notes make terrific souvenir bookmarks for friends at home, and the bundles are great kindling and work out to be cheaper than firelighters.

Despite years and years of sanctions, there is no shortage of anything in Baghdad, so long as you can afford to pay for it. Most ordinary Iraqis, of course, cannot—doctors and engineers are lucky to take home $100 a year. The good news for souvenir hunters with impregnable consciences is that Baghdad's antique shops are a trove of astonishing bargains, as wealthier families bumping down the economic staircase flog off heirlooms to buy bread. Saddam Hussein watches, rugs, clocks, badges, and posters are available in major hotels or in the shops on al-Rashid Street.

**Make sure you get a room with a working television— there's nothing like a few hours of Saddamvision to get you off to sleep.**

In Baghdad, accommodation options revolve around three previously grand but now rather run-down hotels: the Palestine (tel.: (964) 1 887 5641), the Melia Mansur (tel.: (964) 1 537 0041), and the al-Rasheed (tel: (964) 1 886 1000). The latter, famous for its George Bush, Sr. doormat, is the best known, most comfortable, and most expensive hotel, but the rooms are known to be bugged. *DP*'s tip is the Palestine, which has great views over the Tigris River, friendly staff, and shouldn't cost more than $40 a night. If there were any microphones in the lampshades, we couldn't find them. Make sure you get a room with a working television—there's nothing like a few hours of Saddamvision to get you off to sleep.

Eating out in Baghdad is surprisingly good, especially at the specialty restaurants along the Tigris which cook carp in the traditional fashion, known as *masgouf*, in which the carp is killed, cleaned, and filleted on the spot, turned inside out, and roasted slowly in front of an open fire. (Just don't tell any jokes about the president over dinner, or the same might happen to you.) Alcohol is available in most major hotels and a few shops. Electricity is 220V. There are a couple of Internet cafés in Baghdad now, but access to sites is restricted, and you should work on the assumption that anything you mail is being read by a third party.

The United States, Britain, and Canada have no diplomatic representation in Iraq. The U.S. government is not in a position to accord normal consular services to U.S. citizens in Iraq. U.S. government interests are represented by the government of Poland—which, as a protecting power, is able to provide only limited emergency services to U.S. citizens. European citizens in trouble could try throwing themselves on the mercy of the French or Danish missions.

**U.S. Interests Section**
Embassy of Poland
Opposite Foreign Ministry Club
Masbah Quarter
Alwiyah
Baghdad, Iraq
Tel.: (964) 1 718 9267
Fax: (964) 1 718 9297

**Embassy of the Republic of France**
Quarter Abu Nawas
House 102, Street 55
Baghdad, Iraq
Tel.: (964) 1 719 6061

**Royal Danish Consulate General**
House 14, Street 2
929 Hai Babel
Baghdad, Iraq
Tel.: (964) 1 717 0521
Fax: (964) 1 717 0635
latco@uruklink.net
http://www.ambassade-info.dk/
dkiraqbagcg.htm

# Dangerous Days

| | |
|---|---|
| **1/01/03** | 115,000 U.S. troops in region. |
| **12/19/02** | Secretary of State Colin Powell says Iraq fails to meet UN resolution. |
| **11/13/02** | Saddam accepts UN weapons inspectors back into Iraq. |
| **5/14/02** | UN Security Council overhauls sanctions to release more humanitarian aid. |
| **4/8/02** | Iraq announces that it will suspend all oil exports during May in protest against Israeli military action against Palestinian cities on the West Bank. |
| **3/13/02** | George W. Bush promises that Saddam Hussein will be "dealt with." |
| **1/30/02** | The United States restores funding to umbrella opposition group the Iraqi National Congress. |
| **1/30/02** | Iraq accuses the United States of practicing "state terror." |
| **1/29/02** | George W. Bush makes "Axis of Evil" speech. |
| **11/25/01** | Six men are arrested in Baghdad and accused of planning terrorist attacks and working for Iran. |
| **7/11/01** | One person is injured by a bomb explosion in Baghdad. |
| **3/21/01** | Six are injured by a bomb in Baghdad. |

| | |
|---|---|
| 3/15/01 | Two are killed and 20 injured by a bomb at a bus depot in Baghdad. |
| 2/24/01 | One person is injured by a bomb in a residential area of Baghdad. |
| 2/16/01 | U.S. and British aircraft launch slightly heavier raids than usual, attacking 5 antiaircraft radar stations around Baghdad, and 20 others elsewhere in Iraq. |
| 5/01 | Qusay Hussein is elected to the leadership of the Ba'ath party. |
| 2/19/99 | Grand Ayatollah Sayyed Muhammad Sadiq al-Sadr, spiritual leader of Iraq's Shi'a minority, is assassinated in Najaf. |
| 12/16/98 | Operation Desert Fox: Baghdad is bombed for four days after UN weapons inspectors are expelled from Iraq. |
| 11/22/98 | UN weapons inspectors leave Iraq. |
| 12/12/96 | Uday Hussein is seriously injured in an assassination attempt in Baghdad. |
| 8/31/96 | Iraqi forces enter Arbil at the invitation of KDP. |
| 5/96 | Iraq is permitted to sell $2 billion worth of oil over six months to buy food and medicine. |
| 2/23/96 | Saddam's sons-in-law are executed on the orders of Saddam Hussein. |
| 2/20/96 | Saddam's sons-in-law return to Iraq after being promised a pardon by Saddam Hussein. |
| 10/15/95 | Saddam Hussein's presidency is confirmed for another seven years in a referendum. There are no other candidates, and Saddam wins 99.6 percent of the vote. |
| 8/95 | Saddam's sons-in-law, the Industry and Minerals Minister General Hussein Kamil Hasan al-Majid, and the Director of the Military Industrialization Organization Saddam Hussein Kamil Hasan al-Majid, defect from Iraq along with their families. All are granted asylum in Jordan. |
| 4/16/91 | U.S. President George Bush announces that U.S. troops will enter northern Iraq to create a safe haven for displaced Kurds around Zakhu. |
| 3/3/91 | Iraq signs a cease-fire agreement with Allied Forces, ending the Gulf War. |
| 2/27/91 | Kuwait is liberated. Allied Forces in Kuwait and Iraq suspend military operations against Iraq. |
| 2/24/91 | Allied Forces launch the ground assault against Iraqi forces occupying Kuwait. |

IRAQ

| | |
|---|---|
| 2/14/91 | U.S. aircraft strike an air-raid shelter in the Baghdad suburb of Amiriyah, killing more than 300 people. |
| 1/30/91 | Iraqi and multinational force elements have their first combat engagement in Khafji in the Persian Gulf War. |
| 1/17/91 | Operation Desert Storm begins. |
| 11/29/90 | UN Security Council Resolution 678 authorizes "all necessary means" to enforce Resolution 660. |
| 8/8/90 | Iraq announces formal annexation of Kuwait. |
| 8/2/90 | Iraqi forces invade Kuwait. UN Security Council Resolution 660 calls for immediate withdrawal. |
| 3/15/90 | Farzad Bazoft, an Iranian-born reporter for British newspaper *The Observer,* is hanged in Baghdad after being convicted of spying. |
| 8/20/88 | Cease-fire effective between Iraq and Iran. |
| 3/17/88 | Iraq uses chemical weapons in a raid on the Kurdish town of Halabja, killing thousands. |
| 8/15/86 | Turkish troops raid Kurdish rebel camps in Iraq. |
| 6/7/81 | Israeli warplanes attack an Iraqi nuclear research center at Tuwaythah, near Baghdad. |
| 9/4/80 | Iran shells Iraqi towns near the border; Iran-Iraq war begins. |
| 7/16/79 | President al-Bakr resigns, and is succeeded by Vice President Saddam Hussein. |
| 1972 | Iraq nationalizes the Iraq Petroleum Company. |
| 7/17/68 | Abd al-Rahman Muhammad Arif overthrown by a Ba'athist coup. General Ahmad Hasan al-Bakr becomes president. |
| 4/13/66 | Abd al-Salam Muhammad Arif killed in helicopter crash. His brother, Major General Abd al-Rahman Muhammad Arif, becomes president. |
| 11/18/63 | Abd al-Salam Muhammad Arif, along with senior military officers, overthrows the Ba'athist government. |
| 2/8/63 | Qasim overthrown in a coup led by the Ba'ath Party. Former Qasim ally Colonel Abd al-Salam Muhammad Arif becomes president. |
| 7/14/58 | Faisal II is overthrown in a military coup and executed. Brigadier Abd al-Karim Qasim becomes prime minister. |
| 4/8/47 | Iraqi Ba'ath Party founded. |
| 4/3/39 | King Ghazi killed in a suspicious "car accident." |
| 4/28/37 | Saddam Hussein born in Tikrit. |

| 10/3/32 | Iraq becomes an independent nation. |
| 8/23/21 | Faisal I, the son of the Sharif of Mecca, is imported by the British to become Iraq's first king. |
| 4/25/20 | Iraq placed under British mandate. |

## In a Dangerous Place: Baghdad

### IRAQ

Baghdad, like all Arab cities, is an island surrounded by oceans of sand. Anyone who doubts how isolated the Iraqi capital has become from the lack of commercial air traffic over the last decade, needs only to try going there by road.

Iraq's pariah status dates from August 1990, when it invaded Kuwait. Five months of sanctions and threats were followed, in January 1991, by a vast multinational military effort to take Kuwait back. Operation Desert Storm was the first twenty-first-century war: the first conflict covered by round-the-clock television news, the first to see (or, in the case of Iraq's air defenses, not see) the deployment of "stealth" aircraft and "smart" missiles, the first chance since the end of the Cold War for the West, led by the United States, to display its technological superiority over any potential enemy. Iraqi losses were massive, allied casualties minimal: The current conventional wisdom, demonstrated in Yugoslavia and Kosovo in 1999, that we are able to decide that a cause can be worth fighting for but not risking injury for, was born in the Iraqi desert.

Nearly 10 years later, I'm going to Baghdad not because of the war that was fought then, but because of the war that has been fought since, and is being fought now, by missile, by bomb, and by sanction, if not by the light of the world's television cameras. America's longest war since Vietnam, and Britain's longest since Napoleon was dispatched to St. Helena in 1815, is costing billions and killing thousands, and it's lucky if it gets an occasional mention after the stories about a skateboarding parrot and the Ping-Pong results.

It's the 10th anniversary of Desert Storm and, retrospectives aside, the explosions have been loud enough to rouse the BBC and CNN on only a couple of occasions. In 1993, America launched a major aerial offensive on the ridiculous pretext that Iraq had once "plotted to kill" former president George Bush (Cuba somehow overcame a similar temptation to react by bombing Washington). In December 1998, Operation Desert Fox, undertaken with British cooperation, was launched to "degrade," whatever that might mean, Iraq's ability to manufacture weapons of mass destruction (this was apparently less of a concern during the '80s, when Iraq used weapons of mass destruction on neighboring Iran and its own Kurdish population, and Britain and America traded with Iraq quite cheerfully). Today, British and American aircraft patrol, and regularly bomb, "no-fly zones" in the north and south of Iraq. Trade sanctions still apply, in a bid to force Iraq to readmit the UN weapons inspectors it sent packing in 1998.

Our hired Chevrolet truck barrels across Iraq by night, beneath a perfectly black sky decorated by a mesmerizing infinity of stars—it's like looking at a bright light through black silk. On the smooth two-lane highway rebuilt by Iraq after the Gulf War, there are no hazards other than sleep and stray camels. The former is kept at bay by coffee, brewed and poured one-handed by our driver while the cruise control is set at 170 kilometers an hour; as for the latter, we keep our eyes open and our fingers crossed.

The only outpost of anything remotely resembling civilization out here is a truck-stop known as One-Sixty. When we ask our driver to point us to the facilities, he manages to communicate that the toilets at One-Sixty are enough of an ordeal by day, and suggests a rank of oil tankers parked on the forecourt. As we pick a tire each and let it rip, I mutter something about how hilarious it would be if we were interrupted by some swarthy, kaffiyeh-clad figure with a Kalashnikov slung under one arm. No sooner have the titters of agreement started when exactly such an apparition appears.

He freezes, just long enough for me to compose a prayer whose plea is twofold: (1) Please, no, not like this; and (2) Please, please, *please*, make him say, "Sorry to bother you" or "Bunch up, there's room for one more" or "Welcome to Iraq—I kiss you!" or something else that would make an equally perfect conclusion to an opening paragraph. But he just giggles, as well he might, and scuttles back into the shadows.

Though life in Baghdad is hard, there is plenty of it. On al-Rasheed Street, the shopping district that runs by the Tigris River, the work day is the Middle Eastern idea of business as usual, which is to say that when scenes as chaotic as this occur in European cities, they are broken up by riot police. Surreally decrepit cars career in umpteen directions in a cacophony of horns, backfires, and shouts; donkey carts and nervous pedestrians compete for gaps in the traffic. On the crowded footpaths beneath the overhanging buildings, tea vendors carrying silver trays of tulip-shaped glasses weave deftly through the meandering shoppers, never spilling a drop.

You can buy almost anything here. There is the sublime: custom-made suits, antique watches, hand-woven carpets, beautiful copper and silverware, all at the bargain prices common to sanctions-wracked pariah states. There is the ridiculous: 1980 editions of long-defunct British teen magazines *Pink* and *Mates,* with features including "A Night Out with Gary Numan" and "Les McKeown: What's He Been Up To?" There are also the ideal places to pause for refreshments: fabulous fruit juice bars, where delicious liquefied oranges, bananas, strawberries, and pomegranates are poured from luridly colored blenders.

It doesn't look like anyone is suffering a shortage of anything, except for windshield replacements (the view of Baghdad from any taxi is positively kaleidoscopic). But however healthy the city's pulse might feel, Baghdad can never escape the fact that the world—principally the United States and Great Britain—is leaning on several crucial pressure points. In Mackenzie's Bookshop, I get to talking with the proprietor, Lernik Bedrosian. Lernik is an Iraqi of Armenian descent. Besides working in the bookshop, she also presents the English-language bulletins on Iraqi Satellite Television.

"This shop used to be bigger," she explains. "Before."

"Before" is a popular word in Baghdad. It means "before" the epically pointless war with neighboring Iran in the 1980s that left a million dead or wounded, "before" the Gulf War, "before" the decade of sanctions and worse that Iraq has suffered since. If you want to look for the common element in these unhappy occurrences, look to the rise to power of Saddam Hussein.

"We can't get books anymore," says Lernik glumly. "That's why everything in here is so old."

Mackenzie's English-language stock is a random assortment of fifth-hand school texts, dog-eared novels, and musty reference hardbacks. Almost nothing predates 1990.

"We miss that connection with literature," says Lernik. "And our doctors and engineers have to make do with books that are 10, 20 years out of date. Why is this?"

I find a coffee-stained 1978 paperback edition of Tom Stoppard's *Rosencrantz & Guildenstern Are Dead,* and decide it would make a nice keepsake, though I feel uneasy about the idea that my visit to Iraq will result in there being one less book in the country.

Lernik won't take my money. "You are a guest here," she smiles.

This is not the first or last time that photographer Alan Clarke, joining me on assignment for *The Face* magazine, and I are treated with extraordinary—and, all things considered, surprising—generosity and warmth during our visit. It doesn't hurt that we have been helped on our way by British Member of Parliament George Galloway and his antisanctions charity, the Mariam Appeal, who are in town for a conference of solidarity organizations. Since the Mariam Appeal drove an ancient red double-decker bus from London to Baghdad in 1999, Galloway has acquired superstar status in Iraq. He arrived in Baghdad the day before us, on the first flight from Britain since the Gulf War—a private jet, hired from the government of Bulgaria in defiance of the embargo. There hadn't been room for me and Alan on the eight-seater plane, so we'd done it the hard way, on the 11-hour, pedal-to-the-metal cannonball-run across the desert from Amman.

But even when Clarke and I are out by ourselves, we almost wonder whether Saddam has ordered a regimen of overwhelming hospitality, aimed at making visitors feel even more guilty about the sanctions than they might already. A taxi driver invites us home to meet his family, then has to be bullied into accepting payment for his day's labors—twenty dollars—because "I don't take money from friends." The owner of an antique store is nigh tearful on being told we can't stay for lunch because the inescapable kindness of our previous two appointments has already made us an hour late for our next one. A silver-haired gent approaches me in the street, and presses into my hand two new 1973 British 10-pence coins. When we go to a soccer match one evening, to see league leaders al-Zawrah play al-Sinaah, our appearance by the side of the pitch elicits a generous ovation from the grandstand. In front of the Milia Mansur Hotel, the artists constructing a vast sawdust propaganda mosaic on the forecourt talk us through their work in progress every morning; at the end of the week, they have finished a garish purple, green, and gold rendering of Jerusalem's Dome of the Rock, imprisoned by bars made from the stripes of the American flag, and held shut by a padlock marked "Israel."

The only Iraqis who are other than painstakingly obliging are the guards back at the border and the men from the Ministry of Information in Baghdad. The guards hit us for bribes totalling US$150, which we pay up, under threat of baggage searches and blood tests. It would have been more, had some thoughtful soul at the Iraqi consulate in Amman not written Galloway's name, in Arabic, on our visas. And it is the job of the men at the ministry to keep an eye on visitors, especially those with press cards. Clarke and I find ourselves saddled with a camp little chap with an extraordinary comb-over hairdo, whom I'll call Sadoun.

Sadoun is a model company man, down to his gold-plated Saddam Hussein wristwatch. He is very helpful about showing us things like the al-Amiriya air-raid shelter, where American missiles incinerated 408 civilians on Valentine's Day, 1991, and the mosaic of George Bush, Sr. in the floor of the al-Rasheed Hotel—situated so it is impossible to enter the building without treading on Bush's face. He is also solicitous about our request to photograph the grotesque monument to the war with Iran—enormous crossed swords held by immense fists, reputedly modeled on Saddam's, over piles of Iranian army helmets—as long as we do so from an angle that prevents us from seeing "sensitive" installations nearby.

Sadoun is rather less helpful about organizing anything else, especially when it involves his ultimate boss, however tangentially, or either of Saddam's equally delightful sons (Uday, who runs much of Iraq's media, including youth radio station Shebab FM, and Qusay, who is responsible for military and intelligence services). Saddam Hussein is a name that few in Baghdad dare speak. Locals refer furtively to "the president." Some foreigners have taken to using the less-respectful soubriquet Trevor, which allows conversations to proceed normally even in earshot of ministry drones—a necessary diversion, because Trevor is everywhere in Baghdad.

Among things named after Trevor are the airport, a hospital, a suburb, and what will be, when finished, the biggest mosque on earth. The shops in Baghdad's dilapidated "five star" hotels sell Trevor rugs, Trevor watches, Trevor clocks, Trevor plates, Trevor badges, and a six-volume box-set of Trevor's collected ravings, which includes such alluring titles as *On History, Heritage and Revolution*, *The Revolution and Woman In Iraq*, and *One Trench or Two*? (and I thought that he had no sense of humor). Paintings, posters, and mosaics of Trevor cover almost every flat surface in his capital, displaying him in military uniform, traditional robes, business suit, tweed hunting gear, and—my particular favorite—a most fetching beige slacks-and-waistcoat ensemble, with a bouquet of lilies in one arm and a white panama hat tipped raffishly over one eye (I can only hope that the inscription beneath it is Arabic for "Hello, ladies").

Happily, evading the ministry men requires only the most elementary talent for subterfuge. We wander Baghdad unguarded, contentedly picturing Sadoun fuming, "Curse their ingenious pretense of going for a short walk and then staying out all day!" In the shops and cafés, people are reluctant to complain explicitly, but truths lurk in the details. The most minor transaction requires a thick wad of blue 250-dinar notes, all embellished with Trevor's portrait—the currency, trading at around 1,700 dinar to the dollar, is worthless, unless you're buying petrol (when we leave Iraq, we watch our driver fill his 160-litre tank for 3,000 dinar, or about $1.80). Almost every taxi driver we hire is a degree-holding professional (teacher, engineer, radiologist), forced to abandon his vocation because "there was no money in it." The $20 they charge for a few hours' driving is four months' wages for a Baghdad doctor.

The absurdity is that Iraq could be monstrously rich. Beneath it lie what might be the biggest oil reserves in the world, but only a limited amount may be (legally) exported under the UN oil-for-food program—a 1996 amendment to the sanctions which allows Iraq to sell oil to buy food, medicine, and other essentials. It's a nice idea, in theory. In practice, it does what sanctions always do. It makes ill people even sicker, impoverishes the poor still further, and keeps power in the hands of the powerful.

Nonetheless, in the café-bar of one hotel—decorated by a huge oil portrait of Trevor drinking tea—I ask a few people to think the patently unthinkable. If the people of Iraq are caught between the anvil of Trevor's brutal and stupid dictatorship and the hammer of the outside world's stupid and brutal sanctions, then the obvious solution would seem to be a change in leadership, wouldn't it? The responses are startling.

"This is not a police state," says Karim Wasfi, 27 years old. "This is a state where there is a tradition, which we believe in, of offering a certain level of respect to our leaders. There is discussion, but it is respectful. I don't consider the right to call the president names, or know about his private life, necessarily democratic."

Karim is no doctrinaire dupe. Though an Iraqi citizen—and principal cellist in the Iraqi National Symphony Orchestra—he is an American resident, having studied in Indianapolis for four years.

"I wanted to prove myself in the country that attacked me," he says, "but I've come back to take part in cultural life in Iraq." Karim's ambition is to tour Europe, performing works by composers native to each country. "I want to be a bridge between civilizations. If people can communicate, directly, situations like this won't happen."

Karim's sister, Naghin, 20 years old, is an arts reporter for Iraqi Satellite Television. There is no independent media in Iraq, and little access to anything else—the Internet hardly exists, and mobile phones have to be left at a restaurant in Ruwasheid, the last Jordanian town before the border. Asked whether she would like to work for a channel that wasn't state-run, Naghin is also surprisingly sanguine.

"If the media was free, bad ideas would get out as well as good ones. It's not good to have no control."

Naghin introduces me to the extravagantly bearded and bespectacled figure of Khdayr Meri, explaining that he is Baghdad's current literary sensation. *The Days of Madness and Honey,* Meri's memoir of his time in a psychiatric hospital during the Gulf War, is being well reviewed in all the (state-owned) newspapers.

"Freedom must have responsibility," he says.

And a writer's responsibility is to serve the state?

"Sure. That is the sacrifice we make. But what I am concerned with lies beyond politics."

A couple of days later, making conversation in another genial, noisy traffic jam, I ask Karim if he thinks that, in a hypothetical (and unimaginable) free election, Trevor would emerge victorious.

"Yeah, I think so. He knows how to play the game."

While Trevor has, certainly, played it well enough that he is now at war with a second generation of the Bush family, there is at least one vote he wouldn't get. I meet Amir (which isn't his name), 21 years old (which isn't his age), in a shoe shop (which isn't where he works). As he wraps my purchase, he tells me about growing up in Baghdad in the '80s and '90s, of the fear of attack by Iran, of the terror of Desert Storm ("My windows were blown in on the first night"), and of the subsequent air raids in 1993 and 1998 ("I thought they were trying to kill us all"). He tells me about his older brother, who took part in the invasion of Kuwait, and how he'd been unpopular with other soldiers for refusing to participate in the general pillaging ("Our father did not raise us to be thieves"). His brother walked home to Baghdad ("I didn't recognize him"). Kuwaiti loot was not far behind ("I was offered 10 gold Rolexes for 200 dollars, but I didn't take them . . . it might have made this life easier, but I would have to answer to God in the next").

Then he pauses, and looks at me with a huge, exaggerated smile. "Our president," he hisses, grinning wildly, "doesn't care." He winks. I get the hint, start nodding and smiling.

"There is no freedom here," he continues, chuckling merrily, "If anyone heard me talking like this, or even saw me looking serious, after you had gone, they would take not just me, but my whole family."

I ask, all but slapping my thigh, where they would be taken. This gets another big laugh.

"My friend," he says, "I talk to you like this because I am so miserable."

I say I should probably go, and he nods, sadly, and I leave, wondering at the desperation that can drive someone to put the lives of his family in the hands of some scruffy foreigner who has just wandered in off the street.

The West's continuing persecution of Iraq is not accomplishing much, or at least not much good. It does not trouble Iraq's wealthy and powerful, it allows a preposterous tyrant to pass himself off as a heroic leader, and even at the most selfish level, it amounts to commercial hara-kiri on behalf of Western industry—Iraq's oil, and urgent need for modernization, could make someone very rich.

And it kills people. Marwan Khalil Ibrahim, 13 years old, lies on a grubby mattress on a bed in the cancer ward of Trevor Hospital for Children, his face and clothes covered in the blood hemorrhaging from his nose and mouth. His mother, Amonah, her face like stone beneath her veil, flaps flies away from him with a square of cardboard. Marwan was diagnosed with cancer seven years ago, she says, but this is the worst he's ever been. She brought Marwan, who does not appear to pose a meaningful threat to regional security, to the hospital ten days ago. She doesn't know when, or if, she'll be taking him home.

Cancer in Iraqi children, according to the hospital's doctors, has increased 400 percent since the Gulf War—an effect of the depleted uranium munitions dropped by Allied Forces. Now the countries whose shells caused the illness block supplies of the medicines that could treat it; feel free to write to George W. Bush or Tony Blair and congratulate them on this sane and productive use of your money. Bits and pieces do get through, the doctors admit, but the continuity necessary for long-term treatment can't be guaranteed.

At the moment, Marwan depends on a machine called a cell separator. This removes platelets—the cells that cause clotting—from blood. These are then transfused into Marwan in a bid to stop his bleeding; his drip consumes ten 300ml bags every day. There is only one such machine in Baghdad, dating from the '70s, and it frequently breaks down. Iraq cannot import another cell separator, as such machines are deemed "dual use"—it could be used to treat soldiers, or stripped for parts, or dropped out of an airplane onto the heads of Trevor's enemies.

I ask a nearby doctor, who looks uncannily like a gaunt, haunted cousin of Groucho Marx, if there is any particular treatment that he would like to be able to offer Marwan, but cannot because of the sanctions.

"Not at this stage, no," says the doctor.

Back in London, I feel it only fair to allow Her Majesty's government to explain itself. The man charged with defending British policy in Iraq is a foreign office spokesman—let's call him Afos. He begins by recapping what an awfully bad man Saddam Hussein is.

"Saddam Hussein," he explains, "has used horrendous weapons of mass destruction against neighboring nations and his own people."

We can presumably rest assured that he has used the ones he bought from Britain only to keep the rabbits down. A fondness for slaughtering his own citizens en masse is a distinction Saddam shares with Tony Blair's drinking buddy and Russian premier, Vladimir Putin.

"Russia did not use biological or chemical weapons in Chechnya," says Afos, as if this makes much difference to those killed in Grozny by such dreary, conventional methods as aerial bombardment.

"Sanctions work," insists Afos. "Saddam hasn't attacked his own people or neighbors since they were imposed."

This is reminiscent of the joke about the man apprehended while sprinkling a mysterious powder in Trafalgar Square. "Elephant repellent," he explains to the policeman. "There are no elephants here," replies the puzzled cop. "Well," says the man, "it must be good stuff, then."

"As for the Iraqi people," continues Afos, "our quarrel is not with them. We recognize that sanctions cause some suffering."

*Some suffering.* An interesting phrase. Sanctions have contributed directly to the deaths of 500,000 Iraqi children since the end of the Gulf War—5,000 a month, or thereabouts.

"The figures are exaggerated by the Iraqi regime," says Afos.

The figure of half a million comes from UNICEF. Baghdad, for its part, blames 1.3 million deaths on the sanctions. We can therefore infer that "too many dead kids" is a number somewhere between the two figures.

"The Iraqi government plays politics with the suffering of ordinary people."

Pots and kettles call each other black.

"The oil-for-food program means money is available for food and medicine. The Iraqi government stockpiles it."

Two former UN humanitarian coordinators, Denis Halliday and Hans von Sponeck, say otherwise.

"The oil-for-food program has provided £16 billion worth of aid to the Iraqi people. . . . It is making a real difference in northern Iraq, where Saddam doesn't rule." The Royal Air Force are also regular visitors to the north, flying 440 missions in the no-fly zone in 2000, up till November 25.

"We patrol those areas to protect civilians. Saddam hasn't been able to get at them in the same way."

He hasn't had to. In the northern no-fly zone, according to John Nichol, the RAF pilot famously shot down during the Gulf War, Turkish aircraft regularly bomb the Kurdish civilians the zone is supposed to protect from Saddam. In the south, RAF combat aircraft flew 950 missions in 2000 alone, bombing on 31 occasions, to mystifying indifference from British media.

"Iraqi ground defenses attack our planes."

Leaving aside the fact that the Iraqis haven't hit one in ten years of trying, they couldn't amuse themselves by putting RAF jets in missile lock if the planes weren't there in the first place.

"We don't want him to invade his neighbors, or use weapons of mass destruction."

And that's quite right, too. But two UN weapons inspectors, Scott Ritter and Richard Butler, have said that sanctions will not encourage Iraq to open their defense installations to inspectors.

"If Iraq allowed inspectors in today, sanctions would be suspended within a matter of months."

Which is to say, "a matter of months," multiplied by 5,000 dead children. Iraq has offered to allow inspectors in, in return for an immediate lifting of sanctions.

"Our policy is to remove the threat posed by Iraq's weapons and relieve the suffering of Iraqi people."

The policy does neither. And the sanctions are crumbling, anyway—civilian flights from France, Greece, Austria, Jordan, and Russia have all landed in Baghdad recently—and Britain is going to miss out when Iraq is opened up to the world.

"I'm afraid there are other concerns than the purely commercial," says Afos.

Hurray for an ethical foreign policy!

*—Andrew Mueller*

Jerusalem

★ ★ ★ ★
# ISRAEL/PALESTINE

## An Eye for an Eye

One disturbing hallmark of *DP* over the last seven years has been that our Israel chapter stubbornly has refused to change. Frustrated by the region's resistance to our need to update, in *DP4* we had the audacity to suggest that things might get better. Casting a seasoned eye over the region and urged on by a pathetic spasm of optimism, we jauntily viewed the Israelis and the Palestinians as two punch-drunk boxers, warily eyeing each other, realizing that neither side would throw in the towel. Finally, both sides were slowly coming around to the idea that racism, roadblocks, braggadocio, bulldozers, suicide bombers, hot air, air strikes, rubber bullets, and assassinations were not the best means of communicating with each other. Okay, okay, so we can't be right all the time. What was starting to look like "eye to eye" quickly reverted to "an eye for an eye" and since regressed to total blindness. The Holy Land is the only place we can think of where Stalin or even the Khmer

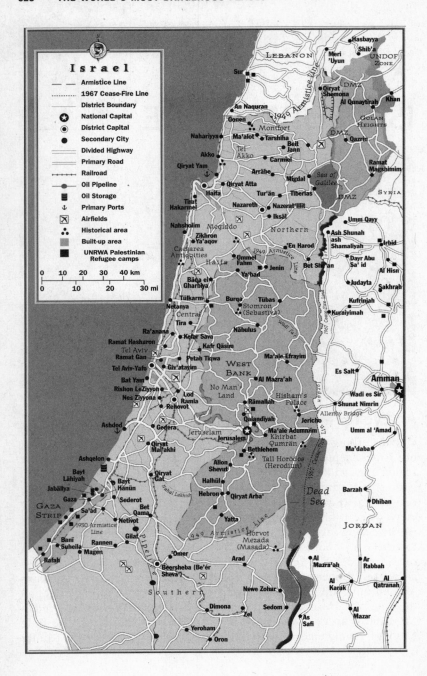

# Israel

| | |
|---|---|
| —— | Armistice Line |
| ·········· | 1967 Cease-Fire Line |
| ·········· | District Boundary |
| ✪ | National Capital |
| ◉ | District Capital |
| ● | Secondary City |
| ═══ | Divided Highway |
| ═══ | Primary Road |
| ┼──┼ | Railroad |
| ●—— | Oil Pipeline |
| ▤ | Oil Storage |
| ↓ | Primary Ports |
| ☒ | Airfields |
| ⁚∴ | Historical area |
| ▨ | Built-up area |
| ■ | UNRWA Palestinian Refugee camps |

0  10  20  30  40 km
0  10  20  30 mi

LEBANON

Hasbayya
Shib'a
Meri 'Uyun
UNDOF ZONE

Sur

An Naquran
Qonen

DMZ

Qiryat Shemona
Al Qunaytirah
Khan

GOLAN HEIGHTS

Nahariyya
Ma'alot
Tarshiha
Beit Jann
DMZ
Qazrin

Akko
Tel Akko
Carmiel
Arräbe
Migdal
Ramat Magshimim

Qiryat Yam
Qiryat Atta
Tur'än
Tiberias
Sea of Galilee

Haifa
Tel Hakarmel
Nazareth
Nazerat'Illit
SYRIA
DMZ

Nahsholim
Megiddo
Zikhron Ya'aqov
Iksäl
Northern
Umm Qayy
Ash Shunah ash Shamaliyah
Irbid

Caesarea Antiquities
Haifa
Ummel Fahm
'En Harod
Dayr Abu Sa'id
Al Hisn

Bäqa el Gharbiya
Ya'bad
Jenin
Bet Shi'an
Judayta
Sakhrah

Tülkarm
Burqa
Tübas
Stomron (Sebastiya)
Kufrinjah
Kuraiyimah

Netanya
Central
Tira
Näbulus
Wadi Fa

Ra'anana
Kefar Sava
Kafr Qäsim
Ma'ale Efrayim
Es Salt
Amman

Ramat Hasharon
Tel Aviv
Ramat Gan
Petah Tiqwa
WEST BANK
Wadi es Sir
Shunat Nimrin

Tel Aviv-Yafo
Giv'atayim
No Man's Land
Al Mazra'ah
Allenby Bridge

Bat Yam
Rishon LeZiyyon
Lod
Ramla
Rämallah
Hisham's Palace
Jericho
Umm al 'Amad

Nes Ziyyona
Rehovot
Qalandiyah
Ma'ale Adummim
Ma'daba

Ashdod
Gedera
Jerusalem
Jerusalem
Khirbat Qumrän

Qiryat Mal'akhi
Bethlehem
Tall Horódos (Herodium)

Ashqelon
Allon Shevut
Dead Sea
Barzah
Dhiban

Bayt Lähiyah
Qiryat Gat
Halhül

Jaballya
Bayt Hänun
Hebron
Qiryat Arba'
JORDAN

GAZA STRIP
Gaza
Sederot
Bet Qama
Yatta

Sa'ad
Netivot
1950 Armistice Line
Gilat
Horvot Mezada (Masada)

Baní Suheila
Rannen
Magen
Arad
Al Mazra'ah
Ar Rabbah

Rafah
'Omer
Al Karak
Al Qatranah

Beersheba (Be'ér Sheva')
Newe Zohar
Al Mazar

Dimona
Zel
Sedom
As Safi

Yeroham
Oron
Southern
JORDAN

1949 Armistice Line
1967 Cease-Fire Line
Pipeline
Nahal Lakhish

Rouge could suggest improvements. The influx of Russian Jews who simply want to have a nice place to live might disagree, but there is an ever-growing group of Israelis and Palestinians who might be willing to put biblical entitlement aside just to be able to go to work or a restaurant without becoming a statistic.

How bad is it? CNN reports that one in every 25,000 Israelis has been killed by a terrorist attack. . . . in a six-month period. That number is sure to be an optimistic understatement by the time you read this. In this remarkably logic-and-compromise-resistant war, both sides are losing. The modern peace process reached its giddy height in September 1994, when Israel's then–Prime Minister Yitzhak Rabin and Palestine Liberation Organization Chairman Yasser Arafat signed a Declaration of Principles in which Israel recognized the PLO, and vice versa. If you had slapped a tea towel on Rabin or thick glasses on Arafat, the diminutive players might have looked like gap-toothed, kissing cousins. Fat checks were cut and things looked rosy. Of course, Israel continued to build settlements on Palestinian land on the West Bank and the Gaza Strip, and while Arafat's wife was out shopping for curtains, militant Palestinian groups declared that their goal of destroying Israel remained unchanged—but still, it was a start. Though a far-right Jewish hard-core group and the likes of Hamas did their best to destroy the fledgling peace process by force—the casualties included Rabin himself, shot dead by a Jewish extremist in November 1995—most people on both sides were weary enough of fighting to give any sort of peace a chance. Peace looked good on the Middle East, like a new paint job on a '72 Pinto or a makeover on an aging truck-stop hooker. Hey, it's still ugly on the inside, but it's not so hard to look at everyday—from the outside at least. Palestinian and Israeli alike also noticed that when they stopped shooting and bombing each other for five minutes, Jerusalem suddenly filled up with American- and European-package tourists, and everyone made a load of money. With airports, casinos, new flags, and uniforms, even Palestine was looking like a potential candidate for an EPCOT pavilion.

Imagine, a nation that demanded the right to a homeland was actually mulling over the idea of allowing the Palestinians to have a homeland . . . even the darkest cynics were getting a little misty eyed. We should have known better.

Then, like in a badly written movie, the plot began to falter. Peace made both sides cocky. Negotiations at Camp David between Israel's then–Prime Minister Ehud Barak and Palestinian leader Yasser Arafat failed. Israel's then-opposition leader, Ariel Sharon, decided to grandstand at the site of a principal bone of contention, the Temple Mount complex in the Old City of Jerusalem, to show that he was further to

## MUPPET INTIFADA?

Israeli television broadcast a homogeneous version of *Sesame Street* called *Rechov Sumsum* beginning in 1982. A few years ago someone thought, hey, why not use the show to promote understanding and tolerance between Arabs and Jews? For four years, the joint Palestinian/Israeli/Jordanian production team tried to patch things up with Hebrew and Arabic segments designed to show that Jews and Arabs can live together (along with the usual education spots). But since the latest Intifada began in September of 2000, things have gone to hell on Sesame Street. Amidst cultural clashes about what characters represent and the growing disbelief that Israelis and Palestinians can live together peacefully, Bin Bertie and Erniewitz are calling it quits. The Palestinian producer thinks it's pointless because it is creating a fiction to show Israelis and Palestinians (even bright, furry ones) living together peacefully. Unlike the polymorphous look of the U.S. version, there are some finer points to consider when showing the characters interacting. The Israeli characters (a porcupine and a monster) have to be invited into Palestine by the rooster and monster puppets. It would appear that a porcupine barging into a rooster's neighborhood is too reminiscent of Israeli settlers.

The replacement: *Sesame Stories*, a series of fairy tales . . . which some say is a much more accurate portrayal of the peace process.

the right than right-of-Attila-the-Hun Binny Netanyahu. Since then, during nearly two years of more or less constant fighting, the toll of dead and injured on both sides is comfortably into five figures. The only ones who don't seem to care are the fat politicians.

The history of Israel has been fraught with grand schemes, messianic figures, violent conflict, and a dark sense of behind-the-scenes duplicity. To be fair, the Jews are just one of many groups from Gypsies to Armenians who have been dumped on by history. But it is the sense of biblical entitlement that has fueled the dogged attempts of the Jews to regain a homeland. The modern genesis for a Jewish return to the Middle East began in 1839 when an English Jew, Sir Moses Montefiore, proposed the idea of resettlement and began donating money so that settlements could be built outside the walls of Jerusalem. Israel was a ragged wasteland where people lived in guarded cities and life outside the walls was short and brutal. The modern state of Israel became closer to reality in the 1917 Balfour Declaration, and then it gained impetus and additional urgency when the Holocaust survivors of Europe demanded a safe place. After World War II, what was the British mandate of Palestine was carved up by the United Nations. The Jews were given part of Palestine, the West Bank of the Jordan River was given to Jordan, Gaza was given to Egypt, and Jerusalem was declared an international territory. All these grand schemes were rife with backroom deals, failed intentions, and dark consequences. If you were to measure success by who got screwed the most and the least, well, there is no doubt the most-screwed award goes to the Palestinians. The Jewish state, a fine idea in theory, was built on land that already belonged to someone in practice—well, actually it belonged to a lot of different people. But in the end, 700,000 people, mostly Palestinians, fled or were driven from land wanted by Israel. Most Palestinians refer to the towns and villages that their grandparents were chased out of as "home." Today, you can meet Jewish teenagers who have grown up in settlements surrounded by hostile Palestinians who wonder exactly when they will have a "home." So far, it's a fast-paced game of musical chairs, with the Israelis holding most of the chairs, playing the music, and kicking off the Palestinians who manage to find an empty chair.

It is not surprising that when the state of Israel was declared in 1948, it found itself at war with its Arab neighbors. Trans-Jordan, Iraq, Egypt, Lebanon, and Syria attacked—and, incredibly, were defeated. Round two followed in 1956, when Egyptian President Colonel Gamal Abdel Nasser nationalized the Suez Canal and banned Israeli shipping from it. Israel was once again victorious, seizing the entire Sinai peninsula, but returned the land to Egypt under pressure from the United States. However, Israeli troops did not have to wait long to wash their socks in the Suez again. In 1967, correctly anticipating another combined Arab attempt to drive the Jewish state into the sea, Israel launched pre-emptive strikes in three directions. In just six days, Israel took the Sinai from Egypt, the Golan Heights from Syria, and East Jerusalem and the West Bank from Jordan, swelling Israel to five times its pre-war size. The Sinai was eventually returned to Egypt in exchange for a peace agreement in 1982, but Israel retains the rest, despite another (humiliatingly unsuccessful) attempt by Egypt and Syria to surprise Israel on the Yom Kippur holiday in 1973. The world held its breath during the Gulf War as Saddam lobbed Scuds and Israelis made gas masks a fashion accessory. In the supposed millennium of the apocalypse, Israel remains the lit cigarette in the tinderbox of the Middle East.

> **S**o far it's a fast-paced game of musical chairs with the Israelis holding most of the chairs, playing the music, and kicking off the Palestinians who manage to find an empty chair.

The crucial deal in the last couple of decades has been one of "land for peace"—how much of the former Israel is willing to yield and what degree of the latter they might expect in return. The problem is that they are trading other people's land as if it were their own. Possession is

10/10ths of the law here. Although Israel and Syria are no closer to an agreement on the Golan Heights, for much of the 1990s it looked as if an accommodation with the Palestinians over the West Bank and Gaza might be possible . . . if there remained any Palestinian land left from which to make a decent state. In an odd ratio of population growth versus quality of life, Palestinians may outbreed the Israelis, but find themselves doing it standing up—Israeli settlements and roads are quickly carving any potential Palestine into useless, arid townships.

In the 1993 Oslo Accords, Israel and the PLO recognized each other as legitimate entities and introduced a limited form of Palestinian rule in the West Bank and Gaza Strip, with an idea of full-fledged statehood at some unspecified point down the road. The two regions were divided into Area A, in which Palestinian authorities had complete control, and Area B, in which Israel still had a hand in security matters (since around April 2002, of course, these distinctions have been irrelevant, at least to the Israeli military). The truth is that the Israelis can invade and occupy where, when, and for however long they choose.

There were two problems with the Oslo Accords. One was that the really tricky points—the right of return for the descendants of the 1948 refugees (still living in Lebanon and Jordan) and the status of Jerusalem—were not resolved to anyone's satisfaction. It was a strip-poker game in which neither side really wanted to win. Barak offered a right of return for 100,000 of the estimated 3.6 million Palestinians classed as refugees, and some sort of compensation for the rest; Arafat failed to respond with a straight answer. Barak went out on a limb to offer Arafat municipal control over some of East Jerusalem and access by tunnel to the al-Aqsa mosque; Arafat upped the ante and wanted all of East Jerusalem and all of the Old City other than the Jewish Quarter. Eventually, Barak lost his pants and Arafat found himself stripped naked by a much uglier, meaner poker partner, Ariel Sharon.

Now the current mode of fighting suits the two old men in charge on both sides. Sharon doesn't have to involve himself in politically delicate—and, no doubt, personally distasteful—discussions with Arabs over Jerusalem and refugees, and Arafat doesn't have to deal with the tedious minutiae of civilian governance and accounting for where all that Palestinian Authority money goes. In the twilight of their lives, both get to portray themselves as staunch defenders of their people and, in classic Middle Eastern style, as victims, and, even sadder, as men who view war as a more flattering existence than peace.

The last word must go to Colonel Sir Ronald Storrs, the British governor of Jerusalem from 1920 to 1926, whose summary remains the only sane response to this eternally vexatious and fascinating region: "Two hours of Arab grievances drive me into the synagogue, while after an intense course of Zionist propaganda, I am prepared to embrace Islam."

***Israel Ministry of Foreign Affairs***
http://www.israel.org/mfa/home.asp

***Palestine Ministry of Tourism and Antiquities***
http://www.visit-palestine.com

# The Scoop

A glib risk assessment of Israel would be that it's perfectly safe except when it isn't—and the appallingly indiscriminate and random nature of Palestinian suicide bombers means that there is nothing at all you can do to protect yourself other than cross your fingers or stay home. Or better yet, stick to the Palestinian territories. At least you can hear a tank or gunship coming and get out of the way.

***Ha'aretz***
http://www.haaretzdaily.com

***The Jerusalem Post***
http://www.jpost.com

***Palestine Media Center***
http://www.palestine-pmc.com

***The Electronic Intifada***
http://electronicintifada.net/new.shtml

# The Players

*Ariel Sharon, aka "The Bulldozer"*

Sharon is prime minister of Israel, and beyond a doubt the most hated figure in the Arab world, which is an unhelpful coincidence. Sharon is both the precipitator and the principal beneficiary of the recent violence in Israel. The current rebellion, the al-Aqsa Intifada, kicked off in September 2000, when Sharon, accompanied by a phalanx of bodyguards, made a willfully tactless visit to the Temple Mount complex in Jerusalem. Within six months, he had been elected prime minister by a frightened and fed-up Israeli public, convinced that Sharon's hard line was the only one left to take. Boy, were they wrong. For the first time, Israelis are now dying faster than Palestinians. Israelis are facing deep divisions, and a smashed Palestinian Authority may be replaced by far more radical elements.

Ariel Sharon was born in Kfar Malal in 1928 into a staunchly Zionist family. Prior to entering politics, he had been a farmer, a lawyer, and, more important, a soldier. At age 14, Sharon was active in the Jewish underground organization Haganah during the last days of the British mandate in Palestine. He was a platoon commander in the 1948 War of Independence, an intelligence officer during Israel's nervous beginnings in the 1950s, a brigade commander during the 1956 Sinai campaign, and a major-general during the 1967 Six-Day War and the 1973 Yom Kippur War.

It was while serving in the military that Sharon acquired a reputation for hotheadedness and ruthlessness. In the early '50s, Sharon's Unit 101, established to carry out retaliatory raids against Arab terrorists operating out of Jordan and Egypt and Arab troops stationed in the Gaza Strip, became infamous for bombing and burning civilian homes, often without giving their inhabitants time to leave. During Yom Kippur, he defied orders to lead troops across the Suez Canal.

Therefore, even before Sharon became Israel's Minister of Defense in 1982, his chances of being awarded the keys to the city of Amman or Cairo or Damascus were pretty remote. But it is his actions in this position during Israel's 1982 invasion of Lebanon that are the primary reason why the mention of his name will be met with a cavalcade of curses at all points from Tangiers to Tehran. On September 15, 1982, Lebanon's Christian president-elect, Bashir Gemayel, was assassinated in a bombing, presumably set by Islamic militants. The following day, Gemayel's Christian Phalangist militias, Israel's allies in the Lebanese war, were allowed into the Palestinian refugee camps of Sabra and Chatila, ostensibly to search for terrorists. The result was a massacre that left hundreds of unarmed Palestinians dead. A subsequent Israeli commission of enquiry found that if Sharon didn't order the slaughter, he didn't try hard enough to stop it, and he was forced to resign as Defense Minister.

Sabra and Chatila continue to haunt Sharon. He successfully sued *Time* magazine over a claim that he had encouraged Gemayel's family to take vengeance against the Palestinians. A civil action against Sharon, brought by survivors of Sabra and Chatila, is under way in Belgium. Intriguingly, the potential star witness, former Christian Phalangist commander Elie Hobeika, was killed by a car bomb in Beirut in 2002, just 48 hours after agreeing to give evidence against Sharon if the matter ever came to trial.

Sharon, twice a widower, lives on a ranch called Havat Hashikmin in the Negev desert, but also maintains a home in Jerusalem. With his typical regard for Arab sensitivities, it is situated overlooking the busiest street in the Muslim Quarter of the Old City and has an enormous Israeli flag hanging from it.

**Prime Minister's Office**
Tel.: (972) 2 670 5555
Fax: (972) 2 670 5475
pm_eng@pmo.gov.il
http://www.pmo.gov.il/english

**Campaign for Justice for the Victims
of Sabra and Chatila**
coordinator@indictsharon.net
http://www.indictsharon.net

## Israeli Defense Forces (IDF)

Israel was founded on the principle that Jews would never again be defenseless victims, and Israeli military doctrine has always been based on the belief that the best form of defense is offense, or more correctly, to be the first to offend. Military service is compulsory for Israeli citizens. The term of service is four years for officers, three years for other ranks, and two years for unmarried women. Annual compulsory reserve duty continues up to the age of 54 for men and 24 for single women. Israel is effectively a country-sized barracks, and the whole nation can be ready to roll in a matter of minutes—as Egypt and Syria discovered to their cost when they attacked Israel on Yom Kippur in 1973. Israel now spends $8.7 billion annually on defense—nearly 10 percent of its total GDP. Without the Israeli army, Israel would cease to exist. There is a thriving conscientious objector movement supported in Israel by folks who are just plain tired of the violence and of their army being used to terrorize or intimidate Palestinians.

**Israel Defense Forces**
info@mail.idf.il
http://www.idf.il

**Israel Ministry of Defense**
public@mod.gov.il
http://www.mod.gov.il

http://www.seruv.org.il/defaulteng.asp

## A VERY DIM LIGHT AT THE END OF A VERY DARK AND LONG TUNNEL

Seif Islam Qaddafi, the son of Libyan leader Muammar Qaddafi, recently shared his pearls of wisdom at the Royal Institute for International Affairs in London. He suggested a Jewish-Arab "Federal Republic of the Holy Land" made up of five regions with Jerusalem as a "city state." Qaddafi did admit that in order to make this work, Israel would have to bring back all the Palestinian refugees, who would then vote on this resolution.

Qaddafi suggested to the audience that Muslims could learn from Jews. "Jews in America do not ask for a separate state. That's why they are stronger. They have influence in a very influential superpower. The Jewish model in America is a good model for Muslims all over the world."

Reliable reports said there was a thunderous ovation of one-hand clapping.

## Mossad

*Mossad* is Hebrew for "Institute" and short for ha-Mossad le-Modiin ule-Tafkidim Meyuhadin, which is Hebrew for "Institute for Intelligence and Special Tasks." (Which is, we suppose, one way of putting it.) Mossad is more or less Israel's equivalent to the CIA and has nearly as global a reach. Mossad has carried out kidnappings in Argentina (Nazi fugitive Adolf Eichmann, who was later hanged in Jerusalem) and Italy (nuclear whistle-blower Mordechai Vanunu, still held in Ashkelon Prison after 16 years, of which more than 11 have been served in solitary confinement), and assassinations in Malta (Islamic Jihad founder Fathi Shaqaqi), Tunisia (senior PLO commander Abu Jihad), and Belgium (Canadian scientist Gerald Bull, who had worked on Iraq's "Supergun" project).

Mossad has agents in the field all over the world. To the enduring anger of various Arab governments, Mossad agents have proved determined, resourceful, and unbelievably brave. One, Eli Cohen, became a confidant of the Syrian defense establishment in the 1960s (he was hanged in public in Damascus when he was caught). Another, Wolfgang Lotz, blew open Egypt's rocket program. They don't get it right all the time, though: They screwed up mightily in 1997, when they tried to bump off senior Hamas leader Khalid Meshaal in Jordan. The Mossad hit-squad got caught with fake Canadian passports, leading to great embarassment in Israel, fury mixed with guffaws across the Arab world and, indirectly, to the release of Hamas founder Sheik Ahmad Yasin from jail in Israel. Although the Arab world blames the Mossad for every possible conspiracy and evil deed from 9/11 to Osama bin Laden, they primarily protect the interests of Israel. (We said "primarily.")

Mossad is believed to have about 1,200 staff members and is known to have a number of different departments: Technology, Research, Lohamah Psichlogit (psychological warfare), Special Operations (wet jobs), Political Action and Liaison (dealing with friendly countries), and Collections (overseas espionage). If you think this sounds like the career for you, Mossad was recently advertising for spooks. You need to be an Israeli citizen and speak Hebrew. Polish up your résumé and send it to jobs_operations@mossad.gov.il. Don't waste your time looking for official Web sites, but try this good conspiracy site.

http://www.fpp.co.uk/BoD/Mossad

## Shin Bet

Shin Bet plays NSA to Mossad's CIA, and is responsible for internal security and counterintelligence. The name is a contraction of *Sherut ha-Bitachon ha-Klali,* which translates roughly as General Security Service. Shin Bet is feared throughout the Palestinian territories and not without reason: for Palestinians who are lifted by Shin Bet, detention without trial, beatings, and torture are common.

Shin Bet's three major arms are Arab Affairs, Non-Arab Affairs, and Protective Security. They are responsible for subverting terrorist groups, spooking foreign embassies, and protecting government buildings and the El Al airline. Looking for a dangerous job? They run a network of informers in the Palestinian territories, who, if found out or even suspected, are often summarily executed.

http://www.fas.org/irp/world/israel/shin_bet/index.html

### Peace Now! and Yesh Gvul

Two Israeli organizations are devoted to the belief that there must be a better way to get along with their neighbors: Peace Now! regularly draws crowds numbering tens of thousands to its demonstrations in Israeli cities, and Yesh Gvul, founded during Israel's 1982 invasion of Lebanon, is a support group for Israeli soldiers who refuse to serve in the occupied territories.

**Peace Now!**
info@peacenow.org.il
http://www.peacenow.org.il

**Yesh Gvul**
peretz@yesh-gvul.org
http://www.yesh-gvul.org/english.html

### Yasser Arafat

More slippery than an eel in a bucket of engine oil, and apparently blessed with more lives than a hundred cats, Yasser is in his final act as the quivering, indignant face and human embodiment of the Palestinian struggle. Now 73, the president of the Palestinian Authority remains a maddening bundle of paradoxes: He is probably the only man capable of bringing mainstream Palestinian opinion to an accommodation with Israel, and yet he is beyond doubt the most risible winner of the Nobel Peace Prize since Henry Kissinger got the gong for napalming Cambodia.

Arafat's official PR claims that he was born in Jerusalem, but the less-poetic truth is that he is the child of a Palestinian merchant family who lived in Cairo. He moved to Jerusalem at age four to live with the family of an uncle after the death of his mother. He returned to Cairo as a teenager to study, but he had already become involved with the Palestinian cause. He spent less time attending lectures than he did attending meetings, giving speeches, and helping run guns to Arab militias who were resisting the imminent foundation of Israel. When war broke out in 1948, Arafat came home and fought—very bravely, by all accounts—against the new state. After the war, he finished his engineering studies at the University of Cairo.

Arafat founded the al-Fateh movement in 1959, while working in Kuwait as a civil engineer. He took up the cause full-time in 1964 and relocated to Jordan, from where he led raids into Israel. He became chairman of the Palestine Liberation Organization (PLO) in 1969; his lasting reputation as a terrorist dates from the period following this, when the PLO succeeded in a number of hijackings. Arafat also developed the PLO into something resembling a government in search of a country, complete with its own armed forces—a situation found intolerable by King Hussein of Jordan, who drove out the PLO in 1971. Arafat then set up shop in Lebanon, with catastrophic consequences for that unfortunate country. After being chased out of Beirut by Israel and their Christian Lebanese allies in 1982, Arafat moved the PLO to Tunisia.

In 1988, Arafat declared that the PLO had renounced terrorism, and though he wasn't drowned out by cheers of agreement and forgiveness, it was the first step down the road that led to Oslo and to Arafat's election, in 1996, to his current position of president of the Palestinian Authority, such as it is. The Peter Principle is in full effect: the PA has 40,000 staff members (mostly security) in 120 different departments, all of whom report directly to Arafat. A Palestinian report estimated that 40 percent of the $800 million annual budget was lost to corruption and mismanagement. There is no official heir (groomed or ungroomed) to the doddering figurehead. If the transition is peaceful, Mahmoud Abbas should take the lead slot. Currently Arafat's headquarters and his organizations are being dismantled by the Israelis, stone by stone.

**Palestinian National Authority**
http://www.pna.org

**Fateh**
http://www.fateh.net

## New-School Terror Groups

These days terror in the Middle East has a distinctive Islamic flavor: A sort of politics-lite, headline-heavy version of what is going on in other Islamic regions. Not surprisingly, the terrorists' funding comes from Gulf patrons and Iran. Syria chips in to get a ringside seat in the fight but really roots for the old-school terror boys. The problem, of course, is that the cure may be worse than the disease, and by the time they get their political agenda together there may be no Palestine left to save. The hard-line stance of Hamas, al-Aqsa, Hizbollah, and others may simply vaporize any moderate (if there can ever be a moderate anything here) Islamic government required to rule the much-touted Palestinian state. Although Uncle Sam doesn't believe it, *DP* predicts this is where the next real leader of the Palestinian state will emerge.

http://web.israelinsider.com
http://www.palestine-info.info

## Hamas

*Hamas* is shorthand for *Harakat al-Muqawama al-Islamiya,* or Islamic Resistance Movement (the word also translates handily into Arabic as "zeal" or "enthusiasm"). They're against pretty much everything: Yasser Arafat, Israel, the United States of America, the peace process, and, it seems safe to assume, mixed dancing and rock music on Sundays. Like its ideological and religious kin Hizbollah in Lebanon, Hamas provides hospitals, schools, mosques, and sports clubs, as well as suicide bombers—it rightly assumes that there is little point waiting for Arafat's hapless Palestinian Authority to organize any such things. Hamas gives hope to the hopeless, help to the helpless, and regular servings of death and destruction to Israeli commuters and shoppers. Among the Palestinians of the West Bank and Gaza Strip, Hamas is immensely, inconveniently, and depressingly popular.

Hamas is led by wheelchair-bound, Gaza-based cleric Sheik Ahmed Yasin, who did eight years in prison on manslaughter charges between 1989 and 1997. Former doctor Abdel Aziz al-Rantisi is another prominent spokesman. Given the numbers of their colleagues who have been dispatched by Israel's so-called targeted killings, neither of them get out much. Hamas's estimated $70 million annual budget comes from the Palestinian diaspora, private donors in Saudi Arabia, well-meaning folks in the West who didn't read the small print before they sent the check to those nice people who were promising to build orphanages for Palestinian children and hutches for Palestinian bunny-wabbits, and so on. In December 2001, the U.S. government seized the assets of America's largest Muslim charity, the Holy Land Foundation, for allegedly funding Hamas.

> **H**amas gives hope to the hopeless, help to the helpless, and regular servings of death and destruction to Israeli commuters and shoppers.

Hamas wants to destroy Israel and establish an Islamic state in a unified Palestine—it's kind of difficult to picture Ariel Sharon signing up for this. To achieve these ends, Hamas began its campaign of violence in 1993 and have scarcely let up since. The armed wing of Hamas is the Izz ad-Din al Qassam Brigade. Several Brigade and Hamas members have been assassinated by Israel in so-called targeted killings—most spectacularly, Hamas's bomb-maker-in-chief, Yehiya "The Engineer" Ayash, whose head was blown off by a booby-trapped mobile phone in 1996. In the meantime, Israel keeps providing enough photo ops and brutal incidents to provoke the zeal that Hamas needs.

## Hizbollah

This Iranian-backed Shi'a group finally drove Israel out of Lebanon in May 2001, ending nearly two decades of a frequently brutal Israeli occupation of their country. They're still swapping shells with the few Israeli troops left in the disputed Shebaa Farms region along Israel's border with Lebanon, but the chances of them steaming into the current quagmire are slight. For the moment, they seem content with a spot on the sidelines, where they can holler encouragement at the likes of Hamas and Islamic Jihad. (See the Lebanon chapter for further details.)

http://www.hizbollah.org

## Islamic Jihad

Everyone knows the name, but nobody really knows much about them. Islamic Jihad was founded in Cairo by three former members of the Egyptian-based Muslim Brotherhood (Ikwhan). They set up shop in Gaza in the mid-'70s to eliminate Israel, unite the Palestinians, and then create a focal point to unify the entire Arab world. Needless to say, that's a tall order that doesn't leave much room for company picnics or soccer tournaments. Although they are Sunni, they look to the Iranian Revolution as a model (Iranians are Shi'a) and reject any Western influence as corrupting.

They are based in Damascus, with finances coming from Iran and some logistical support from Hizbollah in Lebanon. They have conducted several suicide attacks against Israeli military and civilian targets. The founder Fathi Shiqaqi was killed by Mossad in Malta in 1995 (you may also hear of this group being referred to as "al Shiqaqi"). Its current leader, at least until Israel also does to him what it has done to several of his lieutenants, is Dr. Ramadan Abdallah Shalah, who earned his Ph.D. (Islamic economics) at the University of Durham in England and later lectured at South Florida University in Tampa until 1995, when he took over the reins of al-Jihad.

Born in the Saja'iyah refugee camp in Gaza, Shalah is not an intellectual lightweight, and he has attracted an intelligent, educated group of volunteers. They have grown dramatically in the recent intifada and work closely with Hamas and Hizbollah. A sound bite from Shalah gives you better insight: "Our enemy possesses the most sophisticated weapons in the world, and its army is trained to a very high standard. . . . We have nothing with which to repel killing and thuggery against us except the weapon of martyrdom. It is easy and costs us only our lives. . . . Human bombs cannot be defeated, not even by nuclear bombs."

Well, that pretty much guarantees you won't see al-Jihad at the peace tables anytime soon. Oh yeah, here's a safety tip . . . they usually celebrate the assassination of Shiqaqi that occurred in October of '95 by blowing up something . . . preferably something Israeli.

http://www.qudsway.com/nada_e.html

## Al-Aqsa Martyrs' Brigade

This deeply unsavory offshoot of Arafat's Fateh faction emerged in late 2000 soon after the beginning of the current intifada. It is named after the al-Aqsa mosque on Jerusalem's Temple Mount, one of Islam's holiest shrines and the site of the beginning of the current intifada.

The al-Aqsa Martyrs initially claimed that they would target only Israeli soldiers and settlers in Palestinian territories, but, hey . . . it's the Middle East . . . they lied. They swiftly began spreading the joy and their body parts among civilians in Israeli cities, especially after one of their leaders, Raed al-Karmi, was killed by Israeli troops in January 2002. They quickly surpassed the Islamic fundamentalist groups in killing Israelis. And the frightening part is that there are a whole lot of young, impressionable, angry kids in Palestine.

The al-Aqsa Martyrs have claimed responsibility for several massacres, including the suicide bombing of Jerusalem's Moment Café in March 2002 (they were then added to the U.S. State Department's list of terrorist groups), which killed 11 civilians and wounded 50, and a suicide bombing in Jerusalem's ultra-orthodox Beit Israel neighborhood in the same month that killed nine civilians, including six children. The al-Aqsa Martyrs are similar to Hamas and Islamic Jihad in method, but subtly different in ideology: they are Palestinian Nationalist militants, as opposed to Islamic militants—not that it makes much difference to the commuters and shoppers who get blown to bits by their operatives.

Israel claims that the al-Aqsa Martyrs are under the direct command of Yasser Arafat—and, indeed, some al-Aqsa Martyrs leaders have been quoted confirming this. Arafat always makes a show of publicly condemning their outrages, but it is known that many of the group's members are moonlighting in Arafat's security services.

The Brigade's supposed founder and leader is Marwan Barghouti (born June 6, 1958) who, obviously coincidentally, is also the West Bank leader of Arafat's Fateh faction. Barghouti has some experience organizing rock groups (the throwing kind) featuring vocal young Palestinians, and seems to have been successful in recruiting young members of Tanzim (a militant youth movement he leads under Fateh) to become red spray paint. Most of the recruits come from Nablus and Ramallah.

Israel tried to whack Barghouti in August 2001, but the helicopter-launched rockets missed his car and killed his bodyguard. Barghouti was arrested by Israeli troops in April 2002 and is expected to be charged with hundreds of murders; his lawyers claim that he has been tortured while in custody. Another al-Aqsa Martyrs' leader, Walid Sbeh, was shot dead by Israeli soldiers as he drove through Bethlehem in June 2002. Barghouti has been an active militant in Fateh since age 15 and has a bachelor's degree in history and a master's in . . . wait for the snare hit . . . international relations. He lives in Ramallah and is the most likely successor to Arafat (if things don't go well), but this is complicated by the fact that he is on the Israeli most-wanted list and, as we go to press . . . in jail.

http://www.barghouti.com

## Old-School Terror

The PFLP, the DFLP, and the PFLP-GC are the *Life of Brian*-esque confusing, left-winged, similar-acronymed groups formed after the Six-Day War. They are also the classic movie terrorists of the '70s: the ones who hijack planes, pilot rubber boats, cruise in on hang gliders, and generally blow stuff up while wearing goofy ski masks. If you remember, the Soviets were busy in the region and were eager to help anyone who wanted to create mayhem in U.S.-backed countries (i.e., Israel). It's hard for the three groups to generate decent ink, money, or recruits (Syria is the main sponsor, with Iran and others chipping in).

### Popular Front for the Liberation of Palestine (PFLP)

The PFLP had a brief moment of global superstardom on the afternoon of September 11, 2001, when a phone call to a wire service claimed the attacks in New York and Washington on their behalf. This call was swiftly followed by another one denying all involvement, from—one imagines—somewhere beneath a desk at one of the PFLP's offices in Palestine or Lebanon. It's not surprising that the claim was initially taken seriously. In the 1970s, the PFLP were among the first to recognize the political and diplomatic potency of airplane hijacks. It was the PFLP who blew up three (empty) passenger jets in Jordan in 1970; PFLP guerrillas whose jaunt in an Air France jet was memorably ended when Israeli commandos stormed Entebbe Airport in Uganda in 1976; and it was serial PFLP hijacker Leila Khaled who became a poster girl for the kind of student who thought himself a bit above the one of the tennis player with no underwear on.

The PFLP was founded by a pediatrician named Dr. George Habash after Israel's defeat of the Arab armies in the Six-Day War in 1967, and mixes up the standard down-with-Israel shtick with old-school Marxism: Where most of their peers see the destruction of Israel as a holy mission and an end in itself, the PFLP see it as but the first step in removing all Western influence from the Arab world, though they're going to have a heck of a job getting Hizbollah to hand in their Mercedes-Benzes. The PFLP's ideological commitment earned them support from Russia and China, which used the PFLP as a stick to poke America through much of the Cold War.

The checks from Moscow and Beijing dried up in the early '90s, and so did the recruits, as the PFLP learned the hard way that the impressionable young folk of occupied Lebanon and Palestine weren't half as excited about dialectical materialism and a dictatorship of the proletariat as they were about the opportunities for jihad and martyrdom being offered by the likes of Hamas. The PFLP kept their hand in with the occasional bombing and shooting, but their strength had dwindled to an estimated 800 men, and when the Palestinian Authority was formed and a semblance of peace descended on Israel, the PFLP seemed to have outlived their usefulness. It didn't help that George Habash, their founding father, was unwell; he stepped down as leader in 2000, and now lives in Damascus.

Habash was replaced by Abu Ali Mustafa. The Israelis viewed Mustafa as a worryingly hard-line figure, and didn't give him a chance to prove otherwise—Mustafa was killed by a helicopter-launched missile as he sat in his Ramallah office in August 2001. The PFLP responded by shooting dead Israeli Minister for Tourism Rehavam Zeevi in the Hyatt Hotel in Jerusalem. Mustafa's replacement, Ahmed Sadaat, was arrested in Ramallah by Palestinian police, under severe pressure from Israel, in January 2002.

**Popular Front for the Liberation of Palestine**
pflp@p-ol.com
http://www.pflp-pal.org/main.html

**Democratic Palestine**
http://www.democraticpalestine.net

## Popular Front for the Liberation of Palestine-General Command (PFLP-GC)

PFLP-GC's leader, 74-year-old Ahmad Jabril, split from the PFLP in 1968 to focus on killing and maiming, while Habash employed just a little less violence to achieve his ends. Jabril was once a captain in the Syrian army, so it's easy to understand why the PFLP-GC is tighter with Syria than spandex on an aerobics instructor. The PFLP-GC is headquartered in Damascus, with bases in Lebanon. Iran chips in when they run short of funds.

In 1977, the PFLP-GC became the first Palestinian group to use suicide bombers against Israel—three of their volunteers blew up themselves and 18 hostages in the northern Israeli town of Kiryat Shmona. The PFLP-GC later became more famous for its sensational aerial suicide attacks, employing everything from hang gliders to hot-air balloons.

The PFLP-GC are relics of the 1970s school of Palestinian revolutionary nationalism, but they shouldn't be completely written off just yet. They got caught running rockets and missiles to the Gaza Strip in May 2001, and Lebanese authorities arrested six PFLP-GC members for firing rockets into Israel from southern Lebanon in April 2002. Their long-term future is rather less assured—Jabril isn't getting any younger, and his son and heir, Muhammad Jabril, was assassinated by a car bomb in Beirut in May 2002.

### Popular Front for the Liberation of Palestine–Special Command (PFLP-SC)

The PFLP-SC, another PFLP offshoot, set up shop in 1979 under the leadership of Abu Salim. They also operate out of Lebanon, with backing from Iran and Syria. Though it is believed that the PFLP-SC's membership could all go to the annual general meeting in the same taxi, they have a long reach. In 1985, they claimed responsibility for a restaurant bombing in Torrejon, Spain, which missed its intended target of off-duty U.S. servicemen and killed 18 Spanish civilians.

### Democratic Front for the Liberation of Palestine (DFLP)

You may remember a scene in Monty Python's *Life of Brian*, in which members of the People's Front of Judea, having just cursed their rivals in the Judean People's Front, point Brian in the direction of the Judean Popular People's Front—a single old man glumly contemplating the gladiators ("Splitter!"). Meet Naif Hawatmeh, a Jordanian-born Christian who left the PFLP in 1969 because they weren't quite Marxist enough. Not only does Hawatmeh want to liberate Palestine, he also has the overthrow of all the Arab monarchies on his "to do" list.

The DFLP were quite a big noise in the 1970s, most infamously for shooting dead 27 people at a school in Ma'alot, but, like other offshoots of the PFLP, they have lost influence as the Koran has supplanted *Das Kapital* as the angry young Palestinian's preferred bedtime reading. They're now off the U.S. State Department's list of foreign terrorist organizations, but they haven't given up entirely—in August 2001, they claimed responsibility for an attack on an Israeli position in the Gaza Strip that killed three soldiers.

**Democratic Front for the Liberation of Palestine**
info@alhourriah.org
http://www.alhourrlah.org

## Other Groups That Make Things Interesting
### The Chalukah and Gush Emunim

The Chalukah, or "Distribution," is a system of outside donations to encourage Jews to build settlements in occupied or hostile territory. It is also the white-hot center of Palestinian hatred toward the encroachment and ultimate removal of their physical presence and land. After Israel seized the areas of Gaza (from Egypt) and the West Bank (from Jordan), the Gush Emunim, or "Bloc of the Faithful," encouraged hardy Zionists to buy, grab, and build on former Palestinian land.

During Passover of 1968, when Rav Kook, son of the famous rabbi, formed a group to illegally occupy a Hebron hotel, the Labor government backed down and allowed the group to live within a military compound. This was the genesis of the largest settlement the Kiryat Arba settlement and Gush Emunim.

Gush Emunim, founded in 1974, began a policy of transferring occupied land from Arab to Jewish control by whatever means necessary. This has put them at odds with Israel during less confrontational periods and made them heroes when things got aggressive. About half of Israelis support the group's biblically inspired policies while others see it as needlessly confrontational. These Nationalist Zionists (*DP* dare not reduce this to an acronym) are the storm troopers of the movement to take back Israel on the grounds of divine entitlement. A settlement starts as a "garin" and then expands quickly into a jumble of houses, trailers, and barbed-wire fences.

In Gaza today there are 6,900 settlers in 26 settlements, and built-up areas that allow the Israelis to control 40 percent of the region (with all major roads, borders, and checkpoints controlled by Israel), and in the West Bank there are 292 settlements, built-up areas, and roads that have put 59 percent of the territory under the control of Israelis. The settlements are connected by a network of secure roads that cut the Palestinian-controlled areas into disconnected, tiny territories. This is a premeditated campaign that will eventually push out the Palestinians and make the idea of a Palestinian state physically impossible.

Although most people think the policy of using settlers as a way to control and annex land began after the 1967 war, it began 100 years earlier. The land that is now Israel was a poor, miserable place in the mid-19th century. Absentee Turkish landlords who controlled the region of Palestine rented to and taxed land residents through Arab middlemen. The few Jews who lived there had to rely on donations of Chalukah ("the distribution") from European Jews to survive. In 1856, Sir Moses Montefiore, a wealthy English Jew, tried to buy land and donate money so that Jews could settle permanently in the region. Montefiore was a wealthy man (he was married to a Rothschild) who became devoutly religious after his first visit to the region in 1827. He came up with the idea of buying land and restarting Israel. At that time, the Jews lived inside the walls of Jerusalem in the cramped Jewish quarter. Montefiore convinced a small group of Jews to live outside the walls and brave the robbers and lack of facilities. He started small industries and even offered to pay people to stay in the small agricultural settlement if only for one night. In 1878, two more settlements were started and then abandoned (due to malaria).

Today the idea of Torah-banging settlers playing Messianic Monopoly has become the Palestinians' worst nightmare. Through direct government support and foreign donations, settlements are growing two to four times the national rate and the total number of settlers is around 400,000. If you have any doubt the settlements are an aggressive attempt to yank the land out from under the feet of the Palestinians, keep in mind that Ariel Sharon was the Housing and Construction Minister in 1992.

> **T**oday the idea of Torah-banging settlers playing Messianic Monopoly has become the Palestinians' worst nightmare.

Between 1992 and 1999 the area occupied by Israeli settlers in the West Bank doubled in size to 2.6 percent. Since 1993, 70,000 acres of Palestinian land have been stolen, 700 Palestinian homes have been demolished, and 282,000 trees have been destroyed by the Israelis. There exists a number of restrictive rules that are geared toward removal of Palestinians and the encouragement of Jewish settlements. Once small outposts grab a toehold, they are linked by road and quickly blossom into settlements. Even these roads are designed to cut off Palestinians and grab more land.

The Oslo Accords spawned the "bypass" roads, secure highways annexed and built to link settlements and avoid Palestinian areas. The highways include a 50- to 75-meter swath on both sides where construction is prohibited. The number of settlers has gone from 125,000 to over 400,000 with 40,000 new homes built in the same period.

The settlers are fueled by a biblical sense of entitlement and many believe that the Messiah will come when the land is returned to Jews. The result is an uncontiguous collection of Palestinian areas cynically called *Bantustans* after the isolated, desolate townships of apartheid-era South Africa. Bantustans are densely packed groups of poor laborers crowded into areas that have no agricultural value, no industry, and no room to expand. For now the 200,000 (400,000, if you include the 11 settlements in East Jerusalem) Israeli settlers who live in 145 settlements expand by about 2,000 new homes every year and live among the 3 million Palestinians like Custer among the Indians, hungrily eyeing the Sinai . . . and taking measurements.

http://www.uahc.org/rjmag/396ah.html
http://www.ssc.upenn.edu/polisci/faculty/data/lustick/for_the_land/lustick13.html
http://www.peacenow.org/nia/briefs/Settlements0301.html

## Moses and "The Promised Land"

Some folks say that Abraham (son of Noah, whose son Shem spawned the Shemites, or Semites) was the first Jew. The acknowledged origin of Israel comes from Abraham's grandson Jacob, who, after spending a night wrestling with an angel, was given the name Israel, or "one who fights God." Israel's sons created the 12 tribes of Israel (known, not surprisingly, as "the children of Israel"). It of course didn't take long for the squabbling to start and Jacob was sold into slavery in Egypt and the tribes were sent to wander the earth. Hebrew, by the way, comes from *habiru*, or "wandering tribes." A Jew is someone from the tribe of Judah, the fourth son of Jacob (aka Israel) who lived in what is now southern Palestine.

It appears that God played some mean tricks on Moses: he was abandoned as a child, made to wander, given a job without pay, beset by burning bushes. . . . Poor Moses didn't even know he was a Jew until age 40. Oy vey! The story is that Moses, having been raised and educated by the pharaoh, escaped to the Sinai peninsula (now Egypt), where he lived simply until age 80. Moses then heard a voice emanating from a burning bush telling him to bring his people out of bondage and lead them to Mount Sinai, or Jebel Musa. It is said that God showed Moses the Holy Land from Mt. Nebo (now in Jordan). Moses brought the Jews back to Israel in 1250 BC, ending 400 years of slavery to the Egyptians. The Israelites settled in what is now Nablus and along the Jordan valley. Although many different races, religions, and nationalities have come and the cornerstone of the Jewish religion is "The Promised Land," no one knows whether God had his fingers crossed behind his back when he told Moses this.

http://www.fordham.edu/halsall/ancient/asbook06.html

## The Arabs and "The Holy Land"

The original inhabitants of the area known as Palestine were the Canaanites in the third millennium before Christ. They established one of the oldest cities on earth, called Jericho. The area was also the crossroads of a number of trade routes and was invaded many times by, for a start, the Egyptians, Hittites, and Philistines. In 1230 BC, Joshua and the Israelites defeated the Canaanites but failed to usurp the Philistines who controlled Jerusalem. By 1000 BC, King David defeated the Philistines and took Jerusalem as his capital. It was called Israel in the north and Judah in the south. Less than 300 years later, the kingdom was invaded by the Assyrians. In 586 BC, Jerusalem was destroyed and the Jews were expelled into Babylon in chains. They were allowed back and prospered peacefully under Persian rule until 333 BC, when Alexander the Great and his successors ruled under Greek law and religion. The Jews revolted under the Maccabees but were put down brutally. In 63 BC, the Romans entered what was known as Syria Palaistina and reinstalled Herod as King of Judea. Jews fought amongst themselves, as Zealots murdered moderate Jews. Thirty years later Jesus of Nazareth was born (a Jew who spoke Aramaic) and became a teacher of the lessons found in the Old Testament. He was crucified as a heretic. In AD 70, the Romans destroyed the Temple and constructed their own temple on the site. In AD 313, Christianity was legalized and the Holy Land became a site of Christian pilgrimage. The region was a multicultural haven for many religions and cultures. The Arabs invaded and captured the region in 638 and stayed for 1,300 years. The region was known as Filastin, or Palestine. The city of Jerusalem became the third-holiest city of Islam (after Mecca and Medina), and all religions and races were free to practice and prosper within its walls.

There were a number of crusades launched by Christian European armies to free the Holy Land, and the already impoverished region was successively ravaged in the name of God. The area was controlled in later years by the Ottoman Turks, until the end of World War I. At the beginning of World War I, there were around 12,000 Jews in Palestine. In 1897, the first Zionist congress in Basel, Switzerland, encouraged the colonization of Palestine by Jews. By 1917, the Balfour Declaration promised a national home for Jews. Conflicts arose between newly arriving Jews and Arabs who had lived in the region for centuries. The conflicts escalated into war and in April 1947, the UN tried to solve the problem. By now there were 1,3000,000 Palestinians and 600,000 Jews in Palestine. Israel was established on May 14, 1948 and blood has been shed ever since.

http://www.arab.net/palestine

## Getting In —————————————————————

International flights arrive at Ben Gurion International Airport, about 20 kilometers from Tel Aviv. There are plenty of taxis and minibuses to most major cities in Israel—they leave when they're full, but they fill up pretty quickly. Three-month visas for most nationalities will be issued for free upon arrival, but make sure you request that customs refrain from stamping your passport—there are still some countries, including Iraq, Iran, Syria, and Lebanon, that maintain the extremely grown-up policy of refusing to admit visitors with Israeli stamps.

Visitors of Arab nationality or Arab descent, or with Arab visas in their passports, can expect to be questioned at some length upon arrival. This process is moderately tedious but usually fairly polite and respectful, as long as you are. Anyone who has been refused entry to Israel, or experienced difficulties with his/her visa status during a previous visit, can obtain information from the nearest Israeli embassy regarding the advisability of attempting to return to Israel.

Israel can also be entered by road from Jordan—buses and service taxis run regularly from Amman, and between Aqaba and Eilat in the south. For obvious reasons, the Jordan border is subject to delays, especially West Bank crossings, and for equally obvious reasons, you should keep an eye on the news before attempting it.

*Embassy of Israel*
3514 International Drive, NW
Washington, DC 20008
Tel.: (202) 364-5500
Fax: (202) 364-5560
ask@israelemb.org
http://www.israelemb.org

*Embassy of Israel*
2 Palace Green
London W8 4QB, UK
Tel.: (44) 20 7957 9500
Fax: (44) 20 7957 9555
info-assist@london.mfa.gov.il
http://www.israel-embassy.org.uk/
   london

*Embassy of Israel*
50 O'Connor Street, Suite 1005
Ottawa, Ontario K1P 6L2
Canada
Tel.: (613) 567-6450
Fax: (613) 237-8865
embisrott@cyberus.ca

# Getting Around

Israel does have several small domestic airports, but the country is so small that by the time you've factored in preflight security checks, it's quicker to go almost anywhere by road. Although the road system is modern, the driving is old school—every man for himself, and devil take the hindmost.

Intercity travel in Israel is conducted by bus. It is estimated that a quarter of Israel's population uses a bus every day. It is for exactly this reason that buses have become a favorite target of Palestinian suicide bombers. If you're the nervous sort, and your bus ride will be ruined by constant worries that some Allah-addled dingbat with a shirt full of Semtex will decide that the next stop is Paradise, you might want to consider hiring a car.

In the Palestinian territories, people travel by minibus—they cost almost nothing, and leave when they're full. Roadblocks and battles permitting, you can get a ride to almost anywhere on the West Bank from the bus station by Damascus Gate in Jerusalem. Checkpoints and delays are frequent. If you're a journalist, it will help slightly if you have a press card from the Israeli Government Press Office. *DP* useful factoid: There are more journalists per capita in Israel than in any other hot spot. You can apply for a press card by submitting a letter from a recognized media outlet, or from your local embassy, and collect it in Jerusalem. If you don't have access to the necessary documents, *DP* has seen bogus press cards that you can buy for about $5 in Bangkok that can work just as well. Keep in mind that when things get busy, the Israeli military seems to find shooting at journos as entertaining as at Palestinians.

## Getting Out

If you're flying out, arrive at the airport at least three hours before departure—make it four if you've got an Arab surname, an Arab passport, a vaguely Arab appearance, or just a whole load of Arab stamps in your passport. American air travelers who've felt that the post-9/11 security regime in the United States has been strict haven't seen anything yet. Israeli air security is the most stringent in the world—El Al, Israel's national airline, has armed sky marshals posing as passengers on every flight.

You won't be asked any leading questions about your politics, but you will be asked whether you visited the Palestinian territories, why you went, and who you know there. Be cooperative, but, obviously, don't part with any names or addresses. Also, bear in mind that this is not the time or the place to argue about Palestinian statehood—while the questioning can be tiresome, it is usually perfectly courteous, and it's not like they don't have their reasons.

## Dangerous Places

### The Occupied Territories

The Gaza Strip is a 5-by-28-mile sliver that used to belong to Egypt. It is home to a million Palestinians, and none of them are very happy that Israel is their effective landlord and master. The West Bank has two million people and its only claim to fame is that it sucks less than Gaza as a place to live.

## THE ULTIMATE ADVENTURE VACATION

Ever wonder about those foreigners who faked out the Israeli army and nipped into the besieged Church of the Nativity in May 2002? Confused as to why mainstream journalists were calling tourists who were situated inside Arafat's embattled compound in order to get the news? Well, don't be. There is a pacifist group of Jews and Arabs who invite foreign tourists (i.e., you) to visit the occupied areas and act as human shields. . . . Say what? Yes, that's right, human shields. The idea is that the Israeli military will be on their best behavior if foreigners (i.e., residents of countries that contribute billions of dollars) are around. Better yet, if American Jews are found to be in areas that are being occupied or cleansed it makes it very hard to explain why the Israeli army is whacking homeboys. Intrigued?

*The Palestinian Centre for Rapprochement between People*
64 Star Street
P.O. Box 24
Beit Sahour, Palestine
www.rapprochement.org

What do people do to kill time, if they don't have jobs, are young, and live in tight spaces? Well, if you need help, the population of the Occupied Territories is expected to double every 20 years. Consider the growing demand this makes for new housing, and then note that the Israelis figure that since 1987, 2,440 homes have been destoryed in the West Bank as a result of administrative demolition. When you factor in the extraordinary occupancy rates, this means that 16,000 Palestinians have lost their homes.

http://www.btselem.org/English/Statistics/index.asp

*Palestine Red Crescent Society*
http://www.palestinercs.org

*Alaqsaintifada.org*
http://www.alaqsaintifada.org

## Northern Israel

A number of Lebanon-based groups, notably Hizbollah and the PFLP, have the capacity to launch rockets into Northern Israel. Since Israel's withdrawal from Lebanon in 2000, such attacks are less frequent, but there is still concern in some circles that Hizbollah in particular might seek to open up a new front here. They continue to fight sporadically with Israeli troops still stationed in the disputed Shebaa Farms region.

*Anywhere*

Palestinian suicide bombers have targeted bus stations, bus stops, markets, cafés, shops, restaurants, and a pool hall. They're obviously not a threat if you're in the Palestinian territories, but Israeli retaliations for suicide bombings are not always characterized by their precision or proportion.

## Dangerous Things

*"Intifadas"*

If you ever wonder why kids are on the front lines of the war with Israel, it's because 53 percent of Palestinians are under 18. And they are usually from families consisting of at least seven people and whose living conditions make outside a lot better place to be than at home. (The rock throwing part you can figure out.) In Gaza City, half of the population is 14 and under. Two-thirds of Palestinians live on less than $340 a month (the official poverty level). In the Gaza Strip, 84.7 percent of Palestinians live below the poverty level. Unemployment runs over 30 percent. It doesn't take a genius to figure out what happens when they get riled up.

*Intifada* means "waking up from a sleep," "shaking off," or "shivering from a sickness." It began on December 9, 1987, after an Israeli Army truck ran into a group of Palestinians, killing four and injuring seven of them. The world was treated to images of Israeli soldiers gunning down kids who were throwing rocks . . . right around Christmas time. In a PR coup that couldn't have been more poignant, "Horror in the Holy Land" was sprinkled with ads for Christmas cheer. Israeli soldiers beat up doctors and nurses and dragged off wounded Israelis, kids were shot dead live on TV, journos flocked to the intifada like seagulls to a trash barge, and the Palestinians played it up for everything it was worth.

> **I**sraeli soldiers beat up doctors and nurses and dragged off wounded Israelis, kids were shot dead live on TV, journos flocked to the intifada like seagulls to a trash barge.

The first intifada wound down around 1991 and resulted in the deaths of about 1,000 Palestinians—but it was Israel: 0, Palestine: 1. The second intifada (called the al-Aqsa Intifada because it was sparked by Sharon's inflammatory visit to what the Jews call Temple Mount) began on September 29, 2000, and has resulted in the deaths of over 1,300 Palestinians, and Italian journalist and *DP* fan, Raffaele Ciriello. Now it was Israel: 0 and Palestine: 2.

The direct attack on Arafat's compound in Ramallah, set against the background of the War on Terror, swung the pendulum dramatically in the other direction. A series of suicide bombers and the more military approach of the Israelis (and the constant drone of partisan comb-overs like Benny on U.S. cable news networks) repositioned the war as one on terrorism. Now it was Palestine: 0 and Israel: 1. Somehow the counter had been reset.

http://www.palestinemonitor.org/factsheet/Palestinian_intifada_fact_sheet.htm
http://alaqsaintifada.org
http://intifadaonline.com

## Closures

The Israelis never seem to tire of invading or sealing off Palestinian areas. The West Bank is divided into 120 clusters and the Gaza Strip is divided into three. There are 120 Israeli checkpoints in occupied areas and a new $1 million per kilometer security fence going up that will separate the West Bank from East Jerusalem (the intended capital of an independent Palestinian state). The 70-mile fence meanders around the Green Line (the pre-1967 border between Jordan and Israel) and effectively bottles up Palestinians . . . and the Jewish settlers living in the occupied area.

Some Palestinians are given identity numbers and residents can be bottled up in their area for days. The borders to Jordan and Egypt are often closed and the pride of the Palestinian Authority, the Gaza "International" Airport, has been closed since February of 2001.

## Suicide Bombers

There are three Palestinian organizations currently sending suicide bombers into Israel: Hamas, Islamic Jihad, and the al-Aqsa Martyrs' Brigade. From their perspective, the suicide bomber is an ideal weapon on a number of levels: cheap, almost impossible to defend against, terrifying to the enemy, and a galvanizing force in the communities that send them. All Palestinian towns are covered with posters of their martyrs, and their families are revered (the families are also given a bounty of around $5,000 by the organization that sent them, and further donations come from Iraq and Saudi Arabia). The argument can be made that the money donated to a bomber's family is an incentive since it is comparable to two years' wages. Others point to this phenomenon as being proof of the hopelessness of the Palestinian situation.

Most suicide bombers are young men, although the first female suicide bombers were deployed in 2002. They are typically educated and middle-class. Far more volunteer than are accepted—those who are under 18, or have a wife or children, or who are the principal wage earner for their family, are usually turned away.

A well-structured ritual attends the deployment of a suicide bomber, designed to eliminate any doubt in the mind of the volunteer. Two assistants will stay with the bomber—known at this stage as al-Shaheed al Hayy ("The Living Martyr")—throughout the week before the deployment and will report any expressions of doubt or nervousness to a senior cleric.

They will fast and study the Koran intensely—the Baqara, 'Imrans, Anfal, Tawba, Rahman, and Asr chapters are particular favorites. "Never think that those who were slain in the cause of God are dead," reads a verse of the 'Imrans, "they are alive, and well provided for by their Lord; pleased with his gifts and rejoicing that those they left behind, who have not yet joined them, have nothing to fear or to regret; rejoicing in God's grace and bounty. God will not deny the faithful their reward."

Immediately prior to the operation, the bomber records a living will on video. These are both tremendous propaganda—video collections of such testaments are big sellers in markets all over the Middle East—and another psychological means of keeping the bomber on course. (You'd look pretty silly wandering into the party convened to celebrate your obliteration and trying to explain that a dog had eaten your detonator.)

Depressingly, the suicide bomber is not a passing fad. There is no shortage of volunteers, and the organizations that dispatch them have no interest whatsoever in a negotiated peace with Israel. Hamas and Islamic Jihad in particular will settle for nothing less than the Jewish state's abolition or obliteration. Oddly, a question that, to the best of *DP*'s knowledge, has never been asked of Hamas, Islamic Jihad, or the al-Aqsa Martyrs is why, if their members must kill themselves in order to make a point, they don't do it in a place where it won't hurt anyone else: the propaganda value would be colossal, the sympathy it would generate in the West would be immense, and the pressure on Israel would be unbearable. The answer, it can be suspected, is that in a Palestinian state at peace with its neighbor, Hamas, Islamic Jihad, and the al-Aqsa Martyrs might have to go out and get jobs.

http://www.walk4israel.com
http://www.fly-a-cake.com
http://info.jpost.com/1999/Supplements/Tourism2000

## Land Mines

Land mines in many areas of the Golan Heights have not been clearly marked or fenced. Walk only on established roads or trails. Some estimate that there are still 389,000 mines still buried along the border with southern Lebanon. Most of them are along the Blue Line. Look for yellow signs with red triangles.

http://www.icbl.org/lm/2001/israel

## THE WORLD'S MOST DANGEROUS TOURIST

Al-Aqsa is the spot where the prophet Mohammed is said to have ascended to heaven. It is the third most holy site in the Muslim religion (after Mecca and Medina in Saudi Arabia). The area is called al-Haram as-Sharif (the Noble Sanctuary) by Muslims. This is also the spot where Herod built the Great Temple (which was destroyed in AD 70). The Wailing Wall just happens to be Judaism's most holy site.

Israel's Sharon was concerned that Benjamin Netanyahu might appear to be more right-wing. He decided to visit the controversial area and make a speech—an action which launched the second intifada.

http://www.templemountfaithful.org

ISRAEL/PALESTINE

### Being Arrested in the West Bank and Gaza Strip

U.S. citizens arrested or detained in the West Bank or Gaza Strip on suspicion of security offenses often are not permitted to communicate with consular officials, lawyers, or family members during the interrogation period of their case. Over 2,000 Palestinians have been arrested in the latest intifada. The U.S. embassy is not normally notified of the arrests of Americans in the West Bank by Israeli authorities, and access to detainees is frequently delayed.

http://web.amnesty.org/web/ar2001.nsf/webmepcountries/ISRAEL+AND+
    OCCUPIED+TERRITORIES?OpenDocument

## Getting Sick

Medical care and facilities throughout Israel are excellent. Israel has one of the highest doctor-patient ratios in the world, about one doctor for every 339 patients. Travelers can find information in English about emergency medical facilities and after-hours pharmacies in the *Jerusalem Post* newspaper. Water is normally safe to drink, but bottled water is a better choice for the cautious. Tap water outside the main towns is not safe for drinking.

## Nuts and Bolts

Israel is tiny—you could fit all of its 20,700 square kilometers (7,992 square miles) into New Jersey (and you'd never again have to pay for a drink in Ramallah if you did). In addition to its recognized territory, it also partially or completely occupies several other tracts of territory: the Golan Heights, annexed from Syria in 1981 (1,150 square kilometers/444 square miles); the West Bank, annexed from Jordan in 1967

(5,878 square kilometers/2,270 square miles), and the Gaza Strip (363 square kilometers/140 square miles).

Israel's population is just under six million, which includes the 176,000 Israelis who live in the 231 Israeli settlements on the West Bank, the 20,000 in 42 settlements on the Golan Heights, the 6,900 in 25 settlements in the Gaza Strip, and the 173,000 in 29 settlements in East Jerusalem. Around 80 percent of Israel's population are Jews, of whom roughly 32 percent were born in America and Europe, 21 percent in Israel, 15 percent in Africa, and 13 percent in Asia. The rest of Israel's population is made up of Israeli Arabs (mostly Sunni Muslims), Druze, and a very small minority of Christians. The official languages are Hebrew and Arabic, though English is also widely spoken.

> **I**srael is tiny—you could fit all of its 20,700 square kilometers (7,992 square miles) into New Jersey (and you'd never again have to pay for a drink in Ramallah if you did).

Israel is a parliamentary democracy, with the prime minister and largely ceremonial president elected separately. The Israeli parliament is called the Knesset, and 16 different parties currently have sitting members. The currency is the shekel, which is also used in the Palestinian territories.

The weather is arid, warm, and mild most of the year with hot days and cool evenings. Because of its higher elevation, Jerusalem is quite cool, and even cold in the winter. In Tel Aviv and along the coast, the weather is more humid with warmer nights.

The Jewish Sabbath, from Friday dusk until Saturday dusk, is rigorously observed, though slightly less so in Tel Aviv. Most stores close on Friday by 2 PM and do not open again until Sunday morning, and many cinemas and restaurants are closed on Friday night. In most cities during the Sabbath, there is no public transport (except for taxis), postal service, or banking service. It is considered a violation of the Sabbath to smoke in public places, such as restaurants and hotels. The same is true on the six main Jewish religious holidays.

Jewish dietary laws (kashrut) prohibit the mixing of milk products and meat at the same meal. Kashrut is strictly enforced in hotels. Because of this, some restaurants serve only fish and dairy dishes while others serve only meat dishes. Pork is banned under religious laws, but some restaurants serve it, listing it euphemistically as white steak.

Israel calls Jerusalem its eternal and undivided capital, but the claim—especially to East Jerusalem, annexed in 1967—is disputed by most countries. Because of this, most foreign embassies are in Tel Aviv, with some maintaining a diplomatic (in both senses of the world) presence in Arab East Jerusalem, though the United States has been promising to move its embassy to Jerusalem since 1995.

**Embassy of the United States**
71 Hayarkon Street
Tel Aviv 63405, Israel
Tel.: (972) 3 519 7457
Fax: (972) 3 516 4390
webmaster@usembassy-israel.org.il
http://www.usembassy-israel.org.il

**Consulate-General of the United States**
18 Agron Road
Jerusalem 94190, Israel
Tel.: (972) 2 622 7230
Fax: (972) 2 625 9270
jerusalemWeb@pd.state.gov
http://www.uscongen-jerusalem.org

**Embassy of Great Britain**
192 Hayarkon Street
Tel Aviv 63405, Israel
Tel.: (972) 3 725 1222
Fax: (972) 3 527 8574
webmaster.telaviv@fco.gov.uk
http://www.britemb.org.il

**Consulate-General of Great Britain**
19 Nashashibi Street
Sheikh Jarrah
PO Box 19690
East Jerusalem 97200, Israel
Tel.: (972) 2 541 4100
Fax: (972) 2 532 2368
britain@palnet.com
http://www.britishconsulate.org

**Embassy of Canada**
3/5 Nirim Street
Tel Aviv 67060, Israel
Tel.: (972) 3 636 3300
Fax: (972) 3 636 3380
taviv@dfait-maeci.gc.ca
http://www.dfait-maeci.gc.ca/telaviv

**Canadian Representative Office**
Soudah House
12 Mahfal Street
Ramallah, Israel
Tel.: (972) 2 295 8604
Fax: (972) 2 295 8606
rmlah@dfait-maeci.gc.ca

# Dangerous Days

| | |
|---|---|
| 10/12/02 | Israeli tanks enter Nablus, then Gaza City. |
| 7/31/02 | A bomb detonated by a cell phone kills seven (five of them Americans) and injures 86 in the Frank Sinatra Student Center at Hebrew University. |
| 6/21/02 | Israeli troops kill four Palestinians, including three children, in Jenin. |
| 6/20/02 | Palestinian gunman kills six at Itamar, a settlement near Nablus. |
| 6/19/02 | Palestinian suicide bomber kills seven at a bus stop in Jerusalem. |
| 6/19/02 | Israel announces that it will begin reoccupying parts of the West Bank. |
| 6/18/02 | Palestinian suicide bomber kills 20 on a bus in Jerusalem. |

| | |
|---|---|
| 6/14/02 | Israel begins building a concrete fence around Palestinian areas. |
| 6/6/02 | Israeli tanks level Arafat's headquarters in Ramallah. |
| 6/5/02 | Palestinian suicide bomber kills 16 on a bus at Megiddo Junction, in northern Israel. Israeli forces attack Yasser Arafat's headquarters in Ramallah. |
| 5/27/02 | Palestinian suicide bomber kills two in a shopping center in Petah Tikva. |
| 5/22/02 | Palestinian suicide bomber kills one in Rishon Letzion, near Tel Aviv. |
| 5/19/02 | Palestinian suicide bomber disguised as an Israeli soldier kills three at a market in Netanya. |
| 5/17/02 | Israeli troops raid Jenin refugee camp again. |
| 5/9/02 | Siege at Bethlehem's Church of the Nativity ends. Thirteen Palestinian militants sent into exile in various European countries. |
| 5/7/02 | Palestinian suicide bomber kills 16 at a pool hall in Rishon Letzion, near Tel Aviv. |
| 4/29/02 | Israeli attack on a security building in Hebron leaves nine dead, including six civilians. |
| 4/27/02 | Palestinian gunmen kill four, including a child, in a settlement near Hebron. |
| 4/26/02 | Israeli troops attack Qalqiliya. |
| 4/23/02 | Israeli soldiers shoot dead three 14-year-old Palestinian boys, apparently while they are attempting a suicide attack on a settlement in Gaza. |
| 4/22/02 | International Committee of the Red Cross accuses Israel of violating the Geneva Convention during its actions in Jenin. |
| 4/12/02 | Palestinian suicide bomber kills six at a bus stop in Jerusalem. |
| 4/10/02 | Palestinian suicide bomber kills eight on a bus near Haifa. |
| 4/9/02 | Thirteen Israeli soldiers die in an ambush in Jenin. |
| 4/6/02 | President George W. Bush calls on Israel to withdraw from the West Bank "without delay." Israeli planes attack targets in southern Lebanon. |
| 4/3/02 | Bethlehem's Church of the Nativity, reputed site of the birth of Christ, besieged by Israeli troops after armed Palestinians take refuge inside. Hizbollah fires rockets into northern Israel. Syria announces plans to send 20,000 more troops to Lebanon. |
| 4/2/02 | Israel launches air and armor assault on Bethlehem. |

**4/1/02** Israeli tanks surround Bethlehem and Tulkarem.

**3/31/02** Sharon declares Arafat "an enemy of Israel." Palestinian suicide bomber kills 15 in a restaurant in Haifa.

**3/30/02** Palestinian suicide bomber injures 30 in a restaurant in Tel Aviv.

**3/29/02** Palestinian suicide bomber kills two at a supermarket in Jerusalem. Arafat's compound is bulldozed.

**3/29/02** Israeli troops storm Yasser Arafat's headquarters in Ramallah, putting him under siege.

**3/27/02** Palestinian suicide bomber kills 28 at a Passover feast in a hotel in Netanya.

**3/21/02** Palestinian suicide bomber kills two in Jerusalem.

**3/20/02** Palestinian suicide bomber kills seven on a bus near Umm el-Fahem.

**3/12/02** More than 20,000 Israeli troops occupy Ramallah and refugee camps in the Gaza Strip. At least 30 Palestinians killed, and hundreds are evicted from their homes.

**3/11/02** Israeli attack on refugee camp in Gaza kills 17.

**3/10/02** Israel destroys Arafat's headquarters in Gaza City.

**3/9/02** Palestinian suicide bomber kills 11 at a café in Jerusalem.

**3/8/02** Palestinian gunman kills five teenage Israeli officer cadets at Atzmona settlement in the Gaza Strip. Israeli troops kill at least 40 Palestinians in fighting on the West Bank and in Gaza, including Major General Ahmed Mefraj, the deputy commander of Palestinian Authority forces in Gaza.

**3/6/02** Israeli shelling on the Gaza Strip kills seven.

**3/5/02** Palestinian suicide bomber kills one at a bus station in Afula.

**3/4/02** Israeli assaults on Ramallah, Jenin, and Rafah kill 28.

**3/3/02** Palestinian sniper kills ten, including seven Israeli soldiers, at a checkpoint.

**3/2/02** Palestinian suicide bomber kills nine in an ultra-orthodox area of Jerusalem.

**2/28/02** Israel attacks Balata refugee camp from the air, and invades the refugee camp in Jenin.

**2/25/02** Israeli troops shoot dead a 15-year-old Palestinian girl armed with a knife near Tulkarem.

**2/19/02** Palestinian gunmen kill six Israeli soldiers at a checkpoint near Ramallah. Israeli air strikes in response kill 16.

**2/19/02** Israeli missile strikes kill eight.

| 2/18/02 | Palestinian suicide bomber kills a policeman at a checkpoint. |
|---|---|
| 2/16/02 | Palestinian suicide bomber kills two at a pizzeria in Karnei Shomron. |
| 2/15/02 | Palestinian roadside bomb kills three Israeli soldiers, and destroys a Merkava tank. |
| 1/27/02 | Palestinian suicide bomber kills one in a shopping street in Jerusalem. |
| 1/24/02 | Israeli helicopter kills senior Hamas leader Bakr Hamdan and two others. |
| 1/22/02 | Palestinian gunman kills two at a bus stop in Jerusalem. |
| 1/21/02 | Israeli troops occupy Tulkarem, a West Bank town. |
| 1/18/02 | Israeli jets bomb Palestinian Authority police building in Tulkarem, killing one. |
| 1/17/02 | Palestinian gunman kills six at a Bar Mitzvah in Hadera. |
| 1/10/02 | Israeli bulldozers flatten 32 homes in Rafah refugee camp. |
| 1/9/02 | Four Israeli soldiers and two Hamas gunmen die in a shoot-out in Gaza. |
| 1/4/02 | Israeli navy intercepts container ship full of weapons off the coast near Gaza. |
| 12/2/01 | Palestinian suicide bomber kills 15 on a bus in Haifa. |
| 12/1/01 | Palestinian suicide bombers kill ten in a shopping center in Jerusalem. |
| 11/29/01 | Palestinian suicide bomber kills four on a bus in Hadera. |
| 10/16/01 | PFLP gunmen shoot dead Israeli Tourism Minister Rehavam Zeevi in Jerusalem's Hyatt Hotel. |
| 9/27/01 | Israeli tanks kill five Palestinians in a refugee camp in southern Gaza. |
| 9/15/01 | A major Israeli incursion into Gaza kills at least two Palestinians. |
| 9/12/01 | Israeli troops kill at least seven Palestinians in an invasion of Jericho. |
| 9/9/01 | Israeli Arab suicide bomber kills three at a railway station in Naharia. |
| 9/1/01 | Colonel Taiseer Khatab, a Palestinian Authority intelligence aide, is killed by a car bomb in Gaza. |
| 8/27/01 | PFLP leader Abu Ali Mustafa assassinated in his office in Ramallah by an Israeli helicopter-launched missile. |
| 8/22/01 | Israeli commandos kill four Palestinians in Nablus. |

**8/14/01**  Israeli tanks move into Jenin.

**8/12/01**  Palestinian suicide bomber injures 20 at a restaurant near Haifa.

**8/10/01**  Israeli warplanes destroy Palestinian police headquarters in Ramallah, and Israeli troops seize the PLO office in East Jerusalem.

**8/9/01**  Palestinian suicide bomber kills 15 at a pizzeria in Jerusalem.

**8/5/01**  Palestinian gun attacks in Israel and the West Bank kill one Israeli and wound 13. Hamas activist Amer Mansour Habiri killed by an Israeli helicopter-launched missile in Tulkarem.

**7/31/01**  Israeli helicopter attack on Hamas office in Nablus kills eight, including senior Hamas official Jamal Mansour, and two children.

**7/19/01**  Israeli settlers shoot dead three Palestinians, including a three-month-old baby, near Hebron.

**7/17/01**  Israeli troops move into the West Bank. Four more alleged Palestinian militants are assassinated.

**6/10/01**  Israeli tank kills three Bedouin Arab women in a tent in the Gaza Strip.

**6/2/01**  Palestinian suicide bomber kills 21 at a disco in Tel Aviv.

**5/14/01**  Israeli troops kill five Palestinian policemen at a West Bank checkpoint.

**5/8/01**  Four-month-old Iman Hijjo becomes the youngest victim of the intifada so far, when he is killed by shrapnel from an Israeli tank shell at Khan Yunis in the Gaza Strip.

**4/17/01**  Israel reoccupies parts of the Gaza Strip, and closes the border crossing to Egypt.

**4/16/01**  Israel attacks the Gaza Strip from air, land, and sea

**4/15/01**  Israeli aircraft attack a Syrian radar station in Lebanon.

**4/4/01**  Palestinian suicide bomber disguised as an orthodox Jew injures 13 in Jerusalem.

**4/3/01**  Islamic Jihad commander Mohammed Abdel Al killed by a helicopter-launched missile in Gaza.

**3/28/01**  Nail-bomb attack kills three at a bus stop near Kfar Saba.

**2/14/01**  Palestinian bus driver plows into a group at a bus stop, apparently deliberately, killing eight.

**2/6/01**  Ariel Sharon elected prime minister of Israel.

**1/21/01**  A Jewish settler who beat an Arab child to death with a rifle butt is sentenced to six months' community service.

ISRAEL/PALESTINE

| | |
|---|---|
| **11/22/00** | Car bomb kills two in Hadera. |
| **11/2/00** | Car bomb kills two at Mahane Yehuda market in Jerusalem. |
| **10/12/00** | Two Israeli soldiers beaten to death in police station in Ramallah. Massive retaliatory strikes follow. |
| **9/30/00** | 12-year-old Mohammed al-Durrah is shot dead by Israeli troops on the Gaza Strip, becoming a symbol of the intifada. |
| **9/29/00** | Israeli opposition leader Ariel Sharon visits the Temple Mount compound in Jerusalem. Al-Aqsa Intifada begins. |
| **7/25/00** | Talks at Camp David between Ehud Barak and Yasser Arafat break down after 15 days. |
| **5/22/00** | Israel withdraws from southern Lebanon, ending an 18-year occupation. Hizbollah take up positions along Israeli border. Ehud Barak calls off Stockholm peace talks following violence on the West Bank. |
| **2/8/00** | Israel bombs targets in Lebanon after attacks by Hizbollah guerrillas kill five Israeli soldiers. |
| **1/9/00** | Peace talks between Israel and Syria break down after four days. |
| **10/5/99** | Safe passage for Palestinians and foreign visitors begins between Israel and Gaza, and Judea and Samaria. |
| **9/3/99** | Israeli Prime Minister Ehud Barak and Palestinian leader Yasser Arafat sign a peace agreement at Sharm el-Sheikh in Egypt. |
| **9/4/97** | Palestinian suicide bombers kill eight in Jerusalem. |
| **7/30/97** | Palestinian suicide bombers kill 16 at Mahane Yehuda market in Jerusalem. |
| **3/31/97** | Palestinian suicide bomber kills three at a café in Tel Aviv. |
| **4/10/96** | Israel invades Hamas positions and cities within Lebanon after a Hizbollah rocket attack on northern Israel injures 40 people. |
| **3/4/96** | Palestinian suicide bomber kills 13 in Tel Aviv. |
| **3/3/96** | Palestinian suicide bomber kills 19 on a bus in Jerusalem. |
| **2/25/96** | Palestinian suicide bombers kill 26 in Jerusalem and Tel Aviv. |
| **11/4/95** | Prime Minister Yitzhak Rabin assassinated by right-wing Jewish extremist. |
| **8/21/95** | Palestinian suicide bomber kills five on a bus in Jerusalem. |

**7/24/95**   Palestinian suicide bomber kills six on a bus near Tel Aviv.

**4/9/95**   Palestinian suicide bomber kills seven Israeli soldiers and an American tourist in Gaza.

**1/22/95**   Palestinian suicide bombers kill 21 Israeli soldiers near Netanya.

**11/11/94**   Bomb kills three Israeli soldiers at Netzarim settlement near Gaza.

**10/19/94**   Palestinian suicide bomber kills 23 on a bus in Tel Aviv.

**10/11/94**   The Palestine Liberation Organization (PLO) Central Council approves Chairman Yasser Arafat's peace deal with Israel by a vote of 63 to 8, with 11 members abstaining or absent.

**9/13/94**   Israel and the PLO sign a peace agreement in Washington, DC, outlining a plan for Palestinian self-rule in the Israeli Occupied Territories.

**4/13/94**   Palestinian suicide bomber kills five in Hadera.

**4/6/94**   Car bomb kills eight in Afula.

**9/9/93**   The PLO and Israel sign a mutual recognition agreement as part of the Oslo Accords.

**12/17/92**   More than 400 suspected members of Hamas are forcibly expelled from Israel into Lebanon, following the kidnap-murder of an Israeli border policeman. The expellees are refused entry into Lebanon and forced to camp in the Israeli-controlled security zone in south Lebanon.

**12/16/91**   The United Nations General Assembly repeals the 1975 resolution that stated that Zionism is a form of racism.

**1/15/91**   Abu Iyad, the second-ranking PLO leader, and two other high-ranking PLO officials are assassinated by a guard suspected of working for the Abu Nidal Organization (ANO).

**10/8/90**   Eighteen Arabs die during clashes with Israeli police on Temple Mount in Jerusalem.

**5/20/90**   An Israeli gunman kills eight Palestinian laborers in Rishon le Ziyyon, south of Tel Aviv. Nine workers are injured. The gunman is identified as a discharged Israeli soldier.

**12/9/87**   Beginning of the intifada, or uprising, on the West Bank and the Gaza Strip.

**10/1/85**   Israeli Air Force bombs the headquarters of the Palestine Liberation Organization (PLO) in Tunis.

**5/17/83**   Israel signs an accord with Lebanon for the withdrawal of Israeli troops from most of southern Lebanon.

| 3/26/79 | Egyptian-Israeli peace treaty. |
| 9/17/78 | Camp David accords signed. |
| 3/16/78 | Israeli forces invade Lebanon. |
| 7/4/76 | An Israeli raid on Entebbe Airport in Uganda frees 103 hostages from a hijacked Air France airliner. |
| 10/6/73 | The Yom Kippur War begins. |
| 9/6/72 | Palestinian Black September terrorists massacre Israeli athletes at the Munich Olympics. |
| 5/30/72 | Members of the PFLP and Japanese Red Army (JRA) kill 26 people in a massacre at Lod Airport. |
| 2/21/70 | Suspected members of the PFLP-GC place a bomb on a Swissair passenger jet en route from Zurich to Tel Aviv, resulting in the death of all 47 passengers. |
| 7/22/68 | Members of the Popular Front for the Liberation of Palestine (PFLP) hijack an El Al flight en route to Tel Aviv and forced it to land in Algiers. The attack marks the first aircraft hijacking by a Palestinian group. The hijackers are said to have believed that Israeli General Ariel Sharon was on the flight. The passengers and crew are detained by Algeria for six weeks. |
| 6/5/67 | The Six-Day War ends. |
| 5/31/67 | Israeli troops capture East Jerusalem in the Six-Day War. |
| 1/1/64 | Palestine Liberation Organization (PLO) is founded at a meeting in Jerusalem. |
| 5/14/48 | The State of Israel is proclaimed; the date is celebrated in Israel as Independence Day and across the Arab world as al-Nakba ("catastrophe"). |
| 11/2/17 | The Balfour Declaration promises a Jewish homeland in Palestine. Demonstrations in the Occupied Territories and the Gaza Strip still occur on this date. |

# In a Dangerous Place: Israel

### ELECTION WEEK: ISRAEL AND PALESTINE

It's one thing that the movies get right. Whether you're watching a Western in an air-conditioned cinema, or watching a riot from behind a low brick fence on the forecourt of a grocery shop in Ramallah, the shrill twang of a ricocheting bullet sounds exactly the same. It's the first Friday after Israel's elections, the first Muslim holy day after the announcement that Israelis have awarded their prime ministership to Ariel Sharon, probably the most loathed figure in the Arab world.

About 100 meters down the street from where photographer Paul Donohue and I are sheltered, a few bold souls fling rocks at the barricades and armored Jeeps that mark the limit of Israel's authority in the area. The small mob of rioters running this way and that to avoid the Israeli response moves in oddly graceful swirls; it's like watching a lava lamp filled with people and tear gas.

Most of the young Palestinians are heading home, though, stuffing their slings into their pockets and departing in the half-jogging, half-sauntering gait of people trying to look cool while they are, basically, running for it. Bigger boys with bigger toys want to play this afternoon; automatic rifle fire opens up from an abandoned building on the Palestinian side of the line, perhaps 100 meters to our left ("Hamas," explains one of the locals crouching next to us). From somewhere in the retreating throng there's the crisp snap of pistols. When answering fire from the Israeli position starts zinging off the walls around us, we fall back along with everyone else—actually, knowing that we won't be held accountable for our actions in the playground come Monday, we fall back rather ahead of everyone else.

As it happens, nobody really notices us, or our rather undignified retreat. As the Israeli fire intensifies, the only things going in its direction are Palestinian ambulances. Whatever one's doubts about this afternoon's shenanigans—and if it's hard to see what the Palestinians think they are accomplishing by rioting, it's impossible not to believe that if the Israelis just sat tight behind their fortifications, everyone soon would get bored and go home—there is no doubting the bravery of the ambulance crews, mostly female, dressed in their tightly pinned veils and red crescent bibs.

The Friday riot at Ramallah's City Inn junction is more or less a weekly ritual, varying in severity from stone-throwing and tear-gassing to minor battles. Today we've seen the full spectrum. In a car park beneath a building half a block beyond the sightlines of the Israelis, a makeshift field hospital has been established. The medic in charge, Dr. Hassan Basharat, estimates that today's score, at around three in the afternoon, is nine hit by rubber-coated bullets, ten stricken by tear-gas inhalation, and two wounded by live rounds, one seriously—the bullet is lodged under the collarbone, apparently.

The injured are all men, says Dr. Basharat, mostly between 18 and 25 years old. When I ask him if he thinks these victims, and those even younger, really believe they're engaged in a revolutionary national struggle, or if they're basically just kids who are showing off to each other, he offers a kindly shrug.

"What's going on out there," he says, in impeccable, barely accented English, "is always a reflection of the wider political situation. Those are the parameters I work within. When there's trouble between leaders, there's trouble here. When there's not, there isn't."

As Dr. Basharat talks, a middle-aged man in a brown suit is helped to a stretcher, clutching one hip.

"You'd better make that ten by rubber-coated bullets," sighs Dr. Basharat, nodding at my notebook, and goes back to work.

It is customary in all countries that hold elections for those seeking office to suggest that to cast a vote for their opponent is to book a ticket on the next hell-bound handcart. What makes Israel almost refreshingly different is that the candidates mean it: The rhetoric traded in the days before Israelis elected a prime minister on February 6, 2001, was positively apocalyptic.

If the incumbent, Labor Party's Ehud Barak—a former army general and the most decorated soldier in Israel's eventful military history— was to be believed, a vote for his opponent was a vote for Israel's sixth major war with its Arab neighbors since the founding of the state in 1948. To listen to his challenger, Likud's Ariel Sharon—another retired general—Barak was bent on achieving peace by giving away huge swaths of Israeli territory and the holy sites of Jerusalem to a Palestinian entity that had been in open revolt since September, and whose central purpose was driving Israel's Jews into the Mediterranean.

Israelis chose, by a huge margin, to take their chances with Sharon. His accession to Israel's prime ministership is the most remarkable comeback witnessed in the region since Lazarus decided he wasn't feeling so bad after all. As a military commander in the 1950s, Sharon became infamous for punitive raids against Arab troops and civilians alike. As Defense Minister in the '80s, he ran Israel's invasion of Lebanon (the occupation was ended by Barak in 2000), and was removed from the job in 1983 by an Israeli tribunal that found him "indirectly" responsible for the massacres of hundreds of Palestinian civilians in Sabra and Chatila. Ariel Sharon's approach to the Palestinian question has always been best understood by pretending that his surname is "Bombardment."

Sharon sparked the current Palestinian intifada with a provocative visit to Jerusalem's Temple Mount in September 2000. The Temple Mount, known to Muslims as Haram al-Sharif, is the location of The Dome of the Rock, the magnificent shrine built on the lumpy, beige hilltop where Abraham was instructed by Yahweh to sacrifice his son Isaac, and from which Mohammed vaulted into heaven. Temple Mount is also the home of the immense al-Aqsa mosque, and was the original repository for the Ark of the Covenant, believed by many still to be lying around here somewhere, beneath forty turbulent centuries' worth of succeeding rubble.

Temple Mount is sacred to all monotheistic religions in theory, but is a Muslim holy site in practice. Sharon's claim that it was his right as an Israeli citizen to visit what is—or has been since 1967—Israeli territory was accurate but ingenuous: a little like, say, the Reverend Ian Paisley exercising his right as a British citizen to walk the Falls Road in Belfast singing "God Save The Queen." The fact that Israel has nonetheless elected Sharon is an expression of the fear that even many liberal Israelis feel, that their young and undeniably vibrant country is under real threat, either from Arab terrorism or from a peace agreement that would undermine Israel's security.

On Ben Yehuda Street, the pedestrian arcade that is home to what passes for nightlife in Jerusalem's New City, there is a predictably broad spectrum of opinion being offered: Israelis are a fiercely opinionated, splendidly obstinate bunch, and if there are two people in the country who agree on anything, I've only managed to meet one of them.

"For sure, I was happy Sharon won," says Jason, an 18-year-old Yeshiva student originally from New York, as if he's just been asked the silliest question he's ever heard (and maybe he has).

"Barak was giving away the country," he continues. "It's our country, it says so in the Bible, and even aside from that, we won it fair and square in 1948. I think the press has been very unfair about Israel. The Arabs are the ones who are doing the violence. Israel just counters it. The stone-throwing kids have got soldiers with guns behind them. What are Israeli soldiers supposed to do? I understand that the Palestinians had a land, and now they're homeless, but if their Arab brethren care so much about them, why don't they take them in? Jews were exiled for 2,000 years, and when Israel was founded in 1948, we welcomed Jewish people from all over the world. Arabs aren't doing that."

It is difficult, as more experienced mediators than I at higher levels than this have discovered, to argue with people who think they've got God in their corner. Clever chap though the Almighty undoubtedly is, it's hard to resist thinking that putting the holy sites of the rival creeds that claim Him in one neighborhood wasn't one of His brighter ideas.

"Co-existence is impossible," continues Jason. "This land is ours, it was always ours, then they claim something happened with Mohammed, and so it's their land—what if they decided something important to Islam happened in New York? Would they want that as well?"

I don't know. Probably a bridge best crossed when we come to it, I'd have thought.

"And there's nothing in the Koran about Jerusalem."

Actually, there is, though I don't find this out until I look it up later—the "Farther Temple" mentioned in the "Night Journey" chapter of the Koran is a reference to Mohammed's trek to Jerusalem from Mecca in AD 620 ("Glory be to Him who made His servant go by night from the Sacred Temple to the Farther Temple whose surroundings we have blessed.") Jason might be interested to note that the chapter goes on to observe that "We solemnly declared to the Israelites: 'Twice you shall do great evil in the land. You shall become great transgressors.'"

Before I let Jason go, I ask him a question I already know the answer to.

"I don't have any Palestinian friends, no," he replies. "Why would I want any? They want us dead."

About half a second later, I find myself talking to Yonit, a 20-year-old Azerbaijani who has lived in Jerusalem for six years. I had noticed her twitching with annoyance at Jason's sermonizing.

"I was for Barak," she says. "I think the Palestinians have a right to a country of their own, just as we do. For 2,000 years, this was their land and our land, and then we started up with all this Zionism bullshit. We Jews are not the chosen people, not at all. I think we're the people that have been punished the most, and that's made us kind of a fucked-up bunch with really big egos. Sharon goes to Temple Mount, Jews settle in Hebron, Palestinians get frightened and retaliate . . . where does it stop? I don't think people should be dying for this. All that said, I feel that Israel is my country, and that this city is my home. But it's a city that is important to all religions—Judaism, Christianity, and Islam. All should have equal access."

After a couple of hours in and around the pizzerias and cafés on Ben Yehuda Street, I score it roughly a two-to-one win to the Jasons, with his American-born compatriots by far the most hard-line—maybe Azerbaijanis and others with recent experience of living under occupation can muster a little more sympathy for the Palestinians.

There is consensus on one subject, however: business. And here, there is rare agreement among Israelis and across the Israeli-Palestinian divide: It's terrible. The proprietor of Mr T's Disposals on Ben Yehuda Street offers a 35 percent discount before I even ask about his "I Got Stoned in Gaza" T-shirts. In an Italian restaurant on Yosef Rivlin Street, the waitress brings me a complimentary dessert with my bill; when I ask what I've done to deserve it, she replies, "Turned up."

The conflict has had an even more pronounced effect on the Old City. During my last visit to Jerusalem, in July 2000, it had scarcely been possible to move in the Old City's narrow streets because of the shoals of package-tour pilgrims wearing baseball caps that said things like "Regina Tours: 1-800-CATHOLIC" carting crosses in Christ's final footsteps up the Via Dolorosa, and posing for pictures beside the smooth stone slab upon which Jesus is said to have been lain after being removed from the cross ("And here's me and Edna, right next to where our savior perished for our sins").

Now, the Old City is all but deserted. At the Church of the Holy Sepulcher, at the end of the Via Dolorosa, the queues were once legendary ( I once saw two rival tour guides swatting each other about the ears with brochures; they were led outside by a cleric whose resigned demeanor suggested that this was by no means unusual). Today, there is nobody with whom to share the location of the crucifixion but a Greek Orthodox priest and a platoon of Ukrainian soldiers on UN attachment. Many shops in the Christian Quarter are closed, those in the Jewish Quarter give the impression of staying open only to keep up appearances, and while the Palestinian shopkeepers in the Muslim Quarter still tout their incongruous wares of Jewish and Christian religious souvenirs and Israeli army T-shirts, they can hardly be bothered to look up from their backgammon as I walk past.

"It's hopeless," says one. "I've had to borrow money from my father and my brother, just to feed my family. Look, you come here as a friend, you'll have no problems with Arabs—do you have a problem now? Of course not. Sharon, all the Jews, they don't want peace. Do you see Arafat going to the Western Wall?"

If it wasn't for the roadblock, there would be no way of telling where Jerusalem ends and Ramallah begins. The urban sprawl of this part of the West Bank is as solid as it is dingy and dusty, and no obvious break in the jerry-built construction indicates when you've left Israel proper and arrived in the jurisdiction of the Palestine National Authority.

For the visitor, then, the sandbags and soldiers and the huge Israeli flag are a handy reference point. Otherwise, the checkpoint is useless— every vehicle going to or from Ramallah drives around it, joining a slow-moving line of cars, trucks, and buses on a torturous route of narrow, potholed, suspension-wrecking side streets before returning to the highway on the other side of the Israeli post. The checkpoint does not prevent anyone or anything from traveling between Jerusalem and Ramallah: The combined armies of Syria and Iraq could be invading Israel by taxi for all the soldiers under the Star of David would know about it. The only reason for the checkpoint to exist is as a trivial vexation, another minor humiliation designed to remind the West Bank's Palestinian population who's in charge. I sit at the back of a minibus full of Palestinians who are so resigned to the inconvenience that not a single complaint is audible above the radio.

Ramallah, never regarded as a must-see for the Middle Eastern tourist, has had especially lousy press of late. The city provided the definitive media image of the Palestinian uprising in October 2000, when one of its young men was photographed yelling triumphantly from the window of Ramallah's Palestinian Authority police station, his outstretched hands red with the blood of the two Israeli soldiers he'd just helped beat to death. Israel responded with customary severity, destroying the station with helicopter-launched missiles: The wreckage still can be found in the center of town, where the minibuses from Jerusalem drop their passengers.

Ramallah looks just like any other Middle Eastern city—which is to say, like a building site belonging to a company that has gone bust halfway through construction, but with traffic—apart from dozens of posters of young men, smiling and standing against backdrops of the Palestinian flag and Jerusalem's Dome of the Rock. These are memorials to locals who have been killed by Israeli troops since September. Some of the martyrs look every bit the popular image of the Arab extremist, clutching Korans and waving rifles in poses that must have been struck at least partly in anticipation of their eventual display on one of these ad hoc rolls of honor. And some don't: At least one martyr is no more than 12 years old and is pictured wearing something that looks depressingly as though it might be a Boy Scout uniform.

I've come to Ramallah to visit the Popular Art Center in the adjoining municipality of al-Bireit. The Popular Art Center is one of those incongruously cheerful and positive institutions of the sort that often exist in places where dismal and stupid things are happening. With funding provided by a variety of international non-governmental organizations, the PAC's employees travel all over Palestine, to towns and to refugee camps that have been refugee camps so long they've become towns, instructing children in dance and physical education. In the PAC building opposite the al-Ain mosque, they offer yoga and Shaolin classes and maintain a café, a dance studio, and a small movie theater—among the films playing during election week are *The Perfect Storm, High Fidelity, Erin Brockovich,* and, in a Friday night double-bill that is surely too apposite to be deliberate, *The Final Destination* and *Children of Heaven.*

The PAC's activities director, and the only non-Palestinian on its staff, is Nicholas Rowe, one of tragically few people who can answer to the description of Darwin-raised ballet dancer. Now 32 years old, Rowe's career in dance has seen him perform with the Sydney Dance Company, the Australian Ballet, the Finnish National Ballet, and the Royal New Zealand Ballet. It has also taken him, with the Nomad Dance Theatre, to such unlikely habitats for the modern terpsichorean muse as the Philippines, Pakistan, Turkey, and Bosnia-Herzegovina. He fetched up in Palestine nine months ago, before the intifada erupted. He was, he says, wearied of the "decadence" of a ballet dancer's life, and wanted to do something constructive.

Rowe says he has "gone through a few pairs of underpants" since arriving in Ramallah. After the lynching of the Israeli reservists, he spent three days holed up in the PAC office, terrified that the wrath of the mob might be vented upon any passing foreigner. He was once shot at while on the roof of the PAC, probably by a trigger-happy zealot in the nearby Israeli settlement of Psagot who mistook him for a Palestinian sniper. Exchanges of fire between Psagot and Ramallah are common, and the PAC cinema occasionally has to keep customers inside after the late shows when the fighting gets especially bad. They watch videos of *Friends* while they wait for a lull in the shooting.

In the days following the election, I join the PAC's staff as they journey around the West Bank. On Wednesday, we visit a school in Abu Dees, a Palestinian town to the east of Jerusalem—the golden Dome of the Rock is just visible from the school's roof. The primary-age children are divided into groups to perform routines with dancer Maysoun Rafeedie, 22 years old, of Ramallah's internationally renowned El-Fanoun troupe, and play organized team games with PAC volunteer Mohammed Zomlot, 23 years old, whose other occupation is representing Yasser Arafat's Fateh party on the Student Council at Birzeit University, near Ramallah. Mohammed, like a surprising number of Palestinians, expresses a perverse satisfaction with Sharon's victory.

"Barak said he'd give us land," says Mohammed, "said he'd give us Jerusalem, and didn't mean any of it. Sharon says he won't give us anything, and the whole world can see what's going on. Everyone knows about Sharon—about Lebanon, about Sabra, about Chatila. Under the peace process, everyone forgot about Palestine. But everyone knows about us now."

The school visit ends with the kids lining up to have their faces painted by the cool and experienced PAC people and by one panicking, press-ganged journalist desperately hoping he isn't scarring any of them for life, either physically or psychologically. A few nascent nationalists ask for their faces to be painted in the colors of the Palestinian flag, but the most popular request by far is for the Pokémon character Pikáchu. We quickly run out of yellow paint, and are forced to improvise with green.

Thursday's expedition is more ambitious. We leave Ramallah at nine in the morning, hoping to visit a school in the al-Fawwar refugee camp near Hebron. In theory, the drive from Ramallah to Hebron should take around 45 minutes. It takes us a little over three hours. Israeli army checkpoints politely but firmly turn our rented minibus, with its Palestinian license plates, away from the entrances to the main highways. Our driver heads for the back roads that crisscross the rocky, rust-colored, bewilderingly rubbish-strewn hills of Judea, only to find many of them blocked by piles of earth bulldozed into place by Israeli settlers; at one stop, three Palestinian men are struggling to carry an old woman in a wheelchair over the top of the barricade. Every spot of high ground is occupied by Israeli military positions, and Israeli jets make frequent sorties overhead.

The al-Fawwar camp has existed under these conditions since it first was built in 1948. Sixty thousand people have lived here, with their entire lives on hold, determined that al-Fawwar, its brick buildings and sealed roads notwithstanding, is only a temporary arrangement. Ask people in al-Fawwar where they're from, and even if they were born here, and their parents were born here, they'll name villages that are now somewhere in Israel, if they still exist at all: homes they've never known and will probably never see.

"I'm from Dawaima," says Tariq, 20 years old, a policeman with the Palestinian Authority. "I've never been [there], but I've seen the pictures my grandfather took."

"My family is from Biutjibreen, a village near Hebron," says the school's head teacher, Faisa, 51 years old. "My parents left there after the war in 1948, and I was born here in 1949. I think Biutjibreen is used to train Israeli soldiers now. I've never been there, but it is my home. Every day, I hope it is the day I can go back. This is not a good place to live. There's no running water, no telephones, no reliable electricity. People live with 10 people in a room—one room is kitchen, bathroom, bedroom, everything."

"The streets are damaged," adds Zohoun, a 40-year-old volunteer teacher, "there's rubbish everywhere, it's unhealthy. We have no land—only the place we live, and it isn't the same thing. Jews from many lands come here now, but this is my land. Jews live in Palestine, but I don't—and I'm Palestinian. You ask me why we fight—if you lived here, you'd fight. You'd fight to return to your country, and you'd kill anyone who tried to stop you."

When we paint the kids' faces here, there's a design of their own invention to rival Pikáchu and Palestine's flag: a white face flecked with black to resemble a kaffiyeh scarf. They call it "Hizbollah."

I spend most of the day before I leave wandering aimlessly around Jerusalem's Old City—if the intifada has had one positive effect, it is that the consequent devastation of Israel's tourist industry has meant that the Old City seems less like the souvenir stall of a biblical theme park and more like a haven for peaceful reflection, the odd riot notwithstanding.

In Pomerantz, a bookshop nestling in the gleaming new stone construction that defines the Jewish Quarter, a sign on the counter thanks visitors for "showing your support" at "this trying time."

"We're down to about 60 percent of our normal trade," says Max, the shopkeeper, his Australian drawl not softened by 23 years' residence in Israel. "It's only thanks to Yeshiva students buying the religious stuff that we're open at all."

I ask him if he reckons there will ever be an end to this, or whether the Israelis and the Palestinians are, like two men locked together in handcuffs they can't find the keys to, doomed to each other.

"I think there will be a solution," he decides, "maybe in another 50 or 100 years. But I'm an optimist."

—*Andrew Mueller*

# ★ ★
# KURDISTAN

## Blood Kurd'ling

Kurdistan is one of those Alice-in-Wonderland countries that does not officially exist. Numbering somewhere between 20 and 25 million, the Kurds are the largest ethnic group in the world without a country of their own. There are more Kurds than there are Irish, Israelis, Croats, or Eritreans—and all those people have been given their own countries in the last hundred years or so. Who, the Kurds must wonder, in between revolts, rebellions, and uprisings, do they have to blow? Or who, to put it in the context in which most politics in this part of the world are generally conducted, do they have to blow up?

Take a step through the looking glass, and you'll find the Kurds split between modern-day Turkey, Iran, Iraq, and Syria. As many as 15 million Kurds live in southeastern Turkey, 7 million in Iran, 1.5 million in Syria, and about 4 million in northern Iraq. There are also approximately 1.5 million Kurds scattered over the former Soviet Union. (In

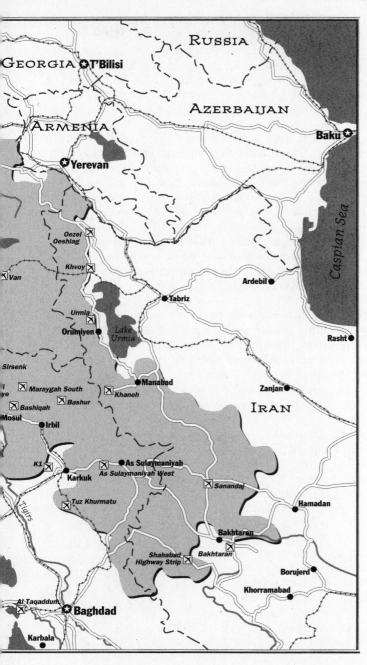

the 1920s, there was a short-lived autonomous Kurdish province known as Red Kurdistan, in what is now Azerbaijan.) Allah knows that Turkey, Iran, Iraq, and Syria have little enough in common, but all do share a dear wish that their resident Kurds would clear off to one of the other three; as the Kurds themselves put it, they have no friends but the mountains. (It should go without saying that the Kurds, in the usual manner of proud and ancient tribal people, don't like each other much.) Welcome to Kurdistan.

Historically, the Kurds have always copped the rough end of the pineapple. When the Ottoman Empire collapsed after World War I, the British promised the Kurds an independent Kurdistan in the 1920 Treaty of Sevres. The treaty was never ratified, however, and by 1923 it had been superseded by the Treaty of Lausanne, which not only failed to mention a Kurdish state, but carved up the land it was supposed to occupy among Turkey, Iraq, and Syria. The British, calculating that they'd rather have an anticommunist Turkey than an unaligned Kurdistan, cut a deal with Turkey's founding president, Mustafa Kemal Ataturk. No less than you'd expect from perfidious Albion, and the betrayal condemned the Kurds to their modern history of repression and rebellion.

Ataturk decided that the Kurds didn't exist. He banned their schools, publications, place names, music, and language. He even banned the very idea of Kurdishness: the Kurds, he announced, were "Mountain Turks," to which the Kurds took about as kindly as Palestinians would to being called "Mountain Israelis." There were major Kurdish revolts and brutal Turkish crackdowns in 1925, 1930, and 1937. In other years, there were merely minor Kurdish revolts and merely unpleasant Turkish crackdowns.

Like many stateless nations, the Kurds thought their moment might have come in the grand global reckoning that followed World War II. With the support of the USSR, they established the Republic of Mahabad in northern Iran. It lasted as long as it took for the USSR to wonder what was in it for them—about a year—and Mahabad was overrun by Iranian troops. Not for the first or last time, the Kurds scattered into the mountains.

The Kurds started getting organized in 1946, when Iraqi Kurd Mullah Mustafa Barzani founded the Kurdistan Democratic Party (KDP). It gave them a rallying point, but it didn't stop people from pushing them around. Syria stripped a fifth of its Kurds of their citizenship in 1962, and Iraq

**T**his would lead, in the 1990s, to an absurd civil war over a country that doesn't even exist—a case, if ever there was one, of two bald men fighting over a comb.

waged full-scale war on them in 1974 when the Kurds raised (not unreasonable) complaints about the fact that the Iraqi idea of an autonomous Kurdish province did not include the province of Kirkuk—or, more to the point, the oil reserves underneath it. The Marxist Patriotic Union of Kurdistan (PUK) was formed in response; in the grand tradition of rebel groups throughout the ages, they hated the KDP even more than they hated the Iraqis. This would lead, in the 1990s, to an absurd civil war over a country that doesn't even exist—a case, if ever there was one, of two bald men fighting over a comb.

Over the border in Turkey, the militancy spread: the Kurdistan Workers' Party (PKK) was formed by Abdullah Ocalan in 1978 and began its armed campaign in 1984. The subsequent two decades of guerrilla war with Turkey left nearly 40,000 dead, but it now seems to be over. Ocalan is in prison in Turkey, under sentence of death, and though he is still leader of the PKK, the PKK won't answer to the name anymore, announcing in April 2002 that all correspondence should be addressed instead to the Congress for Freedom and Democracy in Kurdistan (KADEK).

When Iraq and Iran embarked on their sensationally pointless war with each other in the '80s, the Kurds lost what little of the world's attention they ever had (unlike Iraq and Iran, they had no oil, and therefore not much money, and therefore no ability to buy colossal quantities of armaments from the West). They made some gains while Iraq's military was otherwise engaged, but found themselves fighting with both sides: The Iranians had a crack at taking northeastern Iraq off them, and Iraq launched a major attack against KDP-held areas in 1987. The culmination of this Iraqi pogrom was the infamous chemical weapons attack on Halabja in March 1988, which killed around 5,000 Kurds.

The Kurds were, again, briefly allowed to think their time had come, following the Gulf War. When George Bush the First encouraged the people of Iraq to make Saddam walk the plank, the Kurds and the Shi'ite Arabs in the south took him at his word, naively anticipating that American help might go beyond a "bon voyage" card. It didn't, of course, and the Kurds headed back up into the mountains, with what was left of Iraq's military close behind.

In April 1991, the United States created a safe haven for Kurds in northern Iraq to protect them from nasty old Saddam. In our humble opinion, this was in part due to the efforts of people such as *DP* contributor Coskun Aral, whose photos of Kurds fleeing into the mountains and fighting over bread were published internationally, including in *Time* magazine. These photos, along with graphic TV footage, helped force the United States to instigate the safe-haven policy when the Kurdish rebellion failed. The no-fly zone that still exists in the north of Iraq dates from this time, though it is not unheard of for Turkish jets to use the cover provided by Britain and America to attack suspected PKK bases inside Iraq.

At the same time, Saddam grudgingly agreed to autonomy for Kurdish areas, though the status of Kirkuk remained unresolved. In 1992 Iraqi Kurds held their first-ever free elections. The KDP beat the PUK with a small majority, but, being nice guys, they decided to split the seats in the new parliament evenly. The nice-guy stuff didn't last for long. In 1994 war broke out between the PUK and KDP. The PUK accused the KDP of hogging the cash from the border trade with Turkey. (With as many as 1,000 trucks crossing the border every day, it is estimated that the tax revenue amounts to about US$100 million a year.) Needless to say, the KDP control the border. The KDP said "don't," but the PUK said "do," leveled the antiaircraft guns, and started blasting.

In 1995 the PUK took the self-declared Kurdish capital of Arbil after fierce fighting. There was a breather for a while as the United States brokered an agreement between the two parties in Dublin, but when the United States then refused to put up the cash for the elections (a whole US$2 million), both factions decided to resolve their differences with artillery instead.

This time, though, Barzani's KDP dumped Uncle Sam for Uncle Saddam and invited the latter into Iraqi Kurdistan to kick the PUK out. On August 31, 1996, 10,000 Republican Guards plus tanks rocked up outside the gates of Arbil. Knowing Saddam's elite soldiers were equipped with real bullets, the PUK left in a hurry. Saddam's folks got down to the busy task of blowing up the Iraqi National Congress, rounding up and shooting a number of CIA-trained flunkies, and leaving behind a number of Iraqis who had changed into Kurdish uniforms (see "The Players").

Clinton's election-meisters scrambled to see how they could spin this confrontation. They vaguely remembered that footage of cruise missiles, stealth bombers, and a stern president were good for the opinion polls. What they forgot was that back in 1991, Saddam was choking off our oil supply and Bush had Schwartzkopf in the field with a multinational army instead of Dick Morris in bed with a hooker. Darn, it always worked out so well for the Republicans.

Saddam was unfazed. His new Kurdish allies went on to capture the rest of Kurdistan over the next few days. The PUK retreated to their headquarters in Zahle, way up on the Iranian border, for some counseling and weapons. It didn't take long for the PUK to hatch a plan. A month later they stormed down from the border (with a bit of help from Iran), recapturing most of their traditional areas. This time Saddam didn't come running to Barzani's aid. He simply informed the PUK that if they took the town of Degala then he would enter the conflict again. A tad miffed, the PUK called a halt to the offensive, sat back in Sulymanya, and waited for their next opportunity.

Things really went haywire in October 1997. Earlier in the year the KDP had allied themselves with the Turks in their war against the PKK, operating from the border area. With most of the KDP *peshmerga* tied up along the border, the PUK rubbed their hands with glee and started planning the next offensive. October saw the beginning of the PUK blitzkrieg, and boy, was the KDP in trouble. It was double, double, toil, and trouble, when the PKK kids then moved down from the border and joined in the offensive for a lark. The KDP dialed 911 (or 312, as the case was) and the Turkish military came storming in with everything they had. A month of fighting saw the PUK reluctantly call a halt to the offensive. With the preferred option of exterminating the KDP no longer an option, the PUK decided to negotiate. After months of wrangling, both Kurdish leaders went to Washington in September 1998, where they signed a peace agreement. This left Kurdistan effectively partitioned between two governments—the KDP's, based in Arbil, and the PUK's, based in Sulymanya—but the apparently unwieldy agreement has held up better than anyone dared hope.

However, the Kurds have always been able to provide a problem for every solution: in late 2001, the Ansar al-Islam, a radical Islamist Kurdish group with ties to any or all of Iran, Iraq, and Osama bin Laden, declared that both the PUK and KDP were softies and sellouts, and started hacking up soldiers and civilians to prove it.

## The Scoop

A few years of relative peace and quiet notwithstanding, Kurdistan is a mess. Iraqi Kurds have been fighting successive Baghdad governments as well as other Iraqi Kurds, Turkish Kurds, and the Turkish military. Vast mountainous regions afford plenty of places for the guerrillas of one side to hide and then whack the others. A mishmash of tribal allegiances; political, criminal, and ethnic alliances; and intelligence operatives from half a dozen countries running around make Kurdistan one of the most interesting and potentially dangerous places in the world.

The $64,000 question is, what will happen to the Kurds when something happens to Saddam Hussein—and will the Kurds be asked to be part of the something that happens to him? (In March 2002, Iraqi troops began digging trenches around the Kurdish enclaves in anticipation of such a development.) The Kurds might not have a choice—if it is no longer in the West's interest to tweak Saddam's moustache by enforcing the no-fly zone in the north, there is nothing to stop his successor from reasserting Iraqi hegemony over Kurdistan. And, based on the past, there is no reason whatsoever for the Kurds to expect the West to lift a finger, never mind a missile, to prevent this. But for the first time in Kurdish history, Iraqi Kurds at least control their own destiny, even if that destiny is split between two governments.

**Kurdistan Regional Government (KRG)**
http://www.krg.org

**KRG Representation in the United States**
Tel.: (202) 776-7196
Fax: (202) 887-9168
usrep@krg.org

**KRG Representation in the United Kingdom**
Tel.: (44) 207 828 8616
Fax: (44) 207 828 8526
krguk@aol.com

**KRG Representation at the European Union**
Tel.: (32) 2 513 7228
Fax: (32) 2 513 3679
krg.eu@skynet.be

**KRG Representation in the Nordic Countries**
Tel.: (46) 8 442 05 05
Fax: (46) 8 442 09 05
krg.nordic@telia.com

**KRG Representation in Germany**
Tel.: (49) 30 7974 8491
Fax: (49) 30 7974 8492
krgingermany@netscape.net

# The Players

## The Kurdistan Democratic Party (KDP)

Both the KDP and PUK are estimated to have around 15,000 troops each under arms, or double that if you add in the Kurdish equivalent of security guard/doughnut munchers. The KDP is led by Massoud Barzani, the fourth son of KDP founder Mullah Mustafa Barzani (who led the party from its foundation in 1946 up until his death in 1979). Though clannish and tribal, Massoud is nothing if not politically agile: Under his leadership, the KDP has fought alongside the Turkish army against the Turkish Kurds in the PKK, in step with Iraq's Republican Guard against the KDP's fellow Iraqi Kurds in the PUK, and still manages to command the support of much of Iraq's Kurdish population. Massoud is also a sharp operator in the more traditional sense: In December 2001, it was announced that the KDP had concluded a deal to let the Turkish Petroleum Corporation, as well as Russian oil companies Tatneft and Zarubezhneft, drill wells in KDP-held areas inside Iraq.

You can take a wild guess at how well this has gone over with the KDP's friends in Baghdad.

While Barzani rejoices in the title of President of the KDP's bit of Kurdistan, his prime minister and nephew, Nerchirvan Barzani, is also known for keeping seemingly bizarre company for an Iraqi Kurd. He is a business partner and friend of Saddam Hussein's eldest son, Uday—a man so unpredictably violent and palpably insane that even the rest of his family have noticed.

**Kurdistan Democratic Party**
http://www.kdp.pp.se

**KDP International Relations Committee, Kurdistan**
Central Media & Culture Office
Tel.: (871) 761 610 320
Tel.: (873) 761 610 320
Fax: (873) 761 610 321
Fax: (871) 761 610 321
kdppress@aol.com

**KDP, United States**
770 Little River Turnpike
Suite 302A
Annandale, VA 22003
Tel.: (703) 750-1161
Fax: (703) 750-1106
kdpusa@aol.com

**KDP International Relations Bureau, London**
Tel.: (44) 207 498 2664
Fax: (44) 207 498 2531
kdpeurope@aol.com

**KDP, Turkey**
Kaptanpasa Sokak 59
06700 GOP Ankara
Turkey
Tel.: (90) 312 440 93 40
Fax: (90) 312 447 35 32

**KDP, Spain**
Avda. Papa Negro, 20—1°—105ª
28043 Madrid
Spain
Tel.: (34) 917 599 475
Fax: (34) 913 001 638
kurdi@infonegocio.com

## Patriotic Union of Kurdistan (PUK)

Glasses were first raised to the PUK and all who sail in her back in 1975. The umpteenth Kurdish rebellion had just been ground under heel by well-known champion of the oppressed, Saddam Hussein, who at the same time had placated Iran by giving them the Shatt-al-Arab waterway. The Shah of Iran decided, not altogether coincidentally, that he was no longer terrifically interested in sponsoring Kurdish rebellion, and withdrew all military support from the Kurds—including, presumably, the canoe in which the Kurds might have been able to get back down the creek they were now well and truly up.

A number of Kurds decided it was all the fault of longtime KDP leader Mullah Mustafa Barzani; they decided that his ill-judged dependence on Iran made him a lackey of imperialism, as well as a bit of a twit. This being the '70s, quite a lot of the Kurds had commie tendencies. So, they wrote to Jalal Talabani, who was then Mullah

Barzani's rep in Egypt, asking him to take the reins of the new party, which split from the KDP to become the PUK. The new group cast about for an ideology to go with their territorial ambitions, and decided to plump for Marx with a bit of Lenin thrown in. It was the '70s, and people did things like that.

The PUK's flag is deep green, and its headquarters are at Zahle, in the mountains on the Iranian border (ironically, given its origin, the PUK now gets some military assistance from Iran). The main areas of PUK support are the southeastern parts of northern Iraq. The PUK militia comprises about 25,000 men. About 15,000 of these could put up a half-decent fight. They control their area from Sulymanya, which is a thriving hub of spies and revolutionaries—Turkish intelligence (known as MIT) and the PKK both have offices in Sulymanya, as do the Kurdistan Democratic Party of Iran (KDPI) and Iranian intelligence. In addition, the CIA, MI6, and Saddam's Mukhabarat all have a number of operatives running around town—be careful whom you talk to.

Jalal Talabani is still leader of the PUK, and is something of a talker, which means that if you're interviewing him, as *DP* did, it is often hard to get a word in edgewise. Fluent in English, Jalal will warble on, ad libbing with great charm. There's nothing he likes better than swanning around the international circuit. A summons to Washington will see him making tracks to the airport almost before the invite has hit the doormat. He lives outside Sulymanya and also has a house in Damascus.

The PUK now effectively runs Iraqi Kurdistan in cooperation with the KDP. It took the pair a lot longer than it should have, but they seem to have figured out that there are more productive things than fighting each other. Both have recently declared that they have no interest in attempting to establish a sovereign Kurdish state, but this may or may not have been a ploy to keep the Syrians and Iranians calm while the PUK Kurds and the KDP Kurds wait to see if Uncle Sam is about to provide either or both of them with fresh kit and copies of "What's on in Baghdad."

**Patriotic Union of Kurdistan**
puk@puk.org
http://www.puk.org

**PUK, United States**
1634 Eye Street, NW, Suite 210
Washington, DC 20006
Tel.: (202) 637-2496
Fax: (202) 637-2723
pukusa@puk.org

**PUK, UK**
5 Glasshouse Walk
London SE 11 5ES, UK
Tel.: (44) 207 840 0640
Fax: (44) 207 840 0630

**PUK, Syria**
P.O. Box 12925
Damascus, Syria
Tel.: (963) 11 331 0997
Fax: (963) 11 331 1690

**KURDISTAN**

*PUK, France*
23 Rue Louias Pouey
72800 Puteaux, France
Tel.: (33) 1 4778 7598
Fax: (33) 1 4090 0282

*PUK, Germany*
P.O. Box 210231
10502 Berlin, Germany
Tel.: (49) 30 340 978 50
Fax: (49) 30 340 978 49
PUKOffice@pukg.de

*PUK, Iran*
Tel.: (98) 21 80 72 057
Fax: (98) 21 80 87 972

*PUK, Belgium*
Tel.: (32) 2 779 8984

*PUK, Russia*
Tel./Fax: (7) 095 964 0094

*PUK, Italy*
Tel./Fax: (39) 065 407 227

*PUK, Spain*
Tel./Fax: (34) 91 373 1308

*PUK, Sweden*
Tel.: (46) 891 7693

*PUK, Benelux*
Tel./Fax: (31) 70 389 5832
puk_benlux@msn.com

*PUK, Turkey*
Tel.: (90) 312 440 2199
Fax: (90) 312 440 4549

*PUK, Canada*
Tel.: (519) 572-3509
Fax: (519) 894-0166
PUKCanada@canada.com

*PUK, Australia*
Tel.: (61) 413 959 355
Fax: (61) 297 916 229
pkaus@tig.com.au

## Ansar al-Islam

In a fractured semi-nation struggling to recover from years of out-side oppression and internecine slaughter, it is difficult to imagine any-thing less helpful than the introduction of a militant Islamic guerrilla group into the mix. Fortunately, the Ansar al-Islam (Supporters of Islam) have saved us the trouble of speculation. Initially trading as Jund al-Islam (Soldiers of Islam), the timing of their official founding was, at the very least, interesting—on September 1, 2001, they issued a fatwa declaring jihad against "the secular and apostate forces that are waiting for an opportunity to overpower Islam and the Muslims of Kurdistan, and waiting to implement the sinister plans of the Jewish, Christian and all other apostate leaders." Yeah, uh huh, whatever . . . pleased to meet you, too. On September 23, they killed 42 PUK soldiers in an ambush.

The Ansar al-Islam is composed of malcontent ex-members of the Islamic Unity Movement of Kurdistan (IUMK), an Iranian-backed mob who fought running battles with the PUK throughout the 1990s, even-tually gaining control of the town of Halabja. The PUK claims that al-Qaeda is involved with both the IUMK and Ansar al-Islam—a claim lent credence by the fact that bin Laden's envoy to Kurdistan, Abu

Abdul-Rahman, was killed in fighting with the PUK in November 2001. There have also been reports that Ansar al-Islam's numbers have been bolstered by members of the Taliban and al-Qaeda who decided they'd rather partake of an honest-to-goodness old-school guerrilla war that doesn't involve being carpet-bombed from 35,000 feet. There are also well-placed and altogether believable rumors that Saddam is bunging Ansar al-Islam money and guns in order to annoy the PUK.

The Ansar al-Islam holds several Kurdish villages along the Iranian border, all of which they have Talibanized: burning down schools, beating up women for not dressing like pantomime ghosts, and making everything illegal except beards and praying, both of which are compulsory. The Ansar al-Islam's leader, one Mullah Krekar, has described Osama bin Laden as "the crown on the head of the Islamic nation." The possibility that Mullah Krekar is as crazy as a sackful of ferrets is one that cannot, for the moment, be ruled out. For now you can find these Afghan-trained muj and their leader around the Gulp (yes, we said Gulp) area, most likely wearing "Bomb Me" signs taped to their backs.

## The Kurdish Workers' Party (PKK)

The Parta Kakerin Kurdestan is the only Kurdish group ever to have made the U.S. State Department's A-list of international terror groups—a position they maintain, despite the fact that PKK leader Abdullah Ocalan is in a Turkish prison under sentence of death and the rest of the PKK won't answer to the name PKK (they prefer the much snappier sounding "KADEK"). However, the governments in Ankara, Washington, and Brussels aren't buying the name change or the new-look PKK's renunciation of violence in pursuit of freedom for Turkish Kurds. So, if Osama bin Laden is thinking of ducking America's vengeance by changing al-Qaeda's name to "Laugh with Allah," or something similar, he can forget it.

The PKK got going in 1978 in Siverek. They started off as a Marxist-Leninist organization fighting for independence or autonomy in what they rather wistfully call "northwestern Kurdistan," for which you can read "southeastern Turkey." They were led by Abdullah Ocalan, better known as Apo. He used to be seen on MED-TV (until it, like him, was closed down), which served as a platform for fans to listen to his reasoned calls for dialogue with the Turkish government—or, depending on his mood, long-winded rants. An old-style Marxist, he never really managed glasnost convincingly, though he tuned down his demands for an independent state carved out of Turkey, Iraq, Iran, and Syria. Autonomy, he said, was the goal of the PKK. Get stuffed, said the Turkish military.

At its peak, between 1991 and 1993, PKK guerrillas controlled large sections of southeastern Turkey. There were nightly gun battles in Cizre, Silopi, Nusayabin, and numerous other towns dotted round the southeast. Turkish soldiers were being sent back to the west of the country in boxes at an alarming rate. In Ankara alone, as many as 10 coffins a day would arrive containing bodies of recruits killed by the PKK.

The PKK's campaign began its end in February 1999, when Abdullah Ocalan was captured by Turkish intelligence operatives. In late 1998 the Turks were getting just a bit unhappy with Apo running the show out of a nice little villa in the suburbs of Damascus and they told the Syrians, "Lose the man with the potbelly and the funny moustache or Damascus is history." Rather than lose Damascus, the Syrians lost Apo, who took a plane to southern Cyprus, then slunk off to Russia before landing in Italy on a false passport. The Italians didn't quite know what to do. The Germans did, though, and issued an arrest warrant for Apo—before they realized that maybe they really didn't want 200,000 German Kurds going ape as their leader was hauled through the courts. The extradition order was quietly rubbed off the menu and the German public prosecutor went on a long holiday.

So, for a few weeks Apo had a nice comfy villa on the outskirts of Rome. The Turks were not happy. All those plans and it looked like the bastard was going to end up with better accommodations than they had planned for him. That is, until Apo disappeared from all radar screens. Here one minute, gone the next. Apo had left Italy, said the Italian government, wiping its collective brow with relief. Apo set off on another odyssey to find asylum somewhere other than Turkey. He rocked up in Moscow, only to find the Russkies uninterested. A few Greeks hid him in Greece before carting him off to their ambassador's residence in Nairobi—not the best of choices, perhaps, when you consider that in the aftermath of Mr. bin Laden's little bomb, the place was crawling with CIA and FBI agents.

Needless to say, they were soon listening in to Apo's desperate cellphone calls to anyone who might be able help him. Turkish intelligence, tipped off by Washington, flooded into Kenya. The Greeks told Apo that they were all going for a short ride. Apo's car, though, took a small diversion into the hands of . . . Turkish intelligence. Drugged and rushed to the airport, the next thing poor old Apo knew, he was in a plane heading for Istanbul.

After a quick trial, which was naturally extremely fair and considered all sides of the argument, Apo was sentenced to death. His last-minute plea that he could solve the Kurdish problem in Turkey if his life was spared fell, quite rightly, on deaf ears. As we all know—and as the Turkish government never tires of telling us—there is no Kurdish problem in Turkey. There is only a minor problem of some mindless terrorists, who happen to be Kurds. Sorry, as the Turkish government has just—again, quite correctly—reminded *DP*, these people are Turkish citizens who live in the east and sometimes call themselves Kurdish. There is not a Kurdish problem in Turkey. Get it?

> **S**orry, as the Turkish government has just—again, quite correctly—reminded *DP*, these people are Turkish citizens who live in the east and sometimes call themselves Kurdish. There is not a Kurdish problem in Turkey. Get it?

It wasn't just the PKK, but also quite a lot of ordinary Kurds who were a bit upset by Apo's enforced departure from the scene. Europe was rocked by demonstrations, with young Kurds pouring gasoline over themselves, and there was a wave of panic that support for Apo might get out of hand. In Turkey the PKK began a series of bomb attacks in the west of the country. Turkish tourism plummeted. Department stores were fire-bombed, suicide bombers blew themselves up in the middle of Istanbul, and everyone began to get a little bit nervous. The PKK promised to start a whole new war in west Turkey with plastic explosives on the dining-out menu for most restaurants.

Then, in August 1999, from his prison cell, Apo announced a unilateral cease-fire and the withdrawal of all PKK forces from Turkey. Sporadic clashes continued, however, and the Turkish government said, "No negotiations with terrorists." That said, there have been various noises made about not hanging Ocalan and letting him off with life imprisonment, though these ideas have little to do with any merciful instincts on the part of the Turkish government, and a lot to do with the fact that Turkey wants nothing more than to join the European Union—whose member states regard capital punishment as a cruelty practiced only by barbarians, savages, and Americans. Also, Turkey announced in September 2001 that they wanted to put Ocalan on trial again, on some extra charges of treason, murder, and armed insurgency that they forgot the first time around. (Presumably, when—sorry, if—he's found guilty, they'll announce that they're going to execute him twice.)

Ocalan, the sole prisoner in the island fortress Imrali, may be a poor life-insurance risk with a lousy social life, but he remains nominal leader of KADEK—the rebranded PKK—which has recently issued a statement denouncing terrorism. That's nice.

**Abdullah Ocalan (latest—and probably final—address)**
Imrali Prison
Imrali, Turkey

*American Kurdish Information Network*
2600 Connecticut Avenue, NW, Suite 1
Washington, DC 20008-1558
Tel.: (202) 483-6444
Fax: (202) 483-6476
akin@kurdistan.org
http://www.kurdistan.org

## The Turkish Military and Police Forces

With upward of 350,000 Turkish troops and security personnel in southeastern Turkey at various times over the last couple of decades, you'd have thought that they might be able to keep a lid on it all—but if they have, it's only just. Always a force in politics, the Turkish military has staged three coups in modern Turkish history. There are two things the military hate: Kurds and Islamists. In 1997 the military forced Necmettin Erbakan and his Islamist-led government to resign without actually leaving their barracks.

The Turkish air force, meanwhile, discovered that the no-fly zone in northern Iraq not only protected the Kurds from being bombed by Saddam, but protected their jets from being shot down by Iraq while they were bombing the Kurds themselves. In August 2000, Turkey's own Kurdish allies, the KDP, claimed Turkish jets had bombed a camp of itinerant shepherds, killing 38 people.

Turkish intelligence (known as MIT) operates out of Sulymanya in PUK-held Kurdistan, where it has an office dedicated to monitoring the PKK, which has an office a little further down the road. *DP* wonders what happens if they get stuck in a traffic jam together: a couple of icy smiles, perhaps?

*Turkish Armed Forces*
gnkur@tsk.mil.tr
http://www.tsk.mil.tr/index_eng.htm

## The United States/CIA/Iraqi National Congress/His Munificent Excellency the Very Honorable Saddam Hussein (and Sons)

We come to one of the most entertaining foul-ups in the recent annals of intelligence. In their heady desire to oust Saddam in favor of someone with a prettier face, the CIA decided to dole out the cash to the Arab opposition. Thus, the Iraqi National Congress (INC) was born: a motley crew of more parties than people. Founded by the CIA in a Vienna hotel in 1992 and led by Ahmed Chalabi, a former banker wanted on fraud charges in Jordan, the INC set about the task of collecting Uncle Sam's cash and hatching a plan to depose Saddam.

With a lack of secrecy that Austin Powers would have been proud of, the INC installed itself in the Ankowa district of Arbil and set about plotting the downfall of Saddam. All well and good, you might be thinking. Not quite. Their willingness to welcome defectors from Baghdad—can you see where this is going?—made for more than the usual odd security slipup. Saddam's kids promptly installed themselves at all the right levels, keeping their buddies in Baghdad informed of goings-on. Not a great start. And, as they say, things could only get worse. And boy, did they get worse.

In 1996 the Dublin peace accord, which had been signed by the PUK and KDP, began to fall to pieces. (The Turks told the United States that no way were there going to be any elections in Iraqi Kurdistan: It might give Turkish Kurds ideas of their own. The United States said okay and withdrew support for the elections.) Clashes started between the two factions. The KDP's Massoud Barzani invited Saddam to help him kick the PUK and anyone else he didn't like out of Arbil.

Did the CIA know this was coming? Well, actually, they did. *DP*'s intelligence network in the region says that it was no big secret that Barzani was negotiating with Baghdad. Some in the CIA saw all this as just the opportunity to get rid of Saddam. The thinking among CIA officers on the ground went like this: Saddam comes to Arbil; the Kurds—in the form of the PUK—fight like hell; the United States comes to their aid with massive airstrikes, taking out Saddam's tanks. The Kurds move on to Baghdad and the Iraqi military rebels. It's a re-enactment of 1991, except this time the United States supports the rebellion, and bye-bye Saddam.

That's what they told the PUK. So the PUK—or so they told *DP*—came up with an ultra-cunning plan to defend Arbil, only to find that where the CIA said one thing, the State Department and the Pentagon had other ideas. Whoops! So Saddam rocked into Arbil . . . and, no U.S. support for the PUK, who leg it from town and, well, you know the rest. Bill sends in the missiles and gets the ratings. The PUK get shafted. CIA operatives flee for Turkey. Hundreds of Iraqi spooks and officers who may or may not have been in on the plot get executed. Saddam chuckles.

**Iraqi National Congress**
http://www.inc.org.uk

## Medya-TV

This TV station replaced Med-TV, the station that used to drive the Turkish government wild. Med-TV was the voice of the PKK. To the acute embarrassment of the British government, it was broadcast from London. But the guys overstepped the mark when Osman Ocalan got on the blower after his big brother was snatched by the Turks and in typical Ocalan family style ranted and raved that everything was a "target." The Brits quickly closed it down on the grounds of "incitement to violence." As you may have guessed from the name, Medya-TV is a similar operation, but these days it is based in France.

For millions of Kurds, Medya-TV defines them and gives them a sense of cultural identity. Tune in any time and you'll find Kurdish-language entertainment and news programs, combined with lashings of anti-Turkish polemic.

**Medya-TV**
Kurdish Satellite Television
AB Sat Building
132 Avenue de President Wilson
93213 La Plaine
Saint Denis
Paris, France
Tel.: (33) 1 4917 2449
Fax: (33) 1 4917 2448
medyatv@medyatv.com
http://www.medyatv.com/english/index.htm

# Getting In

To enter Turkey, you need a passport valid for at least six months. Visas are required of U.S., British, and Canadian citizens. Visas for three months are around US$20 and will be given on entry. If you're going on business or want to film anything, you need to apply to your local embassy in advance.

Getting to Turkey's Kurdish areas means either a long bus journey or a short plane ride to Diyarbakir, in the southeast. Once there, travel options are either Turkey's excellent, and cheap, long-haul buses or, for shorter hops, taxis and minibuses (these are also cheap, but often crowded, and occasionally have live goats and chickens strapped to the roof).

Hacks planning a tour of southeastern Turkey should—to avoid tedious hours of questioning by the police—direct inquiries to:

**General Directorate of Press and Information**
Office of the Prime Minister
Ataturk Bulvari 203
Ankara, Turkey
Tel.: (90) 312 455 9000
webadmin@byegm.gov.tr

Alternatively, you can go for the full-blown undercover tour. This means employing a very good taxi driver who knows the game and the checkpoints as well as just about everything else—the drivers can be found through reception desks at hotels in Diyarbakir. If you get spotted, though, expect even more hours of tedious questioning as well as losing all your film. Do not, repeat do not, cheerfully inform the Turkish military or government about your exciting plans to sneak into Iraq . . .

**Embassy of the Republic of Turkey**
2525 Massachusetts Avenue, NW
Washington, DC 20008
Tel.: (202) 612-6700
Fax: (202) 612-6744
info@turkey.org
http://www.turkey.org

**Embassy of the Republic of Turkey**
197 Wurtemburg Street
Ottawa, Ontario K1N 8L9
Canada
Tel.: (613) 789-4044
Fax: (613) 789-3442

**Embassy of the Republic of Turkey**
43 Belgrave Square
London SW1X 8PA, UK
Tel.: (44) 207 393 0202
Fax: (44) 207 393 0066
turkish.embassy@virgin.net
http://www.turkishembassy-
    london.com

Entry to northern Iraq (Iraqi Kurdistan) is next to impossible without some kind of covert contact in the region. *DP* has been tossed out, let in, and then tossed out, depending on the whims of the Kurdish groups.

## Getting Around

This can be a tad hazardous, especially considering that Kurdistan includes two "axis of evil" countries. Though bus services throughout Turkey are excellent, the southeast is still riddled with Turkish military checkpoints, the PKK cease-fire notwithstanding. If they don't like your looks—and they especially don't like the looks of anyone who looks like a journalist—you will be politely but firmly sent back in the direction from whence you came. It should go without saying that traveling by night in Turkey's southeast is for morons and locals only. That said, during a spate of foreign tourist kidnappings in 1995, all the victims were traveling during the day.

In northern Iraq, although the war between the KDP and PKK is more or less over, the area is far from calm—and militant newcomers, the Ansar al-Islam, are probably not going away in a hurry. Expect to find plenty of oddly out-of-place Americans with bad haircuts, and other Bushites, training and coaxing Kurds. Don't go anywhere without someone who knows what they're doing, which in itself should be enough of an adventure. If you want to visit Iraq officially as part of a small group, forget about visiting Kurdistan.

## Dangerous Places

### Northern Iraq (Southern Kurdistan)

Iraqi Kurdistan may now be calmer than it has been for a long time, but nobody's going to confuse it with Switzerland. The cease-fire between the KDP and the PUK seems genuine enough, but the two factions have no great love for each other. The scrapping between the PUK and the recently arrived militants, Ansar al-Islam, could get a whole lot worse, especially if Saddam is serious about using Ansar al-Islam as the agents of destabilization for the entire region.

http://www.hrw.org/wr2k2/mena4.html

### Southeastern Turkey (Northwestern Kurdistan)

Not as bad as it once was, given that the PKK has decided to try playing Mr. Nice Guy to see if it gets them anywhere. In May 2002 Turkey announced that it was ending its 15-year state of emergency in two provinces affected by fighting with the PKK and planned to lift similar restrictions in others if things stayed quiet. Turkish military checkpoints are still frequent, though they generally can't be bothered with hassling foreigners. The usual vigilance necessary for maintaining personal security in the third world should be enough, but if you are a journalist, try to look as little like one as possible: shaving and pulling a comb through your hair should put off suspicious people (they'll think you're a spy, instead). And it won't hurt to keep up to date with current events. For now, much of the focus is on the benefits that the giant dam should bring to the region.

***The Kurdish Observer***
http://www.kurdishobserver.com

***Embassy Safety Briefing***
http://www.usemb-ankara.org.tr/SECURTY/secstb.htm

## Dangerous Things

### Murder

Since the start of the PKK war there have been about 3,000 unsolved murders in southeastern Turkey. As most of the victims were Kurdish activists, suspicion has rather unsurprisingly fallen on the Turkish military. The government tries to blame the PKK. Relatives of victims who try to bring charges against military personnel stand an excellent chance of becoming victims themselves.

http://www.state.gov/g/drl/rls/hrrpt/2001/eur/8358.htm

## Guarding Villages

To root out remaining pockets of rebel resistance in eastern Turkey, the government relocated some 3,000 subsistence farmers who were thought to be PKK sympathizers. Those with the brains to keep their political sympathies to themselves—about 70,000 folks considered loyal to the government—were instructed to defend their villages. Each was rewarded with a gun and $200 a month in cash—hardly night watchman's pay in eastern Turkey. Not a cool job if you want to collect your pension: The biggest PKK massacres, unsurprisingly, have been perpetrated against village guards. On average, 10 village guards are killed every month. On the other hand, there was a time when just under 4,000 village guards were up for 108 cases of extortion, 196 murders, 16 cases of aggravated assault, 208 cases of arms smuggling, 57 kidnappings of women, and 13 rapes. So who is guarding against the village guards?

http://www.hrw.org/press/2000/02/tur0216.htm

## Neighbors

The convoluted tract that is Kurdistan had enough political woes before well-meaning neighbors and outsiders decided to get into the mix. Before, it was pretty straightforward: Kurds were united (well, sort of) in their fight for a homeland. Now Iran, the Whahhabists, and tweaked Afghan muj are threatening to rekindle the flames. Iran-backed and mostly rural Hizbullah is attacking the village-guard, mafia elements of the Kurds; in the country, the Islamic fundamentalist Ansar al-Islam is pounding away at the traditional Kurdish groups with the money and help of . . . Saddam Hussein. Yes, Saddam is making good use of the number of for-hire muj streaming out of Afghanistan and Pakistan and polishing up their flip-flops for a jihad in the north.

http://www.csmonitor.com/2002/0402/p01s03-wome.html

## Memory

Syria has an interesting solution to the Kurdish problem in what is western Kurdistan . . . er, sorry, the Syrian Arab Republic. They simply declared the local and refugee Kurds to be Arabs and took away their lands, their rights, and their language. Simple problem solved.

**Western Kurdistan Association**
Palingswick House, 241 King Street
Hammersmith
London, UK
http://international-friends-of-kurdistan.s5.com/western_kurdistan.htm

## Getting Sick

Medical care is rudimentary and far below Western standards. The only care of any value is given by NGOs operating in the area. Diyarbakir, in eastern Turkey, provides the best medical services in the region. For serious illnesses or injuries, this is where you'll want to start. Then get your ass to Istanbul. Don't drink the water.

## Nuts and Bolts

Kurdistan is the theoretical homeland for the world's 25 million-or-so Kurds. The largest ethnic group in the world without an official country of their own, the Kurds just won't give up fighting for what many consider a lost cause. The Kurdish language is similar to Persian, but centuries of isolation—and internecine hostility—have created a number of dialects. The two main ones are Kurmanji and Sorani. The former is spoken in Turkey and the latter in Iraq and Iran. Another dialect is Zaza, spoken mainly in Turkey. Most Kurds are Sunni Muslims. They are descended from the Medes.

Even though the Kurds are the fourth-largest ethnic group in the Middle East, they are neatly cordoned off into Syria, Iraq, Turkey, and Iran, and then spread around the world. Information is appropriate to the country visited, so visit your local travel bookstore for all countries except Iraq, where *DP* lends a hand. Southeast Turkey is your best bet to see Kurdish culture and get a feel for getting around. Iraq is, and mostly likely will remain, an area in great turmoil, so only war hogs and journos should take the tour. The plight of the Kurds in Syria is a human-rights story that receives very little press, and the Kurds in Iran are the least put-upon. Susan Meiselas' excellent book *Kurdistan: In the Shadow of History* remains the best (and most expensive) source of history and imagery.

Business hours in eastern Turkey are the same as in the rest of the country, from 8:30 A.M.–noon and 1:30 P.M.–5:30 P.M., Monday through Friday. Turkish post offices are recognizable by the black PTT letters on yellow background. Postal service is efficient and modern, as are telecommunications. There are no such luxuries in northern Iraq. There are, however, numerous satellite telephones, which cost about $2 per minute.

Local time in northern Iraq is GMT +3 hours April–September and GMT +2 hours October–March. Electricity is available in most towns and is 220V/50Hz. The currency in Turkey is the Turkish lira (460,000 TL = US$1). In northern Iraq the currency is the dinar (20 ID = US$1). Hotels can be found in Salahudin, Arbil, Dohuk, Zakho, and Sulymanya. The best hotel in Arbil is the Arbil Tower Hotel (tel.: 23797), which costs about US$15 a night, and has a well-stocked bar and decent food. The manager is Mr. Said. If you're in Dohuk, the only place is the Lowkama Hotel, at around the same price. In northern Iraq, it's cash only. Hundred-dollar bills are the currency we advise you to carry. In southeastern Turkey, credit cards can be used in most sizable towns.

www.akakurdistan.com
http://cobblestonepub.com/pages/Kurds.htm
http://www.prio.no/html/osce-kurds.asp

## Dangerous Days

| | |
|---|---|
| 11/13/02 | Kurds announce they are working with the CIA to overthrow Saddam. |
| 4/2/02 | Barham Salih, head of the PUK regional government, escapes an assassination attempt in Sulymanya. |
| 4/16/02 | PKK announces a change of name, to Congress for Freedom and Democracy in Kurdistan (KADEK). |
| 9/23/01 | Ambush by Ansar al-Islam guerillas kills 42 PUK soldiers. |
| 9/1/01 | Militant Iranian-backed Islamic group Jund al-Islam formally announces its existence; later changes its name to Ansar al-Islam. |
| 6/29/99 | Ocalan convicted of treason and sentenced to death. Promises to work toward peaceful solution of Kurdish conflict in return for his life. |
| 5/1/99 | PKK ends its armed struggle against Turkey |
| 3/8/99 | From his prison cell, Ocalan offers a cease-fire and withdrawal of PKK forces from Turkey. |
| 2/15/99 | Turkish intelligence operatives capture PKK leader Abdullah Ocalan in Nairobi, Kenya. He is imprisoned on the island of Imral, site of a maximum-security jail in which he is the only inmate. |
| 9/12/98 | KDP and PUK sign peace agreement in Washington. |
| 3/17/98 | Turkish troops capture Semdin Sakik, PKK regional commander in northern Iraq. |
| 5/14/97 | Turkey sends some 50,000 troops into northern Iraq to destroy PKK bases. An estimated 3,000 people are killed. |
| 8/31/96 | Iraqi Republican Guards take Arbil. |
| 3/30/95 | Medya-TV begins broadcasting. |
| 5/94 | Fighting breaks out between the KDP and PUK in Iraq. |
| 5/4/91 | UN Resolution 688 permits the establishment of safe havens in Kurdish areas of Iraq. |

| | |
|---|---|
| **4/16/91** | U.S. President George Bush announces that U.S. troops will enter northern Iraq to create a safe haven for displaced Kurds around Zakhu. |
| **3/91** | With explicit encouragement from the United States, Kurds in the north of Iraq and Shi'ites in the south launch uprisings against Saddam Hussein. No actual help from the United States is forthcoming, and Saddam crushes both rebellions. Hundreds of thousands of Kurds seek refuge in Turkey (which denies them entry), and more than a million flee to Iran. |
| **3/2/91** | Iraq signs a cease-fire agreement with Allied Forces, ending the Persian Gulf War. The agreement, however, permits them to continue using helicopter gunships. |
| **2/27/91** | Allied Forces in Kuwait and Iraq suspend military operations against Iraq. |
| **1/17/91** | The start of hostilities between the multinational forces and Iraqi forces. The beginning of Operation Desert Storm. |
| **8/2/90** | Iraqi forces invade Kuwait and seize control of the country. |
| **3/16/88** | Iraqi chemical attack on Halabja kills up to 5,000 Kurds. |
| **1987** | Iraq launches major offensive against regions controlled by the KDP. |
| **8/15/86** | Turkish troops raid Kurdish rebel camps in Iraq. |
| **8/84** | PKK begins armed campaign against Turkish government. |
| **9/19/80** | Iran-Iraq war begins. |
| **3/10/79** | Death of Mullah Mustafa Barzani. |
| **1978** | PKK formed. |
| **1975** | PUK formed. |
| **1974** | Iraq-KDP war: 130,000 Kurds take refuge in Iran. |
| **1946** | KDP formed under leadership of Mullah Mustafa Barzani. |
| **1945** | Kurds form independent Republic of Mahabad in Iran. It lasts less than a year. |
| **4/28/37** | Saddam Hussein is born. |
| **1923** | Treaty of Lausanne supersedes Treaty of Sevres: It contains no mention of Kurdistan and divides Kurdish land among Turkey, Iraq, and Syria. |
| **1920** | Treaty of Sevres, agreed among World War I allies in Europe, proposes an independent Kurdistan. |
| **3/21** | Kurdish New Year celebrated. |

**KURDISTAN**

# LEBANON

Beirut

## Deadly Doormat

The U.S. State Department has a list in its little black book of seven nations that it believes harbor or sponsor terrorism. On it are Iran, Iraq, Libya, North Korea, Sudan, Syria, and Cuba. (Those crazy Cubans! Almost as big a threat to the world's security as Mauritius and the Cape Verde Islands.)

There are, of course, any number of nations whose absence from that list seems a little curious to anyone whose moral outlook is more consistent than that of the U.S. State Department—Saudi Arabia, for example (which pays pensions to the families of Palestinian suicide bombers), or Pakistan (which runs dozens of murderous militias in Kashmir and other parts of India). Or, if you want to get really perverse about it, Great Britain (which decided to deal with Irish terrorists by giving them government jobs in the very buildings they'd spent years trying to blow up) or the United States of America (just ask a

Nicaraguan, or an El Salvadoran, or an East Timorese, or a Cambodian, or a Laotian).

But how on Earth has Lebanon missed the cut? What more does a country have to do? Nowhere else do the enemies of the United States operate more openly. Of the U.S. State Department's list of Designated Foreign Terrorist Organizations, all of the following are known or thought to operate in some capacity in, or out of, Lebanon: the Abu Nidal Group, Hizbollah, al-Jihad, the Kurdistan Workers' Party (PKK), the Popular Front for the Liberation of Palestine, the Popular Front for the Liberation of Palestine-General Command, Islamic Jihad, and Hamas.

In Lebanon, these organizations—Hizbollah in particular—go about their business as freely as Western local police, with the possible difference that Hizbollah are more liked and respected on their patch than most American or European cops are in theirs. In Lebanon, the speaker of the parliament, Nabih Berri, is a former commander of the Shi'ite militia Amal and still represents the party today.

> **E**very faction in Lebanon stuck a gun to their own heads and said, "Nobody move, or this guy gets it." And somebody moved.

Bizarre though this may seem, it is by some distance preferable to what came before. Between 1975 and 1990, Lebanon was convulsed by a civil war as murderous as it was bewildering. The complex but civilized ethnic, social, and religious fabric that had earned the country a reputation as an Arab Switzerland was brutally rent; fighting among various combinations of Israelis, Syrians, Palestinians, local Christian militias sponsored by Israel, local Muslim militias sponsored by Iran and Syria, and international peacekeepers who seemed to keep all the peace to themselves, reduced Lebanon to rubble and killed, maimed, or maddened tens of thousands of its people. Every faction in Lebanon stuck a gun to their own heads and said, "Nobody move, or this guy gets it." And somebody moved.

## The Scoop

Lebanon is a country currently hoping that its centuries-long run of shockingly bad luck is finally at an end. Give or take the squabbling between Israel and Hizbollah in the south, things are looking, on the face of it, pretty good. The rubble of downtown Beirut is being bulldozed aside and replaced by new buildings, which are generally surprisingly tasteful replicas of the style that earned prewar Beirut the nickname "the Paris of the East." Major Western brands are all buying

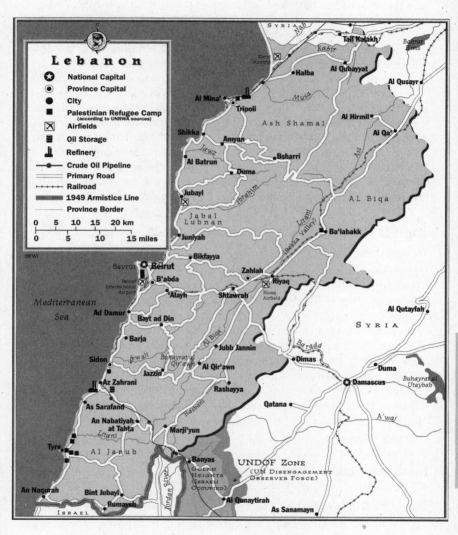

Lebanon

- ★ National Capital
- ◉ Province Capital
- ● City
- ■ Palestinian Refugee Camp
  (according to UNRWA sources)
- ☒ Airfields
- ▤ Oil Storage
- ⚒ Refinery
- ●— Crude Oil Pipeline
- Primary Road
- Railroad
- 1949 Armistice Line
- Province Border

0  5  10  15  20 km
0  5  10  15 miles

©FWI

LEBANON

shop space in the reconstructed downtown as well as in the old battlefields of East and West Beirut, and the seafront is one long construction site, as dozens of resort complexes and marinas start jutting into the water once patrolled by Israeli and American warships. Unfortunately, the intifada that began in neighboring Israel in September 2000 has destroyed the budding tourist business and made new investors nervous. Lebanon has debts of US$17 billion against a US$5 billion a year budget: if it were a car, it would be repossessed.

The long-overdue Israeli withdrawal from southern Lebanon in May 2000 should have been the beginning of Lebanon's formal re-entry into the family of viable nations. However, September 11th and the subsequent global hue and cry against all and any forms of terrorism refocused the world's attention on the fact that Lebanon is home to quite a lot of people whom America would sooner see in cages in Cuba. The challenge facing Lebanon now is to stay on the good side of the rest of the world without provoking uproar at home by selling out the inconveniently popular armed groups who operate on its soil.

# The Players

## The Lebanese Government

Lebanon's peculiar administrative setup is an attempt to reconcile parliamentary democracy with a country whose ethnic and religious divides are more deeply felt than in most. Lebanon's population is about 70 percent Muslim and 30 percent Christian: In an attempt to reflect this, custom has it that the president will be a Christian, the prime minister a Sunni Muslim, and the speaker of the legislature a Shi'a Muslim. Presently, those roles are filled, respectively, by Emile Lahud, Rafiq Hariri, and Nabih Berri—whose previous jobs were, respectively, commander-in-chief of the armed forces, Saudi-based billionaire, and Shi'ite militia commander. The Lebanese parliament is elected by proportional representation along sectarian lines.

**Lebanese Presidency**
http://www.presidency.gov.lb

**Lebanese Parliament**
http://www.lp.gov.lb/english.html

## Hizbollah (Party of God)

The world thinks Hizbollah is a collection of dangerous, marauding terrorists. Hizbollah thinks they're Shriners with artillery. The world and Hizbollah are both about half right.

Hizbollah, which also traded for much of the 1980s under the name Islamic Jihad, are routinely blamed for all of the following: the suicide bombings of the U.S. embassy, U.S. embassy annex, and U.S. Marine barracks in the early 1980s; the kidnappings of several foreign nationals at around the same time; the bombing of the Israeli embassy in Argentina in 1992; the bombing of the Israeli cultural center in Buenos Aires in 1994; and the hijacking of TWA Flight 847 in 1985. Hizbollah's frequent denials of involvement in these attacks have been halfhearted at best. Three Hizbollah members are on the FBI's list of Most Wanted Terrorists—Ali Atwa, Hasan Izz-Al-Din, and Imad Fayez Mugniyah—and if Hizbollah has barred them from the clubhouse, they're being very coy about saying so.

However, Hizbollah cannot be dismissed out of hand as a bunch of sinister, violent fanatics with no interests beyond wreaking death and misery. On their home turf of the Bekaa Valley, South Beirut, and southern Lebanon, Hizbollah funds and runs schools, sports clubs, hospitals, agricultural cooperatives, land-mine awareness campaigns, and veterans' charities, and have massive popular support—in southern Lebanese towns like Nabiteyeh, Hizbollah's green and gold banner is flown from far more windows than the Lebanese national flag. They also have their own newspaper (*al-Ahed*), an award-winning radio station (al-Nour), and a slickly run television channel (al-Manar). Eight Hizbollah members sit as elected deputies in the Lebanese parliament.

Hizbollah was founded in 1982 in reaction to Israel's invasion of Lebanon. Originally a splinter group of Amal, they took their name from the last words of a young mullah who was tortured to death by security services in Qom, Iran, in 1973, and who defied his tormentors with the words "There is only one party, the Party of God." Hizbollah's first secretary-general, Sayyed Abbas Mousawi, was killed by an Israeli helicopter-launched missile in 1983. Today, Hizbollah's secretary-general is Sayyed Hassan Nasrallah, whose other official title is Representative of the Imam Khamenei in Lebanon (Khamenei is the spiritual leader of Iran, a country which continues to pay most of Hizbollah's bills, though money also comes from Syria and Libya). Sheikh Naim Qassem is Sayyed Nasrallah's deputy (the Shi'ite honorific "Sayyed" denotes a direct descendant of Mohammad).

Hizbollah fulfilled its founding purpose in May 2000, when the Israeli military withdrew from southern Lebanon—intermittent fighting between the two sides continues only in the disputed Shebaa Farms region. Today, Hizbollah's twin aims are the establishment of an Islamic state in Lebanon, which they claim they will only pursue through democratic means, and the destruction of Israel, in which case anything goes. Hizbollah has cheerfully admitted swapping intelligence with the Palestinian groups Islamic Jihad and Hamas, and during the Israeli occupation of the West Bank in 2002, stepped up their attacks on Israeli positions in the Shebaa Farms, to which the Israelis responded with air strikes. Other bones of contention between the two sides are the Lebanese nationals still held prisoner inside Israel, and the three Israeli soldiers and one Israeli civilian kidnapped by Hizbollah in 2000. These are side issues, though: The fundamental, and probably unresolvable, core of the dispute is that Hizbollah and Israel each wishes the other didn't exist.

Pro-Hizbollah neighborhoods and cities are denoted by Hizbollah's yellow and gold flag, and by portraits of the young men who died in the war with Israel (one of them is one of Sayyed Nasrallah's sons). Their active military strength is believed to number only a few hundred, and the most sophisticated weapon they own is the haphazard '70s-vintage Russian Katyusha rocket, but they've worked within those limitations with ingenuity and resolve. Hizbollah was the first Arab organization to recognize the strategic possibilities of suicide bombers (the big truck-bomb attacks on U.S. targets in Lebanon in the early '80s were what they call "martyrdom operations"), and are a brilliant guerrilla force by any measure. They are also astute propagandists; video compilations of their operations are big sellers in Shi'ite Lebanon and all over the Middle East.

Today, Hizbollah has acquired a mythical status throughout the Arab world: the only Arab army ever to have defeated Israel on the battlefield.

**Hizbollah Central Information Office**
Sawli Building
Sheik Ragheb Harb Street
Haret Hreik
Beirut, Lebanon
Tel.: (962) 3 83 3442
hizbollahmedia@hizbollah.org
http://www.hizbollah.org/english/
    frames/index_eg.htm

**Homepage of Sayyed Hassan
    Nasrallah**
http://www.nasrallah.net

**Al-Intiqad Newspaper**
http://www.inteqad.com/english

**al-Nour**
Haret Hreik
Beirut, Lebanon
Tel.: (961) 1 54 3555
info@al-nour.net
http://www.alnour.net

**al-Manar**
Abed Al-Nour Street
Haret Hreik
Beirut, Lebanon
Tel.: (961) 3 21 7405
Fax: (961) 1 55 5953
info@manartv.com
http://www.almanar.com.lb

## Amal (Movement of the Dispossessed)

Amal are Hizbollah's sometimes-deadly rivals for the affections of Lebanon's Shi'a Muslims (Hizbollah started out as an Amal splinter group). Their differences are clear enough. Hizbollah is backed by Syria; Amal is Syrian-backed. Where Hizbollah seeks the destruction of

Israel, Amal is pursuing Israel's destruction. Where Hizbollah wants to establish an Islamic state in Lebanon, Amal would prefer to see Lebanon become an Islamic state. Hizbollah's flag is green and yellow, Amal's is green and . . . red! Well, we'd hate to think they were fighting over nothing.

Amal has largely given up the terrorism lark in recent years, restricting its military operations to the occasional bout of shin-kicking and hair-pulling with Hizbollah, but its members were once one of the most-feared militias in Beirut's fearful civil war. Under the leadership of Nabih Berri, now speaker of the Lebanese parliament, Amal fought against the PLO, the U.S.-led multinational forces, the Lebanese army, Fateh, the Israeli army, assorted Druze militias, and Hizbollah. They also fought alongside several of these (it was that kind of war).

Today, Amal is very much Syria's people in Lebanon.

**Amal**
webmaster@amal-movement.com
http://www.amal-movement.com

### United Nations Interim Force in Lebanon (UNIFIL)

That word, "interim," must have seemed like a good idea when UNIFIL was first deployed 24 years ago. They were the world's response to Israel's first invasion of Lebanon in 1978, and their mandate was three-fold: to confirm the withdrawal of Israeli forces; to restore international peace and security; and to assist the government of Lebanon in ensuring the return of its effective authority in the area.

Well, give them points for trying. The Israelis didn't withdraw until May 2000; peace and security might charitably be described as a work in progress; and if you threw a bottle over your shoulder in a truck-stop in Lubbock you'd have a decent chance of hitting someone with more effective authority in southern Lebanon than the Lebanese government (which doesn't mean we recommend it, incidentally). UNIFIL's headquarters is in Naquora in southern Lebanon, and as of March 2002 its members numbered 3,642 strong under the command of Indian Major-General Lalit Mowan Tewari, and included troops from Fiji, France, Ghana, Ireland, Italy, Nepal, Poland, and Ukraine.

Two hundred and forty-three UNIFIL troops or staff members have been killed in Lebanon since their mandate began.

LEBANON

*United Nations Interim Force in Lebanon*
c/o United Nations House
P.O. Box 7476
Bir-Hassan, Beirut, Lebanon
Tel.: (961) 1 82 1450
Fax: (961) 1 42 4118
dpko.unifil.cao@un.org
http://www.un.org/Depts/DPKO/Missions/unifil/unifil_body.htm

## The Lebanese Army

The Lebanese military's principal benefactors are Syria and the United States, and there can't be many people who can claim that. Syria sees them as a bulwark against the Israelis, and America is trying to help Lebanon's legitimate military establish a primacy over Hizbollah—to that end, Uncle Sam has recently donated 750 armored personnel carriers and 3,000 other vehicles. However, cooperation between Lebanese armed forces and Hizbollah in the south is inevitable, commonplace, and ungrudging. In 2001, *DP* was stopped at a Lebanese army checkpoint south of Nabiteyeh; when our Hizbollah guide explained who he worked for, we were waved straight on through.

*Lebanese Armed Forces*
Ministry of Defense
Yarze, Lebanon
Tel.: (961) 5 92 0400
Fax: (961) 1 42 4161
cmdarm@lebarmy.gov.lb
http://www.lebarmy.gov.lb

## Israeli Defense Forces (IDF)

The disputed Shebaa Farms region aside, Israel ended its occupation of southern Lebanon in May 2000, after 18 years and more than a thousand deaths. But, as they like to remind Lebanon with occasional air strikes and regular buzzings, they're only ever as far away as next door.

*Israeli Defense Forces*
http://www.idf.il

## Syria

Syria is not meddling in Lebanon's affairs quite as obviously as it once did, but they pull a lot of strings—especially Nabih Berri's—and there are still 20,000 Syrian troops in the country, in Beirut, the Bekaa Valley, and the north of Lebanon. Lebanon's Christian population wishes they'd take a hike, but at the moment the arrangement is mutually convenient for the governments of Lebanon and Syria, as each sees the other as a deterrent to another Israeli invasion. Just a minor warning: when *DP* called directory information in Damascus and asked for the phone numbers of a variety of terrorist groups, the woman operator was quite adamant that "we don't have any of those people here!" Maybe they moved to Lebanon.

## Solidere

The Solidere company was formed in 1992 to rebuild Beirut's ruined downtown. Its biggest shareholder is Lebanon's billionaire prime minister, Rafiq Hariri—the Lebanese have an attitude toward conflicts of interest that's so relaxed it's almost Texan—but he's suffering alongside the rest of Lebanon's economy as the fighting in Israel scares off tourists and investors. In 2002, Solidere recorded its first-ever annual loss.

http://www.solidere-online.com

# Getting In

A visa is required, but it can be bought with minimal hassle at Beirut Airport or upon entering from Syria, for between US$17 and US$25, depending on how long you want to stay. Bear in mind that if your passport contains any Israeli stamps, or any visas issued in Israel, you'll be put straight back on the plane and sent home.

Taxis from Beirut Airport into Beirut are a racket, but there's not much getting around it—the charge is usually around US$25 for a ride that would cost about a fifth of that over the same distance anywhere else in Beirut (under no circumstances pay more than US$15 for the ride back to the airport—hail a taxi on the street, and bargain hard). Most hotels will send a taxi for you if you ask in advance, and it's a good idea to take them up on it—if you're going to get ripped off, it might as well be by someone you can trace if something goes wrong.

**Embassy of Lebanon**
2560 28th Street NW
Washington, DC 20008
Tel.: (202) 939-6300
Fax: (202) 939-6324
info@lebanonembassy.org
http://www.lebanonembassy.us.org

**Embassy of Lebanon, London**
21 Palace Gardens Mews
London W8 4RA, UK
Tel.: (44) 207 727 6696
Fax: (44) 207 243 1699
emb.leb@btinternet.com

**Embassy of Lebanon, Ottawa**
640 Lyon Street
Ottawa, Ontario K1S 3Z5
Canada
Tel.: (613) 236-5825
Fax: (613) 232-1609
emblebanon@synapse.net
http://www.synapse.net/~emblebanon

LEBANON

## Getting Around

Lebanon is a tiny country, slightly smaller than Connecticut. Most travel is done by shared taxi or bus. Both run on the ad hoc basis common in the Middle East—they leave when they're full, and are cheap. Taxis can be hailed on the street in the cities, but they're usually unmetered—fix a price with the driver before you get in. For longer trips between cities, or tours around the country, a car with a driver can be hired for about US$100 a day—the hotel reception staff will be able to sort this out for you (again, bargain hard). You can also rent your own car, but first you might want to take a few turns on the dodge 'em cars at Beirut's Luna Park fun fair to acclimate yourself to local driving habits.

## Dangerous Places

### Shebaa Farms

The Shebaa Farms are one of those places where history has tripped over geography. The Lebanese government and Hizbollah claim that the 14 farms, covering around 10 square kilometres on the western slopes of Mount Hermon, are Lebanese territory. The Israeli Defense Forces (IDF), who maintain fortified hilltop positions in the mountainous region, says that the area lies on the Syrian side of the Golan Heights—and, because Israel took the Golan Heights off Syria in 1967, the IDF are perfectly entitled to park their soldiers on it, so there. Syria, helpfully, says that the Shebaa Farms are Lebanese territory, despite the fact that Syria fought for them in 1967. The UN's view is that there is no official record of where the border is supposed to be, and so they're screwed if they know, but they think it's probably something Israel and Syria should sort out (*DP*'s suggestion: Pull the name of some other damn country out of a barrel, and give them the Shebaa Farms).

The practical upshot is that a few hundred Israeli reservists are alternately shivering or baking in the mountains while Hizbollah bombs them and fires at them. Fighting escalated during Israel's occupation of the West Bank in 2002, when Hizbollah took the chance to cause Israel further torment, and Israel responded with air strikes. Given the legendary obstinacy of both parties, this conflict is unlikely to be resolved soon. Syria, the putative owner of the region, is more than happy to leave things as they are—while there's still a cutting edge of Israeli forces biting into Lebanon, Damascus has an excuse to keep both its troops in the country and tabs on Lebanon's increasingly lucrative recovery.

http://www.shebaafarms.org

## Bekaa Valley

Hell's boot camp. Among the groups who are operating, or have been known to operate, in the 1,000-meter-high valley between the Lebanon and anti-Lebanon ranges are Hizbollah, three different strains of Popular Front for the Liberation of Palestine (see the Israel/Palestine chapter), the PKK (see the Kurdistan chapter), the Abu Nidal Group, and Hamas. As the war in Afghanistan progressed in late 2001, there were rumors suggesting that senior members of the Taliban and al-Qaeda had decamped to the Bekaa. These reports were strenuously denied by the Lebanese government, which is only what you'd expect—it'd be easy enough for the U.S. Air Force's B-52s to visit Afghanistan and Lebanon in a round trip—but the denials were probably correct: for a start, al-Qaeda and the Taliban are Sunni Muslims, which wouldn't win them too many points with Lebanon's largely Shi'ite militias, and even Hizbollah thinks that Osama bin Laden is a fruitcake.

The militant inhabitants of the Bekaa are all reasonable enough as long as you don't take any pictures. The danger here is from Israel, which would be happier if the whole area, or at least everything in it above ground level, didn't exist. The Israeli Air Force bombed camps belonging to the Popular Front for the Liberation of Palestine (General Command) twice in 2000, and continues to buzz the area regularly, to the voluble irritation of the Lebanese government. This might have something to do with SAM missiles sprouting like weeds . . . and, oh yeah, speaking of weed . . . Bekaa is also a clearinghouse for Lebanon's small but lucrative hashish industry. Despite all this, it is quite a scenic place to visit.

http://www.interline.org.lb/cedarlandtour/htm/bekaa.htm

## South Beirut

This predominantly Shi'ite area is perfectly safe at the time of this writing but would be an obvious target should Israel's anger at Hizbollah lead to a rerun of 1996's Operation Grapes of Wrath. Hizbollah's offices are located here, as well as the buildings that house their television station, al-Manar, and their radio station, al-Nour. These are all protected by armed guards, watchtowers, and thick metal gates, but none of these offer much defense from threats from above. And as the employees of Radio Television Serbia in Belgrade or al-Jazeera in Kabul would be able to confirm, there is no longer much difference, as far as many air-force target selectors are concerned, between hostile media and hostile military.

## Southern Lebanon

Again, at the time of writing the only major hazards were leftover Israeli land mines and Lebanese drivers, but keep an eye on the horizon—while Hizbollah continue to harass Israeli positions in the Shebaa Farms or launch rockets into northern Israel, the Israeli military will have a ready-made excuse to send tanks and aircraft back over the border. It's not like they haven't done it before.

http://www.un.org/Depts/DPKO/Missions/unifil.htm

### Palestinian Refugee Camps

Refugee camps are dotted all over Lebanon, originally dating from the PLO's flight from Jordan in 1970, but some camps like Chatila began in 1949 after the 1948 war. They continue to swell because of subsequent conflicts, despite major remodeling courtesy of Israeli tanks and artillery in 1982. The camps form functional habitats despite their accidental existence. The average Palestinian refugee (if he is one of the lucky 40 percent who have a job) makes about $60 a month. The camps have become cheap residences for nonrefugee Palestinans who can't afford the rapidly escalating prices in other areas, leaving *DP* to wonder if gentrification is far off: refugee chic, if you will.

The most famous camps, for all the wrong reasons, are Sabra and Chatila in Beirut, where Christian Phalangist militia goons, under the supervision of the Israeli army, massacred hundreds of Palestinians, but there are plenty more. The Palestinians in the camps in Lebanon are caught in a particularly hideous Catch-22—they can't go home because the Israelis won't let them, and they can't become Lebanese citizens, because Lebanon doesn't want to give Israel the satisfaction. In 2002, a spate of killings in Palestinian camps, especially around Sidon, hinted at some sort of internecine spat between rival Palestinian groups, which will help their cause no end. This is probably the best bet for the motive behind the car bomb that killed Muhammad Jibril, the son of Popular Front for the Liberation of Palestine (General Command) leader Ahmad Jibril in May 2002. Many Lebanese blamed the Israelis, but the Israelis tend to get blamed for pretty much everything that goes wrong in Lebanon.

http://www.badil.org

## Dangerous Things ━━━━━━━━━━━━━━━━━━━

### Land Mines

The war with Israel may be over, but the unexploded ordnance lingers on, and Lebanon will not be bidding to host any international hopscotch tournaments anytime soon. Despite an intensive clean up effort by the Lebanese army, who cleared 23,293 antipersonnel mines and 4,905 antitank mines between October 1999 and April 2001, UNIFIL's best guess is that there are still 130,000 mines in the part of southern Lebanon once occupied by Israel. Between the Israeli with-drawal and the end of 2001, 132 mine-related injuries, 15 of them fatal, were recorded.

Lebanon has been sown with these ghastly things by Israel, Syria, assorted Lebanese militias, and even the forces that came and went in World War II. There are mines in the Bekaa Valley, North Lebanon, and some parts of Beirut. Anyplace in southern Lebanon should be regarded with extreme caution. The areas immediately surround-ing former Israeli positions in the south are especially dangerous—don't let Hizbollah's heritage-trail-style historical billboards fool you into thinking that these are sanitized tourist attractions, and don't go climbing on the wreckage unless you're with a local who knows what he's doing.

> **P**robably the single most dangerous concept in the Middle East is the idea that some people deserve a home and others don't.

## Al-Nakba

"The Catastrophe," or al-Nakba, is the phrase used to describe the mass displacement of Palestinians from their homes which began in 1948, an event that is commemorated every May 15. Probably the single most dangerous concept in the Middle East is the idea that some people deserve a home and others don't. The total number of registered Palestinian refugees has grown from 914,221 in 1950 to 3,800,000, and increases exponentially each year.

## Having the Goods on Ariel Sharon

Here's an interesting coincidence: On January 22, 2002, the infa-mous Lebanese Christian Phalangist militia commander and former Lebanese government minister Elie Hobeika agreed, at a meeting in a Beirut hotel, to testify against Israeli Prime Minister Ariel Sharon in a civil war-crimes prosecution in a Belgian court. On January 24, 2002, Hobeika and his three bodyguards were blown to pieces by a massive car bomb in the East Beirut suburb of Hazmiyeh.

The list of Lebanese who would cheerfully have seen Hobeika dead is otherwise known as the West and South Beirut telephone directo-ries; it was Hobeika's Phalangist thugs who slaughtered around 1,700 Palestinian civilians in the Sabra and Chatila refugee camps in 1982. But the timing of his murder is startling. Hobeika had agreed with two Belgian senators, Vincent van Quickenborne and Josy Dubie, to appear as a witness at any forthcoming trial involving the refugee camp mas-sacres—massacres carried out with the complicity of Israeli forces under the authority of then-Israeli Defense Minister Ariel Sharon, whose reputation has been clouded by the episode ever since. (The case in Belgium is being brought by 23 survivors of the atrocity.)

Israel denied any involvement with Hobeika's spectacular demise (though it would have been a bit much to expect them to issue a statement reading "Whoo-hoo! Gotcha!"). The killing was claimed by a group called Lebanese for a Free and Independent Lebanon, which nobody had heard of before or has heard of since. But the suspicion that Hobeika was another notch on Ariel Sharon's frayed belt is not going anywhere anytime soon.

## Getting Sick

Lebanese doctors are as good as any, and, as many of them will have been educated overseas, the chances of finding one who speaks English are reasonable. All health care has to be paid for. In case of serious crisis, get yourself to the medical center in the American University of Beirut (tel.: (961) 1 35 0000—any taxi driver will be able to find it). Don't drink the water, and try to resist the considerable temptation posed by seafood.

## Nuts and Bolts

Lebanon's budding tourism industry has taken a battering from the shenanigans in neighboring Israel, so Beirut's dozens of gleaming new hotels are a buyer's market—negotiate by e-mail before you go, especially if you're planning on staying a while. The Commodore Hotel (tel.: (961) 1 35 0400, info@commodore.com.lb, singles from US$80 a night) was the place to stay for hacks covering Lebanon's interminable civil war, but *DP*'s favorite is the smaller Mace Hotel (tel.: (961) 1 34 4626, macehot@cyberia.net.lb) just around the corner—around US$30 a night for a comfortable-enough room just off Rue Hamra in West Beirut is a steal.

Lebanon's principal language is Arabic, though English and French are widely spoken in Beirut (there is an excellent daily English newspaper called *The Daily Star*—http://www.dailystar.com.lb). The currency is the Lebanese pound, which usually trades at around 1,500 to the dollar, and is good for most daily transactions. Hotels will expect to be paid in dollars, and so will some taxi drivers—especially for long trips. Telephones and electricity are mostly reliable, and Internet cafés are plentiful, though Lebanon's Internet connection seems to come and go with the tides. Electricity is 220V.

*Embassy Locations*

**Embassy of the United States**
P.O. Box 70840
Antelias
Beirut, Lebanon
Tel.: (961) 4 54 3600
Fax: (961) 4 54 4136
pas@inco.com.lb
http://www.usembassy.gov.lb

**British Embassy**
Embassies Complex
Army Street, Zkak al-Blat, Serail Hill
P.O. Box 11471
Beirut, Lebanon
Tel.: (961) 1 99 0400
Fax: (961) 1 99 0420
chancery@cyberia.net.lb
http://www.britishembassy.org.lb

**Canadian Embassy**
43 Jal al-Dib Highway
Coolrite Building, 1st Floor
Jal al-Dib
Beirut, Lebanon
Tel.: (961) 4 71 3900
Fax: (961) 4 71 0595
berut.webmaster@dfait-maeci.gc.ca
http://www.canada-lb.org

# Dangerous Days

**5/20/02**  Muhammad Jibril, son of PFLP (GC) leader Ahmad Jibril, killed by a car bomb in Beirut.

**1/24/02**  Former Christian Phalangist Commander Elie Hobeika is killed by a car bomb in Beirut, less than 48 hours after agreeing to testify against Ariel Sharon in a war-crimes prosecution in Belgium.

**5/24/00**  Israel withdraws from southern Lebanon. South Lebanon army collapses.

**4/18/96**  Israel shells UN compound at Qana, killing 106 Lebanese refugees.

**4/11/96**  Israel launches Operation Grapes of Wrath, bombing Beirut, Tyre, and southern Lebanon in response to Hizbollah rocket attacks on northern Israel.

**7/25/93**  Israel launches Operation Accountability, attacking targets in southern Lebanon in response to Hizbollah rocket attacks on northern Israel.

**6/17/92**  The last of the Western hostages held in Lebanon are released.

**2/16/92**  Hizbollah Secretary-General Sayyed Abbas Mousawi is killed, along with his family, when a missile from an Israeli helicopter destroys his car.

**10/90**  Civil war in Lebanon ends.

| 11/22/89 | President-elect Rene Mu'awwad is assassinated. |
| 6/1/87 | Prime Minister Rashid Karami is assassinated. |
| 6/14/85 | TWA Flight 847 from Athens to Rome is hijacked to Beirut. One passenger, U.S. Navy diver Robert Stetham, is killed. Other passengers are dispersed around Beirut; the last 39 are released in Damascus 16 days later. |
| 9/20/84 | Truck bomb in front of U.S. embassy annex in Beirut kills 14 and injures 70. Islamic Jihad claim responsibility. |
| 10/23/83 | Simultaneous truck bombs destroy U.S. Marines barracks and French paratroop barracks in Beirut, killing more than 300. Islamic Jihad claim responsibility. |
| 5/17/83 | Israel and Lebanon end hostilities, agreeing to establish an Israeli-occupied "buffer zone" in southern Lebanon. |
| 4/18/83 | Truck bomb in front of U.S. embassy in Beirut kills 63 and injures 100. Islamic Jihad claim responsibility. |
| 9/16/82 | Hundreds of Palestinians massacred in Sabra and Chatila refugee camps in West Beirut by Israel's Christian Phalangist allies. |
| 9/15/82 | Israeli forces occupy West Beirut. |
| 9/14/82 | President-elect Bashir Gemayel is assassinated. |
| 8/25/82 | U.S. Marines land in Lebanon at the request of Lebanese government. Other international peacekeeping forces follow. |
| 7/19/82 | Kidnappings of foreign nationals in Beirut begin. David Dodge, acting president of the American University of Beirut, is kidnapped by Islamic Jihad (he is released a year later). |
| 6/6/82 | Israel invades Lebanon in Operation Peace for Galilee after attempted murder of Shlomo Argov, Israeli ambassador to Britain. |
| 3/14/78 | Israel occupies southern Lebanon in response to PLO raids, and forms proxy local militia, the South Lebanon Army (SLA). UN force (UNIFIL) makes first deployment. |
| 6/76 | Lebanon invites Syria to intervene as Muslim-Christian fighting worsens. Syria occupies all of Lebanon except the far south. |
| 4/13/75 | Lebanese civil war begins as Christian Phalangists attack Palestinians in Beirut. |
| 4/10/73 | Israeli commandos kill three associates of Yasser Arafat in a raid on Beirut. |
| 1970 | PLO sets up headquarters in Beirut after being driven out of Jordan; begins launching raids on Israel from southern Lebanon. |

| | |
|---|---|
| **12/28/68** | Israel destroys 13 civilian aircraft in a raid on Beirut Airport, in retalitation for an attack on an Israeli plane in Athens by members of the PFLP. |
| **1964** | Palestine Liberation Organization founded. |
| **1958** | Civil war in Lebanon between Muslims supporting Egyptian President Gamul Abdul Nasser's calls for Arab unity, and local Christians. Lebanese President Camille Chamoun asks American President Dwight Eisenhower to send in the Marines. |
| **1948** | State of Israel founded. Exodus of Palestinians into Lebanon and Jordan. |
| **1/1/44** | France transfers power to the government of Lebanon. |
| **11/22/43** | Lebanon declares its independence. |
| **6/41** | Lebanon is taken by British and Free French troops. |
| **1940** | Lebanon falls under control of pro-Nazi Vichy France government. |
| **1920** | France is given mandate for Syria and Lebanon. |
| **1918** | Ottoman rule in Lebanon collapses after the end of World War I. |
| **1860** | French troops land in Lebanon to protect Maronite Christian population, after 12,000 of them are killed in a war with local Druze. |

# In a Dangerous Place: Lebanon

### AT HOME WITH HIZBOLLAH

The South Beirut suburb of Haret Hreik is clearly marked turf. In between the tumbledown high-rises, underneath the cat's cradles of jerry-rigged television cables, the busy, dusty streets are haunted by images from America's recent, and current, foreign policy nightmares: statues of Iran's late spiritual leader Ayatollah Khomeini glowering on corners, posters of Iran's current spiritual leader Ayatollah Khameini hanging from streetlights, and, in every other shop window, portraits of the man whose organization runs this neighborhood: Sayyed Hassan Nasrallah, secretary-general of Hizbollah. Probably the only other places on Earth that look anything like Haret Hreik are Delta Force training camps, though Haret Hreik has considerably more traffic, and just the one Pizza Hut.

I've come to Haret Hreik to meet Hizbollah. I wish I could report that setting this up necessitated weeks of negotiation in Middle Eastern

bazaars, being hustled blindfold to meetings with bearded swashbuck-
lers hunkered amid piles of rifles in sandbagged basements. But actually, I just e-mailed them via their Web site at http://www.hizbollah.org, and
said I'd like to come and visit. Hizbollah replied promptly, saying they'd
be happy to have me.

Say what you will about Hizbollah, but they do have brand recognition. In 20 years of existence, the Arabic name of the Lebanese-based,
Iranian-backed Party of God has become as intractably associated with
terrorism in the Western popular imagination as Coca-Cola has with
soda. The name Hizbollah is a key that instantly unlocks a bank of
news memories: pistols waved from the cockpit of a hijacked airliner; a
colossal hole in the ground that was once a U.S. Marines barracks; the
wreckage of an American embassy blocking a Beirut street; weekly,
then monthly, then yearly updates of the plight of kidnap victims.

On October 5, 2001, the U.S. State Department included Hizbollah
on its list of 28 "Designated Foreign Terrorist Organizations," bracket-
ing them with such unsavory company as Osama bin Laden's al-Qaeda,
Tokyo subway poisoners Aum Shinrikyo, murderous Basque separatists ETA, and the unapologetically violent Palestinian group Hamas.
Of the 22 men on the FBI's list of Most Wanted Terrorists, three—Ali
Atwa, Hasan Izz-Al-Din, and Imad Fayez Mugniyah—are described as
members of Hizbollah; each has $25 million on his head.

All organizations accused of being terrorists object to being called
terrorists, and all accuse those who accused them of being terrorists of
being terrorists themselves; in itself, the term has become all but meaningless with the mind-numbing repetition. Since September 11, however, to be called a terrorist by America is to be put on notice. I
wondered how it felt to know that in the most powerful offices in the
most powerful nation on earth, very clever and very angry people were
planning to freeze your finances, disrupt your communications, infil-
trate your membership, and perhaps, even, dispatch awesome military
force to destroy you.

I also wondered what those on the receiving end might say if they
were asked to explain themselves.

When I find Hizbollah's Central Information Office, located above a
bakery in Haret Hreik, I am greeted by Hizbollah's press officer, Hussein
Naboulsi. A funny, sharp, smartly dressed 35-year-old who has been
working for Hizbollah since the movement began to coalesce following
Israel's invasion of Lebanon in 1982, Hussein begins by apologizing for
not offering refreshments—it is Ramadan, so Muslims are observing
fast during daylight hours. Hussein is intrigued to hear that I'd been to

New York since September 11—he lived there himself for a while, but much preferred Montreal ("It had a much more European feel—a great city"). When I describe the scene at Ground Zero, he shakes his head and agrees that it is terrible and incredible. I wait for the "But . . ." and the litany of American perfidy that has often accompanied halfhearted condemnations of September 11 by the Western Left. It doesn't come. "Terrible," he says, again. "Incredible."

Hizbollah have put together a program for me, Hussein explains. They want me to see what they really do, or at least the part of what they really do that they're happy for journalists to see—my requests to visit the disputed Shebaa Farms region in southern Lebanon, where sporadic fighting with Israeli forces continues, or to see a Hizbollah military base, receive dismissive looks. My request to meet one of Hizbollah's $25 million men provokes delighted, incredulous laughter. The three are accused of the 1985 hijacking of TWA Flight 847, in which one passenger was killed. Like the suicide bombings of the American embassy and U.S. Marines barracks in the early '80s, which killed hundreds, and the kidnappings of Associated Press correspondent Terry Anderson and others—all of which America blames on Hizbollah—the TWA hijacking is a subject Hizbollah does not care to discuss.

"We had no presence back then," says Hussein. "There was a civil war here. Everyone had a gun, and anyone could have kidnapped a journalist."

By coincidence, I have arrived in Beirut on the tenth anniversary of Terry Anderson's release. In an interview published in that morning's edition of Lebanon's English-language paper, *The Daily Star*, Anderson describes the people who held him for nearly seven years as Hizbollah members, and you'd have to imagine that he'd gotten to know his captors fairly well, if only to pass the time.

"We have no connection with what happened in the past," reiterates Hussein, when I mention the article. I will eventually figure out that "the past," as far as Hizbollah is concerned, is any period of time in which something happened that they don't feel happy talking about.

"We are," says Hussein, "the most civilized party in the world. If we were a party with no honor or dignity, a party which practiced violence, nobody would give us their vote. You can't make people love you. Love comes from work on the ground."

Hizbollah's campaign to convince me of their essentially compassionate nature begins with the al-Jarha Establishment in Haret Hreik. The clean, cheerful rooms of al-Jarha are a haven for Hizbollah's wounded veterans and for civilians permanently injured by Lebanon's interminable internecine wars; men in wheelchairs, or on crutches, or missing limbs, build furniture and carve woodcuts which are sold to raise money for the hospice. Their biggest-selling items are wooden sculptures of Hizbollah's logo: a rifle clutched in a fist sprouting from one of the letters of Hizbollah's name.

Abu Ali, 33 years old, was blinded in an operation against Israeli forces in 1986. Despite his disability, he not only weaves baskets at al-Jarha, but teaches others to do so. When he was wounded, he was preparing to go to university to study mathematics, but says he has no regrets.

"It was an honor for me to be a resistance fighter," he says, "and an honor to be injured."

Down the hall, Mohammad Abbas Younis, 32 years old, tells me how, since recovering from a leg wound, he has applied his training as an architect to adapt the homes of disabled veterans. One of those who has benefited from his expertise, 35-year-old Ali Haydar, lost his right arm 10 years ago, but is quick to tell me this has not stopped him from becoming the scourge of al-Jarha's billiard table.

"I fought Israel because they took our land," he says. "That's all we did. And now you see what is implied about us by America."

Hizbollah's rank-and-file seem genuinely perplexed by America's characterization of them as devious enemies of civilization. They insist, repeatedly, and at occasionally exhausting length, that they are no more or less than an army of national liberation, raised in response to foreign occupation of their country—they ask more than once, with gentle indignation, whether I would not have done the same if my country had been invaded. Now that Hizbollah's war with Israel is won—Israel finally ended its frequently brutal occupation of Lebanon in May 2000—Hizbollah are at pains to present themselves as a main-stream political party-cum-religious movement. Hizbollah, as Hizbollah sees it, is kind of a Salvation Army armed with rifles and rockets instead of trombones and tamborines.

Ingenuous though this notion is, there is certainly more to Hizbollah than dimly remembered headlines might lead one to think. Eight Hizbollah members sit as elected deputies in Lebanon's 128-seat parliament. Aside from al-Jarha, Hizbollah own or fund several other hospitals throughout Lebanon, as well as schools, sports clubs, cultural societies, construction companies, agricultural cooperatives, and charities. The doings of all these are chronicled in neatly bound annals, containing details of military and civil operations, photos of the year's martyrs, and press commentary on Hizbollah's activities—some of which are drawn from Hizbollah's weekly newspaper (*al-Ahed*), Hizbollah's television channel (al-Manar), and Hizbollah's radio station (al-Nour).

Al-Nour—the name translates as "the light"—is housed in a labyrinthine basement in Haret Hreik. The underground location was a necessity of wartime, and they plan to move to new offices soon. That said, al-Nour does not feel much like a bastion of revolutionary desperadoes: the walls are freshly painted, the furniture is polished, the equipment is modern, the staff—many of whom are women, as is pointed out to me twice before I've had a chance to ask—are courteous, and a corner table in the office of the general manager, Youseff Al-Zein, is stacked with a couple of dozen awards from Arab broadcasting associations.

"We're here to support the resistance," says Youseff, "but we have all kinds of programs—for women, for children. And we have exclusive rights to the Lebanese soccer league."

Conversation with Youseff is difficult, and not only because it is conducted through a translator. As is the case with almost all Hizbollah members I meet, it is impossible to intercept him before he embarks on a prolonged monologue outlining Israel's serial wrongdoings, and America's complicity in them. For an organization who won't talk about what happened in their own country as recently as the early '80s, they have a remarkable enthusiasm for discussing what happened in the country next door in 1967 and 1948.

There seems to be an assumption that, as a representative of the Western media, I will be naturally inclined to the Israeli point of view, or that some ghastly Jewish conspiracy has heretofore deprived me of the information that, for example, Israel's Christian Phalangist allies slaughtered hundreds of unarmed Palestinians in Beirut's Sabra and Chatila refugee camps in 1982, or that Israeli artillery killed 106 civilians sheltering in a UN base at Qana, in southern Lebanon, in 1996. These (unarguably dreadful) events are Hizbollah's mantra, and however often I tell them that I did my homework before arriving, they evidently believe the lesson cannot be retold too many times. When Youseff eventually draws breath, I manage to deflect him with a question about al-Nour's musical policy.

"We like some European classical composers," says Youseff. "We play Beethoven and Mozart. But we mostly play revolutionary songs, recorded in the current period. These are songs related to the resistance of the occupation of our land, and are targeted to provoke and inspire the people."

I ask to hear a few of these, and am guided to an impressively equipped studio. To my surprise, the three "revolutionary songs" the engineers play for me have no discernible Arabic musical influence. Instead, they borrow heavily from 1980s synthesizer pop. "Hizbollah's Song" resembles a Norwegian Eurovision Song Contest entry. "Hizbollah Are Victorious" sounds like a cross between a military march and, ironically, "The Lebanon"—the Human League's unforgettably asinine commentary on Hizbollah's homeland. "The Resistance Is the Honor of Lebanon" suggests a disco version of the "Knights of the Round Table" singalong from *Monty Python & The Holy Grail.*

They also play me a longer piece—a 20-minute musical dramatization of a 1996 Hizbollah action in which an Israeli patrol near Marjayoun was struck by two roadside bombs, killing four Israeli troops. The accompaniment is samples of Vangelis instrumentals. The narration is provided by the guerrilla who ran the operation, his voice distorted to prevent it from being recognized. A gruesome vérité is added by what I am told are the genuine screams and oaths of injured and terrified Israeli soldiers. There is no reason to disbelieve this—Hizbollah, keen propagandists, are as diligent as the Pentagon about recording their actions (a few days later, Hussein sends one of his colleagues to a market in Haret Hreik to buy me a video called "Heroic Epics: Major Operations of the Islamic Resistance").

Hizbollah's television station, al-Manar—Arabic for "the beacon"— is housed in a new building in Haret Hreik; an armed guard dressed in black stands at the gate, and above the entrance hang colored streamers in honor of Ramadan. While my bag is searched in the marble lobby, I notice a television monitor showing al-Manar's current output: footage of recent fighting between Israelis and Palestinians set to deranged techno music. When the video changes to funerals and soft-focus pictures of maimed Palestinian children, the music shifts to gentle Arabic pop. The screen then fades to a commercial break: the advertised products are both local and foreign—including, startlingly, German chocolate Milka and American detergent Ariel. I idly wonder if anyone has ever tried to sell Israelis a cleaning product called Yasser.

Al-Manar, like al-Nour, is a conspicuously professional enterprise— both admit starting out with financial help from Hizbollah and their backers in Teheran, but now claim to support themselves through advertising and renting their studios. The station broadcasts via satellite to the whole world aside from Southeast Asia and Australia, and they're working on those. Al-Manar is especially proud of its news department, with correspondents in nearly a dozen countries. I ask the chairman of al-Manar's Board of Directors, Nayef Krayem, 37 years old, if al-Manar puts any kind of spin on its news.

"No," he says. "We broadcast what Hamas says, what Arafat says, what the Israelis say, what America says. Our reporting is objective."

The biggest Middle East news story before I arrived had been the Hamas suicide bombers in Jerusalem and Haifa who killed 25 people, all civilians. Nayef immediately objects to the term *suicide bomber.*

"Those were martyrs' operations," he says.

Do you present those martyrs as heroes?

"Of course."

But they killed shoppers, commuters, people every bit as innocent as those murdered by the September 11 hijackers. Did al-Manar offer them the same kind of respect?

"That did not occur in occupied territories, so they are not considered martyrs. Hizbollah is against what happened in America."

This is probably true. The Hizbollah press statement issued on September 16 wasn't the most thundering condemnation of September 11, but it certainly wasn't an endorsement. "We are sorry," the concluding paragraph read, "for any innocent people who are killed anywhere in the world. The Lebanese, who have suffered repeated Zionist massacres in Qana and elsewhere, massacres that the U.S. administration refused to condemn at the UN Security Council, are familiar with the pain and suffering of those who lost their loved ones in bitter events." And what of bin Laden? If he dies fighting America, will al-Manar show montages of scenes from his life, as it does of Khomeini?

"No. Bin Laden is not a hero, and he won't be a martyr."

I ask Nayef how safe he feels here—in the last few years America has twice demonstrated that it regards hostile media organizations as legitimate targets, bombing Radio Television Serbia in Belgrade and the Kabul headquarters of Arab broadcaster al-Jazeera.

"We have another base ready in case that happens," says Nayef, "but if I was killed here, I would be a martyr."

As I leave al-Manar's offices, the channel is broadcasting a cooking show.

"Look, we're not the Taliban," says Abdullah Kassir. Kassir, a 43-year-old father of seven, is a member of Hizbollah's central board, and is now serving his second term as a deputy in Lebanon's parliament. He was once, he confirms, active in Hizbollah's resistance, but won't go into detail.

"We don't deny our Islamic way of thinking," he continues, "but we don't want to make it compulsory. We are happy for Lebanon to be a democracy."

Beirut is now being rebuilt and redeveloped at an astonishing pace. In 10 years, its downtown and seafront will look more like Seattle or Boston than Damascus or Teheran. The streets already contain all the familiar signifiers of international capitalism, except for spoiled students protesting against international capitalism. I ask Abdullah what view Hizbollah takes of this.

"Well, my children will never eat at McDonald's," he laughs. "In our society, unfortunately, there is a tendency to imitate America and the

West in general. We won't fight that aggressively. We just don't think it's a solution."

Was he annoyed about being called a terrorist by America?

"No. Even before September 11, they've always categorized countries and organizations, but never based [it] on facts. They are not the people to categorize the world. They supported terrorism in El Salvador as they support Israeli terrorism now. Hizbollah have never acted as terrorists. We formed to resist terrorism—if it wasn't for Israeli terrorism, Hizbollah wouldn't exist."

Israel's ultimate responsibility for Hizbollah's creation—and Israel's ultimate responsibility for a lot more besides—is taken up a couple of days later by Hizbollah's Deputy Secretary-General, Sheikh Naim Qassem. My translator and I have traveled to my previous appointments in taxis, but for this one we are led to a hidden garage improvised from girders and blankets, and ushered into a black Mercedes with tinted windows—we can see out, but nobody can see in. As I know we're driving to a Hizbollah building a few blocks away, and as I can't imagine that any watching satellites or spies are terribly interested in my comings and goings, I guess this show of secrecy is intended to emphasize Sheikh Qassem's importance.

Sheikh Qassem is the only Hizbollah member I meet who does not wear Western clothes, although the shoes beneath his robes are smart leather loafers. A founding member of Hizbollah, he looks older than his 49 years, but is an affable sort whose gray beard splits frequently with a gleaming white smile. I ask him if anything has changed for Hizbollah since September 11.

"No," he says, "because conditions here didn't change. We are still suffering the same problems—there are still Israelis in Shebaa Farms, there are still Lebanese detainees in their jails, we still have Palestinian refugees here in Lebanon, Israeli planes are still flying in Lebanese airspace and the Israeli navy are still sailing in Lebanese waters."

What did he think, as an avowed enemy of America, when he saw the planes hit the buildings?

"Like the whole world, I was surprised. It was clearly an act against American interests, but because innocent civilians were killed, we issued a declaration expressing our point of view."

Have Hizbollah ever cooperated at any level with al-Qaeda?

"We have no communication with them. We are only interested in what is happening here."

This, for what it may be worth, is in keeping with the rolled eyes and shaken heads with which other Hizbollah members had reacted to the mention of Osama bin Laden (the U.S. State Department nevertheless believes that Hizbollah is harboring al-Qaeda escapees from Afghanistan). I ask Sheikh Qassem if he could explain, then, the moral difference between flying civilian airliners into office blocks, which Hizbollah opposed, and Hamas bombing cafés full of young people drinking on Saturday night in Jerusalem, which Hizbollah supports.

"Hamas," he says, "is part of the Palestinian people, and the Palestinians are surrounded in a very small area. The Israelis are attacking them everywhere. The whole Israeli society is armed."

This shockingly ruthless justification—that killing Israeli civilians is acceptable because nearly all Israelis serve in the Israeli military—is one I have heard from other Hizbollah members, often shortly after they've complained about the killing of Lebanese civilians by Israeli forces pursuing Hizbollah.

"The Palestinians have to defend themselves. As they don't have capabilities equal to the Israeli military, they have no choice but sacrifice."

I ask if Hizbollah cooperates with Hamas. Sheikh Qassem's response is startlingly candid.

"We support their way of operating, we consider that they are right, but their geographic region is different from ours. There is limited cooperation, as conditions permit."

What kind of cooperation?

"Those are details we don't speak about."

Other details Sheikh Qassem doesn't speak about are the three alleged Hizbollah members on the FBI's list, the four Israelis captured by Hizbollah in October 2000, or any of the bombings or hijackings or kidnappings during Lebanon's civil war that are attributed to Hizbollah. I ask if he could at least tell me what he thought, himself, when he heard of these events at the time.

"I don't remember these details. These are part of happenings here that were very complicated."

On the subject of America's view of his party, he is rather more forthcoming.

"For many years, the United States has been describing Hizbollah as terrorists. This is not the first time they have issued such a list."

Things are different now, I say. I don't think they're just calling people names anymore. When he sees what has happened to the Taliban, is he not worried?

"No. This is America's blackmail. It has no effect on us. Our destiny is to continue as a resistance. No one can stop us from taking back our land."

And turning that land into an Islamic state?

"The idea of an Islamic republic is part of our faith. But it depends on the consent of the other parties. God tells us in the Koran that it is not right to impose religion on others. The weapons in our hands are to resist the occupiers, not for use in internal affairs."

But the occupiers are now gone, pretty much, and it's sometimes difficult to believe that Hizbollah's ambitions go no further than that. When I interviewed Abdullah Kassir, he was sitting next to a Hizbollah flag, which has Jerusalem's Dome of the Rock embroidered on a corner of it. Al-Manar's station identification clip shows Hizbollah guerillas on one side of the screen, and Jerusalem's al-Aqsa mosque on the other. The symbolism is not subtle.

"We don't agree with the idea of a Jewish state, because it is on the land of another people. The Israelis came from different parts of the world to take the place of others. The presence of the Israeli state is unjust. The world is imposing Israel by force."

Why would the world do that?

"America is trying to control this region through something which causes fear to everyone else."

I'm not keen to pursue this angle—the idea that history is a chaotic sequence of happenstance and improvisation is not popular in the Middle East, where belief in some grand, malign plot is universal, and I don't want another lecture. So I tell Sheikh Qassem that many people in the West find much to admire about the Islamic world—its emphasis on family, say, its respect for its elders, its hospitality to visitors. Is there anything he finds commendable or enviable about the West?

"What is good in the world is welcome here. We use the Internet, we use the new technology—we'll use anything we can against Israel. We don't agree with everything given to us, but we don't deny everything, either. We have our principles, and we base our judgments on them."

So, I say, briefly relieved, Americans shouldn't think the Arab world hates them.

"No, that's right," he says. "Arabs do hate America, and Hizbollah hates America. This is because of their policies in this region, because of their support for Israel. When confronted with these facts, we don't have time to look for positive things."

Hizbollah is keen that I should see the south of Lebanon. It is the scene of their greatest victory—Hizbollah's mythic status throughout the Arab world derives from its uniqueness as the only Arab force to have defeated Israel on the battlefield. It is also, they tell me, very beautiful, though the weather in the hills might come as a shock after the Mediterranean mildness of Beirut. ("You'll need to wrap up," says Hussein. "Is that the only jacket you brought?")

In Nabiteyeh, Hizbollah's green and gold flag flies from a monument in the city square, and from dozens of windows and roofs. At

Hizbollah's office, in an apartment building not far from the city center, I am introduced to Hassan Abu Hani, a shy, sad-faced man who has been appointed my guide. He is a cameraman—one of the ones who makes Hizbollah's home movies—but disappointingly reluctant to talk about his work.

Nabiteyeh is also festooned with portraits of the young men who have fallen in Hizbollah's war with Israel. I am taken to meet the mother of two of them.

Hajjeh Im Hassan Sabbah lives with her husband and four daughters in a large modern house. The walls of the living room are bare but for two portraits each of her dead children, Hassan and Ali. They were killed exactly three years apart, on February 5, 1987, and 1990, respectively. Both were 21 years old.

"I used to ask Hassan," she says, smiling at the thought of her wayward son as mothers do, "why not get married? Why not lead a normal life? But he hoped that God would choose him for this since he was 13 years old. He always wanted to become a martyr."

It is not unusual for 13-year-old boys to dream of becoming soldiers, even in countries at peace. And all countries revere their war dead. But the single most perplexing aspect of Hizbollah, and one or two like-minded outfits, is not just that they think death preferable to figuring out a way to get on with neighbors, but pursue it with a craving that verges on the ecstatic.

"I have another son," says Hajjeh Sabbah. "He's 33 now, but if they ask for him, they can take him. Me too, if they want."

Outside Nabiteyeh, we are stopped at a Lebanese army checkpoint, but waved through when Hassan explains who he works for. We drive to two former Israeli hilltop positions, al-Bourj and Dabsheh. Both are now abstract sculptures of shattered concrete and twisted metal: Hizbollah blew up al-Bourj after the Israelis withdrew, but the larger Dabsheh base was deliberately destroyed by Israel's own aircraft—to the considerable amusement, Hassan tells me, of watching locals.

Al-Bourj and Dabsheh, like all former Israeli bases in the area, now have billboards alongside them, erected by Hizbollah. These offer, in Arabic and English, a history of the encampments, along with details of their troop strength, weaponry, the number of Hizbollah operations waged against them (242 in 15 years, in Dabsheh's case), and the Israeli casualties these caused (in these two bases alone, Hizbollah's attacks killed 43 and injured 75). The billboards also note, in a somewhat gloating tone, the "Date of ignominous [sic] departure." The more of these we pass, the more the day starts to feel like a coach tour of the sort that regularly roams old battlefields in Europe and America: back in Haret Hreik, I'll tell Hussein that he should buy a green and gold minibus, paint "Hizbollah Tours" on the side and advertise in travel magazines—thrill-seeking tourists would line up around the block.

Our next stop is the prison in the border town of Khiam. The sickly yellow fort was built in the 1930s, when Lebanon was still a French possession, but became justly infamous during the '80s and '90s as a prison run by Israel's Lebanese collaborators, the South Lebanon Army (SLA). Some of those held in Khiam, invariably without trial, were Hizbollah guerrillas. Others were relatives of Hizbollah guerrillas, or otherwise uninvolved locals who just didn't want to cooperate with the SLA. Eighteen months since the last prisoners left, it is still a profoundly depressing place.

Hizbollah has turned Khiam into a shrine. Yellow plastic signs recall the horrors that occurred with a clarity that transcends the clumsy English: "A Room for Investigation and Torturing by Electricity," "The Hall of Torturing: Burying-Kicking-Beating-Applying Electricity-Pouring Hot Water-Placing a Dog Beside" (the skeptical need not take Hizbollah's word for any of this: Amnesty International and The International Red Cross vouch for all of it).

We are shepherded around by Ali Darwich, 26 years old, a young man who radiates a palpable sadness. He was brought to Khiam as a 15-year-old in 1990, when he was captured by the SLA after being wounded while taking part in a Hizbollah operation. He was held for three years, much of it spent in darkness in a room so tiny there was barely room for him and his five cellmates to lie down at once. He shows me into one such hovel, and clangs the door shut behind me. Happily, given Hizbollah's track record with journalists and arbitrary imprisonment, this is for demonstration purposes only.

Ali was also tortured frequently: The scars on his neck reveal systematic excavations from his flesh. Ali returned to Khiam on May 23, 2000, when the SLA guards, fearing reprisals, fled over the border with their Israeli paymasters. I ask him how it felt to come back.

"It was glorious," he says, quietly. "But it was much better than it had been in my time—things changed after the Red Cross came here in 1995. I couldn't believe the prisoners had mattresses."

In the yard, in which Ali had been permitted 10 minutes of exercise and sunlight beneath a chicken-wire ceiling every 20 days, I ask him how he'd coped.

"We are inspired by God to be patient."

There is a small souvenir shop at Khiam, selling Hizbollah videos, flags, key rings, and stickers of Ayatollah Khomeini. Outside the shop is a poster of Sergeant Adi Avitan, Staff Sergeant Benny Avraham, and Staff Sergeant Omer Souad, the three Israeli soldiers captured by

Hizbollah in October 2000—all now officially regarded as dead by Israel—and Elhanan Tannenbaum, taken by Hizbollah at around the same time (Israel claims he was kidnapped while on private business in Switzerland; Hizbollah say he was a Mossad agent who was traveling in Lebanon on a false Belgian passport). The Arabic text alongside their portraits says "Wait for us—who knows when you can expect us?" Hizbollah's sense of humor is possibly an acquired taste. I ask Hassan if he knows where the prisoners are.

"No," he shrugs, and then mutters that nobody ever asks about Lebanese detainees held by Israel. I tell him that if I'm ever in a position to ask the Israeli officials responsible, I will, but I'm asking him because it is his organization that captured the men on the poster.

He shrugs again.

Our excursion finishes at the fortified border that now separates Lebanon from Israel. We walk behind Hassan down the dirt track to the outermost wire fence in careful single file—much of southern Lebanon is still an Israeli minefield. The city limits of the Israeli town of Metulla are maybe 20 meters of fortifications from where we're standing. In the Israeli army observation post behind the wire, we can see soldiers raising their field glasses and leveling their rifles, and I try to imagine a less comfortable place to be than standing next to a member of Hizbollah.

On the Israeli side of the frontier, a white sedan pulls up. From the back seat, someone waves. I wave back. Hassan keeps his hands in his pockets.

—*Andrew Mueller*

## ★★★★★
# LIBERIA

Monrovia

## Black Spot

Liberia is Africa's oldest republic and most ambitious social experiment, and, of course, one of the Dark Continent's most embarrassing examples of equality between blacks and whites. Yes, Africans can do just fine screwing up their own country. Originally established as a homeland for freed slaves, for much of its history Liberia remained relatively stable and prosperous. Not so these days, though. If the world's hellholes ever got together for a party, Liberia would automatically be given the tattered and bloody sash for Least Improved, Most Violent, and Utterly Hopeless. It's the kind of place people are still fighting over long after the last thing there worth fighting over has been sold, stolen, or blown up. Liberia is the best argument in favor of colonialism, intervention, social re-engineering, or just giving everyone a good spanking.

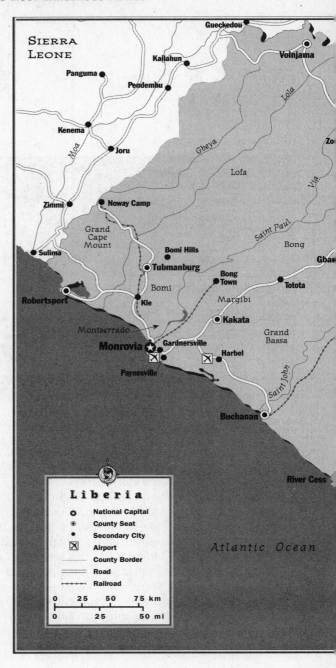

SIERRA
LEONE

Gueckedou

Voinjama

Kailahun

Panguma

Pendembu

Lola

Kenema

Joru

Gbeya

Zo

Lofa

Via

Zimmi

Noway Camp

Saint Paul

Bong

Sulima

Grand
Cape
Mount

Bomi Hills

Tubmanburg

Bong
Town

Gba

Totota

Robertsport

Bomi

Kle

Margibi

Montserrado

Kakata

Grand
Bassa

Monrovia   Gardnersville

Harbel

Saint John

Paynesville

Buchanan

River Cess

**Liberia**

Atlantic Ocean

○ National Capital
◉ County Seat
● Secondary City
☒ Airport
········· County Border
═══ Road
┼┼┼┼ Railroad

0    25    50    75 km

0       25      50 mi

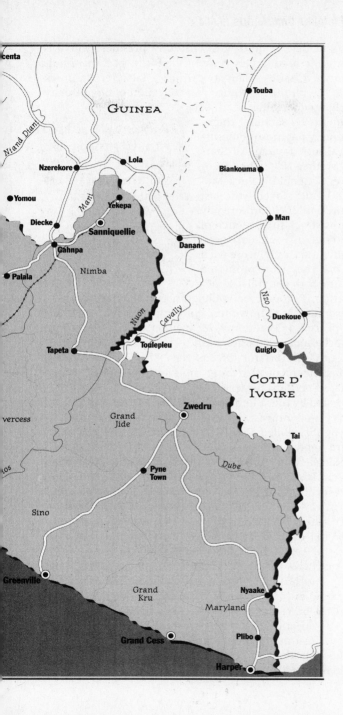

And now, introducing the man who currently presides over this irredeemable dump, the man largely responsible for its present condition—come on down, Charles Ghankay "Chuck" Taaaylorrr! Chuck seized power in 1990 with the assistance of a collection of bloodthirsty brigands who delighted a generation of foreign correspondents by saddling themselves with grotesquely picturesque noms-de-guerre: among Chuck Taylor's All-Stars were General No-Mother-No-Father, General Housebreaker, General Fuck-Me-Quick, and General Butt Naked—the last of whom took to the battlefield armored by no more than tennis shoes and a stench of stale liquor that no bullet would dare penetrate. All these guys, naturally, were such military geniuses that they were promoted straight from volunteer to general—something not even Patton, Rommel, or Wellington ever managed. Much speculation is appropriate as to how these colorful characters made the transition into a "peacetime" economy. *DP* wonders why this colorful affinity for very accurate nicknames hasn't created a Congressman "Swiss Bank Account" or Senator "Needs New Shoes" yet. General Butt Naked was last heard of preaching the word of God on Broad Street in Monrovia, so perhaps there is hope.

> *DP* wonders why we haven't heard of Congressman "Swiss Bank Account" or Senator "Needs New Shoes" yet. General Butt Naked was last heard of preaching the word of God on Broad Street in Monrovia, so perhaps there is hope.

The civil war created by this adorable bunch lasted seven years, until Chuck's position as president was confirmed by a landslide election victory in 1997. The fighting killed about 1 Liberian in 15, and was characterized by torture, rape, punitive amputations, and the mass, forced enlistment of children. In a more robust era, it would have been stopped by some handy colonial power sending in a tiny gunboat and showing the natives who was in charge, but as it is lately unfashionable to point out that Africa's problems are largely the fault of the Africans who run the place, the world ignored Liberia's convulsions as completely as they did the concurrent genocide in Rwanda, and as they have since ignored the war in the Democratic Republic of Congo. Even the copious flow of "Faces of Death"–style war footage couldn't displace water-skiing squirrels or political peccadilloes from the U.S. evening news. We used to care . . . a long time ago.

Founded in 1822, Liberia was an attempt—an experiment, really—by the American Colonization Society to create a homeland in West Africa for freed slaves from the United States (Liberia's capital is called Monrovia after U.S. President James Monroe). It's interesting that a group of individuals so ill-served by the racial strata system of nineteenth-century America chose to re-create the U.S. Constitution on the other side of the Atlantic—Liberia's debut government was modeled directly on the one it sought to escape. By independence in 1847, Liberia had managed to combine the worst elements of their former home (among them corruption, cronyism, slavery, and unbridled greed) with the debilitating effects of the home country (disease, war, pestilence, famine, and lawlessness). The prominent figures of Liberian history, with names like Joseph J. Roberts (Liberia's first president, and illegitimate son of Thomas Jefferson), William V. S. Tubman, Charles Taylor, and William R. Tolbert, Jr., read more like a Palm Beach polo team roster than a struggling, ragtag community of displaced slaves.

The attempt at creating a duplicate America in Africa under Liberia's confusing, lone star and stripes flag never came full circle, mostly because more than a century's worth of efforts at bringing the aboriginal population onto the same playing field as the once-enslaved immigrants proved unsuccessful. Instead of life, liberty, and the pursuit of happiness, by the 1980s Liberia's course had become defined by factional fighting, civil war, partitioning, and bloody coups, led by men with such innocuous, landed-gentryish handles as Doe, Taylor, and Johnson. Sounds like a New York law firm, and, indeed, there are those who would argue that there are other similarities.

Instead of freedom for all, Liberia became a free-for-all, reduced to primal clashes among rival clans, killing each other with old machine guns from the back of ancient, dented jeeps. Bands of marauders cut swaths across the rain forest plateau, donning Halloween masks and bolt-action rifles, as they raped and pillaged in small villages before finally razing them. Calling what happened in Liberia in the '90s a "civil war" is crediting it with too much organization and purpose. The reality was that villagers were slaughtered by tribal-based militias that marked, like dogs pissing on a tree, their territory with the skulls of their victims.

Up until 1980, life was going pretty well—at least, no rock star ever felt the need to make a benefit record on Liberia's behalf. In that year, a coup d'etat, led by a 28-year-old staff sergeant called Samuel Doe, ousted the elected president, William Tolbert, Jr. Doe, a member of the Krahn tribe, had Tolbert and 13 of his ministers executed, suspended Liberia's constitution, and placed Liberia under martial law. If Liberians had any doubt about what sort of man their new leader was, Doe dispelled them by having the executions of Tolbert and the others broadcast on television. Liberia's real life journey up the creek sans paddles makes Conrad's *Heart of Darkness* read like a charming love story.

Doe's gripe with Tolbert had been that, despite Liberia's democratic constitution, power always seemed to end up in the hands of the elite 5 percent of Americo-Liberians who could claim descent from the freed slaves who founded the state and who put on terrible airs and graces as a result. However, Doe clearly didn't see why he should go through the time-consuming hassle of campaigning for office himself. His approach to economics was unorthodox as well. When he noticed that Liberia was flat broke and couldn't pay its debts, he simply printed more money. This, in case any impressionable neophyte leaders of dunned third-world nations are taking careful notes, doesn't work.

Doe's presidency met an end as messy as its beginning on September 10, 1990, when members of Prince Yormie Johnson's Independent Patriotic Front cut Doe's ears off, tortured him to death, and then paraded what was left of him around Monrovia. Johnson fancied himself as Doe's successor by right of conquest, but lost out in factional fighting with Chuck Taylor's National Patriotic Front of Liberia (ya gotta love these political party names). Chuck was previously a flunky of Doe, but had fallen out with his old boss over the matter of US$900,000 looted from Liberia's treasury when he was in charge of purchasing for the Liberian government. Taylor had launched his incursion from neighboring Cote d'Ivoire 10 months previously. The seven-year civil war that followed pitted Chuck's ethnically Gio and Mano NPFL against the Krahn and Mandingo–dominated United Liberation Movement of Liberia for Democracy (ULIMO) and the (mainly Krahn) Armed Forces of Liberia (AFL).

In August 1990, a six-nation West African peacekeeping force called the Economic Community of West African States Cease-Fire Monitoring Group (ECOMOG) had essentially partitioned Liberia into two zones. The first encompassed the capital of Monrovia and was led by President Amos Sawyer. The other, run by Taylor and his NPFL, amounted to about 95 percent of Liberian territory, which it governed, after a fashion, from Gbarnga. Prince Yormie, meanwhile, had rather blindsided himself. He'd agreed to be flown to Ghana for peace talks, and arrived to discover that not only had nobody else shown up, but also that ECOMOG wouldn't fly him back.

Reconciliation and peace agreements were signed and then forgotten, like journalists' bar tabs. A March 1991 conference failed to get anything accomplished except for the re-election of Sawyer as interim president. Despite a peace agreement in 1991, fighting continued to flare. Another peace agreement and cease-fire in July 1993, which established an interim government and set up general democratic elections, crumbled in November. Gambia, Nigeria, Mali, the Ivory Coast, Switzerland,

> **R**econciliation and peace agreements were signed and then forgotten, like journalists' bar tabs.

and Benin all hosted Liberian peace talks, doing wonders for the air-miles accounts of NPFL officials, but accomplishing bugger all else. The 12th agreement, signed in Benin with UN guarantees, seemed the most likely to succeed. However, it ended up in tatters. Only 3,000 of Liberia's estimated 60,000 fighters—many of them teenagers addicted to drugs, as well as killing and raping civilians—were disarmed.

It didn't help that Sierra Leone, while theoretically participating in the ECOMOG peacekeeping operation, allowed dissident groups like the ULIMO to use its territory to launch raids into Liberia. Chuck responded by giving massive support to Foday Sankoh's Revolutionary United Front (RUF) butchers in Sierra Leone, with hideous consequences.

By 1993, the UN had estimated that 150,000 Liberians had died since Chuck launched his crusade, but stopped counting after that (most current estimates are a long way the wrong side of 200,000). A peace accord signed in August 1995 called for countrywide ECOMOG deployment and disarmament of factional fighters, but 10 months later neither of these processes had gotten off the ground. In April 1996, Monrovia again collapsed into lawlessness, when fighting between the rival factions resumed. Thousands fled the capital city in panic; as many as 20,000 Liberians descended upon the residential annex of the U.S. embassy. U.S. commandos evacuated about 2,000 frightened American citizens and other foreigners by chopper to the Sierra Leone capital of Freetown, as Monrovia's airport was destroyed in the fighting. Evacuations continued for at least two months.

In February 1997, the war's 14th peace agreement, the Abuja Accord, was designed by the Economic Community of West African States (ECOWAS) to dissolve Liberia's armed factions, with surprising success—more than 10,000 fighters were demobilized, and 5,000 weapons were recovered. In July 1997, Charles Taylor was elected to the presidency by an impressive margin, though whether this was because people thought he'd be a good president, or because they were scared of what he'd do if he lost, is a moot point. Liberians reportedly explained their choice with the slogan, referring to Chuck, "You kill my pa, you kill my ma, I will vote for you." Strange place, Africa.

Taylor is now fighting (another) brutal war in the north of Liberia, where Liberian LURD rebels backed by Guinea have taken control of over a third of the country. LURD got close enough to Monrovia to suggest that the streets of Taylor's beleaguered capital could run with blood again before too much longer. Until recently, Chuck was still funding the RUF in Sierra Leone—a policy that, in 2001 and again in 2002, has earned Liberia a UN arms embargo and trade sanctions. Chuck has since complained that because of the sanctions, he hasn't got the guns or the money to carry on fighting. It doesn't seem to have occurred to him that this might have been the idea, or that everyone knows the Libyan transport planes landing in Monrovia aren't full of toasted-sandwich makers. For now, Taylor uses RUF mercenary Ukrainian pilots and black market Serbian weapons to tenuously hold onto power.

## The Scoop

Liberia is a country created by former American slaves who brought American presidential surnames and American-style politics to Africa. It was once the most Americanized country in Africa. And, in a way, it still is—racism, guns, and crime are leitmotifs of life here, as well. Liberia now barely functions, except perhaps as living proof that it's not wise to mess with politics or Mother Nature. Like many devolved countries, life is better in the pristine jungles than in the cities. The prolonged civil war has reduced the country to a subsistence economy, and its people to desperation—unemployment is at around 80 percent. Liberia is a truly dangerous place to visit. Every governmental agency on earth advises travelers not to get within a thousand miles of the place, and readers who decide to go anyway may notice a lot of friends and relatives dropping around to write their initials on the bottom of any valuable antiques or decent stereo gear they happen to own. With that said, you could join the ranks of Pat Robertson and Jesse Jackson, and enjoy the squalor with the same eighteenth-century feeling of hopelessness and decay even Conrad couldn't imagine. Well over one-third of the country is in the hands of rebels trying to overthrow a government which barely governs the other two-thirds.

*Liberian Post*
http:/www.liberiannews.com

*The Perspective*
http://www.theperspective.org

*All About Liberia*
http://www.allaboutliberia.com
The government of Liberia sponsors this site: Its brazen propaganda would have given even Goebbels wet dreams.

## The Players

### Dahkpanna Charles McArthur Ghankay Taylor

Chuck's done well for a local boy. He was born on January 28, 1948, in Arthington, to Nelson, his American father (a sharecropper, teacher, and lawyer), and Zoe, a Liberian-American. Though he finally got around to getting himself elected to the job in 1997, he'd considered himself Liberia's top dog since 1990, when he started leading his National Patriotic Front of Liberia (NPFL) in a vicious campaign across Liberia's countryside to the capital, Monrovia. A tactful assessment of Chuck's career to date would be "colorful."

Although Chuck was born just north of Monrovia, he grew up in the United States—he graduated in 1977 from Bentley College in Massachusetts (another tremendous advertisement for America's education system). While there, he'd been preparing for his future role as president by working part-time as a truck driver, security guard, and mechanic, and hanging out with expatriate Liberians who were annoyed that power back in the old country was concentrated in the hands of the elite minority of so-called Americo-Liberians: Liberians who could trace their ancestry back to the freed American slaves who founded Liberia. These privileged oligarchs included such figures as Liberia's then-President William Tolbert and, er . . . uhm, Chuck's mother (who is from the Gola tribe). Just imagine all of the subsequent trouble Liberia could have been saved with the services of a $50-an-hour shrink.

When Tolbert was overthrown and executed by Samuel Doe in 1980, Chuck was already in Liberia. He'd been invited home by Tolbert, who'd been impressed by Chuck when he'd demonstrated against Tolbert during a visit to New York in 1979. Chuck found himself with a choice between returning to Boston to pursue the opportunities (and, if the stories are to be believed, the cheerleaders) that come with an American liberal education, or staying in Liberia to work for a half-mad despot presiding over a broken-down, war-ravaged dump. It was a dilemma that no sane man would be troubled by. However, Chuck is, when all is said and done, as crazy as a square wheel, and so he signed on with Doe.

In just three years as head of Liberia's General Services Agency, in charge of the Liberian government's purchasing, Chuck made a personal fortune, estimated at US$900,000. Sadly for him, Doe's government wanted it back. With the chance of a spell in one of Liberia's delightful prisons beckoning, Chuck legged it back to Boston, where his surprise at learning about Liberia's extradition agreement with America must have been considerable. He was locked up, but escaped after 16 months in the Plymouth House of Corrections—he later bragged about how he sawed through the laundry-room bars after bribing his jailors with $30,000. That economics degree—and a useful connection to the American-Liberian mafia—came in handy after all.

Chuck made his way back to Africa (Libya to be exact), where he started rousing the rabble against his old boss, Doe. Rumor had it he was studying Revolution 101 at the University of Wacky Qaddafi, but he was next seen in Cote d'Ivoire, where he assembled a ragtag army of about 150 men with the help of the Ivorian president—a brother-in-law of William Tolbert, the Liberian president executed by Samuel Doe (it's heartwarming when families help each other out like this). Another 4,000 soldiers—or, at least, men who owned guns—joined from the Gio and Mano tribes of eastern Liberia. Chuck called his merry men the National Patriotic Front of Liberia (NPFL), and blew kick-off on his rebellion on December 24, 1989. Merry Christmas, everybody.

Chuck's uprising was a mixed blessing—good news for him, and bad news for everyone else in Liberia. With President Doe dispatched in September 1990 by another rebel leader, a former comrade of Chuck's, Prince Yormie Johnson (not really a Prince, in case you were wondering), Chuck awarded himself the title of el presidente a month later and swiftly gathered everything in the country under the control of the NPFL. This had the net effect of knocking Liberia's already delicate infrastructure irretrievably into the toilet. The civil war that followed Taylor's assumption of power left 200,000 dead, and more than a million homeless.

Naturally, the great and good of the free and democratic world took a firm line against this blood-soaked tyrant. Or maybe they did in some parallel universe where diplomacy, justice, and common sense speak to each other every so often. Back here on earth, Chuck got a phone call from Bill Clinton, a high-five from well-known friend of the oppressed Jesse Jackson, and a meeting with Jimmy Carter. Actually, we take it back. If *DP* was running some tin-pot African hellhole, we'd cope okay with sanctions or a gunboat . . . but a visit from goofy-tooth? Cruel and unusual punishment, if ever we heard of it. We give up, already.

In fairness to Chuck, when he finally got around to having an election, in July 1997, most international observers conceded that it was more or less fair enough, and that Chuck's whopping 75 percent of the vote was pretty well legitimate, at least relative to the vicissitudes of African democracy. It didn't hurt that Chuck's government ran Liberia's biggest radio station, KISS-FM, and had the money to plaster Liberia with posters of the great man's portrait (a major factor in a country where, because most voters can't read, candidates are identified on the ballot by photograph). And, of course, that most of the groups who didn't support him have been chased out and are living in refugee camps outside his borders.

Chuck is known to be a big fan of the music of Mahalia Jackson and the films of Clint Eastwood. He's not known to be much of an econo-mist. One of his first big revenue-raising ideas was to order all expatriate Liberians to return home to collect new passports—you might remember not hearing a collective cry of "Sure, Chuck, we'll be right there." A similar indifference was roused by Chuck's 2001 offer of amnesty to all rebels who wanted to come home. The rebels in question seemed to think that the welcome might be an uncomfortably warm one. P.S.: Don't plan on sending any fan mail to Chuck; seems that as of December '02, he hasn't paid his country's postal bill.

**Charles Ghankay Taylor**
Executive Mansion
P.O. Box 10-9001
Capitol Hill
1000 Monrovia 10, Liberia
Tel.: (231) 22 8026
emansion@liberia.net

## Liberians United for Reconciliation and Democracy (LURD)

The LURD, a hodge-podge of mostly disenchanted Mandingos and Krahns from the defunct ULIMO rebel group, got off to a bad start by saddling themselves with an acronym that sounds like some sort of cooking fat substitute, but they've developed into the stuff of Chuck Taylor's worst nightmares.

In order to stave off an incursion into southern Guinea by Taylor's forces, the Guinean government armed the LURD as a buffer against Chuck's expansionist ideas. (When the area near Macenta, inside Guinea, was recaptured from Taylor in 1999, Chuck had already started laying down train tracks to help extract minerals and timber—a shame Amtrak isn't so proactive.) After December 2000, and the election of the new LURD leadership, things became a little more concrete: the LURD National Chairman Sekou Damate Conneh, Jr., married the Guinean president's principal advisor. Conneh himself, an affable character of seemingly generous disposition, has a colorful past: previous employment has included used-car sales as well as a spell in the Liberian finance ministry (sound familiar?).

LURD is a force to reckon with. Having started with only 80 men and less than 1,000 rounds of ammunition, the boys have done good; they now control between 30 and 40 percent of Liberia. They are also very well armed: *DP* counted 6 SAM-7 surface-to-air missiles, 3 BZT 14.5 antiaircraft installations, and a number of 12.7 heavy machine guns (you might want to consider swapping that airline ticket for a fishing boat out of Freetown).

By Liberian standards the LURD are reasonably organized and disciplined (the words, "by Liberian standards," are crucial, by the way) and they are now the law of the land in a large swath of northern and central Liberia and seem to have a relatively benign attitude toward the oft-brutalized population.

*DP* found the remnants of Sierra Leone's very baddest bad boys—the West Side Niggaz—fighting with LURD. The West Side "Boys" (as the PC journos called them) kidnapped a number of Brit soldiers and were subsequently attacked by the SAS and then mown down by Hind gunships flown by South African mercenaries. It appears they missed some. Despite the UN's rosy plans for peace in Sierra Leone, Taylor was feeding and arming 7,500 of the supposedly disarmed RUF fighters.

The LURD, if you'll forgive us, moves in mysterious ways: Until *DP* pitched up, not one single journo had ever made it into rebel-held territory. Refugees displaced by the Taylor-engendered upheavals of the '90s formed the movement in Freetown and Conakry in 1999. The predominantly ex-ULIMO founding fathers claimed that Taylor had not honored the 1997 Abuja Peace Accords which ended the civil war: in other words, Taylor kept their slice of the (diamond and timber) pie for himself.

To *DP*, the LURD earnestly claimed an enthusiasm for democracy, law, order, and all the other things that violent guerrilla groups generally claim to be keen on. On closer inspection, this actually seems to be reasonably close to the mark. Suckers, us.

All, however, is not well in the LURD camp. Essentially a reunited ULIMO front, LURD comprises both the old ULIMO-K and -J factions, as well as a rogue's gallery of excombatants identified by an increasingly unintelligible soup of acronyms. Although the chairman of LURD is a Muslim Mandingo, he plays a delicate balancing act between these former friends-cum-enemies-cum-friends again. The LURD chief of staff, Prince Seo (an ex-ULIMO-J Krahn), and most of the rest of the senior military (ex-ULIMO-K Mandingos) each control sections and factions that are currently managing to operate as one army, albeit only just. *DP* has the distinct feeling that the current war is in fact a trailer for *Civil War: The Sequel*, with a surprise guest appearance by Burkina Faso, supported by Muammar Qaddafi.

Since late 2000, the fighting in Liberia has spread down from the north around Voinjama, through the forest, to Fassama, Bopolu, and now into Bomi Hills, a mere grenade's throw away from Monrovia itself. In the west, the town of Foya, held by pro-Taylor RUF mercenaries, has been surrounded by LURD troops for months. Most of the rest of the Sierra Leone border area is subject to ambushes and firefights.

Since September 2001, Chuck has taken to calling LURD "terrorists" and "illegal combatants," but the chances of the Pentagon riding to his rescue are slim. Major battles with them have occurred in the towns of Gbarnga and Tubmanburg.

LURD's motivation is refreshingly clear. There is no cross-eyed frothing leader spouting gibberish, no limbless people, and no pretensions to any great political revolution: just Conte's flunkies kicking the hell out of Taylor's flunkies. It's good, old-fashioned warfare, for a change. And nothing a handful of air-supported peacekeepers couldn't wipe out before lunch . . . but that would leave Taylor in charge, wouldn't it?

**Coalition of Progressive Liberians in**
**the Americas**
bodioh@hotmail.com
http://www.copla.org

**Chairman Sekou Damate Conneh, Jr.**
National Chairman of LURD
lurd_liberia@yahoo.com

## United Liberation Movement of Liberia for Democracy (ULIMO)

ULIMO to its friends, and still fighting after all these years: although officially disbanded in 1997, around 90 percent of LURD's commanders and troops are . . . ex-ULIMO. In fact, the hard-pressed civilian population often refer to LURD as ULIMO. ULIMO's founder, Alhaji Kromah, has also expressed his sympathy for the LURD. The ULIMO splinter faction, ULIMO-J, led by Roosevelt Johnson, spent a while swapping cash, and then lead, with ECOMOG and Chuck Taylor's forces over a diamond concession. This culminated in a three-day battle in Monrovia in September 1998, after which several hundred people lay dead, and Johnson and some of his supporters took refuge in the U.S. embassy. The embassy, with what was surely unnecessary helpfulness, arranged for South African mercenaries to fly them out of the country. Roosevelt Johnson was last heard of living in Nigeria.

## The Special Operations Division (SOD) and Anti-Terrorist Unit (ATU)

Trained by South African mercenaries (please step forward, former Executive Outcomes Colonel Fred Rundle), the SOD and ATU are frequently implicated in human rights abuses. The ATU is a paramilitary security force accountable directly to Chuck, and commanded by none other than the imaginatively named Chucky Taylor, the president's son (and perhaps named after the horror film character, Chucky?). Known for his penchant for underage girls and generally insatiable blood lust, Number 1 son has done a fine job with the ATU. They've tortured and executed hundreds of civilians suspected of being sympathetic to the LURD rebels. The ATU has also been used to kick heads in Monrovia. In March 2001, the SOD and ATU were at the forefront of a raid on the University of Monrovia, where they broke up a meeting of people trying to raise money for the defense of imprisoned journalists. These "elite" troops tortured more than 40 students and raped several of the females. SODs by name, sods by nature. It kind of makes the rebels seem positively romantic.

http://www.charles-taylor.es.org/InnerCircle.php3

## Armed Forces of Liberia (AFL)

The AFL was formerly the national army under the Doe regime and largely made up of ethnic Krahns (Doe was a Krahn). By 1992, as a result of the civil war, the AFL maintained only limited authority and most of its equipment had been destroyed or rendered useless. The Liberian army these days is essentially just another faction, and not a content one. Many of its troops haven't been paid for nearly two years, although it's hard to negotiate a good compensation package when you are 13 years old. And it's altogether plausible that some of the earlier attacks attributed to LURD were in fact made by hungrier elements of the AFL trying to keep body and soul together. Indeed, the AFL has proved so prone to running away and joining the rebels that they have been largely disarmed. Only the navy division (who wear bright yellow T-shirts, for some reason) now seems regularly to be deployed in combat: They bore the brunt of the fighting in Tubmanburg in July 2002.

> **T**he Liberian army these days is essentially just another faction, and not a content one. Many of its troops haven't been paid for nearly two years, although it's hard to negotiate a good compensation package when you are 13 years old.

## Mercenaries

At the moment, Liberia is something of a playground for freelance military professionals. Apart from Libyan advisors, who make sure that the Iraqi and Serbian weapons they are selling Chuck work okay (and are paid for), the Man Himself has a presidential bodyguard consisting of two platoons of Burkinabes recruited in the 1990s—apparently he doesn't trust Liberian soldiers to protect him anymore (wise man). There are also two Ukrainian chopper crews hanging around in Monrovia (Chuck has one Mi-8 in operation; the other was shot down by the LURD in 2001). The South Africans fared less well. Colonel Fred Rundle (ex-EO) was hired to train the ATU. However, reports have it that after their first contact, the new recruits ran in panic, so Rundle was bundled out. The South Africans have since been back, but, judging by the results, they didn't earn their paycheck this time either.

Taylor has recruited RUF mercenaries to fight for him in Foya, near the Sierra Leone border. Led by the murderous (and former dancer and hairdresser) Sam "Mosquito" Bockarie, several hundred RUF troops are currently battling LURD rebels and relying solely on chopper re-supply. The LURD don't seem particularly keen on taking any prisoners.

The LURD, bizarrely, have both ex-Sierra Leonian Civil Defense Force fighters, Kamajors, and RUF fighting with them. *DP* found the remnants of the West Side Boys holding the line (though only just) at Lofa Bridge. Top tip: Jokes about the SAS won't go down all that well.

## Guinea

Chuck Taylor (who took power by invading with a Libyan-backed, ragtag, rebel army) is complaining that neighboring Guinea is invading with their very own ragtag rebel army. Things just aren't sporting anymore in Liberia. The rebels in the north (soon to be in the south) are backed by Guinea's president, Lansana Conte, a blood-and-iron military dictator who makes Chuck Taylor look like Ralph Nader, and he's thoroughly hacked off with the thousands of refugees who have washed up on his doorstep following the wars in Liberia and Sierra Leone. Sierra Leone and the UN, with their half-billion-a-year budget next door, are more than happy to look the other way, though in May 2002 the U.S. government helpfully provided $3 million worth of Special Forces training for the Guinean army and up until October '02 was slipping the occasional fiver in the "overthrow Taylor" collection plate.

Conte and Taylor have been calling each other nasty names for years. Conte thinks Taylor has designs on Guinea's reserves of diamonds, gold, and bauxite—not unreasonable given Taylor's de facto invasion of southeastern Guinea in late 1999—not, to judge by the Guinean average annual income of US$460, that Conte has done much of a job of exploiting them himself. Conte is letting anti-Taylor LURD guerrillas use Guinea as a safe haven and logistical base. Conte's response to this accusation is somewhat terse: "If there are people amongst the refugees who don't like Mr. Taylor," he said, "that's not my fault." He probably forgot the paychecks and weapons he also happens to let them use while they express their dislike of Mr. Taylor.

### Government of Guinea
http://www.guinee.gov.gn

## George Weah

Soccer superstar, and the one Liberian that pretty much every Liberian likes. George Weah, a one-time World Footballer of the Year, and African Player of the Century, is the most famous and most adored Liberian who has ever lived. He has played for some of the biggest clubs in Europe—Monaco, Paris Saint-Germain, AC Milan, and Chelsea—but even though he lives in either whichever European city he's playing in or his adopted New York, he hasn't forgotten where he came from. For a long time, George paid for the kits and travel of the Liberian national team, the Lone Stars, out of his own pocket. He has also set up something called the George Weah Foundation, a charity that helps people affected by Liberia's endemic carnage, and he's a goodwill ambassador for the UN.

Weah is one of the good guys—he's even been spoken of as a future president. Probably for these two reasons, his relations with Chuck Taylor are a little iffy. Chuck made George technical director of the Lone Stars by presidential decree, but Weah may have removed himself permanently from Chuck's Christmas card list in 2000 when he offered to mediate when Chuck locked up a film crew from Britain's Channel 4 and tried to have them charged with spying. In 2001, Weah said that Chuck was jealous of his popularity (to the extent, claimed Weah, that Chuck was planning to kill him) and that he wouldn't come back to Liberia while Chuck was still in charge.

The real flashpoint between the pair was apparently that Taylor tried to overrule Weah's attempts to get sponsorship for the Lone Stars for the 2002 African Nations Cup in Mali: Chuck, it is said, thought the Liberian team would cut more of a dash with their president's face and signature on their shirts, rather than some tiresome corporate logo. No, really?

**George Weah**
http://www.edgesportsintl.com/weah.htm

### The Karate Kid

Do not assume that Chuck's litany of barbarism has gone unnoticed in the rest of the Dark Continent. In August 2002, the Union of African Karate Federations made their feelings about Taylor absolutely unambiguous . . . by awarding him their Gold Peace Medal. Presenting the medal, the clearly confused karate official announced: "You have chosen the path of peace, Mr. President, and history will smile favorably upon you." Incidentally, Chuck is in good company: The first winner of the prize was that well-known, peace-loving democrat, President Denis Sessu Nguessu of Congo Brazzaville.

# Getting In

You're sure about this? You're that tired of anything recognizable as civilization? Well, if you must, you can try to fly directly to Monrovia (the only land crossing officially open is the border with Cote d'Ivoire, and Liberian embassy staff don't recommend that) or via the on-again, off-again air link from Ghana. International and regional airlines frequently suspend flights to Monrovia owing to the proliferation of surface-to-air missiles and antiaircraft artillery in the hands of the rebels. The borders with Guinea and Sierra Leone are free-for-alls, impassable during the rainy season anyway, and best avoided unless you have access to, say, a tank and a large group of armed and desperate men (though this, of course, can be arranged if you've got enough money on you).

You will need a visa to get into Liberia as well. These cost around US$40, and your nearest embassy will tell you what you need to know . . . sort of. The Liberians have a bad habit of telling you not to believe what you read in the news about Taylor's imminent downfall and all that malicious gossip about "rebels on the outskirts of Monrovia." You need to apply for a visa a few weeks in advance, so that your details can be sent to Monrovia for scrutiny. Since there is no postal service, intermittent phone lines, and a general disregard of urgency, don't hold your breath.

If you're a journalist, abandon hope: this is a very, very bad idea. You will not be allowed to leave the airport until the Security and Information Services have vetted you, and you will be confined largely to Monrovia (not that that stopped *DP*). If you piss them off, which you will, you will almost certainly be arrested for spying and/or collaborating with the LURD. All such accusations are dealt with by military tribunals (which can impose the death penalty) and there is no automatic recourse to legal representation. Still, at least you'd know what it feels like to be an Afghan in Guantanamo Bay—great for a color piece in the Sunday magazines.

*Embassy of the Republic of Liberia*
5201 16th Street, N.W.
Washington, DC 20011
Tel.: (202) 723-0437
Fax: (202) 723-0436
info@liberiaemb.org
http://www.liberiaemb.org

*Embassy of the Republic of Liberia*
2 Pembridge Place
London W2 4XB, UK
Tel.: (44) 20 7221 1036

## Getting Around

Are you mad? Didn't you read the damn chapter? Are you blind? Well, if you've got as far as Monrovia, it's a possibility that both possibilities can't be ruled out. If you want to go farther, there are no planes and few trains. The three rail lines in the country are used mostly to take mining produce out of the interior, but the Lamco service between Buchanan and Yekepa takes some passengers. This leaves you with the road, where extreme caution is urged even when roads are open: There are no traffic lights in Liberia, and it wouldn't make much difference if there were. Motorists are frequently hassled at checkpoints manned by bored, stoned, hungry, and unpaid soldiers. Cigarette-rolling papers—indeed, any kind of paper that can be used to make joints with—will increase your popularity immensely, as will booze, cigarettes, and so on.

You'll be able to hire a car and driver through your hotel, but it cannot be overstated what a bad idea it is to travel by road without someone who has done so before, and who knows how to deal with the fighters. As far as payoffs go, there is no rule of thumb—just try to part with as little money as you can get away with. It should go without saying that your Rolex, your Ray-Bans, your cool new iPod, and anything else you didn't want nicked, shouldn't be taken on the plane in the first place. Try to show your papers without actually handing them to the guard.

Above all, stay in after dark.

## Dangerous Places

### Monrovia

Monrovia's crime rate is high, regardless of the level of tensions. Foreigners are targets of street criminals, police, the army, and anyone who wants to advance their financial status. Residential break-ins are common. Just about all officials will ask you for some type of gift. Just act stupid and hand them a Mr. *DP* sticker. If you have to pull their rusty gun barrel out of your nostril, smile and give them your Mr. *DP* hat. Things are very volatile here, so it is really important to check in with your embassy on arrival if you want a chopper ride out if things go to hell again. Remember, the rebels have already launched major attacks within 10 miles of the capital.

Oh, did you know Liberia is offering incentives for people looking to invest in the tourism industry?

http://members.tripod.com/liberian/Post3.html

### Everywhere Else

Once you are outside of Monrovia, you are about as far away from help as you can get. Most of the north, northeast, west, and center of Liberia are partly or completely in rebel hands, or abandoned to the jungle. Numerous government roadblocks will ensure that any item of value will not be yours when you return. Keep in mind that you are in a country full of very tweaked, desperate, and trigger-happy fighters.

## Dangerous Things

### Roadblocks

Roadblocks can be a little difficult to take seriously: Liberia's "soldiers" tend to dress themselves in whatever they stole or found during the last raid and/or pack rape, so it's not unusual for drivers to be bailed up by groups of Kalashnikov-toting teenagers wearing floral dresses. However, the guns are very real, as is the palm wine or beer their owners drink to while away the long hours on patrol. Do be cooperative. Don't have anything with you worth pinching. Do be polite. Don't be in a hurry.

### Ambushes

Helpfully, the LURD frequently ambush all the roads leading to Monrovia, Bomi, and Gbarnga with deadly efficiency. The farther away from Monrovia you venture, the more likely you are to experience firsthand the effects of a thermobaric RPG round dissolving your rental car into a scrap metal and Jell-O mix. With the current exception of the southeast, you should expect to be ambushed anywhere and everywhere at anytime. Do not travel with military personnel, never drive alone or at the head of a convoy of vehicles, and always ask the locals when and where the last ambush was. If the soft stuff hits the fan and your legs aren't already mixed in with this year's cassava crop, get out of the vehicle (very quickly), and lie down by the side of the road. It will all be over in five minutes.

### Children

The UN reckons that about 20,000 Liberian children went to play war for keeps during the '90s: The youngest soldier to gaze poignantly into an award-seeking foreign reporter's camera was six years old. They fought on all sides, though Chuck Taylor's NPFL was the most infamous recruiter of underage warriors, both for his own outfit and for the RUF in Sierra Leone. UNICEF noted that 18 percent of Chuck's NPFL army shouldn't have been allowed out without a note from the folks.

Many of these children were forcibly recruited or were basically bought from their families in exchange for food. They were routinely juiced up with alcohol, speed, and a potent, locally popular stimulant made from cane juice and gunpowder. Their training usually amounted to being forced to participate in tortures, executions, and mass rapes.

These brutalized infants were the most feared of the combatants in Liberia's civil war—obedient and utterly amoral. Many of them were never disarmed: Think about how much you'd enjoy trying to take a loaded rifle off a stoned adolescent. Once again, children are being armed and school-bused to the front line. Both Chuck and the LURD rely heavily on what are locally referred to as "small soldiers." Other than flying them en masse to work as hall monitors in American high schools, it's difficult to know what can be done about them.

*Coalition to Stop the Use of Child Soldiers*
http://www.child-soldiers.org

## Diamonds

Diamonds are the only things in Liberia worth owning—and, as such, are the reason behind a lot of Liberia's carnage. Like neighboring Sierra Leone, Liberia is cursed with a healthy crop of sparkling rocks that desperate people will—and do—kill for. The UN has passed several resolutions to stop the international traffic of these "conflict diamonds" or "blood diamonds," but that doesn't make them any less desirable to the brigands running various patches of Liberia. Now the bad news: Liberia produces a trickle of diamonds compared to Sierra Leone and made most of their money by simply calling smuggled gems "Liberian" rather than Sierra Leonian diamonds. Deprived of his baubles, Taylor has cast his gaze on Liberia's rain forest for his next paycheck. (See the section on Timber.)

http://www.un.org/peace/africa/Diamond.html

## Timber

The UN thought it was being tricky when they cut off Taylor's access to Sierra Leone's diamonds. Ah, but they misjudged the Presidential One. Deprived of his sparkly cash generators, Chuck simply sold off 42 percent of the last remaining rain forest in his country (Liberia used to have 40 percent of all West Africa's rain forest) to a reputed arms- and drug-runner named Gus van Kouwenhoven. Gus and his Oriental Timber Company have exclusive rights to 16,000 square kilometers of tropical timber. Timber? Dangerous . . .? Well, the Global Witness investigations have found that Taylor gets paid for his timber in weapons, which in the hands of his goons are truly dangerous. The sale and control of Liberia's rich timber industry is controlled by the august-sounding Forest Development Authority, which is run by (wait for it) Demetrius Robert Taylor . . . Chuck's brother, a man who has the same amount of knowledge about forestry as his brother does about nuclear physics. Need proof that the embargo on diamonds is working? Timber production was 157,000 cubic meters in 1998 and is now at 1.2 million cubic meters, dropping 100 million green ones a year into Chuck's war purse. Oh, and Chuck's people vehemently deny all of the above. The UN has now partially embargoed timber exports . . . lumber may be exported, but only if the financial proceeds are used for social development programs. God bless the UN. Build a new clinic or live in exile in Ouagadougou? Tough one, no?

www.globalwitness.org

## Juju

Just about everyone around here is more than a little superstitious. Taylor is a numerology freak (seven is his lucky number). On the other side of the border, the deeply paranoid Guinean president's penchant for fortune-telling has shifted his foreign policy firmly behind the rebels. Ayesha Conneh, Lansana Conte's most trusted confidante (and wife of Sekou Conneh, the LURD's National Chairman), rose from humble beginnings as a market trader to the heights of power in 1996 when she had a vision warning the president of a military coup. Ayesha is now apparently universally feared by senior Guinean officials, a number of whom are rumored to have been (permanently) removed from office on the strength of her visions.

Liberians assume that bullets will bounce off them, that witches cast spells, and that white devils walk the forests snatching small children (partly true). Human sacrifice and cannibalism are very real here, but not expected to emerge as the next fast-food franchise concept. It is believed by some that eating an opponent's still-beating heart gives them strength. In wartime, body parts are used as everything from good luck fetishes to signposts, or for impromptu football matches. Will that be white or dark meat with those fries. . . ? Only joking, of course—there are no fries in Liberia.

> **H**uman sacrifice and cannibalism are very real here, but not expected to emerge as the next fast-food franchise concept.

http://www.hrw.org/worldreport99/africa/liberia.html
http://www.intl-crisis-group.org/projects/africa/westafrica/reports/
   A400627_24042002.pdf

## The Love Boats

Liberia vies with Panama to be the world's largest maritime nation. What better place to entrust the safety of your ship than these two stable, democratic countries, which have no history of turmoil and are havens for solid, dependable rulers, and, of course, paragons of law enforcement and accountability in the courts. Liberia began registering ships 50 years ago. The idea is that you set up a Liberian corporation, fill out some forms, pay your per-ton rate (10 cents a ton, with the new, reduced, "Chuck Needs the Cash" sale) and, voilà, after you pay your $3,800 you are one of the 1,700 or so ships registered in the democratic, law-abiding country of Liberia. Liberia registers 35 percent of the world's tanker tonnage and the Maritime Departments' books in Monrovia have not been audited since 1988 (you're kinda guessing where we're going with this, huh?).

So, what do you get for your money? Well, you get tax breaks, Liberian safety inspections, a snappy-looking Liberian flag, and, of course, it's tough as hell for anyone to sue you should you dump a few tons of toxic waste into a maritime park . . . oh, and that fee goes to help out that tiny, nice, "save the slaves" West African country you can't find on a map. According to an October 22, 2001, UN report, the Liberian ship registry is "little more than a cash extraction operation and a cover from which to fund and organize opaque, off-budget expenditures, including for sanction busting." The UN reports that a couple of payments made by the Liberian International Ship and Corporate Registry went directly into United Arab Emirate bank accounts to pay for weapons. When the UN went to audit the books of the Liberian Maritme agency in Monrovia, they were told the generator was broken. Probably not a lie, but the point is that with the LISCR folks making payments to nongovernment accounts, and cash-poor Chuck counting greenbacks at the mansion, it seems like it all could stand a little scrutiny.

And the idea that the vast majority of the cruise industry have their corporate offices in the United States and Europe and cater to Western passengers, but have to live up to Liberian and Panamanian labor laws and safety standards, is something not usually discussed at the captain's table.

The $18 million generated by registering ships accounts for about one-fourth to a third of all Liberia's (or should we say Chuck's?) income. Other sources of income, like clear-cut timber from Liberia's rain forest, also seem to attract controversy (of the Russian mafiya and smuggled weapons kind), and taxes on rice and gas all go into the Executive Mansion Special Projects Accounts. Which, according to Chuck's worst enemies, the LURD, means that people actually deliver cash to Chuck's house, which he in turn doles out—to himself, the government, and goon squads like the Anti-Terrorist Unit (ATU) and the Special Operations Division (SOD). So, no big deal, right? Well, this also means that the next time you take a honeymoon cruise on one of those sexy Liberian registered ships . . . yes, I hate to break it to you, you will have just become a supporter of Charles Taylor and his All Stars. Happy sailing.

**Yoram Cohen, Chief Executive Officer**
Tel. (703) 790-3434
Fax: (703) 790-5655
ycohen@liscr.com

**Liberian International Ship
    and Corporate Registry**
ycohen@liscr.com
http://www.liscr.com

## Getting Sick

Don't. All visitors more than one year old must have a yellow-fever vaccination certificate. Malaria and hepatitis B are widespread, and arthropod-borne diseases, such as river blindness and sleeping sickness, can also be a hazard. There are virtually no medical facilities in Monrovia at all. Most district hospitals have been destroyed in renewed fighting with antigovernment rebels. More succinct advice from the locals: If you start heavin', you better be a'leavin'.

http://www.igo.com/Travel/HTML/liberia/07grw.html

## Nuts and Bolts

Liberia is a hot and nasty place situated on the west coast of Africa, bounded by Guinea and Sierra Leone on the north and Cote d'Ivoire on the east. The country defines the word *fetid*. About 3.2 million people are unfortunate enough to have to live in it. Monrovia, with a population of about half a million, is the capital. The currency is the Liberian dollar. Its value is officially fixed at 45 to the U.S. dollar, but you'll get a much better deal from the ubiquitous moneychangers—anything less than 60 and you've been duped (again).

Liberia has a tropical climate, with temperatures ranging from 65°F to 120°F, and humidity between 70 and 80 percent. The rainy period extends from May through November and is characterized by frequent, prolonged, and often torrential rainfall. All of which means that there's not too much need to worry if your hotel shower doesn't have hot water, which, incidentally, it almost certainly won't.

Around 95 percent of the people who've drawn the losing ticket, that is, Liberian citizenship, are from one of 16 indigenous tribes. These include Kpelle, Bassa, Gio, Kru, Grebo, Mano, Krahn, Gola, Gbandi, Loma, Kissi, Vai, and Bella. The remaining 5 percent are known as Congo people or Americo-Liberians. They are the descendents of former slaves from the United States, which presumably makes them African American Africans. They can be found easily enough; just follow the sound of people cursing the stupidity of their forebears for leaving the richest, healthiest, and most free nation there has ever been to live in a flat-broke, war-torn, mosquito swamp.

Liberia is officially a Christian state, although less than half the population would describe themselves as such. Another 20 percent are Muslim, and the majority subscribe to some or other indigenous belief—try turning up dressed as a giant silver owl and see what you can get away with. English is the official language, and is widely used in business and political circles, but is spoken by only about one Liberian in five. You'll also need to learn the expressions for "For the love of God, don't shoot!" and "For Christ's sake, keep your eyes on the road!" in roughly 20 local dialects derived from the Niger-Congo language group. Only about 40 percent of the population can read or write in any language. Liberian men can expect to live 56 years, and can expect to enjoy almost none of them.

All forms of public utility—water, electricity, fuel, telephone, and mail—are unpredictable to hopeless in Monrovia, and limited to non-existent anywhere else. The capital currently has no electricity or water supply, and fuel is a fond memory of yesteryear. There are a few Internet cafés in Monrovia, but the connection is as reliable as everything else—which is to say, it isn't. Finally, don't spend too much time writing postcards to the folks back home. In July 2002, a group of aggrieved creditors, including the Universal Postal Union, the Pan-African Postal Union, Ghana Airways, and KLM, got tired of Liberia telling them that the check was in the mail, and until Liberia coughs up, the only way to get mail out is to stick it in a bottle and toss it off a wharf.

> **U**ntil Liberia coughs up, the only way to get mail out is to stick it in a bottle and toss it off a wharf.

Finally, a tip for European travelers: Liberia is the only African country to use the American flat, two-pin, 110V plug system—not that there is any power, you understand.

**Embassy of the United States**
111 UN Drive, Mamba Point
1000 Monrovia 10, Liberia
Tel.: (231) 22 6370
Fax: (231) 22 6148
http://usembassy.state.gov/monrovia

**Office of the Honorary British Consul**
British Consulate
EU Aid Coordination Office
UN Drive, Mamba Point
Monrovia, Liberia
Tel.: (231) 22 6056
Fax: (231) 22 6274

## Dangerous Days

| | |
|---|---|
| 10/25/02 | LURD forced back into HQ of Voinjama. |
| 7/02 | The LURD's southern front collapses in a withdrawal from Bomi and Lofa Bridge. |
| 5/11/02 | LURD rebels occupy the strategic town of Tubmanburg, 35 miles north of Monrovia. There are limited attacks on the outskirts of the capital. |
| 5/02 | The UN reimposes an arms embargo, and diamond and timber sanctions. |

| | |
|---|---|
| 2/8/02 | President Taylor declares a state of emergency. |
| 1/02 | More than 50,000 people, both Liberians and refugees from Sierra Leone, flee fighting between Liberian government forces and Guinea-backed LURD rebels. |
| 11/01 | President Charles Taylor orders a new offensive against Guinea-backed LURD rebels. |
| 5/7/01 | The UN Security Council imposes an arms embargo and other sanctions on Liberia to punish President Charles Taylor for interfering in the civil war in neighboring Sierra Leone. |
| 9/00 | Liberian government forces launch a major offensive against Guinea-backed rebels in the north of the country. |
| 9/99 | Liberian government forces cross the border with Guinea in pursuit of rebels. |
| 4/99 | Rebels based in Guinea cross the border into Liberia and attack the town of Voinjama. More than 25,000 people flee the fighting. |
| 9/98 | Fighting in Monrovia between Liberian security forces and rebel leader Roosevelt Johnson kills hundreds. Johnson seeks sanctuary in the U.S. embassy, who arranges for his escape to Nigeria. |
| 7/19/97 | Charles Taylor is elected president with 75 percent of the vote. |
| 4/96 | Fighting continues in Monrovia. |
| 9/90 | Liberian President Samuel Doe is overthrown and executed, along with 16 members of his cabinet. |
| 12/24/89 | Charles Taylor's National Patriotic Front of Liberia begin their uprising, crossing into Liberia from Cote d'Ivoire. |
| 4/12/80 | President William Tolbert is overthrown in a coup d'etat led by Staff Sergeant Samuel Doe, who suspends the constitution and imposes martial law. |

## IN A DANGEROUS PLACE: TUBMANBURG

### THEATRE OF THE ABS-LURD

Let's face it; there are times when war can be fun. Not just amusing, or even humorous, but real, actual *fun*. Not that PC, I admit, and granted, for me at least, the fear-that-becomes-fun is usually wrapped in a whiskey-drenched cloak of ignorance. But there is something to be said for running from a to b (and, crucially, back again) under fire, and taking a few snaps to prove it. It's another great "Whose round is it anyway?" story for the bar back home. And then again, there are times when war is, quite literally, hell. There are times when you forget that you'll probably make it out alive, because no one else seems to be. There are occasions when any kind of optimism would be frankly absurd, because the amphetamine-fueled enemy is only 50 yards away. And there are places to which no one else has been (try as you might to forget this) because there are some places to which no one *should* go. War in Liberia, then, has a special distinction—a hell within Hell.

Tubmanburg is a dilapidated town 35 miles north of Monrovia. It consists of maybe 200 concrete houses huddled around a rare strip of metal road that leads to the capital. Most of these desperate-looking abodes, covered with thin scraps of rusting corrugated zinc, have been raked with machine-gun fire or partially destroyed by armor-piercing RPG shells. Most of the civilians have long since left, preferring near starvation in the relative security of the surrounding, malaria-infested jungles than the urban slaughterhouse they once called home.

There are two things you need to know about Tubmanburg. First, it is controlled by the rebel group Liberians United for Reconciliation and Democracy (whose fantastic acronym LURD makes you realize that rebels can have a sense of humor, too); and second, *DP* picked a bad time to visit.

When I arrived in Tubmanburg, the LURD had been in control for nearly two months; it had subsequently become the fulcrum of their push against President Taylor. One day, LURD had just pitched up out of the forest, and the local government garrison simply fled in disbelief: hardly a shot had been fired. Now, however, quite a few shots were being fired, in a variety of different calibers, on an almost daily basis. Tactically, the LURD seemed to be relying on a fatal mixture of smugness and denial. I was informed by the rebels that they had over 1,000 troops in the town; I counted under a third of that, at least 50 of whom were under the age of 12. Claiming to be "undefeatable" (usually a sign to keep an emergency evacuation bag packed), they simply sat in the town and waited—the LURD had indeed opted to move in a mysterious way. No ambushes on the roads leading to where they knew Taylor's troops were massing, no patrols on the bush roads always used by government troops, and no attempt to conserve any of the ammunition they had to hand-carry over 200 miles to the front line. There's nothing like confidence. And, like clockwork, the rebels were attacked in the town almost every day.

Woken at 6:30 AM by the delicate thud of an incoming RPG, I rolled out from underneath my mosquito net, fully clothed as usual, and pulled on my boots. Escalating rapidly, the morning's assault seemed strangely co-coordinated. It appeared that we were being attacked on three fronts simultaneously, which did not bode well, as clearly there weren't enough troops to defend two fronts successfully. With a rising sense of panic, I picked up my cameras, and waited outside the house where I'd been staying, and tried to assess the situation.

There is much discussion among hacks and other thrill-seekers concerning the relative merits of being able to discern different kinds of firearms from the variety of pops, bangs, and whistles they make, as well as the time-honored debate over whether "that was incoming or outgoing." Knowing the difference, however, can save your life. If at all possible, find out the easy way by going to a firing range and have someone shoot a dozen AK rounds over your head from behind . . . and then from in front (trust is everything).

The main attack was coming in on the Monrovia Highway a thousand yards away, and the sickeningly regular thud-thud-thud, thud-thud-thud of a 12.7 heavy machine gun suggested that someone was serious. Directly behind me, a small-arms firefight was in full flow, out of sight by virtue of a few houses and a low hill. Both sides were also exchanging medium machine-gun fire: dozens of stray rounds (which arguably are in the majority in Africa) found their way into the roof of my house and the limbs of the tree I was leaning against. On the east side of town, more lead was being swapped on the high ground out of town. This provided yet more stray bullets for my roof, though these were slower and droning like alcoholic bees owing to the extra distance they had traveled.

What to do? I squatted on my haunches, and lit a cigarette. The entire town was now thick with high-velocity lead flying from one end of town to the other. Trying to venture out into that would be straightforward suicide. LURD rebels in various shades of confidence began to appear, some in worrying states of confusion or intoxication—for one commander, it had clearly been a long night on the booze. As the fighting behind grew louder, and therefore closer, more rebels rushed to the scene, loading AKs and chanting observations about Charles Taylor's mother as they ran to reinforce their comrades. RPGs now began raining down on the center of town. From where I was sitting, I could see, between clumps of coconut palms, three direct hits on the market. Rebels ran to and fro. An RPG exploded 20 yards away, deafening my left ear, its shrapnel wreaking yet more havoc on the branches overhead.

I noticed with resigned helplessness that most of the town's remaining civilians had decided that I was their best and only ticket out of the enveloping lead storm. A group of women and children gathered around, clinging to bundles of clothes, pots and pans, and even a chimpanzee, edging closer as the pungent stench of cordite grew stronger.

I had two options. One was to run like the devil into the center of the inferno, and see how much progress Chuck's lads had actually made, the other was to sit tight and wait. I sat tight and waited. Two rebels sauntered over and stood nearby. One was wearing a bright green shower cap. "We are your bodyguards. Don't worry, Taylor can't win," they said to me. I smiled weakly and lit another cigarette. "You should stand by the wall though," suggested one of the rebels. "There are lots of bullets today." I obliged, and crouched by the wall of the house opposite my own.

It can be quite tricky to tell how far away fighting really is sometimes. Incoming always sounds closer than it is, outgoing always farther away. I had assumed the fighting behind me was about 200 yards away, but in reality it was over 400 hundred yards away, and despite a rising number of bleeding, screaming rebels, it was not that serious. By contrast, I had underestimated the battle in the town center. Taking a last drag on my Gladstone Extra Mild (you have to admire the irony), I looked up to see one of my bodyguards level his AKM and let out a stream of automatic fire (most rebels in Africa, or anywhere else for that matter, don't realize there actually *is* a single-shot selector).

This was not a good sign. Peeking around the corner of my wall, I saw that the distinctive yellow T-shirts of the Liberian Navy Division were about 70 yards away across the marshy open ground in front of the house. Time to run. Fast. Energetically outpacing the civilians (I am ashamed to say), I wound my way south through narrow back streets that zinged and pinged with copper-jacketed lead ricocheting off concrete, and emerged exhausted on the open tarmac expanse of the Monrovia Highway.

Hurried preparations were in order to get the LURD's one and only ancient 81mm mortar into action. Deeply confused, as if perplexed by some profound religious mystery, Joseph the mortarman was about to have his moment of glory. Apparently unqualified even to light a cigarette, never mind handle light artillery, Joseph made a heroic effort to erect the LURD's only means of taking back the initiative in what was fast becoming a rout. Despite the fact that the sight was left snugly in his belt pouch, that there were no triangulation tables in evidence, and no distance reports from forward fire positions (quite possibly because we *were* the forward fire position), a fully charged bomb was dropped in the tube. "Fire in the hole" someone bellowed (to be honest, I'd always fancied shouting that myself), and the bomb trickled to the bottom with a pathetic plop. Bugger.

After carefully fishing the bomb out again, Joseph tried a second time, with arguably worse results. Unfortunately, he hadn't seen fit to kick in the base-plate. As the charge detonated, the entire mortar dismantled and leapt sideways, sending several pounds of high explosive somewhere into the remaining sector of LURD-controlled Tubman-burg. Subsequent efforts were rewarded with satisfying bangs, at least in the general proximity of government troops. Inexplicably, the tide had turned, and it was time to be brave again. Making my way through the acrid smog of three-hours' combat, I ran back toward the receding front line against a counterflow of dead and dying rebels and prisoners. When the fighting finally died down an hour later, I couldn't find a single rebel with more than five rounds of ammunition. They thought it was all over: It very nearly had been.

—*James Brabazon*

Kathmandu

## ★★
# NEPAL

## Neverest

In June 2001, Nepal had three kings in 48 hours. This game of musical thrones was a result of what became the most spectacular spilling of blue blood since the Romanovs were slaughtered in a Yekaterinburg basement in 1918, and possibly the only simultaneous patricide, matricide, fratricide, suicide, and regicide in history. On June 1, 2001, the Nepalese Royal Family's weekly Friday night dinner in Kathmandu's Narayanhiti Palace developed into a spirited discussion about the love life of Crown Prince Dipendra, the 29-year-old heir to the throne. He'd fallen for a woman called Devyani Rana, who had failed to excite the affection of the rest of the family—to the extent that Dipendra's mother, Queen Aishwarya, had threatened to remove Dipendra from the line of succession unless Dipendra appointed Ms. Rana to the Order of the Boot in short order.

**759**

Dipendra, who'd had a few drinks, stormed off in what looked like a workaday sulk. He returned clad in combat fatigues and armed with a pistol and an automatic rifle. He then proceeded to kill his father, King Birendra, his mother, Queen Aishwarya, his brother, Prince Niranjan, his sister, Princess Shruti, and four other members of the royal family. He then shot himself, but in a rare lapse of aim, succeeded only in putting himself in a coma.

The rules of royal succession contain no contingency plan for such situations, and so the unconscious mass murderer was declared Nepal's new king while connected to a life-support machine. To the immense relief of all concerned, Dipendra's oblivious reign lasted less than 48 hours, and upon his unlamented passing, the crown was passed on to the late king's younger brother, Gyanendra, who'd had the good fortune to be otherwise engaged on the evening of the massacre.

Even in the most staid, predictable, and secure constitutional monarchy in the world, such carnage among the royal family would plunge the country into a mire of fear and doubt—one need only recall the hysterical reaction of Britain to the loss of one princess in a car accident. But the tiny mountain kingdom of Nepal has serious internal security problems, in the shape of an insurgency by committed Maoist guerrillas.

On the face of it, the Communist Party of Nepal (Maoist)—as they prefer to be known, to distinguish themselves from the legitimate, nonviolent Communist Party of Nepal (Unified Marxist-Leninist)— would appear to be the terrorist equivalent of those Japanese soldiers who carried on fighting World War II until the early '70s: after all, even in Beijing, Mao's eternal resting place, the dead maniac's face is seen less often than that of Colonel Sanders. But the communists and their crusade are serious—Nepal's war with the Maoists has cost more than 7,000 lives since it began in 1996.

The manner in which the war has been waged suggests that both sides have learned little from the generations of moccasin-shod peaceniks who have trailed blue clouds of bong smoke over Nepal since the '50s. The Maoists have terrorized villages and businesses, kidnapped opponents, and executed scores of Nepalese security force personnel. The security forces have taken the same attitude to the Maoist-held areas that American troops did to hostile areas of Vietnam—anyone in them is either a terrorist or a sympathizer, and is dealt with accordingly. In November 2001, 11 unarmed farmers were shot dead by an army patrol in a village called Bagadi. Arrests without warrant and detention without trial are also commonplace.

The palace massacre and Maoist insurrection are widely perceived as historical and cultural anomalies. Nepal is, after all, a country best

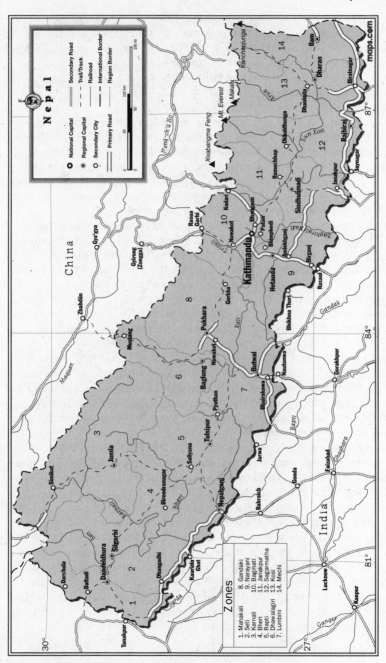

**Nepal**

Zones
1. Mahakali
2. Seti
3. Karnali
4. Bheri
5. Rapti
6. Dhawalagiri
7. Lumbini
8. Gandaki
9. Narayani
10. Bagmati
11. Janakpur
12. Sagarmatha
13. Kosi
14. Mechi

maps.com

known as a cheap, cheerful paradise for climbers looking to get high on mountains, or hippies looking to get high on grass. The truth is that Nepal has a past as impressively blood-soaked as that of any of its Central Asian neighbors.

> The truth is that Nepal has a past as impressively blood-soaked as that of any of its Central Asian neighbors.

Modern Nepal was founded in 1768 by Prithvi Narayan Shah, whose people came from the easterly region of Ghurka—even today, a justly famous Nepalese regiment attached to the British army is called the Ghurkas. Under Prithvi Narayan Shah, Nepal started to throw its weight around, expanding across the region as far as what is now the Indian state of Sikkim, until 1792, when Nepal got a licking from Tibet—another country whose legendary "peaceful" facade belies a spectacularly violent past.

Like the rest of the subcontinent, Nepal experienced a long period of British domination, echoed in the famous Ghurkas and the prominence of the English language but, rather disappointingly, no cricket team worth talking about. As was often the case with their overseas dominions, the British were quite content to let any manner of corrupt and/or demented despot run the place as long as it remained profitable and caused minimal trouble. Fulfilling this role for much of the British period were the Ranas. The first of their line, Jung Bahadur, took care of Prithvi Narayan Shah's descendants with a slaughter of most of Nepal's nobility in Kot in 1846. Propped up by the British, who were grateful for Nepal's support during the Indian Mutiny in 1857, it would be tempting to suggest that the Ranas lived like kings, were it not for the fact that many kings have dreams of living like the Ranas. The actual people of Nepal, needless to say, lived like impoverished, backward, medieval peasants.

The Ranas were never likely to outlive the Empire and were among the least-mourned victims of the subcontinent's emergence into independent states after World War II. Britain had recognized Nepal as an independent nation as far back as 1923, and the Ranas had signally failed to grasp what this might mean for their pampered and redundant lifestyles. A party called the Nepal Democratic Congress, founded by exiled opponents of the Ranas in Calcutta, stirred up a couple of abortive coups in 1949 and 1950, and then allied with the Nepal-based Nepal National Congress to become the Nepali Congress Party. The new group began an armed revolt against the Ranas—with the sympathy, it turned out, of King Tribhuvan, the descendant of the Shahs, whose family had been marginalized by the Ranas. With the support and encouragement of India, Tribhuvan was restored to the throne in 1951.

King Tribhuvan was a democrat of sorts, who ruled through a government containing different political parties. However, his son, Mahendra, who became king upon Tribhuvan's death in 1955, did not share his interest in the popular will. Despite, or perhaps because of, Nepal's first-ever general election in February 1959, King Mahendra decided afterward that the archaic concept of democracy would be surplus to Nepal's requirements. He replaced elected officials with cronies, most of whom were characterized by a reluctance to question the king's edicts and a willingness to help themselves to whatever they could fit in their pockets. This form of government, which continued after Mahendra was succeeded by Birendra in 1972, was known as Panchayat, and was supposed to represent a sort of popular rule by osmosis (it was, in fact, narrowly endorsed by a referendum in 1980); the nearest current adherent of the idea is Colonel Qaddafi in Libya.

In 1989, Nepal threw one of the least remarked-upon revolutions of that extraordinary year. Undoubtedly inspired by the collapse of entrenched oligarchies across Eastern Europe, but also infuriated by sanctions resulting from a trade dispute with India, the Nepalese staged a huge popular protest called the Jana Andolan ("People's Movement"). Within the framework of 1989, it was far closer to the bloodbath of Bucharest than the velvet revolution of Prague—hundreds were killed, arrested, and tortured. King Birendra, doubtless mindful that these sorts of things usually ended badly for whoever was in charge, made dramatic changes. He sacked his self-appointed cabinet, legalized political parties, and invited a once-imprisoned dissident, Krishnaraj Bhatarai, to form an interim government.

Nepal's biggest political parties ever since have been the Nepali Congress Party and the Communist Party of Nepal (Unified Marxist-Leninist). The country remains far from stable. It is still the poorest nation on the subcontinent, the Maoist insurgency shows no sign at all of fizzling out or being defeated, and the latter is not helping the former. The biggest foreign currency earner in Nepal was tourism—and not many people want to holiday in war zones. In June 2002, Nepal's Central Bank said the country's already-stagnating economy was slowing down further—creating, in other words, exactly the conditions in which a left-wing people's militia-cum-ideological cult might flourish.

# The Scoop

Nepal is a nice country with some nasty problems. The reputation it has relied on for years—of being a rustic, untouched Shangri-La equally hospitable to hearty mountain climbers and bong-addled hippies with beads in their beards—is being subsumed beneath an avalanche of headlines about internecine guerrilla war and a royal family even Shakespeare couldn't have dreamed up. A medium-sized war rages in the hills, and there have been bombings in the capital, Kathmandu.

As such, it's no more or less safe than most anywhere else on the subcontinent. If the international community can be persuaded to regard the Maoist insurgents as kin of al-Qaeda, then recovery may come reasonably quickly. If not, all-out civil war remains a real possibility.

**The Kathmandu Post**
http://www.nepalnews.com.np/
ktmpost.htm

**People's Review**
http://www.yomari.com/p-review

**Nepal News**
http://www.nepalnews.com

**Nepal Tourism Board**
http://www.welcomenepal.com

## The Players

### King Gyanendra Bir Bikram Shah Dev

Gyanendra is the younger brother of the late King Birendra. As such, he would never have ascended to Nepal's throne had it not been for the dramatic intervention of his intemperate nephew Dipendra. He has a difficult balancing act to perform. On one side, his people needed reassurance and continuity following the traumatic decimation of their royal family. On the other side is the memory of his older brother: King Birendra reigned for 29 years and was regarded by many Nepalese as a living incarnation of the Hindu god Vishnu. Gyanendra also has to contend with his own son Paras, the new Crown Prince and heir apparent. Paras is a scion who enjoys roughly the same popular esteem in Kathmandu as Uday Hussein does in Baghdad and Marko Milosevic did in Belgrade. The 27-year-old is infamous for indulging his hobbies of simultaneous drinking and driving, and in 2000 he allegedly hit and killed the popular Nepalese singer Praveen Gurung; though 600,000 people signed a petition demanding that then-King Birendra take action against Paras, nothing was done. Paras was winged in Crown Prince Dipendra's onslaught, but this has done little to scotch persistent rumors that it was in fact Paras who was the guilty party—with or without, depending on which conspiracy theory you choose to believe, the assistance of India, China, or the CIA. (There seems to be no shortage of meddlers in Nepal's affairs.)

http://www.stanford.edu/group/tibet/svin/maoist.htm
http://www.nepalhomepage.com/dir/politics

## The Nepalese Army

The Nepalese army's 50,000 troops, and the 60,000 men in the police and reserves, are currently learning the hard way about fighting highly motivated and locally supported guerrillas in hostile terrain. Maoist militias have killed dozens of soldiers and police in raids on military bases. The United States has thrown $20 million at them and taught them to use exciting phrases like "Psy-Ops," but the attacks continue.

**Royal Nepalese Army**
http://www.rna.mil.np

## Nepali Congress Party

The Nepali Congress Party was founded in 1947, formed by a band of young revolutionaries who wanted to rid their homeland of the corrupt Rana oligarchs. The Nepali Congress Party is now a bunch of old guys who occasionally interrupt their squabbling with each other to do a spot of governing. The biggest party in Nepal's congress, they've been falling out with each other furiously over whether or not to extend Nepal's state of emergency in its struggle with the Maoists. It is possible that the party could formally split by the time elections are due in November 2002.

**Nepali Congress Party**
Nepali Congress Central Office
Teku, Kathmandu, Nepal
Tel.: (977) 1 22 7748
Fax: (977) 1 22 7747
ncparty@mos.com.np
http://www.nepalicongress.org.np

## Communist Party of Nepal (Unified Marxist-Leninist) (CPN [UML])

The CPN (UML) is likely to be the major beneficiary of any split in the ranks of their rivals in the Nepali Congress Party. The party, known at the time as the plain old Communist Party of Nepal, was founded in 1949, and also did its bit to help shift the Ranas. The CPN started acquiring extra initials in 1974 when the Jhapa District Committee of the Party's East Koshi Zonal Committee launched an armed uprising (and the networks wonder why nobody watches the New Hampshire primaries). The revolutionaries formed something called the All Nepal Communist Revolutionary Coordination Committee (Marxist-Leninist). Possibly because they feared becoming bankrupt by the expense of printing T-shirts, they signed on as the more-tersely titled CPN in 1978, which then became the CPN (ML).

CPN (ML) became CPN (UML) in 1990 (keep up, there'll be a quiz). The new ingredients this time were the United Left Front, itself an umbrella group already containing the CPN (4th Congress), CPN (Marxist), CPN (Amatya), CPN (Manandhar), and the Nepal Worker and Peasant Party. The CPN (UML) is the second-biggest party in Nepal's parliament. Their slogan is "Oppose Dogmatism and Liquidationalism, Uphold the Banner of Marxism Creatively!"; *DP* has no idea at all what this means, but wishes them well with it. The CPN (UML) publishes a bimonthly English-language magazine, *New Era*, which is possibly the least interesting publication in the world.

**Communist Party of Nepal (Unified Marxist-Leninist)**
P.O. Box 5471
Madan Nagar, Balhku
Kathmandu, Nepal
Tel.: (977) 1 27 8081
Fax: (977) 1 27 8084
uml@ntc.net.np
http://www.cpnuml.org

**The New Era**
http://www.cpnuml.org/newera

## "The Furious One" and the Communist Party of Nepal (Maoist) (CPN [M])

Though even the Chinese now regard Mao Tse-Tung as little more than a trademark on Cultural Revolution souvenirs sold to Western tourists, in Nepal he's the iconic inspiration for a 6-year-old guerrilla war that has claimed at least 4,000 lives. The insurgency started in Nepal's Rolpa district in 1995 with peasant protests and fanned into a full-scale armed revolt when the government responded with guns rather than discussions. They officially began their People's War on February 12, 1996, in five mountainous districts, and their goal is to simply remove the monarchy and establish a Maoist People's government. The CPN (M) are based in the west of Nepal and have effectively become the law in 8 of Nepal's 75 districts—Rolpa, Rukum, Sallyan, Gorkha, Sindhuli, Jajarkot, Kalikot, and Bataidi—and active in all the other districts. On their home turf, they do all the dull municipal stuff like collecting trash and taxes, and running schools and hospitals. Everywhere else, they ambush and kidnap members of Nepal's security forces. The Maoists' troop strength is estimated at around 15,000 in a full-time People's Liberation Army, with another 40,000 militia available. Firefights between the Maoists and security forces leaving dozens dead and injured are common.

The CPN (M) is led by a doctrinaire hard-liner called Pushpa Kamal Dahal, who prefers to be called "Prachanda" or "the Furious One" and who will earn you a bounty of US$64,000 if you bring him in, dead or alive. CPN (M) wants to establish Maoist rule throughout Nepal and, eventually, the world. *DP* would suggest to readers in Europe and America that there's no need to start stocking up on canned goods and ammunition just yet, but the threat to Nepal is real.

The Maoists also have the capacity to make life difficult for tourists, but so far they've been pretty polite about it. When they robbed three groups of climbers near Mount Makalu in April 2002, they wrote out receipts for the kit they'd nicked. The Maoists' most prominent spokesman, a former architect and alleged moderate called Dr. Baburam Bhattarai, another $64,000 man, has even issued an open invitation to tourists to visit not just Nepal, but his motley army in the hills. In March 2002, he faxed the following extraordinary letter to international news organizations:

> **T**he Maoists also have the capacity to make life difficult for tourists, but so far they've been pretty polite about it. When they robbed three groups of climbers near Mount Makalu in April 2002, they wrote out receipts for the kit they'd nicked.

Dear Foreign Tourists,

Welcome to the country on the roof of the world and warmest greetings from the materially poor but spiritually rich people of Nepal! As you very well know, a revolutionary People's War (PW) under the leadership of Communist Party of Nepal (Maoist) is raging in Nepal against a fascist, monarchical state since February 1996.

After getting a severe drubbing from the heroic People's Liberation Army (PLA) in every battle front and losing almost all of the countryside to the advancing revolutionary forces, the fast crumbling reactionary regime headed by hated Gyanendra Shah has imposed a brutal military dictatorship under the guise of the so-called state of emergency in the country since November 2001.

This last desperate act of the tottering regime to save its skin has already backfired on itself and the mass rebellion in the form of the PW has intensified further in recent weeks and will reach a crescendo in the coming days. It is now obvious that two states, two armies, two laws and two cultures, one representing a handful of moribund parasitic classes and the other representing the vast majority of the democratic and progressive working people, are engaged in life and death struggle in the country.

The United Revolutionary People's Council (URPC) is an embryonic Central People's Government Organising Committee in the form of a revolutionary united front headed by the CPN (Maoist). We, therefore, deem it our duty to acquaint you with some of our basic positions and dispel some canards spread against us by the old reactionary state machinery.

What are we basically fighting for? We are fighting for a genuine people's democracy in the country. As you know, in the current political dispensation in Nepal, the real state power vests in the feudal monarchy that effectively controls the royal army, and the parliament is a mere showcase to embellish the hereditary autocracy. Besides, the self-proclaimed current "King" Gyanendra and his son Paras are known criminal gangsters who have usurped the throne in a bloody coup d'etat against King Birendra last June 2001.

Anybody familiar with the Nepalese history will agree that the archaic institution of feudal monarchy is the root cause and bulwark of socio-economic backwardness, abysmal poverty, glaring inequality and all-round underdevelopment plaguing the country, and its abolition is a minimum precondition for ushering in genuine democracy, both political and economic, in the country.

When the English could wage war against their monarchy in the 17th century, or the French in the 18th century, or other civilised peoples in the 19th and 20th century, why can't the Nepalese people do the same even in the 21st century?

And are we against the tourism industry in general and foreign tourists in particular? Nothing could be farther from the truth. We are all for making maximum utilisation of the natural and cultural resources for the rapid economic development and well being of the country and the people. And given the exquisite natural beauty and rich cultural heritage of the country, promotion of tourism obviously comes high in the priority list of the future economic development policy.

As regards the false accusations of our xenophobic inclinations and preference for a closed political system, this is another example of sinister disinformation campaigns deliberately launched by the counter-revolutionary forces. By ideological persuasion we are for the ultimate withering away of all national and state boundaries and creation of a classless and stateless global community of people.

Rather the fake votaries of "globalisation" of capital are mortally against the globalisation of labour as well and hence, in essence, against genuine all-round globalisation. Foreign tourists are, therefore, most welcome in the country and will be so in future as well.

However, we would like to draw your attention to the grossly lopsided nature of current tourism industry in the country and would advise you to take special precautionary measures while travelling during the period of war. Firstly, the tourism industry in Nepal is monopolised by the arch-reactionary Shah-Rana family (related to Nepal's monarchy) and their close courtiers (for example, all the five-star hotels and most of the star hotels and travel business are either owned or controlled by them), and most of the earnings from tourism is said to flow back to foreign countries.

Therefore, it is quite imperative to smash this anti-people and anti-national monopolistic structure of the tourism industry and foreign tourists would be advised not to patronise such tourism services (e.g. hotels, airlines, buses etc.) particularly owned by the hated Shah-Rana families.

Secondly, during wartime the unassuming traveller can be caught between the crossfire of the contending armies. The foreign tourists are, therefore, kindly advised not to venture into areas where active fighting is going on. They are most welcome into the revolutionary base areas, which are firmly under the control of the revolutionary forces.

And a few words to our honoured guests from neighbouring India.

Though the reactionary state media cries hoarse about our so-called anti-India posture, you need not be unduly perturbed. Despite the conspiracy of the ruling classes of both the countries to drive wedges between the people of Nepal and India, we are conscious of the common destiny of the two peoples and are for developing a close and cordial relations between the two.

You are, therefore, most welcome to visit Nepal.

And finally, in view of the 5-day long "Nepal bandh" (general shutdown) from 2 April to 6 April, 2002, and the subsequent surcharged atmosphere in the aftermath, the foreign tourists are well advised to skip the tour itinerary, if any, for the said period.

We deeply regret the inconveniences likely to cause to you all.

Wishing you all the best for a future visit to a democratic, progressive and prosperous People's Republic of Nepal,

Yours sincerely,
Dr Baburam Bhattarai,
Convenor, United Revolutionary
    People's Council
Nepal
15 March, 2002

What next? The GIA running bus tours of Algeria? Al-Qaeda open-ing a Club Med in Cuba? Be sure to read further about holidays among the Maoists in the CPN (M)'s entrancingly tedious magazine, *The Worker*.

**Communist Party of Nepal (Maoist) Online**
http://www.maoistnepal.8m.net/enter.html

**The Worker**
http://www.insof.org/the_worker6/w6_cover1.html

**Wanted Maoists (Nepalese only)**
http://www.nepalpolice.gov.np/atankari/index.htm

# Getting In

By air, you'll arrive at Kathmandu's Tribhuvan Airport; the right-hand side of the aircraft usually affords the best views of the moun-tains, so nervous flyers should ask for a seat on the left, or just wear a blindfold. Those who want to follow the overland hippy trail from India have a choice of four land crossings: Sunauli-Bhairawa, Kakarbhitta-Siliguri, Birganj-Raxaul, and Mahendrenagar-Banbassa. There is a border crossing linking Nepal and Tibet, but it is almost al-ways closed to individual travelers heading into the Chinese province— the U.S. or Chinese embassies in Kathmandu will be able to tell you what the score is.

Visas are required, but can be obtained upon arrival by air or land. If you have the time, however, it's always best to have them in advance. Prices start at around $30 for a 60-day single-entry visa, and they can be extended at the Department of Immigration in Kathmandu or the Immigration Office in Pokhara.

**Royal Nepalese Embassy**
2131 Leroy Place, NW
Washington, DC 20008
Tel.: (202) 667-4550
Fax: (202) 667-5534
info@nepalembassy.org
http://www.nepalembassyusa.org

**Royal Nepalese Embassy**
12A Kensington Palace Gardens
London W8 4QU, UK
Tel.: (44) 20 7229 1594
Fax: (44) 20 7792 9861
info@nepembassy.org.uk
http://www.nepembassy.org.uk

# Getting Around

Going anywhere in Nepal is a severe test for visitors who suffer from vertigo, or just from an acute terror of the last sound you hear in this life being a tinny radio playing awful Asian pop music at a deafening volume, mixed with the screams of your fellow passengers as your bus plunges headlong off a snow-covered bend. There are two sorts of buses: tourist buses, which ply such major routes as Kathmandu to Pokhara, and regular buses, which go everywhere else. On the former, you'll be sharing with backpackers. On the latter, you'll be sharing with pigs, chickens, and goats. Both are slow, and both smell.

Or you can fly—an experience that will test the strength of conviction of any visiting atheist. Delays are frequent, caused by both weather and inefficiency, and when and if the thing does get off the ground, you're liable to wish it hadn't.

**Royal Nepal Airlines**
http://www.royalnepal.com

> **G**oing anywhere in Nepal is a severe test for visitors who suffer from vertigo, or just from an acute terror of the last sound you hear in this life being a tinny radio playing awful Asian pop music at a deafening volume, mixed with the screams of your fellow passengers as your bus plunges headlong off a snow-covered bend.

## Dangerous Places

### Western Nepal

Though the Maoists are a concern almost anywhere outside the Kathmandu Valley, this is their heartland. Open invitation to come visit (see pp. 767–9) aside, this is one of the wildest Wests there is. The war between the Maoists and Nepal's security forces is serious, intense, and being fought without much emphasis on the honor of warriors. Getting between the disputing parties would be a really bad idea.

## Dangerous Things

### Bandhs

A *bandh* is a general strike, and a traditional form of expressing discontent in Nepal—sort of an intifada at altitude. The Maoists have called bandhs on a few occasions in the last few years, and failure to comply often leads to breakages, both of windows and limbs. Bandhs are occasionally associated with violence, but are mostly of concern to travelers who may get off a plane and find there are no taxis, no buses, and no ways to get into town but walking. The goods news is that bandhs are usually announced well in advance, so keep an eye on the papers.

### Public Transport

Badly built roads, badly maintained vehicles, badly trained drivers, mountains, and snow. Bring a blindfold and a bottle of whiskey.

**Nepal Department of Roads**
http://www.dormeu.gov.np

## Wildlife

In June 2002, an elephant killed 13 people over three days on both sides of Nepal's border with India (it was eventually killed by an Indian Forestry Department sharpshooter). Elephants and various kinds of big cats are making more and more frequent inroads into inhabited areas as their natural habitats are whittled back by logging and human settlements. Don't feed them, and don't pat them. Tigers prefer to attack from behind, so try walking away backwards. *DP* has also been told that tigers can be subdued by constructing a ring of white sheeting around them, but we're not too clear on how you keep the cat still while you do it.

**World Wildlife Fund Nepal**
http://www.wwfnepal.org.np

## Journalism

Nepal is another one of those places where the phrase "shooting the messenger" has an unpleasantly literal context. In June 2001, the editor of the Nepali newspaper *Kantipur*, Yubaraj Ghimirey, and two of his colleagues, Binod Raj Gyawali and Kailash Sirohiya, were arrested. Their crime was to have published an (admittedly preposterous) opinion piece by Maoist spokesman Dr. Baburam Bhattarai, in which he accused India and the CIA of being behind the palace massacre. The three were released on bail after nine days following widespread public protests, and the charges were eventually withdrawn, but nobody was left in doubt that the three had been made an example of.

It was an example that went unheeded by Krishna Sen, editor of the pro-Maoist newspaper *Janadisha*. He was one of more than a hundred journalists arrested during 2002—not for the first time, in his case—and hasn't been seen since late May 2002. Some claim he was tortured to death in custody. The government, which had placed a US$32,000 bounty on his head, says he's on the run.

The Maoists themselves aren't always press-friendly, either. In January 2001, Radio Nepal journalist Shambhu Prasad Patel was shot dead in his home by masked men, assumed to be Maoists. In April 2002, *Himalaya Times* reporter Demling Lama was kidnapped from his home in Dushkot. He escaped after four days, but he won't be the last.

**Kantipur Online**
http://www.kantipuronline.com

## BACK TO THE FUTURE

Don't adjust your watch. The Nepali calendar runs a little fast. Each new Nepali year begins in mid-April; there are 12 months starting in the middle of our months. And of course, they are 57 years ahead of us so don't get too worked up; for example, half of 2002 and the first half of 2003 is 2059 according to the Nepali calendar.

## Getting Sick

Your enemies, aside from the standard subcontinental upheavals in the digestive tract, are meningitis in the Kathmandu Valley, malaria in Nepal's less-mountainous areas, and altitude sickness. If you get seriously ill, the nearest hospitals are in Singapore, Bangkok, or Delhi. Make sure your travel insurance covers this eventuality.

## Nuts and Bolts

The Kingdom of Nepal is not very wide or long—it occupies just 140,800 square kilometers, or about as much of the globe as Arkansas—but it is tall. Of the world's 20 highest peaks, 12 are accessible from Nepal, including the biggest of the bunch—Everest, standing 29,035 meters high.

Nepal has a population of just over 25 million and is the only country in the world to have Hinduism as its official religion, though there are small Buddhist and Muslim minorities. The language is Nepali, but many other dialects are spoken. English is reasonably widely understood, especially in government and business circles, and in Kathmandu generally.

The currency is the *rupee*, which was last seen heading for 80 to the dollar. You may do better than that from friendly rug merchants and waiters, but the usual caveats of black-market money-changing apply—be discreet, and make sure you've got their money in your hand before you cough up your greenbacks. There is some reward for honest tourists, though—if you change money at the official rate and get receipts, you'll be able to convert 15 percent of what you've got left back into real money at the Kathmandu airport. Whether that makes up for the disadvantages of the black market is a calculation you'll have to make yourself, but bear in mind that outside Nepal, the rupee is good only for kindling.

Electricity is 220V. Also, aficionados of the bizarre will get a real kick out of setting their watches to local time—Nepal, absurdly, is GMT plus 5 hours and 45 minutes.

**Embassy of the United States**
Panipokhari
Kathmandu, Nepal
Tel.: (977) 1 41 1179
Fax: (977) 1 41 9963

**Embassy of Great Britain**
P.O. Box 106
Lainchaur
Kathmandu, Nepal
Tel.: (977) 1 41 4588
Fax: (977) 1 41 1789
ukconsular@mos.com.np
http://www.britain.gov.np

# Dangerous Days

| | |
|---|---|
| 11/15/02 | Over 100 soldiers and rebels die in a week of violence. |
| 7/5/02 | A bomb in the Kathmandu office of Prime Minister Sher Bahadur Deuba injures 10. |
| 5/27/02 | State of emergency is reimposed in Nepal. |
| 5/10/02 | Maoists offer a one-month truce. The government rejects it. |
| 5/9/02 | Battles around Gam in western Nepal kill around 350 on both sides. |
| 4/02 | General strike called by Maoists brings Nepal to a halt. |
| 4/24/02 | A bomb destroys the family home of Prime Minister Sher Bahadur Deuba in Assigram. |
| 11/26/01 | A state of emergency is declared. |
| 11/23/01 | Maoists break truce with a series of attacks on army and police posts in 42 districts, including the Mount Everest region, that leave more than 150 dead on both sides. |
| 7/23/01 | Peace deal agreed upon between government and Maoists. A truce begins. |
| 6/3/01 | King Dipendra dies in the hospital. Prince Gyanendra becomes king. |
| 6/2/01 | Crown Prince Dipendra named king while on life support. |
| 6/1/01 | Crown Prince Dipendra shoots dead King Birendra, Queen Aishwarya, and seven other relatives, before shooting himself, inflicting critical injuries. |
| 2/96 | Beginning of armed insurrection by the Communist Party of Nepal (Maoist). |
| 1991 | Nepali Congress Party wins general election. |

| | |
|---|---|
| **1989–90** | Prodemocracy uprising results in hundreds of arrests and dozens of deaths. King Birendra agrees to restore democracy and to a new constitution. |
| **1989** | Trade dispute with India results in border blockade. |
| **1960** | King Mahendra suspends parliament and all political parties and seizes power. |
| **1959** | New multiparty constitution adopted. First general elections held, resulting in victory for Nepali Congress Party. |
| **1951** | Monarchy restored under King Tribhuvan. |
| **1950** | Beginning of armed revolt against the Ranas, by promonarchy nationalists of Nepali Congress Party. |
| **1923** | Britain recognizes Nepal's independence, but maintains control of foreign affairs. |
| **1846** | Ruling descendents of Prithvi Shah wiped out in the Kot massacre. Beginning of the rule of the Ranas. |
| **1816** | Nepal becomes British protectorate. |
| **1792** | Nepal reaches limits of expansion, and suffers defeat by Tibet. |
| **1768** | Nepal unified by Ghurka ruler Prithvi Narayan Shah. |

★

# NORTH KOREA

## King of Denial

Kim Il Sung, the Great Leader, departed for the Great Unknown on July 18, 1994, at the age of 82, succumbing to illness that he tried vainly to thwart with a combination of meteorology and herbs.

Myth shrouded the Great Leader. North Koreans are taught that Kim was the inventor of everything from centuries-old scientific theories to such modern conveniences as the automobile and the toaster. Some believe he has walked on the moon. By law, every North Korean household must possess at least two portraits of the Great One. Yet his legendary heroics against the Japanese during World War II, by all historical accounts, never occurred. His great books, the great deeds, the single-handed advancement of North Korea into a leading nation and even his noble birth . . . all are celebrated and, of course, all are terribly false. But what does it matter? Life is good in North Korea . . . isn't it?

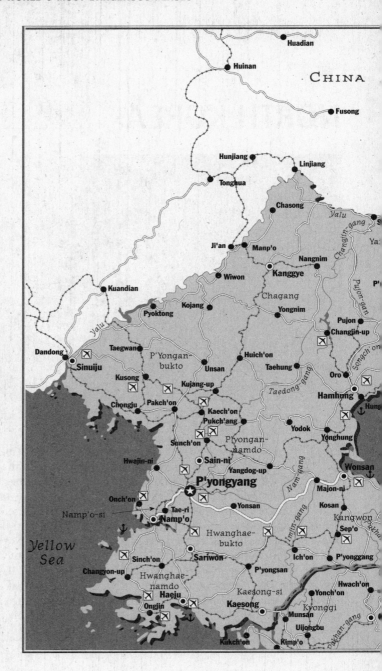

RUSSIA

Sea of Japan

### North Korea

⭐ National Capital
◉ Administrative Capital
● Secondary City
⋯⋯ Administrative Boundary
═══ Primary Road
─── Secondary Road
⊢⊢⊢⊢ Railroad
─ ─ ─ Demarcation Line
▬▬▬ Demilitarized Zone
↓ Primary Ports
⊠ Airfields

| 0 | 25 | 50 | 75 km |
|---|----|----|-------|
| 0 | | 25 | 50 mi |

Ah, life is good in North Korea—the streets are filled with happy smiling people, the cafés echo with laughter, nary a gum wrapper nor beggar is to be found on the scrubbed streets of Pyongyang. Well, that is what the current spate of outside visitors is supposed to see. The truth, once you leave the capital, is of course much different. You will see a quasi-industrialized economy slipping into disaster, with starving children, empty fields, and desperate people. But does it matter? There is nothing anyone can do about it, nothing that you can say that will change anything so why not just keep on smiling through the apocalypse? Twenty-five million North Koreans do so every day. The Great Leader would shed a tear knowing that 48 million Koreans who live below the 38th parallel exist in conditions of abject democracy and appalling financial success.

While citizens wander through the theme-park-like world that is Pyongyang, things are starting to crack at the seams. The sirens at 7 AM, noon, and midnight remind loyal Koreans to get up, have lunch, and go to bed. Bands cheer people on their way to work, large signs provide stirring motivation, giant portraits of Kim spread joy and warmth, and hundreds of manuals written by the Great One urge on flagging comrades lest they need guidance in any professional task.

The burden of bringing North Korea limping optimistically into the '50s is the task of Kim's son, 60-year-old Kim Jong Il, a man who combines stolid Cold War–era dictator-style leisure suits with permed Elvis-style tresses. He's an East Asian version of Larry King stumbling out of a '60s love-in. For Kim, the party never stops. Armed with lifts in his shoes, thick Hollywood-agent glasses, his favorite cognac, and a bevy of Japanese concubines, Kim can communist-party with the best of them. He has outlasted every other Nehru-jacketed dictator, much to the disappointment of Uncle Sam.

> **K**im Jong Il, a man who combines stolid Cold War—era dictator-style leisure suits with permed Elvis-style tresses.

After more than four years of grieving for his dead dad, it was expected that Kim Jong Il would finally get some kind of a promotion—say, to president maybe? No way, José. Instead, on September 5, 1998, Kim Jong Il was named by the Supreme People's Assembly as Chairman of the National Defense Commission, which is, the North Korean officials stress, "the Highest Post of the State." The title of president was awarded in perpetuity to the late Kim Il Sung and, based on the stuck-in-'50s feel of North Korea, it would make perfect sense that progress would create unnecessary overhead.

Detractors of Kim Jong Il say he is both a reported lush and an alleged terrorist. (At least they didn't say he was short and goofy-looking.)

He has been implicated as the mastermind behind a number of terrorist attacks, including the 1983 foiled assassination attempt on the South Korean president in Myanmar that instead blew away 17 high-level South Korean officials, and the Korean Air jetliner explosion that took 115 lives in 1987. He is also believed responsible for North Korea's nuclear program (the bomb part, anyway). It is also thought that North Korea's recent binge in amphetamine and opium was being personally directed by the Chubby One in order to kickstart the moribund economy.

There is convincing evidence that there are disturbing incidents of capitalism being perpetrated by the Leader-loving people. In April 1997, a cache of 154 pounds of amphetamines with a street value of US$95 million was found on a North Korean freighter in port at Hiroshima, Japan. Dope is grown or manufactured in the Democratic People's Republic of Korea (DPRK) and then smuggled through diplomatic channels to Pyongyang's embassies abroad, where it is then sold to domestic dealers or by North Korean diplomats themselves on the street. It is believed that huge quantities of opium go through Russia via North Korean workers commuting to timber projects there.

Late in 1998, the narcotics suppression boys at Bangkok's Don Muang Airport seized 2.5 million tons of ephedrine—a principal ingredient in cheap, garage-lab amphetamines—en route to Pyongyang from India. The pawns of Pyongyang insisted the chemical was intended for the development of bronchodilators. So, we now know that not only are North Koreans starving, they're all suffering from chronic asthma, as well.

But the mythmaking continues. Kim Jong Il was born in Siberia in 1941 while the old man was in exile, but because most North Koreans have never heard of Siberia, it is instead believed that Jong Il was conveniently "reborn" in a log cabin near North Korea's famed Mount Paektu, beneath two rainbows and a bright, previously undiscovered star (Bambi must have been close by). He is reputed to have written hundreds of books, all epic masterpieces, and six operas in the course of two years. He can stop rain (but apparently not flooding), can predict the discovery of natural resources (including, apparently, plutonium), and is credited with designing Pyongyang's Juche Tower (*juche* is the creed of self-reliance devised by Kim Il Sung).

However, the Dear Leader isn't a been-there, done-that type of fellow. He refuses to fly, which rather curtails any ambitions he might harbor of international statesmanship (when he went to Moscow in August 2001, he went by train, taking nine days each way). He doesn't even get out much at home—there was widespread amazement in June 2000 when he turned up at the airport to personally greet the South Korean premier, Kim Dae Jong. In all likelihood, he's met only a couple of Westerners in his entire life, and given that one of those was

Madeleine Albright, it's perhaps not surprising that he regards the outside world with a mix of derision and paranoia.

Trying to get hip in time for his formal ascension to power, Kim, Jr. practiced his English (and probably his Korean, too). His face fills the television screens every night, at all times and on every channel. The man who claims "socialism is not administrative and commanding" may have a different relationship with communism than with alcohol. He is reported to spend nearly three-quarters of a million dollars a year on Hennessy cognac, specifically the Paradis line. That's commanding.

> In all likelihood, he's met only a couple of Westerners in his entire life, and given that one of those was Madeleine Albright, it's perhaps not surprising that he regards the outside world with a mix of derision and paranoia.

Yet, he remains the subject of adulation. Normally bright, responsible scholars and educators from North Korea and abroad reduce themselves to writing driveling, soppy odes to this silver-spooned papa's boy. Sample this, written by a doctor at Delhi University in India:

Dear leader Kim Jong Il
Friend of masses, savior of humanity
Increased efforts of yours inspired
the masses
You have awakened them
To build modern DPRK
Brick by brick
Made them independent and masters
of their own destiny
Dear leader Kim Jong Il
A rising star on the horizon
Shown the path of salvation
Of realism
Removed flunkeyism in the face of
Severe odds
Dear leader Kim Jong Il
A versatile personality
I salute you

Removed flunkeyism? Whoa . . . dude, that's heavy.

In North Korea, propaganda has become an art form. Perhaps the most entertaining reading we've come across at *DP* is the "consumer" magazine that comes out of Pyongyang—*Korea Today*.

There are magnificent book reviews, all of Kim Jong Il's hundreds of books. There's no room for anything else. And no comments such as, "The plot is frayed; the characters develop like a fungus. The author has talent, but should have restricted it to writing flyers for the PTA." Nope, nothing like that. You'd end up in the gulag for a few centuries. The harshest criticism we spotted was surprisingly scathing, though: "Many of the world's people call Kim Jong Il the giant of our times. This means that he is unique and distinguished in all aspects—wisdom, leadership, ability, personality, and achievements." (*Korea Today*, No. 3, 1992.) The writer was anonymous, fearing for his life if his byline were to be published.

There's coverage of some great plays and performing arts shows. One particularly caught our attention, a tear-jerking rendition of *My Automatic Rifle Dance*, performed by two voluptuous (in North Korea, that means fed) actresses prancing about the stage with their AKs. *Korea Today* also publishes cutting-edge, bohemian poetry that mainstream periodicals wouldn't have the balls to print:

My song, echo all the way home from the trenches.
When I smash the American robbers of happiness,
And I return home with glittering medals on my chest,
All my beloved family will be in my arms.

Cool stuff. Want to subscribe? Write: The Foreign Language Magazines, Pyongyang, DPRK.

For more laughs, write The Korean People's Army Publishing House, Pyongyang, DPRK, for a copy of their enormously popular *Panmunjom*, a chronicle of North Korea's innumerable military accomplishments. There are some great combat shots, with captions like "U.S. imperialist troops of aggression training South Korean puppet soldiers to become cannon fodder in their aggressive war against the northern half of Korea." Another innocuous shot of a group of soldiers is depicted as "A U.S. military advisor and the South Korean stooges are on the spot to organize the armed invasion of the northern half of Korea." Another photo shows a 1953 armistice meeting between North Korean and UN officials breaking up, and is appropriately captioned "The U.S. imperialist troops of aggression hastily leave after their crimes have been exposed at a meeting held at the scene of the crime."

But the *DP* runner-up in the book goes to a 1976 shot of an American soldier using a chainsaw to cut down a tree. The caption: "The U.S. imperialist troops of aggression committed a grave provocation, cutting down a tree."

Who knows? For even more knee-slaps, check out the Korean Central News Agency's new Web site (http://www.kcna.co.jp). *DP*'s favorite headline is "U.S. Stands Alone on Land Mine." Although graphically as creative as a pancake, you're sure to howl at the copy, which continually adulates Kim Jong Il as having "perfectly controlled the complicated situation of the world."

Of course, don't expect much on the mess the Leader has perfectly controlled in his own backyard, namely six consecutive years of famine that one UN official said could turn into "one of the biggest humanitarian disasters of our lifetime." Despite the famine, which a U.S. congressional report says has killed up to 2 million people since 1995 (the DPRK admitted in May 1999 to a figure closer to 220,000 between 1995 and 1998), and having been dependent on international aid since the same year, the DPRK appears to have enough food to export. Okryukwan, the North's most famous restaurant and known for its naengmyon—cold buckwheat noodles—opened its first branch in Seoul in May 1999. With the ingredients imported from North Korea, Okryukwan has become Seoul's latest hip, up-market eatery. Regrettably, for most North Koreans, "up-market" is an old lady selling yams by the side of the road in Jian, China. But the hundreds, maybe thousands, of North Korean spies planted in the South finally have a decent place to eat.

What lies ahead for the great dynasty of denial? Not much.

## The Scoop

No one's quite sure—the best travel guide for North Korea was written by George Orwell shortly before the state was founded in 1948. But the rest of the world is getting a clearer picture, as more and more citizens of the DPRK start finding holes in the fence. The trickle of defectors, which has gone on as long as the DPRK has existed, is starting to look like a minor flood. In early 2002, dozens of North Koreans defected to South Korea via the Spanish embassy in Beijing, evoking memories of those first decamping denizens of Eastern Europe who parked themselves in Western embassies in Prague in 1989—and we all know how that ended.

For the moment, though, we're a far way from the grand opening of Pyongyang's first Starbucks, and North Korea is best known as a gold-card member of Dubya's "Axis of Evil"—that coterie of rogue nations, also including Iraq and Iran, whose only common trait is that they had nothing to do with September 11. However, North Korea has been buzzing busily in the Pentagon's bonnet for decades, and not without reason. North Korea spends somewhere between 25 and 33 percent of its total GDP on defense: its military toy box contains missiles capable of striking pretty much anywhere (though the ones people are most worried about are the ones which could travel down the road to Seoul, which Pyongyang could incinerate before any response was possible) and programs to develop nuclear, chemical, and biological weapons.

The question is how far these programs have proceeded—always the case where North Korea is concerned—and everybody is guessing, but nobody knows. The DPRK is the most closed society on the globe. It is also perhaps the most lobotomized—obtaining information from abroad is illegal, as is picking up hitchhikers. Even bicycles were illegal until 1990. North Koreans can't even visit many areas in their own country and talking to a foreigner is grounds for arrest. The DPRK is starting to feel its way into the outside world—missions and embassies have either opened, or are about to, in Australia and Canada, among other countries. The Chubby One shops at the Gap and puts a little mousse in the do.

The ever-laboring subjects have been stung by six years of famine caused by floods and maladroit mismanagement of farmland, and a string of defections, including the high-profile bailing of Hwang Jang Yop in February 1997 (and a number of lesser officials since). Hwang was number 6 (or 26 depending on whom you talk to) in the pecking order, and the architect of Pyongyang's "juche" ideology of self-reliance. How well that concept has worked is evidenced by Pyongyang's willingness to store Taiwan's nuclear waste for US$200 million worth of rice. Not to mention, of course, the US$1 billion admission ticket Pyongyang is trying to sell for a visit to the suspected underground nuclear facility at Kumchang-ri. That's self-reliance. *DP* was going to suggest eBay if the Bouffant One wants to unload some of that Cold War hardware.

## The Players ————————————————————

### *Kim Il Sung (The Great Leader)*

Yeah, he's dead. But long live the Kim. The effects of playing God for 46 years don't go away overnight. The North Koreans still show, and will continue to show for years, blind adoration of their beloved pinko deity—except, perhaps, the estimated 20,000 political prisoners held in the country. But remember—in North Korea, you're a political prisoner if you don't turn on your television in the morning.

Kim Il Sung was born of picturesque peasant stock in 1912 but left Korea as a child when his parents moved to Manchuria. It's not easy to sort out the facts from the tidal waves of bullshit spouted on his behalf by North Korea's propagandists, but it is believed that Kim first took an interest in geopolitics as the 20-year-old leader of a gang of Korean partisans that raided Japanese installations inside Korea. He later fled to the Soviet Union, where he rose to the rank of major in the Red Army, and was chosen to head a provisional government in Soviet-occupied Korea. In 1948, he became the first (and still the only) president of the DPRK.

It wasn't enough for Kim, who fancied gathering all of Korea beneath his cloak. The result was the Korean War: a prototype of future wars, with plenty of dead soldiers, saber rattling, and bizarre peace-keeping armies. Left with only half a country to govern, Kim sulkily sold arms to Libya, Iran, and Syria and plotted the downfall of those dang pesky democrats in the South, in between building statues of himself and orchestrating his hapless people into immense parades in his own honor.

Every bit as batty as the state he created, Kim Il Sung has not yet been formally disencumbered of the responsibilities of head of state, despite being dead for some years.

http://www.korea-dpr.com

## Kim Jong Il (The Dear Leader)

Possibly the least charismatic figure ever to have been the subject of a fully-fledged personality cult, the Dear Leader (not to be confused with his dad the "Great" Leader) is a reclusive and deeply unimpressive figure about whom the kindest thing that can be said is that he does not appear to have as many bats in his belfry as dear dad.

As is always the case with totalitarian heads of government, the view you get of Kim Jong Il rather depends on whom you ask. The North Koreans claim that, in addition to his unparalleled sagacity as a statesman, he is an author, architect, and a composer of world-class genius. Pretty much everyone else on earth thinks he's a vain, slightly dim, and seriously dangerous fruitcake with an assortment of hobbies that are either worrying (his partiality to cognac) or downright unsa-vory (the aforementioned concubines, called "The Pleasure Squad," who may or may not have taken up their positions willingly).

For the moment, Kim's game plan is impossible to fathom. His ten-tative efforts at rapprochement with the South and his epic rail voyage to Moscow raise hopes that perhaps he's beginning to realize that North Korea had better change while it can. But most reports from inside the country suggest it is a place still being tyrannized by a combination of terror and stupidity comparable only with the Cultural Revolution of 1970s China. Kim, incidentally, threw a fit when China first embarked upon free-market reforms, calling even Beijing's repressive geriocracy "traitors to the world socialist movement"—now, that's hard-line.

postmaster@korea-dpr.com

### Kim Jong Nam, the Next Dear Leader?

It is hard to say whether assuming the ever-shrinking mantle is a gift or a curse. The heir apparent looks a lot like Deputy Dog with a pot-belly and bad skin. Born in 1971, Kim Jong Nam is the genetic output of his Marty Allen look-alike dad and an actress/mistress/first wife, Sung Hye-Rim. He was raised in isolation and has a proclivity for geeky things like technology and of course hanging out with all the other bored dictator kids. He can usually be seen cruising Europe with a blonde on his arm. It's good to be the heir apparent. In March of 2001, Kim Jong Nam, the first-born son of the Dear Leader and grandson of the Great Leader, was nabbed on his way to Tokyo Disneyland and deported to China. His crime? Using a false passport . . . from the Dominican Republic.

When is Nam on deck? Don't hold your breath while the people are still singing such snappy tunes as "Benevolent Father of the People" and "The Leader Who Will Always Be with Us" to Daddy. It appears that Kim Jong Nam will have to enjoy his prolonged childhood a little longer.

### The Military

North Korea has approximately 1.2 million troops, the majority of them massed along the border with South Korea. Most are starving and roaming the streets of famine-stricken cities and rural areas with their AKs, hitting the people up at gunpoint for food and money. For the time being, Jong has their support, as the Dear Leader apparently has no plans to socialize the military, whose elite members enjoy such Western luxuries as Mercedes, Marlboros, and mint-flavored Crest. But the military appears to be running out of gas for its 4,000 (whoa!) tanks and 600 combat aircraft. U.S. officials report that the North Korean air force has reduced its training missions near the DMZ by 75 percent.

## Getting In —————————————————

America has no diplomatic representation in North Korea—its interests in the DPRK are handled by the embassy in Beijing, another country not known as "America's friend in need." This is the most colossal pain in the neck, especially if you're American—U.S. citizens weren't admitted at all from 1995 to 2002, and Dubya's "Axis of Evil" nonsense hasn't made the country any more likely to roll out the welcome mat. For everyone else, a passport and visa are required, but that's only the beginning of the fun. Visas must be arranged prior to arrival in Pyongyang, and you must pay for your entire trip before you depart, as you will be part of a government-organized tour. If you're a journalist, you can pretty much forget visiting, except in exceptional circumstances (hacks from the big papers and TV channels are occasionally let in to cover state occasions). If you sign on for a tour pretending not to be a journalist, you'll need to square with your conscience the possibility that the tour company concerned will never work in North Korea again. Also keep a plausible telephone manner handy, as it is common for suspicious North Korean officials to call people at work, to make sure whoever answers the phone doesn't say, "Hello, *Washington Post,* can I help you?" The best person to contact about visiting is Nick Bonner at:

**Koryo Tours**
http://www.koryogroup.com

## Getting Around

You won't have much choice in the matter of getting around. You'll be with a government guide in a government vehicle on a government tour and you'll go where the government wants you to go. Some aid workers, doctors, and the odd foreigner have gained the trust of the higher-ups and traveled more widely (with a political guide), but don't expect any articles by Hunter S. Thompson anytime soon.

There exists only the skeleton of a public transit system in North Korea: very few buses, virtually no cars, and no domestic flights open to foreigners. Travel by train is your best bet next to a car. Again, you'll have no say, but trains usually stop at some of the more popular tourist sites (a three-word oxymoron). There is no bus service between the cities. Pyongyang possesses a two-line metro and regular bus services.

## Dangerous Places

### The Entire Country . . . Not

The North Koreans think all Westerners who visit the country are spies. You will travel in a group and be watched as closely as detectives viewing Sharon Stone's leg-uncrossing move in *Basic Instinct.* North Korea is host to few foreign tourists, and those who do get in will see only areas of the country targeted by the government for them to see. You will be subjected to intense propaganda wherever you go, and you will never be permitted to stray off the beaten path unattended, although you occasionally

> **C**rime is not a problem in North Korea. . . . You will never hear our government mention that North Korea, aka part of the Axis of Evil, is probably the safest place on earth for foreigners.

might be permitted an unattended evening stroll around Pyongyang. Journos have bragged about sneaking out of their hotels, but have failed to mention that their former guide is now breaking small rocks into smaller ones. Needless to say, you won't get many too many opportunities to get into trouble.

Crime is not a problem in North Korea. There is wide speculation that thieves and criminals get the death penalty. You will never hear our government mention that North Korea, aka part of the Axis of Evil, is probably the safest place on earth for foreigners.

## The DMZ

After the Japanese surrender of 1945, Korea was divided into two directorates: The USSR occupied the North, while the United States controlled the South below the 38th parallel. In 1948, the division between the two zones was made permanent. Trade was cut off between the two zones at the advent of the Cold War in the late 1940s. The DPRK is very much a communist nation. The Republic of Southern Korea is very much a democratic, capitalist nation. Before the demise of the Soviet Union, the DPRK imported nearly three-quarters of a million tons of oil from the USSR per year. These supplies have been essentially cut off. North Korea is nearly US$6 billion in debt. Things are a little tense. Oh, and then there is the war. Present tense.

Although the war started on Sunday, June 25, 1950, and lasted only 37 months, it left 2.4 million Koreans, 900,000 Chinese, 37,000 Americans, and 3,000 foreign troops dead. There were 103,000 Americans wounded and massive devastation of both countries.

Despite this punishing experience, the North pretends the war is still going strong and the South is happy to oblige. Like two bar fighters being held back (well, the North is pretending someone is holding it back), the two sides threaten, probe, and pester each other shamelessly. They regularly exchange gunfire and insults, as if the war started yesterday.

Today the 38th parallel dividing North and South Korea is perhaps the most heavily fortified border in the world. On the southern side, some 37,500 U.S. troops sit waiting for Kim Jong Il's horde to come crashing through the gates—in this case, the side of a mountain. For nearly 50 years, the North Korean army has been digging tunnels through the granite mountains on its side of the border into South Korean territory, leaving only a few meters of rock and soil between the North's stockpiled invasion force—artillery equipment, tanks, helicopters, warplanes, and troops—and South Korean "sunshine." War is little more than the tap of an ice pick away.

http://travel.state.gov/nkorea.html

## Dangerous Things ———————————————————

### Juche

*Juche,* or "self-reliance," has been the hallmark of North Korean culture and political style since September 8, 1948. Also known by the snappy name "Kim Il Jongism," it sounds frighteningly like good old American freedom. "Juche means that the masters of the revolution and construction are the masses of the people and they are also the motive force of the revolution and construction. In other words, one is responsible for one's own destiny." Uh, huh; pass the Skoal, and turn up Kid Rock.

The truth is the land above the 38th parallel has become a strange mix of personality cult and Stalinist ideals getting serious wood from the leadership of Kim Il Sung, a former guerrilla-commander-turned-Soviet lackey, turned dictator, turned dead person, turned mythical, immortal leader. His son doesn't inspire the same frenetic worship, but then again he is not the president. His dead dad still is.

North Korea's isolation policy was cemented by the three years of war that began in 1950 when North Korea decided to invade the South. The war ensured that North Korea would simmer in its own "juche" for the next few decades. The support of the communist bloc kept the country ticking along until the early '90s when everything seemed to change . . . for the worse. And the idea of self-reliance was hatched to keep the Great Leader's strain of ideology uninfected by those wild and crazy Soviet and Chinese ideas. The great experiment of communism had dried up, the Great Leader had kicked the bucket, and the outside world was getting a little nervous over rumors about nukes bolted to low-budget commbloc Scud missiles. Power (but not title) was handed down genetically (a first for a commie country), and an aggressive and quite entrepreneurial nuke program began in earnest in 1994. America has managed to bottle up the North while the South makes earnest overtures to the North to kiss and make up.

Recently, the North embarrassingly has been forced to accept handouts of food and money to survive, but they counter the claims of dire need with huge spectaculars that feature up to 100,000 costumed dancers and massive billboards featuring the Great Leader. Makes sense to me. And things haven't been getting better since history, political science, geography, and math whiz George Bush managed to mangle all the aforementioned skills and include North Korea in his "Axis of Evil" speech. Things have been getting a little chillier north of the 38th parallel. Now, be that as it may, you might be surprised to learn that with this track record, juche may be catching on.

**NORTH KOREA**

*The International Institute of the Juche Idea*
http://www.cnet-ta.ne.jp/juche/defaulte.htm
http://www.language-museum.com/jisge

## Bow Shots

In April 1999, the Japanese discovered a pair of North Korean spy trawlers (with Japanese markings) snooping around in their waters, and decided to have a look-see. When the trawlers started high-tailing it back to North Korea, the Japanese got their first taste of a firefight since World War II. But there was a catch. It wasn't an actual firefight. You see, the Japanese are prevented in their post-World War II constitution from using force unless fired upon first. Because the DPRK spy boats didn't shoot at anyone, all the Japanese navy could do was fire bow shots from an armada of warships and helicopters for a few hours as the trawlers raced home unscathed. (If only that had been policy at Pearl Harbor.) No reason anymore for Japan's allies to go to the expense of staging war games with their buddies in the Pacific—the North Koreans will do it for free. And speaking of bow shots, in late August 1998, the DPRK lobbed a Taepo-dong ballistic missile over the Japanese peninsula, with the rocket's cone landing in the Pacific, and the first stage in waters near Alaska. Alaskans didn't complain because Exxon had nothing to do with it, and nothing leaked. But the Japanese and the Pentagon quickly cried foul, while Pyongyang insisted it had merely launched a satellite, which is possibly true, since the Dear Leader had no access to the Playboy Channel.

## Home Rocket Kits

Korea does have an export business, and a very good one at that: build-it-at-home rocket kits. Seems they will sell whatever bits you need to complete your own chemical, high explosives (HE), or nuclear missile program. (Instructions included, please read manufacturer's warning label before operation.) Pakistan's Ghauri and Iran's Shahab-3 missiles are GMC/Chevy-like copies of North Korean protoypes. Iran now can reach out at anyone from Sudan to India to most of Western Europe with its 1,250-mile-range arsenal. Countries like Pakistan simply screw nukes to the top of their Ghauris and voila: an errant over-sized Fourth of July fireworks becomes a Weapon of Mass Destruction. North Korea saves the best for home use. They can fire a missile that would hit anywhere in Southeast Asia, Russia, or the caribou migration in Alaska. That is, if they get the thing pointed in the right direction.

http://www.fas.org/nuke/guide/dprk/index.html

*Famine*

How bad is it? So bad that even the North Korean government admits it's bad. In February 1999, a survey by North Korea's Public Security Ministry found that at least 3 million North Koreans had died since 1995. A third of North Koreans are dependent on food aid, and more than half the population is chronically malnourished. In April 2002, the UN food agency said North Korea would run out of food in three months. Well, they ran out, and they keep running out. In the northern region of Ryangjang, there have been reports of cannibalism.

http://grid2.cr.usgs.gov/map_servers/korea/korea.html

## Getting Sick

North Korea has a shortage of medical supplies, facilities, and doctors. Western medicines and remedies are even more rare. On the plus side, the water is potable, and hygiene and sanitation are very good. You won't, however, find the food stalls that are seen throughout the rest of Asia. North Korea is squeaky-clean and you might enjoy a restful recovery if you are unlucky enough to get sick.

## Nut and Bolts

The country is covered almost entirely by north-to-south mountain ranges and is about the size of Pennsylvania. The language in North Korea is Korean, with indigenous elements in the vocabulary.

Religions in North Korea include Buddhism and Confucianism. However, religious activities within the country basically don't exist. There is no public worshipping of deities in the DPRK, with the obvious exceptions of the Great Leader and the Dear Leader.

The currency is the won. The won equals 100 jon, about 2 to a dollar. Per-capita income is US$1,000.

Electricity is 220V/60Hz. Overseas phone calls can be made from major hotels, and international direct dial (IDD) is available in certain establishments—bear in mind that it is unlikely that your mom and dad are the only people listening to you when you call. Mail can be received at some hotels and at the Korean International Tourist Bureau, but it will be read by the government. Fax services are readily available. Foreign visitors are allowed to link their own computers to the Internet through hotels in Pyongyang. A Chinese company called Silibak opened the first e-mail connection to North Korea in late 2001, but it's off-limits to the general public and expensive for the government agencies and government-approved businesses permitted to use it; sending text e-mails costs about $1.40 each, and photographs cost about $400.

The climate in North Korea is cold and dry in the winter with warm summers. More than 60 percent of the annual rainfall occurs from June through September.

Cell phones and videocameras are verboten. Still cameras are okay, but expect to be told when and where you can photograph. Locals must report photography, and they develop C-41 in Pyongyang. Bring smokes as gifts. American flag pins may be a cute gift idea but probably unwise.

http://lcweb2.loc.gov/frd/cs/kptoc.html

**Embassy of the United States**
3 Xiu Shui Bei Jie
Chaoyang District
100600 Beijing, China
Tel.: (86) 10 6532 3831
Fax: (86) 10 6532 6929
http://www.usembassy-china.org.cn

**Embassy of Great Britain**
Muso Dong District
Pyongyang, North Korea
Tel.: (850) 2 381 7980
Fax: (850) 2 381 7985
*The North Koreans are sort-of speaking to the Brits.*

# Dangerous Days

| | |
|---|---|
| **5/28/02** | Four more North Koreans take shelter in the South Korean embassy in Beijing. |
| **3/02** | A group of 25 North Koreans defect to South Korea via the Spanish embassy in Beijing. |
| **2/1/02** | North Korea calls Bush's speech "little short of a declaration of war" and Bush "a moral leper." |
| **1/29/02** | George W. Bush makes "Axis of Evil" State of the Union speech. |
| **8/01** | The xenophobic Kim Jong Il travels by train to Moscow. |
| **12/17/98** | North Korean spy submarine sunk by South Korean navy. |
| **8/31/98** | Pyongyang launches a ballistic missile over the Japanese peninsula. |
| **7/12/98** | Dead DPRK commando found near South Korea's Tonghae naval base. |
| **6/26/98** | North Korean minisubmarine captured in South Korean waters after becoming tangled in fishing nets. Nine crew, believed to have committed suicide, are found shot dead inside. |
| **2/12/97** | Leading party ideologue Hwang Jang Yop defects to the South Korean embassy in Beijing. |
| **11/12/94** | An American army helicopter is shot down in North Korean airspace. One pilot dies in the crash and the other is repatriated more than two weeks later. |

| | |
|---|---|
| **7/18/94** | Death of the Great Leader, Kim Il Sung. |
| **7/27/53** | Armistice ending the Korean War signed, called by North Korea the "Victory in the Fatherland Liberation War." |
| **9/15/50** | UN Commander General Douglas MacArthur makes an amphibious landing at Inchon, behind North Korean lines, and routs the North Korean army. |
| **6/27/50** | U.S. President Harry Truman orders U.S. combat units into action to enforce the UN condemnation of North Korea's invasion of South Korea. |
| **6/27/50** | The United Nations condemns North Korea's attack of South Korea and demands a withdrawal of the invading forces. |
| **6/25/50** | North Korea mounts a surprise invasion of South Korea. |
| **5/1/48** | The establishment of the Democratic People's Republic of Korea. National Day. |
| **2/16/42** | Birthday of Kim Jong Il (Juche 31). |
| **4/25/32** | Foundation of People's Revolutionary Army. |
| **5/1** | Mayday. |
| **4/12** | Birthday of Kim Il Sung. |

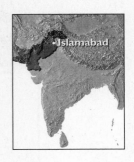

Islamabad

★ ★ ★

# PAKISTAN

## Wackistan

When George W. Bush was running for president in 2000, some enterprising hack decided to test him on his knowledge of foreign affairs. One of the many things in which Dubya demonstrated his thundering ignorance was the name of Pakistan's president, General Pervez Musharaff (and no, we didn't have to look it up). It's amazing how a bunch of Koran-addled yahoos armed with passenger jets can change things. Since about 9:15 on the morning of September 11, 2001, General Musharaff has been pretty close to the top of Dubya's speed-dial list—somewhere between the numbers of Dick Cheney's bunker and the local pizza parlor.

Islami Jamhuria-e-Pakistan (the Islamic Republic of Pakistan) has existed since August 15, 1947, and is the world's first self-proclaimed Islamic state. It was another result of the British fondness for postimperial partition—the same policy that was such a rousing success in

PAKISTAN

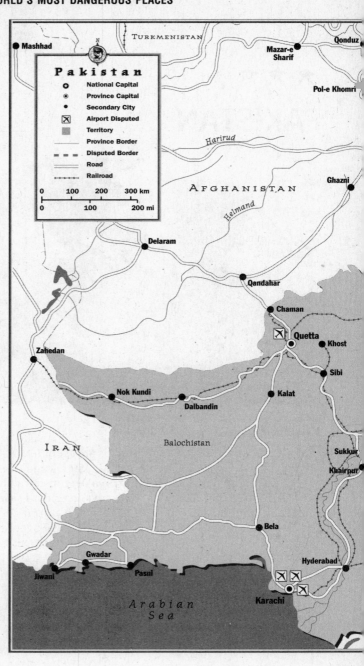

Pakistan

| | National Capital |
| | Province Capital |
| | Secondary City |
| | Airport Disputed |
| | Territory |
| | Province Border |
| | Disputed Border |
| | Road |
| | Railroad |

0    100    200    300 km

0    100    200 mi

Mashhad

TURKMENISTAN

Qonduz

Mazar-e Sharif

Pol-e Khomri

Harirud

AFGHANISTAN

Ghazni

Helmand

Delaram

Qandahar

Chaman

Quetta

Khost

Zahedan

Sibi

Nok Kundi

Kalat

Dalbandin

Balochistan

IRAN

Sukkur

Khairpur

Bela

Gwadar

Hyderabad

Jiwani

Pasni

Karachi

Arabian Sea

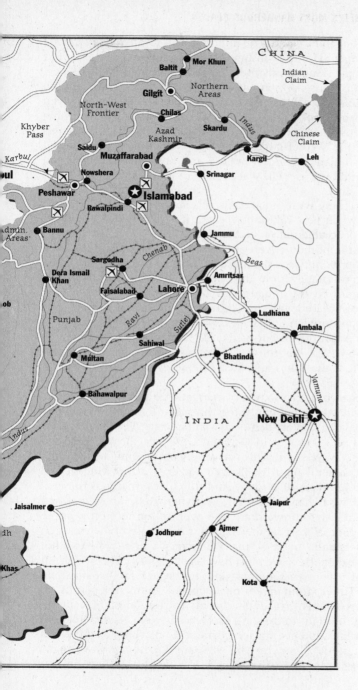

Cyprus, Palestine, and Ireland. The intention was to provide a separate and secure homeland for the Muslims of newly independent India. The result was an epic slaughter as India's Muslims headed for their new homeland, and Hindus—on what was now Pakistani soil—crossed the other way to the safety of India; the death toll comfortably cleared seven figures. When the smoke lifted, Pakistan consisted of two struggling entities on opposite sides of India (West Pakistan and East Pakistan). India still had the second-largest Muslim population on earth, and there was one Indian province—Jammu and Kashmir—that Pakistan thought it should own as well. War broke out immediately, and it has barely stopped since.

As well as fighting with India, Pakistan managed to go to war with itself in 1971, when East Pakistan seceded (it is now the independent and relatively peaceable nation of Bangladesh). Pakistan also became one of the most important covert and overt battlegrounds of the Cold War due to its proximity to Afghanistan; inclined to favor the United States, Pakistan was happy for its Inter Services Intelligence (ISI) to help the CIA run guns to the mujahideen fighting the Russians. When American interest ceased with the USSR's withdrawal from the region, the ISI later sponsored the Taliban's takeover of Afghanistan, until America became abruptly re-engaged on September 11, 2001, at which point Pakistan—which, if nothing else, knows a losing bet when it sees one—decided that the Talibs and their infamous houseguest were on their own.

Pakistan's legal code is a mixture of *sharia* justice and some remnants of British law. Its governmental history has been a similarly unwieldy combination of parliamentary democracy and military dictatorship. General Musharaff seized power in October 1999, overthrowing elected Prime Minister Nawaz Sharif. This was an uncanny echo of the events of 1977, when General Zia ul-Haq seized power, overthrowing elected Prime Minister Zulfikar Ali Bhutto. And this struck many as remarkably similar to what happened in 1958, when General Ayub Khan declared martial law to prevent anyone even trying to elect a prime minister. (The general later claimed he did this because of the weather: "We must understand," he said, "that democracy cannot work in a hot climate. To have democracy we must have a cold climate, like Britain." It is not known if anyone tried pointing out to the general that sunshine didn't stop the Greeks from inventing democracy in the first place.)

What is incredible is that anyone wants to run Pakistan at all, let alone fight for the right to do so. It rarely ends well: Nawaz Sharif is now serving a life sentence for terrorism and hijacking, General Zia died in a "mysterious" plane crash in 1988, Zulfikar Bhutto was hanged after being deposed, Ayub Khan resigned to avoid full-scale revolution, and Pakistan's very first prime minister, Liaquat Ali Khan, was assassinated by an Islamic extremist in 1951. Another prime minister, Bhutto's daughter Benazir, was sacked by the president after two years on the job in 1990 on charges of incompetence and corruption, but returned to power in 1993, only to be sacked again on charges of incompetence and corruption. She finally left the country, leaving her husband behind in prison. The current incumbent, General Pervez Musharaff, seemed, at the time of this writing, to be flirting with going out with the biggest bang imaginable, as Pakistan's interminable squabble with India over Kashmir threatened to go nuclear.

Pakistan could be forgiven, at least, for suffering something of an identity crisis. In the last few years, it has been both a pariah state, suspended from the Commonwealth after the 1999 military coup that brought General Musharaff to power, and the Western world's best friend, a vital ally in the War on Terrorism, which you may remember being in all the papers a while back. However, the truth is that it doesn't much matter what the outside world thinks, or even who is sitting behind the big desk in Islamabad. Much of the country, notably the Northwest Frontier Province that borders Afghanistan, is ungovernable, and the rest of it isn't governed all that much—not competently, anyway.

Pakistan is a crude welding together of four semiautonomous provinces: Punjab, Sind, Northwest Frontier Province (NWFP), and Balochistan. It also encompasses federally administered tribal and northern areas (FATA/FANA) and lays an eternally contentious claim to the Indian-administered but mostly Muslim states of Azad Jammu and Kashmir. Pakistan rates three stars in *DP* because it continues to endure some of the worst political violence of any country that is not—at the risk of tempting fate—in the middle of a declared, full-scale war. The violence began in Karachi in the 1980s, spread to the Punjab, and has recently even infected the previously immune, and reassuringly dull, diplomatic center of Islamabad. Cheap weapons and heroin, freely available from neighboring Afghanistan, have fostered a massive gun culture that almost equals that of the United States. Rampant corruption at all levels of public life hasn't helped.

> Cheap weapons and heroin, freely available from neighboring Afghanistan, have fostered a massive gun culture that almost equals that of the United States.

If you wanna know the "why" for all this, it goes back to the last guy who liked military parades and shoving the politicos on trial: General Zia ul-Haq. He rammed through a whole load of religious laws in the '80s that played well with the Sunni majority, but he caused the 20 percent Shi'a population to get their turbans in severe knots. Haq also set up the madrassahs, or religious schools, for the not-so-rich kids. This probably wasn't the worst idea he'd ever had, but when Saudi Arabian Wahhabist sects began to sponsor the schools, the madrassahs kind of drifted from their remit of Koran study and ended up churning out the Sunni Islamic version of *Terminator II*. (You don't, by the way, get any prizes for guessing where the Taliban emerged from.)

To get the picture here, you've got to see all this happening within the contemporary context of the (predominately Sunni) Afghan jihad against the Soviets, and the (mainly Shi'a) Iranian revolution, and the ensuing Iran-Iraq war. In Pakistan, both Sunni and Shi'a political parties began to get religious, with something of a martial flavor to their daily "let's all tune in to God" meetings. The Sunnis and Shi'as went from tolerating (and even liking) each other to exchanging gunfire. A load of tit-for-tat killings started, which quickly spiraled into all-out massacres. Groups emerged, leaders were killed, more violent splinter groups appeared . . . it's all about as easy to untangle as a couple of mating cobras.

Things are no more peaceful on the foreign-affairs front. While the combined forces of the U.S. Air Force and the Northern Alliance scattered Pakistan's friends, the Taliban, across neighboring Afghanistan, Pakistan went eyeball-to-eyeball across its eastern border with nuclear rival India. If you ever doubted how Pakistan felt about the folks next door, consider that the ballistic missiles Pakistan built to deliver its radioactive goods are named Ghauri, Ghaznavi, and Abdali—all names of Muslim warlords of bygone eras fondly remembered for sweeping across India and putting Hindu believers to the sword and Hindu temples up in flames. Pakistan could hardly have been less subtle if they'd called their delivery systems Calcutta Crusher and Bombay Blaster. The pushing and shoving with the folks next door is over Pakistan's claims to Kashmir. By way of proving their devotion, Pakistan has fought and lost two wars over it and bankrolled Allah-knows-how-many guerrilla groups to carry on the good work. There was a two-month-long semi-war over Kashmir in 1999, which started with the infiltration of a few (thousand) guerrillas from Pakistan, continued with an artillery duel on the border, got a bit heavier as troops from both countries battled it out for a couple of months, but cooled down before either side started fishing around for the instruction manuals for their nukes. For a while in the spring of 2002, it looked like one or both sides was preparing to up the ante—so much so that Western governments advised all their nationals not to travel to India or Pakistan, and told those who were already there to get out.

The situation has cooled off considerably, possibly because Pakistan may have finally apprehended one really important truth: while India, with its vast landmass, dispersed infrastructure, and population of over a billion, might survive a nuclear exchange, Pakistan most certainly would not.

## The Scoop

Pakistan has gone from an adventurer's paradise to a shooting gallery for unlucky foreigners. Along with the danger from anti-Western forces, there are the sensory-numbing amounts of noise, dirt, poverty, temperature extremes, crime, and general mayhem to deal with. But, as Pakistanis never tire of pointing out, India is worse and more expensive.

**Dawn newspaper**
http://dawn.com

**Pakistan Today**
http://www.paktoday.com

**The Nation**
http://www.nation.com.pk

## The Players

### President General Pervez Musharaff

To the debatable extent that anyone can claim to be in charge in Pakistan, it's the guy whose name Dubya couldn't remember. When General Musharaff helped himself to power on October 12, 1999, Western leaders who had taken the time to look his name up denounced him as a tin-pot tyrant, and Pakistan was suspended from the Commonwealth. President Musharaff, as he's now known, would be more than human if, a little less than two years later, he hadn't permitted himself a few chuckles when his antagonists, seeking a convenient ally in their war against Afghanistan, decided he wasn't such a bad chap after all.

Musharaff was born in Delhi, India, on August 11, 1943. His parents were among the millions of Indian Muslims who decided to make their homes in the new Islamic state of Pakistan when it was founded in 1947. His father joined the fledgling nation's diplomatic service, and the young Pervez spent much of his childhood in Turkey. He joined the Pakistan Military Academy as an 18-year-old officer cadet, and after receiving his commission fought in the 1965 war with India, during which he was decorated for bravery, and in the 1971 war with East Pakistan (now Bangladesh). He has two children and, when he isn't playing nuclear chicken with India, enjoys canoeing, badminton, and golf (perhaps he and Vajpayee could sort Kashmir out over 18 holes, in the ultimate Skins game).

Musharaff was appointed to the rank of general and the position of chief of army staff in 1998. In October 1999, while on an official visit to Sri Lanka, he was dismissed from the job by Pakistan's then-prime minister, Nawaz Sharif. If Sharif thought Musharaff would respond by saying "Oh well, fair enough then," and buy a retirement villa in Colombo, he was grievously mistaken. Musharaff got in his plane and flew home. Clearly anxious to avoid a scene, Sharif refused it permission to land. Musharaff ordered the pilot to touch down regardless, and upon arrival in Islamabad told Sharif to clear his desk. (Sharif was later convicted of hijacking and terrorism, but managed to trade his life sentence for exile in Saudi Arabia.)

Musharaff formalized his position at the top of the tree in June 2001, when Pakistan's democratically elected President Tarar retired. Once ensconced behind the big desk, Musharaff made his intentions clear. The elected assemblies, which had been suspended since the coup, were abolished altogether. Musharaff did announce a timetable for restoring democracy by October 2002, which nobody took seriously, least of all Musharaff: In April 2002, he held a referendum seeking to confirm himself as president for another five years. The question put to his people—or to the 50 percent or so of them who could read— was this not-at-all-loaded poser, straight out of the have-you-stopped-beating-your-wife school: "For the survival of the local government system, establishment of democracy, continuity of reforms, end to sectarianism and extremism, and to fulfill the vision of Quaid-e-Azam [that's Pakistan's founder, Mohammed Ali Jinnah, to you], would you like to elect President General Pervez Musharaff as president of Pakistan for five years?"

Well, gee, if you put it like that . . .

Unfortunately for Musharaff's democratic credentials, the referendum was as well-organized as everything else in Pakistan, which is to say it was a total madwoman's custard. The opposition parties told their supporters to boycott it, and nobody really knows how many people were eligible to vote, anyway: The official Election Commission claimed that 42.8 million out of a turnout of 43.9 million voted for five more years, while opposition groups claimed that the official Election Commission were making it up as they went along. *DP*'s money, for what it may be worth, is on the latter hypothesis. It didn't matter: Even if the turnout had been two blokes and a camel, and even if the camel's was the only vote Musharaff got, Musharaff wasn't going anywhere.

Dictator and occasionally maladroit diplomat though he is, Musharaff may be the best chance Pakistan has, provided he doesn't contrive to get it incinerated by its tetchy neighbor. His hero is Mustafa Kemal Ataturk, the founder of modern Turkey, and Musharaff has similar modernizing ambitions—in February 2002, he described the Islamic world as "the poorest, the most illiterate, the most backward, the most unhealthy, the most unenlightened, the most deprived, and the weakest of all the human race" (but he's never been to Florida). Since 9/11, he's also been pretty sharp about weeding fundamentalist elements out of the army and the Inter Services Intelligence (ISI) and has issued a flurry of laws banning various militant groups.

Musharaff is walking a very fine line and is pissing off some very dangerous people; *DP* would not want to be his insurance agent.

**General Pervez Musharaff**
CE@pak.gov.pk

**Islamic Republic of Pakistan**
http://www.pak.gov.pk

### The Army

If you're wondering why the military seems to think they are the only people capable of ruling Pakistan, it's simple . . . it's because they are just about the only people capable of ruling Pakistan. Pakistan is a total shambles, split by ethnic and factional violence, economically on life-support, and chronically corrupt. The military is about the only institution that has the capability and discipline to get anything done in the place, except defend its own country.

> **P**akistan is a total shambles, split by ethnic and factional violence, economically on life-support, and chronically corrupt.

Pakistan has lost every war it has ever fought, but that hasn't stopped them from rattling their rusty colonial-era sabers at the huge Indian army over their eastern border. In Pakistan itself, warring tribes in Balochistan, Sindh, Northwest Frontier Province, and the tribal areas keep the army's bullets from corroding in their clips, while criminals and ethnic terrorists in Karachi, Quetta, and Hyderabad make soldiers sleep with one eye open. Having China as a neighbor to the north and Iran to the west does not make flower-power high on the political agenda, either.

The army has been put through the wringer since 9/11, as General Musharaff has tried to reposition Pakistan's image from a serial sponsor of bearded Koran-waving wackos to a pro-Western enemy of all forms of terror. Musharaff replaced the garrison commanders in the perennially unstable cities of Quetta and Peshawar, appointed a known moderate—General Mohammed Yusuf—his Vice Chief of Army, and packed his former ally, Lieutenant General Mohammed Aziz Khan, off to a ribbon-cutting position as Chairman of the Joint Chiefs of Staff Committee.

The question is whether the army will follow Musharaff or its own hard-line conscience—the stakes, as *DP* scarcely needs to remind you, are apocalyptic. Yes, we know that the Pentagon has expressed satisfaction about nuclear-command-and-control in Pakistan—that's probably because Pakistan's missiles are pointed at India, not at Honolulu.

http://www.pakarmy.gov.pk
http://www.geocities.com/Pentagon/Bunker/5040
http://www.pakarmy.8k.com

**Ministry of Defense**
Defense Division Pak. Secretariat-11
Rawalpindi, Pakistan
Tel: (92) 51 566 203

## *Inter Services Intelligence (ISI)*

The ISI is a very dubious bunch indeed. Then again, most spooks are. Pick any crisis in the region and you can bet that there'll be a shady character from ISI running around somewhere. To a very large extent, they bankrolled the Taliban in Afghanistan. In fact, the Taliban pretty much had been created in the madrasas (religious schools) of Pakistan. The aim, of course, was to secure influence in Afghanistan for Pakistan, but it wasn't working out too well even before the Taliban were bombed into early retirement by the U.S. Air Force. The Talibs were happy to take the cash, but they sure as hell didn't take the orders. Well, not the ones they didn't like, at any rate. The same is true of Kashmir, where the ISI has long been training and arming separatist groups, including the Lashkar-e-Toiba and Harakat-ul-Mujahideen (see the India chapter for further details on these thugs).

The directorate of ISI was founded in 1948 by British army officer Major General R. Cawthome. ISI is mainly made up of military officers—it's a bit like a more overtly military CIA, but with a bit less subtlety than the Langley boys (one shivers at the thought). The ISI is currently believed to have a staff of about 10,000, but that may be in the process of being scaled downward as Musharaff tries to clean Pakistan's fingerprints off the Taliban and their subsidiaries in Kashmir. Musharaff showed the pro-Taliban ISI Director-General, General Mahmood Ahmed, the door in late 2002 and replaced him with the allegedly more moderate Lieutenant General Ehsanul Haq. Musharaff is also said to have closed the ISI division that was responsible for Kashmir.

Reshuffles or not, the ISI remains a riddle inside an enigma, wrapped in a puzzle, and hidden well beyond the ken of most mortals. There are those, including Afghan Interior Minister Younis Qanooni, who believe the ISI is in bed with al-Qaeda and helped Osama bin Laden out of Afghanistan. There are those, including Indian Prime

Minister Atal Vajpayee, who think the ISI are puppet-mastering not only secessionist groups in Kashmir, but also the terrorists who tried to blow up Delhi's parliament building in December 2001. And there are those, including almost everyone who has ever had any dealings with any Pakistani bureaucracy or institution, who doubt that the ISI could run a bath.

http://www.pak.gov.pk

**Inter Services Intelligence Directorate**
Near CDA Office
Islamabad, Pakistan
Tel.: (92) 51 920 1456

## Pakistan People's Party (PPP)

The PPP, founded in 1967, was the party of former Prime Minister Zulfikar Ali Bhutto; since his execution in 1979, it has been led by his daughter, Benazir Bhutto. The Harvard- and Oxford-educated Benazir was only 24 when her father was overthrown in a military coup in 1977, and she spent five years in and out of prison and under house arrest. Whatever people think of her—and in Pakistan the spectrum of opinion covers all points from living saint to she-devil—she is undoubtedly a tough customer.

Benazir has been prime minister of Pakistan twice, from 1988 to 1990, and 1993 to 1996. Both terms ended when the incumbent president sacked her over allegations of corruption, even if sacking Pakistani politicians for being crooks is scarcely less absurd than sacking them for being Pakistani. Benazir's husband, controversial businessman and former Senator Asif Zardari, is in prison in Pakistan, convicted of taking bribes from firms bidding for public contracts. Benazir hasn't set foot in Pakistan since 1999, when she was convicted of similar corruption charges. She currently lives in both London and the United Arab Emirates and travels a lot giving speeches and collecting honorary doctorates. Another triumphal return to Pakistan would be a long shot, but you'd be crazy to bet against it.

**Pakistan People's Party**
Zardari House No. 8, Street 19, F-8/2
Islamabad, Pakistan
Tel.: (92) 51 228 2781
Fax: (92) 51 228 2741
ppp@ppp.org.pk
http://www.ppp.org.pk

**Pakistan People's Party—USA**
http://www.pppusa.com

**Pakistan People's Party—UK**
http://www.pppuk.com

**Benazir Bhutto**
benazir@bhutto.net
http://www.benazir-bhutto.net

**Asif Zardari**
http://www.asif-zardari.com

## Jamaat-e-Islami

The Jamaat-e-Islami are perennially unhappy campers. Pakistan's very first prime minister, Liaquat Ali Khan, was assassinated by a Jamaat-e-Islami supporter as far back as 1951. The Jamaat, Pakistan's biggest and ugliest religious party, are pissed off with pretty much everyone and everything. They think the Iranians are softies for calling off the death sentence on Salman Rushdie, they think Musharaff is a wuss for trying to rein in militants in Kashmir, they're really bloody annoyed about the thought of U.S. Marines stomping all over their country trying to find the Jamaat's old mate Osama bin Laden, and don't get them started on India.

The Jamaat-e-Islami was founded in the 1940s by the religious scholar, author, and journalist Sayyed Abul A'la Maududi. It is now led by Qazi Hussain Ahmad, a man as resolutely hard-line as his beard is long and white. He's had a rough old time of it since Musharaff decided that militant Islam was a beaten dog in the wake of 9/11. Ahmad was locked up for four months in late 2001 on charges of sedition after accusing Musharaff of selling out to America and arrested again in April 2002 after he threatened to lead a march from Lahore to Rawalpindi to protest against the referendum on Musharaff's presidency.

In May 2002, as Pakistan appeared to be edging toward war with India, Ahmad called for Pakistan to establish a government of national unity, including, of course, Jamaat-e-Islami. Musharaff has thus far been conspicuously slow about getting back to Ahmad.

**Jamaat-e-Islami**
Mansoora
Multan Road
Lahore, Pakistan
Tel.: (92) 42 5419520-4
Fax: (92) 54 32194
jipmedia@pol.com.pk
http://www.jamaat.org

## Tehreek-e-Insaf (Movement for Justice)

Tehreek-e-Insaf is led by Imran Khan, a former captain of Pakistan's cricket team and, with the possible exception of Benazir Bhutto, the most famous Pakistani who has ever lived (to get an idea of his public standing within Pakistan, multiply Michael Jordan by Brad Pitt). Imran's party is keen on social justice and against corruption—a bit like every political party that has ever existed. Imran's heart is in the right place, and his bygone heroics on the cricket pitch mean that you'll look long and hard for a Pakistani with an unkind word to say about him, but he's got about as much chance of ever leading Pakistan as General Musharaff has of scoring a century against Australia.

***Tehreek-e-Insaf***
http://www.insaf.org.pk

## The Mujahideen

One of the problems of training people to fight in foreign wars is that they sometimes come home. There are an estimated 10,000 mujahideen (mainly Pakistanis) in Pakistan, excluding those who are still fighting in Afghanistan and Kashmir. There are also hundreds of mujahideen from Libya, Egypt, Yemen, Jordan, Palestine, Algeria, and Tunisia based, recruited, and trained in Peshawar and the border regions between Pakistan and Afghanistan. This was all very well when the nasty old Soviets were running around in Afghanistan. In those days, turban-clad figures ready to do or die for Islam (as long as they killed commies) were positively encouraged by just about everybody. But the Soviets left Afghanistan over a decade ago. The muj haven't quite got round to leaving yet.

***Harakat-ul-Mujahideen***
(See India chapter.)

## Muttahida Quami Movement (MQM)

These guys were known as the Mohajir National Movement until the name change in 1997, but the initials and motivation remain more or less the same. The Mohajirs are the descendants of Urdu-speaking Muslim immigrants from India who arrived in the Karachi area after the partition between Pakistan and India in 1947.

The MQM are the major stirrers of the simmering pot that is Karachi. In the grand tradition of militant groups the world over, their loathing for other groups claiming to represent the same cause far exceeds any objection to their perceived oppressors. The MQM's principal foes are the people now trading as the Mohajir Quami Movement, who split from what is now the Muttahida Quami Movement in 1991, for reasons that no sane person could care less about. The body count in the scrapping between the two factions regularly comes to dozens every week. Oddly, this seems to get far less press than a far-less-deadly war in Israel.

In April 2002, two Muttahida Quami Movement leaders, Mustafa Kamal Rizvi and Dr. Nishat Mallick, were assassinated in Karachi. The Muttahida Quami Movement called a general strike in protest, and a spate of bomb blasts followed, which both MQMs blamed on each other. The Muttahida Quami Movement is led by Altaf Hussein, who skipped Karachi for London in the early 1990s.

*Muttahida Quami Movement*
NINE ZERO
494/8 Azizabad, Federal B. Area
Karachi, Pakistan
Tel.: (92) 21 631 3690
Fax: (92) 21 632 9955
http://www.mqm.com

*Muttahida Quami Movement*
First Floor, 54–58 Elizabeth House
High Street, Edgware
Middlesex HA8 7EJ, UK
Tel.: (44) 20 8905 7300
Fax: (44) 20 8952 9282
mqm@mqm.org

*MQM USA Central Office*
6355 N. Claremont Avenue #203
Chicago, IL 60659
Tel.: (773) 381-0090
Fax: (773) 381-4690
mqmchicago@aol.com

*MQM New York Office*
63–58, Grand Central Parkway
Forest Hills, NY 11375
Tel.: (718) 533-8890
Fax: (718) 205-8900
mqmnewyork@mailcity.com

*MQM Canada Office*
Shoppers World P.O.
3003 Danforth Avenue
P.O. Box 93681
Toronto, Ontario M4C 5R5
Canada
Tel.: (416) 376-3860
Fax: (905) 848-2949
mqmtoronto@usa.net

## Mohajir Quami Movement (MQM)

Previously known as MQM-Haqiqi, or "The Real MQM," to distinguish themselves from their ethnic brethren and political rivals in the other MQM. Led by Afaq Ahmed, this MQM, or MQM-Haqiqi, or "The Real MQM," or the I Can't Believe It's Not MQM, or whatever you want to call them, got in a huff with the other MQM in 1991. The ISI then had the splendid idea of giving this exciting new splinter group a whole bunch of guns, so that they might act as a counterbalance to the original MQM, and the body count has been ticking steadily upward ever since. It's not just for religious reasons that the ISI would be bad people to call if you needed someone to run a booze-up in a brewery.

## The "Afghans"

There are around three million "Afghan" refugees in Pakistan, most living in squalid mud-walled refugee camps outside of Peshawar and Quetta. Many others live in UNHCR tents in small mountainous villages and deserts. They're not popular in Pakistan, especially in the northwest, where they're routinely blamed (and not always without reason) for drug- and gun-related crimes. Their numbers may start dwindling as Afghanistan flirts with civilization.

http://www.hrw.org/campaigns/afghanistan/refugees-facts.htm

## Other Islamic Groups

If you've got a Koran, some guns, and a grievance, there's nowhere you're more likely to meet like-minded folk than in Pakistan. In 2002, President Musharaff formally banned a bunch of self-appointed battalions of the army of the prophet, including Sunni Muslim fruitcakes the Sipah-e-Sahaba, Shi'a Muslim nutters the Tehrik-e-Jafria, and Wahhabist headcases the Tanzeem-e-Nifaz-e-Shariat-e-Mohammadi. There's plenty more where they came from, of course, including the Tanzeem ul-Fuqra (the group that *Wall Street Journal* reporter Daniel Pearl was attempting to interview when he was kidnapped and murdered in Karachi in 2002)

> **I**f you've got a Koran, some guns, and a grievance, there's nowhere you're more likely to meet like-minded folk than in Pakistan.

and newcomers al-Qanoon, who claimed the bombing of the U.S. consulate in Karachi in June 2002. Sectarian violence kills hundreds in Pakistan every year.

## Kashmir

Yes, it's a place, not a player, but much of Pakistan's angst is directly focused on Kashmir from which springs three major players: Harakut ul-Mujahideen (HUM), the Islamic Holy Warriors, aka Harakut-ul-Ansar or Johnny Walker's group. HUM began in the mid-'80s and recruits, trains, and sends muj into Kashmir to pick on Indian troops. In 2000, the bearded ones who were right of right split off to start Jaish-e-Muhammad, or the Army of Muhammad. This group of non-Kashmiris is run by cleric Maulana Masood Ashar. The Lashkar-e-Taiba, or the Army of the Pure, has been around since 1993 and is the military wing of Markaz-ad-Dawa-wal-Irshad, a bosom buddy of the dearly departed Taliban.

http://travel.state.gov/pakistan_warning.html

# Getting In ——————————————————

Passport and visa are required. The visa must be obtained from a Pakistani embassy or consulate before arrival. Tourist visas are around $45 or the equivalent and are generally issued without too much hassle. Business visas require a letter from a sponsoring organization in Pakistan. Journalist visas are usually issued after some moderately irritating questioning at the embassy—you'll also have to sign a declaration that you won't photograph sensitive installations and that you have no problem with some interfering stooge from the Ministry of

**PAKISTAN**

Information annoying the crap out of you the whole time you're there (or words to that effect, anyway).

Vaccinations and certificates are required for people arriving from areas infected by cholera, smallpox, or yellow fever. People wanting to stay in Pakistan more than a year will also have to prove themselves free of HIV infection.

Most visitors to Pakistan arrive by air. There are international airports at Islamabad, Karachi, and Lahore—all of them are basically lunatic asylums with runways. You can also enter from Afghanistan via the Khyber Pass, or from China via the efficient but weather-sensitive Karakoram Highway—the road is open from May 1 to November 30. Buses and trains also travel between Quetta in Pakistan and Taftan and Zahidan in Iran. Coming in from India is by train (Lahore-Wagha) or a four-hour bus ride (Lahore-Amritsar), but check ahead—the India-Pakistan border is infamous for sudden closures. If the train is running, a first-class seat from Delhi to Lahore costs around $10.

**Embassy of Pakistan**
2315 Massachusetts Avenue, NW
Washington, DC 20008
Tel.: (202) 939-6200
Fax: (202) 387-0484
http://www.pakistan-embassy.com

**Consulate of Pakistan**
12 East 65th Street
New York, NY 10021
Tel.: (212) 879-5800

**Consulate of Pakistan**
10850 Wilshire Boulevard, Suite 1100
Los Angeles, CA 90024
Tel.: (310) 441-5114

**High Commission of Pakistan**
35–36 Lowndes Square
London SW1X 9JN, UK
Tel.: (44) 20 7664 9200
Fax: (44) 20 7664 9224
informationdivision@highcommission-uk.
  gov.pk

**High Commission of Pakistan**
151 Slater Street
Burnside Building, Suite 608
Ottawa, Ontario K1P 5H3
Canada
Tel.: (613) 238-7881
Fax: (613) 238-7296
hcpak@pakistan.ca
http://www.geocities.com/pakdiplomat

**Consulate of Pakistan**
5734 Yonge Street, Suite 600
Toronto, Ontario M2M 4E7
Canada
Tel.: (416) 250-1255
Fax: (416) 250-1321
cgpakt@pakistan.ca

**Consulate of Pakistan**
3241 Peel Street
Montreal, Quebec H3A 1W7
Canada
Tel.: (514) 845-2297
Fax: (514) 845-1354
cgpakm@pakistan.ca

# Getting Around

Travel inside Pakistan is subject to weather, regional idiosyncrasies, and plain luck—or, Pakistan being what it is, the desires of the big guy upstairs. You'll get used to hearing the word *Inshallah* ("If God wills it"), whether you're on a plane approaching a runway at the kind of angle that makes you wonder if the pilot is the same guy who was flying the plane when you took off, or in a motorized rickshaw that is screaming toward the gap between an oncoming bus and a herd of goats. The good news is that traveling around Pakistan is pretty cheap.

Most visitors end up going by road, which is what you could call "an experience," if you survive it. The World Bank gave Pakistan millions to upgrade its highways, but no one was taught to drive. The visitor with no experience of subcontinental traffic is in for a shock—in the civilized world, they charge people money to watch stuff like this and call it Demolition Derby. In the cities, yellow taxis are cheap and should be hired round-trip, since they tend to gravitate to hotels and are hard to find elsewhere. Wildly decorated buses are cheaper, but remember they expect you to jump on (and off) while they are moving. Don't forget that the seats by the driver are for women, and don't be shy about yelling before your stop.

Transit between cities in minivans or open-sided buses costs next to nothing, and that's about all it is worth. You might want to hire your own yammering driver and death-trap car. Hotels and tourist information centers should be able to point you in the right direction. Rates are around $20 a day, not including petrol, depending on where you're going, for how long, and what sort of car you want.

There is moderately less of a chance of ending up smeared across the pavement like jam across bread if you go by rail—the downside is that most of Pakistan's trains proceed at the pace of an elderly and footsore mule carrying a grand piano. You'll have a choice between second-, economy-, first-, and air-conditioned classes. Go for the air-con class—it won't cost much; you'll stand a better chance of meeting English-speaking Pakistanis; and all the other classes are hell on wheels.

But if you want to avoid the mind-numbing terror of Pakistan's roads and the bottom-numbing torpor of Pakistan's railways, there's an aerial option. (Readers should probably imagine an evil chuckle at this point.) Regional airlines in the north have to fly below and between some of the world's tallest mountaintops, and flights, particularly to the northern areas, are often disrupted due to weather conditions. Dust, high winds, turbulence, downdrafts and updrafts, and the

> **T**here is moderately less of a chance of ending up smeared across the pavement like jam across bread if you go by rail—the downside is that most of Pakistan's trains proceed at the pace of an elderly and footsore mule carrying a grand piano.

extra maintenance required to keep planes airborne may be the reasons why the landing announcement is a Muslim prayer: "Ladies and gentlemen, Inshallah (God willing), we will shortly be landing." Don't be surprised to find other passengers—or even yourself—praying fervently on rough flights.

Domestic air tickets are, at least, laughably cheap—you can fly pretty much anywhere within Pakistan for less than $80. Before you fork out, though, you might consider that the national carrier, Pakistan International Airlines, is the inspiration for a parlor game popular with frequent flyers. The PIA Game, as it is known, is played by inventing as many appropriate explanations for the initials as you can. Here are some of *DP*'s favorites:

Pilot Is Asleep
Parachute Is Advisable
Plane Isn't Airworthy
Postponement, Inconvenience, Aggravation
Perhaps I'll Arrive
Panic In Airport
Please Inform Allah

http://www.tourism.gov.pk/car_rental.html

**Pakistan International Airlines**
http://www.piac.com.pk

## Trekking

Since many of the major historical sites have been pounded to rubble by invading armies, and the vast deserts to the south do not inspire too many nature photographers, Pakistan realizes that most of its tourism is related to its spectacular northern mountain scenery. You will find this area of Pakistani tourism well run and efficient. In a country where you would have a hard time finding a decent motor-coach tour, you can climb a major mountain with great ease (or at least in making the preparations). To facilitate understanding and access, tourism officials define *trekking* as walking anywhere below 6,000 meters (travel above that point is classified as mountaineering and requires a separate permit), and have divided the country into open, restricted, and closed zones for trekkers. Open and closed zones are exactly that, and restricted zones are accessible only with a permit and a licensed guide. All this can be organized by the tour company you book with.

http://www.tourism.gov.pk/trekking_in_pakistan.html

## Climbing

Of the 100 highest mountains in the world, 33 are either in Pakistan or in the parts of Kashmir that Pakistan claims. Among these are five peaks over 8,000 meters, including the world's second highest, the 8,611-meter K2. There are also hundreds of peaks that have never been climbed by anyone. To climb anything over 6,000 meters in Pakistan, you must have a permit from the Ministry of Tourism, which will be processed in 24 hours or 14 days, depending on whether the mountain you want to climb is classed as "open" or "restricted." Needless to say, none of this is cheap. A permit for a party of 5 for K2 costs $12,000, with another $3,000 for each additional climber.

**Mountaineering and Expeditions Department**
Ministry of Minorities, Culture, Sports, Tourism, and Youth Affairs
Pakistan Sports Complex
Shahrah-e-Kashmir, near Aabpara
Islamabad, Pakistan
Tel.: (92) 51 920 3509
Fax: (92) 51 920 2347
http://www.tourism.gov.pk/mountaineering.html

# Getting Out

Leaving Pakistan can be a bit like trying to dump someone who just won't let go—difficult to accomplish without a lot of determination and screaming. (That said, how much easier would life be if inconvenient exes could be bought off with 20 bucks?) If you've stayed in Pakistan longer than 30 days, you'll need an exit visa, which you should apply for before you leave (you'll need to get it validated at a police station prior to departure).

The airports, as previously noted, are hopeless—you'll have to negotiate your way to departures through swarms of pestering porters—a huge throng of them gather outside subcontinental airports for no discernible reason at all—and then you may need to buy your way past the customs guards and check-in staff. The most common wheezes for airport staff trying to bump up their pay packet are to claim that you need to pay "export duty" on some item or other that you've bought, or to tell you that you've been bumped off your flight for failing to confirm your book in triplicate six years earlier. It's probably best just to cough up for the customs officers—they have an almost limitless power to ruin your trip—but *DP* has found that baksheesh-seeking check-in staff can be prodded into doing their jobs by bellowing, in a voice loud enough to be heard at the end of the runway, that you're not going to bribe this idiot to do the job he's supposed to do.

If you are carrying anything that can be interpreted as being an antiquity, you are in trouble again. You'll need an export permit for rugs, and don't think for a moment that the nifty pen-gun you bought in Darra Adam Khel is not going to be spotted and confiscated. If you're even thinking of bringing some smoking green back with you, have a long and hard think about what Pakistani jails must be like—Karachi, Lahore, and Islamabad airports are patrolled by sniffer dogs who get plenty of practice rumbling idiot hippies.

There is a departure tax of between 400 and 600 rupees, if anyone remembers to collect it. Also, make sure you keep all your credit-card receipts—*DP* was surprised, in 1998, to receive a Visa charge for a hotel in Islamabad that was almost enough to buy the place outright. When *DP* queried this, the hotel's receipt proved to have a signature on it that looked like it had been forged by a chimpanzee with rickets.

## Dangerous Places

### Karachi, Hyderabad, and Sindh Province

Some consider Karachi, the dirty, bustling port town and capital of Sindh, the most dangerous city in the world. Robbery and kidnapping are common. Bombings occur at Pakistan government facilities and public utilities. Vehicular hijacking and armed theft are regular occurrences. Persons resisting have very often been shot and killed. Unnecessarily gory reports of murders, bombings, robberies, and assassinations fill the papers every day. Sectarian feuding between majority Sunni and minority Shi'a Muslims, plus internecine squabbling between the rival breeds of MQM (see The Players), kill dozens of people every week. In the first few weeks of 2002, Shi'a doctors became a particular target, with more than a dozen being shot.

In an exciting new development, Karachi has also become the battlefield of choice for extremist Islamic elements infuriated by America's war against al-Qaeda, and Pakistan's cooperation with it. *Wall Street Journal* reporter Daniel Pearl was kidnapped and murdered in Karachi in early 2002. On May 8, 2002, a suicide car-bomb outside Karachi's Sheraton Hotel killed 15 people, including 12 French technicians employed by the Pakistani navy. On June 14, 2002, another suicide car-bomb outside Karachi's U.S. consulate killed 11 and injured dozens more.

> **I**n an exciting new development, Karachi has also become the battlefield of choice for extremist Islamic elements infuriated by America's war against al-Qaeda.

In Hyderabad, there have been recurring outbreaks of ethnic and sectarian violence, which have been characterized by random bombings, shootings, and mass demonstrations. Recent incidents have resulted in several deaths and the unofficial imposition of curfews. There have also been numerous incidents of kidnapping for ransom.

It's hardly less hectic in the countryside. Hundreds of years ago, travelers called Sindh province the Unhappy Valley because of its burning deserts, freezing mountain peaks, dust, lack of water, and a general fear of the predatory tribes. Today, it should perhaps be called the Very Unhappy Valley. Competing groups of Sunnis and Shi'as, Mohajirs, and Sindhis all try their best to lower the population of the other groups. Anyone contemplating travel into the Sindh interior should first contact the American Consulate (see Nuts and Bolts for contact details). Gunmen can be hired from travel groups or on the street (not advised) for about 4,000 rupees a day. You will have to pay for your bodyguard's room and board. Sindh province still has a fairly healthy kidnappings-for-ransom business.

**Government of Sindh**
http://sindh.gov.pk

**Sindh Today**
http://www.sindhtoday.com

**Sindh resource page**
http://www.freesindh.org

**Indus Tribune**
http://www.ibratgroup.com/industribune

**Daily Kawish**
http://kawish.com

## The Northwest Frontier Province (NWFP)/Khyber Pass

An area created in 1901 by the British, who could never figure how to "civilize" the many tribes and clans, the NWFP is still the land of *badal*, or revenge. It is the oldest continuously lawless area in the world. Home to the "wily Pathans," this rugged land of green valleys and snow-capped mountains has never been fully conquered, by Alexander, the Moguls, the Sikhs, the Brits, or even the Russians. It is currently even more tense than usual, due to the fact that it is the obvious refuge for any Taliban or al-Qaeda, up to and including Osama bin Laden, fleeing Afghanistan. Any Westerners in the area who are not obviously journalists are likely to be perceived as spies.

The Northwest Frontier Province has an affinity with Afghanistan in the west and is known for its well-armed populace. It's a place where the local farmers like to guard their crops with antiaircraft guns, with Stinger missiles inside the house for emergencies. Not a big surprise, really, when the "crops" in question happen to be hash and opium.

Peshawar, the largest city and capital of the province, is not quite like the Dodge City with turbans it used to be—weapons are no longer carried or sold openly on the streets, and if you hear gunfire at night, it's more likely to be someone celebrating a wedding than a shoot-out. If you're in town and want to find a decent watering hole, the best (and only) place is the American Club, but you'll need someone to sign you in.

It would be an understatement to say that it is dangerous to travel overland through the tribal areas along the Khyber Pass from Peshawar to the Afghan border. The Northwest Frontier areas are ruled by the Afridi tribes and are not under the control of the Pakistani government or police. There are many deadly tribal feuds over things as important as stolen goats or errant wives, so lightening some dumb foreigner of his vehicle or belongings does not even appear on their list of "things not to do." Car hijackings and the abduction of foreigners are occasionally reported from the tribal areas, but not as often as they once were.

To enter the tribal areas, you'll need a permit from the nearest office of the Home Department—your hotel staff will be able to point you in the right direction—and the department may require that an armed escort accompany the visitor. The local army barracks will provide the guard, who will be either a clueless young private or a half-asleep sergeant clutching a rifle that looks like it's been buried in someone's garden since the Indian Mutiny and who would be less than no help if some bunch of Kalashnikov-wielding hillbillies decided to spoil your day out, but there's no getting around it. You'll be expected to tip your protector a few rupees at journey's end.

**The Frontier Post**
http://www.frontierpost.com.pk

## Islamabad and Rawalpindi

Welcome to the Twin Cities: squeaky-clean Islamabad, the capital of Pakistan, and dirty Rawalpindi are only 10 kilometers and two worlds apart. Islamabad is the showcase city for the embassy folks, and Rawalpindi is where all the real people live. The crime rate in Islamabad is lower than in most parts of Pakistan, but it is on the increase, especially since Pakistan signed on for Dubya's War on Terror. In March 2002, five people were killed in a grenade attack on Islamabad's Protestant International Church. Rawalpindi has experienced some bombings in public areas, such as markets, cinemas, and parks.

**The Pakistan Observer**
http://www.pakobserver.com

**Daily Hot News**
http://www.dailyhotnews.com

## Lahore and Punjab Province

Lahore, Punjab's capital, is placid but famous for rip-offs of tourists in cheap hotels, bogus traveler's checks, and other tourist-related crime. Out in the Punjab hinterland, a low-level sectarian war fizzes and crackles. Shi'a mosques are bombed by Sunnis, and vice versa, while the police lash out at both sides (in May 2002, Riaz Basra, founder of the militant Sunni group Lashkar-e-Jhangvi, was shot dead in a police raid). Punjab's small Christian population has also been on the receiving end of sectarian hatred—in October 2001, 16 Christians were killed in the town of Bahawalpur when Islamic militants opened fire on a church service.

**Government of Punjab**
http://www.punjab.gov.pk

**The Friday Times**
http://www.thefridaytimes.com.pk

## Kashmir

Once upon a time, Kashmir was one of the most popular tourist destinations in the world. Not any more. Instead, Kashmir now takes up a rather large slice of both Pakistan and India's defense budget, with both sides playing artillery volleyball along the 700-kilometer-long Line of Control.

The Kashmir problem originated in 1947, the year of partition between India and Pakistan, when the princes who ran the "princely states" cut a quick deal with mainly Hindu India and screwed their predominately Muslim subjects. The dispute, which caused the 1948 and 1965 wars with India (Pakistan was whipped both times), remains unresolved. The Simla Agreement after the 1971 Pakistan-Bangladesh war adjusted the boundary between the Indian state of Jammu and Kashmir and the Pakistani state of Azad Kashmir. The Muslims in the Indian state of Jammu and Kashmir demand greater autonomy from Hindu India. The separatist elements in the province (see the India chapter for full details) openly receive training and equipment from Pakistan.

India and Pakistan have nearly had a third full-scale war over Kashmir twice in recent years, which, since both now have the happy combination of nuclear weapons and somewhat haphazard command-and-control structures, is tremendous news all around. In 1999, Indian soldiers went back up the Siachen glacier as the snow melted to find that the high ground had been taken by a large number of guerrillas who had infiltrated from Pakistan. In nearly two months of subsequent fighting there were an estimated 3,500 casualties. In early 2002, there was open discussion of the possible consequences of nuclear war after India blamed Pakistan for a series of terrorist attacks in Kashmir and elsewhere in India, including a suicide attack on India's parliament building in Delhi in December 2001.

**Pakistan Government Kashmir Page**
http://www.pak.gov.pk/public/kashmir/kashmir.htm

**Kashmir Times**
http://www.kashmirtimes.com

**Kashmir Observer**
http://www.kashmirobserver.com

**Jammu & Kashmir Knowledge Base**
http://www.jammu-kashmir.com

### Quetta and Balochistan Province

Quetta became a bit of a boomtown in late 2001, when the world's media used it as a launching pad for expeditions into southern Afghanistan. This didn't do much to improve the province—*DP* would be tempted to say that nothing would improve Quetta apart from a series of large explosions, but the locals have been trying that for years, and that hasn't helped either. To make matters even worse, a sizable percentage of the population of southern Afghanistan headed for Quetta when the skies started raining bombs in late 2001—and, needless to say, most of these people weren't terrifically pleased with the United States. There have since been many protests, some of them violent, a few bus bombings, some unexplained rocket attacks, and a bit of a shoot-out at the airport.

Balochistan borders on Iran and Afghanistan and has always been notorious for cross-border smuggling operations—the major drug smugglers run large truck and even camel caravans from Afghanistan to the coast. Those considering travel into the Baloch interior should first notify the province's home secretary, arrange to travel in a group, round up some reliable armed security, limit travel to daylight hours, and see a psychiatrist. Although the Pakistani government tells *DP* that permission from the provincial authorities is required for travel into some interior locations, we can't help but wonder which government folks would be around to check.

**Balochistan Express**
http://www.balochistanexpress.com

**Balochistan Post**
http://www.balochistanpost.com

## Dangerous Things

### Crime

Pakistan is a special place when it comes to crime. There are three levels of crime: The first is the friendly, constant pressure to relieve the unwitting of their possessions. Just as the wind and rain can erode granite mountains, the traveler to Pakistan will find his or her money slowly slipping from him or her. Perhaps this is not a crime, since the victim is consensual, but it nevertheless is not an honest transfer of funds—for weeks after leaving, you'll hear the word "Baksheesh!" echoing in your head like tinnitus after an AC/DC concert.

> **J**ust as the wind and rain can erode granite mountains, the traveler to Pakistan will find his or her money slowly slipping from him or her.

The second level is petty crime: the fingers rummaging through your baggage, the wallet that leaves your pocket, or the camera that disappears from the chair next to you. Everyone will caution you about petty theft. Here, theft is an art, almost a learned skill. These crimes happen to the unwary and unprepared. Lock your zippers, do not leave anything of value in your hotel room, and do not tell people your schedule. The luggage of most airline and bus passengers looks like a Houdini act with locks, rope, sewn-up sacks, and even steel boxes used to keep out curious fingers. Mail must be sent in a sewn-up sack to prevent theft. Naturally, thieves love the many-zippered, unlocked backpacks of foreign trekkers. The best solution is to put your luggage in a canvas or vinyl duffel bag and keep all valuables on your person. Do not carry any money in pockets, and use money belts as well as decoy wallets when traveling. (Decoy wallets are cheap wallets containing old credit cards, pictures and addresses of your worst enemy, and wads of Iraqi dinars.)

The third level is where Pakistan outshines many other areas: The cold, calculated arts of kidnapping, extortion, and robbery. There is little any traveler can do to prevent this crime in certain areas. Any people who have regular schedules, who travel to crowded markets along well-known paths, or who do not have good security are at risk. Check State Department reports and contact the local embassy for the latest horror stories. All large cities have security agencies that can provide advice, drivers, and bodyguards for reasonable daily rates.

*U.S. State Department Consular Information Sheet*
http://travel.state.gov/pakistan.html

## Dacoits

Being a *dacoit* is possibly the most lucrative night job in Pakistan. Many dacoits are professional bandits aligned along tribal lines who hold normal day jobs and then head out into the country for a little extra cash at night. Unlike the greasy thugs of Russia or the gold-toothed banditos of Mexico, dacoits are usually bad guys for hire led by educated or civil-service-level young men. They cannot find employment, so they use their organizing and planning skills to support political parties, back up rebel units, raise operating funds, and expand operations areas.

Despite the genteel background of the leaders, the actions of their members are bloody and crude. Dacoits will stop buses and trains, rob, rape, and murder, and generally create a bloody mess. They also use kidnapping as a way to generate funds and flip the bird to the local government. Expect to be a well-treated but powerless pawn, as the dacoits negotiate with the strapped local government (not your fat, rich, home government) for payment for your release. Your biggest problem may be a heavy-handed (but fiscally efficient) rescue attempt staged by the government on your behalf. Stay out of remote tribal areas or areas known for dacoitry.

http://www.peshawarpolice.gov.pk
http://www.sindhpolice.gov.pk

## Cheap Guns

The border regions of Pakistan are Wild West regions, with most tribal, ethnic, and criminal groups well armed with cheap weapons brought in from Afghanistan or manufactured on demand. There are few tribes that don't possess large arsenals, but all have fierce rivalries with one another. Most urban residents employ *chowkidaars,* or private guards, for protection. If you are not caught in the middle of a firefight, you may be worse off at a wedding or party—in the tribal areas, Pathans have a bad habit of celebrating weddings using their AK-47s as firecrackers and shooting bursts into the air, ignorant of the Newtonian fundamentals of falling bullets.

The famous arms bazaar at Darra Adam Khel is theoretically off-limits to foreigners, but accessible enough with a guide (look for *DP*'s friend Poppa, who usually hangs around outside Green's Hotel, and tell him we said hello). *DP* was the first to tip off journos to Sakahot, 25 miles north of Darra Adam Khel. At the first gun shop, ask the owner to invite the police to escort you, and a little baksheesh will get you a guided tour and a wave out of town. You can't actually buy the guns, but you can fire them. Choose a Chinese- or Russian-made gun to fire since the locally made ones can explode in your face.

http://www.worldpress.org/cover1.htm

## Roads

Despite everything you've read here about dacoits and civil unrest, the greatest potential for injury while traveling through Pakistan is being involved in a car crash or being smacked like a cricket ball when crossing the street. To give pedestrians and other drivers a chance, Pakistanis decorate their vehicles with as many bright and shiny objects as possible—though it is possible that the national fondness for painting lurid murals all over their windshields doesn't help matters (at least, we assume the lurid murals are paint—they might be pedestrians). If you do happen to take a bus around the country, *DP* advises you to keep your eyes closed, unless you really are after a thrill a minute.

> **I**f you do happen to take a bus around the country, *DP* advises you to keep your eyes closed, unless you really are after a thrill a minute.

http://www.pakroadusers.com

## Polo

One of Pakistan's most famous exports (besides drugs and terrorists) is polo. Afghans and Pakistanis love polo, a violent-spirited game that is as close to horse-mounted warfare as one can get. The British picked it up while stationed here and it quickly became the upper-class macho sport of Britain. You can still see polo games played by soldiers, cops, and just regular folks in Chitral and Gilgit. Polo is a sort of PG-rated version of the Afghan game buzkashi—the difference being that in polo the game is played with a ball, not the headless body of a calf.

http://www.sports.gov.pk/html/polo.html

# Getting Sick _____

There are good medical facilities in all major towns in Pakistan. You may need them after your first fly-blown kabobfest. Pakistan may not be the dirtiest place in the world, but it can make some Siberian mining towns look positively pristine. Expect to get the runs, unless you have a PVC gastrointestinal tract. Some folks go gaga over the spicy food, and other folks end up crouched over a grubby pit toilet, learning the hard way that fiery spices and peppers burn as bad going out as they do going down. Take the normal precautions you would take in any third-world country and carry medicine for diarrhea.

Immunizations against typhoid, polio, and meningitis are recommended, as are prophylactic antimalarial drugs—malaria is present throughout Pakistan at altitudes below 2,000 meters. Even if you are heading straight for the mountains, you can still get bitten in the airport lounge in Karachi. Hepatitis and tetanus are further health risks, as are amoebic dysentery and worms. Bilharzia (schistosomiasis) and elephantiasis (filariasis) are also endemic diseases, although not widespread. Follow the usual precautions for countries with poor sanitation. Military hospitals, frequently open to fee-paying local civilians and foreigners, often provide the best facilities.

## Nuts and Bolts

With a population of 145 million, Pakistan is the largest Muslim country in the world—97 percent of its population is Muslim, of which 77 percent are Sunnis and 20 percent Shi'a. There are also tiny Hindu and Christian minorities. The principal ethnic group is Punjabi (66 percent), with significant minorities of Sindhis (13 percent), Pakhtuns (11 percent), Mohajirs (8 percent), and Balochis (2 percent). The official language is English, and while it is widely spoken, day-to-day Pakistani life is conducted in Urdu, Punjabi, Pashto, Sindhi, Saraiki, and Balochi. Approximately half of Pakistani men and two-thirds of women cannot read or write.

Pakistan is a land of hard extremes. The climate is generally arid and very hot (very, very hot), except in the northern mountains, where the summers are hot and winters are very cold (very, very cold). In general, the weather is at its least beastly between October and February. During the rest of the year, the climate is like a restaurant kitchen.

The currency is the rupee; at the time of writing, a dollar would buy about 60 of these. The rupee is best purchased at a bank, not at your hotel, and definitely not from money changers—the benefits are negligible, and many will try to foist dirty and faded notes on you, which nobody else will take. Also, you won't get a receipt, and you will need to carry around the paperwork you get when you swap dollars for rupees, in case of tedious questions from bribe-seeking customs officers when you try to leave. Credit cards are worthless outside the major cities, but AMEX has offices in Islamabad, Rawalpindi, Lahore, and Karachi.

"Baksheesh" is the Pakistani version of tipping, but it applies to anyone who helps you out, not just taxi drivers and waiters. When people help you, it's normal and expected that you will drop a few rupees in their palm. If you're buying anything significant, haggle, haggle, and haggle. Don't be polite about it—feel free to start by offering 10 percent of the first price you're quoted. Having a local guide do your haggling for you (shopping, bus, hotel, air fares, taxis, bribes, souvenirs) can easily save you his fee. You can bring in as much foreign currency as you want, but it must be declared upon arrival.

Electricity is 220V/50Hz. The electrical system can only be described as deadly, and shorts and blowouts are common. Be careful plugging in appliances around wet areas. Many water heaters are electric. Do not turn lights or appliances off with your bare feet or while in the shower.

Normal office hours from Saturday to Wednesday are from 9:00 AM to 2:00 PM, with at least one hour for lunch. Offices close earlier on Thursdays, usually at lunchtime. Friday is the weekly Muslim holiday. Banks are open from 9:00 AM to 1:30 PM from Saturday to Wednesday, and until 11:00 AM on Thursday. If you're trying to accomplish anything involving any sort of Pakistani institution or bureaucracy, allow way more time than you think you could possibly need—nothing, aside from driving, gets done quickly in Pakistan, and losing your temper won't help.

Alcohol is illegal in Pakistan, but you can order hard liquor and beer by the bottle through room service at the swank hotels in the large cities or over the bar in private members' clubs. You must first fill out a form that declares that you are not a Muslim and that you need it for medical purposes, and you will need to pay a small fee (about a dollar). Don't try taking your own booze in—it is illegal.

**U.S. Embassy**
Diplomatic Enclave
Ramna 5
Islamabad, Pakistan
Tel.: (92) 51 208 0000
Fax: (92) 51 227 6427
http://usembassy.state.gov/islamabad

**U.S. Consulate, Karachi**
8 Abdullah Haroon Road
Karachi, Pakistan
Tel.: (92) 21 568 5170
Fax: (92) 21 568 3089
http://usembassy.state.gov/karachi

**U.S. Consulate, Lahore**
50 Empress Road
Lahore, Pakistan
Tel.: (92) 42 636 5530

Fax: (92) 42 636 5177
http://usembassy.state.gov/lahore

**U.S. Consulate, Peshawar**
11 Hospital Road
Peshawar, Pakistan
Tel.: (92) 91 279 801
Fax: (92) 91 276 712

**British High Commission, Islamabad**
Diplomatic Enclave
Ramna 5
P.O. Box 1122
Islamabad, Pakistan
Tel.: (92) 51 220 6071
Fax: (92) 51 282 3439
bhcmedia@isb.comsats.net.pk
http://britainonline.org.pk

**British Deputy High Commission, Karachi**
Shahrah-e-Iran
Clifton
Karachi 75600, Pakistan
Tel.: (92) 21 587 2431
Fax: (92) 21 587 4014
bdhc@crestarnet.net

**Canadian High Commission, Islamabad**
Diplomatic Enclave
Sector G5
Islamabad, Pakistan
Tel.: (92) 51 227 9100
Fax: (92) 51 227 9110

**Canadian High Commission, Karachi**
Beach Luxury Hotel, 3rd Floor
Moulvi Tamiz Uddin Khan Road
Karachi 74000, Pakistan
Tel.: (92) 21 561 0685
Fax: (92) 21 561 0673
honcon@khi.comsats.net.pk

**Canadian High Commission, Lahore**
PAAF Building, 5th Floor
7-D, Kashmir Egerton Road
Lahore, Pakistan
Tel:: (92) 42 636 6230
Fax: (92) 42 636 5086
honcon@lhr.comsats.net.pk

## Dangerous Days

| | |
|---|---|
| **9/13/02** | 9/11 planner Ramzi bin al-Shibh is arrested in Karachi. |
| **6/14/02** | Suicide car bomb outside U.S. consulate in Karachi kills 11 and injures dozens. |
| **6/7/02** | Pakistani jets shoot down an unmanned Indian spy aircraft near Raja Jang, in Pakistani Punjab. |
| **5/27/02** | Musharaff promises to respond "with full force" if Pakistan is attacked by India. |
| **5/24/02** | Pakistan begins a series of tests of mid-range ballistic missiles. |
| **5/18/02** | Pakistan's High Commissioner in India is expelled. |
| **5/7/02** | Suicide car bomb near the Sheraton Hotel in Karachi kills 15, including 12 French nationals. |
| **4/30/02** | General Musharaff's presidency confirmed for another five years in referendum. |
| **3/16/02** | Grenade attack on Protestant church in Islamabad kills five. |
| **2/21/02** | Kidnapped *Wall Street Journal* reporter Daniel Pearl is confirmed dead. |
| **12/01** | Pakistan and India both move troops and missiles to border as tensions over Kashmir grow. |
| **10/01** | India fires on Pakistani positions along the line of control in Kashmir. |
| **10/12/99** | General Pervez Musharraf overthrows Prime Minister Nawaz Sharif. |

PAKISTAN

| | |
|---|---|
| **4/14/99** | Pakistan responds to Indian missile test by test-firing its Ghauri II long-range missile. |
| **4/11/99** | India test-fires long-range version of its nuclear-capable Agni missile. |
| **11/5/98** | Fresh attempts at negotiations in New Dehli amid tense military standoff on Kashmir's Siachen glacier, the world's highest battlefield. |
| **6/12/98** | Pakistan and India invite each other for talks, but fail to agree on agenda. |
| **5/28/98** | Pakistan says it has conducted five nuclear tests in response to India's tests weeks before. |
| **4/6/98** | Pakistan tests long-range (1,500 km) Ghauri missile. |
| **9/19/96** | Benazir Bhutto's brother, Murtaza Bhutto, killed in a shoot-out with police in Karachi. |
| **5/11/96** | Benazir Bhutto sacked as prime minister, again on charges of corruption and incompetence. |
| **10/93** | Benazir Bhutto re-elected prime minister. |
| **2/6/92** | Pakistan declares capability to build nuclear bomb, but vows not to build the bomb. |
| **1991** | Islamic Sharia law formally incorporated into Pakistan's legal code by Prime Minister Nawaz Sharif. |
| **8/6/90** | Benazir Bhutto sacked as prime minister on charges of corruption and incompetence. |
| **11/88** | Benazir Bhutto elected prime minister. |
| **8/5/88** | Arif Hussain al-Hussaini, a leading Shiite religious and political leader in Pakistan, is shot to death in Peshawar. |
| **7/17/88** | An airplane carrying President Zia Ul-Haq and U.S. Ambassador Arnold Raphel crashes, killing everyone aboard. |
| **9/5/86** | Nineteen people, including two Americans, are killed in an abortive hijacking of Pan Am Flight 73 by four Palestinian gunmen at Karachi Airport. |
| **4/10/86** | Daughter of former President Bhutto, Benazir Bhutto, returns from exile in Europe. |
| **7/18/85** | Shahnawaz Bhutto, son of executed President Zulfikar Bhutto and younger brother of Pakistani People's Party leader Benazir Bhutto, dies in mysterious circumstances in France. |
| **1985** | Martial law lifted, along with a ban on political parties. |
| **3/2/81** | AZO guerillas hijack a PIA airliner to Kabul. One passenger is killed. |

PAKISTAN

| | |
|---|---|
| 4/4/79 | Former President Bhutto executed on the orders of President Zia. Bhutto's sons, Shahnawaz and Murtaza, form a resistance organization called al-Zulfikar (AZO). |
| 7/5/77 | Army Chief of Staff General Mohammad Zia ul-Haq seizes power in a military coup, deposing Zulfikar Ali Bhutto and reimposing martial law. |
| 8/14/73 | New constitution takes effect. Zulfikar Ali Bhutto becomes prime minister. |
| 12/20/71 | General Yahya Khan resigns presidency and hands it over to Zulfikar Ali Bhutto. |
| 1971 | East Pakistan, now known as Bangladesh, attempts to secede from Pakistan. Civil war follows, with India intervening in support of East Pakistan. |
| 3/25/69 | General Ayub Khan hands over power to General Yahya Khan. Martial law reimposed. |
| 1965 | Second war with India over Kashmir. |
| 6/8/62 | Martial law, imposed in 1958, is lifted and the national assembly convenes. |
| 3/23/62 | A new constitution is promulgated by President Ayub Khan. |
| 10/27/58 | President Mirza is ousted by General Ayub Khan, who declares himself president. |
| 10/7/58 | President Iskander Mirza, supported by senior military officers, imposes martial law. |
| 3/23/56 | The national assembly adopts a new constitution that rejects Pakistan's status as a dominion and becomes an "Islamic Republic" within the commonwealth. Also known as Pakistan Day. |
| 10/16/51 | Pakistan's first prime minister, Liaquat Ali Khan, is assassinated in Rawalpindi. |
| 1948 | First war with India over Kashmir. |
| 8/14/47 | Independence Day. Pakistan becomes a self-governing dominion within the British Commonwealth. |
| 1947 | Foundation of Pakistan. Hundreds of thousands are killed in sectarian fighting as India is partitioned between its Hindu and Muslim populations. |

## ★ ★ ★

# THE PHILIPPINES

## A Marriage of Inconvenience

Filipinos seem to have both accepted and rejected the cultures and influences that have swept through their country. These 80 million (and growing by 1.7 million a year), laid-back Malays can somehow embrace and combine rabid fundamentalism, sex tourism, fanatic Roman Catholicism, Spanish machismo, Russian communism, Asian traffic, American jeepneys, and bad '80s lounge music, and still survive the occasional devastating natural catastrophe with a smile and a shrug. The first-time visitor to these 7,000 islands would find it hard to believe that this is also an island of pirates, kidnappers, assassins, and rebels, as well as Jolly Bee, Mickey D, and a rebel group called the RPM-P/RPA/ABB (some bad boys who seriously need a name make-over).

In the '50s, the Philippines had the strongest economy in Southeast Asia, if not all of Asia, surpassing even the economies of South Korea, Japan, Thailand, and Malaysia. Today, however, nearly half of all

827

Filipinos live on or below the poverty line. The Philippines is rapidly spiraling from being an enterprising mini-America to being a third-world country. Accordingly, there are problems in the land of the crescent and the cross. The biggest headache (if you ignore the Filipinos' love for Las Vegas–style lounge music and chrome jitneys) is the desire of the Moros to be separate from the North. But it's not a real war. It's more like a forced marriage of inconvenience. The current Muslim uprising in the Philippines has been going on for a quarter of a century and has killed more than 120,000 people.

The Muslim separatists of Mindanao have been around for a while. It all started when the King of Spain had a cow when his vanguard found Muslims (or Moors, as in Moros) in the Far East just a few years after they had finally expelled the Umayaids from Granada. The Spanish tried for 300 years to extinguish the flame of Allah; they couldn't— and neither could the Americans during their 50-year rule of the islands; and nor could the Japanese during their occupation of the country during World War II. Although various Philippine governments have negotiated with the principal Muslim extremist group— the Moro National Liberation Front (MNLF)—with varying degrees of success, an even nastier, deadlier faction emerged: the Moro Islamic Liberation Front (MILF).

The Philippine military claims the MILF is only about 60,000 poorly trained guerrillas, yet has stationed most of the government's 115,000-soldier army on Mindanao to contain the separatists. The MILF itself claims 120,000 troops, but the number is closer to 40,000 combatants, only about a third of whom are on "active duty" at any given time. Even at that number, the MILF is far stronger than the communist New People's Army (NPA) of the mid-'80s. And, just to give the movement a little international flavor and foreign intrigue, as many as 1,000 MILF members were sent to fight in Afghanistan in the 1980s.

The government could easily eradicate the MILF or the NPA, but they choose not to. It is partly because the groups distract the people's attention from the lousy economy and also because the government gets so much damn military aid to fight the nonwar.

Muslims comprise only about 5 percent of the population: There are 4 million Muslims in the Philippines, which is 83 percent Catholic, and the only Christian state in Southeast Asia. Because of active settlement by Christians in Mindanao, the Moros are greatly outnumbered by government supporters. The government manages to keep most of its 115,000 troops in Mindanao. Since the 1987 constitution was ratified, any secession or autonomy move must be approved by a plebiscite, and both Moro groups would lose handily on Mindanao. So, it looks like the south will be jihadland for a while longer.

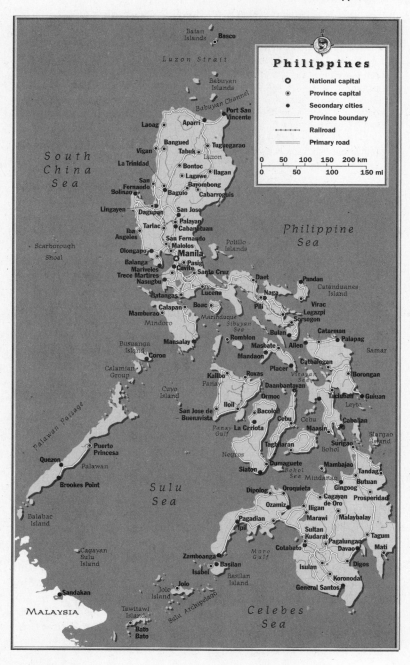

Batan
Islands
Basco

*Luzon Strait*

Babuyan
Islands

*Babuyan Channel*

Port San
Vincente

Laoag
Aparri

Bangued
Vigan      Tabuk      Tuguegarao
La Trinidad           *Luzon*
Bontoc      Ilagan
Lagawe
San        Bayombong
Fernando    Baguio    Cabarroguis
Bolinao

Lingayen    Dagupan    San Jose
Palayan
Iba      Tarlac    Cabanatuan
Angeles    San Fernando
Malolos
Olongapo                Polillo
Balanga            **Manila**    Islands
Mariveles          Pasig
Trece Martires    Cavite
Nasugbu          Santa Cruz    Daet      Pandan
Batangas                        Naga      Catanduanes
Calapan    Lucena            Pili      Virac  Island
Mamburao    Boac          Legazpi
*Mindoro*    *Marinduque*    Sorsogon
                *Sibuyan    Bulan
                 Sea*    Allen    Catarman
Mansalay        Romblon                Palapag
Busuanga        Masbate    Aillen
Island    Coron    Mandaon            Catbalogan    *Samar*
Calamian                Placer    *Virayan
Group                            Sea*    Borongan
        *Cuyo*    Kalibo    Roxas
        *Island*    *Panay*    Daanbantayan    Tacloban  Guiuan
                            Ormoc    *Leyte*
    San Jose de    Iloilo    Bacolod
    Buenavista            Cebu    Cebu    Cabalian
                *Panay*    La Carlota        Maasin
Puerto          *Gulf*            Tagbilaran    *Bohol*    *Siargao
Princesa                                        Island*
Quezon                  *Negros*    Dumaguete        Surigao    Tandag
                            Siaton    Mambajao
Brookes Point                            *Bohol    Butuan
                                        Sea*  *Mindanao*  Gingoog
        Dipolog    Oroquieta            Prosperidad
                Ozamiz    Cagayan
                    Iligan    de Oro
Balabac                Pagadian    Marawi    Malaybalay
Island                Ipil    Sultan
                        Kudarat    Pagalungan    Tagum
Cagayan                Cotabato    Davao    Mati
Sulu
Island            Zamboanga        Isulan    Digos
                Isabel            Koronodal
        Jolo    Basilan    *Basilan    General Santos
Sandakan  Jolo        *Island*
        *Island*
        *Sulu Archipelago*
**MALAYSIA**    Tawitawi
        Island        *Celebes
        Bato            Sea*
        Bato

*South
China
Sea*

Scarborough
Shoal

*Philippine
Sea*

*Palawan Passage*

Palawan

*Sulu
Sea*

*Moro
Gulf*

**THE PHILIPPINES**

## WAR? HELL, IT'S JUST NEW YEAR'S EVE!

New Year's Eve is a dangerous time in the jungles of Mindanao. Because of the high number of injuries caused by "happy" fire on New Year's, the MILF has decided to crack down on the festivities. Ghazali Jaafar, deputy chairman of the MILF, said the movement's fighters have been warned they will be punished for firing their weapons to commemorate the New Year. "For every bullet fired, the penalty would be equivalent to planting at least 20 banana plants," Jaafar said. The government retaliated by ordering their soldiers not to fire their weapons during New Year celebrations or they will be dismissed.

Mindanao is one of the more tense places that *DP* has visited. Checkpoint after checkpoint was manned by loosely identified gun-carrying men. There is always some form of peace treaty in place, and there is always some sort of fighting.

It seems that despite, or because of, the number of armed men, violent crime and kidnapping (or "stealing people," as it is called here) is the biggest cause for fear.

The fear meter really gets turned up when you enter the Sulu Sea. Foreigners are registered (but not offered any protection) as they leave airports, and locals will go out of their way to warn you of the crime here. Our driver packed a .45 in his cowboy boot even when he entered a heavily armed bank, "for his personal protection." Yeehaa.

The real no-go parts of the Philippines are Basilan and Jolo, where the rapidly dwindling tweaker-boys' club of Abu Sayyaf slowly is being picked off by Uncle Sam's new Boy Scouts.

Up north in the provinces, you are bound to hear of the communist New People's Army. This consists of the remnants of the Huk rebellion, who fought with the Americans against the Japanese. We thanked them by hunting them down and creating an army of 25,000 in 1987. The NPA is down to about 5,000 now, and depending on which way the economy goes, the army will shrink or grow as angered and impoverished youths take to the hills. The New People's Army is a spent force which sporadically makes the headlines these days with an assassination or kidnapping or two.

Don't be fooled by the modern veneer of the Philippines. It is a have and have-not country where outsiders are spared much of the brutality and injustice. Muslim and communist separatists have been battling various Manila governments for nearly 30 years (okay, so the Muslims have been fighting for six centuries), resulting in more than 10,000 firefights between insurgents and government troops during that time. More than 120,000 people have been killed.

## THE HOURS SUCK, BUT THINK OF THE ACCRUED HOLIDAYS

Hiro Onada makes the Energizer Bunny look like a piker. Second Lieutenant Onada fought World War II for 30 years. Nobody bothered to tell him that Japan had surrendered in 1945, and he kept hanging on until 1974. The 73-year-old Onada hid out on the island of Lubang in the Philippines, living off wild animals and plants. A Japanese journalist found Onada in 1952, but Onada thought the journalist was a U.S. spy. In a way, you can't blame him, because he could see the activity at Subic Bay and the constant U.S. military activity in the area, which made him believe that the war raged on. Onada's orders were to stay in Lubang if the Americans captured it and to wage a guerrilla campaign. His only companion, Private Kinshinchi Kozuka, was shot by Philippine police after 19 years on the island.

Onada was finally convinced to give up his fight when Norio Suzuki, a Japanese adventurer, conveyed a direct order from his commander to surrender. He now teaches at an outdoor survival school in the Fukushima prefecture of Japan.

The government has kept a relative lid on the extremist problem—in the interest of promoting tourism—until the mid-'90s discovery of an al-Qaeda-linked terrorist plot to kill the Pope and blow up numerous airliners simultaneously. When American Special Forces landed to help fight Abu Sayyaf, the Americans found themselves playing Wyatt Earp against a ragtag group of bad-boy islanders. For now, it's déjà vu time for Uncle Sam as we find ourselves once again fighting drug-crazed Moros in the Sulu Seas.

## The Scoop ─────────────────────────

America's only former colony is a happy, poor, shopworn place with commies in the north (and south) and Muslims fighting in the south (and north). Crime in the south is more of a problem than getting caught in the middle of a jihad. The north and center are not really dangerous, and when your kidnappers pose you for your photo, they will at least smile.

http://www.abs-cbnnews.com
http://www.manilatimes.net
http://www.philstar.com
http://www.sunstar.com.ph

## The Players ————————————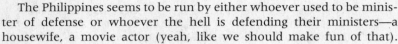

### The Government

The Philippines seems to be run by either whoever used to be minister of defense or whoever the hell is defending their ministers—a housewife, a movie actor (yeah, like we should make fun of that). Erap, the Wayne Newton clone, has been replaced by a much cuter and hopefully less corrupt president, Gloria Macapagal-Arroyo. She is the daughter of a former president, a former classmate of Bill Clinton, and a standing member (along with Omar Bongo and Vladimir Putin) of the Short World Leaders club. Like most Filipino presidents before her, it is doubtful that she will make much progress or effect any meaningful change. If you think politics are dull, check out the September issue of the *Philippine Tattler* featuring Arroyo and four members of her administrations decked out à la *Men in Black*. The goal was to show her fun side, according to the society-rag editor. If you forget, the movie *Men in Black* is about a secret force that arbitrarily hunts and executes alien invaders.

> **I**f you think politics are dull, check out the September issue of the *Philippine Tattler* featuring Arroyo and four members of her administration decked out à la *Men in Black*.

### President of the Philippines
opnet@ops.gov.ph
http://www.kgma.org
http://www.opnet.ops.gov.ph
http://www.gov.ph

### Tourism
http://www.tourism.gov.ph

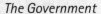

## REBEL PRIMER

It's pretty easy to figure out the rebels in the Philippines. The commies are urban-based intellectuals with links to union groups. They feed off the sugarcane workers, who have lost their jobs, and inner-city refugees. They also incorporate the negrito and mestizo elements, but really don't have any ethnic or linguistic links to them other than Tagalog. The Islamic groups in the south are more interesting. The MNLF is made up primarily of Tausags; the breakaway MILF is made up of Maguindanaoans, found in large numbers in the Cotabatao area; and the Abu Sayyaf group is a mix of different tribes—Tausugs, Samals, Badjaos, and Yakans from the islands of Sulu and Basilan.

## Salamat Hashim and the Moro Islamic Liberation Front (MILF)/ Bangsamoro Islamic Armed Forces (BIAF)

Salamat Hashim (b. July 7, 1942) and his MILF snuck into the Philippine political scene just before they closed the barn door. He's not radical enough (like Abu Sayyaf) to attract the wrath of Crusaders. He's not big enough to have any political clout, but just restrained enough in his violence to prevent wholesale attacks from looking like ethnic cleansing. His establishment of the BIAF, or the uniformed army of the MILF, shows that he is serious in his threat to liberate his Muslim homeland . . . if, of course, the Christians and missionaries don't out-religion him first.

Salamat Hashim is a tough guy to get hold of. Many military commanders and many of the front's other fighters have never set eyes on Salamat. He received his religious and, by default, his political training in Egypt and Pakistan in the 1960s (he was heavily influenced by Malauna Syed Abul Ala Maududi of Pakistan's Jamaat-e-Islami Party and Syed Outh of Egypt's Muslim Brotherhood) and formed the MNLF in 1970. His training in the Middle East gained him a lot of bearded jihad buddies with bombs, so he had no problem arming his spin-off movement when he founded the MILF. His beef was that the MNLF had sold out and his regional and ethnic group wasn't getting their fair share.

Hashim is one of seven kids from a family in the Municipality of Pagalungan, Maguindanao. A bright kid, he was able to go on haj (visit Mecca) at the age of 16. After a year in a Saudi madrassah, Salamat decided to go to Cairo and study theology and philosophy (both apparently big money-making careers back in the Philippines). He became part of the revolutionary movement of the Ikwhan, and after he got his master's degree in 1969, he returned to the Philippines to begin organizing a Moro revolutionary movement. He arranged for the first group of Moros to be trained as fighters. This was the "Batch 90" that began the fight. It is no coincidence that Salamat Hashim, much like the leaders of early Palestinian groups, combines '60s-era Marxi-babble with jihad-jingoism. The underlying truth is that this movement is primarily ethnic rather than religious. His support base is in Maguindanao and Lanao del Sur.

> **I**t is no coincidence that Salamat Hashim, much like the leaders of early Palestinian groups, combines '60s-era Marxi-babble with jihad-jingoism.

An offshoot of the primarily Tausag MNLF that sprang up in 1978 in the wake of the Tripoli-brokered autonomy agreement between Manila and the Moros, the Maguindanaoan MILF felt its people were being marginalized. MILF troop strength is estimated at between 20,000 and

40,000 by independent analysts, but no one seems to know for sure. The MILF itself claims a force of 120,000 members, 80,000 of them armed in 13 major camps in 7 provinces. The Philippine government says the group numbers no more than 8,000, the military guesstimates 60,000, and *DP* estimates that the MILF is about 12,000 active fighters with plenty more on call. More than 1,000 Filipino Muslims in its ranks fought against the Soviets during the war in Afghanistan, although Philippine military intelligence says no more than 300 did. When *DP* paid a visit, we found Hashim, aka the Amir of the Bangsamoro Mujahideen and Chairman of the MILF, to be cautious and cranky, but no dummy. Salamat's MILF is highly disciplined and as radical as can be expected, given his background and the political pressures against fundamentalism. They are not that thrilled with the wild-ass violent tactics of the Abu Sayyaf group, which gets support from Jolo and Basilan. The MILF (which pulls supporters from Mindanao) doesn't simply seek autonomy (as the more moderate Sulu-supported MNLF has claimed), but complete secession of Mindanao from the Philippines and the creation of a fundamentalist Islamic state—and will settle for no less. The front's military commander, Al-haj Murad, a genial and modest man, boasts of possessing six full divisions of soldiers; however, it seems to be a rotating army, with only two divisions on duty at any given time. This may explain the massive gaps in estimates of the group's strength. From 1994 to 2000, the MILF operated out of highly visible camps in central Mindanao (the largest was the 10,000-hectare Camp Abu Bakar) from March until June of 2000. Former President Estrada decided to attack the MILF, and the MILF wisely decided to abandon their camps and begin a guerrilla war. Camp Abu Bakar (named after the first Sultan of Sulu, who spread Islam in Mindanao) is now called Camp Duma Sinsuat (after a local, government-friendly, Muslim politician) and is the home of the 603rd Philippine Army Brigade. Hashim returned from a two-year exile in Saudi Arabia in March of 2002 to renew the war against the government.

**Al-haj Murad**
Vice Chairman for Military Affairs, Central Committee, and Chief of Staff
Bangsamoro Islamic Armed Forces (BIAF)
Tel.: (064) 421 34 86
alhijrah@microweb.com.ph

Or, for the latest in rebel dish, subscribe to:

**MILF Maradika**
The Editor
P.O. Box 535
9600 Cotabato City, The Philippines
http://www.fas.org/irp/world/para/docs/ph2.htm

## The Abu Sayyaf Group (ASG)

These days the Abus are a gang of Tausag tweakers turned faux revolutionaries turned body-bag stuffers, who have terrorized missionaries, businessmen, and tourists for too long.

> **T**hese days the Abus are a gang of Tausag tweakers turned faux revolutionaries turned body-bag stuffers.

The ASG roots are found in the actions of al-Islami Tabliq ("spread the word"), an organization founded in 1972 by Iranian missionaries who came to the Philippines to spread the doctrines of Ayatollah Ruholla Khomeini—an interesting mirror action of the missionaries who first brought Islam here 500 years ago. The Tabliq (also funded by Pakistan and Saudi Arabia) figured the poor Muslim communities of the Philippines were a good place to spread the word, and sponsored bright young men to study overseas. Abdurajak Janjalani Abubakar, a mestizo Ilongoo-Tausag and son of a fisherman, was sent from his village of Tabuk to madrassahs in Saudi Arabia and Libya and then later fought in Afghanistan under Professor Abdul Rasul Abu Sayyaf in 1986. Upon his return to the Philippines, he thought he would create an Islamic state. Janjalani went by his mentor's jihad handle of Abu Sayyaf. The early members of Janjalani's group were sons of MNLF leaders who wanted a more hardcore group and had fewer political sensibilities. The eight founding fathers (mostly from the now-pacified MNLF) gathered together about a dozen other members and called themselves Al Harakatul al Islamiya, or the Islamic Movement.

Although most sources will tell you that Abu Sayyaf means "Father of the Sword," its real meaning refers to someone who is a master at wielding a sword. It also means an executioner in the traditional Sharia practice of beheading criminals or enemies. During the 10 years under Janjalani, Abu Sayyaf was a Basilan-based group that worked to push out Christian missionaries, earn money by kidnapping Chinese-Filipino merchants, and attack military installations; nothing on a global scale or even anything that seemed to make international papers.

Janjalani (who had a price on his head of $37,000) was killed in combat by government troops in Lamitan on Basilan Island on December 18, 1998; the group never really recovered under the leadership of his brother, Khaddaffy Janjalani (named after guess who?). Khaddaffy (with the emphasis on "daffy") was neither educated, nor disciplined, nor charismatic, and the group lost its central focus and theological purpose.

This group first appeared in August 1991 on Basilan. It is a loose affiliation of minority ethnic groups from Jolo and Basilan and also comprises members with affiliations to criminal groups that work as pirates and kidnappers. Originally their attacks were against Christian missionaries, churches, and schools. They have targeted foreigners since their very first attack in 1991 killed two foreign women. Their money came from Mohammed Jamal Khalifa, a Saudi and brother-in-law of bin Laden. The first hard evidence of links to bin Laden came when Ramsi Youseff showed up in 1994 to train the Abus in explosives.

In December 11, 1994, they claimed responsibility for a test explosion aboard a Philippine airliner. Youseff's Manila-based cell was busy planning to assassinate the Pope when he visited the Philippines and to crash a hijacked plane into CIA headquarters. Project Bojinka (a Serbian word, which gives you some idea of the international links) was Youseff's most ambitious project. The multiple and simultaneous hijacking of 12 airliners and blowing them up was modified by an Algerian cell's concept of flying them into national monuments, and an Egyptian cell's obsession with toppling the World Trade Center. Strange that it took this much turban-scratching to reinvent something that was very familiar in the Philippines's military history: World War II Japanese kamikaze attacks on U.S. aircraft carriers. Youseff was busted when a fire broke out at headquarters and Manila police found the contents of his computer to be a little incriminating.

In April of 1995, the group had grown to about 600 men and had become more military in their actions. They attacked the Christian town of Ipil, killing 53 civilians and soldiers. At this point, it was assumed that weapons were coming from Libya and money was coming from the Gulf states (via a Saudi hothead named Osama), but Abu Sayyaf was still basically a Philippine government problem. Despite foreign visitors and money, the group was down to less than a hundred men. Then the Abu's went big time. On April 23, 2000, a three-engined speedboat driven by some more-seasoned members of ASG, under the cell leaders Ghalib Andang (aka Commander Robot) and Aldam Tilao (aka Abu Sabaya), zipped over to the tiny speck called Sipadan Island (*DP*'s favorite dive resort) off the east coast of Borneo and snagged 21 victims (a UN of dive tourists that included South Africans, Finns, Lebanese, and local workers). The speedboat was found abandoned in the area of Cagayan de Tawi-Tawi.

The Abu's cleared an estimated $20 million in ransoms when they handed back the foreigners, and an ugly cash-business opportunity was created (paid out by Libya, who brokered and cashed-out the deal).

A month later, on May 27, 2001, Abu's showed up at Dos Palmas resort on Palawan and grabbed another 20 vacationers. This time they snagged three Americans. Guillermo Sobero from Corona, California (who was beheaded by his captors in early June) and the two other

Yanks—-Wichita, Kansas, missionaries Martin and Gracia Burnham—
were kept as hostages on the island of Basilan, 560 miles south of
Manila.

Then, to make sure that there was no doubt about their links to bin
Laden's group, they snagged the docile and curious Jeffrey Schilling
(an American convert to Islam married to a local wife) and demanded
the release of Ramsi Youseff, Sheikh Adel Omar Rahman, and Abu
Haidal from U.S. jails. In September of 2001, they grabbed three people
from a dive resort on Pandanan Island, pretty much ending dive tourism
in the Philippines and sparking a military campaign against their bases
in Jolo. Their timing sucked: September 11 finally made it clear to folks
that obscure causes, funny names, and a remote location don't insulate
Americans from terrorism. Bingo . . . the Abu's became number two
with a bullet (Afghanistan was number one, Yemen number three).

The Pentagon sent a 25-man U.S. Special Operations Assessment
Team to visit the Philippines for two weeks in October and immediately
sent in helicopters, comms gear, night-vision equipment, covert surveillance gear, and even bloodhounds, and of course, a check for $19
million, to take out the Abu's. Previous military assistance from Washington was a paltry $1.9 million.

The newest ex-leader of Abu Sayyaf was Abu Sabaya. He was caught
in a boat near Zaomboango around 4 AM on June 22, 2000, and was
gunned down in the water by soldiers (using the same speedboat Abu
Sabaya had used to kidnap the Sipadan tourists). Abu was shot in the
back from 12 yards and sank to the bottom of the ocean. It was too late
for the Burnhams, though: the husband was shot and killed on a rescue attempt on the Zoambonga peninsula on June 7. With the little
help of 650 U.S. Special Forces troops, for now the Abus are on the run,
but nothing has been done to remove the underlying problem that
spawned them.

http://home.online.no/~erfalch/basilan.htm
http://www.ict.org.il/inter_ter/orgdet.cfm?orgid=3
http://www.cnn.com/SPECIALS/2001/abusayyaf
http://www.inquirer.net

## The Moro National Liberation Front (MNLF)

A formidable and brutal Muslim insurgency group for a quarter-
century is now a paper tiger. It was created in the early '70s to defend
Muslims from the government's plan to populate the region with
Christian refugees and to defend their rights and heritage. Four million
Muslims are found in 7 of the Philippines's 24 provinces. The other 17
provinces are home to 11 million Christians.

The MNLF signed a peace agreement with the Ramos government on September 2, 1996. Today, the MNLF is a mainstream political entity that has spawned the more-militant MILF. Some 7,500 former guerrillas are now being trained and paid to fight alongside government troops to battle the even-nastier MILF and the remnants of the Abu Sayyaf group. The former guerrillas get $170 and a monthly allowance of $30. The MNLF chairman, Nur Misuari, is now in charge of a four-province autonomous region in Muslim Mindanao.

The MNLF was doing just fine under a UN peace agreement and Nur Misuari was even governor of the autonomous region. Nur was elected after the 1996 peace accord. Unfortunately, he was dumped as a candidate by his own group for the November 26, 2001, election, and he and a small group of supporters chose to return to their militant ways. They attacked an army camp and grabbed hostages. His grand design was foiled and Nur hoofed it to Malaysia and was arrested. His peeps decided to join with Abu Sayyaff.

http://mnlf.net
http://pw1.netcom.com/~okonw/Jolo25d.html

## The New People's Army (NPA)

The communist NPA is an outgrowth of the Maoist Communist Party of the Philippines, founded in 1968. In 1969, they created an armed group called the New People's Army, once the most powerful insurgent group in the Philippines. At their peak in 1988, there were 26,000 guerrillas and supporters, but government fighting, assassinations, amnesties, and defections have whittled them down. Also the biggest bane of rebel groups, a good economy, has cooled their ardor for war. Once figured to be an anachronism, a recent government study found that the NPA have increased the number of guerrillas to 6,700, up 10 percent from 1996. *DP* figures the hard-core members number only about 3,000. They are gaining members in Mindanao and losing them in the north. It's really all about economics here. Former President Fidel Ramos's principal objective was to pursue peace with the NPA, and that has been largely accomplished. José María "Joma" Sison is now in exile in the Netherlands. Ramos scored a success when he was able to persuade another NPA leader, Leopoldo Mabilangan, to leave the group. Mabilangan was later assassinated by NPA operatives. In August of 2002, the Communist People's Party and their military wing, the NPA, were declared terrorist organizations by the U.S. State Department.

**New People's Army**
NDF International Office
P.O. Box 19195
3501 DD Utrecht
The Netherlands
Tel.: (31) 30 23 10 431
Fax: (31) 30 23 22 989
ndf@antenna.nl
http://www.geocities.com/bukluran

## Revolutionary People's Army/Sparrows/Rebolusyonaryong Partido ng Manggagawa-Alex Boncayao Brigade (RPM-P/RPA/ABB)

A mix of a Maoist hit squad (see Sparrows below), Marxist agrarian land-reform group, pissed-off college kids, and farm boys, this tongue-twisting rebel group is active on the island of Negros. *DP* just happened to be the first one to ever film them. We didn't have the heart to tell the guy with the bright orange Nike basketball outfit about the benefits of camouflage, but they are a serious bunch, despite having a hard time coming up with any snappy socialist sayings that rhyme with RPM-P/RPA/ABB.

They are working to pressure the landowners and the military for land reform, and they promised me they wouldn't hurt tourists. The "Sparrows," or, as they are really called, "The Alex Boncayao Brigade" (ABB), have gone straight. The ABB is a lethal leftist death squad led by Sergio Romero (whose real name is Nilo de la Cruz) that has taken scores of lives in its 10-year history. These guys are supposed to be the assassin branch of the Communist Party of the Philippines, but in reality they don't get along with the more-moderate NPA. Most recently, the group has been offing Chinese businessmen in sort of an ethnic cleansing of the ranks of the Philippines's industrialists. The leader, Nilo, who was charged with 200 murders, was nabbed and is awaiting trial and sentencing. They have reduced his sentence so that no judges or government officials wake up with horse heads in their beds. The government has drawn up a list of more than 160 ABB members targeted for arrest. Right now they are down to about 20 active members. As Nilo told me, "Thank goodness for pro bono human rights lawyers."

These days Nilo is involved with peace talks following the December 6, 2000, peace agreement with the government.

## Uncle Sam

You were just waiting for some postcolonial angst, weren't you? The Philippines were America's only colony, an odd side effect of the

Spanish-American War. Commodore Dewey sent a cable to President McKinley after sinking the Spanish fleet in Manila Bay: "Have taken Manila, what shall I do with it?" That wasn't the bad part. The troublesome part in the south was initially going to be swapped for a much nicer piece of real estate, but McKinley was convinced by Methodists that if the United States hung on to Bangsamoro, they would convert the little brown buggers. Bad advice.

After we fought a war with the Moros and fought with the communist rebels against the Japanese, we glued the southern area of Mindanao onto the other islands to create one big happy Philippines and gave them independence. In 1915, the Americans allowed Christian northerners to settle in the lands of the Muslim south. In April of 1940, the sultanate of Bangsamoro was recognized and incorporated into the independent country of the Philippines. We got a few military bases and a whole lot of pissed-off Moros who would be just as happy being left alone. If you hang around the south long enough without being kidnapped, you'll get an earful in the mosques. The kicker? Some of the Moros want us to intervene militarily against the Philippine government for their independence. In October of 2001, a group of Special Forces brass went to the area and recommended that we get waist-deep in a war we fought 100 years ago. In 2002, we did.

http://www.pacom.mil

### Sex Workers

Rene Ofreneo of the University of the Philippines estimates that there are 400,000 to 500,000 prostitutes in the country—equal to the number of its factory workers.

http://worldsexguide.org
http://www.ecpat.org

### Pirates

Pirates are a very real part of the southern Philippines. Zamboanga is a historic trading center, where luxury goods from Indonesia, Malaysia, Singapore, and China are as plentiful as the raw materials from the sea and jungles that surround the city. The goods are brought in on tora-toras. These flat-bottom boats are usually loaded to the gunnels with cheap TVs, beer, cigarettes, and other prized items.

The "pirate" ships are an assortment of rusting freighters, aging ferries, modern speedboats, basligs (which are large boats with outriggers to avoid capsizing in the heavy seas), and speedy canoe-like vintas with their colorful sails.

The amount of trade in high-ticket items from duty-free ports, such as Labuan in Brunei, make legitimate traders easy targets for pirates who employ everything from parangs (machetes) to machine guns to kill their victims.

**IMB Piracy Reporting Centre**
Kuala Lumpur, Malaysia
Tel.: (60) 3 2078 5763
Fax: (60) 3 2078 5769
Telex: MA31880 IMBPCI
Twenty-four-hour antipiracy helpline: Tel.: (60) 3 2031 0014
imbkl@icc-ccs.org.uk
http://www.iccwbo.org/ccs/menu_imb_piracy.asp
http://www.maritimesecurity.com
http://www.iccwbo.org/ccs/imb_piracy/weekly_piracy_report.asp

## Radio Commentaries

The media has a strange and tangled relationship with rebels in the Philippines. There are many communist sympathizers in the main Manila media outlets and plenty of Muslim sympathizers down south. It is not uncommon for kidnappers to give media interviews showing off kidnap victims, for police to set up enough extra-violent warrants to match a news program's need to get bigger ratings, or even for the rebels to demand a TV star or journalist to act as a hostage negotiator. There have also been a number of murders of journalists who were too talkative or friendly to rebels.

http://www.rsf.org/article.php3?id_article=1443

# Getting In ———————————————————

A passport and onward/return ticket are required to enter the Philippines. For entry by Manila International Airport, a visa is not required for a transit/tourist stay up to 21 days. Visas are required for longer stays; the maximum stay is 59 days. When applying for a visa, you'll need to fill out an application and provide one photo, at no charge. A company letter is needed for a business visa. An AIDS test is required for permanent residency; a U.S. test is accepted. For more information contact the following:

**Embassy of the Philippines**
1600 Massachusetts Avenue, N.W.
Washington, DC 20036
Tel.: (202) 467-9300

Or, contact the nearest consulate general at the following numbers:

Hawaii  Tel.: (808) 595-6316     New York  Tel.: (212) 764-1330
Illinois  Tel.: (312) 332-6458     California  Tel.: (213) 930-3220, or (415) 433-6666

Arrival into the Philippines from abroad is primarily through Manila's Ninoy Aquino International Airport, which is a modern facility with 14 jetways and is named after the man who was gunned down there, by the way. Located in nearby Pasay City, the airport is less than 30 minutes away by car to any major hotel and services an average of 170 international flights weekly. Manila is just over an hour by air from Hong Kong, 3 hours from Singapore, 5 hours from Tokyo, 17 hours from San Francisco, and 22 hours from New York.

Several Southeast Asian regional carriers have direct flights into Zamboanga and Mindanao, and proposed international airports are due for Cebu City and Zamboanga.

PTICs are located at Ninoy Aquino International Airport (tel.: 828-4791 or 828-1511), Nayong Pilipino Complex, Airport Road (tel.: 828-2219), and on the ground floor of the Philippine Ministry of Tourism (Ermita) building near Rizal Park in Metro Manila (tel.: 501-703 or 501-928). Field offices are situated in Pampanga, Baguio, Legazpi, La Union, Bacolod, Cebu, Iloilo, Tacloban, Cagayan de Oro City Davao, Marawi, and Zamboanga. The Department of Tourism hotline is 501-660 or 507-728.

In North America, the Philippine Tourist Office has the following locations:

**Philippine Center**
556 Fifth Avenue
New York, NY 10036
Tel.: (212) 575-7915

30 North Michigan Avenue, Suite 1111
Chicago, IL 60602
Tel.: (312) 782-1707

3460 Wilshire Boulevard, Suite 1212
Los Angeles, CA 90010
Tel.: (213) 487-4525

The Philippines might be the world's second-most-popular sex tourist destination after Thailand. Although the U.S. military bases have packed up and shipped out, horny foreigners keep the hookers gainfully employed in places like Angeles, Sabang, and Subic City. If this is your thing, get hold of Asia File and subscribe to their newsletter, which handles the particulars of these places pretty thoroughly.

> **A**lthough the U.S. military bases have packed up and shipped out, horny foreigners keep the hookers gainfully employed in places like Angeles, Sabang, and Subic City.

**Asia File**
P.O. Box 278537
Sacramento, CA 95827-8537
Fax: (916) 361-2364
asiafile@earthlink.net

## Getting Around

Accommodations, food, and travel in the Philippines offer some of the best bargains found in Asia. It can be terribly unexotic compared to other hot spots. Around the archipelago, there are inter-island sea vessels with first-class accommodations that sail between several different ports daily.

## Getting Out

If you find yourself in a pinch, or need quick transport out of the Philippines, you can charter a boat from Sitangkai for the 40-kilometer trip to Semporna in the Malaysian state of Sabah. This, of course, is completely illegal. However, there are a slew of boats that make the trip from the Philippines to the busy market in Semporna. Keep in mind that Sabah has its own customs and immigration requirements, so you'll need a separate stamp when you move back and forth from Sabah to peninsular Malaysia. These waters are also home to Sulu pirates (who are actually a combination of minor smugglers and armed thugs) who prey on large commercial vessels. Pirates have also been known to rob banks and terrorize entire towns in coastal Sabah; just inquire at any fishing village or dockside hangout in Sitangkai. Usually, you'll have to cross at night, and don't be surprised to pay two to three times the normal rate of P$150. Going the other way is also easy; there are boatmen who can hook you up with the many speedboats that are for rent in Semporna. Be careful dealing with the Ray-Banned entrepreneurs you meet along the docks. They might turn you in for the reward money and simply pocket the sizable fee you paid them to get you across.

Leaving from Ninoy Aquino International or Domestic Airport can be a drag due to the tight security inspections. The airport taxes are P$500 for international flights and P$25 for domestic flights.

## Dangerous Places

### Mindanao

More than 10,000 firefights between government soldiers and rebel separatists as well as countless bombings and other politically motivated slayings have left 50,000 people dead over the last 30 years in the Philippines—most of them on the island of Mindanao. Sultan Kudarat is particularly dangerous. Government soldiers are regularly attacked by MILF guerrillas in this area, and surrounding parcels of land change hands regularly. Dangerous as well is Zamboanga, where a wave of bombing attacks by ASG terrorists rattled the city for six days in March 1996.

http://www.mindanao.com

### Basilan

This island is the stronghold of Abu Sayyaf, but it is in an area where law and order are strictly homemade. Inquire at the local mosques and civil centers to understand just exactly what the crisis of the moment is. Best advice . . . let the locals steer you clear of the kidnapping and attacks on foreigners that occur here.

http://www.alumni.net/Asia/Philippines/Basilan
http://www.pacom.mil/imagery/archive/0202photos/basilanisland.html

### The Spratlys

Okay, okay, so the worst thing that happened to *DP* when we finally made it to the Spratlys was that we got sunburned. The minister of defense flew us out on a tourist junket to see the newest thing in eco-tourism. Well, it's not bad if you don't mind a lot of drunken soldiers, chopped-down palm trees, rusty antiaircraft guns, abandoned military gear, and old bunkers. As for danger . . . well, the air force pilot said he wouldn't buzz the brand-new Chinese Motel 6s on Mischief Reef "because sometimes they throw their garbage at us." Lock and load the Glad bags gunny . . . we're going in.

http://www.fmprc.gov.cn

## Dangerous Things

### Crime

Crime is high throughout the Philippines, particularly in urban areas. Many stores employ armed guards. There are 30 murders and 3 rapes per 100,000 people. There are 72 thefts for every 100,000 people.

http://www.nscb.gov.ph

### Kidnapping

The kidnapping rate in the Philippines has risen 48 percent over the last year. If you're a Chinese businessman living and/or working in the Philippines, consider wearing a mask or seeing a plastic surgeon, as you're the favorite target of kidnappers. Kidnappers like snatching Chinese for ransom because their companies/embassies/families invariably pay up. Kidnappers realize that if they take a Westerner, they'll have to feed the poor SOB for a couple of months, only to end up being stormed by police commandos. In 1995, more than 160 people were abducted in the Philippines (many of them belonging to rich ethnic Chinese families), hauling in more than a US$3.6 million booty for the kidnappers. One syndicate demands 50 million pesos ($1.2 million), and gets it, for their victims. Now that's positive cash-flow. During the first eight weeks of 1997, kidnap gangs had seized 42 victims—again, most of them ethnic Chinese—making the Philippines the kidnapping capital of Asia. The official kidnap rate in the Philippines is about 13.5 victims per month (most anticrime groups say the figure is much higher: about 1,000 people kidnapped every year in the Philippines). There are an estimated 40 different kidnapping syndicates in Manila alone. In 1997, kidnap gangs in the Philippines collected a total ransom of $7.1 million from 249 victims, nearly triple the $2.5 million they earned from 241 victims in 1996. These days kidnapping is supposed to be down, but nobody believes it. The latest twist is that victims must provide the name and address of another prime kidnap victim before they are released.

http://www.worldpress.org/profiles/Philippines.cfm

## KIDNAPPING BY THE NUMBERS

Kidnapping has become such a way of life in the Philippines that gangs now accept checks to cover their ransom demands. At least three Filipino-Chinese businessmen were quickly freed by kidnappers after they issued checks ranging from US$11,500 to US$38,000. One anticrime watch official stated that he doubts "if they gave stop-payment instructions, because the kidnappers would certainly have gotten back to them."

## Getting Sick

Shots for smallpox and cholera are not required for entry, but cholera shots are suggested when the Philippines appears on a weekly summary of infected areas (according to the World Health Organization). Yellow-fever vaccinations are required of all travelers arriving from infected areas. There is one doctor for every 6,413 people in the Philippines. Medical care in the Philippines outside of Manila can be below Western standards, with some shortages of basic medical supplies. Access to the quality facilities that exist in major cities sometimes requires cash-dollar payment upon admission. Most of the general hospitals are run privately. Malaria, once a big problem in the Philippines, has been eradicated in all but the most rural regions. Tuberculosis and respiratory and diarrheal diseases pose the biggest threats to travelers. The U.S. embassy and consulates maintain lists of health facilities and English-speaking doctors. Drinking only boiled or bottled water will help to guard against cholera, which has been reported, as well as other diseases. More complete and updated information on health matters can be obtained from the Centers for Disease Control's international travelers' hotline, tel.: (404) 332-4559.

## Nuts and Bolts

The world's second-largest archipelago after Indonesia, the Republic of the Philippines comprises 300,000 square kilometers (777,001 square miles) on 7,107 islands in the South China Sea between Borneo to the southwest and Taiwan to the north; only 4,600 islands are named and a mere 1,000 are inhabited. The islands are in three main groups: the Luzon group, the Mindanao group, and the Sulu and Visayan group. The country's 65.2 million inhabitants speak Tagalog and English. Roman Catholics comprise 83 percent of the population; Protestants, 9 percent; Muslims, 5 percent; and Buddhists, 3 percent. There are more than 100 ethnic groups in the country.

The Philippines has one of the developing world's highest literacy rates. Nearly every child in the country finishes primary school and nearly three-quarters of the population completes secondary school. The education system is based on the U.S. model. Although relatively highly educated, about 50 percent of Filipinos live at or below the poverty line, mainly because economic expansion falls short of the country's population growth rate. The official currency is the Philippine peso. Approximately 26 pesos equal US$1. Hard foreign currency and traveler's checks are easily exchanged at banks, hotels, and authorized moneychangers throughout the country. Credit cards are also widely accepted.

The local water is generally potable, except in remote rural areas. Hours of business in the Philippines are from 8 AM to 5 PM Monday through Friday, with most offices closed from noon to 1 PM or so. Banks are open from 9 AM to 4 PM Monday through Friday. Shops in major tourist centers are open at 9 or 10 AM until at least 7 PM daily.

Telephone, telex, and fax services in the Philippines are surprisingly poor, and communication with the outside world is slower than you'll find in other parts of the Far East. Overseas calls take from 30 minutes to an hour to put through and are expensive, although IDD has arrived at the better hotels.

The local current is 220V/50Hz—sometimes. One of the biggest infrastructural problems in the Philippines is electricity. The country experiences frequent and lengthy power outages on 258 out of the 297 working days each year.

**United States Embassy**
1201 Roxas Boulevard-Ermita 1000
Manila
Philippines
Tel.: (63-2) 523 1001
Fax: (63-2) 522 4361
http://usembassy.state.gov/posts/rp1/
    wwwhmain.html

**The Canadian Consulate**
Allied Bank Centre, 9th Floor
6754 Ayala Avenue
1226 Makati
Metro Manila
Philippines
Tel.: (63-2) 867-001
Fax: (63-2) 810-4299

# Dangerous Days

| | |
|---|---|
| 11/11/02 | MILF rejects amnesty; government persuades United States not to label MILF a terrorist group. |
| 10/29/02 | The MNLF and MILF join forces. |
| 8/22/02 | Two members of a Jehovah's Witness Christian sect are beheaded two days after being kidnapped in Patikul on Jolo Island by Muslim rebels in the southern Philippines. |
| 6/22/02 | Abu Sabaya, Abu Sayyaf Commander, is killed. |
| 6/7/02 | Kidnapped U.S. missionary and a Filipino are killed. |
| 1/30/02 | U.S. troops arrive in southern Philippines. |
| 8/5/01 | Abu Sayyaf militants behead hostages. |
| 7/9/01 | Top Abu Sayyaf leader is arrested in the Philippines. |
| 6/1/01 | Philippine forces clash with Abu Sayyaf hostage-takers. |
| 4/12/01 | Philippine troops rescue an American hostage. |
| 9/16/00 | The Philippine military launches an assault on the Abu Sayyaf group. |
| 9/12/00 | Abu Sayyaf kidnaps three people from the Pandanan Island diving resort and takes them to Sulu. |
| 8/30/00 | U.S. citizens are taken hostage by Abu Sayyaf. |
| 8/29/00 | Abu Sayyaf militants abduct Jeffrey Craig Schilling, an American Muslim convert who came to visit their Jolo Island stronghold. Leader, Abu Sabaya, demands the release of Ramsi Youssef, Sheikh Adel Omar Rahman, and Abu Haidal from American jails. |
| 7/26/00 | Eighteen are injured in a Jolo Island grenade attack. |
| 5/21/00 | One dead and 14 are wounded in a blast at Manila shopping mall. |
| 4/23/00 | The Philippine military launches a hostage rescue operation on Jolo Island. |

| | |
|---|---|
| **4/23/00** | Twenty-one hostages are kidnapped from Sipadan Island—a Malaysian dive resort. |
| **4/17/00** | Abu Sayyaf demands the release of Ramsi Youseff. |
| **3/20/00** | Abu Sayyaf grabs 53 hostages, which include 22 school children, 5 teachers, and a priest, from 2 schools in Basilan. |
| **1/3/99** | To avenge the death of their leader, Abu Sayyaf throws a grenade into a crowd watching firefighters battle a supermarket fire. Ten are killed and 74 are injured. |
| **12/19/98** | Janjalani, founder of ASG, is killed in a gunfight with Philippine police. |
| **9/9/97** | The ASG kidnaps a German business executive in Zamboanga City. The hostage is released December 26. |
| **9/2/96** | A peace agreement is reached between MNLF and the Philippine government. |
| **12/11/94** | The ASG and Ramsi Youseff plant a bomb aboard a Philippine airliner, killing a Japanese citizen and injuring 10 others. |
| **11/14/93** | The ASG kidnaps U.S. missionary Charles M. Watson on Pangutaran Island, Sulu Batu. He is released in Manila on December 7. |
| **2/25/86** | Marcos flees into exile in the United States. |
| **8/21/83** | Opposition leader Benigno Aquino is shot to death by military police as he arrives in Manila after returning from self-exile. |
| **1/17/81** | President Ferdinand Marcos ends eight years of martial law. |
| **7/4/46** | The Philippines gains independence. |
| **12/8/41** | Japan invades the Philippines. |
| **10/26/1898** | President McKinley decides to annex the southern Philippines. |
| **6/12/1898** | Filipino General Emilo Aguinaldo declares the Philippines independent (witnessed by U.S. Artillery Colonel L. M. Johnson). |
| **5/1/1898** | Commodore Dewey defeats the Spanish fleet in Manila Bay and is promoted to admiral on March 13, 1899. |
| **6/1578** | Rodriguez de Fibreroa and Jesuit priest Juan del Campo are the first Europeans to arrive at Sulu. |
| **3/16/1521** | Portuguese explorer Magellan arrives on Samar Island and raises a wooden cross. |
| **12/1450** | Johore-born Arab, Abu Bakar, arrives in Sulu and begins Islamic sultanates. |

THE PHILIPPINES

# In a Dangerous Place: Negros

## THE PHANTOMS

I am to meet a company of NPA rebels on the run from the military, a group that has never been photographed before, and the odds are good that they may all be dead by the time I get there. They are on the run from the army, so they say they can only wait and talk to us for an hour, no longer. Then they must move on.

Making my covert contact with the rebels is easier than I thought. When I arrive at the airport on the island of Negros, there is a man with a withered hand and a big, toothy smile holding a large sign that says "Robert Telkon and Company."

Our four guides use aliases when they greet us, and then talk to each other using their real names. Oops. So much for security.

The trip will be delayed. There are troop movements by the Special Action force. The rebel camp is on the move. This is better for us because the camp is now only two hours away, instead of seven.

There are three battalions of the Philippine military on the island, about 3,000 troops in all. Two are here in Bacolod, one is in the south. The special forces group is in the south, and they are carrying out an operation today. There are rebels here because there is sugarcane. Sugarcane is a peasant crop, and like coffee or cotton crops, that means hard, seasonal, manual labor, and low pay.

There are 25,000 haciendas, or sugarcane plantations. There are 50 families that are the major landowners. The biggest landowner, the Cojuanco, owns thousands of hectares. The cane cutters are indentured laborers, and the landlords call the shots. The cane cutters tell us they get 600 pesos per hectare—not for each person, but for however many people and days it takes to finish. It takes them two days to weed a hectare, and if there are nine people working, they each get the equivalent of 30 cents a day. Agricultural workers, by Philippine law, should get 100 pesos a day.

We are in the newest, swankiest hotel in town, which costs a mere $20 a night. I don't even want to figure out how long it would take a sugarworker to afford a night here. It might sound strange that we hole up in a businessman's hotel, but it is the place where we will stand out the least. Our guides leave us here, to watch four overweight golfers load a mountain of golf bags into the back of a shiny Chevy dual-cab pickup truck, as our guides roar away on their motorbikes.

Negros is split down the middle both by culture and by a ragged, denuded cordillera. The people align themselves with the people on the facing slope of the neighboring island. We are in Negros occidental, where they speak Ilokano; the other side of the island speaks Cebuano.

The Victoria Sugar Mill is the largest sugar mill in Southeast Asia. It has been in operation for 78 years. It's more a small town than just a mill. Gray flakes of burnt sugar float down like snow. Everybody is gone because it's Sunday.

On the morning we are to meet our peripatetic rebels (at a secret location, of course), our guide zooms up on a very noisy dirt bike. He doesn't hang around long, but zooms up and down the street like a buzzing fly. For once, everybody is on time. We head out into the cool dawn and begin our journey high up into the mountains.

The odds of an ambush by the military are high in the dawn hours, so it is probably the worst time, place, and conditions to visit rebels on the run. The people in the hills know our escorts well. There is lots of handshaking and welcoming when we pass through villages.

The most striking things about the mountains are the cool air and that they have been completely devastated by clear-cutting. There is simply nothing left that would resemble the triple-canopy rain forest that covered this archipelago. In place of jungle are scrubby ferns and a hodgepodge of trees among scattered villages and plantations.

The road winds up and down and round and round. I pull out my GPS to figure out exactly where we are going. My contact says my GPS is making our rebel contacts nervous. I look over to see them sleeping, their heads bobbing in time to the sways in the road. Uh huh.

Needless to say, the rebels are in the hills, but exactly where is unknown. Originally we were told that we would drive seven hours and then walk for three. Then it became drive five, walk two. When we arrive on Negros, there is a development. The rebels have been chased closer to us.

Soon a blue arc of sky forms and the clouds are painted a dusty pink. A 300-meter waterfall appears. We see steep volcanic canyons and black boulders sitting like sculptures in reflective rice paddies. It takes about three hours and a few backtracks to avoid the military, but we soon arrive on the slope of a mountain with a few ramshackle nipa huts. Then, like the first sighting of big game on a safari, rebels appear. They're attired in faded green camouflage, festooned with worn and polished weapons, and are wearing canvas sneakers with red shoelaces. We have a brief powwow to set up filming. This group is a company of the Revolutionary Proletariat Army/Alex Boncayao Brigade, or RPA/ABB, a breakaway faction of the NPA formed in 1996 who work with the urban members of the Alex Boncayao hit squad. There are about three dozen men, mostly in their twenties and thirties. There are three *manara*, the local name for black-skinned mestizo Filipinos.

The troops are lined up in threes and go through their drill for us. They get most of it right, and it is easy to see that the military skills lie with the two or three leaders. They play "rebel in the jungle," posing for us with their battered rifles, stolen from the Philippine army. They also have some newer M-16s with grenade launchers, obviously stolen or captured from the special forces groups.

They kill a pig in our honor, and just as lunch is getting ready, we learn that an RP special forces group is now in the village we just passed and heading our way. We have to disperse fast, as a blocking force is sent down the road to protect us. We quickly pack up our gear and begin humping up the mountain. The camp followers carry the cooking pot and the soldiers listen carefully to the radio communication of the Philippine army. They also smoke homemade cigarettes. We have a sit-down chat with the local commander, his military head, and his spokesperson.

Essentially, they split with the NPA because they want a more functional solution to the plight of the poor. They also consider the landowners and warlords to be their enemy. I ask why they attack the military instead of the kids in the military. They say the military does the bidding of the landowners. We have a pretty low-key conversation on whether having an insurgency actually harms the people because of lack of investment. They welcome investors (although I heard the word "capitalist" used as a form of insult many times). Would they harm or kidnap foreigners? Not at all. Their fight is with the landowners (although the ABB takes considerable pride in having assassinated the station chief of the CIA in Manila). It's a good interview. The right questions. The right answers. How do they feel when they kill a brother Filipino in the military? They are forced to do so because their reaction is to defend themselves. Do they initiate attacks on the military? Yes, but only as part of the greater revolutionary struggle and in conjunction with their comrades' political agenda. Uh huh.

They decide to ask me a few questions. They want to know what people think of them. I tell them that acronyms and socialist dogma are the quickest way to get people to turn off. There is no shortage of revolutionary groups here, so their revolution-lite formula is going to get lost in the mix. (Wastes great, less killing?)

They are obviously thrilled to see a camera crew from the United States, but they don't quite know what to do. They set up their ever-present red flag with the unpronounceable Tagalog long-form name of their group behind every interview and they make a bad-boy motif in the background with all the best weapons and meanest-looking fighters. The guy with orange day-glo basketball shorts and lime-green shirt probably needs a little jungle camouflage training.

When things quiet down, they invite us to a meal of greasy pig and rice. Then the rebels get to do their laundry.

Seven days later, three of our newly made friends die in a shootout with the military.

*—RYP*

# RUSSIA

Moscow

## Red 'n' Dead

Russia has tumbled from first-world superpower to third-world life-support patient in a mere decade. Or from red to dead without even gaining an ounce of the octane that has driven the success of some of its former republics: While Estonia and Lithuania in particular have swiftly reinvented themselves as bright, efficient, prosperous, and freshly scrubbed annexes of Scandinavia, Russia has found ways to become even more gloomy, incompetent, broke, and filthy than Stalin's USSR ever was. The government of this beached-whale of a country, once all things to all of its 146 million citizens, has been reduced to a cabal of old men stuffing their pockets with tattered rubles as fast as they can, while the real money is being made by people who never see the inside of the Kremlin: gangsters, businessmen, killers, and even rebels.

Commonwealth of
Independent States

1. Adygea
2. Karachay-Cherkessia
3. Kabardino-Balkaria
4. North Ossetia
5. Checheno-Ingushetia

| 0 | 400 km |
| 0 | 400 mi |

SVALBARD
(NORWAY)

Arkhangel'sk

Barents
Sea

Kara
Sea

Baltic
Sea

FINLAND

Murmansk

Arkhangel'sk

Karelia

White Sea

Pechorskoye
More

KALININGRAD  ESTONIA

LATVIA

St. Petersburg

Nenetsia
AOk

LITHUANIA

Leningrad
Oblast

Pskov

Arkhangel'sk

Novgorod

BELARUS

Vologda

Tver'

Komi

Yamalia
AOk

Smolensk

Yaroslavl'

Bryansk

Kaluga

Moscow

Ivanovo  Kostroma

Tula

Moscow

Vladimir

Permyakia
AOk

Khantia
Mansia
AOk

UKRAINE

Orel

Ryazan'

Nizhniy-
Novgorod

Kirov

Kursk

Lipetsk

Mordovi

Mari El

Perm'

Belgorod

Tambov

Chuvashia

Udmurtia

Voronezh

Penza

Tatarstan

Sverdlovsk
Oblast

Ul'yanovsk

Saratov

Samara

Bashkortostan

Tyumen'

Tomsk

Rostov

Volgograd

Chelyabinsk

Krasnodar
Kray

Orenburg

Kurgan

Omsk

1

Kalmy

Novosibirsk

Kemerov

Stavropol'
Kray

2

Astrakhan'

3

4  5

Altay Kray  Kha

GEORGIA

Dagestan

KAZAKHSTAN

Gorno-
Altay

ARMENIA

AZERBAIJAN

Aral Sea

Lake Balkhash

Caspian Sea

IRAN

TURKMENISTAN

UZBEKISTAN

CHINA

RUSSIA

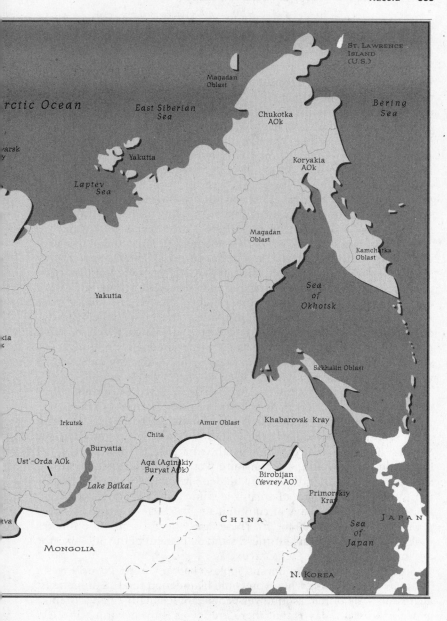

Russians may put more rubles in their pockets than when they were under the hammer and sickle (John Q. Sixpackovitch takes home an average of US$112 a month), but prices have beaten them to any gains. To make sure they don't miss the cruel joke, they're actually living shorter lives than under communist rule. War, disease, drugs, unemployment, crime, poverty, and all those other frills of freedom are taking their toll on the previously resilient Russians with a vengeance. Male life expectancy has fallen to 58, down seven years since the flag of freedom was hoisted over the Kremlin. Men in Russia today live 15 to 17 fewer years than their counterparts in the United States and Western Europe and are 20 times more likely to be murdered. Russian women now outlive men by 13 years (the norm is 7 years). The bright side? Russian men lived to an average age of only 40 before the revolution. The decline can be directly attributed to smoking, drinking, drugs, bad health care, and poor diet. Oh, and there is the violence and crime. . . .

When the USSR imploded in '91, nobody leapt into the power vacuum faster than the *mafiyas*. They'd functioned in some shape or form since the czar's time and flourished in the '50s: running Western cigarettes, booze, electronic equipment, and clothes to people who were fed up with smoking tobacco that smelled like ground tractor-tires (which it might well have been), drinking vodka better suited to powering lawnmowers (not that it stopped them), putting up with scratchy, monophonic sound systems (though these could only improve the sound of Russian pop music), and dressing like Bulgarian air stewards (even if most of the population still do so).

In those days, the mafiosi had to do their work with a certain discretion—the penalty for being rumbled was a one-way ticket to the Siberian salt pile. When most sorts of economic and legal authority collapsed, they came out of hiding, and were able to live out all their Scorcese-inspired dreams. Suddenly, the smartest restaurants and hotel lobbies in Moscow and St. Petersburg were filled with men in striped suits parading girlfriends clad in faux leopard skin. In '94, the interior minister said the number of organized crime groups in Russia had risen from 785 in the last days of communism to 5,691—a figure that was revised upward to 8,000 in '96. These days, the government estimates that 40 percent of private businesses and 60 percent of the public sector are in the hands of the *Goodfellas* extras.

Suddenly communism doesn't look so bad anymore. Poverty was a lot easier to cope with when you could blame it on the U.S. imperialist aggressors. The only reason fewer people are feeling the pangs of indigence in Russia today is that there are fewer Russians around to feel anything. There have been a million more deaths than births each year in Russia since the days when there were crowds at Lenin's tomb—the population is down 2 percent since 1992. And like Ex-Lax to a dysentery victim . . . it's getting worse every year. "Mother Russia" is truly a mother. Even worse is that the lack of new Russians will mean that in 20 years there will be one working Russian for each elderly pensioner. Just another cheery thought that will drive more young Russians to drink.

In December 1991, the Cold War ended when the Soviet Union collapsed. The jagged pieces of the Soviet dream numbered 12: Armenia, Azerbaijan, Belarus, Georgia, Kazakhstan, Kyrgyzstan, Moldova, Russia, Tajikistan, Turkmenistan, Ukraine, and Uzbekistan, with Russia by far the largest. Some of these states are still going through secondary breakups, as ethnic and religious factions fight for sovereignty, usually with the help or antagonism of "Mother Russia," outsiders, or gangsters. Europe and America began pumping in cash to create instant capitalism, but decades of learning how to outfox the system rapidly created the largest criminal empire on earth. It seems that it was easier to steal, price-fix, and monopolize than to actually work for money.

Although then-President Boris Yeltsin survived a national referendum on his ability to lead Russia in '93, he dissolved the legislative bodies still left dangling from the Soviet era. On October 3, 1993, tensions between the executive and legislative branches of the government escalated into armed conflict. Yeltsin stood on a tank, waved his fist, and barricaded himself in Moscow's parliament building, there to make a last stand against the forces who sought to strangle Russian democracy in its cradle. Thanks to the indiscreet recollections of former Soviet Foreign Minister Eduard Shevardnadze, now president of Georgia, who met with the besieged Russian president, we now know that Yeltsin was utterly, incapably plastered during the entire episode (as, indeed, it seems he was for much of his term in office). But it worked. Yeltsin kept his job.

In December '94, Mother Russia attempted to stop Chechnya from deserting her dirty, threadbare skirts. Russia decided to spank the Chechens and found its arm torn off. The attack on Grozny, the capital of the rebel Republic of Chechnya, resulted in a rout of the Russian forces and revealed how full of puffery and incompetence the Russian military had become. Renegade commanders refused to follow orders or never received them, Russian soldiers captured by the insurgent Chechens revealed that they were without food or maps, and Russian corpses littered Grozny streets like dead worms after a heavy rain. The numerically superior but tactically inferior Russian forces eventually took the Chechen capital in February '95, only to retreat in disarray in August '96.

They had another go in October '99, when 100,000 Russian soldiers thundered into Chechnya. The number of troops that have since limped or been carried back out is continually obfuscated by Moscow, but it is known to run into the thousands—and there's no ignoring the legions of legless young men begging on the platforms of Moscow's Metro stations. For this and other reasons, Yeltsin left his political cabinet to spend more time with his liquor cabinet on New Year's Eve '99.

Yeltsin was replaced by Vladimir Putin. Putin (the name translates into a variety of rude terms in foreign languages) is a dour and tiny former KGB drone whose election platform consisted of unloading immense tonnages of ordnance on old people and children in Chechnya. An odd genetic combination of Mini Me and Dr. Evil, Putin's also made a similarly ineffectual song and dance about fixing Russia's chronic crime plague, criticizing "feeble" law enforcement while completely castrating Russia's wild-and-woolly free press. Well, at least he's sober when he fibs.

Things *are* looking up; after all, it's hard to imagine Russia sinking any lower. Oil may be the biggest domestic resource, but crime may be Russia's biggest export in the next decade. The brutal control of a central government has been reborn in the form of Russian *mafiyas*. In an average year there are 3 million crimes recorded in Russia, and 7,000 murders remained unsolved, many of which were committed with silencers and at close range, using the same weapons issued to the police and the

> **T**hings *are* looking up; after all, it's hard to imagine Russia sinking any lower.

military—one clue as to why they've remained unsolved. (It is common for Russia's underpaid police and military to moonlight as security guards and enforcers for the *mafiya*.)

There is worse afoot than just thuggery in Russia. Tired of polishing their ICBMs and rotating their nuclear weapons, some army units have decided to strip the nukes down into more economically attractive components and generate a little cash. In early 2002, former U.S. Senate majority leader Howard Baker summed up the situation rather well: "It really boggles my mind," he told the Senate Foreign Relations Committee, "that there could be 40,000 nuclear weapons, or maybe 80,000, in the former Soviet Union, poorly controlled and poorly stored, and that the world isn't in a state of near hysteria about the danger."

A few years back, Yeltsin's national security bagman, the late General Alexander Lebed, admitted that of the KGB's stock of 100 suitcase nukes, 40 appeared to have gone missing. Whoops. Around the same time, the U.S. government did what so many of the world's ne'er-do-wells have been trying to do and bought a considerable pile of enriched uranium from the Russians, reasoning that it was better locked up in

Oak Ridge, Tennessee, than being sold at yard sales in Kazakhstan. In 2002, a report by the Stanford Database on Nuclear Smuggling, Theft, and Orphan Radiation Sources (DSTO) listed 830 incidents of nuclear material being smuggled and reckoned that around 40 kilograms of weapons-grade uranium and plutonium had been lifted in the ex-USSR since the USSR became ex—more than enough, in capable hands, to utterly ruin large tracts of Europe or America. The DSTO compilers admitted, however, that for all anyone really knows, it could be 10 times that, which is more than enough to ruin the eternity of everyone.

Once you leave the glitz and bustle of Moscow and other major cities, Russia is a sad, empty place that lives day by day. It's a country where the citizens disco in an alcoholic fog by night and rattle their tin cups in the cold light of day. Oh, and can you lend us a fiver 'til Tuesday?

**It's a country where the citizens disco in an alcoholic fog by night and rattle their tin cups in the cold light of day.**

## The Scoop

Russia's myriad woes and extended death-rattle defy being capsulized. The country mimics a condemned man awaiting execution. Drink, cigarettes, sex, drugs, crime, insane nightlife, and a wild abandon all contrast the drab, desperate pessimism of life in modern Russia.

But, hey, there's nothing like an eviction party or bankruptcy sale for great opportunities. Within certain limits, Russia is not an unpleasant place to visit—Moscow and St. Petersburg are beautiful, especially in the winter, and the trans-Siberian railway is still something every traveler should do at least once (if for no other reasons than that it's clean and comfortable and it works, unlike everything else in Russia). In the normal run of things, Russia is fairly safe—while it's not unheard of for tourists to get caught in the crossfire of Moscow and St. Petersburg's turf wars, it is highly unusual. Should you venture into the uglier parts of Russia's violent self-destruction, expect the worst.

## The Players

### President Vladimir Putin

Charmless little man who was appointed president by the outgoing Boris "Mine's-a-Treble" Yeltsin in December '99. (Given Yeltsin's usual vodka-sodden state, we should probably count ourselves lucky he didn't give the job to Bill Clinton, David Hasselhoff, or a pink elephant.) Putin's appointment was rubber-stamped by Russia's voters at an election in May 2000.

Born on October 7, 1952, Putin was a career spook who joined the KGB right after gaining a law degree at what was then called Leningrad University. (He worked in foreign intelligence, specializing in the Cold War's most fraught front line, Germany, but he won't talk about what he was doing there.) Putin moved into politics in 1990, becoming deputy mayor of what was by then St. Petersburg in 1994, where he smoothly handled the various criminal, political, and financial dons. He then became deputy head of management in Yeltsin's presidential administration in Moscow in 1996. In a rare moment of clarity, Yeltsin put him in charge of the KGB's successor, the Federal Security Service (FSB), where Putin did little but shore up his own political powerbase. It worked—he was prime minister, and natural heir to Yeltsin, by August 1999.

The Western world still seems to be having trouble taking the dour, diminutive Putin seriously, and not without reason. He looks exactly like the wimp who was snapped by too many towels in the men's shower at high school. He has had a black belt in judo since age 18 and likes to be photographed at the front lines in his own personal war on Chechnya. Putin had noticed that when Russian generals didn't have a war, they tended to turn their weapons on whoever was running Russia. He also noticed that Russians need an enemy to focus their complaints on: America, Afghanistan, and now Chechnya. His attack on the Russian media (for lying), the oligarchy (for stealing), and his own people (for being uppity), if done by an American president would have quickly ended any support, but in Putin's case he has gained the support of the Russian people. Imagine if Bush had pardoned Bill Clinton, shut down CBS, took Ross Perot to court, and invaded California . . . well, you get the point. But the Russians suck it up. Smart guy, this Putin. George Orwell would have been proud.

His enthusiasm for free-market reform seems genuine enough—he is forever proclaiming his admiration for Margaret Thatcher, which should be enough to put anyone off, but he is also a committed Russian nationalist. In December 2000 he signed a law abolishing the (admittedly rather weedy) new Russian national anthem that Yeltsin had selected and replacing it with the old Soviet one; the lyrics extolling Lenin and Stalin were tactfully rewritten. This was at least partly in response to a complaint from Russian footballers, who worried that they were in danger of nodding off during the prematch formalities.

Putin's total failure to impose any sort of law and order on Russia—which, in fairness, is a task that Hercules would have balked at—should not be misinterpreted as softheartedness. He has continued to pulverize Chechnya on pretexts that most of us wouldn't dare offer as excuses for a late math assignment, and has shown a Milosevic-esque fondness for harassing media organizations that have the temerity to question his judgment. ("We interpret freedom of expression in different ways," Vlad once glumly replied when journalists tackled him about his lack of enthusiasm for the U.S. First Amendment.)

In January 2002, Russia's fourth-largest station, TV6, was closed on the order of Moscow's Higher Arbitration Court because of (all together now) "financial irregularities." It is possibly completely coincidental that 75 percent of TV6 is owned by relentless Putin critic Boris Berezovsky—who has claimed, among other things, that the 1999 apartment-block bombings in Russia which killed 300 people and were the pretext for Russia's renewed war on Chechnya, were the work of Russian security forces, not Chechen extremists. And it's possibly by-the-by that TV6 hired a lot of the journalists who'd quit NTV, Russia's last remaining independent television network, when the Russian government bought it out in April 2001. And it may be utterly irrelevant that the minority shareholder who demanded TV6 be closed for failing to turn a profit was Lukoil-Garant, a company that is partly owned by the Russian government. And if you believe any of that, you'll never understand Russian politics (or any politics, come to that). Putin was best described to *DP* by now-deceased Chechen terrorist Abu Mosayev, who held out his thumb and index finger to measure an inch: "The problem with Putin is that the distance from his heart to his asshole is too short."

Putin's mastery of the dark arts, sure grasp of Stalinist politics, and successful destruction of those who oppose him seem to indicate that he will be around for a very long time.

**Russian Government**
http://www.gov.ru
president@gov.ru

**Federal Security Service**
http://www.fsb.ru (Russian only)

## The Russian Mafia (Organizatsiya or Mafiya)

If you ever wonder who really runs Russia, look no further. The gangs that seized Russia's economy in 1991 cannot be accused of being small-time: in the mid-'90s, one gang attempted to sell a surplus ex-Soviet submarine to Colombian drug-runners . . . until the Colombians could build their own from stolen Russian plans. Hey, it's a free country, right? There are many estimates as to the number of criminal gangs operating in Russia, most of which fall between 8,000 and 10,000, but the exact number isn't important: What matters is that the mafias control around half of the total Russian economy, such as it is, and may now be so entrenched that cleaning Russia up will be impossible. The mafia extort protection money from Russian businesses ranging from hot dog sellers to banks (the standard rate is apparently 20 to 30 percent of turnover). It is also widely speculated that they know in advance the results of Russian soccer and hockey matches (a strategy some players have allegedly brought to the European soccer leagues and the NHL).

The bad news is that the *mafiya* is expanding faster than Starbucks. They launder money through front businesses in Israel (gangsters pretend to be Jewish in order to obtain Israeli passports). They have annexed many of the lucrative Bering Strait fisheries. Their presence in Eastern Europe is such that the FBI has now opened an office in Budapest. They are also key players in Eastern Europe's booming vice industry—a UN report in 2000 estimated that every year half a million women arrive in Europe from the former USSR to work as prostitutes. The competition posed by Russia prompted hookers in the French city of Lyon to complain to then-Prime Minister Lionel Jospin that these women were undercutting them.

http://gangstersinc.tripod.com/Rus.html

## The Russian Army

Although Yelstin shrank the military from 2.7 million to 1.2 million, Putin's army is still as disheveled and unruly as a Monday Moscow drunk. Each year 200,000 young men are called up to defend what's left of Russia. What they can expect is a dollar a day—if it ever gets to them—and a life of brutality, broken equipment, and misery.

Over 80 percent of military gear has been in use for 10 years. Half of all combat planes and tanks don't work and 80 percent of assault helicopters won't fly. The situation is so bad that the defense minister plans on sacking 200,000 soldiers a year for three years to scrape together enough money to buy new weapons. That number doesn't include the 70,000 conscripts who are rejected for health reasons.

While Uncle Sam peels off about $180,000 per soldier per year, Uncle Ivan squeaks by with just $4,000. And it's probably not really about the money anyway. If you are looking for blood, guts, and violence, you'll find it in the Russian military. Problem is, it will be your own.

The rank-and-file military here is made up of drunken lifers brutalizing ill-trained farmboys working for corrupt mafia-controlled generals. Beatings and hazings are so common that troops pay a portion of their meager pay to avoid the pain, and those who don't . . . let's just say there are more injuries from beatings within the military than in combat. About 57 soldiers are killed, 3,000 are injured, and many more die unaccounted for. *Dedovshchina*, or the practice of bullying, causes an estimated 2,000 to 3,000 deaths a year, most of them suicides. There are an estimated 500 homicides each year. *DP* even met a poor, pumpkin-headed recruit in the Chechen bunkers who thought he would be better off with his sworn enemy than his brutal commander.

In some areas, army commanders rent out weapons and men are hired out as mercenaries to the highest bidder. It's not a very tightly run ship. More than 6,000 crimes involving corruption and embezzlement were committed in the Russian armed forces. More than 20 generals were being investigated, many in housing schemes. An estimated 110,000 troops lack proper housing, and about 500 soldiers commit suicide every year—Russian roulette, after all, was invented by Russian conscripts during World War I.

There are also chronic shortages of money (it is not unusual for troops to go months without being paid) and food, with reports of Russian troops reduced to begging for food or foraging in forests. Perhaps unsurprisingly, an increasing number of young Russians have decided that it all sounds like no fun at all and are either dodging the draft or deserting. When a partial amnesty was offered in 1998, 11,478 soldiers who'd gone AWOL turned themselves in.

When Russian troops stormed the Pristina Airport at the end of NATO's war in Kosovo in 1999, the politicians were red-faced. Seems that the generals were doing a little freelance foreign-policy planning. When the Kremlin made some mumbles about easing off in Chechnya in the fall of 1999, the military made it clear that they could run the country just fine without the benefit of spineless politicians. The good news is that Russia is now a member of NATO.

**Ministry of Foreign Affairs**
http://www.mid.ru

## The Russian Navy

It seems the Russian navy has more submarines stuck on the bottom of the ocean than moving through it. Of the 42 nuke subs of the Northern fleet, only three can go out at any one time. And it appears that there are about 100 nukester subs lying on the bottom of the ocean bordering Norway. Not a pleasant bedtime story. Can anyone spell Kursk?

http://www.webcom.com/~amraam/rnav.html

## Soldiers' Mothers St. Petersburg (SMSP)

Since its foundation in St. Petersburg in 1989, this redoubtable organization has terrorized the Russian military establishment almost as badly as the Chechens. The SMSP is what it says it is—a sorority of implacable Russian matriarchs concerned (and quite rightly so) about the welfare of their little Ivans. The SMSP has sent more than 20 groups of mothers to Chechnya to bury dead soldiers and harangue their sons' commanders, negotiate with Chechens for the release of POWs, stage protests against the war, and assist thousands of deserters. It may be heartening to know that during the second Chechen war the Russians found hundreds of war dead in refrigerated railcars. The problem is that they were from the first Chechen war—6 to 8 years earlier.

**Soldiers' Mothers St. Petersburg**
info@soldiersmothers.spb.org
http://www.soldiersmothers.spb.org

## The Communist Party (KPRF)

Remember them? Under the leadership of failed presidential aspirant Gennadiy Zyuganov, they're now the party with the biggest bloc in the Russian state parliament, the Duma. However, one shouldn't read too much into the names of Russian political parties—the Liberal Democratic Party of Russia is led by fascist dingbat Vladimir Zhirinovsky, for example—and the communists are no longer quite as communist as they used to be.

**Russian Communist Party**
http://www.kprf.ru (Russian only)

## Perestrelka

No, not *perestroika*, a word used by Mikhail Gorbachev to symbolize reforms. *Perestrelka* means "shoot-out" in Russian and is a better description of what is going on in Russia today.

The military vacuum in Russia has allowed the rise of the *vory v zakone* (literally "thieves-in-law" or "thieves who follow a code"). A class of thugs created before the revolution and toughened in Soviet gulags, these gangsters are enamored with pomp and circumstance and even possess private jets. They are roughly one-third Russian, one-third Georgian, and one-third descended from ethnic minorities. Typically they are between 25 and 40 years old and they live by their unique law (*vorovskaia spravedlivost*). They even have their own courts, which, along with Russia not having any penal reform system, may be why you don't see too many old gangsters.

The government estimates that there are 289 thieves-in-law operating in Russia and 58 other countries around the world. You will be pleased to know that there are about 15 Russian criminal groups with about 5,000 to 6,000 members operating in America. Their main export? Violence, of course.

Below these very wealthy and powerful mafia figures are the gangs. There are about 20 criminal brigades, or gangs, that control Moscow, identified by the L.A.-style monikers they use for their neighborhoods.

There are estimated to be 5,800 gang members in Russia. The gangs aren't quick enough or smart enough to control the country, so it's left to the *vory v zakone* to reap the profits of absolute control.

There are four levels of mafia in Russia. The lowest stratum consists of shopkeepers who sell goods at inflated prices to raise protection money. The enforcers are burly, loud men with a fancy for imported cars (usually stolen). They'll also double as pimps, gun-runners, or drug dealers. The businessmen are unfettered capitalists who steer most of the lucrative deals the mafia's way.

Finally, at the top of the food chain, is the "state mafia." They are the controllers of a large percentage of the money earned by the lesser mafia. These politicians/gangsters allow the lower echelons to operate in peace and without fear of prosecution. They have driven away a lot of Western investment and businessmen who find themselves forced to retain a local "partner" in their enterprises.

http://www.tandemnews.com/viewstory.php?storyid=93
http://www.ojp.usdoj.gov/nij/international/russian.html

## Big Business

It should come as no surprise that a handful of "czars" call the shots in the Kremlin. Their only competition is the high-ranking members of the Russian military. How did they get this rich? Well, think Enron. When the Soviet Union made the transition from state control of industry to deregulation, these folks were there quicker than tweakers through a concert fence.

If you look at how American robber barons made their piles of money at the turn of the 19th century, you can figure it out. Anyway, in the end, it doesn't matter how you get it, it's how much you have that counts.

**Russia's oligarchs**
http://www.megastories.com/russia/oligarchs/glossary.htm

## The Roof/Krysha

You simply don't do business in Russia without a "roof"—a protector who guarantees that you stay alive long enough to pay your monthly dues. These groups are usually affiliated with FSB and local authorities. Naturally, you also make an accommodation with the local mafia. In a concession to modern economics, many of these groups will only dip their beaks into your profits, giving you a chance to get into the black. If you try to outsmart them, you'll of course end up in the red. Or the river.

http://www.eurasianet.org/departments/insight/articles/eav013102.shtml

## MAKIT BIG RUBLES NOW . . . ASKIT ME HOW!

Forget Mary Kay, forget no money down. The big business in Russia is corruption. Fire and sanitary inspectors in Moscow can expect an average gratuity of around $5,000 a year to let the rats play undisturbed around your corroded wiring. (Payments are broken into two easy installments.)

Business licensing is a snap with the average handout of $4,600, and traffic cops have adopted a high-volume, low-price policy that allows them to rake in $350 million a year (about $300 per employee). The typical traffic officer makes $64 a month, when he or she is paid.

But the best gigs by far are in health care and education, where $602 million is provided to ensure prompt medical (or any) attention, and college students fork out a cumulative half a billion a year so they can be educated enough to figure out how much they will have to pay in bribes once they graduate. Oh, and the legal system manages to pocket a quarter of a billion to sneak a peek from under the blindfold.

Source: World Bank

# Getting In

Visas are required for all foreigners traveling to or transiting through Russia by any means of transportation, including train, car, or airplane. While under certain circumstances travelers who hold valid visas to some countries of the former Soviet Union may not need a visa to transit Russia, such exceptions are inconsistently applied. Travelers who arrive without an entry visa may be subject to large fines, days of processing requirements by Russian officials, and/or immediate departure by route of entry (at the traveler's expense). Carry a photocopy of passports and visas to facilitate replacement should your passport be stolen.

Getting a visa for Russia is not quite as big a pain in the nads as it used to be, but it's still not much fun—there are a bewildering array of visas available, and you may need to provide evidence of sponsorship from a Russian individual or organization. Or you may not. It depends on what sort of mood the person behind the glass screen at the embassy is in, whether Dynamo Moscow won over the weekend, and other such imponderables. *DP* recommends that you invest a few extra dollars, save yourself a whole load of bother, and get a visa agency to sort it all out for you.

*Visa agencies in the United States and Europe*

http://www.visatorussia.com/russianvisa.nsf/agents.html

*Embassy of the Russian Federation*
2650 Wisconsin Avenue, NW
Washington, DC 20007
Tel.: (202) 298-5700
Fax: (202) 298-5735
http://www.russianembassy.org

*Embassy of the Russian Federation*
13 Kensington Palace Gardens
London W8 4QX, UK
Tel.: (44) 207 229 2666
Fax: (44) 207 727 8625

*Embassy of the Russian Federation*
285 Charlotte Street
Ottawa, Ontario K1N 8L5
Canada
Tel.: (613) 235-4341
Fax: (613) 236-6342
rusemb@intranet.ca
http://www.magma.ca/~rusemb

# Getting Around

Unlike the old days, when visitors to Russia had to spend their days being directed from one statue of Lenin to the next by Intourist guides spouting lies about tractor production, you can now go just about anywhere you want. You don't even need Intourist to get around.

Internal travel, especially by air, can be erratic and may be disrupted by fuel shortages, overcrowding of flights, and various other problems. Travelers may need to cross great distances, especially in Siberia and the Far East, to obtain services from Russian government organizations or from the U.S. embassy or its consulates. Russia stretches over 6,000 miles east to west and 2,500 miles north to south. Winter can last a long time.

The cheapest way into Moscow from the airport is via the regular bus. You can use rubles. Taxis are preposterously expensive—even if you don't get scammed, expect to pay $50 to $60 in real money. And make sure you arrange your taxi with one of the booths in the arrivals section rather than going with one of the freelancers, who will plague you as soon as you clear customs—their pricing structure is rather more fluid and depends on such factors as how badly you want your luggage to be removed from the trunk once you get to the hotel.

About half the roads in Russia are paved. The worst time to traverse Russian roads is during the spring, when the rural roads become muddy rivers. About 20 percent of the roads are simple tracks. The railways are the major means of transport, with most routes spreading out from Moscow on 11 major trunk lines. There are 32 railway subsystems within the former Soviet Union. The main route is the passenger

## CHIMPS TO CHUMPS

Have $20 million burning a hole in your pocket? Why not be an astronaut? Seems that the International Space Station needs to replenish their supplies of smokes and vodka every six months. A Soyuz spacecraft must be sent to the International Space Station with at least two professional astronauts on board. Since there are three seats on the Soyuz spacecraft, that leaves a spot for some rich, smiling goof to blast off every October/November or April/May. You need to be checked out by 48 Russian doctors (see Bribery) and you have to speak Russian. Seems we have come a long way from our first noble space pioneers . . . the Central African chimpanzee. Pretty much sums up the accomplishment.

Now everyone from pop stars to TV producers who want to test out Russian engineering can do so . . . at their own risk. A word of warning: The Americans scrapped their space tourist idea after the Challenger disaster.

*Chimponauts*
http://www.savethechimps.org/space.asp

artery through Russia along the Trans-Siberian Railway, which travels east from Moscow across Siberia to the Pacific and China, Mongolia, and Korea. The food on Russian trains is appalling even by Russian standards, and the pickings on the railway platforms are slim, so stock up with fresh stuff before leaving: a bottle of reasonably good Scotch will help you win friends and influence people. Traveling by sea is also an efficient way to get around Russia, particularly in the Baltic region. Twenty-seven former Soviet passenger ships form the largest passenger fleet in the world.

Russian airlines serve 3,600 population centers inside Russia, and you can gener-

> **A** bottle of reasonably good Scotch will help you win friends and influence people.

ally spot Westerners who've flown with Russian domestic airlines from a way off—they blink a bit more than the rest of us and have the haunted demeanor of people who've seen too much. Do as the locals do, and get yourself anesthetically sloshed before takeoff. Some airlines are adding new Western aircraft to the various Russian airlines, so ask what kind of plane you'll be on. The severe winters can affect schedules and flights into places like Tajikistan, and airlines are subject to fuel shortages.

The telecommunications infrastructure remains underdeveloped. Only 30 percent of urban and 9 percent of rural families have telephones. More than 17 million customers have ordered telephones, but are still waiting (sometimes for years) to have them installed. On the plus side, this means that long train journeys can be enjoyed in peace and quiet, without having to endure the teeth-grindingly banal conversations of self-important jackasses with mobile phones, which have ruined railway travel in the West.

**Trans-Siberian Railway**
http://www.sokoltours.com
http://www.transsib-travel.com

## Getting Out

All items which may appear to have historical or cultural value—icons, art, rugs, antiques, and so on—may be taken out of Russia only with prior written approval of the Ministry of Culture and payment of a 100 percent duty. Goods that are purchased from street vendors can be problematic and expensive to export. Russian customs laws state that any item for export valued at more than 300,000 rubles (value is established by customs officials at the time of export—for example, just prior to a traveler's departing flight) is subject to a 600 percent export tax. Items purchased from government-licensed shops, where prices are openly marked in hard currency, are not subject to the tax. Request a receipt when making any purchase. Caviar may be taken out of Russia only with a receipt indicating that it was bought in a store licensed to sell to foreigners. Failure to follow the customs regulations may result in temporary or permanent confiscation of the property in question.

## Dangerous Places

### The Caucasus

There is little to recommend travel in the rotting row of quasi-breakaway republics along Mother Russia's dirty skirt hem. The military and internal police (excuse the pun) call the shots here and foreigners snooping around are considered to be spies, journalists, or walking cash machines.

The situation remains unsettled in Russia's northern Caucasus area, which is located in southern Russia along its border with Georgia, and travel to this area is considered dangerous. The regions of the Chechen Republic, the Ingush Republic, and the North Ossetian Republic have experienced continued armed violence and have a state of emergency and curfew in effect. Vladikavkaz, the capital of North Ossetia, has suffered several fatal bombings of markets and other public places.

**Chechen "Rebels"**
http://www.kavkaz.org

## Moscow

In Moscow alone there are 5,000 murders and 20,000 incidents of violent crime every year. In 2001 serious crimes jumped 14 percent and burglaries rose 23 percent and half of them will most likely go unsolved. With senior detectives making around $60 a month, it's not surprising they find other, more profitable things to do, like work for the local *mafiya* dons or prey on businessmen and tourists. The local population quickly recognizes foreign tourists and business travelers because of their clothing, accessories, and behavior. Western visitors tend to experience a relatively high incidence of certain types of crime, such as physical assaults and pickpocketing of wallets, passports, and cameras on the street, in hotels, in restaurants, and in high-density tourist areas. Police will not release statistics related to "xenophobic" crimes or break-ins against embassies and foreigners. Could they be bad for tourism?

**The Moscow Times**
http://www.themoscowtimes.com

## St. Petersburg

St. Petersburg has an even higher crime rate than Moscow. The area around Gostiny Dvor and the underground passage on Nevsky Prospekt, as well as train stations, food markets, flea markets, and the so-called "art park," are frequent stages for street crime against foreigners. Most crimes are committed in broad daylight, because the police will do little, if anything, to help you or track down your assailants. If you are staying in one of the better hotels in St. Petersburg, ask the desk to send a car to pick you up at the airport. To give the tourism folks equal time:

> We ask you to forget all that you have read. Look around you. You will see a beautiful city with faultless architecture and a high level of culture. The people of this city are attentive, kind, and well educated. Many speak English, German, or French . . .

"Donnez your friggen wallet, Liebschen." The truth? St. Petersburg has a robbery rate 50 to 100 times that of Moscow's and a mugging rate 200 to 400 times greater.

**The St. Petersburg Times**
http://www.sptimesrussia.com

# Dangerous Things

*Flight, or the Sudden Lack Thereof . . .*

All the horror stories you've heard are true. You've a greater chance in Russia than in any other country of your flight ending more quickly than you'd anticipated. In 1991 the state airline Aeroflot was broken up into 400 smaller companies, few of whom could afford to properly maintain their aircraft—elderly Tupolev 154s, as often as not—or pay their pilots. It hasn't helped that air traffic control in some parts of Russia is still only a step up from people using broom handles to push model planes around on a map.

Russian airlines are now using Yankee tin and change is coming slowly. There were no Russian airline accidents in '98 and '99 . . . because they crashed in other countries and the statistics do not cover charter flights. But, to be fair, Russian air travel is heading into the yellow safety zone with annual deaths dropping from an average of 800 to less than 50. . . . Oh, did we tell you that, coincidentally, airline traffic dropped from 140 million to less than 20 million?

Then there is that touchy little subject of cargo flights. In one instance, an IL-76 was loaded with 60 tons of cargo . . . the capacity is only 40. And then there is that bribery business. . . .

If these weren't sufficient reasons for even the most blasé traveler to keep their St. Christopher medal gripped in his or her sweaty palm, Russia's workaday air disasters are puncuated by accidents straight out of the "Only in Russia" file. In March 1997, 50 died when the tail fell off a chartered An-24 in mid-flight. Most incredible of all, in March 1994, an Aeroflot Airbus A-310 crashed near Novokuznetsk, killing all 70 aboard, after the pilot decided to let his 11-year-old son have a go at flying it. In July of 2001, 145 people died when the pilot simply flew his TU-154 straight into the ground at full throttle. After analysis of the voice cockpit recorder it was determined that "There was a lot of shouting, loud shouting." Have a nice flight.

**Aeroflot**
aeroflot@russia.net
http://www.aeroflot.org

**Air Disaster**
http://www.airdisaster.com

*Safety, or the Sudden Lack Thereof . . .*

In a place where hiring a hit man to kill someone costs only $200, you had better watch your step. Foreigners are favorite

> **I**n a place where hiring a hit man to kill someone costs only $200, you had better watch your step.

targets of crime in Russia, especially in major cities. Why? Because that's where the money is, silly.

Pickpocketing and muggings occur both day and night. Street crimes are most frequent in train stations, airports, and open markets, and when hailing taxis or traveling by the Metro late at night. Groups of children who beg for money sometimes pickpocket and assault tourists. (Anyone who has visited Italy will be familiar with the routine—one snot-encrusted delinquent is suddenly joined by a dozen more, and there are hands in every one of your pockets faster than you can say "Bugger off, you little bastards"; the correct drill is to kick the smallest one as hard as you can, and then run for it.)

Hotel rooms and residences have been targeted—lock your doors and keep your wallet under the flowerpot. The Moscow–St. Petersburg overnight train is another favorite target—travel first class (it's not that expensive) and secure your compartment from the inside with a bicycle or luggage lock-chain. The police, should you need to resort to them, are worse than useless. If you decide that the best thing to do is hire security, there are quite a few choices, but bear in mind that of the 5,000 such firms investigated by the Ministry of the Interior in the mid-'90s, 10 percent had convicted criminals among their staff.

**Mariguard security**
http://www.mariguardgroup.ru/eng_versia/index.htm

## Jail

Given that conditions in Russia's army are worse than in most countries' jails, you'd imagine that things in Russia's jails must be very grim indeed. And you'd be right. More than a million Russians are currently guests of the penal system, and overcrowding is rampant—it is common for 10 men to live in cells that were built for two, sleeping in shifts or sharing bunks. According to Russia's Justice Ministry, more than 4,000 inmates are HIV-positive and another 100,000 are down with tuberculosis, of whom 10,000 die every year. Little wonder that in a survey of Russian prisoners whose death sentences had been commuted to life terms, 20 percent said they'd rather be dead.

If you are silly enough or unlucky enough to earn yourself a custodial sentence in Russia, try to make sure you've got a few rubles saved up, and it won't be so unpleasant. In 2001, the city of Kursk opened what might be the world's first luxury prison. Aimed at the rare "businessman" who manages to fall foul of the law—almost invariably as a result of failing to pay off the right people—the new lockup offers televisions, refrigerators, and single-occupancy cells, as long as the inmate is able to pay for it.

## GANGSTER RAP

You won't get much of a chance to chit-chat if the *mafiya* visits you, but you can give it a shot.

**akademiya**    jail, or prison, but really means "school."
**babki**    money, originally a term used with soup bones.
**blat**    clout, someone who has connections.
**boyevik**    home boy, or member of a gang.
**buks**    money, usually American cash rather than rubles.
**fartsofshchik**    black-market fence or dealer.
**frayeri**    suckers, the pigeons, and so on.
**kidali**    con man.
**krestnii otets**    big boss or godfather.
**lomshchiki**    short-changers who usually cheat when changing money.
**mafiya**    the Russian version of organized crime but used more generally as a term to describe any disliked group.
**organizatsiya**    organization or *mafiya.*
**razborka**    shootouts, or settling scores by gangsters.
**shestyorka**    mob flunky.
**suka**    bitch, a police or military insider who works with the police.
**volk**    cop who can't be bribed (wolf).
**vorovskoi obshak**    bribes.

*Source:* Chicago Tribune

## Water

We wouldn't drink it. It's not the source, it's those old pipes. Drink water out of bottles only.

## Vodka, or the Lack Thereof

Vodka is a preferred beverage, which many Russians drink as if it were water. If you must join in, stick to recognized brands and make sure the bottle is sealed. On no account sample the stuff sold by roadside kiosks—the kind that comes out of unlabeled bottles with tinfoil lids, a packaging method that is also used to sell diesel and gas, if you doubt our sage advice. In 1997, some 340,000 cases of counterfeit vodka that were brought to Moscow aboard 70 railroad cars were sent to a chemical plant for reprocessing into windshield cleanser

**N**eed a handy recipe for bootleg Russian vodka? Just mix stolen medical alcohol with tap water and flavor with machine oil, wood alcohol, or brake fluid; bottle and serve chilled....

and brake fluid. Need a handy recipe for bootleg Russian vodka? Just mix stolen medical alcohol with tap water and flavor with machine oil, wood alcohol, or brake fluid; bottle and serve chilled. . . . Suffice it to say that around 30,000 people die of acute alcohol poisoning each year (compared to about 300 people in the United States).

**Stolichnaya Vodka**
http://www.stoli.com

## The Afghan Curse

If there is any doubt that the Afghans stuck it to the Russians, take a look at the dramatic increase in the use of injected drugs. It seems the Russian army quickly figured out that cheap heroin and empty military cargo planes on return flights could be combined for an exciting new business opportunity.

Heroin usage is so serious that 6 percent of 16- to 25-year-olds in Moscow have tried heroin at least once. Since the end of the Afghan war, registered drug users have increased 400 percent (the real number is estimated to be eight or ten times this number). Even the government admits that around 3 million Russians, or 2.1 percent of its citizens, are drug users. Along with this lust for heroin comes an explosion in HIV/AIDS cases. In 1999 there were 130,000 Russians with HIV/AIDs. Two years later there were a million. By the time you read this, the numbers will have jumped exponentially.

http://usinfo.state.gov/topical/pol/terror/01111313.htm
http://www.avert.org/ecstatee.htm

## Knowing Where You Are

Seems the Russians just can't get used to Westerners using their GPSs to figure out the confusing road system. They take knowing where you are very seriously and have penalties of up to 20 years for using GPS systems to map sensitive locations. If you think you are being tricky telling them it's a cell phone . . . there are also rules about importing cell phones, radio transmitters, and so on.

http://travel.state.gov/gps.html

## Being Born Again . . . and Again

It seems that the Russian government has an interesting way of calculating the losses in the latest Russian war. In June 2002, the official tally of military casualties in the second Chechen war since October '99 was 2,410 killed and 6,053 wounded. The problem is that a year ago the official number was 3,433 dead and two years earlier it was 2,304. All this in a war where 5 to 10 Russian soldiers continue to die every week. Obviously Russian military medicine has progressed to the point where dead troops are brought back to life within two or three years. *DP* is happy to report that everyone killed in the Russian military should be in good health and back on the job. . . .

http://www.chechnyanews.com

### Baksheesh, or the Lack Thereof . . .

Before we get too high on our horse, it should be remembered that capitalism and corruption are virtually one and the same in today's Russia. The idea of keeping careful track of money earned, refusing to give in to extortionary demands, and then faithfully sending in a tax check every year would elicit peals of laughter in modern Russia. In a country where the former president lived like a pasha on his official US$30,000 a year and his supposedly squeaky-clean successor passed laws to prevent criminal prosecution for corruption, there is little hope for reform. In fact, Putin's crackdown on corruption is assumed to be a way to make sure the bribe money ends up in its rightful place . . . as government bribes.

The bribery process has simply replaced the need to pay salaries or benefits to police, government, military, and other state entities. So it impressed us all to heck when a Danish think tank (funded by the World Bank) figured out that Russians paid $36 billion in bribes every year (more than half of total government spending, or 12 percent of GNP). Even Transparency International gave a heads-up that Russian companies are the most likely to pay bribes to win business. Bribes are a normal line item in deals, usually running about 10 percent of the total bid. Although most bribes are paid to low-level government employees, it was determined that 99 percent of the Russian executive branch accepted bribes. Just for a hoot, next time you are in Russia make the bold decision not to pay off a traffic cop or minor official and watch the wheels go to work. Within minutes your minor obstacle or infraction will have increased from simple tea money to a major violation costing hundreds of dollars. You will soon learn to go with the flow.

The Indem report estimates that 82 percent of Russian companies and businessmen normally pay bribes. Perhaps the most surprising result of the study is that 18 percent of companies *don't* pay bribes—and just who, exactly, is that 1 percent of the government that won't accept bribes?

http://www.transparency.org

# Getting Sick

An Australian newspaper is reputed to have kept a database for foreign correspondents, containing useful numbers and addresses in

## DUCK HUNTING

A Russian TU-154 airliner vanished over the Black Sea, killing all 77 souls. Investigators couldn't help noticing hundreds of steel pellets penetrating the engines, bodies, and fuselage. Investigations revealed that a Ukrainian S200 missile had been fired as part of a test. Perhaps the military decided that the Sibir jet was an intriguing target. After initially denying responsibility, the Ukrainian military was fingered by the Russians because "there were no other versions left."

The story about overzealous Crimean duck hunters was not accepted as an alternate possibility. The government of the Ukraine has yet to pay one ruble to the victims' families.

every country on earth that could be contacted in the event of one disaster or another. For Russia, under "Emergencies," the database stated "Don't have one." Medical care in Russia is usually far below Western standards, with severe shortages of basic supplies. Access to the few quality facilities that exist in major cities usually requires payment in dollars at Western rates upon admission. The U.S. embassy and consulates have a list of good facilities and English-speaking doctors. Many expats travel outside Russia for their medical needs. Travelers may wish to check their insurance coverage and consider supplemental coverage for medical evacuation. On the other hand, Russian health care is very low cost and there are plenty of Soviet-era-trained medical doctors.

Typhoid can be a concern for those who plan to travel extensively in Russia. Drinking only boiled or bottled water will help to guard against cholera, which has been reported, as well as other diseases.

***Centers for Disease Control and Prevention***
http://www.cdc.gov/travel/easteurp.htm

## Nuts and Bolts ———————————————

The Russian Federation is noticeably smaller than the USSR, but it's still a big place—with 17,075,200 square kilometers, it's almost twice the size of the United States. Moscow, with nearly 9 million residents, is the largest city.

The Russian Federation officially came into existence in December 1991. Russia is a presidential republic, containing 22 autonomous republics that maintain an uneasy balance between the Russian president and the Congress of People's Deputies (parliament). In practice, the power base is much more complex. Russia's vast size and population (148 million) could make the region ripe for exploitation by Western investors; however, the corrupt infrastructure makes business profits unlikely for years to come.

Russian is the official language, although there are many regional ethnic tongues. English is widely read but not yet fluently spoken. Translators of varying abilities will be found in all sizable organizations. The country boasts a nearly 100 percent literacy rate.

Business hours are from 9:00 A.M. to 1:00 P.M., with a break for the typical heavy Russian lunch between 1:00 and 2:00 P.M. Some stores close from 2:00 to 3:00 P.M. Banks are open from 9:30 A.M. to 12:30 P.M., with currency exchanges open longer. You can change money at Sheremetyevo II International Airport in Moscow 24 hours a day. Also, the American Express office in Moscow can cash your AMEX traveler's checks.

Russia is $163 billion in debt but still manages to keep finding major oil fields. Gas comes from western Siberia; the largest areas are Urengoi and Yamburg. New fields on the Yamal peninsula are waiting for development. The former USSR was the world's third-largest coal producer (after China and the United States). Russia possesses the world's largest explored reserves of copper, lead, zinc, nickel, mercury, and tungsten. It also has about 40 percent of the world's reserves of iron ore and manganese. Figures released in September 1990 show confirmed iron reserves of 33.1 billion tons. The world's largest gold deposits, at the Sukhoi Log reserves, are estimated at more than 1,000 tons: gold continues to be smuggled out of Russia through the Baltic states. Russia is also trying to retain more control over its diamond reserves. The government created the Federal Diamond Center, granting parliament more control over the industry. The intent is to undermine the control over Russia's diamonds by De Beers, which has operated a supply cartel and maintained Russia's output at 7,500,000 carats per year.

## OH, THOSE WACKY SIBERIANS

In Barnaul, the Altai region of southern Siberia, a police officer was found guilty of beating a man with an axe and kicking him to death. The policeman and his partner originally responded to a complaint that a drunken man had stolen a neighbor's dog and eaten it. In true Russian style, the two cops broke into the dog chef's house, hit him on the head with an axe, and kicked him until his liver ripped in two, causing his death. We recommend the squirrel next time.

Russia will be a net food importer for some time to come. Even when there are record harvests, shortages of labor leave the crops to rot in the fields. Arms sales continue to be an important part of Russia's exports, although there is worldwide concern that a lot of high-tech systems are getting into the wrong hands.

The official currency is the ruble; it's pointless to post the ruble's rate against the U.S. dollar because it changes as frequently as most people change their underwear. U.S. currency is still preferred in Russia for major purchases, but rubles are now acceptable for almost all transactions. There are 100 kopeks to the ruble. Traveler's checks and credit cards are not widely accepted in Russia; in many cities, credit cards are accepted only at establishments catering to Westerners. Old, or very worn, dollar bills are often not accepted, even at banks. Major hotels or the American Express offices in Moscow or St. Petersburg may be able to suggest locations for cashing traveler's checks or obtaining cash advances on credit cards. Western Union has agents in Moscow, St. Petersburg, and some other large cities that can disburse money wired from the United States.

Electricity is 220V/50Hz.

## Embassy and Consulate Locations

### U.S. Diplomatic Mission to Russia
Novinskiy Bulvar 19/23
123242 Moscow, Russia
Tel.: (7) 95 728 5000
Tel.: (7) 95 728 5025 (after-hours emergency)
Fax: (7) 95 728 50 84
consulmo@state.gov
http://usembassy.state.gov/moscow.html

### U.S. Consulate General in St. Petersburg
Ulitsa Furshtadtskaya 15
191028 St. Petersburg, Russia
Tel.: (7) 812 275-1701
Fax: (7) 812 110 7022
http://usembassy.state.gov /stpetersburg

### U.S. Consulate General in Yekaterinburg
Gogolya ul. 15
Yekaterinberg, Russia
Tel.: (7) 3432 62 9888
Fax: (7) 3432 56 4515
uscgyekat@state.gov
http://www.uscgyekat.ur.ru

### U.S. Consulate General in Vladivostok
Pushkinskaya 32
69001 Vladivostok, Russia
Tel.: (7) 4232 30 0070
Fax: (7) 4232 30 0091
pavlad@state.gov
http://usembassy.state.gov/vladivostok

### British Embassy
Smolenskaya Naberezhnaya
121099 Moscow, Russia
Tel.: (7) 95 956 7301
Fax: (7) 95 956 7328
consular.moscow@fco.gov.uk
http://www.britemb.msk.ru

### British Consulate General in St. Petersburg
Proletarskoy Diktatury 5
193124 St. Petersburg, Russia
Tel.: (7) 812 320 3200
Fax: (7) 812 320 3211
bcgspb@peterlink.ru
http://www.britain.spb.ru

**British Consulate General in Yekaterinburg**
4th floor, Gogol ul. 15a
Yekaterinburg 620075, Russia
Tel.: (7) 3432 56 4931
Fax: (7) 3432 59 2901
brit@sky.ru
http://www.britain.sky.ru

**Canadian Embassy**
Starokonyushenny Pereulok 23
121002 Moscow, Russia
Tel.: (7) 95 956 6666
Fax: (7) 95 956 1577
mosco@dfait-maeci.gc.ca

*Web Resources*

**ITAR-TASS**
http://www.itar-tass.com/news.asp

**All about Russia**
http://www.russianinfo.com

**Russia Today**
http://www.innews.com/russia

**Voice of Russia radio**
http://www.vor.ru

**Canadian Consulate General, St. Petersburg**
Malodetskoselski Prospekt 32
198013 St. Petersburg, Russia
Tel.: (7) 812 325 8448
Fax: (7) 812 325 8393
spurg@dfait-maeci.gc.ca

**Center for Policy Studies in Russia**
http://www.pircenter.org/english/index.htm

**Glasnost Defense Foundation**
http://www.gdf.ru/english/index.shtml

*Emergency Numbers*

Fire: 01
Police: 02
Ambulance: 03
Special police service for foreigners: 164 9787 (St. Petersburg)
International Medical Clinic: 280 8388 (Moscow)

# Dangerous Days

| | |
|---|---|
| 10/29/02 | 117 hostages die, most from gas used in rescue attempt. |
| 10/26/02 | Chechen rebels take over 800 people hostage in a Moscow theater. |
| 10/4/02 | Russian airliner flying between Tel Aviv and Irkutsk accidentally shot down by Ukrainian navy over Black Sea. |
| 5/9/02 | Pipe bomb in Vladikavkaz kills 34 people. |
| 1/02 | Russia's last independent national TV station, TV-6, forced to stop broadcasting. |

| | |
|---|---|
| 3/23/01 | Three car bombs kill 20 in towns in the Stavropol region, near Chechnya. |
| 3/15/01 | Russian airliner hijacked from Istanbul to Medina. |
| 12/19/00 | Moscow's deputy mayor, Iosif Ordzhonikidze, is wounded in an assassination attempt; his driver is killed. |
| 8/12/00 | Nuclear submarine Kursk sinks in Barents Sea, killing all 118 crew members. |
| 3/27/00 | Vladimir Putin elected president. |
| 12/31/99 | Yeltsin announces his retirement. Vladimir Putin appointed acting president. |
| 9/9/99 | A series of explosions in Moscow apartments is blamed on Chechens; Russian troops sent back into Chechnya. |
| 8/10/99 | Southern Dagestan declares independence, but the Russian military change their mind. |
| 3/19/99 | Bomb in a busy marketplace in Vladikavkaz kills 60 and injures more than 100. |
| 8/98 | The ruble collapses. |
| 7/2/96 | Yeltsin wins Soviet election. |
| 10/93 | Yeltsin uses the army to attack and recapture the parliament. Rutskoy arrested, along with the speaker, Ruslan Khasbulatov. |
| 9/93 | Yeltsin suspends parliament. MPs barricade themselves inside parliament building in Moscow, and name Vice President Aleksandr Ruskoy acting president. |
| 12/31/91 | President Bush recognizes the independence of all 12 former Soviet republics and proposes the establishment of full diplomatic relations with 6 of them, including Russia. Russian President Yeltsin responds formally and positively on December 31. |
| 1991 | The year officially considered to be when the United States established formal diplomatic relations with Russia. |
| 12/25/91 | Mikhail Gorbachev resigns as president of the Soviet Union and transfers control of the Soviet nuclear arsenal to Russian President Boris Yeltsin. A few hours later, the United States recognizes Russia as the successor state to the Soviet Union. These actions mark the end of the Soviet Union, 74 years after the Bolshevik revolution. |
| 12/21/91 | Russia joins with 10 other former republics of the Soviet Union (which ceased to exist on December 25, 1991) in establishing the Commonwealth of Independent States. The Commonwealth was expected to have military and economic coordinating functions and would be headquartered in Minsk, Belarus. |

| 8/19/91 | Coup attempt fails, symbolizing the end of communism in Russia and the breakup of the Soviet Union. |
|---|---|
| 5/2/45 | Berlin falls to the Soviets. |
| 2/1/43 | Germany's 6th Army surrenders to Soviet forces in Stalingrad. |
| 6/22/41 | German invasion of USSR. |
| 11/7/17 | Revolution Day, considered the most sacred day by Russian communists. |

## In a DANGEROUS PLACE: RUSSIA

### IF YOU'RE LOOKING FOR RUBLE

*Ambulance Chasing with* Highway Patrol, *Moscow*
*March 1996*

In Moscow, as everywhere else, midnight is where bad television goes to die. Freezing on a spring night in a cheap hotel, I'm keeping warm by getting up every few minutes and walking across the room to change channels. On channel 1, capitalist pornography—a low-rent game show tottering on a set that wobbles perceptibly every time one of the contestants leans on a buzzer. On channel 2, a dismal documentary involving a surely unnecessary number of pictures of tractors. On channels 3 and 4, music videos in a proportion of roughly four parts balls-achingly awful Russian ballad singers to one part the only thing worse: Phil Collins. On channel 5, grainy highlights of an ice hockey game, apparently filmed on an aging Super-8 camera by someone who had one or two drinks before reporting to work.

And over on channel 6, a ghostly pale face leers from the screen, its bloodshot eyes divided by a ragged gash running from forehead to nose. A trickle of dark blood dribbles from the cut into a froth-encrusted, furiously yammering mouth which emits a frantic, babbled commentary as the camera pans dispassionately around the room in which this apparition is sitting, revealing the detritus of a quiet night that has clearly gone badly, badly wrong: pizza crusts of various vintages in cardboard trays, empty bottles strewn across the mildewed carpet, two spent syringes in a vase full of dirty water, and, slumped in the far corner, the scene's other protagonist. His left eye has been neatly replaced by a bullet hole, and the contents of his head are splashed across the wallpaper behind him.

The camera dwells on the corpse just that little bit too long, as if it can't quite believe what it's seeing, then pulls suddenly away, just like a human eye flinching from something unsightly. It rests again on the hysterical narrator, as he's handcuffed by the police and hustled from view. A date—today's—appears along the bottom of the screen in type, followed by a time, about six hours ago. The picture fades to a shot of a sponsor-spangled white BMW Estate leaving the site, and the credits roll. So ends another episode of *Highway Patrol*, the most popular television program in Russia, and one of the most-watched in the world.

*Highway Patrol* is a bona fide broadcasting phenomenon, boasting 70 million viewers in Russia, Belarus, Estonia, Latvia, Lithuania, Kazakhstan, and, through some unfathomable miracle of syndication, Israel. The idea is hardly unique: most countries with sufficiently noteworthy crime rates entertain and appall themselves with footage retrieved by ambulance-chasing camera crews (*Cops* in America, *Blues & Twos* in Britain).

*Highway Patrol* is different, however. It is broadcast with an inescapable frequency, producing a daily 15-minute show which is shown at midnight every night and repeated twice the following day, in addition to an irregular roundup of mafia activity—all too literally, a Greatest Hits. *Highway Patrol* also has a pitiless attitude toward broadcasting the grisliest of material, though they do have their limits, as I eventually found out the hard way.

Most important, *Highway Patrol* has a firm touch on the pulse of its home city. Postcommunist Moscow is a 1990s version of Al Capone's Chicago—a city where the gangsters don't bother to conceal their weapons, and where the police don't bother to change out of uniform when they go to their other jobs, such as doorman at one of Moscow's mafia-controlled nightclubs. Muscovites talk about crime the way Londoners talk about the weather, nodding wearily and muttering to each other that it's bad, it's going to get worse, and nobody's going to do anything about it.

*Highway Patrol* began broadcasting in January 1995, the bright idea of television producer Kirill Legat and businessman Dmitri Koriavov. Koriavov, an amiable sort somewhere in his late 30s, is typical of what is often sneeringly referred to as a New Russian: one who has been cunning enough to ride out the uncertainties of the post-communist years and to manufacture cash from chaos. When Mikhail Gorbachev started talking about *glasnost* and *perestroika* in 1985, Koriavov was a mathematician at a Soviet scientific institute, where his job was constructing climactic models intended to predict the effects of nuclear winter. In one sense or another, he knew which way the wind was blowing—by 1989, he'd gone into private business, selling computers and importing luxury cars, before branching into television. His production company, Aladdin, makes *Highway Patrol*.

When I meet Koriavov at Aladdin's offices, he is predictably unrepentant about the view his program presents of Moscow ("A city of opportunity," he calls it) and the relentless frequency with which it does so—it's not like he's making this stuff up, after all. "This is real information about our lives in this city," he says. "It does good, as well, for sure. Two years ago, I used to, you know, drive home after I'd been drinking. But now, never. Because, three times a day, five times a week, I see what results when people do that."

Koriavov recalls that the first few weeks of *Highway Patrol* were characterized by mutual antipathy and suspicion between his film crews and Moscow's emergency services, but says that relations have improved—Aladdin's offices are abundantly decorated with certificates and awards presented by the city's police and fire departments in recognition of the illustrations that *Highway Patrol* has provided of the dangers of smoking while drunk in bed; its stark depictions of the consequences of drinking and driving; and its role in enlisting public response to police enquiries. The relationship is now so close that a lot of the program's information about new crimes comes from contacts within the police force. Otherwise, *Highway Patrol* relies on calls from viewers or its own monitoring of police radio frequencies.

"We don't judge," says Koriavov. "We don't criticize. We don't praise. We just show what happens."

Koriavov leads me out of his office and up the hall to meet the crew who've agreed to take me out for the night. The three of them sit around a table in a small, smoke-filled room, pouring an occasional slug from an unlabeled vodka bottle into shot-sized paper cups. This is what they do until something interesting comes in on the radio or telephone. I'm extended the same welcome usually granted to an itinerant angler or visiting surfer: "You should have been here yesterday."

It had been, at least from the journalistic point of view, a good one—a black Volvo, driving up a busy road around the corner from the American embassy, had been cut off by a Jeep charging out of a side alley. According to a street full of eyewitnesses, the occupants of the Jeep had fired 30 or 40 shots from two automatic rifles into the windshield of the Volvo, killing both occupants, before driving off and disappearing into the traffic. A classic mafia hit.

I'm shown the unedited footage by the crew's reporter/presenter, Vladimir Yemelyanov, a ruddy-cheeked 25-year-old bearing an astonishing and, frankly, disturbing resemblance to David Platt.

"I wonder who did it," he muses, to nobody in particular.

Without thinking, I suggest that it won't be too hard for the police to find the perpetrators of a murder carried out in broad daylight on a busy street in rush hour. Vladimir laughs a mirthless laugh, and I try to cover my tracks by smiling the sort of smile you smile when you've just said something idiotic and you're trying to make it look like you were joking.

The average Moscow police officer gets paid about £100 a month. Moscow is not much cheaper a place to live than most European capitals. So, Moscow policemen have to find other work, and a moonlighting cop will find the easiest and steadiest employment from the kind of person who wants not only armed muscle, but the added advantage of a reasonable guarantee that the person's not going to look too closely during his own day job. A month before I arrived in Russia, a Scottish lawyer was killed by crossfire in a St. Petersburg café when two balaclava-clad hitmen attempted to assassinate a local crime boss. Two other men died in the attack: Both were St. Petersburg policemen working at their after-hours gigs, as bodyguards to the gangster.

I talk more with Vladimir while we sit and await the call to action— he gets one of Aladdin's receptionist's to help him with his halting English through the more complicated questions. He happily confirms that he gets paid considerably better than any of the policemen, firemen, and paramedics he follows around, and says that he enjoys his job, although he gets rattled and "has some trouble sleeping" on nights after they've done a story in which a child has been on the receiving end. He wears a pistol on his belt, and I wonder if that's because *Highway Patrol* crews often arrive at crime scenes before the police—their new BMW is quicker than a rusty Lada patrol car.

"No, the job is not dangerous," Vladimir says. "But none of us have our own cars, and sometimes we have to walk home late at night."

I run a few standard knee-jerk reactions to his job past Vladimir: that he's a vulture with a camera crew; that he's making gruesome violence look like an acceptable part of everyday life; that he's encouraging the weak-willed to emulate what they see on the screen; that he's profiting from the misfortune of others. I don't believe much of this myself: *Highway Patrol,* like other amoral cultural signifiers, such as tabloid newspapers, slasher films, gangsta rap, and heavy metal music, exists because people like it and are willing to pay for it. Perhaps I feel he could be guilty of profiting from the misfortune of others, but as that's a fair, if cynical, definition of journalism, I'm in no position to criticize. Vladimir's heard it all before, anyway.

"Our program doesn't do any of that," he says. "There are lots of stupid action movies shown on television every day that are much, much worse. It's just that whenever people see death—I mean real death, of real people—they are surprised. Nothing more than that. Death happens every day, but people are surprised when they see it. I was surprised the first time I saw Lenin in the mausoleum."

The crew's driver, Sacha, puts down his mobile phone and announces that we're off: He's heard something from one of his contacts. Vladimir throws me a spare *Highway Patrol* parka, and while I struggle into it, he draws his pistol from its holster and points it at the temple of Leon, the cameraman. Leon looks up briefly, finishes his coffee with exaggerated serenity, and walks down to the carpark with us.

Sacha weaves the BMW through Moscow's comically potholed streets with the bravado of one who believes that the rules of the road were written for lesser mortals. Perhaps they were: Policemen on point duty wave as the famous car passes, and one holds up traffic at an intersection to allow us through against the lights. We fetch up at a police station amid the crumbling tower blocks of Moscow's southern suburbs. Like every other public building I've visited in Moscow, including the office block that houses Aladdin, the cop shop is a dank, musty shambles that gives the impression of having been recently abandoned by a previous owner and hurriedly occupied by squatters.

The police trot out a singularly gormless-looking youth who has, they explain, been apprehended at the unpromising beginning of his criminal career: He was caught burgling a flat in the same block his family lives in. Vladimir interviews the kid, and then the station chief, but his heart's obviously not in it, and his thoughts are easy to read on his face: This is no big deal, a dull little morality play, strictly filler stuff, of use only if this turns out to be an especially dull shift. Whether his disappointment is normal, or whether he was hoping for something a bit more hair-raising to show the visitor, Vladimir descends into a gale-force sulk, fidgeting irritably with the car radio all the way back to base. He cheers up only when a motorcycle policeman, evidently no fan of *Highway Patrol*, pulls us over in front of the White House (the former home of the Russian parliament, which was shattered during the attempted coup of 1991) and books Sacha for speeding.

The next day means a new shift, and a renewed optimism among the crew that they'll come up with something really horrible to show me. They explain that they average one call to a proper underworld execution every day, so it's only going to be a matter of time. Nevertheless, we have to start somewhere, and so we start in what remains of a flat above a Hyundai spares shop, not far from the Aladdin offices. The resident of the flat obviously wasn't watching the last time *Highway Patrol* warned about the perils of falling asleep drunk while smoking: he's fallen asleep drunk while smoking and incinerated himself. It looks bad, and smells worse, but there's a strange calm about the proceedings. Firemen quietly lay down planks so that we can walk through the water they've sprayed into the place without getting our shoes muddy. A policeman pours me coffee from a thermos while Leon and Vladimir set up for Vladimir's piece-to-camera. Sacha tuts at me for getting paint on the *Highway Patrol* jacket I'm wearing, and wipes me down with turpentine—a scene that will baffle Moscow's viewing public later this evening.

As it turns out, this shift yields no decapitated hitmen, kneecapped stool pigeons, cement-flippered informers, or horse's heads in anyone's beds. There aren't even any workaday domestic catastrophes: no road smashes, clumsy drinkers, Metro-jumpers, or overdoses. We get called to only one more story, and it's something much worse than any of these, at least insofar as one fatal tragedy can be said to be much worse than any other.

In a courtyard between three dung-colored tower blocks, in the snow next to a rubbish skip, someone has left a baby boy. I get close enough to see how blue the naked form is, and how purple the vestige of umbilical cord trailing from its midriff, before I work out exactly what it is I'm looking at, and then I don't believe it, and when I do believe it, I don't want to. The *Highway Patrol* crew and a forensic scientist in a white fur coat hunch over the dead child; the scene looks like some grotesque parody of the Nativity.

Vladimir shoots me a look; he's not enjoying this one, and neither am I. I wander off and stare very determinedly at anything else at all. He and I seem to be the only people here who are remotely perturbed. Leon and Sacha fiddle about with the camera cables. The forensic team discusses whether or not the boy was alive when he was left here, or if perhaps he was thrown from one of the balconies overlooking the square. There's one policeman in attendance, and he sits in his car, reading a paper, smoking, keeping warm, doing nothing to shoo away passersby—but this is exactly what they do: they pass by. This is a busy pedestrian route, and though people look over, and raise an eyebrow or two beneath their fur hats, they don't seem any more curious than I might be if someone parked an expensive sports car on my street. Despite what Vladimir has said about death being a surprise, these people are behaving as if a dead child on the footpath is about as surprising as the sun coming up. Nobody weeps or wails; no teeth are gnashed, no garments rent.

That said, I don't know the neighborhood. Maybe people leave dead kids lying around here every day of the week; maybe it isn't that interesting. Or perhaps it's just that Russia has never been an easy place to live, and that maybe Muscovites have a hardened attitude toward death, caused by centuries of proximity to it.

"Don't know," says Vladimir, as we drive off. In the end, it doesn't matter anyway. Tomorrow is Women's Day, the Russian equivalent of Mother's Day, and a story like this is hardly going to make for suitable family-holiday viewing. So Sacha drives us to a nearby flower market and we take some pictures of that, instead.

*—Andrew Mueller*

★★★

# SOUTH AFRICA

## So'sweat-o

Of all the African countries, South Africa was ruled by the white inter-loper the longest. It is also where discrimination in favor of the minor-ity was most brutally upheld by law. Little wonder that when South Africa made the adjustment to democracy in the '90s, so many people expected a bloodbath. Indeed, it's fair to say that much of the world would have taken a barely disguised satisfaction in seeing South Africa's privileged, pale-skinned overlords dangling by their ankles in front of dancing mobs of the black majority they'd held hostage for so long. South Africa's legal enshrinement of a policy called *apartheid*, which explicitly and unapologetically named the black majority as second-class citizens, had made it the one country that the rest of the divided Cold-War world had been able to agree to abhor.

From Russia (whose record on its minorities is, uh, interesting), to the United States (where, when Muhammad Ali first became Heavyweight

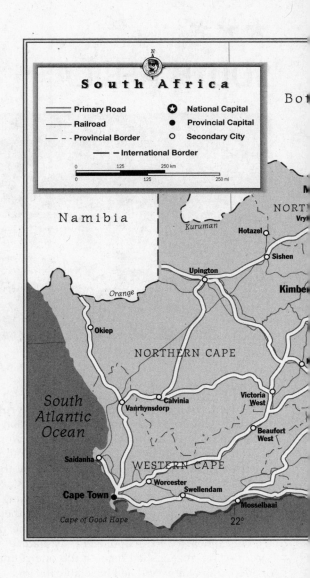

Champion of the World, he couldn't get served in most restaurants), to Australia (where citizenship was not extended to its aboriginals until 1967), countries around the world could all declare that the white South Africans were a sack of assholes, and congratulate themselves on their moral superiority. This is not to say that the white South Africans weren't a sack of assholes (with a few heroic exceptions, such as newspaper editor Donald Woods, they most certainly were), but apartheid was so patently bigoted that it always seemed a bit much when people outside South Africa claimed credit for opposing it: It was like expecting a round of applause for declaring yourself against hitting kittens with shovels or burning down orphanages for the blind.

At the dance of nations, South Africa was the wallflower who couldn't ever find a partner. Ordinary people all over the world wouldn't buy its apples or wines. Sports teams boycotted it (a few tennis and cricket players, to their shame, took advantage and accepted huge sums of money to break the embargo). Pop stars got together as Artists United Against Apartheid to sing "(I Ain't Gonna Play) Sun City," referring to the whites-only resort complex in the nominal black homeland of Bophuthatswana (unbelievably, however, a few unprincipled bottom-feeders were quite happy to take the filthy lucre that was on offer, precisely because of the stand taken by their fellows—Queen, Rod Stewart, Elton John, Liza Minelli, and Status Quo, to name five). In Britain, The Special AKA had a hit with a song called "Free Nelson Mandela," and the makers of the satirical program *Spitting Image* topped the singles charts with a memorable ditty called "I've Never Met a Nice South African." All together, now:

I've seen a flying pig in a quite convincing wig,
but I've never met a nice South African.

But you get the point. South Africa's status as the world's least-popular country dated from 1948, when apartheid was signed into law in the former British dominion by the governing National Party. The Dutch and German immigrants along with their traditional nemeses, the more la-di-da English immigrants, seemed to agree on one thing: that the natives were restless and needed to be penned up at night. (It's a *kraal* but necessary thing, don't you know.) An assortment of preposterous laws were passed to maintain the purity of South Africa's whites, and, more to the point, to maintain the privilege of South Africa's whites. The Group Areas Act specified different living areas for blacks and whites. The Immorality Act banned sexual relations across the color bar. The only contact between white and black was to be the contact between master and servant. The system was propped up with ruthlessness and brutality.

This nonsense finally began to unravel in the late '80s, when hard-line President P. W. Botha was replaced by F. W. De Klerk. There is an extent to which the praise De Klerk later received—including a Nobel Peace Prize—was akin to congratulating a rooster on crowing at the dawn, but like Mikhail Gorbachev in the USSR at around the same time, De Klerk was able to see that his country's situation was no longer tenable. De Klerk was facing pressure from abroad and upheavals within. In his first year as president, De Klerk oversaw the desegregation of public facilities and met with Nelson Mandela, the long-imprisoned figurehead of the banned African National Congress party and internationally adored symbol of the struggle against apartheid. De Klerk recognized that without Mandela on board, he could not bring South Africa into the light. Mandela recognized that De Klerk recognized this. Had these two men not occupied these two positions at this point, South Africa could have wound up like Zimbabwe today, or even Rwanda in 1994.

## MADE IN ENGLAND

*Apartheid* is one of those words that needs no translation. It is a unique Afrikaaner word that describes the systematic separation and control of racial or ethnic groups as part of government policy. The system was put in place in South Africa in 1948, but was actually a rough copy of what the British did to the Boers at the turn of the century during the Boer War. Knowing that the Boers could never be defeated, the Brits simply corralled the Boer women and children and put them in concentration camps. Neglect and disease thinned their ranks until the Boers realized they would become extinct. It is a policy that has been repeated in Germany, Vietnam, Israel, Chechnya, and other dirty wars around the world.

With the last vestiges of apartheid finally abolished in 1991, and Mandela elected president in South Africa's first all-races election in 1994, the country looked set fair. For the first time in its life, South Africa basked in the goodwill of the rest of the world. The sanctions, which had been in place for decades, were lifted, its passionately supported sports teams were readmitted to international federations, and it was allowed back into the Commonwealth, which it had left in a huff in 1961. It wasn't perfect: An institutional injustice like apartheid can't be rectified overnight, and it didn't help that the two biggest black parties, Mandela's African National Congress (ANC) and the Zulu In-khata movement, celebrated the defeat of the common enemy by embarking on a small-scale civil war with each other. But it looked like a better bet for foreign investment and tourism than any other country in Africa.

It still looks that way, but the question is, for how much longer? Mandela has retired from politics, leaving South Africa's government in the hands of people who are merely human. The Lonely Planet crowds stream through Soweto as it becomes the newest human zoo for PC tourists. South Africans put on great shows of freedom and triumph, but at night the bodies of the murdered pile up and nothing seems to get better. For the meantime, it's a little sweaty in Soweto.

## The Scoop

South Africa is rare among countries listed in *DP* in that it's a civilized, democratic, and more or less first-world country with a functioning infrastructure. It's also a popular tourist destination, where millions of people go on vacation and have an absolute whale of a time. However, South Africa is being eaten away from within by two problems, AIDS and crime, which are eroding its wealth, draining its resources, killing its people, and persuading increasing numbers of its educated and wealthy that they might be better off elsewhere. If South Africa does not get a grip on both of these problems soon, it may be unrecognizable within two or three generations, and it may have two or three more stars in its *DP* rating.

**South African Tourism**
http://www.southafrica.net

**Mail & Guardian**
http://www.mg.co.za

## The Players

### The Boers

Damned if a bunch of white guys didn't start this whole mess. As with most things African, white people are blamed for pretty much everything, and yet you don't see any Africans locking their condos and moving back to a hut in the bush. The Boers (Boer is the Dutch word for "farmer") were Dutch immigrants who came in 1652 (uncomfortably close to a similar scenario in America). Of course, there were people there when they arrived, but they were nomadic Bantu tribesmen and the last thing they wanted to do was build nice little houses and plant crops. The Boers soon began to spread north from Cape Town and look for grazing land and ranches for their cattle. Some of the Bantu fought back, but it was the old sticks-against-rifles thing (sound familiar?) and the Boers soon put the Bantus to work.

Things were going swimmingly (for the Boers at least) until a Napoleonic War screw-up meant that their new landlord was England. The British outlawed slavery in 1835 and a diamond rush in 1867 flooded the country with "saltpricks," or Brits. The Zulus went on a rampage against other tribes and the Brits, and threw the country into disarray in the mid-1800s. In 1836 the Voortrekkers set out to colonize the land and could not come to an agreement with the Zulus, who did not want the settlers expanding out of Natal. They launched a savage war against each other. On December 16, 1838, 464 Boers defeated more than 10,000 Zulus without suffering a single fatality. The Boers took it as a sign from God that they were meant to have the land.

Then the British and the Boers got into it, and in 1844 Natal become a Crown Colony. In 1879 the British simply declared Zululand to be their territory, and immediately had their butts kicked by 20,000 Zulus at Isandlwana. Eventually enough Brits showed up to win in 1887, but there was never that undeniable tension that comes from being outnumbered. The Boers continued to spread out and create what is now knwn as South Africa. On February 11, 1899, the British finally started a war pitting 450,000 men under British command against 52,000 Boers, or Afrikaaners. At first the Boers won, but eventually they were reduced to a guerrilla style of warfare.

The Boers fought back in "commandos," or small attack groups, from 1899 to 1902, but gave up when the British came up with the idea of rounding up all the Boer women and children in a nifty new invention called a concentration camp (an idea that Brits stole from the U.S. war against the Indians) and starving them to death. Over 27,000 women and children died from disease and starvation. This essentially created three classes in South Africa: the British ruling and wealthy classes; the poor, agrarian Boers; and the segregated blacks—a recipe for disaster if ever there was one.

The reality is that the Boers are a tough, gregarious bunch of people who are suspicious of outsiders but intensely loyal once they get to know you. They know their hard-learned lessons about Africa are frowned upon by the more naive PC crowd. Today the Afrikaaners are in demand as low-wage, highly functional professionals who are not afraid to work in the worst parts of Africa.

http://rapidttp.com/milhist/index.html

## Nelson Mandela

Nelson's not president anymore, but he's still the most important man in South Africa, and arguably the most important man in the

entire African continent. In an age dominated by corrupt or compromised politicians, suspicious and prurient media, and
cynical and apathetic publics, Nelson
Rolihlahla Mandela is that rarest of things:
an undisputed, untarnished, honest-to-
goodness hero. Not only has he borne his
personal travails with awesome grace and
good humor, he was the principal reason
that postapartheid South Africa didn't
drown in a sea of blood, and he has continued to work hard, if not always success-

> In an age dominated by corrupt or compromised politicians, suspicious and prurient media, and cynical and apathetic publics, Nelson Rolihlahla Mandela is that rarest of things: an undisputed, untarnished, honest-to-goodness hero.

fully, at hauling the rest of Africa into the light. Maybe some of the
press hailing him as a secular saint can get to be a bit much, but it's
really not much more than he deserves.

Mandela was born on July 18, 1918, near a village called Umtata in
Transkei province. In 1942, while studying for a law degree in Johannesburg, he joined the African National Congress (ANC). At the time,
the ANC was pursuing a policy of gently lobbying and petitioning
South Africa's white rulers for a fairer shake for South Africa's black
majority. Mandela was among those who thought this approach inade-
quate, especially after apartheid was enshrined in law in 1948. The
more radical ANC faction that Mandela helped found in 1944, the
African National Congress Youth League, became the guiding force of
the ANC as a whole, directing its focus to boycotts, strikes, and nonco-
operation with South Africa's white authorities.

Mandela spent the '50s traveling, agitating, organizing, and being
continually harassed and occasionally imprisoned by the white authorities. They finally nailed him in November 1962, sending him to prison
for five years for incitement to strike and leaving the country illegally
(he'd been receiving paramilitary training in Algeria), and then adding
a life sentence for sabotage. He spent just over 27 years in prison: on
Robben Island off Cape Town until 1984, then Pollsmoor Prison in Cape
Town until 1988, and finally in Victor Verster Prison near Paarl, from
where he was released in February 1990.

When South Africa had its first all-races election in May 1994, there
was only ever going to be one winner. As president, Mandela strove for
reconciliation with the white minority rather than revenge against
them, and the moral authority lent by his suffering at the hands of the
apartheid regime brought his country along with him. One needs only
look north to Zimbabwe to see how badly it could have turned out.

Mandela stepped down as president in June 1999, but has continued to work as a broker in other African conflicts and on behalf of

South Africans with AIDS (to the occasional annoyance of his successor, Thabo Mbeki). The new South Africa, the country he did more
than anyone to invent, is far from perfect, but nothing that's wrong
with it is his fault. Having divorced the charismatic but erratic Winnie
Madikizela-Mandela in 1996, he is now married to his third wife,
Graca Machel, the widow of a former president of Mozambique. He is a
fan of Handel, Tchaikovsky, Paul Robeson, and porridge. He lives near
his birthplace in Transkei.

**African National Congress**
http://www.anc.org.za

## Thabo Mbeki

If you've ever felt like you've had a tough act to follow, spare a
thought for Thabo Mbeki, who became president of South Africa
in 1999 following the resignation of the sainted Nelson Mandela.
Mbeki has all the right revolutionary credentials. He was not only an
ANC activist in Britain, Russia, Zimbabwe, and Nigeria during the
apartheid years, but he was also a member of the South African communist party. However, he lacks Mandela's beatific aura and general
likeability. He's also prone to occasional rushes of blood, which have
led a few people to worry if he might have more in common with the
increasingly demented Robert Mugabe than with Mandela. For example, he criticized the Truth and Reconciliation Commission, the rock
on which South Africa's postapartheid reconciliation was built, for
pointing out that the ANC had perpetrated its fair share of torture and
murder during its struggle against white minority rule, and with its
Inkhata rivals. Everyone seems to have a few skeletons in their closet
here.

Mbeki's presidency—and South Africa's very future—will ultimately be defined by his performance on one issue: AIDS. It is estimated that 20 percent of South Africans are HIV-positive, with new
infections running at 1,500 a day, and between 70,000 and 100,000
HIV-positive babies born annually. It is the most fundamental and
grievous crisis a country could face, and Mbeki's views on the subject
are, to put it mildly, unorthodox. He's not convinced that HIV causes
AIDS. He thinks AIDS has more to do with poverty, poor food, and bad
housing. Mbeki has restricted the availability of antiretroviral drugs,
because he thinks they are poisonous, too expensive, and don't work
(in July 2002, South Africa's constitutional court overruled Mbeki, and
ordered that the antiretroviral drug Nevirapine be made available at
public clinics).

What's even more worrying is that in his own cabinet, Mbeki is
pretty much a moderate on the AIDS issue. In 1999, his Minister for

Health, Manto Tshabalala-Msimang, distributed to her provincial counterparts a chapter of William Cooper's conspiracist tract *Behold, A Pale Horse*, which posits that AIDS was introduced to Africa by the Illuminati (that is, a cabal of foreign bankers and/or generals and/or Jews and/or freemasons), possibly in collusion with extraterrestrial beings.

**Office of the President**
Private Bag X1000
Pretoria, South Africa
Tel.: (27) 12 300 5200
Fax: (27) 12 323 8246
president@po.gov.za
http://www.gov.za/president

**President Mbeki Petition of Support**
http://www.virusmyth.net/aids/news/mbeki.htm

## Treatment Action Campaign (TAC)

The TAC have the highest profile of the lobby groups trying to bring Mbeki's thinking on HIV and AIDS somewhere close to the realms of scientific consensus. It was their court action in July 2002 that forced the South African government to provide the antiretroviral drug Nevirapine to public hospitals and clinics. Nevirapine helps prevent the transmission of AIDS from infected mothers to newborn children, but Mbeki had dismissed it as unsafe, unproven, and too expensive. Between 70,000 and 100,000 HIV-positive babies are born in South Africa every year.

**Treatment Action Campaign**
http://www.tac.org.za

## Truth and Reconciliation Commission (TRC)

The TRC was chaired by 1985 Nobel Peace Prize laureate Archbishop Desmond Tutu, who was acutely aware that the last thing post-apartheid South Africa needed was to seek or to exact revenge, judicial or otherwise. Everyone was going to have to figure out how to live together, and the cause would not be helped by rerunning Nuremberg. The idea was that the TRC would listen to testimonies of apartheid's victims and perpetrators, and in some cases, reward full disclosures by the perpetrators with amnesties from prosecution (of 7,000 applications for amnesty, the TRC turned down more than 4,500 flat, so they weren't giving them away).

The TRC's highest profile cases were white, which was to be expected, given that apartheid was a crime committed by white people. Former President P. W. Botha was fined for refusing to appear, and former police commander Eugene De Kock was sentenced to more than 200 years in prison. But the TRC did not shy from criticizing those who fought apartheid. Nelson Mandela's ex-wife, Winnie, was found "responsible

for gross violations of human rights" (her bodyguards, the so-called
Mandela United Football Club, had waged Winnie's vendettas with a
combination of kidnappings, beatings, arson, and murders). Mango-
suthu Buthelezi, leader of the Inkhata Freedom Party (and currently
Minister for Home Affairs), was held responsible for atrocities committed by his followers.

The TRC has officially shut up shop now, but its effects resonate, not
just in South Africa, but in other recently conflict-torn countries where
this idea of a paralegal confessional has been adopted. At the time of
writing, TRCs based on the South African model were underway, or
being planned, in Peru, Venezuela, Sierra Leone, Yugoslavia, East
Timor, and Sri Lanka.

**Truth and Reconciliation Commission**
http://www.doj.gov.za/trc

## People against Gangsterism and Drugs (PAGAD)

South Africa's combination of rampant crime and hopeless police
has inevitably led some to take matters into their own hands, and,
equally inevitably, these vigilante groups have been scarcely distin-
guishable from the criminals they set out to destroy. The Muslim-
dominated PAGAD started life in the Cape Flats area of Cape Town in
1996 and takes roughly the same view of Western society in general
that it does of local hoodlums. In addition to meting out frontier justice
to drug dealers and thieves, PAGAD has carried out bombings of syna-
gogues, mosques favored by more-moderate Muslims, gay clubs, and
tourist attractions (including, many believe, the attack on the Cape
Town branch of Planet Hollywood in 1998). PAGAD's mouthpiece is
the Cape Town radio station Radio 786.

**People against Gangsterism and Drugs**
http://www.pagad.co.za

**Radio 786**
http://www.radio786.co.za

## Afrikaaner Resistance Movement (AWB)

Included here more for comic relief
than anything else, the Afrikaaner Weer-
standsbeweging (AWB) are the white
South African equivalent of those Japanese soldiers who carried on fighting World
War II until the early '70s. According to the
AWB's haphazardly spelled and edited Web
site—it looks kind of like someone accidentally put on a sheet without any holes

> **M**ore for comic relief than
> anything else, the Afrikaaner
> Weerstandsbeweging (AWB)
> are the white South African
> equivalent of those Japanese
> soldiers who carried on
> fighting World War II until
> the early '70s.

in it before he typed it—the AWB was formed either in 1970 or 1973. Their heartland is Ventersdorp, a horrible little farming town to the west of Johannesburg. The AWB claim that what they want is an independent homeland for the Boers, the descendants of South African settlers from Holland who fought a long and ugly war with the British at the beginning of the twentieth century. However, if the AWB's behavior is anything to judge by, they're rather more interested in reclaiming what was once their legally ordained right to treat black people like farm animals.

The AWB peaked in the mid-'90s, during South Africa's run-up to its first all-races elections. Their leader, a belligerent buffoon named Eugene Terre'blanche, became a staple of international television news reports, addressing rallies of fellow hay-eating rednecks while surrounded by his black-clad retinue of Iron Guards and leading marches of khaki-clad dim-bulbs chanting "Hang Mandela!" while wearing armbands bearing an unpleasantly familiar insignia. (The official explanation for the AWB's three-pointed swastika is that it is three linked sevens, demonstrating a superiority over the devil's number of 666 and all that it represents, like, presumably, democracy, and so on.) When AWB members attempted an invasion of the black homeland of Bophuthatswana, they succeeded only in providing an eloquent symbol of the demise of all they stood for: three fat, bearded, white oafs in "let's play soldier" costumes begging for their lives on the road before being shot dead by a black policeman.

Terre'blanche is in jail now, serving a sentence for assaulting a black security guard. He did make an appearance before the TRC, confessing to his role in the AWB's car-bombing campaign before the 1994 elections, which left 17 people dead. Unbelievably, the commission failed to extract any remorse for the far more serious offense of his poetry (CDs of which are available from the AWB Web site, though to judge by the pitiful total on their visitor counter, most of which was racked up by *DP* researching this, they're not being knocked down in the rush). The AWB at this point are pretty much a national joke, and nobody pays any attention but smartass European documentary makers and war-zone travel guides looking for cheap laughs.

**Afrikaaner Resistance Movement**
http://www.awb.co.za/english.htm

# Getting In

If you're a citizen of the United States, Canada, or the European Union, you don't need a visa to go to South Africa, unless you are a concert performer, stage artist, musician, religious worker, journalist, or photographer. Anyone who meets one or more of these descriptions should contact their local embassy, who'll tell you precisely how big a pain in the neck getting a visa is going to be.

Most international flights to South Africa land at Johannesburg and do their best to get away before somebody takes the wheels off them. A few other flights park at Cape Town and Durban. Accessing South Africa by road from Namibia, Botswana, or Mozambique is easy enough, but *DP* wouldn't bank on the border between South Africa and Zimbabwe, if only because the road is likely to be jammed solid by network news crews filing their reports on Mugabe's latest idiocy from as close to Harare as they're allowed get.

**Embassy of the Republic of South Africa**
3051 Massachusetts Avenue, N.W.
Washington, DC 20008
Tel.: (202) 232-4400
Fax: (202) 165-1607
http://www.saembassy.org

**Consulate-General of South Africa**
333 East 38th Street
New York, NY 10016
Tel.: (212) 213-4880
Fax: (212) 213-0102
sacg@southafrica-newyork.net
http://www.southafrica-newyork.net

**Consulate-General of South Africa**
6300 Wilshire Boulevard, Suite 600
Los Angeles, CA 90048
Tel.: (323) 651-0902
Fax: (323) 651-5969
sacgla@link2sa.com
http://www.link2southafrica.com

**Consulate-General of South Africa**
200 South Michigan Avenue, Suite 600
Chicago, IL 60604
Tel.: (312) 939-7929
Fax: (312) 939-2588
sacongenchicago@worldnet.att.net

**High Commission for the Republic of South Africa**
South Africa House
Trafalgar Square
London WC2N 5DP, UK
Tel.: (44) 20 7451 7299
Fax: (44) 20 7451 7284
general@southafricahouse.com
http://www.southafricahouse.com

**High Commission for the Republic of South Africa**
15 Sussex Drive
Ottawa, Ontario K1M 1M8
Canada
Tel.: (613) 744-0330
Fax: (613) 741-1639
rsafrica@sympatico.ca
http://www.docuweb.ca/southafrica

**Consulate-General of the Republic of South Africa**
Suite 2615
1 Place Ville Marie
Montreal, Quebec H3B 4S3
Canada
Tel.: (514) 878-9217
Fax: (514) 878-4751
sacongen@total.net

# Getting Around

South Africa is serviced by a comprehensive network of planes, trains, and automobiles. The latter are by far the most popular, in no small part because intercity trains are favorite targets of thieves and muggers. The best way to get around is to hire a car, or even, the rand being in the wretched state it is, buy one. The best place to look for a car is Cape Town, where a lot of people sell off their four-wheel drives at the completion of their African adventure. If you do decide to drive yourself, you should also make sure you've got a mobile phone, in case of remote breakdowns or carjackings.

**South African Airways**
http://www.saa.co.za

**Intercape Travel**
http://www.intercape.co.za

**Greyhound Bus Lines**
http://www.greyhound.co.za

## Dangerous Places ——————————

### Johannesburg

Johannesburg, known to the locals as Jo'burg, is increasingly known to foreign visitors as the city you fly into and then get out of as fast as possible, with your bankroll stashed in your boots and all other valuables buried under as many layers of clothing as you can bear to wear. Jo'burg has acquired a reputation as an African Dodge City, and not entirely without reason.

Locals will tell you that Jo'burg has changed beyond recognition in the short time between the dismantling of the old South Africa and the establishment of the new. The city center, once the financial and social hub, has been deserted by the white middle class and the institutions they built: homes have disappeared behind high fences, security cameras, and metal gates in Jo'burg's northern suburbs, and businesses have migrated north to Sandton.

Crime is rampant in Jo'burg. Your best chances of not being added to its astonishing statistics are to take all the usual precautions, but more so. Try to look as little like a tourist as possible. Don't have anything valuable where anyone could possibly grab it. Leave your passports and spare cash in a hotel safe, and save the fancy new digital video camera for the safari. Keep out of the city center altogether at night and on weekends, and avoid commuter trains. Above all, if you do get mugged, just give your assailant what he wants. The chances that he won't have a gun are not so good that you'd want to risk your life.

If one crime has become popularly associated with Jo'burg, it's carjacking. So, when stopped at traffic lights, leave enough room between your car and the one in front so you can get away if need be. Don't leave valuables on display, and keep the windows up, however hot it is. Ignore people asking for directions, or trying to tell you there's something wrong with your car. If you get a flat tire, keep driving until you find a garage.

The latest trend for Jo'burg's legion of criminals is to dress up in an official uniform and "help" tourists using ATMs. Politely but firmly decline (it should go without saying that you should not use an ATM at night, or out of sight of other people).

**City Press**
http://www.news24.com/City_Press/Home

**The Star**
http://www.iol.co.za/html/frame_thestar.php

## All Other Cities and Townships

Johannesburg merits its reputation as South Africa's crime capital, but in Cape Town they joke that anyone on the street after dark is a tourist or a mugger, and we wouldn't go flashing the Rolex in Durban, or Pretoria, or Soweto, either.

## Squatter Camps

More than 7 million South Africans lack proper housing, and many of them have congregated in shanty towns on the edges of South Africa's big cities. Squatter camps are unhappy and volatile places. A small opposition party, the Pan-African Congress, tried to encourage squatters to seize unoccupied or unutilized land, but were slapped down by a new law making land occupation a criminal offense. Mbeki has been a little woolly about Mugabe's encouragement of similar seizures in Zimbabwe, but he seems determined that the same won't happen on his patch. South Africa's police have used rubber bullets to disperse squatters.

**Pan-African Congress**
http://www.paca.org.za

# Dangerous Things

## Crime

Here are some numbers to think about as you leaf through the brochures of safari organizers. In South Africa between January and September 2001, there were 15,054 murders, 21,207 attempted murders, 87,610 violent robberies, 188,961 serious assaults, 182,110 common assaults, and 37,711 reported rapes. You stand a better chance of being murdered in South Africa than in Colombia, Russia, Zimbabwe, or even the trigger-happy United States. South Africa has the highest per capita crime rate in the world.

These numbers only relate to reported crimes and are likely to be understatements, especially where rape is concerned. According to figures published by SpeakOut, an organization set up to help rape victims, half of all South African women can expect to be raped at some stage in their lives; only 7 percent of reported rapes result in prosecutions; and 75 percent of rapes in South Africa are gang rapes, involving between 3 and 30 men. Sexual attacks on children and babies are also becoming more common, due to a widespread myth that sex with an infant will cure AIDS.

Wealthier South Africans are increasingly responding to this crime tsunami by walling themselves off. Private security is one of South Africa's boom industries, employing more than 200,000 guards at 5,000 firms. The inner cities and poorer areas are effectively being abandoned to the criminals, which is unlikely to improve matters.

**SpeakOut**
http://www.speakout.org.za

**Crime Victims**
http://www.crimevictims.co.za

**Business against Crime**
http://www.bac.co.za

## The Police

South Africa's police are no longer quite the feared and loathed instrument of state oppression that they were during the apartheid years. Back then they had carte blanche to terrorize and torture, and black activists frequently suffered fatal falls down stairs or out of windows during routine questioning. But the reconstruction of South Africa's 121,000-strong police force still has a way to go. In March 2001, the Independent Complaints Directorate, which handles accusations of police misconduct, reported 650 deaths in custody or as a consequence of police action in the previous 12 months. Allegations of torture by beating, suffocation, and electric shock are regular occurrences.

Visitors to South Africa are relatively unlikely to be kicked to death in a lock-up, but should be aware that South African police on remote country roads are notorious for imposing "fines" on "speeding" motorists. Make sure you get the number on the officer's badge, and feel free to add it to the Independent Complaints Directorate's overflowing in-box.

**South African Police Service**
http://www.saps.org.za

**Independent Complaints Directorate**
http://www.icd.gov.za

## AIDS

While there is considerable dispute about the precise numbers of South Africans with HIV and AIDS, and even more argument about what is causing it, nobody disputes that it's a problem of catastrophic proportions. Estimates of the number of HIV-positive South Africans run as high as 20 percent of the population. Projections of the epidemic anticipate 500,000 deaths every year by 2008, and a life expectancy dropping below 40 within a decade. The epidemic has been fanned by South Africa's endemic rape, by official and social denial of the realities of homosexuality and teenage sexual activity, and by a consequent lack of education.

There are some signs that South Africa is finally beginning to face up to the crisis. Some corporations, led by the mining giant Anglo-American, are providing their staff with free anti-AIDS drugs (more than a quarter of Anglo-American's 90,000 employees are HIV-positive). South African Breweries, which makes 90 percent of South Africa's beer, has a full-time AIDS manager, charged with promoting awareness among his staff. Starting in September 2002, the cast of South Africa's version of *Sesame Street* was due to be joined by an HIV-positive muppet.

AIDS has not been all bad news for South African business. In 2002, South Africa's largest insurance company, Old Mutual, announced that an AIDS-inspired upsurge in sales of funeral plans had allowed it to buck the fall of the worldwide stock market.

**AIDS Foundation of South Africa**
http://www.aids.org.za

**The Joint UN Program on HIV/AIDS**
http://www.unaids.org

## Brain Drain

Under apartheid, South Africa's white, liberal, educated middle class left the country to get their kids out of compulsory service in the justly loathed South African military. Now, South Africa's white, liberal, educated middle class is leaving the country, while their rands are still worth something, to get themselves out of the reach of crime, AIDS, unemployment, and the possible consequences of the fact that Thabo Mbeki is no Nelson Mandela. Between 1999 and 2002, more than 100,000 South Africans (including 8,000 teachers) left South Africa, and 70 percent of South Africans of all colors classed as skilled workers said they wanted to go.

*Wildlife*

In the bush, zip your tent up before you go to sleep, and give your boots a shake before putting them on. In safari parks, stay in the damn car. Lions are faster and stronger than you are, as several illegal immigrants from Mozambique trying to cross into South Africa through the Kruger National Park have learned the hard way.

## Getting Sick

By the standards of sub-Saharan Africa, South Africa is clean, hygienic, and relatively lacking in weird viruses that will make your ears leak blood, though there is a small risk of malaria in the eastern part of the country, and occasional outbreaks of bilharzia throughout South Africa. Ask locals before drinking or swimming in water. By far the most potentially worrisome risk to your health is AIDS; while there's no need to buy a HazMat suit or wear rubber gloves throughout your stay, make very, very sure that you don't attempt anything intimate without a condom. Roughly one South African in five is HIV-positive: The odds are better in Russian roulette.

If you do get ill, medical facilities in South Africa's cities, and at tourist-frequented game reserves, are of first-world standard. In the bush, things will be a little more rudimentary, but as long as you can be kept together long enough to get to a big hospital, you'll be fine.

## Nuts and Bolts

There are 43.6 million South Africans. About 75 percent are black Africans, 14 percent are descendants of white Europeans, and roughly 9 percent are what used to be described as "colored," that is, officially accorded a sort of semihuman status under the boneheaded strictures of apartheid. About 70 percent of all South Africans are Christian, with animist and indigenous faiths observed by most of the rest. There are also tiny Muslim, Jewish, and Hindu minorities. South Africa's eclectic make-up is reflected in the fact that it has no less than 11 official languages: English, Afrikaans, Ndebele, Pedi, Sotho, Tsonga, Swazi, Venda, Tswana, Xhosa, and Zulu. South Africa's capital city is Pretoria, but the legislature is based in Cape Town and the judiciary in Bloemfontein.

South Africa's currency is the rand, which has suffered a slow but nonetheless spectacular collapse over the last couple of years, from about 6 to the U.S. dollar at the end of 2000 to 12 to the dollar by January 2002. At the time of writing, it was hovering between 10 and 11, and for visitors from the United States and United Kingdom especially, everything in South Africa will seem a frankly unbelievable bargain.

Infrastructure and communications in the cities are generally of first-world standard. Infrastructure and communications outside the cities are extremely variable.

**Embassy of the United States**
877 Pretorius Street
Pretoria, South Africa
Tel.: (27) 12 342 1048
Fax: (27) 12 342 2244
embassy@pd.state.gov
http://usembassy.state.gov/posts/sf1/
wwwhmain.html

**Consulate-General of the United States**
Broadway Industries Center
Heerengracht
Foreshore
Cape Town, South Africa
Tel.: (27) 21 421 4280
Fax: (27) 21 425 3014

**Consulate-General of the United States**
1 River Street
Killarney
Johannesburg, South Africa
Tel.: (27) 11 644 8000
Fax: (27) 11 646 6916

**Consulate-General of the United States**
Old Mutual Building, 31st Floor
333 Smith Street
Durban, South Africa
Tel.: (27) 31 305-7600
Fax: (27) 31 305-7691

**British High Commission**
255 Hill Street
Arcadia 0002
Pretoria, South Africa
Tel.: (27) 12 483 1200
Fax: (27) 12 483 1302
pta.visaenquiries@fco.gov.uk
http://www.britain.org.za

**British Consulate General**
Southern Life Centre
8 Rieback Street, 15th Floor

91 Parliament Street
Cape Town 8001, South Africa
Tel.: (27) 21 405 2400
Fax: (27) 21 425 1427
bhcppa@iafrica.com

**British Trade and Investment**
275 Jan Smuts Avenue
Dunkeld West
Johannesburg 2196, South Africa
Tel.: (27) 11 537 7206
Fax: (27) 11 537 7253

**Canadian High Commission**
1103 Arcadia Street
Hatfield 0028
Pretoria, South Africa
Tel.: (27) 12 422 3000
Fax: (27) 12 422 3052
pret@dfait-maeci.gc.ca
http://www.dfait-
    maeci.gc.ca/southafrica/
    menu-en.asp

**Canadian High Commission**
Reserve Bank Building, 19th Floor
60 St. George's Mall
Cape Town 8001, South Africa
Tel.: (27) 21 423 5240
Fax: (27) 21 423 4893
cptwn@dfait-maeci.gc.ca

**Canadian High Commission**
Cradock Place, 1st Floor
10 Arnold Road
Rosebank
Johannesburg 2196, South Africa
Tel.: (27) 11 442 3130
Fax: (27) 11 442 3325
jobrg@dfait-maeci.gc.ca

*Consulate of Canada*
14 Nuttall Gardens
Morningside
Durban 4001, South Africa
Tel.: (27) 31 303 9695
Fax: (27) 31 309 9694
vnaidu@trematon.co.za

# Dangerous Days

| | |
|---|---|
| **6/30/01** | South African Catholic bishops denounce condoms as an "immoral and misguided" means of preventing AIDS. |
| **4/11/01** | A stampede at a soccer game at Ellis Park Stadium kills 43. |
| **1/01** | Cholera outbreak in KwaZulu-Natal kills more than 50. |
| **5/28/00** | Themba Khoza, leader of the Inkhata Freedom Party, dies of AIDS at the age of 41. |
| **11/99** | Fighting between rival taxi operators in Empangeni leaves 10 dead and 24 wounded. |
| **5/14/99** | The ruling ANC party signs a peace agreement with longtime rivals, Inkhata Freedom Party. |
| **8/25/98** | A bomb in Planet Hollywood restaurant in Cape Town kills two and injures 24. |
| **8/21/98** | Apartheid-era President P. W. Botha is convicted of refusing to testify before the TRC. He is fined and given a suspended sentence. |
| **7/31/98** | The TRC closes after conducting two years of hearings into apartheid-era atrocities. |
| **12/25/95** | A mob of Inkhata supporters kills 14 ANC supporters in KwaZulu-Natal. |
| **5/10/94** | Nelson Mandela is sworn in as South Africa's first black president. |
| **5/1/94** | South Africa's first all-races elections are held. |
| **4/25/94** | Bombs set near polling stations by Afrikaaner extremists kill 21 people. |
| **3/94** | An attempted coup by far-right AWB in Boputhatswana. |
| **3/28/94** | A march by Zulu nationalists in Johannesburg escalates into a riot that leaves 50 dead. |
| **10/15/93** | Nelson Mandela and F. W. De Klerk are named joint winners of the Nobel Peace Prize. |
| **10/8/93** | The last UN sanctions against South Africa are lifted. |

| | |
|---|---|
| **9/7/92** | South African troops shoot dead 28 ANC supporters and injure 200 more near Transkei homeland. |
| **5/13/91** | Winnie Mandela is convicted of assault and kidnapping. |
| **2/11/90** | Nelson Mandela is freed from prison after 27 years. |
| **3/21/60** | Sharpeville massacre. South African police open fire on a demonstration against South Africa's Pass Laws, shooting dead 56 black South Africans and injuring another 162. A subsequent inquiry reveals that most were shot in the back. |
| **1949** | Establishment of apartheid. |

# ★★★
# SUDAN

Khartoum

## Black Moon Rising

On the map, Sudan is the largest country in Africa. On terra firma, it is actually two countries. There is the north—a dry, arid, Islamic Arab land. And there is the south—a lush, green nation of black-skinned Christian and animist Nilotes. These two cultures have never dwelled in harmony, and they never will, as long as the north persists in imposing its political and religious will on the south. The current civil war, between the government forces based in the north and the Sudan Peoples' Liberation Army (SPLA) rebels who hold the south, is nearing its 20th anniversary—which no one is celebrating. Bilal al-Sudan (land of the blacks), or New Sudan, may emerge from the two-decade war. Peace talks are being held, but there's little cause for optimism—an earlier insurrection in the south lasted 17 years, from 1955 to 1972. It's possible that the shooting will only stop when the inevitable is

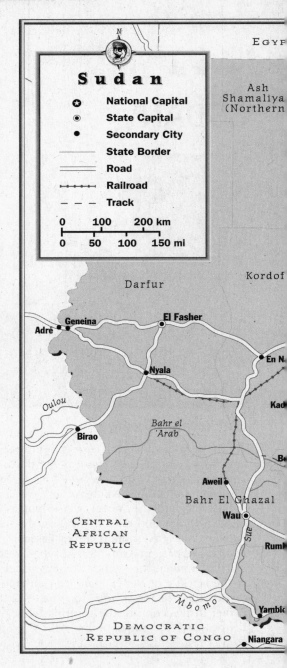

accepted and Sudan splits in two. This is unlikely to happen for a variety of reasons (see The Scoop).

Sudan, like Zimbabwe, Uganda, DR Congo, Nigeria, Sierra Leone, Liberia, like . . . aw, heck, like just about every other country in Africa, has it well within its power to be a prosperous, secure, and happy place. Unfortunately, Sudan, like just about every other country in Africa, has spent most of its time since independence being governed by crooks, psychopaths, dunderheads, and lunatics. Sudan's current incumbent, General Omar Hassan Ahmed al-Bashir, is a depressing combination of all four. Al-Bashir's been in charge since 1989, when he seized power with the help of a sort of Islamic Jimmy Swaggart called Hassan al-Turabi. Al-Bashir fell out with al-Turabi in 2001 and had him arrested, but before then the pair had contrived to make Sudan a flat-broke war zone with nearly a third of its territory in the hands of a rebel army.

Sudan became independent in 1956. Before that, it was chiefly noteworthy as the canvas upon which was painted most of the modern-day liberal mythology of British empire-building—that is, of aristocratic Englishmen with gold-braided uniforms and immense moustaches ordering the machine-gunning of ranks of witless, turban-clad natives armed with nothing much more threatening than pointy sticks. This is actually a reasonably accurate depiction of the Battle of Omdurman, which took place just outside Khartoum in 1898 (and in which one of the minor protagonists was an impetuous lieutenant named Winston Churchill). In an uncanny preview of Operation Desert Storm nearly a century later, the superior weaponry of Western troops allowed them to pile up thousands of dead Arabs while suffering less than a dozen casualties.

> **A**ristocratic Englishmen with gold-braided uniforms and immense moustaches order the machine-gunning of ranks of witless, turban-clad natives armed with nothing more than threatening pointy sticks.

Sudan embarked upon independence with every intention of becoming a civilized and democratic nation. Unfortunately, it became swiftly apparent that the only people capable of running the place properly had gone back to London, and in November 1958 Sudan experienced the first of a series of military coups. By 1964 it had been decided to give democracy another go. This time, it lasted four years before another bunch of army officers, under General Gaafar Nimeiri, seized power.

In 1972, Nimeiri negotiated a deal that ended a rebellion rumbling in the south since 1955. Sudan's Christian and animist south was unhappy then (as it is now) about being pushed around by the Muslim and Arab north. Sadly, Nimeiri, who was also to an extent a glove puppet of al-Turabi, undid his good work in 1983 by imposing Sharia law over all of Sudan—Muslim, Christian, or miscellaneous. The south re-organized and re-armed, and the SPLA, the military wing of the Sudan Peoples' Liberation Movement, was born. They're still with us. Nimeiri's reign was wounded further by his economic incompetence—remarkable even by African standards. And so, in 1985, Nimeiri, who had seized power in a coup, was himself overthrown in a coup led by General Dahab. Dahab organized elections, which brought in a government headed by Sadiq al-Mahdi, who was unable to get together either a working coalition or Sudan's economic act, and al-Bashir unloaded him in 1989, which is where we came in.

Allah alone knows how al-Bashir has avoided getting the same kind of press as Saddam Hussein. He has harbored and sponsored terrorists (Carlos the Jackal and Osama bin Laden are both former residents of Khartoum), killed millions of his own people, arrested and tortured uncountable dissidents, and has a really stupid moustache. But instead of sending bombers, the United States has sent peace envoys: Jimmy Carter in 1995 and 1997 ("Dammit," you can imagine them muttering at the State Department, "we keep sending him, and he keeps coming back.") and Missouri Republican Senator John Danforth in 2001. Granted, America clobbered a pharmaceutical plant in Khartoum with cruise missiles in 1998, but there were really important reasons for that, like keeping the president's girlfriend out of the headlines.

Expect Sudan to figure more and more on America's radar. Sudan has two things America desperately wants—bottomless reserves of oil, and equally plentiful intelligence on Islamic terrorists, many of whom have been, or remain, residents in this vexatious country. Because the rebels came uncomfortably close to the North's oil supplies, a mildly meaningful series of meetings and signed agreements may allow us to toss this depressing chapter out of *DP* forever.

> **S**udan has two things America desperately wants—bottomless reserves of oil, and equally plentiful intelligence on Islamic terrorists, many of whom have been, or remain, residents in this vexatious country.

## The Scoop

Sudan is a country at war with itself on a number of levels, and in several locations: The Sudanese civil war has lingered on for 19 years and has reduced the Sudanese population by a little over 2 million. It multiplies the worst of ancient sectarian hatred between the Muslim north and the Christian and animist south with extremely modern differences over the ownership of Sudan's immense oil deposits. If Sudan ever gets its act together, it could become the richest nation in Africa—there's more than enough black gold there for everyone, and at the time of writing the two sides were at least talking to each other, which is a start.

Unfortunately, the U.S.-brokered peace plan currently on the table isn't likely to stop the shooting anytime soon. The sticking point is that it provides southern Sudan with the option to secede from Sudan within six years—something that won't be popular with the north, who don't want to see half of Sudan's oil in the hands of a separate (and possibly hostile) country, or with Sudan's Arab neighbors, for a variety of reasons. In Libya, Colonel Qaddafi would view an oil-rich Christian-dominated southern Sudan as the basis for a rival bloc in his fondly imagined united Africa. In Egypt, they'd be none too delighted at the prospect of the upper reaches of the Nile—still Egypt's pulmonary artery—falling into the hands of the infidel.

**Sudanese Ministry of Foreign Affairs**
http://www.sudmer.net

**Sudan News Agency**
http://www.sunanews.net

**The Khartoum Monitor**
http://www.khartoummonitor.com

## The Players ————————————————

### President Omar Hassan Ahmed al-Bashir

Omar has been president of Sudan for 13 years, and is more entrenched than ever, following his sacking and imprisonment of Sudan's spiritual leader and former al-Bashir ally, Sheikh Hassan al-Turabi, in February 2001. Al-Bashir is a military dictator of the most tin-pot sort—a bellicose, violent, self-aggrandizing thug who peddles a deeply tiresome line of anti-Semitic conspiracy theory (the usual "Jews-run-America" nonsense, if you're at all interested, though there's no reason why you should be). He was last re-elected in 2000, receiving 87 percent of the vote in one of those comedy elections that is a specialty of Africa, the Middle East, and Florida.

Al-Bashir was born in 1947 in Hosh Bannaga, a two-goat village north of Khartoum. He joined the military when still young and showed promise in his initial training as a pilot, before learning his trade as a paratrooper at military college in Cairo and testing his knowledge in the field on secondment to the Egyptian army during the disastrous 1973 Yom Kippur assault on Israel—as salutary a lesson in how not to wage war as can be imagined. Before seizing power, he was commander of the Sudanese army's 8th Brigade, known for their zealousness in scorching the earth on which the SPLA and their sympathizers in the south were trying to live.

Once in power, al-Bashir set about bringing Sudan under Islamic Sharia law, with the connivance and encouragement of Sheikh Hassan al-Turabi (see below). Al-Bashir has continued to prosecute a war against his own people in the south, which has killed 2 million Sudanese and displaced more than 4 million more. His dismal behavior, and his harboring of such jolly folk as Carlos the Jackal and Osama bin Laden, has earned Sudan some UN sanctions (recently lifted, although unilateral U.S. sanctions remain) and suspension of World Bank aid. But as long as the guns keep coming—and they do, from Iran, Iraq, and China—al-Bashir's not bothered.

The secret to al-Bashir's insouciance is Sudan's colossal oil reserves, which he knows are deep enough to buy him out of just about anything. Among the Western companies who seem only too happy to give this unrepentant murderer and ethnic cleanser the wherewithal to purchase further destructive force are Canada's Talisman Energy, Malaysia's Petronas, Austria's OMV, and Sweden's Lundin Oil. Lundin pulled out of Sudan in March 2002—not due to any crisis of conscience, but because the fighting was getting a little close to their compounds for comfort, poor lambs. Perhaps you might care to drop one of these upstanding corporations a line and ask them how they sleep.

**Talisman Energy**
http://www.talisman-energy.com

**OMV**
http://www.omv.com

**Petronas**
http://www.petronas.com.my

**Lundin Oil**
http://www.lundin-petroleum.com

## Sheikh Hassan al-Turabi

Last time out, *DP* described al-Turabi, Sudan's chief Islamist ideologue and speaker of its parliament, as the man who was really pulling the strings in Khartoum. Maybe President al-Bashir read that and got jealous. In February 2001, al-Bashir had his old mate al-Turabi arrested, accusing him of undermining his authority, plotting to overthrow his government, and bedding the rebels of the SPLA. It wasn't the first time that al-Turabi had tasted prison gruel, and if he stages an apparently unlikely comeback, there would be ample precedent for that, as well. Al-Turabi may well be a three-parts-crazy fundamentalist intent on yoking the entire Islamic world into a joyless theocracy ruled by fear of Allah and the lash, but he's also a heck of an operator.

Al-Turabi was born 70-odd years ago, and educated at the University of Khartoum, where he gained a law degree, in Britain, and at the

Sorbonne in Paris. In the 1960s, he became leader of what was then a small group of religious nuts called the Muslim Brotherhood. His timing was not ideal. In 1969, power was seized by Gaafar Nimeiri, a Sudanese general with marxist leanings who took a dim view of al-Turabi's Allah-bothering. Nimeiri dissolved the Muslim Brotherhood and had many of its members arrested. Al-Turabi lit out for Saudi Arabia, always a popular refuge for dangerous cranks whose own countries have gotten sick of them, and found a ready audience, and a ready source of funds, among the 350,000 Sudanese expats. Al-Turabi used their money to create the Islamic Relief Association and the Faisal Islamic Bank, and to send bright Muslim kids to university—the idea being that these young doctors and lawyers would spread al-Turabi's version of the word of Mohammed when they got home.

Nimeiri eventually had a change of heart about hard-line Islam in general and al-Turabi in particular, and appointed him attorney-general in 1977. Although many perceived al-Turabi's hand at play when Nimeiri imposed Sharia law on Sudan in 1983, it was apparently due to a vivid dream the general had—that'll teach him to eat cheese before going to bed. Whatever the truth, it gave al-Turabi license to string up felons in public and hack bits off minor miscreants. This, along with the economic catastrophe caused by Nimeiri's Koran-inspired decision to abolish interest rates and income tax, won a mixed response—that is, anger mixed with bewilderment—from the Sudanese. With his country US$8 billion in the hole and defaulting all over the shop, Nimeiri blamed al-Turabi, then fired him and slung him in the hoosegow. It didn't help. Nimeiri was eventually bundled out of office in a bloodless coup in 1985. When Sudan had a crack at democracy the following year, al-Turabi rebranded his Muslim Brotherhood as the National Islamic Front (NIF), and won enough seats to lead the third-biggest party in the newly constituted National Assembly.

It wasn't enough for al-Turabi, who still harbored dreams of placing Sudan, and then the rest of the world, under the rule of the Koran, and setting up shop as a sort of Islamic pope. In 1989, he was a major player in the coup that brought to power his ally—and now jailer—General Omar al-Bashir. Until al-Bashir locked him up in February 2001, al-Turabi was allowed a free hand. He recruited NIF militias who enforced al-Turabi's ideas with brutal ruthlessness. He set up, and became secretary-general of, the Popular Arab Islamic Conference, a sort of UN for angry, bearded men that organized training in Sudan for aggrieved hankie-heads from Palestine, Egypt, and Algeria, and facilitated the five-year residency in Sudan of the son about whom Mr. and Mrs. bin Laden prefer not to talk.

For now, al-Turabi is under house arrest in Khartoum, rereading the Koran and his beloved Shakespeare, though the charges against him have been dropped. His detention is partly for the obvious reasons—as speaker of the National Assembly and (lately) secretary-general of the majority National Congress Party, he was certainly a threat to al-Bashir's authority, especially if he was consorting with the SPLA. But also, since September 11, al-Bashir must be acutely aware that Sudan is, in some shape or form, on the U.S. State Department and Pentagon's "to do" list. The last thing he needs is al-Turabi running around blithering about jihad.

**Popular National Congress Party**
webmaster@ncsudan.org
http://www.ncsudan.org

## Sudan Peoples' Liberation Movement/Sudan Peoples' Liberation Army (SPLM/SPLA)

The peace talks are not stopping the SPLA, officially the military wing of the Sudan Peoples' Liberation Movement (they haven't stopped the Sudanese army, either, so this is probably fair enough). In June 2002, they captured the strategically important town of Kapoeta, near Sudan's borders with Uganda and Kenya. The SPLA now holds a sizable chunk of Sudan's south, amounting to nearly a third of the country. The SPLM is the closest thing to a civil authority in the provinces of Equatoria, Upper Nile, Bahr El Ghazal, Southern Blue Nile, and Kordofan—an area about the size of France. They are also stepping up attacks on foreign oil installations in the region. Not without reason, the SPLM/SPLA regard the oil corporations as accomplices in the war that Sudan's Muslim north has been waging against its animist and Christian south since 1983.

The SPLM/SPLA is headed by Dr. John Garang, who had been part of the Anya Nya rebellion in Sudan's south in the '60s, but had since risen to the rank of colonel in the Sudanese Army. One day in 1983, he was sent south to put down a mutiny of southern troops, and never came back—instead, he turned that mutiny into a rebellion into what is now Africa's longest-running war. Garang (b. 1950), is a complicated mix of sky-worshipping Dinka tribesman and modern military academic (his Ph.D. in agricultural economics is from Grinnell College, Iowa, and he is also a graduate of the Infantry Officers' Advanced Course at Fort Benning, Georgia). He is both a presentable diplomatic presence and a ruthless bush warrior—there are numerous pits filled by people whose last act on this earth was to disagree with him. Garang's chunk of real estate in the south is rich in gold, hardwood, cotton, tea, coffee, and tobacco. The fertility of the soil is such that farmers sympathetic to the SPLA are able to feed the guerrillas with surpluses of rice, corn, sorghum, goats, and cattle.

The SPLM/SPLA want the current regime in Sudan removed and replaced with, as their manifesto has it, a New Sudan based on "the liberation of the individual and society from all forms of political, economic, social, and natural constraints to freedom, development, the pursuit of happiness and self-fulfilment, social justice, democracy, human rights, and equality for all irrespective of ethnicity, religion, or gender." Maybe it was the stuff about the pursuit of happiness that got the boys at Langley all misty-eyed, because the SPLA have had help from the CIA. In 1996, US$20 million was sent via Ethiopia, Eritrea, and Uganda to help Garang's lot, and unconfirmed reports suggest that several Operational Detachments-Alpha (or A teams) of the U.S. Army were in the field on the SPLA's side. They've also had help from Ethiopia, Eritrea, Uganda, and Israel.

The SPLA has about 60,000 troops—or more, since formally amalgamating with another rebel militia, the Sudanese Alliance Forces, in 2002. The SPLM, meanwhile, is becoming more and more like a proper government— in 2002, they were planning to launch their own bank based in Yambo, on the border with the imaginatively named Central African Republic, and print their own currency. In July 2002, Garang met with Sudanese President Omar al-Bashir for the first time, in talks chaired by Ugandan President Yoweri Museveni in Kampala. Both al-Bashir and Garang said that peace would be, you know, nice, but not just yet.

> **B**oth al-Bashir and Garang said that peace would be, you know, nice, but not just yet.

**Sudan Peoples' Liberation Movement**
splana@newsudan.com
http://www.newsudanweb.com

**Sudan Alliance Forces**
safsudan@safsudan.org
http://www.safsudan.com

## National Democratic Alliance (NDA)

The NDA is an awkward coalition of the Christian-led SPLA and ten mostly Muslim parties: the Democratic Unionist Party, the Union of Sudan African Parties, the Communist Party of Sudan, the General Council of Trade Union Federations, the Legitimate Command of the Sudanese Armed Forces, the Beja Congress, the Federal Democratic Alliance, the Free Lions Association, the Ba'ath Socialist Party, and the Sudanese National Party—all of which not only supported the imposition of Sharia law on the south, but also opposed southern autonomy or secession prior to the 1989 coup.

The NDA's president is Moulana al-Sayed Mohammed Osman al-Mirghani, and the NDA is based in Asmara, Eritrea. The NDA have a military component, which bugs the hell out of Khartoum by staging frequent attacks on the road that links Sudan's oilfields to Port Sudan on the Red Sea coast, especially around Kassala—a city which has changed hands between the Sudanese government and NDA forces a few times. Khartoum's nightmare scenario is the NDA getting a major military boost from the Eritreans and making a bid to overrun Sudan's vital Red Sea coast.

**National Democratic Alliance**
chairman@ndasudan.org
http://www.ndasudan.org

## Umma

The Umma is a party/militia led by former prime minister Sadiq al-Mahdi—the one who got rolled by the al-Bashir/al-Turabi coup back in 1989. Al-Mahdi is the great-grandson of the legendary El Mahdi, the Sudanese leader who united the tribes in the 19th century and gave Sudan's British imperial masters merry hell for years, until the Brits invented machine guns and put an end to El Mahdi's shenanigans with a hideous slaughter at Omdurman in 1898. (El Mahdi's "fuzzy-wuzzies," as the British called them, were a little slow on the uptake in their assessment of the new British weapon, and continued to charge at it waving swords.) Sadiq spent seven years under house arrest after the 1989 coup, and then four years in exile, before returning to Khartoum to a rapturous welcome in 2000. Umma broke ranks with the NDA in 1999—which may have been part of a bargain struck with al-Bashir to allow Sadiq to come home. Sadiq currently claims he's not interested in power, but in peace, pluralism, and all that sort of thing. He's worth keeping an eye on.

> **E**l Mahdi's "fuzzy-wuzzies," as the British called them, were a little slow on the uptake in their assessment of the new British weapon, and continued to charge at it waving swords.

**Umma (Arabic only)**
http://www.umma.org

## The Beja

The Beja are nomads, reputedly descended from Noah's grandson, Cush. Though a few now work on the docks in Port Sudan, most of Sudan's 2 million Beja still wander the north and east of the country, living a life changed little by the passing millennia. Or possibly they just keep on the move to get away from the Christian missionaries who have been trying, with an amusing lack of success, to "enlighten" them for years. The Beja are keen on Islam and Sharia law, but not keen on serving in the Sudanese military, which is why the party that represents them, the Beja Congress, has signed on with the NDA.

### The Lord's Resistance Army (LRA)

Christian fundamentalist loonies who've been using Sudan as a base from which to pester Uganda for years. Sudan finally withdrew its support for them in 2001 and even allowed Ugandan troops to enter Sudan in hot pursuit, so the LRA may be meeting their maker soon—bet he can't wait. (See the Great Lakes chapter for further details.)

### Uganda

Uganda has 10,000 troops in southern Sudan trying to smite the Lord's Resistance Army into the next world. Off the battlefield, Ugandan president Museveni is helping to drive peace talks between Sudan's government and the SPLA.

### Libya

Colonel Qaddafi—or The Golden Leader, as he now prefers to be addressed—sees bringing peace to Sudan as part of his long-term quest to unite the African continent under his own visionary leadership. Peace talks in January 2000 were held in Tripoli.

### Senator John Danforth

The Missouri Republican—ain't they the best kind?—was appointed Dubya's official envoy for peace in Sudan on September 6, 2001—interesting timing that would have sent *DP* hog-wild if we believed in conspiracy theories (Danforth headed the WACO review in 1999). Senator Danforth's job appears to consist of junketing off to Sudan every so often to remind all concerned that war and slavery and terrorism are, like, bad. Someday, someone will explain to *DP* why Sudan (an oil-rich nation run by a violent maniac who rules by fear, persecutes minorities, and sponsors terrorists) gets a Presidential Envoy for Peace and why Iraq (an oil-rich nation run by a violent maniac who rules by fear, persecutes minorities, and sponsors terrorists) gets cast as the star of *Desert Storm II: This Time It's Personal.*

# Getting In

Is a question that has to be answered in two parts. If you're flying to Khartoum, or entering the portion of Sudan actually controlled by

## THE SEVEN-FOOT-SEVEN REBEL

Manute Bol, the forty-year-old, seven-foot-seven Dinka from Turalie, Sudan, has a new job. The former NBA star is going to be a hockey player with the Indianapolis Ice (Central Hockey League). Manute has never skated and the owner of the Ice admits that hiring him is a charitable act combined with a publicity stunt. You see, Manute Bol gave away all the money he made to support projects in his home-nation of Sudan and the SPLA. It is estimated that he has donated over $4 million toward the Sudanese rebel movement and its people.

In 1985 Manute was the first foreign player drafted by the NBA and was so tall he could dunk a basket without lifting his heels. After he retired in 1995 his fans were shocked to find out that he had donated all his money to relieve the suffering of the Sudanese people and kept no money for himself. Bol was also a headliner on Fox's *Celebrity Boxing:* He beat William "The Refrigerator" Perry and donated even that prize money to southern Sudanese children.

Bol will make $350 a week for his one-season contract.

*Source:* http://www.angelfire.com/sports/manutebol

Sudan's government, your passport must be valid for six months from your proposed date of entry into Sudan, and free of any Israeli stamps. You'll also need to show a return ticket and evidence that you've got sufficient funds to pay your way. Visas for U.S. citizens cost US$50; other nationalities should contact the nearest Sudanese embassy.

If you're going to the part of Sudan controlled by the SPLM/SPLA, you'll need permission from them in advance (see The Players for contact details) and an NGO willing to give you a lift—something they're extremely unlikely to do for tourists or anyone else who doesn't have accreditation from the SPLA. The most common entry point to the SPLM/SPLA-held region is the Ugandan border from Adjumani, Moyo, or Koboko (see the Great Lakes chapter for details of how to get into Uganda), or from Lokichogio in Kenya.

Accessing the south from Khartoum is impossible, especially using a letter from the SPLA. You will be arrested, tried under every law the Sudanese can think of, and jailed forever in the deepest, darkest dungeon in Islamdom.

**Embassy of the Republic of Sudan**
2210 Massachusetts Avenue, NW
Washington, DC 20008
Tel.: (202) 338-8565
Fax: (202) 667-2406
info@sudanembassy.org
http://www.sudanembassy.org

*Embassy of the Republic of Sudan*
3 Cleveland Row
St. James's
London SW1A 1DD, UK
Tel.: (44) 20 7839 8080
Fax: (44) 20 7839 7560
zb24@pipex.com

*Embassy of the Republic of Sudan*
354 Stewart Street
Ottawa, Ontario K1N 6K8
Canada
Tel.: (613) 235-4000
Fax: (613) 235-6880
sudanembassy-canada@rogers.com
http://www.sudanca.com

## Getting Around

Most travel is done by road—given that Sudanese roads, vehicles, and drivers are a mix of all that is the worst about African and Middle Eastern roads, vehicles, and drivers, the religious fervor of the locals may come to make a lot of sense. There is, ironically, little to no fuel in the south, and vehicles must be hired from Uganda or other neighboring countries. Roads are mined, as is much of the countryside. Food is brought in through aid groups but there are times when no food is available. Outsiders may travel in the south only with the permission of the SPLA, which you will need to get in advance.

If you'd rather rise above this and fly, Sudan's carrier is Sudan Air, whose crash-prone Web site is not a happy omen. Unforeseen circumstances, such as sandstorms (April and September) and electrical outages, may cause flight delays. The Khartoum Airport arrival and departure procedures are lengthy: Passengers should allow three hours for pre-departure security and other processing.

*Sudan Air*
http://www.sudanair.com

## Dangerous Places

### The Entire South of the Country

Peace talks or no peace talks, all of SPLA-held Sudan remains a war zone. The Nuba mountains and the province of Bahr El Ghazal are especially dangerous.

### Relief Centers

The Antonov bombers and helicopter gunships of Sudan's military do not discriminate much between military and civilian targets. In February 2002 alone, the air force of the Sudanese government twice attacked depots belonging to the World Food Program—once in a village called Bieh, killing 17 people, and once near the town of Akuem, killing two children. The international medical charity Médecins Sans

Frontières has also accused Khartoum of deliberately targeting hospitals in the south.

**Médecins Sans Frontières**
http://www.msf.org

*Khartoum*

In 2000, a London-based human-resources consultant named William M. Mercer called Khartoum the third worst city in the world in which to live—better than Brazzaville or Pointe Noire, about equal with Baghdad, and worse than Bangui, Luanda, Ougadougou, or Kinshasa.

## Dangerous Things

*Oil*

Sudan's oil reserves are estimated to be at least as big as those of Saudi Arabia, and the country currently produces 185,000 barrels a day. A 1,600-kilometer pipeline to the Red Sea was constructed in 1998—thousands of homes in the Upper Nile region in Sudan's south were torched to make this possible, generally without the consent of the occupants. Sudan only started exporting oil in 1999, so it'll be a while before the real money starts flooding in—though whether it flows much further than Omar al-Bashir's personal checking account remains to be seen.

Sudan's black gold is the not-terribly-well-hidden agenda for Sudan's civil war—al-Bashir's troops clear the land of such inconveniences as the people who live on it with a combination of aerial bombardment and old-fashioned house-to-house terrorizing; the oil companies build roads, bridges, and airstrips; and al-Bashir's troops use the new roads, bridges, and airstrips to empty more land of its residents. The Nuer and Dinka tribes in particular are catching the rough end of this, which is why you'll find so many of both in the SPLA.

Reports of the roles of foreign oil companies—if it waddles like a duck and quacks like a duck, let's call it a duck—in this genocide do not make for edifying reading. The opening of the Red Sea pipeline was presided over by Omar al-Bashir, a blood-soaked tyrant, and James Buckee, CEO of the largest Western oil company working in Sudan, the Calgary-based Talisman: By their friends shall ye know them. The 10th and 15th Divisions of the Sudanese army have been contracted as "security" for Talisman's operations.

One under-reported side effect of 9/11 was the sparing of foreign oil companies working in Sudan from punishment by the United States, because Bush was anxious for Sudan's support in his War on Terror. On June 13, 2001, the House of Representatives had passed—by 422 votes to two—the Sudan Peace Act, which would have banned foreign corporations working in Sudan from being listed on American stock exchanges. On September 20, 2001, Dubya killed the act.

**Oil Development in Sudan**
http://www.sudanoil.net

### Slavery

Slavery remains a reality in Sudan. The slave traders strike during dry weather in carefully planned raids, with the Bahr El Ghazal province a particularly regular hunting ground. Various estimates suggest that up to 20,000 people, overwhelmingly women and children, have been kidnapped to be sold off as domestics (read unpaid maids and prostitutes) and cheap labor. In response to this problem, President al-Bashir is going with the la-la-la-la-I've-got-my-fingers-in-my-ears-I-can't-hear-you tactic. In 2002 he shrugged aside the many well-documented reports of slavery in Sudan as "mere media propaganda." To prove his point, he locked up the editor of the independent Sudanese newspaper *The Khartoum Monitor*, Nhial Bol, who had written a story about how slave traders were using the government-run armed train between Wau and Babanusa to carry out their raids. Bol and the *Monitor* were convicted of "propagation of false news" and fined. Well, that'll help.

**Anti-Slavery International**
http://www.antislavery.org

### Drought

The rains have been staying away from Sudan these last few years, causing massive crop failures. Relief efforts have been hampered by the continuing conflict. Nobody knows exactly how many people starved to death in Bahr El Ghazal province in 1998 because the NGOs were kept away by the fighting, but all the guesses start with five figures.

**United Nations World Food Program**
Plot 79, Gezira Road
Khartoum 2, Sudan
Tel.: (249) 11 47 5829
Fax: (249) 11 47 5826
wfp.khartoum@wfp.org
http://www.wfp.org

## House Guests

It's possible that Omar al-Bashir is looking at winding up Sudan's reputation as a preferred travel destination for terrorists now that Dubya is getting his posse together, but there's no denying that Sudan has provided hospitality to some rum customers over the years: Khartoum's African International University was the Fort Benning of Islamic terror. Three guys wanted for a 1995 attempt to assassinate Egyptian President Hosni Mubarak are still in Khartoum getting their nails done and watching the V channel, despite UN diplomatic and travel sanctions (now lifted). Ilich Ramirez Sanchez, aka Carlos the Jackal, was living in Khartoum when he was lifted in 1994: His three-decade-long résumé of murder, bombing, kidnapping, and hijacking had not, apparently, been enough to get him refused a Sudanese visa.

Then, of course, there's the intriguing case of Osama bin Laden, a resident of Sudan from 1991 to 1996. Osama owned several business in Sudan, including a construction company called al-Hajira and a farming concern called Wadi al-Aqiq, which covered thousands of acres in the central province of Gezira; most of his business was done with Sudan's government (al-Hajira, for example, built the highway north out of Khartoum to Atbarah). He also had an office in McNimr Street in Khartoum, a house in the Riyadh district of the city, and a farm outside town, where he lived with three horses, four wives, and several children. It wasn't all "Little Tent in the Desert," though. In 1995, he survived an assassination attempt by, not CIA hitmen, but militant Egyptian Islamists, who—are you sitting down?—didn't think Osama was quite militant enough. "Allah on a bicycle," you can imagine Osama thinking as his bodyguards gunned down the assailants, "you really can't please some people."

For obvious-enough reasons, since 9/11 the Sudanese government have been keen to stress that they were as surprised as anyone to discover that this munificent businessman was a terrorist mastermind with a psychotic grudge against the West. They're being a little ingenuous. Not only was Osama funneling guns to al-Bashir's militias fighting the SPLA, but he was running camel convoys and boat deliveries of weapons to kindred spirits in Egypt, Palestine, Chechnya, Tajikistan, and Turkey. Sudan finally deported Osama in 1996, under intense pressure from America. He chartered a plane to Afghanistan, bought himself a nice big cave in the country, and settled down to plot the downfall of the United States. The Sudanese claim, incidentally, that it was this expulsion that sent Osama over the edge and turned the honest entrepreneur they remember into the World's Most Wanted. It is,

SUDAN

*DP* supposes, statistically possible that someone out there believes them.

The truth is that Osama wasn't alone in Sudan, and he wouldn't be now. The country remains the world's biggest terrorist training ground, housing an estimated 15,000 fighters from organizations including Jamaat-e-Islami, Islamic Jihad, Hamas, Hizbollah, and al-Qaeda. Many of their camps were originally built by the United States, to train CIA-backed Afghan mujahideen in the '80s. Funny old world.

## Getting Sick

Medical facilities are as scarce as literate Sudanese outside Khartoum. Don't expect squat in the rebel-held south. Some health care is provided free of charge through any NGOs, especially in the south, but keep in mind that al-Bashir's forces from the north love to bomb hospitals (they use that nice red X on the roof to line up on before they kick the 500-pounders out the back of the Antonovs).

Malaria, typhoid, rabies, and polio are endemic. Bilharzia is also present—visitors should stay out of slow-moving freshwater. Other prominent diseases include amoebic and bacterial dysentery, cerebral malaria, giardiasis (a hemorrhagic fever similar to Ebola), and guinea worm. The latter affliction is particularly nasty—the eggs of the worm are ingested through river water and, after hatching, the larvae cruise the blood system until they find a suitable home, where they mature before eating their way out of the body.

## Nuts and Bolts

The largest country in Africa is home to 36 million Sudanese. Just over half are black Africans, 39 percent are Arabs, and 6 percent belong to the Beja people. Sudan is 70 percent Muslim, reflected in its strict Sharia legal code. The Christians, accounting for only about 5 percent of Sudan's population, are a small but militant minority. The only official language is Arabic—English is reasonably widely spoken in the cities, with Nubian, Ta Bedawie, and some Nilotic, Nilo-Hamitic, and Sudanic dialects spoken in the country, but the Khartoum government is trying to eradicate all these as part of its "Arabization" program. Less than half the population of Sudan is literate.

Sudan's arid north is mainly desert, with greener, agricultural areas on the banks of the Nile. Crops can be grown only during the rainy season (July to September). The south is mainly swamp and tropical jungle. The most important features are the White and the Blue Niles. The

Blue Nile is prone to severe flooding. Mid-April to the end of June is the hot, dry season, with temperatures regularly above 110°F.

The currency is the Sudanese dinar, which replaced the pound a few years back, of which you'll get 270 for your dollar. Electricity, communications, and everything else you might regard as basic signifiers of civilization are erratic in the extreme.

**Embassy of the United States**
Sharia Ali Abdul Latif
Khartoum, Sudan
Tel.: (249) 11 77 4611
Fax: (249) 11 77 4137
> Note: U.S. embassy officials for Sudan are now stationed in the embassies in Nairobi and Cairo, and make only occasional visits to Khartoum; the U.S. Consular Officer in Cairo can be contacted at (20) 2 795 7371 or consularcairo@state.gov.

**Embassy of Great Britain**
10th Street
Off Sharia-al-Baladia
Khartoum, Sudan
Tel.: (249) 11 77 7105
Fax: (249) 11 77 6457
information.khartoum@fco.gov.uk

**Embassy of Canada**
10th Street
Off Sharia-al-Baladia
Khartoum, Sudan
Tel.: (249) 11 79 0320

# Dangerous Days

| | |
|---|---|
| 11/20/02 | U.S. government says it is encouraged by peace talks in Sudan. |
| 4/20/02 | Sudanese military launch major offensive against the SPLA. |
| 2/21/01 | Hassan al-Turabi is arrested after calling for a general uprising against President al-Bashir. |
| 6/5/00 | President al-Bashir dismisses Hassan al-Turabi as secretary-general of the ruling National Congress Party. |
| 12/12/99 | President Omar al-Bashir declares a State of Emergency and dissolves the National Assembly, following a power struggle with Sheikh Hassan al-Turabi. |
| 8/20/98 | Al-Shifa chemical plant in Khartoum destroyed by U.S. cruise missiles. |
| 2/96 | U.S. embassy in Khartoum closed for security reasons. |
| 8/14/94 | Ilich Ramirez Sanchez, aka Carlos the Jackal, arrested in Khartoum. |
| 1991 | Founding of the National Democratic Alliance. |
| 6/30/89 | Elected coalition government of Sadiq al-Mahdi overthrown by General Omar al-Bashir and the National Islamic Front of Sheikh Hassan al-Turabi. |

| | |
|---|---|
| **1986** | General elections return coalition government under Sadiq al-Mahdi. |
| **4/4/85** | President Gaafar Nimeiri overthrown in a coup d'etat by General Dahab. |
| **5/16/83** | Formation of the Sudan Peoples' Liberation Army. |
| **1983** | Civil war reignites after imposition of Sharia law by the Khartoum government. |
| **1978** | Oil discovered in Bentiu, in southern Sudan. |
| **3/2/73** | Black September terrorists execute U.S. Ambassador Cleo Noel, U.S. Deputy Ambassador George Curtis Moore, and Belgian Charge d'Affaires Guy Eid in Khartoum. |
| **3/3/72** | Addis Ababa accords end the southern insurgency, granting substantial autonomy to the south. |
| **5/69** | General Gaafar Nimeiri seizes power in a coup. |
| **10/64** | General Abboud overthrown in a popular revolt and replaced with a national government. |
| **1962** | Civil war begins in Sudan, launched by the Anya Nya movement in the south. |
| **1958** | Civilian government elected at independence overthrown in a coup by General Abboud. |
| **1/1/56** | Sudan becomes independent from Great Britain. |
| **1955** | Fighting between north and south Sudan along religious and ethnic lines—Arab Muslims in the north, black Christians in the south. |
| **2/9/1898** | Battle of Omdurman. British forces machine-gun a futile frontal charge by Dervish warriors, killing or wounding thousands of the enemy while suffering less than a dozen casualties. Among the British troops is Lieutenant Winston Churchill. |
| **9/1896** | British forces under General Horatio Kitchener begin the British reconquest of Sudan. |
| **1/26/1885** | General George "Chinese" Gordon, British Governor-General of Sudan, killed in Khartoum by the Dervish forces of El Mahdi. |
| **1880s** | El Mahdi unites the tribes of Sudan. |

# THE UNITED
# STATES OF AMERICA

## Home of the Brave

Ah, America . . . Land of the free and home of the brave. And you'd better be damned brave, because the people here are free to do pretty much anything they please. The foundation of a nation based on individual freedom is still one of the boldest and best ideas human beings have ever had, and it has worked, by and large. The problem with constitutionally guaranteeing Americans' basic rights to life, liberty, and the pursuit of happiness is that the United States of America has legally enshrined the right of 280 million people to emulate the lifestyles of daytime talk-show guests and syndicated cop shows.

Most Americans have little conception of how unfathomable and bizarre their country appears to the rest of the world. The "Only in America" file is a large and bulging one: religious cults being incinerated by federal agents using tanks, trench-coated kids running wild

THE UNITED STATES
OF AMERICA

**United States**

- ⊙ National capital
- ⊙ State capital
- ● Secondary city
- ═══ Primary road
- ⊢•⊢•⊢ Railroad
- ⋯⋯ State border

800 km

500 mi

with assault weapons in high school cafeterias, guilty people being acquitted because their lawyers are more famous than their prosecutors, innocent people being executed because they're poor, corporations built on hot air, a congress that thinks lying about having an affair is an impeachable offense, but killing foreign civilians to try to distract media attention from the fact

> **H**owever, if the rest of the world thinks America is a weird place, its incomprehension is mild compared to what America thinks of the rest of the world.

that you're having an affair is just politics, and a president who manages to get elected with fewer votes than his rival.

The patent insanity and enduring appeal of America was summed up long ago by one of its most astute journalistic chroniclers, H. L. Mencken. "Here, more than anywhere that I know of or have heard of," he wrote, "the daily panorama of human existence, of private and commercial folly—the unending procession of governmental extortions and chicaneries, of commercial brigandages and throat-slittings, of theological buffooneries and aesthetic ribaldries, of legal swindles and harlotries, of miscellaneous rogueries, villainies, imbecilities, grotesqueries and extravagances—is so inordinately gross and preposterous, so steadily enriched with an almost fabulous daring and originality, that only the man who was born with a petrified diaphragm can fail to laugh himself to sleep every night." Naturally, there are far too many big words for this quote to run in an American publication or on TV, but you get the general idea. They love us and they hate us, and ultimately, they all want to be us.

However, if the rest of the world thinks America is a weird place, its incomprehension is mild compared to what America thinks of the rest of the world. This might explain why America's many and varied foreign interventions tend to arouse at least as much hostility and suspicion as gratitude. The English historian Arnold Toynbee said that "America is a large, friendly dog in a small room. Every time it wags its tail it knocks a chair over." Americans are not great travelers, either physically or mentally—fewer than 20 percent of Americans own passports, and American newspapers and television news networks tend to regard the world beyond America's shores as interesting only when it directly affects America. A war in Africa might kill millions of Africans, but it won't play on Fox unless American tourists get caught in the cross fire, and seeing as how four in five Americans never leave the country, what are the chances of that? Perhaps the long-standing singular existence and baffled amusement caused by *DP* is a testament to America's xenophobic traits. This is an odd dilemma for a country whose citizenship is literally made up from every other nation and every continent on earth. The conventional wisdom is that the world changed on September 11, 2001. The reality is that the world on September 12 was every bit as nasty, dangerous, and complicated as it had been on September 10—it was just that America was treated to the ultimate infomercial. Had September 11 not been televised live, darker cynics might wonder what had transpired.

Before now, the United States of America has faced four major threats to its security: the Confederate states, Nazi Germany, Imperial Japan, and the Soviet Union. Only the last of these was barely able to match the firepower of the United States, which is why America chose to make the most of its economic advantages: it fought the Cold War, and won it, by outspending the Soviets. In the other three cases, where America was confident in its military superiority, America physically destroyed its enemy, absolutely and utterly, and then spent millions on rebuilding the vanquished foe in America's image. This strategy was remarkably successful for Japan and Germany (arguably, our foreign enemies fared much better than the Confederacy). In keeping with America's new strategy of declaring wars without actually having any tangible victory in sight, the War on Terrorism could prove to be our longest and most expensive foray into our dark culture of violence. Currently American taxpayers are spending over 1 billion dollars . . . a day . . . on war. Now, that is dangerous.

## The Scoop

The United States is the wealthiest and most powerful nation that has ever existed. Sadly, despite this blessing, it is some distance from being the safest. There are more than 200 million guns in the possession of Americans, and few of them are owned by upright pioneers seeking to defend their wagons from marauding Indians.

Though terrorist acts, from 9/11 to the assassinations of doctors employed by abortion clinics, are highly publicized, they are not a likely threat to travelers. And, though America has been nearly constantly at war since it was founded, its own territory has only been seriously attacked by foreign forces twice: by Japan in 1941,

> **T**here are more than 200 million guns in the possession of Americans, and few of them are owned by upright pioneers seeking to defend their wagons from marauding Indians.

and by mostly Saudi Arabian terrorists in 2001. Statistically, there is an argument to be made that you are more likely to be killed by an American outside of America as we pursue our various and ever-changing foreign policies, armed with the world's most devastating arsenal.

Visitors to the United States are in much more realistic danger of robbery or other violent crimes in inner cities. This sort of crime is random by nature, but the chances of falling victim to it can be minimized with proper precautions.

## The Players

### George Walker Bush, President

Only *DP* has the cojones to tell you that George W. Bush (b. July 6, 1946) is actually a Yankee. George came into this world in New Haven, Connecticut. And yes, he has a history degree from Yale and an MBA in business from Harvard. Yes, he did grow up in Odessa, Texas, but he spent a decade as an Ivy Leaguer . . . and, even more damning . . . what good ol' boy plays rugby?

Once you toss the God-fearing, "plain-talking," Texas oil-man image out the window and replace it with a more realistic image, more akin to a yuppie Gordon Gecko, you might get a better handle on GWB.

He won the 2000 presidential election in much the same way that a boxer "wins" a fight if, at some point in the 12th round, his brother steps into the ring and smacks his opponent over the head with a chair. Some time after the Supreme Court of the United States lived up to the satirical vision of an article in *The Onion* by ruling the American people unfit to govern on December 9, 2000, and handing the presidency to Bush, it was announced that in the crucial state of Florida, Bush had polled 537 more votes than Al Gore.

Interestingly, before the election, the state of Florida (Governor Jeb Bush) had removed from its electoral rolls 173,000 registered voters, some of whom were convicted felons, but many of whom were wholly innocent people who just had the same or similar names or Social Security numbers as people who were convicted felons, and most of whom were black, and therefore (according to polling), 90 percent likely to be Gore voters. This is to say nothing of at least 3,000 myopic Jews who voted accidentally for Pat Buchanan when they were trying to vote for Gore, and several hundred extremely dubious postal votes for Bush. It is also beyond dispute that fewer Americans wanted Bush to be their 43rd president than wanted Gore: The nationwide vote was 50,456,169 for Bush and 50,996,116 for Gore. If this had happened in some Central American banana republic, the United States would have sent a peacekeeping force.

Nevertheless, it was Dubya who got to have a turn at being the most powerful person on earth, and you can't say he hasn't been making the most of it. The confetti of shredded agreements and treaties that surrounds him has made him look like a figurine in a souvenir snowglobe.

Dubya has thumbed his nose at the European Union over carbon dioxide emissions and steel tariffs, got the United States bounced from the UN's Human Rights Commission, refused to sign a UN declaration on childrens' rights because it mentioned S-E-X education, pulled out of the Kyoto Protocol on global warming signed by 178 other countries, and overrode the objections of pretty much every other nation on earth by pressing ahead with his "Son of Star Wars" missile defense program (though he's been pretty quiet about that since 9/11 demonstrated that America's skies were already full of missiles—they'd just been more benignly directed before then).

It is, of course, 9/11 and its aftermath that will end up defining the George W. Bush presidency. Before the attacks on New York and Washington, Bush was settling happily into a presidency that intended to pursue indifferent isolationism abroad (candidate Bush, remember, couldn't name the heads of government of two of the world's nuclear-armed states) and rapacious philistinism at home. Bush, who has always been happy to be presented as a man with more horses than books (despite being married to an ex-librarian) cut federal spending on libraries, cut research on renewable energy resources, cut health care for the uninsured . . . and cut taxes for the rich. He also decided to drill for oil in the wildernesses of Alaska and Montana.

Rarely have a president's chickens have come home to roost quite so quickly. Domestically, it was discovered that the corporations who'd been the engines of America's prosperity—and donors to the Bush campaign—had a lot of sand in their tanks. On the foreign policy front, 9/11 forced Bush to engage with the outside world, and, it has to be said, he's done slightly better than might have been expected. He deserves some credit for not launching an apocalyptic blitz in the immediate aftermath of 9/11 when tempers and fears were running high. But since then his War on Terror has started to resemble some endless Orwellian conflict against vaguely defined enemies for very vaguely defined reasons. It isn't helping that Bush doesn't appear to have the remotest understanding of, or interest in, Middle Eastern politics, despite being the first U.S. president to openly endorse Palestinian statehood. Bush seems genuinely surprised that his unstinting and unquestioning support of Israel isn't making the region any calmer. The one sure thing is that the corporations who churn out the weapons, machines, and supplies that fuel the War on Terror have never had it so good.

Bush has taken care of the tobacco, mining, banking, and oil supporters, and the War on Terror (which stretches conveniently from America to Colombia to Iraq to North Korea to the southern Philippines). For now George practices mangling simple phrases and coming up with new and more wonderful ways to wage war on America's enemies.

### President of the United States
http://www.whitehouse.gov

## Dick Cheney, Vice President

Believed by most observers to be vice president, Dick Cheney (b. January 30, 1941) has been studying hard at the Howard Hughes School of Publicity. The possibility that he is, in fact, running the United States from inside a hollowed-out volcano while stroking a large white cat cannot be ruled out. It is common knowledge that the media's obsession with his health problems has caused Cheney to be methodically and continuously robotized (Darth Vader style), one body part at a time. His speech delivery has always been robotic, and of course, he is safeguarding GWB's brain, which he keeps in a very small test tube. There is no truth to the rumor that Dick Cheney doesn't need a pacemaker because doctors discovered that he doesn't actually have a heart.

For more than 30 years, nothing short of fumigation or Democratic administrations has been sufficient to keep this Lincoln, Nebraska, boy out of the White House. In a frightening attack of déjà vu, Cheney was Donald Rumsfeld's special assistant . . . in 1969. He was a Deputy White House Counsel during the Nixon presidency, Chief of Staff under Ford (where Rumsfeld was Secretary of Defense), and Defense Secretary under George Bush the first, and, of course, he is now heir to the throne under George Bush the Younger (where Rumsfeld is Secretary of Defense). Cheney has yet to be seen in public wearing Nehru jackets and holding his pinkie to his mouth. Rumsfeld has privately confided that Cheney is actually Mini-Me and that it is he who is in charge.

Either way you look at it, Dick is Mr. Big, in more ways than one. In between Bush presidencies, Dick passed the time serving on the boards of various impressively vast corporations. One of these, an oil company (surprise!) called Halliburton, signed contracts through two subsidiaries, Dresser-Rand and Ingersoll Dresser Pump Company, to sell $73 million worth of production equipment to . . . Iraq, while Cheney was CEO. This was technically legal, but politically embarrassing, so Cheney simply proclaimed that this wasn't the case. When told that it was the case, he decreed that he just didn't know about it.

Of course, Cheney divested himself of all his Halliburton holdings before ascending to the vice presidency. In August 2000, he unloaded his shares in the company at around $52 a go, trousering $18.5 million as a result. Just 60 days later, Halliburton told its investors that it wasn't doing as brilliantly as it thought, and that a grand jury wanted a word with it for gouging the federal government. The shares dropped by 11 percent. Then, Halliburton realized it was in the soup over liability for asbestos-related claims, and the Securities and Exchange Commission was taking an interest in its accounting. By July 2002, Halliburton shares were limping along at $13.

There is naturally no suggestion that Cheney had the remotest inkling that anything funny was going on. He was only the CEO.

**Dick Cheney**
Presidential Emergency Operations Center
"A Secure, Undisclosed Location"
Somewhere, USA
http://www.isdickcheneydeadyet.com

## Colin Powell, Secretary of State

The popular image of Colin Powell (b. April 5, 1937) is pretty much the same as the character that Morgan Freeman plays in every film he's cast in: wise, thoughtful, reserved, and restrained. Make no mistake about it: Powell is about image, a fair-skinned intellectual touted as an African American (whose parents, he is quick to remind you, came from Jamaica, not Africa). This Bronx boy is a real rags-to-almost-riches story and he embodies all the elements that make America what it should be.

Powell may be a Clintonesque token to some, but he is probably the man who should be running the country: intelligent, sage, pragmatic, proven under fire, and eager to get the hell out of the public spotlight once he has made his nest egg. Which is why he never will.

Since 9/11, the world's liberals have tried to comfort themselves with the idea of Powell holding grimly onto the ankles of Bush, Cheney, and Rumsfeld as they try to launch themselves at another opponent. It is not surprising that Powell is looking to get out of the Beltway nightmare. The former chairman of the Joint Chiefs of Staff is not so much the black man that southern right-wingers would begrudge him as the Bush appointee, and not enough the black man that northern left-wingers don't want to put a boot through the television screen. His creed of caution, which governed the 1991 Gulf War, is known as the Powell Doctrine, which, simply put, means that unless the American military can go in with overwhelming force, an explicit idea of its objectives, and some idea when it plans to come home, it shouldn't go anywhere. Powell, unlike his boss, is a Vietnam veteran with enough ground time to know what a dead American soldier looks like.

Powell's softly-softly approach is widely credited—or blamed—for delaying American intervention in Bosnia. It may also have been the reason that the United States didn't respond to 9/11 by turning sand into glass from Tangiers to Tehran. It should be mentioned that there were those in the Bush cabinet who advocated the immediate and comprehensive clobbering of Iraq, Afghanistan, Syria, and the Bekaa Valley in Lebanon. Powell is possibly alone in Washington's upper echelon in believing that the world is an essentially complicated place. He probably even reads books.

Of course, this son of Jamaican immigrants hasn't got where he is without playing politics. As a young officer in Vietnam, he managed to compile an investigation of the My Lai massacre that didn't mention the My Lai massacre. In the Reagan White House, he was an Assistant to the Defense Secretary and National Security Advisor during the invasion of Grenada, the bombing of Libya, and America's wholly dubious shenanigans in El Salvador, Guatemala, Honduras, and Nicaragua. Powell was a big fan of the contras, and spouted some fabulous obfuscatory twaddle to the enquiry into why America was flogging guns to its sworn enemies in Tehran to fund paramilitary thuggery in Central America.

Powell was once touted as a presidential candidate, and this is not yet completely beyond the realms of possibility, though, at 65, he wouldn't want to leave his run until much later. Of course, he could just retire to spend more time with his money. He cleaned up when AOL, where he was a board member, merged with Time Warner. By a happy coincidence, Powell's son, Michael Powell, was a member of the Federal Communications Commission at the time, and he argued that the merger should be permitted without question.

For now, Powell proudly trumpets, "America stands ready to help any country that wishes to join the democratic world," but sadly never takes the calls from Somalia, Chechnya, DR Congo, and other DPs. Proof perhaps that politics and common sense really don't mix.

**Colin Powell**
U.S. Department of State
2201 C Street, N.W.
Washington, DC 20520
Tel.: (202) 647-4000, Press: (202) 647-6575
http://www.state.gov

## Condoleezza Rice, National Security Advisor

Condi (47), like almost everyone else in the Bush White House, has ties to both George Bush the Elder (she was part of his National Security setup) and big oil (Chevron, where she once served on the board and named a 130,000-ton oil tanker after herself). She is the daughter of a preacher and a former figure skater and concert pianist. She is apparently intellectually and morally more qualified to run the country than her boss (which is a testament to George senior's skills in running the country while his son housesits in the White House). Condi is a political science academic whose focus was the Evil Empire.

Ms. Rice, it is said, is the second person Dubya speaks to every morning, next to the good lady wife. (And no, Condi's not in the room at the time. Hey, this isn't the Clinton administration.)

**Condoleezza Rice**
National Security Advisor
The White House
1600 Pennsylvania Avenue, N.W.
Washington, DC 20500
Tel.: (202) 456-1414
Fax: (202) 456-2461
http://www.rice2008.com
http://www-hoover.stanford.edu/BIOS/rice.html

## Donald Rumsfeld, Secretary of Defense

The ultra-hawkish (b. 1932) Secretary of Defense, Donald Rumsfeld, was a wrestler back at Princeton, and has a similar hawkish approach to diplomacy. Along with his ultra-ultra-right-right-right-wing deputy, Paul Wolfowitz, Rumsfeld has led the Pentagon's charge for wide-ranging military action against anyone who has ever looked at America funny, against the more cautious approach advocated by Powell's State Department. The full-scale implementation of the Rumsfeld/Wolfowitz response would have involved Special Forces actions and/or air strikes against not just Afghanistan, but Iraq, Syria, the Bekaa Valley in Lebanon, and possibly even selected left-wing political groups in the States. It's impossible to imagine that any other country but Israel, and possibly the reliably subservient Great Britain, would go along with Rumsfeld's response, but it's not impossible to imagine that it might happen, especially if Dubya's polling starts to look a bit rickety before 2004.

Rumsfeld has also signed off on a classified report, the Nuclear Posture Review, that warns that the United States must be ready and able to use nuclear weapons against any or all of Iraq, Iran, North Korea, Libya, Syria, China, and . . . Russia (hey, welcome back, guys). Rumsfeld is eyeing the big red button as a response to three possible contingencies: against targets which can withstand conventional weapons; in retaliation for nuclear, biological, or chemical attack; or "in the event of surprising military developments." You may (or may not) be comforted to learn that defense spending is expected to reach $451 billion by 2007.

*Honorable Donald H. Rumsfeld*
Secretary of Defense
1000 Defense Pentagon
Washington, DC 20301
http://www.defenselink.mil

## John Ashcroft, Attorney General

In a sick, Ted Koll-like joke, the man (b. May 9, 1942) charged with protecting America's freedoms as it prosecutes a war against religious fundamentalism is a religious fundamentalist. Mullah Omar move over . . . meet Attorney-General John Ashcroft, the bastard child of J. Edgar Hoover and Ned Flanders from *The Simpsons*, a man who was only available to take the job because he lost his seat in the U.S. Senate to a corpse (Ashcroft's opponent, Democratic Governor Mel Carnahan, died in a plane crash shortly before the election). *DP* humbly submits that it's time that a law was passed precluding from high public office anyone whose home state has ever passed him or her over in favor of sending a dead guy to Washington.

Ashcroft is the son and the grandson of Pentecostal Assemblies of God ministers, and it shows. On arriving in the Department of Justice, he ordered a blue curtain to cover the naked forms of two statues, the bare-breasted Spirit of Justice and the indecorously clad Majesty of Law. He is against drinking, gambling, and dancing, and according to some unconfirmed reports, believes tabby cats are emissaries of the devil. Most famously, he fancies himself as a latter-day George Cohan—although, obviously, not as Jewish. Among his catalog of self-penned patriotic anthems, which his long-suffering staff are encouraged to sing along to, is a rousing ditty called "Let the Eagle Soar." (The clip of Ashcroft bellowing this fearful nonsense at some reception or other must be the most-forwarded non-pornographic video attachment in the history of the Internet.)

Since 9/11, the well-meaning but internationally ignorant Ashcroft has told some entertaining whoppers about half-assed Chicago gang members building nuclear weapons in their garages, and proved to be a big fan of warrantless wiretaps and secret detention without charge. He also believes that anyone who points out that such tactics are, you know, illegal and unconstitutional and all that kind of stuff, might just as well sign on with Osama bin Laden and have done with it ("Those who scare peace-loving people with phantoms of lost liberty," he thundered before Congress, "only aid terrorists."). Naturally, *DP* would never be so disrespectful as to suggest that the nation's senior law officer might be a couple of chapters short of a full gospel. To his credit, and despite being the favorite son of a preppy pro-business administration, Ashcroft now finds himself declaring jihad on corporate fat cats. In calling in fire on his own position, accusations against Cheney and Bush, Jr. have rained down. Perhaps for his efforts the Bush gang will eagerly reward Big John with a diplomatic post in . . . let's say . . . Central Africa?

**Office of the Attorney General**
U.S. Department of Justice
950 Pennsylvania Avenue, N.W.
Washington, DC 20530-0001
Tel.: (202) 353-1555
http://www.usdoj.gov/ag

## The Military Industrial Complex

Be afraid. Be very afraid. This White House has turned an attack by a ragtag collection of flip-flopped jihadis into a global conflict of World War III proportions. Never mind that the military could not identify the enemy accurately; it couldn't even find its purported high-profile (he is well over 6 feet tall) leader, Osama bin Laden. When pressed on the world's most powerful nation's inability to find a scrawny Saudi megalomaniac in Afghanistan, Rummy decided that Binny was not relevant to the War on Terror. Oookaay.

While Donald Rumsfeld continues to fling ever more darts at his office map of the Middle East and Central Asia, the U.S. military is enjoying a concomitant budget blowout. America's allowance request for "blowing things up" is up to $379 billion and expected to grow 30 percent over the next five years. Despite the lack of traditional enemies, U.S. taxpayers continue to ante up for nuke-tipped missiles, $8 billion for antimissile systems, half a billion dollars for archaic mobile howitzers (with the inconvenient name "Crusader"), and a tidy rounded-up sum of $10 billion in mad money for the president to spend on a whim.

It may not have escaped our eagle-eyed readers of *DP* that we could purchase the entire Axis of Evil with this amount on credit and sell timeshares. The GDP for the entire country of Afghanistan is only $21 billion. For North Korea it is $22 billion and for Iraq (owner of 10 percent of the world's oil reserves), it is an anemic $50 billion.

For now, the U.S. military budget buys America a total of 1,398,238 active military personnel, with 667,715 civilians in ancilliary roles. Perhaps in recognition of the fact that that's a whole bunch of uniformed folks to have to keep in one place, America likes to spread them around—in 149 different countries, at last count. Major deployments include 71,000 in Germany, 40,000 in Japan, 38,000 in South Korea, 4,300 in Kuwait, 12,000 in Italy, 3,000 in Bosnia-Herzegovina, 4,800 in Saudi Arabia, 5,200 in Kosovo, and 11,000 in the United Kingdom. Oh, and a thought should be spared for the 1,700 personnel stationed at the NATO base at Keflavik in Iceland, chowing on smoked fish and puffin and bathing in sulphurous tap water just so you can rest easy from worries that the Soviet Union's Arctic Fleet is going to get together for a reunion tour.

**United States Army**
http://www.army.mil

**United States Navy**
http://www.navy.mil

**United States Air Force**
http://www.af.mil

**United States Marine Corps**
http://www.usmc.mil

## Central Intelligence Agency (CIA)

It's not easy being a spook. The nature of the job dictates that the CIA can't claim credit for their successes, so all you ever hear about is the mistakes—or, at least, the mistakes they can't cover up. (Or is this just disinformation designed to distract you from the real screw-ups?) The CIA has been responsible for some classics over the years: mounting an absurd invasion of Cuba, failing to notice that the Indians were building an atomic bomb, carrying on in Iraq in a manner rather more reminiscent of Inspector Clouseau than Jack Ryan, and targeting the Chinese embassy in Belgrade, a lone building in a huge block of land and clearly identified for what it is, even in *Let's Go Europe*. And then there was the very difficult to ignore, Laurel and Hardy noninterrogation of John Walker Lindh, who somehow seemed to be quite chatty to *DP*.

Presently, the CIA is trying to dampen the firestorm of criticism that has erupted over what probably represents the biggest failure in the company's history. Prior to 9/11, the CIA did not have a single agent within a thousand miles of Osama bin Laden. Granted that spending years living in a cave deprived of the company of women, eating boiled goat, and discussing the Koran and beard-care tips with a bunch of ill-educated cranks isn't the most glamorous of gigs, but someone should have been doing it; and someone could have been doing it. John Walker Lindh, a muj wannabe with no resources at all, only had to turn up and ask if he could be in Osama's gang, and *DP* was invited to join the Taliban more than once.

The CIA is currently headed by George Tenet. The agency won't tell anyone how many people work for it, or how much money it spends; however, in 1997, the CIA let it be known that the budget for "Black Ops" alone was a staggering $26.6 billion. It is probably safe to assume that this figure has increased dramatically. To underline their renewed seriousness of purpose, the CIA's Web site now advises that it has suspended its practice of sending congratulatory certificates to "the fine young Americans" who have become Eagle Scouts, "in order for us to concentrate on the War on Terrorism." Presumably this means that Saddam Hussein, Ayatollah Khatami, and Kim Jong Il will be receiving their Axis of Evil certificates any day now.

### Central Intelligence Agency
http://www.cia.gov

### CIA Freedom of Information Act Reading Room
http://www.foia.cia.gov
http://www.fas.org/irp/cia/ciabud.htm

## National Security Agency (NSA)

The NSA, like the CIA, was signed into existence by President Harry S. Truman during the tempestuous beginnings of the communism craze that was popular in some sections of the world in the twentieth century. The NSA's particular area of responsibility is cryptology, or, in other words, trying to read everyone else's e-mails and signals while making sure that nobody else reads theirs. The NSA doesn't go into details about its budget or personnel either, but their Web site coyly suggests the scale of their enterprise by admitting that if the NSA were a private corporation, it would be in the top 50 of the Fortune 500. The NSA is based in Maryland, and its current director is Lieutenant General Michael Hayden.

### National Security Agency
http://www.nsa.gov

## Federal Bureau of Investigation (FBI)

The Feds currently have 11,400 special agents and 16,400 other employees staffing 56 field offices, 400 satellite offices, and 40 foreign liaison posts. At the moment, their principal enterprise is explaining their baffling failure to think there was anything weird about reports of young Arab men turning up for flight training and asking to skip the dull stuff about takeoff and landing.

The FBI had known since its investigations into the 1993 World Trade Center bombing that al-Qaeda was planning to use hijacked passenger aircraft as missiles. Despite this, the head office ignored a warning from an agent in Minneapolis about a flight school student called Zacarias Moussaoui, which said that Moussaoui was the kind of guy who could, you know, just as a random example, fly a hijacked plane into the Twin Towers.

Moussaoui has since become the only person charged in connection with the 9/11 attacks. The agent in question, Coleen Rowley, has since accused the FBI of being hamstrung by "a climate of fear which has chilled aggressive law enforcement action"—the inference here being that the FBI buried the report on Moussaoui because they didn't want to be seen to be picking on Arabs. What is worse is that a second memo, from Phoenix, warning of potential hijackers, was also ignored. That political correctness was the reason the FBI dropped the ball seems unbelievable, but it is either that or the sort of incompetence that would put you off from asking someone to water your plants while you were away, never mind maintain the security of the nation.

FBI Director Robert Mueller has admitted that Rowley's tip was a lead that the Bureau "should have pursued more aggressively." If there's ever an Academy Award for Understatement, bet your farm on this guy.

**Federal Bureau of Investigation**
http://www.fbi.gov

### Department of Homeland Security

This new department is the bureaucratic response to 9/11. Run by former Pennsylvania Governor Tom Ridge, its mission is to prevent further terrorist attacks in the United States and deal with whatever attacks it can't prevent. Its four divisions are Border and Transportation Security; Emergency Preparedness and Response; Chemical, Biological, Radiological, and Nuclear Countermeasures; and Information Analysis and Infrastructure Protection. All of which begs the question of what the already fabulously expensive FBI, CIA, and NSA are doing all day. It is reassuring to know that these agencies need $38 billion a year to issue meaningless, but cute, color warnings. But the more profound horror is the idea that a country built on a ready and armed militia (and owners of 220 million guns) is now to be defended by a very large, toothless, inept, centralized bureaucracy.

**Department of Homeland Security**
http://www.whitehouse.gov/homeland

# Getting In ————————————

You must have a passport to enter the United States. The United States has over 20 different types of visas indicating different reasons for travel . . . all of which are designed to keep people out. Visa type and length varies by country. Travelers from favored countries can stay for up to 90 days without a visa. Contact the nearest U.S. embassy or consulate to obtain visa information and requirements. ·

**Embassy of the United States**
24 Grosvenor Square
London W1A 1AE, UK
Tel.: (44) 20 7499 9000
http://www.usembassy.org.uk

**Consulate-General of the United States**
3 Regent Terrace
Edinburgh
Scotland EH7 5BW, UK
Tel.: (44) 131 556 8315
Fax: (44) 131 557 6023
http://www.usembassy.org.uk/scotland/
   index.htm

**Consulate-General of the United States**
14 Queen Street
Belfast
Northern Ireland BT1 6EQ, UK
Tel.: (44) 28 9032 8239
Fax: (44) 28 9024 8482

**Embassy of the United States**
490 Sussex Drive
Ottawa, Ontario K1N 1G8
Canada
Tel.: (613) 238-5355
Fax: (613) 688-3097
http://www.usembassycanada.gov

**Consulate of the United States**
360 University Avenue
Toronto, Ontario M5G 1S4
Canada
Tel.: (416) 595-1700
Fax: (416) 595-0051

**Consulate of the United States**
1095 West Pender Street, Mezzanine
Vancouver, British Columbia V6E 2M6
Canada
Tel.: (604) 685-4311
Fax: (604) 685-5285

**Consulate of the United States**
615 MacLeod Trail, S.E., Suite 1000
Calgary, Alberta T2G 4T8
Canada
Tel.: (403) 266-8962
Fax: (403) 264-6630

**Consulate of the United States**
Purdy's Wharf Tower II, Suite 904
1969 Upper Water Street
Halifax, Nova Scotia B3J 3R7
Canada
Tel.: (902) 429-2485
Fax: (902) 423-6861

**Consulate of the United States**
1155 St. Alexandre Street
Montréal, Quebec H2Z 1Z2
Canada
Tel.: (514) 398-9695
Fax: (514) 398-0973

**Consulate of the United States**
1, rue Ste-Geneviève
2 Place Terrasse Dufferin
C.P. 939
Quebec City, Quebec G1R 4T9
Canada
Tel.: (418) 692-2095
Fax: (418) 692-4640

# Getting Around

The United States possesses perhaps the most modern and comprehensive transportation systems in the world, yet is surprisingly bereft of clean, timely, and efficient public transportation. Airlines and rental cars are the preferred method of travel. You should know that 40,000 people die on the nation's highways each year, usually equal to the number of homicides. Crime is present in inner-city areas at night and in some heavily touristed spots. Overall, America is safe, with disturbingly random outbreaks of violent gun-related crime.

# Dangerous Places

## Schools

Few things about America seem more alien to the foreign visitor than the idea of schools with armed security and metal detectors. In most developed countries, the greatest hazard faced by a high school student is the occasional locker-room wedgie. In the United States in 1999, the last year for which complete statistics are available, students aged between 12 and 18 were the victims of roughly 2.5 million crimes, including 186,000 instances of rape, sexual assault, aggravated assault or robbery, and 47 violent deaths, including 38 murders—which, of course, included the 12 killed at Columbine High School in Colorado in April 1999 by two students who also killed a teacher, and then themselves. Every year, 8 percent of students in grades 9 through 12 report being threatened or attacked with a weapon on school premises.

Want to identify a potential school killer? Well, he or she is typically of above-average intelligence and is obsessed with violent popular culture such as violent video games and heavy metal rock bands. Sounds just like the average American teenager.

http://www.ardemgaz.com/prev/jonesboro/index.asp

## Office Buildings

In December 2000, Michael McDermott shot dead seven people at an Internet company in Wakefield, Massachusetts. In November 1999, two people were gunned down in a shipyard in Seattle, and seven in a Xerox office in Honolulu. In August 1999, three more bit the dust in Pelham, Alabama, and a little over a week before that disgruntled Atlanta day-trader Mark Barton killed nine people in two stockbroker offices, having first done the same for his wife and kids. And so on, and so on, and so on. In 1999, 645 Americans were murdered at work. The phenomenon of workplace shootings seems especially prevalent in the U.S. Mail service, giving the English language a new phrase for violent loss of control: "going postal."

http://www.ojp.usdoj.gov/bjs/abstract/vw99.htm

## Jails

The United States imprisons a higher proportion of its population than any other country in the world. In 2000, nearly 6.5 million Americans were in the brig, on parole, or on probation: 1 adult in 32. More than 2 million of those were actually behind bars, of which 62.6 percent were black or Hispanic. The $40 billion spent annually on keeping these people locked up sounds like a lot, but most U.S. prisons are overcrowded, badly maintained, and riven with drugs and gangs. In

1999, nearly 8,000 prisoners needed medical attention after assaults by other inmates. One survey of seven prisons concluded that 21 percent of male prisoners had been raped at least once.

http://www.ojp.usdoj.gov/bjs/prisons.htm

### The Mexican Border

This is the only frontier on Earth where the first world directly abuts the third. As a result, it gets crossed slightly more often than Fifth Avenue, except that the traffic is all one way. In 2000, 499 would-be immigrants died trying to reach the home of minimum wage and the land of plentiful work for itinerant dishwashers, either through drowning or exposure.

http://www.usembassy-mexico.gov/eborder-mechs.htm

## Dangerous Things ——————————————————

### Terrorists

The felling of Manhattan's highest man-made peaks by criminals armed with the weapons of a Mail Boxes Etc. clerk demonstrated that there were . . . uh, gaps . . . in U.S. security. So, the big question these days is when exactly will the other shoe . . . or building . . . drop? This is the question currently vexing America's hydra-headed law-enforcement apparatus, and the unspeakable truth is that if a rerun of 9/11 is in the offing, there is almost certainly nothing law enforcement can do about it: trying to act against an enemy with no targetable infrastructure, and whose operatives do not fear death, is a little like trying to put a fence around a cloud. If the terrorists are dedicated, professional, and have a rudimentary talent for concealment, or even if they are (as they truly are) incompetent, bumbling, and lucky, there is no reason why they'd be found until it was too late.

However, what has distinguished the terrorists who have struck America in the last couple of years is that while they are certainly dedicated, they are about as good at concealing their true intentions as a fox in a Foghorn Leghorn costume. The odd behavior of the 9/11 hijackers at their flight schools registered instantly with their instructors, who informed the authorities, who, in turn, did nothing. Indeed, six weeks after the attacks, the Immigration and Naturalization Service sent an official notice to the Florida flight school where two of the hijackers had trained that, to point out the fine skills of government, informed the school that the long-dead terrorists were happily approved for visas. In March 2002, the Federal Aviation Authority sent its regional pilots' newsletter to the Fort Lauderdale address of Ziad

Samir Jarrah, who had flown United Flight 93. One wonders what pouring more money into this gaping maw of incompetence will produce.

The hijackers' dress rehearsals were similarly badly disguised. About a month before 9/11, the actor James Woods caught a flight from Boston to Los Angeles, which was the same routing as the flight that crashed into the Twin Towers. The only other people in the first-class section on that flight were four Middle Eastern–looking men who, Woods noticed, boarded without any cabin baggage, books, magazines, or computers, and instead spent the six-hour flight whispering to each other. Woods reported his observations to airport authorities, who responded with something less than zeal. Only in America can an actor who plays a cop do better detective work than the real cops.

It is also noteworthy that al-Qaeda's claimed or admitted operations since 9/11 have not been noteworthy for their intelligence. Zacarias Moussaoui has put up a brilliant legal defense. Nizar Nawar tried to destroy the La Ghriba synagogue on the Tunisian island of Djerba, but succeeded only in killing a bunch of German tourists. Still, at least Nawar got his bombs to go off, which is more than can be said for Richard Reid, the British-born idiot who tried to detonate his crudely made shoe-bombs in full view of his fellow passengers on American Flight 63 from Paris to Miami. If al-Qaeda sent Reid to blow up a bus instead of a plane, perhaps he'd have burnt his beard on the exhaust pipe.

> **I**f al-Qaeda sent Reid to blow up a bus instead of a plane, perhaps he'd have burnt his beard on the exhaust pipe.

http://story.news.yahoo.com/fc?cid=34&tmpl=fc&in=US&cat=Terrorism

## Guns

"Guns don't kill people," observes the hoary NRA canard. "People kill people." Despite this backyard wisdom, few coroners insist on typing "Death by People" on 26,000 to 30,000 or so gunshot death certificates issued every year in America. Guns just make the death process a little quicker and more likely . . . something our less-armed Euro and Canuck neighbors have been whining about for years. There are more than 220 million constitutionally protected firearms owned by Americans, and they use them. In 2000, 10,417 Americans were murdered with firearms—that's 28 every day. Another 16,418 individuals killed themselves with firearms, and 808 were killed in accidents with firearms. In the twentieth century, more Americans were killed by guns in America than were killed by guns on foreign battlefields.

*National Rifle Association*
http://www.nra.org

*Gun Owners of America*
http://www.gunowners.org

*The Brady Campaign to Prevent Gun Violence*
http://www.handguncontrol.org

## Hate Groups

According to the Southern Poverty Law Center, there are 602 active hate groups in the United States. That is, there are 602 groups of people who've found nothing better to do with their time than to sit around and complain about how everything that's wrong with their lives is the fault of people who aren't the same color, religion, or sexual orientation as they are. We could list all the URLs for these groups here, but we reckon that these dim-witted, ignorant hicks would be far too busy eating squirrels, molesting their cousins, and scattering auto parts all over their trailer parks to answer your e-mails anyway.

*Southern Poverty Law Center*
http://www.splcenter.org

## Gangs

America's willingness to absorb large masses of refugees has resulted in the importing of some of the nastiest and hardest street gangs in any Western country. In New York, rival gangs don't actually break out into spontaneous choreography when they want to settle a dispute: *West Side Story* has become *Apocalypse Now*. In Los Angeles, fast cars and even faster weapons have elevated gangs into small armies. The weapons of choice are assault weapons, like the AK-47, Tec 9, MAC, or Uzi.

Most gangs are created along ethnic and neighborhood lines. The Bloods and the Crips are the new Hatfields and McCoys. The gangsta look has become big business now. Baggy pants, work shirts, short hair, and that unique gangsta lean have all been adopted by freckle-faced kids from Iowa. Gangsta music has towheaded kids reciting tales of inner-city woes just as ably their parents can sing "Itsy Bitsy Teenie Weenie Yellow Polka-Dot Bikini." The new proponents of this violent/hip culture seem to live life a little too close to their lyrics. Rappers Tupac Shakur and Notorious B.I.G. both probably wish they had been singing Barney's theme of "I love you, you love me."

In Los Angeles, there are over 800 gangs with 30,000 members. There are at least 1,000 homicides every year and well over 1,000 drive-by shootings. According to figures presented to the White House, there are 500,000 gang members in 16,000 gangs in the United States. Eight hundred American cities are homes to these gangs, compared to 100 in 1970. Fifty-seven percent of towns with over 25,000 residents have reported gang-related incidents.

But gangsterism in America is not merely black, white, or Hispanic. Gang members come in all flavors. The most dangerous gangs in America are the new Asian gangs: groups of Cambodian, Vietnamese, Laotian, and Filipino youths whose families came from the refugee camps, killing fields, and dung heaps of Southeast Asia. Chinese-American gang members are being blamed for the February 25, 1996, murder of Cambodian actor Dr. Haing Ngor, a former refugee of the Khmer Rouge and the star of the 1984 movie *The Killing Fields*. After enduring 4 years of savage brutality under the Khmer Rouge during the guerrilla group's reign of terror between 1975 and 1979, the Academy Award winner was ironically slain in the land of the free, for the sake of a Buddhist amulet.

**Street Gangs**
http://www.streetgangs.com

## Militias

There are more than 70 active militias in America, ranging from reasonably well-organized paramilitary groups to (rather more often) gaggles of web-footed yokels who get together on weekends to drink beer and shoot off a few rounds at cardboard cut-outs of federal agents. Ignored by the press until the Oklahoma City bombing in 1995, militias were free to dress in army surplus gear and stomp about the swamps of Florida or the mountains of Colorado. Now the more colorful members realize that being on TV doesn't do much other than get you a fat FBI file. Most of these individuals are now hiding out in the woods waiting in relative silence for the New World Order's black helicopters to arrive.

Divisive, unruly, and as media-savvy as Reggie Jackson, the militias were quickly demonized and ostracized after Tim McVeigh blew most of the Alfred P. Murrah Federal Building into a different zip code. Given a few more longnecks and a couple of pinches of Skoal, the more colorful and mercenary of the bunch could come up with a coherent political agenda. But that is just the cartoon version the Feds would like you to believe. Militias are a very pervasive and deep-rooted movement. As one leader told *DP*, "You are not going to see a real militiaman on TV, but we're here . . . waiting."

> **G**iven a few more longnecks and a couple of pinches of Skoal, the more colorful and mercenary of the bunch could come up with a coherent political agenda.

The point is that militias don't exist to sell videotapes, parade around in designer cammo, and fondle guns. The lifeblood of the American militia movement flows from the forebears who thumped King John and tossed the British under King George, and they insist they become visible when our government forgets that. The militia movement has become the repository for feelings that rarely dare speak their name in polite company anymore—part of the process of registering online with the California militia is certifying that you are heterosexual (in California, of all states, just think of what they are missing out on).

**7th Missouri Militia**
http://users.mo-net.com/
    mlindste/7momilit.html

**51st Missouri Militia**
http://www.mo51st.org

**California Militia**
http://geocities.com/slk299/
    welcome2.html

**Citizens' Militia of Maryland**
http://www.expage.com/page/citizensmi
    litiaofmaryland

**Connecticut 51st Militia**
http://ctmilitia.homestead.com

**Indiana Citizens' Volunteer Militia**
http://www.icvmilitia.homestead.com

**Kentucky State Militia**
http://www.kysm.org

**Maine Constitutional Militia**
http://mainemilitia.homestead.com

**Marietta Pennsylvania Militia**
http://mariettapa.com/marietta_militia.
    html

**Militia of East Tennessee 3rd Brigade**
http://www.geocities.com/met3rdbrigade

**Militia of Montana**
http://www.militiaofmontana.com

**North Carolina Citizen Militia**
http://www.ncmilitia.org

**Ohio Unorganized Militia Assistance
    and Advisory Committee**
http://www.oumaac.com

**Virginia Citizens Militia**
http://vcm.freeservers.com

## Christian Fundamentalists

Or, specifically, the hard-core group of God-botherers who express their distaste for the killing of unborn people by killing born people. The National Abortion Federation has logged 3,849 acts of violence against abortion clinics and doctors since 1977, including 7 murders, 17 attempted murders, 41 bombings, and 166 instances of arson. It was Christians, not Muslims, who were first responsible for threatening to deliver anthrax by mail. During the anthrax scare of late 2001, more than 500 abortion clinics and pro-choice organizations in the United States received envelopes of white powder and threatening letters, many signed by someone claiming to represent the Army of God.

The Army of God, also grandly styling itself as the American Holocaust Resistance Movement, is the most militant of the antiabortion groups. Their Web site includes a photo gallery called "Heroes of the Faith," which consists of activists who have committed acts of violence against clinics and doctors, and some deeply tiresome ranting about the satanic propensities of gays and Muslims. It is a cruel irony that those who are the most voluble opponents of abortion are generally the best advertisements for the idea.

**National Abortion Federation**
http://www.prochoice.org

**Army of God**
http://www.armyofgod.com

## Muslim Fundamentalists, or "Those Dark-Skinned Guys with Beards"

After 9/11, the U.S. government detained more than 1,100 people. The government refused to make public their names, locations, the charges against them, or even the precise numbers arrested, but it is known that most were Arab or Muslim men. Attorney-General Ashcroft eventually announced that 548 were being held on immigration charges and 104 were facing criminal charges, none of which had anything to do with 9/11. Many others who'd been living otherwise unremarkable suburban existences found themselves abruptly removed to war-ravaged home countries, including Somalia.

The legislative response to 9/11, the risibly named October 26, 2001 Patriot Act, makes it more likely that there will be further sweeps of people whose faces don't quite fit. Noncitizens can now be detained for up to a week if the attorney-general has reasonable grounds to believe that they are a threat to national security. This might sound more reasonable if the incumbent attorney-general didn't believe that unclothed statues were a threat to national morality. Let's hope John doesn't read his *DP* bio.

http://www.eff.org/Privacy/Surveillance/Terrorism_militias/20011031_eff_usa_
    patriot_analysis.html

## Being Black, or "Those Dark-Skinned Guys without Beards"

In America the idea that all men are created equal is a long way from the statistical reality, despite annual government spending of $185 billion on various minority programs. Life expectancy at birth for white Americans is 77.4 years. Life expectancy at birth for black Americans is 71.8 years. Infant mortality in whites is 5.7 per 1,000 births. Infant mortality in blacks is 14 per 1,000 births. Black people are 8 times more likely to be murdered than white people, 9 times more likely to go to jail (in 2000, 10 percent of black men between the ages of 25 and 29 were behind bars), and their children are 3.5 times more likely to live in poverty than those of white people.

http://www.ethnicmajority.com/Healthcare.htm

*Being President*

There have been 43 presidents of the United States, of whom 10 have been shot, or shot at. James Garfield, Abraham Lincoln, William McKinley, and John Kennedy were all killed. Ronald Reagan was seriously wounded, Theodore Roosevelt slightly less so. Franklin Roosevelt and Gerald Ford both had the good fortune to be the targets of people who, respectively, couldn't have hit a barn door with a handful of wheat (Giuseppe Zengara missed Roosevelt and killed the mayor of Chicago instead), didn't really understand how guns work (Lynette Fromme might have done Ford more damage if she'd put a bullet in the chamber first), and couldn't have hit a cow's backside with a banjo (just two weeks later, Sarah Jane Moore missed Ford from 10 yards). Harry Truman survived an assassination attempt by two Puerto Rican nationalists, which was long on ambition but short on common sense (one of his assailants was killed by security guards, the other seriously wounded). This is, of course, to say nothing of Robert Kennedy and George Wallace, both of whom were shot while campaigning for the job—the former was killed, the latter paralyzed.

Okay, so the money's not bad and the perks are pretty cool, but would you take a job that came with a 23 percent chance of being gunned down by an angry loner?

http://www.near-death.com/experiences/origen9.html

## Getting Sick ─────────────────────────

Excellent but expensive health care is available throughout the United States. Medical facilities and supplies, including medicines, are in abundance, and so is the demand for payment and/or proof of insurance. The level of training of U.S. doctors is the best in the world. When presented with their medical bill, foreign visitors without medical insurance will quickly learn why America attracts the best and the brightest.

http://www.worldwidemedical.com

## Nuts and Bolts ─────────────────────────

There are 280 million people entitled to take the Pledge of Allegiance with a straight face. About 83 percent of these are white and 12 percent black, with the difference being made up by minorities from, or descended from, Asia and the subcontinent. Descendants of the original inhabitants of the United States account for less than 1 percent of the population. The United States is a substantially Christian nation, with 56 percent of its population subscribing to one or another variation of Protestantism and 28 percent to Roman Catholicism, and equal numbers of Jews and Muslims.

The official language is English, though dozens of other languages are spoken, especially Spanish and Creole in the South. The currency is the dollar. There is really nothing you need to figure out; just bring credit cards and cash.

### Embassy of Great Britain
3100 Massachusetts Avenue
Washington, DC 20008
Tel.: (202) 588-6500
Fax: (202) 588-7850
http://www.britainusa.com/embassy

### Consulate-General of Great Britain
845 3rd Avenue
New York, NY 10022
Tel.: (212) 745-0200
Fax: (212) 754-3062
http://www.britainusa.com/ny

### Consulate-General of Great Britain
The Wrigley Building, 13th Floor
400 North Michigan Avenue
Chicago, IL 60611
Tel.: (312) 970-3800
Fax: (312) 970-3852
http://www.britainusa.com/chicago

### Consulate-General of Great Britain
11766 Wilshire Boulevard, Suite 1200
Los Angeles, CA 90025-6538
Tel.: (310) 481-2900
Fax: (310) 481-2961
http://www.britainusa.com/la

### Consulate-General of Great Britain
Wells Fargo Plaza
1000 Louisiana, Suite 1900
Houston, TX 77002
Tel.: (713) 659-6270
Fax: (713) 659-7094
http://www.britainusa.com/houston

### Embassy of Canada
501 Pennsylvania Avenue, N.W.
Washington, DC 20001
Tel.: (202) 682-1740
Fax: (202) 682-7726
wshdc-outpack@dfait-maeci.gc.ca

### Consulate-General of Canada
1251 Avenue of the Americas
New York, NY 10020-1175
Tel.: (212) 596-1628
Fax: (212) 596-1790
cngny@dfait-maeci.gc.ca

### Consulate-General of Canada
550 South Hope Street, 9th Floor
Los Angeles, CA 90071-2627
Tel.: (213) 346-2700
Fax: (213) 346-2767
lngls-td@dfait-maeci.gc.ca

### Consulate-General of Canada
100 Colony Square, Suite 1700
1175 Peachtree Street, N.E.
Atlanta, GA 30361-6205
Tel.: (404) 532-2000
Fax: (404) 532-2050
atnta-td@dfait-maeci.gc.ca

### Consulate-General of Canada
2 Prudential Plaza, Suite 2400
180 North Stetson Avenue
Chicago, IL 60601
Tel.: (312) 616 1860
Fax: (312) 616 1878
chcgo-td@dfait-maeci.gc.ca

*Consulate-General of Canada*
750 North St. Paul Street, Suite 1700
Dallas, TX 75201
Tel.: (214) 922-9806
Fax: (214) 922-9815
dalas-td@dfait-maeci.gc.ca

# Dangerous Days

| | |
|---|---|
| **10/24/02** | Two arrested in sniper spree. |
| **3/2/02** | Operation Anaconda begins. Seven U.S. servicemen killed and 50 wounded. |
| **3/1/02** | U.S. Advisor sent to Yemen. |
| **2/27/02** | U.S. Advisor sent to Georgia. |
| **2/18/02** | U.S. Advisor sent to the Philippines. |
| **12/7/01** | Kamdaha falls to the United States. Last Talib-held city cleared. |
| **12/1/01** | John Walker Lindh is found and interviewed by Robert Young Pelton. |
| **11/25/01** | Battle of Qal-I-Janji. CIA paramilitary Mike Spann becomes first U.S. casualty of war in Afghanistan. |
| **11/25/01** | Taliban surrender to General Dostum in Kunduz. |
| **11/13/01** | Kabul falls. |
| **11/9/01** | Mazar-I-Sharif falls. |
| **10/7/01** | War in Afghanistan begins. |
| **10/01** | U.S. senators and media organizations receive letters contaminated with anthrax. |
| **9/11/01** | Two hijacked airliners are flown into the Twin Towers of the World Trade Center in New York. Another airliner hits the Pentagon in Washington. A fourth plane, believed bound for the White House, crashes in a field in Pennsylvania when its passengers overpower the hijackers. Nearly 3,000 people are killed in the attacks. |
| **4/20/99** | Twelve students and a teacher are killed, and 23 others are wounded, when teenage gunmen Eric Harris and Dylan Klebold go on a rampage at Columbine High School in Littleton, Colorado. Harris and Klebold also kill themselves. |
| **4/19/95** | A truck bomb destroys the Alfred P. Murrah Federal Building in Oklahoma City, killing 167 and injuring more than 400. Timothy McVeigh, a Gulf War veteran, is later convicted of the bombing and is executed. |
| **4/19/93** | FBI agents and U.S. soldiers attack the Branch Davidian compound in Waco, Texas, starting a fire which kills 74 people. |

**THE UNITED STATES OF AMERICA**

**2/28/93**   Agents of the Bureau of Alcohol, Tobacco, and Firearms attack the Branch Davidian compound in Waco, Texas. Four agents and six Branch Davidians are killed.

**2/26/93**   A bomb in the car park beneath the World Trade Center in New York kills six and injures more than a thousand.

**3/30/81**   President Ronald Reagan is wounded in an assassination attempt in Washington, DC.

**6/5/68**   Presidential candidate Robert F. Kennedy is assassinated in Los Angeles.

**4/5/68**   The Reverend Martin Luther King, Jr. is assassinated in Memphis.

**11/22/63**   President John F. Kennedy is assassinated in Dallas.

**12/7/41**   The U.S. Navy's Pacific fleet in Pearl Harbor, Hawaii, is attacked by 353 aircraft belonging to the Imperial Japanese Navy. More than 2,000 sailors, soldiers, and civilians are killed, 21 ships are sunk or damaged, and 164 aircraft are destroyed.

**9/6/1901**   President William McKinley is assassinated in Buffalo.

**7/2/1881**   President James A. Garfield is assassinated in Elberon.

**4/14/1865**   President Abraham Lincoln is assassinated in Washington, DC.

**1861–65**   The U.S. Civil War kills 620,000 Americans, more than any other war in American history.

**7/4/76**   The United States of America declares independence from Great Britain.

★★★

# YEMEN

## Blamin' Yemen

In the vagaries of history, it would have been hard to predict that this tiny, sunburned chunk of dirt would be the root cause of all our recent problems or even that it would be such an obsession of the United States. But it is. Yemen pops up in almost every bad-news terror headline: The hijackers of 9/11, the USS *Cole* bombing, American Taliban John Walker Lindh, secret terror cells in Lackawanna, embassy bombings in East Africa, Afghan jihadis, kidnappings and deaths of foreign tourists . . . the list goes on. Oh yeah, and that guy . . . darn . . . what's his name? . . . oh yeah, . . . bin Laden. An online search for "terrorism" and "Yemen" will give you 67,000 hits. That's not quite as many as the number of bomb attacks and embassy shutdowns America experiences in Sana'a in a year, but it's a good indication of the love Yemenis have toward the Great Satan (yes, that's the term used in some radical madrassahs to describe their new best friend).

959

If you want a more specific idea of the anger some Yemenis have against America, just visit the very popular Dar al-Hadith, or House of the Prophet's Sayings and Deeds, in the northern city of Dhammar. The school has cranked out over 3,000 very militant folks from around the world and its founder was said to be one of bin Laden's heroes. Of course, the curriculum at this Salafist (an old-school form of Islam that literally means "ancestor") school includes weapon training as well as old-fashioned religious tutoring.

If you are looking for the seeds of discord, you can't do much better than in Yemen. This is where the Palestinians holed up in the '70s; where Hamas has an office; where bin Laden's pappy sprang from; where gun love runs rampant; where fundamentalism runs riot; where kidnapping is a tourist draw; where blood feuds keep things, well, bloody; and where America chooses to fight a minicrusade. Attention, reality show producers: Yemen is a bubbling, laugh-a-minute mix of Marxist hard-liners, Islamic fundamentalists, angry tribes, and impoverished youth all smacked together by a brutal government—a government that seems very similar to Iraq, Syria, Jordan, Saudi Arabia, and all those other enlightened dirt patches. Bluntly put, Yemen is a place held together by whoever can whip out more guns 'n' daggers faster and in greater numbers than the other guy. Here the oratory of politics is replaced with the more violent tactic of kidnapping, stern editorials in the *Yemeni Times* are replaced by grenade blasts, and security is as solid as the shifting sands of the north or tribal allegiances.

Yemen has the dubious honor of being chosen (along with Georgia, the Philippines, Afghanistan, and Iraq) as a new battleground for our ambitious, ambiguous, and never-ending War on Terror. (*Wheel of Fortune* fans have forsaken the Gameshow Channel for CNN as they tune in each week to see who will make it to the new AXIS OF TERROR!) *DP* sure can't keep up with our new foreign policy. It might be important to note that when the Pentagon decided to send 800 Special Operations troops to help fight the war in Yemen, they decided to base them in a place they considered safer and more hospitable—the deadly and arid wasteland of nearby Djibouti. Well, maybe the food's better in that French outpost.

*Wheel of Fortune* fans have forsaken the Gameshow Channel for CNN as they tune in each week to see who will make it to the new AXIS OF TERROR!

Yemen is a good-kid-gone-bad story. Despite its good points (climate, Queen of Sheba stuff, and regal hospitality), you could say Yemen just grew up in a bad part of town. In spite of being known as the fertile bit of the Arabian peninsula (hence its former Roman name of Arabia Felix),

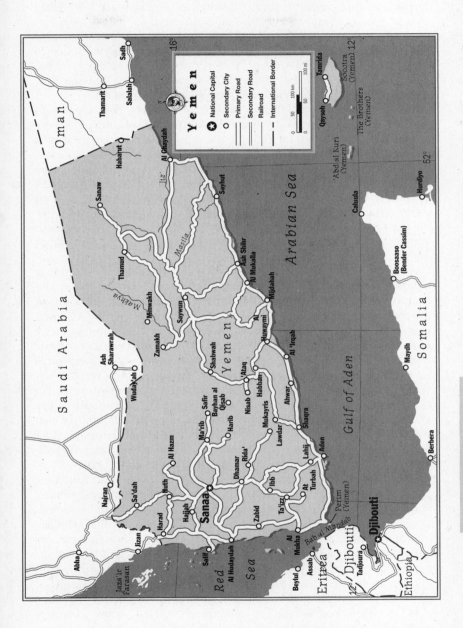

its next-door neighbors (Eritrea, Djibouti, and Somalia) are less "felix," or happy, areas. Even Saudi Arabia and Oman have warred over Yemen's border, but essentially Yemen has always been a wild and woolly place; a place where, let's say, even a Somali warlord might feel nervous. People don't come here for the scenery. Yemen's position at the elbow of the Arabian Peninsula and at the tight little sphincter of the Red Sea have always made it an important chess piece for colonial powers.

So you could probably blame history for Yemen's troubles. Yemen was originally a trade route that fed warring nomadic tribes. Like a Somali barmaid, Yemen has had the usual list of ancient conquerors. It did settle down and get married until it became part of the Ottoman Empire, and it was made even more important when the Suez Canal was completed in 1869, and then released from its bad marriage in 1918. The British were concerned about protecting the port of Aden (bugger the hinterland, was their philosophy) and kept a watchful eye on the sea lane until their departure in 1967, which created South Yemen, a place that the Russians just had to have even if they didn't have the gumption to take it themselves.

In 1970, Russia's need to control key strategic points resulted in a Marxist government for South Yemen. Marxist persecution of the Islamist rebels created a mass migration of Yemenis from the south to the more traditional north. On May 22, 1990, the Republic of Yemen was created between these two warring concepts. The Islamic country of North Yemen and the Marxist region of PDRY (People's Democratic Republic of Yemen) somehow combined their two disparate worlds into one. A cute side benefit of this new republic is that the Marxist PDRY vanished off the U.S. State Department's sponsors-of-terror list even though the terrorists didn't go anywhere. The remnants of the PDRY army and the ruling Yemeni Socialist Party started another civil war against the Islamic government in 1994 and were soundly defeated, leaving the army commanded by former North Yemeni President Ali Abdallah Saleh and occupying what had been the PDRY.

Although there is little chance of another civil war, all is not completely calm; disputes on its 1,458-kilometer-long border were resolved with Saudi Arabia in 2000, but have yet to be marked and manned. There are skirmishes between government soldiers and tribes who are opposed to their lands being ceded to Saudi Arabia. Although President Saleh has always kept a hands-off approach with the hard-line fundamentalists (remember the complaints about his not being forthcoming enough in the USS *Cole* investigation?), he is being forced to crack down on elements that have plenty of support in his country.

Al Jumhuriyah al Yamaniyah (as Yemen is officially known) consists of 18 million people occupying only half a million square kilometers.

The country has no surface water, little to no industry, some of the hottest desert in the world, blinding summer dust-storms, and a sliver of usable land. It's a land with 30 percent unemployment, continual hardships, constant tribal spats, and now Americans running around with helicopters and machine guns looking for Islamic terrorists. Things should get interesting.

## The Scoop

Yemen is among the poorest countries in the world (stop me if you have heard this one before) and is a hotbed of Islamic fundamentalism as well as a major supplier of scrawny jihadis to various wars around the world. So it's no surprise that it has become one of our rapidly expanding "Make Big Money Fighting al-Qaeda" franchises. Normally hard-line Islamic states are being drenched with American dollars, weapons, and technology and instantly becoming fast allies against their own people (see Pakistan), with of course the usual destabilizing results. Yemen's favorite homeboy, Osama bin Laden (whose father was from Yemen), is proof that local boys can make good (or bad, depending on your perspective). Despite its fundamentalist roots, honed by kicking foreigners out (see Afghanistan), and if you ignore its support of Iraq in the Gulf War, this little scruffy knee-bend of a country could be our next newest best friend. Like Pakistan, Saudi Arabia, Egypt, and other paragons of democratic, fair, level-headed, secular nations, Yemen is now with "us" and is against "them." In this case, "them" is themselves, because the government has always relied on the good graces of Saudi Arabia and its way-too-orthodox Islamists to stay in power. Yemen is so safe and welcoming that the U.S. embassy shuts down more often than a Bulgarian pacemaker, and even the heavily armed U.S. Special Operations troops sent to hunt terrorists in the country are stationed in . . . Djibouti. As in most poor, Islamic countries, hospitality in Yemen seems to make regular world headlines. Kidnapping has morphed from a social function and tourist attraction to a deadly crime.

http://www.yementimes.com

## The Players

### President Field Marshall Ali Abdallah Saleh/ General People's Congress (GPC)

The man in charge and more than likely to stay in charge for a while is Ali Abdallah Saleh (b. March 21, 1942, in Bait al-Ahmar village in Sana'a Governorate), the local hero, founder, warrior, statesman, poster boy, and, well, boss. He attended a religious school in Kuttah and joined the army at age 16. He was bumped into officer candidate school two years later in 1960. He then helped plan the September 26, 1962, revolution. He stayed in the military and specialized in armored warfare until he became president of the Yemen Arab Republic and commander in chief of the armed forces on June 24, 1978 (oddly, his bio trumpets his promotion to colonel as occurring a year later, even though that means he technically reported to himself). When Yemen unified, Saleh became president on May 22, 1990, and was elected by the shura on April 27, 1993, and again by the parliament on October 1, 1994, and by a public vote on September 23, 1999. Others might point out that he came to power in 1978 after the yet-to-be-solved assassinations of his two predecessors. Ali held on to the job with a magical 96 percent of faithful subjects agreeing that he was indeed the right man for the job. Of course, Ali gets more negative press on human rights abuses, torture, and suppression of free speech than Britney gets about having fake boobs. But hey, that's why they have jails for journalists, right?

> **A**li gets more negative press on human rights abuses, torture, and suppression of free speech than Britney gets about having fake boobs. But hey, that's why they have jails for journalists, right?

Since then, there have been two rounds of elections and everyone seems happy with the status quo. Shaykh Abdallah bin Husayn al-Ahmar's Islamic Reform Grouping, or Islah, has been in a partnership with Saleh since the end of the civil war in 1994. So expect Saleh to be on the posters for a while longer.

http://www.presidentsaleh.ye
http://www.yemeninfo.gov.ye/english/home.htm
http://www.gpc.org.ye
http://www.parliament.gov.ye
parliament.ye@y.net.ye
Tel.: (967) 01 277 049

## Colonel Ahmad Ali Abdullah Saleh

Every Middle East dictator . . . er, sorry, democratically elected official, must have an heir apparent . . . er, we mean, preferred candidate for the next election, right? Well, Saleh, Sr. luckily has Saleh, Jr. Thank God junior seems to be actually educated and competent. The eldest son of the Yemeni president has a degree in political science and administration from the United States. He was elected as a member of the parliament in 1997 and received military training in Jordan and at the British Royal Military Academy. In October of 1999, Saleh, Sr. decided to create a special forces unit to combat internal threats and after an exhaustive search based solely on merit and experience . . . put his number-one son in charge.

How is Junior doing? Well, on December 18, 2001, Ali, Jr. showed what he was made of and attacked a "bin Laden hideout." The locals were understandably perturbed at being attacked by their own government's troops and helicopter gunships, and fought back, resulting in the death of 18 soldiers and only one tribesmen. Oh well, back to the drawing board.

The unit commanded by Saleh, Jr. was the finest that the Yemen military has to offer and is mandated to fight riots, combat kidnapping, chase terrorists, and of course make sure that Daddy . . . er, we mean President Saleh, will remain in charge—regardless of which generation decides to overthrow him. In March of 2002, approximately 200 Green Berets arrived to begin training this group and the Republican Guard, whose main job is also to protect the president and is also led by Saleh, Jr. (Dad is also a major general). In September of 2002, another 800 Green Berets, plus an assault ship packed with Marines and helos arrived as well. Both dad and son can sleep tight at night.

http://www.fas.org/terrorism/at/docs/HR%20report/Yemen.htm

### The Aden-Abyan Islamic Army (AAIA)/Jaysh Adan-Abiyan al-Islami

An offshoot of Islamic Jihad, this fundamentalist group seems to dislike British and U.S. interests in the Arabian peninsula. They attacked Yemeni socialists before the 1993 parliamentary elections and were behind the December 28, 1998, kidnapping of 16 Western tourists. Just to keep things jumping, they have been behind a number of bomb attacks in and around the southern port of Aden. Many Yemenis came home as hard-core fundamentalists of the "Salafi" or "Wahhabi" versions of Islam.

There are two other groups found in Yemen: the Islamic Deterrence Forces (IDF) and Muhammad's Army (MA)—both of whom took credit for the attack on the USS *Cole*. It is assumed that the AAIA, IDF, and MA are simply alphabet soup for bin Laden's "We don't like infidels" glee club. Why would we put forward such a radical theory? Well, the organizations also praised the August 1998 U.S. embassy bombings in East Africa, and called upon Yemenis to attack Americans after the cruise missile attacks on the Afghan training camps, and think bin Laden is just swell.

You can also connect the dots to the hook-handed Abu Hamza al-Masri, the cleric at the Finsbury Park, London, mosque who is a fan of

Yemen and considers it the last Islamic country. It is assumed that al-Masri and founder and former leader of this group, al-Hassan, fought together. It is also believed that al-Masri was an exile in Yemen for a while.

Abu al-Hassan, a 32-year-old Salafist from Shabwan province (real name: Zein al-Abidine al-Mihdar), was executed for the 1998 kidnapping of 16 foreigners on October 18, 1999. He was the first person to be executed (by firing squad) under a law that mandated the death penalty for kidnapping, which was passed four months before the kidnapping. Timing is everything.

http://www.csmonitor.com/2002/0205/p01s04-wome.html

## Osama bin Laden

Fashion-trend spotters could not help but notice that in the video that bin Laden sent out three weeks before the USS *Cole* bombing, Binny was decked out in a Yemeni dish-dasha gown and was wearing a dagger common to the Hadhramaut region. Hadhramaut is in southeast Yemen, where the Quaiti and Kathiri sultanates are found, and of course is the place from where bin Laden's father, Muhammad bin Laden, left in the '30s to become a porter in Saudi Arabia. (Muhammad bin Laden left Yemen in 1931 with a battered suitcase and ended up owning one of the Arabian Gulf's largest construction companies and fathering over 50 children . . . one of them a tall, shy boy named Osama.)

In this region, the Hadranis farm wheat, coffee, and dates, while Bedouins raise sheep and goats. Bin Laden senior came from al-Rubat ("the tent") in Wadi Doan. Bin Laden, Jr. grew up in Jiddah, but he married a girl from a prominent family in Hadhramaut. Not surprisingly, links to this region were found during the USS *Cole* investigation and just about every other anti-U.S. terror plot in the region over the last 10 years.

http://dailynews.yahoo.com/fc/World/Osama_Bin_Laden

## Sheik Muqbel bin Hadi al-Wadie/Salafism

Salafists are Sunni Muslims who adhere to the teachings of the "forefathers" or al-Salaf al Salah. Salafism dates from the ninth century and calls for a return to the customs and lifestyle of the period during the life of Mohammed (definitely a retro look, with brown and tan being the predominant decorating colors). It is unusual in that its original teacher, Taqi al-Din Ahmad Ibh Tamiya (who died in 1328), called for jihad against other Muslims who did not share his orthodox and retro views. Back then, Taqi declared war against Mongols, who he believed were not true Muslims. This is strangely similar to the Taliban (who followed the Deoband school of Islam in India) warring against other Afghans, and bin Laden declaring jihad on the Sa'uds. My fundo is more fundo than your fundo, we guess. From the Salafist movement sprung the Wahhabist movement in the eighteenth century, which was a missionary-type movement that included the original Sa'ud family. The Sa'uds did not believe you could war against other Muslim nations.

For a full dose of modern-day Salafist dogma, all roads lead to Sheik Muqbel bin Hadi al-Wadie, the now-deceased sheik in the north of Yemen, who started a number of schools, or madrassahs, to crank out folks with missionary zeal and that dour holier-than-thou look all warring fundos seem to have. He ran a Salafist school that teaches locals and foreigners the most austere form of Islam and an intolerance for Jews and Christians that borders on rabid: lots of references to "dogs" and "pigs" during heated sermons. Salafism is the predominant root of the al-Qaeda network that has united Egyptian, Yemeni, Saudi, Algerian, and other dissidents. One of the elements of Salafism is *taqiyyeh*, or concealment of the belief from enemies.

The angry sheik provided willing recruits not only to the jihad in Afghanistan, but other dirty wars, from Algeria to Kashmir to the Philippines. His school, the Dar al-Hadith (House of the Prophet's Sayings and Deeds), teaches the only version of Islam that is more creaky and bleak than the old-school version of Islam, other than the missionary-style Wahhabism that is popular in Saudi Arabia.

Followers of Salafism try to get back to the history or ancestry of Islam, forsaking modern conveniences . . . like democracy, as well as electricity, women, photographs, and music—very Taliban-chic and sadly lacking in snappy gospel tunes. The deceased chic sheik apparently has his detractors. There have been bomb attacks outside his mosques in Sana'a and Aden. He also allegedly had some famous students, like John Walker Lindh, who left dull language training in Sana'a for a more debilitating form of Islam. Lindh (aka Abdul Hamid) ended up traveling from the Dar al-Hadith to a madrassah in Bannu and then into the arms of bin Laden, and then, of course, to *DP*. He was a party kind of guy. Lindh now has a couple of decades to ponder his educational choices and why his brand of religion required him to kill brother Muslims. He will, of course, be in a federal prison and surrounded by plenty of Muslims, many with the nickname "Bubba."

Muqbel had always been a teacher of Islam in Saudi Arabia and Yemen, when he wasn't stirring things up or in jail. He was linked to the fundamentalist group that occupied the Great Mosque in Mecca in November of 1979 and spent three months in jail. His views are shared by many of the tribal leaders in the north and have attracted foreign students from around the world, some of whom have been arrested for their efforts. There are now six training centers in Yemen. The man who currently carries on the angry tradition of demonizing Jews and Christians is probably Abdel Meguid al-Zindani. He is a member of Sheikh Abdullah al-Ahmar's "Islah" party, the country's second-largest political party. Zindani also runs the al Iman University in Sana'a, which cranks out dissidents and jihadis. His school was not only supported by the Yemeni government (i.e., Saleh), but by Gulf and Turkish donors, too.

http://muslim-canada.org/binladendawn.html
http://www.terrorismcentral.com/Library/Biographies/BiographyList.html

### Al Jihad et al.

Long before al-Qaeda was the buzzword in terrorism circles, there was al Jihad. (Both sound very odd when pronounced with a nasal Texas accent.) Readers of *DP* probably realize that terrorist groups make up and use more handles than a tone-deaf Ibiza Club DJ. Most of these groups can trace their roots to the Ikwhan, or Brotherhood, in Egypt in the early part of the twentieth century. Yemen's proximity to Saudi Arabia, and the need to have friends, has resulted in a disproportionate number of extremists from Yemen. The political and economic climate in Yemen has been perfect for hatching terrorists. Combine the Marxists' crackdown on the Islamic religion in the '80s, the live-fire training in

> **R**eaders of *DP* probably realize that terrorist groups make up and use more handles than a tone-deaf Ibiza Club DJ.

Afghanistan that many of the young Yemenis received, rich expat and Saudi sponsors, and then the brutal tactics of the military dictatorship of Saleh; and voilà! A snake's nest of seething anger and violence. Then, of course, there is Yemeni homeboy (once removed) Osama bin Laden who said it was a toss-up whether he should pick Afghanistan or Yemen as his next base when he was asked to leave Sudan.

Yemen is a natural resting and training place for terrorist groups. A weak central government, heavily armed tribal control, and more religious fundamentalists than at a Dukabour barn burning make it the ideal spot. Al Jihad has split into three smaller groups and is responsible for low-level threats and attacks against U.S. interests in the south and around Sana'a. But take comfort in the notion that even if the group doesn't have the same name, it's always playing the same game.

http://www.fas.org/irp/world/para/iaa.htm
http://cns.miis.edu/research/wtc01/aljihad.htm
http://www.fas.org/irp/world/para/jihad.htm

## Old/New/North/South/East/West

The key to understanding Yemen is in its geography and history. Without traveling very far a visitor can experience places that run the gamut from tropical to arid, frigid to hot, wet to dry, and, of course, safe to dangerous. Politics are simpler. The north is tribal and Islamic in nature and the south has been Marxist (a legacy of the National Liberation Front, which began in 1963) and colonial (until the British left Aden in 1967). The south ran out of steam (and money) with the death of the Soviet Union and merged with the Islamist north in 1990. To make things trickier, what is called the traditional region of Yemen, or the north, is actually geographically to the west (makes it harder to rail against "Western values," *DP* guesses); the south, or the old British protectorate turned Marxist haven, actually runs east and, yes, north. Although the government of the south was Marxist, there was always a thriving mujahideen insurgency funded by Saudi Arabia and others. These days Yemen is an extraordinary blend of old (its 2,000-year-old tribal cultures and unique eight-story brick-and-mud high rises) and new (Special Forces and Predator unmanned planes cruising around looking for al-Qaeda). But it's all one big happy Yemen now . . . right?

http://www.yemennetwork.com

## Getting In

You need a visa and a couple of photos, a return ticket, and a health certificate (yellow fever required) to get into Yemen. Evidence of a visit to Israel in your passport will get your entry refused. Flights to Sana'a originate from Europe on Yemen Airlines.

http://home.earthlink.net/~yemenair

**Embassy of the Republic of Yemen**
2600 Virginia Avenue, N.W., Suite 705
Washington, DC 20037
Tel.: (202) 965-4760
Fax: (202) 337-2017
http://www.yemenembassy.org.

**Yemen Mission to the U.N.**
866 United Nations Plaza, Room 435
New York, NY 10017
Tel.: (212) 355-1730
http://www.traveldocs.com/ye
http://travel.state.gov/yemen.html

**U.S. Embassy in Sana'a**
Dhahr Himyar Zone
Sheraton Hotel District
P.O. Box 22347
Sana'a, Yemen
Tel.: (967) 1 303 155, ext. 118, 265, or 266
Emergency: (967) 1 303 166
Fax: (967) 1 303 175
Open between 8:30 and 10:30 AM, Saturday through Wednesday

YEMEN

## Getting Around

Once you leave the cities, you lose the comfortable sense that the government is in control. Most kidnappings occur on the main road and in the remote provinces. (Shabwa and Abyan provinces are kidnap spots, but kidnappings have also occurred on the Sana'a–Dhamar–Aden road.) The best method of travel is to hire a car and driver from a travel agency. For cheapskates who don't need to travel far, there are dhabars, or black-striped minibuses, in the north, or the blue buses in the south. Longer trips require the service taxis, which wait until each seat is full before leaving. More practical travelers will fly between major cities.

Americans in Yemen are urged to register with the American Embassy in Sana'a and remain in contact with the embassy for updated security information at (967) 1 238 843 through 238 852.

http://www.travel-guide.com/data/yem/yem.asp

## Dangerous Places

### The South

When the Marxists drove the British from Aden in 1967, they also kicked out the Sultan of Abyan and other wealthy landowners. Marxism is not the most fertile environment for the wealthy or religious (things that go hand-in-hand in Yemen). The closure of the Suez Canal helped to turn the south and Aden into a slum and the Marxist politics of South Yemen didn't help. Saudi Arabia covertly funded Islamic groups to fight against the Marxists.

The People's Democratic Republic of Yemen (PDRY) was a major hangout for Russian-backed Palestinian terrorists in the '70s and even made it onto the U.S. State Department's list of countries that sponsor terrorism (it was the Soviet kind of terrorism, back then). Naturally, Marxism and Islam mixed like oil and water and large numbers of Yemenis traveled to the north as well as to Saudi Arabia and other Middle East countries, creating a large Yemeni diaspora. Among these travelers were bin Laden's remaining relatives. A disproportionate number of these Yemenis ended up fighting the Soviets in Afghanistan, in the jihad, and, of course, many of them went through bin Laden's camps. Even in December of 2001, Yemenis made up one of the largest national groups that were captured in Afghanistan and sent to Guantanamo Bay. These days the tribal areas are a hotbed of dissent as the government tries to show how tough it can get over fundamentalists, tribal law, and crime. Naturally, no one outside the city limits of Aden takes it very seriously.

http://www.geographyiq.com/countries/ym/Yemen_us_relations_summary.htm

## Dangerous Things

### Kidnapping

Although Colombia is the kidnap king, Yemen seems to do it with far more style and with the comfort of foreigners in mind. Even by 1991, over 250 foreigners had been kidnapped inside Yemen. Tour guides paid about $150 per vehicle to avoid the inconvenience of having their customers detained. Kidnapping started to be in vogue in 1994, and by 1997 there were 84,000 foreign visitors to Yemen willing to run the gauntlet.

Before things got ugly, tourism generated around $70 million a year and the numbers were skyrocketing. Estimates since 9/11 figure that Yemen has lost $1.5 billion in tourism. It wasn't too hard for tribesmen and fundamentalists to find victims. Many tourists took adventure tours to Yemen with the giddy hopes that they would be kidnapped. Back in the good old days, kidnap victims were shown great hospitality, put up for free, given gifts, and handed back when the tribesmen's grievances were addressed. Usually unpaved roads, schools, or complaints to police about unfair treatment were the source of their problems. Then, in 1998, the death penalty was passed for kidnapping. Now things are a little more serious.

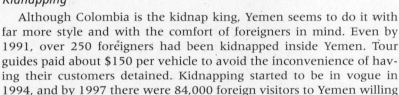

**B**ack in the good old days, kidnap victims were shown great hospitality, put up for free, given gifts, and handed back when the tribesmen's grievances were addressed.

Kidnapping was fun until three Brits and one Aussie were killed (along with two of the kidnappers) in 1998. On December 12, 16 foreign tourists were snagged by an armed group calling themselves the Islamic Army of Aden-Abyan, led by a bin Laden buddy and fellow jihadi. It was supposed to be a Christmas/New Year trip put together by UK-based Explore Worldwide. Around 11:00 AM, the convoy of five SUVs was ambushed five kilometers outside Lahmar and armed men were taken captive. Twelve Britons, two Australians, two Americans, and four Yemeni drivers were captured by men belonging to the Islamic Army of Aden-Abyan, an offshoot of Jihad, led by Abu al-Hassan al-Mihdar. British Islamic cleric, Abu Hamza, was also involved in the aftermath of the attacks and reportedly was upset that there were not more Americans in the convoy. According to Abu al-Hassan, the UK cleric advised him not to harm the hostages and urged him to exchange them for nine Islamists who were under arrest in Yemen. The nine prisoners consisted of two groups: Sheikh Saleh Haidara al-Atawi and his two brothers who had been arrested at the beginning of December, and the six men (five Britons and an Algerian living in Britain) who had been arrested on December 23 and 24.

On December 29, the government attacked (after initial attempts to negotiate failed) and the shootout began.

If the tourists had just done a little research, they might have read bin Laden's February 23, 1998, fatwa urging Muslims "to kill the Americans and plunder their money wherever and whenever they find it," noticed the embassy attacks in East Africa, the cruise missile attacks on the Afghan camps, and bin Laden's December 24 interview on ABC news, and perhaps determined the timing . . . er . . . slightly dangerous.

Tour companies like Explore Worldwide still toss around slogans like "Expect the Unexpected," and even promote "spending a few days with tribal people in their villages." Now that, even by *DP*'s standards, is truth in advertising.

That doesn't stop hordes of Germans, Italians, and adventure-bus tourists from taking advantage of rock-bottom tourist prices. Four tourists can hire a driver with a four-wheel drive for $40 a day, and hotels are offering double rooms with breakfast for $7.00 a day.

http://www.exploreworldwide.com

## WHATEVER HAPPENED TO MARLIN PERKINS AND MUTUAL OF OMAHA?

It seems that the new business is extortion. Alhed Saleh al-Khawlani was knocking on people's doors just south of Sana'a and showing them his marketing presentation—a simple sales pitch consisting of revealing to potential customers the grenades he had hidden under his clothing. He then demanded protection money or he would set off the grenades . . . probably not the first time an insurance salesman used the threat of impending doom to sell policies. You do, however, have to admire Alhed's ability to encapsulate sales, marketing, threat assessment, and security in a simple, convincing presentation.

Then one day the Yemeni police found Alhed splattered all over the street. It seems he had accidentally detonated his own grenades. *DP* speculates that perhaps he had forgotten to take out an insurance policy in his own name?

## Qat

Khat, Chat, or African tea. The buds on fresh leaves of the *catha edulis* shrub keep the Yemenis happy. Well, more specifically, *qat*, or *khat*, delivers mild, tweaker-like feelings of euphoria, hallucinations, mental clarity, paranoia, and anxiety. Mix that with a deep fondness for guns and tribal spats, and you have a crazy cocktail.

Qat is grown in Yemen on irrigated terraces or flown from Kenya and Ethiopia in large bundles. It is potent when fresh, and most locals start chewing it in the afternoon, resulting in green slobbering bursts of gibberish around late afternoon. Qat comes in a wide variety of qualities and the longer the branch, the better the buzz. You can also slum it and try *qatal*, the working man's buzz, but be warned it can be addictive. Normally there are social activities connected to chewing qat. Devotees meet at a "makyal" for a "kailah," or group chew. Besides reducing hunger, chasing sleep, and delivering a sense of well-being, it has some negative side effects. Gunmen use qat to get ready for a firefight and odd and strange things are done under its influence. Those who are hooked on qat are referred to as *mawalaee*, or *mawali'a* in the singular.

*DP* trivia: Qat is legal in the United Kingdom and if you are so inclined to sample the leaf, drop an e-mail to:

qatman@al-bab.com
http://www.somaliawatch.org/archive/000410201.htm

## Guns

In Yemen there are an estimated 60 million guns spread out over 4 million adult males. No one has actually counted the weapons, and the number seems to grow with each telling. Even if you spread out that number of guns among babies, women, and old men, you would still have three guns for each citizen. An AK costs around $100 and there is no shortage of anything, from colonial-era blunderbusses to Russian-made antiaircraft guns. You can thank the Russians for flooding the country with guns during the 1994 civil war, and of course the old tribal need to use or brandish them for a variety of self-serving reasons.

Sadly for you *High Noon* types, carrying guns on the streets of Sana'a was banned in February of 2002. You can, however, still sport a *jambiya*, or the traditional curved dagger that Yemeni men earn at age 14. Those in the know realize that the curved handle of the Arabic knife is used for hanging a bag of qat.

http://arms2armor.com/knives/knives.htm

## Sand

Although Yemen is as old as dirt, Sana'a was supposedly founded by Noah's son Shem. Back then there weren't really any borders. It seems no one got around to figuring out where Arabia Felix (happy Arabia) ended and Arabia Deserta (you figure it out) began. One of the sore spots for Yemen has been the northern border with Saudi Arabia. This frying-pan world of rocks and shifting sand is important more for any potential oil deposits that might be found than for strategic needs. Although the actual location of the border was determined and agreed to in 2000, it seems the actual process of marking the border is fraught with problems. The Dahm tribe (and others) has resisted any clear demarcation of the Saudi-Yemeni border (they want compensation for their land, which is being annexed by Saudi Arabia as part of the border disputes), and has been attacking the German company hired to do the job. Accordingly, the Yemeni military has held captive some Dahm tribesmen who were injured in an attack on the German company's workers. A virtual state of war exists.

http://www.historyguy.com/Saudi_Yemen_Conflict.html

## Being a Journo

In Yemen, libel is punished with 80 lashes. If a local writes an article that disagrees with the president's opinion, he can get three years and a $20 fine (yes, that is 20 U.S. dollars). One journo who criticized the government's lack of concern about preserving historical sites faced a two-year prison term.

http://www.freemedia.at/wpfr/yemen.htm
http://www.rsf.fr/rubrique.php3?id_rubrique=43

# Getting Sick ─────────────────────────────

Yemen requires the usual raft of shots and has outbreaks of Rift Valley fever. Malaria is found at low elevations. Hospitals in the main cities are passable for minor stuff, and the French military hospital in Djibouti might work in a pinch. Hospitals include the Yemeni German Hospital, tel.: (967) 418-686/9, 418-690/1 (Hadda Road, near 60-Meter Road); The Azal, tel.: (967) 200-000/ 213-870 (60-Meter Road, close to Mathbahr vegetable market); The Al-Moyad, tel.: (967) 323-760 (on Airport Road, near elevated walkway); The Al-Thawra, tel.: (967) 246-966/ 246-983 (Al-Khoulan Street, near Bab Al-Yemen); and the Military Hospital, tel.: (967) 222-513/4 (Bab Shaoub area).

http://www.usembassy.ye/doctors.htm
http://mosquito.who.int/docs/country_updates/yemen.htm
http://www.mdtravelhealth.com/destinations/asia/yemen.html

# Nuts and Bolts

The Yemeni rial seems to be pegged to Martha Stewart's popularity index. These days, 164.590 Yemeni rials will get you 1 U.S. dollar, but expect much less by the time you get there. The legal system can be a conundrum because it is a mishmash of Sharia, Turkish law, English common law, and local tribal customary law, and, of course, however much money it takes to skirt all of the above.

Yemen is a land of extremes, particularly in temperatures. The best time to avoid the heat or cold is in spring and fall. April and August are the wet months. Yemeni holidays are May 22, Day of National Unity; September 26, Revolution Day; October 14, National Day; and November 30, Independence Day.

# Dangerous Days

| | |
|---|---|
| 4/23/02 | Large bomb explosion at the Civil Aviation Authority building. |
| 4/12/02 | A bomb explodes outside U.S. embassy. |
| 3/15/02 | Yemeni throws grenade at U.S. embassy in Sana'a. |
| 1/3/02 | The United States announces plans to send advisors to train Yemeni troops. |
| 12/18/01 | Yemen's attempts to capture Mohammad Hamdi al-Ahdal and 20 others results in the death of 18 government troops and 4 villagers. |
| 9/26/01 | President Saleh insists he will not let foreign troops use Yemen territory to fight the war on terrorism. |
| 10/12/00 | The USS *Cole* is attacked; 17 U.S. sailors are killed. |
| 1999 | Zein al-Abidine al-Mihdar, leader of Yemen's militant Aden-Abyan Islamic Army, is executed after being convicted of abducting 16 Western tourists, resulting in the deaths of four of them. |
| 1999 | Thirty foreigners are kidnapped. |
| 1998 | Sixty foreigners are kidnapped. |
| 5/94 | The civil war between North and South ends. |
| 1/93 | All U.S. military are pulled out of Yemen. |
| 5/22/90 | The Republic of Yemen was created from the union of the south (The People's Democratic Republic of Yemen) and the north (Yemen Arab Republic). |
| 1991 | Yemen opposes U.S. military action against Iraq in the Gulf War. |

YEMEN

**1990** Yemen is unified.

**1986** Friction between extreme Marxist elements of the government in The People's Democratic Republic of Yemen leads to civil war. The Marxists create a new government.

**6/24/78** President Ahmed Al-Ghashmi is assassinated by a briefcase bomb planted by the socialist party in Aden, South Yemen.

**1997** The second round of democratic elections for the unified country is held. Islamic fundamentalists lose 13 seats.

**1972** Border clashes between North and South Yemen. The Arab League brokers a cease-fire.

**1967** Marxist guerrillas revolt against British in South Yemen. The People's Democratic Republic of Yemen (PDRY) is formed.

**1962** A coup after the leader dies results in Egyptian-backed communists replacing the Royalists. Yemen Arab Republic is created and the Royalists create division between north and south.

**1948** Rebels assassinate the ruler of North Yemen.

**11/18** North Yemen becomes independent after dissolution of the Ottoman Empire.

**1905** The Ottomans attempt to take over Yemen but end up controlling the north while the British control the south. The Violent Line separates the two powers.

**1869** The Suez Canal opens.

**1839** The British take over Aden and provide protection to local sheikhs under treaty.

**1517** The Ottomans control Aden and are forced out by the Zayidis in 1636.

**1513** The Portuguese take over Aden and are expelled by the Ottomans.

**1454** The Kathrids come to power in the south and rule until 1967.

**897** The Zayidis come to power in the north and rule until 1962.

**628** Islam comes to Saba and is strictly followed in the north by the Zayidis in 897.

**575** Persia takes over Saba.

**AD 396** Romans institute Christianity, stop the frankincense business, and in 570 the dam at Ma'rib bursts. Saba goes into decline.

**1000 BC** Irrigation and frankincense create the affluent state of Saba.

Harare

# ★★★
# ZIMBABWE

## Farmageddon

Zimbabwe was the last of Britain's African colonies to become independent, hoisting its green, yellow, red, and black beach-towel of a flag above the expectant heads of its liberated citizens in April 1980. Naturally, within months its economy, security, and future prospects went careening into the third-world abyss like an unsnapped bungee jumper at Batoka Gorge.

Social scientists might opine that Zim's present troubles are "the encapsulation of the central dichotomy of modern African politics," but here at *DP* we sum it up as just old-fashioned greed, incompetence, hatred, and stupidity, put into high gear. A once-glorious African kingdom, turned British colonial showcase, has now become a blood-soaked bankrupt dictatorship. African politicians routinely blame the continent's woes on the mendacity of Western corporations, or the paternalism of Western aid, or the fetters of Western loan repayments, or the legacy of Western colonialism. Funny how no one mentions that the prehistoric, all-African Great Zimbabwe kingdom, after which

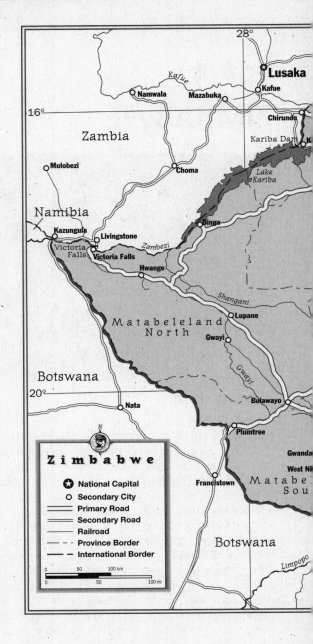

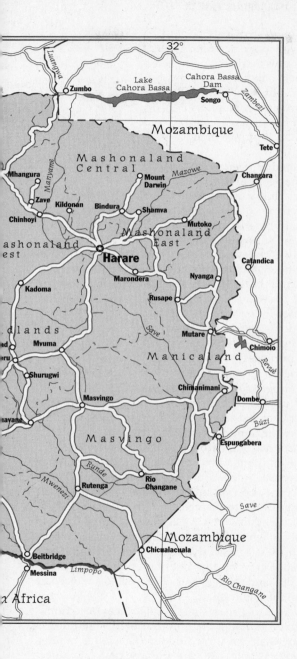

modern Zim is named, managed to self-implode in the 1500s with nary a white man in sight. In present-day markets and bars, you'll hear a much simpler truth: Africa's agonies have far more to do with the idiocy, incompetence, and corruption of the African leaders who are trying to pin the rap on whitey while stuffing their pockets.

> **A**frica's agonies have far more to do with the idiocy, incompetence, and corruption of the African leaders who are trying to pin the rap on whitey while stuffing their pockets.

Founded in 1890 amid a frenzy of expectation over potential gold and mineral deposits, Rhodesia, as Zimbabwe was known before independence, yielded little but excellent farmland and plentiful southern African *lebensraum* for British and South African farmers. The consequent influx of white settlers, and subsequent mass land acquisitions, bedevils the country to this day. Rhodesia developed from a combination of Queen Victoria's high-minded maternalism and the dubious rapaciousness of Cecil Rhodes, and became the second-most healthy and wealthy country in southern Africa at independence.

Zimbabwe's leader since independence, President Robert "Robber" Mugabe, is not, frankly, doing a great job. His country has an economy that has shrunk 22 percent since 2000, and an AIDS epidemic which could, to all intents and purposes, destroy Zimbabwe within a generation. One might reasonably assume that someone who'd been in charge for 22 years might bear some slight responsibility for this, but Bob is not, to put it tactfully, a reasonable man. As he sees it, if Zimbabwe is now an irretrievable basket-case—and, by most rational analyses, it is—it's entirely the fault of Great Britain.

No, really. When the International Monetary Fund suspended aid to Zimbabwe in 1999, accusing Zimbabwe of running guns and money and sending troops to the war in the Democratic Republic of Congo, Mugabe said Britain had put the IMF up to it. When Zimbabwe suffered a severe fuel shortage, Mugabe blamed it on British banks hoarding foreign exchange. Even Zimbabwe's AIDS crisis is, apparently, all Britain's fault. When Britain, which has spent millions trying to combat the spread of AIDS in Africa, suggested that African leaders could be a little more helpful, Mugabe threw his toys out of his pram in spectacular fashion. Apparently, the land that gave us Oscar Wilde and Freddie Mercury has an even more insidious plan.

"If Tony Blair wants to turn Britain into a United gay Kingdom," bleated Bob in 1999, "that is a matter for him. But he should not lecture other countries. Tony Blair has three homosexuals in his cabinet. This is a gay organization. People who are homosexuals are queer because they think differently." *DP* naturally hesitates to advance the old chestnut that those who are most volubly antigay are protesting that little bit too much, but Bob, who passed a law which punishes "unnatural sex acts" with up to 10 years in prison, sounds like a man with issues he urgently needs to address.

Before it achieved independence in 1980, Zimbabwe was a British colony variously called Southern Rhodesia, the Central African Federation, Rhodesia, and Zimbabwe-Rhodesia (if it wasn't complicated, it wouldn't be African, now would it?). Rhodesia was named after Cecil Rhodes, a figure that no author of swashbuckler novels would have dared invent: Originally sent to Africa from England for the improvement of his frail health, he went on to found the De Beers diamond mines, become prime minister of the Cape Colony (now part of South Africa), and secure what became Southern Rhodesia as land chartered for the British South Africa Company.

The British South Africa Company ran Southern Rhodesia like a national business corporation, the occasionally violent objections of the local Ndebele tribespeople notwithstanding, until 1922. A British colonial government followed, which in 1930 passed a law whose ramifications are continuing to vex Zimbabwe today—the Land Apportionment Act, which restricted native ownership of land. From 1953 to 1963, Southern Rhodesia was incorporated into a British creation called the Central African Federation (described by one eminent historian as "a sad case of total failure"), which included Northern Rhodesia and Nyasaland. When the latter two became the independent nations of Zambia and Malawi, respectively, the federation split up.

Sensing somehow that the British government's tendency to grant its former colonies independence at the drop of a hat did not bode well for them, the (white) Rhodesians voted into office the newly formed Rhodesian Front (RF) in 1962, dedicated to demanding full independence from the United Kingdom with the retention of the existing minority-rule constitution. When the United Kingdom refused independence on this basis, the RF appointed the intransigent Ian Smith as prime minister. In November 1965, Smith carried out the long-threatened unilateral declaration of independence (UDI), renaming the territory just "Rhodesia."

The rest of the world reacted much as they reacted to South Africa afterwards. Economic sanctions were imposed, and Smith's options for foreign holidays narrowed dramatically. Curiously, Smith, a World War II fighter ace who once vowed that whites would rule Rhodesia for "a thousand years," still lives in Zimbabwe. (Historically speaking, the "thousand year" claim doesn't bode well for far-right oppressive regimes.) Smith, who still foams at the mouth at the slightest mention of the despicable commies that stitched him up, claims to support the opposition party, Movement for Democratic Change.

Black resentment of white rule simmered gently enough until boiling over in the Marxist '60s, with the convenient arrival on the scene of armed nationalist groups such as the Russian-sponsored Zimbabwe African Peoples' Union (ZAPU), run by Joshua Nkomo, and the Chinese-backed Zimbabwe African National Union (ZANU), founded by Nkomo protégé Robert Mugabe. In 1972, the battle began in earnest.

From 1976 onward, a combined struggle was waged in the name of the Patriotic Front (PF), an uneasy alliance formed by ZAPU and ZANU, which was aided and abetted by sympathetic governments in Zambia and the newly independent Mozambique. By the late '70s, the Rhodesian bush war had escalated into a savannah bloodbath with an estimated 30 to 50 people dying on a daily basis. When hostilities finally ended, over 20,000 Rhodesians of all hues had been fatally wounded; atrocities and murder had become commonplace on both sides. While Mugabe's soldiers routinely butchered locals suspected of collaborating with Smith, the Rhodesian army (backed by South African special forces after 1967) packed hundreds of locals into "protected areas" (de facto concentration camps), occasionally dropping napalm on villages that didn't cooperate. Inevitably, the war widened into Mozambique and Zambia, where Rhodesian SAS units and South African *Recces* attempted to disrupt ZANU PF's logistical network. Eventually bowing to U.S. pressure, South Africa ended its military-technical support for the illegal regime, giving the guerrillas a vital leg-up. Bereft of supplies, the undoubtedly superior troops of the Rhodesian armed forces were obliged to capitulate: by 1979, elite Rhodesian Light Infantry troops were forced into battle with a mere 6 rounds of ammunition each.

In 1979, mounting economic difficulties, resulting in large part from the imposition of economic sanctions by the international community, together with declining white morale and guerrilla inroads in the rural areas, led the Smith regime to fashion what was termed an "internal settlement." This took the form of a black surrogate regime under the leadership of Bishop Abel Muzorewa, and the foundation of the brief-as-it-was-unsuccessful state of Zimbabwe-Rhodesia. Within less than a year all the parties in the conflict agreed to participate in the Lancaster House constitutional conference in London, which led to the emergence of the independent state of Zimbabwe on April 18, 1980. Much to the dismay of the British, who favored Nkomo for the job, Robert Mugabe was elected leader with a landslide majority, and has occupied the big desk ever since.

Zimbabwe could have become the great success story of postcolonial Africa. Yet in a very crowded field, Mugabe, raised by Jesuits, a former staunch Marxist now turned devout Roman Catholic, is swiftly ascending to the very top ranks of the Batty African Tyrants club. Though he is not quite as monstrously profligate as Mobutu was, or as psychopathically murderous as Kabila, or indeed as out-and-out-howling-at-the-moon cracked as Idi Amin, he's getting there. His rule is one of pettiness, vanity, and extreme violence.

Why this has surprised anyone is unclear: His first and sustained act of domestic policy involved the massacre of tens of thousands of his own citizens, creating a wound in the Zimbabwean psyche that still bleeds today. Shortly after this killing spree, he changed Zimbabwe's constitution so that he could call himself "President" instead of merely "Prime Minister." More recently, he bankrupted his country by bribing a disreputable gang of bullies masquerading as war veterans to kick the heads of the country's only foreign-exchange earners; sent his army into a profligate war in the Democratic Republic of Congo; and fixed a presidential election.

Zimbabwe is now flat broke and facing a serious famine, while Mugabe passes laws effectively making it illegal to grow food if you're white. One day, the UN will wake up to the fact that its peacekeeping forces could all be replaced by a plain van with a padded interior, staffed by half-a-dozen determined operatives, and armed with a butterfly net and a straitjacket (*DP* top tip: you can find Bob most Sundays at Harare's Catholic Cathedral).

## The Scoop

Zimbabwe is going to hell on a sled, and all the faster for said vehicle being steered by a lunatic nuttier than a weapons-grade fruitcake. With all the usual caveats of third-world travel, it's still a *reasonably* safe place to visit, unless someone suspects you of being a journalist; but if you're going to go, go (very) soon. You'll have all the advantages of being a tourist in a place that's had lousy press—no crowds, cheap hotels—and, more important, travel to Zimbabwe may soon become impossible or unacceptably dangerous. Zimbabwe's short-term prospects are dismal—famine, bankruptcy, sectarian thuggery, racial violence, and an aging president with only one oar in the water. Meanwhile, Western donors, including the World Bank and IMF, are refusing to help until Barmy Bob stops chewing his desk, so your tourist dollars are probably the only hard currency they will see this year. But don't have too much fun: just one example of Zim's long-term prospects is that at least 35 percent of the population is HIV-positive. Not bad for the country that once boasted sub-Saharan Africa's highest literacy rate.

*The Zimbabwe Independent*
http://www.independent.co.zw

*The Daily News*
http://www.dailynews.co.zw

## The Players ────────────────────────

*Robert Gabriel Mugabe*

The silly old Shona bastard is 78 years old, and some say he is as crazy as a rat in a coffee tin. Despite persistent rumors that he suffers from tertiary syphilis (check out the incessant hand-wringing at public speeches), he appears in dishearteningly good health, possibly owing to the fact that he's married to his 38-year-old former secretary. Like many who fought for black-majority rule of African colonies during the '60s and '70s, he was once regarded internationally as a hero and a freedom fighter. And, like many such figures who end up getting their hands on power, he's not been a conspicuous improvement on what he replaced.

Bob was born just outside Salisbury (renamed Harare), in Kutama. A bright kid, he was educated in a Jesuit mission in what was then the British possession of Southern Rhodesia. After finishing school, he attended Fort Hare University in South Africa and became a teacher in Ghana. He appears to have undergone some sort of political awakening during this period, and he returned to Southern Rhodesia in 1960, becoming a PR flak for the pro-independence National Democratic Party (NDP), then led by Joshua Nkomo (the NDP later morphed into the Zimbabwe African Peoples' Union—ZAPU—to evade a banning order, but was banned again, anyway). Bob split from ZAPU in 1963, and set up a more radical party, the Zimbabwe African National Union (ZANU), in cooperation with the always carefully typed and slowly pronounced Ndabaningi Sithole. ZANU was also banned by the Rhodesian authorities, and Mugabe spent 10 years in the slammer from 1964 onward.

In prison, Mugabe completed two law degrees by correspondence and became—difficult though this is to imagine now—a globally renowned martyr-saint in the manner of a made-for-TV version of Nelson Mandela. When he was released in 1974, Rhodesia was at war—ZAPU and ZANU guerrillas had been fighting the forces of Ian Smith's white colonial government since 1972. Mugabe was an active figure on and off the battlefield, leading guerrilla raids and infusing ZANU with an old-school Marxism (it was the '70s . . . at least he wasn't listening to Pink Floyd).

In 1976, Mugabe became ZANU's secretary-general (poor old Sithole was never going to cut it as a serious icon of popular liberation with a name like that—he later stood against Mugabe in the 1996 presidential election, but was "mysteriously" persuaded to withdraw a week before the poll, and later jailed in a sh. . . . Oh hell, we can't say it). ZANU and ZAPU amalgamated to form the Patriotic Front, which finally prevailed in 1980 as Zimbabwe held its first free elections. Robert Mugabe, now leader of the Zimbabwe African National Union—Patriotic Front (ZANU-PF), was elected prime minister (to the chagrin of the Brits), with a whopping 63 percent of the vote.

With the defeat of their common enemy, white rule, Zimbabweans were now free to start fighting each other, and did so. During 1982, dissidents from Joshua Nkomo's former ZAPU guerrilla army, and former colleagues who had deserted from the new national army, perpetrated numerous indiscriminate acts of violence. Although their exact links with Nkomo and his party could not be fully established, the government held ZAPU largely to blame for the worsening situation, and Joshua got the sack. Mugabe, whose support was largely from the northern region of Mashonaland, ordered his notorious 5th Brigade into Nkomo's Ndebele-speaking Matabeleland. It wasn't pretty. Trained by the wise and gentle North Korean army, his red berets set about killing more than 20,000 people, interring them in mass graves or unused mine shafts. The slaughter continued unabated for three years, culminating, after a brief pause, in November 1987 with yet another brutal massacre in Matabeleland. A "surprise" accommodation was reached with ZAPU, which was incorporated once again into ZANU-PF.

According to the agreement, the new party was to be committed to the establishment of a one-party state with a Marxist-Leninist doctrine (this far-sighted decision was reached in December 1987, by the way, a mere three years before the Berlin Wall came down). The party was to be led—surprise, surprise—by Mugabe, with Nkomo as one of two vice presidents (African politics is in reality very straightforward).

Meanwhile, huge constitutional changes dragged Zimbabwe nearer to becoming the Holy Grail of every Great African Dictator: a one-party state. In 1987, parliament adopted another sinister constitutional reform. The ceremonial presidency was replaced by an executive presidency incorporating the post of prime minister. Bob was nominated as sole candidate for the office, and yes, you guessed it, was duly inaugurated as Zimbabwe's first executive president.

Mugabe remains the only executive leader the young state of Zimbabwe has ever had, and a change is long overdue; at least, that's what the majority of Zimbabweans seem to think. In late 1999, Mugabe was defeated in a referendum on constitutional reform designed to further entrench his power. Blaming Zim's white population for fomenting opposition, his populist (read *draconian*) wheeze ever since has been encouraging the forcible eviction of white farmers from their land. With a population on the brink of famine, this is possibly not an opportune moment to demand, as Mugabe did in June 2002, that 2,900 (white) commercial farmers cease all production and vacate their properties, or face imprisonment.

Barking Bob was reelected president in March 2002, in an election that even George W. Bush called "flawed" (and correct though he was, the global guffaws that greeted such a statement, from him of all people, must have been audible from Neptune—Mugabe even considerately offered to send Zimbabwean election observers to the United States to help ensure a free and fair result). The count gave Mugabe 54 percent of the vote, and Movement for Democratic Change (MDC) leader Morgan Tsvangirai 40 percent. It was condemned as unfair by the Norwegian observer mission and the Zimbabwean Election Support Network (a European Union observer mission was thrown out of the country before voting started). The Organization of African Unity described the elections as "transparent, credible, free and fair," but this announcement was drowned out by the incredulous laughter of journalists attending the OAU's press conference.

Mugabe's response to the assertion that his election was not completely lawful was not subtle: 1,400 MDC agents and monitors were arrested, and many more were prevented from observing the polling. Insufficient polling stations were laid on in Harare and other places where the MDC were known to be strong, and extra polling stations were set up in rural areas where traditional supporters of Mugabe were in the majority. Straightforward violence and intimidation were also common. In a significant contribution to democratic freedom of the press, Mugabe had earlier resolved the problem of unfair election coverage by ensuring that very few journos were allowed in at all. A cabinet reshuffle in August 2002 eliminated any voice of dissent within a government so hard-line it makes Ian Smith's regime look positively progressive.

Mugabe's antics have got him and his government banned from the United States and Europe, and his country bounced out of the Commonwealth; one can only hope that his actions make some sort of sense to him. Some here might say that Mugabe is as mad as a cut snake (and what's up with that Hitleresque mini-moustache?), but you don't need to take *DP*'s word for it—we're happy to concede that Archbishop Desmond Tutu is a better judge of men and morals than us. "It is a great sadness what has happened to President Mugabe," the anti-apartheid campaigner and 1984 Nobel Peace Prize laureate told a South African newspaper. "He was one of Africa's best leaders, a bright spark, a debonair, well-spoken and well-read person . . . but he seems to have gone bonkers in a big way."

*Zimbabwe Government Online*
http://www.gta.gov.zw

*ZANU PF*
Corner Rotten Row and Samora Machel Avenue
Harare, Zimbabwe
Tel.: (263) 4 75 3329
zanupf@africaonline.co.zw
http://www.zanupfpub.co.zw

## War Veterans

The shock troops of Mugabe's land reform, who have been responsible for the seizures of dozens of white-owned farms—and the injury or death of several of their owners. Though many of the so-called veterans possibly saw service in Zimbabwe's struggle for independence, the vast majority of them were hardly born when Zimbabwe became independent. Most are indubitably hooligans and thugs who've spotted a chance to help themselves to something for nothing. Recruited from seething high-density townships like Porter Farm near Harare, their machetes and petrol bombs are also backed by government Kalashnikovs. They were apparently paid—$15 million by some accounts—to act as muscle for Mugabe during the 2002 presidential election. So far they have attacked over 1,000 white farms and homes.

The veterans' momentum was arrested slightly in June 2001 by the death, more than likely from AIDS, of their iconic former leader, Chenjerai "Hitler" Hunzvi. That he chose his nickname himself pretty much renders any other biographical data redundant, but here goes: A bonafide veteran of the independence struggle and a qualified doctor, he shored up a power base in the mid-'90s by issuing certificates of disability to thousands of fellow veterans, who were then able to claim compensation from the government (a couple of those who benefited were cabinet ministers).

As chairman of the Zimbabwe Liberation War Veterans Association (ZLWVA), Hunzvi campaigned, often violently, to prize further largesse from Mugabe's government. In 1997, Mugabe—not coincidentally, the Patron of the ZLWVA—coughed up Z$5 billion (Zimbabwean dollars), including one-off payments equivalent to US$2,500 and monthly pensions of US$100, for 50,000 ZLWVA members (the minimum wage in Zimbabwe is around US$30 a month). It was money Zimbabwe didn't have. What to do? The solution, as any serious student of *DP* will by now realize (you've made it to Z, after all), was simple: print more. Zimbabwe's current economic crisis dates from this sorry intersection of Hunzvi's greed and Mugabe's irresponsibility.

To nobody's surprise, Hunzvi was eventually charged with lifting Z\$45 million from the war veterans' funds, and for fraudulently signing disability forms (the trial, mysteriously postponed on several occasions, was never held). The infamous invasions of white-owned farms by veterans was Hunzvi's plan to extract his nads from the mangle, and to rescue Mugabe when his attempts at constitutional reform went off in his face. Hunzvi also personally directed assaults and tortures of dozens of members of the opposition Movement for Democratic Change. His fellow ZLWVA members eventually moved to eject him from office, but he was elected to Zimbabwe's parliament in 2000.

The current secretary general of the ZLWVA is Andy Mhlanga, who was recently heard demanding a 150 percent increase in his members' monthly pensions. Zimbabwe can no more afford this than it can a space program, but Mugabe is scared of the veterans, and wants to keep them on his side so they can continue to scare everyone else on his behalf.

**Zimbabwe Liberation War Veterans Association**
Postal Bag 237
Harare, Zimbabwe
Tel.: (263) 4 75 8360

## Movement for Democratic Change (MDC)

The MDC is the principal opposition to Mugabe. Its sudden rise to prominence since its foundation in 1999 is a clear indication of the rising swell of disenchantment with Mugabe. In Zimbabwe's parliamentary elections in 2000, the MDC won 57 seats, just behind the 62 won by ZANU-PF. In a country that has been a virtual one-party state since independence, this was extraordinary.

The MDC is led by Morgan Tsvangirai, a former head of Zimbabwe's Congress of Trade Unions. He has proved a persistent, if naïve, fly in Mugabe's porridge, helping to defeat the government on its 1999 constitutional reform referendum. Mugabe wanted to enshrine in law the practice of seizing white-owned farms without compensating their owners—the practice continues, but thanks to Tsvangirai, Mugabe can't pretend it's legal. Not, you understand, that the MDC are against equitable land redistribution. It's just that they'd rather do it in a way that doesn't lead to the needless suffering of countless millions of their own people.

Mugabe, in keeping with his habit of blaming everything he dislikes on Britain, has called Tsvangirai a British puppet. He's also had Tsvangirai charged with high treason—an offence that carries the death penalty. Tsvangirai was arrested just after he "lost" the March 2002 presidential election, and was accused of conspiring to assassinate Mugabe. The basis for the charge is a videotape, filmed in secret, of a meeting between Tsvangirai and a business strategist in Canada with links to Mugabe's ZANU-PF, in which the violent removal of Mugabe is apparently discussed. Although obviously a clumsy propaganda hatchet-job, it doesn't say much about the MDC's research department. Another *DP* tip: don't seek sensitive strategic advice from your enemy's pals.

MDC supporters are routinely arrested, beaten, tortured, raped—and worse. By February 2002, the MDC's Roll of Honor, commemorating its supporters who have died or disappeared, was 103 names long.

*Movement for Democratic Change*
6th Floor, Harvest House
Corner Angwa Street and Nelson Mandela Avenue
Harare, Zimbabwe
Tel.: (263) 4 78 1138
mdcinfo@zol.co.zw
http://www.mdczimbabwe.com

## White Farmers

Zimbabwe's farmers have borne the brunt of Bob's demented efforts to deflect blame for Zimbabwe's problems away from himself. There are currently only about 80,000 white Zimbabweans still in residence and less than a tenth of them are farmers. They are an easy group to stir resentment against, seeing as how they look different from most of the population (they're white) and are conspicuously wealthier than most: according to government figures published before the current crisis, some 4, 400 whites owned 32 percent of Zimbabwe's agricultural land, while about one million black peasant families farmed around 38 percent.

Mugabe's case is that they are parasitic colonialists who wouldn't even be here if Britain had never subjugated Africa, so there. This may well be true, but many of the farming families have been there for generations, and are no less African than any of the people their land is being "redistributed" to—by Mugabe's logic, the European-descended populations of the United States, Canada, Australia, and South America have no legitimate claim to their own territory.

Still, no politician ever lost ground by telling poor people that their poverty wasn't their fault. Mugabe announced in July 2000 that he was seeking to appropriate 5,872 white-owned farms, to be divided among 162,000 black families, within four years. Not even someone as cuckoo as Mugabe could think this was logistically possible, but he certainly would have recognized it as a license for his new-found "war veteran" supporters to raise hell, and they did—some farmers and a lot of livestock were killed, equipment was destroyed. Crucially, it has been black farmworkers who have suffered the most at the hands of the "war vets": hundreds have been brutalized and left impoverished as their livelihoods vanish. Funnily enough, of the land titles that have been allocated, nearly half have gone to pro-Mugabe politicians and bureaucrats.

In June 2002, with crops awaiting harvest and Zimbabwe facing famine, Mugabe passed a law insisting that most white farmers stop work and surrender their property, or face prison. Some are staying and continue to work in defiance of this idiocy—though as a result at least 133 farmers have been arrested so far. Others are taking up the opportunities offered by Zimbabwe's neighbors, who are quite happy to relieve Mugabe of the farmers' money and expertise—Angola has made an initial 10,000 hectares available to fleeing white Zimbabweans, and Mozambique has also put out the welcome mat.

**Commercial Farmers Union of Zimbabwe**
Agriculture House
Corner Marlborough Drive and Adylinn Road
Harare, Zimbabwe
Tel.: (263) 4 30 9800
Fax: (263) 4 30 9874
aisd1@cfu.co.zw
http://www.samara.co.zw/cfu

## Central Intelligence Organization (CIO)

Originally the secret police of the former Rhodesian regime, the CIO has been expanded since independence. Despite regularly declaiming that "Zimbabwe will never be a colony again," Mugabe has rigorously reinforced the single most successful instrument of colonial repression the Rhodesians possessed. Indeed, one of the most famous cases of abuse of the presidential pardon occurred in 1993, when President Mugabe used his power to intervene in the punishment of a CIO agent who attempted to kill an opposition candidate. According to Amnesty International, the CIO has been party to a litany of human rights abuses that have recently increased in ferocity. Harassment of MDC members is commonplace—cars have been stopped at gunpoint and their drivers burned to death—and beatings are routine.

If you check into any of the larger hotels in Harare, be aware that the management is obliged to pass details about you on to the CIO, who will then follow you to see if you are really a tourist (which you aren't). If you are arrested *on spec,* a bribe is worth a (careful) shot— US$300 should see you right. Tentatively raise the possibility of a beer and a quiet chat about the rising cost of living. If you are the calculated target of political vitriol, you're probably going to end up with a sphincter like a clown's pocket.

**Amnesty International** .
http://web.amnesty.org

**Zimbabwe Human Rights Forum**
http://www.hrforumzim.com

## Professor Jonathan Moyo

Zimbabwe's Minister for Information and Chief Government Spokesman has been called many things, possibly the most insightful of which is "Black Goebbels." All successful press accreditations are personally issued by him, and they are rare indeed.

Moyo is the architect of Zimbabwe's ultra-repressive Access to Information and Protection of Privacy Act, and the draconian Public Order and Security Act, which makes it an offense to "undermine the authority of the president" or "engender hostility" towards him. His career has been varied, to say the least.

Until July 1999, Moyo was a highly respected academic and scathing critic of Batty Bob's descent into dictatorship, yet, almost overnight, the curiously camp Moyo ditched the prestige of the Witwatersrand University for the sadistic embrace of powermonger Mugabe. Thanks to Moyo, journalists now face up to two years in prison for doing their job, further cementing the Committee to Protect Journalists' ranking of Zimbabwe as one of the world's 10 worst places to be a journalist. He's also currently being pursued by the Ford Foundation for the trifling matter of US$100,000 that he is accused of stealing during his tenure in Nairobi.

Moyo's notoriously anticolonial rhetoric has not, however, stopped him from resurrecting the colonial-era Censorship and Entertainment Control Act as a means of controlling the press. This precolonial act is so outdated that it is unclear whether the prosecuting Censorship Board even still exists.

**Scotch Tagwireyi**
Information and Communications Officer
Freedom of Expression Institute
Republic of South Africa
Tel.: (27) 11 4038403
Cell Tel.: (27) 82 8210756
Fax: (27) 11 4038309
http://fxi.org.za

## Muammar Qaddafi

Yup, the Wacky One has cast the shadow of his padded Bedouin tent south of the Zambezi. Riding to the rescue of Zimbabwe's fuel crisis, the Libyans have pumped over US$360 million worth of petroleum into

Mugabe's empty tanks—a massive 70 percent of Zim's entire supply. The problem is that Bankrupt Bob can't pay for it (no white-owned tobacco farms equals no foreign exchange) and not even The Colonel is mad enough to accept Zim dollars as anything other than wallpaper or white gold. Answer? Give him the land whose confiscation bankrupted the country in the first place. Here at *DP*, we hold our heads in our hands and sigh—even by African standards, this is going some. By informed estimates, Qaddafi is now the largest landowner in Zimbabwe. Are you a starving, landless war veteran? Sorry pal, but a multi-billionaire Arab who lives 5,000 miles away has just beaten you to it.

## Victoria Fails: Misadventure Sports

It appears that Zim was destined to join the select group of dysfunctional ragged African postcolonial countries that seem to attract tourists like a dead wildebeest attracts flies. Almost two million tourists a year used to flock here (most from neighboring South Africa and Zambia) for the adventure sports, fishing, and safaris that centered on a trip to Victoria Falls. Tourism brought in US$400 million in hard currency (6 percent of the GDP) and employed 200,000 people. Then the first white farmer was killed in April 2000, and tourists began to realize that there might be a little too much adventure in Zim, as the death toll began to mount. Tourism is down 75 percent and that's the optimistic estimate. The government's solution, of course, is to include white-owned tourist resorts and hotels in their seizure program—many of which have also been used to pay off the Libyans. Although we could thrill you with plenty of stories, like the one about the 19-year-old Brit safari guide who was dragged by a lioness from his tent in Matusadona Park and killed, or the good news that the land mines around the Victoria Falls' tourist resorts are almost cleaned up, *DP* would like to suggest that perhaps farm-stays should replace rafting and bungee jumping as new Zim adventure vacations. Remember that most of Zim's rivers are thick with crocs, and home to lots of hippos—Africa's number-one tourist killer. For now most visitors to Victoria Falls stick to the Zambian side . . . a place, by the way, where 67 percent of the hookers are HIV-positive.

> **R**emember that most of Zim's rivers are thick with crocs, and home to lots of hippos—Africa's number-one tourist killer. For now most visitors to Victoria Falls stick to the Zambian side . . . a place, by the way, where 67 percent of the hookers are HIV-positive.

http://www.zim-sight.co.zw
http://www.haz.co.zw

### Reverend Canaan Banana

Not really a player any more, but frankly, we just couldn't resist listing him. The splendidly named Canaan Banana, Methodist minister, former Marxist, and erstwhile secretary to the ANC, became the first leader of independent Zimbabwe. After his association with the outlawed ANC during the struggle against Ian Smith, Banana peeled off to the United States until 1975, when he returned home only to be grabbed by the cops and stuck in the pokey. Here he languished until 1979 when he became Zim's first, and mostly ceremonial, president. Mugabe replaced him seven years later, after making the presidency an executive position—not that this has saved Zimbabwe from becoming a Banana republic.

Subsequently, Mugabe squeezed Banana out for good. In 1996, the year after Mugabe made a speech about homosexuals being worse than pigs and dogs, Banana was arrested for molesting (male) staff members. Mrs. Banana had learned of her husband's alleged sexual proclivity from her bodyguard.

In a fit of pique, Mrs. Banana's bodyguard shot to death a policeman who called him "Banana's wife." In a bid to redeem himself, the bodyguard told a tale of boozing, dancing, and gambling . . . and being assaulted by a stiff Banana in the State House library. Although Banana tried to slip out of the charges, he was stuck with 11 counts of sodomy. Banana then split to South Africa before sentencing, lending credence to the phrase, "Yes, we have no Banana." All in all, a case which, while sad and sordid, briefly made the world's subeditors feel like all their Christmases had come at once. Some of the better headlines included "Banana Denies Buggery," "Banana Forced Officer To Have Sex," "Mugabe Slips On Banana," and, when the disgraced ex-president fled during the case, "Fruitless Search for Banana," and "Banana Splits."

His wife, Jan Banana (c'mon, we're not making this up, at least she is not named Anna), lives on $65 a week in dole money in London. She arrived with $60 in her pocket, asking for asylum. Her husband is supposedly loafing in Zim, perhaps waiting for the day he can find a bunch of supporters.

# Getting In

Visas are required for U.S. citizens, but not yet for Britons or Canadians (a complete breakdown of who needs Zimbabwean visas and who doesn't can be found at the Web site of Zimbabwe's embassy in Washington). For Americans, single-entry visas are $50, and can be organized in advance, or granted at the border or airport. It's worth considering a double-entry visa if you're planning to venture into

## WHAT'S IN A NAME?

Zimbabweans are justly famous for their extraordinary names, often expressing the hopes of the mother during birth. Here is a list of *DP* favorites (seriously):

| | | |
|---|---|---|
| Stalin Mau Mau | Big Boy | Lucky |
| Learnmore | Welshman | Nomore |
| Lovely | Talent | Help |
| Lovemore | Eveready | Atlast |
| Gift | Surprise | Trymore |
| Jealous | Goodenough | Cloud |

All of these, however, pale into insignificance compared to the stunning name of the baby called after the last words her mother heard the doctor say before the birth (and we promise this is genuine). Step forward: Fullydilated.

neighboring Botswana on safari, or cross the bridge into Zambia at Victoria Falls, for example.

Things are slightly more complicated if you're a journalist, and virtually impossible if you're a British journalist. The Zimbabweans would be a good deal happier, basically, if you went and reported on somewhere else. All visiting journalists have to apply for a temporary work permit from the Ministry of Information in Harare (Fax: (263) 4 70 8557) and send a copy of their application to their local embassy. There is no fixed idea of how long the application should take to process, but we'd suggest giving it at least two weeks—that's assuming you're allowed in at all. If you are, expect to be followed. If you go without a work permit, and you're caught, you'll be deported if you're lucky.

Brits wanting to spill the beans on Barking Bob should be aware that they may be accused of working for the BBC (which is banned in Zim). Owing to the recent influx of "tourists" with expensive Nikons and laptop computers who seem to be more interested in visiting MDC headquarters than safari lodges, unaccredited hacks and actual holidaymakers have increasingly been refused entry and sent packing on the next flight.

*Embassy of Zimbabwe*
1608 New Hampshire Avenue, N.W.
Washington, DC 20009
Tel.: (202) 332-7100
Fax: (202) 483-9326
zimemb@erols.com
http://www.zimembassy-usa.org

**High Commission of Zimbabwe**
Zimbabwe House
429 The Strand
London WC2R 0QE, UK
Tel.: (44) 20 7836 7755
Fax: (44) 20 7379 1167
zimlondon@callnetuk.com

**High Commission of Zimbabwe**
332 Somerset Street West
Ottawa, Ontario K2P OJ9
Canada
Tel.: (613) 237-4388
Fax: (613) 563-8269
zim.highcomm@sympatico.ca
http://www.docuweb.ca/zimbabwe

## Getting Around

Zimbabwe's main cities and tourist attractions—Harare, Bulawayo, Mutare, and Victoria Falls—are serviced by air and rail. Hire cars are available from the airport and the Meikles Hotel in downtown Harare, though carjackings are on the rise—with the added twist that many stolen 4 x 4s have ended up in the DR Congo as ad hoc military transports. Buses go everywhere else. Most foreign visitors used to travel on the scheduled tourist buses, which are comfortable, run according to timetables, and leave from town centers. Local buses, which depart whenever they're (very) full from so-called "Township" bus stations, are cheap but accident-prone; if you're white, you will find yourself in a minority of one once aboard—a consideration if visiting rural areas. All transport, including aviation, is subject to Zim's frequent fuel shortages.

The former tourist-stuffed train between Harare, Bulawayo, and Victoria Falls is regarded as something of a casino by local brigands. Keep your possessions away from open windows at stations, and take a bicycle chain to lock compartment doors if traveling at night. Oh, did we mention that this train likes to have head-ons every once in a while?

**Air Zimbabwe**
http://www.airzimbabwe.com

**Blue Arrow Buses**
http://www.bluearrow.co.zw

## Dangerous Places

### Large Plots of Dirt

Lovingly described as "unrepentant racists and fascists" by Zim's Agriculture Minister, most white commercial farmers were given a month to get lost. Trouble is, these farmers have lived and farmed here for decades—as one farmer put it, "you can't wind up 50 years of farming in 45 days." As you can guess, this is not an orderly process, as gangs of "war veterans"—groups made up of random combinations of armed, unpredictable, and drunken youths—intimidate and threaten their fellow citizens. Several farmers have been killed or injured during these seizures; many journalists have been intimidated and physically abused while reporting on them. As expected, the takeover of a well-run farm by a hundred subsistence farmers has not helped the catastrophic food shortage blighting the country's 13 million people. Naturally, the government blames the food shortage on a "carefully planned conspiracy" by white farmers. The UN figures that Zim will need to import about 2 million tons of grain to survive. Mugabe has claimed to solve the food shortage by ordering the 2,900 commercial farmworkers harvesting what little crops there are to stop work—officially, there is no shortage. That'll show 'em.

Travel through most parts of rural Zimbabwe has become increasingly unsafe, especially in areas settled or targeted by "war vets." Particularly bad areas include most of Matabeleland, where the Zimbabwean Army is now redeploying after its withdrawal from DR Congo, and Buhera Province in the east, a ZANU hot spot. Traveling in pick-ups or any other kind of traditional white farmer transport is likely to raise hackles, and occasionally machetes. For detailed local knowledge, you could do worse than a call to the Commercial Farmers Union or MDC rep.

*Commercial Farmers Union of*
*    Zimbabwe*
Agriculture House
Corner Marlborough Drive and Adylinn
    Road
Marlborough
Box WGT390, Westgate
Harare, Zimbabwe
Tel.: (263) 4 309800
Fax: (263) 4 309874
aisd1@cfu.co.zw

*Lao Watson-Smith, Administrator*
ZAWT (Zimbabwe Agricultural Welfare
    Trust)
P.O. Box 168
Woodbridge
Suffolk IP 13 8WE, UK
http://www.zawt.org

## Borders

In case you forgot, there used to be a war here. There are still thousands of land mines along Zimbabwe's borders with Mozambique (near Mutare) and Zambia (near Vic Falls), planted by the pre-independence Rhodesian government to deter guerrilla incursions. Stick to the path, and stay particularly alert after heavy rainfalls, which can dislodge previously buried munitions.

http://maic.jmu.edu/research/searches/countries/zimbabwe.htm

# Dangerous Things ——————————————

*Truth*

Reporting on Zimbabwean politics is the kind of occupation you take up when base-jumping, skiing blindfolded, and teasing crocodiles just aren't giving you the adrenaline rush they used to. In December 2001, Mugabe's government approved the amusingly named Access to Information and Protection of Privacy Bill. Under the terms of this bill, journalists have to apply for a license to work—you can take a wild guess as to who issues the licenses. Also, all journalists resident in Zimbabwe, including locally based correspondents for foreign news organizations, must be Zimbabwean citizens (in July 2001, Zimbabwe suspended the credentials of all BBC correspondents in the country, doubtless feeling that the BBC was part of the sinister British plot that Mugabe imagines is plaguing him). Foreign media companies wishing to open bureaus in Zimbabwe have to pay US$12,000 for the privilege.

Not content with legislative hindrances, sometimes Mugabe or his proxies prefer to take direct action. Dozens of reporters have been threatened, attacked, or arrested for committing journalism; some have fled the country in fear of their lives. *The Daily News*, Zimbabwe's only privately owned daily newspaper, has come in for special punishment. In April 2000, a bomb exploded in the art gallery below its Harare office. In January 2001, another bomb destroyed its printing press. A little over a year later, *The Daily News* office in Bulawayo was hit by petrol bombs. Whatever happened to a stern letter to the editor?

In yet another lovely little episode that shows just how much freedom of the press is cherished in Zimbabwe, on August 29, 2002, "someone" blew up the offices of the independent radio station, Voice of the People. This followed hard on the heels of the state closure of Joy TV, Zim's only independent television station, and the passing of the Public Order and Security Act. So far, 22 journalists have been charged under the new legislation, and further crackdowns are expected. If you get busted and think you can flee south, think again: Mugabe has an extradition treaty with South Africa. Nice one, Mbeki.

**Zimbabwe Union of Journalists**
P.O. Box 66070, Kopjc
Harare, Zimbabwe
Tel.: (263) 4 781 032
Fax: (263) 4 752 831

**Sizani Weza**
Media Monitoring Project Zimbabwe
monitors@mweb.co.zw
http://mmpz.icon.co.zw

**Media Institute of Southern Africa (MISA)**
Private Bag 13386
Windhoek, Namibia
Tel.: (264) 61 232975,
Fax: (264) 61 248016
http://www.misanet.org

## Your Wallet

Like many spots in Africa, street crime has increased in direct relationship to the plunging employment rate. Zimbabwe's economy continues to do its impression of Mickey Rourke's acting career with the resultant demand for snatch-and-grab professionals. Most of it is common- or garden-variety pickpocketing and bag-snatching, but guns and knives are occasionally produced by way of incentive to part with your wallet. The usual rules apply—keep most of your cash (US$ or British pounds are favored) in a money belt or in your shoes, and don't wear your camera around your neck. Credit cards are still accepted, though all transactions will be calculated at the official exchange rate, making any purchases over six times more expensive.

**Zimbabwe Association of Crime Prevention and
Rehabilitation of the Offender (ZACRO)**
P.O. Box MSK 260
Mbare
Harare, Zimbabwe
Tel./Fax: (263) 4 770046

## Using Your Willy

Forty-two percent of Zimbabwe's productive population is HIV-positive (the rate is believed to be as high as 80 percent in the military). Life expectancy at birth is 43 years, and falling. Between two and five thousand Zimbabweans die of AIDS-related diseases every week. Yes, *every week*—that's a bare minimum of 100,000 each year, and rising. In a country of 13 million, an estimated 900,000 are children orphaned by AIDS—an entire generation. You might well think this renders all other concerns entirely meaningless, but you're not Robert Mugabe.

**Zimbabwe AIDS Network**
228 Herbert Chitepo Avenue
Harare, Zimbabwe
Tel.: (263) 4 70 3819
Fax: (263) 4 70 0330
zansec@zol.co.zw

**Joint UN Program on HIV/AIDS**
http://www.unaids.org

# Getting Sick

Make sure you're up to date with inoculations for bilharzia, rabies, malaria, cholera, and yellow fever. Don't take any risks whatsoever where HIV is concerned—this is not the country for carefree holiday romances or emergency blood transfusions—odd, considering all the adventure sports Zim is famous for. In bigger cities, like Harare and Bulawayo, or major tourist sites such as Victoria Falls, English-speaking doctors shouldn't be too difficult to find, though medical facilities are extremely limited. In 2001, Harare General Hospital, once a showcase of southern African medicine, had no surgical gloves, replacement light bulbs, or regular supplies of anesthetic. Doctors were forced to perform emergency surgery by candlelight with plastic bags on their hands—and that was *before* the government went broke. Take your own supply of syringes and any prescription medicines.

## Nuts and Bolts

Zimbabwe has a population of 13 million, of whom 70 percent are ethnically Shona and 20 percent Ndebele. The official language is English, but the overwhelming majority of Zimbabweans are native speakers of Shona or Ndebele. Most Zimbabweans would describe themselves as Christian, though a traditional animist faith known as Mwari is still popular. The currency is the Zimbabwe dollar (Z$), which trades officially at around 56 to the U.S. dollar. Unofficially, you will get up to Z$1,000 for your George Washington: just ask the Bureau De Change clerk, with all the wide-eyed naïveté you can muster, what his "best rate" is. If that doesn't work, ask the nearest whitey to help out—hard currency is desperately sought by would-be émigrés. Don't change money in the street, as you might well be trading with an undercover cop. Prices in Zimbabwe are prone to massive fluctuation—in the first half of 2002, food prices rose from 400 to 1,000 percent. Almost nobody in Zimbabwe, incidentally, takes American Express. Electricity is 220V. Fuel supplies can be erratic, with sales lines over a mile long not unknown in Harare. Diesel fuel is harder to find than gasoline.

*Embassy of the United States*
172 Herbert Chitepo Avenue
Harare, Zimbabwe
Tel.: (263) 4 25 0593
Fax: (263) 4 79 6488
http://www.usembassy.state.gov/
zimbabwe

*British High Commission*
7th Floor, Corner House
Corner Samora Machel Avenue and
Leopold Takawira Street
Harare, Zimbabwe
Tel.: (263) 4 77 2990
Fax: (263) 4 77 4617
british.info@fco.gov.uk
http://www.britainzw.org

*Canadian High Commission*
45 Baines Avenue
Harare, Zimbabwe
Tel.: (263) 4 73 3881
Fax: (263) 4 73 2917
harare@dfait-maeci.gc.ca

## Dangerous Days

| | |
|---|---|
| **8/29/02** | A bomb destroys the independent radio station, Voice of the People, in Harare. |
| **6/24/02** | Mugabe announces a law threatening 2,900 white farmers with imprisonment unless they stop working their land and surrender their properties within 45 days. |
| **4/02** | State of disaster declared as food shortages worsen. |
| **3/20/02** | Defeated presidential candidate Morgan Tsvangirai is arrested and charged with treason; he is accused of plotting to assassinate Mugabe. |
| **3/19/02** | Zimbabwe suspended from the Commonwealth for at least one year. |
| **3/13/02** | Mugabe declared the victor. Many observers describe the poll as flawed. |
| **3/9/02** | Polling opens in presidential election. |
| **2/02** | European Union imposes sanctions on Zimbabwe. Restrictive new press laws passed. |
| **1/11/02** | Presidential elections called for March. Mugabe passes laws making criticism of his leadership illegal. Army announces that the only result they will accept is a Mugabe victory. |
| **8/16/01** | Zimbabwean government announces plans to use the army to help with the seizures of white-owned farms. |
| **8/9/01** | After further intimidation and violence against white-owned farms by "war veterans," 20 white farmers are charged with assault. |
| **1/28/01** | A bomb destroys the printing press of *The Daily News*, Zimbabwe's only privately owned daily newspaper. *The Daily News* has often been critical of the government of Robert Mugabe. No one is arrested in connection with the blast. |
| **10/16/01** | Three days of food riots begin in Harare. |
| **2/00** | Groups of "war veterans," with the tacit support of the government, begin violently occupying white-owned farms. |
| **9/11/99** | Opposition movement, Movement for Democratic Change, formed in Harare. |
| **12/31/87** | Mugabe merges the roles of prime minister and ceremonial president and dissolves the senate to become Zimbabwe's first executive president. |

| | |
|---|---|
| **1982–1987** | Rebellion in Midlands and Matabeleland provinces by guerrillas loyal to ZAPU leader Joshua Nkomo. Mugabe's ZANU-PF crush the rebellion, killing over 20,000 civilians. |
| **4/18/80** | Zimbabwe becomes an independent state. Robert Mugabe elected prime minister. |
| **9/03/78** | Joshua Nkomo's ZAPU rebels shoot down a Rhodesian Viscount airliner, using a Soviet-made SAM-7 missile. Of the 56 civilians on board, 18 survived the crash—a further ten were executed on the ground. |
| **1976** | Robert Mugabe's ZANU and Joshua Nkomo's ZAPU merge to form the ZANU Patriotic Front. |
| **12/72** | Sporadic attacks led by Robert Mugabe, Joshua Nkomo, and Ndabaningi Sithole against Rhodesia's white-minority government develop into full-scale war. |
| **11/11/65** | Rhodesian Prime Minister Ian Smith illegally severs ties to Great Britain with a Unilateral Declaration of Independence (UDI). UN sanctions are applied. |
| **9/12/1890** | A British pioneer column from Bechuanaland reaches the site of the future capital of Rhodesia without incident. |
| **AD 9th Century** | Foundation of the Bantu Great Zimbabwe civilization. |

## IN A DANGEROUS PLACE: ZIMBABWE

### THE CROCODILE HUNTER

"Whatever you do, don't let go of its mouth." Those are the last words I remember Rich Fergusson, Africa's crocodile-catcher extraordinaire, telling me as he passed a five-foot croc into my shaking hands. Within seconds I would be in agony, covered in my own blood, my right arm barely intact.

In the freezing cold blackness of a Zimbabwe night, the croc felt massive and dangerous. It was as much as I could do to carry the animal out of the fetid, waist-deep water where we had caught him and put him on dry land for closer inspection. Strangely docile and lethargic, the animal was easy to handle. With my left hand tightly clamped around the base of its jaw, and my right hand gripping its right hind leg for dear life, it seemed handling crocs really wasn't so bad after all. The headlights from our Land Rover illuminated the patch of dry grass where we had set up operations for the night, drowning out the spotlight of my miner's lamp and bringing the night into sharp relief. Bending forward to put the animal on the ground so that Rich could measure and tag it, I began to breathe a sigh of relief. Time to relax, and let Rich take over. But you can never relax with crocs, and I was about to pay a high price for my complacency.

Suddenly I felt a sharp, stinging slap to the back that knocked me off balance. The croc's tail flailed at my neck and shoulders. Five feet of armor-plated muscle, with skin as hard as wood and scales as sharp as a bread knife, had decided that it was dinner time. *Don't let go of its mouth.* I half dropped to my knees, half fell. Following me out of the blackness of the lake onto the shore was a nameless terror, engulfing my mind, paralyzing my actions. The croc began to roll, and I fell with it. My right arm clamped down hard over its body, as I tried desperately to contain its writhing determination to break loose. *Don't let go of its mouth.* And then suddenly its head was free, and 35 kilos of evolutionary assassin snapped round my arm to do what it does best.

My footing now completely lost, I stumbled and fell sideways. Rich's words came back to me: "Even if you have to dive on it, don't let it roll with you." I was rolling. Somehow I managed to keep a grip on its leg. I watched its head glance over my forearm, and saw my skin part and split. A deep wound opened up through muscle and tendons. "Get this fucking thing off me!" I started to kick, no weapon but my feet. The blood was flowing now, the night darker and more threatening. I was on my back, right forearm up to protect my face, blood soaking into my trousers and shirt. No pain yet. I kicked again, and looked up. It was on me, lying on me, its front teeth through the muscle of my arm. Illuminated in the headlights, and in the glare of the miner's lamp, its eyes were cold and brutal, staring without compassion or mercy into my eyes, the eyes of its prey. Mustering all the will I could, I threw a left into the side of its head, and collapsed back to earth. Finished. Spent. Adrenaline pumping through me so fast I could see patterns swirling in the sky above. Claws ripped through my clothing, scratching my thighs and stomach. This wasn't going to be quick, or painless. I was going to die in agony on the shores of a godforsaken lake in the middle of nowhere. I felt sick and alone and defeated.

"Gotcha!" Suddenly Rich was there. What had seemed endless, the march of hours, had been in reality a few seconds of blind panic. Running full tilt out of the water, he dived on the croc, flattening it to the ground. Within moments the croc was subdued, and I found myself standing up looking most of the way through my arm. "Are you okay?" he was asking. "No," came the reply. "I am a very long way from being okay." What happened next was nothing short of miraculous. I was sat down and given a quick but vital field assessment by Rich. "No major arteries severed; fingers still moving; minor cuts here and there; one major laceration. Fine. You'll live. And remember, next time, don't let go of its mouth." And with that he removed his shirt, tightly bandaging the wound. The drive that followed was only marginally better than the attack itself. Crashing through the undergrowth, overtaking lorries on the inside and then speeding through Harare, we arrived at the trauma clinic in record time. Within an hour I had been shot full of drugs, my muscles sutured, and my arm stitched up.

Two weeks previously, I had been on the telephone with my editor in London. The magazine had originally sent me to Zimbabwe to cover the violence that erupted around the recent elections, but after three weeks of African doom and gloom, they had decided to change tack. "Crocodiles. We want crocodiles. You're in Africa, so it can't be that hard. Go and wrestle some."

Two days later I was having a beer with Rich Fergusson, executive manager of the Crocodile Farmers Association of Zimbabwe. Rich, I later discovered, is something of a legend not only in his native Zimbabwe, but internationally as well. He is respected worldwide for his fearless pursuit of crocodiles in the wild, and also for the pioneering scientific work that motivates his interest in observing and monitoring our reptilian friends.

I wondered aloud if I might be able to participate in some of this research. I mean, what exactly did it all entail, anyway? "Why don't you come and find out?" Rich smiled. "You might find it interesting." Rich was prepared to take me to Lake Kyle, a four-hour drive southwest of Harare, to carry out a survey of crocs in the wild in that region for the first time. He didn't know what we'd find, but it would be an exclusive story no matter what. Not only had Kyle never been assessed before, but Rich had never previously been photographed in the line of duty: "No one's ever had the guts."

Sitting in a boat in Lake Kyle later that week, I began to wonder if it had all been an idiotic lapse of judgment on my part. Here I was, scarcely able to swim, in the middle of a lake the size of the English Channel, about to offer myself up as some kind of British crocodile snack-food specialty. Clearly, we wouldn't actually be getting in the water, would we now?

Okay, so we had to get in the water. How else could you catch them? Stupid me. Well, at least it's a nice, hot, sunny day. We'll be able to see them coming from miles off, won't we? Rich was laughing uncontrollably by now. Apparently, you don't catch crocs during the day. While it's nice and hot they sun themselves on the banks, well hidden, and well poised for a quick attack and/or escape. No, it's during the day that all the reconnaissance work is done: favorite haunts and nest sites are discovered and the creeks and pools where they hunt and play are located and recorded for later visits. Crocs are *caught* at night, in the dark, just the crocs and you in the water. The prospect of being mobbed by political protesters with automatic weapons on burning farms seemed strangely appealing. In fact, automatic weapons seemed like a good idea all round.

Rich works unaided as regards weapons, though. "I've thought about it, but ultimately it wouldn't work. A knife is as good as useless against an angry croc. If you had an automatic pistol in a sprung holster between your shoulder blades, that might work. To be honest, though, it all happens so fast that you'd never get the chance to use it."

How right he was. In fact, Rich has had a lot of experience with things happening fast. I noticed that his lower legs, wrists, and hands were a mess of criss-crossed scar tissue. "Nothing too serious, but it's a risk you run. Your best defense is to know what you are doing, and know your limitations. You can't catch a croc over six feet long in the wild without taking a chance of it going wrong. We're not here to take chances, we're here to do a job, and to keep coming back to do it." That was all very well for him, but I had the teensiest suspicion that this may be a one-off for me.

The day's recce went well. Armed with a GPS satellite positioning system, field glasses, and minutely detailed maps, we built up a series of references that would allow us to explore the lake in the dead of night without relying on sight-markers. How on earth was all this done before GPS? Answer: "We got lost a lot."

I learned that the program of observation would involve catching baby and yearling crocodiles (up to six feet long) in the shallows of the lake near the shoreline. We would find them by picking out their reflective red eyes with spotlights, and then bring them aboard for tagging, measuring, weighing, sexing, and general examination.

As the day receded behind the mountains ringing the lake, the temperature plummeted. By the time the sunset had faded and the stars were out, the ambient temperature was down to almost zero degrees centigrade. Rich began changing into a wet suit. Christ on a bike, here we go.

Combing the water with powerful halogen spotlights, we spent four hours plying the backwaters that we had investigated earlier. Just as we were preparing to call it a night, two glowing eyes lit up in the darkness ahead. "Jesus!" exclaimed Rich, "it's massive." How could he possibly tell at such a distance? "You have to relate the gap between the eyes and the distance from the eyes to the nose, which sticks out of the water. He's about fifteen foot long." Fifteen feet? The boat was barely eight feet long. Time to turn back, then? No. Time to follow it, apparently. But surely this was insanity? When we were on top of the croc, I realized I would never be able to get into that lake, no matter what. Enormous, slow, and methodical, the gigantic croc swished its way across the surface of the water. Rich made a series of strangled barking noises, emulating the sound of a distressed infant croc, to stop the monster from diving under. Instantly, the lake, previously beautiful and shimmering under the full moon, became a repository of evil. All around me the black rippling waters beckoned disaster, as the nameless menace of nightmares took on the form of a ton of green-scaled destructive energy.

The following two nights took on a similar pattern. Huge prehistoric beasts would slip down from the banks to glide into the water, circling the boat, causing it to sway as they explored its keel. For Rich, the trip was a great success. Noting down adult numbers and drawing up maps of population concentration provided him with a valuable resource for future exploration. All the baby crocs, though, had gone to ground in their nests in a bid to escape the bitterly cold nights. With this in mind, Rich suggested another trip, this time just north of Harare, to a smaller lake where we could work from the shore in a vehicle. I agreed, and so after three roasting days and three frigid nights we left Kyle for the warmer environs of Harare.

After a brief visit to the capital, we made our way out onto the Kariba road. Setting up camp on the shore was a joyfully easy process in comparison to the tight confines of the dinghy, though it was with a certain sense of foreboding that I unpacked and photographed the medical kit.

Within a couple of hours we were in the water, up to our waists in weeds and slime, shining flashlights out into the darkness. As I waited, sinking in mud, for something to happen, I remembered the power and majesty of the vast creatures in Kyle. Involuntarily, I could feel myself edging back toward the shore, while Rich began barking croc-speak into the night air. I froze. The weeds seemed to close in around my legs, the mud holding me fast. And then Rich emerged from a frenzy of splashing with a four-foot yearling tucked under his arm. Easy.

On dry land, we measured and tagged the croc, recording all its scaly vital statistics. Rich asked if I would like to hold it. "This is at your own risk. I don't really recommend this at all, but, well, you've come a long way to see all this . . ." He passed the croc over, and in this miniature killer I could see and sense all the power of its brutal potential. Relieved finally to have handled a wild croc, I handed it back to Rich, and the hunt continued. Ten minutes later, half-submerged in silt and spluttering in the filthy water, Rich was handing me another. "Are you sure?" "Yes," I said, "just hand it over. It's quite good fun really." "Okay," Rich grunted, "there you go. This one's a bit bigger, though. Whatever you do, don't let go of its mouth."

—*James Brabazon*

# Mr. *DP*'s
# Little Black Book

# SAVE THE WORLD

## Patching the Apocalypse

Civilization is a machine that does not offer an instruction manual. Worse, there isn't even a repair manual. It's not worth going into the various woes of the world, but the UN has defined 1.3 billion poor people (poor is a relative word) who probably could use a little help. You could also focus on the 42 so-called Highly Indebted Poor Countries (HIPCs), where people die sooner, work harder, eat less, get ill, and just plain have a tenuous hold on the dirty end of the stick. The good news is that these are countries where a two-week visit can make an extraordinary

**Y**our cherished vacation budget spent at Disney World doesn't really make a dent in the overall scheme of things. Two weeks in a small village in Africa will change those people's lives (and yours) forever.

difference. Your cherished vacation budget spent at Disney World doesn't really make a dent in the overall scheme of things. Two weeks in a small village in Africa will change those people's lives (and yours) forever.

So why isn't everyone parking their Winnebagos in Colombia or pitching their North Face tents in Somalia? These days, the hides of Americans are thicker than that of the endangered rhino. Reality TV shows have spawned like flies from maggots, and the affluent can watch the pain and suffering of total strangers intermingled with cheerful commercials selling online trading Web sites and new SUVs. The 4 o'clock, 6 o'clock, 7 o'clock, 8 o'clock, 9 o'clock, and 10 o'clock news cut together the world's woes and wars into 15 minutes, complete with snazzy graphics, logos, and maps. Designed to stop channel surfers and to fire up

> **T**elevision zooms in with nice clean images of blood, explosions, screaming, and "you are there" action. The trouble is, you aren't there.

freaks, television zooms in with nice clean images of blood, explosions, screaming, and "you are there" action. The trouble is, you aren't there, and even if you are, television makes it seem more distant and less painful. Anything too disturbing can be cast away with a simple click of the remote control. Hey, it's not my problem. Or is it?

You can't save the world; you can't convince Bush to stop whacking Iraqis and vice versa; you can't convince the Pope that birth control might actually be a good idea in some countries; and you probably also won't get far telling our government to stop messing in other countries' affairs.

You might even be of the opinion that those knock-kneed little tykes are going to bite the bullet anyway, so why waste your time? Corrupt governments, civil war, and plain old poverty aren't new in these places.

If you actually go there, you might find things are very different from what you see on those hand-wringing infomercials and news stories. Most people get by—they don't have much, but they get by. They might have to walk a mile to get water, make shoes out of truck tires, or even share one tattered textbook in an open-air school, but they get by. This is the secret. Anything you can do for these people makes their lives a little better. Giving a box of books, teaching farming skills, organizing governments, donating an old computer to publish a newspaper, or even pitching in to build a schoolhouse, are all real contributions.

People helping people can make a difference—one-on-one, face-to-face, or even by mail. Whether it be teaching kids a song or working for 10 years for their indigenous rights, every time you do something for someone, you change his or her life. Dangerous places need people who can help push back the danger. You don't need to be a bomb-disposal expert or a facial-reconstructive surgeon to make a difference; by simply picking up a shovel you can do wonders.

So, back to how you can connect. Don't assume that being a "charity tourist" is the solution (as one Mexican anthropologist in Tijuana said to me in disgust, visiting poor countries on the weekends with bags of faded T-shirts and Kraft macaroni dinners is not the best way to approach poverty). You need to understand the unique needs of the region you are interested in. The United Nations Development Program (http://www.undp.org) specializes in analyzing problems of the developing world. InterAction (American Council for Voluntary International Action) publishes a biweekly newsletter called *Monday Developments,* which lists dozens of job opportunities at international organizations in each issue (http://www.interaction.org). They also have a directory of groups you can contact.

Your first step should be to contact NGO Web sites and country Web sites that provide background information. You will find that they come in two flavors: long-term relief and emergency relief groups. Then look into how you can help.

**InterAction**
A coalition of over 150 nonprofit groups working worldwide with excellent resources for addresses and background information.
http://www.interaction.org

**University of Wales, Department of International Politics**
http://www.aber.ac.uk/interpol/home.html
This is a link site to nongovernmental agencies and relief organizations.

**Doctors of the World (links page)**
http://www.doctorsoftheworld.org

**Relief Web Directory of Humanitarian Organizations**
http://www.reliefweb.int/library/contacts/dirhomepage.html

**AlertNet**
http://www.alertnet.org
The Reuters Foundation's news and communications service for the emergency relief community.

**Disaster Relief**
http://www.disasterrelief.org
Worldwide disaster aid and information via the Internet. News page and links.

**Links to emergency response groups**
http://www.interaction.org/monday

**ReliefWeb**
http://www.notes.reliefweb.int
News and links to the humanitarian relief community.

## Working Overseas

Once you get into the idea of helping people around the world, your tiny vacation may not be enough. How about making it your life's passion? Be forewarned: Working overseas is a lot more romantic-sounding than it is financially rewarding. Yes, there are professional folks at the UN and big-money groups that just want to make that tax-free "nut" of around a million dollars to buy that condo in Key West. But most people who work have to sacrifice to make it happen. Most people just don't want to chuck it all for a life of misery and poverty. Jobs overseas require training and lengthy job searches. There are some shortcuts: the military, the diplomatic corps, multinational corporations, even foreign correspondents; all will guarantee you frequent-flier miles and broken marriages. There are also short deals, like the Peace Corps, or contract work, or even Club Med. In any case, the world will be your workplace, and you will develop an understanding and enjoyment of the world that few people will ever appreciate.

## International Volunteer Program Opportunities in Europe and America

### Société Française de Bienfaisance Mutuelle
210 Post Street, Suite 502
San Francisco, CA 94108
Tel.: (415) 477-3667
Fax: (415) 477-3669
rjewell@ivpsf.org
http://www.ivpsf.org

### Expat Network
Rose House
109a South End
Croydon CR0 1BG, UK
Tel.: (44) (0) 20  8760 5100
Fax: (44) (0) 20 8760 0469
expats@expatnetwork.com
http://www.expatnetwork.co.uk
A 5,000-plus member organization of mostly UK expats, the Expat Network also provides a directory of recruitment companies for overseas work. It costs about $150 to join.

### Vacation Work Publications
9 Park End Street
Oxford OX1 1HJ, UK
Tel.: (44) (865) 241978
Fax: (44) (865) 790885
vacationwork@vacationwork.co.uk
http://www.vacationwork.co.uk

A British source for publications on summer jobs, volunteer positions, and other new ways to travel and work. If you cover the postage, they will send you their latest catalog of books and specific publications on subjects that cover teaching or living and working in various countries around the world. A small sampling of publications can show you how to teach English in Japan, work on a kibbutz in Israel, choose an adventure holiday, get au pair and nanny jobs, find summer employment in France, and much more.

### Institute for Global Communications (IGC)
P.O. Box 29904
San Francisco, CA 94129-0904
Tel.: (415) 561-6100
Fax: (415) 561-6101
support@igc.apc.org
http://www.igc.org
A central clearinghouse for "people who are changing the world." A little left of left, this site provides good information on a broad range of global subjects. Sites include

AntiRacismNet, WomensNet, EcoNet, and PeaceNet. Not a direct job source, but a good way to keep up on global events and meet others.

### The Federation of American Women's Clubs Overseas Inc. (FAWCO)
vp-reps@fawco.org
http://www.fawco.org
This group is an international network of 76 independent clubs with a combined membership of over 17,000 women in 34 countries throughout the world. It serves as a support network for American women living and working abroad with a particular interest and involvement in the areas of U.S. citizens' concerns, education, environmental protection, and women's and children's rights.

### Overseas Jobs
12 Robinson Road
Sagamore Beach, MA 02562
info@overseasjobs.com
http://www.overseasjobs.com
This site provides online recruitment information as well as career resources and employment opportunities. Everyone from high school and college students to expats, international job seekers, part-time workers, and adventure travelers will find this site a useful source for employment opportunities worldwide.

### Club Med
Club Med—North America
75 Valencia Avenue, 12th Floor
Coral Gables, FL 33134
Fax: (305) 476-4100
Canada Fax: (514) 937-9661
resumes@clubmed.com
http://www.clubmedjobs.com
Okay, you're not going to save the world, but you can at least get some training wheels at one of the 120-plus resorts run by Club Med. The idea is that you can travel to some of the most godforsaken places in the world and then contact the locals after your six-month gig is up. By then you should have made enough contacts to get a meaningful job. The Club Med recruitment and interview schedule can be found on their Web site.

### Transitions Abroad
P.O. Box 1300
Amherst, MA 01004-1300
Tel.: (413) 256-3414
Fax: (413) 256-0373
info@TransitionsAbroad.com
http://www.transitionsabroad.com
This bimonthly magazine full of practical information is targeted for people who want to live and work in a foreign country. It includes a directory of international volunteer positions available as well as job opportunities in many areas, including teaching and technical positions. The cost for six issues is: U.S. $28; Canada $32; overseas surface mail $46; overseas air mail $56.

### Job Search Overseas
P.O. Box 35
Falmouth
Cornwall TR11 3UB, UK
Tel.: (44) 0872 870070
Fax: (44) 0872 870071
http://garlic.aitec.edu.au/~bwechner/Do
    cuments/Travel/Lists/Journals.html
This monthly paper contains international job ads collected from other sources and geared toward the working traveler. There are also articles and classified ads to keep travelers in touch.

*Overseas Employment Newsletter*
P.O. Box 460
Town of Mount Royal
Quebec City, Quebec H3P 3C7
Canada
Tel.: (514) 739 1108
Fax: (514) 739 0795
http://www.overseasjobs.com
Also:
http://www.escapeartist.com
http://www.joyjobs.com

This newsletter is published by Overseas Employment Services every two weeks. It contains detailed descriptions of the current jobs available in a broad range of skills, careers, and positions in the many developing nations and industrialized countries of the world. This group also publishes a variety of useful books on the same topic.

## Student Travel and Work Exchange Contacts

*International Student Travel
    Confederation*
Herengracht 479
1017 BS Amsterdam
The Netherlands
Tel.: (31) 20 421 28 00
Fax: (31) 20 421 28 10
istcinfo@istc.org
http://www.istc.org
The ISTC was created in 1949 as a way to make travel more affordable to students and to allow them to become connected globally. Today, there are over 70 organizations that specialize in student travel and student services. The ISTC has evolved into an international network of 5,000 offices in more than 100 countries, and provides information and services to 10 million students and youth every year.

*Center for Study Abroad (CSA)*
325 Washington Avenue South, #93
Kent, WA 98032
Tel. (info): (206) 726-1498
Tel. (office): (206) 583-8191
Fax: (253) 850-0454
info@centerforstudyabroad.com
http://www.centerforstudyabroad.com
CSA has been providing affordable, high-quality, fully accredited programs overseas to students, working

adults, and retirees worldwide since 1990. There are programs available to all adults throughout the world. Check out the informative Web site for more information.

*STA Travel*
Toll-free Tel.: (800) 781-4040
go@statravel.com.
http://www.sta-travel.com
Travelers can get experienced assistance and information to plan a trip for work or play 365 days a year, 24 hours a day. To stay completely up to date on travel news, STA offers a monthly e-mail newsletter.

*Global Citizens Network*
130 North Howell Street
St. Paul, MN 55104
Tel.: (651) 644-0960
Toll-free tel.: (800) 644-9292
info@globalcitizens.org
http://www.globalcitizens.org
Global Citizens Network sends small teams of volunteers to rural communities around the world. Volunteers immerse themselves in the daily life of the local culture from one to three weeks, depending upon the location and the project needs. Teams work on

community projects initiated by the local people. This may involve planting trees, digging irrigation trenches, organizing a school, building a school, or teaching various skills required for the community to sustain itself.

## AFS
### (formerly American Field Service)
71 West 23rd Street, 17th Floor
New York, NY 10010
Tel.: (212) 807-8686
Fax: (212) 807-1001
info@afs.org
http://www.afs.org
From its origins as a volunteer ambulance corps in 1914 through the present, AFS remains a global leader in promoting intercultural understanding through student exchange programs. AFS is one of the world's largest community-based volunteer organizations, dedicated to building a more just and peaceful world through international student exchange. Students can choose from more than 100 programs in over 50 countries around the world. They live and study abroad for a year or a semester, or they can take time out between high school and college to do valuable community service work in another country. AFS also offers opportunities for families and high schools in the United States to host selected students from 50 countries who come to live and study in America for a semester or a year. More than 10,000 students, young adults, and teachers participate in AFS exchange programs each year.

## Volunteers for Peace
1034 Tiffany Road
Belmont, VT 05730
Tel.: (802) 259-2759
Fax: (802) 259-2922
vfp@vfp.org
http://www.vfp.org
This group offers over 2,000 affordable and short-term international voluntary service programs in 80 countries. The programs are usually from two to three weeks in duration and the cost to participate is between $200 and $400.

## World Learning Inc.
Kipling Road, P.O. Box 676
Brattleboro, VT 05302-0676
Tel.: (802) 257-7751
Fax: (802) 258-3248
info@worldlearning.org
http://www.worldlearning.org
This organization offers a school for international training in teaching languages, intercultural management, and world issues as well as college semester abroad programs in over 40 countries. Citizen exchange and language programs include summer abroad programs for students and seniors, corporate language projects, and youth adventure camps. Au pair arrangements and exchange programs are also offered. Projects in international development and training focus on the improvement of economic and social conditions around the world.

### Youth Exchange Service (YES)
1600 Dove Street, Suite 460
Newport Beach, CA 92660
Tel.: (949) 955-2030
Toll Free Tel.: (800) 848-2121
Fax: (949) 955-0232
yes1@ix.netcom.com
http://www.yesint.com
This international teenage exchange-student program is dedicated to world peace. If you are interested in hosting an international teenage "ambassador," contact this group.

### ·United Nations Volunteers Program (UNV)
Postfach 260 111
D-53153 Bonn, Germany
Tel.: (49) 228 815 2000
Fax: (49) 228 815 2001
information@unvolunteers.org
http://www.unv.org
The UNV was created by the United Nations General Assembly in 1970 to promote volunteerism. Each year there are 5,000 volunteers from over 150 nations working in the developing countries of the world.

### The Council on International Educational Exchange (CIEE)
633 Third Avenue, 20th Floor
New York, NY 10017-6706
Toll-free Tel.: (800) 40-STUDY
Fax: (212) 822-2779
info@ciee.org
http://www.ciee.org
Since 1947 the mission of the Council on International Educational Exchange, known as CIEE and formerly as Council, has been "to help people gain understanding, acquire knowledge, and develop skills for living in a globally interdependent and culturally diverse world." CIEE offers more than 60 Study Center Programs in 29 coun-tries throughout the world for students as well as volunteers who have the option to work in archaeology, nature conservation, construction and renovation, or social service. You can write for a directory or for more information, or check out their very informative Web site.

### Operation Crossroads Africa
P.O. Box 5570
New York, NY 10027
Tel.: (212) 289-1949
Fax: (212) 289-2526
oca.icg.org
http://oca.igc.org/web/index.html
Operation Crossroads Africa offers volunteer opportunities in several African countries as well as the Caribbean and Brazil. Since 1957, 11,000 Crossroads participants have traveled to 35 African countries, 12 Caribbean countries, and Brazil in the pursuit of creating a better world through understanding and communicating. Being a Crossroads volunteer is an intense living, working, and learning experience at the grassroots level.

### ACDI/VOCA
Headquarters
50 F Street, NW, Suite 1075
Washington, DC 20001
Tel.: (202) 383-4961
Fax: (202) 783-7204
webmaster@acdivoca.org
http://www.acdivoca.org
ACDI/VOCA is the result of the 1997 merger of Agricultural Co-operative Development International and Volunteers in Overseas Cooperative Assistance. ACDI/VOCA helps people learn how to sustain themselves with the resources available to them and to rebuild and maintain their way of

life. Over 600 volunteers a year work worldwide assisting where needed.

### Friendship Force International
34 Peachtree Street, Suite 900
Atlanta, GA 30303
Tel.: (404) 522-9490
Fax: (404) 688-6148
info@friendshipforce.org
http://www.friendshipforce.org
The Friendship Force is a private, nonprofit organization whose purpose is to create an environment where personal friendships can be established across the international barriers that separate people.

### Peacework
Programs in International Volunteer
   Service
209 Otey Street
Blacksburg, VA 24060-7426
Tel.: (540) 953-1376
Fax: (540) 953-0300
mail@peacework.org
http://www.peacework.org
Peacework arranges international volunteer service projects around the world. Its programs offer volunteers the opportunity to learn about different cultures and customs and to gain insight into developing communities around the world.

### The International Partnership for
   Service-Learning
815 Second Avenue, Suite 315
New York, NY 10017
Tel.: (212) 986-0989
info@ipsl.org
http://www.ipsl.org
Offers programs that combine structured academic studies with volunteer community service for a summer, a semester, a year, or a 3-week session.

### International Cultural Youth Exchange
   (ICYE)
ICYE International Office
Große Hamburger Str 30
D-10115 Berlin, Germany
Tel.: (49) 30 28390550
Fax: (49) 30 28390552
icye@icye.org
http://www.icye.org
ICYE is an international nonprofit youth exchange organization with 35 Member Committees in Africa, Asia-Pacific, Europe, and Latin America. Its purpose is the promotion of intercultural learning and international voluntary service. Both short- and long-term exchanges that combine homestays with voluntary service in a variety of community service projects are available in over 30 countries throughout the world. ICYE headquarters are located in Berlin, Germany.

### JustAct: Youth Action for Global
   Justice
### (Formerly Overseas Development
   Network)
333 Valencia Street, Suite 101
San Francisco, CA 94130
Tel.: (415) 431-4204
Fax: (415) 431-5953
info@justact.org
http://www.justact.org
This organization was founded in 1983 as the Overseas Development Network. It is primarily for students who want to work overseas in an intern (read "no pay") position. This is also called "alternative tourism" in the San Francisco area. The benefit is that you have the opportunity to get in there and do something about hunger, poverty, and social injustice. The almost 20-year-old organization has placed over 200

interns overseas and in the Appalachian area of the United States (yes, third-world standards do still exist in America). If you want to do your good deeds even closer to home, JustAct will introduce you to other like-minded students. There are also positions with the organization that require about 12 to 20 hours a week. You can gain experience organizing, promoting, writing, and marketing and get a good "foot in the door" position if you want to get serious about global affairs. All positions are unpaid and require a minimum commitment of eight hours a week for three months. You can take part in a local chapter, work to build sustainable locally initiated development programs within your local community, or just contribute to the ongoing programs.

### Peace Corps
### The Paul D. Coverdell Peace Corps
###   Headquarters
1111 20th Street, NW
Washington, DC 20526
Toll-free Tel.: (800) 424-8580
Fax: (202) 692-1201
hrmjobs@peacecorps.gov
http://www.peacecorps.gov

When most people in the '60s and '70s thought about how they could change the world, the Peace Corps came to mind. It may surprise you to know that the Vietnam-era hearts-and-minds division of the U.S. government is still hard at work making the world a better place without any killing or maiming.

The Peace Corps is pure American do-goodism from its Woodstock-style logo (the Peace Corps was formed in 1961) to its Puritan slogan, "The Toughest Job You'll Ever Love," and goes straight to the soul of every Midwestern farm boy. The Corps appeals to the American love of doing good things in bad places. In the over 40 years of the Peace Corps' existence, 140,000 Americans have heeded the call and the world has truly benefited from such an outpouring of American know-how. Last year there were about 10,000 volunteers spread out in over 130 countries. What do you get? Well, the answer is better stated as, What do you give? Successful applicants go through two to three months of language, technical, and cultural training for each "tour." You get a small allowance for housing, food, and clothing, airfare to and from your posting, and 24 days of vacation a year.

While in-country, you will work with a local counterpart and may be completely on your own in a small rural village or major city. The payoff is that you can actually make things happen, understand a different culture, and say that you did something to help the world. Does the reality meet the fantasy? Apparently it does. The average length of time spent in the Peace Corps is six years, with nine months of training. That works out to three two-year tours with the minimum training. All ex-Peace Corps volunteers we talked to said their Peace Corps years were among the most rewarding of their lives. Getting in is not that easy, but once in, you join a club that can greatly benefit you in your career. Being an ex-Peace Corps member says that you are about giving and hard work and that you are a little more worldly than most.

You must be a U.S. citizen, at least 18 years old, and healthy. Most successful applicants have a bachelor's degree. You must also have a minimum 2.5 grade point average for educational assignments or experience in the field you want to enter. Although there is no age limit, the Peace Corps is typically a younger person's game and is considered to be an excellent way to get a leg up in government and private sector employment. At the end of your service as a volunteer, you will receive a "readjustment allowance" of $225 for each month of service to the Peace Corps. The government will give you $6,075 upon completion of your full term of service, find you a job in the government on a noncompetitive basis, and even help you apply for the over 50 special scholarships available for ex-Peace Corps members.

The emphasis is on training and education in the agricultural, construction, and educational areas. There are not too many fine arts requirements, although they do have a category for art teacher. Couples with dependents are a no-no, and couples are strongly discouraged. It helps if you know a foreign language, have overseas experience, and have a teaching/tutoring background.

The Peace Corps does not mess around in countries that are overtly hostile or dangerous to Americans. Also, you will not be posted to Monaco or Paris. You can be posted to Fiji, Thailand, Central Africa, or

most countries in the CIS. If you are curious, the Peace Corps recruiters hold two-hour evening seminars at their regional offices. Don't be put off by the slightly '80s banner reading "Globalize Your Résumé." You can meet with returning volunteers and ask all the questions you want.

## CARE

### Worldwide Headquarters
151 Ellis Street
Atlanta, GA 30303
Tel.: (404) 681-2552
Fax: (404) 589-2651
info@care.org
http://www.care.org

CARE was founded in 1945 when 22 American organizations joined forces to help European survivors of World War II. It is one of the world's largest private international humanitarian organizations. CARE is committed to helping families in poor communities improve their lives and ultimately overcome poverty. There are programs for disaster relief, food distribution, primary health care, agriculture and natural resource management, population, girls' education, family planning, and small-business support. Ongoing self-help projects are in place in over 60 countries around the world, including some of the least developed countries of Africa, Asia, and Latin America. CARE responds to disasters overseas and sends emergency aid to victims of famine and war worldwide.

**Save the Children**
54 Wilton Road
Westport, CT 06880
Tel.: (203) 221-4000
Toll-free Tel.: (800) 728-3843
Fax: (203) 221-4077
twebster@savechildren.org
http://www.savethechildren.org
Save the Children is a nonprofit,
nonsectarian organization founded
in 1932. Its purpose is to make positive and lasting differences in the
lives of disadvantaged children,
both in the United States and
abroad. During its 70-plus years,
Save the Children has provided
emergency relief and community
development assistance in over 45
countries and throughout the
United States. The group targets the
four key sectors of: (1) health/
population/nutrition, (2) education, (3) economic opportunities,
and (4) commodity-assisted
development/emergency response.

**UNICEF**
**UNICEF House**
3 United Nations Plaza
New York, NY 10017
Tel.: (212) 326-7000
Toll-free Tel.: (800) FOR-KIDS
Fax: (212) 887-7465
netmaster@unicef.org
http://www.unicef.org
UNICEF is the leading advocate for
children throughout the world, and
provides vaccines, clean water,
medicine, nutrition, emergency
relief, and basic education for
children in more than 160 nations.
This organization is an integral but
semi-autonomous agency of the
United Nations with its own executive board. Financial support for its
work comes entirely from voluntary contributions. UNICEF's

budget is not part of the dues paid
by the member governments of the
United Nations. An extensive
network of volunteers work for
UNICEF throughout the world, and
local volunteers are always needed.

**U.S. Committee for Refugees**
1717 Massachusetts Avenue, NW
Suite 200
Washington, DC 20036
Tel.: (202) 347-3507
Fax: (202) 347-3418
uscr@irsa-uscr.org
http://www.refugees.org
Founded in 1958, the U.S.
Committee for Refugees is a
nongovernmental, nonprofit agency
dedicated to defending the rights of
displaced peoples worldwide. The
U.S. Committee documents and
defends the rights of refugees
throughout the world, regardless of
their nationality, race, religion,
ideology, or social group. USCR
hires interns for its national office in
Washington, D.C., who work closely
with members of the staff on
refugee and asylum issues. Intern-
ships in region-specific research,
government relations, media relations, development, and fundraising
are offered for the fall, spring, and
summer semesters. Interns are generally a diverse group of students
and professionals who wish to
increase their exposure to humanitarian advocacy. They come from all
areas of the country and the world.
Interns are required to commit a
minimum of 20 hours per week for
10 weeks to USCR. In return they
receive reimbursement for local
travel expenses as well as a
stipend—the amount of which
depends on the number of hours
worked.

**Soros Foundations Network**
400 West 59th Street
New York, NY 10019
Tel.: (212) 548-0668
http://www.soros.org
Investor George Soros is chairman
of the Open Society Institute and
the founder of a network of philanthropic organizations that are active in more than 50 countries.
These foundations are dedicated to
building and maintaining the infrastructure and institutions of an
open society. This group of autonomous organizations operates around
the world, principally in Central
and Eastern Europe and the former
Soviet Union, and also in Guatemala, Haiti, Mongolia, southern
Africa, and the United States. All of
the national foundations share the
common mission of supporting the
development of open society. The
Soros network supports efforts in
civil society, education, media, public health, and human and
women's rights, as well as social,
legal, and economic reform.

**The Carter Center**
One Copenhill
453 Freedom Parkway
Atlanta, GA 30307
Tel.: (404) 420-5109
Fax: (404) 688-1709
carterweb@emory.edu
http://www.cartercenter.org
Former President Jimmy Carter has
been busy since he left office. His
peace negotiations throughout the
world have been effective in achieving short-term results, as well as
angering many hard-liners, with
his friendly approach to our enemies. Carter shows that a mild-
mannered, ever-smiling good ol'
boy from the South can play the

perfect good cop to the U.S. military's bad cop. Jimmy Carter has
been working overtime defending
humanity and peace throughout
the world. In August 1999, he was
awarded America's highest civilian
honor, and he very deservedly was
awarded the Nobel Peace Prize in
October 2002. Carter works tire-
lessly because he really believes
that all people have good in them
and he personally has a responsibility to make the world a better
place. Jimmy and Rosalynn's "keep
busy and do good" organization is
known as the Carter Center. One of
the Carter Center's big events is
building homes in poor countries
(with the help of hundreds of
volunteers like you). Carter works
out of a 100,000-square-foot
complex, complete with chapel,
library, conference facilities, and
museum fighting disease, hunger,
poverty, conflict, and oppression
worldwide. The center is always
happy to receive donations and
résumés from motivated individuals who want to volunteer
their time.

**BBB Wise Giving Alliance
(formerly Philanthropic Advisory
    Service [PAS] of the Council of
    Better Business Bureau)**
4200 Wilson Blvd, Suite 800
Arlington, VA 22203
Tel.: (703) 276-0100
Fax: (703) 525-8277
http://www.give.org
A merger of the National Charities
Information Bureau and the Coun-
cil of Better Business Bureau's
Foundation and its Philanthropic
Advisory Service has created the
BBB Wise Giving Alliance. This
organization promotes ethical

standards of business practices and strives to protect consumers through voluntary self-regulation and monitoring activities. They publish a bimonthly list of philanthropic organizations that meet the Council of Better Business Bureau's Standards for Charitable Solicitations. Donors who contribute $45 or more receive four issues of the quarterly *BBB Wise Giving Guide,* a magazine summarizing the Alliance's current charity evaluations and containing articles about accountability. The standards include Public Accountability, Use of Funds, Solicitations and Informational Materials, Fund-Raising Practices, and Governance. Consumers can also subscribe to the monthly electronic newsletter, *The Wise Consumer,* for $24 per year. It contains advice about common danger signs and ways to defend yourself from fraudulent charities. Many of the groups in the newsletter have e-mail addresses, databases, and online services.

## Human Rights Groups

### Amnesty International USA
322 Eighth Avenue
New York, NY 10001
Tel.: (212) 807-8400
Fax: (212) 463-9193
admin-us@aiusa.org
http://www.amnesty.org

Amnesty International was founded by British lawyer Peter Benenson in London in 1961 and so far claim they have come to the rescue of over 43,000 prisoners. More than 350 staff members and over 100 volunteers from more than 50 countries around the world monitor news, information, and communications from around the world to seek out cases of mistreatment. Their goal is to pressure governments to end torture, executions, political killings, and disappearances; to ensure speedy trials for all political prisoners; and to affect the release of prisoners of conscience provided they have neither used nor advocated violence. Their method is simple and easy. They coordinate the writing and mailing of letters to the captors of prisoners of conscience. These methods have been proven successful, and the international group was awarded the Nobel Peace Prize in 1977 for their efforts to promote observance of the UN Universal Declaration of Human Rights. Amnesty International membership exceeds 1 million people in over 140 countries. Together, they can create an avalanche of mail and global protest over the mistreatment of prisoners.

### Cultural Survival, Inc.
215 Prospect Street
Cambridge, MA 02139
Tel.: (617) 441-5400
Fax: (617) 441-5417
csinc@cs.org
http://www.culturalsurvival.org

There are about 40 ethnic groups at risk around the world. But there is more talk about saving the rain forest than about the people who live in it. Nomadic forest dwellers have no money, own no land, and in many cases do not integrate into the societies that are pushing them out of their homeland. Having seen the havoc wreaked on our own native Indians and Inuit, it is difficult to come up with viable alternatives to their eventual extinction.

Cultural Survival is an organization of anthropologists and researchers whose goal is to help indigenous peoples (like tropical rain forest dwellers) develop at their own pace and with their own cultures intact. Cultural Survival's weapon is the almighty dollar, and they put it in the hands of the groups they help. Working with indigenous peoples and ethnic minorities, they import sustainably harvested, nontimber forest products. What are those, you ask? Well, handicrafts, cashew nuts and Brazil nuts, babassu oil, rubber, bananas, even beeswax. The end result is that indigenous peoples gain land, develop cash crops, and don't have to live in shantytowns or timber camps to support themselves.

Founded in 1972, Cultural Survival has a variety of methods for achieving its goals: educational programs, importing and selling products, providing expertise to larger aid groups, and providing technical assistance to local groups seeking economic viability. The organization has projects worldwide. The membership fee of $45 gets you a yearly subscription to the quarterly journal *Cultural Survival Quarterly* (CSQ; an award-winning journal) and *Cultural Survival Voices*. By joining Cultural Survival, you will directly support their work with special projects worldwide and expand the reach of

their educational program. If you would like to work as an intern, CS is looking for people to help crank out the newsletter, raise funds, handle the office work, and expand the network of indigenous groups and supporters. To receive an application, contact:

**Pia Maybury-Lewis**
Coordinator, Intern Program
Cultural Survival
215 Prospect Street
Cambridge, Massachusetts 02139
Tel.: (617) 441-5403
pia@cs.org
You can also fax your résumé, along with a letter explaining your personal interests, to (617) 441-5417.

**Human Rights Watch**
350 Fifth Avenue, 34th Floor
New York, NY 10118-3299
Tel.: (212) 290-4700
Fax: (212) 736-1300
hrwnyc@hrw.org
http://www.hrw.org
The Human Rights Watch is dedicated to protecting the human rights of people around the world. It serves as an umbrella organization to Africa Watch, Asia Watch, Americas Watch, Middle East Watch, Helsinki Watch, and the Fund for Free Expression. Human Rights Watch tracks developments in more than 70 countries around the world and follows issues in women's rights, children's rights, and the flow of arms to abusive forces. Other special projects include academic freedom, the human rights sibilities of corporations, international justice, prisons, drugs, and refugees. Check out their very informative Web site.

### UNHCR

United Nations High Commissioner for
   Refugees
P.O. Box 2500
1211 Geneva 2 Depot
Switzerland
Tel.: (41) 22-739-8111
http://www.unhcr.ch

The United Nations High Commission for Refugees works to prevent refugees from being forcibly
returned to countries where they
could face death or imprisonment.
It also assists with food, shelter, and
medical care. *Refugees* magazine
focuses on a different refugee
movement each month. The UN
defines a refugee as anyone who
flees his home country in fear of
loss of life or liberty.

### Peace Brigades International

International Office
Unit 5, 89-93 Fonthill Road
London N4 3HT, UK
Tel.: (44) (0) 20-7561-9141
Fax: (44) (0) 20-7281-3181
info@peacebrigades.org
http://www.peacebrigades.org

The Peace Brigades work to prevent
human rights violations by escort-
ing individuals at threat, carrying a
camera, holding all-night vigils,
and other nonviolent actions. This
is an interesting way to make a nonviolent stand. Volunteers act as human shields or witnesses in areas
where locals' lives are at risk. Partly
funded by British-based Christian
Aid.

### War Resisters' International (WRI)

5 Caledonian Road
London N1 9DX, UK
Tel.: (44) 20-7278 4040
Fax: (44) 20-7278 0444
info@wri-irg.org
http://wri-irg.org

The purpose of War Resisters'
International is to promote nonviolent action against war. This group
supports and also connects people
around the world who refuse to
take part in war. "WRI works for a
world without war."

### Reporters Sans Frontières (Reporters Without Borders)

International Secretariat
5 rue Geoffroy-Marie
75009 Paris, France
Tel.: (33) 1-44-83-84-84
Fax: (33) 1-45-23-11-51
rsf@rsf.org
http://www.rsf.org

RSF was founded in 1985 to defend
the rights of journalists and
freedom of the press. They defend
imprisoned journalists and members of the press around the world.
Their annual report offers tips for
journalists on over 150 countries,
including the ones where journalists have been harassed, threatened,
and murdered. The annual report is
available for US$20. RSF will send
protest letters and provide lawyers
(if possible) and contribute other
forms of assistance to reporters in
jail. If you want to convert to
journalism after you are jailed,
these folks can't help you.

**The Journal of Humanitarian Assistance**
Department of Peace Studies
Bradford University
Bradford BD7 1DP, UK
Tel.: (44) 01274 235239
Fax: (44) 01274 235240
editors@jha.ac
http://www.jha.ac

The *Journal* was started in 1995 and exists as a communication device whereby practitioners and analysts worldwide can support their common goal of contributing to the humanitarian cause. The *Journal* is freely accessible to all readers via the Internet.

## Peace Groups

These are comprised of mostly university or privately funded think-tanks concerned with developing peaceful solutions to conflict.

**The Albert Einstein Institution**
http://www.aeinstein.org

**The Center for Defense Information**
http://www.cdi.org

**The Commission on Global Governance**
http://www.cgg.ch

**The Conflict Research Consortium**
http://www.colorado.edu/conflict

**The Peace and Justice Studies Association (Formerly Consortium on Peace Research, Education and Development)**
http://www.evergreen.edu/pjsa

**The Cyprus Peace Center**
http://www.peace-cyprus.org

**Fellowship of Reconciliation**
http://www.forusa.org

**The Foundation for the Prevention and Early Resolution of Conflict (PERC)**
http://www.conflictresolution.org

**Harvard University: Program on Nonviolent Sanctions and Cultural Survival (PONSACS)**
http://www.wcfia.harvard.edu/ponsacs

**Initiative on Conflict Resolution and Ethnicity**
http://www.incore.ulst.ac.uk

**Institute for Conflict Analysis and Resolution**
http://www.gmu.edu/departments/ICAR

**War Child**
http://www.warchild.org

**UNICEF**
http://www.unicef.org

**Human Rights Watch**
http://www.hrw.org

**World Disasters Report (IFRC)**
http://www.ifrc.org/publicat/wdr2002

**Institute for Global Communications: AntiRacismNet, EcoNet, PeaceNet, WomensNet**
http://www.igc.org

**International Peace Research Association (IPRA)**
http://www.human.mie-u.ac.jp/~peace/about-ipra.htm

**Stockholm International Peace Research Institute (SIPRI)**
http://www.sipri.se

**Network of Communities for Peacemaking and Conflict Resolution**
http://www.apeacemaker.net

**Peace Brigades International**
http://www.peacebrigades.org

**ReliefWeb, a project of the UNDHA**
http://www.reliefweb.int

**Tampere Peace Research Institute, University of Tampere, Finland**
http://www.uta.fi/laitokset/tapri

**United States Institute of Peace**
http://www.usip.org

**University of California: Institute on Global Conflict and Cooperation (IGCC)**
http://www.isop.ucla.edu/eas/fellowships/UC-igcc.htm

**The Disaster Response Unit of InterAction (The American Council for Voluntary International Action)**
http://www.interaction.org/disaster

**United Nations High Commissioner for Refugees (UNHCR)**
http://www.unhcr.ch

**United States Department of State Human Rights Report**
http://www.state.gov/www/global/human_rights

## Medical Aid Groups

There are angels in Rwanda, Somalia, Angola, Afghanistan, and Iraq. They are not there to convert souls or play harps. They are not soldiers or politicians, but white-coated volunteers who sew limbs back onto bodies, pull out shrapnel from babies' heads, and minister to the sick and dying. They are the men and women who try to ease the suffering caused by violent actions. Natural disasters also tax the resources and stamina of aid workers to the limit. If you don't mind stacking bodies like firewood or can live with the ever-present stench of too many sick people in one place, you will do just fine. The world needs people who are capable of cleaning up the mess caused by governments. If there is a disaster, chances are you will see these folks in there long before the journalists and the politicians arrive. These are nondenominational groups that are found in the world's most dangerous places. If you have medical skills and want to save more lives in a day than a tentful of TV evangelists do in a lifetime, this is the place to be. Conditions are beyond primitive, usually makeshift refugee camps on the edges of emerging conflicts. Many groups will walk or helicopter into war-torn regions to assist in treating victims. Many aid workers have been targeted for death because of their policy of helping both sides. There is constant danger from rocket attacks, land mines, communicable diseases, and riots. These people are not ashamed to stagger out of a tent after being up 48 hours straight, have a good cry, and then get back to work saving more lives. It hurts, but it feels good. Contact the following organizations for more information:

## International Committee of the Red Cross

19 avenue de la Paix
CH-1202 Geneva
Switzerland
Tel.: (41) (22) 734 60 01
Fax: (41) (22) 733 20 57 (ICRC Info
  Centre)
webmaster.gva@icrc.org
http://www.icrc.org

The International Committee of the Red Cross (ICRC) is an impartial, neutral, and independent organization whose exclusively humanitarian mission is to protect the lives and dignity of victims of war and internal violence and to provide them with assistance. It directs and coordinates the international relief activities conducted by the movement in situations of conflict. It also endeavors to prevent suffering by promoting and strengthening humanitarian law and universal humanitarian principles. Established in 1863, the ICRC is the origin of the International Red Cross and Red Crescent Movements.

## ICRC Regional Delegation for U.S.A and Canada

2100 Pennsylvania Avenue, NW
Suite 545
Washington, DC 20037
washington.was@icrc.org

## ICRC Delegation to the UN

801 Second Avenue, 18th Floor,
New York, NY 10017-4706
mail@icrc.delnyc.org

## American Red Cross

National Headquarters
431 18th Street, NW, 2nd floor
Washington, DC 20006
Tel.: (202) 639-3520
http://www.redcross.org

Since 1881, whenever there has been a disaster or war, these folks have been on the scene knee-deep in bandages, blood, and cots, helping the injured and consoling those who have just lost everything. They always have a need for volunteers, particularly people with medical and technical skills. If you can't volunteer your time or skills, blood donors are always desperately needed.

## Doctors of the World

Doctors of the World—USA
375 West Broadway, 4th Floor
New York, NY 10012
Tel.: (212) 226-9890
Toll-free Tel.: (888) 817-HELP
Fax: (212) 226-7026
info@dowusa.org
http://www.doctorsoftheworld.org

Doctors of the World is a nonsectarian, international organization working in the United States and abroad providing humanitarian assistance to those in the greatest need.

## AmeriCares

161 Cherry Street
New Canaan, CT 06840
Tel.: (203) 966-5195
Toll-free Tel.: (800) 486-4357
info@americares.org
http://www.americares.org

AmeriCares is a private, nonprofit disaster relief and humanitarian aid organization that provides immediate response to emergency medical needs. The organization supports long-term health care programs for people around the world irrespective of race, color, creed, or political persuasion. Since its inception in 1982, AmeriCares has delivered more than $1.4 billion worth of medical and disaster aid around the world. AmeriCares works with corporate America to secure large donations of supplies and materials. Cash contributions are used primarily for logistical costs. For every $1 donated, AmeriCares is able to deliver $22 worth of relief supplies.

### Refugee Relief International; Inc.
2995 Woodside Road
Suite 400-244
Woodside, CA 94062
info@refugeerelief.org
http://www.refugeerelief.org

One of DP's favorite group of guys, this organization was founded in 1982 to provide medical supplies and other aid for refugees and war victims. There is no salaried staff and volunteers pay their own expenses. All administrative offices are donated. RRI has assisted people in Afghanistan, Myanmar, the Balkans, Thailand, and Cambodia. This small group of ex-Special Forces guys will guarantee that every dollar you spend gets sent up to the front lines, where civilians need medical attention the most. A unique operation.

### Physicians for Peace
223 West Bute Street, Suite 900
Norfolk, VA 23510
Tel.: (757) 625-7569
Fax: (757) 625-7680
info@global corps.com
http://www.globalcorps.com/orgs/ngo/
    pfp/pfp.html

PFP is an apolitical, nonprofit organization that helps foster international peace and cooperation by improving health care. It is part of the Global Corps network of humanitarian assistance.

### Doctors Without Borders (Médecins Sans Frontières)
U.S. Headquarters
6 East 39th Street, 8th floor
New York, NY 10016
Tel.: (212) 679-6800
Fax: (212) 679-7016
doctors@newyork.msf.org
http://www.doctorswithoutborders.org

### International Headquarters
Rue de la Tourelle 39
1040 Brussels, Belgium
Tel.: (32) 2 280 1881
Fax: (32) 2 280 0173
http://www.msf.org

Doctors Without Borders, founded in 1971, is the largest international emergency medical organization in the world. Every year, around 3,000 volunteers leave for three to six months of service in more than 80 countries around the world. Many of the countries are in a state of war. Sixty percent of the volunteers are medically trained and come from 45 countries worldwide. Most volunteers are 25 to 35 years old. The organization assists victims of natural disasters and health crises like Ebola; it also ministers to refugees and war victims. In order to deploy people as quickly as possible (the goal is within 24 hours), special emergency kits were created with strict operational and medical procedures. Today, these kits and manuals are used by other international organizations around the world.

**International Medical Corps**
Headquarters
11500 West Olympic Boulevard, Suite
  506
Los Angeles, CA 90064
Tel.: (310) 826-7800
Fax: (310) 442-6622
imc@imcworldwide.org
http://www.imc-la.com

IMC is a private, nonsectarian, nonpolitical, nonprofit organization established in 1984 by U.S. physicians and nurses to provide emergency medical relief and health care training to devastated regions worldwide.

# SAVE YOURSELF

## Stay Alive! (At Least Until You Get Home)

There is much ink and many photons about survival being wasted on adventure and travel these days. Most are knee-jerk stories about what victimized people should have done, written by people in the comfort of their media offices. Yemen, Chechnya, Uganda, Guatemala, Colombia, the Philippines, and other countries have been the site of tourist and expat disasters. After talking to a number of people involved in these highly publicized kidnappings, murders, rapes, and attacks, I can tell you that no amount of training would have predicted, prevented, or averted what happened. Most of these people are smart, fearful, cautious, and took a lot of precautions. What does come out of these incidents is that knowing what to do in a worst-case scenario does make the difference between being able to talk about it on *Oprah* versus being a statistic.

Armies have long known that training can replace thinking with ingrained reaction. The brain has a bad habit of pushing your "Holy shit, what are we going to do now?" button every time it hears a loud noise. This button immediately sets into motion helpful self-defense devices like shaky knees, dry mouth, buggy eyes, stammering, slack jaw, and mental confusion.

> **T**he brain has a bad habit of pushing your "Holy shit, what are we going to do now?" button every time it hears a loud noise.

There is the other side of the coin, described as "blissful ignorance," where backpackers think antiaircraft fire and wildly erratic *katushyas* are just charming native celebrations. Both can lead to a condition called "sudden reality check." This is caused by a rapid education in the truths and evils of not being prepared for danger.

Can you really train for the myriad horrors that are out there? No. But you can dramatically shave the odds. I sat down to communicate what I have learned and I wrote a whole book on survival called *Come Back Alive* (Doubleday). When I turned it in, it was 64 chapters and over 700 single-spaced pages long. The publisher, of course, cut it in half, which means that you don't know the half of it.

The point is that there are a lot of very simple things that you can do to save your life. There are also many courses and experts who can convey that information to you.

What does that have to do with survival training? First of all, most people have never been in a life-threatening situation. We've seen movies, been challenged by bullies, or read other people's accounts, but it is always different. Often people will use the word "dreamlike" to describe the event—a natural outcome of heightened senses and information overload playing things out in slow motion, but more like the look a rat has when a snake towers over it. Training can at least help you to recognize situations, react intelligently, and minimize the trauma.

## Journalist Safety Training

Many of these courses and all this information are also available to nonjournalists. There is a blurred line between tourists, stringers, and journalists these days with small DV cameras and a trend in khaki adventure wear. The courses are expensive, but obviously worth whatever your hide is. The U.S. government has joined in with ad hoc training programs for military-related reporters.

Groups such as Frontline, CPJ, and Reporters Respond have no interest in providing travel planning tips to civvies, but if you are trying to break into the impecunious business of war reportage, they can offer some advice.

# BA BOOM . . . THUNK

There are six universal types of soft body-armor you can choose from in the field. They are heavy, hot, and sweaty and provide little protection from mines, shrapnel, or multiple gunshots . . . but they can improve the odds or save your life. Most journos should consider Level III or Level IV for war zones.

| CLASS | STOPS | NOTES | COST |
|---|---|---|---|
| Level I | 22 LR and .38 Special | Offers minimal protection from the smallest types of pistols. Will stop a .38 Special at 850 fps or a .22 at 1,050 fps. Will not stop military rifle ammunition. | $175–$250 |
| Level IIA | Low-velocity .357 Magnum; 9mm | Will stop low-powered ammunition from standard handguns: 9 mm at 1,090 fps or a .357 Magnum at 1,250 fps. Will not stop military rifle ammunition. | $250–$700 |
| Level II | High-velocity .357; 9mm | Will stop high-powered ammunition from standard handguns, such as a 9 mm FMJ (full metal jacket) at 1,175 fps or a .357 Magnum at 1,395 fps. Will not stop military rifle ammunition. | $750 |
| Level IIIA | .44 Magnum; sub-machine gun; 9mm | Will stop high-velocity 9mm FMJ or .44 Magnum ammunition at 1,400 fps. Will not stop military rifle ammunition. | $800–$900 |
| Level III | High-powered rifle | Will stop 7.62mm, 5.56mm (.223), .30 cal military rifle ammunition at 2,750 fps, and shotgun slugs (with plate added). Some Level III vests can be upgraded with ceramic plates. Figure on spending around $1,600 for a top-of-the-line jacket. | $250–$275 |
| Level IV | Armor-piercing rifle | Will stop armor-piercing ammunition from high-velocity military rifles. This type of jacket is very heavy but will protect the chest from .30-06 sniper hits. | $300+ |
| Trauma Plates (Steel or Ceramic Groin Plate) | Upgrades front and rear protection significantly as well as increasing weight | Vests provide different amounts of coverage in the groin and arm area. A trauma plate is a solid piece of ceramic steel, or layered Kevlar that stops high-velocity rounds aimed at the heart or groin. Note: Kevlar can be penetrated by knives or sharp weapons. | |

http://www.bulletproofme.com
http://www.mpscompany.com

### Centurion Risk Assessment Services Ltd.

P.O. Box 1740
Andover, Hants SP11 7PE, UK
Tel.: (44) (0) 1264 355255
Tel.: (44) (0) 7000 221221
Fax: (44) (0) 1264 355322
Fax: (44) (0) 7000 221222
Mobile: (44) (0) 7785 248934
main@centurion-riskservices.co.uk
http://www.centurion-riskservices.co.uk
Founded in 1995, Centurion provides survival training for journalists as well as businesspeople working worldwide. Body armor and helmet rental are also available.

### AKE Group

UK Office:
AKE Limited
Mortimer House
Holmer Road, Hereford HR4 9TA, UK
Tel.: (44) (0) 1432 267111
Fax: (44) (0) 1432 350227
services@ake.co.uk
http://www.akegroup.com

U.S. Office
AKE LLC
1825 I Street NW, Suite 400
Washington, DC 20006
Tel.: (202) 974-6556
services@akellc.com
http://www.akegroup.com
Since 1991 this company has been teaching journalists and travelers how to survive in hostile regions. It also provides protection and security services.

# Adventure/Recreation Schools

### The School for Field Studies

16 Broadway
Beverly, MA 01915-4435
Tel.: (800) 989-4418
Fax: (978) 927-5127
For info about admissions/programs:
admissions@fieldstudies.org
http://www.fieldstudies.org
This nonprofit group was founded in 1980. Since then, over 10,000 college and high school students have participated in this program that focuses on hands-on, community-based, environmental fieldwork. The world is the SFS classroom. Students can choose to study in any of the six field study centers located in Australia, British Columbia, British West Indies/ Turks & Caicos Islands, Costa Rica, Baja in Mexico, and Kenya. There is a wide choice of topics—from marine mammals to coral reefs to wildlife management. Students live and study in some of the most beautiful, as well as the most threatened, ecosystems in the world while earning a college degree. SFS offers fall and spring semester programs and also 30-day summer courses at each field center. Students gain invaluable knowledge of the environment and the community in which they are working as well as an opportunity to learn more about the world by doing. Financial aid is available.

# HACKS, SAVE YOUR SKIN

AKE Group is one of two British companies running Hostile Environment Courses (HECs) for journos. Based in Hereford on the Welsh border, the course is run by Andrew Kain and Paul Brown, both of whom spent over a decade in the British army's elite Special Air Service.

The course is structured as if the participants have never been near a war zone. It consists of five days of intensive lectures and a final day of field work (theoretically evacuating and treating severely wounded people from a war zone). Divided into two sections, the course concentrates on weaponry, the damage it can do, the accuracy of different types of weaponry, and the (different) men behind the guns. Thereafter, the course consists of a series of intensive lectures on emergency medical procedures and recognizing various diseases.

Andrew Kain takes participants through the various tactics employed by different armies, from guerrilla forces to former Eastern Bloc and NATO forces, with useful tips for recognizing military tactics and what to do in some of the more predictable situations. Paul Brown, a former SAS medic, lectures on everything from hypothermia and snake bites to open fractures and gunshot wounds. Almost half of the medical course is practical, with the participants learning how to splint broken arms and legs, treat burns, and (all-important in a war zone) treat gunshot wounds.

Lectures on antipersonnel mines, the different types and how they are placed and recognized, combined with what to do if you step on one (from a medical perspective), make the course a must for hacks venturing into war zones. While the course organizers readily acknowledge that five days is the bare minimum needed for the course, it covers almost every life-threatening risk you are likely to encounter. It might not be nice being threatened by a thug with a pistol, but it's nice to hear from the experts that if the thug in question is more than 65 feet (20 meters) away, his chances of hitting you are about zilch, and even less if you're running. AKE also has offices in Washington, D.C.

## Stonehearth Open Learning Opportunities (SOLO)

P.O. Box 3150
Conway, NH 03818
Tel.: (603) 447-6711
Fax: (603) 447-2310
info@soloschools.com
http://www.stonehearth.com

A school for professionals, SOLO is designed to teach wilderness guides what to do in an emergency. They offer a variety of course options from which to choose, including the four-week Wilderness Emergency Medical Technician (WEMT) course, which costs about $2,200. This will get you on the preferred list of just about any expedition. Other courses offered include Wilderness First Responder (WEMT Part 1), WEMT Part 2, and Wilderness/Rural EMT Module. Shorter seminars covering a wide variety of topics are taught around the country. The areas of specialization are wilderness emergencies (frostbite, hypothermia, animal and insect bites, and altitude sickness), climbing rescue, and emergency medicine (wounds, broken limbs, shock, and allergy). Participants are expected to have a basic grounding in climbing and outdoor skills. Check the Web site for detailed information on the intensive training courses available.

### National Outdoor Leadership School (NOLS)
284 Lincoln Street
Lander, WY 82520-2848
Tel.: (307) 332-5300
Fax: (307) 332-1220
admissions@nols.edu
http://www.nols.edu
This school gets past the superficial imagery of some survival schools and right down to business. People who want to make money in the outdoor adventure business come here to learn not only survival aspects, but also the nuts and bolts of adventure travel outfitting. You can take the 35-day, $3,600 NOLS instructor's class once you have passed a basic wilderness class. The emphasis here is on safety, since your future charges will be less than amused if they end up living off the land because you forgot to pack their favorite pudding. Choose from sea kayaking, winter camping, Telemark skiing, backpacking, or mountaineering. Some courses qualify for college credit.

Entry-level classes are in reality great adventure vacations depending on your area of interest. Mountaineering classes are taught in Alaska, British Columbia, and even Kenya. Expect to spend two weeks to three months on location learning the specialized skills you will need to lead other groups. If you want to cram in a class on your vacation, then opt for their selection of two-week courses on horse-packing, winter skiing, rock climbing or canoeing. If you flunk, well, you had a good time on a well-organized adventure tour.

## Adventure Experience Organizations

### British Schools Exploring Society (BSES Expeditions)
BSES Expeditions at
The Royal Geographical Society
1 Kensington Gore
London SW7 2AR, UK
Tel.: (44) (0) 20 7591 3141
Fax: (44) (0) 20 7591 3140
bses@rgs.org
http://www.bses.org.uk
BSES sets up an expedition for young people between the ages of 16-1/2 and 20 every year. The four- to six-week expeditions are usually to the Arctic and subarctic regions such as Greenland, Alaska, and Svalbard during the summer holidays. However, in the past years, they have been sneaking in expeditions to tropical climes like Botswana, Kenya, India, Zimbabwe, Queensland, Morocco, and the Amazon. Since 1932 over 3,000 people have taken part in these adventures of a lifetime. Participants pay a fee to cover costs and membership to BSES is by election after the successful completion of a BSES expedition.

### Earth Skills
1113 Cougar Court
Frazier Park, CA 93225
Tel.: (661) 245-0318
jlowery@frazmtn.com
http://www.earthskills.org

There is a school where you can learn tracking, survival, plant uses, and general bush lore. The Earth Skills school was founded in 1987 by Jim Lowery to introduce people to the great outdoors in a very practical way. Most of the classes are over a three-day weekend and run between $60 and $250. The wilderness skill course is a three-day class that will teach you how to trap, identify edible plants, weave baskets, build shelters, start a fire with an Indian bow, make primitive weapons, purify water, and generally learn how to survive more than 50 miles from a 7-Eleven. There are also some one-day classes that teach the basics of plant identification and tracking.

### Outward Bound
Outward Bound U.S.A.
100 Mystery Point Road
Garrison, NY 10524
Tel.: (888) 88BOUND
info@obusa.com
http://www.outwardbound.com

Do you want to develop that calm, steely-eyed approach, that strong warmth that exudes from those '40s male movie stars with an unshakable faith in your abilities and courage? All right, how about just being able to sleep without your Mickey Mouse nightlight on?

Outward Bound starts with training the mind, and the body follows. The program has been used with the handicapped, the criminal, and the infirm, and it creates magical transformations in all. What is the secret? Well, like the little engine that said, "I think I can, I think I can," OB teaches you to motivate yourself, trust your companions, and step past your self-imposed limits. What emerges is self-confidence and a greater understanding of your fellow man. The idea for the school was developed in 1941. Today, there are 40 Outward Bound schools around the world, with five wilderness schools in North America: Colorado, Maine, North Carolina, Oregon, and Minnesota. The national headquarters is in Garrison, New York, 50 miles north of New York City.

Outward Bound has expanded to include executive training courses, but the results are not as glorious as anticipated. The story goes, in one of the sessions, instructors in England divided executives into two groups and told them to rescue two injured people on the side of a mountain. One group then proceeded to steal the other's stretcher, brought their "victim" to safety, then stood and cheered while the other victim lay stranded on the mountain. Oh, well. Maybe learning to survive the urban jungle makes men tougher than we thought.

# Survival Training

### Boulder Outdoor Survival School (BOSS)
P.O. Box 1590
Boulder, CO 80306
Tel.: (303) 444-9779
Fax: (303) 442-7425
info@boss-inc.com
http://www.boss-inc.com
If you want to live like a native (no, they do not offer casino management courses), check out the BOSS program. The big one is the 28-day course (also offered in seven- and 14-day segments) in the southern Utah Mountains, where you will go through four phases. For openers, you will spend five days traveling without food or water. The second phase is 12 days spent with the group learning and practicing your survival skills. The third phase has you spending three to four days on a solo survival quest with minimal tools (no credit cards or Walkmans), living off the land until you finally make the grade by spending five days in the wild while traveling a substantial distance. Graduation ceremonies are somewhat informal and muddy. Naturally, food, accommodations, and transportation are not included. One added benefit is that most participants lose about 5 to 8 percent of their body weight after taking the month-long course.

For those who don't have a month to spend on a forced weight-loss system, there are one- to three-week courses that range from basic earth skills and aboriginal knowledge to winter survival courses that include making snowshoes, mushing dogsleds, and cold-weather first aid. The one that appeals to me is the seven-day desert and marine (as in water) survival course held in the Kino Bay area of Sonora, Mexico. This course teaches you how to find your food underwater and on land, find fresh water, what there is to eat in arid lands, and gives you general desert survival knowledge. BOSS is consistently held above the others as the toughest and most rewarding survival school.

### Gryphon Group Security Solutions, Inc.
100 Rialto Place, Suite 709
Melbourne, FL 32901
Tel.: (321) 952-4948
Fax: (321) 952-4951
info@gryphonsecurity.com
http://www.ssdd.com
Over 800 corporations have sent their personnel over the past two decades to learn evasive and survival driving from the experts in this company. This intensive three-day course teaches incident avoidance through awareness and planning.

### Executive Security International (ESI)
Gun Barrel Square
2128 Railroad Avenue, Dept. Web
Rifle, CO 81650
Toll-free Tel.: (888) 718-3105
ESI@esi-lifeforce.com
http://www.esi-lifeforce.com
ESI was established in 1980 and offers an intensive training program for bodyguards, protection specialists, or protective intelligence operatives.

**Enviro-Tech International**
P.O. Box 2135
Montrose, CO 81402
Tel.: (970) 249-7590
Toll-free Tel.: (800) 994-2434
info@etisurvival.com
http://www.etisurvival.com

ETI offers a number of survival training programs that cover a wide range of environmental conditions and terrain that teach participants how to survive in arctic, as well as desert, conditions. Custom training programs can also be arranged in just plain old survival.

## Travel Insurance

Go ahead, pick up the phone, tell the toothy Rotarian with the bad comb-over that you are going to Chechnya and are worried about losing your camera. Can he write a travel insurance policy? Not likely. Sure, a few years ago the disclaimer on your insurance pretty much guaranteed that the only thing insurance companies would pay for would be the cost of the postage to cancel your insurance, after they explain all the things they didn't cover. Things like terrorism, acts of God, and even things like theft or loss without a police report. Good luck trying to find a cop, let alone a piece of paper and pencil in the places *DP* travels to. In most cases, it's the cops that arrange to have our stuff stolen.

But things have changed. And, of course, so have the premiums. You can get kidnap insurance, AIDS insurance, cancellation insurance, and I guess you could probably buy insurance in case something happens to your insurance company while you are away.

Tips for buyers: Use a broker and be up front about the type of coverage you need. Read the fine print and check the quality of medical treatment coverage (including any caps) and demand replacement value of your expensive items.

**Access America Travel Protection Products**
http://www.accessamerica.com

**Travel Guard**
http://www.travel-guard.com

**CSA Travel Protection**
http://www.travelsecure.com

**Kidnap, Rescue, Extraction**
http://www.black-fox.com

**Travel Insurance**
http://www.chubb.com

**Long-Term Travel Insurance**
http://www.worldwidemedical.com

**Extreme Sports Coverage**
https://www.worldcover.com/NASApp/wcd/WCDServlet

**Medical Coverage**
http://www.intsos.com

## Emergency/Rescue

If you become seriously ill or injured abroad, a U.S. consular officer can provide assistance in finding medical services and informing your next-of-kin, family, or friends. A consular officer can also assist in the transfer of funds from the United States, but payment of hospital and other expenses is your responsibility.

It is wise to learn what medical services your health insurance will cover overseas before you leave on your trip. If you do have applicable insurance, don't forget to carry both your insurance policy identity card as proof of such insurance, and a claim form. Many health insurance companies will pay customary and reasonable hospital costs abroad, but most require a rider for a Medevac flight back to the States. This is usually done via private plane or by removing airline seats. You will be accompanied by a nurse or medical assistant who will also fly back to the country of origin. Medevacs can burn money as fast as the Lear Jet you charter, so plan on spending a minimum of five grand and up to $30,000. If you are really banged up, you may need more medical technicians, special equipment, and a higher level of care during your flight. The Social Security Medicare program does not provide for payment of hospital or medical services outside the United States.

If you're getting toward the back end of your adventuring career, the American Association of Retired Persons (AARP) offers foreign medical care coverage at no extra charge with its Medicare supplement plans. This coverage is restricted to treatments considered eligible under Medicare. In general, it covers 80 percent of the customary and reasonable charges, subject to a $50 deductible for the covered care during the first 60 days. There is a ceiling of $25,000 per trip. This is a reimbursement plan, so you must pay the bills first and then obtain receipts for submission to the plan. Keep in mind that many insurance policies may not cover you if you were injured in a war zone.

To facilitate identification in case of an accident, complete the information page on the inside of your passport; provide the name, address, and telephone number of someone to be contacted in an emergency. The name given should not be the same as your traveling companions, in case the entire party is involved in the same accident. Travelers going abroad with any preexisting medical problems should carry a letter from their attending physician. The letter should describe their condition and include information about any prescription medications, including the generic name of any prescribed drugs that they need to take.

Any medications being carried overseas should be left in their original containers and should be clearly labeled. Travelers should check with the foreign embassy of the country they are visiting to make sure any required medications are not considered to be illegal narcotics in that country.

**International SOS Assistance**
Worldwide Headquarters
International SOS Pte., Ltd.
331 North Bridge Road
#17-00 Odeon Towers
Singapore 188720
Tel.: (65) 6338 2311
Fax: (65) 6338 7611
Alarm Center Tel.: (65) 6338 7800
corpcomm@internationalsos.com
http://www.intsos.com

**Access America, Inc.**
P.O. Box 90315
Richmond, VA 23286-4991
Toll-free Tel.: (866) 807-3982
Toll-free Fax: (800) 346-9265
service@accessamerica.com
http://www.accessamerica.com

**Air Ambulance Inc.**
Hayward, CA 94540
Tel.: (800) 982-5806
Aero Ambulance International
4631 Northwest 31st Street, Suite 220
Fort Lauderdale, FL 33309
Tel.: (800) 443-8042, (305) 776-6800

**Air Ambulance Network**
905 Martin Luther King Jr. Drive, #330
Tarpon Springs, FL 34689
Toll-free Tel.: (800) 327-1966
Fax: (727) 937-0276
airambulance@airambulancenetwork.com
http://www.airambulancenetwork.com

**Air-Evac International**
8665 Gibbs Drive, Suite 202
San Diego, CA 92123
Toll-free Tel.: (800) 854-2569
Toll-free Tel.: (800) 321-9522
Tel.: (619) 278-3822

**Air Medic—Air Ambulance of America**
P.O. Box 538
Washington, PA 15301
Toll-free Tel.: (800) 245-9987

**American Aero-Med**
1575 West Commercial Blvd.
Hanger 36B
Fort Lauderdale, FL 33309
Tel.: (800) 443-8042

**Euro-Flite**
3000 Weslayan, Suite 200
Houston, TX 77027
Tel.: (713) 961-5200
Fax: (713) 961-4088

**Euro-Flite Air Ambulance**
P.O. Box 86
FIN-01531
Vantaa, Finland
24-hour Alarm Center:
Tel.: (358) 9-8702544
Fax: (358) 9-8702507
http://www.jetflite.fi

**Air Ambulance America**
P.O. Box 4051
Austin, TX 78765-4051
Toll-free Tel.: (800) 222-3564
Or call collect: (512) 479-8000
Fax: (512) 472-8810
dispatch@airambulance.com
http://airambulance.com

**Care Flight International**
14609 Airport Parkway
Clearwater, FL
Toll-free Tel.: (800) 282-6878
Tel.: (727) 530-7972
info@careflight.com
http://www.careflight.com

**National Air Ambulance**
3495 S.W. 9th Avenue
Fort Lauderdale, FL 33315
Toll-free Tel.: (800) 327-3710
Tel.: (954) 359-9900
Fax: (954) 359-0039
http://www.nationaljets.com

*International Medivac Transport*
Phoenix, AZ
Toll-free Tel.: (800) 468-1911
Tel.: (602) 678-4444

*International SOS Assistance, Inc.*
Eight Neshaminy Interplex
Suite 207
Trevose, PA 19053-6956
Tel.: (215) 244-1500 or (215) 245-4707
Alarm Center:
Toll-free Tel.: (800) 523-8930
http://www.internationalsos.com/contact

*Mercy Medical Airlift*
National Headquarters:
9998 Wakefield Drive, Suite 110
Manassas, VA 20110
Toll-free Tel.: (800) 296-1191/ Ext. 23
Tel.: (703) 296-1191/Ext. 23
Fax: (703) 257-1642

Patient Assistance Center:
4620 Haygood Road, Suite 1
Virginia Beach, VA 23455
Toll-free Tel.: (888) 675-1405
Tel.: (757) 318-9175
Fax: (757) 318-9107
mercymedical@erols.com
http://www.mercymedical.org

*AIRescue*
7435 Valjean Avenue
Van Nuys, CA 91406
Toll-free Tel.: (800) 922-4911,
Tel.: (818) 994-0911 (Call collect world-
   wide)
Fax: (818) 994-0180
airescue@msn.com

# Trauma Counseling

Here at *DP* we think it's good to talk, but don't just take our word for it: The armed forces, police departments, and health services of practically every country in the developed world recommend trauma counseling for those who have been involved in or witnessed a life-threatening situation.

If you have experienced or witnessed an event or episode that involved actual or threatened death or serious injury, or a threat to the physical integrity of yourself or others, and felt intense fear, helplessness, or horror (not being able to get a tall, skinny, vanilla cappuccino to go in New Jersey doesn't count, by the way) you could experience post-traumatic stress reaction (PTSR), which can develop into the more serious post–traumatic stress disorder (PTSD).

The following are typical reactions that might indicate PTSR:

- Hyperactivity and oversensitivity (for example, being easily startled)
- Having distressing dreams about the event
- Disturbed sleep
- Feeling on edge
- Feeling isolated, numb, or guilty
- Flashbacks (sudden vivid and distressing mental pictures connected with the event)
- Avoiding things, people, conversations, and situations connected with the event
- Irritability or bursts of anger

These reactions can begin immediately, or are occasionally triggered as long as 50 years after the event in question (in the case of some World War II survivors). If detected in its early stages, PTSR can be treated easily and effectively, sometimes with only one counseling or debriefing session. Also, remember that if you meet a survivor of traumatic events and ask about what happened, there is a chance that you'll witness—and may even precipitate—PTSD.

Post–traumatic stress disorder was first coined in 1980 after extensive studies of Vietnam veterans revealed an identifiable cluster of related symptoms that had affected 20 percent of all U.S. combat troops in Southeast Asia.

**Dart Center for Journalism and Trauma**
University of Washington
School of Communications
Box 353740
Seattle, WA 98195-3740
Tel: (206) 616-3223
Fax: (206) 543-9285
uwdart@u.washington.edu
http://dartcenter.org/resource.html

**Ticehurst Trauma Unit**
The Priory Ticehurst House
Ticehurst
Wadhurst
East Sussex TN5 7HU, UK
Tel.: (44) 1580 202206
Fax: (44) 1580 201006
http://www.prioryhealthcare.co.uk/
    patinfo/servicefram.htm

# WHAT TO PACK

## Use It or Lose It

You really cannot give solid advice on what to pack. If you say travel light, people feel cheated. If you provide a five-page list of gizmos, you get yelled at for being a gadget hawker. I have traveled with nothing (after all my luggage was stolen) and lots (on assignment, complete with tripod, tape recorders, video cameras, and camera), and traveling with nothing is the way to go. Most travelers travel with less and less as they gain experience or as they get mugged and pickpocketed. You choose: Lose it now or later. The only exception would be specialized expeditions, where you are expected to come back with footage or samples of your discoveries. Even if you consider porters for your gear, maintain your credo of traveling light. The Web sites listed are some of my resources, but not endorsements (yes, I get just as mad as you at high prices, low quality, and fashion extras invading the adventure business). Anybody want to hire me to create decent equipment?

## Luggage

What separates you from the locals is your baggage (not to mention that ridiculous hat you're wearing). I prefer a frameless black military bergen, a camera bag that snaps around my waist, and a mountaineer fanny pack. I tell people to avoid outside pockets, but I must have 20 of them, filled with dirty laundry and cold-weather gear. Sometimes I squash everything into a UN flour sack when checking in on nasty airlines. Having multiple bags that attach to me keeps my hands free, confuses the hell out of customs inspectors, and gives a thief something to think about when it's all carabinered together. Locks and twist-ties from garbage bags are a good way to slow down thieves. Put everything inside large heavy-duty Ziploc freezer bags, and then put those inside large garbage bags. Bring some spares of both types of bags. Some people like to use thick rubber "rafting" sacks, but in my experience they are useless, being neither waterproof nor durable. Inside my pack, I like to put a small Pelican case with the delicates and expensives. I also carry a second fanny pack for toiletries and personal stuff. I use clear Tupperware containers to store first-aid supplies, medicines, and other assorted small objects. Don't scrimp on your pack, but remember it will come back foul-smelling, ripped, and covered in dirt.

http://www.eagleindustries.com
http://www.eaglecreek.com
http://www.letravelstore.com
http://www.timberland.com
http://www.tamrac.com

### Tent

Do you really need a tent? Consider a hammock, a bug net, or even a simple plastic tarp. You can substitute a groundsheet with rope for warmer climes, or a jungle hammock for swamps. Or you can get extra friendly and crash with the locals.

http://gorp.com/gorp/gear/bg_tents.htm
http://www.junglehammock.com

### Sleeping Bag

Get a light, cotton-lined sleeping bag that has anything but down stuffing. A flannel sheet will do just fine in the summer. Down does not insulate when wet, so look into thin synthetics. I have never used a sleeping bag in DPs, since most people will provide a sheet or blanket.

http://www.outdoorreview.com/reviewscrx.aspx
http://www.hitthetrail.com/sleepbag.htm
http://www.backpacking.net/gearbags.html

## Toiletry Kit

Combination comb/brush, toothbrush, toothpaste, floss, deodorant, toilet paper, tampons, condoms, small Swiss-Army knife with scissors and nail file, razor, shampoo, liquid soap . . . tiny, tiny, tiny, and all stuck in a Tupperware container.

http://www.tupperware.com

## Compass/GPS

Even if you don't know how to use a compass, you should have one. If you take along the manual, you'll easily learn how to use your compass to tell time, measure maps, navigate by the stars, signal airplanes, and, God forbid, even plot your course if you get lost. The best compasses are made by Silva. I love the Garmin GPSs with the built-in maps. Military checkpoints and rebels don't. Some countries consider GPSs to be military equipment, so ask before you go.

http://www.titansystemscorp.com
http://igscb.jpl.nasa.gov
http://joe.mehaffey.com
http://www.silva.se

## Flashlight

You should carry three flashlights: (1) a tiny single-cell key; (2) an AA-battery Maglight or other waterproof flashlight (get two or three because they make great gifts); and (3) a Petzl or REI waterproof head-mounted flashlight. Get lots of AA batteries.

http://www.petzl.com
http://www.meiresearch.com
http://www.leeco.com/page021.htm

## Mosquito Netting

REI sells a nifty mosquito tent that will cover your head and arms. Mosquitoes like to start feeding as soon as you drift off to sleep, so this light tentlike mesh will keep your head and arms safe. It can also be used to catch fish, strain chunks out of water, and strain gasoline. Bring bug repellent with the highest DEET content. Wash it off, though, because it otherwise may cause some nasty rashes. In hotel rooms, mosquito coils can make life bearable. They do not scare off large rats, however.

## Clothing

There is much debate on fabrics and clothing styles. In the arid tropics, cotton is about the only fabric worth wearing, but synthetics are preferred by others. In tropical countries, be careful of the germ buildup that synthetics create. Try loose-fitting, light cotton shirts rather than T-shirts. After one week, everything you own will be stinky, damp, and wrinkled, so it's best to rotate three shirts, three T-shirts, two pairs of pants, one pair of shorts, three pairs of socks, three sets of underwear, a hat, a poncho, one pair of sneakers, hiking boots, and flip-flops. And that's it.

http://www.actiongear.com
http://www.cabelas.com

## Pants

The plain khaki army fatigues made in Korea are your best bet. Others swear by convertible short/pant combos. Be careful of shorts. Many Muslim countries don't think the sight of your naked legs is all that sexy. You'll get cut, dirty, and burned as well. Cabellas, safari catalogs, Travelsmith, and army surplus stores are all excellent sources for outdoor clothing.

http://www.royalrobbins.com
http://www.imsplus.com/ims_catalog_index.html

## Light, Cotton T-shirts

Preferably with the name of where you are from or a *DP* shirt (you can use them as gifts later). Plan on buying your T-shirts where you travel to and pick up a few semiformal shirts. In some countries they will make you an entire wardrobe in a day . . . and for pennies. Some people prefer synthetics for wicking and ease of washing.

http://www.patagonia.com

## Wool Socks

I avoid synthetic socks (and cotton socks). I like wool, or at least a good wool blend. You want your socks to maintain their shape and breathe, and good wool does that. Take three pairs—one to wear, one to wash, and another to wear because you forgot to wash the first pair. Do not get the high-tech synthetic socks, just the funky rag type. After a few weeks you'll be wearing flip-flops sans socks, anyway.

http://www.mtbr.com/reviews/Socks
http://www.thorlo.com

## Underwear

Loose cotton boxers; get groovy-looking ones so they can double as swim trunks. Speedos are for the French and strip clubs.

http://www.topdrawers.com

## Shirts

Long-sleeved cotton, and not too butch-looking, so you can wear it to dinner. Safari-style is fine because people expect you to look adventurous.

## Poncho

One heavy vinyl, another cheap plastic, to protect your pack and camera gear and to sleep on.

## Hat

Wide-brimmed canvas hat. Tilleys are the best, but who wants to look like a geriatric on safari? Another choice is to pick up a cheap straw hat when you get to where you're going—natty and disposable.

http://www.tilley.com
http://www.thingzoz.com/hats/bushhats.htm

## Hiking Boots

Lightweight mesh and canvas or leather; no foam padding if possible. Go for leather or canvas with replaceable soles so they can be repaired on the road. If you are doing some rugged work in remote regions, think about repair. Leather and separate Vibram soles can be patched; some of the new designs can't. I go custom with Viberg, the people who made my logging boots (still in perfect condition after over 20 years).

http://www.viberg.com
http://www.raichle.com
http://www.hi-tec.com

## Sneakers

I use Chuck Taylor's Converse in beige (over 500 million pairs have been sold since 1917). Get 'em one size larger 'cause your feet will swell up. These are the world's greatest (and cheapest) jungle boots. Others swear by simple boots and shoes like the classic Timberlands or Rockports.

http://www.converse.com
http://www.rockport.com
http://www.timberland.com

## TIPS FOR WOMEN BY WOMEN

1. **Emergency Contraception:** A little pack of hormone pills that, when taken within 72 hours of unprepared-for (and, therefore, probably unprotected) intercourse (whether it's unexpected romance or unfortunate rape), will very reliably prevent pregnancy. It's easily available over the counter or by prescription in North America and Europe (or put it together yourself anywhere you can get birth control pills). It does *not* prevent STD transmission. It is *not* an abortifacient—if the woman is already pregnant but unaware of it, this medication will not abort or damage the embryo or fetus. The worst side effect is nausea and/or vomiting. The last thing a woman wants (in my opinion) while traveling, is to put her life in the hands of a third-world abortionist or bear the child of some scum-of-the-earth assailant.
2. **Hormone Pills:** A pack of birth control pills for perimenopausal women (the 45 to 55 age group), who might unexpectedly experience a gynecological hemorrhage for a variety of hormonal or pathological reasons. Taking 2 to 4 pills a day can sometimes (depending on the cause) stem the flow of blood long enough to evacuate to an adequate health care facility, and perhaps avoid the need for a blood transfusion (oh God, who wants a blood transfusion in Thailand or Botswana?).
3. **Urine Pregnancy Test:** An over-the-counter test for any woman who might be pregnant and is experiencing abdominal pain; ruling out pregnancy is *vital*. If a woman is pregnant, it could be an ectopic (commonly known as a "tubal") pregnancy, and if the fallopian tube ruptures, the woman can bleed to death internally in a matter of hours. Also, lots of places don't even *have* pregnancy tests (pregnancy is sometimes diagnosed at birth); so, bring your own. They are extremely accurate 10+ days after conception.

Naturally, all this advice is not a substitute for discussing these issues with a health care provider while preparing for a trip.

*Source:* Karen Hays, CNM ARNP (Certified Nurse-Midwife, Advanced Registered Nurse-Practitioner), University of Washington Medical Center, Seattle, WA.

## Food

It's not worth bringing a cooking kit. Even in the most devastated of places, someone prepares food. I do recommend bringing beef jerky, gum, energy bars, bags of nuts, and other high-protein/high-fat munchies. Also, hot sauce is indispensable in eating that third-world slop.

http://www.ofd.com/mh
http://theepicenter.com/mre_freeze_dried_dehydrated_foods.html

## First-Aid Kit

A prescription from your doctor or a letter describing the drugs you are carrying can help. Pack wads of antidiarrheal medications, electrolyte powder, antibiotics, an insect-sting kit, antacids, antihistamines (for itching and colds), antibiotic ointment, iodine, water purifier, foot powder, antifungal ointment, and a syringe or two. Also look into items like Vagisil, which can be used to dry feet out; Superglue, to seal cuts; and other home remedies. Ask your doctor to prescribe any drugs you might need to complete your kit. Single-sided razor blades, a lighter, condoms, rubber gloves, IV drip (needle and bag) and small first-aid kits are good to have.

http://gearreview.com/firstaidrev99.asp
http://www.adventuremedicalkits.com
http://www.destinationoutdoors.com
http://www.orgear.com
http://www.sawyerproducts.com
http://www.siriusmed.com

## Camera/Video/Binoculars

Bring the smallest, simplest camera that uses standard negative film. You would be surprised where they have 1-hour processing. Bring two if it matters. Hi-8 cameras or tapes are now common worldwide (don't forget the PAL, SECAM, and NTSC problem), but DV is now the way to go. Some of the pocket-sized cameras from Sony and Canon are broadcast quality and can also double as a digital tape recorder and a still camera. You won't find tape or batteries unless you check the duty-free shop at the airport. I have added a Fuji digital camera to my camera collection and it's extremely easy to use, takes great pictures that you can download onto your computer later, and you don't need to worry about film. But you do need battery storage, and electricity to charge everything. Don't bring binoculars. You can always bum somebody else's unless you are going to Africa or want to avoid gunships—then they are a must. Leica and Zeiss roof prisms are the only ones to consider.

http://www.canon.com
http://www.leica.com
http://www.sel.sony.com
http://www.nikonusa.com
http://www.fujifilm.com
http://www.i-zone.com

## Survival Kit

Survival kits are like an African fetish. We hope that just having these items around means we will never have to use them. Remember to keep this kit separate from your main pack, ideally in a belt-mounted bag. Your entire pack should consist of a first-aid kit, two space blankets, Bic lighters, Swiss-Army knife (get the one with the saw), a whistle, Power Bars (get one of each flavor), string, extra money, your photocopied ID, fishing line with hooks (not too helpful in the desert), candle butts, Stop Trot or any other electrolyte replacement product, and headache pills. Also bring a sewing kit, and buy a surgical needle shaped like a fishhook. You will need this to sew up your skin (sterilized with a lighter first) if you suffer a severe gash. Baby wipes are handy for many uses. Hydrogen peroxide is a nasty but useful disinfectant. Reader Trond M. Vagen from Norway also suggests tampons (for wounds), a small magnet (for a makeshift compass with needles or razorblades), a magnesium fire-starting kit, and, to cap it off, a small survival guide so you figure out how you got so lost.

http://sharplink.com/jkits
http://www.gutz.com
http://www.equipped.com/survlkit.htm
http://www.baproducts.com/survkit.htm

WHAT TO PACK

## Water Bottle/Purifiers

Bring a metal water bottle that can be used to boil water in a pinch. The kind they sell as fuel bottles are fine and you should carry a small MSR stove for the purpose of disinfecting questionable water supplies. Purifiers and filters are helpful depending on whether you will be near sterile water supplies. The new Camelbak-style "hydration systems" are fine until they freeze, puncture, and leak all over your clothes or get contaminated. They are fine for external use and make a great addition to carry water but beware of their limitations. The new filtration canteens and drip purifiers are a godsend.

http://www.msrcorp.com
http://www.camelbak.com
http://www.generalecology.com

## Essentials

Your passport, airline tickets, money, credit cards, traveler's checks, driver's license, malaria pills, sunscreen, lip balm, spare contacts, glasses, sunglasses are the essentials. Make two copies of all documents, including credit cards. Leave one at home, take one with you, and keep it in a separate place from the originals.

## Letters of Recommendation

If you get in a jam or need special dispensation, it doesn't hurt to have plenty of glowing letters about you on fancy stationery. Lots of official stamps help, too. Money is better.

*Equipment Resources*
http://www.gorp.com
http://www.out-there.com
http://www.gorefabrics.com
http://www.rei.com
http://www.ems.com
http://www.fogdog.com
http://www.magellans.com

# Gifts

Most of the third world views you as a rich, capitalist pig. Just because you think you are a *poor*, capitalist pig doesn't let you off the hook when it comes to giving gifts. Keep it simple and memorable and have plenty to go around. Mirrors, beads, and shiny paper were big in Columbus' time, but you are expected to do better than that today. Here are a few suggestions to make you the hit of the village:

> Just because you think you are a *poor*, capitalist pig doesn't let you off the hook when it comes to giving gifts.

### Pens

Call an advertising specialty company to get cheap pens printed with your name and message on them. They will still be as cheap as drugstore Bics and a lot cooler as gifts.

### Stickers/Cards

Buy a bag of them from party stores; if you can't resist a little self-promotion, have your own stickers printed up on foil and give 'em out to the eager hordes. You can also have your photo printed on stickers or use your computer, color printer, and adhesive paper to make your own. At the least, you'll have a bunch of cards made up with your photo, name, and e-mail address to hand out. Polaroid also makes iZone sticker photo film.

http://www.kinkos.com

### Cigarettes

I know it is not cool to smoke, but passing around smokes is a successful way to initiate male bonding in the rest of the world. In the Muslim world, where men don't drink, they smoke enough to make up for it. Even if you don't smoke, carry a

> In the Muslim world, where men don't drink, they smoke enough to make up for it.

couple of packs of cigarettes as gifts and icebreakers. I know for a fact that people's intentions to shoot me have been altered by the speed with which I have offered up the smokes.

## Weird Stuff No Adventurer Should Be Without

Everyone tells you to pack light (including me), so here are all the little items that can make your day or night in the bush:

### Psion Palm Computer

I used to carry a laptop but this baby fits in your pocket, runs on AA batteries for a month, and has everything, including spreadsheets, language software, calculator, word processing, drawing, and much more. You offload your files onto a static memory chip so even if you get busted, your precious words of wisdom are safe. No longer made but available on eBay.

http://www.ebay.com

### Adventurer Watch

A number of companies make waterproof watches with all sorts of gee-whiz features including alarms, compasses, and dual dials for different time zones. My favorite is the Casio series with built-in compass, altimeter, and more.

http://www.web-watches-casio.com

### Books

Buy them by thickness. My faves are *Information Please Almanac,* the *Book of Lists,* Penguin compendiums of classic stories, and fat, chunky adventure novels like *The Three Musketeers* or *Les Misérables.* The *Bible* or the *Koran* will do in a pinch, and I have been known to write a book out of boredom. Trade 'em or give them away as gifts along the way. We hope the first thing you pack is a guidebook. Also think about phrase books, survival manuals, and even poetry for those times you know all is lost. Address books are useful, too.

http://www.amazon.com

### Maps

Good maps are very difficult to get in third-world countries. Especially in war zones. Spraying them with a spray fixative available at any art store will help to waterproof them. Consider the new GPS hand receivers that let you download digital maps.

http://www.maps.com
http://www.maptown.com
http://www.lib.utexas.edu/maps/index.html
http://www.reliefweb.int/mapc/index.html
http://www.un.org/Depts/Cartographic/english/htmain.htm
http://plasma.nationalgeographic.com/mapmachine

## Business or Calling Cards

If you are the sociable type, have a bunch of cheap cards with plasti-cized ink made up (be sure moisture doesn't make the ink run). Look in the phonebook for a translator if you would like them in two lan-guages. Leave enough room for your new friends to write their names and addresses on them. Make sure you also bring plenty of extra pass-port photos.

www.kinkos.com

## Shortwave Radio

Now that Sony makes those teensy-weensy shortwave receivers, you need never spend a 10-hour bus ride without entertainment.

http://www.grundig.com/produkte/audio/welt.html
http://tekgallery.site.yahoo.net/tekgallery/shorrad.html

## Notebook and Pens

For the non-technical, a notebook is an indispensable part of the travel experience. You will have plenty of time to wax poetic and cap-ture your thoughts.

## Carabiners

Use them to snap your pack to a bus rail or bike frame, hold items on your belt, hang things from trees, rescue people, and to use as a belt when you lose weight.

http://www.omegapac.com

## Yellow and Black Danger Zone Tape

I use the heavy-striped tape to mark my luggage, tape rips, pack boxes, and even fix my runners. I just point at the yellow tape on my waist bag, hold up the number of fingers for how many pieces of lug-gage, and presto, instant recognition.

## Syringes

Just visit a third-world hospital.

## Razor Blades

Boils, slivers, infected cuts—all may require a little field surgery.

## Hydrogen Peroxide

Cleans out cuts, hurts like hell, stops major infections.

## Credit Card Survival Kits

### Tool Logic

http://www.toollogic.com

Credit card–sized knife, compass, screwdriver, etc. Ideal for gifts or backup survival. Also made by Victorinot.

## Ziploc Freezer Bags

Organize, hold anything, waterproof everything from passports to cameras. Use them for everything but food. The plastic transmits an icky plastic taste to food when used in hot climates.

## Trash Bags

Heavy-duty garbage bags make great waterproofers. They also double as ponchos, groundcovers, umbrellas, water catchers, spare windows, sails, and even garbage bags.

## Tupperware

It organizes and waterproofs, and you can eat out of it or give it away as gifts. Get the clear stuff and size it to the pockets or corners in your luggage.

http://www.tupperware.com

## Bubblegum

Get the kind that Amerol makes in the tape form. It's sold in a plastic dispenser. Get the dayglo pink stuff; it drives the natives crazy to watch you blow those bubbles.

http://www.topps.com
http://www.bubblegum.com

## Empty Film Canisters

Take the clear kind that Fuji film comes in. Take the tops off, squeeze them, and they act like suction cups. Squeeze them with the tops on and they are like tiny popguns. You can amuse the little ones for hours.

http://www.fujifilm.com

## Polaroid Camera (iZone)

I could create peace in the world and brotherly love if I just had enough Polaroid film to take pictures of every headhunter, mercenary,

WHAT TO PACK

tribal warrior, soldier, and politician. They love it, and smiles break out all around. Think about it: How many times does somebody take your picture where you work and actually give you a copy?

http://www.i-zone.com
http://www.polaroid.com

If any of our rabid readers have more gizmos or tips send them to:

ryp@comebackalive.com.

*Resources*

http://www.rei.com
http://www.ems.com
http://www.fogdog.com
http://www.gorp.com

## Those Hard-to-Find Items

**Camouflage Passports**
http://www.scopebooks.com

**Bulletproof Rain Coat**
http://www.counterspyshop.com

**Hostage Tracking Sensors**
http://www.spooktech.com

**Pith Helmet**
http://www.actiongear.com

**Nightvision**
http://www.73.com/a/0111.shtml

**Female Bodyguards**
http://www.execops.com/execops.htm

**Tracked Military Vehicles, heavy weapons, jets, etc.**
http://www.angelfire.com/biz/troopsupport/index.html

# INDEX

# World's Most Dangerous Places: Photo Credits

**ROBERT YOUNG PELTON'S**
# COME BACK ALIVE

**The Web site your mother doesn't want you to visit...**
**RYP's DP5 and Come Back Alive, now online as a searchable**
**database with swag, updates, adventure forum, and links.**

### Need Gear?
Mr. DP's Travel Gear...the real thing, worn by rebels, muj, specfors, and
people of dubious character and intent. T-shirts, hats, stickers,
patches, survival stuff and more...

### Seeking Co-Conspirators?
Black Flag Café is where DP'ers hang out and swap info,
insults, and stories, as well as meet the like-minded and motivated.

### Getting Soft? Waiting for a Mission?
Chase away that PTSD and boredom with videos, DVDs,
books, signed gear, and whatever other crazy stuff we think of.

**ROBERT YOUNG PELTON'S**

**WWW.COMEBACKALIVE.COM**